North-Ea

a Lonely Planet shoestring guide

**Robert Storey
Chris Taylor
Clem Lindenmayer**

North-East Asia

4th edition

Published by
  Lonely Planet Publications
  Head Office: PO Box 617, Hawthorn, Vic 3122, Australia
  Branches: 155 Filbert St, Suite 251, Oakland, CA 94607, USA
              10 Barley Mow Passage, Chiswick, London W4 4PH, UK
              71 bis rue du Cardinal Lemoine, 75005 Paris, France

Printed by
  Colorcraft Ltd, Hong Kong

Photographs by
  Front Cover: Saké Barrels at Oagata-jinja Shrine, Japan (Richard I'Anson)

First Published
  August 1985

This Edition
  January 1995

Although the authors and publisher have tried to make the information as accurate as possible, they accept no responsibility for any loss, injury or inconvenience sustained by any person using this book.

National Library of Australia Cataloguing in Publication Data

Storey, Robert
  North East Asia on a shoestring.

  4th ed.
  Includes index.
  ISBN 0 86442 250 4.

  1. East Asia – Guide-books.
  I. Taylor, Chris, 1961- . II. Wheeler, Tony, 1946- . III. Title. (Series: Lonely Planet on a shoestring).

915.04429

Robert Storey

Robert has had a number of distinguished careers, including monkeykeeper at a zoo and slot machine repairman in a Las Vegas casino. After obtaining a worthless liberal arts degree, he wandered the world in search of a decent job. While doing a stint as an English teacher in Taiwan, Robert wrote Lonely Planet's guide to *Taiwan* and thus his present career was born. He is now a respectable citizen and a pillar of the community.

Chris Taylor

Chris Taylor spent his early years in England. He emigrated to Australia with his family in the '70s. After frittering away his youth in a variety of occupations, travelling and working on a useless BA, Chris joined Lonely Planet to work on the phrasebook series. He has since co-authored Lonely Planet's guides to *China* and *Japan* and written the *Mandarin Chinese* phrasebook and city guides for *Tokyo* and *Seoul*. He is currently somewhere in North-East Asia.

Clem Lindenmayer

Clem's decidedly scattered 'career' has ranged from dishwasher and telex operator to layabout and habitual traveller. Mountains and languages are his pivotal interests, and for both reasons China eventually caught his attention. Having made the fateful resolution to learn Chinese while on a lengthy solo trek through Lapland, he studied the language intermittently for several years in Australia and China before working on the update for this book. Clem is also the author of Lonely Planet's *Trekking in the Patagonian Andes* and a contributing author of Lonely Planet's *China*.

This Book

Lonely Planet's shoestring guides are designed with the budget traveller in mind and give compact, essential information on the countries of a particular region. This guide was compiled from research gathered for our series of travel survival kits, which give in-depth coverage of a single country for a range of budgets.

North-East Asia combines the talents of a battalion of Lonely Planet authors. The first edition was put together by Alan Samalgalski and Michael Buckley (China), Tony Wheeler (Hong Kong and Macau), Ian McQueen (Japan) and Geoff Crowther (Korea). The second edition was assembled by Laurie Fullerton, with new research by the same team plus Robert Strauss (China)

and Robert Storey (Taiwan). Robert Storey went back to the region to update the third edition and add a chapter on Mongolia. This fourth edition draws on the new research in Lonely Planet's guides to individual countries in North-East Asia written by Robert Storey, Chris Taylor and Clem Lindenmayer; Robert returned to the region to update the information and was responsible for co-ordinating the book.

From the Publisher

This edition was edited by Kristin Odijk and Rob Flynn. Adrienne Costanzo, David Collins, Frith Pike and Diana Saad assisted with proofing, and Ann Jeffree with index tagging. Mapping, design and layout of this edition were coordinated by Richard Stewart. Maps were also contributed by David Kemp, Chris Klep, Adam McCrow, Andrew Smith, Andrew Tudor and Angus Williams. Margaret Jung produced the title page and Jane Hart was responsible for the cover.

Thanks must also go to Diana Saad and Tom Smallman for editorial guidance; Valerie Tellini for design assistance; Dan Levin for help with soft softs; and Yoko Speirs for typesetting the Japanese script.

Thanks

We are deeply grateful to a number of local residents whose assistance in this mammoth project greatly enhanced the quality of the book. With apologies to any who were left out, special thanks go to Trish Conville & Scott Foster (USA), Bryan L Smith (Taiwan), Craig Soucie (China), Harvey Kline (Japan), Jenny Chan (Hong Kong), Kim Sung-hee (Korea) and Ariunbat (Mongolia).

Many others out there on the road took the time and trouble to write to Lonely Planet with new information. We'd like to thank the following people:

Palmer Acheson (C), Mark Anderson, Pam Bowers (UK), Eddie Coleman (SA), David Fleming (NZ), Rich Freewalt (USA), Elizabeth Freund (USA), Nathan Funk (USA), Mike Gagin, Mary Gallacher (UK), Wayne Garbutt (C), Floki Halldorsson (Ice), Howard Hattersley (UK), Wolfgang Hutt (D), Christopher Jacques (UK), Gabriel Lafitte (Aus), Jasper Lloyd (UK), Michael Masters (USA), David Matton (C), Kate McGregor (Aus), Martin Novak (Cz), Ivor Roberts (UK), Mark Rosenfeld, Sarajean Rossitto (Jap), George Roth (USA), Paul Sherrard (Aus), Nicola Skudder (UK), Dianne Street (Aus), Kim Szabo, Jen & Caroline Taylor (USA), Mark Turrin, James Wilcox (C), Michelle Williams (Aus), Peter Yore (Irl)

C – Canada, Cz – Czech, D – Germany, Jap – Japan, Ice – Iceland, SA – South Africa

Warning & Request

Things change – prices go up, schedules change, good places go bad and bad places go bankrupt – nothing stays the same. So if you find things better or worse, recently opened or long since closed, please write and tell us and help make the next edition better!

Your letters will be used to help update future editions and, where possible, important changes will also be included as a Stop Press section in reprints.

All information is greatly appreciated and the best letters will receive a free copy of the next edition, or any other Lonely Planet book of your choice.

Contents

INTRODUCTION...9

FACTS FOR THE VISITOR...11

Planning......................11	Electricity..................17	Work..........................25
Visas..........................14	Health.......................18	Accommodation...........26
Documents...................15	Dangers & Annoyances....23	Food..........................26
Money........................16	Activities...................24	

GETTING THERE & AWAY...28

Air...........................28	Overland...................34	Sea...........................42

GETTING AROUND...43

Air...........................43	Land........................46	Sea...........................47

CHINA..53

Facts about the Country ... **53**	**Anhui**..........................**146**	Xishuangbanna 191
Facts for the Visitor **67**	Hefei..........................146	**Sichuan** **192**
Getting There & Away.......**82**	Huangshan City 146	Chengdu.......................192
Getting Around.................**85**	Huangshan 146	Around Chengdu..............196
Beijing..........................**89**	**Zhejiang**......................**148**	Emeishan......................196
Around Beijing................**105**	Hangzhou.....................148	Leshan.........................197
The Great Wall 105	**Fujian**........................**151**	Chongqing.....................197
Ming Tombs...................106	Xiamen........................151	Downriver on the Yangzi....200
Western Hills 106	**Jiangxi**.......................**155**	Dazu...........................200
Shidu..........................107	Lushan........................155	Jiuzhaigou 200
Tianjin........................**107**	**Hubei**.........................**157**	**Inner Mongolia**.............**201**
Hebei..........................**110**	Wuhan.........................157	Hohhot.........................201
Chengde.......................110	**Hunan**.........................**161**	The Grasslands...............202
Beidaihe.......................111	Changsha......................161	Dongsheng 202
Shanhaiguan...................111	Shaoshan......................162	**Ningxia** **203**
Liaoning......................**111**	**Guangdong** **162**	Yinchuan......................203
Shenyang......................112	Shenzhen......................162	**Gansu** **204**
Jilin...........................**112**	Zhuhai.........................164	Lanzhou.......................204
Changchun.....................112	Guangzhou....................164	Around Lanzhou..............206
Jilin...........................112	Shantou 171	Xiahe..........................206
Heilongjiang **114**	Zhanjiang 172	Dunhuang.....................207
Jingbo Lake 114	**Hainan**........................**172**	**Xinjiang** **208**
Shanxi........................**115**	Haikou.........................172	Turpan.........................208
Datong.........................115	Sanya..........................175	Ürümqi........................209
Hanging Monastery.............116	**Guangxi**......................**176**	Tianchi........................212
Shaanxi......................**117**	Wuzhou........................176	Kashgar.......................212
Henan.........................**122**	Yangshuo......................180	Karakoram Highway..........214
Kaifeng........................122	**Guizhou**......................**182**	**Tibet**..........................**215**
Luoyang........................122	Guiyang........................182	Yarlong Valley................218
Shandong **123**	Huangguoshu Falls 183	Shigatse.......................218
Taishan........................127	Anshun.........................183	Gyantse.......................218
Qufu...........................128	**Yunnan**.......................**184**	Sakya..........................218
Jiangsu.......................**130**	Kunming.......................184	**Qinghai**......................**219**
The Grand Canal 130	The Stone Forest 188	Xining.........................219
Suzhou........................130	Dali...........................188	Ta'er Lamasery 219
Nanjing........................135	Lijiang........................190	Qinghai Lake..................220
Shanghai.....................**138**	Tiger Leap Gorge 191	Golmud........................220

HONG KONG...222

Facts about the Country ... 222	Kowloon 249	Places to Stay 263
Facts for the Visitor 228	Hong Kong Island (Nth side) ... 251	Places to Eat..........................273
Getting There & Away 241	Hong Kong Island (Sth side) 254	Hong Kong Island – Central ... 278
Getting Around.................. 244	New Territories 256	
Around the Country......... 249	The Outlying Islands 260	

NORTH KOREA 284

Facts about the Country ... 285	**P'yŏngyang 296**	Kŭmgangsan 302
Facts for the Visitor 288	**Around the Country......... 301**	Paekdusan 303
Getting There & Away...... 294	Myohyangsan...........................301	
Getting Around.................. 295	Kaesŏng 302	

SOUTH KOREA..304

Facts about the Country ... 304	Odaesan National Park 350	Maisan Provincial Park............361
Facts for the Visitor 316	**East-Central Korea 351**	Naejangsan National Park 361
Getting There & Away...... 328	Kyŏngju 351	Sŏnunsan Provincial Park........361
Getting Around.................. 328	Taegu 354	Kwangju...................................363
Seoul.................................. 332	Kayasan National Park 354	**Chejudo 363**
Around Seoul 347	Ullŭngdo 354	Cheju City 364
Suwon 348	**South-East Korea 355**	Around the Island....................365
Korean Folk Village 348	Pusan 355	**West-Central Korea 368**
Yŏju 348	Around Pusan 358	Taejŏn.....................................368
North-East Korea 348	**South-West Korea 358**	Taedunsan Provincial Park 369
Sŏraksan National Park...........349	Yŏsu 358	Songnisan National Park.........369
Naksan 349	Moaksan Provincial Park........359	Kongju.....................................369

MACAU 371

Facts about the Country ... 371	**Getting Around 385**
Getting There & Away...... 384	**Around Macau.................. 386**

MONGOLIA...394

Facts about the Country ... 394	**Ulaan Baatar...................... 413**	South Gobi 421
Facts for the Visitor 401	**Around the Country......... 420**	Hovsgol Nuur...........................421
Getting There & Away...... 411	Ulaan Baatar Environs............. 420	Hovd.......................................421
Getting Around.................. 411	Harhorin.................................420	

TAIWAN 423

Facts about the Country ... 423	Taichung 459	Taitung 467
Facts for the Visitor 431	Kukuan..................................459	Lanyu......................................470
Getting There & Away...... 443	Lishan 462	Kenting....................................471
Getting Around.................. 444	Wuling Farm 463	Chiayi......................................473
Taipei.................................. 446	Hohuanshan...........................464	Alishan....................................476
Around the Country......... 458	Tienhsiang..............................465	
Central Cross-Island Highway 458	Hualien...................................466	

JAPAN 479

Facts about the Country ... 480	Mt Fuji 530	Nagano 543
Facts for the Visitor 489	Nikkō 532	Hakuba 543
Getting There & Away...... 501	Yokohama 535	Matsumoto 544
Getting Around.................. 503	Kamakura 535	Kamikōchi 545
Tokyo 507	Nagoya 537	Kanazawa 546
Around Tokyo.................... 527	Takayama 539	Kyoto......................................548
Izu-Hantō Peninsula 527	Shōkawa Valley 541	Osaka......................................559
Hakone...................................527	Kiso Valley Region 542	Kōbe..562

Himeji	564	Mt Hakkōda-san	584	Tokushima	604
Nara	564	Hirosaki	584	Kōchi	605
Kurashiki	567	Mt Iwaki-san	585	Cape Muroto-misaki	606
Hiroshima	569	Kakunodate	585	Cape Ashizuri-misaki	606
Miya-jima Island	573	Tsuruoka	586	Matsuyama	606
Shimonoseki	574	Dewa Sanzan	586	Mt Ishizuchi-san	608
Matsue	575	Niigata	587	Uwajima	608
Izumo	575	Hakodate	588	Dazaifu	612
Tsuwano	575	Sapporo	589	Nagasaki	613
Hagi	576	Wakkanai	593	Kumamoto	616
Aizu Wakamatsu	576	Rishiri-tō Island	594	Mt Aso Area	617
Mt Bandai-san &		Rebun-tō Island	594	Kirishima National Park	619
Sendai	579	Daisetsuzan National Park	595	Kagoshima	620
Matsushima	580	**Shiretoko National Park**	**597**	Sakurajima	621
Kinkazan Island	581	Bihoro	598	Takachiho	622
Hiraizumi	582	Kushiro	598	Okinawa Island	623
Morioka	582	Akan National Park	599	Islands Around Okinawa	625
Mt Iwate-san	583	Shikotsu-tōya National Park	600	Other Islands	625
Mt Osore-zan	583	Takamatsu	603		
Aomori	583	Kotohira	604		

APPENDIX **626**

INDEX **629**

Maps	629	Text	629

Map Legend

BOUNDARIES

.... International Boundary
.... Internal Boundary
.... Disputed Boundary

ROUTES

.... Freeway
.... Highway, Major Road
.... City Road, City Street
.... Railway
.... Private Railway
.... JR Shinkasen (Japan)
.... Underground Railway
.... Tram
.... Walking Track
.... Walking Tour
.... Ferry Route
.... Cable Car or Chairlift

AREA FEATURES

.... Park, Gardens
.... National Park
.... Built-Up Area
.... Pedestrian Mall
.... Market
.... Christian Cemetery
.... Non-Christian Cemetery
.... Beach or Desert
.... Rocks

HYDROGRAPHIC FEATURES

.... Coastline
.... River, Creek
.... Intermittent River or Creek
.... Lake, Intermittent Lake
.... Canal
.... Swamp

SYMBOLS

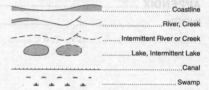

○ CAPITAL		National Capital
◉ Capital		Provincial Capital
● CITY		Major City
● City		City
● Town		Town
● Village		Village
■		Place to Stay
▼		Place to Eat
♟		Pub, Bar
✉	☎	Post Office, Telephone
❶	❽	Tourist Information, Bank
⊖	℗	Transport, Parking
🏛	🏠	Museum, Youth Hostel
🏕	🛆	Caravan Park, Camping Ground
†	☩	Church, Cathedral
☪	✡	Mosque, Synagogue
卍	卐	Buddhist Temple, Shinto Shrine

⊕	★	Hospital, Police Station
✈	✝	Airport, Airfield
▭	✿	Swimming Pool, Gardens
❖	🐘	Shopping Centre, Zoo
☕	⛱	Cafe, Picnic Site
←	A25	One Way Street, Route Number
∴		Archaeological Site or Ruins
🏛	🗼	Stately Home, Monument
♖	▣	Castle, Tomb
⌒	⌂	Cave, Hut or Chalet
▲	※	Mountain or Hill, Lookout
🗼	⚓	Lighthouse, Shipwreck
)(	⚡	Pass, Spring
		Ancient or City Wall
		Rapids, Waterfalls
		Cliff or Escarpment, Tunnel
		Railway Station

Note: not all symbols displayed above appear in this book

Introduction

North-East Asia is many different and contrasting things: high-energy Hong Kong, a British colony nervously watching the countdown for its return to China; tiny Macau, a curious and colourful colonial relic; Japan, the economic powerhouse of the world, with myriad glimpses of a picture-postcard rural side still to be found; Mongolia, once the world's largest empire but now one of Asia's least visited backwaters; Korea, exotic and dynamic but split into two violently opposed halves; Taiwan, another dynamic economy but also uneasy about the intentions of its huge would-be parent; and finally China, ancient, vast, varied and stumbling towards modernisation.

Hong Kong, with its superb natural harbour, is the key to this whole region, the centre from which to explore other parts of North-East Asia. This over-populated city-state, offset by beautiful and sparsely populated islands, wins this role through its central position and its reputation as an office for issuing visas and a supermarket for cheap air fares.

Just an hour away by jetfoil is Macau, the oldest European settlement in the East and an interesting contrast to the bustle of Hong Kong. Yet it offers one form of modernisation that Hong Kong lacks – casino gambling.

Individual travel in China will provide you with a host of impressions: a giant statue of Mickey Mouse (adored by the Chinese), the ancient splendour of the Forbidden City and the Great Wall, or the hackwork that is creating modern China. And every so often China throws up something that takes you completely by surprise – like a village lifted lock, stock and barrel out of Switzerland and grafted onto a Chinese mountaintop.

In Japan, despite overwhelming modernisation, you can still find the traditional way of life. In Tohoku in northern Honshu there are towns with old thatched-roof buildings that have survived earthquakes and wars. Despite its comprehensive transport system, Japan is still a country of heavily beaten highways and barely visited back roads.

Taiwan also remains a land of sharp contrasts – heavy industrialisation has taken its toll on the urban environment, yet the rural areas remain amazingly unspoilt. The island is extremely mountainous and offers some of the best hiking opportunities in the region. Traditional Chinese culture flourishes and is in fact better preserved in Taiwan than on the Chinese mainland.

Although parts of North-East Asia are the most advanced and developed in the whole of Asia, others are as backward as you'll come across. Travellers have been beating a shoestring path across Hong Kong and China for years, but South Korea and Taiwan are relatively little known. Tales of high costs have scared many travellers away from Japan, while Mongolia and North Korea have until recently been about as isolated as the South Pole. North-East Asia is waiting for you to explore it.

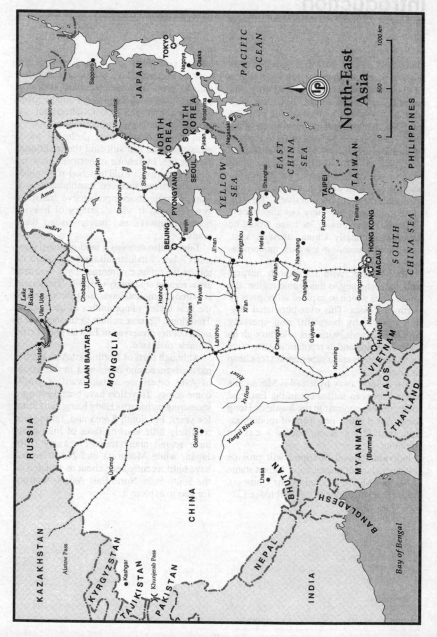

North-East Asia

Facts for the Visitor

PLANNING
When, How Much & How Long?
The lunar new year is a week-long holiday falling roughly in late January or February – it's a time to avoid! Nothing exciting happens at this time, but it's a family holiday so everything is closed and public transport is jam-packed. If you have to stay in North-East Asia at this time, stock up with food and reading matter and wait for the chaos to end. Lunar new year falls on 31 January in 1995, 19 February 1996, 7 February 1997, 28 January 1998 and on 16 February 1999. A similar but less severe week of chaos occurs during Chinese Easter, known as the Qing Ming Festival or Tomb Sweep Day. This usually falls in early April.

The season that most travellers try to avoid is winter. The northernmost regions of China, Mongolia, Korea and Japan experience frigid temperatures, as low as -45°C. On the other hand, northern winters are very dry and the snow makes for good scenery, but as you move south towards central China and southern Japan, winters tend to be chilly and rainy. The only places in North-East Asia that have pleasant winters are south-west Taiwan, the southern half of China's Hainan Island and Yunnan Province in south-west China.

The spring brings moderate temperatures but the weather is fickle – the temperature can plunge suddenly whenever the monsoonal winds blow in from Siberia. Spring is the time to see the various cherry-blossom festivals in Japan, South Korea and Taiwan. Unfortunately, the flowering season only lasts a few weeks and varies from year to year, so it isn't wise to plan your trip around this elusive phenomenon.

Summer is hot throughout the region except high in the mountains. High humidity and rains plague the regions near the Pacific Ocean, but it's much drier as one travels north-west. Indeed, much of north-west China and Mongolia is desert. Summer is also the beginning of typhoon season, but this won't affect you if you keep at least 200 km inland.

Autumn is the best season for the entire region. Temperatures tend to be mild and the weather is dry.

Sporting enthusiasts may have different ideas about what is ideal weather. If you're a skier, January and February are the best months for a visit to the far north. Trekkers have a longer season – spring through autumn. Beach lovers should of course aim for the summer. Other than that, plan your trip according to the most comfortable seasons and your available funds.

Your budget will depend on how you live and travel. If you're moving around fast, going to lots of places and spending time in the big cities, then your day-to-day living costs are going to be quite high, and sometimes there is no alternative to paying up – being too tight with your money can spoil your trip as much as being robbed can.

Comparative Costs in North-East Asia
The bad news is that prices have been rising rapidly. While parts of China might qualify as inexpensive, in general no country in North-East Asia can be described as cheap. Some countries (Japan, for example) are frightfully expensive. The following should give some basis for comparison:

What Kind of Trip?
Your finances and commitments are likely to affect the kind of trip you have. Those who are working full-time will most likely have to make a mad dash or even settle for a tour. Travelling this way will of course only allow you to catch a glimpse of a foreign culture. Some travellers compensate for this by concentrating on a special interest, such as skiing, mountain climbing or temple viewing.

Most travellers using this book will have more time than money. If you fall into this

COMPARATIVE COSTS TABLE
(All prices in US$)

	China	Hong Kong	Japan	Macau	S Korea	Taiwan
100 km by bus	1.50		13.88		3.80	4.58
100 km by train	1.40		14.38		3.80	5.80
Big Mac	1.03	1.19	3.65	1.18	2.85	2.36
Cheap hotel	15.00	32.00	40.00	20.00	12.00	19.00
Cheap restaurant	1.50	3.89	6.75	3.00	3.50	2.10
Glass of beer	0.20	5.00	4.50	4.00	2.50	3.45
Hostel	2.80	10.38	19.65	4.50	8.00	6.87
Loaf of bread	0.40	0.70	2.25	0.60	1.75	1.00
Local phone call	0.02	0.13	0.09	0.12	0.04	0.04
One litre petrol	0.30	1.05	1.36	1.10	0.75	0.62
Time magazine	3.30	3.89	6.19	3.89	3.75	4.18

Mongolia
With budget accommodation and no tour, as low as $20 per day. With tours, US$30 to $100 per day
North Korea
$100 to $180 per person per day

category, you're part of a time-honoured tradition. Spending more time in one place is preferable to a mad dash, but if finances become a problem, you might have to either cut the trip short or turn your journey into a working holiday.

What to Bring

Bring as little as possible as it's better to start with too little rather than too much – you may surprise yourself with how little you need.

A backpack is still the most popular carrying container as it is commodious and the only way to go if you have to do any walking. On the debit side a backpack is awkward to load on and off buses and trains and doesn't offer much protection for your valuables.

An alternative is a travel pack, which is a combination backpack and shoulder bag. They're not really suitable for long hiking trips but they're much easier to carry than a bag. In either case get some tabs sewn on so you can semi-thief-proof it with small padlocks. Forget suitcases.

Inside? Lightweight and compact are two words that should be etched in your mind when you're deciding what to bring. Saw the handle off your toothbrush if you have to –

anything to keep the weight down! You only need two sets of clothes – one to wear and one to wash. You will, no doubt, be buying clothes along the way – except for Japan and possibly Taiwan, clothing is cheap in Asia, and you can find some real bargains in Hong Kong and China. However, don't believe sizes as 'large' in Asia is often equivalent to 'medium' in the West.

Nylon sports shoes are best as they're comfortable, washable and lightweight. If you're going to be in cold weather, buy them oversized and wear heavy wool socks – it's better than carrying a pair of boots. Of course, if you're going to be in really bitter cold weather, you'll need insulated shoes or boots, but get something lightweight. A pair of thongs (flip-flops) are useful footwear for indoors and in shower rooms.

A Swiss army knife (even if not made in Switzerland) comes in handy, but you don't need one with 27 separate functions. Basically, you need one small, sharp blade, a can opener and bottle opener – a built-in magnifying glass or backscratcher isn't necessary.

It's wise to bring a few recent passport-size photos (5x5 cm). See the Visas section later in this chapter for further information.

The secret of successful packing is plastic bags or 'stuff bags' – they keep things not only separate and clean but also dry.

The following is a checklist of other things you might consider packing.

Passport, money, address book, business cards, visa photos, passport photos, electric immersion coil (for making hot water), cup, padlock, camera & accessories, sunglasses, alarm clock, leakproof water bottle, torch (flashlight), comb, compass, daypack, long pants, short pants, long shirt, T-shirt, nylon jacket, overcoat, sweater, woollen stocking cap, mittens, raincover for backpack, rainsuit or poncho, razor, razor blades, shaving cream, sewing kit, spoon, sunhat, sunscreen, toilet paper, tampons, toothbrush, toothpaste, dental floss, deodorant, shampoo, long underwear, socks, nail clipper, tweezers, mosquito repellent, vitamins, painkillers, laxative, anti-diarrhoeal drugs, contraceptives (including condoms) and any special medications you use plus a copy of the prescription.

The padlock will lock your bag to a train or bus luggage rack and will also fortify your hotel room, which often has a place to attach the padlock. It will come in handy at some youth hostels which have lockers. You'll need a medium-sized padlock, as a heavy-duty one will not fit through the latches usually provided.

A final thought: airlines do lose bags from time to time and you've got a much better chance of it not being yours if it is tagged with your name and address *inside* the bag as well as outside. Other tags can always fall off or be removed.

Appearances & Conduct

Although Asians expect madness from foreigners and will make allowances, there are certain standards of dress and behaviour which are expected. Knowing some of these common courtesies will make your trip smoother.

Fitting in rates higher among Asians than standing out – children who are naturally left-handed are taught to use the right hand just to avoid being 'odd'! Western notions about individuality can cause offence in the Orient – a punk haircut and tattered jeans will not win you any points with most Asians,

especially immigration officers and other figures of authority.

Wearing shorts is OK in all the countries of this book except Korea and Mongolia, but long trousers are more acceptable. People dress more formally in big cities than in the countryside. Very short shorts, miniskirts and see-through clothing can easily cause offence except maybe in ultra-fashionable Hong Kong. Public nudity is simply not on, unless you want to see the inside of an Asian police station or prison.

Thongs should never be worn outdoors in public places, but a regular sandal with a strap across the back of the ankle will be OK. This is somewhat less true in the hottest regions during summer, but even in such places you may not be allowed to enter restaurants or theatres if your feet aren't 'strapped-in'.

One quaint sign spotted in Korea said, 'Please don't wear shoes in this room – thank you very big'. Bad English or not, the point to remember is that in Japan, Korea and Taiwan, shoes are generally not worn in homes or some hotel rooms, especially where the floor is carpeted or covered with tatami mats. If you see shoes piled up next to the doorway, that's a sure sign that you should remove yours too.

Abrasive Western reactions to incompetence, delays, mistakes and dishonesty are totally unpalatable to Asians, who are acutely aware of loss of face. Should this occur in front of others it can have a devastating effect. You'll get a lot further with government officials, ticket agents and hotel clerks if you keep smiling and bowing – even when you hate them. Bear this in mind while you are in Asia – if you have a sharp tongue, keep it in check.

When handing a piece of paper, a business card, or a gift to someone, always use both hands – this shows respect. If you must use one hand, be sure it's the right hand.

When you want to set down a pair of chopsticks, place them horizontally across the top of your bowl. Never leave a pair of chopsticks sticking vertically in your food. This resembles two sticks of incense placed vertically in an incense burner which is a universal death sign in most countries of the Orient.

If you write a letter or note to anyone, avoid writing in red ink. A note written in red is considered unfriendly, and in many countries it signifies that the writer is going to die soon. If you get stuck and must write something in red, be sure to apologise to the person receiving the note, explaining that your other pen stopped working.

In Japan, Korea and Taiwan, it's considered rude to eat something while walking on the street. It's OK to eat something while standing next to a foodstall or sitting on a park bench, but not while walking. The Japanese are particularly strict about this, although they seem to make an exception for ice-cream cones, to which they are thoroughly addicted.

Death, divorce and other such negative matters are not suitable topics for discussion except with close friends and relatives. Asians will often ask if you're married – if you're divorced or widowed, just say you're not married and let it go at that.

When you meet people for the first time, give them a business card – if you don't have any, get some made and always carry them. Except in very poor places like rural China or Mongolia, most people have business cards and hand them out like confetti. Even if your last job was working the counter at McDonald's, try to come up with something impressive – *Joe Smith, Customer Relations Specialist*. Business cards can be printed in Asia easily enough, but be sure to check the spelling after they've done the typesetting as mistakes when typing English are very common. Hong Kong has business card machines in some of the major train and ferry terminals.

Lastly, there is a special etiquette concerning toilets because the plumbing systems in much of Asia cannot handle toilet paper. If you see a wastebasket right next to the toilet, in most cases this is where the used toilet paper goes. In some hotels the owners will be quite angry if you flush paper down the toilet and jam up the system.

The Top 10
1. Nara, Japan, where deer will eat out of your hand
2. Sorak-san National Park, South Korea, but only when the kids are in school
3. The Ice Lantern Festival in Harbin, China
4. The Forbidden City in Beijing
5. The Turpan oasis in China's Xinjiang Province
6. Dali in China's Yunnan Province
7. The walk up Hohuanshan in Taiwan
8. Hong Kong's Victoria Peak at night
9. Winning big in a Macau casino
10. Chinese food

The Bottom 10
Thumbs Down Awards go to:

1. The Lunar New Year
2. Hong Kong's money-grubbing shopkeepers
3. Taiwan's Window On China
4. Japan's Beppu Hot Springs
5. The China International Travel Service (CITS)
6. Nightlife in North Korea
7. South Korea's immigration office
8. Losing big in a Macau casino
9. Japanese prices
10. Mongolian food

VISAS
Visas can be annoying, expensive and time-consuming pieces of red tape. Many countries do not require a visa for short stays – see the section on visas under the individual countries in this book.

Effectively, a visa is a permit to enter a country. Normally, these are stamped in your passport, though they're occasionally issued on separate pieces of paper. You can either get them before you go or along the way. The advantage of predeparture collection is that it doesn't waste travelling time, the post office can do the legwork, and occasionally 'difficult' embassies are less difficult in your own country. The two main drawbacks are that some countries may not even be represented in your own country, and often visas have a limited lifespan – it is no good getting a visa that will expire in three months if you are not going to be in the country until four months later.

You can always get a visa at an embassy or a consulate in a neighbouring or nearby country, and sometimes it is available at the border or at the airport on arrival. It is often cheaper to get visas in neighbouring countries. Be aware that embassies and consulates are notorious for using the flimsiest excuse to take a day off: during all local holidays, holidays 'back home' (wherever that is), during the ambassador's birthday or when the moon is full. You need to pay attention to these details – if you buy an air ticket for next day departure, you may find yourself out of luck if you require a visa straight away.

You normally need a photograph of yourself to apply for a visa – some countries even require three photos for one visa. Almost all countries will accept cheapie prints you can get from a machine, but at least one country (South Korea) wants passport-quality photos (5x5 cm). To save time, it would be prudent to keep about 10 cheapie and three passport-quality photos with you while travelling – you can always get more made later.

Some visas are issued free while others will cost you money. There may be other requirements too, like having a certain amount of money or travellers' cheques. You may have to provide the dreaded 'ticket out', which means before you can obtain a visa to enter the country you must have a ticket to leave it. This can often be a real nuisance if you should want to leave by some obscure method for which tickets are only available within the country, or want to keep your travel plans flexible. In fact, few countries in North-East Asia require a ticket out unless you stay too long, return too many times or hold a passport from a Third World country. If you fall into these categories, the answer is to get the cheapest ticket out with a reputable airline and have it refunded later.

There are many types of visas – tourist, transit, business, student, working, resident etc. In most cases, you should apply for a tourist visa. There are also single-entry versus multiple-entry visas. Multiple-entry visas are usually easier to obtain in your home country, and some are valid for up to five years. These are worthwhile getting if you plan a long trip with a lot of zig-zagging across Asia rather than a straight through quick journey. Some countries don't care if you work or study on a tourist visa, but others are very strict. South Korea, for example, has become really sticky – even if you have a working visa, they will not allow you to enrol in a language course because that requires a student visa. Furthermore, these rules are enforced with hefty fines and occasional prison sentences. Regulations do change periodically – when in doubt, check with the immigration authorities.

DOCUMENTS
A passport is essential, and if yours is within a few months of expiry get a new one now, as many countries will not issue a visa if your passport has less than six months of validity remaining. Also, be sure it has plenty of space for visas and entry and exit stamps. It could be embarrassing to run out of blank pages when you are too far away from an embassy to get a new passport issued or extra pages added.

Losing your passport is very bad news – getting a new one takes time and money. It helps if you have a separate record of the passport number, issue date and a photocopy of your birth certificate. While you're compiling that information, add the serial numbers of your travellers' cheques, details of health insurance and US$100 or so as emergency cash, and keep all that material totally separate from your passport, cheques and other cash.

If your passport is stolen, you'll need to make your way to the nearest embassy or consulate representing your country. Don't expect much help beyond replacing your passport – embassy staff are notorious for leaving travellers twisting in the wind.

If you plan to be driving abroad get an International Driving Permit from your local automobile association. They are usually valid for one year only. Even if you're on a tight budget, there are a few areas where you might want to rent or buy a motorcycle, such as Taiwan and Japan.

A Hostelling International (HI) card can be useful in Japan, Korea and Hong Kong. Although some Asian hostels don't require that you belong to the HI, they will sometimes charge less if you're a card-carrying member.

If you plan to pick up some cash by teaching, photocopies of university diplomas, transcripts and letters of recommendation could prove helpful. If you're travelling with your spouse, a photocopy of your marriage licence just might come in handy should you become involved with the law, hospitals or other bureaucratic authorities. Useful (though not essential) is an International Health Certificate – see Immunisations in the Health section later in this chapter for more details.

The International Student Identity Card (ISIC) can perform all sorts of miracles, such as getting you a discount on some international and domestic flights, as well as discounts at museums, parks etc. Small wonder there is a worldwide trade in fake cards, but the authorities have tightened up on the abuse of student cards in several ways. You may be required to provide additional proof of student status, such as having 'student' marked in your passport or a letter from your university or college stating that you are a student. Additionally, there are now maximum age limits (usually 26) for some concessions. Nevertheless fake cards are still widely available and useable, but some are of quite poor quality.

Remember that a student is a very respectable thing to be, and if your passport has a blank space for an occupation you are much better off having 'student' there than something awkward like 'journalist' or 'photographer'.

MONEY
Estimate how much money you think you'll need, then multiply by three. You should have some money in hard cash (US dollars are the favourite) but most should be in travellers' cheques. American Express,

Thomas Cook or Visa travellers' cheques are probably the best to carry because of their 'instant replacement' policies. The main idea of carrying cheques rather than cash is the protection they offer from theft, but it doesn't do a lot of good if you have to go back home first to get the refund. American Express has offices in many big cities in the region, but the replacement is not always as instant as the adverts would have you think. Keeping a record of the cheque numbers is vital, and it's very helpful to have the initial purchase receipts. Without these you may well find that 'instant' takes a very long time.

Credit cards are accepted easily in some places (Hong Kong), but in others (Mongolia) they are only just gaining acceptance so they may not be of much use to you. In Japan they tend to be accepted only by the more expensive shops. Americans are prohibited by their government from using credit cards in North Korea.

Travellers' cheques, including American Express, are often available in yen – if you're going to spend a long time in Japan they might be a good idea. Travellers' cheques are available in Hong Kong dollars but these are *not* a good idea, except in Hong Kong.

Money from China, South Korea and Taiwan can be changed in Hong Kong but can be difficult to get rid of elsewhere. North Korean and Mongolian currency isn't worth the paper it's printed on once you leave those countries.

When exchanging money for local currency remember to keep your transaction receipts as you will need these to convert the local currency back to hard currency, especially in China, Korea and Taiwan. There are no restrictions on money-changing in Hong Kong and Macau.

The Hong Kong dollar is as readily accepted as the Macau dollar in Macau, but the Macau pataca is difficult to unload in Hong Kong – only a few banks will do it.

It's a good idea to take some travellers' cheques, some hard cash and some local currency. Carry some cheques in small denominations for last-minute conversions. As you may be charged a service fee for each cheque, don't have it all in small amounts. It is often worth checking around a couple of banks as exchange rates do vary and there are those hidden extras like service fees. Most airports are good for changing money, except Hong Kong airport where the exchange rate is terrible. Banks are usually your best bet.

Cash is very useful for emergency non-bank transactions you have to make from time to time, but forget about black market money-changing – it's virtually disappeared in North-East Asia, except Mongolia where *everybody* does it.

The only safe place to carry all this money is next to your skin. A money belt or pouch or an extra pocket inside your jeans will help to keep things with their rightful owner. Remember that if you lose cash you have lost it forever, so don't go overboard on the convenience of cash over cheques. Try to have a totally separate emergency stash for use if everything else disappears.

If you have to have money sent to you, ask your home bank to send you a telegraphic transfer and specify the city and the bank you want the money transferred to. If your bank prefers to nominate its own correspondent bank, ask it to advise you of the address. Hong Kong, for example, seems to have banks on every street corner, and tracking down the one with your money could take a long time.

Money sent by telegraphic transfer should reach you in a couple of days, but some countries (China) are horribly slow – just what they do with the money while you're waiting is anybody's guess. Cheques sent by mail could take a month or more to clear. When you finally get the cash you can usually have it in US dollar travellers' cheques or converted into local currency – foreign currency is not often available. Hong Kong is exceptional – it's the banking centre of Asia and you can be paid in everything from Swiss francs to Indonesian rupiah.

ELECTRICITY

In Asia, electric power comes in a variety of voltages and different plug designs. Try to avoid dealing with it – life will be simpler if

you can manage without your electric hair dryer or radio. In some countries you'll find two standard voltages in use (South Korea, Japan & Taiwan), or maybe just one voltage but a variety of plug designs (Hong Kong & China) – see the individual country chapters of this book for details. The following chart gives a quick rundown of the different voltages and illustrates the types of plugs required:

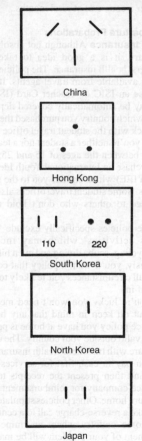

China

Hong Kong

110   220

South Korea

North Korea

Japan

The plugs for Mongolia & Taiwan are found in the Facts for the Visitor section of their respective chapters.

HEALTH

Health and fitness while travelling depend on several things – your predeparture protection (immunisations), diet, sanitation and exposure to people infected with nasty diseases. North-East Asia is generally quite a healthy region to travel in and it's unlikely you'll have any serious problems if you exercise proper precautions. Plan your immunisations ahead – some must be spaced out over a course of several months.

Predeparture Preparations

Health Insurance Although not absolutely necessary, it is a good idea to take out travellers' health insurance. The policies are usually available from travel agents. If you purchase an ISIC or Teacher Card (ISTC), you may be automatically covered depending on which country you purchased the card in. Check with the student travel office to be sure. If you're neither a student nor a teacher but are between the ages of 15 and 25, you can purchase an International Youth Identity Card (YIEE) which entitles you to the same benefits. Some student travel offices also sell insurance to others who don't hold these cards.

Some policies specifically exclude 'dangerous activities' which may include motorcycling, scuba diving and even hiking. Obviously, you'll want a policy that covers you in all circumstances you're likely to find yourself in.

If you're lucky you won't need medical care, but do keep in mind that any health insurance policy you have at home is probably not valid outside your country. The usual procedure with travellers' health insurance is that you pay in cash first for services rendered and then present the receipts to the insurance company for reimbursement after you return home. Other policies stipulate that you make a reverse-charge call to a centre in your home country where an immediate assessment of your problem will be made.

The best policies cover the expense of flying you home in a dire emergency.

Medical Kit Carry a small, straightforward medical kit with any necessary medicines, anti-diarrhoeal drugs (Lomotil, Imodium), a laxative, tweezers (for removing splinters), plasters, antiseptic, paracetamol (Panadol, Tylenol etc) and a thermometer. Rehydration kits can be useful if you suffer from severe diarrhoea. In South Korea, Taiwan and China, you'll usually find that if a medicine is available at all it will generally be available over the counter and will be much cheaper than in the West.

Immunisations Some countries require vaccinations against cholera if you arrive within five days of leaving an infected area – ditto for yellow fever.

Though not required, some vaccinations which might prove useful include influenza, tetanus, hepatitis B, tuberculosis, and (for Tibet) rabies. If you're bringing children, be sure they've had all the usual childhood vaccines such as polio, diphtheria, whooping cough, measles, mumps, rubella etc.

As proof of all these scratches, jabs and punctures, you'd be wise to get an International Health Certificate to be signed and stamped by your doctor and local health authority. Although you'll seldom be asked to show it, if you pass through an epidemic area it might suddenly become compulsory. In some countries (Australia, the UK and many countries in Asia) immunisations are available from airport or government health centres. Travel agents or airline offices will tell you where they are. In Japan the least expensive place for vaccinations is the Tokyo Port Authority or the health facility at Narita Airport.

Basic Rules

Most food in North-East Asia is pretty healthy. The main thing to look out for is the cleanliness of the utensils – disposable chopsticks are widely available throughout the region and it would be wise to use them or carry your own. Take care about what you eat – make sure food is well cooked and hasn't been sitting around. Make sure fresh food has been properly cleaned. Uncooked food is a problem in China – avoid salads and always peel fruit before eating.

Water poses a bigger problem than food. In Japan and Hong Kong there is no problem at all. Korea is also pretty safe, but Taiwan is marginal and in China water should definitely be boiled. Freezing things doesn't kill germs, so don't trust ice cubes. Bottled water, beer and soft drinks should be safe. Hotels do provide vacuum flasks of boiled water for guests so finding something to drink is not too difficult. Water purification tablets could be worth taking for emergencies, but you probably won't have trouble finding boiled water or bottled drinks anywhere.

It is best to bring your spectacle prescription with you, though in many Asian countries you get a free eye examination when you buy spectacles. If you need glasses you can get them made up cheaply and efficiently in Hong Kong, but avoid the eyeglass shops in tourist-trap ghettoes like Tsimshatsui.

Do yourself a favour and get your teeth checked before you depart. Dental problems in remote areas are no fun.

Medical Problems & Treatment

If you're going to get sick in North-East Asia, you're probably best advised to do it in Taiwan where medical care is excellent and reasonably priced. South Korea probably comes in second place. Of course, Japan has outstanding health facilities charging outstanding prices. Hong Kong has modern facilities and moderate prices, but as the 1997 deadline for China's takeover approaches, qualified health care professionals are emigrating in droves. Macau isn't too bad, though not recommended for major surgery. China's hospitals are fine if you don't mind 1950s technology. Mongolia is not a good place to get sick, while North Korea remains a big unknown. All of the above applies to dental care too, except that Hong Kong is unusually expensive.

If you need medical help your embassy or consulate can usually advise on a good place to go, but don't count on it – just getting

through the layers of bureaucrats and security guards to talk to somebody can make you sick. Your best bet for advice on hospitals and clinics is usually your hotel or the local English-speaking tourist bureau.

Tetanus & Typhoid Both are serious illnesses best treated by a doctor. Prevention is the best option and there are three types of vaccinations available: plain typhoid protection; TAB, which protects against typhoid and paratyphoid A and B; and TABT, which protects you against the lot and also against tetanus. TABT lasts for three years.

Diarrhoea Intestinal upsets are usually due simply to a change of diet or a system unused to spicy food. Many times, however, contaminated food or water is the problem. If prevention fails and you do get a stomach upset, the simplest treatment is to do nothing. If your system can fight off the invaders naturally you'll probably build up some immunity. Eat lightly, and stick to hot water or herb tea – regular tea, coffee, cola or anything else containing caffeine may increase diarrhoea. Your diet should be as free as possible of roughage and spices – if you start eating beans with hot sauce, you're going to regret it. If you do decide to resort to modern medicines don't do so too readily and don't overdo them; if you start a course of antibiotics follow it through to the end.

There are various over-the-counter cures like the popular Lomotil. The name indicates that it 'lowers motility'; it simply slows your system down and lets it work things out. Imodium is also effective, but even plain codeine will often do as well. Antibiotics will attack the bacterial invaders, but also kill off friendly bacteria as well, which is why you shouldn't resort to them at the first sign of illness.

Dysentery The word 'dysentery' is used far too casually by many travellers. If you've just got loose movements, then you've got diarrhoea. If blood or pus are also present then you probably have dysentery. If on top of that you have a fever then it's probably bacillary dysentery and you need an antibiotic like tetracycline or ampicillin. If there is no fever, then it could be amoebic dysentery, a potentially serious illness which must be treated with an anti-amoebic drug like Tinidazole, known as Fasigyn, or metronidazole (Flagyl). If you take Flagyl, do not under any circumstances consume alcohol at the same time – not a drop! Similar to amoebic dysentery, but not as dangerous, is giardia, which is also treated with Flagyl.

Whether you just have travellers' diarrhoea or something worse, it's important to keep your fluid and salt intake up to avoid dehydration.

Constipation Ironically, some travellers are afflicted with the opposite problem, constipation. This is especially true when visiting northern Asia in the winter when fresh fruits, vegetables and other high-fibre foods are scarce. Obviously, the best solution is to try and eat more fibre – carry some bran if you have this problem. Having a laxative in your first-aid kit wouldn't be a bad idea, though these can easily be bought along the way if you can communicate your needs to a local pharmacist. Failing that, strong coffee and tea often have a mildly laxative effect on many people.

Some travellers speculate that you can cure constipation by eating at the dirtiest, scuzziest restaurant or street stall you can find, thus inducing diarrhoea. Although the theory sounds logical, this is generally *not* a good idea.

Hepatitis The hep comes in many varieties, most commonly A and B. The best preventive measure against hepatitis A is to eat food that is clean and well cooked, and to use disposable chopsticks. A vaccine exists, Havrix, but is not readily available.

The disease is spread by contaminated food or water. The symptoms are fever, chills, headache, fatigue, feelings of weakness and aches and pains, followed by loss of appetite, nausea, vomiting, abdominal pain, dark urine, light-coloured faeces and jaundiced skin, and the whites of eyes may turn yellow. In some cases you may feel unwell, tired, have no appetite and experience aches and pains. If you should be so unfortunate as to get the dreaded hepatitis you should seek medical advice, but in general there is not much you can do apart from rest, drink lots of fluids, eat lightly and avoid fatty foods. People who have had hepatitis must forego alcohol for six months after the illness, as hepatitis attacks the liver and it needs that amount of time to recover.

Hepatitis B is usually transmitted in the same three ways as the AIDS virus: by sexual intercourse; contaminated needles; or inherited by an infant from an infected mother. For reasons unknown, infection rates are very high in China, Hong Kong and Taiwan, but it is probably a case of being passed down from mother to child and then spread sexually. In recent years, it has also been spreading rapidly in developed countries through casual sex and drug use. Innocent use of needles – ear piercing, tattooing and acupuncture – can also spread the disease. The symptoms of type B are much the same as for type A except that they are more severe and may lead to irreparable liver damage or even liver cancer.

Although there is no treatment for hepatitis B, there is a very effective vaccine, but it must be given before you've been exposed. Once you've got the virus, you're a carrier for life and the vaccine is useless. Therefore you need a blood test before the vaccine is administered to determine whether you're a carrier. The immunisation schedule requires two injections at least a month apart followed by a third dose five months after the second.

Hepatitis Non-A and Non-B is a blanket term formerly used for several different strains of hepatitis, which have now been separately identified. Hepatitis C is similar to B but is less common. Hepatitis D (the 'delta particle') is also similar to B and always occurs in concert with it; its occurrence is currently limited to intravenous drug users. Hepatitis E, however, is similar to A and is spread in the same manner, by water or food contamination.

Tests are available for these strands, but

are very expensive. Travellers shouldn't be too paranoid about this proliferation of hepatitis strains; they are fairly rare (so far) and following the same precautions as for A and B should be all that's necessary to avoid them.

Rabies It's very rare, but rabies is such a deadly disease that it's worthy of your attention. You're probably most at risk of catching it in Tibet, where packs of wild dogs roam the streets of major towns and villages. Other mammals, such as monkeys and rats, can also transmit the rabies virus to humans. If you are bitten by a rabid animal, try to get the wound flushed out and scrubbed immediately with soapy water and then alcohol. It would be prudent to seek professional treatment since rabies carries a 100% fatality rate if it reaches the brain. How long you have from the time of being bitten until it's too late varies – anywhere from 10 days to a year depending on where the bite occurred. Those bitten around the face and upper part of the body are in the most immediate danger. Don't wait for symptoms to occur – if you think there's a good chance that you've been bitten by a rabid animal, get medical attention promptly even if it means cancelling your trip.

A vaccine for rabies exists though few people bother to get it because the risk of infection is so low. The vaccine will not give you 100% immunity, but will extend the time you have for seeking treatment, and the treatment will not need to be nearly so extensive.

Tuberculosis Tuberculosis (TB) bacteria are transmitted by inhalation. Coughing spreads infectious droplets into the air. In closed, crowded spaces with poor ventilation (like a train compartment), the air can remain contaminated for some time. Especially in overcrowded China, where the custom is to cough and spit in every direction, it's not hard to see why infection rates remain high.

Many carriers of TB experience no symptoms. The disease is opportunistic – the patient feels fine, but the disease suddenly becomes active when the body is weakened by other factors such as injury, poor nutrition, surgery or old age. People who are in good health are less likely to catch the disease. TB strikes at the lungs and the fatality rate is about 10%.

There are good drugs to treat TB, but prevention is the best cure. If you're only travelling for a short time there is no need to be overly worried, as it is usually contracted after repeated exposures.

The effective vaccine for TB is called BCG and is most often given to school children because it must be taken before infection occurs. Once you have TB, you carry it for life. If you want to be vaccinated, you first must be tested to see if you're a carrier – if you are, the vaccination will do no good. The only disadvantage of the vaccine is that, once given, the recipient will always test positive with the TB skin test. Even if you never travel, the tuberculosis vaccine could be useful as the disease is increasing worldwide.

Skin Problems Hot, humid weather can lead to fungal infections of the skin. Bathe twice daily and dry yourself thoroughly before getting dressed. Standing in front of an electric fan is a good way to get thoroughly dry. Apply an anti-fungal ointment or powder (ointments are better) to the affected area – popular brand names are Desenex, Tinactin or Mycota, all available in Hong Kong. The Chinese have equivalent medications but you may have a hard time getting this across to a pharmacist who doesn't speak English. Wear light cotton underwear or very thin nylon that is 'breathable' – maybe even no underwear at all if the condition gets serious. Wear the lightest and loosest outer clothing possible when the weather is really hot and humid. For athlete's foot, wearing open-toed sandals will often solve the problem without further treatment. It also helps to clean between the toes with warm soapy water and an old toothbrush.

Influenza & Bronchitis You may have heard of the 'Shanghai flu', but it's a lot more than just a case of the sniffles. China is one vast reservoir of influenza viruses and many travellers find it impossible to get well until they leave the country. After a week of the flu you may well be left with bronchitis, which is characterised by almost constant coughing that brings up large quantities of thick phlegm. The Chinese have made a national sport of spitting this gob in every direction which helps spread the disease.

Bronchitis can be very distressing – it is usually worse at night, making it impossible to sleep. You can attack the virus with antibiotics, but unpleasant side effects may result so it's wise to try more conservative treatments first. Drinking hot fluids helps, as does keeping warm and resting in bed. Keep your head elevated at night with pillows – otherwise, the phlegm tends to creep up into the throat and set off a coughing fit. Cigarette smoke is a disaster – keep away from it. If all this fails, give your battered lungs a vacation – a warm beach in Thailand may be what you need.

Vaccinations for influenza are often hard to come by – different strains appear annually. Vaccines are usually available in the autumn only from public health services in Western countries and the shot is good for no more than a year.

Sexually Transmitted Diseases Sexual contact with an infected partner spreads these diseases, and while abstinence is the only 100% preventative, use of a condom is also effective. Gonorrhea and syphilis are the commonest, and sores, blisters or rashes around the genitals, discharges, or pain when urinating are common symptoms. Symptoms may be less marked or not observed at all in women. Syphilis symptoms eventually disappear completely but the disease continues and can cause severe problems in later years. Treatment of gonorrhea and syphilis is by antibiotics.

There are numerous other sexually transmitted diseases, for most of which effective treatment is available. There is no cure for herpes or AIDS. Carry condoms when you're travelling, and avoid any sexual practice that involves the exchange of body fluids.

AIDS can be spread through infected blood transfusions (most developing countries do not screen blood for transfusions) or by dirty needles – vaccinations, acupuncture and tattooing are as dangerous as intravenous drug use if the equipment is not clean. If you do need an injection it may be a good idea to buy a new syringe from a pharmacy and ask the doctor to use it.

Malaria While malaria is not a severe problem in North-East Asia, there have been periodic outbreaks, especially in rural parts of southern China. The problem is most serious in the summer. Prevention consists of weekly doses of chloroquine, but there are chloroquine-resistant strains of malaria around. Other drugs used to prevent malaria are daily doses of doxycycline or paludrine, but both have side effects and should only be used for the short term. Ask your doctor before gobbling any anti-malarial pills. Should you be so unfortunate as to catch malaria the same tablets in much greater doses are also the cure. Don't take chances – see a doctor if you suspect you've got malaria. Blood tests are needed to determine if you've been cured, otherwise the disease may recur. Where there are mosquitoes around, mosquito nets, mosquito coils and insect repellent all offer some protection.

Women's Health
Gynaecological Problems An inadequate diet, lowered resistance through the use of antibiotics for stomach upsets and even contraceptive pills can lead to vaginal infections when travelling in hot climates. Keeping the genital area clean, and wearing skirts or loose-fitting trousers and cotton underwear will help to prevent infections.

Yeast infections, characterised by a rash, itch and discharge, can be treated with a vinegar or even lemon-juice douche or with yoghurt. Nystatin suppositories are the usual medical prescription – these can be hard to find in China or Mongolia, so bring them. Trichomonas is a more serious infection;

symptoms are a discharge and a burning sensation when urinating. Sexual partners must also be treated. If a vinegar-water douche is not effective medical attention should be sought. Metronidazole (Flagyl) is the prescribed drug.

Pregnancy Most miscarriages occur during the first three months of pregnancy, so this is the most risky time to travel as far as your own health is concerned. Miscarriage is not uncommon, and can occasionally lead to severe bleeding. The last three months should also be spent within reasonable distance of good medical care. A baby born as early as 24 weeks stands a chance of survival, but only in a good modern hospital. Pregnant women should avoid all unnecessary medication, but vaccinations and malarial prophylactics should still be taken where possible. Additional care should be taken to prevent illness and particular attention should be paid to diet and nutrition. Alcohol and nicotine, for example, should be avoided.

Women travellers often find that their periods become irregular or even cease while they're on the road. Remember that a missed period in these circumstances doesn't necessarily indicate pregnancy. There are hospitals, health posts or Family Planning clinics in many small and large urban centres in Asian countries, where you can seek advice and have a urine test to determine whether you are pregnant.

DANGERS & ANNOYANCES
Theft
The situation has worsened in recent years. Places like South Korea and Taiwan, once perfectly safe, have become increasingly dangerous, though nowhere near as bad as China. Theft in North-East Asia is rarely violent – the biggest threat comes from pickpockets and bag slashers.

The most important things to avoid getting stolen are your passport, papers, tickets and money. It's best always to carry these next to your skin or in a sturdy leather pouch on your belt. Be especially careful on buses and trains and even in hotels – don't leave valuables lying around in your room. Be a little wary of your fellow travellers too – unfortunately not everybody on the road is scrupulously honest.

Dope
It is around, both in its light and heavy varieties, and everybody, including the authorities, knows about it. In North-East Asia cannabis is not part of the local culture in the way it is in some other parts of Asia, and nowhere in the region is it legal. Although enforcement is sporadic, occasionally the authorities decide to 'make an example' out of some traveller. If you want to do first-hand research on the human rights situation in Asian prisons, using and selling drugs is one way to do it.

Mosquitoes
Aside from being annoying, some types of mosquitoes spread malaria and dengue fever. Mosquito incense coils are widely available in Asia, and these not only scare off mosquitoes, but actually kill them. Unfortunately, the smoke is not particularly good for your lungs, so if you're going to resort to chemical weapons, at least keep a window open. Somewhat less irritating to the lungs are mosquito pads – chemically treated cardboard placed in a small electric heater. The heat causes the chemical to slowly evaporate, thus driving off or killing the mosquitoes. Both the heater and the mosquito pads are widely available in the region from grocery and department stores.

Even safer is insect repellent, especially if it contains the magic ingredient diethyl toluamide, commonly known as 'deet'. Autan and OFF! are popular brands widely available in Western countries and Asia. In areas where malaria is common, it wouldn't hurt to use both incense coils and insect repellent simultaneously.

A mosquito net can be too bulky to carry, and is of no use unless you have a way to suspend it over your bed. Some hotels supply mosquito nets, but this is rare.

Snakes

We speak here not of Hong Kong shopkeepers, but of the kind that crawl around on their bellies and make hissing noises. Asia has a fairly thorough assortment of poisonous snakes, most commonly in subtropical regions such as south-east China, Taiwan and the southernmost islands of Japan.

There are several poisonous species such as the cobra, habu and bamboo snake. All sea snakes are poisonous and are readily identified by their flat tails. Taiwan has an interesting snake called the '100 pacer', so called because if it bites, you can expect to walk about 100 paces before dropping dead.

Fortunately, you probably won't get to see many poisonous snakes in North-East Asia, except on your dinner plate in Guangzhou's exotic Snake Restaurant. Snakes tend to be shy, and – contrary to popular rumour – do not eat people. Most snake-bite victims are people who accidentally step on a snake. Be careful about walking through subtropical areas with a lot of undergrowth. Wearing boots gives a little more protection than running shoes.

Should you be so unfortunate as to get bitten, try to remain calm (sounds easier than it really is) and not run around. The conventional wisdom is to rest and allow the poison to be absorbed slowly. Tying a rag or towel around the limb to apply pressure slows down the poison, but the use of tourniquets is not advisable because it can cut off circulation and cause gangrene. Cutting the skin and sucking out the poison has also been widely discredited. Immersion in cold water is also considered useless.

Treatment in a hospital with an antivenin would be ideal. However, getting the victim to a hospital is only half the battle – you will also need to identify the snake. In this particular case, it might be worthwhile to kill the snake and take its body along, but don't attempt that if it means getting bitten again. Try to transport the victim on a makeshift stretcher.

All this may sound discouraging, but the simple fact is that there is very little first-aid treatment you can give which will do much

good. Fortunately, snake bite is rare and the vast majority of victims survive even without medical treatment.

ACTIVITIES

Hiking

Local hiking clubs are active in Hong Kong, Japan, South Korea and Taiwan. Most trips are day hikes, though overnight treks are possible in the more remote regions of these small countries. Hiking, trekking and rock climbing equipment is widely available, and is quite cheap in South Korea and Taiwan.

Given the tiny land area and urban congestion, Hong Kong has a surprisingly large number of hiking enthusiasts. Hong Kong is fairly mountainous, though you'd be hard pressed to find a wilderness area for an overnight trip.

Hiking in China is a mixed bag. There are undoubtedly unlimited possibilities for trekking through some of the most ruggedly beautiful and remote territory on earth. The problem is that the best areas (remote corners of Tibet for example) are mostly closed to foreigners. There are no local hiking clubs that foreigners can join, and you won't find the sort of free trekking that is so popular in Nepal. For most travellers, hiking in China means climbing some of the 'sacred mountains' which are criss-crossed with stone steps and dotted with temples, pavilions and statues. These hikes are worth doing, but they're not exactly a wilderness experience.

Mongolia has tremendous potential for hiking, but this activity is hampered by the lack of transport to the countryside.

Surfing

Surfing is possible in most countries mentioned in this book, though you can forget it in Mongolia. China and North Korea both seem pretty hopeless for renting equipment. Hong Kong and Taiwan are the most likely venues for surfers, though Japan and Korea are possible if you can tolerate cold water.

Skiing

Downhill skiing is popular in Japan and

catching on in South Korea and costs are slightly lower than in the West. It's cheaper in north-east China though the facilities leave much to be desired. As long as you don't have enormous feet, equipment rentals should not be a problem, but devoted skiers might want to bring their own boots.

Cross-country skiing is not well known in Asia even though there are some excellent places for pursuing this hobby – bringing your own equipment is strongly advised.

Whitewater Rafting

A quick glance at the map of North-East Asia makes it obvious that China has what whitewater enthusiasts crave – high mountains cut by long rivers, most of which have not yet been damned by dams. Indeed, China offers some of the most challenging whitewater runs in the world, and Western river runners have been beating a path to the People's Republic ever since it opened up to the outside world.

Sad to say, success has spoiled China's rafting and kayaking scene. Not that the rivers have become jam-packed with paddle-toting tourists – far from it. The problem is that greedy Chinese officials were quick to sense the lunacy of well-moneyed thrill-seekers, and now charge outrageous fees for the privilege of floating downstream. Certain popular venues like the Yangzi River are pretty much off limits to all but millionaires. To add insult to injury, there are plans to dam China's unspoilt rivers, including the Yangzi.

There are a few commercial whitewater outfitters in Japan, and even fewer in Taiwan – don't worry, all equipment is supplied. In South Korea, a few hardy souls have been exploring the remaining meagre unspoilt rivers on the east coast. The problem is that all these countries are small and their rivers have either been dammed or are too short to offer more than a few hours of excitement. Needless to say, it's mostly a summer activity, though Taiwan's rafting season is a little longer than that of most other countries in the region.

Courses

Language courses have been attracting a steady stream of devotees to Japan, China, Taiwan and South Korea, and the flow has increased along with the growing economic importance of North-East Asia. However, there are other regional specialities in the Orient which are worth investigating. Martial arts enthusiasts have for years been flocking to Japan and South Korea. Now that China has opened up, curious Westerners have come to study acupuncture, herbal medicine, calligraphy and Chinese watercolour painting.

WORK

It is possible to work in North-East Asia, and a few countries (Japan, South Korea and Taiwan) pay good salaries for teaching English. Some of these jobs are advertised in the English-language newspapers in various Asian countries. Many other jobs can be obtained through word of mouth – youth hostels are the likely place to enquire.

The big hurdle is the legalities. Most teaching jobs are illegal and you could get fined or deported. Enforcement varies – South Korea has clamped down with an iron fist. Taiwan, Japan and Hong Kong are tightening up, but it is still possible to work legally after battling mountains of red tape. Once your visa expires you may have a hard time renewing it – the authorities probably won't believe you want to be a tourist for six months or a year. You can often get around this by becoming a student in a legally recognised language school, but you'll have to pay tuition and attend class. Still, teaching English and studying an Asian language is not a bad thing to do if you want the experience of living in a foreign culture.

Arranging a work visa is usually possible if you're patient. The bureaucratic procedures take a few months to complete. The requirements are usually that you sign a one-year contract, pay income tax and test negative for the AIDS virus. It also helps to have impressive pieces of paper to show that you are qualified; a university diploma in almost any subject will do. If you change jobs, you have to go through the whole lengthy procedure again. If you quit or get fired, your work visa will be cancelled and you will be given just a few days to leave the country. Some foreigners have run into the problem of being cheated by their employers, especially in South Korea. The main question is whether you're willing to make a long-term commitment to this line of work.

Teaching English in China is feasible, but salaries are very low by Western standards, though still much higher than what a Chinese teacher would get for doing the same job. Enquire at Chinese embassies or universities if interested.

It's possible to teach English in Hong Kong, but the large number of expatriates keeps salaries low.

Attractive Western women can pick up good money working as bar hostesses or cocktail waitresses. In most cases, these are legitimate (though illegal) jobs and do not involve prostitution. Nevertheless, any woman entering these professions should have it made clear from the outset just what is expected of her.

If you have a special skill (accounting, computer programming) you may find it easy to land a good legal job with a big company on a long-term contract, but most budget travellers do not fall into this category.

Busking is a possibility for the desperate in Japan, Taiwan and Hong Kong. Others try selling paintings, jewellery and other goods on the street, and a few foreigners resort to begging. All this has not gone unnoticed by the police, who occasionally crack down with arrests, fines and deportations.

Some travellers reckon that they can earn a living buying and selling. That is, they buy something in a country where it's cheap and resell it in a country where it's more expensive. A nice theory, but it seldom works in practice. Whenever you find two neighbouring countries with widely differing prices for goods – Hong Kong and China, for instance – the locals quickly latch on to the idea and set up their own smuggling operations, and do not welcome foreign competition.

ACCOMMODATION

Accommodation in North-East Asia is generally not as straightforward or as cheap as in other parts of Asia. In China the places where Westerners can stay are strictly defined and limited, and while not horrendously expensive they're not nearly as cheap as places travellers head for in South-East Asia or West Asia. There are, however, dormitories in many hotels, although getting into them can involve some ingenuity.

Inflation has hit Hong Kong hard, and the few remaining cheap places tend to be closet-sized dormitories. In Japan if you're trying to travel on a shoestring you will either have to go camping or stay in the youth hostels, of which there is an extensive and well-organised chain. Other cheapish possibilities are the traditional *ryokan* (hotel) and *minshuku* (a family-run private home, like a B&B), but there are few bargains around.

In South Korea relatively cheap accommodation can be found at the traditional *yogwan* (hotel) and *yoinsuk* (guesthouse) where you sleep on the floor. In Taiwan, hotels are generally priced in the mid-range, but there are youth hostels in a few convenient spots. Macau isn't too outrageously expensive if you hit it during the off season (winter) – forget it during holiday weekends. More details about the budget hotel scene are provided in the individual country chapters of this book.

FOOD

One of the great treats of travelling in Asia is the quality and variety of food. It's also reasonably cheap in most of the countries in this book except Japan, where you pay the earth for stingy portions. In general, Chinese and Korean food continues to get rave reviews; opinions about Japanese food are decidedly mixed; and Mongolian food is at the bottom of the list when you buy it in Mongolia, though Mongolian hotpot is a favourite dish throughout the region. Another problem is that Mongolia currently suffers from a food shortage.

If you're on a tight budget, look for cheap food stalls along major streets and back alleys. There are times when you may break down and head for Western fast-food restaurants – after months of rice and noodles, a Big Mac can suddenly look like exotic, foreign cuisine.

Self-catering is a distinct possibility, and is probably the only way you can afford to eat in Japan. Peanut butter makes good backpacking food – stock up before heading into China or Mongolia where it's a rare commodity. But be aware that insects and even rats can be a problem – if you leave food lying around your hotel room, you might have unwelcome nocturnal visitors!

Getting There & Away

Air

An air ticket alone can gouge a great slice out of anyone's budget, but you can reduce the cost by finding discounted fares. You will have to choose between buying a ticket to Hong Kong only and then making other arrangements when you arrive, and buying a ticket allowing stopovers around Asia. For example, such a ticket could fly you from Los Angeles to Singapore with stopovers in Tokyo, Taipei, Hong Kong and Bangkok. This almost always works out cheaper than buying individual tickets along the way.

A variation on this theme is round-the-world (RTW) tickets. These are offered by an airline or combination of airlines, and let you take your time (six months to a year) moving from point to point on their routes for the price of one ticket. The main restriction is that you have to keep moving in the same direction; a drawback is that because you are usually booking individual flights as you go, and can't switch carriers, you can get caught out by flight availabilities. However, booking this kind of a ticket is usually cheaper than buying individual tickets from point to point.

There are a host of other deals which travel agents will offer in order to sell you a cheaper ticket. Fares will vary according to your point of departure, the time of year, how direct the flight is and how flexible you can be. Whatever you do, buy air tickets from a travel agent. The airlines don't deal directly in discount tickets, only the travel agents do. However, not every travel agent offers discount tickets, and among those that do, there is a wide range of deals on offer. It's a good idea to call the airline first and see what their cheapest ticket costs – use that as your starting point when talking to travel agents. Thanks to intense competition, most tickets sold these days are discounted.

It's important to realise that when you buy a discounted air ticket from a travel agent, you must also go back to that agent if you want to obtain a refund – the airlines will not refund you directly unless you paid full fare. While this is no problem if you don't change your travel plans, it can be quite a hassle if you decide to change the route halfway through your trip. In that case, you'd have to return to the place where you originally purchased the ticket to refund the unused portion of the journey. Of course, if you had a reliable friend whom you could mail the ticket to, that person could possibly obtain the refund for you, but don't count on it. It's also true that some travel agents (and airlines) are extremely slow to issue refunds. Some travellers have waited a full year!

Most airlines divide the year into 'peak' (expensive), 'shoulder' (less expensive) and 'off' (cheapest) seasons. In the northern hemisphere, peak season is June to September and off season is November to February. However, holidays (Christmas and Chinese New Year) will be treated as peak season even though they occur during the off season. In the southern hemisphere, the seasons are reversed. If you leave home with a round-trip ticket during the off season, you might find that the airline will not honour the return portion of your ticket if you want to return in peak season. In such a case, you could be forced to upgrade at additional cost. Be sure to ask your travel agent if such a restriction applies.

Despite the name, normal economy-class tickets are *not* the most economical way to go. Essentially, these are full-fare tickets. On the other hand, they do give you maximum flexibility and the tickets are valid for 12 months. Also, if you don't use them they are fully refundable by the airlines as are unused sectors of a multiple ticket.

Group tickets are well worth considering. You usually do *not* need to travel with a group. However, once the departure date is booked it may be impossible to change – you can only depart when the 'group' departs, even if you never meet or see another group member. The good news is that the return date can usually be left open, but there could be other restrictions – you might have to complete the trip in 60 days, or perhaps can only in the fly off season or during weekdays. It's important to ask the travel agent what conditions and restrictions apply to any tickets you intend to buy.

One thing to avoid is a 'back-to-front' ticket. These are best explained by example: if you want to fly from Japan (where tickets are relatively expensive) to Hong Kong (where tickets are much cheaper), you can pay by check or credit card and have a friend or travel agent in the Hong Kong mail the ticket to you. The problem is that the airlines have computers and will know that the ticket was issued in Hong Kong rather than Japan, and they will refuse to honour it. Consumer groups have filed lawsuits over this practice with mixed results, but in most countries the law protects the airlines, not consumers. In short, the ticket is only valid starting from the country where it was issued. The only exception to this rule is if you purchase a full-fare (non-discounted) ticket, but of course that robs you of the advantage you gain by purchasing a back-to-front ticket.

If the ticket is issued in a third location (such as the USA), the same rule applies. You cannot fly from Japan to Hong Kong with a ticket mailed to you from the USA – if you buy a ticket in the USA, you can fly from the USA to Japan and then to Hong Kong and thus enjoy a discounted price, but you can't start the journey from Japan. Again, an exception is made if you pay full fare and thus negate your savings.

'Frequent flyer' plans have proliferated in recent years and are now offered by most airlines, even some budget ones. Basically, these allow you a free ticket if you chalk up so many km with the same airline. The plans aren't always as good as they sound – some airlines require you to use all your frequent flyer credits within one year or you lose the lot. Sometimes you find yourself flying on a particular airline just to get frequent flyer credits, but the ticket is considerably more expensive than what you might have bought from a discount airline without a frequent flyer bonus. Most airlines have 'blackout' periods – peak times when you cannot use the free tickets you obtained under the frequent flyer programme. When you purchase the ticket be sure to give the ticket agent your frequent flyer membership number, and again when you check in for your flight. A common complaint seems to be that airlines forget to record your frequent flyer credits when you fly, so save all your boarding passes and ticket receipts and be prepared to push if no bonus is forthcoming. In general, American carriers are the most generous with frequent flyer credits. North west Airlines, for example, offers a free ticket after you've flown 32,000 km (20,000 miles).

Some airlines offer student discounts on their tickets of up to 25% to student card holders. In some countries, an official-looking letter from the school is also needed. You also must be aged 26 or younger. These discounts are generally only available on ordinary economy-class fares. You wouldn't get one, for instance, on an APEX or a RTW ticket since these are already discounted.

Courier flights can be a bargain if you're lucky enough to find one. The way it works is that an airfreight company takes over your entire checked baggage allowance. You are permitted to bring along a carry-on bag, but that's all. In return, you get a steeply discounted ticket. These arrangements usually have to be made a month or more in advance and are only available on certain routes. Such flights are sometimes advertised in the newspapers, or contact airfreight companies listed in the phone book.

Airlines usually carry babies up to two years of age at 10% of the relevant adult fare and a few carry them free of charge. Reputable international airlines usually provide nappies (diapers), tissues, talcum and all the other paraphernalia needed to keep babies clean, dry and half-happy. For children between the ages of four and 12 the fare on international flights is usually 50% of the regular fare or 67% of a discounted fare.

To/From the USA

There are some very good open tickets which remain valid for six months or one year (opt for the latter), but don't lock you into any

fixed dates of departure and allow multiple stopoffs. For example, there are cheap tickets between the US west coast and Hong Kong with stop offs in Japan and Korea and continuing on to Hong Kong for very little extra money – the departure dates can be changed and you have one year to complete the

Air Travel Glossary

Apex *A*-dvance *P*-urchase *E*-xcursion is a discounted ticket which must be paid for in advance. There are penalties if you wish to change it.

Baggage Allowance This will be written on your ticket: usually one 20 kg item to go in the hold, plus one item of hand luggage.

Bucket Shop An unbonded travel agency specialising in discounted airline tickets.

Bumped Just because you have a confirmed seat doesn't mean you're going to get on the plane; see Overbooking.

Cancellation Penalties If you have to cancel or change an Apex ticket there are often heavy penalties involved, insurance can sometimes be taken out against these penalties. Some airlines impose penalties on regular tickets as well, particularly against 'no show' passengers.

Check In Airlines ask you to check in a certain time ahead of the flight departure (usually 1½ hours on international flights). If you fail to check in on time and the flight is overbooked the airline can cancel your booking and give your seat to somebody else.

Confirmation Having a ticket written out with the flight and date you want doesn't mean you have a seat until the agent has checked with the airline that your status is 'OK' or confirmed. Meanwhile you could just be 'on request'.

Discounted Tickets There are two types of discounted fares – officially discounted (see Promotional Fares) and unofficially discounted. The lowest prices often impose drawbacks like flying with unpopular airlines, inconvenient schedules, or unpleasant routes and connections. A discounted ticket can save you other things than money – you may be able to pay Apex prices without the associated Apex advance booking and other requirements. Discounted tickets only exist where there is fierce competition.

Full Fares Airlines traditionally offer first class (coded F), business class (coded J) and economy class (coded Y) tickets. These days there are so many promotional and discounted fares available from the regular economy class that few passengers pay full economy fare.

Lost Tickets If you lose your airline ticket an airline will usually treat it like a travellers' cheque and, after enquiries, issue you with another one. Legally, however, an airline is entitled to treat it like cash and if you lose it then it's gone forever. Take good care of your tickets.

No Shows No shows are passengers who fail to show up for their flight, sometimes due to unexpected delays or disasters, sometimes due to simply forgetting, sometimes because they made more than one booking and didn't bother to cancel the one they didn't want. Full fare passengers who fail to turn up are sometimes entitled to travel on a later flight. The rest of us are penalised (see Cancellation Penalties).

On Request An unconfirmed booking for a flight, see Confirmation.

journey. However, remember that it's easy to get locked out during Chinese New Year and other peak times.

Usually, and not surprisingly, the cheapest fare to whatever country is offered by a discount travel agency owned by someone of that particular ethnic origin. San Francisco is the travel discount capital of the USA, though some good deals can be found in Los Angeles, New York and other cities. Discounters can be found through the Yellow Pages or the major daily newspapers. Those listed in both Roman and Oriental scripts are invariably discounters. A more direct way is

Open Jaws A return ticket where you fly out to one place but return from another. If available this can save you backtracking to your arrival point.

Overbooking Airlines hate to fly empty seats and since every flight has some passengers who fail to show up (see No Shows) airlines often book more passengers than they have seats. Usually the excess passengers balance those who fail to show up but occasionally somebody gets bumped. If this happens guess who it is most likely to be? The passengers who check in late.

Promotional Fares Officially discounted fares like Apex fares which are available from travel agents or direct from the airline.

Reconfirmation At least 72 hours prior to departure time of an onward or return flight you must contact the airline and 'reconfirm' that you intend to be on the flight. If you don't do this the airline can delete your name from the passenger list and you could lose your seat. You don't have to reconfirm the first flight on your itinerary or if your stopover is less than 72 hours. It doesn't hurt to reconfirm more than once.

Restrictions Discounted tickets often have various restrictions on them – advance purchase is the most usual one (see Apex). Others are restrictions on the minimum and maximum period you must be away, such as a minimum of 14 days or a maximum of one year. See Cancellation Penalties.

Standby A discounted ticket where you only fly if there is a seat free at the last moment. Standby fares are usually only available on domestic routes.

Tickets Out An entry requirement for many countries is that you have an onward or return ticket, in other words, a ticket out of the country. If you're not sure what you intend to do next, the easiest solution is to buy the cheapest onward ticket to a neighbouring country or a ticket from a reliable airline which can later be refunded if you do not use it.

Transferred Tickets Airline tickets cannot be transferred from one person to another. Travellers sometimes try to sell the return half of their ticket, but officials can ask you to prove that you are the person named on the ticket. This is unlikely to happen on domestic flights, on an international flight tickets may be compared with passports.

Travel Agencies Travel agencies vary widely and you should ensure you use one that suits your needs. Some simply handle tours while full-service agencies handle everything from tours and tickets to car rental and hotel bookings. A good one will do all these things and can save you a lot of money but if all you want is a ticket at the lowest possible price, then you really need an agency specialising in discounted tickets. A discounted ticket agency, however, may not be useful for other things, like hotel bookings.

Travel Periods (Seasons) Some officially discounted fares, Apex fares in particular, vary with the time of year. There is often a low (off-peak) season and a high (peak) season. Sometimes there's an intermediate or shoulder season as well. At peak times, when everyone wants to fly, not only will the officially discounted fares be higher but so will unofficially discounted fares or there may simply be no discounted tickets available. Usually the fare depends on your outward flight – if you depart in the high season and return in the low season, you pay the high-season fare. ■

to wander around San Francisco's China-town where most of the shops are, especially in the Clay St and Waverly Place area. Many of these are staffed by recent arrivals from Hong Kong and Taiwan who speak little English. Enquiries are best made in person. One place popular with budget travellers is Wahlock Travel in the Bank of America Building on Stockton St.

It's not advisable to send money or even cheques through the post unless the agent is very well established – some travellers have reported being ripped off by fly-by-night mail order ticket agents. Nor is it wise to hand over the full amount to Shady Deal Travel Services unless they can give you the ticket straight away – most US travel agencies have computers that can spit out the ticket on the spot.

Council Travel is the largest student travel organisation, and, though you don't have to be a student to use them, they do have specially discounted student tickets. Council Travel has an extensive network in all major US cities and is listed in the telephone book. There are also Student Travel Network offices which are associated with STA Travel.

One of the cheapest and most reliable travel agents on the west coast is Overseas Tours (☎ 800-222 5292), 475 El Camino Real, room 206, Millbrae, CA 94030. Another good agent is Gateway Travel (☎ 214-960 2000, 800-441 1183), 4201 Spring Valley Rd, suite 104, Dallas, TX 75244. Both of these places seem to be trust-worthy for mail-order tickets.

The price of flights is obviously affected by which US city you start out from. The lowest one-way/return fares to Hong Kong are as follows: Honolulu US$376/727; Los Angeles US$428/675; and New York US$496/870.

To/From Canada

Getting discount tickets in Canada is the same as in the USA – go to the travel agents and shop around until you find a good deal.

CUTS is Canada's national student bureau and has offices in a number of Canadian cities, including Vancouver, Edmonton, Toronto and Ottawa; you don't necessarily have to be a student. There are a number of good agents in Vancouver for cheap tickets.

The cheapest one-way/return Vancouver-Hong Kong ticket is US$392/678.

To/From Australia

As an alternative to flying direct between Australia and Hong Kong, you can often get free stop offs in either Singapore or Bangkok, especially if you fly with Singapore Airlines or THAI Airways respectively.

Australia is not a cheap place to fly out of, and air fares between Australia and Asia are absurdly expensive considering the distances flown. However, there are a few ways of cutting the costs.

Among the cheapest regular tickets available in Australia are APEX tickets. The cost depends on your departure date from Australia. It's possible to get reductions on cost of APEX and other fares by going to the student travel offices and/or some of the travel agents in Australia that specialise in discounting.

The weekend travel sections of papers like *The Age* (Melbourne) or the *Sydney Morning Herald* are good sources of travel information. Also look at *Student Traveller*, a free newspaper published by STA Travel, the student travel organisation which has offices worldwide. STA Travel has offices all around Australia (check your phone directory) and you definitely do not have to be a student to use them.

Also well worth trying is the Flight Shop (☎ 03-670 0477) at 386 Little Bourke St, Melbourne. They also have branches under the name of the Flight Centre in Sydney (☎ 02-233 2296) and Brisbane (☎ 07-229 9958).

A one-way/return Sydney-Hong Kong discounted ticket starts from US$570/825.

To/From New Zealand

Air New Zealand and Cathay Pacific fly directly from Auckland to Hong Kong. APEX fares are the cheapest way to go, but you have to pay for your ticket at least 21 days in advance and spend a minimum of six days overseas. The lowest-priced one-way/return tickets available on the Hong Kong-Auckland run are US$574/898.

To/From Europe

The Netherlands, Brussels and Antwerp are good places for buying discount air tickets. In Antwerp, WATS has been recommended. In Zurich, try SOF Travel and Sindbad. In Geneva, try Stohl Travel. In the Netherlands, NBBS is a reputable agency. Frankfurt is Germany's major gateway to Asia with direct flights on Lufthansa.

From most major cities in Western Europe, rock bottom one-way/return fares to Hong Kong begin at US$375/725.

To/From the UK

In recent years, British Airways in particular has become a very competitive airline, offering fares that can match many Asian budget airlines. Cut-throat competition is also forcing British Caledonian, Cathay Pacific and other airlines to offer big discounts. The best bargains are on the London-Hong Kong route. Flying directly from London to Beijing also makes sense as long as you don't buy the ticket in China, where it's very expensive.

As elsewhere, travel agents give bigger discounts than the airlines themselves. To find out what's on the market, there are a number of magazines in the UK which have good information about flights and agents. These include *Trailfinder*, free from the Trailfinders Travel Centre in Earls Court, and *Time Out* and *City Limits*, the London weekly entertainment guides widely available in the UK. A good source of information is *Business Traveller*, which is available in UK and Hong Kong editions.

Two reliable London bucket shops are Trailfinders, in Earls Court, and STA Travel, which has several offices. In Bristol, look up Regent Holidays.

Flights from London and Manchester to East Asian destinations are cheapest on THAI Airways, Singapore Airlines, Malaysian Airlines Systems (MAS) and Cathay Pacific. These airlines do not charge extra if passengers want to stop over en route, and in fact offer stopover packages which encourage it.

To/From Guam

Guam has emerged as a popular honeymoon and holiday spot for the well-to-do in Japan, Hong Kong and Taiwan. Guam is about four hours' flight time from all these places. Continental Airlines Micronesia has most of these routes sewn up. Return tickets are almost the same price as a one-way fare. For example, one-way/return Hong Kong-Guam fares are US$455/476!

To/From Other Asian Countries

To/From Indonesia Garuda Airlines has direct flights from Jakarta to Hong Kong, and from Denpasar to Hong Kong via Jakarta. Cheap discount air tickets out of Indonesia can be bought from travel agents in Kuta Beach in Bali and in Jakarta. There are numerous airline ticket discounters around Kuta Beach, including several on the main strip, Jalan Legian. You can also buy discount tickets in Kuta for departure from Jakarta. In Jakarta the cheapest tickets are available from agents along Jalan Jaksa.

To/From Malaysia Kuala Lumpur and Penang both have international airports with direct flights to Hong Kong. Malaysian Airlines Systems (MAS) has a flight from Kuala Lumpur to Seoul via Taipei. You can fly directly from Penang to Guangzhou.

To/From Myanmar (Burma) There is a once-weekly flight from Rangoon to Kunming. Your stay in Myanmar (formerly known as Burma) is limited to two weeks and you usually must have an air ticket out of the country before they'll issue you a visa. At the time of writing, Myanmar was experiencing serious political chaos and civil unrest, so visits to that country are an uncertain proposition.

To/From Nepal There are direct flights between Kathmandu and Lhasa twice weekly. Visas for China are currently not available in Kathmandu. If entering China this way you have to book through expensive tour agencies. It's much less expensive if you just want to exit Tibet this way.

To/From the Philippines Manila is well connected with Hong Kong, Taipei and Tokyo. There are also direct flights from Manila to Beijing, Guangzhou and Xiamen.

To/From Singapore Singapore is a major Asian transport hub, with flights to Hong Kong, Seoul, Taipei and Tokyo. There are flights from Singapore to Beijing, Guangzhou, Shanghai and Xiamen.

A good place for buying cheap air tickets in Singapore is Airmaster Travel Centre. Also try STA Travel. Other agents advertise in the *Straits Times* classified columns.

To/From Thailand There are flights from Bangkok to numerous cities in North-East Asia, including Hong Kong, Seoul, Taipei and Tokyo. There are also flights from Bangkok to several destinations in China, including Beijing, Guangzhou, Kunming and Shantou, and there is a very popular flight between Chiang Mai and Kunming.

In Bangkok, STA Travel in the Thai Hotel is helpful and efficient.

To/From Vietnam Direct flights operate to both Hanoi and Ho Chi Minh City. From both cities there are daily flights to Hong Kong and Taipei. There are overpriced flights between Vietnam and the Chinese cities of Beijing, Guangzhou and Nanning.

Overland

CHINA-VIETNAM BORDER

Entering Vietnam overland from China requires a special visa. It's not difficult to get, but costs twice as much and takes twice as long to issue as a standard visa. Travellers who have attempted to use a standard visa to enter Vietnam overland have fared poorly – some have managed it only after paying huge bribes, only to be given a one-week rather than a one-month stay. Exiting Vietnam overland poses no such problem, but the correct exit point must be marked on the visa – alternations can easily be made in Hanoi.

There are two places where you can enter or exit Vietnam: Dong Dang and Lao Cai.

Dong Dang

This is the more popular of the two options. Dong Dang is 20 km north of Lang Son in north-east Vietnam. The nearest major Chinese city to this border crossing is Nanning, capital of Guangxi Province. The border crossing is called 'Friendship Pass', and at one time there was regular train service between Vietnam and China at this crossing. However, both the friendship and the train service came to an end in 1979 when China attacked Vietnam to 'teach the Vietnamese a lesson'. Just what lesson the Vietnamese learned is not clear, but the Chinese learned that Vietnam's combat-hardened troops were no easy pushover. Although China's forces were withdrawn after 17 days and the operation was officially declared a 'great success', most observers soon realised that China's People's Liberation Army (PLA) had been badly mauled by the Vietnamese. The PLA is believed to have suffered 20,000 casualties in the 2½ weeks of fighting.

Officially, all such 'misunderstandings' are ancient history. Chinese Prime Minister Li Peng visited Hanoi in December 1992 to formally end the Sino-Vietnamese rift. It was all toothy smiles and warm handshakes in front of the cameras, but in reality relations between Vietnam and China still remain very tense. Nevertheless, trade across the Chinese-Vietnamese border is booming and both countries publicly profess to be 'good neighbours'.

The border reopened to foreign travellers in 1992. The railway link is also destined to be resurrected soon, perhaps even by the time you read this. At the time of writing, foreigners still had to travel the 20 km between Dong Dang and Lang Son by bus. The border crossing itself has to be done on foot, a walk of about 600 metres. On the Chinese side, it's a 20-minute drive between the border and Pinxiang. Pinxiang is connected to Nanning by trains and buses.

Lao Cai

The other border crossing is at Lao Cai in north-west Vietnam, opposite the Chinese border town of Hekou. Lao Cai lies on the rail line between Hanoi and Kunming in China's Yunnan Province.

Probably for security reasons, passenger trains from Hanoi currently do not go all the way to Lao Cai but terminate at Pho Lu, 40 km away. While there are trains going all the way to Lao Cai from Hanoi, these are only for hauling freight.

There are three trains daily from Hanoi to Pho Lu, but two arrive in the middle of the night. The most useful train departs Hanoi at 7 am and arrives in Pho Lu at 5.30 pm. Be careful about falling asleep on this train – foreigners have woken up to find that their pockets had been picked! In Pho Lu, you can transfer to another train that is waiting at the station. This is a very basic train with only small wooden benches on the long sides of the carriages and takes about an hour to get to a tiny village about 10 km from Lao Cai. The best way to get from the village to Lao Cai is to hire a motorbike for about US$2.

This border only opened to foreigners in 1993 and things are changing fast. There was no place to stay near the border at the time of writing, but a hotel was under construction on the Chinese side of the border. It's possible that there will be improvements on the transport situation too. In other words, the preceding information should not be regarded as engraved in stone – most likely things will continue to get easier for travellers.

TRANS-SIBERIAN RAILWAY

The ever-popular Trans-Siberian Railway is a great way to start or finish your trip to Asia. Compared with the cost of a boring old flight, the train ride is competitively priced and infinitely more interesting. However, organising visas and railway tickets is a far more complex affair than simply flying straight through.

There is some confusion of terms here – there are, in fact, three railways. The 'true' Trans-Siberian line, the Trans-Manchurian and the Trans-Mongolian.

Trans-Siberian Railway Entertainment

Unless you travel in a group, the selection of travelling companions for the journey is delightfully or excruciatingly random – a judgement upon which you have five or six days to ponder.

On the trip you can get stuck in the crossfire of political debates, retreat to a chess game, an epic novel or epic paralytic drinking bouts, or teach English to the train attendant. The scenery is mostly melancholic birch trees, but there are some occasionally fascinating views, such as the snow on the Mongolian Desert and the scenery around Lake Baikal, the deepest lake in the world. At sub-zero temperatures you can exercise along the platform, start snowball fights or wonder about the destination of teenage recruits milling around a troop train. In these stations, make sure your luggage is secure – during the few minutes that you're out on the platform a thief could pinch your camera and other valuables.

A chess set soon makes friends. The Russians produce not only talented players but also courteous ones – perhaps as a gesture of friendship they'll quickly cede the first game but the rest are won with monotonous regularity. Prodigious amounts of alcohol disappear down Russian throats, so expect a delighted interest in consuming your hoard of Chinese alcohol, for which there is plenty of time. On the other hand, if you want to repulse freeloaders you might try injecting them with a bottle of one of those ghastly Chinese liquors – the recipient is either going to stagger out in absolute revulsion or remain vaccinated and your stock is doomed.

For those interested in barter or fund-raising, bring along tea, watches, jeans and Walkman cassette recorders – they are are all sources of inspiration to passengers. ∎

The Trans-Siberian line runs from Moscow to the eastern Siberian ports of Nakhodka and Vladivostok, from where you can catch a boat to Japan. There is a seldom-used option, the Baikal-Amur Mainline (BAM) which runs through Siberia north of Lake Baikal – very few foreign travellers go that way. Neither the main Trans-Siberian route nor the BAM railway line go through China or Mongolia. Most readers of this book are not interested in the 'true' Trans-Siberian since it excludes China. Another problem is that the boats from Japan to Siberia are notoriously unreliable. Perhaps a better option is to take the Trans-Siberian from Moscow to the Siberian city of Khabarovsk, from where you can fly to Japan on the Russian airline Aeroflot. There are also flights from Khabarovsk to Harbin in north-east China.

Most travellers prefer to take either the Trans-Manchurian or the Trans-Mongolian trains. The Trans-Manchurian line crosses the Russia-China border at Zabaikalsk-Manzhouli, completely bypassing Mongolia (which saves you the small hassle of getting a Mongolian transit visa). The Trans-Mongolian line connects Beijing to Moscow, passing through the Mongolian capital city, Ulaan Baatar.

There are different classes but all are acceptably comfortable. Deluxe (also called 'soft-sleeper') class is only available on the Chinese-run trains and has two beds per cabin plus an attached shower. First class is available on all non-Chinese trains and has two beds per cabin but no shower. Second class is available on all trains and has four beds per cabin and no shower. Tickets and train schedules carry a numerical designation which indicates the class and number of beds per cabin: 1/2 means '1st class, two beds per cabin' while 2/4 means '2nd class, four beds per cabin'. On the trains between Moscow and Western Europe you might find the designation 2/3, meaning '2nd class, three beds per cabin'. Easy.

Which direction you go in makes a difference in cost and travelling time. The trains from Beijing take 1½ days to reach Ulaan Baatar. The journey from Moscow to Ulaan Baatar is four days.

There are major delays (six to ten hours) at both the China-Mongolia and Russia-Mongolia borders thanks to rigorous customs inspection of all the freight being

---

Money for Nothing

Many of your fellow passengers are likely to be traders travelling 'on business'. They take advantage of the economic disparities between China, Russia, Eastern Europe and Mongolia. The traders buy up ridiculously cheap subsidised goods in Russia and Mongolia for sale in China and elsewhere, and then purchase inexpensive Chinese goods like clothing for sale in Mongolia, Russia and Poland. Because of the scarcity of goods in Russia, there tends to be more freight moving from China to Eastern Europe than the other way around. However, some valuable items move from West to East, such as deer antlers and Siberian tigers' testicles which figure prominently in Chinese aphrodisiac recipes.

Among the more bizarre (and cruel) cargo items are puppies. The puppies are bought in Russia, drugged, stuffed into bags and smuggled into China – not all survive this rough treatment. It's illegal to own dogs in Beijing, but China's nouveaux riches (especially the wives of cadres) are apparently willing to pay a premium for cutesy, furry little animals to keep around the house, and so the black market exists. Sadly, once the cutesy little puppies grow up and become decidedly less cute, they are often abandoned.

In the recent past, a four-bed passenger compartment typically had only one person travelling with four passenger tickets, with the entire compartment stacked to the ceiling with boxes, bags and shipping crates. Needless to say, this created considerable chaos at the railway stations when 'passengers' tried to board the train with tonnes of luggage. The railway staff have now cracked down, and passengers are limited to 35 kg of luggage. However, the traders often bribe their way through. In other words, you may still be sharing your compartment with one passenger and half a tonne of merchandise. ■

carried by 'passengers'. Very little is confiscated, but customs officers try to extract import duty from the traders. On the other hand, those holding passports from Western countries typically sail right through customs without their bags even being opened, which is one reason why people on the train will approach you and ask if you'll carry some of their luggage across the border. During this time, you can get off the train and wander around the station, which is just as well since the toilets on the train are locked during the whole inspection procedure. You will not have your passport at this time, as the authorities take it away for stamping. When it is returned, inspect it closely because sometimes they make errors like cancelling your return visa for China.

At the Chinese-Russian or Chinese-Mongolian borders, about two hours are spent changing the bogies (undercarriage wheels). This is necessary because Russia, Mongolia and all former Eastern bloc countries use a wider rail gauge than China and the rest of the world. The reason has to do with security – it seems the Russians feared an invasion by train.

Security

There is much theft on the train, so never leave your luggage unattended, even if the compartment is locked. Make sure that at least one person stays in the compartment while the others go to the dining car or toilet. A lot of theft is committed by Russian gangs who have master keys to the compartments, so don't assume that a 'Western face' means honesty. You are much safer if travelling with a group. Indeed, many travel agents that sell Trans-Siberian tickets insist that you book into one of their group tours for just this reason. Travel agents who simply sell you a ticket are, in a sense, just throwing you to the wolves.

The Chinese train is slightly more upmarket than the Russian train (at least in deluxe carriages), and is also more popular with traders. For these reasons, passengers are likely to be carrying large amounts of cash, which means this train is a prime target for theft. Sometimes, looking poor and humble can be a virtue.

Tickets

From Europe Logically, you would think that you could simply drop in at any European railway office and purchase a ticket from London or Berlin to Beijing. However, 'logic' is not the term that comes to mind when attempting to buy a Trans-Siberian ticket. More descriptive terms would include 'shortages', 'bureaucracy' and 'inefficiency'. The western terminal of the Trans-Siberian is Moscow, so you have to go to Moscow to buy the ticket. Of course, you need a Russian visa before you can go to Moscow, but the visa won't be issued until you have your ticket! If by some chance you do get to Moscow, you'll almost certainly find that the waiting list for tickets is two months long. Needless to say, hanging around Moscow for a few months just to catch a train can be a real drag.

So what's a traveller to do? The answer is to purchase a ticket through a travel agent. Many travel agents offer Trans-Siberian tickets, but both prices and the standards of service vary enormously. The better agents can help you organise both the tickets and the requisite visas. Furthermore, a reputable agent will sell you a group ticket, which means you share a berth with other foreign travellers rather than with Russian traders.

In the UK, one of the experts in budget rail travel is Regent Holidays (UK) Ltd (☎ 0117 9-211711; telex 444606; fax 0117 9-254866), 15 John St, Bristol BS1 2HR. Another agency geared towards budget travellers is Progressive Tours (☎ 0171-2621676), 12 Porchester Place, Connaught Square, London W2 2BS.

Several travellers have recommended Scandinavian Student Travel Service (SSTS), 117 Hauchsvej, 1825 Copenhagen V, Denmark. This organisation has branch offices in Europe and the USA, and provides a range of basic tours for student or budget travellers, mostly during summer.

Travel Service Asia (☎ 07-371 4963; fax 07-371 4769), Kirchberg 15, 7948 Dürmentingen, Germany, is one place for tickets. Mongolia Tourist Information Service (MTIS) (☎ 030-784 8057), also known as Lernidee-Reisen, is very knowledgeable and can be contacted at Postfach 62 05 29, D-1000 Berlin 62.

From China In theory, the cheapest place to buy a ticket is at the office of China International Travel Service (CITS) in the Beijing International Hotel. The problem with this theory is that CITS doesn't make advance reservations by phone, fax or through its Hong Kong office. In other words, you first must go to Beijing and fight like everyone else for a ticket, with a very good chance that the next seat available will be two months later. This could work if you want to visit Beijing, buy a ticket, travel in China for two months, and then return to Beijing. Of course, very few travellers want to do this since backtracking to Beijing eats up much time and money. Tickets are noticeably easier to purchase during winter, but not many people want to cross Siberia when the mercury hovers around -50°C. The cheapest Beijing-Moscow ticket (if you can get one) costs US$175. Contrary to what CITS brochures say, Trans-Siberian tickets bought from Beijing CITS are basically nonrefundable – after a vociferous argument, you might get back 20% of the purchase price if you're lucky.

Your other alternative is to buy from a private travel agent. This will always be more expensive than CITS because the agents must purchase their tickets from CITS too. However, it may well work out cheaper to go through a travel agent – hanging around Beijing for months or making a separate trip to Beijing just to buy a ticket will also cost you money. Almost all of these agents are based in Hong Kong.

The best organised of the Trans-Siberian ticket vendors is Monkey Business, officially known as Moonsky Star (☎ 7231376; fax 7236653, CompuServe 100267, 2570), 4th floor, Block E, Flat 6, Chungking Mansions, 30 Nathan Rd, Tsimshatsui, Kowloon. Monkey Business also maintains an infor-mation office in Beijing at the Qiaoyuan Hotel (new building), room 716 (☎ 301-2244 ext 716), but it's best to book through their Hong Kong office as far in advance as possible. A booking can be done by telephone or fax and a deposit can be wired to them. One advantage of booking through them is that they keep all their passengers in a group (for mutual protection against theft). Monkey Business can also arrange visas and stopover tours to Mongolia and Irkutsk (Siberia), but such services cost extra. The cheapest ticket available from Monkey Business is a direct Beijing to Moscow berth for US$270.

Wallem Travel (☎ 5286514), 46th floor, Hopewell Centre, 183 Queen's Rd East, Wanchai, Hong Kong, also books tours but is very pricey.

There are a number of other Hong Kong-based agencies that can sell you an individual budget Trans-Siberian ticket, but don't offer visa services or group tickets. However, it might work out OK if you round up a couple of other travellers to accompany you (for safety reasons) and don't mind doing the visa legwork. One agency offering Trans-Siberian tickets is Phoenix Services (☎ 7227378), room B, 6th floor, Milton Mansion, 96 Nathan Rd, Tsimshatsui, Kowloon. Another agency is Time Travel (☎ 3666222; fax 7395413). They are located on the 16th floor, Block A, Chungking Mansions, 30 Nathan Rd, Tsimshatsui, Kowloon.

Black Market Tickets Once upon a time, black-market tickets were so common that it seemed like everyone on the train had one. Indeed, you were almost a fool not to buy one. The way it worked was that people with connections would go to Budapest and buy Beijing-Moscow tickets in bulk for around US$50 a piece, then take the tickets to Beijing and sell them for about US$150. A nice little business, while it lasted.

The good old days are gone. Eastern European countries no longer sell tickets for ridiculously cheap subsidised prices. Not that the black market has disappeared – it's still around. The problem is that the black-market scene has turned ugly. Rather than being cheaper, black-market tickets are now more expensive than tickets you could buy yourself – it's simply the law of supply and demand. In Moscow and Beijing, gangsters buy up big blocks of tickets and sell them at whatever price the market will bear. In order for anyone to be able to buy up so many tickets, connections on the inside are needed, which requires the payment of considerable bribes.

If you attempt to buy a ticket from CITS, it's likely you'll be asked to 'come back tomorrow'. When you come back, you'll probably be told again to 'come back tomorrow'. This may continue for five days or so, at the end of which time you *might* get a ticket (in the dead of winter), but probably not. If you do succeed in getting a ticket, you'll be told that somebody 'cancelled' and that's why the ticket is suddenly available. This is nonsense – nobody cancels because CITS doesn't refund cancelled tickets. What really happens is that CITS sells the tickets out the back door to black marketeers at a premium price – if any remain unsold, the black marketeers return them on the very last day and CITS tries to flog them off to the hopeful 'come back tomorrow' people. Unfortunately, there is very little chance of scoring an unsold ticket outside the winter slow season.

CITS has pulled a few other dirty tricks on travellers. Persistent 'come back tomorrow' people have sometimes been sold tickets to the Siberian city of Chita. The CITS people will assure you that in Chita you can buy a ticket on a local train to Moscow. The problem is that the Russian Embassy requires that you have a through ticket to Moscow before a visa will be issued, and tickets to Chita are *not* acceptable.

There is also a problem with cheaper Russian tickets which are valid for Russian passport holders only. Black marketeers sell these Russian tickets to gullible foreigners who then find they can't use them. There has also been a problem with forged tickets. Once you try to get to the railway station and

realise that your ticket is worthless, just try filing a complaint with your local black marketeer.

Black marketeers hang out around the CITS booking office in Beijing and will hustle any likely looking customers. We suggest that you ignore them.

Visas

Russia Obtaining a Russian visa is a headache. You have a choice between getting a transit visa or a tourist visa. There is a very big difference between the two. Transit visas are valid for a maximum of 10 days and tourist visas are required if your journey is broken. In practice, you can stay in Moscow for three days on a transit visa and apply for an extension when you arrive. This only really works if you're going from Beijing to Moscow rather than the other way round – otherwise you'll miss your train to Beijing. Trying to extend a tourist visa is much more expensive – the hotel 'service bureau' will do it for you through Intourist, but only with expensive hotel bookings.

With a tourist visa, you can stay in Russia much longer, but you will pay heavily for the privilege. All hotels must be booked through Intourist before you arrive. The attitude of Intourist is to milk travellers for every cent they can get. For a two-star hotel, expect to pay around US$65 outside of Moscow, and US$135 a day in Moscow. The hotel bookings must be confirmed by telex (which you will also have to pay for) and the whole bureaucratic procedure takes about three weeks. On a transit visa, you can sleep in the station or in one of the rapidly proliferating cheap private hostels.

Before you can get a transit visa, you must have a ticket in hand or a ticket voucher. A transit visa can be issued the same day or take two to five days depending on how much you pay. There are two fees you must pay: a visa application fee and a bizarre 'consular fee' for certain nationalities. Visa application fees are US$40 for a visa issued in three working days, US$50 if issued in two days and US$60 if issued the same day. The consular fee varies according to which passport you hold; it's free for Aussies, Kiwis, Canadians, Brits and Americans, but it's US$12 for the Dutch and Belgians, US$18 for Swiss citizens and US$18 for Austrians. Three photos are required. The embassy does not keep your passport, so you are free to travel while your application is being processed.

Someone can apply for the visa on your behalf and use a photocopy of your passport (all relevant pages must be included). If you want to change an already-issued transit visa, this will cost you US$20. Reasons for changing could be if you want go on a different date or change the final destination. Russian embassies are closed during all Russian public holidays: New Year's Day (1 & 2 January), Eastern Orthodox Christmas (7 January), Women's Day (8 March), Labour Day (2 & 3 May), Victory Day (9 May), Independence Day (7 June) plus spontaneous holidays (the ambassador's daughter's birthday?).

In Beijing, the Russian Embassy (☎ 5322051, 5321267) is at Beizhongjie 4, just off Dongzhimen and west of the Sanlitun Embassy Compound. Opening hours are Monday to Friday from 9 am to noon. This embassy is particularly notorious for rotten service – expect long queues, intimidation from the security guards and bureaucratic inertia from the staff. Conditions are noticeably better at the Russian Consulate (☎ 3242682) in Shanghai, 20 Huangpu Lu, opposite the Pujiang Hotel. Unfortunately, their opening hours are brief: Tuesday and Thursday from 10 am until 12.30 pm.

The Russian Consulate in Budapest is at Nepkoztarsasag utca 104 (open Monday, Wednesday and Friday from 10 am to 1 pm).

Mongolia The Mongolian Embassy in Beijing is open all day, but the visa section keeps short hours – only on Monday, Tuesday, Thursday and Friday from 8.30 am to 11.30 am. It closes for all Mongolian holidays, and shuts down completely for the entire week of National Day (*Naadam*), which officially falls on 11-13 July. In the UK, the Mongolian Embassy (☎ (0171)

9370150, 9375235) is at 7 Kensington Court, London W85 DL.

Visas cost US$20 if picked up on the third day, or US$25 for same-day delivery. Tourist visas cost US$25 if processed in three days, or US$30 for same-day delivery. Some nationalities can get visas for free (India, Finland etc). Two photos are required, and visas *must* be paid for in US dollars cash.

It's easy enough to get a transit visa, but obtaining a tourist visa requires the same bureaucratic somersaults as required for a Russian tourist visa.

Poland Travellers between Berlin and Moscow go via Poland, though there are alternative routes via Finland or Hungary which avoid Poland altogether. A Polish visa is not needed for nationals of the USA and Western Europe (except Spain and Portugal). Polish visas are required for Australians, Britons, Canadians and New Zealanders. You get a discount on these fees if you have a student (ISIC) card. Visas cost US$18 for most nationalities, but Canadians are charged more.

In China, there is a Polish Embassy in Beijing and Polish consulates in Guangzhou and Hong Kong (☎ 8400779). Poland has embassies in most Western European capitals. Two photos are needed.

Czech & Slovakia Except for Albanians and Turks, West Europeans are exempt from visa requirements. Australians, Canadians, New Zealanders, Israelis and South Africans do need a visa. Visas cost US$21 and are issued in two working days. Two photos are required.

Hungary West Europeans (except Greeks and Portuguese) do not need a visa. Americans and Canadians are also visa exempt, but Australians and New Zealanders do need a visa. Two photos are required and the visa is issued the next working day.

Ukraine Trains between Moscow and Budapest or Prague cross the Ukraine. Transit visas cost US$15 and are issued in five working days, or the same day for a much higher fee. A tourist visa can only be obtained in Moscow or Kiev and costs US$50. To get a Ukrainian transit visa, you first must show the visa for the next country you will visit (if that country requires a visa). Two photos are needed.

Other Former Soviet Republics No visa is required for Belorussia if you're on an international train going directly between Moscow and Berlin or Prague. If you're going on a 'local' train between St Petersburg and Western Europe, there are all sorts of visa hassles that are best avoided.

The three Baltic republics (Estonia, Latvia and Lithuania) require visas. However, a visa for any one is valid for all three.

Predeparture Tips
Bring plenty of cash US dollars in small denominations for the journey – only in China can you readily use the local currency. In China, good food is plentiful and readily available from both the train's dining car and vendors in railway stations. In both Russia and Mongolia, food quality is poorer, but barely edible meals are available on the train.

Once you get off the train it's a different story – food can be extremely difficult to buy in Russia, Mongolia, the Ukraine and other former Soviet republics. If you don't want to starve, bring plenty of munchies like biscuits, instant noodles, chocolate and fruit.

It's important to realise that food in the dining car is priced in local currency. This is true even in Mongolia or Russia. Many foreigners have the mistaken impression that they must pay in US dollars. The railway staff will gladly accept your dollars instead of roubles or togrogs at some ridiculous exchange rate, which means you'll be paying many times the real price. There are black-market moneychangers at border railway stations, but all the usual dangers of black-market exchanges apply.

Except for Chinese beer, most alcohol available on the train tastes like low-grade jet fuel and you'd be wise to purchase your own stash before boarding.

Showers are only available in the deluxe carriages on the Chinese train. In economy class, there is a washroom. You can manage a bath with a sponge but it's best to bring a large metal cup (available in most Chinese railway stations) and use it as a scoop to pour water over yourself from the washbasin. The metal cup is also ideal for making coffee, tea and instant soup. Hot water is available on the trains.

Books
A popular book about this journey is the *Trans-Siberian Handbook* by Bryn Thomas (Trailblazer Publications), distributed through Roger Lascelles in the UK. *The Trans-Siberian Rail Guide* by Robert Strauss (Compass Publications) also covers the journey.

THE SILK ROUTE
As an alternative to the Trans-Siberian railway, some travellers have started exploring the so called 'Silk Route', which roughly follows the ancient Silk Road. The railway runs between Alma Ata in Kazakhstan (a republic of the former Soviet Union) and Ürümqi in China's Xinjiang Province. Alma Ata is connected to the Russian railway network and Ürümqi is connected by rail to the rest of China, so with a change of trains you can travel from Beijing to Moscow and vice versa.

The main obstacles on this route are the lack of an express international train (such as the Beijing-Moscow express) plus the visa complications. This route has only recently opened to foreigners and travel agents are just starting to experiment with it.

At present, Russian visas are valid for entry to Kazakhstan. However, this could change once Kazakhstan establishes its own embassies. A new book entitled *Silk Route by Rail* by Dominic Streatfeild-James is due to be published soon, and should cover this journey in detail.

Sea

Unless you're wealthy enough to travel on luxury cruisers, there are few chances to arrive or depart from North-East Asia on a ship. If you really can afford US$200 a day and up, check out some of the cruise ships that call into Hong Kong, Shangai and Yokohama; travel agents can advise you.

One possible option for budget travellers is the ferry between Japan and Russia, which will mostly be of interest to travellers taking the Trans-Siberian Railway (see the previous Overland section in this chapter). However, this boat is not reliable, cheap or safe – think of it as an 'adventure'.

The Japan-Russia ferry runs every week starting in June and terminates service sometime in September. It departs from the Russian port of Nakhodka or Vladivostok. On the Japanese side it alternates between Niigata and Takaoka (Fushiki). The journey takes three days and costs from Y31,400 (Japanese price, which works out over US$300). Information in Japan can be obtained from the shipping company in Tokyo (☎3475-2841).

Getting Around

AIR

Air services are very well developed in North-East Asia, except for a few blank spots. Macau does not have an airport yet, but one is under construction. Except for hijackings, there is no direct air service between China and Taiwan. With the exception of the flight to Beijing, North Korea is cut off from the world.

International air tickets purchased in China and Japan are expensive, often double what you'd pay elsewhere. Hong Kong, the freest free market in the world, is cheapest for air tickets. Taiwan and South Korea are still not terribly cheap, but gradually becoming increasingly competitive as their economies liberalise.

China-Hong Kong

Only Civil Aviation Administration of China (CAAC) and Dragonair are permitted to fly between Hong Kong and China. Because the Chinese government owns CAAC outright and has a majority stake in Dragonair, China effectively has a monopolist position on all air routes between Hong Kong and China. Foreign airlines simply cannot fly these routes, which means prices stay high. There is no discounting on these routes – everyone pays full fare and a return ticket costs exactly double the price of a one-way ticket. Since Dragonair is a joint venture with Hong Kong's Cathay Pacific Airlines, it offers better service at slightly lower prices. Most travellers prefer to fly on Dragonair, but CAAC has most of the routes sewn up by government edict.

CAAC runs numerous direct flights between Hong Kong and every major city in China. Many of these flights are technically called 'charter flights' and therefore do not appear in the CAAC timetable, even though they operate according to a fixed regular schedule. It's important to know if your flight is designated a 'charter' because it means that the tickets have fixed-date departures and are nonrefundable.

The following are the one-way fares between China and Hong Kong on CAAC, and flights marked with an asterisk are 'charters':

Beijing	US$292
Changsha*	US$182
Chengdu*	US$272
Chongqing*	US$272
Dalian	US$309
Fuzhou	US$197
Guangzhou	US$85
Guilin*	US$164
Guiyang*	US$210
Haikou*	US$151
Hangzhou	US$197
Harbin*	US$342
Hefei*	US$194
Ji'nan*	US$269
Kunming	US$203
Meixian*	US$148
Nanchang*	US$184
Nanjing*	US$216
Nanning*	US$158
Ningbo	US$205
Qingdao*	US$285
Shanghai	US$215
Shantou	US$145
Shenyang	US$343
Tianjin	US$293
Wuhan*	US$185
Xi'an	US$254
Xiamen	US$166
Zhanjiang*	US$152
Zhengzhou*	US$246

Dragonair typically charges US$12 to US$25 less than CAAC on one-way tickets, and double that amount for return tickets. Dragonair has flights from Hong Kong to 14 cities in China: Beijing, Changsha, Chengdu, Dalian, Guilin, Haikou, Hangzhou, Kunming, Nanjing, Ningbo, Shanghai, Tianjin, Xi'an and Xiamen.

China-Japan

CAAC, Japan Airlines (JAL) and All Nippon Airways serve the China-Japan market.

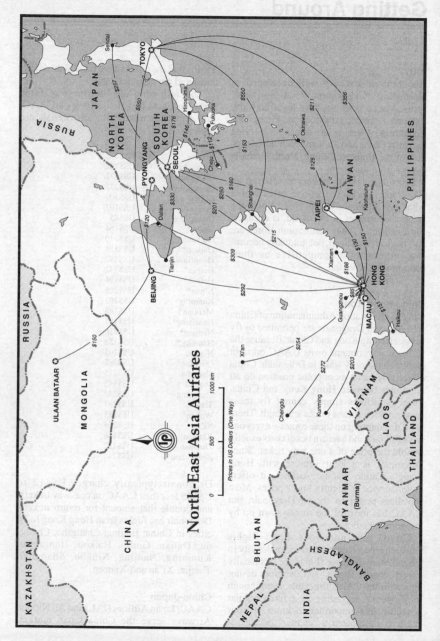

North-East Asia Airfares

Prices in US Dollars (One Way)

Flights between Beijing and Tokyo cost US$550. Flights between Shanghai and Tokyo cost the same. There are flights between Dalian and Fukuoka/Tokyo on All Nippon Airways.

Chinese visas obtained in Japan are outrageously expensive – US$80 to US$120 depending on which agent you use. You'll save money if you can obtain the visa elsewhere.

China-Mongolia

MIAT (Mongolia's airline) runs four flights weekly between Beijing and Ulaan Baatar for US$150 one way. The flight schedule may be reduced during winter.

CAAC has two flights weekly in both directions between Beijing and Ulaan Baatar. There are also two return flights weekly between Ulaan Baatar and Hohhot (the capital of China's Inner Mongolia Province). Presently, these flights are on Tuesday and Friday, but the schedule could change. The one-way airfare is US$150.

China-North Korea

If you can get a visa for North Korea (a big *if*), you'll probably fly from China. Getting a seat should be no problem as the planes are mostly empty. However, you're advised to book as far in advance as possible because delegations of diplomats occasionally descend on Pyongyang for some special event and seats suddenly become scarce.

There are flights between Beijing and Pyongyang by either CAAC once weekly, or the North Korean airline Korean Airways (also known as Chosonminhang) twice weekly. The flight takes less than two hours.

The airfares are insane. The one-way Beijing-Pyongyang ticket costs US$120 in Pyongyang, but a one-way Pyongyang-Beijing flight is US$274 if the ticket is bought in China! This is because CAAC calculates the fare using the absurd 'external exchange rate' of US$1 = W0.97. To make it more absurd, a round-trip Beijing-Pyongyang-Beijing air ticket bought in China costs US$220, or US$54 less than a one-way ticket.

China-South Korea

Asiana Airlines offers direct flights between Seoul, South Korea and the Chinese port of Tianjin for US$330. Korean Air flies Seoul-Shanghai for US$250.

Hong Kong-Japan

Tickets purchased in Hong Kong will typically be 50% cheaper than if purchased in Japan. If purchased in Hong Kong, the cheapest one-way/return fares to Tokyo are US$356/550. It's certainly cheaper to fly Hong Kong-Osaka, where fares start at US$246/378.

Hong Kong-Macau

The vast majority of people travelling between Hong Kong and Macau do so by boat. However, for people in a hurry to lose their money, East Asia Airlines runs a helicopter service. Flying time from Hong Kong is 20 minutes at a cost of US$140 on weekdays, US$160 on weekends – quite an expense just to save the extra 30 minutes required by boat. There are at least 12 flights daily in each direction, and departures are from the ferry piers in both Hong Kong and Macau. You can get the tickets in Hong Kong (☎ 8593359) at Shun Tak Centre, 200 Connaught Rd, Sheung Wan, Hong Kong Island. In Macau, you can book at the Jetfoil Pier (☎ 572983, 550777).

Hong Kong-South Korea

Many discount travel agents in Seoul offer tickets that are priced competitively, but Hong Kong is still somewhat cheaper. One-way/return fares on the Hong Kong-Seoul route start at US$200/285.

Hong Kong-Taiwan

Air tickets sold in Taiwan have been steadily falling in price, but Hong Kong is still a better place to pick up a cheap 'group ticket'. Bottom-end one-way/return fares on the Hong Kong-Taipei route are US$130/215. You can also fly Hong Kong-Kaohsiung, though fewer discounts are available on that route.

Japan-South Korea

Airfares are definitely cheaper if you purchase your ticket in Korea. The following are the cheapest prices you can expect on tickets booked in Seoul:

Route	One Way	Return
Fukuoka-Cheju	US$112	US$224
Fukuoka-Pusan	US$76	US$192
Fukuoka-Seoul	US$105	US$210
Hiroshima-Seoul	US$146	US$292
Nagoya-Seoul	US$170	US$240
Okinawa-Seoul	US$153	US$306
Sendai-Cheju	US$269	US$538
Sendai-Pusan	US$231	US$462
Sendai-Seoul	US$257	US$514
Takamatsu-Seoul	US$158	US$316
Tokyo-Seoul	US$176	US$352
Toyama-Seoul	US$199	US$398

LAND

Within the region there are only a few places where you can cross borders by land – China to Hong Kong, Macau, Mongolia or North Korea. Don't even think about crossing the border between the two Koreas.

China-Hong Kong

The express train between Hong Kong and Guangzhou is fast and comfortable. The adult fare is US$25 one way. Timetables change, so check departure times. There are usually three or four express trains daily, and the whole trip takes a bit less than three hours.

In Hong Kong, tickets can be booked up to seven days before departure at CTS. On the day of departure, tickets can be bought from Hunghom railway station. Return tickets are also sold, but only between seven and 30 days before departure. Bicycles can be carried in the freight car.

A cheaper alternative to the express train is the local train. The trains start running early in the morning, and the border stays open until 10 pm (11 pm during daylight savings time in China). You can take it from Hunghom station (Kowloon) to the Hong Kong/China border at Lo Wu, then walk across the border bridge to Shenzhen and pick up the local train to Guangzhou. The fare from Kowloon to Lo Wu is US$4.80.

There are about a dozen local trains a day between Shenzhen and Guangzhou. Tourist-price hard-seat is US$6.60 and soft-seat is US$8.55. The Shenzhen-Guangzhou journey takes about 2½ to 3½ hours.

China-Macau

Macau is just over the border from China's Special Economic Zone of Zhuhai. The border post is at Gongbei. The Macau-Gongbei border is open from 7 am to 9 pm. Cyclists can ride across. There are buses from the long-distance bus station in Guangzhou to Gongbei (five hours). There is also an express bus service from Macau.

China-Mongolia

There are direct international trains running several times a week between Beijing and Ulaan Baatar. The schedule varies according to the season. From either end, tickets can be very hard to get on short notice, especially during the summer peak season. Tickets start at US$85 and the journey takes 1½ days. Mongolians boarding the train have mountains of luggage – if you share a compartment with them you'll have to battle for turf.

In theory at least, you can take a domestic train from either Beijing or Ulaan Baatar to the border, cross by bus, and continue onwards by domestic train. In practice, this is extremely difficult because of chronic overcrowding on the bus. Plenty of Mongolians use this method, but there always seems to be five times as many passengers as there are seats. Many foreigners have tried to cross this way, but most have failed and it's certainly not advised. The situation could change if the Chinese and Mongolians could learn to cooperate on improving the cross-border bus service, but don't hold your breath.

China-North Korea

There are four trains per week in either direction between Beijing and Pyongyang via Tianjin, Tangshan, Jinxi, Dandong and Sinuiju. The Chinese trains leave on Monday and Thursday and the North Korean trains leave on Wednesday and Saturday. All these trains leave Beijing at 4.48 pm and arrive at Pyongyang the next day at 3.55 pm. Going the other way, trains depart from Pyongyang at noon on Monday, Wednesday, Thursday and Saturday. The cost is US$77 one way.

Chinese trains are more comfortable than the North Korean ones. North Korean trains don't have air-conditioning even in the soft sleeper section, and the windows are locked so ventilation is nonexistent.

The North Korean train is actually just two carriages attached to the main Beijing-Dandong train, which are detached at Dandong (Chinese side) and then taken across the Yalu River bridge to Sinuiju (Korean side), where more carriages are added for local people. Non-Koreans remain in their original carriages.

Customs and immigration on both sides of the border are relatively casual and your passport will be taken away for stamping. The trains spend about four hours at the border for customs and immigration — two hours at Dandong and two hours at Sinŭiju. You are permitted to wander around the stations but you should not attempt to go beyond the entrance gate.

Sinŭiju station will be your first introduction to North Korea and the contrasts with China will be quite marked. Everything is squeaky clean and there are no vendors plying their goods. A portrait of the Great Leader looks down from the top of this station, and at all other railway stations in North Korea. You may wander around the station and take photos. One of the buildings is a rest area for foreign passengers, and here you will encounter the first of many billboards with photos and captions in English: 'The US Aggression Troops Transferring Missiles'; 'South Korean Puppet Police'; 'US Imperialists and South Korean Stooges' etc.

Soon after departing Sinŭiju, you will be presented with a menu (complete with colour photographs) of what's for dinner. The food is excellent and the service is fine. It's all very civilised. Make sure you have some small denomination US dollar bills to pay for the meal, as this is not included in the package deal you paid for in advance. There are no facilities for changing money at Sinŭiju or on the train. The dining car is for the use of non-Koreans only.

Your guide will meet you on arrival at Pyongyang railway station and accompany you to your hotel. Likewise, when you leave North Korea, your guide will bid you farewell at Pyongyang Railway Station or the airport and you travel to China unaccompanied.

SEA

There are regular daily ferries between Japan and South Korea. Between Hong Kong and Macau, there is a steady stream of ferries, jetfoils and jet-powered catamarans. Ferries running the Hong Kong-China and Macau-China routes are also frequent. Less frequent are ferries plying the Japan-China, China-South Korea and Okinawa-Taiwan routes.

China-Hong Kong

You can get tickets in Hong Kong most easily from CTS for a US$4 surcharge. Otherwise, go to the ticket windows at China Hong Kong City on Canton Rd in Tsimshatsui. You can also buy tickets directly from the China Merchants Steam Navigation Company (☎ 5440558, 543 0945), 18th floor, 152-155 Connaught Rd, Central. There are substantial discounts (around 40%) for children under five years of age. Children under the age of two travel for free.

Hong Kong – Guangzhou

The Hong Kong-Guangzhou boat is one of the most popular ways to enter or exit China. The journey takes about 10 hours, and the boats leave at 9 pm from China Hong Kong City in Kowloon and from the Zhoutouzui Wharf in Guangzhou. There is no service on the 31st day of each month.

Class	From HK	From Guangzhou
Special	US$37	US$35
1st	US$32	US$30
2nd	US$27	US$24
3rd	US$23	US$20

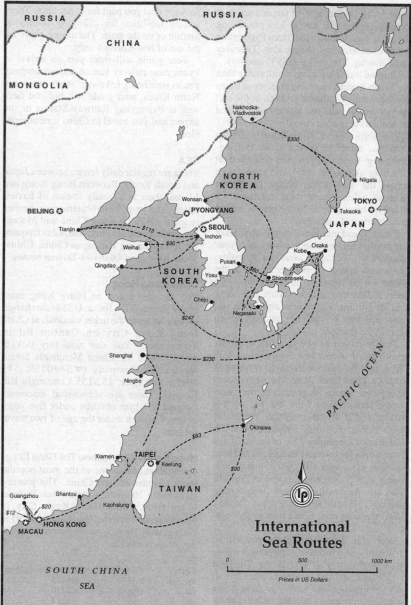

There is also a jet-powered catamaran which completes the journey in just four hours. Departures from Hong Kong are daily at 8.15 am, and from Guangzhou at 1 pm. The fare from Hong Kong is US$31, and from Guangzhou it's US$30.

Hong Kong-Haikou There are five trips monthly. Departures are from China Hong Kong City in Tsimshatsui, and the journey takes 24 hours. In Hong Kong, check-in is from noon to 12.45 pm. In Haikou, check-in is from 7 to 8 am.

Class	From HK	From Haikou
Special A	HK$496	HK$446
Special B	HK$471	HK$416
1st	HK$446	HK$366
2nd	HK$362	HK$346
3rd	HK$306	HK$266

Hong Kong-Ningbo There is one trip at half-month intervals, and the journey takes 55 hours. The departure from Hong Kong is at 10 am. From Ningbo, departure time is at 9 am.

Class	From HK	From Ningbo
Special	HK$1212	HK$932
1st	HK$1021	HK$541
2nd	HK$894	HK$437
3rd	HK$822	HK$441

Hong Kong-Shanghai There is one trip every five days and the journey takes 62 hours. In Hong Kong check-in time is at noon, but in Shanghai departure time is not fixed, so ask.

In Shanghai, tickets can be bought from CITS or the China Ocean Shipping Agency (☎ 216327 ext 79) at 255 Jiangxi Rd.

Class	From HK	From Shanghai
Special A	HK$1309	HK$1029
Special B	HK$1212	HK$925
1st	HK$1021	HK$799
2nd	HK$894	HK$697
3rd	HK$753	HK$584
Economy	HK$649	HK$501

Hong Kong-Shantou The journey takes 15

hours. Departures are at 5 pm from either Hong Kong or Shantou.

Class	From HK	From Shantou
Special A	HK$446	HK$433
Special B	HK$416	HK$383
1st	HK$366	HK$333
2nd	HK$346	HK$313
3rd	HK$266	HK$233

Hong Kong-Shekou Shekou is the main port for the Shenzhen Special Economic Zone, just north of Hong Kong. The hovercraft departs seven times daily, taking one hour to complete the journey. In Hong Kong, the one-way fare is HK$104. In Shekou, it costs HK$81.

Hong Kong-Shenzhen Airport The jet-powered catamaran departs six times daily in each direction. Although the journey *officially* takes one hour, it usually takes two hours so you must depart Hong Kong at least three hours before your scheduled flight time.

Class	From HK	From Shenzhen
VIP	HK$1578	HK$1428
1st	HK$263	HK$238
Economy	HK$163	HK$138

Hong Kong-Taiping (Opium War Museum) The jet-powered catamaran takes two hours (minimum) to complete the journey. Departures from Hong Kong are daily at 9.15 am and 2.20 pm. Departures from Taiping are at 11.50 am and 4.50 pm. Fares from Hong Kong are HK$226 and HK$186. Fares from Taiping are HK$158.

Hong Kong-Wuzhou The journey takes 12 hours, and departures from Hong Kong are at 8 am on even-numbered dates. Departures from Wuzhou are at 7.30 am on odd-numbered dates. The fare from Hong Kong is HK$360, and from Wuzhou it's HK$350.

Hong Kong-Xiamen The journey takes 22 hours. Hong Kong check-in time is Tuesday or Friday from 12.30 pm to 1 pm, and departures are at 2 pm. In Xiamen, departures are on Monday or Thursday at 3 pm.

Class	From HK	From Xiamen
Special A	HK$845	HK$580
Special B	HK$745	HK$510
1st	HK$595	HK$445
2nd	HK$545	HK$370
3rd	HK$495	HK$335
Seat	HK$435	HK$295

Hong Kong-Zhaoqing The journey takes 12 hours. Departures from Hong Kong are on odd-numbered dates at 7.30 pm, with no service available on the 31st day of the month. Departures from Zhaoqing are on even-numbered dates at 7 pm.

Class	From HK	From Zhaoqing
Special A	HK$624	
Special B	HK$361	
1st	HK$321	HK$288
2nd	HK$286	HK$253
3rd	HK$231	HK$198

There is also a jet-powered catamaran which completes the journey in five hours. Departures from Hong Kong are at 7.45 am on even-numbered dates. From Zhaoqing departures are at 2 pm on odd-numbered dates, with no service available on the 31st day of the month.

Class	From HK	From Zhaoqing
Special	HK$306	
1st	HK$286	HK$263
Economy	HK$276	HK$253

China-Japan
There is a ferry between Shanghai and Osaka/Kobe. It leaves once weekly, alternating between Osaka and Kobe, taking two days for a one-way trip. There is another ship running between Yokohama and Shanghai, leaving twice monthly. For a berth in a cabin with four beds, the fare is US$330 (from Japan) or US$230 (from China).

Passenger ships also ply the route from Kobe to Tianjin (the port is called Tanggu). Departures from Kobe are every Thursday at noon, arriving in Tianjin the next day. Economy/1st class tickets cost US$247/333.

The food on this boat gets poor reviews so bring a few emergency munchies. Tickets can be bought in Tianjin from the shipping office (☎ 312243) at 89 Munan Dao, Heping District. In Kobe, the office is at the port (☎ 3215791).

China-Macau
There is a direct overnight ferry between Macau and Guangzhou. There are two ships which run on alternate days, the *Dongshanhu* and the *Xiangshanhu*.

In Macau, departures are from the pier near the Floating Casino (*not* the Jetfoil Pier). The boat leaves Macau at 8.30 pm and arrives in Guangzhou the next morning at 7.30 am. Fares are US$12 in 2nd class, US$15 in 1st class and special class costs US$22. There is an extra US$1 charge on holidays.

In Guangzhou, departures are from Zhoutouzui Wharf. Fares are exactly the same as in Macau. From Guangzhou, the boat departs at 8.30 pm.

China-South Korea
Also useful is the boat between the South Korean port of Inch'ŏn and Weihai in China's Shandong Province. The cost is US$90 in economy class, US$110 (2nd class), US$130 (1st class) and US$150 (special 1st class). In China, tickets are available from Weihai China International Travel Service (CITS).

There is also a twice-weekly boat running between the South Korean port of Inch'ŏn and Tianjin (Tanggu). This costs US$115 in economy class but rises to US$350 in 1st class. The trip takes 28 hours and the boat arrives in Tianjin at 7 pm. Given the ridiculously high cost of accommodation in Tianjin, you'd be wise to hop the first train to Beijing if you're on a budget.

The Inch'ŏn International Ferry Terminal is the next to last stop on the Inch'ŏn-Seoul commuter train (red subway line from downtown). The commute takes one hour and from the station it's either a long walk or short taxi ride to the terminal. You must arrive at the terminal at least one hour before departure or you won't be allowed to board.

In Seoul, tickets for any boats to China can be bought from the Universal Travel Service (UTS) behind City Hall, just near the Seoul City Tourist Information Centre.

Hong Kong-Macau

Although Macau is separated from Hong Kong by 65 km of water, the journey can be made in as little as one hour. There are frequent departures throughout the day from 7 am to 9.30 pm.

You have a wide selection of boats to choose from. There are jetfoils, hoverferries, jumbocats (jet-powered large catamarans) and high-speed ferries. The fastest and most popular boats are the jetfoils and jumbocats.

For reasons only understood by the geniuses of marketing management, the jumbocats have now been renamed the 'super-shuttle'. The jumbocats are marginally more comfortable than the jetfoils, but neither this nor the catchy 'super-shuttle' slogan has been able to increase market share. The jetfoils remain far more popular with the Hong Kongers apparently because of the big 10 minutes they save. Perhaps the management of the super-shuttle should try another marketing gimic, like a karaoke lounge or an on-board casino.

Smoking is prohibited on the jetfoils and super-shuttle. Most of the boats depart from the huge Macau Ferry Pier next to Shun Tak Centre at 200 Connaught Rd, Sheung Wan, Hong Kong Island. This is easily reached by MTR to the Sheung Wan Station.

Hoverferries depart from the China Hong Kong City ferry pier in Tsimshatsui. However, these are far less numerous than jetfoils.

Luggage space on the jetfoils is limited to what you can carry. You'll be OK just carrying a backpack or one suitcase, but no way will they let you on with a trunk or something requiring two people to move it.

If you have to return to Hong Kong the same day as departure, you'd be wise to book your return ticket in advance because the boats are sometimes full, especially on weekends and holidays. Even Monday mornings can be difficult for getting seats back to Hong Kong. If you can't get on the jetfoil or super-shuttle, you might have a chance with the high-speed ferries which have a lot more room.

Jetfoil tickets can be purchased up to 28 days in advance in Hong Kong at the pier and at Ticketmate offices in some MTR stations, or booked by phone (☎ 8595696) if you have a credit card. Super-shuttle bookings (☎ 5599255) can be made 35 days in advance by telephone if you pay with plastic.

There are three different classes on the high-speed ferries (economy, tourist and 1st). The jetfoils have two classes (economy and 1st). All other boats have only one class. The Hong Kong government charges HK$26 (US$3.40) departure tax which is included in the price of your ticket. Macau charges M$20 (US$2.50), also included in the ticket price.

Japan-South Korea

There are several ferries linking Japan to South Korea. Purchasing a return ticket gains you a 10% discount on the return half, but fares from Japan are higher and there is a Y600 departure tax in Japan. Korea-Japan-Korea tickets work out to be the same or less than a straight one-way Japan-Korea ticket. So for the numerous travellers who work in

Hong Kong-Macau Boat Prices				
Vessel	Travel Time	Weekday	Weekend	Night
High-speed Ferry	95 minutes	US$8/10/12	US$10/13/15	
Hoverferry	80 minutes	US$1	US$1	US$16
Jetfoil	55 minutes	US$14/16	US$15/17	US$18/20
Super-Shuttle	65 minutes	US$1	US$17	

Naha-Keelung-Kaohsiung Fares					
From	To	1st	2nd	3rd	Student
Naha	Keelung	US$195	US$166	US$139	US$111
Naha	Kaohsiung	US$217	US$187	US$161	US$129
Keelung	Naha	US$124	US$98	US$83	US$68
Kaohsiung	Naha	US$135	US$109	US$90	US$75

Japan and need to make visa runs, consider taking a one-way to Korea the first time if you intend to cross the waters more than once a year.

The most popular boat is the Pukwan (Pusan-Shimonoseki) Ferry which takes 14½ hours. Daily departures from either Pusan (South Korea) or Shimonoseki (Japan) are at 6 pm and arrival is at 8.30 am. Fares on tickets bought in Korea for 1st class are US$80 to $90; 2nd class costs US$55 to $65. Students can receive a 20% discount and bicycles are carried free. Tickets are available in Shimonoseki (☎ 0832-243000) and Pusan (☎ 051-4633161) or Seoul (☎ 02-7380055). In addition, there are combination ferry-train tickets allowing you to make the Tokyo-Seoul run without taking to the air. Many travel agents can sell these – try contacting the Nippon Travel Agency (☎ 06-3120451), Osaka, or Aju Travel Service (☎ 02-7535051), Seoul.

Korea Ferry (Pusan ☎ 051-4667799, Hakata ☎ 092-2622323) plies three times weekly between Pusan and Hakata in 16 hours for US$55-110 with similar discounts to the Pukwan Ferry.

There are also hydrofoils daily from Pusan to Shimonoseki (3½ hours, US$62-88, Korean prices) and to Hakata (three hours, US$62). Departure from Hakata is at 10 am, arriving in Pusan at 12.55 pm; departure from Pusan is at 2 pm, arriving in Hakata at 4.55 pm. Note that the name of the wharf for Pusan (and for boats to Okinawa) is Chuo Futoh and it is across the bay, a long walk from Hakata Futoh (bayside place) which has other domestic boats.

The Kuk Jae Ferry connects both Kobe and Osaka with Pusan. The trip takes 22 hours and tickets cost from US$90 to US$200. A 20% student discount is available in 2nd class. Departures from Osaka (☎ 06-2661111) are on Wednesday and Saturday at noon, and from Pusan (☎ 051-4637000) to Osaka on Monday and Thursday at 5 pm. Departures from Kobe are on Monday and Friday and from Pusan to Kobe on Wednesday and Saturday. Tickets can be purchased in Seoul (☎ 02-7547786), 8th floor, Centre Building, 118 Namdaemunno 2-ga, Chung-gu.

Japan-Taiwan
There is a weekly passenger ferry that operates between Taiwan and Naha on the Japanese island of Okinawa. The ship departs from Okinawa and arrives in Taiwan the next day. Sometimes the ship will make brief stops at the islands of Miyako and Ishigaki, but the schedule for this is irregular. The ship alternates between the Taiwanese ports of Keelung and Kaohsiung, twice monthly from each port. Departures from Okinawa are on Thursday or Friday; departures from Taiwan are usually on Monday. See the above Naha-Keelung-Kaohsiung Fares table for prices.

Arimura Line has an office in Naha (☎ 098-8640087) and Osaka (☎ 06-5319269). In Taiwan, you can buy tickets from Yeong An Maritime Company (☎ 02-7715911), 11 Jenai Rd, Section 3, Taipei. You can also buy tickets in Kaohsiung (☎ 07-5510281) and Keelung (☎ 02-4248151).

China

China is a sleeping giant. Let her lie and sleep, for when she awakes, she will astonish the world.
Napoleon

After being shut down for 30 years of revolutionary fervour, China flung open its doors to tourism in 1981. Prior to that time, individuals could travel to the People's Republic of China (PRC) by invitation only, but now visas are being issued to all and sundry.

China is not always an easy country for the individual to travel in. Foreigners are generally unhappy with the Chinese government's pricing formula (foreigners should pay triple or more), severe transport bottlenecks (particularly on the railways) and the nagging feeling that xenophobia lurks just behind the official smile. But after centuries of isolation, the Middle Kingdom is trying to modernise and catch up with the West. No matter what you might think of the place, it's worth remembering what Cold War military planners in the 1950s used to say: China is a country that cannot be ignored.

Facts about the Country

HISTORY
Early China
The first Chinese dynasty, the Xia, was formed about 4000 years ago; it was followed by the Shang Dynasty from the 16th to 11th centuries BC, which established the area around the Yellow River as the cradle of Chinese civilisation. During the Zhou Dynasty of the 11th to 5th centuries BC, the most enduring feature of Chinese thinking was formulated: the concept of the 'mandate of heaven' raising the emperor to god-like status. As the Zhou Dynasty declined the Warring States period began. Confucius lived in this era, around 500 BC, and his response to turmoil was to advocate a return to what he saw as the dependable ways of the past.

In the 3rd century BC the short-lived Qin Dynasty, marked by the extreme cruelty of its emperor, laid the foundations for a unified empire. Under the succeeding Han Dynasty, which ruled until 220 AD, the empire reached its zenith and Confucianism became the basis of education for almost the next 2000 years. In the period of disunity that followed the collapse of the Han Dynasty, Buddhism spread throughout China. In the 6th century AD, the country was reunited under the short-lived Sui Dynasty, which was succeeded in 618 AD by the Tang Dynasty. This is now regarded as China's golden age. The capital at Chang'an (today's Xi'an) was one of the greatest cities in the world.

In 1211, Mongol tribes under Genghis Khan swept over the Great Wall and by 1279 Genghis' grandson Kublai controlled southern China and had founded the Yuan Dynasty. It was to the China of the Mongols that Europeans like Marco Polo came – and their books revealed the splendours of Asia to an amazed Europe. After Kublai died in 1294, the Mongol hold on China disintegrated, and the Ming Dynasty came to power. Buddhism and Taoism were made state religions. The Ming emperors, who saw China as both culturally superior to the outside world and economically self-sufficient, closed the doors to Europe just when the Europeans were entering their most dynamic phase since the Roman Empire.

In 1628 a famine and ensuing turmoil led the Manchus to invade China and found the Qing Dynasty.

The Impact of the West
Meanwhile, the Europeans were about to expand their power on a scale undreamt of by the isolated Chinese. The Portuguese arrived in China in 1516 and, in 1557, set up a trading base in Macau. In the next century

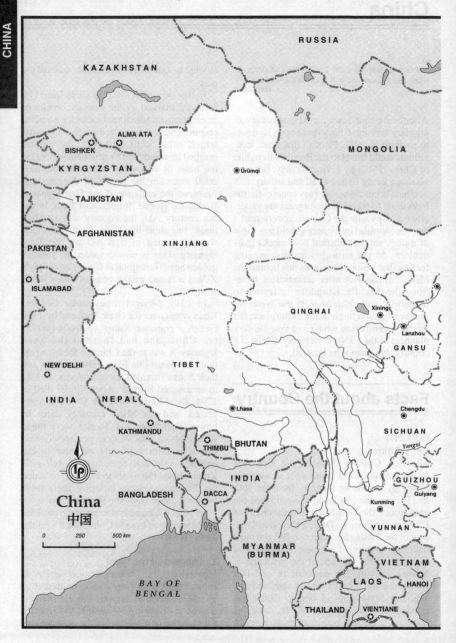

China
中国
0   250   500 km

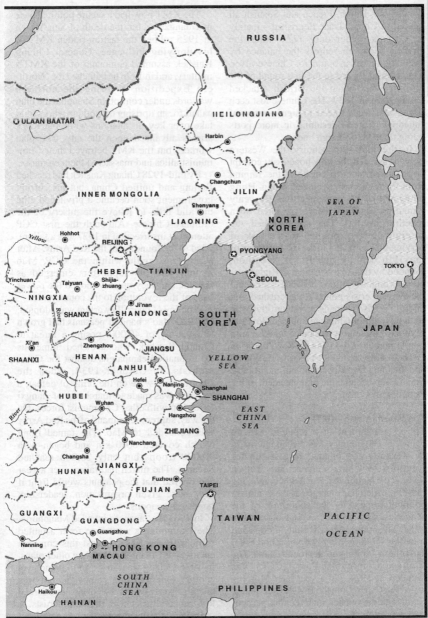

the British, Dutch, French and Spanish all landed in China. Trade flourished – mainly in China's favour until 1773, when the British began to redress the balance by exchanging Indian opium for Chinese silver. This eventually led to the first round of the Opium Wars when the British attacked Guangzhou in 1839. The Chinese lost each round and were forced to sign a series of 'unequal treaties', resulting in more ports being opened to foreign trade.

In the mid-19th century, the Western powers assisted the now hopelessly corrupt Qing government to put down the Taiping Rebellion, which occurred when Hong Xiuquan and his movement the 'Heavenly Kingdom of Great Peace' declared open rebellion in 1851. That accomplished, the foreign powers returned to the task of carving up China; but in the last few years of the 19th century, the Boxer Rebellion, founded by the Boxers United in Righteousness, brought relations between China and the West to crisis point. It was crushed, but laid the seeds for many secret anti-dynastic societies within China and abroad. In 1905 several of these groups banded together into the Alliance for the Chinese Revolution; in 1911 an army uprising spread from Wuhan and the Qing Dynasty crumbled; and in 1912 Sun Yatsen became the first president of the Republic of China.

The Kuomintang (KMT)

The establishment of a republic was no panacea. The country was racked internally by warlords and looting. In a search for solutions to China's crises, Sun Yatsen revived the Nationalist Party, or Kuomintang (KMT), which had emerged as the dominant political force after the abdication of the Manchus, and based it in Guangzhou in 1917. Meanwhile Marxist study groups and societies – led by Mao Zedong, Zhou Enlai and others – sprang up all around China. The Chinese Communist Party (CCP) was founded in 1921, but a year later Moscow urged the CCP to join the KMT to strengthen China against outside intervention, particularly from Japan.

The KMT now had a secure political base in Guangzhou, but the death of Sun Yatsen in 1925 robbed the faction-ridden KMT of his unifying influence. General Chiang Kaishek assumed command of the KMT's military, and in 1926 he launched the 'Northern 'Expedition' to bring the northern warlords under control. In Shanghai the plan called for an uprising of workers who would take over key installations while the KMT armies advanced upon the city. The plan worked, but the KMT betrayed their Communist allies and massacred them en masse.

By mid-1928 Chiang Kaishek had reached Beijing and unified China, but his corrupt government soon became a privileged elite that did little to relieve the misery of the ordinary Chinese. Although the first CCP attempt at insurrection in 1927 was a failure, it led to the founding of the Red Army. After a power struggle within the CCP, Mao Zedong and his supporters emerged as leaders, and they quickly moved the power base of the revolution to the countryside.

A policy of guerrilla warfare was adopted; by 1930 Mao's band of peasants had grown to an army of 40,000, posing a threat to Chiang Kaishek, who launched numerous extermination campaigns against the Communists. In October 1934, when the Communists were on the brink of defeat, a decision was made to march out of Jiangxi to join up with other Communist forces. On the way, supreme command of the Red Army was conceded to Mao. The famed Long March covered 8000 km and began with 90,000 troops but only 20,000 reached Shaanxi. The march had taken over a year and proved that the peasants would fight if they were given organisation, leadership, hope and weapons.

In 1931 the Japanese invaded Manchuria. The Communists wanted to form a united front with the KMT against this common enemy, but Chiang Kaishek had other plans. In 1936 Chiang went to Xi'an to launch yet another extermination campaign, but was taken prisoner by his own troops and forced to form an alliance with the Communists.

In 1937 the Japanese launched an all-out

invasion of China, and by 1939 controlled all of eastern China. The KMT and Communists scrambled for position after the Japanese surrendered in 1945. US-trained and equipped KMT forces went to battle with the Red Army which, together with its support units, had grown to several million.

The turning point came between 1948 and 1949 when whole divisions of the KMT went over to the Communist side. On 1 October 1949 Mao Zedong proclaimed the formation of the People's Republic of China while the KMT fled to Taiwan with about 1½ million supporters.

Communist China

The People's Republic began as a bankrupt nation decimated by war. Yet the Communists recall the 1950s as a successful period because of the elation of victory, the reconstruction of the country and because they fought the Americans to a standstill in the Korean War. By 1953 inflation had been halted, industrial production restored to prewar levels and land redistributed to peasants. But the desire to fulfil speedily the promise of the revolution led to the ill-fated Great Leap Forward in the mid-1950s. Peasants were set to work on small-scale industrial projects like 'backyard' steel furnaces, and gigantic rural communes were established; the resulting misdirected agricultural and industrial output caused a disastrous slump in useful production. Floods and drought ruined the harvests of 1959 and 1960, resulting in widespread famine. Political disputes with the Russians led to the withdrawal of Soviet aid and advisers in 1960.

The power of Liu Shaoqi, Deng Xiaoping and their supporters, who held pragmatic economic views, increased at Mao's expense. Incentives much like those being tried today were instituted, and by 1965 the economy had recovered some of its equilibrium. For Mao these policies reeked of capitalism.

In 1966 the Party Central Committee launched the Cultural Revolution 'to struggle against and crush those persons in authority who are taking the capitalist road'.

Many of Mao's opponents (including Deng Xiaoping) were purged, but the whole exercise soon turned into a colossal disaster. Mao was quick to recognise the disruptive potential of the Red Guards who materialised in 1966. Millions of teenagers were suddenly given the opportunity to attack and humiliate teachers, scientists and other 'stinking intellectuals'. People were beaten, imprisoned, tortured and killed for being 'capitalist roaders'. It wasn't long before Red Guard factions battled each other and the country moved towards civil war. In 1967, Mao had to call in the army to put down the Red Guards, but not before they had destroyed or vandalised anything that was a physical reminder of China's past or 'evil foreign influence'. By this time, Mao was raised to a god-like status and anyone who wanted to stay healthy quoted frequently from his Little Red Book.

Zhou Enlai assumed the number two position in China – and with the health of Mao (aged 79) declining, it was Zhou (73) who soon took over the reins and began to steer a more pragmatic and rational course. Fear of the Soviet Union prompted a reconciliation with the USA, and in 1973 Zhou managed to return to power none other than Deng Xiaoping, who had been vilified during the Cultural Revolution.

Zhou died in early 1976 and Deng disappeared from public view. Mao died on 9 September 1976 and a month later the 'Gang of Four' (including Jiang Qing, Mao's widow) were arrested and blamed for the horrors of the Cultural Revolution. Deng Xiaoping was once more returned to power in mid-1977 and China embarked on its current path of modernisation.

The 1980s saw a decade of rapid economic progress and liberalisation, but it ended on a bitter note. Pro-democracy demonstrators rallied in Beijing in April 1989. The demonstrations quickly grew into a full-scale movement involving over half a million people who marched through the streets of Beijing and camped out in Tiananmen Square. While vehemently denouncing the demonstrations, Communist Party leaders showed surprising restraint for a while, but martial law was declared on 20 May. Then Party General Secretary Zhao Ziyang openly sided with the student demonstrators. On 4 June, tanks and troops moved into Tiananmen Square and crushed the pro-democracy movement. Zhao Ziyang was arrested along with thousands of others accused of 'counter-revolutionary crimes'. Disgusted by China's brutality, many Western countries imposed economic sanctions but most were lifted within two years. However, continuing reports of human rights abuses and a total lack of democracy has left many wondering if much has changed since the last emperor was dethroned.

GEOGRAPHY

China is the third-largest country in the world, after the Soviet Union and Canada. The government also regards Taiwan, Hong Kong and Macau as territory belonging to the People's Republic.

Western China is dominated by the high plateaus of Tibet and Qinghai, 4500 metres above sea level. The east is dominated by plains – the most important agricultural areas of the country and heavily populated. The north-west region of the country is a sparsely inhabited desert.

The environment has taken a heavy beating in some parts of the country – chimneys belching out thick, black smoke are not an uncommon sight.

CLIMATE

China gets a lot of it. Spread over such a vast area, the country is subject to the worst extremes of temperature, from bitterly cold to sizzling hot.

In the north, December to March is a period of incredibly cold and windy weather. Beijing's temperature doesn't rise above 0°C though it is generally dry and sunny. North of the Great Wall and into Inner Mongolia and Heilongjiang the temperature can drop to as low as minus 45°C. Summer in the north is from May to August and temperatures can rise to 38°C or more. July and August are also the rainy months in the eastern region, but

the west is a vast desert and humidity is never a problem. Spring and autumn are the best times for visiting the north, with temperatures in the 20 to 30°C range.

In the central region (including Shanghai) summers are long, hot and humid – the area is known as China's oven. Winters are short and cold, but the weather can also be wet and miserable at any time other than summer.

In the south, April to September is a hot, humid period. Heavy rains are common, and typhoons are liable to hit the south-eastern coast between July and September. The short winter from January to March is nowhere near as bad as in the north. See the Beijing, Shanghai and Guangzhou climate charts in the Appendix later in this book.

GOVERNMENT

Every revolution evaporates, leaving behind only the slime of a new bureaucracy.
Franz Kafka

Although no one person rules all of China, there is little in the Chinese political system that resembles a democracy. Highest authority rests with the 25-member Politburo. Below it is the 210-member Central Committee. The Party's chain of command moves through different layers right down to universities, government offices and industries, thus ensuring strict central control. Officials are appointed – not elected – and there is a tendency for the sons and daughters of high-ranking officials to inherit positions of privilege and power just as in feudal times.

The day-to-day running of the country lies with the State Council, which is directly under the control of the Communist Party. The State Council is headed by the Premier. Rubber-stamping the decisions of the Communist Party leadership is the National People's Congress (NPC).

The great stumbling block of the Chinese political system is the bureaucracy. The term 'cadre' is usually applied to all powerful bureaucrats.

The role of the army should also not be forgotten. Mao held that 'political power grows out of the barrel of a gun'. China's leadership is riven with mutually antagonistic factions, but ultimately those who control the military have the final say.

At grass-roots level the basic unit of social organisation outside the family is the work unit. Every Chinese is a member of one. Many Westerners may admire the cooperative spirit this system is supposed to engender, but they would cringe if their own lives were so intricately controlled. Work units decide if a couple may marry or divorce and when they can have a child. It assigns housing, sets salaries, handles mail, recruits Party members, keeps files on each unit member, transfers people to other jobs or other parts of the country (often against their will) and gives permission to travel abroad. The work unit's control extends into every part of the individual's life.

ECONOMY

Mao feared economic ties with other countries would bring dependency, and China under his rule became economically isolated. Since his death, however, this approach has been radically altered. Foreign trade is the key to China's economic modernisation. While inefficient state-owned enterprises continue to hobble the economy, individuals are now actively encouraged to set up their own businesses.

Especially since 1991, when most restrictions were lifted, China has seen spectacular rates of economic growth. However, the economy remains fragile. Inflation has become a severe problem, and consumer demand is putting a serious strain on China's supply of infrastructure (highways, railroads, seaports, electrical power capacity and so on). China is also reportedly on the verge of a banking crisis, with money supply and shoddy accounting practices threatening to spiral out of control. But many firmly believe that China is destined to become a major world economic power.

POPULATION & PEOPLE

With 1.2 billion people, China is the world's most populous nation. Of that total, 93% is Han Chinese and the rest is composed of China's 55 or so minority groups.

China's birth control policies are the strictest in the world – every couple is only allowed one child. This policy is strongly enforced in the cities, but in rural areas – where 80% of the people live – enforcement is much less effective. Although the rate of increase is slowing, China's population continues to grow and is expected to hit 1.25 billion by the year 2000.

ARTS

Calligraphy – writing Chinese characters with brush pens and ink – is one of China's ancient art forms. Closely related is Chinese watercolour painting. Pottery, bronze vessels and funerary objects also have a long history in China.

Taijiquan (slow-motion shadow boxing) has in recent years become quite trendy in Western countries – it has been popular in China for centuries. *Gongfu* (previously spelled *kungfu*) differs from taijiquan in that it is performed at much higher speed and with the intention of doing bodily harm. Gongfu also often employs weapons.

Then there is *qigong* not easily described in Western terms but it's rather like faith healing. *Qi* represents life's vital energy and *gong* is from gongfu. Qigong can be thought of as energy management and healing. Practitioners try to project their qi to perform various miracles, including driving nails through boards (an indication of its martial arts origins) as well as healing others.

One of the highlights of a visit to China is to see a Beijing opera – obviously, most easily accomplished in Beijing.

CULTURE

The usual standards of Asian decorum apply, but in some ways China is a relief after fashion-conscious Tokyo, Seoul and Hong Kong. In other words, you can get away with being a slob in China – most backpackers will fit right in! However, fashion consciousness is on the increase in large cities like Guangzhou and Shanghai.

The Chinese place little importance on

CHINA

what foreigners wear, as long as it's within acceptable levels of modesty. While shorts are less acceptable for women, plenty of Chinese women wear them. Skirts and dresses are frequently worn in the cities – in Beijing, miniskirts are in vogue and many young women have started wearing skin-hugging tights. However, bikinis have still not made their debut in China, and public nudity is absolutely taboo.

RELIGION

Traditional Chinese religions – Taoism, Buddhism and Confucianism – are in a dismal state. During the Cultural Revolution, rampaging Red Guards swept through China like a laxative, purging the People's Republic of religion and its practitioners. Temples and monasteries were ransacked and often levelled, and monks and priests were imprisoned, murdered or sent to the countryside to labour in the fields. In Tibet, for example, the theocracy which had ruled the country for 1000 years was wiped out virtually overnight. Muslims were often given the job of raising pigs.

The present Chinese government professes atheism and considers religion to be a superstition, but religious freedom is guaranteed under the Chinese constitution and worshippers are on the increase. Temples which were ransacked during the Cultural Revolution have now mostly been repaired, often with funds donated by overseas Chinese. On the other hand, many of the temples appear to be tourist attractions – devoid of worshippers and admission fees are collected at the gate. Furthermore, those who hold allegiance to a church, mosque or temple are not permitted to join the Communist Party.

These days, the people who still practise their religion sincerely in China are mainly ethnic minorities such as the Muslim Uigurs in Xinjiang or Lama Buddhists in Tibet. Many Tibetan monks and nuns are currently serving long prison sentences for 'counter-revolutionary activities'. There's a growing minority of Christians, but their numbers are small. Catholics have had a particularly hard time since loyalty to the Pope is still considered sacrilegious by the Communist Party. Indeed, the government has established a separate Beijing Catholic Church which does not recognise the Holy See.

LANGUAGE

The official language is the Beijing dialect, known as Mandarin in the West and as *putonghua* or 'common speech' in China. About 70% of the population speaks Mandarin but there are many other Chinese dialects.

Written Chinese has something like 50,000 characters – but only about 5000 are in common use and about 2000 are needed to read a newspaper easily. The Communist government has simplified the written script – about 50% of the strokes were eliminated, which also makes it simpler to learn and much faster to write. However, the simplified characters differ significantly from those used in Taiwan and Hong Kong, and any serious student of Chinese now must learn both systems!

In 1958 the Chinese officially adopted a system known as *pinyin* to enable them to write using the Roman alphabet, but don't expect all literate Chinese to know pinyin. However, it's commonly used on shop fronts, street signs and advertising billboards. Basically the sounds are pronounced as in English, with a few exceptions:

Vowels

a	like the 'a' in 'father'
ai	like the 'i' in 'I'
ao	like the 'ow' in 'cow'
e	like the 'u' in 'blur'
ei	like the 'ei' in 'weigh'
i	like the 'ee' in 'meet'; or the 'oo'in 'book' when it occurs after c, ch, r, s, sh, z, zh
ian	like in 'yen'
ie	like the English word 'yeah'
o	like the 'o' in 'or'
ou	like the 'oa' in 'boat'
u	like the 'u' in 'flute'
ui	like 'way'
uo	like 'w' followed by an 'o' like in 'or'

yu like German umlaut 'ü' or French 'u' in 'union'

ü like German umlaut 'ü'

Consonants

c like the 'ts' in 'bits'

ch like in English, but with the tongue curled back

h like in English, but articulated from the throat

q like the 'ch' in 'chicken'

r like the 's' in 'pleasure'

sh like in English, but with the tongue curled back

x like the 'sh' in 'shine'

z like the 'ds' in 'suds'

zh like the 'j' in 'judge' but with the tongue curled back

Consonants can never appear at the end of a syllable except for **n, ng** and **r**.

In pinyin, apostrophes are occasionally used to separate syllables. So, you can write *ping'an* to prevent the word being pronounced as *pin'gan*.

Tones

Their are four basic tones used in Mandarin Chinese, while other dialects such as Cantonese can have as many as seven. For example, in Mandarin Chinese the word *ma* can have four distinct meanings depending on which tone is used:

high tone	*mā* is mother
rising tone	*má* is hemp or numb
falling-rising tone	*mǎ* is horse
falling tone	*mà* is to scold or swear

In the tourist hotels and at travel agencies catering to foreigners there is nearly always someone around who speaks a little English. In many universities, there are 'English corners' where the students go to practice – foreigners are enthusiastically welcomed. Phrase books are invaluable – you may want to pick up Lonely Planet's *Mandarin Chinese Phrasebook*. A small dictionary in English, pinyin and Chinese characters will come in handy – these are readily available from the Xinhua Bookstore which has branches all over China.

Greetings & Civilities

Hello.
Nǐ hǎo.
你好
name card
míng piàn
名片
Goodbye.
Zài jiàn.
再见
Thank you.
Xiè xie.
谢谢
Thank you very much.
Duō xie.
多谢
You're welcome.
Bú kè qì.
不客气
Yes/Have.
Yǒu.
有
No/Don't have.
Méi yǒu.
没有
Maybe (it's possible).
Yǒu kě néng.
有可能
I'm sorry (excuse me).
Duì bù qǐ.
对不起

Useful Expressions

Do you speak English?
Nǐ huì jiǎng yīng wén ma?
你会讲英文吗
Does anyone speak English?
Yǒu méi yǒu rén huì jiǎng yīng wén?
有没有人会讲英文
I don't understand.
Wǒ tīng bù dǒng.
我听不懂
Just a moment.
Děng yī xià.
等一下

Please write it down.
Qǐng nǐ xiě xià lái.
请你写下来

I want to change money.
Wǒ yào huàn qián.
我要换钱

How much is it?
Duō shǎo qián?
多少钱

Too expensive.
Tài guì le.
太贵了

Air Transport

airport
fēi jī chǎng
飞机场

CAAC
zhōng guó mín háng
中国民航

ticket office
shòu piào chù
售票处

reserve a seat
dìng wèi zǐ
定位子

cancel
qǔ xiāo
取消

ticket
piào
票

one-way (ticket)
dān chéng piào
单程票

return (ticket)
lái huí piào
来回票

buy a ticket
mǎi piào
买票

refund a ticket
tuì piào
退票

reconfirm air ticket
què rèn
确认

boarding pass
dēng jì kǎ
登记卡

Rail Transport

train
huǒ chē
火车

railway station
huǒ chē zhàn
火车站

main railway station
zhǔ yào huǒ chē zhàn
主要火车站

timetable
shí kè biǎo
时刻表

ticket office
huǒ chē shòu piào chù
火车售票处

upgrade ticket (on train)
bǔ piào
补票

hard-seat
yìng xí, yìng zuò
硬席/硬座

soft-seat
ruǎn xí, ruǎn zuò
软席/软座

hard-sleeper
yìng wò
硬卧

soft-sleeper
ruǎn wò
软卧

middle berth
zhōng pù
中铺

upper berth
shàng pù
上铺

lower berth
xià pù
下铺

1st-class waiting room
tóu děng hòu chē lóu
头等候车楼

platform ticket
zhàn tái piào
站台票

Which platform?
Dì jǐ hào zhàn tái?
第几号台

luggage storage room
  jì cún chù
  寄存处
subway (underground) station
  dì tiě zhàn
  地铁站

Other Public Transport

What time is the...?
  ...jǐ diǎn zhōng?
  ...几点钟
    first
      dì yī ge
      第一个
    last
      zuì hòu
      最後
    next
      xià yī ge
      下一个
bus
  gōng gòng qì chē
  公共汽车
minibus
  xiǎo gōng gòng qì chē
  小公共汽车
long-distance bus station
  cháng tú qì chē zhàn
  长途汽车站
boat
  chuán
  船
pier
  mǎ tóu
  码头
taxi
  chū zù chē
  计程车
I want to get off (bus or taxi).
  Xià chē.
  下车

Directions

Where is the toilet?
  Cè suǒ zài nǎ lǐ?
  厕所在哪里
I'm lost.
  Wǒ mí lù.
  我迷路

I want to buy a map.
  Wǒ yào mǎi dì tú.
  我要买地图
I want to go to...
  Wǒ yào qù...
  我要去...
    China International Travel Service (CITS)
      zhōng guó guó jì lü xíng shè
      中国国际旅行社
    China Travel Service (CTS)
      zhōng guó lü xíng shè
      中国旅行社
    China Youth Travel Service (CYTS)
      zhōng guó qīng nián lü xíng shè
      中国青年旅行社
    embassy
      dà shǐ guǎn
      大使馆
    Foreign Language Bookstore
      wài wén shū diàn
      外文书店
    Xinhua Bookstore
      xīn huá shū diàn
      新华书店

Please show me where we are on the map.
  Wǒ mén xiàn zài de wèi zhì zài dì tú shàng de nǎlǐ.
  我们现在的位置在地图上的哪裡
Turn right.
  Yòu zhuǎn.
  右转
Turn left.
  Zuǒ zhuǎn.
  左转
Go straight.
  Yì zhí zǒu.
  一直走
Turn around.
  Xiàng huí zǒu.
  向回走
far
  yuǎn
  远
near
  jìn
  近

alley
xiàng, hú tóng
巷/胡同

road
lù
路

boulevard
dà dào
大道

section
duàn
段

street
jiē, dà jiē
街/大街

No 21
21 hào
21号

Accommodation

hotel
lü guǎn
旅馆

hostel
zhāo dài suǒ
招待所

big hotel
jiǔ diàn, bīn guǎn
酒店/宾馆

room
fáng jiān
房间

dormitory
duō rén fáng
多人房

single room (1 bed)
dān rén fáng
单人房

double room (2 beds)
shuāng rén fáng
双人房

bed
chuáng wèi
床位

economy room
jīng jì fáng
经济房

economy room with bath
jīng jì tào fáng
经济套房

standard room with bath
biāo zhǔn tào fáng
标准套房

luxury room with bath
háo huá tào fáng
豪华套房

book the whole room
bāo fáng
包房

reserve a room
dìng fáng jiān
定房间

deposit
yā jīn
押金

check-in (register)
dēng jì
登记

check-out
tuì fáng
退房

Please give me a name card for this hotel.
Qǐng gěi wǒ lü guǎn de míng piàn.
请给我旅馆的名片

How much per person?
Yī ge rén duō shǎo qián?
一个人多少钱

How much for a room?
Yī jiān fáng jiān duō shǎo qián?
一间房间多少钱

Please let me see the room first.
Qǐng xiān gěi wǒ kàn fáng jiān.
请先给我看房间

Necessities

bathroom (washroom)
xǐ shǒu jiān
洗手间

mosquito incense coils
wén xiāng
蚊香

mosquito mats
dìan wén xiāng
电蚊香

sanitary pads (Kotex)
wèi shēng mián
卫生棉

sunscreen (UV) lotion
fáng shài yóu
防晒油
tampons
wèi shēng mián tiáo
卫生棉条
tissue paper
miàn zhǐ
面纸
toilet paper
wèi shēng zhǐ
卫生纸
wash clothes
xǐ yī fú
洗衣服

Post

aerogramme
háng kōng yóu jiǎn
航空邮简
airmail
háng kōng xìn
航空信
envelope
xìn fēng
信封
International Express Mail (EMS)
guó jì kuài jié
国际快捷
Main Post Office (GPO)
zǒng yóu jú
总邮局
package
bāo guǒ
包裹
postcard
míng xìn piàn
明信片
poste restante
cún jú hòu lǐng lán
存局候领栏
post office
yóu jú
邮局
printed matter
yìn shuā pǐn
印刷品
registered mail
guà hào
挂号

stamp
yóu piào
邮票
surface mail
píng yóu
平邮
telegram
diàn bào
电报

Telecommunications

collect call
duì fāng fù qián
对方付钱
direct dial
zhí bō diàn huà
直拨电话
fax
chuán zhēn
传真
international call
guó jì diàn huà
国际电话
telephone
diàn huà
电话
telephone card
diàn huà kǎ
电话卡
telephone office
diàn xùn dà lóu
电讯大楼
telex
diàn chuán
电传

Visas & Documents

passport
hù zhào
护照
visa
qiān zhèng
签证
visa extension
yán cháng qiān zhèng
延长签证
Public Security Bureau
gōng ān jú
公安局

CHINA

Foreign Affairs Branch
wài shì kē
外事科

Medical

I'm sick.
Wǒ shēng bìng.
我生病

I'm injured.
Wǒ shòu shāng.
我受伤

I want to see a doctor.
Wǒ yào kàn yī shēng.
我要看医生

I want to go to the hospital.
Wǒ yào qù yī yuàn.
我要去医院

Please call an ambulance.
Qǐng nǐ zhǎo jiù hù chē.
请你找救护车

I'm allergic to...
Wǒ duì...hěn guò mǐn.
我对...很过敏

I'm a diabetic.
Wǒ yǒu táng niào bìng.
我有糖尿病

antibiotics
kàng jūn sù
抗菌素

anti-diarrhoeal drug
huáng liǎn sù
黄连素

diarrhoea
lā dù zi
拉肚子

emergency room
jí zhěn
急诊

fever
fā shāo
发烧

giardia
ā mǐ bā fù xiè
阿米巴腹泻

hepatitis
gān yán
肝炎

influenza
liú xíng xìng gǎn maò
流行性感冒

laxative
xiè yào
泻药

malaria
nüè jì
疟疾

penicillin
qīng méi sù
青霉素

pharmacy
yào diàn
药店

rabies
kuáng quǎn bìng
狂犬病

Emergencies

Please call the police.
Qǐng nǐ zhǎo jǐng chá.
请你找警察

Fire!
Huǒ zāi!
火灾

Help!
Jiù mìng a!
救命啊

Thief!
Xiǎo tōu!
小偷

pickpocket
pá shǒu
扒手

rapist
qiáng jiān fàn
强奸犯

Time

When?
Shén me shí hòu?
甚麼时候

What is the time now?
Xiàn zài jǐ diǎn zhōng?
现在几点钟

What time does it open?
Jǐ diǎn kāi shǐ yíng yè?
几点开始营业

Today what time does it close?
Jīn tiān yíng yè dào jǐ diǎn?
今天营业到几点

7.15 am
zǎo shàng 7 diǎn 15 fēn
早上7点15分

7.15 pm
wǎn shàng 7 diǎn 15 fēn
晚上7点15分

now
xiàn zài
现在

today
jīn tiān
今天

tomorrow
míng tiān
明天

Sunday
Xīng qī tiān
星期天

Monday
Xīng qī yī
星期一

Tuesday
Xīng qī er
星期二

Wednesday
Xīng qī sān
星期叁

Thursday
Xīng qī sì
星期四

Friday
Xīng qī wǔ
星期五

Saturday
Xīng qī liù
星期六

Numbers

0	*líng*	零
1	*yī, yào*	一
2	*èr, liǎng*	二 两
3	*sān*	叁
4	*sì*	四
5	*wǔ*	五
6	*liù*	六
7	*qī*	七
8	*bā*	八
9	*jiǔ*	九

10	*shí*	十
11	*shí yī*	十一
12	*shí èr*	十二
20	*èr shí*	二十
21	*èr shí yī*	二十一
100	*yì bǎi*	一百
200	*liǎng bǎi*	两百
1000	*yì qiān*	一千
2000	*liǎng qiān*	两千
10,000	*yí wàn*	一万
20,000	*liǎng wàn*	两万
100,000	*shí wàn*	十万
200,000	*èr shí wàn*	二十万

Facts for the Visitor

VISAS & EMBASSIES

Visas for individual travel are readily available from many agents in Hong Kong and can be issued the same day for an extra fee. One photo is required and there must be a blank page in your passport. The visa length is normally one month from the date of entry that you've written on the application, but can be issued for up to three months (on request) if you apply through a travel agent.

The cost of the visa ranges from HK$90 to HK$250, depending on how quickly you want it and where you get it. More expensive are the two-entry visas. Multiple-entry visas are expensive (HK$700), and you can stay for just 30 days at a time (no extensions permitted), but the visa remains valid for six months. It will only be issued if you've already been to China at least once and have stamps in your passport to prove it.

Many travel agents provide speedy visa service, but it's cheapest if you do it yourself at the Visa Office of the Ministry of Foreign Affairs of the People's Republic of China (☎ 8939812), 5th floor, Low Block, China Resources Building, 26 Harbour Rd, Wanchai, Hong Kong Island. The office is open Monday to Friday from 9 am to 12.30 pm and 2 to 5 pm, and Saturday until 12.30 pm. This place issues the cheapest visas. A three-month visa issued in two days costs HK$90.

In Macau, you can get Chinese visas at China Travel Service (☎ 700888), Xinhua Building, Rua de Nagasaki.

Chinese Embassies

Following are the addresses of Chinese embassies in major cities around the world.

Australia
   247 Federal Highway, Watson, Canberra, 2600 ACT (☎ 06-273 4780)
   Consulate: Melbourne (☎ 03-822 0604)
Austria
   Metterrichgasse 4, A-1030 Vienna (☎ 06-75 31 49, 713 67 06)
Belgium
   443-445, Avenue de Tervueren, 1150 Brussels (☎ 02-771 33 09, 771 26 81)
Canada
   515 St Patrick St, Ottawa, Ontario KIN 5H3 (☎ 613-234 2706)
Denmark
   25 Oeregaards alle, DK 2900 Hellerup, Copenhagen 2900 (☎ 1-62 58 06, 61 10 13)
France
   11 Ave George V, Paris 75008 (☎ 1-47.23.36.77, 47.36.77.90)
Germany
   Kurfürstenallee 12, 5300 Bonn 2 (Bad Godesberg) (☎ 0228-36 10 95, 36 23 50)
Italy
   56 Via Bruxelles, Rome 56-00198 (☎ 06-841 34 58, 841 34 67)
Japan
   3-4-33 Moto-Azabu, Minato-ku, Tokyo (106) (☎ 03-3403 3380, 3403 3381)
Netherlands
   Adriaan Goehooplaan 7, 2517 JX The Hague, (☎ 070-355 15 15, 355 92 09)
New Zealand
   2-6 Glenmore St, Kelburr, Wellington (☎ 472 1382, 472 1384)
South Korea
   83, Myong-dong 2-ga, Chung-gu
Spain
   C/Arturo Soria, 113 28043 Madrid (☎ 01-519 4242, 519 3672)
Sweden
   Lidovagen 8, 115 25 Stockholm (☎ 08-783 6730)
Switzerland
   Kalecheggweg 10, 3006 Berne (☎ 031-44 73 33, 43 45 93)
UK
   49-15 Portland Place, London WIN 3AH (☎ 0171-636 2580, 636 8845)
USA
   Embassy: 2300 Connecticut Ave NW, Washington, DC 20008 (☎ 328 2500, 328 2517)
   Consulates: 3417 Montrose Blvd, Houston, TX 77006
   104 South Michigan Ave, Suite 1200, Chicago, IL 60603
   1450 Laguna St, San Francisco, CA 94115
   520 12th Ave, New York, NY 10036

Visa Extensions

Visa extensions are handled by the Foreign Affairs Section of the local Public Security Bureaus (the police force). The general rule is that you can get one extension of one month's duration.

DOCUMENTS

To travel to closed places an official 'Alien's Travel Permit' is required. These are obtainable from the Foreign Affairs Office of the Public Security Bureau. However, there are very few places in China that are closed to foreigners anymore. Permits are required for visiting sensitive regions prone to ethnic unrest like parts of Tibet and Qinghai. The rules change from time to time, but in general the trend is towards opening up everything to foreign travellers. How do you know if a particular place is closed? In general, a place is open if the staff at the local bus station or airline will sell you a ticket to go there.

CUSTOMS

Customs is pretty much a formality these days. Customs declaration forms seem to be a thing of the past.

You can take in 600 cigarettes, two litres of alcohol, approximately half a litre of perfume and 72 rolls of film. 'Subversive literature' (literature that makes the Chinese government look bad) cannot be brought in. Customs will also seize pornography.

When you leave China, antiques (or things which look antique) may be confiscated unless you have an official receipt. Some herbs are also prohibited exports.

MONEY

Inflation in China has been so rapid (20% to 30% a year) that we've decided to quote most prices in this chapter in US$.

Currency

The basic unit of Chinese currency is the yuan (Y), which is divided into *jiao* and *fen*. Ten fen make up one jiao (usually pronounced *mao*), and 10 jiao make up one yuan. The Chinese unit of currency is also known as the Renminbi (RMB), which means 'the people's money'.

Foreign currency and travellers' cheques can be changed at the main centres of the Bank of China, at tourist hotels and some Friendship Stores. Credit cards are now becoming accepted in the big cities, but don't rely on plastic – most places don't have machines to process cards.

Black market moneychangers congregate around places where gullible travellers hang out. The 'moneychangers' are mostly expert thieves and you are advised not to deal with them.

Exchange Rates

Australia	A$1	=	Y5.95
Canada	C$1	=	Y6.59
France	Ffr1	=	Y1.46
Germany	DM1	=	Y4.98
Hong Kong	HK$1	=	Y1.13
Japan	¥100	=	Y7.70
New Zealand	NZ$1	=	Y4.85
Singapore	S$1	=	Y5.44
Switzerland	Sfr1	=	Y5.87
Taiwan	NT$1	=	Y0.32
Thailand	B1	=	Y0.35
UK	UK£1	=	Y12.88
USA	US$1	=	Y8.70

Costs

While China qualifies as the cheapest country covered in this book, it's not going to be nearly as cheap as India, the Philippines or many other places in Asia. This is because the Chinese government has made it a policy to milk every dollar it can from foreigners. With the full cooperation of the police and other authorities, foreigners are usually forced to stay in the most expensive accommodation, charged triple or more for train and plane tickets and charged up to 30 times the Chinese price for admission to tourist spots like museums and scenic areas. Some

foreigners have joked that the Chinese government must tell people it's their patriotic duty to bilk foreigners. In fact, it's not a joke – students at Beijing's School of Hotel Management are told just that. With the government's enthusiastic encouragement, everyone from travel agents to pedicab drivers feel that it is perfectly OK to rip off foreign tourists.

All of which makes cheap travel in China continuous combat. Costs per day start at around US$15, assuming you live in dormitories, take hard-seat trains, pay Chinese prices for tickets (possible but not easy), eat at street stalls etc. Figure two or three times that if you want to have a comfortable double room, eat well and occasionally take a domestic flight. You *can* travel cheaply in China, but it's hard work. On the other hand, your journey can be a miserable experience if you're constantly worried about how far your money is going to stretch and if you force yourself to live in perpetual discomfort. At some point it's just better to pay the tariff and enjoy a little luxury.

Tipping

Tipping is not normally a custom. Bribery is another matter.

Bargaining

There's a lot of room to bargain in China – for hotel rooms, in private shops and even with the police if you are fined. Always be polite and smiling when bargaining – nastiness will cause the Chinese to lose face, in which case they'll dig their heels in and you'll come out the loser.

WHEN TO GO

There is really no best time to visit China. The immense size of the country means that when the weather is rotten in one place it will be good in another. The Chinese New Year is the worst time to visit China.

WHAT TO BRING

A medical kit is important. This is discussed in detail in the introductory Health section in the Facts for the Visitor chapter at the beginning of this book.

Sunglasses are needed for the Xinjiang desert or the high altitudes of Tibet. Ditto for UV (sunblock) lotion. If you wear contact lenses, bring your own cleaning solution, eye drops and other accessories.

Shaving cream and good razor blades are rare items. Mosquito repellent guards against malaria. Chinese nail clippers are poor quality and deodorant is unknown. Dental floss and tampons are hard to find in China. Condoms are widely available but not always reliable.

An alarm clock is essential for catching early-morning trains. A lightweight digital model is best – make sure the battery is OK because you'll have trouble finding replacements in China.

Good batteries are hard to come by in China – bring what you need for your camera. While rechargeable batteries are available, Chinese rechargers (220 volts) are bulky and not very suitable for travel.

A gluestick is convenient for sealing envelopes and pasting on stamps. The Chinese equivalent is a leaky bottle of glue.

Having something to read will help preserve your sanity as well as pass the time.

Chinese green tea is sold everywhere. If you need the Indian black variety you'd better bring it.

If you want to give someone a gift, English books and magazines are much in demand. Most young Chinese women are very interested in fashion magazines from Hong Kong and Taiwan. Many Chinese people are avid stamp collectors, and also desire foreign postcards (including photos of Hong Kong). Pictures of you and your family also make good gifts.

TOURIST OFFICES
Local Tourist Offices

China's government-owned 'tourist offices' are really self-supporting travel agencies well known for shoddy service and extreme avarice. Although you can sometimes get pamphlets and useful information from them, don't expect too much. Mostly they sell pricey tours, but you can also buy air, train and boat tickets from these offices.

CITS China International Travel Service organises travel arrangements and staff are supposed to speak English. Service varies from good to abysmal. CITS usually has at least one office in the major tourist hotel of each city.

CTS China Travel Service was originally set up for people of Chinese ancestry only. Those with a Western face were excluded from their tours (only China could get away with institutionalised racism like this). CTS has had a change of heart and now solicits business from Westerners too, though a major effort is expended to keep ethnic Chinese and Westerners on separate tours. The CTS offices in Hong Kong and Macau are under separate management from those in China itself, and most foreigners find the Hong Kong CTS to be particularly useful for booking air, rail and boat tickets.

CYTS Despite the name, China Youth Travel Service prefers older clients with lots of money.

Overseas Reps
CITS Outside of China and Hong Kong, CITS is usually known as China National Tourist Office.

Australia
    China National Tourist Office, 11th floor, 55 Clarence St, Sydney NSW 2000 (☎ 02-299 4057)
France
    China National Tourist Office, 51 Rue Saint-Anne, 75002 Paris (☎ 1-42.96.95.48)
Germany
    China National Tourist Office, Eschenheimer Anlage 28, D-6000 Frankfurt (☎ 069-55 52 92)
Hong Kong
    Main Office, 6th floor, Tower Two, South Seas Centre, 75 Mody Rd, Tsimshatsui East, Kowloon (☎ 732 5888)
    Central Branch, Room 1018, Swire House, 11 Chater Rd, Central (☎ 810 4282)

Japan
China National Tourist Office, 6F Hachidal Hamamatsu-cho Building, 1-27-13 Hamamatsu-cho Minato-ku, Tokyo (☎ 03-3433 1461)
UK
China National Tourist Office, 4 Glentworth St, London NW1 (☎ 0171-935 9427)
USA
China National Tourist Office, Los Angeles Branch, 333 West Broadway, Suite 201, Glendale, CA 91204 (☎ 818-545 7505)
New York Branch, Lincoln Building, 60E, 42nd St, Suite 3126, New York, NY 10165 (☎ 212-867 0271)

CTS In Hong Kong, the Tsimshatsui branch office of CTS is open on Sunday and public holidays.

Australia
Ground floor, 757-759 George St, Sydney, NSW 2000 (☎ 02-211 2633)
Canada
556 West Broadway, Vancouver, BC V5Z 1E9 (☎ 604-872 8787)
France
10 Rue de Rome, 75008, Paris (☎ 1-45.22.92.72)
Germany
Düsseldorfer Strasse 14 6000, Frankfurt 1 (☎ 069-25 05 15)
Hong Kong
Main Office, 4th floor, CTS House, 78-83 Connaught Rd, Central (☎ 853 3888; fax 541 9777)
Central Branch, 2nd floor, China Travel Building, 77 Queen's Road, Central (☎ 525 2284; fax 868 4970)
Tsimshatsui Branch, 1st floor, Alpha House, 27-33 Nathan Rd, Tsimshatsui (☎ 721 1331; fax 721 7757)
Japan
Nihombashi-Settsu Building, 2-2-4, Nihombashi, Chuo-Ku, Tokyo (☎ 03-3273 5512)
Macau
Edificio Xinhua, Rua de Nagasaki (☎ 700888; fax 706611)
Philippines
489 San Fernando St, Binondo, Manila (☎ 2-474187)
Thailand
559 Yaowaraj Rd, Bangkok 10500 (☎ 2-2260041)
UK
24 Cambridge Circus, London WC2H 8HD (☎ 0171-836 9911)

USA
2nd floor, 212 Sutter St, San Francisco, CA 94108 (☎ 800-332 2831, 415-398 6627)
Los Angeles Branch, Suite 138, 223 East Garvey Ave, Monterey Park, CA 91754 (☎ 818-288 8222)

USEFUL ORGANISATIONS
Public Security Bureau (PSB) is the name given to China's police force. In any large city, the PSB has a Foreign Affairs Office at their headquarters. This office issues visa extensions and (rarely) Alien Travel Permits.

BUSINESS HOURS & HOLIDAYS
In China, nobody moves slower than a government employee, except a dead government employee. As a rough guide only, government offices are open Monday to Friday from around 8 to 9 am, close for two hours around noon and then re-open until 5 or 6 pm. Offices are supposed to also open on Saturday morning and close at noon, while Sunday is a public holiday. Some businesses are open Sunday morning and make up for this by closing on another day.

Government restaurants are open for early morning breakfast (sometimes as early as 5.30 am) until about 7.30 am, then open for lunch and again for dinner. Privately run restaurants are usually open all day and often late into the night, especially around railway stations.

Long-distance bus stations and railway stations open their ticket offices around 5 or 5.30 am before the first trains and buses pull out. Apart from a one or two-hour break in the middle of the day, they often stay open until late at night.

There are nine national holidays during the year, as follows: New Year's Day, 1 January; Chinese Lunar New Year, usually in February – sheer chaos for one week (avoid it); International Working Women's Day, 8 March; International Labour Day, 1 May; Youth Day, 4 May; Children's Day, 1 June; Anniversary of the founding of the Communist Party of China, 1 July; Anniversary of the founding of the People's Libera-tion Army, 1 August; and National Day, 1 October.

CULTURAL EVENTS

The ice festival is magnificent in the north-eastern city of Harbin during January and February – so long as you're prepared for temperatures of minus 40°C.

Down in Yunnan Province, the Water-Splashing Festival is held around mid-April (usually 13-15 April).

The birthday of Confucius (28 September) would be the best time to visit the Confucius Temple in the great sage's home town of Qufu, Shandong Province.

POST & TELECOMMUNICATIONS
Postal Rates

International postcards cost Y1.10 by surface mail and Y1.60 by air mail to any-where in the world. Aerogrammes are Y1.90 to anywhere in the world. There are dis-counts for printed matter, small packets and parcels.

The following are the rates to send inter-national letters by surface mail, but add Y0.50 for airmail:

Weight		Rate
0-20 grams	=	Y1.50
20-50 grams	=	Y2.90
50-100 grams	=	Y4.50
100-250 grams	=	Y8.80
250-500 grams	=	Y17.90
500-1000 grams	=	Y34.90
1000-2000 grams	=	Y49.40

International Express Mail Service (EMS) charges vary. EMS to Hong Kong starts at US$8.70, but for Europe, Canada and the USA it's US$16.50. EMS is not available to every country.

Air freight service is available from DHL and UPS. Express document and parcel service is offered by two other foreign carri-ers, Federal Express and TNT Skypak. Air freight service is only offered in major cities and doesn't come cheap – costs start at around US$50.

Sending Mail

Some have reported that their outgoing mail has been opened and read. This seems to affect tourists less, although letters with enclosures will almost certainly be opened. Your mail is less likely to be opened if it's sent from cities that handle high volumes of mail, like Beijing.

Receiving Mail

It's worth noting that some foreigners living in China have had their mail opened or parcels pilfered before receipt. Officially, the People's Republic prohibits several items from being mailed to it, including books, magazines, notes and manuscripts. Poste restante seems to work OK in large cities.

Telephone

Many hotel rooms are equipped with phones from which local calls are free. Local calls can be made from public payphones (there are some around but not many). China's budding entrepreneurs try to fill the gap – people with private phones run a long cord out the window and stand on street corners, allowing you to use their phone to place local calls for around Y0.50 each – long-distance domestic and international calls are not always possible on these phones, but ask. In the lobbies of many hotels, the reception desks have a similar system – free calls for guests, Y0.50 for non-guests, and long-dis-tance calls are charged by the minute.

You can place both domestic and inter-national long-distance phone calls from main telecommunications offices. This is sometimes cheaper, but usually not.

Domestic long-distance rates in China vary according to distance, but are cheap. By contrast, international calls are expensive. Rates for station-to-station calls to most countries in the world are typically US$2 to US$3 per minute. Hong Kong is somewhat cheaper at US$1.40 to US$2 per minute. There is a minimum charge of three minutes. Reverse-charge calls are often cheaper than calls paid for in China. Time the call yourself – the operator will not break in to tell you that your minimum period of three minutes is approaching. After you hang up, the operator will ring back to tell you how much it cost. There is no call cancellation fee.

If you are expecting a call – either international or domestic – try to advise the caller beforehand of your hotel room number. The operators frequently have difficulty understanding Western names, and the hotel receptionist may not be able to locate you. If this can't be done, then try to inform the operator that you are expecting the call and write down your name and room number – this increases your chances of success.

Direct Dialling Domestic Direct Dialling (DDD) and International Direct Dialling (IDD) calls are cheapest if you can find a phone which accepts magnetic cards. These phones are usually available in the lobbies of major hotels, at least in big cities, and the hotel's front desk should also sell the phone cards. These cards come in two denominations, Y20, Y100 and Y200 – for an international call, you'll need at least Y100.

To make an IDD call, dial 00 (the international access code – always the same throughout China) followed by the country code, area code and the number you want to reach. If the area code begins with zero (like '03' for Melbourne, Australia) omit the first zero.

If card phones aren't available, you can usually dial direct from the phones in the business centres found in most luxury hotels. Hotels and telephone centres almost always charge a minimum of three minutes even if you only talk 10 seconds.

If your hotel lacks card phones or a business centres, you should be able to direct dial from your hotel room. You'll have to ask the staff at your hotel what's the dial-out code for a direct line (usually a '7' on most switchboards, or sometimes a combination like '78'). Once you have the outside line, you dial 00 + country code + area code + the final number.

There are a few things to be careful about. The equipment used on most hotel switchboards is not very sophisticated – it's often a simple timer and it begins charging you starting from 30 seconds after you dial '7' (or '78' or whatever) – the timer does not know if your call succeeds or not so you get charged if you stay on the line over 30 seconds, even if you just let the phone ring repeatedly or get a busy signal! On the other hand, if you complete your conversation within 30 seconds and hang up, you don't get charged at all. The hotel switchboard timer keeps running until you hang up, not when the other party hangs up, so replace the receiver immediately when the conversation ends.

The usual procedure is for you to make the call and someone comes to your room five or 10 minutes later to collect the cash. If the hotel does not have IDD, you can usually book calls from your room through the switchboard and the operator will call you back, but this procedure will be more expensive.

With DDD it's useful to know the area codes of China's cities. These all begin with zero, but if you're dialling into China from abroad, omit the first zero from each code. China's country code is 86. The codes for provincial capitals and municipalities are as follows, listed in alphabetical order by province:

Anhui, Hefei	(0551)
Beijing	(01)
Fujian, Fuzhou	(0591)
Gansu, Lanzhou	(0931)
Guangdong, Guangzhou	(020)
Guangxi, Nanning	(0771)
Guizhou, Guiyang	(0851)
Hainan, Haikou	(0750)
Hebei, Shijiazhuang	(0311)
Heilongjiang, Harbin	(0451)
Henan, Zhengzhou	(0371)
Hubei, Wuhan	(027)
Hunan, Changsha	(0731)
Inner Mongolia, Hohhot	(0471)
Jiangsu, Nanjing	(025)
Jiangxi, Nanchang	(0791)
Jilin, Changchun	(0431)
Liaoning, Shenyang	(024)
Ningxia, Yinchuan	(0951)
Qinghai, Xining	(0971)
Shaanxi, Xi'an	(029)
Shandong, Ji'nan	(0531)
Shanghai	(021)
Shanxi, Taiyuan	(0351)

Sichuan, Chengdu	(028)
Tianjin	(022)
Tibet, Lhasa	(0891)
Xinjiang, Ürümqi	(0991)
Yunnan, Kunming	(0871)
Zhejiang, Hangzhou	(0571)

Essential Numbers There are several telephone numbers which are the same for all major cities. The problem is that the person answering the phone will most likely be Chinese-speaking only:

local directory assistance	☎ 114
long-distance directory assistance	☎ 113, 173
HK & Macau directory assistance	☎ 115
police hot line	☎ 110
fire hot line	☎ 119
phone repair	☎ 112

Fax, Telex & Telegraph
Big hotels that have international telephone service usually also have fax machines and – more rarely – telex service. Telegrams can be sent from the central telecommunication offices in major cities.

TIME
As ridiculous as it may seem, China is one big time zone – Greenwich Mean Time plus eight hours.

When it is noon in China it is also noon in Singapore, Hong Kong, Taiwan and Perth; 2 pm in Sydney; 8 pm the previous day in Los Angeles; 11 pm the previous day in New York; and 4 am in London.

Daylight-saving time was experimented with, but unceremoniously dropped in 1992.

LAUNDRY
Almost all tourist hotels have a laundry service, but tend to be expensive. If the hotel doesn't have a laundry, staff can usually direct you to one. Expensive garments have a tendency to disappear.

WEIGHTS & MEASURES
China uses the metric system, but some traditional measures can still be found.

Metric	Chinese	Imperial
1 metre	3 chi	3.28 feet

1 km	2 li	0.62 miles
1 hectare	15 mu	2.47 acres
1 litre	1 gongsheng	0.22 gallons
1 kg	2 jin	2.20 pounds

ELECTRICITY
Electricity is 220 V, 50 cycles AC. Power blackouts occur most often during summer.

BOOKS & MAPS
The best known English fiction about China is *The Good Earth* by Pearl S Buck.

The Soong Dynasty by Sterling Seagrave (Sidgwick & Jackson) is one of the most popular books on the corrupt Kuomintang period. The classic book on the Chinese revolution is *Red Star Over China* by Edgar Snow, an idealistic account by a Western journalist who visited the Red Army and its leaders during the 1930s.

The Search for Modern China by Jonathan D Spence is the definitive work, often used as a textbook in college courses. If you want to understand the People's Republic, this is the book to read.

A chilling best seller about the Cultural Revolution is *Life and Death in Shanghai* by Nien Cheng (Grafton). Franz Kafka's *The Trial* wasn't written with China in mind, yet his book is a potent reminder of the helplessness of individuals against the all-powerful state bureaucracy.

Bitter Winds; My Life in the Chinese Gulag by Harry Wu (Wu Hongda) provides an unforgettable dose of reality. Arrested just after graduating from university, Mr Wu spent 19 years in forced labour camps because he was labelled a 'counter-revolutionary rightist'.

Random House publishers is due to soon release *My Life with Chairman Mao*. The author, Dr Li Zhisui, was the personal physician of Mao Zedong. Despite the Communist Party's attempts to depict Mao as a paragon of virtue, Dr Li asserts that the old chairman in his later years spent nearly all his free time in bed with young teenage girls. If true, it could be argued that Mao differed little from the emperors he replaced, who were notorious for keeping legions of concubines.

A moving and now popular book is *Wild Swans* by Jung Chang. The author traces the lives of three Chinese women – the author's grandmother (an escaped concubine with bound feet), her mother and herself.

Lonely Planet's *China – a travel survival kit* gives a complete rundown on the country. More specialised Lonely Planet guides include *Tibet – a travel survival kit* and the *Beijing City Guide*.

The most useful map of China is published by Cartographic Publishing House in Beijing and is called the *Map of the People's Republic of China*.

MEDIA
Newspapers & Magazines
The only English-language daily newspaper is the *China Daily*. The *Beijing Review* is a weekly magazine on political and current affairs. *China Today* is a monthly magazine founded in 1952, previously called *China Reconstructs*. The name was changed in 1989 because – as one official said – '37 years is a hell of a long time to be reconstructing your country'.

Foreign magazines can be found in major hotels in large cities – elsewhere, forget it. If you need something to read, bring it yourself.

Radio & TV
If you want to keep up with foreign news, bring a short-wave radio.

There are some imported English-language shows, but the majority are in Chinese only. In fancy hotels, in-house video and satellite TV are available. Most Chinese find their public TV boring, which explains the extreme popularity of video tape players.

FILM & PHOTOGRAPHY
Colour print film is available, but slide film is hard to get except in large cities. The quality of photoprocessing facilities varies. Controversial photos sometimes get 'lost'.

Obviously, don't film anything that looks like it has a military function.

In Tibetan temples, photography is often prohibited (ask if not sure) – some of those monks can rip film out of a camera so fast you'll swear they must possess special martial arts skills.

HEALTH
China now requires HIV (AIDS) certificates before granting work permits. Useful (though not required) vaccines could include influenza, cholera, meningitis, rabies, hepatitis A, hepatitis B, BCG (tuberculosis), polio, and TABT (protects against typhoid, paratyphoid A and B, and tetanus) and diphtheria. There is a small risk of malaria in the south-western provinces near the Burmese border. Bring your own condoms; the local product is unreliable.

Tibet presents a few special problems of its own. One is the nasty giardia amoeba which infects drinking water supplies. Another issue are the dogs which roam in packs around monasteries and towns – several foreigners have been badly bitten, and there have been reports of rabies.

More details about health are included in the Health section in the introductory Facts for the Visitor chapter earlier in this book.

WOMEN TRAVELLERS
Women report relatively little sexual harassment except in Muslim areas like Xinjiang, where it is best to dress conservatively.

Women may need to take special precautions with their health. For example, if you're prone to yeast infections, bring your own medication (Nystatin suppositories). Tampons are seldom available and Chinese sanitary pads are big and bulky.

DANGERS & ANNOYANCES
China is the most dangerous country in this book in terms of theft. Be especially wary of pickpockets, especially on buses and other crowded areas. Thieves often slash pockets with razor blades in order to get at valuables, occasionally causing injuries to the victim. Violent robberies are increasing, especially on trains and some remote back-country hiking trails where witnesses are not around.

The PSB can issue a loss report which will be needed if you want to make an insurance claim.

To less sophisticated Chinese people, staring at a foreigner is better than TV. Staring squads are most common in places where foreigners are scarce. Staring back doesn't seem to help – indeed, the crowd will love it. The best bet is to keep moving so a crowd of enthusiastic onlookers can't get organised.

Spitting is a national sport. Everyone does it, anytime and anywhere, so try not to get caught in the crossfire. Some cities (notably Beijing) have tried to enforce short-lived anti-spitting campaigns, especially when some important foreign dignitary is in town.

China officially condemns racism and sexism, but the reality is somewhat different. Western men should avoid situations in which they are alone in a room with a closed door with a Chinese woman – even if nothing is going on but polite conversation. There have been numerous cases of the police bursting into a foreign man's hotel room, accusing him of 'insulting Chinese women' and then hauling him down to the police station to pay a huge fine. The woman may also be punished. In xenophobic Beijing, the sex police have even arrested foreign men for riding in the same taxi with a Chinese woman. Race seems to be the deciding factor – a Japanese or Korean man accompanying a Chinese woman rarely provokes trouble with the police, but when the man is Western the situation changes drastically. And if the man is Black, that's the most heinous crime of all as far as the police are concerned. The opposite situation – where a foreign woman accompanies a Chinese man – does not seem to be a problem in male-oriented China.

WORK

There are opportunities to teach English and other languages, or even other technical skills. The pay is generally poor. The main reason to do it is to experience living and working in China. If interested, contact a Chinese embassy or the universities directly.

ACTIVITIES
Hiking
China is somewhat disappointing for hiking and camping. Those areas which would be most interesting – like Tibet – can be difficult to reach. Those areas which are accessible tend to be intensively cultivated. Probably your best bet is to climb some of the 'sacred mountains' like Emeishan and Taishan.

Skiing
Don't expect to find another Aspen or St Moritz, but you can pursue the art of sliding downhill in China. Westerners may have trouble renting ski boots which are large enough. In north-east China, 16 km from Jilin town (Jilin Province) are the Songhua Lake skifields. A more advanced skifield is at Tonghua. The best skifields are near Harbin in Heilongjiang Province.

Language Courses
Studying Chinese is indeed possible, though many come to the conclusion that Taiwan is better because it's easier to make friends with individual Chinese there. Most major universities welcome foreign students but often charge high prices.

HIGHLIGHTS
Opinions differ, but Yunnan Province probably rates first for the sheer number of scenic wonders and pleasant people. Some popular places in Yunnan include Dali and Xishuangbanna.

Jiuzhaigou National Park in Sichuan could well be the most beautiful place in China, but is difficult to get to. Far more accessible are Guilin and neighbouring Yangshuo, scenic wonders in Guangxi Province.

The nation's capital – Beijing – is also China's cultural capital. The Forbidden City is just as fascinating now as it was 500 years ago.

Remote Xinjiang in China's rugged north-west offers unique scenery and culture. Highlights of this region include Turpan and Kashgar, plus the trip to Pakistan over Khunjerab Pass (4800 metres).

ACCOMMODATION

Hotels are a source of constant frustration in China. There are plenty of cheap places to stay for the Chinese, but the PSB has placed most of them off limits to foreigners. Consequently, you may be forced to pay for luxury you don't really need or want.

Segregation is not universally enforced, and there are times when you will be able to stay in a 'Chinese-only' hotel. In very small towns, for example, there may only be one hotel so everyone stays there. In many hotels there is a Chinese section and a foreigners section.

Generally foreigners will pay triple what a Chinese would pay for the same room. The price of rooms varies enormously and often illogically – sometimes you pay exorbitant rates for a dump, and at other times you bask in luxury at rock-bottom prices. You *can* bargain the price for a room in many hotels, but do so politely. Dormitory accommodation *(duō rén fáng)* is still available in many places, but the trend is definitely towards fancy rooms and fancy prices.

FOOD

Chinese food comes in a wide variety of styles, depending in part on which region of the country it originated in. Probably most familiar to foreigners is the Cantonese variety, prevalent in Hong Kong and Guangdong Province. The emphasis is on steaming, pot boiling and stir frying, with lots of vegetables, roast pork, chicken, steamed fish and fried rice. The Cantonese are famous for their ability to eat almost anything, including snake, monkey, pangolin (an armadillo-like creature), bear, giant salamander and raccoon, not to mention more mundane dog, cat and rat dishes.

Beijing (Peking) and Shandong food originated in one of the coldest parts of China and use heaps of spices to warm the body. Bread and noodles are often used instead of rice. The chief speciality is Beijing duck, of which the crisp skin is the prized part. Another speciality is a Mongolian barbecue – assorted barbecued meats and vegetables mixed in a hotpot.

Sichuan (Szechuan) food is the hottest of the categories and is characterised by the heavy use of spices and peppers. The *mapo doufu*, or spicy bean curd, is a Sichuan classic.

Shanghai cuisine is the least popular with foreigners. While there are some tasty dishes, Shanghainese food is so oily it slides off the plate. Given the fact that Shanghai is a major seaport, it's not surprising that seafood plays an important role. The big speciality of Shanghai food is the strange hairy crab which arrives in September or October and keeps the gourmets happy for three months or so. The crabs are beyond the budget of most shoestring travellers.

Incidentally, fortune cookies are a foreign invention – you won't find them in China.

Chinese food is generally good, but be prepared for the occasional disappointment. Chinese bread, for example, tends to taste like a damp sponge.

Always ask the price of what you're ordering before you eat it. There have been horror stories of foreigners ordering food without first asking the price, and then being presented with an outrageous bill. It happens even in government-run restaurants.

Useful Expressions

I'm a vegetarian.
    Wǒ shì chī sù de. 我是吃素的
I don't eat meat.
    Wǒ bù chī ròu. 我不吃肉
I don't eat pork.
    Wǒ bù cha zhū ròu. 我不吃猪肉
I cannot eat spicy food.
    Wǒ bù néng chī là. 我不能吃辣

Rice

plain white rice
    mǐ fàn 米饭
watery rice porridge
    xī fàn 稀饭

rice noodles
  mǐ fěn 米粉

Bread, Buns & Dumplings

fried roll
  yín sī juǎn 银丝卷
steamed buns
  mán tóu 馒头
steamed meat buns
  bāo zi 包子
fried bread stick
  yóu tiáo 油条
boiled dumplings
  jiǎo zi 饺子
prawn cracker
  lóng xiā piàn 龙虾片

Vegetable Dishes

fried rice with vegetables
  shū cài chǎo fàn 蔬菜炒饭
fried noodles with vegetables
  shū cài chǎo miàn 蔬菜炒面
spicy peanuts
  wǔ xiāng huā shēng mǐ 五香花生米
fried peanuts
  yóu zhà huā shēng mǐ 油炸花生米
spiced cold vegetables
  liáng bàn shí jǐn 凉拌什锦
Chinese salad
  jiā cháng liáng cài 家常凉菜
fried rape in oyster sauce
  háo yóu pá cài dǎn 蚝油扒菜胆
fried rape with mushrooms
  dōng gū pá cài dǎn 冬菇扒菜胆
fried bean curd in oyster sauce
  háo yóu dòu fǔ 蚝油豆腐
spicy hot bean curd
  má pó dòu fǔ 麻婆豆腐
bean curd casserole
  shā guō dòu fǔ 沙锅豆腐
bean curd & mushrooms
  mó gū dòu fǔ 磨菇豆腐
garlic & morning glory
  dà suàn kōng xīn cài 大蒜空心菜
fried garlic
  sù chǎo dà suàn 素炒大蒜
fried eggplant
  sù shāo qié zi 素烧茄子

fried beansprouts
  sù chǎo dòu yá 素炒豆芽
fried green vegetables
  sù chǎo qīng cài 素炒青菜
fried green beans
  sù chǎo biǎn dòu 素炒扁豆
fried cauliflower & tomato
  fān qié cài huā 炒蕃茄菜花
broiled mushroom
  sù chǎo xiān me 素炒鲜蘑
black fungus & mushroom
  mù ěr huá kǒu mó 木耳滑口蘑
fried white radish patty
  luó bo gāo 萝卜糕
assorted hors d'oeuvre
  shíjǐn pīn pán 什锦拼盘
assorted vegetarian food
  sù shí jǐn 素什锦

Egg Dishes

preserved egg
  sōng huā dàn 松花蛋
fried rice with egg
  jī dàn chǎo fàn 鸡蛋炒饭
fried tomatoes & eggs
  xī hóng shì chǎo jī dàn 西红柿炒鸡蛋
egg & flour omelette
  jiān bǐng 煎饼

Beef Dishes

fried rice with beef
  niú ròu sī chǎo fàn 牛肉丝炒饭
noodles with beef (soupy)
  niú ròu tāng miàn 牛肉汤面
spiced noodles with beef
  niú ròu gān miàn 牛肉干面
fried noodles with beef
  niú ròu chǎo miàn 牛肉炒面
beef with white rice
  niúròu fàn 牛肉饭
beef platter
  niú ròu tiě bǎn 牛肉铁板
beef with oyster sauce
  háo yóu niú ròu 蚝油牛肉
beef braised in soy sauce
  hóng shāo niú ròu 红烧牛肉
beef with tomatoes
  fān qié niú ròu piàn 蕃茄牛肉片

beef with green peppers
qīng jiāo niú ròu piàn 青椒牛肉片
beef curry & rice
gā lǐ jī ròu fàn 咖哩牛肉饭
beef curry & noodles
gā lǐ jī ròu miàn 咖哩牛肉面

Chicken Dishes
fried rice with chicken
jī sī chǎo fàn 鸡丝炒饭
noodles with chicken (soupy)
jī sī tāng miàn 鸡丝汤面
fried noodles with chicken
jī sī chǎo miàn 鸡丝炒面
chicken leg with white rice
jī tuǐ fàn 鸡腿饭
spicy hot chicken & peanuts
gōng bào jī dīng 宫爆鸡丁
fruit kernel with chicken
guǒ wèi jī dīng 果味鸡丁
sweet & sour chicken
táng cù jī dīng 糖醋鸡丁
sauteed spicy chicken pieces
là zi jī dīng 辣子鸡丁
sauteed chicken with green peppers
jiàng bào jī dīng 酱爆鸡丁
chicken slices & tomato sauce
fān qié jī dīng 蕃茄鸡丁
mushrooms & chicken
cǎomó jī dīng 草蘑鸡丁
chicken pieces in oyster sauce
háo yóu jī dīng 蚝油鸡丁
chicken braised in soy sauce
hóng shāo jī kuài 红烧鸡块
sauteed chicken with water chestnuts
nán jiè jī piàn 南芥鸡片
sliced chicken with crispy rice
jī piàn guō bā 鸡片锅巴
chicken curry
gā lǐ jī ròu 咖哩鸡肉
chicken curry & rice
gā lǐ jī ròu fàn 咖哩鸡肉饭
chicken curry & noodles
gā lǐ jī ròu miàn 咖哩鸡肉面

Duck Dishes
Beijing duck
běi jīng kǎoyā 北京烤鸭

duck with white rice
yā ròu fàn 鸭肉饭
duck with noodles
yā ròu miàn 鸭肉面
duk with fried noodles
yā ròu chǎo miàn 鸭肉炒面

Pork Dishes
pork chop with white rice
pái gǔ fàn 排骨饭
fried rice with pork
ròu sī chǎo fàn 肉丝炒饭
fried noodles with pork
ròu sī chǎo miàn 肉丝炒面
pork & mustard greens
zhà cài ròu sī 榨菜肉丝
noodles, pork & mustard greens
zhà cài ròu sī miàn 榨菜肉丝面
pork with crispy rice
ròu piàn guō bā 肉片锅巴
sweet & sour pork fillet
táng cù zhū ròu piàn 糖醋猪肉片
sweet & sour pork fillet
táng cù lǐ jī 糖醋里肌
pork fillet with white sauce
huá liū lǐ jī 滑溜里肌
shredded pork fillet
chǎo lǐ jī sī 炒里肌丝
soft pork fillet
ruǎn zhá lǐ jī 软炸里肌
spicy hot pork pieces
gōng bào ròu dīng 宫爆肉丁
fried black pork pieces
yuán bào lǐ jī 芫爆里肌
sauteed diced pork & soy sauce
jiàng bào ròu dīng 酱爆肉丁
spicy pork cubelets
là zi ròu dīng 辣子肉丁
pork cubelets & cucumber
huáng guā ròu dīng 黄瓜肉丁
golden pork slices
jīn yín ròu sī 金银肉丝
sauteed shredded pork
qīng chǎo ròu sī 清炒肉丝
shredded pork & hot sauce
yú xiāng ròu sī 鱼香肉丝
shredded pork & green peppers
qīng jiāo ròu sī 青椒肉丝
shredded pork & bamboo shoots
dōng sǔn ròu sī 冬笋肉丝

shredded pork & green beans
biǎn dòu ròu sī 扁豆肉丝
pork with oyster sauce
háo yóu ròu sī 蚝油肉丝
boiled pork slices
shuǐ zhǔ ròu piàn 水煮肉片
pork, eggs & black fungus
mù xū ròu 木须肉
pork & fried onions
yáng cōng chǎo ròu piàn 洋葱炒肉片
fried rice (assorted)
shíjǐn chǎo fàn 什锦炒饭
Cantonese fried rice
guǎng zhōu chǎo fàn 广州炒饭

Seafood Dishes

fried rice with shrimp
xiā rén chǎo fàn 虾仁炒饭
fried noodles with shrimp
xiā rén chǎo miàn 虾仁炒面
diced shrimp with peanuts
gōng bào xiā rén 宫爆虾仁
sauteed shrimp
qīng chǎo xiā rén 清炒虾仁
deep-fried shrimp
zhà xiā rén 炸虾仁
fried shrimp with mushroom
xiān mó xiā rén 鲜蘑虾仁
squid with crispy rice
yóu yú guō bā 鱿鱼锅巴
sweet & sour squid roll
sūan là yóu yú juàn 酸辣鱿鱼卷
fish braised in soy sauce
hóng shāo yú 红烧鱼
braised sea cucumber
hóng shāo hǎi shēn 红烧海参
clams
gé 蛤
crab
páng xiè 螃蟹
lobster
lóng xiā 龙虾

Soup

three kinds seafood soup
sān xiān tāng 三鲜汤
squid soup
yóu yú tāng 鱿鱼汤

sweet & sour soup
suān là tāng 酸辣汤
tomato & egg soup
xī hóng shì dàn tāng 西红柿蛋汤
corn & egg thick soup
fèng huáng lì mǐ gēng 凤凰栗米羹
egg & vegetable soup
dàn huā tāng 蛋花汤
mushroom & egg soup
mó gu dàn huā tāng 蘑菇蛋花汤
fresh fish soup
shēng yú tāng 生鱼汤
vegetable soup
shū cài tāng 蔬菜汤
cream of tomato soup
nǎi yóu fān qié tāng 奶油蕃茄汤
cream of mushroom soup
nǎi yóu xiān mó tāng 奶油鲜蘑汤
pickled mustard green soup
zhà cài tāng 榨菜汤
bean curd & vegetable soup
dòu fū cài tāng 豆腐菜汤
wanton soup
hún dùn tāng 馄饨汤
clear soup
qīng tāng 清汤

Miscellanea & Exotica

deermeat (venison)
lù ròu 鹿肉
dogmeat
gǒu ròu 狗肉
goat, mutton
yáng ròu 羊肉
kebab
ròu chuàn 肉串
Mongolian hotpot
huǒ guō 火锅
ratmeat
lǎo shǔ ròu 老鼠肉
snake
shé ròu 蛇肉

Condiments

black pepper
hú jiāo 胡椒
butter
huáng yóu 黄油
garlic
dà suàn 大蒜

honey
fēng mì 蜂蜜
hot pepper
là jiāo 辣椒
hot sauce
là jiāo jiàng 辣椒酱
jam
guǒ jiàng 果酱
ketchup
fān qié jiàng 蕃茄酱
MSG
wèi jīng 味精
salt
yán 盐
sesame seed oil
zhī má yóu 芝麻油
soy sauce
jiàng yóu 酱油
sugar
táng 糖
vinegar
cù 醋

DRINKS

Green tea is the most common drink while black tea is relatively scarce. Coffee is seldom available in restaurants but big jars of the instant variety can be bought in any shop. Delicious yoghurt is served like a drink (in milk bottles and slurped through a straw) and can be bought from kiosks everywhere.

The top-brand Chinese beer, Tsingtao (Qingdao), is premium stuff – but it's really a German beer, since the brewery dates back to the days of the foreign concessions. Local beers of varying but generally good quality are found all over China. Stronger brews have the exquisite, subtle flavour of rocket-fuel.

Drinks Vocabulary
tea
chá 茶
jasmine tea
mò lì huā chá 茉莉花茶
oolong tea
wū lóng chá 乌龙茶
coffee
kā fēi 咖啡
water
kāi shuǐ 开水

mineral water
kuàng quán shuǐ 矿泉水
fizzy drink (soda)
qì shuǐ 汽水
Coca-Cola
kě kǒu kě lè 可口可乐
Sprite
xuě bì 雪碧
yogurt drink
suān nǎi 酸奶
beer
pí jiǔ 啤酒
San Miguel Beer
shēng lì pí 生力啤
Tsingtao Beer
qīng dǎo pí jiǔ 青岛啤酒
whiskey
wēi shì jì jiǔ 威士忌酒
vodka
fú tè jiā jiǔ 伏特加酒
red grape wine
hóng pú táo jiǔ 红葡萄酒
white grape wine
bái pú táo jiǔ 白葡萄酒
hot
rè de 热的
ice cold
bīng de 冰的

ENTERTAINMENT

Some of the big hotels have expensive discos which attract affluent foreigners and the occasional hip Chinese or Hong Konger. Budget travellers in China try to create their own nightlife. In places where foreigners are numerous, there are sometimes late-night restaurants where travellers congregate to sip beer or Cokes and swap yarns – that's about as thrilling as it gets.

Like elsewhere in North-East Asia, karaoke is the big rage with the locals. Besides any mental damage you may suffer from listening to karaoke, these places can be ruinous to your budget. There have been disturbing reports that the 'Tokyo Nightclub Syndrome' has hit China. Basically, foreigners (chiefly male) sitting in a karaoke bar are suddenly joined by attractive young woman (or maybe several women) who 'just want to talk'. A few drinks are ordered – maybe just

CHINA

Coke or orange juice – and at the end of an hour's conversation a bill of perhaps US$500 or so is presented to the hapless foreigner. The drinks might only cost US$10, while the other US$490 is a 'service charge' for talking to the women, who are in fact bar hostesses.

Even more sinister is that these women sometimes approach foreigners on the street, ostensibly just to 'practice their English'. Somewhere in the conversation they suggest going to a 'nice place', which happens to be a karaoke bar. What they fail to mention is that they work for the bar and get a percentage of the profits for every sucker they bring in.

It needs to be mentioned that the victims of these schemes are not only foreigners. Overseas Chinese, Hong Kongers, Taiwanese and even mainland Chinese who appear to have money are also targeted. This rip-off system seems to be spreading – we've heard complaints so far from travellers in Guangzhou, Guilin, Hangzhou and Xi'an.

THINGS TO BUY

The Chinese do produce some interesting items for export – tea, clothing, Silkworm missiles – the latter not generally for sale to tourists.

Unfortunately, quality has not kept pace with quantity. There is an awful lot of junk on sale – zippers which break literally the first time you use them, stereos which last a week, lamps that can electrocute you etc. Given this state of affairs, you might wonder how China manages to successfully export so much – the simple fact is that export items are made to a much higher standard while junk is dumped on the local markets. Always test zippers, examine stitching, and in the case of electrical appliances, plug it in and make sure it won't go up in smoke before handing over the cash. Chinese sales clerks expect you to do this – they'll consider you a fool if you don't.

The real bargain in China is clothing. It's so much cheaper than in the West that you could just about pay for your trip if you go home with a new Chinese-made wardrobe. In particular, check out the leather goods and down jackets. Fine silk shirts and silk underwear cost a fraction of what you would pay at home. Again, examine the quality before you buy because all sales are final.

Jade, bronzes, jewellery, reproduction antiques, scroll paintings, vases, papercuts, calligraphy brushes, wood carvings plus other arts & crafts are some of China's specialities. 'Friendship Stores', which cater to tourists, tend to be pricey but are worth visiting to get an idea of what is available and to compare prices. The lowest prices are at the Chinese department stores where the masses shop, rather than touristy outlets.

Branches of the Xinhua Bookstore not only sell books, but also maps, atlases, art supplies and posters. Various Foreign Language Bookstores in major cities (especially Beijing) have books in English plus textbooks for learning Chinese, music tapes and CDs. Copies of the Little Red Book and Mao caps are available at street markets.

Getting There & Away

AIR

As a general rule, tickets to Hong Kong are cheaper than tickets directly to China. While Hong Kong is a great place to find cheap air fares, China is not – tickets purchased within China are invariably more expensive (usually much more) than those purchased elsewhere. This reflects the fact that there is practically no free-market competition in China, so the government can fix the price at the highest level the market will bear. Thus, a London to Beijing ticket is likely to be half the price of a Beijing to London ticket!

On the other hand, Hong Kong is becoming more expensive for accommodation. Many budget travellers now prefer to fly directly to China and then exit via Hong Kong where there are cheap air tickets to fly elsewhere.

The China Aviation Administration of China, usually known as CAAC, is the official flag carrier. Well known for poor service, hijackings and frequent crashes, the government has attempted to polish CAAC's image by breaking it up into smaller subsidiaries with a variety of names. Three CAAC spin-offs are currently authorised to offer international flights – China Eastern Airlines, China Southern Airlines and Air China (not to be confused with China Airlines which belongs to Taiwan). There have been definite improvements over the years, but CAAC's reputation is still tarnished – in 1993 the International Air Passengers Association named China the most dangerous country in which to fly.

China's other major airline is Dragonair, a joint venture between China and Hong Kong's Cathay Pacific Airlines. Given a choice, most travellers would prefer to fly on Dragonair. For this reason, Dragonair's flights are often heavily booked and you might have no choice but to fly on CAAC. Dragonair's prices are identical to CAAC's because the Chinese government controls both airlines.

To/From Asian Countries

For details of travel between China and other cities in North-East Asia see the introductory Getting Around chapter at the beginning of this book. The following information is for other countries in Asia:

To/From Bangladesh Dragonair has flights from Dhaka to Kunming.

To/From Indonesia CAAC has flights originating in Jakarta which continue onwards to Surabaya and then to Guangzhou, Xiamen or Beijing. Tickets to Hong Kong are likely to be much cheaper.

To/From Kazakhstan From Ürümqi in China's Xinjiang Province, there are twice-weekly international flights to Alma Ata, the capital of the former Soviet republic of Kazakhstan.

To/From Laos CAAC offers a scarcely used flight between Vientiane and Kunming.

To/From Malaysia Penang is one of the cheapest places in the world to purchase air tickets. CAAC has direct flights from Penang to Guangzhou and Xiamen.

To/From Myanmar (Burma) There is a once-weekly flight from Beijing to Rangoon (now officially called Yangon) with a stopover in Kunming. You can pick up the flight in Kunming too, but you must have a visa for Myanmar which is available in Beijing, not Kunming.

To/From Nepal There are direct flights between Lhasa and Kathmandu twice a week, but you need to get the Chinese visa somewhere besides Kathmandu.

To/From Pakistan CAAC has direct flights from Beijing to Karachi three times weekly.

To/From Philippines CAAC and Philippine Airlines offer flights from Manila to Beijing, Guangzhou and Manila. The Manila-Xiamen flight is particularly popular.

To/From Russia CAAC has flights from Beijing to Moscow but there are no bargain fares. Any air ticket you buy in Russia is likely to be expensive. You're not paying for fine service, you're paying for the lack of competition. Aeroflot (formerly the only Russian airline) and new Russian airlines are well known for frequent cancellations, high prices, poor safety and lost or stolen luggage. A direct Moscow to Beijing flight costs US$1200, and foreigners are required to pay in dollars even for domestic flights within Russia – forget any rumours you've heard about cheap rouble-denominated tickets. Nevertheless, there are a couple of tricks for reducing the cost significantly. One of the best ways is to take a domestic flight from Moscow to the Siberian city of Irkutsk, then fly internationally from Irkutsk to Shenyang in north-east China. The combined Moscow-Irkutsk-Shenyang ticket costs US$495. From Shenyang, you can take a domestic flight to Beijing on CAAC for US$38. Taking this circuitous route may be less convenient, but the saving of over US$700 is a powerful incentive.

To/From Singapore CAAC has flights from Singapore to Beijing, Guangzhou and Xiamen.

To/From Thailand Bangkok is one of Asia's hot spots when it comes to finding bargain basement prices on air tickets.

There is a twice-weekly flight from Beijing to Bangkok via Guangzhou (you can pick up the flight in Guangzhou too), but it's not cheap at 9100 baht one way. There is also a very popular flight from Kunming to Bangkok via Chiang Mai on Thai Airways. A typical one-way fare from Bangkok to Kunming is 4000 baht; return 45-day tickets are 5100 baht. Some of the Bangkok-Guangzhou flights continue on to Shantou in China's Guangdong Province.

To/From Turkey There is a once-weekly flight between Beijing and Istanbul, stopping at Ürümqi en route. This ticket is outrageously expensive if bought in China (over US$1000), but travel agents in Istanbul can give generous discounts.

To/From Uzbekistan Once weekly there are flights between Ürümqi in China's Xinjiang Province and Tashkent, the capital of the former Soviet republic of Uzbekistan.

To/From Vietnam China Southern Airlines (a CAAC spin-off) flies jointly with Vietnam Airlines between Ho Chi Minh City and Guangzhou via Hanoi. The Guangzhou-Hanoi flight takes 1½ hours; Guangzhou-Ho Chi Minh City (US$270 one way) takes 4½ hours.

The Beijing-Hanoi flight on China Southern Airlines now stops at Nanning (capital of China's Guangxi Province) en route – you can board or exit the plane there.

To/From Australia

The cheapest way into China is via Hong Kong. Hong Kong is a convenient transit point for southern China, but too far south if you just want to get to Beijing or the north of the country.

The cheapest return tickets to Beijing are with Malaysian Air Systems (MAS) from Melbourne or Sydney. The fare is A$1305/A$1410 in the off/high season, but you will have to overnight at your own expense in Kuala Lumpur. CAAC flies direct from Sydney to Beijing (stopping for a Customs check at Guangzhou) for $A1450 return.

Nippon Airlines has a 90-day ticket to Beijing or Shanghai for A$1499 (A$1699 peak season), which includes one night's accommodation in Tokyo.

To/From New Zealand

Flying to Hong Kong is certainly a better deal than flying straight to China. The cheapest one-way tickets to Beijing are with Japan Airlines via Tokyo for NZ$1821/1925 in the low/high season.

To/From Europe

CAAC has flights from Beijing to Belgrade, Bucharest, Frankfurt, London, Paris, Athens, Istanbul and Zurich. Other international airlines operate flights out of Beijing but there are very few, if any, cut-rate fares from the Chinese end.

To/From the UK

A standard-price one-way ticket with CAAC from London to Beijing will cost £300 (£550 return). This is more than you'd pay for a flight to Hong Kong, but it's a better deal if you just want to visit northern China.

To/From the USA & Canada

For direct flights from the USA to China the general route is from San Francisco (with connections from New York, Los Angeles and Vancouver in Canada) to Tokyo, then Beijing, Shanghai or several other cities in China. It's entirely possible to go through to Beijing and then pick up the return flight in Shanghai. Tickets from the USA directly to China will cost around US$200 to US$300 more than tickets to Hong Kong, even though the flying distance is actually shorter.

In general, airfares from Vancouver to

Hong Kong or China will cost about 5% to 10% more than tickets from the US west coast. Besides numerous flights to Hong Kong, CAAC has two flights weekly which originate in Toronto, then fly onward to Vancouver, Shanghai and Beijing (in that order).

LAND

There are overland border crossings between China and other countries in North-East Asia, including Hong Kong, Macau, Mongolia and North Korea. See the introductory Getting Around chapter for details.

To/From Russia

A great way to start or finish your China trip is to travel on the Trans-Siberian Railway. More information on this journey is provided in the Getting There & Away chapter at the beginning of this book.

A railway exists between the former Soviet republic of Kazakhstan and Xinjiang in north-west China via the Alataw Pass. Since Kazakhstan has rail connections to Russia, in theory you could travel this route between Europe and China. In practice, travellers have had a very difficult time getting visas to make this crossing.

To/From Pakistan

The journey between Pakistan and Kashgar in China's north-west takes you through the Khunjerab Pass in the spectacular Karakoram Mountains. This trip is only possible during the warm months, and the Chinese have at times closed the route because of anti-government rioting in Kashgar.

To/From Nepal

The road between Nepal and Tibet has been periodically closed due to landslides and political earthquakes. At the moment it is open again, who knows for how long?

The road connecting Lhasa with Nepal is officially called the Friendship Highway and runs from Lhasa to Zhangmu (the Chinese border post) via Gyantse and Shigatse.

Very few people do the Nepal trip by local bus nowadays, mainly because you have no control over your itinerary this way. By far

the most popular option is renting a 4WD through the Yak Hotel and sorting out a private itinerary with the driver. A popular option is a seven to eight-day jaunt taking in Gyantse, Shigatse, Sakya, the Everest base camp, Tingri and on to the border. Prices are very reasonable – reckon on around US$125 per person for the 4WD.

The Yak Hotel operation is a reliable option and you can generally trust your driver to hold to a spoken agreement. If you go for one of the other operators in town, it would probably be a good idea to get everything down in writing. Check with the people at the Yak for the latest on permit requirements. At the time of writing, only the Everest base camp required a permit for the above itinerary.

Travelling from Nepal to Lhasa, the only transport for foreigners is arranged through tour agencies. If you already have a Chinese visa, you can try turning up at the border. The occasional traveller slips through this way. At Zhangmu (Khasa) you can hunt around for buses, minibuses, 4WDs or trucks heading towards Lhasa. Unfortunately, you currently cannot get Chinese visas in Nepal.

LEAVING CHINA

Airport departure tax is officially US$10, but many airports stick all sorts of weird extra fees on top of this. You'd be wise to keep a spare Y200 (in Chinese currency) handy when you check in. There is no departure tax if you leave by ship.

Getting Around

AIR

The CAAC, for many years China's only domestic and international carrier, has officially been broken up and private carriers have been allowed to set up operations in China. This doesn't mean that CAAC is out of business – it now assumes the role of 'umbrella organisation' (nothing to do with umbrella manufacturing) for its numerous subsidiaries. The seven major divisions of

CHINA

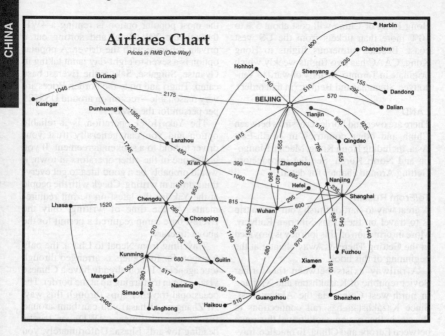

CAAC are CAAC, China Eastern, China Southern, China Northern, China Southwest, China Northwest and Xinjiang Airlines.

In its role as 'umbrella organisation', CAAC still publishes a combined international and domestic timetable in both English and Chinese in April and November each year. These can be bought at most CAAC offices in China, but they're more easily obtained from the two CAAC offices in Hong Kong.

In addition to the divisions of the CAAC network, there is also a bewildering array of private lines taking to the Chinese skies. Many of thes lines serve a small number of destinations, linking one major city with other major cities around China (as is the case with Shanghai Airlines), but others, such as Yunnan Airlines, have extensive routings.

Foreigners pay a surcharge of 75% of the fare charged to local Chinese people. Unlike the situation with trains, there is no way past this CAAC regulation, unless you are a foreign expert or have a residence permit. If you do somehow happen to get the Chinese price and it's discovered, your ticket will be confiscated and no refund given. Children over 12 are charged adult fare.

Cancellation fees depend on how long before departure you cancel. On domestic flights, if you cancel 24 hours before departure you lose 10% of the fare; if you cancel between two and 24 hours before the flight you lose 20%; and if you cancel less than two hours before the flight you lose 30%. If you don't show up for a domestic flight, you are entitled to a refund of 50%.

Domestic departure tax is roughly US$3 but take this with a grain of salt. Each airport seems to have its own rules and adds extra fees. Sometimes you even pay the fee twice – when you check in and when you reach the departure gate!

BUS

The long-distance bus service in China is reasonably good, although the roads are like washboards and accidents are an effective method of population control. The price of a bus seat is comparable to a hard-seat on a train. The seats are numbered and tickets are bought at long-distance bus stations. There is very little room on the bus, certainly not enough for a bulky backpack, so travel light.

There are now some night buses, but rides can be reckless and uncomfortable with gongfu videos blaring all through the night.

TRAIN

Trains are the best way of getting around in reasonable speed and comfort. Food is available on trains or from vendors at stations. You can get boiled water at the end of each carriage but on long runs they sometimes run out.

Classes

Despite the fact that China is a 'classless society', train tickets are designated as hard-seat, soft-seat, hard-sleeper and soft-sleeper. A hard-seat is actually padded, but you'll get no sleep; the carriages are crowded and uncomfortable. Soft-seats are cleaner and less crowded and cost the same as hard-sleepers. Soft-seats are usually only available for short journeys, never on overnight trips.

Hard-sleepers are comfortable, doorless compartments with six bunks in three tiers. Sheets, pillows and blankets are provided. Go for a middle bunk, as the top ones can be near loudspeakers and the bottom ones get taken over by people wanting to sit. Soft-sleepers are the luxury class; closed compartments with four bunks, lace curtains, pot plants and often air-conditioning. You can even turn the loudspeakers off.

Reservations

Tickets can be bought one to four days in advance at CTS or CITS, usually found in major tourist hotels. They charge for this service and they are often slow. You can do it yourself faster at the railway station either on the day of departure or the night before. However, CITS can often get sleeping berths even when tickets are 'sold out'.

Stations in large cities often have notoriously long queues (more like riots), but there is often a special ticket window for foreigners. Indeed, you may be forced to use it – the other windows will probably be Chinese-only. Although you'll have to pay triple, the foreigners' window allows you to avoid the horrors of the queues.

There is such a thing as black market tickets. Essentially, locals with connections on the inside buy up large quantities of tickets and sell them at a significant profit to those in need. But watch out – some of the tickets are fake.

Depending on the distance to the destination, hard-seat tickets are valid for one to seven days:

250 km	– one day
500 km	– two days
1000 km	– three days
2000 km	– six days
2200 km	– about seven days

On some lines this system is not followed.

This system enables you to break your journey and board the next day without booking again or claiming refunds.

Costs

Calculating prices is a complex business and depends on many rational and irrational factors. Foreigners are usually charged three times as much as locals, but it is often possible to get a Chinese-priced ticket. Just go up to the ticket window, shove the money in front of the clerk and say what you want – this will work about 50% of the time. You may be charged triple, but of course there will be no problem if a Chinese person buys the ticket for you.

You can always get local prices by using an official PRC student card. However, the proliferation of fake student cards has made railway workers suspicious to the point where they sometimes reject legitimate student cards. If you manage to buy a cheap ticket at the station, the conductor may still ask you to make up the difference on the train, though this rarely happens.

BOAT

The most famous boat trip in China is the three-day ride down the Yangzi River from Chongqing to Wuhan. Although the trip itself is a bit dull, it's a great way to get from Chongqing to Wuhan and makes a change from trains. You can travel all the way to Shanghai this way if you want to.

There is a very popular route from Guangzhou upriver to Wuzhou, where you can catch a bus to Guilin or Yangshuo.

LOCAL TRANSPORT

Around the cities buses are the most common means of transport apart from bicycles. Walking is often not practicable as Chinese cities are usually very spread out, but you may find yourself doing a lot of legwork anyway.

Streets are sometimes split into sectors. Each sector is given a number or (more usually) labelled according to its position relative to the other sectors and to the points of the compass. For example Zhongshan Lu (Zhongshan Rd) might be split into an east and a west sector. The east sector will be designated Zhongshan Donglu and the west will be Zhongshan Xilu.

Bus

These are almost always horribly crowded and somewhat slow, but you rarely pay more than two jiao per trip unless you get your pocket picked. Good maps of Chinese cities, complete with bus routes, are generally available. Contrary to popular belief, buses are not colour coded – the bus maps are.

Minibus

These are an excellent alternative to the horrors of Chinese buses. Minibuses cost about 10 times more, but are still reasonable at less than US$1 per journey. They generally follow the major bus routes.

Pedicabs

Pedicabs (pedal-powered tricycles) congre-

gate outside train and bus stations, and sometimes outside tourist hotels. The drivers are so dishonest that you have to question whether or not they are worth bothering with.

Almost without exception a reasonable fare will be quoted, but when you arrive at your destination it'll be multiplied by 10. So if you're quoted a fare of Y20 it will become Y200. Another trick is to ask for US$ upon arrival when you were originally quoted a price in Chinese money. The best bet is to write it down, get the driver to agree three or four times, and then when he tries to multiply by 10, hand over the exact change and walk away. At this point the smiling friendly driver will suddenly be transformed into an exceedingly menacing creature – you just have to stand your ground. It's worse if there are two of them, so *never* get into a pedicab if the driver wants his 'brother' to come along for the ride (a common situation). The 'brother' is there to threaten and bully you into paying up when you inevitably balk at being ripped off.

Motortricycle (Auto-Pedicab)

These are similar to pedicabs but are powered by an engine. The drivers are *usually* honest and will charge you whatever fare was agreed to in advance.

Taxi

These are widely available in major cities but scarce in small cities and the countryside. If there is no meter, make sure the fare is agreed to in advance.

Motorcycle Taxi

If you turn a blind eye to the hazards, it's a quick and cheap way of getting around. The deal is that you get a ride on the back of someone's motorcycle. Most rides cost only a few yuan and drivers provide a helmet. Obviously, there is no meter so fares must be agreed to in advance.

Bicycle

This is the main mode of private transport in China. It is possible to rent a bike for around US$1 per day and rental places usually want a deposit or a passport for security. Check that the bike is in good working order, has brakes and that the tyres are well pumped up. Bicycles can be left in bicycle parks for a small charge. Otherwise they could be towed away. Around 9 pm, when bicycle parks close down, the proprietor stores the bike until you come to claim it – a hassle best avoided! Chain locks with keys are sold at department stores and are highly recommended.

TOURS

CITS, CTS and big tourist hotels always have tours but these are usually expensive. Much cheaper is to go with a local Chinese tour group. There are many such one-day tours to all the major attractions, but don't expect anyone to speak English.

Beijing 北京

China revolves around Beijing; all Chinese time is set to Beijing time, and putonghua, the Beijing dialect, is the official national language. From here the great monolith is controlled.

All cities in China are equal, but some are more equal than others. Beijing has the best of everything: food, hotels, education and temples. If Beijing is all you see of China, you will probably be convinced that the Chinese are living pretty well. For a more realistic impression of China, go down to Beijing railway station where newly arrived destitute peasants from the countryside squat on the pavement, wondering what their next move should be. Or better still, get out into the countryside yourself.

Orientation

The independently administered Beijing Municipality sprawls about 80 km from the city centre. Although it might not seem like it in the chaos of arrival, Beijing is a city of very orderly design with long straight boulevards. Streets in the central area end with the suffix *nei* meaning 'inner' (eg, Jianguomennei). Moving farther afield, the suffix becomes *wai* meaning 'outer' (eg, Jianguomenwai). Unfortunately, the name of a major boulevard may change six or eight times along its length. The city is looped by a number of major freeway-like 'ring roads'.

Information

Tourist Offices CITS has two offices. One is in the Beijing Tourist Tower (☎ 5158570), 28 Jianguomenwai – the large building just behind the New Otani Hotel. The other one (☎ 5120509) is in the Beijing International Hotel *(guó jì fàn diàn)* on Jianguomennei, the large tower just one block north of the Beijing railway station.

Money Almost every hotel can change money. The most useful branch of the Bank of China is on Dong'anmen Dajie – just to the east of the Forbidden City and west of Wangfujing near the Foreign Languages Bookstore. Better service is offered by CITIC, International Building, 19 Jianguomenwai, which is across from the Friendship Store. Either of these two banks can cash travellers' cheques and pay you in US$ cash.

Post & Telecommunications The International Post & Telecommunications Building is on Jianguomen Beidajie, slightly north-west from the Friendship Store. All letters and parcels marked 'Poste Restante, GPO Beijing' will wind up here. Hours are from 8 am to 7 pm daily.

Embassies & Consulates These are concentrated in the two compounds of Jianguomenwai and Sanlitun in Beijing. The Jianguomenwai Compound is in the vicinity of the Friendship Store. Some embassies located here are:

Austria
    5 Xiushui Nanjie (☎ 5322061)

CHINA

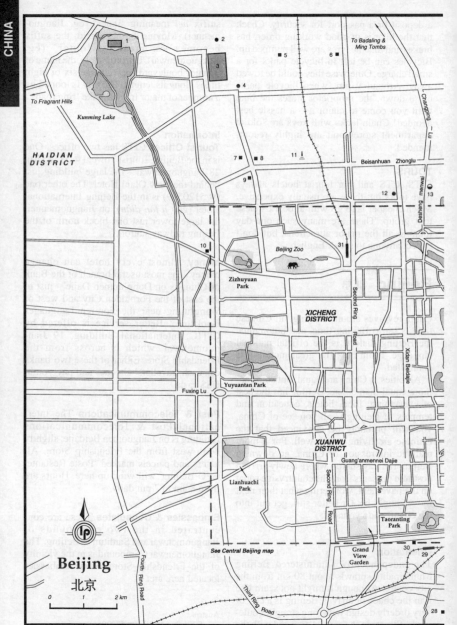

To Badaling &
Ming Tombs

To Fragrant Hills

Kunming Lake

Changping Lu

HAIDIAN
DISTRICT

Beisanhuan Zhonglu

Deshengmenwai

Beijing Zoo

Zizhuyuan
Park

Second Ring
Road

XICHENG
DISTRICT

Xidan Beidajie

Fuxing Lu

Yuyuantan Park

Lianhuachi
Park

XUANWU
DISTRICT

Guang'anmennei Dajie

Niu Jie

Second Ring
Road

See Central Beijing map

Grand
View
Garden

Taoranting
Park

Beijing
北京

0   1   2 km

Fourth Ring Road

Third Ring Road

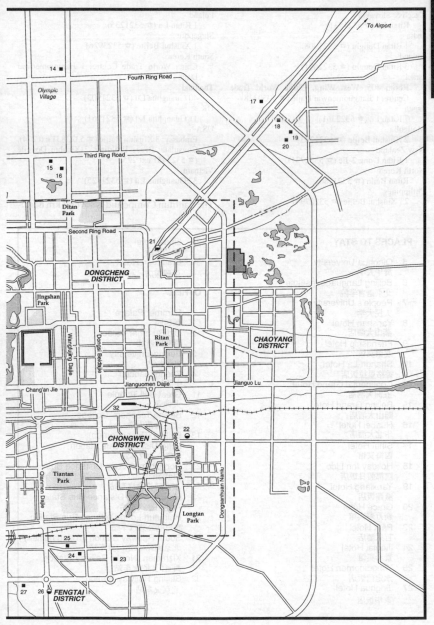

Czech & Slovakia
  Ritan Lu (☎ 5321531)
India
  1 Ritan Donglu (☎ 5321908)
Ireland
  3 Ritan Donglu (☎ 5322691)
Israel
  Room 405, West Wing, China World Trade Centre, 1 Jianguomenwai Dajie (☎ 5050328)
Japan
  7 Ritan Lu (☎ 5322361)
Mongolia
  2 Xiushui Beijie (☎ 5321203)
New Zealand
  1 Ritan Dong 2-Jie (☎ 5322731)
North Korea
  Ritan Beilu (☎ 5321186)
Philippines
  23 Xiushui Beijie (☎ 5322794)

Poland
  1 Ritan Lu (☎ 5321235)
Singapore
  1 Xiushui Beijie (☎ 5323926)
South Korea
  China World Trade Centre, 1 Jianguomenwai Dajie (☎ 5052608)
Thailand
  40 Guanghua Lu (☎ 5321903)
UK
  11 Guanghua Lu (☎ 5321961)
USA
  Embassy: 3 Xiushui Beijie (☎ 5323831 ext 274), Consulate: Bruce Building, 2 Xiushui Dongjie (☎ 5323431 ext 225)
Vietnam
  32 Guanghua Lu (☎ 5321125)

The Sanlitun Compound is several km north-

PLACES TO STAY

5 Qinghua University
   清华大学
6 Beijing Language Institute
   北京语言学院
7 People's University
   人民大学
8 Yanshan Hotel
   燕山大酒店
9 Friendship Hotel
   友谊宾馆
10 Shangri-La Hotel
   香格里拉饭店
14 Continental Grand Hotel
   五洲大酒店
15 Beijing Grand Hotel
   圆山大酒店
16 Huabei Hotel
   华北大酒店
17 Sihai Hotel
   四海宾馆
18 Holiday Inn Lido
   丽都假日饭店
19 Yanxiang Hotel
   燕翔饭店
20 Grace Hotel
   新万寿宾馆
23 Park Hotel
   百乐酒店
24 Jingtai Hotel
   景泰宾馆
25 Yongdingmen Hotel
   永定门饭店
27 Jinghua Hotel
   京华饭店

28 Lihua Hotel
   丽华饭店
30 Qiaoyuan Hotel
   侨园饭店

OTHER

1 Summer Palace
   颐和园
2 Old Summer Palace
   圆明园遗址
3 Beijing University
   北京大学
4 Zhongguancun
   中关村
11 Great Bell Temple
   大钟寺
12 Beijing Teachers' College
   北京师范大学
13 Beijiao (Deshengmen) Long-Distance Bus Station
   北郊长途汽车站
21 Dongzhimen Long-Distance Bus Station
   东直门长途汽车站
22 Majuan Long-Distance Bus Station
   马圈长途汽车站
26 Haihutun Long-Distance Bus Station
   海户屯公共汽车站
29 South Railway Station (Yongdingmen)
   北京南站/永定门火车站
31 Xizhimen (North) Railway Station
   西直门(北)火车站
32 Beijing Railway Station
   北京火车站

east of Jianguomenwai, near the Agricultural Exhibition Hall:

Australia
    21 Dongzhimenwai Dajie (☎ 5322331)
Belgium
    6 Sanlitun Lu (☎ 5321736)
Cambodia
    9 Dongzhimenwai Dajie (☎ 5321889)
Canada
    19 Dongzhimenwai Dajie (☎ 5323536)
Denmark
    1 Sanlitun Dong 5-Jie (☎ 5322431)
Finland
    Tayuan Building, 14 Liangmahe Nanlu (☎ 5321817)
France
    3 Sanlitun Dong 3-Jie (☎ 5321331)
Germany
    5 Dongzhimenwai Dajie (☎ 5322161)
Hungary
    10 Dongzhimenwai Dajie (☎ 5321431)
Kazakhstan
    13th floor, Tayuan Building, 14 Liangmahe Nanlu (☎ 5326182)
Kyrgyzstan
    4th floor, Tayuan Building, 14 Liangmahe Nanlu (☎ 5326458)
Malaysia
    13 Dongzhimenwai Dajie (☎ 5322531)
Myanmar (Burma)
    6 Dongzhimenwai Dajie (☎ 5321584)
Nepal
    1 Sanlitun Xi 6-Jie (☎ 5321795)
Netherlands
    1-15-2 Tayuan Building, 14 Liangmahe Nanlu (☎ 5321131)
Norway
    1 Sanlitun Dong 1-Jie (☎ 5322261)
Pakistan
    1 Dongzhimenwai Dajie (☎ 5322504)
Russia
    4 Dongzhimen Beizhongjie, west of the Sanlitun in a separate compound (☎ 5322051)
Sweden
    3 Dongzhimenwai Dajie (☎ 5323331)
Switzerland
    3 Sanlitun Dong 5-Jie (☎ 5322736)
Ukraine
    Tayan Compound, Building 4, Entrance 1, 9th floor (☎ 5326359)

Medical Services Beijing's best medical care (including emergency service) is at the Sino-German Policlinic (☎ 5011983), Landmark Tower B-1, adjacent to the Sheraton Great Wall Hotel (*cháng chéng fàn diàn*).

There is a foreigners clinic and emergency room at the Beijing Union Medical College (☎ 5127733 ext 217) (*xié hé yī yuàn*), 1 Shifuyuan, Wangfujing. There is also a foreigners' clinic at the Friendship Hospital (☎ 4221122) (*yǒu yí yī yuàn*), 95 Yong'an Lu (west side of Tiantan Park in the Tianqiao area).

Bookshops The Friendship Store is a gold mine of US, British and European magazines, newspapers, books and other saddle-bag material. Also try the Foreign Language Bookstore on Wangfujing.

Emergency The PSB (☎ 5122471) is at 85 Beichizi Dajie.

Things to See

The enormous open space in the heart of Beijing is **Tiananmen Square** (*tiān ān mén guǎng chǎng*). It was Mao's creation and has since been the scene of many of China's dramatic political events. The square gained its greatest fame in 1989 when the government suppressed pro-democracy demonstrators here with tanks and troops. Surrounding the square are numerous monuments to Chinese history. On the east side of Tiananmen Square are the **History Museum & Museum of the Revolution** (*zhōng guó gé mìng lì shǐ bó wù guǎn*), both housed in the same building.

The body of the Great Chairman himself is housed on the south side of the square in the **Mao Zedong Memorial Mausoleum** (*máo zhǔ xí jì niàn táng*). CITS guides freely quote the official Party line that Mao was 70% right and 30% wrong (what, one wonders, are the figures for CITS itself?). Still farther to the south is **Qianmen** (Front Gate). Qianmen guarded the wall division between the ancient Inner City and the outer suburban zone, and dates back to the reign of Emperor Yong Le in the 15th century. With the disappearance of the city walls, the gate has had its context removed, but it's still an impressive sight. For US$0.30 you can go upstairs to the top of the gate.

Tiananmen Square should not be confused

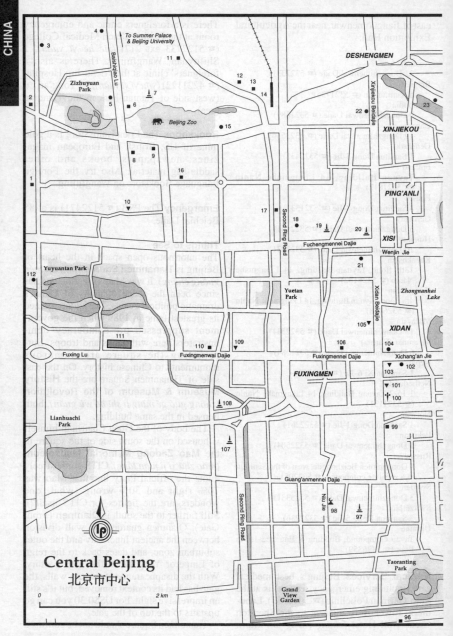

DESHENGMEN

To Summer Palace
& Beijing University

Baishiqiao Lu

Zizhuyuan
Park

Xinjiekou Beidajie

XINJIEKOU

Beijing Zoo

PING'ANLI

XISI

Second Ring Road

Fuchengmennei Dajie

Wenjin Jie

Xidan Beidajie

Zhongnanhai
Lake

Yuyuantan Park

Yuetan
Park

XIDAN

Xichang'an Jie

Fuxing Lu

Fuxingmenwai Dajie

Fuxingmennei Dajie

FUXINGMEN

Lianhuachi
Park

Guang'anmennei Dajie

Niu Jie

Second Ring Road

Central Beijing
北京市中心

0   1   2 km

Taoranting
Park

Grand
View
Garden

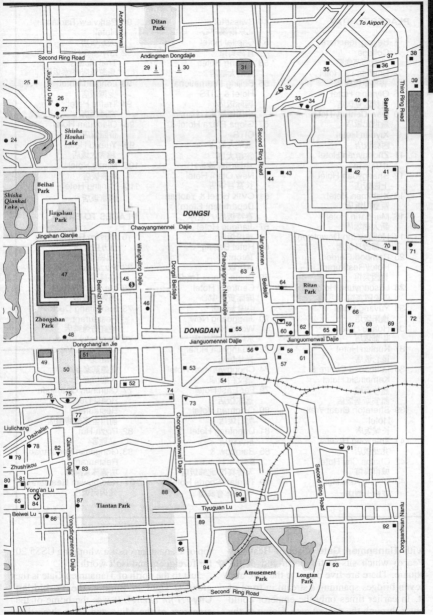

Ditan Park

Andingmenwai

Second Ring Road

Andingmen Dongdajie

To Airport

29 30

31

37

38

36

35

39

Sanlitun

Third Ring Road

32

25

Jingxiou Dajie

26

27

33 34

40

Shisha Houhai Lake

24

28

42

41

Beihai Park

43

44

Shisha Qianhai Lake

Jingshan Park

70

71

DONGSI

Jingshan Qianjie

Chaoyangmennei Dajie

Second Ring Road

Jianguomen

47

Wangfujing Dajie

Beichizi Dajie

Dongsi Beidajie

Chaoyangmen Namxiajie

Jianguomen Beidajie

63

64

Ritan Park

45

46

66

Zhongshan Park

48

DONGDAN

55

59

62

65

67 68 69

72

60

Dongchang'an Jie

Jianguomennei Dajie

Jianguomenwai Dajie

49

50

51

56

58

57

61

52

53

54

76 75

74

73

77

91

Liulichang

Dazhalan

78

82

Zhushikou

79

83

Changwanmenwai Dajie

Second Ring Road

80 81

Yong'an Lu

84

87

88

Tiantan Park

90

Tiyuguan Lu

85

86

Yongdingmennei Dajie

89

92

Dongbianmen

95

94

93

Amusement Park

Longtan Park

Second Ring Road

PLACES TO STAY

1 Beijing Teachers'
College
北京师范学院
2 Shangri-La Hotel
香格里拉饭店
6 Olympic Hotel
奥林匹克饭店
8 New Century Hotel
新世纪饭店
9 Xiyuan Hotel
西苑饭店
11 Zhongyuan Hotel
中苑宾馆
12 Shangyuan Hotel
上园饭店
13 Xizhimen Hotel
西直门饭店
16 Mandarin Hotel
新大都饭店
17 Holiday Inn Downtown
金都假日饭店
25 Bamboo Garden
Hotel/Restaurant
竹园宾馆
28 Lüsongyuan Hotel
侣松园宾馆
35 Yuyang Hotel
渔阳饭店
36 Huadu Hotel
华都饭店
37 Kunlun Hotel
昆仑饭店
38 Lufthansa Centre &
Kempinski Hotel
燕沙商城/
凯宾斯基饭店
39 Sheraton Great Wall
Hotel
长城饭店
41 Zhaolong Hotel
兆龙饭店
42 Chains City Hotel
城市宾馆
43 Beijing Asia Hotel
亚洲大酒店

44 Swissotel
北京港澳中心
52 Capital Hotel
首都宾馆
53 Jinlang Hotel
金朗大酒店
55 Beijing International
Hotel & CITS
国际饭店/
中国国际旅行社
57 Gloria Plaza Hotel &
CITS
凯莱大酒店/
旅游大厦/
中国国际旅行社
58 New Otani Hotel
长富宫饭店
61 CVIK Hotel & Yaohan
Department Store
赛特饭店/八佰伴
67 Jianguo Hotel
建国饭店
68 Hotel Beijing
Toronto
京伦饭店
69 China World Trade
Centre & Hotel
国际贸易中心/
中国大饭店
70 Jingguang New
World Hotel
京广新世界饭店
72 Guanghua Hotel
光华饭店
74 Chongwenmen Hotel
崇文门饭店
79 Far East Hotel
远东饭店
80 Qianmen Hotel
前门饭店
81 Dongfang Hotel
东方饭店
85 Rainbow &
Beiwei Hotels
天桥宾馆/北纬饭店
89 Tiantan Sports Hotel
天坛体育宾馆

90 Parkview Tiantan
Hotel
天坛饭店
92 Leyou & Hua
Thai Hotels
乐游饭店/华泰饭店
93 Longtan Hotel
龙潭饭店
94 Traffic Hotel
交通饭店
96 Qiaoyuan Hotel
侨园饭店
99 Yuexiu Hotel
越秀大饭店
106 Minzu Hotel
民族饭店
110 Yanjing Hotel
燕京饭店

PLACES TO EAT

10 Muslim Restaurants
百万庄西路
(回民餐馆)
33 Pizza Hut
必胜客
66 Mexican Wave
墨西哥波涛
73 Bianyifang Duck
Restaurant
便宜坊烤鸭店
76 Kentucky Fried
Chicken & Vie de
France
肯德基家乡鸡/
大磨坊面包
77 Qianmen Quanjude
Roast Duck
Restaurant
前门全聚德烤鸭店
82 Pizza Hut
必胜客
83 Gongdelin Vegetarian
Restaurant
功德林素菜馆
101 Kaorouwan Restaurant
烤肉宛饭庄

with **Tiananmen Gate** (Gate of Heavenly Peace) which sits at the north end of the square. There are five doors to the gate and seven bridges spanning a stream in front of it. In earlier times only the emperor could enter through the central gate. Going to the top of Tiananmen costs a whopping US$5.20 for foreigners and isn't worth it.

Just to the north of Tiananmen Gate is the grandest sight in Beijing, the **Forbidden City** (zǐ jìn chéng). It was the home of the emperors of the Ming and Qing dynasties.

103 Vie de France Bakery
大磨坊面包
105 Quyuan Restaurant
曲园酒楼
109 McDonald's II
麦当劳

OTHER

3 China Grand Theatre
中国剧院
4 Central Nationalities
Institute
中央民族学院
5 National Library
北京图书馆
7 Wuta Temple
五塔寺
14 Xizhimen (North)
Railway Station
西直门火车站
15 Beijing Exhibition
Centre
北京展览馆
18 Lu Xun Museum
鲁迅博物馆
19 White Dagoba Temple
白塔寺
20 Guangji Temple
广济寺
21 Dizhi Cinema Hall
地质礼堂
22 Xu Beihong
Museum
徐悲鸿博物馆
23 Song Qingling
Museum
宋庆龄故居
24 Prince Gong's
Residence
恭王府
26 Bell Tower
钟楼
27 Drum Tower
鼓楼
29 Confucius Temple
孔庙

30 Lama Temple
雍和宫
31 Russian Embassy
苏联大使馆
32 Dongzhimen
Long-Distance Bus
Station
东直门长途汽车站
34 Australian Embassy
奥大利亚大使馆
40 Friendship
Supermarket
友谊超级商场
45 Bank of China
中国银行
46 Beijing Union Medical
College
协和医院
47 Forbidden City
紫禁城
48 Tiananmen Gate
天安门
49 Great Hall of the
People
人民大会堂
50 Tiananmen Square
天安门广场
51 History Museum &
Museum of the
Revolution
中国革命历史博物馆
54 Beijing Railway
Station
北京火车站
56 Ancient Observatory
古观象台
59 International Post &
Telecommunications
Office
国际邮局局
60 International Club
国际俱乐部
62 Friendship Store &
CITIC
友谊商店/国际大厦
63 Black Temple
智化寺

64 Yabao Lu Clothing
Market
雅宝路
65 Xiushui Silk Market
秀水东街
71 Chaoyang Theatre
朝阳剧场
75 Qianmen
前门
78 Sun City
Department Store
太阳城百货
84 Friendship
Hospital
友谊医院
86 Tianqiao Theatre
天桥剧场
87 Natural History
Museum
自然博物馆
88 Hongqiao Market
红桥商场
91 Majuan
Long-Distance Bus
Station
马圈长途汽车站
95 Harmony Club
幸福俱乐部
97 Fayuan Temple
法源寺
98 Niujie Mosque
牛街礼拜寺
100 South Cathedral
南堂
102 Shoudu Cinema
首都电影院
104 Aviation Building
(CAAC & Airport Bus)
民航营业大厦
107 Tianning Temple
天宁寺
108 White Cloud Temple
白云观
111 Military Museum
军事博物馆
112 TV Tower
电视台

The 'city' got its name because it was off-limits to uninvited visitors (even with a CITS tour) for 500 years. That has all changed and the Forbidden City is now open daily from 8.30 am to 5 pm – last admission tickets are sold at 3.30 pm. Two hundred years ago the admission price would have been instant death, but this has dropped considerably to US$7.80 for foreigners and US$2 for Chinese. Your US$7.80 includes rental of a cassette tape player and tape for a self-guided tour – the tape player requires a refundable US$17 deposit, but you can use your own tape player instead. For the tape to make sense you must enter the Forbidden City from the south gate and exit from the north.

Just north-west of the Forbidden City is **Beihai Park** (*běi hǎi gōng yuán*), the former playground of the emperors and of Mao's wife Jiang Qing (No 1 of the 'Gang of Four'). The park covers 68 hectares, half of which is a lake that freezes up in winter and becomes the venue for ice skating.

Back in the Cultural Revolution days one of the safest hobbies for an artist was to retouch classical-type landscapes with red flags, belching factory chimneys or bright red tractors. You can get some idea of the current state of the arts in the **China Art Gallery** (*zhōng guó měi shù guǎn*). There's still a fair bit of communist drivel – one painting shows five teenage girls with ecstatic expressions effortlessly lifting an enormous boulder out of a quarry. There are occasionally outstanding exhibitions – check the *China Daily* for current listings. The arts & crafts shop inside has an excellent range of woodblock prints and papercuts. The gallery is west of Dongsi intersection.

The Temple of Heaven, a perfect example of Ming architecture, is in **Tiantan Park** (*tiān tán gōng yuán*). The temple appears in endless advertisements and as a brand name for a wide range of products. Set in the 267-hectare park in the south of the city, it has four gates at the compass points and walls to the north and east.

The beautiful **Lama Temple** (*yōng hé gōng*) is a monument to Tibetan Buddhism featuring gardens, stunning frescoes and tapestries and incredible carpentry. Open daily from 9 am to 4 pm, the temple is in active use again, though some say a few monks look suspiciously like undercover Public Security agents. Prayers are held early in the morning, but are not public. It's off Dongsi Beidajie – get there by subway to the Yonghegong station.

Just down the lane opposite the gates of the Lama Temple is the **Confucius Temple** (*kǒng miào*). Formerly the Imperial College,

this is the largest Confucius Temple in China after the one at Qufu.

The **Summer Palace** (*yí hé yúan*) competes with the Forbidden City as one of Beijing's top attractions. Set in an immense park, the site was enlarged and embellished in the 18th century by Emperor Qianlong. Empress Dowager Cixi did a major renovation in 1888 using money that was supposedly reserved for the construction of a modern navy – but she did restore a marble boat that sits immobile at the edge of the lake. In 1900 foreign troops, annoyed by the Boxer Rebellion, had a go at razing the Summer Palace. Restorations took place a few years later and a major renovation occurred after 1949. Three-quarters of the park is occupied by Kunming Lake. You can get around the lake by rowboat, or on a pair of ice skates in winter. The park is about 12 km north-west of the centre of Beijing. The easiest way to get there is to take the subway to Xizhimen (close to the zoo), then a minibus for less than US$1. Bus No 332 from the zoo is slower but will get you there eventually. There are heaps of minibuses returning to the city centre from the Summer Palace.

Nearby is the original **Old Summer Palace** (*yuán míng yuán*), which was laid out in the 12th century. In the second Opium War (1860), British and French troops destroyed the palace and sent the booty abroad. The ruins have long been a favourite picnic spot for foreign residents and Chinese twosomes seeking a bit of privacy. More recently, the government has decided to slowly restore the gardens, moats and buildings. Minibuses connect the new Summer Palace with the old one. There are some slower but pleasant trips you can do around the area by public transport. Take bus No 332 from the zoo to the Old Summer Palace and to the Summer Palace; change to bus No 333 for the Fragrant Hills; and change to bus No 360 to go directly back to the zoo. Another round-trip route is to take the subway to Pingguoyuan (the last stop in the west) and then take bus No 318 to the Fragrant Hills; change to No 333 for the Summer Palace;

and then to No 332 for the zoo. Admission for foreigners costs US$3.

Blockbuster Bicycle Tour

Walking tours are close to impossible in sprawling Beijing. You can walk a bit in certain neighbourhoods like Wangfujing, Dazhalan and Jianguomenwai, but the city is so spread out that the obvious way to go is by bicycle. A proposed route follows:

Tiantan Park (west side) – Natural History Museum – Dazhalan – Qianmen – Tiananmen Square – History Museum & Museum of the Revolution – Great Hall of the People – Tiananmen Gate – Forbidden City – Beihai Park – Jingshan Park – Song Qingling Museum – Drum Tower – Bell Tower – Confucius Temple & Imperial College – Lama Temple – China Art Gallery – Kentucky Fried Chicken or McDonald's – Wangfujing – Tiantan Park (east side) – Home?

Obviously this is far too much to attempt in one day. But if you start out early (like dawn) you can see a good chunk of town and take in some of Beijing's many moods, and you can always continue the tour the next day.

For this tour, nonstop cycling time is about 2½ hours – Chinese bike, Western legs, average pace. The starting point is the west side of Tiantan Park – the finishing point is the east side of the same park.

The southern end of Qianmen Dajie is called Yongdingmennei Dajie – it's here that you'll find the west entrance of Tiantan Park. The park is certainly worth exploring, but you can do that on the way back. Right now, our goal is just a little to the north, the Natural History Museum on the east side of Yongdingmennei Dajie.

After you've had your dose of natural history, continue north to where Yongdingmennie Dajie becomes Qianmen Dajie. Coming up on your left is Dazhalan, one of Beijing's most intriguing *hutongs* (alleys). Bikes cannot be ridden into this particular hutong, though you can explore most others on two wheels.

Slightly more than a stone's throw to the north is Qianmen, the front gate to the vast expanse of Tiananmen Square. Traffic is one way for north-south avenues on either side

of the square. If you want to go to Tiananmen, dismount after the archway and wheel the bike to the parking areas along the footpath. Bicycles cannot be ridden across Tiananmen Square (apparently tanks are OK), but you can walk the bike. Nearby are the History Museum, Museum of the Revolution, Great Hall of the People, Mao's Mausoleum, Tiananmen Gate and the Forbidden City itself.

Over to the west side of the old Forbidden City is the new Forbidden City, the Zhongnanhai compound where top Party members live and work. On the right, going up Beichang Jie, you pass some older housing that lines the moat. On the left is a high wall that shields Zhongnanhai from public view.

Then it's Beihai Park, which by this time of day should be bustling with activity. You can exercise your arms as well as your legs – hire a rowboat.

Back on the bike and you'll soon bump into Jingshan Park. There's bicycle parking by the entrance. Jingshan Park is a splendid place to survey the smog of Beijing, get your bearings with 360° views and enjoy a good overview of the russet roofing of the Forbidden City opposite. There are snack bars both in the park and at the north end of the Forbidden City.

North of Jingshan Park it gets a bit tricky. You want to get off the main road into the small alleys running around the Shisha Hai Lakes. Worth checking out is Prince Gong's Residence (*gōng wáng fǔ*), which lies more or less at the centre of the arc created by the lakes running from north to south. It's one of the largest private residential compounds in Beijing, with a nine-courtyard layout, high walls and elaborate gardens. Prince Gong was the son of a Qing emperor.

The lake district is steeped in history; if you consult a Beijing map you will see that the set of lakes connects from north to south. The lakes have been used for pleasure boating, and were bordered by the residences of high officials.

The larger lake to the north-west is the Shisha Houhai (Lake of the Ten Back Mon-

CHINA

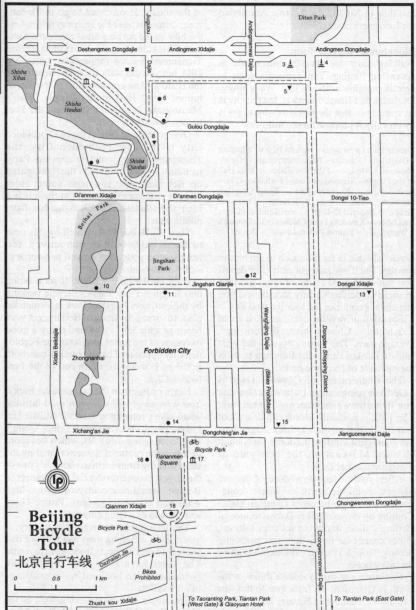

Beijing
Bicycle
Tour
北京自行车线

0   0.5   1 km

Ditan Park

Deshengmen Dongdajie   Andingmen Xidajie   Andingmen Dongdajie

Shisha
Xihai

■ 2

Dajie

■ 3 ⚲

⚲ 4

Shisha
Houhai

● 6

▼ 5

● 7

■ 8
▼

Gulou Dongdajie

● 9

Shisha
Qianhai

Di'anmen Xidajie   Di'anmen Dongdajie   Dongsi 10-Tiao

Beihai Park

Jingshan
Park

● 12

Dongsi Xidajie

● 10

13 ▼

● 11

Jingshan Qianjie

Xidan Beidajie

Zhongnanhai

Forbidden City

Wangfujing Dajie
(Bikes Prohibited)

Dongdan Shopping District

● 14

Xichang'an Jie   Dongchang'an Jie   Jianguomennei Dajie

▼ 15

🚲
Bicycle Park

● 16   🏛 17

Tiananmen
Square

Chongwenmennei Dajie

Chongwenmen Dongdajie

Qianmen Xidajie   ● 18

🚲
Bicycle Park

Dazhalan Jie

Bikes
Prohibited

Zhushi kou Xidajie

To Taoranting Park, Tiantan Park
(West Gate) & Qiaoyuan Hotel

To Tiantan Park (East Gate)

1	Song Qingling Museum 宋庆龄故居
2	Bamboo Garden Hotel 竹园宾馆
3	Confucius Temple 孔庙
4	Lama Temple 雍和宫
5	Confucius Restaurant 孔子餐厅
6	Bell Tower 钟楼
7	Drum Tower 鼓楼
8	Kaorouji Restaurant 北京烤肉季
9	Prince Gong's Residence 恭王府
10	Beihai Park Main Entrance 北海公园北门
11	Forbidden City Rear Gate 故宫北门
12	China Art Gallery 中国美术馆
13	Kentucky Fried Chicken 肯德基家乡鸡
14	Tiananmen Gate 天安门
15	McDonald's 麦当劳
16	Great Hall of the People 人民大会堂
17	History Museum & Museum of the Revolution 中国革命历史博物馆
18	Qianmen 前门

asteries). Below that is the Shisha Qianhai (Lake of the Ten Front Monasteries). Also around the lakes you'll find the Song Qinqing Museum, the retirement residence of Sun Yatsen's respected second wife.

Make a small detour here. If you go northeast through the hutongs you will arrive at the Bamboo Garden Hotel, which is a wonderful illustration of the surprises that hutongs hold. This was originally the personal garden of Sheng Xuanhuai, an important Qing official.

Another small detour brings you to the

Kaorouji Restaurant – not necessarily the cheapest place, but the balcony dining in summer is pleasant enough.

Back on the main drag and you come to the Drum Tower (gǔ lóu). It was built in 1420 and has several drums which were beaten to mark the hours of the day – in effect the Big Ben of Beijing.

Behind the Drum Tower, down an alley directly north, is the Bell Tower (zhōng lóu), which was originally built at the same time as the Drum Tower but burnt down. The present structure is 18th-century, and the gigantic bell which used to hang there has been moved to the Drum Tower.

Back on the road and you'll reach the former Confucius Temple & Imperial College, now a museum/library complex. Unless you can read stele-calligraphy, you probably won't spend much time.

By contrast, just down the road is the Lama Temple, one of Beijing's finest.

This is the northernmost point of today's journey (you're still with us, aren't you?). Head south, and if you're still ready for another museum there's the China Art Gallery, a slight detour to the west at the northern end of Wangfujing. Unfortunately, Wangfujing itself is closed to cyclists, so head back to the east on Dongsi Dajie and you'll find Kentucky Fried Chicken. If the Colonel's finger-lickin' chicken isn't what you had in mind, you could try McDonald's at the southern end of Wangfujing. No matter what you think of the food, these restaurants are at least as popular as the Forbidden City – and just remember that none of China's emperors ever had the chance to taste a Big Mac, Thickshake or Egg McMuffin.

Launch yourself into the sea of cyclists, throw your legs into cruising speed, and cycle the length of Dongdan south to the east entrance of Tiantan Park. If this is still Day One of your bike tour, you're probably too exhausted to walk inside to see the Temple of Heaven – well, there's always tomorrow.

Places to Stay
Famous for broken plumbing and surly staff, the *Qiaoyuan Hotel (qiáo yuán fàn diàn)* has

been low-budget headquarters for years. There are different phone numbers for the front building (☎ 3038861) and rear building (☎ 3012244). Dorm beds are US$4.30, double rooms cost from US$10 to US$14 with shower. To get there take bus No 20 or 54 from the main Beijing station to the terminus (Yongdingmen railway station) and walk for about 10 minutes along the canal to the hotel, or from just north of the Beijing railway station take a minibus to Yongdingmen station.

A good alternative is the *Jingtai Hotel* (☎ 7212476) (*jīng tài bīn guǎn*) at 65 Yongwai Jingtaixi, a small alley running off Anlelin Lu in the south of the city. Dorm beds cost US$3.50; doubles/triples without bath US$9/11; and doubles with bath US$12, US$16 and US$21. From the railway station take bus No 39 to the first stop after it crosses the canal – the name of the bus stop is 'Puhuangyu'. From there, you've got a 10-minute walk west on Anlelin Lu. Alternatively, bus No 45 will drop you off at the intersection of Yongdingmennei Jie and Anlelin Lu, also a 10-minute walk from the hotel. Bus No 25 goes right down Anlelin Lu and will drop you off near the hotel – this bus both terminates and starts at the Anlelin Lu's east end.

Just a two-minute walk from the Jingtai Hotel is the *Yongdingmen Hotel* (☎ 721-2125, 7213344) (*yǒng dìng mén fàn diàn*) at 77 Anlelin Lu. This place is not as good as the Jingtai, but if you arrive during the busy season and the Jingtai is packed out, it beats sleeping on the streets. Doubles/triples are US$11/13. Take bus No 39 from the railway station.

The *Jinghua Hotel* (☎ 7222211) (*jīng huá fàn diàn*) is on Nansanhuan Xilu, the southern part of the third ring road around Beijing. It's an adequate and friendly place to stay, but the neighbourhood may leave you cold with its ugly apartment blocks. Doubles with private bath cost US$9 and US$11. Bus Nos 2 and 17 from Qianmen drop you off nearby. This place is also very convenient for the Haihutun long-distance bus station (buses to cities south of Beijing).

Within walking distance of the Jinghua is the *Lihua Hotel* (☎ 7211144) (*lì huá fàn diàn*) at 71 Yangqiao, Yongdingmenwai. Dorms cost US$4 and doubles are US$16. Bus No 343 is the easiest to get you there but No 14 will also do.

The *Longtan Hotel* (☎ 7711602) (*lóng tán fàn diàn*), 15 Panjiayuan Nanli, Chaoyang District, is an excellent alternative to all of the preceding and many budget travellers now stay here. The staff are friendly and there is a good (but not cheap) restaurant. Beds go for US$5 in three-bed rooms or US$4 in a five-bed room – the communal baths deserve honorable mention for being in extraordinarily good condition. Doubles cost US$14. The hotel is opposite Longtan Park in the south of the city, close to a hospital. Bus No 51 (to the last stop) lets you out near the hotel, but bus No 63 from the railway station is somewhat more frequent.

The *Traffic Hotel* (☎ 7011114) (*jiāo tōng fàn diàn*), 35 Dongsi Kuaiyu Nanjie, has 82 comfortable rooms but no dorms. Doubles with shared bath are US$11; with private bath they're US$17. The hotel is in a narrow alley running south from Tiyuguan Lu – signs in English point the way. Bus No 41 runs along Tiyuguan Lu and drops you off at the alley's entrance.

The *Tiantan Sports Hotel* (☎ 7013388) (*tiān tán tǐ yù bīn guǎn*), 10 Tiyuguan Lu, falls in the mid-range. Doubles are US$17 and it's a good place to stay if you want something comfortable but not ridiculously expensive. Take the subway one stop from Beijing Main Station to Chongwenmen, then take bus No 39, 41 or 43.

The *Beiwei Hotel* (☎ 3012266) (*běi wěi fàn diàn*) is at 13 Xijing Lu, Xuanwu District – on the west side of Tiantan Park. Standard rooms are US$23, superior US$26 and suites are US$34. Take the subway to Qianmen, then bus No 5 south; you can take bus No 20 direct from the main railway station. This place belongs to the neighbouring Rainbow Hotel but is cheaper.

The *Chongwenmen Hotel* (☎ 5122211) (*chóng wén mén fàn diàn*) is at 2 Chongwenmen Xi Dajie. It is a good, mid-range place and has a very central location that makes the five-star hotels jealous. Standard rooms are US$33, and suites cost US$45 to US$52.

Places to Eat

Travellers residing in the Qiaoyuan Hotel or thereabouts can choose from a wide selection of cheapie restaurants which have sprung up to milk the backpacker market. English menus are a nice feature in this neighbourhood, plus the locals have learned to make decidedly un-Chinese specialities such as banana muesli.

Otherwise known as the 'Big Duck', the *Qianmen Quanjude Roast Duck Restaurant* (☎ 7011379) *(qián mén quàn jù dé kǎo yā diàn)* is at 32 Qianmen Dajie, on the east side, near Qianmen subway. Next door you'll find the *Lili* (☎ 751242) *(lì lì cān tīng)* at 30 Qianmen, specialising in Sichuan food and superb dumplings.

The Yangzhou-style *Gongdelin Vegetarian Restaurant (gōng dé lín sù cài guǎn)* at 158 Qianmen Dajie has some of the best vegetarian food in the city.

Muslim food is not only excellent, but dirt-cheap if you know the right place to look for it. The right place is a little street called Baiwanzhuangxi Lu in a neighbourhood known as Ganjiakou (not far south of the zoo). This is where Beijing's Uigur minority congregates – if you didn't know better you'd swear you were walking down a side street in Ürümqi. Restaurants here are very specialised – you'll probably have to collect your meal from several proprietors.

Fast-food fanatics will find *McDonald's (mài dāng láo)* on the south end of Wangfujing opposite the Beijing Hotel. *Pizza Hut (bì shèng kè)* has arrived on the Beijing fast-food scene with three branches – the easiest to find is at the Friendship Store.

Entertainment

Discos *Alfredos* in the Sara Hotel *(huá qiáo dà shà)* at 2 Wangfujing Dajie is normally a mellow Mexican restaurant, but on Monday nights after 9 pm or so, the heavy metal is rolled out and the volume is turned up loud enough to shatter a taco chip, not to mention eardrums.

The *Pig & Whistle* (☎ 5006688 ext 1976) on the ground floor of the Holiday Inn Lido is the most British thing in Beijing besides the UK Embassy. Operating hours are from 5 pm until 1 am on weekdays, or noon until 1 am on weekends and holidays.

Cultural The *China Daily* carries a listing of cultural evenings recommended for foreigners – also worth checking is the *Beijing Weekend* published once weekly. Offerings include concerts, theatre, minority dancing and some cinema. You can reserve ahead by phoning the box office via your hotel, or pick up tickets at CITS (for a surcharge) – or take a risk and just roll up at the theatre.

Seeing the Beijing opera *(píng jù)* is one of the reasons for coming to Beijing. The most reliable (but most expensive) performances are put on for foreigners nightly at the Liyuan Theatre (☎ 3016688, ext 8860 or 8986) – this is in fact inside the Qianmen Hotel *(qián mén fàn diàn)* at 175 Yong'an Lu. Ticket prices depend on seat location, starting at US$1. For US$3 you can sit at a table and enjoy snacks and tea while watching the show. For US$7 you get better snacks and a table with a good location. Performances here last just one hour with sporadic translations flashed on an electronic signboard – the attempts at English translations are often funnier than the dialogue.

Two thousand years old, and one of the few art forms condoned by Mao, acrobatics *(tè jì biǎo yǎn)* is the best deal in town. Acts take place in various locations, normally advertised in the *China Daily*. The International Club (☎ 5322188) *(guó jì jù lè bù)*, 21 Jianguomenwai Dajie (west of the Friendship Store) has performances for US$3. Another venue for acrobatics is the Chaoyang *(cháo yáng xì yuàn)* at Dong sanhuan Beilu and Chaoyang Beilu out in the north-east part of the city. Shows start around 7 pm and acts change nightly.

Things to Buy

There are several notable Chinese shopping

CHINA

districts offering abundant goods and low prices. Chief amongst them is Wangfujing – also known as McDonald's St – to the east of the Forbidden City and Beijing Hotel. On the south side of Tiananmen Square is the Qianmen shopping area which includes the Dazhalan hutong. A bit farther south is Liulichang, a lane known for its mostly fake antiques. West of the Forbidden City is Xidan which aspires to be another Wangfujing. Pricier but more luxurious shopping areas can be found in the embassy ghettos of Jianguomenwai and Sanlitun. The Hongqiao Market at the north-east corner of Tiantan Park is notable for cute items like Mao caps, English-language versions of the Little Red Book and 'youth of China' alarm clocks.

Getting There & Away

Air Beijing has by far the largest collection of foreign carriers in China. While CITS can book you on domestic and some international flights, you might do better going directly to the airlines. The partially computerised CAAC ticket office (☎ 4014441 for domestic reservations; ☎ 4012221 for international reservations; and ☎ 554415 for enquires) is in the Aviation Building (Mínháng Dàshà) on Xi Chang'an Jie, Xidan District. Other airlines include:

Aeroflot
  Hotel Beijing-Toronto, Jianguomenwai (☎ 5002412)
Air France
  2716 China World Trade Centre, 1 Jianguomenwai (☎ 5051818)
Alitalia
  Room 139, Jianguo Hotel, 5 Jianguomenwai (☎ 5002233 ext 139)
All Nippon Airways
  Room 1510, China World Trade Centre, 1 Jianguomenwai (☎ 5053311)
Asiana Airlines
  Room 134, Jianguo Hotel, 5 Jianguomenwai (☎ 5002233 ext 134)
British Airways
  Room 210, 2nd floor, SCITE Tower, 22 Jianguomenwai (☎ 5124070)
Canadian Airlines
  Room 135, Jianguo Hotel, 5 Jianguomenwai (☎ 5003950)

Dragonair
  1st floor, L107, World Trade Tower, 1 Jianguomenwai (☎ 5054343)
Finnair
  SCITE Tower, 22 Jianguomenwai (☎ 5127180)
Iran Air
  Room 701, CITIC Building, 19 Jianguomenwai (☎ 5124940)
Japan Airlines (JAL)
  Ground floor, Changfugong Office Building, Hotel New Otani, 26A Jianguomenwai (☎ 5130888)
Yugoslav Airlines (JAT)
  Room 414, Kunlun Hotel, 2 Xinyuan Nanlu (☎ 5003388 ext 414)
Polish Airlines (LOT)
  Room 102, West Wing Office Block, China World Trade Centre, 1 Jianguomenwai (☎ 5050136)
Lufthansa
  Lufthansa Centre, 50 Liangmaqiao Lu (☎ 4654488)
Mongolian Airlines (MIAT)
  Jing Guang Centre, 8th floor, room 06, Hujia Lou, Chaoyang Qu (☎ 5014544)
  Lot 115A/B Level One, West Wing Office Block, China World Trade Centre (☎ 5052681)
  Room 104, China World Trade Centre, 1 Jianguomenwai (☎ 5053505)
Pakistan International
  Room 106, China World Trade Centre, 1 Jianguomenwai (☎ 5051681)
Philippine Airlines
  12-53 Jianguomenwai (☎ 5323992)
Qantas Airways
  5th floor, Hotel Beijing-Toronto, 3 Jianguomenwai (☎ 5002235)
Romanian Air Transport
  Room 109, Jianguo Hotel, 5 Jianguomenwai (☎ 5002233 ext 109)
Scandinavian Airlines (SAS)
  18th floor, SCITE Tower, 22 Jianguomenwai (☎ 5120575)
Singapore Airlines
  Room 109, China World Trade Centre, Jianguomenwai (☎ 5052233)
Swissair
  Room 201, SCITE Tower, 22 Jianguomenwai (☎ 5123555)
Thai International
  Room 207, SCITE Tower, 22 Jianguomenwai (☎ 5123881)
United Airlines
  Room 204, SCITE Tower, 22 Jianguomenwai (☎ 5128888)

Bus The basic rule is that long-distance bus stations are on the perimeter of the city in the direction you want to go. The four major ones are at Dongzhimen (north-east), Haihutun (south), Beijiao (north – also called Deshengmen) and Majuan (east). In addition, there is a tiny bus station in the car park in front of Beijing railway station – this is where you catch buses to Tianjin and the Great Wall at Badaling. Another tiny bus station is in the car park of the Workers' Stadium – this is mainly geared towards buses for destinations within Beijing Municipality (like Miyun Reservoir).

Train There's a Foreigners' Ticketing Office at the main railway station, to the left and through a door at the back of the main entrance hall. Look for the sign saying 'International Passenger Booking Office'. The ticketing office is inside the foreigners' waiting room. It's open daily from 5.30 to 7.30 am and 8 am to 5.30 pm, and from 7 pm to 12.30 am. At least those are the official times – foreigners have often found the staff unwilling to sell tickets in the early morning. International trains must be booked through CITS or other travel agents.

Getting Around

To/From the Airport The airport is 25 km from the Forbidden City, but add another 10 km if you're going to the southern end of town.

For US$1 you can catch the airport shuttle bus from the Aviation Building *(mín háng dà shà)* on Xi Chang'an Jie, Xidan District – this is the location of CAAC and China North-West Airlines.

At the airport, you can catch this shuttle bus in front of the terminal building – buy the bus ticket from the counter inside the terminal building, not on the bus itself. The bus terminates at the Aviation Building in Xidan, but makes several stops en route – get off at the second stop (Swissotel-Hong Kong Macau Centre) if you want to take the subway.

A taxi from the airport to the Forbidden City area costs around US$10, or US$13 to the Qiaoyuan Hotel area in the southern side of town.

Bus One or two-digit buses are city central, series 100 are trolley buses and series 300 are suburban lines. If you can work out how to combine subways and buses (get a bus map) you will speed things up considerably.

There are privately operated minibuses with fixed fees, about US$1 minimum.

Underground Better than the buses, the subway is less crowded. Platform signs are in pinyin and the fare is five jiao regardless of distance. The subway is open from 5 am to 11 pm.

Taxi The vehicles usually have a sticker on the window indicating their per km charge, which varies all the way from Y1 to Y2 with a Y10 minimum. If you don't get one with a meter, negotiate the fare in advance.

Bicycle Bicycles can be hired nearby the Qiaoyuan Hotel for about US$1 per day. The Rainbow Hotel has bikes in top-notch condition but wants US$3 per day. The renter may demand you leave your passport, but a deposit of about US$20 will usually do. Bike parks are everywhere and cost peanuts – compulsory peanuts since your trusty steed can otherwise be towed away.

Pedicab Beijing's pedicab drivers are absolute thieves – the worst in China. No matter what price is agreed on in advance, it will be multiplied by 10 when you arrive at your destination.

Around Beijing

THE GREAT WALL
(cháng chéng) 长城

China's greatest public works project, the Great Wall stretches 6000 km across the country. Although construction began 2000 years ago, it was periodically allowed to crumble, then rebuilt and allowed to fall apart again. The wall has now reached its greatest height as a tourist attraction. The wall never really did perform its function as a defence line to keep invaders out.

Most foreigners see the wall at Badaling, 70 km north-west of Beijing. Unfortunately, Badaling has become a tourist circus and much of the overflow crowd has been diverted to a more impressive section at Mutianyu, 90 km north-east of Beijing. Unfortunately, that too is starting to become a carnival and the latest place where everyone goes to escape everyone else is Simatai, a mostly undeveloped section of the wall 110 km north-east of Beijing.

Getting There & Away

CITS, CTS, big hotels and everyone else in the tourist business does a tour to Badaling. Prices border on the ridiculous, with some hotels asking over US$55 per person.

Local buses also ply the route to Badaling but it's slow going; take bus No 5 or 44 to Deshengmen, then No 345 to the terminal (Changping), then a numberless bus to the wall (alternatively, bus No 357 goes part of the way along the route and you then hitch). Another route is bus No 14 to Beijiao's long-distance bus station, which is north of Deshengmen, then a numberless bus to the wall. Going on local buses saves some money but it's a headache even if you speak Chinese – if you don't it's a migraine.

You can reach Badaling by express train from Beijing's main railway station, getting off at Qinglongqiao. There are actually three stations within one km of the wall – Qinglongqiao, New Qinglongqiao and Badaling, but the first is by far the closest to your destination.

The Qiaoyuan Hotel operates a bus directly to the wall at Mutianyu for US$6, and it's about the easiest way to get there. A small number of Chinese tour buses also go to Mutianyu – look for them near the Kentucky Fried Chicken near Tiananmen Square, the Beijing railway station or the Workers' Stadium. Entrance to the wall at Mutianyu costs US$3. The cable car ride costs US$5 one way or US$7 return.

Simatai is not easy to visit. Hiring a microbus taxi for the day would cost at least US$55, but getting a group together makes it more affordable. Buses to Simatai cost US$2 for the round trip and depart just once daily from the Dongzhimen bus station at 7 am. The journey takes from two to three hours, and the bus departs Simatai at 3 pm (but ask to be sure). Even once you get to Simatai there is much walking to do and some of the slopes are steep and dangerous.

MING TOMBS

(shí sān líng) 明陵

Dying is a big deal in China, especially if you're an emperor. There are several burial plots for China's former rulers, of which the Ming Tombs are far and away most famous. Most travellers find the tombs boring, but the views along the way are pleasant.

Aware of the fact that many visitors have found the tombs disappointing, the Beijing municipal government is busy dressing up the area. New facilities include a golf course, the Dingling Museum (with a wax Genghis Khan), the Nine Dragons Amusement Park, archery and rifle range, shops, cafes, a 350-room hotel, swimming pool, aquarium, campground, picnic area, a fountain (with 200-metre waterjet), fishing pier (on the Ming Tombs Reservoir) and a bicycle racing velodrome. There are also helicopter rides over the tombs and the nearby Great Wall. Plans call for the construction of additional facilities, including a horse-racing track, cross-country skiing area and Mongolian yurts for use as a summer hotel.

The tombs lie 50 km north-west of Beijing and four km from the small town of Changping. The tour buses usually combine them with a visit to the Great Wall at Badaling. You can also get there by local bus. Take bus No 5 or 44 to Deshengmen terminal. West of the flyover (overpass) is the terminal of bus No 345 which you take to Changping, a one-hour ride. Then take bus No 314 to the tombs (or hitch the last stretch).

WESTERN HILLS

(xī shān) 西山

Within striking distance of the Summer

Palace, and often combined with it on a tour, are the Western Hills, another former villa-resort area. The part of the Western Hills closest to Beijing is known as the **Fragrant Hills Park** (xiāng shān gōng yuán). This is the last stop for the city buses – if you want to get farther into the mountains, you'll have to walk, bicycle or take a taxi.

About half way between the Fragrant Hills and the Summer Palace is the **Temple of the Sleeping Buddha** (wò fó sì). About two km east of Fragrant Hills Park and just to the south of the Temple of the Reclining Buddha is the new **Xiangshan Botanical Gardens** (xiāng shān zhí wù yuán).

There are a couple of ways of getting to the Fragrant Hills by public transport: bus No 333 from the Summer Palace, bus No 360 from the zoo and bus No 318 from Pingguoyuan (the last stop in the west on the subway).

SHIDU
(shí dù) 十渡

This is Beijing's answer to Guilin. The pinnacle-shaped rock formations, small rivers and general beauty of the place makes it a favourite spot with expatriates like foreign students, diplomats and business people.

Shidu means 'ten ferries' or 'ten crossings'. At least before the new road and bridges were built, it was necessary to cross the Juma River 10 times while travelling along the gorge between Zhangfang and Shidu village.

Down near Jiudu (the 'ninth ferry') there is a campground, conveniently located on a flood-plain. This is one of the few scenic areas outside of Beijing which can be easily reached by train.

Departures are from the south railway station (Yongdingmen) near the Qiaoyuan

Hotel – not to be confused with Beijing's main station. If you take the morning train, the trip can be done in one day. The schedule is as follows:

Tianjin 天津

Tianjin is the nearest port to Beijing and as such was too attractive to be ignored by foreign nations. The Europeans and Japanese set up concessions here around 1895 to 1900. The remaining Western architecture is still in evidence, though much of it is crumbling. Hotels are absurdly expensive in this city, but Tianjin is close enough to be visited as a day trip from Beijing.

Things to See
The enormous **Antique Market** (gǔ wán shì chǎng) on Shenyang Dao operates daily from 7.30 am until 3 pm, but reaches its zenith on Sunday. The **Ancient Culture St** (gǔ wén huà jiē) is a colourful attempt to recreate the appearance of an ancient Chinese city. Only one block away is Tianjin's **Confucius Temple** (wén miào). Although it has a Chinese look, the **Grand Mosque** (qīng zhēn sì) is an active place of worship for Tianjin's Muslims. **Dabeiyuan Monastery** (dà bēi yuàn) is one of the largest and best preserved temples in the city. The **Catholic Church** (xī kāi jiāo táng) with its twin onion domes is one of the most bizarre looking churches you'll ever see.

The **Hai River Park** (hǎi hé gōng yuán) along the Hai River has a peculiarly Parisian feel, in part due to the fact that some of the railing and bridge work is French. The pride and joy of Tianjin residents, the **TV Tower**

Train Timetable for Yongdingmen (Beijing South Railway Station) to Shidu				
Train No	*From*	*To*	*Depart*	*Arrive*
595	Yongdingmen	Shidu	6.07 am	8.40 am
597	Yongdingmen	Shidu	5.40 pm	8 pm
596	Shidu	Yongdingmen	6.41 pm	9.03 pm
598	Shidu	Yongdingmen	10.41 am	1.05 pm

CHINA

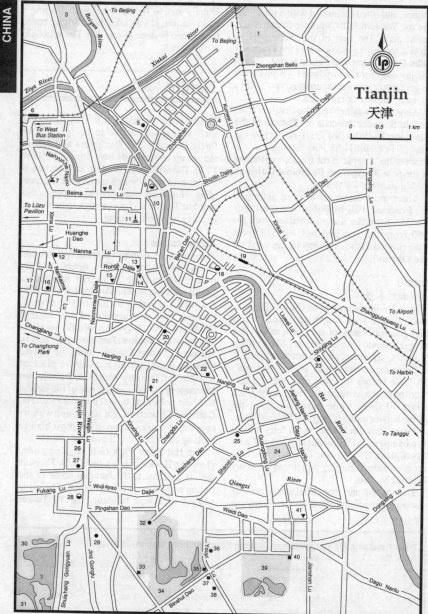

Tianjin
天津

0   0.5   1 km

To Beijing
To Beijing

Braqun River
Xinkai River
Ziya River

To West Bus Station

Nanyunhe Nanlu

To Lüzu Pavilion

Huanghe Dao
Nanma Lu

To Changhong Park

Weijin River

To Changhong Park

Zhongshan Beilu
Zhongshan Lu
Kunwei Lu
Jinzhonge Dajie

Shizilin Dajie

Zhenli Dao
Hongqiao Lu

Beima Lu
Shizilin Dajie

Balan Dao

Xinkai Lu

Nanmenwai Dajie
Nankaima

Rongli Dajie

Zhangguizhuang Lu
To Airport

Changjiang Lu

Liuwei Lu

Shijing Lu

To Harbin

Nanjing Lu

Nanjing Lu

Jiefang Nanlu
Hai River
Dagu Nanlu
To Tanggu

Xinxing Lu
Chengdu Lu
Machang Dao
Shaoxing Lu

Guangdong Lu

Qiangzi River

Dongxing Lu

Wujiayao
Dajie

Fukang Lu

Pingshan Dao

Weidi Dao

Jinz Gonglu
Shuishang Gongyuan

You...

Binshui Dao

Dagu Nanlu
Jianshan Lu

PLACES TO STAY

22 Friendship Hotel
友谊宾馆

23 Furama Hotel
富丽华大酒店

33 Sheraton Hotel
喜来登大酒店

35 Crystal Palace Hotel
水晶宫饭店

37 Tianjin Grand Hotel
天津宾馆

38 Geneva Hotel
津利华大酒店

40 Park Hotel
乐园饭店

PLACES TO EAT

8 Eardrum Fried Spongecake Shop
耳朵眼炸糕店

13 Yanchunlou Restaurant
燕春楼饭庄

14 Quanjude Restaurant
全聚德烤鸭店

15 Food Street
食品街

41 18th Street Dough Twists Shop
桂发祥麻花店

OTHER

1 Beining Park
北宁公园

2 North Railway Station
北火车站

3 Xigu Park
西沽公园

4 Zhongshan Park
中山公园

5 Dabeiyuan Monastery
大悲院

6 West Railway Station
西火车站

7 Grand Mosque
清真寺

9 North East Bus Station
东北角发车站

10 Ancient Culture Street
古文化街

11 Confucius Temple
文庙

12 5th Subway Exit
地下铁第五站

16 Zhou Enlai Memorial Hall
周恩来记念馆

17 Nankai Park
南开公园

18 Buses to Beijing
往北京汽车站

19 Main Railway Station
天津火车站

20 Antique Market
古玩市场

21 Catholic Church
西开教堂

24 Renmin Park
人民公园

25 Foreign Languages Bookstore
外文书店

26 Tianjin University
天津大学

27 Nankai University
南开大学

28 South Bus Station
八里台发车站

29 TV Tower
电视台

30 Shuishang Park
水上公园

31 Zoo
动物园

32 Natural History Museum
& Cadre Club
自然博物馆 / 干部俱乐部

34 Cadre Club Park
干部俱乐部公园

36 Friendship Store
友谊商店

39 Children's Park
青年儿童活动中心

(diàn shì tái) dominates the horizon on the south side of town and tourists can visit the top for a US$10 fee. Nearby is **Shuishang Park** (shuǐ shàng gōng yuán), where the main activity is renting rowboats and

pedalboats. The **Art Museum** (yì shù bó wù guǎn) at 77 Jiefang Beilu, is one stop on bus No 13 from the main railway station. It is easy to get to and is pleasant to stroll around.

Zhou Enlai attended school in Tianjin, so

his classroom is enshrined at the **Zhou Enlai Memorial Hall** (*zhōu ēn lái jì niàn guǎn*).

Places to Stay

Cheapest is the huge *Tianjin Grand Hotel* (☎ 359000) (*tiān jīn bīn guǎn*) on Youyi Lu, but it's nearly always full. Doubles cost from US$21. Take bus No 13 from the main railway station.

It's much easier to get a room at the *Tianjin No 1 Hotel* (*tiān jīn dì yī fàn diàn*) (☎ 310707) at 198 Jiefang Beilu, directly opposite the Hyatt Hotel. Doubles are US$65 but try bargaining. Take bus No 13 three stops from the main railway station and walk south.

If you're taking the ferry to Korea, it's best to stay in the port district of Tanggu (50 km from downtown Tianjin). Cheapest and most convenient is the *International Seamen's Club* (☎ 973897) (*guó jì hǎi yuán jù lè bù*), where rooms cost US$13.

Places to Eat

The place to go is *Food St* (*shí pǐn jiē*), a covered alley with two levels of restaurants.

Getting There & Away

Air CAAC (☎ 704045) is at 242 Heping Lu. There are daily international flights to Hong Kong and Seoul, plus domestic flights to Guangzhou and Shanghai.

Bus Buses to Beijing depart from in front of the Tianjin main railway station. In Beijing, catch the bus to Tianjin from the west side of the car park in front of the Beijing main railway station.

Train Tianjin's main railway station has frequent trains to Beijing. At Tianjin station foreigners can avoid the horrible queues by purchasing tickets on the 2nd floor at the soft-seat ticket office.

Hebei 河北

This province is often viewed as an extension of Beijing and Tianjin – and they do take up a fair slice of the pie. In fact, Tianjin used to be the provincial capital but is now a separate municipality. The province boasts a few fine beaches, a slice of the Great Wall and other monuments to ancient Chinese history.

CHENGDE
(*chéng dé*)   承德

Chengde is an 18th-century imperial resort area. In 1703 Emperor Kangxi began building a summer palace here, and by 1790 it had grown to the size of Beijing's Summer Palace and the Forbidden City combined. Once emperors fell out of fashion, the place was allowed to decay. Now Chengde's splendour is being restored, in some cases from the base up, in the interests of a projected increase in tourism.

Important sites worth visiting include the **Imperial Summer Villa** (*bì shǔ shān zhuāng*), the **Eight Outer Temples** (*wài bā miào*), numerous other temples and the oddly shaped **Hammer Rock** (*bàng chuí shān*).

Places to Stay

Hotel reps try to capture travellers at the railway station, and it's not a bad idea to go with them if you first negotiate a suitable price. The best bargain in town is the splendid *Mountain Villa Hotel* (☎ 223501) (*shān zhuāng bīn guǎn*) at 127 Lizhenmen Lu, where doubles cost US$13 to US$28. The *Xinhua Hotel* (☎ 225880) (*xīn huá fàn diàn*), 4 Xinhua Lu Bei, is a reliable cheapie with rooms for US$12.

Getting There & Away

The regular approach to Chengde is by train from Beijing. The fast train (No 11) departs Beijing at 7.17 am and arrives in Chengde at 11.51 am. Soft-seat for tickets for foreigners cost US$12 – this is a non-smoking car! The same train gets renamed No 12 when it returns to Beijing, departing Chengde at 2.31 pm. The one-way trip takes less than five hours. There are slower trains which take over seven hours. Tickets for trains leaving Chengde are only sold on the day of departure. Your hotel can buy your ticket, but this usually requires a small fee and you need to trust the staff with your passport (or old expired passport).

Getting Around

There are occasional taxis and pedicabs around town, but most travellers wind up booking a minibus tour from a hotel. Most of these tours start out at 8 am, but a few begin in the afternoon just after lunch, around 1.30 pm. The cheapest sightseeing bus tours are Chinese-speaking only and cost US$4. Tours can be booked at the Lizheng men Hotel *(lì zhèng mén lü guăn)*.

BEIDAIHE

(bĕi dài hé) 北戴河

This seaside resort is part of the Beidaihe, Qinhuangdao and Shanhaiguan districts, which stretch 35 km along the coast. Bikinis have not made their debut but bare thighs are now in vogue. High-ranking officials gather here in summer for 'meetings' at government expense. There are shark nets – it's questionable whether sharks can live at this latitude, so maybe they're submarine nets. Beidaihe has large numbers of sanatoriums where patients can get away from the noise of the city – if you've been in China any length of time, you may wish to join them.

That's about all you need to know about Beidaihe. The Chinese have tried to categorise the rocks and decide whether they're shaped like dragons, tigers or steamed bread, and immortalise the place where Mao sat and wrote lines about fishing boats disappearing. Nobody gives a damn – they come for the beaches and so should you.

Places to Stay

There are only three places that accept foreigners. The *Guest House for Diplomatic Missions* (☎ 441587) *(wài jiāo rén yuán bīn guăn)* has triples for US$11. The splashy tourist place in town is the *Jinshan Guest House* (☎ 441678) *(jīn shān bīn guăn)* where

doubles cost US$31. Right on the beachfront is the *Haibin Hotel* (☎ 441373) *(hăi bīn fàn diàn)* which is only open during summer.

Getting There & Away

The three railway stations of Beidaihe, Qinhuangdao and Shanhaiguan are all accessible by train from Beijing, Tianjin or Shenyang. The trains are frequent but don't always stop at all three stations. The usual stop is Shanhaiguan; several skip Beidaihe. If you arrive during daylight there are plenty of minibuses that meet incoming trains at Beidaihe Station. If you're going to arrive in the dead of night, it's better to do it at Shanhaiguan.

SHANHAIGUAN

(shān hăi guān) 山海关

Shanhaiguan is a city of considerable charm. It's where the Great Wall meets the sea. A major attraction is the **First Pass Under Heaven** *(tiān xià dì yī guān)*, also known as the **East Gate** *(dōng mén)*. The Great Wall meets the sea at **Old Dragon Head** *(lăo lóng tóu)*.

Places to Stay

The cheapest place to stay is the *North Street Hotel (bĕi jiē zhāo dài suŏ)* where doubles are US$9. The hotel is right near the First Pass (East Gate).

Also in the same neighbourhood is the pleasant *Jingshan Hotel* (☎ 551130) *(jīng shān bīn guăn)* where doubles are US$16.

Liaoning 辽宁

Liaoning, Jilin and Heilongjiang provinces comprise what used to be called Manchuria. Overall, travellers tend to find the north-east disappointing. There are a couple of scenic natural areas, but mostly it's prairies, farms, oil wells and petrochemical plants. To add insult to injury, this part of China has the most expensive accommodation.

SHENYANG
(shěn yáng) 沈阳

Shenyang is the only city in the north-east to have some historical interest. The cradle of the Manchus, it became their capital by the 17th century. With the Manchu conquest of Beijing in 1644, Shenyang became a secondary capital under the Manchu name of Mukden.

These days Shenyang is a major industrial city and the capital of Liaoning Province, but there are a couple of sights worth seeing.

Things to See
The **Mao Statue** in Zhongshan Square is one of the largest monuments to the personality cult and follies of the Cultural Revolution still remaining in China.

The **North Tomb** *(běi líng)* is the finest sight in Shenyang. Set in a magnificent park, the North Tomb is the burial place of Huang Taiji (1592-1643), who founded the Qing Dynasty. Take bus No 220 from the railway station.

The **Imperial Palace** *(gù gōng)* is a much scaled-down version of Beijing's Forbidden City. The main structures were started by Nurhachi, leader of the Manchus, and completed in 1636 by his son, Huang Taiji. You can take bus No 213 from the North Tomb or bus No 10 from the railway station.

Places to Stay
The *Hua Sha Hotel (húa shà fàn diàn)* is near the railway station at No 3 Zhongshan Lu. Singles/doubles are US$26/31.

The *Zhongxing Hotel* (☎ 338188) *(zhōng xīng bīn guǎn)*, 86 Taiyuan Beijie, is the brick-red pyramid-shaped skyscraper in the main market area a couple of blocks south of the railway station. Singles cost US$24.

Getting There & Away
Air CAAC (☎ 363705) is at 31 Zhonghua Lu, Section 3. Useful flights include those to Hong Kong, Beijing, Chengdu, Guangzhou, Kunming, Shanghai, Xi'an and Xiamen. Aeroflot has international flights to Irkutsk.

Train All train services to Beijing, Harbin and Dalian connect here.

Jilin 吉林

The most scenic of the north-eastern provinces, Jilin offers winter skiing and summer hiking; however, the summer season is short and like elsewhere in China's north-east, prices are high.

CHANGCHUN
(cháng chūn) 长春

Changchun, capital of Jilin *(jí lín)* Province, has little of interest but makes a useful transit point for trips to Tianchi, the one outstanding scenic spot in north-east China.

Places to Stay & Eat
The *Chunyi Guest House* (☎ 279966) *(chūn yí bīn guǎn)*, 2 Sidalin Dajie, is one block south of the railway station and costs a ridiculous US$42.

The main tourist place is the *Changbaishan Hotel* (☎ 883551; fax 882003) *(cháng bái shān bīn guǎn)*. Doubles cost US$50. CITS has its office here. It's nine km from the railway station – take trolley bus No 62 or 63.

Getting There & Away
Air CAAC (☎ 39772) is at 2 Liaoning Lu. There are daily flights to Beijing and Guangzhou.

Train There are frequent trains heading north to Harbin (four hours) and south to Shenyang (five hours). There is an overnight train for Yanji (depart 6.40 pm, arrive 6.30 am), which is the route you take to Tianchi.

JILIN
(jí lín) 吉林

East of Changchun is the city of Jilin. It's not a terribly exciting place, but in winter boasts the **Songhuahu Qingshan Ski Resort** *(sōng huā hú qīng shān huá xuě cháng)*, 16 km south-east of town. January is the time to see the **ice-rimmed trees** *(shù guà* or *wù sōng)* – trees near the Songhua River which are draped in icicles by steam rising from the river. Jilin also boasts an **Ice Lantern Festival** *(bīng dēng jié)*, though not as spectacular as the one farther out in Harbin.

Places to Stay

The *Milky Way Hotel* (☎ 241780) *(yín hé dà shà)*, 175 Songjiang Lu, is reasonable (by Jilin standards) if you get one of the standard rooms for US$31. Suites cost US$49.

The *Dongguan Hotel* (☎ 454272) *(dōng guān bīn guǎn)*, 223 Songjiang Lu, costs US$39 for threadbare rooms. The hotel is about three km from the railway station – take trolley bus No 10 or a taxi for US$2.

Adjacent to the Dongguan Hotel is the up market *Jiangcheng Hotel* (☎ 457721) *(jiāng chéng bīn guǎn)*. Living conditions are cosy here, but the US$42 price for a double may cause you to hesitate.

Getting There & Away
Air There is an international flight from Jilin to Seoul, South Korea, via Tianjin. CAAC flies between Jilin and Beijing, Guangzhou, Shanghai and Shenyang.

Bus There are buses between Jilin and Changchun approximately once every 20 minutes throughout the day. The trip takes 2½ hours. The long-distance bus station *(chà lù xiāng)* is one long block west of the railway station.

Train There is a direct rail service between Jilin and Changchun nearly once every hour in each direction. There are also direct trains to Harbin (four hours) and Yanji.

TIANCHI
(tiān chí) 天池
Tianchi – the Lake of Heaven – is in the Changbaishan (Ever-White Mountains) Nature Reserve. The reserve is China's largest, covering 210,000 hectares of dense virgin forest.

Tianchi is north-east China's prime scenic spot. It's a volcanic crater lake at an elevation of 2194 metres. Three rivers run off the lake, and a roaring 68-metre waterfall is the source of the Songhua and Tumen rivers. Hiking at the lake is limited by sharp and dangerous peaks and surrounding rocky debris, and also because the lake overlaps China's border with North Korea.

One unpleasant aspect of Tianchi is the Chinese habit of filling up the volcanic crater with rubbish.

Places to Stay
There are many cheap places to stay but all of these are off-limits to foreigners. Big noses are herded into one of five official tourist hotels, all charging a standard US$38. Presently, your options include the *Birch Hotel (yuè huá lóu)*, the *Nature Reserve Bureau Hotel (bǎo hù jú bīn guǎn)*, *Meilinsong Guest House (měi lín sōng bīn guǎn)*, *Yalin Hotel (yǎ lín bīn guǎn)* and the *Tianchi Hotel (tiān chí fàn diàn)*.

Getting There & Away
The Changbaishan area is remote, and a journey there somewhat expeditionary. The *only* season in terms of transport access is late June to September. The transit point is the town of Baihe – 40 km and two hours by bus from Tianchi.

Antu Route There are trains to Antu from Changchun – the trip takes 10 hours. The evening train departs from Changchun at 6.40 pm. There are sleepers but you might have to book them all the way to Yanji. There is a small hotel in Antu. Buses for Baihe depart from 7.20 to 10.30 am. You can also get buses to Baihe from Yanji (farther down the rail line) but then you'll have to backtrack. From Antu it takes five hours to travel the 125 km. Unless you arrive early in Baihe, you may find yourself waiting till the next morning for transport to Tianchi. Special tourist buses run from Antu to the Changbaishan Hot Springs area in July and August but they may be crowded.

Tonghua Route The morning train leaves Shenyang at 6.30 am for Tonghua; from Dandong there are buses to Tonghua departing at 6.30 am. Tonghua to Baihe is 277 km or about 10 hours by train. The two daily trains between Tonghua and Baihe have no sleepers, and soft-seat is recommended.

Heilongjiang 黑龙江

The northernmost piece of Chinese real estate, Heilongjiang can boast sub-arctic forests plus a few neat lakes and wildlife reserves. The problem is that these areas are difficult to reach, expensive to visit and few travellers bother. If you can survive temperatures of minus 40°C, winter sports are a possibility.

HARBIN
(hā ěr bīn) 哈尔滨
This city is known for its freezing winters, but also hosts the dazzling Ice Lantern Festival. Most foreign visitors are Russians who come for shopping and 'doing business' (smuggling).

Things to See
If you don't mind the cold then try not to miss Harbin's No 1 drawcard, the **Ice Lantern Festival** *(bīng dēng jié)*, held from 1 January to early March (Lunar New Year) in Zhaolin Park.

Down by the river, **Stalin Park** *(sī dà lín gōng yuán)* is a tacky strip stacked with statues. Opposite Stalin Park and reached by a ferry hop is **Sun Island** *(tài yáng dǎo gōng yuán)*, a recreational zone. The sandy banks of the Songhua take on a beach atmosphere in summer complete with boat tours. During winter the Songhua is a road of ice – the perfect venue for hockey, skating, ice-sailing, sledding and sleighing. The ice toys can be rented.

Crumbling Soviet architecture is still much in evidence in Harbin, with spires, cupolas and scalloped turreting. The area

known as **Daoliqu** – near Zhongyang Lu – is especially good to investigate.

The **Japanese Germ Warfare Experimental Base** *(rì běn xì jūn shí yàn jī dì)* is not for the faint of heart. In 1939 the Japanese army set up a top-secret, germ warfare research centre here with horrific results. Take bus No 338 from the main railway station to the terminus, which is close to Pingfangqu.

Places to Stay
The *Beiyuan Hotel* (☎ 340128) *(běi yuàn fàn diàn)* directly faces the railway station and dishes up doubles for US$10 and US$15. Unfortunately, it's often filled to the rooftop with Russians visiting Harbin 'on business' and there have been reports of things being stolen from rooms. If you stay here, keep your valuables with you or store them in the left-luggage rooms at the railway station.

As you exit the railway station, just off to your right is the 19-storey *Tianzhu Hotel* (☎ 3432725, 343720) *(tiān zhú bīn guǎn)*. This is an excellent place to stay, although doubles cost US$18.

Getting There & Away
Air CAAC (☎ 52334) has its office at 87 Zhongshan Lu close to the Swan Hotel. There are flights to Beijing, Guangzhou, Chengdu, Shanghai and Xi'an.

Train There are frequent departures to Beijing, Shanghai and points in between. Harbin to Changchun takes four hours; to Shenyang, nine hours; and to Beijing, 18 hours. Rail connections to Qiqihar, Mudanjiang and Jiamusi are regular but slow.

For travellers on the Trans-Siberian Railway, Harbin is a possible starting or finishing point.

JINGBO LAKE
(jìng bó hú) 镜泊湖
The name means Mirror Lake, and it's probably the most impressive sight in Heilongjiang. The area includes forests, hills, streams, pools and cliffs around the

lake and there is a lava cave in the area. Peak season (July and August) is crowded – autumn is nice when the leaves are turning. Get out on the lake in a rowing boat – loads of stars at night. Slightly to the north of Jingbo Villa, Diaoshuilou Waterfall offers an opportunity to jump off into the pools below and amaze the Chinese.

Places to Stay

The centre of operations is *Jingbo Villa (jìng bó shān zhuāng)*, at the north end of the lake, and the new *Jingbo Lake Hotel (jìng bó hú bīn guǎn)*. There are other, cheaper hotels around the lake but they aren't allowed to take foreigners.

Getting There & Away

The best approach is by rail from Harbin. Take a train to Dongjing *(dōng jīng)*. From there, it's one hour by minibus to the lake.

Some trains only go as far as Mudanjiang. If you get off at Mudanjiang, it's three hours by bus to Jingbo Lake. Buses depart between 6 and 7 am from the square in front of Mudanjiang station, during summer only (from June to September). There are two or three trains a day between Harbin and Mudanjiang.

Shanxi 山西

Shanxi counts for about a third of China's known coal deposits, and cities such as Datong and Taiyuan are major industrial centres. But the province's greatest wealth lies in its history. It was one of the earliest centres of Chinese civilisation, and is still a gold mine of temples, cave-temples and monasteries. The main attraction is the Yungang Buddhist Caves at Datong.

DATONG
(dà tóng) 大同

The Northern Wei Dynasty established its capital here. Now Datong is a grotty town,

but it's also the site of the outstanding Yungang Buddhist Caves.

Information

Datong has two CITS offices: a branch at the railway station (☎ 624464 ext 3755) and another at the Yungang Hotel (☎ 522265). CITS runs regular tours of the city and Yungang Caves.

The most convenient branch of the Bank of China is on Caochangcheng Jie. The Yungang Hotel also offers a money-changing service.

The main post and telephone office is the large central building with the clock tower.

The PSB is next to the large department store on Xinjian Beilu.

Things to See

Yungang Caves *(yún gāng shí kū)* This is the reason for coming to Datong. These fine caves are cut into the southern cliffs of Wuzhou Mountain 16 km west of Datong, next to the pass leading to Inner Mongolia. The caves contain over 50,000 statues and stretch for about one km east to west.

Buses No 3 and No 10 from the terminal at Xinkaili on the western edge of Datong go past Yungang Caves. You can get to Xinkaili on bus No 2 from the railway station or bus No 17 from outside the Datong Hotel. From Xinkaili it's half an hour's ride to the caves.

Places to Stay

Only two hotels in Datong are officially allowed to take foreigners, but the helpful CITS at the railway station can get you into one of the inexpensive Chinese hotels if no other cheap accommodation is available.

The *Yungang Hotel* (☎ (0352) 521601) *(yún gāng bīn guǎn)* at 21 Yingbin Donglu has doubles from US$31. There is a dormitory on the 3rd floor of the separate CITS building to the right from the compound gate. It has beds in three-person rooms for US$5 and hot showers in the evening.

The *Datong Hotel* (☎ (0352) 232476) *(dà tóng bīn guǎn)* was undergoing a total facelift when we checked, but is expected to have doubles with bath for around US$35 after

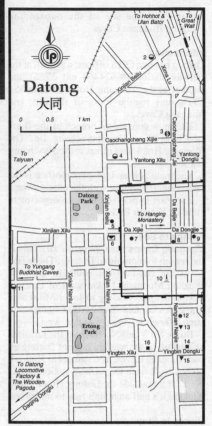

Datong
大同

1	Railway Station & CITS 火车站/中国国际旅行社
2	Old Long-Distance Bus Station 长途汽车站旧址
3	Bank of China 中国银行
4	New Long-Distance Bus Station 新长途汽车站
5	PSB 公安局
6	Main Post & Telephone Office 邮电大楼
7	Huayan Monastery 华严寺
8	Drum Tower 鼓楼
9	Nine Dragon Screen 九龙壁
10	Shanhua Temple 善化寺
11	Xinkaili (Buses to Yungang Caves) 新开里
12	CAAC 中国民航
13	Yaxuyuan Restaurant 雅叙园酒家
14	Yungang Hotel & CITS 云冈宾馆/中国国际旅行社
15	Hongqi Restaurant 红旗大酒店
16	Datong Hotel 大同宾馆

reopening. It will probably have dorm beds too.

To get to either of the hotels take bus No 15 from the railway station.

Getting There & Away
There are daily express trains to Taiyuan (seven to nine hours), Beijing (seven to 8½ hours) and Hohhot (five to six hours).

HANGING MONASTERY 悬空寺
Perched on Jinlong Canyon in the mountains 75 km from Datong is the peculiar Hanging Monastery (*xuán kōng sì*). It's more than 1400 years old but has been rebuilt several times.

The CITS in Datong runs regular tours, with an English-speaking guide, to the Hanging Monastery and the Wooden Pagoda for US$10. They can also arrange tours for around US$45 per car or minibus, so for larger groups it often works out cheaper per person. Chinese tours costing US$3 and taking four to five hours leave from around 7 am, near the long-distance bus station on Yantong Xilu.

Alternatively, you can take a direct public bus from Datong to Hunyuan, just 3.5 km from the Hanging Monastery. The earliest bus leaves at 9 am and the last bus back to Datong leaves Hunyuan at 3.30 pm. Some travellers stay overnight in Hunyuan and return to Datong the next day.

Shaanxi 陕西

Shaanxi was the political heart of China until the 9th century AD. The great Sui and Tang dynasty capital of Chang'an (modern-day Xi'an) was built there, and the province was a crossroads on the trading routes from eastern China to central Asia. Its history over the next thousand years, however, was punctuated by famines and rebellions, and by the 1920s the Shaanxi peasants were ready to give enthusiastic support to the Communists, who established their base in the remote town of Yan'an, at the end of the Long March.

XI'AN
(xi an) 西安

Known as Chang'an in ancient times, Xi'an was once the gateway to the Silk Road and was one of the greatest cities in the world, rivalling Rome and Constantinople. These days it attracts a steady stream of travellers who come to marvel at the thousands of terracotta soldiers who guard the tomb of Qin Shihuang, the first emperor of unified China.

On the down side, Xi'an has become exceedingly commercialised, and this ruins it for many travellers. Every time the locals see a foreigner, all they seem to think about is how to stick a vacuum cleaner into his or her pockets and suck the money out. Every site has an admission fee and anyone with a big nose is charged 10 to 20 times the Chinese price. If you've got a student card, real or fake, Xi'an is a good place to use it.

Information
The main CITS (☎ 735600) office is on Chang'an Beilu, a few minutes' walk south of the Xi'an Hotel. There are more central CITS branches at the Jiefang Hotel (☎ 713329 ext 237) and the Bell Tower Hotel (☎ 775046).

The main Bank of China (☎ 772312) is at 223 Jiefang Lu, just up from Dong 5-Lu. Two other useful branches where foreigners can change money are on Xi Dajie and Dong Dajie. Xi'an is a rip-off in a number of respects, and that includes the banks – a hefty 7½% service charge is demanded for cashing travellers' cheques. Many of the hotels also have money-changing services and may waive the service charge, but they often refuse to serve non-guests.

The PSB is at 138 Xi Dajie, a 10-minute walk west of the Bell Tower.

Things to See
There are a number of things to see in Xi'an itself, but the most interesting sights are far out of town. There are plenty of tours available and these are probably worthwhile. See Getting Around later in this section for details.

In the south of Xi'an is **Big Goose Pagoda** *(dà yàn tǎ)*, originally built in 652 AD. It's an impressive, fortress-like building of wood and brick which rises 64 metres. It was built to house the Buddhist scriptures brought back from India by the travelling monk Xuan Zang, who then set about translating them into 1335 Chinese volumes. The pagoda is at the end of Yanta Lu, at the southern edge of Xi'an. Bus No 41 from the railway station goes straight there. The entrance is on the southern side of the temple grounds. Foreigners pay US$2 at the main gate, plus US$3 to climb the pagoda.

On the east side of the temple is the newly built **Tang Dynasty Arts Museum** *(táng dài yì shù bó wù guǎn)*, with a collection specifically devoted to the Tang period in Xi'an (admission US$1).

The **Bell Tower** *(zhōng lóu)* is a huge structure at the centre of Xi'an. The **Drum Tower** *(gǔ lóu)* is a smaller structure to the west of the Bell Tower and it marks the Muslim quarter of Xi'an.

The **Great Mosque** *(qīng zhēn dà sì)* is one of the largest in China. Still an active place of worship, the mosque holds several prayer services each day. It stands north-west of the Drum Tower.

The **Shaanxi Provincial Museum** *(shǎn xī bó wù guǎn)* was once the temple of Confucius and houses a large collection of relics

CHINA

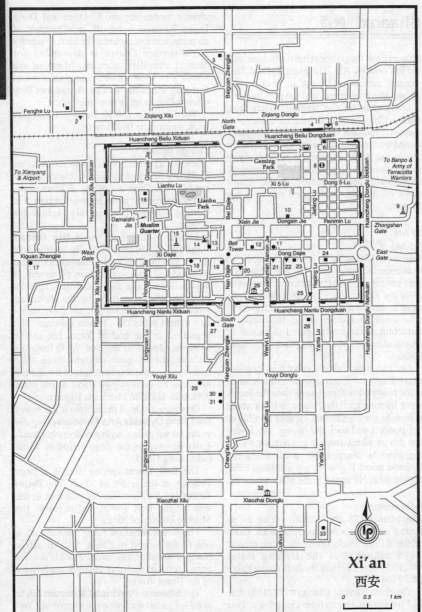

Xi'an
西安

Beiguan Zhengjie

Fenghe Lu
Ziqiang Xilu   Ziqiang Donglu

North Gate

Huancheng Beilu Xiduan   Huancheng Beilu Dongduan

Qianwei Jie

Geming Park

To Xianyang & Airport

Lianhu Lu   Xi 5-Lu   Dong 5-Lu

Huancheng Xilu Beiduan

Lianhu Park

Bei Dajie

Jiefang Lu   Renmin Lu   Huancheng Donglu Beiduan

Damaishi Jie   Muslim Quarter   Xixin Jie   Dongxin Jie

Zhongshan Gate

To Banpo & Army of Terracotta Warriors

Xiguan Zhengjie   Xi Dajie   Bell Tower   Dong Dajie

West Gate   East Gate

Hongguang Jie   Nan Dajie   Duanlumen Nanxin Jie   Heping Lu

Huancheng Xilu Nanduan

Huancheng Nanlu Xiduan   South Gate   Huancheng Nanlu Dongduan

Huancheng Donglu Nanduan

Lingyuan Lu   Nanguan Zhengjie   Wenyi Lu   Yanta Lu

Youyi Xilu   Youyi Donglu

Cuihua Lu   Chang'an Lu   Yanta Lu

Lingyuan Lu

Xiaozhai Xilu   Xiaozhai Donglu

Cuihua Lu

0   0.5   1 km

PLACES TO STAY

1 Flats of Renmin Hotel
人民大厦公寓
3 Golden Dragon Hotel
金龙大酒店
6 Jiefang Hotel
解放饭店
10 People's (Renmin) Hotel
人民大厦
12 May First Hotel
五一饭店
16 Grand New World Hotel
古都大酒店
19 Bell Tower Hotel
钟楼饭店
23 Hotel Royal
西安皇城宾馆
24 Hyatt Hotel
凯悦宾馆
27 Grand Castle Hotel
长安城堡大酒店
28 Victory Hotel
胜利饭店
30 Xi'an Hotel
西安宾馆

PLACES TO EAT

2 Dad's Home Cooking
20 East Asia Restaurant
东亚饭店
21 Laosunjia Restaurant
老孙家饭庄
22 Xi'an Restaurant
西安饭庄
25 Small World Restaurant
小世界餐厅

OTHER

4 Railway Station
火车站
5 Post Office
邮电局
7 Long-Distance Bus Station
长途汽车站
8 Bank of China
中国银行
9 Temple of the Eight Immortals
八仙安
11 Friendship Store
友谊商店
13 Drum Tower
鼓楼
14 Great Mosque
大清真寺
15 City God's Temple
城隍庙
17 CAAC (China Northwest Airlines)
中国西北航空公司
18 PSB
公安局
26 Shaanxi Provincial Museum
陕西省博物馆
29 Little Goose Pagoda
小雁塔
31 CITS
中国国际旅行社
32 Shaanxi History Museum
陕西历史博物馆
33 Big Goose Pagoda
大雁塔

from the Zhou, Qin, Han, Sui and Tang dynasties, including a collection of rare relics unearthed in Shaanxi Province. The 'Forest of Steles' is an extraordinary exhibit of engraved stone tablets spanning 2000 years. The museum is open daily, except Monday, from 8.30 am to 6 pm. Admission for foreigners is US$3.

For most visitors, the compelling reason to come to Xi'an is to see the terracotta warriors at the **Tomb of Qin Shihuang** (*qín shǐ huáng líng*). When the Emperor took the throne, work on his tomb began immediately and continued for 36 years, until the year before his death. The necropolis extends for

many km but most of it has still not been excavated. The most fantastic find thus far has been the underground vault holding 6000 life-size terracotta figures representing an army of warriors and their horses in battle formation. It's certainly worth seeing, but admission is steep at US$9 plus an additional US$2 for the museum. It's forbidden to take photos and your film will be confiscated if you get caught (helps prop up the postcard industry). The tomb is near the town of Lintong – 30 km east of Xi'an. To reach Lintong, take a bus from the eastern side of the Xi'an railway station. Some trains also stop in Lintong. From Lintong take another

CHINA

bus an additional five km to the Tomb of Qin Shihuang.

The **Banpo Neolithic Village** *(bàn pǒ bó wù guǎn)* is the second best sight in Xi'an after the terracotta warriors. The ruins of this 6000-year-old settlement are the earliest signs of human habitation around Xi'an. There's a museum at the site. Tours to see the terracotta warriors take in a stop at Banpo. The best way of getting there by public transport is the No 105 trolley bus from just north of the Bell Tower or bus No 11 from the railway station, both of which pass the Banpo site. To get to the warriors from Banpo, catch a bus to Lintong from the stop 50 metres north of the main road (Changdong Donglu), then change at Lintong. Foreigners pay US$2 to get in.

The **Huaqing Pool** *(huá qīng chí)* is 30 km east of Xi'an below Lishan. Water from hot springs is funnelled into public bathhouses that have 60 pools accommodating 400 people. During the Tang Dynasty these natural hot baths were a favoured retreat of emperors, who often came here to relax with their concubines. The Huaqing Pool leaves most visitors cold, but going for a dip is well worthwhile. If you don't fancy strolling around the gardens with swarms of excited Chinese tourists, try the museum up the road or take a walk on one of the paths leading up through the forest behind the complex. A visit to this place is almost mandatory if you sign onto a tour. Admission to the site costs US$3 for foreigners, plus an additional US$2 for entry to the bathhouse.

Xianyang is a little town half an hour's bus ride from Xi'an. The chief attraction is **Xianyang City Museum** *(xián yáng shì bó wù guǎn)*, which houses a remarkable collection of 3000 miniature terracotta soldiers and horses, discovered in 1965. Each figure is about half a metre high. Admission to the Entombed Warriors is US$5, with an extra ticket needed for entry to the special exhibition hall. Take bus No 3 from the Xi'an railway station to the terminal and then get bus No 59, get off at the terminal in Xianyang, but you'll still have a 20-minute walk.

Organised Tours

One-day tours allow you to the see all the sights around Xi'an more quickly and conveniently than if you do it yourself. Itineraries differ somewhat, but there are two basic tours: a 'Western Tour' and an 'Eastern Tour'. There are also tours of the sights within the city area that leave from the square in front of the railway station. CITS-organised tours are more expensive than those run by other operators, but the cheaper tours usually won't leave until they have enough people and tend to give you less time at each place.

The **Eastern Tour** *(dōng xiàn yóu lǎn)* is the most popular since it includes the Army of Terracotta Warriors as well as the Tomb of Qin Shihuang, Banpo Museum and Huaqing Pool. The CITS-run Eastern Tour costs US$16 with transport only, or US$36 including lunch and all entry tickets. The coach leaves Xi'an around 9 am and returns by 5 pm, and will pick you up from your hotel. An English-speaking guide is provided and you usually get two hours at the warriors and Qin Shihuang's tomb, although many tourists complain that the CITS tour spends too long at the boring Huaqing Pool. Essentially the same tour can be done for far less by taking one of the Chinese minibus tours; you can buy tickets for US$3 at a kiosk in front of the railway station or outside the Bell Tower Hotel. The Jiefang Hotel also does the Eastern Tour (excluding Banpo Museum) for US$4.

The longer **Western Tour** *(xī xiàn yóu lǎn)* includes the Xianyang City Museum, some of the Imperial Tombs, the Qian Tomb and sometimes also Famen Temple. The CITS organises a Western tour costing US$21, but it doesn't leave every day. The cheapest minibus tours are US$4 and depart from outside the railway station. The Jiefang Hotel runs buses on the standard Western Tour for US$5, or US$7 including Famen Temple.

Places to Stay

The *Flats of Remin Hotel* (☎ 722352) *(rén mín dà shà gōng yù)* is at No 9 Fenghe Lu.

Beds in mini-dorms go for US$3, doubles with bathroom are US$14. The place is north-west of the city outside the old walls, but the hotel regularly sends its own scout with a minibus to snap up arriving train passengers – otherwise take bus No 9 from the railway station and get off after six stops. You can rent bikes from reception for US$1 a day.

The *Victory Hotel* (☎ 713184) (*shèng lì fàn diàn*) is just south of Heping Gate. Rooms are grotty and the toilets quite disgusting, but beds in simple triples start at US$3 and doubles with bathroom are US$14. Buses No 5 and No 41 (among others) go past the hotel from the railway station.

The *May First Hotel* (☎ 712212) (*wǔ yī fàn diàn*) is at 351 Dong Dajie, a short distance from the Bell Tower. Foreigners favour this place for its friendliness and central location. A double with private bath costs US$17.

Places to Eat

A good night-food street is Dongxin Jie between Jiefang Lu and Zhongshan Gate.

Two popular meeting places for foreign backpackers are *Dad's Home Cooking* near the Flats of Renmin and the *Small World Restaurant (xiǎo shì jiè cān tīng)* on Heping Lu just inside the city wall.

The cheap downstairs restaurant in the *May First Hotel (wǔ yī fàn diàn)* is good for staple food like pork dumplings and hearty bowls of noodles. Upstairs is a more upmarket restaurant with an English menu listing 'barbecued gourd in honey' and other delicacies.

Things to Buy

Huajue Xiang is a narrow alley running beside the Great Mosque with many small souvenir and 'antique' shops – it's great for browsing. This is one of the best places in China to pick up souvenirs like name chops or a pair of chiming steel balls. Bargaining is the order of the day.

Getting There & Away

Air Xi'an is one of the best connected cities

in China. Here, CAAC is called 'China Northwest Airlines' (☎ 42264) (*zhōng guó xī běi háng kōng gōng sī*), and its booking office is on the south-eastern corner of Xiguan Zhengjie and Laodong Lu, 1.5 km from West Gate. It's a fair way out, but you can get there on trolley bus No 101 from the railway station or the Bell Tower. It may be more convenient to buy air tickets from CITS. There's also another CAAC-affiliated company calling itself 'Shaanxi United Airlines', whose small booking office is conveniently located beside the People's (Renmin) Hotel gate.

Bus The most central long-distance bus station is opposite Xi'an railway station. Some useful connections are to Huashan, Ankang, Yan'an and Ruicheng (southwestern Shanxi). Evening buses with sleeping berths go to Zhengzhou, Yichang, Yinchuan and Luoyang.

Train There are direct trains from Xi'an to Ürümqi, Beijing, Shanghai, Chengdu, Taiyuan, Hefei, Qingdao and Wuhan. The foreigners' ticket office is on the 2nd floor of the railway station above the ticket office for Chinese.

Getting Around

To/From the Airport The new airport is 40-odd km north-west of Xi'an. CAAC's shuttle buses run only between the airport and their ticket office (50 minutes). For a taxi expect to pay about US$20.

Bus Buses are packed and pickpockets do a brisk business. Much better are the ubiquitous minibuses.

HUASHAN

(*húa shān*) 华山
Huashan, one of the sacred mountains of China, is 2200 metres high. It lies just south of the Xi'an-Luoyang railway line. There's only one route to the top, a north-south path about 15 km long.

CHINA

Places to Stay

Huashan village has plenty of budget and mid-range accommodation. There is a good CITS-run hotel on the left 20 metres before you come to the entrance gate; doubles with bath cost US$5 per person and singles are US$8. The *Xiyue Hotel (xī yuè fàn diàn)*, a short way down the street, has dorm beds from US$2.

Getting There & Away

Bus Xi'an is a good jumping off point. There is a direct bus to Huashan.

Train You can take a train from Xi'an to Huashan station (two hours). However, few trains stop there, so you may have to take a train to Mengyuan, which is one station farther down the line, and from there get a bus to Huashan.

Henan 河南

The unruly Yellow River snakes its way across the north of Henan, where it all began. About 3500 years ago the Chinese were turning their primitive settlements into an urban-centred civilisation governed by the Shang Dynasty. Zhengzhou was their capital for a while, and the ancient city walls are still visible.

Today, Zhengzhou is the provincial capital but is basically a dump which isn't worth visiting. The biggest drawcard for travellers is the Longmen Caves near Luoyang.

KAIFENG

(kāi fēng) 开封

Kaifeng was once the imperial capital of China. This honour came to an end in 1127 when the Song Dynasty fled south. These days, travellers come here as a stopover on the route between Qufu and Luoyang.

Chief among the sights is the **Xiangguo Monastery** *(xiàng guó sì)* in the centre of town, originally founded in 555 AD but completely destroyed in 1644. Other sights

include the **Iron Pagoda** *(tiě tǎ)* and **Long-ting Park** *(lóng tíng gōng yuán).*

Places to Stay

The Chinese hotels here all seem to accept foreigners, and private hotels send runners to meet incoming trains.

The *Bianliang Hotel (biàn liáng lǚ shè)* on Zhongshan Lu, about 100 metres up from the railway station, has doubles with crude bathrooms for US$6 and dorm beds from US$1 to US$2. A similarly priced place is the *Dongfeng Hotel (dōng fēng lǚ shè)* across the road, with single rooms without bathroom for US$2.

The *Bian Hotel (biàn dà lǚ shè)* is the big four-storey building you see to the left as you leave the bus station. Basic singles start from US$2 and doubles for US$3.

Another good-value place is the *Dajintai Hotel (dà jīn tái lǚ guǎn)* on Gulou Jie (nearly opposite the Bank of China). It's a central yet quiet location in a small courtyard just behind the street front, and offers double rooms with bath for US$5.

LUOYANG

(luò yáng) 洛阳

Founded in 1200 BC, Luoyang was the capital of 10 dynasties, until the 10th century when the Jin emperor moved the capital to Kaifeng. The main attraction here is the Longmen Cave Temples.

Information

The CITS office (☎ 413701) is on the 2nd floor of the ugly white building immediately behind the Friendship Guest House. There is also a CITS branch in the Peony Hotel.

The PSB is on the corner of Kaixuan Lu and Tiyuchang Lu.

Things to See

The magnificent **Longmen Cave Temples** *(lóng mén shí kū)* are among the best in China. Work began on the cave temples from 494 AD onwards, and over the next 200 years or so more than 100,000 images and statues of Buddha and his disciples were carved into cliff walls on the banks of the Yi River, 16 km south of the city. They represent one of the high points of Buddhist cave art.

From the Luoyang railway station area, bus No 81 goes to the Longmen Caves. From the Friendship Guest House, take bus No 60 which leaves from the far side of the small park opposite the hotel. Bus No 53 from Xiguan traffic circle also runs past the caves.

Half-day minibus tours including the Longmen Caves, White Horse Temple and possibly other sights around Luoyang depart sporadically from in front of the railway station. The price is negotiable, but Chinese tourists seem to pay about US$3. Some hotels run their own tours out to the caves as well.

Places to Stay
Directly opposite the railway station is the depressing *Luoyang Hotel (luò yáng lü shè),* where doubles without bath cost US$7.

Far more pleasant is the *Huacheng Hotel (huá chéng fàn diàn),* 49 Zhongzhou Xilu, which has beds in triple rooms for US$3 and doubles from US$7. Bus Nos 2, 4 and 11 will get you there.

Around the corner from the railway station is the *Tianxiang Hotel* (☎ 337846) *(tiān xiāng lü shè)* on Jinguyuan Lu. The cheapest dorm beds are US$2, simple doubles US$7 and doubles with bathroom US$14 or US$17.

The *Xuangong Hotel (xuán gōng dà shà)* is in a central location on Zhongzhou Lu near its junction with Jinguyuan Lu. This tower block has doubles from US$27.

The *Friendship Guest House* (☎ 412780) *(yǒu yí bīn guǎn)* at 6 Xiyuan Lu is where foreign tour groups generally stay. It charges US$34/45 for singles/doubles.

Getting There & Away
Air The CAAC office (☎ 335301) is up a short lane off Dao Beilu. Bus No 83 passes it on the way to the small Luoyang Airport.

Bus The long-distance bus station is diagonally opposite the main railway station.

There are frequent buses to Zhengzhou. Night coaches head for Xi'an, Taiyuan, Wuhan and Yantai (Shandong Province).

Train From Luoyang there are direct trains to Beijing via Zhengzhou, to Shanghai and Xi'an.

Getting Around
Luoyang is ideal for getting around by bicycle. Bikes can be rented outside the Tianxiang Hotel and around the railway station.

Shandong 山东

Shandong is overpopulated and plagued by the rotten Yellow River, which has changed direction 26 times in its known history. In the late 19th century the Boxers arose out of Shandong and their rebellion set all of China ablaze.

Travellers tend to gloss over this province, which is a shame since it has much to offer, with the coastal port of Qingdao, the splendour of Qufu and the sacred mountain of Taishan.

QINGDAO
(qīng dǎo) 青岛
Qingdao is a remarkable replica of a Bavarian village dropped onto the coast of China. At least it was like that – modernity is starting to intrude. Nevertheless, the city has a distinctive flavour not found elsewhere in the PRC. It's best visited in summer when you can enjoy its white, sandy beaches. Tsingtao, the local beer, is China's most famous brew.

Information
The PSB is at 29 Hubei Lu in a beautiful old building with a clock tower, very close to the Overseas Chinese Hotel.

Things to See
If you're here when the weather is warm, put

CHINA

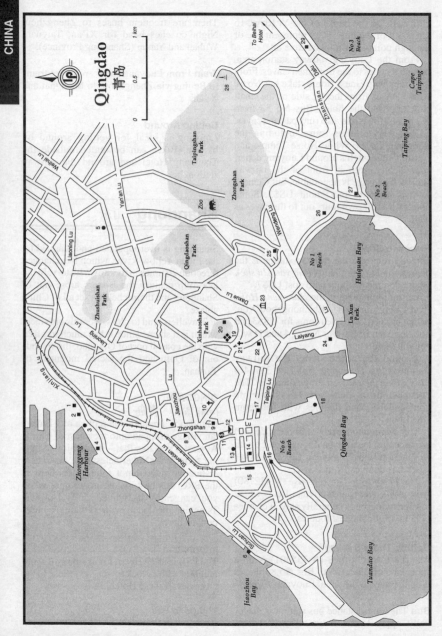

Qingdao
青岛

PLACES TO STAY

1   Peace Hotel
    和平宾馆
2   Friendship Store & Hotel
    友谊商店
4   Jingshan Hotel
    晶山宾馆
9   Qingdao Hotel
    青岛饭店
14 Overseas Chinese Hotel
    华侨饭店
15 Railway Hotel & Railway Station
    铁道大厦
16 Qingdao Pharmaceutical
    Building (Hotel)
    医药大厦
17 Zhanqiao Guesthouse
    栈桥宾馆
20 Xinhao Hill Hotel
    信号山迎宾馆
22 Dongfang Hotel
    东方饭店
24 Haiqing Hotel
    海青宾馆
25 Yellow Sea Hotel &
    China Eastern Airlines
    黄海饭店/东方航空公司
26 Huiquan Dynasty Hotel & CITS
    汇泉王朝大酒店/
    国际旅行社¢
27 Badaguan Hotel
    八大关宾馆

29 Haitian Hotel
    海天大酒店

OTHER

3   Passenger Ferry Terminal
    青岛港客运站
5   Brewery
    青岛啤酒厂
6   Local Ferry
    青岛轮渡站
7   Xinhua Bookstore
    新华书店
8   Chunhelou Restaurant
    春和楼饭店
10 Catholic Church
    天主教堂
11 Bank of China
    中国银行
12 Main Post Office
    邮电局
13 PSB
    公安局外事科
18 Huilan Pavilion
    回澜阁
19 Longshan Underground Market
    龙山地下商业
21 Protestant Church
    基督教堂
23 Qingdao Museum
    青岛博物馆
28 Zhanshan Temple
    湛山寺

the beaches high on your list. Swimming areas are marked off with buoys and shark nets, though the increasingly polluted water makes sunbathing rather than swimming the main attraction.

Qingdao's city parks are amongst the best in China. **Xinhaoshan Park** (*xìn hào shān gōng yuán*) is notable for its fine views of Bavarian architecture. At the highest point in the park are the three red golfball-shaped towers known as the **Mushroom Buildings** (*mógu lóu*). The **Longshan Underground Market** (*lóng shān dì xià shāng yè jiē*) is an amazing shopping arcade built in a tunnel right under the park. Close to this market is the **Protestant Church** (*jī dū jiào táng*), a single-spired structure with a clock tower. Off Zhongshan Lu, up a steep hill, is a structure now simply known as the **Catholic Church** (*tiān zhǔ jiào táng*) – its double spires can be spotted a long way off.

Zhongshan Park (*zhōng shān gōng yuán*) is north of the Huiquan Dynasty Hotel, covers 80 hectares, has a teahouse and temple, and in springtime is a heavily wooded profusion of flowering shrubs and plants. The **City Zoo** (*dòng wù yuán*) is also within the park's boundaries.

The mountainous area north-east of Zhongshan Park is called **Taipingshan Park** (*tài píng shān gōng yuán*), an area of walking paths, pavilions and the magnificent Zhanshan Temple (*zhàn shān sì*). This is the best place in town for hiking.

Places to Stay

The *Railway Hotel* (☎ 269963) (*tiě dào dà shà*), 2 Tai'an Lu, is right in front of the

CHINA

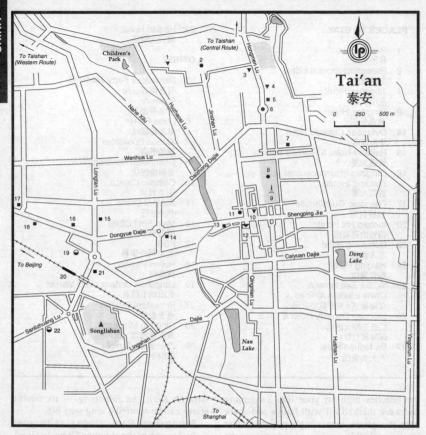

Tai'an
泰安

0   250   500 m

To Taishan
(Central Route)

To Taishan
(Western Route)

Children's
Park

To Beijing

Songlishan

To
Shanghai

railway station. The 24-storey hotel has 224 rooms, including dormitories for US$5 and US$7. Doubles are US$27 and US$33.

The *Friendship Hotel* (☎ 227021) *(yǒu yí bīn guǎn)* is in the same building as the Friendship Store, next door to the Ferry Terminal on Xinjiang Lu. The Friendship Hotel is popular with budget travellers, though it's in a dumpy neighbourhood. Double rooms are US$10. If you arrive in Qingdao by boat, the hotel is just a step away. If you arrive by train it's best to take a motor-tri-cycle.

In the same neighbourhood, but more pleasant, is the *Jingshan Hotel (jīng shān bīn*

guǎn) on Xiaogang 2-Lu. Dormitories (a shared double room) are US$10, or book the whole room for US$20. The hotel is a five-minute walk from the Passenger Ferry Terminal.

Stradling the border between budget and mid-range accommodation, the *Qingdao Pharmaceutical Building (yī yào dà shà)* is that large high-rise on No 6 beach with the circular 'VW' sign on the roof. Singles/doubles are US$17/21, but there are no dor-mitories. Prices might shoot up during the summer peak season.

The *Overseas Chinese Hotel* (☎ 279092) *(húa qiáo fàn diàn)*, 72 Hunan Lu, is cen-

PLACES TO STAY

5 Taishan Guesthouse & CITS
泰山宾馆 / 中国国际旅行社
7 Taishan Grand Hotel
泰山大酒店
13 Overseas Chinese Hotel
华侨大厦
14 Waimao Dasha (Hotel)
外贸大厦
15 Longtan Binguan (Hotel)
龙潭宾馆
16 Liangmao Dasha (Hotel)
粮贸大厦
17 Baiyun Binguan (Hotel)
白云宾馆
18 Tiedao Binguan (Hotel)
铁道宾馆
21 Tai'an Binguan (Hotel)
泰安宾馆

PLACES TO EAT

1 Jinshan Seafood Restaurant
金山渔村
3 Dafugui Restaurant
大富贵酒店

4 Sinaike Restaurant
斯奈克酒店
10 Buyecheng Restaurant
不夜城

OTHER

2 Martyrs' Tomb
烈士陵园
6 Daizong Arohway
岱宗坊
8 Museum
博物馆
9 Dai Temple
岱庙
11 PSB
公安局外事科
12 Post Office
邮局
19 Minibuses to Ji'nan &
Bus No 3 (to Taishan)
往济南汽车 / 三路汽车
20 Railway Station
火车站
22 Long-Distance Bus Station
长途汽车站

trally located near the railway station, but pricey at US$43.

Getting There & Away

Air The CAAC office (☎ 286047) is at 29 Zhongshan Lu. The booking office of China Eastern Airlines (☎ 270215) is adjacent to the Yellow Sea Hotel at 75 Yan'an 1-Lu. There are flights to Hong Kong and plans to add flights to Seoul, South Korea.

Train All trains to Qingdao go through the provincial capital of Ji'nan, except for the direct Qingdao to Yantai trains. There are direct trains to Beijing (17 hours).

JI'NAN
(jì nán) 济南
Ji'nan, the capital of Shandong Province, is a dull city but is an important transport hub for Qufu and Taishan.

TAISHAN
(tài shān) 泰山
Taishan is the most revered of the five sacred mountains of China, adopted in turn by Taoists, Buddhists, Confucians and Maoists. Taishan does not offer the mountain-climbing you might expect, but it's an engrossing experience and certainly worthwhile.

TAI'AN
(tāi'ān) 泰安
The town of Tai'an lies at the foot of Taishan and is the gateway to the mountain.

Information
CITS (☎ 337020) is on the 5th floor of the Taishan Guesthouse. It's one of the most helpful and friendly CITS offices in China. It offers an interesting qigong tour for US$3 with an English-speaking guide – this tour has become very popular with travellers.

The PSB (☎ 224004) is just up the road from the GPO on Qingnian Lu.

CHINA

Things to See

Before climbing Taishan, check out the **Dai Temple** *(dài miào)* at the foot of the mountain south of the Taishan Guesthouse.

The biggest attraction is climbing **Taishan**. Allow at least eight hours up and down at the minimum. The mountain is 1545 metres above sea level, with a climbing distance of 7.5 km from base to summit on the central route. You can also cheat your way to the top – minibuses run from the Tai'an railway station to Zhongtianmen, halfway up Taishan, with several departures each morning. From Zhongtianmen there is a cable car to the summit.

Places to Stay

The most popular place in town with budget travellers is the three-star *Taishan Guesthouse* (☎ 224678) *(tài shān bīn guǎn)*. What makes it popular is the dormitory which costs US$6 per person. It's a good place to round up a small group for an assault on the mountain. Comfy double rooms with private bath are also available for US$24. The hotel is four km from the railway station and just a short walk from the start of the central route trail up Taishan. You can deposit your bags at the hotel's luggage room while you climb the mountain. To get to the hotel, take bus No 3 or the No 3 minibus from the railway station to the second-last stop. A taxi is US$2, or you can charter a whole minibus for the same price.

On Taishan itself, you can stay at the *Zhongtianmen Guest House* midway up or the *Daiding Guest House* on the summit.

Getting There & Away

Buses connect Tai'an to Qufu and there are trains to Ji'nan.

QUFU

(qū fù) 曲阜

Qufu is the birthplace of Confucius (551 to 479 BC) who began and ended his life here. During the Cultural Revolution Confucian teachings were out of favour (to put it mildly), and in the 1960s a contingent of Red

1	Tomb of Confucius
	孔墓
2	Hall for Memorial Ceremony
	祭奠堂
3	Ruins of the Ancient Lu State
	鲁国址
4	Zhougong Temple
	周公庙
5	Yanhui Temple
	颜庙
6	Confucius Mansions
	孔府
7	Drum Tower
	鼓楼
8	Queli Hotel
	阙里宾舍
9	Bell Tower
	钟楼
10	Tourist Souvenior Market
	旅游事业市场
11	Restaurants & Street Market
	餐厅/商业街
12	Yangjingmen Gate
	仰经门
13	Yingshi Binguan (Hotel)
	影视宾馆
14	Bus Station
	汽车站
15	Luyou Binguan (Hotel)
	旅游宾馆
16	Kongfu Fandian (Hotel)
	孔府饭店

Guards came on a mission of destruction. The leader of the ransacking guards, Tan Houlan, was jailed in 1978 and tried in 1982. Confucian ethics have made a comeback, and respect and obedience are being promoted to instil civic-mindedness. In 1979 the Qufu temples were renovated and reopened. Capitalism has also made a comeback – the souvenir vendors are just barely outnumbered by the tourists.

Things to See

The **Confucius Temple** *(kǒng miào)* takes up one-fifth of Qufu. It is more than one-km long and the entrance, Star Gate, is at the south. The dominant features are clusters of twisted pines and cypresses, and the rows of

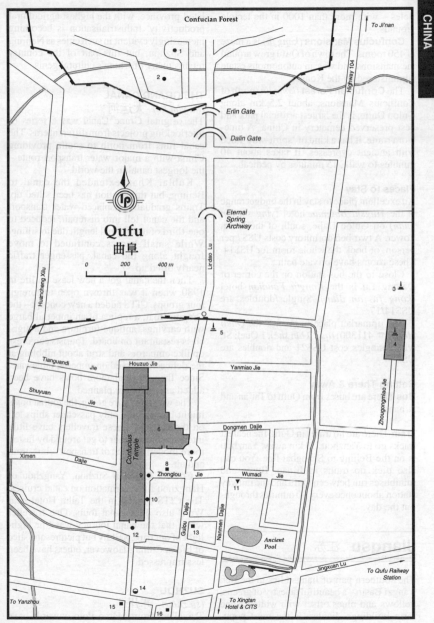

steles – with more than 1000 in the temple grounds.

Confucius Mansions (*kǒng fǔ*) is a maze of 450 rooms. The town of Qufu grew around the mansions and was an autonomous estate administered by the Kongs.

The **Confucian Forest** (*kǒng lín*) north of Confucius Mansions, about 2.5 km along Gulou Dajie, is the largest artificial park and best preserved cemetery in China. A time-worn route, it has a kind of 'spirit-way' lined with ancient cypresses. It takes about 40 minutes to walk, 15 minutes by pedicab.

Places to Stay

An excellent place to stay in the budget range is the *Yingshi Bingnan* hotel (*yǐng shì bīn guǎn*) on Gulou Dajie, south of the Drum Tower. A two-bed dormitory costs US$7 per person, or book the whole room for US$14. These rooms have private bath.

Close to the bus station on the corner of Datong Lu is the *Kongfu Fandian* hotel (*kǒng fǔ fàn diàn*). Singles/doubles are US$14/17.

The upmarket place in town is the *Queli Hotel* (☎ 411300) (*què lǐ bīn shè*), 1 Queli St, where singles cost US$21 and doubles are US$33.

Getting There & Away

Bus There are buses from Qufu to Tai'an and Ji'nan.

Train There are no trains in Qufu; the nearest tracks go to Yanzhou, 13 km away. Yanzhou is on the Beijing to Shanghai line. You can also pick up trains in Ji'nan. Buses and minibuses run between Qufu and the railway station about once every 30 minutes throughout the day.

Jiangsu 江苏

The southern part of Jiangsu lies in the rich Yangzi Basin – a beautiful tapestry of greens, yellows and blues offset with whitewashed farm buildings. Jiangsu is the most popu-lated province, with the highest agricultural productivity. Industrialisation is becoming increasingly evident in such cities as Nanjing and Suzhou, but this part of the country retains many of China's cultural gems.

THE GRAND CANAL
(*dà yùn hé*) 大运河

The original Grand Canal was a series of interlocking projects from different eras. The canal runs from north to south, providing China with a major water transport route – the longest canal in the world.

Kublai Khan extended the canal to Beijing, but this section has been silted up. Trains gradually displaced water transport and the canal fell into disrepair, reduced to one-third of its original length due to silting. While small barges continued to move freight along the canal, passenger traffic nearly dried up.

Then the canal got a new lease on life in 1980 when it was thrown open to foreign tour groups. CITS added a new concept – the Dragon Boat, a replica of an imperial barge with carvings, antique furniture and a high-class restaurant on board. Tourists can dress up like emperors and strut about nibbling at the delicacies served on imperial tableware. Since then, several more boats have been added and more are planned.

The way things are going, the tourist boats might become the only passenger ships left on the canal. Chinese travellers have little interest – most prefer to get around by faster, more modern means of transport – bus, train and air.

Contact CITS in Suzhou, Yangzhou or Hangzhou for information on canal cruises. The CITS branch in the Taihu Hotel near Wuxi also does canal tours. One traveller wrote that the canal journey was 'the high-light of our trip...a filthy but picturesque slice of life in China'. However, others have been less impressed.

SUZHOU
(*sū zhōu*) 苏州

Travellers from Marco Polo onwards have

rated this as one of the finest places in China. Marco Polo's Suzhou was inhabited by beautiful maidens, rich merchants, artists, artisans and magicians. It has been variously dubbed the 'Venice of the East' and the 'Garden City', and seems to have survived the Cultural Revolution largely intact.

Sericulture – raising silkworms – has been the town's major industry since time immemorial and is largely responsible for its continued prosperity. However, industrialisation is starting to impinge on the scenery.

Information
Both CITS (☎ 222681) and CTS (☎ 225583) are ensconced in a separate building in the Suzhou Hotel compound.

The PSB is at 7 Dashitou Xiang.

Things to See
Suzhou is a great place to walk or bicycle around, particularly along the bridges over the main moat to the west of the Grand Canal. The best preserved city gate, **Panmen**, is next to the **Wumen Bridge** which is the largest single-arched stone bridge in Suzhou.

At the northern end of Renmin Lu is the **North Temple** *(běi sì tǎ)*, a nine-storey structure dating from the 17th century. You can climb to the top for a superb aerial view.

Some blocks east is the **Suzhou Museum** *(sū zhōu bó wù guǎn)*, once the residence of the Taiping leader Li Xiucheng. It is open daily from 8 am to 5 pm.

The area surrounding Guanqian Jie – the **Suzhou Bazaar** *(sū zhōu shāng chǎng)* – has numerous restaurants, theatres, speciality shops, street vendors, hairdressing salons, noodle dispensaries, silk merchants etc. Bicycles and buses are banned in the back alleys during the daytime. At the heart of the bazaar is the Taoist **Temple of Mystery** *(xuán miào guān)*, founded in the 3rd century AD.

Suzhou's gardens are looked upon as works of art. The gardens are usually open from early morning to dusk (7.30 am to 5 pm) and there is a small admission charge.

The **Humble Administrator's Garden** *(zhuó zhèng yuán)* in northern Suzhou was built in the 1500s. In 1350 the monk Tian Ru built the **Lion Grove** *(shī zi lín)* just up the street. The **Garden of Harmony** *(yí yuán)* is off Renmin Lu, just south of Guanqian.

The smallest but perhaps most pleasant garden is the **Master of the Nets** *(wǎng shī yuán)*, laid out in the 12th century and restored in the 18th. It may be hard to find, as the entrance is a narrow alley just west of the Suzhou Hotel.

The **Blue Wave Pavilion** *(cāng làng tíng)* is a bit on the wild side with winding creeks and luxuriant trees. It's on the east side of Renmin Lu on the south side of town.

The **Garden for Lingering In** *(liú yuán)* covers over three hectares, making it one of the largest Suzhou gardens. The garden is about one km west of the old city walls. The bus there will take you over bridges looking down on the busy water traffic.

Places to Stay
We can tell which place *used to* be the cheapest and best – without a doubt it was the *Lexiang Hotel* (☎ 223898) *(lè xiāng fàn diàn)*, where dorm beds were US$5 and doubles US$31. The problem is that the hotel was being renovated at the time of our visit, and it's likely that prices will also be renovated when it reopens. The Lexiang Hotel is right in the city centre at 18 Dajing Xiang, an alley which runs off Renmin Lu near the Guanqian markets. To get there take bus No 1 from the railway station.

Closest to the railway station is the *Foreign Trade Guesthouse* (wài mào bīn guǎn), 684 Renmin Lu. Good-looking doubles/triples go for US$21/23.

The south-east corner of town has a goldmine of mid-range accommodation. One to consider is the *Friendship Hotel* (☎ 773518) *(yǒu yí bīn guǎn)*, Zhuhui Lu. An 'ordinary' double is US$22 and a 'standard' is US$29.

Just down the street is the newly opened *Xiangwang Hotel* (☎ 231162) *(xiāng wáng bīn guǎn)*. All double rooms cost US$22. The hotel is on the north-west corner of Xiangwang Lu and Zhuhui Lu.

CHINA

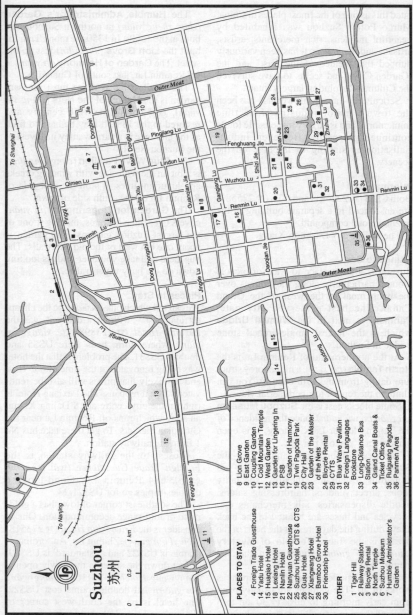

Suzhou 苏州

To Shanghai

To Nanjing

Outer Moat

Outer Moat

Dongbei Jie

Pingjiang Lu

Fenghuang Jie

Lindun Lu

Baita Donglu

Shizi Jie

Shiquan Jie

Zhuhui Lu

Qimen Lu

Baita Xilu

Wuzhou Lu

Renmin Lu

Renmin Lu

Guanqian Jie

Gangqiang Lu

Daoqian Jie

Jingde Lu

Pingli Lu

Dong Zhongshi

Guang Lu

Renmin Lu

Fengqiao Lu

Sujing Lu

PLACES TO STAY

- 4 Foreign Trade Guesthouse
- 14 Yadu Hotel
- 15 Huaqiao Hotel
- 21 Lexiang Hotel
- 21 Nanlin Hotel
- 22 Nanyuan Guesthouse
- 25 Suzhou Hotel, CITS & CTS
- 26 Gusu Hotel
- 27 Xiangwang Hotel
- 28 Bamboo Grove Hotel
- 30 Friendship Hotel

OTHER

- 1 Tiger Hill
- 2 Railway Station
- 3 Bicycle Rental
- 5 North Temple
- 6 Suzhou Museum
- 7 Humble Administrator's
     Garden
- 8 Lion Grove
- 9 East Garden
- 10 Coupling Garden
- 11 Cold Mountain Temple
- 12 West Garden
- 13 Garden for Lingering In
- 16 PSB
- 17 Garden of Harmony
- 19 Twin Pagoda Park
- 20 City Hall
- 23 Garden of the Master
      of the Nets
- 24 Blue Wave Pavilion
- 29 CYTS
- 32 Foreign Languages
      Bookstore
- 33 Long-Distance Bus
      Station
- 34 Grand Canal Boats &
      Ticket Office
- 35 Ruiguang Pagoda
- 36 Panmen Area

0   0.5   1 km

PLACES TO STAY

4 外贸宾馆
14 雅都大酒店
15 华侨饭店
18 乐乡饭店
21 南林饭店
22 南园宾馆
25 苏州饭店/中国国际旅行社/
    中国旅行社
26 姑苏饭店
27 相王宾馆
28 竹辉宾馆
30 友谊宾馆

OTHER

1 虎丘山
2 火车站
3 租自行车店
5 北寺塔

6 苏州博物馆
7 拙政园
8 狮子林
9 东园
10 耦园
11 寒山寺
12 西园
13 留园
16 公安局外事科
17 怡园
19 双塔院
20 市政府
23 网师园
24 租自行车店
29 中国青旅旅
31 沧浪亭
32 外文书店
33 南门汽车站
34 轮船站
35 瑞光塔
36 盘门三景

Walk around the corner and you'll reach the entrance of the *Gusu Hotel* (☎ 224689) *(gū sū fàn diàn)*, 5 Xiangwang Lu Shiquan Jie. Doubles cost US$28.

The *Nanlin Hotel* (☎ 224641) *(nán lín fàn diàn)* is at 22 Gunxiufang off Shiquan Jie. Its very pleasant gardens include a small section with outdoor ceramic tables and chairs. Doubles cost US$31 or US$48. The Nanlin is not to be confused with its more expensive neighbour, the Nanyuan.

Things to Buy
Suzhou-style embroidery, calligraphy, painting, sandalwood fans, writing brushes and silk lingerie are for sale nearly everywhere, probably even in the gift shop of your hotel.

Another Suzhou speciality is hair-embroidery. The technique uses human hair worked onto a silk backing.

Forgetting artistic pursuits for a moment, check out the Suzhou Foreign Language Bookstore near the long-distance bus station. This place has a treasure trove of English-language paperbacks – just the thing to preserve your sanity in hard-seat hell when

all your fellow passengers stare at you and spit for 12 hours.

Getting There & Away
Bus The long-distance bus station is at the south end of Renmin Lu. Considering that Suzhou is relatively prosperous and supposedly a major tourist attraction, the bus station is a surprising third-world horror. There are connections between Suzhou and just about every major place in the region, including Shanghai, Hangzhou, Wuxi, Yangzhou and Yixing.

Train Suzhou is on the Nanjing-Shanghai line, and there are frequent express services.

Boat Along the Grand Canal it's six hours to Wuxi and 14 hours to Hangzhou.

Getting Around
Bicycle You can rent a bike from a shop just opposite the entrance to the Suzhou Hotel. Another bike rental place is at the very northern end of Renmin Lu, just east of the railway station.

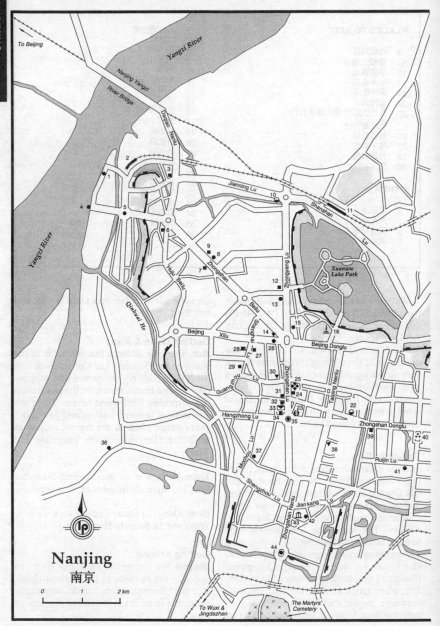

To Beijing

Yangzi River

Nanjing Yangzi
River Bridge

Daqiao Nanlu

Yangzi River

Qinhuai He

Jianning Lu

Shanshan
Lu

Xuanwu
Lake Park

Zhongyang Lu

Zhongshan

Hujiu Beilu

Beilu

Zhongshan

Zhongshan Beilu

Beijing

Xilu

Guangzhou Lu

Zhongshan Lu

Beijing Donglu

Taiping Nanlu

Zhongshan Donglu

Ruijin Lu

Hangzhong Lu

Moshou Lu

Shengzhou Lu

Zhongshan Nanlu

Jian kang Lu

Nanjing
南京

0   1   2 km

To Wuxi &
Jingdezhen

The Martyrs'
Cemetery

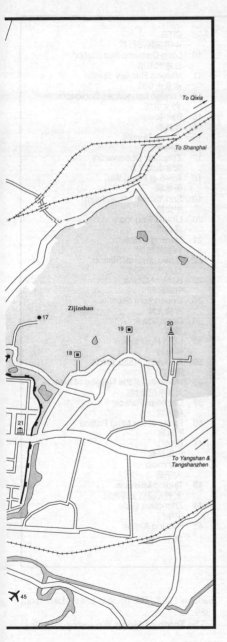

To Qixia

To Shanghai

Zijinshan

● 17

19 ▣

20

18 ▣

21

To Yangshan &
Tangshanzhen

✈ 45

NANJING

(nán jīng) 南京

Nanjing means 'southern capital'. It was China's capital under the first Ming emperor, and also under the Kuomintang. In fact, maps produced in Taiwan still show this as China's capital city.

Nanjing is a very green and pleasant place, with broad boulevards lined with thousands of trees. Most things to see are to the east of Nanjing, in or around Zijinshan *(zǐ jīn shān)*, meaning 'Purple Mountain'.

Information

CITS (☎ 631125) is at 202/1 Zhongshan Beilu and offers free maps with places of interest to tourists shown in English.

The Bank of China is at 3 Zhongshan Donglu, just east of Xinjiekou traffic circle. You can also change money at the Jinling and Central hotels.

The main post office is at 19 Zhongshan Lu, just north of Xinjiekou. The more upmarket tourist hotels also offer postal services. There is a large telephone and telegram office just north of the Drum Tower traffic circle.

Things to See

The exhibits at the **Memorial of the Nanjing Massacre** *(dà tú shā jì niàn guǎn)* document the atrocities committed by Japanese soldiers against the civilian population during the occupation of Nanjing in 1937.

Just west of Zhongshan Gate on Zhongshan Lu, the **Nanjing Museum** *(nán jīng bó wù guǎn)* houses an array of artefacts from Neolithic times through to the Communist period.

The **Ming City Wall** is the longest city wall ever built in the world, measuring over 33 km. Some of the original 13 **Ming City Gates** remain, including Heping Gate in the north and Zhonghua Gate in the south.

Built in 1382, the **Drum Tower** *(gǔ lóu)* is in the city centre in the middle of a traffic circle on Beijing Xilu. Drums were usually beaten to give directions for the change of the night watches and in rare instances to

PLACES TO STAY

3 Daqiao Hotel
   大桥饭店
6 Shuangmenlou Hotel
   双门楼宾馆
7 Nanjing Hotel
   南京饭店
9 Hongqiao Hotel
   虹桥饭店
12 Xuanwu Hotel
    玄武饭店
24 Jingu Hotel
    金谷大厦
27 Nanjing University/
    Foreign Students' Dormitory
    南京大学的外国留学生宿舍
29 Nanjing Normal University/
    Nanshan Hotel
    南京师范大学的南山宾馆
31 Central Hotel
    中心大酒店
32 Shengli Hotel
    胜利饭店
34 Jinling Hotel
    金陵饭店
39 Xihuamen Hotel
    西华门饭店

PLACES TO EAT

14 Maxiangxing Restaurant
    马祥兴菜馆
28 Black Cat Cafe
    黑猫餐馆
30 Sprite Freeze
    梧州酒家
38 Sichuan Restaurant
    四川酒家

OTHER

1 No 4 Dock
   四号码头
2 Nanjing West Railway Station
   南京西站
4 Zhongshan Dock
   中山码头
5 Monument to the Crossing of the
   Yangzi River
   渡江纪念碑

8 CITS
   中国国际旅行社
10 Long-Distance Bus Station
    长途汽车站
11 Nanjing Railway Station
    南京火车站
13 Foreign Languages Bookstore
    外文书店
15 Bell Tower
    大钟亭
16 Jiming Temple
    鸡鸣寺
17 Zijinshan Observatory
    紫金山天文台
18 Tomb of Hong Wu
    明孝陵
19 Sun Yatsen Mausoleum
    中山陵
20 Linggu Pagoda
    灵谷塔
21 Nanjing Museum
    南京博物馆
22 Hanfu Jie Bus Station
    汉府街汽车站
23 Bank of China
    中国银行
25 Department Store
    百货大楼
26 Drum Tower
    鼓楼
33 Main Post Office
    邮电局
35 Xinjiekou Traffic Circle
    新街口
36 Memorial of the Nanjing Massacre
    大屠杀纪念馆
37 Chaotian Palace
    朝天宫
40 Ruins of the Ming Palace
    明故宫
41 CAAC
    中国民航
42 Fuzimiao
    夫子庙
43 Taiping Museum
    太平天国历史博物馆
44 Zhonghua Gate
    中华门
45 Nanjing Airport
    南京机场

warn the populace of impending danger. North-east of the Drum Tower, the **Bell Tower** (zhōng lóu) houses an enormous bell

made in 1388. The present tower dates from 1889.

The **Tomb of Hong Wu** (míng xiào líng)

lies east of the city on the southern slope of Zijinshan. Hong Wu was the first emperor of the Ming Dynasty (1368-1644).

Sun Yatsen, called the 'father of modern China', died in 1925 and wished to be buried in Nanjing. Less than a year after his death construction of the immense **Sun Yatsen Mausoleum** (zhōng shān líng) began at the southern foot of Zijinshan. No doubt he would have preferred greater simplicity than the Ming-style tomb which his successors built for him.

To the east of the city by Zijinshan is **Linggu Park** (líng gǔ gōng yuán) with an assortment of sights. A road leads either side of the **Beamless Hall** (wú liáng diàn) and up two flights of steps to the **Pine Wind Pavilion**, originally dedicated to the Goddess of Mercy as part of the Linggu Temple. The **Linggu Temple** (líng gǔ sì) and its memorial hall to Xuan Zang is close by. Xuan Zang was the Buddhist monk who travelled to India and brought back the Buddhist scriptures. After you pass through the Beamless Hall, turn right and follow the pathway. Close by is the **Linggu Pagoda** (líng gǔ tǎ), which was built in the 1930s under the direction of an American architect. It's an octagonal building 60 metres high and has nine storeys.

Fuzimiao (fū zǐ miào) is a district in the south of the city, centred around the site of an ancient Confucian temple. Today, Fuzimiao has become Nanjing's main amusement quarter, and is a particularly lively and crowded place on weekends and holidays. There are restaurants, silk stores, souvenir shops, art exhibitions and tacky shows in old halls. You can get to the Fuzimiao area from Nanjing west railway station by bus No 16, from the docks by trolley bus No 31 and from Xinjiekou by bus No 2.

Also in the south of town is the **Taiping Museum** (tài píng tiān guó lì shǐ bó wù guǎn). The museum has an interesting collection of documents, books and artefacts relating to the rebellion.

Enter **Xuanwu Park** (xuán wǔ gōng yuán) from the main gate off Zhongyang Lu. This park is almost entirely covered by the waters of a large urban lake and boats are available.

Places to Stay

The *Nanjing University Foreign Students' Dormitory* (nán jīng dà xué wài guó liú xué shēng sù shè) is the large white building on Shanghai Lu, just south of Beijing Xilu. Doubles with communal facilities cost US$6 or US$3 per bed. Take the No 13 bus from the railway or the long-distance bus station, or you can take a No 3 trolley bus down Zhongshan Lu and get off just after Beijing Lu.

If it's full, try the *Nanjing Normal University Nanshan Hotel* (nán jīng shī fàn dà xué nán shān bīn guǎn). Doubles with private bath cost US$10. To get there from the Nanjing University dorm, walk half a km south along Shanghai Lu. Turn right into a short market lane, then take the first road left to the main gate of Nanjing Normal University. The hotel is 500 metres inside the campus compound, left of the large grassy quadrangle.

Daqiao Hotel (dà qiáo fàn diàn) is in the far north-west of the city at the corner of Daqiao Nanlu and Jianning Lu. A bed in a basic triple costs US$3, or US$5 in a double with attached bath. Take bus No 10 either west-bound from the railway station or from the Yangzi ferry terminal.

Xihuamen Hotel (xī huá mén fàn diàn) is 1.5 km east of Xianjiekou on Zhongshan Donglu. Doubles start at US$12. Take bus No 5 east from Xinjiekou.

Places to Eat

Some of Nanjing's livelier eating houses are in the Fuzimiao quarter. The *Yongheyuan Restaurant* (☎ 623836) (yǒng hé yuán chá diàn shè) at 122 Gongyuan Jie specialises in sweet and savoury steamed pastries. Nearby is the *Lao Zhengxing Restaurant* (laǒ zhèng xìng cài guǎn) at 119 Gongyuan Jie, just east of the main square by the river. You can get your fingers greasy at Fuzimiao's new *Kentucky Fried Chicken* (kěn dé jī jiā xiāng jī).

Getting There & Away

Air Nanjing has flights to all major cities in China. The main CAAC office (☎ 649275) is at 52 Ruijin Lu (near the terminal of bus route No 4), but you can also buy tickets at the CITS office or at the Jinling or Central Hotel.

Bus The long-distance bus station is west of the main railway station, south-east of the wide bridged intersection with Zhongyang Lu.

Train Nanjing is a major stop on the Beijing-Shanghai railway line. The foreigners' booking office is on the right as you approach the railway station near the entrance to the soft-sleeper waiting room.

Boat Ferries cruise along the Yangzi River east towards Shanghai and west towards Wuhan. Most ferries leave from No 4 dock (*sì hào mǎ tóu*), one km north of Zhongshan dock at the western end of Zhongshan Beilu.

Shanghai 上海

Shanghai is the name which more than any other evokes images of the mystic, inscrutable East of the 1930s and 1940s – in the days when Hollywood thought slums were romantic.

Shanghai had its heyday under the Kuomintang. At that time there were more cars cruising the Shanghai streets than in the whole of the rest of China; powerful Western financial institutions opened offices; and foreign ships and submarines patrolled the coast. There was money and corruption in abundance – child labour, 30,000 prostitutes, gangsters, opium dens, casinos, bars and dance halls.

Under the Communists the opium dens, night clubs and brothels quickly disappeared, but the city remained stuck in a 1940s time warp for more than four decades. That changed in 1990 with the announcement of massive plans to develop Pudong on

the east side of the Huangpu River. Foreign companies have been tripping over themselves to get involved – the city's hotels are overflowing with foreign financiers working on one project or another. Along with Guangzhou and Shenzhen, Shanghai is now one of China's hottest economic prospects. New skyscrapers seem to pop up overnight, bridges and tunnels are being built while factories belch out smoke and finished goods for export.

Orientation

Shanghai municipality covers a huge area (6300 sq km), but the city proper is a more modest 375 sq km. There are four main areas of interest in the city: the Bund from Suzhou Creek to the Shanghai Harbour Passenger Terminal (Shiliupu Wharf); Nanjing Donglu (a very colourful neighbourhood); French-town, which includes Huaihai Zhonglu and Ruijin Lu (an even more colourful neighbourhood); and the Jade Buddha Temple and the side strip along Suzhou Creek.

Information

The headquarters of CITS (☎ 3217200) is at 33 Zhongshan Dong 1-Lu (on the Bund), but more useful is the CITS ticket office (☎ 3234067) at 66 Nanjing Donglu (next door to the Peace Hotel). The office remains open Saturday and for half a day on Sunday.

International express mail service and poste restante are at 276 Bei Suzhou Lu. The International Post & Telecommunications Office is at the corner of Sichuan Beilu and Bei Suzhou Lu.

There are several foreign consulates in Shanghai. If you're doing the Trans-Siberian journey and have booked a definite departure date, it's much better to get your Russian visa here than face the horrible queues at the Russian Embassy in Beijing. Consulates include:

Australia
17 Fuxing Xilu (☎ 4334604; fax 4331732)

Czech & Slovak
  5th floor, New Town Mansion, 55 Loushanguan Lu, Hongqiao (☎ 2757203; fax 2759033)
France
  Room 2008, Ruijin Building, 205 Maoming Nanlu (☎ 4336273; fax 4336286)
Germany
  181 Yongfu Lu (☎ 4336951; fax 4714448)
Hungary
  Room 1810, Union Building, 100 Yan'an Donglu (☎ 3261815; fax 3202855)
Italy
  127 Wuyi Lu (☎ 2524373)
Japan
  1517 Huaihai Zhonglu (☎ 4336639; fax 4331008)
Poland
  618 Jianguo Xilu (☎ 4339288)
Russia
  20 Huangpu Lu (☎ 3242682; fax 3069982)
Singapore
  400 Wulumuqi Zhonglu (☎ 4331362; fax 4334150)
UK
  244 Yongfu Lu (☎ 4330508; fax 4333115)
USA
  1469 Huaihai Zhonglu (☎ 4336880; fax 4314122)

Shanghai's medical facilities are among the most advanced in China. Foreigners are referred to Shanghai No 1 People's Hospital (☎ 3240100) (shàng hǎi shì dì yī rén mín yī yuàn) at 190 Bei Suzhou Lu; or Ruijin Hospital (☎ 4370045) (ruì jīn yī yuàn) at 197 Ruijin 2-Lu.

The PSB is at 210 Hankou Lu.

Things to See & Do

Shanghai starts as early as 5 am, with people exercising in the streets or concentrating on their taijiquan and other martial arts. Markets abound. The atmosphere in Shanghai in the early hours is enjoyable, before its millions begin to crowd the streets.

The Bund (wài tān) is an Anglo-Indian term for the embankment of a muddy waterfront. It's Shanghai's most scenic street and a popular hangout for locals and foreigners. The facades of the buildings along the Bund are a mix of neo-classical 1930s Chicago with a hint of Egyptian. They were used as trading houses, hotels, residences and clubs – and some still are.

Some of the best views of Shanghai are seen from the water. **River tour boats** depart from the dock on the Bund, slightly north of the Peace Hotel. There are several decks on the boat with varying prices. The schedule may become more erratic when the weather doesn't cooperate, but cruises are most frequent during summer. Tickets can be purchased in advance from CITS at the Peace Hotel (there's a small surcharge), or at the boat dock.

During the colonial era, **Huangpu Park** at the north-western end of the Bund was called the British Public Gardens. At that time a notorious sign by the gate said 'No Dogs or Chinese Allowed', a humiliation which the Chinese have neither forgotten nor forgiven.

In the city centre, the commercial golden mile of **Nanjing Lu** was originally home to restaurants, nightclubs and coffin makers. Prestigious stores of bygone eras still trade, now under different names. Wing On has become the No 10 Department Store; Sun Sun is the No 1 Food Store; and The Sun is the No 1 Department Store. During the day, Nanjing Lu is closed to all motor vehicles except buses.

The **Shanghai Museum** (shàng hǎi bó wù guǎn) is on Henan Nanlu, just off Yan'an Donglu. It houses a good collection of bronzes, ceramics, paintings and a few terracotta figures from Xi'an. It's open from 9 am to 3.30 pm.

Mandarin Gardens Bazaar (yù yuán shāng chǎng) is at the north-eastern end of the old Chinese city and includes the Temple of the Town Gods. Many foreigners consider this to be one of the most interesting places in Shanghai, but it gets some 200,000 visitors daily – avoid it on weekends! While there's nothing of historical interest left, it's one of those great places where people just come to gawk, mix, buy, sell and eat

If you want to visit the famous **Jade Buddha Temple** (yù fó sì), bus No 16 from the Mandarin Gardens Bazaar takes you there, travelling across half of Shanghai. The centrepiece is a white-jade buddha almost two metres high, which was brought from Burma in 1882. Photographs are not

CHINA

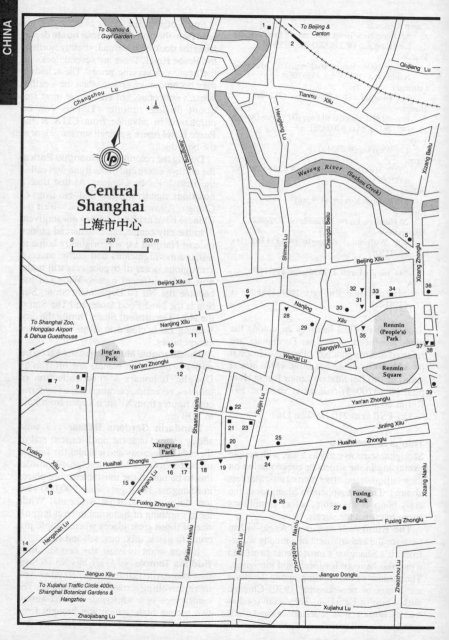

Central Shanghai

上海市中心

0   250   500 m

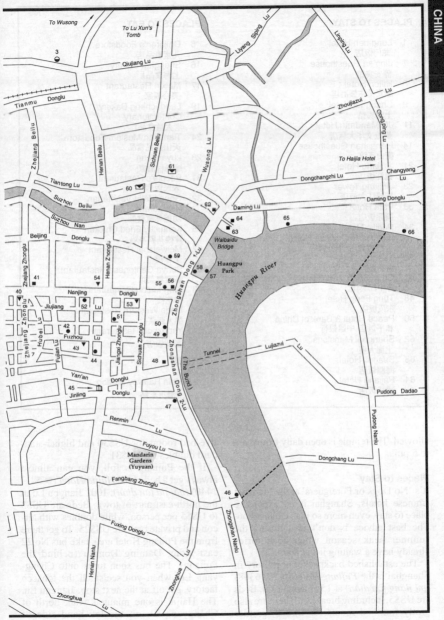

PLACES TO STAY

1   Longmen Hotel
    龙门饭店
7   Jing'an Guesthouse
    静安宾馆
8   Hilton Hotel
    静安希尔顿酒店
9   Shanghai Hotel
    上海宾馆
11 JC Mandarin Hotel
    锦沧文华大酒店
14 Hengshan Guesthouse
    衡山宾馆
21 Jinjiang Hotel
    锦江饭店
23 Jinjiang Tower
    新锦江大酒店
33 Park Hotel
    国际饭店
34 Pacific Hotel
    (Overseas Chinese Hotel)
    金门大酒店/华侨饭店
38 Yangtze Hotel
    扬子饭店
41 Chun Shen Jiang Hotel
    春中江宾馆
48 Tung Feng Hotel
    东风饭店
56 Peace Hotel & Bank of China
    和平饭店/中国银行
62 Shanghai Mansions
    上海大厦
63 Seagull Hotel
    海鸥饭店
64 Pujiang Hotel
    浦江饭店

PLACES TO EAT

6   Children's Foodstore
    儿童食品店
16 Shanghai Bakery
    上海食品厂
17 Meixin Restaurant
    美心酒家
19 Laodacheng Bakery/
    Confectionary
    老大昌食品厂
24 Tianshan Moslem Foodstore
    天山回民食品
28 Luyangcun
    绿扬村酒家
31 People's Restaurant
    人民饭店
32 Gongedelin Vegetarian
    Restaurant
    功德林蔬食处
35 Kentucky Fried Chicken
    肯德基家乡鸡
37 Meiweizhai Restaurant
    美味斋
40 Sunya Cantonese Restaurant
    新雅粤菜馆
43 Xinghualou Restaurant
    杏花楼
53 Deda Western Restaurant
    德大西菜社
54 Yangzhou Restaurant
    扬州饭店

OTHER

2   Main Railway Station
    上海火车站

---

allowed. The temple is open daily from 8 am to 5 pm.

Places to Stay

It's 'No Dogs or Foreigners' at the low-cost Chinese hotels. Shanghai is an expensive place to stay, even more so than Guangzhou. The best advice is don't visit during the summer peak season when dormitories already have a waiting list at 8 am.

The established backpacker dormitory in Shanghai is the *Pujiang Hotel* (☎ 3246388) (*pǔ jiāng fàn diàn*) at 15 Huangpu Lu. Beds are US$5, including breakfast. There are also grotty four-bed rooms for US$28, grottier five-bed rooms for US$30 and higher-standard doubles for US$31.

If the Pujiang is full, you can almost always get a bed at the *Haijia Hotel* (☎ 541-1440) (*hǎi jiā fàn diàn*), 1001 Jiangpu Lu in the north-east part of town. Beds are US$3 to US$5 per person, while doubles with air-con and private bath are US$25. To get there from the Pujiang Hotel area, take bus No 22 east along Daming Donglu (behind the Pujiang). The bus soon turns onto Chang-yang Lu; when you see/smell the tobacco factory, get off at the next stop, Jiangpu Lu. The Haijia is one minute's walk north of Changyang Lu on the left-hand side of

3	Long-Distance Bus Station 长途汽车站	42	Foreign Languages Bookstore 外文书店
4	Jade Buddha Temple 玉佛寺	44	Shanghai Antique & Curio Store 文物商店
5	24-Hour Department Store 二十四百货商店	45	Shanghai Museum 上海博物馆
10	Exhibition Centre 上海展览中心	46	Shiliupu Wharf 十六浦码头
12	CAAC 中国民航	47	Booking Office for Yangzi River & Coastal Boats 轮船售票处 (长江)
13	US Consulate 美国领事馆	49	City Hall 上海市人民政府
15	Conservatory of Music 音乐学院	50	Customs House 海关楼
18	Gongtai Fruit Store 公泰水果店	51	PSB 公安局外事科
20	Guotai Theatre 国泰剧院	52	Xinhua Bookstore 新华书店
22	Shanghai Art Theatre 艺术剧院	55	CITS (Ticket Office) 中国国际旅行社
25	Shanghai Art Academy Exhibition Hall 画院美术馆	57	Wharf for Huangpu Tour Boats 浦江游船码头
26	Former Residence of Sun Yatsen 孙中山故居	58	CITS (Administrative Office) 国际旅行社总部
27	Site of First National Congress of the CCP 中共一大会址	59	Friendship Store 友谊商店
29	TV Tower 电视台	60	International Post Office 国际邮局
30	Shanghai Acrobatics Theatre 杂技场	61	Post Office (Poste Restante) 总邮局
36	No 1 Department Store 第一百货商店	65	International Passenger Terminal 国际客运站
39	Great World 大世界	66	Gongpinglu Wharf 公平路码头

Jiangpu Lu. Coming from the main Shanghai railway station, bus No 310 or 70 stop almost in front of the hotel.

In the same neighbourhood is the *Changyang Hotel* (☎ 5434890) *(cháng yáng fàn diàn)*, 1800 Changyang Lu. The hotel is very modern but quite a bargain with singles/doubles for US$17/20. Bus No 22 from the Bund area runs right past the hotel.

Also good is the *Conservatory of Music* (☎ 4372577) *(yīn yuè xué yuàn)*, 20 Fenyang Lu off Huaihai Zhonglu. The foreign student dorm will take non-students when there's room, but it's often full (best bet is during the summer when the students are gone). The

cost is US$4 per person for a double with shared bath. To find the dorms, take the first left after passing through the main gate.

Everything else is mid to upper range. A good example is the *Yangtze Hotel* (☎ 3207880) *(yáng zi fàn diàn)*, 740 Hankou Lu (one block east of People's Park). Doubles cost US$34 to US$42. Take bus No 109 from the railway station to People's Park on Nanjing Donglu.

Places to Eat

If you're staying in a budget hotel, you might as well eat there – Shanghai's restaurants are universally packed and often not all that good. Shanghai has a couple of its own specialities and is noted for its seafood (such as the freshwater crab that appears around October to December). Most Chinese food tends towards the oily side, but Shanghai-style cooking is the Persian Gulf of Chinese cuisine.

For Chinese-style snacks there's nowhere better than the *Mandarin Gardens Bazaar (yù yuán lǜ yóu shāng chéng)*. Officially, it's at 41 Jiujiaochang Lu, the west side of Mandarin Gardens. It serves nanxiang dumplings (served in a bamboo steamer), pigeon-egg dumplings (shaped like a pigeon egg in summer), vegetarian buns, spicy cold noodles etc.

The *Jade Buddha Temple Vegetarian Restaurant* (☎ 2585596) *(yù fó sì sù zhāi)* at 170 Anyuan Lu certainly has an authentic and congenial atmosphere, not to mention good food.

The *Gongdelin* (☎ 3271532) *(gōng dé lín shū shí chù)* at 43 Huanghe Lu is a branch of the Beijing establishment with the same name. It's a government-run place featuring mock seafood, mock duck and roasted bran-dough. The restaurant is just around the corner from the Park Hotel on Nanjing Xilu.

A couple of shops specialise in vegetarian food; these include the *Hongkouqu Grain Store* (☎ 3240514) at 62 Linping Lu, which is good for fresh peanut butter, tahini, grains, beans and vegetable oils. The *Sanjiaodi Vegetable Market* at 250 Tanggu Lu in the Hongkou District, north of the Bund, is a large indoor market selling fresh vegetables and bean-curd products, and ready-to-cook dinners, fish and meat.

Kentucky Fried Chicken (☎ 3275947) *(kěn dé jī jiā xiāng jī)* has made its debut at 231 Nanjing Xilu, and if imitation is the sincerest form of flattery, the Colonel should be proud of the fake Chinese Kentucky Fried Chicken just next door. There is another Kentucky Fried in the Tung Feng Hotel (right on the Bund) at 3 Zhongshan Dong 1-Lu.

Entertainment

Back in the pre-revolutionary days the acrid smell of opium hung in the streets, bevies of bar girls from the four corners draped themselves over the rich; there were casinos, greyhound and horse-racing tracks, strings of nightclubs, thousands of brothels, lavish dinners and several hundred ballrooms.

Shanghai has quietened down a lot since the 1920s and 1930s. The missionaries had a go at reducing the nightlife, but it was the Communists who finally succeeded. Only in the 1990s have things picked up again, but now it's karaoke bars. These are easy to find – try any hotel.

Each of the elite Euro-American-style hotels (eg, the Sheraton Huating, Shanghai Hilton and Yangtze New World) has at least one international nightclub where business people and tech reps shake it as best they can. One place worth checking out might be the Trader's Pub (☎ 2791888 ext 5307) in the Shanghai JC Mandarin Hotel – open from 7 pm to 1 am nightly, except Monday.

The Shanghai Acrobatics Theatre *(shàng hǎi zájì chǎng)* has stunning shows almost every evening. Some people find the animal acts a bit sad, but in general reactions to the shows have been enthusiastic. Sometimes performing tigers and pandas (not together) show up as an added bonus. Tickets for the regular shows are around US$1, but scalpers buy them up ahead of time to resell on the day of the show for US$10 or more. Some suckers pay, but you can bargain with scalpers – if you wait until the very last minute, the price drops dramatically (US$2 is easily possible as they have no use for an unsold ticket). Buying from the ticket office doesn't seem to work – it's permanently 'sold out' even though the show is rarely half full. CITS will also book seats for a fee. Performances start around 7 pm. The theatre is on Nanjing Xilu, a short walk west of the Park Hotel on the same side of the street.

Things to Buy

Good buys in Shanghai are clothing (silks, down jackets, traditional Chinese clothing), stencilled T-shirts, embroidered clothing), antiques (real or otherwise), tea (chrysanthemum and Dragon Well tea from Hangzhou), stationery...the list goes on and on, so just regard this place as one big department store.

Major shopping areas in Shanghai besides crowded Nanjing Donglu are Huaihai Zhonglu, Ruijin Lu, Sichuan Beilu, Jinling Donglu and Nanjing Xilu.

One good place to look for down jackets is Zhongya Down & Feather Products Store (☎ 2582261) at 990-2 Nanjing Xilu.

The Friendship Store (*yǒu yí shāng diàn*), once housed in the former British consulate on the Bund, has moved around the corner to a multistorey building at 40 Beijing Donglu. This place sells a lot of touristy junk, but useful things too like books in English, maps, silk underwear and other goodies. The Friendship Store also houses a Western-style supermarket.

The Shanghai Antique and Curios Store (☎ 3210019) (*wén wù shāng diàn*) at 192-226 Guangdong Lu is a major tourist outlet.

Getting There & Away

Air CAAC's useful international flights include those to Brussels, Fukuoka, Hong Kong, Los Angeles, Nagasaki, Nagoya, New York, Osaka, Paris, San Francisco, Tokyo, Toronto and Vancouver. CAAC has announced plans to add direct flights from Shanghai to Seoul, Bangkok and Singapore in the near future. Dragonair also flies between Shanghai and Hong Kong. Northwest and United fly to the USA (with a brief change of aircraft in Tokyo), and Canadian International can get you to Canada.

Daily (usually several times daily) domestic flights connect Shanghai to every major city in China.

Several international airlines maintain Shanghai offices:

Aeroflot
    East Lake Hotel, Donghu Lu
Air France
    Hongqiao Airport (☎ 2558866)
Canadian Airlines International
    Room 109, Jinjiang Hotel, 59 Maoming Nanlu (☎ 2582582)
Dragonair
    Room 123, North Wing, Jinjiang Hotel, 59 Maoming Nanlu (☎ 4336435)

Japan Airlines
    Room 201, Ruijin Building, 205 Maoming Lu, 1202 Huaihai Zhonglu (☎ 4333000)
Korean Air
    Rooms 104 & 105, Hotel Equatorial, 65 Yan'an Xilu (☎ 2588450)
Northwest Airlines
    Room 207, level 2, East Podium, Jinjiang Hotel, 59 Maoming Nanlu (☎ 2798100)
Singapore Airlines
    Room 208, East Wing, Shanghai Centre, 1376 Nanjing Xilu (☎ 2798000)
United Airlines
    Shanghai Hilton Shopping Arcade, 250 Huashan Lu (☎ 2553333)

Bus The long-distance bus station is on Qiujiang Lu west of Henan Beilu. There are several buses a day to Hangzhou, Wuxi and Changzhou.

Train Shanghai is at a major rail junction and you can reach just about anyplace in China from here.

Your train may arrive or depart from either the main station or the west station. For departures, be sure you know which is which.

Getting Chinese-priced tickets is difficult in Shanghai if you don't have a Chinese face. Having a Chinese person buy it for you is one option – otherwise, consider plastic surgery.

There are three locations for foreigners to buy tickets, and though you'll have to pay foreigner prices, you can at least avoid the horrible queues in the station. The soft-seat waiting room in the Shanghai railway station is the best place to purchase tickets on short-notice (even same-day departures). For next-day departures, you can also try the Longmen Hotel (☎ 3170000 ext 5315) next to the railway station at 777 Hengfeng Lu (the ticket office is open from 2.30 until 9 pm). Your third option is CITS adjacent to the Peace Hotel, but that office asks for six days' notice, though it can sometimes be managed in three days.

Boat One of the cheapest and best ways of getting to or leaving Shanghai is by boat. Tickets to Hong Kong are available through CITS, but they charge a commission. In Hong Kong you buy the tickets from CTS.

There are also boats along the Yangzi River. The main destinations are Nantong, Nanjing, Wuhu, Guichi, Jiujiang and Wuhan. Tickets for all domestic passenger shipping out of Shanghai can be bought from CITS or the main booking office at 1 Jinling Donglu.

Getting Around

To/From the Airport Hongqiao Airport is 18 km from the Bund and getting there takes about 30 minutes if you're lucky, or over an hour if you're not. There is a bus from the CAAC office on Yan'an Lu to the airport. Major hotels like the Jinjiang have an airport shuttle. Taxis from the Bund will cost approximately US$8. A new airport is to be constructed in the Pudong New Area but no word yet on when it will open.

Bus Shanghai's buses are about the most crowded in China, but if you don't get crushed they'll get you where you want to go.

There are trolley buses (Nos 1 to 30), and city buses (Nos 31 to 99). Nos 201 to 220 are peak-hour city buses, and Nos 301 to 321 are all-night buses.

No 18 runs north-south from the front of the north railway station to the Huangpu River. No 65 goes to the Bund; No 49 from the PSB goes west along Yan'an Lu; No 11 travels the ring road of the old Chinese city; and No 16 runs from the Jade Buddha Temple to Yuyuan Bazaar, then on to a ferry hop over the Huangpu River.

Underground The Shanghai subway is being built at a feverish pace and portions of it could be in operation by the time you read this. The authorities say that the first section to be opened will run along Huaihai Zhonglu.

Anhui 安徽

Northern Anhui forms part of the North China Plain, where the Han Chinese settled in large numbers during the Han Dynasty.

The southern area, below the Yangzi, was not settled until the 7th and 8th centuries AD.

Most of the tourist attractions are in the south, and are more easily accessible from Hangzhou or Shanghai than from the provincial capital of Hefei. The Yangzi River ports of Guichi and Wuhu are convenient jumping-off points for the spectacular Huangshan mountains.

HEFEI

(hé féi) 合肥
A nondescript industrial town, the capital of Anhui is not really worth a visit. The only real attraction is the local Provincial Museum whose prize possession is a 2000-year-old burial suit made of jade pieces held together by silver thread.

Hefei is connected by train with Ji'nan, Beijing and Zhengzhou, with the Yangzi River port of Wuhu to the south and with Xi'an to the west.

HUANGSHAN CITY

(huáng shān shì) 黄山市
The old town of Tunxi *(tún xī)* has now been rechristened Huangshan City. Whatever the correct name, it's significant to travellers only as a jumping-off point for the climb up Huangshan (Yellow Mountain).

Regular buses run between Huangshan City and Tangkou in the Huangshan mountains. There are other scheduled bus services to Shanghai, Hangzhou, Hefei, Nanjing and Jingdezhen, and direct trains to Hefei, Yingtan (via Jingdezhen) and Wuhu. The local airport receives many weekly flights from Beijing, Guangzhou and Shanghai as well as other regional Chinese cities.

HUANGSHAN

(huáng shān) 黄山
Huangshan (Yellow Mountain) is the collective name of a range of 72 peaks in the south of Anhui Province, 280 km west of Hangzhou. The highest is the Lotus Flower Peak *(lián huā fēng)* at 1800 metres.

Public buses from Huangshan City drop you off at the terminal near Huangshan Gate in upper Tangkou *(tāng kǒu)*, the main village at the foot of the range. This is the most convenient place to pick up a mountain map, store your excess baggage or buy some snacks. Clustered around the hot springs 2.5 km farther up the valley is another resort built on both sides of the gushing Taohua (Peach Blossom) Stream, where you'll find tourist hotels, sanatoriums, a bank and a post office. The road ends halfway up the mountain at the lower cable-car station where the eastern steps begin.

Information
CITS has an office in the Peach Blossom Hotel (☎ 562666) *(táo yuán bīn guǎn)*, near the hot springs resort.

Scaling the Heights
The eight-minute cable-car ride is the least painful way up. For US$1 minibuses take you from Huangshan Gate to the lower cable-car station. From here the round-trip cable-car fare is US$6 for foreigners. The queues can get quite long, with waiting times often exceeding one hour.

There are two basic walking routes up Huangshan: the western steps (15 km) from above the hot springs, and the eastern steps (7.5 km, three hours one-way) which lead up below the cable-car line. The most scenic way is to ascend the eastern steps and descend by the western steps.

Guides are not really necessary since the mountain paths are very easy to follow and you can't get lost for long.

Places to Stay & Eat
There are five locations with hotels and restaurants in the Huangshan area. Prices and availability of beds can vary a lot according to seasonal demand. Summer is the peak season.

Tangkou You'll find the cheapest and most accessible hotels in Tangkou.

The *Tiandu Hotel* (☎ 562160) *(tiān dǔ shān zhuāng)*, 700 metres downhill from Huangshan Gate, charges US$7 for a bed in a three-person room and US$28 for an air-con double. It's the closest place to the bus terminal.

The *Tangkou Hotel* (☎ 562400) *(tāng kǒu bīn guǎn)* is at the bottom end of the village, 200 metres off the main road. If you intend staying in Tangkou you can ask to be dropped off here rather than at the bus terminal a few km uphill at Huangshan Gate. Doubles go for US$7 to US$21.

Hot Springs Around the hot springs resort 2.5 km farther uphill are several more hotels. Beside the hot springs bathhouse is the *Huangshan Hotel* (☎ 562320) *(huáng shān bīn guǎn)*, which has beds in basic quads for US$4 and beds in doubles for US$6. For a wash you'll have to go next door.

Just across the bridge is the *Huang Mountain Wenquan Hotel* (☎ 562788) *(huáng shān wén quán dà jiǔ diàn)*. Doubles are US$21 to US$35.

Lower Cable-Car Station The *Yungu Hotel* (☎ 562444) *(yún gǔ shān zhuāng)* is down the steps from the car park in front of the station. It has doubles for US$31.

Summit Area There are two tourist hotels within easy walking distance of the upper cable-car station. During the summer tourist season especially, it's advisable to reserve a room as these hotels are very popular with foreign and Chinese tourists alike. Most of the other places on the mountain are cheaper and don't have any showering facilities.

The *Beihai Hotel* (☎ 562555) *(bě i hǎi bīn guǎn)* has doubles from US$7 to US$34, and the *Xihai Hotel* (☎ 262132/3) *(xī hǎi bīn guǎn)*, farther west along the trail, is a real 'mountain hotel' designed by Swedish architects. Doubles start at US$100.

Western Steps Highest up is the *Tianhai Hotel (tiān hǎi bīn guǎn)*, just down from Bright Top Peak, with dorm beds from US$5 and doubles for US$10.

Farther down the mountain at a spectacular 1660-metre-high lookout near Heavenly Capital Peak is the *Jade Screen Tower Hotel* (☎ 562540) *(yù píng lóu bīn guǎn)*. A simple

CHINA

double is US$26, and washing arrangements are basic indeed. The next place you'll come to is the small *Mid-Level Temple (bàn shān sì)* at 1340 metres. It only has a small dorm, and is best considered as emergency accommodation.

Getting There & Away
Air The airport serving Huangshan is at Tunxi (Huangshan City).

Bus Buses from Tunxi (Huangshan City) take 2½ hours to reach Huangshan Gate. In summer other direct buses come from Hefei (eight hours), Shanghai (10 hours), Hangzhou, Suzhou and Jingdezhen.

Zhejiang 镇江

North of Hangzhou, Zhejiang Province is part of the lush Yangzi River delta. The land has been intensively farmed for 1000 years, and the plain has a dense network of waterways, canals and irrigation channels. To the south, the province is mountainous.

Hangzhou, Ningbo and Shaoxing have been important trading centres and ports since the 8th century AD. Today Zhejiang is one of China's most prosperous provinces.

HANGZHOU
(háng zhōu) 杭州
Hangzhou is the provincial capital and a well-known Chinese tourist resort. It's famous for its West Lake, set among hills, gardens, pavilions and temples. Being close to Shanghai, it packs out on weekends and holidays and is best avoided at such times.

Information
CITS (☎ 552888) is at 1 Shihan Lu in a charming old building near the Wanghu Hotel *(wàng hú lóu)* .
The PSB is at the junction of Dingan Lu and Huimin Lu.

Things to See
West Lake *(xī hú)*, upon which Hangzhou is built, is about three km long and wide, and split into sections by two causeways. In the middle of the lake are some islands; the largest is Solitary Hill, where you'll find the Provincial Museum, the Louwailou Restaurant and Zhongshan Park. There are a number of sightseeing cruisers plying the lake. You can also hire paddle boats.

The **Zhejiang Provincial Museum** *(zhè jiāng bó wù guǎn)* is on Solitary Hill Island *(gǔ shān)*, a short walk from the Hangzhou Shangri-La Hotel.

The **Temple of Inspired Seclusion** *(líng yǐn sì)* dates from 326 AD, but has been restored 16 times since then. Take bus No 7 to the terminus at the foot of the hills west of Hangzhou.

Facing the temple is the **Peak that Flew from Afar** *(fēi lái fēng)*. This name, so the story goes, came from an Indian monk who visited Hangzhou in the 3rd century and said that the hill looked exactly like one in India and asked when it had flown to China. The peak's sides are covered with sculptures dating from 951 AD.

Northern Peak *(běi fēng)* is behind the Temple of Inspired Seclusion and is reached by a cable car. You can get a good view across the lake to the city below.

The **Mausoleum of General Yue Fei** *(yuè fēi mù)*, commemorating a soldier hero, was ransacked during the Cultural Revolution but has been restored. It's in a compound surrounded by a large brick wall, just a few minutes' walk west of the Hangzhou Shangri-La Hotel.

Six Harmonies Pagoda *(liù hé tǎ)* is in the south-west of the city close to the railway bridge, which spans the Qiantang River. The pagoda was built in 970 AD as a lighthouse tower, and escaped demolition during the Cultural Revolution because of its sheer size.

The original Protect Chu Tower *(bǎo chù tǎ)* was erected on **Precious Stone Hill** *(bǎo shí shān)* in 938 during the Song Dynasty. It was built to ensure the safe return of Hangzhou's Prince Qian Chu from an audience with the emperor. In China there is an

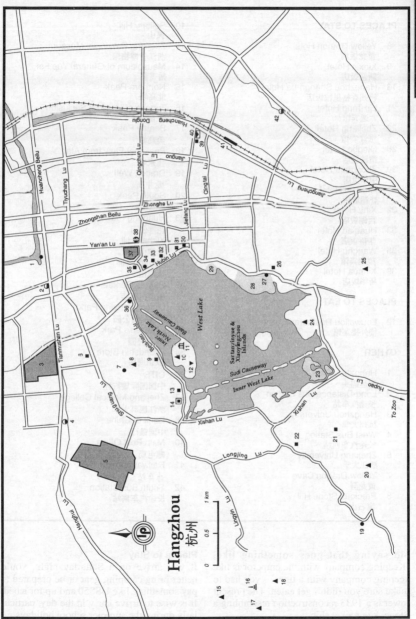

Hangzhou
杭州

West Lake
Sandanyinyue & Xuiayuezhou Islands
Inner West Lake
Sudi Causeway
Inner West Lake
Bebai Causeway
Inner West Lake

To Zoo

Huancheng Beilu
Tiyuchang
Qingchun Lu
Huancheng Donglu
Jianguo Lu
Zhonghe Lu
Zhongshan Beilu
Jiefang Lu
Qingtai Lu
Jianchong Lu
Yan'an Lu
Hubin Lu
Tianmushan Lu
Shuguang Lu
Xishan Lu
Longjing Lu
Xishan Lu
Hupao Lu
Hangtu Lu
Lingyin Lu

0   0.5   1 km

CHINA

PLACES TO STAY

6   Yellow Dragon Hotel
    黄龙饭店
9   Xinxin Hotel
    新新饭店
13 Hangzhou Shangri-La Hotel
    杭州香格里拉饭店
21 Liu Tong Hotel
    六通宾馆
22 Zhejiang Hotel
    浙江宾馆
26 Qingbo Hotel
    清波饭店
30 Zhonghua Hotel
    中华饭店
31 Huanhu Hotel
    环湖饭店
32 Xihu Hotel
    西湖饭店
33 Huaqiao Hotel
    华侨饭店
35 Wanghu Hotel
    望湖宾馆
39 Xinhua Hotel
    新华饭店

PLACES TO EAT

12 Louwailou Restaurant
    楼外楼菜馆

OTHER

1   Hangzhou Passenger Wharf
    客运码头
2   Long-Distance Bus Station
    长途汽车站
3   Hangzhou University
    杭州大学
4   West Bus Station
    长途汽车西站
5   Zhejiang University
    浙江大学
7   Yellow Dragon Cave
    黄龙洞
8   Precious Stone Hill
    宝石山
10 Solitary Hill
    孤山
11 Zhejiang Provincial Museum
    浙江省博物馆
14 Mausoleum of General Yue Fei
    岳飞墓
15 Northern Peak
    北高峰
16 Temple of Inspired Seclusion
    灵隐寺
17 Beauty Peak
    美高峰
18 Peak that Flew from Afar
    飞来峰
19 Dragon Well
    龙井
20 South Peak
    南高峰
23 Huagang Park
    花港公园
24 Xizhao Hill
    夕照山
25 Phoenix Hill
    风凰山
27 Bicycle Rentals
    租自行车店
28 Liulangwenying Park
    柳浪问莺公园
29 Children's Park
    儿童公园
34 Friendship Store
    友谊商店
36 CITS
    中国国际旅行社
37 Zhejiang Medical College
    浙江医科大学
38 Bank of China
    中国银行
40 Main Post Office
    邮电局
41 Railway Station
    火车站
42 South Bus Station
    长途汽车南站

old saying that goes something like, 'Keeping company with the emperor is like keeping company with a tiger' – you had to make sure you didn't get eaten. The present tower is a 1933 reconstruction resembling a Stone Age rocket ship.

Places to Stay

If you arrive on a Saturday night, you'd better bring camping gear or be prepared to pay something like US$50 and up for a bed. It is wise to arrive early in the day, particularly during the summer school holidays.

At the bottom of the market is the *Xihu Hotel* (☎ 761601) *(xī hú fàn diàn)*, 89 Hubin Lu. Room prices start at US$6. Despite the low cost, the hotel is just across the street from the lake.

Also right on the east side of the lake is the colonial-style *Huanhu Hotel* (☎ 765491) *(huán hú fàn diàn)*, 54 Hubin Lu. Standard double rooms go for US$15.

The *Xinhua Hotel (xīn huá fàn diàn)* on the eastern end of Jiefang Lu is next to the post office and convenient for the railway station. Rooms cost US$10, US$14 and US$24.

The *Xinxin Hotel* (☎ 777101) *(xīn xīn fàn diàn)*, 58 Beishan Lu, on the north shore of the lake looks like a good place to stay and is reasonable at US$34. However, this places seems to be almost permanently 'all full'.

Getting There & Away
Air The CAAC office (☎ 554259) is at 160 Tiyuchang Lu. Dragonair (☎ 554488 ext 2040) has a representative in the Yellow Dragon Hotel *(huáng lóng fàn diàn)* on Shuguang Lu, but booking at CITS might be more convenient. Both CAAC and Dragonair offer daily flights to/from Hong Kong. There are domestic flights to all major cities in China.

Bus The long-distance bus station is on Hushu Nanlu just north of the intersection with Huancheng Lu. Here buses leave for Shanghai, Huangshan (Tunxi), Hefei and Ningbo.

Train There are trains to Fuzhou, Nanchang, Shanghai and Guangzhou, and east to Shaoxing and Ningbo. For trains to the north you must first go to Shanghai.

Boat You can travel by boat up the Grand Canal to Suzhou. The boat leaves from the dock near the corner of Huancheng Lu and Changzheng Lu in the northern part of town. The trip takes 12 hours.

Getting Around
To/From the Airport Hangzhou's airport is 15 km from the city centre and taxi drivers want around US$8 for the trip.

Bus A very useful bus is No 7 connecting the railway station to the major hotel area on the east side of the lake. Bus No 1 connects the long-distance bus station to the east shore and bus No 28 connects it to the lake's west side. Bus No 27 is useful for getting between the east and west sides of the lake.

Taxi Metered taxis are ubiquitous, but the drivers are cut-throats. They will often take you for a complete drive around the lake when the place you want to get to is only a couple of blocks away.

Fujian 福建

The coastal region of Fujian has well-established trading ports, which for centuries enjoyed substantial contact with the outside world. The interior is lush and attractive. About 80% of Taiwanese families trace their roots to Fujian and can speak the local lingo, making this province a favourite with tourists from Taiwan. Foreigners are relatively few, but most visitors seem to enjoy the coastal city of Xiamen.

XIAMEN
(xià mén) 厦门
Formerly known as Amoy, Xiamen is an important port on China's south-east coast. European influence has been heavy and this is reflected in the interesting architecture.

Xiamen was opened to the tourist trade in 1980, and became a Special Economic Zone in 1981. Fishing boats from Taiwan do a good deal of smuggling around here, and if the trade is ever legalised Xiamen's fortunes could rise once again.

Orientation
Xiamen is on an island, connected to the

CHINA

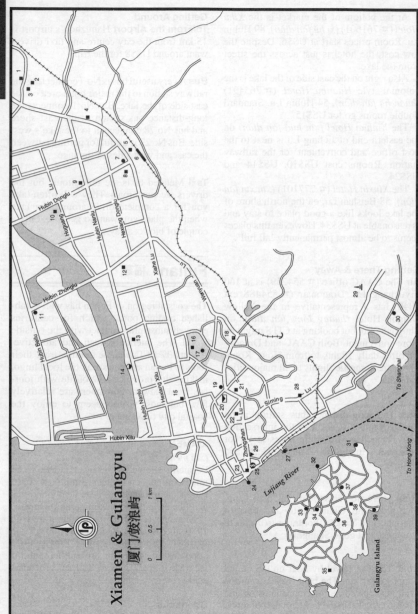

Xiamen & Gulangyu
厦门/鼓浪屿

0   0.5   1 km

PLACES TO STAY

1 Xiamen Aviation Hotel
   厦门航空宾馆
2 China Forestry Hotel
   中林宾馆
3 China North Hotel
   北方宾馆
4 Jinghua Hotel
   京华饭店
5 Xiamen Plaza Hotel
   东南亚大酒店
8 Tingzhou Hotel
   汀州大厦
9 United Fujian Hotel
   福联大饭店
10 Taiwan Hotel
   台湾酒店
12 Hubin Hotel
   湖滨饭店
13 Haixia Hotel
   海峡酒店
15 Bailan Hotel
   白兰饭店
16 Singapore Hotel
   新加坡酒店
18 Xiamen Hotel
   夏门宾馆
21 Xinqiao Hotel
   新侨酒店
22 Xiaxi Hotel
   夏西饭店
23 Lujiang & East Ocean hotels
   鹭江大厦/东海大厦酒店
28 Holiday Inn
   假日大酒店
35 Gulang Hotel
   鼓浪别墅
38 Gulangyu Binguan Hotel
   鼓浪屿宾馆

PLACES TO EAT

26 McDonald's
   麦当劳

OTHER

6 Railway Station
   厦门火车站
7 Friendship Store
   友谊商场
11 CITS
   中国国际旅行社
14 Long-Distance Bus Station
   长途汽车站
17 Zhongshan Park
   中山公园
19 PSB
   公安局外事科
20 Main Post & Telephone Office
   邮电局
24 Ferry Terminal (to Gulangyu)
   轮渡码头 (往鼓浪屿)
25 Bank of China
   中国银行
27 Heping Pier (to Hong Kong)
   和平码头 (往香港)
29 Nanputuo Temple
   南普陀寺
30 Xiamen University
   厦门大学
31 Statue of Koxinga
   郑成功塑像
32 Ferry Terminal (to Xiamen)
   轮渡码头 (往厦门)
33 Zheng Chenggong Memorial Hall
   郑成功纪念馆
34 Bank of China
   中国银行
36 Sunlight Rock
   日光岩
37 Musical Hall
   音乐厅
39 Shuzhuang Garden
   菽庄花园

mainland by a long causeway. On the mainland side of the causeway is Jimei which has a number of attractive buildings. The interesting part of Xiamen itself is the western (waterfront) district directly opposite the small island of Gulangyu. This is the old area of town, known for its quaint architecture, parks and winding streets. Gulangyu can be reached by ferry, and this remarkable island is perhaps the only place in China where *all* vehicles (motorised and pedalled) are banned.

Information
CITS (☎ 551825) is on the 15th floor of the Zhenxing Building (*zhèn xīng dà shà*), Hubin Beilu. This CITS office has its act together – the staff are knowledgeable and

CHINA

friendly, though they are geared towards group tours. You can book air tickets here.

The Bank of China is at 10 Zhongshan Lu, near the Lujiang Hotel.

Opposite the Xinqiao Hotel is a large, red-brick building; the wide footpath on the right-hand side (as you face it) leads to the PSB.

Things to See

First developed by Westerners in the 1840s, **Gulangyu Island** (gǔ làng yǔ) retains the charming old colonial buildings. A ferry to Gulangyu leaves from the pier just north of the Lujiang Hotel in Xiamen. Ferries run from about 5 am to midnight. Transport around Gulangyu is by foot; there are no buses, cars or pedicabs. It's a small island and the sights are within easy walking distance of each other.

The **Zheng Chenggong Memorial Hall** (zhèng chéng gōng jì niàn guǎn) on Gulangyu is dedicated to the memory of Zheng Chenggong, known in the West as Koxinga. A general allied to the Ming Dynasty, he used Xiamen as a base from which to fight the invading Manchus. His efforts came to naught and he had to flee to Taiwan with his troops in 1661. While in Taiwan, he took the opportunity to expel the Dutch colonists, thus making himself into a national hero. Zheng Chenggong died just one year later and Manchu armies captured Taiwan in 1682. The museum is open daily from 8 to 11 am and 2 to 5 pm.

Nanputuo Temple (nán pǔ tuó sì), on the southern outskirts of Xiamen, is a Buddhist temple originally built during the Tang Dynasty more than 1000 years ago. Take bus No 1 from the stop outside the Xinqiao Hotel, or bus No 2 from the intersection of Zhongshan Lu and Lujiang Lu. Both stop outside the temple.

Xiamen University (xià mén dà xué) is next to the temple. It was established with overseas Chinese funds, and some of the old buildings have charm. The Museum of Anthropology is on the campus – it houses a large collection of prehistoric stones, pottery, clothing, sculpture and paintings from the Shang through to the Qing Dynasty.

Jimei School Village (jí měi xué xiào cūn) is a much-touted tourist attraction on the mainland north of Xiamen Island. The school is a conglomeration of separate schools and colleges set up by Tan Kahkee (1874-1961). Tan was a native of the area who migrated to Singapore and became a rich industrialist. He set a fine example for other overseas Chinese by returning some of that wealth to his homeland. The school now has around 20,000 students, and the Chinese-style architecture has a certain appeal which makes a visit worthwhile.

Places to Stay

The Xiaxi Hotel (xià xī fàn diàn), next to Xiaxi Market off Zhongshan Lu, is the cheapest place in the charming western part of town. Doubles cost US$10. To get there from the railway station take a minibus.

The bottom end of the market belongs to the Hubin Hotel (☎ 225202; fax 229964) (hú bīn fàn diàn), where very basic singles are US$5 and more salubrious accommodation costs US$10 and US$11. The hotel's location on Huzhong Lu is not the best but it's acceptable.

The Taiwan Hotel (☎ 553808) (tái wān jiǔ diàn) on Hubin Donglu has very reasonably priced doubles for US$14. The Haixia Hotel (hǎi xiá jiǔ bīn), near the long-distance bus station, has doubles for US$14 and US$16.

A really excellent place to stay is the Xiamen Hotel (☎ 222265; fax 221765) (xià mén bīn guǎn), 16 Huyuan Lu. The location can't be beat – the hotel is built in a park. There is also a swimming pool and disco. All this luxury costs US$19/28 for singles/doubles.

The Lujiang Hotel (☎ 223235) (lù jiāng dà shà) at 3 Haihou Lu, is opposite the Gulangyu ferry pier. Singles/doubles cost US$23/28. Bus No 3 from the railway station and minibuses terminate at the Gulangyu ferry pier just outside the hotel.

The Bailan Hotel (bái lán fàn diàn) is a small but very clean place on Gugong Lu. Rooms start at US$20.

Xinqiao Hotel (☎ 238388; fax 238765) *(xīn qiáo jiǔ diàn)* is an old but classy place at 444 Zhongshan Lu. Singles range from US$28 to US$38 and doubles from US$40.

There are two tourist hotels on Gulangyu Island, neither of which does very good business because of the inconvenience of carrying luggage where there are no vehicles. Most convenient (closest to the ferry) is the *Gulangyu Binguan* (☎ 231856) *(gǔ làng yǔ bīn guǎn)*, 25 Huangyan Lu, which has doubles for US$24. On the west side of the island is the *Gulang Hotel (gǔ làng bié shù)* which is more expensive but often empty.

Places to Eat

Xiamen is 'seafood city', with many seafood restaurants along Zhongshan Lu and its side streets. It's hardly worth recommending any one place in particular; all look good.

Xiamen holds the distinction of being the third city in China to acquire a *McDonalds* (after Shenzhen and Beijing).

Getting There & Away

Air Xiamen Airlines is what CAAC calls itself in this part of China. CITS books air tickets, as do some major hotels. The CAAC office (☎ 225942) is at 230 Hubin Nanlu.

Xiamen is well connected to major cities in China. CAAC offers international flights to Hong Kong, Jakarta, Manila, Penang and Singapore. You can also fly between Xiamen and Manila with Philippine Airlines (☎ 225456), 4th floor, Flat J, Seaside Building, Lujiang Dao. On the same floor in Flat F you'll find Dragonair (☎ 225433), which offers Xiamen to Hong Kong flights.

Bus Buses to the towns on the south-east coast depart from the long-distance bus station. Destinations include Fuzhou, Quanzhou and Shantou. You can also get buses straight through to Guangzhou and Shenzhen.

Train The railway line from Xiamen heads north and connects the city with the main Shanghai-Guangzhou line at Yingtan junc-

tion. There are also direct lines to Zhengzhou, Yingtan, Shanghai and Fuzhou.

Boat Ships to Hong Kong leave from the Passenger Station of Amoy Port Administration on Tongwen Lu, about a 10-minute walk from the Lujiang Hotel.

Getting Around

To/From the Airport The airport is 15 km east of the waterfront district, or about eight km from the Eastern District. Taxis charge around US$6.

Bus & Minibus Frequent minibuses run between the railway station and Lujiang Hotel. Bus No 3 runs from the railway station and the long-distance bus station to the Lujiang Hotel, but it's packed to the rooftop and beyond. Walking around the western part of town is enjoyable, and on Gulangyu no motor vehicles are allowed.

Jiangxi 江西

Jiangxi was sparsely populated until the 8th century AD, when the Grand Canal opened it up as a trade route from Guangdong. It declined in the 19th century, with the opening of coastal ports to foreign shipping. The province was one of the most famous Communist guerrilla bases; the Kuomintang took several years to drive them out onto the Long March to Shaanxi.

LUSHAN

(lú shān) 庐山

Every now and then, China throws up something that takes you completely by surprise. One such place would have to be Lushan, a Swiss-style village grafted onto the side of a Chinese mountain. Lushan, in the very north of Jiangxi Province, is regarded as one of the most beautiful mountains in China. The hill resort here was established by Europeans in the 19th century and features European-style hotels, churches and stone cottages.

CHINA

Although perhaps a symbol of China's ruthless exploitation by foreign powers, the country's post-1949 revolutionaries favoured these cool uplands as a site for Party conferences.

The bus ride from the plains of Jiangxi to the top of Lushan is dramatic – and slightly nerve-racking – as the road winds its way around the mountainsides, looking down on sheer cliffs. Over the long drop below you can see vast expanses of patchwork fields.

Orientation & Information

The point of arrival in Lushan is the charming resort village of Guling (gǔ lǐng), perched 1167 metres high at the northern end of the range. Two km before Guling is the entrance gate, where you must pay an entry fee (US$2 for foreigners). Guling village is where the shops, post office, bank and the long-distance bus station are located. Nestled into the surrounding hills are scores of tourist hotels, sanatoriums and factory work units' holiday hostels.

The CITS office, uphill from the Lushan Hotel, is quite well organised and helpful.

Things to See

Built by Chiang Kaishek in the 1930s as a summer getaway, **Meilu Villa** (měi lú bié shù) was named after the general's wife.

The **Peoples' Hall** (rén mín jù yuàn), built in 1936 and the venue for the Chinese Communist Party's historic 1959 and 1970 get-togethers, has been turned into a museum.

At Lushan's north-western rim, the land falls away abruptly to give some spectacular views across the densely settled plains of Jiangxi. A long walking track south around these precipitous slopes passes the **Fairy Cave** (xiān rén dòng) and continues to the **Dragon Head Cliff** (lóng shǒuyá).

A place of interest to Chinese visitors is the **Three Ancient Trees** (sān bǎo shù) not far by foot from Lulin Lake, which were planted by Buddhist monks 500 years ago.

The **Lushan Museum** (lú shān bó wù guǎn) beside Lulin Lake commemorates the historic 1970 meeting with a photo collection and Mao's huge bed.

The **Botanical Gardens** (zhí wù yuán) are mainly devoted to sub-alpine tropical plants that thrive in the cooler highland climate.

Places to Stay

The Guling Hotel (gǔ lǐng fàn diàn) is the cheapest place for foreigners. It's right in Guling village around the corner from the bus terminal. Beds are US$2 in dorms or US$3 in very basic doubles, and US$35 in deluxe doubles.

Just uphill from the original Meilu Villa is Meilu Villa Hotel (měi lú bié shù), with a number of cottages scattered throughout lovely old pine forest. Doubles start at US$17.

The Lushan Hotel (☎ 282932) (lú shān bīn guǎn) is a large old colonial-era hotel now managed as a joint venture. Singles/doubles start at US$11/35. It's a 20-minute downhill walk from the bus station.

The Yunzhong Guest House (☎ 282547) (yún zhōng bīn guǎn) is on the wooded slopes above Guling. Doubles with bath start at US$17. The Yunzhong is most easily reached via the road past the Lushan Hotel. It's a tiring uphill trudge.

Next door to the People's Hall is Lushan Mansion (☎ (0792) 282860) (lú shān dà shà). The hotel is on the open sunny side of the valley and is a good base for walks into the surrounding hills. The cheapest rooms here are US$26 a double. It's 10 minutes' walk downhill from where the local bus drops you off.

Situated on the slopes overlooking Lulin Lake is the Lulin Hotel (☎ 282424) (lú lín fàn diàn). Doubles/triples cost US$30/36. The setting is very peaceful, but several km from Guling. The local public bus passes the hotel turn-off, from where it's a one-km walk.

Getting There & Away

In summer there are daily buses to Nanchang (US$5) and Jiujiang (US$1), but from November to late March direct buses to Nanchang from here are sporadic. During the tourist season numbers can be very high, so try to arrive early in the day to get a room.

Getting Around
In season you can pick up a half-day tour in Lushan for around US$2 at the bus station, the Lushan Hotel or through CITS. From Jiujiang, return day trips cost US$4 and give you about five hours in Lushan, one hotel in Jiujiang that has regular tours is the Bailu Hotel. Tours normally include several of the pavilions, a nature hike and the museum. Even if you don't know any Chinese, it's a good way to take in most of the sights without having to arrange step-by-step transport.

Hubei 湖北

Eastern Hubei is a low plain drained by the Yangzi. To the west are mountains with small cultivated valleys, which divide Hubei from Sichuan. The province was settled by the Han Chinese 3000 years ago. In the 19th century it was the first inland province to industrialise. Economically, it's still one of China's most important provinces. For travellers, it's mainly an important crossroads to get somewhere else.

WUHAN
(wǔ hàn) 武汉
Wuhan is one of the largest cities in China. It's actually a conglomeration of what were once three independent cities: Hankou, Hanyang and Wuchang. The terminus for Yangzi ferries from Chongqing, it's *the* major transit point in this province.

Orientation
Wuhan is divided by the Yangzi River: Wuchang lies on the eastern bank, Hankou is the centre of things, while Hanyang is on the western bank, south of Hankou. The main road is Zhongshan Dadao, parallel to the Yangzi River.

Information
CITS (☎ 238340) is in Hankou at No 48 Jianghan Yilu (opposite the Xuan Gong Hotel).

The main branch of the Bank of China is in Hankou on the corner of Zhongshan Dadao and Jianghan Lu. Tourist hotels, such as the Qingchuan and Jianghan, also have money-changing services.

The main post office is on Zhongshan Dadao near the Bank of China.

The PSB is at 206 Shengli Lu, a 10-minute walk north-east of the Jianghan Hotel.

Things to See
Since Hankou was a foreign concession area, there are quite a few European-style buildings, particularly along Yanjiang Dadao.

Guiyuan Temple *(guī yuǎn sì)* is across the river in Hanyang. This Buddhist temple dates from the late Ming Dynasty, and is slowly being restored. The chief attraction is the main hall, featuring numerous seated statues of Buddha's disciples (often in comical poses).

Wuhan's **Yangzi Bridge** *(wǔ hàn cháng jiāng dà qiáo)* is over 1100 metres long and 80 metres high. The completion of the bridge in 1957 marked one of Communist China's first great engineering achievements, because until then all road and rail traffic had been laboriously ferried across the river. East of the bridge in Wuchang is **Hongshan** (Red Hill), noted for its nine-storey, 1000-year-old Buddhist pagoda.

Hubei Provincial Museum *(hú běi shěng bó wù guǎn)* is a must if you're interested in archaeology. The museum is beside Donghu (East Lake) in Wuchang. Take bus No 14 from the Wuchang ferry (the dock closest to the bridge) to the terminal.

In summer you can do a scenic day trip that includes the museum, taking a ferry over from Hankou to Wuchang, then boarding bus No 36 to Moshan Hill. Take another ferry across the lake to East Lake Park, walk to the museum, then get bus No 14 to Yellow Crane Tower, and finally a ferry back to Hankou.

Places to Stay
To your right as you exit Hankou railway

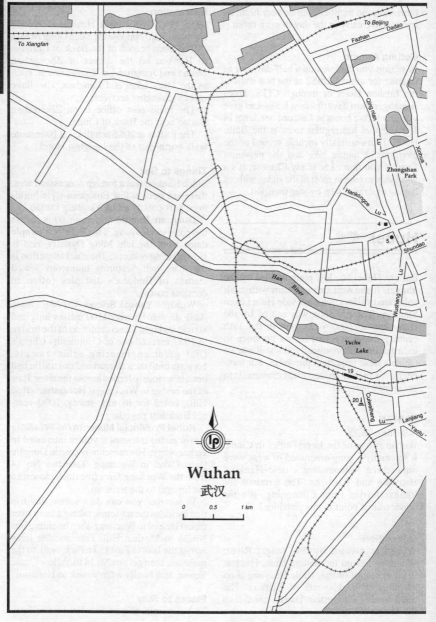

Wuhan
武汉

0   0.5   1 km

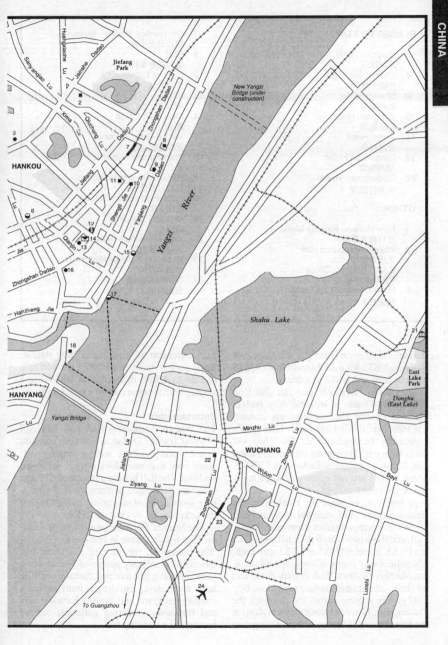

CHINA

PLACES TO STAY

2 Huaqiao Hotel
花桥饭店
4 Changjiang Hotel
长江大酒店
8 Shengli Hotel
胜利饭店
10 Jianghan Hotel
江汉饭店
11 Aiguo Hotel
爱国饭店
18 Qingchuan Hotel
晴川宾馆
22 Dadongmen Hotel
大东门饭店

OTHER

1 New Hankou Railway Station
汉口新火车站
3 Wuhan Acrobatics Hall
武汉杂技厅
5 CAAC Booking Office
中国民航售票处
6 Long-Distance Bus Station
长途汽车站
7 Old Hankou Railway Station
汉口旧火车站
9 PSB
公安局外事科
12 Bank of China
中国银行
13 CITS
中国国际旅行社
14 Main Post Office
邮局
15 Yangzi Ferry Terminal
武汉港客运站
16 The Masses' Paradise
民众乐园
17 Hankou-Wuchang Ferries
汉口武昌渡船
19 Hanyang Railway Station
汉阳火车站
20 Guiyuan Temple
归园寺
21 Hubei Provincial Museum
湖北省博物馆
23 Wuchang Railway Station
武昌火车站
24 Nanhu Airport
南湖机场

station is the *Jinyan Hotel (jīn yàn fàn diàn)*. Beds are US$5 for a double with bath, US$3 without bath and US$2 in a dorm.

The *Aiguo Hotel (ài guó fàn diàn)* on Zhongshan Dadao is still the only budget place in central Hankou that lets in non-Chinese, but this filthy, damp hole is not especially recommended. The cheapest dorm beds with communal shower and toilet cost US$4, and singles/doubles are US$5/7. Some rooms are not quite so disgusting – check yours beforehand.

A much nicer place in Hankou is the *Huaqiao Hotel (huá qiáo fàn diàn)* on Huiji Lu. It's in a narrow market street near Jiefang Park and there is no English sign. Dorm beds are US$3, doubles US$5 or US$7 with bath. It's quite a way north of the centre of town, but bus Nos 68 (from Wuhan ferry dock) and 24 (from Zhongshan Dadao) pass close by.

If you're staying across the river, try the *Dadongmen Hotel (dà dōng mén fàn diàn)* at the intersection of Wuluo Lu and Zhongshan

Lu, convenient to Wuchang railway station. Basic rooms range from US$3 per bed in a double to US$2 in quads, or US$4 for a single. Traffic noise can be a problem here.

Entertainment

The Wuhan Acrobatics Hall *(wǔ hàn zájì tíng)* on Jianshe Dadao in northern Hankou is a circular building with a striking red-dome roof that resembles a small enclosed stadium. The hall houses a troupe of Chinese acrobats. Scheduled performances are irregular, so make local enquiries at your hotel or the ticket office, or contact CITS.

The Masses' Paradise *(mín zhòng lè yuán)* on Zhongshan Dadao in Hankou is a kind of 'fun palace' in the best of sideshow traditions. The ordinary people of Wuhan often come here at night to enjoy themselves. The large three-storey building is built around a central courtyard and houses karaoke bars and teahouses, shooting galleries, billiard rooms and a dancing hall.

Getting There & Away

Air CAAC (☎ 357949) has its main ticket office in Hankou at 217 Liji Beilu. It offers air connections to virtually all major cities in China

Train Wuhan is on the main Beijing to Guangzhou railway line.

Boat Ferries travel the Yangzi from Wuhan to Shanghai via Nanjing, a trip which takes 48 hours in all. Tickets can be bought in Wuhan at the CITS office, the booking office at the river port or the tourist hotel service desks.

The first major town in Jiangxi is Jiujiang, the departure point for nearby Lushan. The first large city in Jiangsu Province is Nanjing, followed by Zhenjiang and the port of Nantong. The ferry proceeds down the Yangzi to Shanghai.

Hunan 湖南

Hunan Province – birthplace of Mao Zedong – lies on some of the richest agricultural land in China; under the Ming and Qing dynasties it was one of the empire's granaries. By the 19th century, however, it was suffering from land shortage and landlordism, and the increasingly desperate economic situation led to the massive Taiping Rebellion of the 1850s and 1860s. The Communists took refuge on the mountainous Hunan-Jiangxi border in 1927.

CHANGSHA
(cháng shā) 长沙

Changsha is the capital of Hunan Province and is an important transit point for travellers. Historically, the city is of some interest. It was here that Mao studied at the Teachers' Training College and set up the 'New People's Study Society' with a group of 70 or 80 students. It was in Changsha in 1927 that Mao organised the 'Autumn Harvest Uprising' with troops drawn from

the peasantry, the Hengyang miners and rebel Kuomintang soldiers.

Orientation
Most of Changsha lies on the eastern bank of the Xiang River. The railway station is at the far east of the city.

Information
CITS (☎ 439757) is on the 4th floor of the building behind the Lotus Hotel. The Xiangjiang Hotel can assist with transport bookings as well.

The Bank of China is next to the CAAC office on Wuyi Donglu. You can also change money at the Xiangjiang Hotel and the Lotus Hotel.

The PSB is in a big cream-tiled building on Huangxing Lu, over on the western end of town just south of Jiefang Lu.

Things to See
Apart from lots of Mao-bilia, it is worth seeing the mummified remains of a Han Dynasty woman in the **Hunan Provincial Museum** *(hú nán bó wù guǎn)*. She was excavated from a tomb 2100 years old.

Maoist pilgrimage spots are scattered around the city and include the **Hunan No 1 Teachers' Training College** *(dì yī shī fàn xué xiào)*. You can get to it on bus No 1 from the Xiangjiang Guest House. There is also the **Museum of the Former Office of the Hunan Communist Party Committee** *(zhōng guó gòng chǎn dǎng zǎo qī huó dòng de dì fang)*. Most of these places feature photographs and historical items from the 1920s.

Places to Stay
There's plenty of good, cheap accommodation for locals, but staff are quite determined in excluding non-Chinese from their registers. One Chinese hotel that will probably accept you (if you beg) is the *Binhua Hotel (bīn huá bīn guǎn)* on Bayi Lu. Beds go for US$3 to US$7.

The *Lotus Hotel (fú róng bīn guǎn)* (☎ 401888), is a high-rise favoured by foreigners because of its central location.

Bottom-range singles cost US$20 and doubles are from US$21 to US$39.

The *Xiangjiang Hotel* (☎ 408888) *(xiāng jiāng bīn guǎn)* is at 2 Zhongshan Donglu. The cheapest standard doubles are US$48. To get there, take bus No 1 from the railway station and get off at the fourth stop, which is just outside the hotel.

Getting There & Away
Air The main CAAC office (☎ 23820) is at 5 Wuyi Donglu, around the corner from the railway station. The Lotus Hotel also has a CAAC booking office.

Bus The long-distance bus station is conveniently located near the railway station.

Train Important routes via Changsha are Beijing-Kunming-Guilin, Guangzhou-Xian-Lanzhou and Shanghai-Changsha. Not all trains to Shanghai, Kunming and Guilin stop in Changsha, so it may be necessary to go to Zhuzhou first and change there. There is also a train daily to Shaoshan (US$1), leaving at 7 am. Counter No 6 at the Changsha railway station is for foreigners.

SHAOSHAN
(sháo shān) 韶山
This obscure village would hardly be worth a footnote were it not for the fact that Mao Zedong was born here in 1893. He was the son of poor peasants who made their way in the world to become rich peasants. Mao went to school and worked on his father's farm here. He also witnessed peasant resentment – sometimes directed against his father.

Things to See
Although Shaoshan is a national shrine, a trip here is really an excuse to see some of the Chinese countryside. Shaoshan is set in a pretty valley amidst sleepy little villages. The principal shrine is **Mao's Childhood House** *(máo zé dōng tóng zhì gù jū)*.

More information about the life of Mao can be found in the **Museum of Comrade Mao** *(máo zé dōng tóng zhì jì niàn guǎn)*,

which features graphic exhibits but no English explanations.

Places to Stay & Eat
The centrally located *Shaoshan Guest House (sháo shān bīn guǎn)* (☎ 682127) has doubles for US$14 or US$7 per bed. Up the road is the cheaper *Hongri Hotel (hóng rì fàn diàn)*, with no-frills accommodation for US$1 per bed in small dorms.

Back in the new town many good cheap places can be found close to the bus station. The *Entertainment City Hotel (yù lè chéng dà jiǔ diàn)*, on the corner opposite the park, offers doubles for US$5 and beds for US$2.

Getting There & Away
Bus Between Changsha and Shaoshan there are two morning buses and one afternoon bus in either direction daily.

Train There is one train daily from Changsha. The train leaves at 7 am and departs from Shaoshan station at 3.40 pm, so you can easily do Shaoshan as a day trip.

Guangdong 广东

Guangdong is the wealthiest and most progressive province in China. The main force behind this development is neighbouring Hong Kong from which flows investment, tourism, capitalist ideas and various other 'corrupting' influences.

SHENZHEN
(shēn zhèn) 深圳
Just north of Hong Kong is China's most important Special Economic Zone (SEZ). The SEZs were set up with reduced taxation schemes, low wages and (supposedly) minimal interference from the government to encourage investment. The Shenzhen SEZ was little more than farmland when it was established in 1979. It is now China's fastest growing city.

Shenzhen resembles Hong Kong in a

number of ways, including high-rise buildings and high prices. Shenzhen's airport can be useful for getting to various destinations in China, but few foreigners spend much time in the city itself. However, Shenzhen is worth a look – if only a brief one – to see what China's drive for modernisation is all about. A visit to Shenzhen can easily be done as a day trip from Hong Kong.

Information
CITS is at 2 Chuanbu Jie, just west of Heping Lu.

The GPO is at the north end of Jianshe Lu and is often packed out – a great place to practice sumo wrestling.

The PSB (☎ 5572114) is on the west end of Jiefang Lu, north side of the street.

Things to See
The tourist brochure for **Splendid China** (jǐn xiù zhōng huá) says 'visit all of China in one day'. The whole concept was cloned from Taiwan's 'Window on China', which was built to give the Taiwanese a chance to see the mainland without actually going there. You get to see Beijing's Forbidden City, the Great Wall, Tibet's Potala Palace and so on – the catch is that everything is reduced to one-fifteenth of life size. Many travellers denounce it as a 'bad Disneyland without the rides' but the Chinese are crazy about the place.

Just next door is the **China Folk Culture Villages** (zhōng guó mín sú wén huà cūn). This place seeks to accomplish the same thing as Splendid China – give you a chance to see all of China in one day. In this case, rather than admiring miniaturised temples and palaces, you get to see full-sized ethnic minorities. To add to the effect, there are over 20 re-creations of minority villages.

Both of the preceding attractions are in the western end of the SEZ, near Shenzhen Bay. From the railway station there are frequent minibuses.

Places to Stay
Shenzhen's hotels are not cheap. One of the cheapest is the *Yat Wah Hotel* (rì huá bīn

guǎn) on the north-west corner of Shennan Lu and Heping Lu, just to the west of the railroad tracks. Rooms start at US$33.

The *Jinghu Hotel* (jīng hú dà jiǔ diàn) has no English sign but is easy to find and centrally located on Renmin Nanlu just south of Cunfeng Lu. Singles/doubles are US$21/40 but the single rooms seem to be permanently 'all full'.

Relatively good value is offered by the *Oriental Hotel* (☎ 2234118) (dōng fāng jiǔ diàn) at 136 Shennan Donglu. Singles/doubles cost US$29/38.

Also recommended is the *Heping Hotel* (☎ 2252111) (hé píng jiǔ diàn), 63 Chuanbu Jie, near CITS. Comfortable doubles start at US$34.

The *Shenzhen Hotel* (☎ 2238000; fax 2222284) (shēn zhèn jiǔ diàn) at 156 Shennan Donglu has doubles for US$38 and US$43.

The *Overseas Chinese Hotel* (☎ 5573811) (huáqiáo dà shà) costs US$41 for a double. Its one real advantage is the location on Heping Lu, very close to the railway station.

For a convenient location, you can hardly beat the *Dragon Inn* (☎ 2229228) (gǎng lóng dà jiǔ diàn) which is on the ground floor of the railway station. Doubles are US$44 to US$51.

Getting There & Away
Shenzhen is just across the border from Hong Kong. The border closes at 11 pm and reopens at 7 am. There can be long waits in the immigration queues during weekends and holidays. Rush hours can also be problematic – quite a few people commute across this border in both directions.

Air Shenzhen's Huangtian Airport is north-west of town and is one of China's busiest.

Bus Outside Shenzhen railway station you can get minibuses to Guangzhou. There are also buses to towns on the south-east coast including Shantou and Xiamen.

Train There are about a dozen local trains a

day between Guangzhou and Shenzhen. Go upstairs to the 2nd floor to buy a ticket.

At Shenzhen you pass through customs and catch the train to Kowloon. The border closes at 10 pm (11 pm daylight savings time).

There are *no* money changing facilities on the Hong Kong side. If you are entering Hong Kong this way, change some money on the Shenzhen side. You need at least HK$37 to get into Kowloon by train from the border area.

Boat There are hoverferries between the port of Shekou (in western Shenzhen) and Hong Kong. Departures are from two places in Hong Kong: China Hong Kong City on Canton Rd in Tsimshatsui, Kowloon, and also from the Macau Ferry Pier on Hong Kong Island.

There are high-speed ferries between Shenzhen and the Zhuhai SEZ north of Macau.

Getting Around
To/From the Airport There are shuttle buses between the airport and the Airlines Hotel (*háng kōng dà jiǔ diàn*) at 130 Shennan Donglu.

If you want to travel directly between the airport and Hong Kong, there is now a rapid boat service (jet-powered catamaran) that takes 60 minutes to complete the journey, at least twice as fast as the bus. The sole ticketing agent in Hong Kong is the branch office of CTS (☎ 7361863) in Kowloon's China-Hong Kong City Ferry Terminal on Canton Rd. In Shenzhen, you can purchase tickets right at the airport.

ZHUHAI
(*zhū hǎi*) 珠海
Zhuhai is a SEZ just across the border from Macau. Not long ago, it was a picturesque rural area with attractive beaches. Unfortunately, Zhuhai's charms are fast being paved over in the mad rush towards industrialisation.

Zhuhai is a possible entry and exit point for China – you simply cross the border by

foot. Visas for China are available from CTS in Macau. There are high-speed boats between Zhuhai and Shenzhen as well as Zhuhai and Hong Kong. Minibuses between Zhuhai and Guangzhou are frequent.

GUANGZHOU
(*guǎng zhōu*) 广州
Formerly known as Canton (and sometimes still called that), Guangzhou occupies a key position on the Pearl River Delta, 120 km north-west of Hong Kong.

Guangzhou has been one of the main gateways to China for over 1000 years. It was here that the British set up trading relations with China in the late 18th century. The European influence can still be seen in some of the city's old buildings.

Today, Guangzhou's population stands at over five million and it's one of the most prosperous cities in China. Unfortunately, it's also one of the most congested, with horrendous traffic and pollution. There are some serious social problems too, such as the large number of vagrants who drift into the city from the poverty-stricken countryside in hopes of finding work. Many wind up living on the streets, and the desperately poor turn to begging, prostitution and theft.

Despite all this, Guangzhou does have a few worthwhile sights. It's also an important transit point and many travellers pass through. However, few foreigners care to linger here.

Orientation
Guangzhou owes its existence to the Pearl River, a major transport artery which flows through the city. Everything of interest to travellers is on the north bank, except for the Zhoutouzui ferry wharf.

Information
There is an enormous CITS office (☎ 6677151) at 179 Huanshi Lu next to the main railway station, but they have little information. It's one big ticket office and the only thing the overworked clerks are likely to say to you is 'next please'. You can buy

tickets here for trains, planes hovercraft and ships.

Adjacent to the main railway station is the GPO, locally known as the Liuhua Post Office (☎ 6662735) (liú huā yóu jú). You can collect poste restante letters here.

There are several useful consulates in Guangzhou, including:

Japan
    Garden Hotel Tower, 368 Huanshi Donglu (☎ 3338999)
Poland
    Shamian Island near the White Swan Hotel
Thailand
    Rooms 309-310 and 303-316, White Swan Hotel, Shamian Island (☎ 8886968)
USA
    1 Shamian Nanjie, Shamian Island (☎ 8882222)

If you get sick you can go to one of the hospitals or to the medical clinic for foreigners – Guangzhou No 1 People's Hospital (☎ 3333090) (dì yī rén mín yī yuàn), 602 Renmin Beilu.

The PSB (☎ 3331060) is at 863 Jiefang Beilu, opposite the road which leads up to the Zhenhai Tower.

Things to See

The **Sun Yatsen Memorial Hall** (sūn zhōng shān jì niàn táng) on Dongfeng Lu was built in honour of Sun Yatsen, with donations from locals and overseas Chinese.

There are a number of interesting temples in Guangzhou. The **Temple of the Six Banyan Trees** (liù róng sì huā tǎ) is the most significant. It was rebuilt at the end of the 10th century after being destroyed by fire. Within the temple compound is the octagonal-shaped Flower Pagoda built in the 6th century, the oldest and tallest pagoda in the city.

The **Bright Filial Piety Temple** (guāng xiào sì) is near the Temple of the Six Banyan Trees, and was founded in the 4th century AD. The present buildings of **Five Genies Temple** (wǔ xiān guān) are comparatively recent. The temple is at the back of a lane off Xianyang Lu.

Qingping Market (qīng píng shì chǎng),

near the north side of Shamian Island with an entrance from Liu'ersan Lu, is one of the most unusual sights in Guangzhou. As you wander farther in, the market starts to resemble a take-away zoo featuring such delicacies as owls, pigeons, pangolins, dogs, rats, monkeys and raccoons.

Yuexiu Park (yuè xiù gōng yuán) is the biggest park in Guangzhou. It contains the Zhenhai Tower which is the only part of the city wall that remains. The tower, which provides good views, also houses the City Museum. South of the tower is Sun Yatsen's Monument, which is also good for views.

The **Southern Yue Tomb Museum** (nán yuè wáng mù) is built on the site of the palace of the second ruler of the Nanyue Kingdom dating back to 100 BC. The Nanyue Kingdom is what the area around Guangzhou was called back in the Han Dynasty. It's on Jiefang Beilu south of the China Hotel.

The **Chen Clan Academy** (chén shì shū yuàn or chén jiā cí) is an academy of classical learning housed in a large compound built between 1890 and 1894. The compound encloses 19 traditional-style buildings along with numerous courtyards, stone carvings and sculptures.

In the north-eastern suburbs of Guangzhou are the **White Cloud Hills** (běi yún shān). This is where you'll get the best views of the seething metropolis below. The highest peak in the White Cloud Hills is Star Touching Hill (mō xīng líng) at 382 metres. Express buses leave from Guangwei Lu for the White Cloud Hills every 15 minutes. The bus trip takes about an hour (most of that fighting Guangzhou's traffic).

Lotus Mountain (lián huā shān) is an old quarry site 46 km south-east of Guangzhou. The stone cutting ceased several hundred years ago and the cliffs have eroded to the point where they look almost natural. They have been dressed up with pagodas and pavilions – most travellers find it a pleasant excursion. You can get to Lotus Mountain by either bus or boat, but the boat is more interesting. The once-daily boat leaves Guangzhou around 8 am and takes about 2½ hours to reach Lotus Mountain, depart-

CHINA

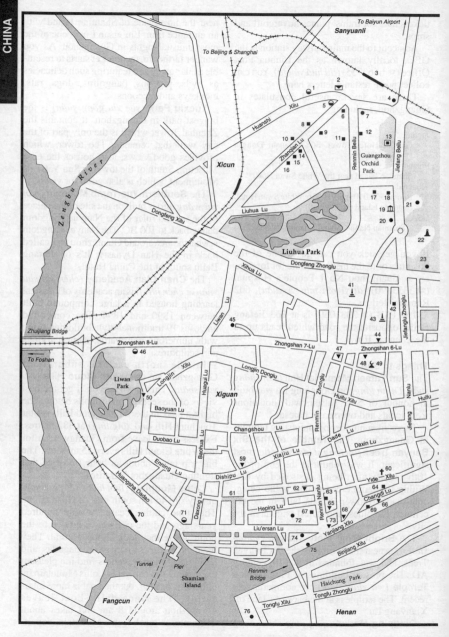

To Baiyun Airport
Sanyuanli

To Beijing & Shanghai

Huanshi

Xilu

Xicun

Zhangjian Lu

Zengbu River

Liuhua Lu

Dongfeng Xilu

Renmin Beilu

Jiefang Beilu

Guangzhou
Orchid Park

Liuhua Park

Dongfeng Zhonglu

Xihua Lu

Liwan Lu

Jiefanglu Zhonglu

Zhuijiang Bridge

Zhongshan 8-Lu

To Foshan

Zhongshan 7-Lu

Zhongshan 6-Lu

**Liwan
Park**

Longjin Xilu

Longjin Donglu

Xiguan

Huagui Lu

Renmin Zhonglu

Huifu Xilu

Naniu

Jiefang

Huifu

Baoyuan Lu

Changshou   Lu

Dade   Lu

Duobao Lu

Baohua Lu

Daxin Lu

Enning   Lu

Xiajiu Lu

Yide   Xilu

Changdi Lu

Dishipu   Lu

Heping Lu

Renmin Nanlu

Yanjiang Xilu

Huangsha Dadao

Daxong Lu

Liu'ersan Lu

Tunnel   Pier

**Shamian
Island**

Renmin
Bridge

Binjiang Xilu

Haichung   Park

Tongfu Xilu

Tongfu Zhonglu

Fangcun

Henan

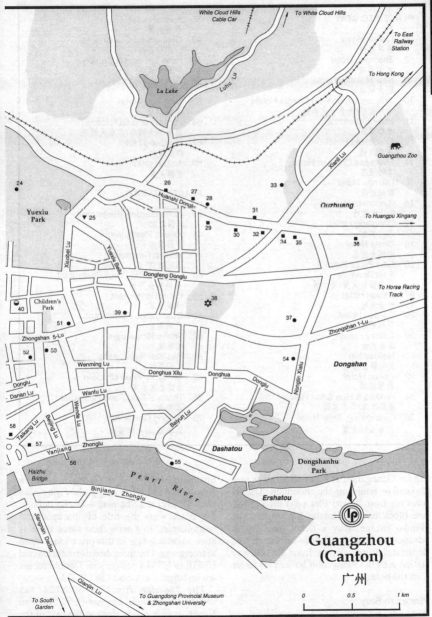

White Cloud Hills
Cable Car

To White Cloud Hills

To East
Railway
Station

To Hong Kong

Lu Lake

Luhu Lu

Guangzhou Zoo

Xianli Lu

24

26

27

28

33

Huanshi Donglu

Ouzhuang

Yuexiu
Park

25

31

To Huangpu Xingang

29

30

32

Xiaobei Lu

Yuexiu Beilu

34

35

36

Dongfeng Donglu

To Horse Racing
Track

38

37

40

Children's
Park

39

Zhongshan 1-Lu

51

Zhongshan 5-Lu

Dongshan

52

53

54

Wenming Lu

Donghua Xilu

Donghua

Dongiu

Donglu

Wanfu Lu

Danan Lu

Baiyun Lu

Nonglin Xialu

Dongiu

Wende Lu

Beijing Lu

Zhonglu

58

Taikang Lu

Yanjiang

Dashatou

Dongshanhu
Park

57

55

56

Haizhu
Bridge

Pearl River

Binjiang Zhonglu

Jiangnan Dadao

Ershatou

Guangzhou
(Canton)

广州

Qianjin Lu

To South
Garden

To Guangdong Provincial Museum
& Zhongshan University

0   0.5   1 km

CHINA

PLACES TO STAY

6　Liuhua Hotel
　　流花宾馆
8　Zhanqian Hotel
　　站前酒店
9　New Mainland Hotel
　　新大地宾馆
10　Jinhuan & Maoming Shihua Hotels
　　金环酒店/茂名石化宾馆
11　Hotel Equatorial
　　贵都酒店
12　Friendship Hotel
　　友谊宾馆
14　Overseas Chinese Hotel
　　华侨酒店
15　Leizhou Hotel
　　雷州酒店
16　Sinochem Hotel
　　中化大酒店
17　Dongfang Hotel
　　东方宾馆
18　China Hotel
　　中国大酒店
26　Gitic Plaza Hotel
　　& McDonald's
　　广东国际大厦/麦当劳
27　Baiyun Hotel
　　白云宾馆
29　Garden Hotel
　　花园酒店
30　Cathay Hotel
　　国泰宾馆
31　Holiday Inn
　　文化假日酒店
32　Ocean Hotel
　　远洋宾馆
34　Hakkas & Hua Shan Hotels
　　嘉应宾馆/华山宾馆
35　Guangdong Jinye Hotel
　　广东金叶大厦

36　Yuehai Hotel
　　粤海大厦
42　Guangdong Guesthouse
　　广东迎宾馆
57　Hotel Landmark Canton
　　华厦大酒店
58　Guangzhou Hotel
　　广州宾馆
63　New Asia Hotel
　　新亚酒店
64　Furama and GD Hotels
　　富丽华大酒店/广东大酒店
67　Bai Gong Hotel
　　白宫酒店
69　Aiqun Hotel
　　爱群大厦

PLACES TO EAT

25　North Garden Restaurant
　　北园酒家
44　Xiyuan Restaurant
　　西园饭店
47　Muslim Restaurant
　　回民饭店
48　Caigenxiang (Veg) Restaurant
　　菜根香素菜馆
50　Panxi Restaurant
　　泮溪酒家
59　Guangzhou Restaurant
　　广州酒家
62　Snake Restaurant
　　蛇餐馆
65　Yan Yan Restaurant
　　人人菜馆
66　Kentucky Fried Chicken
　　肯德基家乡鸡
68　Timmy's Fast Food Restaurant
　　添美食
73　Datong Restaurant
　　新华酒店/大同饭店

ing for Guangzhou at 4 pm. That gives you about five hours on the mountain. Departures are from Tianzi Pier on Yanjiang Lu, one block east of Haizhu Square and the Haizhu Bridge. Buy a ticket one day in advance to avoid long lines on the day of departure. Buses depart from the railway station area in Guangzhou but are no faster than the boat.

Places to Stay

Near the massive White Swan Hotel on Shamian Island is the *Guangzhou Youth Hostel* (☎ 8884298) *(guǎng zhōu qīng nián zhāo dài suǒ)* at 2 Shamian 4-Jie. By default, this place wins the title of 'backpackers' headquarters' in Guangzhou since there is almost nothing else in this price range open to foreigners. The three-bed dormitories cost US$10 to US$14 per person. Double rooms are no bargain at US$24 to US$32.

The *Shamian Hotel* (☎ 8888124; fax 8861068) *(shā miàn bīn guǎn)*, 50 Shamian Nanjie, is only a few steps to the east of the

OTHER

1 Long-Distance Bus Station
广东省汽车客运站

2 GPO
邮政总局 (流花邮局)

3 Guangzhou Railway Station
广州火车站

4 CAAC/CITS
中国民航/国际旅行社

5 Minibus Station
小公共汽车站

7 Telecommunications Office
国际电话大楼

13 Mohammedan Tomb
穆罕默德墓

19 Southern Yue Tomb Museum
南越王汉墓

20 PSB
公安局外事科

21 Sculpture of the Five Rams
五羊石像

22 Sun Yatsen Monument
孙中山纪念碑

23 Sun Yatsen Memorial Hall
孙中山纪念堂

24 Zhenhai Tower
镇海楼

28 Friendship Store
友谊商店

33 Mausoleum of the 72 Martyrs
黄花岗七十二烈士墓

37 Zhongshan Medical College
中山医科大学

38 Memorial Garden to the Martyrs
烈士陵园

39 Peasant Movement Institute
农民运动讲习所

40 Buses to White Cloud Hills
开往白云山的汽车站

41 Bright Filial Piety Temple
光孝寺

43 Temple of the Six Banyan Trees
六榕寺花塔

45 Chen Clan Academy
陈氏书院/陈家祠

46 Buses to Foshan & Xiqiao Hills
广佛车站

49 Huaisheng Mosque
怀圣寺光塔

51 Down jacket & sleeping bag store
工农服装场

52 Guangzhou Department Store
广州百货大楼

53 Foreign Language Bookstore
外文书店

54 Dongshan Department Store
东山百货大楼

55 Dashatou Wharf
大沙头码头

56 Tianzi Pier
天字码头

60 Sacred Heart Church
石室教堂

61 Qingping Market
清平市场

70 South Station (Cargo Only)
南站(货运站)

71 Huangsha Bus Station
黄沙车站

72 Cultural Park
文化公园

74 Nanfang Department Store
南方大厦

75 No 1 Pier
一号码头

76 Zhoutouzui Wharf
洲头嘴码头

Guangzhou Youth Hostel. Doubles with twin beds start at US$23.

The *Bai Gong Hotel* (☎ 8882313; fax 8889161) *(bái gōng jiǔ diàn)* is a pleasant place to stay but little English is spoken. It's near the river at 17 Renmin Nanlu. Singles/doubles are US$17/25. From the railway station, take bus No 31 and get off when you come to the river.

Near the railway station is the *Zhanqian Hotel* (☎ 6670348) *(zhàn qián jiǔ diàn)* at 81 Zhanqian Lu. This place is positively a

bargain (for Guangzhou at least), with twin rooms costing US$17. Just down the street is the *Leizhou Hotel* (☎ 6681688) *(léi zhōu jiǔ diàn)* at 88 Zhanqian Lu. Rooms are priced between US$24 and US$41. Also in the neighbourhood is the *Maoming Shihua Hotel* (☎ 6688388; fax 6682722) *(mào míng shī huà bīn guǎn)* at 101 Zhanqian Lu. Doubles here are US$21 to US$25. In the very same building is the *Jinhuan Hotel* (☎ 6689510; fax 6662778) *(jīn huán jiǔ diàn)*, where doubles are US$26 to US$38.

Places to Eat

On Shamian Island, most budget travellers head for *Li Qin Restaurant (lì qún yǐn shí diàn)* on Shamian Dajie near the Victory Hotel – distinguished by a large tree growing right inside the restaurant and out through the roof.

The *Pearl Inn (yè míng zhū jiǔ diàn)* is just to your right as you face the Shamian Hotel on Shamian Nanjie. This place has good and cheap dim sum breakfast and lunches in the ground floor restaurant.

There are a couple of good places close to the riverfront. Foremost is the *Datong* (☎ 8888988) *(dà tóng jiǔ jiā)* at 63 Yanjiang Xilu, just around the corner from Renmin Lu. The restaurant occupies all of an eight-storey building overlooking the river. It's by no means the cheapest place in town, though the morning dim sum is reasonably priced.

Over near the railway station are heaps of places to eat. Within the Zhanqian Hotel at 81 Zhanqian Lu is the *Chuan Caiguan*, which serves cheap but excellent Sichuan food. However, you can forget about English menus in this place.

Entertainment

That most bourgeois of capitalist activities, gambling, has staged a comeback in Guangzhou with the opening of the horse racing track *(pǎo mǎ chǎng)*. Chairman Mao is no doubt doing somersaults in his grave. Races are held in the evening twice weekly during the racing season, which is winter, but the exact times are subject to change. The track is east of town along Huangpu Dadao.

Getting There & Away

Guangzhou is a major transport hub with connections to almost every city in China.

Air CAAC is at 181 Huanshi Lu, to your left as you come out of the railway station. There are separate telephone numbers for domestic (☎ 6662969) and international (☎ 6661803) flights. You can also book air tickets at the travel agencies in the White Swan Hotel and China Hotel. The CAAC office is open from 8 am to 8 pm daily.

There are at least four daily flights (usually more) from Hong Kong on CAAC and Dragonair. There are direct flights between Guangzhou and a number of other foreign cities including: Bangkok, Hanoi, Jakarta, Kuala Lumpur, Manila, Melbourne, Penang, Singapore, Surabaya and Sydney.

Singapore Airlines (☎ 3358886) is at room 1056, Garden Tower, Garden Hotel, 368 Huanshi Donglu. Malaysian Airline System (☎ 3358828) is also in the Garden Hotel, Shop M04-05.

Bus The long-distance bus station is on Huanshi Xilu, a 10-minute walk west of the railway station. From there you can get buses to many places in and beyond Guangdong Province. The first major town on the route up the south-east coast is Shantou. Night buses head west to Zhanjiang from where you can get a bus/boat connection to Haikou on Hainan Island. There is a direct bus to Guilin, which has an overnight stop in Wuzhou. There are frequent minibus departures to Zhuhai (next to Macau) and Shenzhen (next to Hong Kong).

Train The fastest express to Beijing takes about 33 hours. The express trip to Shanghai takes about 24 hours. CITS in Guangzhou sells train tickets but *not* for same-day departure. Same-day tickets can be bought to your right as you enter the railway station on the 1st floor of the 'Express Departure Area'.

The express train between Hong Kong and Guangzhou is comfortable and convenient. The train covers the 182-km route in 2½ hours. However, it is much cheaper to take a local train to Shenzhen and then another local train to Guangzhou.

Boat Guangzhou has two main wharves – Zhoutouzui and Dashatou – and a harbour, Huangpu (formerly Whampoa), 25 km east. The ticket office for ferries and hovercraft to Hong Kong and Macau is at the gateway of Zhoutouzui.

Boats and jet-powered catamarans to Hong Kong, Macau and Hainan Island leave from Zhoutouzui on the south side of the Pearl River.

Boats to Wuzhou leave from Dashatou on Yanjiang Donglu, in eastern Guangzhou. From Wuzhou you can continue by bus to Yangshuo or Guilin. This is a very popular route.

Getting Around
To/From the Airport Guangzhou's Baiyun Airport is 12 km north of the city centre. The facilities are pretty grotty, but a new airport is under construction with a projected opening date sometime in 1997. A cheap bus makes frequent runs from the CAAC office to the airport.

Bus Bus No 31 runs along Hongde Lu, across Renmin Bridge and straight up Renmin Lu to the main railway station.

Bus No 30 runs from the main railway station, passing both the Baiyun Hotel and the New Garden Hotel.

Bus No 5 takes a route similar to bus No 31, but goes along Liu'ersan Lu on the north side of the canal which separates the city from Shamian Island. Get off here and walk across the small bridge to the island.

Bicycle You can rent bicycles on Shamian Island directly across the street from the Guangzhou Youth Hostel.

SHANTOU
(shàn tóu) 汕头
Shantou is the chief port of eastern Guangdong Province and now one of China's SEZs. Shantou is the first major stop on the long haul along the coast road from Guangzhou to Fujian. The town itself is not of any special interest, but it's a useful transit point.

Information
CTS (☎ 233966) is in the Huaqiao Hotel. Here you can buy bus tickets to Guangzhou, Shenzhen and Xiamen, boat tickets to Hong Kong and air tickets to wherever CAAC flies.

The PSB is on Yuejin Lu, near the corner with Nanmai Lu.

Places to Stay
The *Swatow Peninsula Hotel* (☎ 231261, 316668; fax 25013) *(tuó dǎo bīn guǎn)* on Jinsha Lu is no relation to the Hong Kong Peninsula, but is the best bargain in town. Very comfortable rooms with private bath and no TV (what a blessing!) are US$11. If you want to pay extra to have your eardrums blasted by your neighbours' gongfu movies, TV-equipped rooms cost US$19 to US$48.

Another cheapie but goodie is the friendly *Xinhua Hotel* (☎ 273710) *(xīn huá jiǔ diàn)* at 121 Waima Lu. Doubles are US$14 to US$27.

Just next door is the *Taiwan Hotel* (☎ 276400) *(tái wān bīn guǎn)*. Fortunately, it does not charge Taiwanese prices. Singles/doubles are reasonable at US$24/29, with higher-class rooms costing US$32, US$43 and US$54.

The *Hualian Hotel* (☎ 228389) *(huá lián jiǔ diàn)*, 2 Hushan Lu, is just opposite the main bus station. Built right over a department store, you'll also have no trouble finding a place to shop. Doubles are US$20 and US$23.

The *Huaqiao Hotel* (☎ 319888) *(huá qiáo dà shà)* on Shanzhang Lu is the home of CTS. Singles are US$22 to US$27 and doubles are US$25 to US$36.

Getting There & Away
Air The CAAC office (☎ 251915) is at 46 Shanzhang Lu, a few minutes' walk south of the intersection with Jinsha Lu.

Shantou has international flights three times weekly to Bangkok via Guangzhou, and twice daily direct to Hong Kong.

Bus There are frequent departures to Guangzhou (nine hours), Shenzhen (eight hours) and Xiamen (eight hours). It's a confused situation with bus terminals – there are several scattered around town and they seem to move periodically. Not to worry – most tourist hotels (including the cheapies) offer some sort of bus booking service but you should book the night before. The buses come around and collect passengers at the hotel booking offices.

Boat There are boats to Guangzhou and Hong Kong.

ZHANJIANG
(zhàn jiāng) 湛江
Zhanjiang is the largest Chinese port west of Guangzhou. You're most likely to come to Zhanjiang if you're on your way from Guangzhou or Nanning to Hainan Island. It's a good place to wander around at night when the crowds are out and the lights are bright, but is rather boring during the day – too many concrete blocks and drab streets.

Orientation
Zhanjiang is divided into two widely separated parts. The north section is called the Chikan District *(chì kǎn qū)* and the south is Xiashan *(xiá shān qū)*. Xiashan is where most travellers stay.

Information
CTS (☎ 228775) maintains a small office in the Canton Bay Hotel, 16 Renmin Lu.

Places to Stay
The *Canton Bay Hotel* (☎ 281966), 16 Renmin Lu, offers both cheap and luxurious rooms. Budget doubles with electric fan and private bath cost US$8. With air-con and carpeting, the tariff for double rooms is US$19 to US$27. This is probably the best of the lot in the low to mid price range.

Zhanjiang Traffic Hotel (☎ 221129) *(zhàn jiāng jiāo tōng lǚ diàn)*, 33 Jiefang Donglu, is convenient for the railway station. At the moment, it's a grotty place undergoing renovation.

The *Friendship Hotel* is a popular place in the centre of town. Singles/doubles/triples are US$9/14/16.

Cuiyuan Fandian (☎ 221688, 225167), 124 Minzhi Lu, has no English name and is a small but very comfortable hotel. Rooms cost US$14, US$16 and US$17.

Haiwan Hotel on Renmin Lu is also the location of the International Seamen's Club and boasts a karaoke bar. Double rooms cost US$18 and US$23. Just around the corner is the *Zhangang Hotel* with similar prices.

Getting There & Away
Air The CAAC office (☎ 224415) is at 23 Renmin Nan Dadao, but CTS in the Canton Bay Hotel can arrange tickets for you. There are three weekly flights between Zhanjiang and Hong Kong. Daily flights connect Zhanjiang to Guangzhou and Shenzhen.

Bus There are heaps of night buses to Guangzhou from both the north and south bus stations, as well as from the Canton Bay Hotel (CTS office) and elsewhere.

Train From Zhanjiang south railway station trains depart for Guilin (a 13-hour trip) and for Nanning (9½ hours).

Boat You can take a bus-boat combination to Haikou on Hainan Island. A bus takes you from Zhanjiang to Hai'an on the Leizhou Peninsula (five hours), where you take a boat to Haikou (two hours).

Hainan 海南岛

China's tropical island province, Hainan is also a SEZ. The beaches on the southern shore of the island are a popular winter retreat for busy Hong Kongers, weary travellers and cadres attending beachside 'meetings' at government expense.

HAIKOU
(hǎi kǒu) 海口
The capital of Hainan Island, Haikou is a busy place that travellers try to pass through quickly on the way to beaches farther south.

Information
The main CTS office (☎ 773288) is hidden

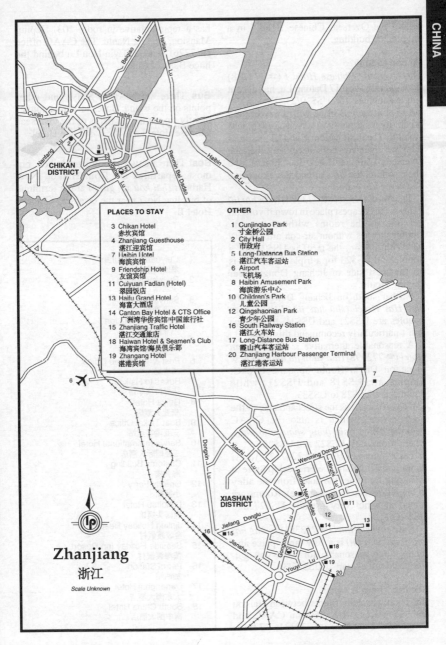

PLACES TO STAY

3 Chikan Hotel
赤坎宾馆
4 Zhanjiang Guesthouse
湛江迎宾馆
7 Haibin Hotel
海滨宾馆
9 Friendship Hotel
友谊宾馆
11 Cuiyuan Fadian (Hotel)
翠园饭店
13 Haifu Grand Hotel
海富大酒店
14 Canton Bay Hotel & CTS Office
广州湾华侨宾馆·中国旅行社
15 Zhanjiang Traffic Hotel
湛江交通旅店
18 Haiwan Hotel & Seamen's Club
海湾宾馆·海员俱乐部
19 Zhangang Hotel
湛港宾馆

OTHER

1 Cunjinqiao Park
寸金桥公园
2 City Hall
市政府
5 Long-Distance Bus Station
湛江汽车客运站
6 Airport
飞机场
8 Haibin Amusement Park
海滨游乐中心
10 Children's Park
儿童公园
12 Qingshaonian Park
青少年公园
16 South Railway Station
湛江火车站
17 Long-Distance Bus Station
霞山汽车客运站
20 Zhanjiang Harbour Passenger Terminal
湛江港客运站

CHIKAN
DISTRICT

XIASHAN
DISTRICT

Zhanjiang
浙江

Scale Unknown

behind the Overseas Chinese Hotel I in a dilapidated building.

Places to Stay

The *Overseas Chinese Hotel I* (☎ 773288) *(huá qiáo dà shà)*, 17 Datong Lu, has decent singles/doubles for US$19/23. Be careful not to confuse this place with a newer (and much more expensive) Overseas Chinese Hotel II. The designation 'I' and 'II' is something we invented – both places are called the Overseas Chinese Hotel. In Chinese, the cheap one is the *dà shà* and the expensive one is the *bīn guǎn*.

The *Nanhai Hotel* (☎ 773474) *(nán hǎi jiǔ diàn)* is the cheapest place in town if you can get one of the rooms without air-con. Doubles/triples without air-con are US$10/13. With air-con, the tariff is US$21 for a double and US$23 for a triple. The hotel is on the west side of Jichang Donglu near Daying Houlu.

Farther south on Jichang Donglu is the *Shu Hai Hotel* *(shǔ hǎi jiǔ diàn)* where doubles are US$21 and US$31, though we don't particularly recommend this place.

A reasonable alternative is the *Taoyuan Hotel* (☎ 772998) *(táo yuán jiǔ diàn)*, a new place on Dayin Houlu opposite CAAC. Singles are US$18 and US$21, while doubles are US$28 to US$33.

Or you can cross the street and stay at the *CAAC Hotel*, which is also the CAAC booking office *(mín háng shòu piào chù)*, where rooms cost US$22 and US$28.

The *Friendship Hotel* (☎ 224712) *(yǒu yì dà jiǔ diàn)* is behind the Friendship Store at 2 Datong Lu (enter the hotel from the alley to the left as you face the store). Rooms are priced at a not very friendly US$27 and US$41.

The *Seaview Hotel* (☎ 773381) *(wàng hǎi guó jì dà jiǔ diàn)* is a very fancy place and seems quite reasonable for what you get. Singles/doubles start at US$26/36.

Getting There & Away

Air There are daily flights between Haikou and Hong Kong (HK$960) on CAAC and Dragonair. Dragonair (☎ 338131, 772117)

has a representative in room 103, Heping Mansion, Heping Nanlu. The CAAC office (☎ 772615) is on Dayin Hou Lu behind the huge Bank of China.

Bus There are buses to Sanya and other points on the island. Buses to Sanya conveniently stop at the car parks of the Overseas Chinese Hotel I and the East Lake Hotel.

Boat There are two harbours in Haikou, but most departures are from Haikou New Harbour *(hǎi kǒu xīn gǎng)* at the terminus of bus line No 7 near the Overseas Chinese Hotel II.

1	Cuiyuan Restaurant 翠园酒家
2	Railway Station 火车站
3	Sanya Market 三亚商场
4	Sanya Bus Station 三亚汽车站
5	Sanya Hotel 三亚宾馆
6	Post & Telephone Office 邮店局
7	Buses to Haikou 往海口汽车站
8	Guiya Hotel 贵亚大酒店
9	Boat Ticket Office 三亚港客运站
10	Sanya International Hotel 三亚国际大酒店
11	Customs Building 海关楼
12	Granny Ferry 小渡船
13	Luhuitou Hotel 鹿回头宾馆
14	Jinling Holiday Resort 金陵渡假村
15	Seaside Holiday Inn Resort 滨海渡假村
16	Petrol Station 加油站
17	Dadonghai Hotel 大东海大酒店
18	South China Hotel 南中国大酒店

Boats leave Haikou about once an hour for the 1½-hour trip to Hai'an on the Leizhou Peninsula, where you get connecting transport to Zhanjiang. There are direct boats daily between Haikou and Guangzhou.

SANYA
(sān yà) 三亚

Sanya is a busy port and tourist resort on the southern tip of Hainan Island. It's one of the few places in China that has a tropical climate. The most popular sandy beach is at Dadonghai *(dà dōng hǎi)*, but it's rapidly

turning into a carnival complete with speedboats, massage parlours and admission fees. The Luhuitou Peninsula *(lù huí tóu)* has a beautiful beach that is mostly undeveloped, but it's too rocky for swimming.

Places to Stay & Eat

If you're willing to share a room with two other people, there are three-bed dorms in the *Seaside Holiday Inn Resort (bīn hǎi dù jià cūn)* in Dadonghai. You can also book the whole room for US$16 or live in a regular air-con double for US$21.

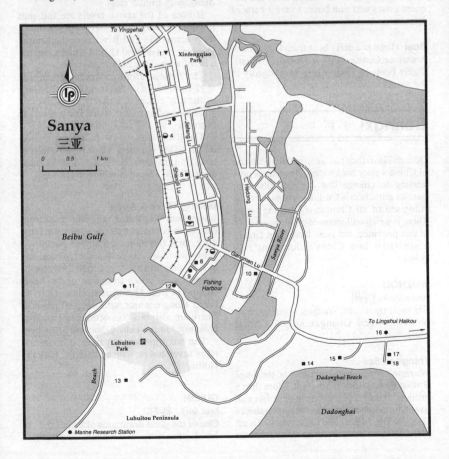

Over on Luhuitou Peninsula, the *Luhuitou Hotel* (☎ 214659) *(lù huí tóu bīn guǎn)* sits in secluded semi-splendour. The mini-villas in lush gardens are a great place to rest, well worth the occasional hassle with the frosty receptionists. Singles/doubles cost US$16/ 20.

Getting There & Away

Air Sanya's airport is being renovated and should soon offer flights direct to Hong Kong and Guangzhou.

Bus From Sanya bus station there are frequent buses and minibuses to most parts of Hainan.

Boat There is a daily boat from Guangzhou departing Guangzhou's Zhoutouzui Wharf. Direct boats to Hong Kong are allegedly in the works.

Guangxi 广西

Guangxi Province has traditionally been one of China's poor backwaters. Tourism is now starting to change that – Guangxi's most famous attraction is Guilin, perhaps the most eulogised of all Chinese sightseeing areas. There is a rich collection of ethnic minorities in this province, but most have been largely assimilated into China's dominant Han culture.

WUZHOU

(wú zhōu) 梧州

For most travellers, Wuzhou is just a transit point between Guangzhou and Guilin/ Yangshuo.

Things to See

Wuzhou's one claim to fame is the huge **Snake Repository** *(shé cáng)*. More than a million snakes a year are sent here from all over China for transport to the restaurants of Hong Kong, Macau and Guangzhou. To get there, take the road that runs away from the

river next to the Wuzhou Hotel; it's about one km away. The repository is open daily, but closed during lunch (11.30 am to 2.30 pm).

Places to Stay

The *Yuanjiang Hotel (yuān jiāng jiǔ diàn)* on Xijiang Lu is a five-minute walk down from the bus station and ferry dock area. Singles/doubles with attached bathroom range from US$6/10, while singles/doubles with common washing facilities are US$4/6. There are also dorm-style triples for US$3. Close by is the gloomy *Xinxi Hotel (xīn xī lü diàn)*, with similar rates.

If both of the above hotels are full (not likely), try the *Hebin Hotel (hé bīn fàn diàn)*, west across the Gui River near the bridge. Doubles cost around US$14 a night, but it's a bit of a concrete hulk.

The *Beishan Hotel (běi shān fàn diàn)* is at 12 Beishan Lu up Dazhong Lu to the north of the city centre. It's overly expensive for what they offer, and is also a fair trudge out of town.

The *Wuzhou Hotel* (☎ 222193) *(wú zhōu dà jiǔ diàn)* is a new place rapidly falling apart. It's also overpriced, with doubles starting at HK$132 and climbing to HK$332.

Getting There & Away

Buses from Wuzhou to Yangshuo leave from the two bus stations to the left of the ferry dock area (for Guangzhou and Nanning). Buses leave at 7.20, 8.20 and 11.30 am, and at 6.40 pm, making it generally possible to connect with buses from any of the boats coming in from Guangzhou. Hovercrafts to Hong Kong connect with the 6.40 pm bus. There are also bus connections to Liuzhou, Nanning, Guilin, Guangzhou and Shenzhen.

The bus trip from Wuzhou to Yangshuo takes seven hours, with another 1½ hours to Guilin.

GUILIN

(guì lín) 桂林

One of the great drawcards of China and the No 1 attraction of Guangxi Province is

Guilin. It is famous for its landscape of high karsts (limestone peaks).

The town of Guilin is surrounded by huge limestone pinnacles jutting out of the rice fields.

Travellers' coffee shops, bicycle rentals and one or two fledgling discount-tour-ticket operators got off to an early start here. Guilin was, and still is, a great place to learn about capitalism!

If Guilin is too crowded you can break away to Yangshuo – a couple of hours down the Li River – and enjoy similar scenery without the tourist hype.

Warning Many travellers in both Guilin and Yangshuo have been approached by young people wanting to 'practice their English'. Unfortunately, after some friendly conversation the 'English students' suggest going to a nice restaurant which turns out to be horribly expensive. In fact, the 'students' get a sizeable commission for every sucker they bring in.

Orientation
Most of Guilin lies on the west bank of the Li River. For the best views of the surrounding karst formations you either have to climb to the top of the hills or get out of the town altogether.

Information
CITS (☎ 222648) is at 14 Ronghu Beilu, facing Banyan Lake.

All tourist hotels change money. The Bank of China is on Ronghu Beilu.

The Post & Telecommunications Building is on Zhongshan Lu. Another post and telecommunications office is by the large square in front of the railway station, and offers a convenient international direct-dial phone service.

The PSB is on Sanduo Lu, a side street which runs west off Zhongshan Lu, in the area between Banyan Lake and Jiefang Lu.

Things to See
In the centre of town is **Solitary Beauty Peak** (dú xiù fēng), a 152-metre-high pin-

nacle. At its foot is the gate of a palace built in the 14th century. Bus No 2 from the Guilin railway station goes past the peak.

The best scenery lies outside the town, and good views of the area can be seen from the top of the Li River Hotel.

Seven Star Park (qī xīng gōng yuán) is on the eastern side of the Li River. Cross Liberation Bridge and the Ming Dynasty Flower Bridge to the park. To get to the park take bus No 9, 10 or 11 from the railway station. From the park, bus No 13 runs back across the Li River, past **Wave-Subduing Hill** (fú bō shān) and down to **Reed Flute Cave** (lú dí yán). North of Solitary Beauty Peak is **Folded Brocade Hill** (dié cǎi shān). Climb the stone pathway which takes you through the **Wind Cave**, with walls decked with inscriptions and Buddhist sculptures.

There's a good view of **Old Man Hill** (lǎo rén shān), a curiously shaped hill to the north-east of Wave-Subduing Hill. The best way to get there is by bicycle as buses don't go past it.

At the southern end of town, one of Guilin's best known sights is **Elephant Trunk Hill** (xiàng bí shān), which stands next to the Li River. It's basically a large lump of rock with a big hole in it.

Also at the southern end of Guilin, **South Park** (nán gōng yuán) is a pretty place. You can contemplate the mythological immortal who is said to have lived in one of the caves here; look for his statue.

There are two lakes near the city centre, **Banyan Lake** (róng hú) on the western side and **Fir Lake** (shān hú) on the eastern side.

Places to Stay
There's a real shortage of budget accommodation in Guilin, the lower end of the market being served primarily by Yangshuo. Backpackers usually choose the *Overseas Chinese Hotel* (huá qiáo dà shà), where a bed in a three-bed room is US$4. There are also doubles available for US$7 with shared bath and US$10 with private bath,

The only other budget option in Guilin is the *Dahua Hotel* (dá huá jiǔ diàn), a 20-minute hike north of the railway station up

CHINA

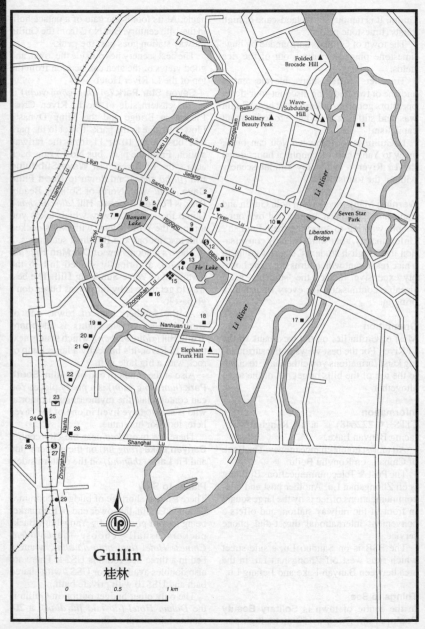

Folded
Brocade Hill ▲

Beilu

Wave-
Subduing
Hill ▲

Solitary ▲
Beauty Peak

Zhongshan

Legun Lu

Yiwu Lu

Lijun Lu

Huancei Lu

Jiefang Lu

Sanduo Lu

Ronghu Lu

Xinyi Lu

Banyan
Lake

Yiren Lu

Seven Star
Park

Liberation
Bridge

Li River

Beilu

Fir Lake

Zhongshan Lu

Nanhuan Lu

Elephant ▲
Trunk Hill

Nanlu

Shanghai Lu

Zhongshan

Li River

Guilin

桂林

0   0.5   1 km

PLACES TO STAY

1   Guilin Royal Garden Hotel
    帝苑酒店
2   Dahua Hotel
    达华大酒店
3   Hotel Universal
    环球大酒店
7   Ronghu Hotel
    榕湖饭店
8   Holiday Inn Hotel
    桂林宾馆
9   Hubin Hotel
    湖滨饭店
10 Sheraton Hotel
    文华大酒店
11 Li River Hotel
    漓江饭店
16 Tailian Hotel
    台联酒店
17 Guishan Hotel
    桂山大酒店
18 Yu Gui Hotel
    榆桂饭店
19 Osmanthus Hotel
    丹桂大酒店
20 Taihe Hotel
    泰和饭店
22 Hidden Hill Hotel
    隐山饭店
26 Guilin Garland Hotel
    凯悦酒店

28 Hong Kong Hotel
    香江饭店

OTHER

4   PSB
    公安局
5   Ancient South Gate
    古南门
6   CITS
    中国国际旅行社
12 Bank of China
    中国银行
13 Xinhua Bookstore
    新华书店
14 CAAC
    中国民航
15 Guilin Department Store
    桂林百货大楼
21 Long-Distance Bus Station
    长途汽车站
23 Post Office/International Phones
    邮电局
24 Yangqiao Bus Station
    城南站
25 Guilin Railway Station
    火车站
27 Bank of China
    中国银行
29 Overseas Chinese Mansion
    华侨大厦

Zhongshan Lu. Dorms with attached bathroom cost US$4 and doubles with the same features cost US$12.

There are plenty of other hotels in Guilin, but none offer dormitories.

Places to Eat

Guilin food is basically Cantonese. Traditionally the town is noted for its snake soup, wild cat or bamboo rat, washed down with snake-bile wine. A lot of endangered species are on the menus, and command high prices. But generally the most exotic stuff you should come across is eels, catfish, pigeons and dog.

Overseas Chinese with fistful's of dollars have pushed many restaurant prices to Hong Kong levels, and the problem is compounded by overcharging in the smaller

restaurants. If prices are not listed make a point of asking first.

If you are just after a quick bite to eat, your best bet is to wander north of the railway station up Zhongshan Lu. There are a couple of places between the railway station and the long-distance bus station with reasonable prices and English menus. Don't worry too much about finding these places; the staff normally dash into the crowd and drag you off the street.

Getting There & Away

Guilin is connected to many places by air, bus, train and boat. Give serious thought to flying in or out of this place, as train connections are not good.

Air CAAC has an office (☎ 223063) at 144

CHINA

Zhongshan Lu, just to the south of the intersection of Zhongshan Lu and Shahu Beilu. The most popular travellers' option is the Guilin to Kunming flight. There are direct air connections to Hong Kong.

Bus For short local runs (eg, Yangshuo), minibuses depart regularly from the railway station. The long-distance bus station is just north of the railway station on Zhongshan Lu. For Wuzhou and Guangzhou both ordinary and deluxe buses are available – the deluxe buses offer a bit more legroom, a feature not to be sneezed at over a long distance, though it's a comfort that nearly doubles the price of the trip.

Train There are useful train connections to Guilin, but some tend to involve hauls in incredibly crowded carriages. Guilin railway station has a separate ticket office for foreigners which helps you avoid the long queues. Sleepers to Kunming tend to book out, but it's relatively easy to get one to Guangzhou.

Boat There is a boat trip from Guilin down the Li River to Yangshuo, but tickets cost an outrageous US$57. There is a bus/boat combination ticket which takes you by bus to Wuzhou and then by boat to Guangzhou.

Getting Around
Bicycles are definitely the best way to get around Guilin. Just look around Zhongshan Lu for bike-hire shop signs.

YANGSHUO
(yáng shuò) 杨州
Yangshuo is a tiny town on the west bank of the Li River, 80 km south of Guilin. You can explore the limestone peaks and small villages from Yangshuo and avoid the hordes of packaged tourists at Guilin. Not that you'll avoid foreigners – Yangshuo has become one of China's foremost backpacker hang-outs.

Information
CITS is on the grounds of the Yangshuo

Hotel and has another office next to the Sihai Hotel. You can buy useful maps here.

The Bank of China is on Binjiang Lu.

Things to See
The main peak in Yangshuo is **Green Lotus Peak** (bì lián fēng), which stands next to the Li River in the south-eastern corner of the town.

Yangshuo-Gongyan Park (yáng shuò gōng yuán) is in the western part of the town, and here you'll find **Man Hill** (xī láng shān), which is supposed to resemble a young man bowing and scraping to a shy young girl represented by **Lady Hill** (xiǎo gǔ shān). The other hills are named after animals: **Crab Hill, Swan Hill, Dragon Head Hill** etc. Sights along the Li River in the vicinity of Yangshuo include the hills, **Green Frog Watching** & **Enjoying the Moon**.

The highway from Guilin turns southward at Yangshuo and after a couple of km crosses the Jingbao River. South of this river and just to the west of the highway is **Moon Hill** (yuè liàng shān), a limestone pinnacle with a moon-shaped hole. To get to Moon Hill by bicycle, take the main road out of town towards the river, turn right on the road about 200 metres before the bridge and cycle for about 50 minutes. Moon Hill is on your right and the views from the top are incredible!

A series of caves have been opened up not far from Moon Hill, including the **Black Buddha Caves** (hēi fó dòng). If you head out to Moon Hill, you will undoubtedly be intercepted and invited to visit the caves. Tours cost in the vicinity of US$3 per head, though prices go down the more of you there are. Be prepared for a wet and muddy experience.

A popular riverboat trip is to the picturesque village of **Fuli**, a short distance down the Li River. There are a couple of boats daily to Fuli from Yangshuo, although most people tend to cycle there. A new alternative mode of transport to Fuli is by inner-tube. Inner-tube hire is available at Minnie Mao's cafe for about US$1 per day. It takes around three or four hours to get to Fuli this way. There

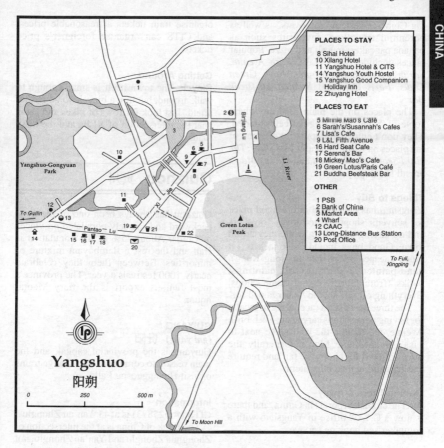

PLACES TO STAY
8 Sihai Hotel
10 Xilang Hotel
11 Yangshuo Hotel & CITS
14 Yangshuo Youth Hostel
15 Yangshuo Good Companion
   Holiday Inn
22 Zhuyang Hotel

PLACES TO EAT
5 Minnie Mao's Café
6 Sarah's/Susannah's Cafes
7 Lisa's Cafe
9 L&L Fifth Avenue
16 Hard Seat Cafe
17 Serena's Bar
18 Mickey Mao's Cafe
19 Green Lotus/Paris Café
21 Buddha Beefsteak Bar

OTHER
1 PSB
2 Bank of China
3 Market Area
4 Wharf
12 CAAC
13 Long-Distance Bus Station
20 Post Office

Yangshuo
阳朔

have been many reports of foreigners having had their pockets picked in Fuli – be careful in crowded market areas.

Places to Stay

The three most popular places to stay in Yangshuo are the *Yangshuo Youth Hostel*, opposite the bus station, the *Yangshuo Good Companion Holiday Inn*, not far from the youth hostel, and the *Sihai Hotel* (also known as the Good Companion Holiday Inn just to confuse things), nestled in among all the travellers' hang-outs on Xi Jie. All three offer very similar standards and can be noisy.

Dorm beds cost between US$1 and US$2, while singles/doubles are around US$4.

Travellers coming in on the night bus from Wuzhou are often dropped off outside the *Zhuyang Hotel*, where singles/doubles are US$3/4. The *Xilang Hotel* is quiet and friendly. Singles/doubles are US$2/5.

The *Yangshuo Hotel* is shabbily upmarket, offering damp doubles with attached bathroom for US$5 and air-con doubles/triples for US$12/15.

Places to Eat

Xi Jie teems with tiny cafes offering interesting Chinese/Western crossovers, as well as perennial travellers' favourites such as banana pancakes, muesli and pizza. Popular places include *Lisa's*, *L&L Fifth Avenue*, *Sarah's*, *Susannah's*, *Minnie Mao's*, *Green Lotus*, *Paris Café* and *Buddha Beefsteak Bar*.

The places on the main road are where some of Yangshuo's original cafes started. They don't enjoy the popularity of some of the places on Xi Jie, but cafes like *Slims*, *The Hard Seat Cafe*, *Serena's* and *Mickey Mao's* are all friendly spots.

Things to Buy

Yangshuo has developed into a good place for souvenir shopping and many travellers end up buying something while they are in town. Good buys include silk jackets (at much cheaper prices than in Hong Kong), hand-painted T-shirts, scroll paintings, batiks (from Guizhou) and name chops. Everything on sale should be bargained for.

The three best places (according to locals) for having name chops carved are L&L Fifth Avenue, the hole-in-the-wall place next to Lisa's and Minnie Mao's. Generally the prices offered for chops are fair and require less bargaining than other items.

Getting There & Away

Air The closest airport is in Guilin, and there is now a CAAC office in Yangshuo with a computerised booking service.

Bus To Guilin there is frequent minibus service which operates from the square in front of the Yangshuo bus station.

If you're heading to Guangzhou you can take a bus/boat combination from Yangshuo; buses to Wuzhou leave at 6.40 am and 5.30 pm, and cost US$5. The morning bus allows you to connect with the evening boat from Wuzhou; the evening bus is less convenient as it leaves you to sit out in the wee small hours of the morning waiting for the first boat of the day.

Train The nearest railway station is in Guilin. A number of cafes around Yangshuo will

organise train tickets at reasonable prices, and CITS can organise foreigner's price tickets.

Getting Around

Bicycle The town itself is small enough to walk around, but hire a bicycle to go farther afield. Just look for rows of bikes and signs near the intersection of Xi Jie and the main road.

Guizhou 贵州

Guizhou has always been one of the most backward and sparsely populated provinces of China. About 75% of the population is Han and the rest a flamboyant mixture of minorities. Between them they celebrate nearly 1000 festivals a year. The province's most famous export is the fiery Maotai liquor.

GUIYANG
(guì yáng) 贵阳

Guiyang is the provincial capital, and the main reason to come here is to change trains or visit Huangguoshu Falls.

Information

CITS (☎ 525873) is at 11 Yan'an Zhonglu.

The Bank of China is at the intersection of Zhonghua Zhonglu and Yan'an Zhonglu, not far from CITS. CAAC also has a foreign-exchange counter and ditto for the Guiyang Plaza Hotel.

The post and telecommunications building is at the intersection of Zunyi Lu and Zhonghua Lu.

Places to Stay & Eat

If you don't mind dirt and noise, try the *Chaoyang Hotel (cháo yáng fàn diàn)* on Zunyi Lu, just a few minutes' walk from the railway station. There are dorm beds here for US$2 and doubles for US$8.

The only other cheapie is the *Jinqiao Hotel* (☎ 27921) *(jīn qiáo fàn diàn)*, inconveniently located on Ruijin Zhonglu, a good 25 minutes' walk from the railway station. Four-bed dorms here cost US$3; doubles are US$15. Bus Nos 1 and 2 run from the railway station past the hotel.

The *Sports Hotel* (☎ 522470) *(tǐ yù bīn guǎn)*, on the grounds of the Guizhou Gymnasium, is good value. Enormous and very clean doubles with TV and bathroom start from US$19. The hotel is just a short walk from the railway station.

The *Overseas Chinese Friendship Guest House (qiáo yì dà jiǔ diàn)* was closed for renovations at the time of writing, and is likely to be fairly pricey when it's resurrected.

Getting There & Away
Air The CAAC office (☎ 522300) is at 170 Zunyi Lu. There are daily flights to Beijing and Guangzhou.

Bus The long-distance bus station is quite a long way from the railway station, and you're better off using the bus services that operate from the railway station. There are two buses a day to Xingyi (from where there are onward buses to Kunming). Minibuses run through the day every 20 minutes to Anshun (near Huangguoshu Falls), Kaili and Zunyi.

It's also possible to take tour buses to Huangguoshu Falls from the railway station. These depart at 7 am and cost US$4.

Train Direct trains run to Kunming, Guilin, Chongqing and Nanning.

HUANGGUOSHU FALLS
(huáng guǒ shù dà pù bù)
黄果树大瀑布
Forty-three km south-west of Anshun, Huangguoshu (Yellow Fruit Tree) Falls is China's premier cataract. It has a width of 81 metres and a drop of 74 metres.

Nearby hiking is superb. At the edge of the falls is **Water Curtain Cave** *(shuǐ lián dòng)*, where you can view the rushing water from the inside of the waterfall. One km above the

main falls is **Steep Slope Falls** *(dǒu pō pù bù)*, 105 metres wide and 23 metres high. Eight km below Huangguoshu Falls is **Star Bridge Falls** *(tiān xīng qiáo)*. In all there are about 18 falls, four subterranean rivers and 100 caves in the area.

About 32 km from Anshun is a spectacular series of underground caverns called **Longgong**, or Dragon Palace, which form a network through some 20 mountains. Charter boats tour one of the largest waterfilled caves, often called the 'Dragon Cave'. The caverns are at the town of Longtan (Dragon Pool). Other scenic caves in the vicinity include **Daji Dong**, **Chuan Dong** and **Linlang Dong**.

The dry season lasts from November to April, so during March and April the flow of water can become a less impressive trickle.

The region is also the homeland of the Bouyei, the 'aboriginals of Guizhou'. Of Thai origin, the Bouyei are related to the Zhuang of Guangxi. Batik (cloth wax-dyeing) is one of the skills of the Bouyei. The masonry at Huangguoshu is also intriguing – stone blocks comprise the housing, but no plaster is used; the roofs are finished in stone slates. There is a Bouyei festival in Huangguoshu lasting 10 days during the first lunar month (usually February or early March).

Places to Stay & Eat
At the bus park near the Huangguoshu Falls are some food stalls. Nearby is the *Huangguoshu Guest House (huáng guǒ shù bīn guǎn)*, where dorm beds are US$5 per person. Its decent restaurant charges from US$1 to US$5 for set meals; buy tickets at the reception desk.

Just before the bridge on the way into town from Anshun is the *Tianxing Hotel (tiān xīng fàn diàn)* with accommodation for US$3 per person.

ANSHUN
(ān shùn) 安顺
Once an opium-trading centre, Anshun remains the commercial hub of western

Guizhou and is now known for its batiks. The town lies on the Guiyang-Kunming railway line, a two-hour ride from Guiyang, and is probably the best place to stop en route to Huangguoshu Falls.

Information

CITS (☎ 3173) has an office at the Hongshan Hotel which organises trips to Huangguoshu and the surrounding area. From town, the bus station and the railway station are four and three km away respectively. The Hongshan Hotel minibus charges about US$1 per person for transfer to the railway station.

Places to Stay

The *Xixiushan Hotel (xī xiù shān bīn guǎn)*, just around the corner and up the road from the bus station, has cheap dorm beds but is sometimes reluctant to let to foreigners. Doubles cost around US$7. Behind the bus station, a guesthouse *(qì chē zhàn zhāo dài suǒ)* has very cheap six-bed dorms. Again, they are often not keen on taking foreigners.

The *Minzu Hotel (mín zú fàn diàn)* on Tashan Donglu, on the eastern side of town near the highway to Guiyang, has doubles for US$8. Ask about rooms in the old building *(jiù lóu)*, which are substantially cheaper.

The main tourist joint, inconveniently located on the northern outskirts of Anshun, is the *Hongshan Hotel (☎ 23435) (hóng shān bīn guǎn)* at 39 Baihong Lu. Its cheapest rooms cost US$23.

Getting There & Away

Minibuses run to Anshun from the Guiyang railway station every 20 minutes.

Yunnan 云南

Geographically, Yunnan is the most varied of all China's provinces, with terrain ranging from tropical rainforest to icy Tibetan highlands. It is the home of a third of all China's ethnic minorities, and it harbours half of all China's plant and animal species. The province is a favourite with travellers.

KUNMING

(kūn míng) 昆明

Kunming is the provincial capital. In the tropics but at 1890 metres above sea level, the city has a mild climate year-round. Sadly, much of the quaint wooden architecture is being bulldozed in the interests of 'progress'. Nevertheless, it's a pleasant city and an excellent staging post for fascinating trips farther afield.

Information

CITS (☎ 3132895) is just east of Beijing Lu on Huancheng Nanlu.

The Kunming, Green Lake, Camellia, King World, Sakura Holiday Inn and Golden Dragon hotels all have foreign-exchange counters.

The international post office on the east side of Beijing Lu is halfway between Tuodong Lu and Huancheng Nanlu. This is where you collect poste restante letters.

The Yan'an Hospital *(yán ān yī yuàn)* is on Jiaosanqiao Lu, about one km north-east of the Kunming Hotel, and has a foreigners' clinic (☎ 22390).

The PSB is at 525 Beijing Lu.

Things to See

To the south of Jinbi Lu are two Tang pagodas, of which the **West Pagoda** *(xī sì tǎ)* is a must-see. The **Yunnan Provincial Museum** *(yún nán shěng bó wù guǎn)* on Wuyi Lu houses an exhibition centred around Yunnan's minorities. The **Yuantong Temple** *(yuán tōng sì)*, to the north-east of the Green Lake Hotel, is the largest Buddhist complex in Kunming. Close to Yuantong Temple is the zoo *(dòng wù yuán)*, but animal lovers had best give it a miss. A short distance south-west of the zoo, **Cuihu Park** has free Chinese opera performances on Sunday.

The **Ancient Mosque** *(nán chéng qīng zhēn gǔ sì)* is a ramshackle 400-year-old building at the city centre, next to the Kunming Department Store at 51 Zhengyi Lu. It was turned into a factory during the

Cultural Revolution but is now getting some overdue renovation.

The rest of Kunming's major sights are spread out within a 15-km radius of the city. Local transport to these places is awkward, crowded and time-consuming; it tends to be an out-and-back job, with few crossovers for combined touring. If you wish to take in everything, you'd be looking at something like five return trips, which would consume three days or more. You can simplify this by pushing Black Dragon Pool, Anning Hot Springs and the Golden Temple to the background, and concentrating on the trips of high interest – the Bamboo Temple and Western Hills, both of which have decent transport connections with special express buses in the mornings. Lake Dian presents some engrossing circular-tour possibilities on its own. Better yet, buy a map, hire a good bicycle and tour the area by bike.

The **Bamboo Temple** (qióng zhú sì) is 12 km north-west of Kunming and dates from the Tang Dynasty. **Lake Dian** (diān chí), to the south of Kunming, is dotted with settlements, farms and fisheries; the lake covers 300 sq km and is 150 km in circumference and 40 km long. At the northernmost tip of Lake Dian is the 60-hectare **Daguan Park**, three km south-west of the city. **Daguan Tower** provides a vantage point over Lake Dian. The **Western Hills** (xī shān) spread out across a long wedge of parkland on the western side of Lake Dian.

Places to Stay

Most popular with travellers is the *Camellia Hotel (chá huā bīn guǎn)* on Dongfeng Donglu. Beds in a dorm cost US$2, while basic doubles are US$7. More upmarket doubles range from US$21 to US$35.

The *Three Leaves Hotel (sān yè fàn diàn)* is a short walk from Kunming's main railway station and directly opposite the long-distance bus station on Beijing Lu. At the time of writing the hotel was undergoing renovations, which normally spells one thing: massive price hikes.

The *Kunhu Hotel* (☎ 3133737) *(kūn hú fàn diàn)* is a bit farther up Beijing Lu from

the railway station, just north of Huancheng Nanlu and the Golden Dragon Hotel. The surly staff have been driving away travellers, but some rooms are still good value. The hotel is two stops from the railway station on bus No 3, 23 or 25.

The *Yunnan Hotel* (☎ 3130258) *(yún nán fàn diàn)* on Dongfeng Xilu is an unfriendly place and is only recommended in the unlikely event of everything else being booked up. Doubles with attached bath range from US$14 to US$21.

Close to the Yunnan Hotel is the *Spring City Hotel (chūn chéng fàn diàn)*. Not many foreigners stay here, but it has some clean, cheapish rooms. Dorms are US$3 to US$4, and doubles are US$15.

Places to Eat

One of the best options on Dongfeng Donglu is the *Yunnan Typical Local Food Restaurant*. It has a good range of dishes, including across-the-bridge noodles, a local speciality. Almost next door is the fine *New Land Restaurant*.

Several small restaurants in the vicinity of Yunnan University's main gate are highly recommended, especially the popular *Tong Da Li Restaurant*. Coming out of the Yunnan University gate, go left on the main road and then take the first left onto a small back street; Tong Da Li is the first restaurant on the right. This area is about 15 minutes' walk north from the lavish Green Lake Hotel.

The best Muslim food in Kunming is reportedly served at the *Yingjianglou Muslim Restaurant* (☎ 3165198) *(yìng jiāng lóu fàn diàn)* at 360 Changchun Lu.

Entertainment

The most popular foreigners' hang-out is the *Groove Garden* next to the Three Leaves Hotel. It's a tiny place with seating at the bar and in a dark room upstairs.

Getting There & Away

Air CAAC (☎ 3137465) is at 146 Dongfeng Donglu, next door to the Kunming Hotel. CAAC has international flights to Hong

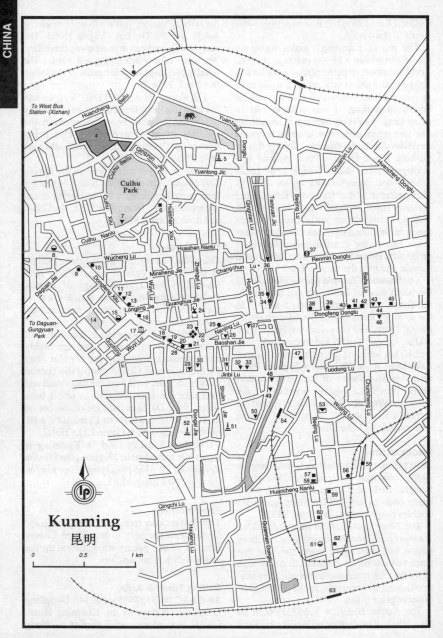

To West Bus
Station (Xizhan)

Huancheng Beilu

Bellu

1

3

2

Yuantong Donglu

Qingyun Jie

Cuihu Beilu

4

Chuanjin Lu

Huancheng Donglu

5

Yuantong Jie

Qingnian Lu

Taoyuan Jie

Beijing Lu

Cuihu
Park

7

6

Huashan Xilu

Cuihu Xilu

Huashan Nanlu

Cuihu Nanlu

Zhengyi Lu

Changchun Lu

36

37

Renmin Donglu

8

Wucheng Lu

Baita Lu

10

Minsheng Jie

Wuyi Lu

9

Daguan Jie

Dongfeng Xilu

Huguo Lu

35

34

38 39 40 41 42 43 45

44

Guanghua Jie

11
12
13

Longjing Jie

24

46

Dongfeng Donglu

To Daguan-
Gungyuan
Park

15

14

16

25

26

Nanjing Lu

27

47

Guofang Lu

17

18

23

22

Baoshan Jie

19 20

21

Wuyi Lu

28

29 30

31

32 33

Tuodong Lu

Jinbi Lu

48

Shulin Jie

49

Dongsi Jie

50

53

Wujing Lu

Chunecheng Lu

52

54

51

Beijing Lu

57
58

56 55

59

Huancheng Nanlu

60

Guanman Donglu

Qingchi Lu

Haugeng Lu

61 62

Kunming
昆明

0   0.5   1 km

63

PLACES TO STAY

6 Cuihu Guesthouse
翠湖宾馆
16 Yunnan Hotel
云南饭店
21 Spring City
(Chuncheng) Hotel
春城饭店
41 Kunming Hotel
昆明饭店
45 Camellia Hotel
茶花宾馆
57 Kunhu Hotel
昆湖饭店
59 Golden Dragon Hotel
金龙饭店
60 King World Hotel
锦华大酒店
62 Three Leaves Hotel/
Groove Garden
三叶饭店

PLACES TO EAT

7 Laozhiqing Restaurant
老知食馆
11 Blue Skies Duck
Restaurant
蓝天烤鸭店
12 Shanghai Noodle
Restaurant
上海面店
18 Qiaoxiangyuan
Restaurant
桥香园饭店
23 Ice Cream Shop
冰淇淋店
26 Beijing Restaurant
北京饭店
27 Minsheng Restaurant
民生饭店
28 Muslim Restaurants
清真饭店
29 California Noodle
King USA
美国加州牛肉面大王ó
30 Yunnan Across the
Bridge Noodles
Restaurant
云南过桥米线
31 Chuanwei Sichuan
Restaurant
川味饭店
32 Nanlaisheng Coffee
Shop
南来盛咖啡馆

33 Mengbai Across the
Bridge Noodles
蒙白过桥米线
36 Yingjianglou Muslim
Restaurant
映江楼饭店
43 Yunnan Typical Local
Food Restaurant
根兴饭店
44 New Land Restaurant
新大陆饭店
46 Cooking School
学厨校
48 Guanshengyuan
Restaurant
冠生园饭店
49 Pan Se Seng
Restaurant
班色酒村
50 Yingjianglou
Restaurant (No 2)
映江楼饭店
58 Happy Cafe
快乐食馆

OTHER

1 Yunnan Minorities
Institute
云南少数民族学院
2 Kunming Zoo
昆明动物园
3 North Railway Station
火车北站
4 Yunnan University
云南大学
5 Yuantong Temple
圆通寺
8 Xiaoximen Bus Station
小西门汽车客运站
9 Yunnan Arts &
Crafts Store
云南工艺美术服务部
10 Dongfeng Department
Store
东风百货商店
13 Arts Theatre
艺术剧院
14 Guofang Sports
Ground
国防体育场
15 Wacang Lu Minibuses
(for Western Hills,
Bamboo Temple etc)
瓦仓南路小型车站

17 Yunnan Provincial
Museum
云南省博物馆
19 Wuhua Mansions
Department Store
五华大厦
20 Kunming United
Airlines
昆明联合航空公司
22 Kunming Department
Store
昆明百货商店
24 Ancient Mosque
南城清真古寺
25 Xinhua Bookstore
新华书店
34 Yunnan Antique Store
云南文物商店
35 Foreign Languages
Bookstore
外文书店
37 Bank of China
中国银行
38 Post & Telephone
Office
邮电局
39 Golden Triangle Bar
金角酒吧
40 Shanghai Airlines
上海航空公司
42 CAAC
中国民航售票处
47 PSB
公安局
51 East Pagoda
东寺塔
52 West Pagoda
西寺塔
53 International
Post Office
国际邮局
54 South Railway
Station
明南火车站
55 Thai Airways
泰国航空公司
56 CITS
中国国际旅行社
61 Long-Distance
Bus Station
长途汽车总站
63 Main Railway
Station
火车站

Kong, Bangkok, Rangoon (Yangon) and Vientiane.

For internal flights, alternatives to CAAC are Shanghai Airlines (☎ 3038502), close to CAAC on Dongfeng Donglu, which has flights to Shanghai, and United Airlines on Dongfeng Xilu, which has flights to Beijing.

Thai Airways (☎ 3133315) has three weekly flights to Chiang Mai and Bangkok. The office is at 32 Chuncheng Lu. Dragonair (☎ 3133104) has an office in the Golden Dragon Hotel and has flights to Hong Kong.

Bus The long-distance bus station on Beijing Lu is the main centre of operations, and this is the best place to organise bus tickets to almost anywhere. Exceptions to this are more local destinations like Lake Dian. A further exception is the bus trip to Xishuangbanna, for which many travellers use the bus service from the Three Leaves Hotel (this may not still be operating though, owing to the hotel's renovations).

Train Rail options out of Kunming include Beijing (via Guiyang, Changsha and Zhengzhou), Shanghai, Guangzhou, Chengdu and Chongqing. Kunming can become a real trap for railway travellers, as trains are often fully booked, so book your tickets at least four days in advance.

Getting Around
Bus Local transport is awkward, crowded and time-consuming, though there are tour buses to the sights. Another option for getting out to the sights around Kunming is to head over to Wacang Lu, the first street on the left on Dongfeng Xilu after the Yunnan Provincial Museum. Minibuses run here to all the major sights, including the Golden Temple, Black Dragon Pool, Bamboo Temple, Lake Dian, Daguan Park and the Western Hills.

Bicycle Bikes are a fast way to get around town. Both the Kunming and Camellia hotels offer bikes for US$2 per day. The

bikes for hire at the Happy Cafe look like they've seen better days.

THE STONE FOREST
(shí lín) 石林
The Stone Forest is an exotic collection of grey limestone pillars, fissured by rainwater and eroded into their present fanciful forms. The tallest are about 30 metres high. The whole area is a giant rock garden with pavilions and pathways.

There are actually several stone forests in the region – the section open to foreign tourists covers 80 hectares. Twelve km to the north-east is a larger (300-hectare) rock series called Fungi Forest.

Places to Stay
The *Shilin Hotel (shí lín bīn guǎn)*, near the main entrance to the Stone Forest, has singles/doubles for US$10/17. The same prices are charged at the *Yunlin Hotel (yún lín fàn diàn)*, but rooms are concrete cells with beds for US$2. The Yunlin is off the road that forks to the right in front of the entrance.

Near the bus terminal are several smaller hotels with basic rooms for US$2 per person.

Getting There & Away
It takes about 3½ hours to get to the Stone Forest from Kunming. Buses depart Kunming's long-distance bus station at 7.45 and 8 am. Alternatively, the west bus station has two buses a day which depart at 7.15 am and 1.30 pm.

DALI
(dà lǐ) 大理
Dali lies on the western edge of Erhai Lake, with the imposing Cangshan mountain range behind it. The main inhabitants of the region are the Bai people. Dali is a popular haven for foreigners who want to slow down and relax in one of China's most peaceful spots.

Thousands of people converge on Dali during the Third Moon Fair *(sān yuè jíe)*, which begins on the 15th day of the third

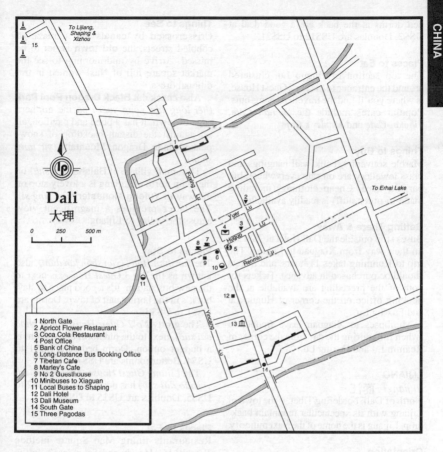

Dali
大理

0   250   500 m

To Lijiang,
Shaping &
Xizhou

To Erhai Lake

1 North Gate
2 Apricot Flower Restaurant
3 Coca Cola Restaurant
4 Post Office
5 Bank of China
6 Long-Distance Bus Booking Office
7 Tibetan Cafe
8 Marley's Cafe
9 No 2 Guesthouse
10 Minibuses to Xiaguan
11 Local Buses to Shaping
12 Dali Hotel
13 Dali Museum
14 South Gate
15 Three Pagodas

lunar month (usually April) and ends on the 21st day.

Information

The Bank of China is in the centre of town, at the corner of Huguo Lu and Fuxing Lu. The PSB is at the northern end of the block behind the No 2 Guest House.

Things To See

The **Three Pagodas** *(sān tǎ sì)* stand on the hillside behind Dali and look particularly beautiful reflected in the nearby lake.

Erhai Lake *(ér hǎi)* is a 40-minute walk

from town where you can watch the large sailing junks or the smaller boats with their captive cormorants.

Places to Stay

Just about everyone who makes it to Dali heads for the *No 2 Guest House (dì èr zhāo dài suǒ)* on Huguo Lu in the centre of town. It's an unfriendly dump but cheap with dorms for US$2 to US$3 and doubles for US$5.

The *Dali Hotel (dà lǐ bīn guǎn)* on Fuxing Lu is the sole alternative to the No 1 Guest House, and it's not much better. The three-bed dorms at the back are a good deal at US$2. Doubles are US$12 to US$21.

Places to Eat

The top section of Huguo Lu, clustered around the entrance to the No 2 Guest House, is where you'll find the travellers' hang-outs. Popular cafes include the *Yunnan Cafe*, *Tibetan Cafe* and *Marley's Cafe*.

Things to Buy

Marble souvenirs, batik wall hangings and brass jewellery are on sale everywhere, but bargain hard. Cheap clothing (including made-to-order stuff) is readily available.

Getting There & Away

Buses stop outside the Dali Hotel at 7.20 am on their way from Xiaguan to Lijiang. The trip to Kunming takes 11 hours, and tickets should be purchased in advance. Tickets for both of the preceding are available at the booking office on the corner of Huguo Lu and Fuxing Lu.

Minibuses to Xiaguan leave frequently (when full) during the day from the corner of Renmin Lu and Fuxing Lu.

LIJIANG

(lì jiāng) 丽江

North of Dali, bordering Tibet, is the town of Lijiang with its spectacular mountain backdrop. Lijiang is the home of the Naxi minority.

Orientation

Lijiang is divided into a boring Chinese section and an old town full of character, cobbled streets and market life. The approximate line of division is a hill topped with a radio mast. Everything west of the hill is the new town, and everything east of the hill is the old town.

Information

The PSB is across from the Lijiang Guest House. The Bank of China is on Xin Dajie almost opposite the intersection of the road that leads off to the Lijiang Hotel and the PSB.

Things to See

Crisscrossed by canals and a maze of cobbled streets, the **old town** is not to be missed. Arrive by mid-morning to see the market square full of Naxi women in traditional dress.

Also check out **Black Dragon Pool Park** *(hēi lóng tán gōng yuán)* on the northern edge of town; it has a pond and pavilion, all set against the distant backdrop of snow-peaked Jade Dragon Mountain *(yù lóng shān)*.

The small village of **Baisha** *(bái shā)* on the plain north of Lijiang is a lovely stop on the way to **Yufeng Monastery** *(yù fēng sì)*. The latter provides a magnificent view across the valley to Lijiang.

Places to Stay

The *Yunshan Hotel (yún shān fàn diàn)*, also known as the *No 3 Guest House*, is next to the new bus station. It's a good place to stay, but it's in the boring part of town. Dorms are US$1 to US$3.

The grotty *No 2 Guest House (dì èr zhāo dài suǒ)*, next to the old north bus station, is a budget option. Dorm beds are US$1 to US$4. Better rooms are US$7 to US$17.

The *Lijiang Guest House (No 1 Hotel) (dì yī zhāo dài suǒ)* has dorm beds for US$2 to US$5. Doubles are US$5 to US$12.

Places to Eat

Restaurants lining Mao Square include *Peter's*, *Ma Ma Hu* and *Salvadore's*. In the old town look for *Mimi's Cafe*, *Kele* and the *No 40 Restaurant*.

Getting There & Away

Air An airport is under construction, which threatens to change the character of this laid-back region forever.

Bus Buses run daily between Lijiang and Dali. There is a connection between Lijiang and Jinjiang, a town on the Chengdu-Kunming railway line. The bus trip to the railway takes nine hours from Lijiang.

TIGER LEAP GORGE
(hǔ tiào xiá) 虎越峡

Tiger Leap Gorge is a 16-km gorge on the Yangzi where cliffs drop nearly 300 metres to the river below. A narrow path clings to vertical walls at a height of over 3900 metres above sea level. Many travellers have become sick on the trek so it's a good idea to bring your own bottled water.

Tiger Leap Gorge is 94 km from Lijiang. At one end of the gorge is the town of Qiaotou and at the other end is Daju. A walk through the gorge usually takes two days, with an overnight stay at Walnut Grove where there are two hotels. There is one mandatory ferry crossing, and the ferryman is known to charge foreigners ridiculously high prices.

Buses run to Qiaotou daily from the south long distance bus station in Lijiang at 1 pm (the No 2 shuttle bus runs from the north station at 12.45 pm to connect with it), and theoretically minibuses run every second day from Daju back to Lijiang.

XISHUANGBANNA
(xī shuāng bǎn nà) 西双版纳

In the deep south of Yunnan Province, next to the Burmese and Laotian borders, is the region of Xishuangbanna. The Han Chinese and the Dai people make up a third of the population, the rest are a hotchpotch of minorities including the Miao, Zhuang, Yao and lesser known hill tribes.

Xishuangbanna attracts Han Chinese tourists who come in droves for the sunshine.

Jingchong
(jǐng hóng) 景洪

Jingchong is the capital of Xishuangbanna prefecture. The Water-Splashing Festival held around mid-April (usually 13-15 April) is a major tourist event which makes finding a hotel room very difficult.

Information CITS (☎ 2708) is on the Banna Hotel grounds. The Bank of China is on Jinghong Xilu opposite the post office. The PSB is opposite Peacock Park in the centre of town.

Places to Stay & Eat The *Banna Hotel (bǎn nà bīn guǎn)* in the centre of town has dorms for US$2 and doubles for US$8 to US$21. Nearby is the *Banna Mansion (bǎn nà dà shà)* with doubles for US$15.

The *Communications Hotel (jiāo tōng fàn diàn)*, next to the long-distance bus station, is a good option. Dorm beds are US$1 to US$2 and doubles are US$6 to US$9.

Along Manting Lu (25 minutes by foot from the bus station) are numerous Dai homes that double as restaurants and guesthouses. Basic rooms cost US$1 per person and facilities are primitive. Two such places are the *Lotus Hotel* and *Wanli Dai Restaurant*. The latter is an excellent place to eat dinner.

Actually, the whole of Manting Lu is lined with Dai restaurants, but it seems as if the Westerners have marked the Wanli as their own and left the rest for the busloads of Chinese tourists.

Getting There & Away There are daily flights to Kunming. Buses leave daily for Kunming and the trip takes two days; the road is beautiful but dangerous.

Getting Around The Banna Hotel hires out bikes for US$1 a day, and there's a place across the road that is even cheaper.

Around Jingchong

The possibilities for day trips and longer excursions out of Jingchong are endless. Some travellers have hiked and hitched from Menghai to Damenglong, and some have cycled up to Menghai and Mengzhe on mountain bikes.

Mengyang is 34 km east of Jingchong on the road to Simao. It's a centre for the Hani and Floral-Belt Dai.

Ganlanba (Menghan) lies on the Mekong south-east of Jinghong. The town itself is fairly forgettable, but if you come on a bike (it is also possible to hire one in Ganlanba) there is plenty of scope for exploration in the

CHINA

neighbourhood. Check the visitors' book in the Dai Bamboo House for some ideas.

Sichuan 四川

Sichuan supports 100 million people and is the largest and most heavily populated province in China. The eastern region, the great Chengdu Plain, has one of the densest rural populations in the world, while the regions to the west are mountainous, remote and populated mainly by Tibetans.

CHENGDU
(chéng dū) 成都

The capital of Sichuan, Chengdu is the stepping stone to the rest of the province.

Warning Theft is definitely on the increase. In particular there have been a couple of incidents (one foreigner was stabbed) on the riverside pathway between the Jinjiang and Traffic hotels.

Orientation
It's not unusual when following street numbers in one direction to meet another set coming the other way, often leaving the poor family in the middle with five sets of numbers over their doorway. Street names also seem to change every 100 metres or so.

Information
CITS in the Jinjiang Hotel is useless. Staff in the main office (☎ 25042) on Renmin Nanlu opposite the Jinjiang Hotel are friendlier but can't book train tickets or domestic flights and have been trained to say 'Tibet is closed'. However, they can book flights to Hong Kong on Dragonair.

The GPO is on the corner of Huaxinzhen Jie and Shuwa Beijie. Poste restante is at the window marked 'International Post'.

The US Consulate (☎ 582222) is in the Jinjiang Hotel.

The PSB is on Xinhua Donglu, east of the intersection with Renmin Lu.

Things to See
Renmin Park *(rén mín gōng yuán)* is one of the great parks in China. **Wenhua Park** *(wén huà gōng yuán)* is home to **Qingyang Palace** *(qīng yáng gōng)*, the oldest and most extensive Taoist temple in Chengdu. Nearby is **Du Fu Cottage** *(dù fǔ cǎo táng)*, the thatched cottage of the celebrated poet Du Fu (712 to 770 AD).

The **Temple of Wuhou** *(wǔ hòu sì)* in Nanjiao Park was named after a famous military strategist of the Three Kingdoms period (220 to 265 AD). He was the prime minister of the state of Shu when Chengdu was the capital.

Wenshu Monastery *(wén shū yuàn)* is overcrowded with worshippers and best avoided at weekends. The monastery's Buddhist statue was made in Tibet. The monastery, on an alley running eastwards off Renmin Zhonglu, is open from 8 am to 8 pm.

The **Sichuan Museum** *(sì chuān shěng bó wù guǎn)* is the largest provincial museum in China's south-west, with more than 150,000 items on display. The **Sichuan University Museum** *(sì dà bó wù guǎn)* is on the 1st and 3rd floors of Sichuan University's Liberal Arts building. The collection is particularly strong in the fields of ethnology, folklore and traditional arts.

Chengdu Zoo *(chéng dū dòng wù yuán)* is the best place in China to see pandas. It's six km from the city, reachable by minibuses from the north railway station. Next door to the zoo is the interesting **Zhaojue Temple** *(zhào jué sì)*.

Places to Stay
The *Traffic Hotel* (☎ 554962) *(jiāo tōng fàn diàn)* next to Xinnanmen bus terminal is most popular with budget travellers. Dorm beds start at US$4 while better rooms go for US$15 to US$17.

The nearby *Black Coffee Hotel (hēi kā fēi fàn diàn)* is unique for having been built in an old bomb shelter, but otherwise it's a

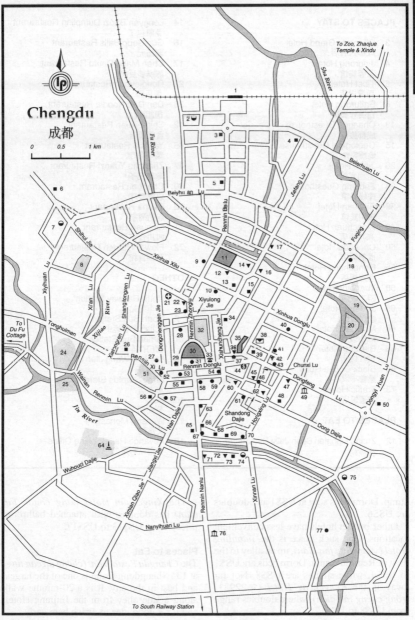

CHINA

PLACES TO STAY

3   Chengdu Grand Hotel
    成都大酒店
4   Jingrong Hotel
    京蓉宾馆
5   Tibet Hotel
    西藏饭店
6   Baifurong Hotel
    白芙蓉宾馆
13 Chengdu Guesthouse
    成都旅馆
15 Geological Guesthouse
    地质宾馆
26 Jinhe Hotel
    金河宾馆
34 Zhufeng Guesthouse
    珠峰宾馆
39 Sichuan Hotel
    四川宾馆
48 Xingchuan Hotel
    兴川饭店
50 Chengdu Hotel
    成都饭店
55 Rongcheng Hotel
    蓉成饭店
56 Yuanding Hotel
    园丁饭店
65 Jinjiang Hotel
    锦江宾馆
66 Minshan Hotel
    岷山饭店
68 Binjiang Hotel
    滨江饭店
69 Black Coffee Hotel
    黑咖啡饭店
73 Traffic Hotel
    交通饭店

PLACES TO EAT

12 Zhang Liangfen Bean Jelly Restaurant
    张凉粉

14 Longyan Baozi Dumpling Restaurant
    龙眼包子
16 Guo Soup Balls Restaurant
    郭汤元
17 Chen Mapo Doufu Restaurant
    陈麻婆豆腐
22 Rongleyuan Restaurant
    荣乐园
36 Dan Dan Noodle Restaurant
    担担面
42 Shimeixuan Restaurant
    食美饭店
45 Yaohua Restaurant
    耀华餐厅
47 Zhenzhu Yuanzi Restaurant
    珍珠元子
60 Chengdu Restaurant
    成都餐厅
62 Banna Restaurant
    版纳酒家
71 Sichuan Restaurant
    四川食馆
72 Flower Garden Restaurant
    花园食馆

OTHER

1   North Railway Station
    火车北站
2   North Bus Station
    城北汽车客运中心
7   Ximen Bus Station
    西门汽车站
8   Tomb of Wang Jian
    王建墓
9   Army Surplus Store
    军衣店
10 PSB
    公安局
11 Wenshu Monastery
    文殊院
18 Advance Rail Booking Office
    火车站售票处

dump. Dorm beds start at US$1 and doubles are US$6.

Other budget hotels have less convenient locations. One such place is the *Yuanding Hotel (yuán dīng fàn diàn)*, up an alley to the west of Renmin Nanlu. Dorm beds are US$1 to US$4, while singles are US$8. Not far away is the *Rongcheng Hotel (☎ 22931) (róng chéng fàn diàn)*, where doubles range from US$8 to US$17.

The *Xingchuan Hotel (xīng chuān fàn diàn)* has doubles with attached bathroom priced from US$13 to US$17.

Places to Eat
The *Chengdu Restaurant (chéng dū cān tīng)* at 134 Shangdong Dajie is one of the largest and best in the city. It is a 20-minute walk along a side alley from the Jinjiang Hotel, and it's a good idea to arrive here early.

19	Fun Park 市游乐园	46	Chunxi Commercial District 春熙路商业区
20	Mengzhuiwan Swimming Pool 猛追湾游泳池	49	Municipal Museum 市博物馆
21	No 3 Hospital 三医院	51	Renmin Park 人民公园
23	Tape Shop 音像书店	52	Sichuan Antique Store 文物店
24	Qingyang Palace (Wenhua Park) 青羊宫/文化公园	53	Dental Hospital 牙科医院
25	Baihuatan Park 百华潭公园	54	People's Market 人民商场
27	Sichuan Fine Arts Exihibition Hall 四川美术展览馆	57	Provincial PSB 省公安局
28	Advance Rail Booking Office 火车站售票处	58	Chengdu Department Store 成都百货大楼
29	Chengdu Folk Arts Exhibition Centre ('Hell World') 鬼城	59	Advance Rail Booking Office 火车站售票处
30	Sichuan Exhibition Centre 省展览馆	61	Friendship Store 友谊商店
31	Mao Statue 毛主席像	63	China Southwest Airlines/Pubs 中国西南航空公司
32	Municipal Sports Stadium 市体育场	64	Temple of Wuhou (Nanjiao Park) 武候祠/南郊公园
33	Telecommunications Centre 电话电报大楼	67	CAAC 中国国际旅行社
35	Cultural Palace 文化宫	70	China Southwest Airlines Booking Office 中国西南航空售票处
37	Hongqi Market 红旗商场	74	Xinnanmen Bus Station 新南门汽车站
38	GPO 市电信局	75	Jiuyanqiao Bus Station 九眼桥汽车站
40	Stock Market 红庙子	76	Sichuan Museum 省博物馆
41	Jinjiang Theatre 锦江剧场	77	Sichuan University 四川大学
43	Sichuan Foreign Language Bookshop 省外文书店	78	River Viewing Pavilion Park 望江楼公园
44	Bank of China 银行大厦		

Another main-course restaurant in the heart of the city is the *Yaohua Restaurant* (*yào huá fàn diàn*) at 22 Chunxi Lu. A visit by Mao himself in 1958 clinched the restaurant's reputation.

Along the south side of the Jin River between the Jinjiang and Traffic hotels is a short string of restaurants and teahouses with outdoor tables, and all serve Sichuan specialities. Perhaps the best is the *Jinjiang*

Restaurant. Down at the very end of the row, close to the Traffic Hotel, is the popular *Flower Garden Restaurant* where most travellers hang out. Also on the same stretch of road and popular with travellers is the *YS Restaurant*.

Things to Buy
Chunxi Lu is the main shopping artery. At No 10 is the Arts & Crafts Service depart-

ment store (chéng dū měi shù pǐn fú wù bù), dealing in most of the Sichuan specialities.

Getting There & Away
Air China Southwest Airlines (☎ 23991) is diagonally opposite the Jinjiang Hotel. The smaller Sichuan Provincial Airlines also has an office nearby.

Domestic flights from Chengdu are extensive. Dragonair offers flights to Hong Kong.

Bus The main bus station, Xinnanmen bus station, next to the Traffic Hotel, sells tickets to most destinations around Sichuan but not to the north. For northern destinations you will need to head over to the Ximen bus station in the north-west of the city.

For Emeishan, the best option is the 9.30 am bus that runs direct to Baoguo Temple. Buy tickets one day in advance.

The Ximen bus station is really only of interest to travellers heading up to Jiuzhaigou or taking the overland route to Xiahe in Gansu Province by way of northern Sichuan.

Train Getting train tickets out of Chengdu is no easy feat. Many travellers simply give up on the idea and get locals at either the Flower Garden or YS restaurants to fix tickets up for them. This is fine if you don't mind paying extra for their services.

Getting Around
Bus Bus No 16, which runs from the north railway station to the south railway station, is the most useful for getting around.

Bicycle Bike hire is readily available at the Traffic Hotel.

AROUND CHENGDU
Monastery of Divine Light
(bǎo guāng sì) 宝光寺
The Monastery of Divine Light is an active Buddhist monastery near Xindu, a small town 18 km north of Chengdu. It comprises five halls and 16 courtyards surrounded by bamboo. The temple was founded in the 9th century and reconstructed in the 17th.

Getting There & Away Buses run from 6.20 am to 6.30 pm from the terminal of the No 1 trolley bus (in front of the north railway station). The trip takes just under one hour. On a bicycle the whole trip would take four hours.

EMEISHAN
(é méi shān) 峨眉山
One of China's four famous Buddhist mountains (the others are Putuo, Wutai and Jiuhua), Emeishan is the site of annual pilgrimages for young and old.

The hiking is spectacular – craggy rocks, dense fir forest, azaleas, butterflies, rain and fog. For the Chinese, the goal is to view sunrise over the sea of clouds at the summit.

The best time to visit is from May to October. You should be prepared for sudden changes in weather, as Emeishan is 3099 metres high. There is no heating or insulation in the monasteries, although blankets are provided. You will also need a good pair of rough-soled shoes, as the going becomes slippery higher up the mountain.

Places to Stay & Eat
Two to three days on the mountain is enough. The old monasteries provide food and shelter but they often ask ridiculous prices from foreigners – bargain! Prices should range from US$1 for a bed in a very large dormitory, but these are usually off limits to foreigners. Single rooms cost around US$3. There are eight monastery guesthouses – at Baoguo Temple, Qingyin Pavilion, Wannian Temple, Xixiang Pond, Xianfeng Temple, Hongchunping, Fuhu Temple and Leiyin Temple.

At the foot of Emeishan is the *Hongzhushan Hotel (hóng zhū shān bīn guǎn)*, with dorm/singles at US$3/$6 and up. About 400 metres uphill from the Baoguo-Leshan bus station is *Xi Xiang Hotel (xī xiàng fàn diàn)*, where comfortable dorms cost US$3 per person.

Getting There & Away

The hubs of the transport links to Emeishan are Baoguo village and Emei town. Emei town itself is best skipped, though it does have cheap dorms at the Emei Hotel. Emei town lies 3.5 km from the railway station. Baoguo is another 6.5 km from Emei town. At Emei station, buses will be waiting for train arrivals. There are also direct buses running from Baoguo to Leshan and Chengdu.

LESHAN

(lè shān) 乐山

Apart from providing an insight into village life in China, Leshan is the home of the Grand Buddha *(dà fó)*, 71 metres high and carved from the cliff face overlooking the confluence of the Dadu and Min rivers. It's the largest buddha in the world. You can climb to the top or descend to the foot, but every part of the Buddha seems to have an admission fee.

Places to Stay & Eat

The *Leshan Educational Research Centre* (☎ 22964) *(lè shān jiào yù yán jiu suǒ)* at 156 Liren is around the corner from the bus station in the town centre. Doubles are US$7.

Near the Wuyou Temple is the *Da Du He Hotel (dà dù hé fàn diàn)*. Beds cost US$2.

There are two Chinese hostelries in the area above the head of the Grand Buddha; *Nanlou Guest House (nán lóu bīn guǎn)* and *Jiurifeng Guest House (jiǔ rì fēng bīn guǎn)*. Prices run between US$4 and US$17.

Getting There & Away

Bus There are three bus stations in Leshan, which complicates matters. The main one for travellers is the Leshan long-distance bus station. There are numerous daily buses running to Chengdu and the 165-km trip takes over five hours.

There are soft-seat coaches which leave at 7.30 am and 4.40 pm for Chongqing, and take 12 hours.

From Leshan to Emeishan is 30 km. Buses run to Emei town and Baoguo Temple.

CHONGQING

(chóng qìng) 重庆

This big city is heavily industrialised, but Chongqing retains vestiges of old China – neighbourhoods of ancient stone steps and alleys, and crumbling tiled rooftops.

For many travellers, the main attraction here is that Chongqing is the starting point for the boat trip down China's greatest river, the Yangzi.

Information

CITS (☎ 350188) is in the Renmin Hotel compound.

The PSB is on Linjiang Lu. Bus No 13 from the front of the Renmin Hotel goes there.

Things to See

Chongqing has few real sights of interest, though walking around the back alleys of this hilly city can be interesting. **Pipa Shan Park** *(pí pá shān gōng yuán)* at 345 metres marks the highest point on the Chongqing Peninsula. The Hongxing Pavilion at the top of the park provides good views.

There are **cable cars** spanning both of the rivers that cut through Chongqing: the Jialing River and the Yangzi River. Both are within walking distance of the Liberation Monument.

Red Cliff Village *(hóng yán cūn)* just outside Chongqing was used as the offices and living quarters of Communist representatives during the tenuous alliance between the Communists and the Kuomintang. Take bus No 104 from its terminal on Beiqu Lu just north of the Liberation monument.

The **Northern Hot Springs** *(běi wēn quán gōng yuán)* are on the site of a Buddhist temple in the large park overlooking the Jialing River to the north-east of the city. There is a big public pool plus private rooms with large hot baths. Swimsuits can be rented. Take bus No 306 from the Liberation monument.

Places to Stay

Chongqing's hotels are mostly expensive. The cheapest dorms cost US$6 at the

CHINA

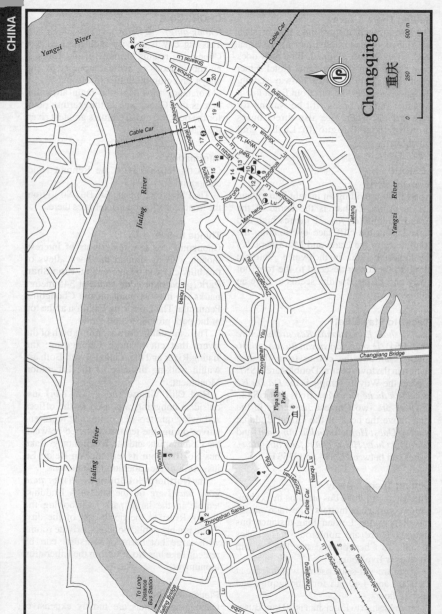

PLACES TO STAY

3 Renmin Hotel
   人民宾馆
7 Chongqing Guesthouse
   重庆宾馆
11 Yudu Hotel
    愉都宾馆
16 Huixianlou Hotel
    合仙楼宾馆
20 Chung King Hotel
    重庆饭店
21 Three Gorges Hotel
    三峡宾馆

PLACES TO EAT

14 Huleyuan Restaurant
    湖乐园
18 Lamb Restaurant
    羊肉馆

OTHER

1 Buses to SACO Prisons
   至中美合作所汽车站
2 CAAC
   中国民船

3 CITS
   中国国际旅行社
4 Cultural Palace of the
   LabouringPeople
   劳动人民文化宫
5 Railway Station
   火车站
6 Chongqing Museum
   博物馆
8 Long-Distance Bus
   Station (for Dazu)
   长途汽车站(往大足)
9 Foreign Languages Bookstore
   外文书店
10 Post Office
    邮电局
12 Xinhua Bookstore
    新华书店
13 Liberation Monument
    解放碑
15 PSB
    公安局外事科
17 Bank of China
    中国银行
19 Luohan Temple
    罗汉寺
22 Chaotianmen Dock (Booking Hall)
    朝天门码头(售票处)

Huixianlou Hotel (☎ 44135) *(huī xiān bīn guǎn)*, close to the Liberation Monument. From the railway station, walk up to Zhongshan Lu and take bus No 405 to the Liberation Monument *(jiě fàng bēi)*.

At the time of writing the *Three Gorges Hotel* (☎ 331112) *(sān xiá bīn guǎn)*, down by the Chaotianmen dock, had applied to take foreign guests. This would be a cheap alternative.

The palatial *Renmin Hotel* (☎ 351421) *(rén mín bīn guǎn)* is one of the most incredible hotels in China, but costs US$28 to US$38 for doubles.

Places to Eat

The central business district in the eastern section of the city near the docks abounds with small restaurants and street vendors. For tasty noodles and baozi, check out Xinhua Lu and Shaanxi Lu towards Chao-

tianmen dock. Behind the Huixianlou Hotel in the vicinity of Luohan Temple and in the area of the Yudu Hotel are some good night markets.

Getting There & Away

Air The CAAC office (☎ 55824) is on the corner of Zhongshan Sanlu and Renmin Lu. You can also book flights at the Chung King Hotel.

Bus The long-distance bus station is on the northern side of the Jialing River, across the Jialing Bridge.

Train There are direct trains to Beijing, Chengdu and Guiyang. Change at Chengdu for Kunming and at Guiyang for Guilin.

Boat You can take a boat trip from Chongqing to Wuhan down the Yangzi River – an interesting break from the trains.

DOWNRIVER ON THE YANGZI

The Yangzi is the third-longest river in the world, flowing from the Tanggulashan mountains to the East China Sea. The three gorges between Fengjie and Yichang provide some of the most exciting scenery. Enjoy it while you can; the government has plans to build a dam and flood these gorges to generate hydroelectric power.

The trip downriver from Chongqing to Wuhan takes three days and two nights, but the upriver journey takes five days. It's possible to leave the boat at Yichang, and take the train north to Xiangfan and Luoyang, or at Yueyang, where you can catch the train to Guangzhou.

CITS sells these tickets, but is badly organised. You can do better yourself booking at Chaotianmen Dock. You usually have to book two or three days in advance. Second class is a two-berth cabin, 3rd class is a four to eight-berth cabin and 4th class is a 24-bed cabin with communal showers and toilet. There is no 1st class.

Boats depart Chongqing at approximately 7 am from Chaotianmen Dock. You can sleep on the boat the night before departure for US$3 – easier than rushing to the dock in the morning. There are different boats departing at different times at different piers – make sure you've got the right one.

If you want to go farther down the Yangzi to Nanjing or Shanghai, you must change boats at Wuhan.

There are restaurants on each boat, but it's not a bad idea to bring some food – just make sure it's in *rat-proof* containers!

DAZU

(dà zú) 大足

The grotto art of Dazu County, 160 km north-west of Chongqing, is among the best in China. The main groupings of rock carvings and cave paintings are at Beishan (North Hill) and the more interesting Baoding. They

date from the Tang Dynasty (9th century) to the Song Dynasty (13th century).

Places to Stay & Eat

The *Dazu Guest House (dà zú bīn guǎn)* is the official abode for foreigners. Accommodation costs from US$3 to US$15.

Getting There & Away

There are several options by bus. The first is the direct bus from Chongqing to Dazu which leaves at 7.20 am from Chongqing's north-west bus station; there are seven buses a day. The second is the Kangfulai (KFL) bus company, which has three ticket offices and pickup points: next to the Chongqing Guesthouse, the railway station and the Renmin Hotel.

JIUZHAIGOU

(jiǔ zhài gōu) 九寨沟

Jiuzhaigou in northern Sichuan Province has several Tibetan settlements and a number of dazzling features. It's a spectacular nature reserve with mountains, forests and pristine lakes. You should calculate between a week and 10 days for the round trip; two to three days to get there and several more for hiking and exploring. The rainy season is from June to August, but there are tours available even at this time.

Getting There & Away

Air Plans are in the works to construct a small airport, but no word yet on when this will happen.

Bus Tours are booked out of Chengdu, but be careful, some of these tour companies have acquired a reputation for rotten service.

Public transport is not plentiful, so if you board en route rather than catching a bus at its originating point, be prepared for some tough competition for seats. To maximise your chances of a seat on a bus out of Jiuzhaigou, it's best to book your ticket three days in advance at the entrance to the reserve.

The road is dangerous and accidents are

frequent. The ticket office at the Ximen bus station in Chengdu requires that foreigners present a People Insurance Company of China (PICC) card certifying that they're carrying a PICC insurance policy for bus travel in northern Sichuan (the same applies for most of Gansu Province farther north). The card costs US$3 for one month's cover and is available from the PICC office *(zhōng guó rén mín bǎo xiǎn gōng sī)* on Shudu Dadao (Renmin Donglu), just down the road from the Hongqi Market in Chengdu. It's a good idea to have this card with you at all times while travelling in northern Sichuan – any bus driver could ask to see it.

Inner Mongolia 内蒙古

The nomadic Mongol tribes were united by Genghis Khan in 1206, and under his leadership conquered China and most of the known world. The vast Mongol Empire crumbled around 1368. The Qing emperors took control of the area in the 18th century, and the Russians set up a protectorate over the northern part of Mongolia. These divisions were set in concrete in the 1940s and the Chinese region is known as Inner Mongolia. Today, Han Chinese constitute the majority of Inner Mongolia's population.

HOHHOT
(hū hé hào tè) 呼和浩特
Hohhot became the capital of Inner Mongolia in 1952. The name means 'blue city' in Mongolian. It can be bleak in the dead of winter, but it's comfortable enough in summer, and is certainly one of China's more pleasant cities.

Information
CITS (☎ 624494) is in the lobby of the Inner Mongolia Hotel. However, we have found CTS (☎ 626774) on the 3rd floor of the rear building to be more helpful. You might need CTS to get a sleeper on the trains.

The PSB is in the vicinity of the Renmin

Park, near the corner of Zhongshan Lu and Xilin Guole Lu.

Things to See
The biggest attraction in town is the **Inner Mongolia Museum** *(nèi méng gǔ bó wù guǎn)* at 1 Xinhua Dajie. The museum includes a large mammoth skeleton, Mongolian costumery, archery equipment, saddles and a yurt.

The **Five Pagoda Temple** *(wǔ tǎ sì)* dates back to 1740 but is now bereft of its temple, leaving the Five Pagodas standing on a rectangular block. The Five Pagodas are on the bus No 1 route.

The **Great Mosque** *(qīng zhēn dà sì)* is not so great and is in sad shape. South of the mosque is **Xiletuzhao Temple** *(xí lè tú zhào)* and **Dazhao Temple** *(dà zhào)*.

The **Wang Zhaojun Tomb** *(zhào jūn mù)* is nine km from the city on the bus No 14 route. The tomb honors the Han Dynasty concubine of Emperor Yuandi (1st century BC).

Places to Stay
Most popular is the *Xincheng Hotel (xīn chéng bīn guǎn)* (☎ 663322), with nice dorms with three beds each for US$3. Double rooms with private bath go for US$17. It's two km from the railway station. You can take bus No 5 two stops from the station to get within 10 minutes' walking distance of the hotel.

Just next door is the *Inner Mongolia Hotel (nèi méng gǔ fàn diàn)*. Dorms in a three-bed room cost US$7 per person; doubles are US$26 and US$35.

The *Hohhot Hotel (hū hé hào tè bīn guǎn)* is near the railway station and has dorms for US$11 and doubles for US$22.

The *Zhaojun Hotel* (☎ 662211; fax 668825) *(zhào jūn dà jiǔ diàn)*, 11 Xinhua Dajie, is a fancy Hong Kong joint venture. Doubles cost US$38 and US$45.

Entertainment
Just east of the intersection of Xinhua Dajie and Hulunbei'er Lu is the Bailing Market *(bǎi líng shāng cháng)*. As you face the

market, on the right side of the building is a theatre where you can see brilliant Mongolian song and dance performances at night. Tickets are sold at all the big hotels for US$1.

Getting There & Away

Air CAAC (☎ 664103) is on Xilin Guole Lu. Air tickets between Hohhot and Beijing are harder to find than the Holy Grail. You might have more success with flights to Guangzhou or Wuhan.

Bus There are sporadic bus connections between Hohhot and Datong. Buses to Baotou leave every 30 minutes or so. The most useful bus connection for travellers is to Dongsheng, departing at 7.40 am.

Train Hohhot is on the Beijing to Lanzhou railway line that cuts a long loop through Inner Mongolia.

THE GRASSLANDS 草原

This is what most travellers come to see in Inner Mongolia. As for visions of the descendants of the mighty Khan riding the endless plains, the herds of wild horses etc – remember that this is still China. The independent nation of Mongolia is where the real Mongolians live, though getting there imposes some severe difficulties (see the Mongolia chapter later in this book for details).

There are three grasslands targeted for CITS and CTS tours: Xilamuren, 80 km from Hohhot; Gegentala, 170 km away in Siziwang Qi; and Huitengxile, 120 km from Hohhot, the most beautiful but least visited.

Legally speaking, all tours must be arranged through an authorised travel agency like CTS, CITS or some of the others catering to mainly Chinese tourists (eg, China Comfort Inner Mongolia Travel Service in the Hohhot Hotel). There are some fledgling private travel agents who try to solicit business in the lobbies of the tourist hotels; you can talk to them and discuss prices.

There are also individual taxi drivers around the railway station who do self-styled grassland tours for around US$35 per

person, which includes an overnight stay in a yurt belonging to the driver's family. These unofficial tours are technically illegal and get mixed reviews – one traveller was served a wretched meal in a yurt and got food poisoning. As you'll discover if you explore the Mongolian hinterland, sanitation is not a strong point.

If the price of a tour seems too hefty, you can see some of the same things at Dongsheng and even stay there in a yurt for a fraction of what CITS charges.

DONGSHENG

(dōng shèng) 东胜

Dongsheng lies south-west of Hohhot and serves as a staging post for the site of **Genghis Khan's Mausoleum** *(chéng jí sī hàn líng yuán)*, which was built as recently as 1954, when his supposed ashes were brought from Qinghai, where they had been taken to keep them from the invading Japanese.

Places to Stay

The *Foreign Trade Hotel (wài mào dà jiǔ diàn)* has double rooms for US$5. Many travellers also stay at the cheapie *Yimeng Binguan* for US$3. The most upmarket place in town is the *Ordos Hotel* (☎ 26301) *(è ěr duō sī fàn diàn)*, with doubles for US$21.

There are two places to stay right by the mausoleum itself. One is a tourist yurt campground *(méng gǔ bāo)* that costs US$5. The other place is a hostel *(chéng jí sī hàn líng zhāo dài suǒ)* with no English name. However, most travellers prefer to stay in Dongsheng.

Getting There & Away

There is a bus directly from Hohhot (5½ hours) departing at 7.40 am. More frequent buses connect Dongsheng to Baotou, a depressing city to the west of Hohhot. After spending a night in Dongsheng, most travellers head for the mausoleum. The first bus leaves Dongsheng at 7 am, but there are several throughout the day. The journey from Dongsheng to the mausoleum takes 1½ hours. The mausoleum is in the middle of nowhere.

Another strategy is to take a bus to Ejin Horo Qi *(yī jīn huò luò qí)*, which is 25 km from the mausoleum, and then switch to a minibus which takes 30 minutes to complete the journey.

Ningxia 宁夏

Much of arid Ningxia is populated by a few hardy nomads who make their living grazing sheep and goats. The Yellow River is Ningxia's lifeline. Most of the population live near it or the irrigation channels that run off it.

About a third of the population are Hui, the Muslim descendants of Arab traders who travelled to China during the Tang Dynasty and of later immigrants from Central Asia.

YINCHUAN
(yín chuān) 银川
Yinchuan was once the capital of the Western Xia, a mysterious kingdom founded during the 11th century. Today it's the capital of tiny Ningxia Province.

Orientation
Yinchuan is divided into two parts: a new industrial section close to the railway station and the old town about four km away. The railway station is in the new town, but everything worth seeing and the hotels are in the old town.

Information
The main CITS/CTS office (☎ 544485) is upstairs at 150 Jiefang Xijie. There is also a small CITS office in room 129 of the Ningxia Hotel.

The main Bank of China is at 102 Jiefang Jie in a white-tiled building near the Ningxia Hotel.

The PSB is in a white building on Jiefang Xijie.

Things to See
The **North Pagoda** *(běi tǎ)* is easy to spot, standing like a stone spaceship to the north of town. There is no public transport; other than walking, you can reach the pagoda by bicycle or taxi. The distance from the Oasis Hotel is 2.5 km.

The **Regional Museum** *(qū bó wù guǎn)* is on Jinning Jie, three blocks south of Jiefang Lu. Its collection includes Western Xia and Northern Zhou historical relics as well as material covering the Hui culture. Within the leafy courtyard is the **West Pagoda** *(xī tǎ)*.

The **Drum Tower** *(gǔ lóu)* is similar to other drum towers you find in China. Just to the east of the Drum Tower is the **Yuhuang Pavilion** *(yù húang gé)*. It is 400 years old but has been restored.

The **South Gate** *(nán mén)* is a mini-model of Tiananmen gate in Beijing, complete with Mao portrait. Close to the South Gate is the **Mosque** *(qīng zhēn sì)*, which features a huge water fountain in the front.

Places to Stay
If you want to stay in the new city, there's the *Alashan Hotel* (☎ 366723) *(ā lā shān fàn diàn)*, a friendly Chinese hotel just west of the traffic circle at Tie Dongjie and Xincheng Jie. Doubles are US$8. Across the intersection is the *Xincheng Hotel (xīn chéng fàn diàn)* which has similar rates. The No 1 bus stops almost outside.

Bus No 1 also stops near the *Oasis Hotel* (☎ 546351) *(lü zhōu fàn diàn)* on Jiefang Xijie, easily distinguished by the 'rocket ship' on the roof. Dorm beds cost US$2 and singles/doubles are US$6/7.

One block south you'll find the *Xinxi Hotel (xìn xī fàn diàn)* which has good dorm beds for US$1 and singles for US$7.

The *Ningxia Hotel* (☎ 545131) *(níng xià bīn guǎn)* at 3 Gongyuan Jie near Zhongshan Park is a classy place starting at US$17 for a double.

Getting There & Away
Air CAAC (☎ 622143) is at 14 Minzu Beijie.

CHINA

There's a branch of the CAAC-clone United China Airlines (☎ 631625) at 24 Zhongshan Beilu, north of Jiefang Lu. There are flights to Beijing, Xi'an and Lanzhou.

Bus Buses connect Yinchuan with major towns in Ningxia such as Zhongwei, Tongxin and Guyuan. There are also buses to Xi'an and Lanzhou. The bus station is in the south-east part of town near Nanmen Square.

Yinchuan lies on the Lanzhou-Beijing railway which runs through Baotou, Hohhot and Datong.

Getting Around
Bus Buses and minibuses connect the old town to the railway station.

Bicycle The Oasis, Xinxi and Ningxia hotels have a few rental bicycles, but only for their own guests.

Gansu 甘肃

Gansu is a barren province, made up of mostly mountains and deserts. But through this impoverished region ran the Silk Road, along which camel caravans carried goods in and out of China. The Great Wall ends here. Traditionally, towns were established in the oases where agriculture was possible; these days, manufacturing, mining and tourism contribute to the economy.

LANZHOU
(lán zhōu) 兰州
Lanzhou, the capital and only city in Gansu, has been an important garrison town and transport centre since ancient times.

Orientation
Lanzhou stretches for 20 km along the Yellow River. The eastern segment of town harbours the railway station and most of the tourist facilities.

```
┌──────────────────────────────────────┐
│ PLACES TO STAY                         │
│                                        │
│  3   Friendship Hotel                  │
│      友谊饭店                           │
│  5   Victory Hotel                     │
│      胜利宾馆                           │
│ 14   Ningwozhuang Guesthouse           │
│      宁卧庄宾馆                         │
│ 15   Jincheng Hotel                    │
│      金城饭店                           │
│ 16   Lanzhou Hotel                     │
│      兰州饭店                           │
│                                        │
│ OTHER                                  │
│                                        │
│  1   West Railway Station              │
│      火车西站                           │
│  2   Gansu Provincial Museum           │
│      甘肃省博物馆                       │
│  4   West Bus Station                  │
│      汽车西站                           │
│  6   PSB (City Office)                 │
│      市公安局                           │
│  7   Telephone & Telegram Office       │
│      电信大楼                           │
│  8   The East is Red Square            │
│      东方红广场                         │
│  9   PSB (Provincial Office)           │
│      省公安局                           │
│ 10   Bank of China                     │
│      中国银行                           │
│ 11   Post & Telephone Office           │
│      邮电局                             │
│ 12   CAAC                              │
│      中国民航                           │
│ 13   CITS                              │
│      中国国际旅行社                     │
│ 17   Lanzhou University                │
│      兰州大学                           │
│ 18   Main Railway Station              │
│      火车总站                           │
│ 19   Chairlift to Lanshan              │
│      兰山索道                           │
└──────────────────────────────────────┘
```

Information
CITS (☎ 23055) is on Nongmin Xiang, the lane running behind the Jincheng Hotel.

The Bank of China is just north of The East is Red Square on Pingliang Lu.

There are two PSB offices. The provincial office is at 38 Qingyang Lu on The East is Red Square. The PSB's smaller 'city' office is at 132 Wudu Lu on the right as you enter the compound.

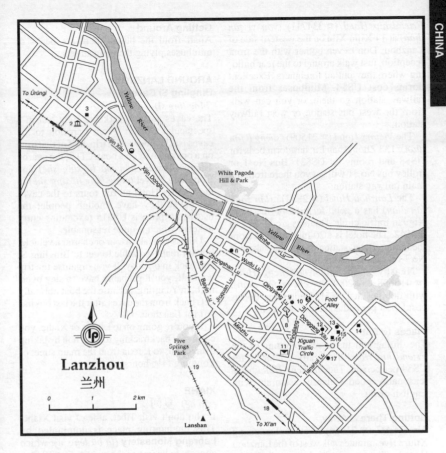

Lanzhou
兰州

0   1   2 km

To Ürümqi

Yellow River

Xijin Xilu

Xijin Donglu

White Pagoda
Hill & Park

Yellow River

Zhongshan Lu

Wudu Lu

Binhe Lu

Baiyin Lu

Jiuquan Lu

Minzhu Lu

Qingyang Lu

Dongang Xilu

Tianshui Lu

Food
Alley

Xiguan
Traffic
Circle

Five
Springs
Park

Lanshan

To Xi'an

Things to See

The **Gansu Provincial Museum** *(gān sù shěng bó wù guǎn)* is across the street from the Friendship Hotel, and is among the best of China's smaller provincial museums.

You'll find three mosques, two pagodas, numerous pavilions and a large, white Buddhist shrine at **White Pagoda Hill** *(bái tǎ shān)*. Bus No 7 from the railway station goes there. You have to cross a bridge, but there is also an occasional ferry. Admission is US$1 for foreigners.

Lanshan Park *(lán shān gōng yuán)* is part of a mountain range rising steeply to the south of Lanzhou, reaching over 2000 metres. The quickest and nicest way up is by chairlift from behind **Five Springs Park** *(wǔ quán gōng yuán)*.

Places to Stay

The *Lanzhou Mansions (lán zhōu dà shà)*, the big tower immediately left as you leave the railway station, charges US$7 per bed or US$24 for doubles. In the big yellow building opposite the station square is the *Lanshan Guest House (lán shān bīn guǎn)*, with doubles for US$21.

An old favourite of budget travellers is the

CHINA

Friendship Hotel (☎ 334711) (*yǒu yì fàn diàn*) at 14 Xijin Xilu on the western side of Lanzhou. Don't even bother with the front reception, just walk around to the rear building where they put all foreigners. Excellent dorms cost US$4. Minibuses from the railway station go there, or you can walk from the west bus station or west railway station.

The *Victory Hotel* (☎ 21509) (*shèng lì fàn diàn*), 133 Zhongshan Lu, has dorm beds for US$8 and rooms for US$21. Bus No 1 or trolley bus No 31 will get you there from the main railway station.

The *Lanzhou Hotel* (☎ 28321) (*lán zhōu fàn diàn*) has a good location on the large Xiguan traffic circle. Doubles are US$14 to US$42. The hotel is a 20-minute walk from the main railway station or you can take bus No 1 or 7 for two stops.

Nearby is the plush *Jincheng Hotel* (☎ 416638 ext 200) (*jīn chéng fàn diàn*), with doubles at US$51. Depressing dorms cost US$4 per bed and aren't worth it.

Places to Eat

The dining hall in the rear building of the *Friendship Hotel* has hearty set meals for US$4 per person. The *Jincheng Hotel* has a reasonably good Chinese restaurant with English menu.

Getting There & Away

Air CAAC (☎ 21964) is at 46 Donggang Xilu, a five-minute walk west of the Lanzhou Hotel. There are flights to Beijing, Guangzhou, Chengdu, Dunhuang, Xi'an and Ürümqi.

Bus The west bus station handles departures to Linxia and Xiahe. As in Sichuan Province, foreigners travelling by bus in Gansu must purchase insurance from the People's Insurance Company of China (PICC). In Lanzhou you can buy insurance at the PICC office (☎ 416422 ext 114) at 150 Qingyang Lu, the CITS office and most of the tourist hotels.

Train Trains run to Ürümqi, Beijing, Xi'an and Shanghai.

Getting Around

Apart from the buses, there are heaps of minibuses plying the main streets.

AROUND LANZHOU
Bingling Si Caves

(*bǐng líng sì*)

The caves are a remarkable sight, set in a spectacular canyon. From Lanzhou to the caves is a 12-hour round trip, half of that time on a bus and half on a boat. CITS, the nearby Tianma Travel (*tiān mǎ lǚ xíng shè*) and Dongfang Travel (*dōng fāng lǚ xíng shè*) in the Victory Hotel all run tours to the caves whenever they have enough people; the usual tour price is US$15 (excluding entry tickets), which is quite reasonable.

Unless you take a tour or charter a vehicle, it's not really possible to get to Bingling Si and back in one day. If you organise the trip yourself, you'll probably have to stay overnight in Yongjing, because the boat normally gets back from the caves after the last bus has left for Lanzhou.

If you're going on to Linxia or Xiahe, you can avoid backtracking to Lanzhou by taking a direct bus to Linxia from the main street of Yongjing (4½ hours).

XIAHE

(*xià hé*) 夏河

If you don't visit Tibet, at least visit Xiahe. This enchanting place is dominated by **Labrang Monastery** (*lā bǔ lèng sì*), which appears to be one of the most active Tibetan communities in existence. Entry to the monastery is by tour only and costs US$3.

Xiahe is a great place for hiking amidst mountains, temples and grazing land. Be careful of dogs which run loose all over the town – carrying a large stick is advised.

Information

CITS is at the Labrang Hotel. There is no adequate place to change travellers' cheques here. Small antique shops along the main street will give you a reasonable rate for US$ cash. There is a small post office a short way up from the Minzu Hotel. The PSB is directly opposite the hotel. If you need to buy insurance for bus travel, there is a PICC office in a compound just across the first bridge. You can rent bikes at several of the restaurants along the main road for about US$2 a day.

Places to Stay

The *Dasha Hotel (dà shà bīn guǎn)* near the bridge charges US$3 in quads or US$4 in triples; average doubles with bathroom are US$14. Opposite is the *Xinhua Hostel (xīn huá zhāo dài suǒ)*, where beds in doubles/triples are US$3/2.

The *Waterworks Hostel (zì lái shuǐ zhāo dài suǒ)* has beds from US$1.

The *Labrang Monastery Guest House (lā bǔ lèng sì zhāo dài suǒ)* has beds for US$2 in double and triple rooms.

The *Labrang Hotel (☎ 21849) (lā bǔ lèng bīn guǎn)* is by the river a few km up the valley from the village. A double suite is US$25; other doubles with bath cost US$20 and US$12. Beds in triples are US$2. You can get here by motortricycle for about US$1, or walk for 45 minutes. The hotel rents out bicycles for US$3 a day.

The *Minzu Hotel* near the lower bus station was undergoing renovations at the time of our visit.

Things to Buy

The shops along Xiahe's main street are a surprisingly good place to pick up Tibetan handicrafts. Needless to say, prices are highly negotiable.

Getting There & Away

Most travellers arrive from Lanzhou, but some visit Xiahe as a stop en route between Gansu and Sichuan. From Lanzhou, there is only one direct daily bus departing from the west bus station at 7.30 am. If you can't get a direct ticket from Lanzhou to Xiahe, then take a morning bus to Linxia and change there.

DUNHUANG

(dūn húang) 敦皇

Dunhuang is a large oasis in one of the most arid regions of China. Travellers come here because of the superb Buddhist art on view in the nearby Mogao Caves. The area has a certain haunting beauty, especially at night under a star-studded sky.

Information

The main CITS office is on the 2nd floor of the Dunhuang Hotel (Binguan) at the southern end of Dingzi Lu, almost opposite the Western Region Hotel. The PSB is on Xi Dajie, near the Bank of China.

Things to See

Virtually all the sights are outside the town itself. One which isn't is the interesting **Dunhuang County Museum** *(dūn húang xiàn bó wù guǎn)* on Dong Dajie east of the main traffic circle.

Of the sights to see around Dunhuang, recommended spots include the Mogao Caves, the Old City Movie Set, White Horse Dagoba and Crescent Moon Lake. To charter a small minibus to the above-mentioned places you'll pay around US$26.

The **Mogao Caves** *(mò gāo kū)* are the highlight of Dunhuang. These Buddhist caves are set into desert cliffs above a river valley about 25 km south-east of Dunhuang. Admission is US$2 or US$8 depending on how many caves you want to see. There are only two scheduled public buses daily – the first departs at 8 am and returns at 11 am. The afternoon bus departs at 1.30 pm and returns at 4 pm.

The **Old City Movie Set** *(diàn yǐng gǔ chéng)* was built in 1987 as a movie set for a Sino-Japanese co-production titled *Dunhuang*. Standing isolated out in the desert some 20 km south-west of Dunhuang, from a distance the Old City has a dramatic and strikingly realistic appearance. From close up, though, the place is starting to look a bit shabby. To travel there, minibuses leave from the side street one block north of Dunhuang bus station. They charge only US$2, but generally stay far too long. You can get there by bicycle.

The **White Horse Dagoba** *(bái mǎ tǎ)* is something of an anticlimax. The dagoba is four km west of town and is easily combined with the trip out to the Old City Movie Set. It makes a good place for a short bicycle excursion.

Crescent Moon Lake (*yùe yá qúan*) is just a pond, but it's well worth visiting. Nestled among the giant sand dunes on the south side of the oasis, the setting is dramatic. Camel riding, 'dune surfing' and paragliding are additional attractions. There is a once-daily bus which departs the bus terminal at 6 pm and returns at 8 pm.

Places to Stay
The *Western Region Hotel* (*xī yù bīn guǎn*) is a white-tiled building a few doors south of the bus station. Dorms/doubles are US$3/7.

Almost directly opposite the bus station is the *Feitian Hotel* (☎ 22726) (*fēi tiān bīn guǎn*), which has dorms/doubles for US$3/17.

Close by is the crumbling *Mingshan Hotel* (☎ 22132) (*míng shān bīn guǎn*), with dorm beds for US$2 and doubles for US$8 to US$19.

There are two places called the Dunhuang Hotel in English, but with different Chinese names. The smaller *Dunhuang Hotel* (*dūn huáng fàn diàn*) charges US$2 per bed in simple quads and US$14 for doubles. This place has clearly seen better days.

A second, much larger *Dunhuang Hotel* (☎ 22415) (*dūn huáng bīn guǎn*) is a slick tourist hotel at No 1 Dong Dajie on the eastern side of town. There is a wide range of rooms with varying prices. Dorms bottom out at US$2, with doubles from US$21 to US$59.

Getting There & Away
Air In the peak season from July to October there are daily flights to/from Lanzhou and Xi'an and less frequent air services to Beijing and Ürümqi.

Bus Buses to Liuyuan (130 km) depart eight times daily from the bus station between 7.30 am and 6 pm, taking 2½ hours. There are scheduled public buses to Jiayuguan (seven hours). Minibuses cover these routes too.

There is one bus daily to Golmud departing at 6.30 am; the trip takes 13 hours.

Train Liuyuan (on the Lanzhou-Ürümqi line) is the jumping-off point for Dunhuang.

Xinjiang 新疆

Xinjiang is divided by the east-west Tianshan range into two major regions. To the south of the range is the Tarim Basin, and to the north is the Junggar Basin. To the east is the huge salt marsh and lake of Lop Nur, which is almost uninhabited and used by the Chinese for nuclear weapons tests. The climate tends towards extremes – sizzling summers and frigid winters. The population used to be mostly Uigur, but with large-scale Chinese immigration to the north, the Uigurs now number less than half the total, plus Kirghiz, Kazakhs and other minorities.

TURPAN
(*tǔ lǔ fān*) 吐鲁番
Turpan is unique – a stronghold of one of China's most interesting minorities, the Turkish-speaking Muslim Uigurs. They are not Chinese at all and could easily pass for southern Europeans or Arabs. Donkey carts, grapevines, mosques, two ancient ruined cities and numerous other sights make Turpan an exotic place to visit.

If the culture is exotic, the geography is bizarre – Turpan is an oasis situated in a basin 154 metres below sea level. It's the lowest spot in China and the second-lowest depression in the world. It's also the hottest place in China, with a record temperature of 49.6°C. Yet this barren desert is a rich agricultural region thanks to melting snow from the nearby mountains.

Orientation
The centre of the Turpan oasis is little more than a few main roads and a couple of side streets. The centre is called Old City (*lǎo chéng*) and the western part is New City (*xīn*

chéng). Most of the sights are scattered on the outskirts of the oasis or in the surrounding desert.

Information

CITS (☎ 22768) is at the Oasis Hotel.

The most convenient place to change money is the Oasis Hotel. There is also a Bank of China about a 10-minute walk from the hotel.

The PSB is one block west of the Bank of China.

Things to See

The **Bazaar** *(nóng mào shì chǎng)* is one of the most fascinating markets in China. It's just opposite the bus station.

CITS puts on a traditional Uigur **Song & Dance Show** almost every night during the summer in the courtyard of the Turpan Guest House at 10 pm. Tour groups usually put up the money but most travellers get to watch for free.

Most of the best sights are around Turpan and you need to book a minibus tour to see them. This requires a full day. You won't have to find the minibuses, they'll find you. Drivers typically expect US$35 for the bus (bargain!) for a whole day. Since a minibus holds six to eight people, you can split the cost. A typical trip should include the **Atsana Graves** *(ā sī tǎ nà),* **Gaochang Ruins** *(gāo chāng gù chéng),* **Bezeklik Caves** *(bó zī kè lǐ qiān fó dòng),* **Grape Valley** *(pú táo gōu),* **Emin Minaret** *(é mǐn tǎ),* **Underground Irrigation Channels** *(dì xià shuǐ)* and **Jiaohe Ruins** *(jiāo hé gù chéng)* – usually in that order.

Places to Stay

The *Oasis Hotel (lü zhōu bīn guǎn)* is the best place in town. Dorm beds are US$3, though there is talk of pushing this up to US$7 during the busy summer months. Doubles range from US$26 to US$35. All rooms, including dorms, have air-con.

The *Turpan Guest House (tǔ lǔ fān bīn guǎn)* is known for surly staff. In the shade of the vine trellises is a good place to sit while saturating yourself with cold drinks (try the watermelon juice). Rates are US$3 for a dormitory bed and US$17 minimum for a double in one of the new wings.

The *Jiaotong Hotel (jiāo tōng bīn guǎn)* is right next to the bus station and market – a busy, noisy place. Dorms are US$2 and doubles cost US$14.

The *Tulufan Hotel (tǔ lǔ fān fàn diàn)* doesn't really have a lot going for it, but it does have dorms/doubles for US$3/8.

Places to Eat

Opposite the Turpan Hotel is *John's Cafe,* which also has a branch in Kashgar. It's a good place to hang out and has an English menu and reasonable prices.

Opposite the Oasis Hotel is the *Silk Road Restaurant* with a menu made up mainly of Chinese dishes. The area around the *Yanye Restaurant* is also a good place to eat.

Getting There & Away

Bus There are bus connections between Turpan and Ürümqi or Daheyan. In Turpan, the bus station is near the market. Make sure you get to the station an hour before departure because there is invariably a long queue for tickets.

There are at least four buses daily to Ürümqi plus private minibuses about once every hour.

Train The nearest railway line is the Ürümqi-Lanzhou line north of Turpan. The nearest railway station is at Daheyan. There are buses between Daheyan and Turpan.

ÜRÜMQI
(wū lǔ mù qí) 乌鲁木齐

Ürümqi is Xinjiang's capital and basically a Chinese city, though there is a considerable Uigur presence. It's an interesting place to visit but the best sights are in the surrounding areas.

Information

CITS is in a compound on the east side of Renmin Square, and has a reputation for avarice and incompetence. Much better is CYTS on the 1st floor of the Hongshan

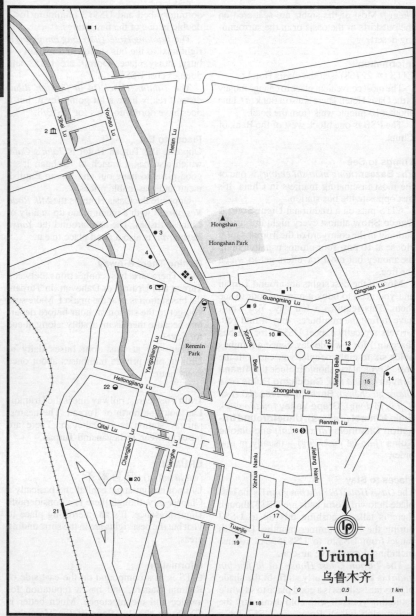

Hongshan

Hongshan Park

Renmin Park

Xibei Lu

Youhao Lu

Hetan Lu

Qingnian Lu

Guangming Lu

Xinhua Beilu

Jiefang Beilu

Zhongshan Lu

Renmin Lu

Yangzijiang Lu

Heilongjiang Lu

Qitai Lu

Changjiang Lu

Huanghe Lu

Xinhua Nanlu

Jiefang Nanlu

Tuanjie Lu

Ürümqi

乌鲁木齐

0   0.5   1 km

PLACES TO STAY

1. Kunlun Guesthouse
   昆仑宾馆
8. Holiday Inn Urumqi
   假日大酒店
9. Hongshan Hotel & CYTS
   红山宾馆
10. Laiyuan Hotel
    休远宾馆
11. Bogda Hotel
    博格达宾馆
18. Overseas Chinese Hotel
    华侨宾馆
20. Xinjiang Hotel
    新疆饭店

PLACES TO EAT

12. Hongchunyuan Restaurants
    鸿春园饭店
19. Guangdong Jiujia
    广东酒家

OTHER

2. Xinjiang Autonomous Region Museum
   新疆维吾尔自治区博物馆

3. CAAC
   中国民航
4. Hongshan Market
   红山市场
5. Hongshan Department Store
   红山商场
6. GPO
   邮局
7. Buses to Tianchi & Baiyanggou
   往天池/白扬沟汽车
13. PSB
    公安局外事科
14. CITS
    中国国际旅行社
15. Renmin Square
    人民广场
16. Bank of China
    中国银行
17. Erdaoqlao Market
    二道桥市场
21. Railway Station
    火车站
22. Long-Distance Bus Station
    长途汽车站

Hotel. CYTS can do rail tickets, provide maps and other information.

The GPO is a big Corinthian-colonnaded building directly across the traffic circle from the Hongshan Department Store.

The PSB is a 10-minute walk from the CITS office, in a large government building just to the north-west of Renmin Square.

Things to See

About one km in length, **Renmin Park** (*rén mín gōng yuán*) can be entered from either the north or south gates. Avoid it on Sunday when the Chinese descend on the place and hold 'who can make the most noise and throw the most rubbish' contests.

Just to the north of Renmin Park is **Hongshan Park** (*hóng shān gōng yuán*) with its distinctive pagoda. It's not exactly one of the world's seven wonders, but the pagoda sits on top of a big hill and affords sweeping views of the city.

Places to Stay

The *Hongshan Hotel* (☎ 24761) (*hóng shān bīn guǎn*) is favoured by backpackers. The dorms cost US$4 in a three-bed room without private bath. For US$8 there are two-bed dorms with private bath – good value if you don't mind paying a little more for the luxury.

Just around the corner from the Hongshan is the *Bogda Hotel* (*bó gé dá bīn guǎn*). Prices here are basically the same as those at the Hongshan, with three-bed dormitories for US$4 per person.

The *Xinjiang Hotel* (☎ 552511) (*xīn jiāng fàn diàn*) at the southern end of Changjiang Lu is the only accommodation within walking distance of the railway station. Dorms cost US$2 per person and doubles are US$6 per bed. The only rooms here with attached bath cost US$26.

The *Overseas Chinese Hotel* (☎ 260845) (*huá qiáo bīn guǎn*) is much farther from the

CHINA

town centre than the others but still easy to reach with bus No 7. Doubles here look good but are not cheap at US$17.

Places to Eat
For traditional Uigur foods (shish kebab, flatbread), try the *Hongshan Market* across from the Hongshan Department Store. An even better place is the *Erdaoqiao Market* near the Overseas Chinese Hotel.

Entertainment
On the 2nd floor of the Holiday Inn is Silks, a disco that's open until 2 am. The cover charge is an exorbitant US$7 if you're not a guest.

Getting There & Away
Air The CAAC office (☎ 217942) is on Youhao Lu, just up the road from the post office. Bus Nos 1 and 2 go past the office. Useful domestic flights include those to Beijing, Guangzhou, Chengdu, Kashgar, Shanghai and Xi'an.

There are some international flights too, including flights to Tashkent and Alma Ata in the former Soviet Union.

Bus The long-distance bus station is in the western part of town. The departure time given on your ticket is usually Beijing time, check if you're not sure. Foreigners are charged at least double what locals pay.

Train From Ürümqi there are eastbound trains at least six times daily.

TIANCHI
(tiān chí) 天池
Tianchi (Lake of Heaven) is a sight you'll never forget. Halfway up a mountain in the middle of a desert, it looks like a chunk of Switzerland or Canada that's been exiled to western China.

The lake is 115 km east of Ürümqi at an elevation of 1900 metres. Horses are also offered at US$10 to US$17 per day for a trek to the snow line. The trek to the snow line and back takes 10 hours. There's a hotel at the lake that has dorms for US$2 and there are also yurts for rent.

Getting There & Away
Buses leave Ürümqi at around 8 am from both the north and south gates of Renmin Park – the north side is more convenient if you're staying at the Hongshan Hotel. Departures are from where the sign says in English 'Taxi Service'. Buy your ticket about 30 minutes ahead of time to assure getting a seat. The trip takes over three hours. The bus will probably drop you off at the end of the lake, and from there it's a 20-minute walk to the hotel on the banks.

KASHGAR
(kā shí) 喀什
Kashgar is a giant oasis and one of those bizarre end-of-the-earth places like Timbuktu, where time seems frozen in a different age. The culture is heavily Muslim and relations between the Uigur majority and the Han rulers are tense.

Information
CITS is in Chini Bagh Hotel (☎ 23156) but has little understanding of the needs of travellers. John's Information & Cafe opposite the Seman Hotel is probably the best place to get the lowdown on travelling to Pakistan and seeing the sights around Kashgar. John himself is a mine of information and he offers competitive rates for minibus and 4WD hire.

The Bank of China (☎ 2461) is on Renmin Xilu near the post office.

Things to See
The focus of activity is the bazaar and the **Id Kah Mosque** *(ài tí gǎáér qīng zhēn sì)*.

The **Abakh Hoja Tomb** *(xiāng fēi mù)* is a strange construction in the eastern part of the oasis. It looks something like a stubby, multicoloured miniature of the Taj Mahal. The tomb is the burial place of Hidajetulla Hoja, a Muslim missionary and saint. It's an hour's walk east from the Kashgar Guesthouse.

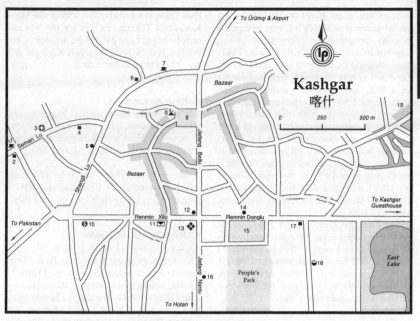

Kashgar
喀什

To Ūrūmqi & Airport

Bazaar

Bazaar

To Pakistan

To Hotan

To Kashgar Guesthouse

East Lake

People's Park

PLACES TO STAY	OTHER	
2 Seman Hotel 色满宾馆	3 Minorities Hospital 民族医院	14 Mao Statue 毛泽东塑像
4 Silk Road Hotel 丝绸之路饭店	5 PSB 公安局	15 People's (Renmin) Square 人民广场
6 Chini Bagh Hotel 其尼巴合宾馆	8 Id Kah Mosque 艾提尕清真寺	16 CAAC 中国民航
17 Tiannan Hotel 天南饭店	9 Id Kah Square 艾提尕广场	18 Long-Distance Bus Station 长途汽车站
PLACES TO EAT	10 Bank of China 中国银行	19 Sunday Market 星期日市场
1 John's Information & Cafe 咖啡馆	11 Post Office 邮电大楼	
7 Le Bistro Cafe 咖啡馆	12 Cinema 电影院	
	13 Department Store 百货大楼	

You should not miss the **Sunday Market**
(*jià rì jí shì*) on the eastern fringe of town.
Hundreds of donkey carts, horsemen, pedestrians and animals thunder into town for a
bargaining extravaganza.

Places to Stay
The *Seman Hotel* (☎ 2129) (*sè mǎn bīn
guǎn*) is on the western edge of town. A double
with bath costs US$10, but check the plumb-
ing first. A bed in the dormitory costs US$3.

The *Chini Bagh Hotel* (☎ 2291) *(qí ní bā hé bīn guǎn)* is probably the next best place to stay, though it gets very noisy in the summer months when it fills up with Pakistani traders. Doubles with bath cost US$14; three-bed dorms are US$5; four-bed dorms are US$5; and a bed in a chaotic six-bed room costs US$2. The shower block is a slime pit. Travellers, both male and female, have complained of sexual harassment here.

The *Tiannan Hotel (tiān nán fàn diàn)* near the bus station is a bit of a dive, but it has bicycle hire, a laundry service and reasonably priced rooms. Beds in a double are US$3 and in a four-bed dorm US$3. There are also suites for US$21 and twins with bath for US$10.

The *Kashgar Guesthouse* (☎ 2367) *(kā shí gě ěr bīn guǎn)* is the top-rated hotel but is far from the town centre – the main intersection is a good hour's walk away and there's no bus. You can usually wave down a jeep. Double rooms with private bath go for US$17. Dorm beds cost US$4.

Places to Eat

The Seman Hotel has a nice little restaurant out the back with tables outside. There are also a couple of good places to eat opposite the Seman Hotel, the pick of them being *John's Information & Cafe*.

Make a point of heading down to *Le Bistro*, just down the road from the Chini Bagh Hotel. This place has good coffee and cakes and an extensive English menu.

For a wide variety of Uigur foods, pop into the food market close to the Id Kah Mosque. There you can try shish kebab, rice and mutton. Whatever you buy, pay for it when you get it and take it with you – there have been reports of travellers eating first and then being overcharged (and physically threatened if they didn't pay up).

Getting There & Away

Air CAAC (☎ 22113) is on Jiefang Beilu north of the Id Kah Mosque. There are daily flights from Kashgar to Ürümqi.

Bus There is a daily bus to Ürümqi via Aksu, Korla and Toksun. Tickets for the bus can only be bought one day before departure, and the bus is scheduled to depart Kashgar at 8 am. The trip takes three days.

Getting Around

The city buses are of no use; to get around you have to walk, hire a bike or charter a jeep or minibus. Most travellers prefer bicycles. Donkey carts have been banned from the streets.

The Tiannan Hotel has bike hire, and John's Information & Cafe may also have a bike hire service by the time you read this.

KARAKORAM HIGHWAY

(zhōng bā gōng lù) 中巴公路
This highway over Khunjerab Pass (4800 metres) offers splendid scenery. From 15 April to late October buses run daily from the Chini Bagh Hotel in Kashgar to Tashkurgan, which is where the Chinese customs are located. Be warned: although the highway is officially open, it still remains a relatively dangerous trip. Landslides are common, and in 1992 at least one traveller was killed by falling rocks – take your hard hat.

Take warm clothing, food and drink on board with you – once stowed on the roof of the bus your baggage is not easily accessible.

For information or advice, contact the Pakistan Tourism Development Corporation at H-2, St 61, F – 7/4, Islamabad, Pakistan. CITS in Ürümqi has no maps, no knowledge of the highway and no interest other than to sell you an outrageously expensive tour.

Once again, John's Information & Cafe in Kashgar is probably the best place to catch up with the latest developments on the highway situation. The CITS office is only interested in hiring minibuses for the trip, and is not forthcoming on the situation with public buses.

Alternatively, you can go from Kashgar as far as Pirali just for the trip (or some hiking en route) without crossing the border.

Tibet 西藏

Most of Tibet is an immense plateau which lies at an altitude of 4000 to 5000 metres, often nicknamed the 'rooftop of the world'. It's completely barren apart from some poor grasslands to the south-east. The Qamdo region to the east is lower, wetter and warmer; some agriculture is possible, and most of the population lives here.

The Chinese officially opened Tibet to foreigners in late 1984. In late 1987 the situation changed dramatically when Tibetans held anti-Chinese demonstrations in Lhasa which turned into a virtual uprising. The military clamped down, there were a number of deaths and many arrests, and Tibet was closed to foreigners once again.

In 1993, Tibet once again opened to individual travellers. However, the police presence is heavy. Many of the police are in plain clothes, so don't think that they aren't there even if their presence isn't always obvious. Travellers to the region are advised to avoid conversations about politics and religion – even if you don't get arrested, the person you're talking to might. More than in any other part of China, Tibet is a police state. The police know they have absolute authority and sometimes abuse it – one hapless traveller was fined US$170 simply for wandering into the PSB office and asking for a visa extension.

The government's ultimate solution to the crisis in Tibet is assimilation. Han Chinese settlers are being encouraged to move to Tibet en masse, and are given financial incentives for doing so. On the positive side, the influx of money and skills is helping the local economy. On the negative side, Tibet's unique culture is being severely undermined.

Despite the ethnic tensions that lie just below the surface, Tibet is a fascinating and worthwhile place to visit. There is no place quite like it in the world, and it remains one of China's highlights.

LHASA
(lā sà) 拉萨

Lhasa has long been the capital of Tibet and remains the political centre, the most important city and the showpiece of the region.

Orientation
The city lies 3683 metres above sea level. Towering above Lhasa is the Potala Palace, and forming the nucleus of the Tibetan part of the city is the Jokhang Temple.

Information
CITS has an office opposite the Holiday Inn but it's a total waste of time going there. Currently, the best place for the latest on Tibetan individual travel is the Yak Hotel or a table in Tashi's Restaurant.

The Nepalese Consulate (☎ 22880) is at 13 Norbulingka Lu. Visa-issuing hours are Monday to Saturday from 9.30 am to 12.30 pm.

The PSB has two offices – one behind the Potala Palace and the other on Linkuo Lu in the direction of Sera Monastery. The Linkuo Lu branch is the place to do your business as the other gets consistently bad reports from travellers.

Things to See
The most imposing attraction of Lhasa is the **Potala Palace** *(bù dǎ lā gōng)*, once the centre of the Tibetan government and the winter residence of the Dalai Lama. One of the architectural wonders of the world, this huge 17th-century edifice was built on the site of its 7th-century forerunner and contains thousands of rooms, shrines and statues. The Potala is open daily except Sunday.

At the foot of the Potala is the **Exhibition Hall**, open from 9 am to 4 pm on Monday, Thursday and Sunday only. The rooms devoted to Tibetan ethnography, monastic life, handicrafts and daily life are well worth a visit.

The golden-roofed **Jokhang Temple** *(dà zhāo sì)* is 1300 years old and one of Tibet's holiest shrines. The Jokhang is east of the Potala and best visited early in the morning.

Around the periphery of the Jokhang is the **Barkhor Market**, always a hive of activity.

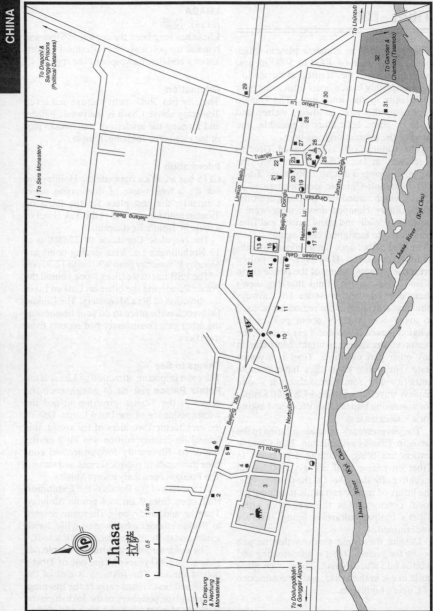

Lhasa
拉萨

To Drapchi &
Sangyip Prisons
(Political Detainees)

To Sera Monastery

To Drepung &
Nechung
Monasteries

To Dolungdêqên &
Gongar Airport

0   0.5   1 km

Jiefang Beilu

Linkuo Beilu

Tuanjie Lu

Beijing Donglu

Qinghai Lu

Linjuo Lu

Jinzhu Dônglu

Renmin Lu

Dosenn Gelu

Norbulingka Lu

Beijing Xilu

Minzu Lu

To Lhünzub

To Ganden &
Chamdo (Tsiamdo)

Lhasa River (Kyi Chu)

Lhasa
River
(Kyi Chu)

PLACES TO STAY

2 Tibet Hotel
西藏宾馆

5 Lhasa Holiday Inn
拉萨饭店

22 Yak Hotel
亚客旅社

23 Snowlands Hotel
雪城旅馆

27 Kirey Hotel
吉日旅社

28 Banak Shol Hotel
八郎学旅社

29 Plateau Hotel
高原旅馆

31 Himalaya Hotel
喜玛拉亚宾馆

PLACES TO EAT

11 Good Jmells Restaurant
好味菜馆

20 Tashi's Restaurant
咖啡馆

24 Barkhor Cafe
八廓咖啡馆

OTHER

1 Zoo
动物园

3 Norbu Lingka
罗布杯卡

4 Nepalese Consulate
尼泊尔大使馆

6 CITS
中国国际旅行社

7 Bus Station
汽车站

8 Bank of China
中国银行

9 Yak Statue
毛牛像

10 Transmitter Mast
电视台

12 Potala Palace
布达拉宫

13 CAAC
中国民航

14 Exhibition Hall
展览馆

15 Post & Telephone Office
邮电局

16 Worker's Cultural Palace
劳动人民文化宫

17 Xinhua Bookstore
新华书店

18 Bus Ticket Office
汽车售票处

19 Minibus Stand
小型车站

21 Lilac Bar
咖啡馆

25 Ganden Bus Tickets
汽车售票处

26 Jokhang Temple
大昭寺

30 PSB
公安局

32 Tibet University
西藏大学

About three km west of the Potala is the **Norbu Lingka** (*luó bù lín kǎ*), once the summer residence of the Dalai Lama. The gardens are a favourite picnic spot for the Tibetans.

Places to Stay

The *Yak Hotel (yǎ lü shè)* has become the current backpackers' centre. Dorms/doubles are US$2/10.

The *Snowlands Hotel* (☎ 23687) *(xuě yù lü guǎn)*, close to the Jokhang Temple, is a friendly place. Beds cost US$2.

The *Banak Shol* (☎ 23829) *(bā láng xuě lü shè)* is on Beijing Donglu near the Barkhor. It's a friendly place with a good location. Dorms/doubles are US$2/4.

The *Kirey Hotel (jí rì lü guǎn)*, close to the Banak Shol, has dorms/doubles for US$2/5.

Inconveniently located down Linkuo Lu is the *Himalaya Hotel (xī mǎ lā yǎ fàn diàn)*, with doubles for US$10.

The *Lhasa Holiday Inn* (☎ 32221) *(lā sà fàn diàn)* is the lap of Lhasa luxury. Doubles start at US$55.

Places to Eat

Number one on the backpackers' dining circuit at present is *Tashi's Restaurant*, just up the road from Snowlands on the corner of Beijing Lu.

Snowlands has a very decent pick-and-choose restaurant, but you need to be there early if you want anything to eat. Up the road from the Yak Hotel in the direction of the Potala is the *Lilac Bar*, which can produce a semi-decent plate of greasy chips. The Banak Shol Restaurant also goes under the moniker *Kailash Restaurant* and the food is consistently good. Alternatively, Lhasa also abounds with very good Chinese-style restaurants, though many foreigners consider it ideologically unsound to eat there.

Getting There & Away

Air Lhasa is not really well connected with anywhere in China except Chengdu. There is a once-weekly (Sunday) direct flight to Beijing. Chengdu flights leave twice a day at 8 and 8.30 am (figure that one out). Buses to the airport leave at 4.30 pm the previous afternoon, providing a major source of revenue for the airport hotel. Rooms at the airport are reasonable but the food is inedible. Flights to Kathmandu operate on Tuesday and Saturday.

The CAAC office (☎ 22417) at 88 Jiefang Lu is fairly well organised.

Bus Although there are five major road routes to Lhasa, foreigners are officially allowed to use only the Nepal and Qinghai (Golmud) routes. Travellers are warned *not* to charter a minibus from CITS in Golmud – the minibuses invariably break down and no refund is issued.

The bus station is four km out of town, near the Norbu Lingka. Buy your tickets several days in advance and roll up early. Alternatively, buy your tickets at the ticket office a few doors down from the Xinhua Bookstore.

There are daily departures in the early morning for Gyantse, Shigatse, Zétang and Golmud.

Beware of well-dressed pickpockets operating around the buses, and a word of warning, tickets sold to foreigners at the bus station are foreigner's tickets, and if that's what you paid for you should check that you have actually been issued a foreigner's ticket. Foreigners pay double.

Jeep Very few foreigners travel the Lhasa-Nepal road by public bus. Far better is jeep rental, which is easily arranged in Lhasa. The Yak Hotel is a good place to make these arrangements. Prices are very reasonable; reckon on around US$120 to US$170 per person for the vehicle. Travelling from Nepal to Lhasa, the only transport for foreigners is arranged through tour agencies. On the Nepal road, you can visit the historic and attractive towns of Shigatse, Gyantse and Sakya.

YARLONG VALLEY
(yǎ lǔ liú yù) 雅鲁流域
About 190 km east of Lhasa, the Yarlong Valley is considered to be the birthplace of Tibetan culture. Within a radius of the adjacent towns of Zétang and Nedong, which form the administrative centre of the region, are several sites of religious importance: the Samye Monastery, Yumbu Lhakang (the legendary first building in Tibet) and the Tombs of the Kings.

SHIGATSE
(rì kā zé) 日喀则
The second-largest urban centre in Tibet is Shigatse. This is the seat of the Panchen Lama, a reincarnation of Amitabha (Buddha of Infinite Light), who ranks close to the Dalai Lama. The most recent Panchen, the 10th, was taken to Beijing during the 1960s, and lived a largely puppet existence there, visiting Tibet only occasionally until he died.

GYANTSE
(jiāng zī) 江孜
Gyantse is one of southern Tibet's chief centres, although its scale is that of a small village which retains some Tibetan charm.

SAKYA
(sà jiā) 萨迦
Sakya is 152 km west of Shigatse and about 25 km south of the main road. The huge, brooding monastery at Sakya was Tibet's most powerful 700 years ago and once the centre for the Sakyapa sect which was founded in the 11th century. The monastery

probably contains the finest collection of Tibetan religious relics remaining in Tibet – but the monks may restrict you to a couple of halls.

Qinghai 青海

Historically Qinghai was part of Tibet – its separate existence is one of the great cartographical constructions of our time. Although conditions have improved considerably since the Cultural Revolution, Qinghai still has a reputation as China's Gulag where common criminals and political prisoners are incarcerated in remote labour camps.

XINING

(xī níng) 西宁

Xining is the only large city in Qinghai and is the capital of the province. It serves as a stopover for foreigners following the route between Qinghai and Tibet.

Information

CITS (☎ 45901 ext 1109) is in the front building of the Xining Guest House. The PSB is on Bei Dajie near the Xining Guest House.

Things to See

Xining has nothing exceptional to see, but it is a convenient point for visiting Ta'er Lamasery and Qinghai Lake.

The **Great Mosque** (qīng zhēn dà sì) is on Dongguan Dajie. The **Beishan Temple** (běi shān sì) is about a 45-minute walk up the mountainside west of the Xining Hotel.

Places to Stay

The *Yongfu Hotel* (yǒng fù bīn guǎn), just down the road from the railway station, is the best place to stay. A bed in a double costs US$4 and triples are US$4.

The *Xining Dasha* (xī níng dà shà) is gloomy, but it has the advantages of being cheap and close to the station. Dorms are

US$1. Doubles range from US$2 to US$4 per bed, singles US$10. Take bus No 1 from the station and get off at the second stop. Walking takes 10 minutes.

The *Xining Hotel* (☎ 45901) (xī níng bīn guǎn) is overpriced. Triples are US$7 per bed and doubles are US$19 to US$33. Take bus No 9 from opposite the railway station for five km.

The new *Qinghai Hotel* (☎ 44888) (qīng hǎi bīn guǎn) costs US$40 for doubles, while the best room in the house fetches a staggering US$1000. The hotel is nearly nine km from the railway station.

Getting There & Away

Air CAAC is on the 1st floor of the Qinghai Hotel, and it would be difficult to find a more confused office.

Bus The main bus station, opposite the railway station, has daily departures in the morning for Hcimahe (near Qinghai Lake), Golmud (1½ days) and the Ta'er Monastery. Between 8.30 am and noon there are three buses running to Tongren. From Tongren it is possible to take onward buses to Xiahe in Gansu Province. There are buses to Lanzhou at 7.30 am.

Train Xining has frequent rail connections to Lanzhou (4½ hours). There are two trains to Golmud; the afternoon train is six hours faster than the morning train.

TA'ER LAMASERY

(tǎ ěr sì) 塔尔寺

This is a large Tibetan monastery, one of the six great monasteries of the Yellow Hat sect of Tibetan Buddhism, located in the town of Huangzhong about 25 km south-east of Xining.

Places to Stay & Eat

The monastery has a couple of buildings which have been converted from monks' quarters into tourist accommodation. A bed in a three-bed room costs US$2.

The *Ta'er Hotel* (tǎ ěr sì bīn guǎn) is just

opposite the Tibetan hospital and charges US$14 for a double.

The food at the monastery is good. For a change, take a wander down the hill towards town and try some noodles in a Muslim restaurant. Stalls on the approach road to the monastery sell great yoghurt and peaches.

Getting There & Away

Buses to Huangzhong leave Ximen station in Xining about every 10 minutes between 7 am and 6.30 pm. Minibuses also do the trip faster.

Catch your return bus or minibus to Xining from the square in Huangzhong.

QINGHAI LAKE

(qīng hǎi hú) 青海湖

Qinghai Lake, known as the 'Western Sea' in ancient times, is a somewhat surreal-looking saline lake lying 300 km west of Xining and 3200 metres above sea level. It's the largest lake in China and produces copious quantities of fish.

The main attraction is **Bird Island** (niǎo dǎo), a breeding ground for all manner of species. You will only see birds in any quantity during the mating and breeding season between March and early June.

Getting There & Away

It's a hassle. The north shore is accessible by train, but Bird Island (on the south shore) has no public transport. Every Saturday and Sunday during the summer months only, there is a day trip from Xining to Bird Island for only US$7. Buses depart at 7 am from Ximen bus station (xī mén qì chē zhàn) and return at 9 pm. Don't expect a tranquil nature experience – you may want to bring earplugs.

CITS organises a three-day trip to Bird Island which costs US$26 based on a minimum of 10 passengers. This price is for the bus only; meals and accommodation cost more.

GOLMUD

(gé ěr mù) 格尔木

Golmud is a town on the high, desolate plateau of central Qinghai. The residents will be the first to tell you that from here to hell is a local call, but the moonscape is scenic in its own eerie way. The town owes its existence to the potash mining industry. Golmud is the main overland gateway to Tibet, assuming you can get in.

Information

CITS (☎ 2001 ext 254) is in the Golmud Hotel. The best advice we can give is to avoid the place, but this is difficult to do as Mr Hou will probably be waiting for you at the railway station to make sure you don't jump on the nearest bus to Lhasa. Officially, all travellers with their eyes set on Tibet should register with CITS, which will charge you US$7 for the service. In practice, however, some travellers have gone directly to the Tibet bus station and registered there instead.

The post office is on the corner of Chaidamu Lu and Jiangyuan Lu. The Bank of China is on the corner of Kunlun Lu and Chaidaimu Lu. The PSB is in the Golmud Hotel.

Places to Stay

There's only one place accepting foreigners, the Golmud Hotel (☎ 2817) (gé ěr mù bīn guǎn). Dorms in the old building cost US$2 and doubles are US$8 per bed. The staff are unbelievably surly and the hot water supply is erratic. The new wing is more expensive, with triples at US$7 per bed and doubles for US$10 per bed. There's a free bus service from the railway station to the hotel. Walking takes about 35 minutes.

Places to Eat

Just outside the gate of the Golmud Hotel is the Golmud Hotel Restaurant. The food is good and very cheap. Down the road towards the Bank of China is The Best Cafe, a friendly place (in Golmud!) with a decent English menu. It's on the 2nd floor – look for the sign.

Getting There & Away

Air Despite the existence of a much-touted airport, there are no flights to Golmud.

Bus The bus station is opposite the railway station. Golmud to Dunhuang takes 13 hours and departures are at 6.30 am. Buy your ticket a day in advance. The bus departs from behind the station, not in front, and no one will bother to tell you this.

Buses for Lhasa leave from the Tibet bus station on Xizang Lu. There's a special foreigner's section inside where they charge special foreigner's prices – at least they do it with a smile. Prices seem to vary from day to day, but the average seems to be US$80 on the Chinese bus and US$89 on the Japanese bus (if it's running). To this you'll probably have to add a US$7 registration fee.

Train From Xining there are two trains, one express and one local. The local runs in the morning, the express in the afternoon. From Golmud back to Xining, the express train runs at around 2 pm, and the local train at around 8.30 pm. The express train is around six hours quicker than the local.

Hong Kong

Precariously perched on the edge of China, Hong Kong is a curious anomaly. It's an energetic paragon of the virtues of capitalism but nevertheless gets the unofficial blessing of the largest Communist country in the world – on which it is dependent for its very existence. The countdown to 1997, when Hong Kong is due to be handed back to the People's Republic of China, has made it an even more volatile and intriguing enigma.

Facts about the Country

HISTORY

Hong Kong must stand as one of the more successful results of dope running. The dope was opium and the runners were backed by the British government. European trade with China goes back over 400 years. As the trade mushroomed during the 18th century and European demand for Chinese tea and silk grew, the balance of trade became more and more unfavourable to the Europeans until they started to run opium into the country.

The Middle Kingdom grew alarmed at this turn of events and attempted to throw the 'foreign devils' out. The war of words ended when British gunboats were sent in. There were only two of them, but they managed to demolish a Chinese fleet of 29 ships. The ensuing First Opium War went much the same way and, at its close in 1842, the island of Hong Kong was ceded to the British.

Following the Second Opium War in 1860, Britain took possession of the Kowloon Peninsula. Finally, in 1898, a 99-year lease was granted for the New Territories. What would happen after the lease ended on 1 July 1997 was the subject of considerable speculation. Although the British supposedly had possession of Hong Kong Island and the Kowloon Peninsula for all eternity, it was pretty clear that if they

handed back the New Territories, China would want the rest as well.

In late 1984, an agreement was finally reached that China would take over the entire colony lock, stock and skyscrapers, but that Hong Kong's unique free enterprise economy would be maintained for at least 50 years. It would be a tiny enclave of all-out capitalism within the Chinese sphere. However, many of Hong Kong's population – well aware of China's broken promises and erratic policies of the past – aren't yet buying it. The emigration queues at the embassies of Australia, Canada, New Zealand and the USA grow longer all the time.

The reality of the situation has always been, of course, that China could reclaim Hong Kong any time it wanted to. Hong Kong has survived so long already simply because it's useful. It acts as a funnel for Chinese goods to the West and for Western goods into China. Also, it is a valuable source of both foreign exchange and information, without the need for China to let corrupting foreign influences across the borders.

GEOGRAPHY

Hong Kong's 1070 sq km is divided into four main areas – Kowloon, Hong Kong Island, the New Territories and the outlying islands.

Hong Kong Island is the economic heart of the colony, but covers only 7% of Hong Kong's land area. Kowloon is the densely populated peninsula to the north. The New Territories, which include the outlying islands, occupy 91% of Hong Kong's land area. Much of it is rural and charming, but tourists seldom visit this scenic part of Hong Kong.

The southern tip of the peninsula is Tsimshatsui, the tourist centre of Kowloon.

CLIMATE

Although it never gets below freezing, Hong Kong is certainly colder than South-East Asian capitals like Bangkok, Singapore,

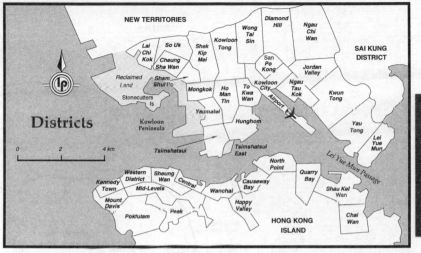

Jakarta and Manila. More than a few travellers have arrived in the dead of winter wearing shorts and T-shirts, and barely survived the experience! Summer is hot and humid, and thunderstorms often force visitors to scamper for cover. From June to October, Hong Kong is occasionally hit by typhoons. Autumn is the most pleasant time of the year. See the Hong Kong climate chart in the Appendix later in this book.

GOVERNMENT

Hong Kong is not a democracy, and China is determined that it doesn't become one. At the moment, Hong Kong is a British colony.

Heading Hong Kong's administration is a governor who presides over meetings of both the Executive Council (EXCO) and the Legislative Council (LEGCO). The Urban Council and Regional Council are in charge of the day-to-day running of services like street cleaning and garbage collection. The enormous Hong Kong Civil Service does the rest.

ECONOMY

Trade with both the West and China has always been the cornerstone of the Hong Kong economy. Service industries such as banking, insurance, telecommunications and tourism now employ 75% of Hong Kong residents. All the polluting sweatshop factories have moved across the border to China.

Part of the reason for Hong Kong's prosperity is that it is a capitalist's dream: it has lax controls and a maximum tax rate of 15%. Even with less than three years to go until the handover, fortunes are still being made, new skyscrapers are still being hurled up, and new BMWs and Mercedes are still pouring out of the showrooms. You can smell wealth in the air.

POPULATION & PEOPLE

At the end of WW II, the population was slightly over half a million. Today it stands at six million, most of it squeezed on to Hong Kong Island, Kowloon and the so-called 'new towns' in the New Territories.

About 98% of Hong Kong's population is ethnic Chinese, most of whom have their origins in China's Guangdong Province. About 60% were born in the colony.

Over 300,000 expats permanently reside (legally) in Hong Kong, plus an unknown number of illegals who stay until they get

HONG KONG

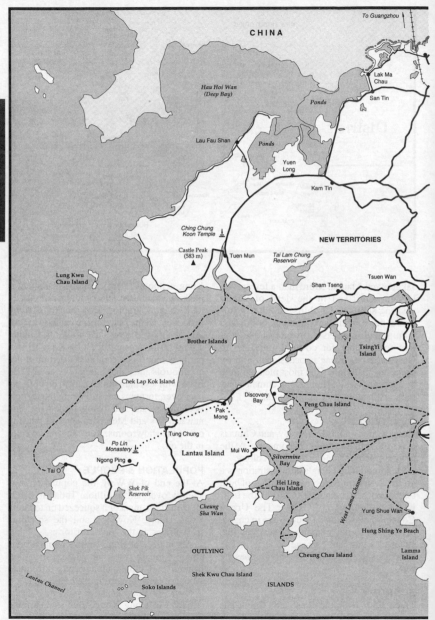

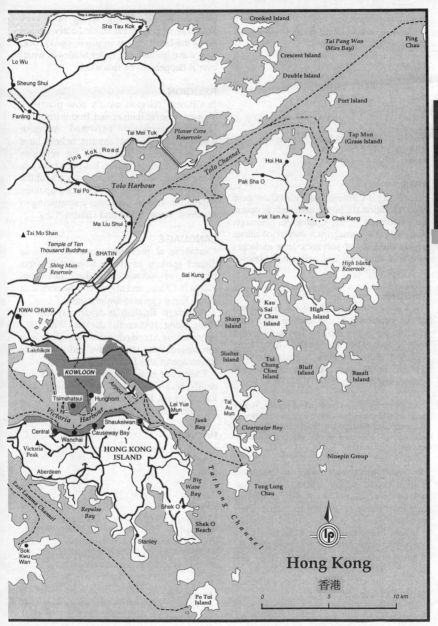

HONG KONG

Hong Kong

香港

0   5   10 km

caught. In descending order, the breakdown of expats living in Hong Kong (both legally and illegally) is as follows:

Filipinos	106,000
Americans	27,000
British	22,000
Thai	20,000
Canadians	20,000
Indians	19,000
Australians	17,000
Japanese	15,000
Malaysians	13,000
Others	65,000

ARTS

Hong Kong is Chinese, but with a Cantonese twist. Traditional Chinese arts, such as opera, are performed in the Cantonese language. Hong Kong's homegrown variety of music largely consists of soft rock love melodies sung in Cantonese, and collectively known as 'Canto-Pop'.

CULTURE

The Cantonese people have always existed on the periphery of the empire, and their relationship with Beijing has not always been good. The northerners have long regarded their southern compatriots with disdain, or as one 19th-century northern account put it:

The Cantonese...are a coarse set of people...Before the times of Han and Tang, this country was quite wild and waste, and these people have sprung forth from unconnected, unsettled vagabonds that wandered here from the north.

The traditional stereotype of the Cantonese is of a proud people, frank in criticism, lacking in restraint, oriented to defending their own interests and hot tempered. They are also regarded as shrewd in business and as quick, lively and clever in catching on to new skills, which for the most part are those of small traders and craftspeople. They also have the reputation of being willing to eat anything, including dog, cat, rat, snake and monkey's brain.

Of all the Chinese, the Cantonese have probably been the most influenced by the outside world. Hong Kong is a very Westernised place that immediately latches on to the latest crazes in disco, punk, rock, new wave, miniskirts, roller blades or whatever it happens to be this week.

RELIGION

In Chinese religion as it's now practised, Taoism, Confucianism and Buddhism have become inextricably entwined. Ancestor worship and ancient animist beliefs have also been incorporated into the religious milieu. Foreign influence has been heavy in Hong Kong, which explains why 9% of the population are Christians. The cosmopolitan population also incorporates a smattering of Muslims, Jews, Sikhs and Hindus.

LANGUAGE

Cantonese is the most common Chinese dialect spoken in Hong Kong. Mandarin Chinese, or *putonghua*, is the official language in China, and about half the people in Hong Kong can also understand it.

Although English is widely spoken in Hong Kong, it is on the decline. With 1997 approaching, those educated in English have the easiest time emigrating and are taking advantage of this fact.

Cantonese is difficult for *gwailos* (foreign devils) because it's tonal – the meaning varies with the tone. Few gwailos gain fluency, but here are a few phrases to have a go with:

Pronouns

I
 ngo
 我
you
 nei
 你
he, she, it
 keui
 他
we, us
 ngodei
 我們
you (plural)
 neidei
 你們

they, them
keuidei
他們

Greetings & Civilities
Hello, how are you?
Nei hou ma?
你好
Good morning.
Jou san.
早晨
Goodbye.
Joi gin.
再見
Thank you.
M goido zei.
唔該/多謝
You're welcome.
M saihaakhei.
不客氣
I'm sorry/excuse me.
Deuimjyu.
對不起

Useful Expressions
I want...
Ngo yiu...
我要
I want to buy...
Ngo yiu maai...
我要買…
Yes/Have.
Yau.
有
No/Don't have.
M yau.
沒有
How much does it cost?
Gei siu chin.
多少錢
Too expensive.
Taai gwaige.
太貴
Waiter, the bill.
Fogei, maai daan.
伙記埋單
I don't understand.
Ngo m meng ba.
我聽不懂

Wait a moment.
Deng chan.
等一下

Necessities
laundry service
sai yee chung sum
洗衣中心
sanitary pads (Kotex)
wai seng gan
衛生巾
sunscreen (UV) lotion
tai you yau
太陽油
tampons
wai sang ming tiu
衛生棉條
tissue paper
ji gan
紙巾
toilet paper
chi ji
廁紙

Getting Around
I want to go to the...
Ngo you hoi...
我要去…
    airport
    fei gei chang
    飛機場
    MTR station
    dei tip zam
    地鐵站
    KCR station
    fo chei zam
    火車站
    LRT station
    heng bin ti lou
    輕便鐵路
    Star Ferry
    ting seng ma tau
    天星碼頭
I'm lost.
Ngo dong sat lou.
我蕩失路
Where is the...?
...hai bin dou?
在那裡

HONG KONG

HONG KONG

telephone
din wah
電話
post office
yau go
郵局
toilet
ji sou
廁所
I want to hire a bicycle.
Ngo yu jo daan chei.
我要租單車

Turn right
Yau jwin
右轉
Turn left
Jwo jwin
左轉
Go straight
Yet zet zau
一直走
Turn around
Jwin gou wan
轉個彎

Time
What is the time?
Gei dim?
幾點
hour
dim
點
minute
fan
分

Numbers

0	*leng*	零
1	*yet*	一
2	*yi, leung*	二, 兩
3	*sam*	三
4	*sei*	四
5	*m*	五
6	*lok*	六
7	*chat*	七
8	*ba*	八
9	*gau*	九
10	*sap*	十
11	*sap yet*	十一

12	*sap yi*	十二
20	*yi sap*	二十
21	*yi sam yet*	二十一
100	*yet ba*	一百
200	*leung ba*	兩百
1000	*yet chin*	一千
2000	*leung chin*	兩千
10,000	*yet man*	一萬
20,000	*leung man*	兩萬
100,000	*sap man*	十萬
200,000	*yi sap man*	二十萬

Emergencies
I'm sick.
Ngo beng la.
我生病
I'm injured.
Ngo sau cheung.
我受傷
Fire!
Fo jok!
火燭
Help!
Gau meng ah!
救命啊
Thief!
Siu tau!
小偷
hospital
yi yun
醫院
pickpocket
pa sau
扒手
police
geng cha
警察
rapist
keng gan ze
強姦者

Facts for the Visitor

VISAS & EMBASSIES
Most visitors do not need a visa for Hong Kong. British passport holders are permitted to stay visa-free for 12 months, citizens of all Western European nations can stay for three

months, and citizens of the USA and most other countries get one month. Visas are still required for Eastern Europeans and for citizens of all communist countries.

Hong Kong is the usual launching pad for excursions into China, though Macau is also a possibility. Chinese visas can be obtained in Hong Kong in one or two days.

Visa Extensions
For visa extensions, you should enquire at the Immigration Department (☎ 8246111), 2nd floor, Wanchai Tower Two, 7 Gloucester Rd, Wanchai. In general, it does not like to grant extensions unless there are special circumstances – cancelled flights, illness, registration in a legitimate course of study, legal employment, marriage to a local etc.

DOCUMENTS
Visitors and residents are advised to carry identification at all times in Hong Kong. It needn't be a passport, anything with a photo on it will do.

MONEY
Hong Kong is a dream come true for money changing. Any major trading currency, and even many insignificant currencies, can be exchanged. All major international credit cards are accepted.

Banks give the best exchange rates by far, but it varies from bank to bank. One of the best banks is Wing Lung Bank, 4 Carnarvon Rd, Tsimshatsui, next to the New Astor Hotel. Another good bank for changing money is Hang Seng Bank which has numerous branches all over the city. The main Tsimshatsui branch is at 18 Carnarvon Rd. The small branches in the MTR stations do not change money.

The Hongkong Bank gives relatively poor rates for a bank, and in addition tacks on a HK$20 service charge for each transaction.

Bank hours are from 9 am to 4 pm Monday to Friday, and until noon or 1 pm on Saturday. When the banks are closed, you have to deal with the private moneychangers.

Licensed moneychangers in the tourist districts operate 24 hours a day, but give relatively poor exchange rates which are clearly posted. However, you can almost always get a much better rate by bargaining! Moneychangers are no longer allowed to charge commissions.

Some of the best rates are given by the moneychangers in Chungking Mansions at 36-44 Nathan Rd, Tsimshatsui.

Try not to change any money at the airport as the exchange rate there is pathetic.

Currency
Hong Kong's unit of currency is the HK$, divided into 100 cents. Bills are issued in denominations of $10, $20, $50, $100, $500 and $1000. Coins are issued in denominations of $5, $2, $1, 50 cents, 20 cents and 10 cents.

Exchange Rates

Australia	A$1	=	HK$5.28
Canada	C$1	=	HK$5.85
China	Y1	=	HK$0.89
France	Ffr1	=	HK$1.30
Germany	DM1	=	HK$4.42
Japan	¥100	=	HK$6.90
New Zealand	NZ$1	=	HK$4.31
Singapore	S$1	=	HK$4.83
Switzerland	Sfr1	=	HK$5.21
Taiwan	NT$1	=	HK$0.29
Thailand	B1	=	HK$0.31
UK	UK£1	=	HK$11.43
USA	US$1	=	HK$7.72

Costs
Apart from Japan, Hong Kong is the most expensive city covered in this book – it's a result of the continuing economic boom and the ever-increasing cost of land. Accommodation is the biggest expense, though food is reasonably priced and transport is cheap. If you stay in dormitories, eat budget meals and resist the urge to shop, you can survive on under HK$200 per day. However, most travellers will spend more.

Tipping
In general, tipping is not expected in Hong Kong. A 10% service charge is usually added to restaurant bills in upmarket establish-

HONG KONG

ments, and this is a mandatory 'tip'. With taxis you should round the fare up to the nearest HK$0.50 or dollar.

Bargaining

If you shop for cameras, electronics and other big ticket items in the tourist ghetto of Tsimshatsui, bargaining is essential because the shops will try to charge you double. However, bargaining is *not* the norm in Hong Kong. It's only normal in places where the tourists congregate. In suburban shopping malls or the street markets of Mongkok and Shamshuipo, everything has a price tag and there is little scope for bargaining.

Consumer Taxes

Hong Kong is a duty-free port, and the only imported goods on which duty is paid are alcohol, tobacco, perfumes, cosmetics, cars and some petroleum products. Although many shops in Hong Kong display a big sign proclaiming 'Duty-Free Goods', there is little reason to bother with them as they cater mostly to a Japanese clientele who are already accustomed to being ripped off.

The only true 'duty-free' shops in Hong Kong are those in the exit area of Kai Tak Airport. However, the prices charged are so ridiculously high that you would be better off buying your booze and cigarettes at 7 Eleven.

TOURIST OFFICES
Local Tourist Offices

The enterprising Hong Kong Tourist Association (HKTA) is definitely worth a visit. They're efficient and helpful and have reams of printed information, free or fairly cheap.

You can call the HKTA hotline (☎ 8017177) from 8 am to 6 pm Monday to Friday, or from 9 am to 5 pm on weekends and holidays. For shopping advice and enquiries on HKTA members, there's a different phone (☎ 8017278) staffed from 9 am to 5 pm Monday to Friday, and until 12.45 pm on Saturday (not operating on Sunday and holidays). You'll find HKTA offices at:

Star Ferry Terminal
    Tsimshatsui, Kowloon – open from 8 am to 6 pm Monday to Friday, and 9 am to 5 pm weekends and holidays
Shop 8
    Basement, Jardine House, 1 Connaught Place, Central – open from 9 am to 6 pm weekdays, until 1 pm on Saturday and closed on Sunday and holidays
Buffer Hall
    Kai Tak Airport, Kowloon – open from 8 am to 10.30 pm daily. Information is provided for arriving passengers only.
Head Office
    35th floor, Jardine House, 1 Connaught Place, Central (☎ 8017111). This is a business office and is not for normal tourist enquiries.

Overseas Reps

Overseas offices of the HKTA include:

Australia
    Level 5, 55 Harrington St, The Rocks, Sydney (☎ 02-251 2855, outside Sydney 008-25 1071)
Canada
    347 Bay St, suite 909, Toronto, Ontario M5H 2R7 (☎ 416-366 2389)
France
    Escalier C, 8ème étage, 53 rue Francois 1er, 75008, Paris (☎ 01-47.20.39.54)
Germany
    Weisenau 1, 60323 Frankfurt am Main (☎ 069-722841)
Italy
    c/o Sergat Italia Sr1, Casella Postale 620, 00100 Roma Centro (☎ 06-68801336)
Japan
    4th floor, Toho Twin Tower Building, 1-5-2 Yurakucho, Chiyoda-ku, Tokyo 100 (☎ 03-35030735)
    8th floor, Osaka Saitama Building, 3-5-13 Awaji-machi, Chuo-ku, Osaka 541 (☎ 06-2299240)
Korea
    c/o HK PR, suite 1204, Sungji Building, 538 Dowha-Dong, Mapo-gu, Seoul (☎ 02-706 5818)
New Zealand
    PO Box 2120, Auckland (☎ 09-520 3316)
South Africa
    c/o Development Promotions Pty Ltd, PO Box 9874, Johannesburg 2000 (☎ 011-339 4865)
Singapore
    13th floor, 13-08 Ocean Building, 10 Collyer Quay, Singapore 0104 (☎ 532 3668)
Taiwan
    7th floor, 18 Chang'an E Rd, Section 1, Taipei (☎ 02-5812967)
    Hong Kong Information Service (☎ 02-581 6061)

Spain
c/o Sergat Espana SL, Pau Casals 4, 08021 Barcelona (☎ 3-414 1794)

UK
5th floor, 125 Pall Mall, London, SW1Y 5EA (☎ 0171-930 4775)

USA
333 North Michigan Ave, suite 2400, Chicago, IL 60601-3966 (☎ 312-782 3872)
5th floor, 590 Fifth Ave, New York, NY 10036-4706 (☎ 212 869 5008)
10940 Wilshire Blvd, suite 1220, Los Angeles, CA 90024 (☎ 213-208 4582)

USEFUL ORGANISATIONS

Since the likelihood of getting ripped off by shopkeepers is high, it's good to know about the Hong Kong Consumer Council (☎ 7363322). The main office is in China Hong Kong City, Canton Rd, Tsimshatsui, Kowloon. It has a complaints and advice hot line (☎ 7363636) and an Advice Centre (☎ 5411422) at 38 Pier Rd, Central.

If you get genuinely ripped off by robbers, you can obtain a loss report for insurance purposes at the Central Police Station, 10 Hollywood Rd (at Pottinger St) in Central. There are always English-speaking staff here.

The Royal Asiatic Society (RAS) (☎ 551-0300), GPO Box 3864, is dedicated to helping its members or visitors learn more about the history and culture of Hong Kong. The RAS organises lectures and field trips, operates a lending library and puts out publications of its own. The RAS was founded in London in 1823 and has branches in several Asian countries.

St John's Cathedral Counselling Service (☎ 5257202) provides help to all those in need.

If you're interested in doing business in Hong Kong, you might want to consult the Hong Kong Chamber of Commerce (☎ 5237177), 902 Swire House, 9-25 Chater Rd, Central. Perhaps even more to the point is the Hong Kong Trade Development Council (☎ 5844333), 38th floor, Office Tower Convention Plaza, 1 Harbour Rd, Wanchai.

Know any government officials you want to get rid of? Call the Report Centre of the Independent Commission Against Corruption (☎ 5266366).

Other organisations which could do you some good include the American Chamber of Commerce (☎ 5260165), 1030 Swire House, Central, and the British Council (☎ 8795138), ground floor, Easey Commercial Building, 255 Hennessy Rd, Wanchai

BUSINESS HOURS & HOLIDAYS

Office hours are Monday to Friday from 9 am to 5 pm, and on Saturday until noon. The lunch hour is from 1 to 2 pm and many offices simply shut down and lock the door at this time.

Stores and restaurants that cater to the tourist trade keep longer hours, but almost nothing except 7 Eleven opens before 9 am. Even tourist-related businesses shut down by 9 or 10 pm. Only the late-night pubs and restaurants in places like Lan Kwai Fong and Wanchai stay open after midnight. Most places close for major holidays, especially Chinese New Year.

Western and Chinese culture combine to create an interesting mix of holidays. The first day of the first moon (late January or early February) is Chinese New Year. Only the first three days of this are a public holiday, but everything pretty much shuts down for a week and all flights out of Hong Kong are booked solid for at least two weeks.

The other big public holiday to avoid is Ching Ming (visits to ancestors' graves), which falls around Easter time.

The mid-year Dragon Boat (Tuen Ng) Festival is a dramatic sight culminating in the international races. The time to enjoy moon cakes is during the Mid-Autumn Festival (15th night of the eighth moon).

The last public holidays are Christmas (25 December) and Boxing Day (26 December), when the lights of Hong Kong are bright and the streets are packed.

CULTURAL EVENTS

There are literally hundreds of cultural events throughout the year, but the exact dates vary. The Hong Kong Tourist Association publishes a complete schedule every

HONG KONG

month. If you want to time your visit to Hong Kong to coincide with a particular event, it would be wise to contact the HKTA beforehand. A brief rundown of important annual events includes:

HK Arts Festival – An assortment of exhibitions and shows usually held in January.

Orientation Competition – Sponsored by the Urban Council, this event is usually staged in January in Tai Tam Country Park.

HK Festival Fringe – The Fringe Club supports upcoming artists and performers from Hong Kong and elsewhere. This three-week festival occurs from late January to February.

HK Golf Open – This is held at the Royal Hong Kong Golf Club, usually in February.

HK International Marathon – Organised by the Hong Kong Amateur Athletic Association, this major event is held in Shatin, usually in March.

HK Food Festival – Sponsored by the HKTA, this festival is usually held in March.

HK International Film Festival – Organised by the Urban Council, this event usually occurs in March or April.

HK International Handball Invitation Tournament – Organised by the Hong Kong Amateur Handball Association, this event is in March or April.

Sotheby's Auction – This usually occurs in April.

International Dragon Boat Festival – Usually falling in June, the international festival is usually held the week after the Chinese dragon boat races.

Davis Cup – This tennis tournament is usually held in July.

International Arts Carnival – This unusual summer festival promotes performances by children's groups. The carnival usually falls in July or August.

Asian Regatta – Organised by the Hong Kong Yachting Association, this event usually occurs in October.

Festival of Asian Arts – This is one of Asia's major international events, attracting performers from Australia as well as nearby countries. This festival usually occurs in October or November.

Some colourful nonpublic holidays include the birthdays of Tin Hau (the goddess of fisherfolk), Tam Kung (another patron saint of seafarers) and Lord Buddha. The Cheung Chau Bun Festival features raucous fun on the island of Cheung Chau, and there's the Yue Lan Festival of Hungry Ghosts (in late August or September) which is a great time to visit Taoist temples.

POST & TELECOMMUNICATIONS
Postal Rates
Local Mail Rates for Hong Kong mail are as follows:

Weight Not Over	Letters & Postcards	Printed Matter
30 grams	HK$1.00	HK$0.90
50 grams	HK$1.70	HK$1.30
100 grams	HK$2.40	HK$1.90
250 grams	HK$3.50	HK$2.80
500 grams	HK$7.10	HK$5.70
1 kg	HK$15.00	HK$9.00
2 kg	HK$25.00	

International Airmail The Hong Kong postal service divides the world into two distinct zones. Zone 1 is China, Japan, Taiwan, South Korea, South-East Asia, Indonesia and India. The rates are as follows:

Letters & Postcards	Zone 1	Zone 2
first 10 grams	HK$1.90	HK$2.40
each additional 10 grams	HK$1.00	HK$1.10
Aerogrammes	HK$1.90	HK$1.90
Printed Matter		
first 10 grams	HK$1.30	HK$1.80
each additional 10 grams	HK$0.60	HK$0.80

Speedpost The rates for international express mail service vary enormously according to destination country but there is little relation to actual distance. For example, a 250 g Speedpost letter to Australia costs HK$85 but to China it's HK$90 and to Singapore HK$65! The main factors seem to be the availability of air transport and efficiency of mail handling at the destination country. Every post office has a schedule of fees and timetable for Speedpost delivery available on request.

Sending Mail
All post offices are open Monday to Saturday from 8 am to 6 pm, and are closed on Sunday and public holidays.

Receiving Mail
The GPO is where you go to collect poste restante letters – it's in Central just to the

west of the Star Ferry Terminal. In Tsimshatsui, there are two convenient post offices just east of Nathan Rd: one at 10 Middle Rd and another in the basement of the Albion Plaza, 2-6 Granville Rd.

Telephone

From 2 January 1995, a '2' will be added to the beginning of all existing seven-digit telephone numbers. This applies to all telephone numbers listed in this book.

If you want to phone overseas, it's cheapest to use an International Direct Dialling (IDD) telephone. You can place an IDD call from most phone boxes but you'll need stacks of coins. An alternative is to buy a 'Phonecard', which comes in denominations of HK\$50, HK\$100 or HK\$250. You can find these IDD phones in shops, on the street or at a Hong Kong Telecom office. There's a HK Telecom at 10 Middle Rd in Tsimshatsui and another at Exchange Square No 1 Building, west of the GPO in Central.

For calls to countries that do not have IDD service, you can call from a HK Telecom office – first pay a deposit and they will hook you up (minimum three minutes) and give you your change after the call is completed.

Some useful phone numbers and prefixes include the following:

Ambulance, Fire, Police, Emergency	☎ 999
Calls to China	☎ 012
Credit Card Billing	☎ 011
Crime Report, Police Business	☎ 5277177
Directory Assistance	☎ 1081
Hong Kong's Country Code	☎ 852
IDD Prefix	☎ 001
International Dialling Assistance	☎ 013
Reverse Billing	☎ 010
Taxi Complaints	☎ 5277177
Time & Weather	☎ 18501

Fax, Telex & Telegraph

All your telecommunication needs can be taken care of at Hongkong Telecom. The charge to send a one-page (A4 size) fax is HK\$10 within Hong Kong; HK\$30 for South-East Asia; HK\$35 to Australia, New Zealand, Canada, USA and UK; and HK\$45 to all other countries. For HK\$10 you can receive a fax here.

Many hotels and even hostels have fax facilities and will allow you to both send and receive for a reasonable service charge.

TIME

The time in Hong Kong is GMT/UTC plus eight hours. When it is noon in Hong Kong, it is also noon in Singapore and Perth; 2 pm in Sydney; 8 pm in Los Angeles; 11 pm in New York; and 4 am in London. Daylight-saving time is not observed.

LAUNDRY

Many hotels, even the cheap youth hostels, have a laundry service. If they don't, just ask where one is. Prices are normally HK\$25 for three kg. If you have less than three kg, you still pay the same, so you might want to throw your clothes together with a friend's.

Two convenient laundry services in Tsimshatsui are Carlye Steam Laundry, Golden Crown Court, 66-70 Nathan Rd, and Purity Laundry, 25 Chungking Arcade, Chungking Mansions, 30 Nathan Rd.

WEIGHTS & MEASURES

The international metric system is in official use in Hong Kong. In practice, traditional Chinese weights and measures are still common.

If you want to shop in the local markets, become familiar with Chinese units of weight. Things are sold by the *leung*, which is equivalent to 37.5 grams, or in *catty*, where one catty is about 600 grams. There are 16 leung to the catty.

BOOKS & MAPS

The Government's annual report is titled *Hong Kong 1993, Hong Kong 1994* etc. In addition to the excellent photographs, the text is a gold mine of information.

A cynical antidote to the government's upbeat version of events is *The Other Hong Kong Report* (Chinese University Press).

Maurice Collin's *Foreign Mud* (Faber & Faber, UK, 1946) tells the sordid story of the Opium Wars.

Novels to dip into include the readable *Tai-pan* by James Clavell, which is (very) loosely based on the Jardine-Matheson organisation in its early days. Richard Mason's *The World of Suzie Wong* is also interesting, after all she was Hong Kong's best known citizen.

If you want more information on Hong Kong and the surrounding area, check out the Lonely Planet guidebook *Hong Kong, Macau & Guangzhou – a travel survival kit*.

The giveaway maps provided by the HKTA are adequate for finding your way around most places in Kowloon or the city part of Hong Kong Island. The Government Publications Centre in the GPO sells far more detailed maps.

Bookshops

Good bookshops in Hong Kong include:

Bookazine Company, basement, Jardine House, Connaught Rd, Central, Hong Kong Island (opposite HKTA office)

Government Publications Centre, GPO building, Central (near Star Ferry pier)

Peace Book Company, 35 Kimberly Rd, Tsimshatsui

South China Morning Post Bookshop, Star Ferry pier, Central, Hong Kong Island

Swindon Books, 13 Lock Rd, Tsimshatsui

The Book Centre (☎ 5227064), Basement, 25 Des Voeux Rd, Central

Times Books, Shop C, 96 Nathan Rd, entrance on Granville Rd, Tsimshatsui

Wanderlust Books, 30 Hollywood Rd, Central (good travel book section)

Libraries

The main library is at City Hall, High Block, Central, just one street to the east of the Star Ferry Terminal. However, they will not let you make photocopies of anything which is copyrighted (which means just about everything). As a result, most of their reference books have pages ripped out of them by frustrated students.

The American Library (☎ 5299661), 1st floor, United Centre, 95 Queensway, Admiralty, has good research facilities and *does* allow you to make photocopies.

MEDIA
Newspapers & Magazines

The three main local English-language newspapers are the *South China Morning Post*, *Hong Kong Standard* and *Eastern Express*. All three are of reasonably good quality and there is no real equivalent to the scandalous tabloids produced in many Western countries.

Hong Kong Magazine is the final word in nightlife and entertainment in this city. The magazine is published once every two weeks and is free. The best place to find it is around pubs frequented by gwailos. For subscription information, contact the office (☎ 575 5065; fax 5730914).

Hong Kong is Asia's regional printing and distribution centre of major international magazines, including *Time*, *Newsweek* and the *Far Eastern Economic Review*.

Radio & TV

Radio Television Hong Kong (RTHK) operates three stations: RTHK (Radio 3) at AM 567 kHz and 1584 kHz, and FM 97.9 mHz; RTHK (Radio 4) at 97.6 mHz and 98.9 mHz FM; and RTHK (Radio 6) with the BBC World Service relay at AM 675 kHz. Commercial Radio (CR) is at AM 864 kHz. The British Forces Broadcasting Service (BFBS) is at FM 93.1, 95.4, 96.6, 102, 104.8 and 107.4 mHz. Metro Broadcast has the news channel at AM 1044 kHz and regular programming at FM 104 MHz. Hit Radio is at FM 99.2 mHz. The English-language newspapers publish a daily guide to radio programmes.

Hong Kong's TV stations are run by two companies, Television Broadcasts Ltd (TVB) and Asia Television Ltd (ATV). Each company operates one English-language and one Cantonese-language channel, making a total of four stations in Hong Kong. The two English stations are TVB Pearl (channel 3) and ATV World (channel 4). The two Cantonese stations are called TVB Jade (channel 1) and ATV Home (channel 2). The programme is listed daily in the English-language newspapers.

FILM & PHOTOGRAPHY

Almost everything you could possibly need in the way of film, camera and photographic accessories is available in Hong Kong. Stanley St on Hong Kong Island is the place to look for reputable camera stores.

A word about buying film – Kodachrome slide film can be bought in Hong Kong with the processing included. Check the box to make sure that the offer is valid in your home country. The price is HK$50. Slide processing is particularly expensive in Europe so it turns out to be a good deal if Europe is where you are heading.

For security reasons (terrorism?), you cannot take photographs of the runways at Kai Tak Airport or of the security procedures (x-ray machines, metal detectors, machine gun-toting airport police etc).

HEALTH

Hong Kong is a very healthy place. You can drink water straight from the tap, and even the street markets are reasonably clean despite their dubious appearance.

Public hospitals charge reasonable fees, but Hong Kong residents pay less than foreign visitors. Public hospitals include: Queen Elizabeth Hospital (☎ 7102111), Wylie Rd, Yaumatei, Kowloon; Princess Margaret Hospital (☎ 3103111), Lai Chi Kok, Kowloon; Queen Mary Hospital (☎ 8192111), Pokfulam Rd; and Prince of Wales Hospital (☎ 6362211), 30-32 Ngan Shing St, Shatin, New Territories.

Private doctors usually charge reasonable fees, but it pays to make some enquiries first. Most large hotels have resident doctors.

Hong Kong has a shortage of dentists and fees are consequently very high. If the next stop on your itinerary is Taiwan, you might want to wait because the cost for dental treatment is much lower there.

Most pharmacies in Hong Kong are open from 9 am to 6 pm daily, with some open until 8 pm.

DANGERS & ANNOYANCES

In a form of poetic Chinese justice, the colony's opium-based foundation has rebounded and Hong Kong has a serious dope problem. Like elsewhere, addicts turn to crime to finance their habit. For the most part, it's non-violent crime: pickpocketing, burglaries and (in the case of addicts) prostitution. However, muggings do occasionally occur, though seldom in tourist areas since these are heavily patrolled by the police.

More visitors have been ripped off by their fellow travellers than by Hong Kong residents. Be careful with your valuables, especially if you're staying in a dormitory.

The biggest annoyance in Hong Kong is the appalling rudeness of shopkeepers, especially in the Tsimshatsui tourist combat zone. The HKTA is aware of the problem, and has attempted to educate sales clerks not to bite the tourists. They've tried all sorts of catchy slogans: 'Smile at our foreign friends' etc. Unfortunately, most shopkeepers prefer the motto 'Give us your money and get the hell out!'

WORK

Legally speaking, there are only three groups of foreigners who do not need employment visas for Hong Kong: UK citizens, British passport holders or registered British subjects.

As for foreign nationals, including Australians, Americans and Canadians, you must get an employment visa from the Hong Kong Immigration Department before you arrive if you want to work in Hong Kong. This is no longer very easy to arrange as you need a job skill which cannot easily be performed by a local, and your employer must be willing to sponsor you.

As for under-the-table employment, that certainly exists too. Plenty of Westerners do find temporary illegal work in Hong Kong, but there are risks and discretion is strongly advised!

Some suggest registering with Hong Kong personnel agencies, and others suggest checking the classified sections of the local newspapers. However, most foreigners who have found work in Hong Kong have done so by going door to door and asking. A good place to start looking is at bars and Western restaurants in Lan Kwai Fong, Wanchai and Tsimshatsui. Besides finding opportunities to be a bartender or waitress, people in gwailo bars and restaurants may have tips on English-teaching opportunities, modeling jobs, secretarial work and so on.

ACTIVITIES
Anyone who is serious about sports should contact the South China Athletic Association (☎ 5776932), Caroline Hill Rd, Causeway Bay, Hong Kong Island. The SCAA has numerous indoor facilities such as bowling, tennis, ping pong tables, an exercise room, yoga, karate and other classes.

Billiards & Snooker
The most accessible venues are in Tsimshatsui East, including the Peninsula Billiards Club (☎ 7390638), 3rd floor, Peninsula Centre, and the Castle Billiards Club (☎ 3679071), Houston Centre.

In Central you can check out the Olympic Billiard Association (☎ 8150456), Hollywood Commercial Centre, on the corner of Hollywood Rd & Old Bailey St. In Wanchai, there are two good places, Jim Mei White Snooker (☎ 8336628), 339 Jaffe Rd, and Winsor Billiard Company (☎ 5755505), 10 Canal Rd West.

Cycling
There are bicycle paths in the New Territories, mostly around Tolo Harbour. The paths run from Shatin to Tai Po and continue up to Tai Mei Tuk. You can rent bicycles in these three places, but it's very crowded on weekends. On a weekday you may have the paths to yourself.

Bicycle rentals are also available at Shek O on Hong Kong Island and Mui Wo on Lantau Island.

Hiking
Hong Kong has some excellent walks. Practically everyone does the walk around Victoria Peak. The MacLehose Trail in the New Territories is 100 km long and goes over the summit of Hong Kong's highest peak, Tai

Mo Shan. Almost equally challenging is the 70-km Lantau Trail on Lantau Island.

Horse Racing
The racing season is from late September to June. Normally, races at Shatin are held on Saturday from 1 to 6 pm. At Happy Valley, races are normally on Wednesday evening from about 7 to 11 pm.

Ice Skating
One of the best ice skating rinks in Hong Kong is on the 1st floor of Cityplaza-Two (☎ 8854697), Cityplaza Shopping Centre, 18 Tai Koo Shing Rd, Quarry Bay. The easiest way to get there is to take the MTR to the Tai Koo station.

On the Kowloon side, the best rink is Whampoa Super Ice (☎ 7744899) in basement two of the Whampoa Gardens shopping complex in Hunghom. Farther afield is Riviera Ice Chalet (☎ 4071100), 3rd floor, Riviera Plaza, 28 Wing Shun St, Tsuen Wan, New Territories.

Running
If you'd like a morning jog with spectacular views, nothing beats the path around Victoria Peak on Harlech and Lugard roads. Part of this is a 'fitness trail' with various exercise machines (parallel bars etc). Almost as spectacular is the jog along Bowen Rd, which is closed to traffic and runs in an east-west direction in the hills above Wanchai. As long as there are no races at the time, the horse racing track at Happy Valley is an excellent place to run. There is also a running track in Victoria Park in Causeway Bay.

On the Kowloon side, a popular place to run is the Promenade along the waterfront in Tsimshatsui East. The problem here is that it's not a very long run, but the views are good and it's close to many of the hotels.

The Hong Kong International Marathon is held on the second day of the Chinese New Year. This has become a cross-border event, with part of the running course passing through China. The Coast of China Marathon is held in March. Contact the HKTA for more information on upcoming marathons.

If you like easy runs followed by beer and good company, consider joining Hash House Harriers (☎ 376229; fax 8136517), 3rd floor, 74 Chung Hom Kok Rd, Stanley, Hong Kong Island. You do not need to be in particularly good shape to participate. The Hash is an international organisation geared towards young people and the young at heart.

If you're looking for people to run with, call the Distance Runners Club (☎ 8296254; fax 8241220), GPO Box 10368. There is a Ladies Road Runners Club (☎ 3175933; fax 3175920), PO Box 20613, Hennessy Rd Post Office, Wanchai.

Swimming

Except for Kowloon and the north side of Hong Kong Island, there are good beaches spread throughout the colony. The most accessible beaches are on the south side of Hong Kong Island but some of these are becoming increasingly polluted. The best beaches can be found on the outlying islands and in the New Territories. (See those sections later in this chapter for details.) The longest beach in Hong Kong is Cheung Sha on Lantau Island. There is an official swimming season from 1 April to 31 October when lifeguards are available.

Hong Kong's Urban Council operates 13 public swimming pools. During school term weekdays the pools are nearly empty so this is the best time to go. There's an excellent pool in Kowloon Park, Tsimshatusi, and Victoria Park, Causeway Bay.

Waterworld, next to Ocean Park in Aberdeen, offers outdoor pools and waterslides.

Windsurfing

The best months for windsurfing are September through December when a steady north-east monsoon blows. Windsurfing during a typhoon is not recommended!

Equipment rentals are available in the New Territories at the Windsurfing Centre (☎ 7925605), Sha Ha (just past Sai Kung). Also check out Tai Po Sailboard Centre, Chan Uk Chuen, 77 Ting Kok Rd, Tai Po, New Territories. Ditto for the Tai Mei Tuk Water Sports Centre (☎ 6653591), Regional

Council, Tai Mei Tuk, Tai Po, New Territories.

Perhaps the best spot for rentals is on Cheung Chau Island at the Outdoor Cafe (☎ 9818316), Tungwan Beach. Costs are HK$70 for two hours or HK$200 for a full day. Tuition (if you need it) costs HK$450 for five hours.

At Stanley Main Beach on Hong Kong Island you can try the Pro Shop (pager 1128238-287) and Wind Surf Pro Motion (☎ 8132372). Shek O is another good place on Hong Kong Island for windsurfing.

Rental fees are typically from HK$50 to HK$80 per hour. Around December, Stanley Beach becomes the venue of the Hong Kong Open Windsurfing Championship.

HIGHLIGHTS

The trip on the Peak Tram to Victoria Peak has been practically mandatory for visitors since it opened in 1888. A 30-minute ride on a sampan through Aberdeen Harbour is equally intriguing. Lunch at a good dim sum restaurant is one of the great pleasures of the Orient, and of course, shopping is what Hong Kong is all about. The relatively undeveloped outlying islands are in some ways the most surprising and enjoyable part of Hong Kong.

ACCOMMODATION

Prices are rising to absurd levels. There are a couple of YHA dormitories which charge only HK$50 per bed, but most are very inconveniently located. The same is true for camping sites – they exist, but you'll spend an hour or more commuting to the city. You cannot camp at beaches which are patrolled by lifeguards, though it should be OK at remote sites.

You'll need a YHA card to stay at any of the hostels. If you arrive in Hong Kong without a YHA card and wish to join, the local representative is Hong Kong Youth Hostels Association (☎ 7881638), room 225, block 19, Shek Kip Mei Estate, Kowloon. This office is inconveniently located in a hideous housing estate near the Shek Kip Mei MTR station. HI cards cost

HK$80 for Hong Kong residents or HK$150 for nonresidents.

Guesthouses are the salvation of most budget travellers. Some guesthouses (not many) have dormitories where beds go for HK$70 to HK$100, with discounts for long-term (one week or more) rentals. Private rooms the size of closets are available for as little as HK$150 but you can easily spend twice that. Again, long-term discounts can be negotiated. It definitely pays for two people to share a room as this costs little or no extra. Mid-range hotels start at around HK$400 and go up to around HK$800.

For information on exactly where to stay in Hong Kong, see Places to Stay in the Around the Country section later in this chapter.

FOOD & DRINKS

Hong Kong offers incredible variety when it comes to eating. By all means you should try *dim sum*, a uniquely Cantonese dish served only for breakfast or lunch, but never dinner. Dim sum delicacies are normally steamed in a small bamboo basket. Typically, each basket contains four identical pieces, so four people would be an ideal number for a dim sum meal. You pay by the number of baskets you order. The baskets are stacked up on pushcarts and rolled around the dining room. You choose whatever you like from the carts, so no menu is needed.

In Chinese restaurants tea is often served free of charge, or at most you'll pay HK$1 for a big pot which can be refilled indefinitely. On the other hand, coffee is seldom available except in Western restaurants or coffee shops, and is never free.

Beer is extremely popular among the Chinese. The brands made in China are excellent, the most popular being Tsingtao, now a major export.

Food Vocabulary
Dim Sum
barbecued pork buns
  cha siu bau   叉燒飽
bean-curd chicken roll
  gai chuk   雞紮

bean-curd pork roll
  seen chuk guen   鮮竹卷
fried spring rolls
  tsun guen   春卷
fried green pepper
  yeung chen chiu   叉燒飽
fried rice flour triangle
  ham shui kok   咸水餃
fried taro puff
  woo kok   芋角
fried chicken feet
  fung jau   鳳爪
fried flour triangle
  jar fun gwor   炸粉果
minced pork dumpling
  guon tong gau   灌湯餃
pork & shrimp dumplings
  siu mai   燒賣
rice flour triangle
  fun gwor   粉果
rice wrapped in lotus leaf
  ho yip fan   荷葉飯
rice dumpling in bamboo leaf
  gwor ching chung   裹蒸粽
rice flour & shrimp roll
  har cheung   蝦腸粉
shark's fin dumpling
  yee chi gau   魚翅餃
spicy spare ribs
  pai gwat   排骨
steamed shrimp dumplings
  har gau   蝦餃
steamed tripe
  ngau pak yip   牛柏葉
steamed meat buns
  siu lung bau   小龍飽
steamed minced-beef balls
  au yuk   山竹牛肉

Dim Sum Desserts
coconut pudding cubes
  yeh jap go   椰汁糕
coconut snowball
  nor mai chi   糯米茲
custard tart
  daan tart   蛋撻
steamed egg pudding
  dun gai daan   炖雞蛋
steamed lotus-paste bun
  lin yung bau   蓮蓉飽

HONG KONG

sticky cake & nuts
  ma chai 馬仔
sweet red-bean porridge
  hung dow sa 紅豆沙
wrapped coconut, peanut & sesame
  pun yip kok 蘋葉角

Fruits

carambola
  yong tou 楊桃
durian
  laulin 榴蓮
jackfruit
  taishui boluo 大樹菠蘿
longan
  long an 龍眼
lychee
  lai chi 荔枝
mangosteen
  san jop 山竹
mango
  mong gow 芒果
papaya
  mok gwa 木瓜
pomelo
  sa tin yau 沙田柚
rambutan
  fan gwai lo lai chi 番鬼佬荔枝

Useful Phrase

I'm a vegetarian.
  ou sek zai

Drinks Vocabulary

ice cold
  dong 凍
ice cubes
  bingfai 冰塊
hot
  yit 熱

Cold Drinks

water
  soi 水
mineral water
  kong chwin soi 礦泉水
fizzy drink (soda)
  hesoi 汽水
Coca-Cola
  hohau holok 可口可樂

Diet Coke
  gamfei holok 減肥可樂
Fanta
  fantat changchap 芬達橙汁
Sprite
  shwe bae 雪碧
lemon tea (cold)
  dong lengmeng cha 凍檸檬茶
carrot juice
  hong lobak chap 紅蘿蔔汁
orange juice
  chang chap 橙汁
starfruit juice
  yong tou chap 楊桃汁
sugarcane juice
  gam chei chap 廿蔗汁
papaya milkshake
  mougwa aulai 木瓜牛奶
pineapple milkshake
  boluo laisek 菠蘿奶昔
watermelon milkshake
  saigwa laisek 西瓜奶昔

Fleecy

Red Bean
  hongdau bing 紅豆冰
Green Bean
  lokdau bing 綠豆冰
Black Grass Jelly
  leungfan 涼粉
Fruit Punch
  zap gou bing 雜果冰
Pineapple
  boluo bing 菠蘿冰

Tea & Coffee

tea
  cha 茶
black tea
  zai cha 齋茶
tea with milk
  lai cha 奶茶
lemon tea
  lengmeng cha 檸檬茶
green tea
  luk cha 綠茶
chrysanthemum tea
  gukfa cha 菊花茶
jasmine tea
  heung pin cha 茉莉花茶

HONG KONG

oolong tea
 oolong cha   烏龍茶
hot chocolate
 ye jugulek   熱朱古力
Ovaltine
 ye ouwahtin   熱呵華田
Horlicks
 ye holahak   熱好立克
coffee with milk
 gafei   熱咖啡
black coffee
 zai fei   齋啡

Alcohol
beer
 beijau   啤酒
Carlsberg Beer
 gasiba   加士百
Lowenbrau Beer
 lowenbo   盧雲堡
San Miguel Beer
 sangle bei   生力啤
Tsingtao Beer
 chingdo beijau   青島啤酒
whisky
 waisigei   威士忌
vodka
 fukte ga   伏特加
red grape wine
 hung jau   紅酒
white grape wine
 ba jau   白酒
rice wine
 mai jau   米酒
Mao Tai
 mao toi   茅台

ENTERTAINMENT
Apart from sitting around the hostels and smashing cockroaches with a rolled up newspaper, most forms of amusement require money. The street markets in Kowloon cost nothing to wander around, and there are some cheap eats from pushcarts. English-language movies are shown at most cinemas, check the newspapers for listings. The HKTA has a publication entitled *Culture* which includes a monthly schedule of events such as performances by Chinese opera troupes and piano recitals.

Discos are concentrated mostly in the Wanchai district of Hong Kong Island, see that section later in this chapter for details. Pubs are heavily concentrated in the Lan Kwai Fong neighbourhood in Central, Hong Kong Island, and in Tsimshatsui.

The consensus of opinion is that the so-called 'girlie bars' around Tsimshatsui are rip-off schemes. Enticing photos at the entrances and promises of cheap beers (HK$25 or so) have lured many travellers, who only belatedly are told about the HK$400 'service charge'!

THINGS TO BUY
Oh yeah, shopping, some people do come to Hong Kong for that. 'Shop till you drop' is the motto of many tourists, but you should pause before embarking on a buying binge. It's very easy in Hong Kong to decide suddenly that you need all sorts of consumer goods you don't really need at all.

Hong Kong resembles one gigantic shopping mall, but a quick look at price tags should convince you that the city is not quite the bargain it's cracked up to be. Imported goods like Japanese-made cameras and electronic gadgets can be bought for roughly the same price in many Western countries. However, what makes Hong Kong shine is the variety – if you can't find it in Hong Kong, it probably doesn't exist.

The worst neighbourhood for shopping happens to be the place where most tourists shop. Tsimshatsui, the tourist ghetto of Kowloon, is the most likely place to be cheated. Notice that none of the cameras or other big ticket items have price tags. This is *not* common practice elsewhere in Hong Kong. If you go out to the Chinese neighbourhoods where the locals shop, you'll find price tags on everything.

Clothing is the best buy in Hong Kong. All the cheap stuff comes from China and most is decent quality, but check zippers and stitching carefully as there is some real junk around. You'll find the best buys at the street markets at Tong Choi St in Mongkok and Apliu St in Shamshuipo. If you want to search around Tsimshatsui, the best deals are generally found on the eastern end of Granville Rd. Another good place for clothes is the mezzanine floor of Chungking Mansions (not the ground floor). Two Chinese chainstores with Italian names, Giordano's and Bossini, offer quality clothing at reasonable prices.

Yue Hwa Chinese Products at 301 Nathan Rd, Yaumatei (corner of Nathan and Jordan Rds), is a good place to pick up everyday consumer goods. It's also one of the best places to get eyeglasses made.

The Golden Shopping Centre, Basement, 146-152 Fuk Wah St, Shamshuipo, has the cheapest collection of desktop computers, accessories and components in Hong Kong.

If it's a camera you need, don't even waste your time on Nathan Rd in Tsimshatsui. Photo Scientific (☎ 5221903), 6 Stanley St, Central, is the favourite of Hong Kong's resident professional photographers. But if you're in a hurry and want to buy in Tsimshatsui, the best seems to be Kimberley Camera Company (☎ 7212308), Champagne Court, 16 Kimberley Rd.

Apliu St in Shamshuipo has the best collection of electronics shops selling Walkmans, CD players etc.

You can find cheap CDs and music tapes in the night markets of Temple St, Tong Choi St and Apliu St, but selection is very limited. Tower Records (☎ 5060811), 7th floor, shop 701, Times Square, Matheson St, Causeway Bay, offers the widest selection of recorded music in Hong Kong. KPS is a good chain store for discounted CDs and tapes, with shops at: Prince's Building, 9-25 Chater Rd, Central; Far East Finance Centre, Central, which is just next to the Admiralty MTR station; Ocean Gallery, No 233-235 Harbour City on Canton Rd, Tsimshatsui; and another at Inter-Continental Plaza, Granville Rd, Tsimshatsui East.

The sports-minded might want to visit Flying Ball Bicycle Shop (☎ 3815919), 201 Tung Choi St (near Prince Edward MTR station), Mongkok.

Hong Kong is a good place to pick up a decent backpack, sleeping bag, tent and other gear for hiking, camping and travelling. Mongkok is by far the best neighbourhood to look for this stuff, though there are a couple of odd places in nearby Yaumatei. Some places worth checking out include:

Grade IV Alpine, 13 Saigon St, Yaumatei (☎ 7820202)
Mountaineer Supermarket, 395 Portland St, Mongkok (☎ 3970585)
Rose Sporting Goods, 39 Fa Yuen St, Mongkok (☎ 7811809)
Sportsman Shop, 72 Sai Yee St, Mongkok (☎ 3956405)
Tang Fai Kee Military, 248 Reclamation St, Mongkok (☎ 3855169)
Three Military Equipment Company, 83 Sai Yee St, Mongkok (☎ 3914019, 7894326)

If you want to visit a good shopping mall where the locals go, visit Cityplaza in Quarry Bay. Take the MTR to the Tai Koo station.

Getting There & Away

AIR

For most travellers, the normal arrival point will be Kai Tak Airport – with its runway sticking out from Kowloon into the harbour it makes a pretty dramatic entrance.

Hong Kong is a good place to buy discounted air tickets, but watch out! There are a few real swindlers in the travel business. The most common trick is a request for a non-refundable deposit on an air ticket. So you pay a deposit for the booking, but when you go to pick up the tickets they say that the flight is no longer available, but that there is another flight at a higher price, sometimes 50% more!

It is best not to pay a deposit, but rather to pay for the ticket in full and get a receipt clearly showing that there is no balance due, and that the full amount is refundable if no ticket is issued. Tickets are normally issued the next day after booking, but for the really cheap tickets (actually group tickets) you must pick these up yourself at the airport from the 'tour leader' (who you will never see again once you've got the ticket). One caution; when you get the ticket from the tour leader, check it carefully. Occasionally, there are errors, such as you're issued a ticket with the return portion valid for only 60 days when you paid for a ticket valid for one year etc.

Some budget fares available in Hong Kong follow, but realise that these are discounted fares and will have various restrictions upon their use:

Destination	One Way	Return
Auckland	US$574	US$898
Bangkok	US$155	US$220
Beijing	US$267	US$532
Guam	US$455	US$476
Guangzhou	US$57	US$114
Ho Chi Minh City	US$294	US$589
Honolulu	US$376	US$727
Jakarta	US$227	US$415
Frankfurt	US$375	US$725
Kuala Lumpur	US$188	US$314
London	US$375	US$725
Manila	US$115	US$193
New York	US$496	US$870
Pnomh Penh	US$272	US$532
Rangoon	US$367	US$735
San Francisco	US$428	US$675
Seoul	US$201	US$272
Singapore	US$216	US$275
Sydney	US$570	US$825
Taipei	US$127	US$214
Tokyo	US$279	US$487
Vancouver	US$392	US$678

Airline Offices

You do need to ring up or visit the airlines to reconfirm flights out of Hong Kong. Listed are some of the airlines which fly into Hong Kong, along with the addresses of ticketing offices on both sides of the harbour. The reservation and reconfirmation telephone number (Res) is followed by the flight information telephone number (Info). A few airlines have only one telephone number.

Aeroflot
    (Res ☎ 8454232, Info 7698111)
Air France
    Room 2104, Alexandra House, 7 Des Voeux Rd Central (Res ☎ 5248145, Info 7696662)
Air India
    10th floor, Gloucester Tower, 11 Pedder St, Central (Res ☎ 5221176, Info 7696539)

Air Lanka
    Room 602, Peregrine Tower, Lippo Centre, Central (☎ 5210708)
Air Mauritius
    c/o Mercury Travel Ltd, St George's Building, Ice House St & Connaught Rd, Central (☎ 5231114)
Air New Zealand
    Suite 902, 3 Exchange Square, 8 Connaught Place, Central (Res ☎ 5249041, Info 7698111)
Air Niugini
    Room 705, Century Square, 1-13 D'Aguilar St, Central (Res ☎ 5242151, Info 7477888)
Air Seychelles, Hopewell Centre, Queen's Rd East, Wanchai (☎ 8213881)
Alitalia
    Room 2101, Hutchison House, 10 Harcourt Rd, Central (Res ☎ 5237047, Info 7697417)
All Nippon
    Room 2512, Pacific Place Two, 88 Queensway, Admiralty (Res ☎ 8107100, Info 7698606)
British Airways
    30th floor, Alexandra House, 7 Des Voeux Rd Central (Res ☎ 8680303, Info 8680768)
    Room 112, Royal Garden Hotel, 69 Mody Rd, Tsimshatsui East (☎ 3689255)
Civil Aviation Administration of China (CAAC)
    Ground floor, 17 Queen's Rd, Central, Hong Kong Island (☎ 8401199)
    Ground floor, Mirador Mansion, 54-64B Nathan Rd, Tsimshatsui (☎ 7390022)
Canadian Airlines International
    Ground floor, Swire House, 9-25 Chater Rd, Central (Res ☎ 8683123, Info 7697113)
Cathay Pacific
    Ground floor, Swire House, 9-25 Chater Rd, Central
    Room 1126, 11th floor, Ocean Centre, Tsimshatsui
    Shop 109, 1st floor, Royal Garden Hotel, 69 Mody Rd, Tsimshatsui East (Res ☎ 7471888, Info 7471234)
China Airlines (Taiwan)
    Ground floor, St George's Building, the corner of Ice House St & Connaught Rd, Central
    G5-6 Tsimshatsui Centre, Tsimshatsui East (Res ☎ 8682299, Info 8439800)
Dragonair
    Room 1843, Swire House, 9 Connaught Rd, Central
    12th floor, Tower 6, China Hong Kong City, 33 Canton Rd, Tsimshatsui (☎ Res 5901188, Info 7697727)
Eupo-Air
    Swire House, 9 Connaught Rd, Central (☎ 542-3633)
Garuda Indonesia
    2nd floor, Sing Pao Centre, 8 Queen's Rd, Central (Res ☎ 8400000, Info 7696681)

Gulf Air
    Room 2508, Caroline Centre, 28 Yun Ping Rd, Causeway Bay (☎ Res 8822892, Info 7698337)
Japan Air Lines
    20th floor, Gloucester Tower, 11 Pedder St, Central
    Harbour View Holiday Inn, Mody Rd, Tsimshatsui East (Res ☎ 5230081, Info 7696524)
Japan Asia
    20th floor, Gloucester Tower, 11 Pedder St, Central (Res ☎ 5218102)
Jardine's
    Alexandra House, 7 Des Voeux Rd Central (☎ Res 8680303, Info 8680768)
KLM Royal Dutch Airlines
    Room 701-5, Jardine House, 1 Connaught Place, Central (☎ Res 8228111, Info 8228118)
Korean Air
    Ground floor, St George's Building, the corner of Ice House St & Connaught Rd, Central
    11th floor, South Seas Centre, Tower II, 75 Mody Rd, Tsimshatsui East
    G12-15 Tsimshatsui Centre, Salisbury Rd, Tsimshatsui East (☎ 3686221)
Lauda (Austria)
    M1, New Henry House, 10 Ice House St, Central (Res ☎ 5246178, Info 7697017)
Lufthansa German Airlines
    6th floor, Landmark East, 12 Ice House St, Central (Res ☎ 8682313, Info 7696560)
Malaysian Airline System (MAS)
    Room 1306, Prince's Building, 9-25 Chater Rd, Central (Res ☎ 5218181, Info 7697967)
Northwest Airlines
    29th floor, Alexandra House, 7 Des Voeux Rd Central, Central (☎ 8104288)
Philippine Airlines
    Room 603, West Tower, Bond Centre, Central (Res ☎ 5249216)
    Room 6, Ground floor, East Ocean Centre, 98 Granville Rd, Tsimshatsui East (Res ☎ 3694521, Info 7696263)
Qantas Airways
    Room 1422, Swire House, 9-25 Chater Rd, Central (Res ☎ 5242101, Info 5256206)
Royal Brunei Airlines
    Room 1406, Central Building, 3 Pedder St, Central (☎ 8698608)
Royal Nepal Airlines
    Room 704, Lippo Sun Plaza, 28 Canton Rd, Tsimshatsui (☎ 3759151)
Singapore Airlines
    United Centre, Queensway, Central (☎ Res 5202233, Info 7696387)
South African Airways
    30th floor, Alexandra House, Central (Res ☎ 8773277, Info 8680768)

Swissair
    8th floor, Tower II, Admiralty Centre, 18 Harcourt Rd, Central (Res ☎ 5293670, Info 769-8864)
THAI Airways
    United Centre, Two Pacific Place, Queensway, Central
    Shop 124, 1st floor, World Wide Plaza, the corner of Des Voeux Rd and Pedder St, Central
    Shop 105-6, Omni, The Hongkong Hotel, 3 Canton Rd, Tsimshatsui (☎ Res 5295601, Info 7697421)
United Airlines
    29th floor, The Landmark, Gloucester Tower, Des Voeux Rd & Pedder St, Central
    Ground floor, Empire Centre, Mody Rd, Tsimshatsui East (Res ☎ 8104888, Info 7697279)

Travel Agencies

Some agencies we've personally tried and found to offer competitive prices include:

Phoenix Services
    Room B, 6th floor, Milton Mansion, 96 Nathan Rd, Tsimshatsui (☎ 7227378; fax 3698884)
Shoestring Travel
    Flat A, 4th floor, Alpha House, 27-33 Nathan Rd, Tsimshatsui (☎ 7232306; fax 7212085)
Traveller Services
    Room 1012, Silvercord Tower 1, 30 Canton Rd, Tsimshatsui (☎ 3752222; fax 3752233)
Victoria Travel (connected with Victoria Hostel)
    1st floor, 33 Hankow Rd, Tsimshatsui (☎ 3760621; fax 3762609)

Departure Tax

The airport departure tax was previously a hefty HK$150 but was dropped to HK$50 in 1994, though this might only be a temporary pre-1997 public relations exercise. If you're departing by ship to Macau or China, departure tax is HK$26 but it's included in the purchase price of the ticket.

LAND

If you just want a brief guided visit to the People's Republic of China, you can do that quite easily. There are plenty of one-day cross-the-border jaunts available from Hong Kong or Macau, and slightly longer Guangzhou quickies which give you a few days in the neighbouring city.

A train to Lo Wu at the border will cost

you just HK$37. You walk across the border to the city of Shenzhen, and from there you can take a local train to Guangzhou and beyond.

If you're entering Hong Kong from Shenzhen, it's very important to realise that there is no moneychanger on the Hong Kong side – many travellers have been stuck! You can change money on the Chinese side, but be sure you have at least HK$37 (preferably a little more) so you can get into the city.

Alternatively, you can take an express train straight through from Hunghom station in Kowloon to Guangzhou for HK$182.

SEA

Hong Kong has one of the most spectacular harbours in the world, so it's a shame that there's not much of a chance of arriving by boat – unless you're rich and on a cruise liner. It may still be possible though for budget travellers, if you want to take a boat from China. See the introductory Getting Around chapter earlier in this book for details.

Getting Around

Hong Kong has a varied and frequent public transport system. Fastest is the Mass Transit Railway (MTR), but slower and much more fun are the ferries. Before setting out to travel anywhere by bus, ensure you have a good pocketful of small change – the exact fare normally must be deposited in a cash box and nobody has change. However, change is readily available for the MTR and ferries.

AIR
To/From the Airport

The Airbus (airport bus) services are very convenient and are significantly cheaper than taxis. There are four services: the A1 to Tsimshatsui (HK$9); the A2 to Wanchai, Central and the Macau Ferry Terminal (HK$14); the A3 to Causeway Bay (HK$14); and the A5 to Quarry Bay (also HK$14). The previously existing A4 went bankrupt some years ago. The buses operate

every 15 to 20 minutes from 7 am to midnight, except the A5 which runs from 9 am to 11 pm. There's plenty of luggage space on board and they go past most major hotels.

The A1 service to Tsimshatsui in Kowloon goes down Nathan Rd right in front of Chungking Mansions, then turns around at the Star Ferry Terminal and heads back, making numerous stops en route. There is an Airbus brochure at the departure area with a map showing the bus routes.

BUS

There are plenty of buses with fares starting from HK$1.80 and going up to HK$12 for the longest ride you can take in the New Territories. You pay the fare as you enter the bus so make sure you have the exact change ready. The double-decker buses are blue and cream on Hong Kong Island (operated by China Motor Bus) or red and cream in Kowloon (operated by Kowloon Motor Bus).

Most services stop around 11 pm or midnight, but buses Nos 121 and 122 are 'Cross Harbour Recreation Routes' which operate through the Cross-Harbour Tunnel every 15 minutes from 12.45 to 5 am. Bus No 121 runs from Macau Ferry Terminal on Hong Kong Island, then through the tunnel to Chatham Rd in Tsimshatsui East before continuing on to Choi Hung on the east side of the airport.

Bus No 122 runs from North Point on Hong Kong Island, through the Cross-Harbour Tunnel to Chatham Rd in Tsimshatsui East, the northern part of Nathan Rd and on to Laichikok in the north-west part of Kowloon.

MINIBUS & MAXICAB

Small red and yellow minibuses supplement the regular bus services. They are a little more expensive (generally from HK$2 to HK$6), and generally don't run such regular routes but you can get on or off almost anywhere. If you know where you are going and where they are going, you may well find them both fast and convenient.

Maxicabs are just like minibuses except they are green and yellow and do run regular routes. Two popular ones depart from the

HONG KONG

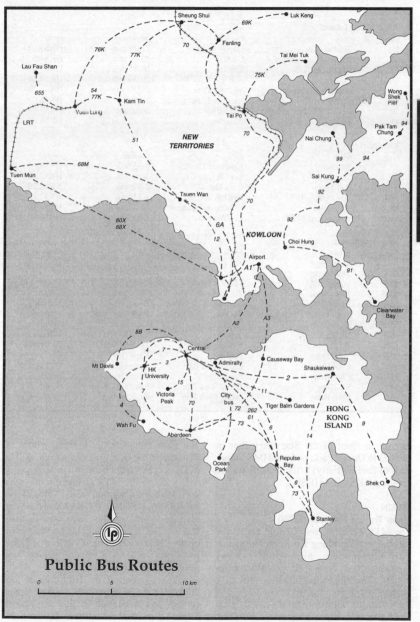

Public Bus Routes

0   5   10 km

Hong Kong Island

bus	from	to	frequency	cost
1	Central (Rumsey St)	Happy Valley	12-20 min	HK$3.80
6	Repulse Bay/Stanley	Central	10-20 min	HK$4/6
7	Aberdeen	Central	10-15 min	HK$3.20
14	Sai Wan Ho	Stanley	20-30 min	HK$4.80
15	Central (Exchange Sq)	Victoria Peak	15-30 min	HK$5.20
15B	Causeway Bay	Victoria Peak	20 min	HK$6.00
70	Central (Exchange Sq)	Aberdeen	5-10 min	HK$3.60
73	Stanley	Aberdeen	15-30 min	HK$4.80

Kowloon

bus	from	to	frequency	cost
1A	Star Ferry	Kowloon City	6-13 min	HK$3.00
2	Star Ferry	Lei Cheung Uk	5-10 min	HK$2.10
5	Star Ferry	Choi Hung	3-8 min	HK$2.10
6A	Star Ferry	Laichikok	8-15 min	HK$2.10
8A	Jordan Rd	Whampoa Gardens	12-20 min	HK$2.10
14C	Kwun Tong MTR	Lei Yue Mun	13-25 min	HK$1.80

New Territories

bus	from	to	via	frequency
51	Tsuen Wan	Kam Tin	Route Twisk	10-20 min
52X	Shamshuipo	Tuen Mun	Tsuen Wan	12-20 min
54	Yuen Long	Sheung Tsuen	Kam Tin	15-25 min
60M	Tsuen Wan	Tuen Mun	Ma Wan Pier	5-10 min
60X	Jordan Rd	Tuen Mun	Tsuen Wan	5-20 min
64K	Yuen Long	Tai Po	Kam Tin	5-15 min
68M	Tsuen Wan	Yuen Long	Tuen Mun	4-14 min
68X	Jordan Rd	Yuen Long	Tuen Mun	9-16 min
75K	Tai Po	Plover Cove Res	Tai Mei Tuk	13-25 min
77K	Yuen Long	Fanling	Kam Tin	14-25 min
91	Choi Hung	Clearwater Bay	Hang Hau	12-16 min
92	Choi Hung	Sai Kung	Hebe Haven	6-15 min
94	Sai Kung	Wong Shek Pier	Pak Tam Chung	60 min
96R	Choi Hung	Wong Shek Pier	Sai Kung	holidays

carpark in front of the Star Ferry Pier in Central to Ocean Park, or from HMS Tamar (east of the Star Ferry) to the Peak. Fares are between HK$1 and HK$8.

TRAIN
Mass Transit Railway (MTR)

The MTR operates from Central across the harbour and up along Kowloon Peninsula. This ultramodern, high-speed subway system has been quite a hit with office commuters. The ticket machines do not give change (get it from the ticket windows) and the tickets are valid only for the day they are purchased. Once you go past the turnstile, you must complete the journey within 90 minutes or the ticket becomes invalid. The MTR operates from 6 am to 1 am.

If you use the MTR frequently, it's very useful to buy a Common Stored Value Ticket for HK$70, HK$100 or HK$200. These can also be used on the Kowloon-Canton Railway (KCR), except for the Lo Wu station on the China border. The MTR Tourist Ticket is a rip-off at HK$25 because it gives you only HK$20 worth of fares!

Smoking, eating or drinking are not allowed in the MTR stations or on the trains (makes you wonder about all those Maxim Cake Shops in the stations). The fine for

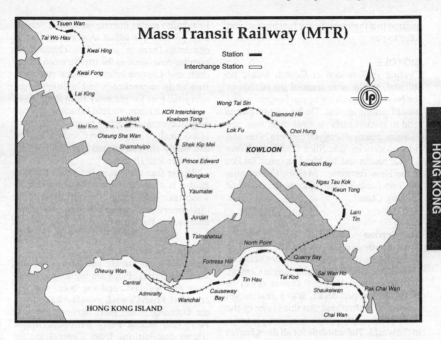

HONG KONG

eating or drinking is HK$1000, while smoking will set you back HK$2000. Busking, selling and soliciting are forbidden. There are no toilets in the MTR stations.

Kowloon-Canton Railway (KCR)

The KCR runs from Kowloon's Hunghom station right up to the border at Lo Wu where visitors to China usually walk across the bridge to Shenzhen. From Shenzhen, there are buses and trains to Guangzhou (Canton) and beyond. There are also four express trains daily which run right through from Kowloon to Guangzhou. Apart from being one of the best ways of entering China, it's also an excellent alternative to buses for getting into the New Territories. There is no place to visit in Lo Wu itself, you are not even supposed to go to this station unless you intend to cross into China.

TRAM

The tram runs east-west along the northern side of Hong Kong Island. As well as being ridiculously picturesque and fun to travel on, the tram is quite a bargain at HK$1 for any distance. You pay when you get off.

There is just one major line, plus a spur route off to Happy Valley. Some trams don't run the full length of the line, but basically you can just get on any tram that comes by. They pass frequently and there always seem to be half a dozen trams in sight.

TAXI

On Hong Kong Island and Kowloon, the flagfall is HK$9 for the first two km and an extra 90c for every additional 0.2 km. In the New Territories, flagfall is HK$8 for the first two km, thereafter 80c for every 0.2 km. There is a luggage fee of HK$4 per bag but not all drivers insist on this.

If you go through either the Cross-Harbour Tunnel or Eastern Harbour Tunnel, you'll be charged an extra HK$20. The toll is only HK$10, but drivers are allowed to assume that they won't get a fare back so you have to pay.

BICYCLE

Cycling in Kowloon or Central would be suicidal, but in quiet areas of the islands or the New Territories a bike can be quite a nice way of getting around. The bike rental places tend to run out early on weekends.

Some places where you can rent bikes and ride in safety include: Shek O on Hong Kong Island; Shatin and Tai Mei Tuk (near Tai Po) in the New Territories; Mui Wo (Silvermine Bay) on Lantau Island; and on the island of Cheung Chau.

BOAT
Star Ferries

There are three routes on the Star Ferry, but by far the most popular one shuttles between Tsimshatsui and Edinburgh Place in Central. Costing a mere HK$1.20 (lower deck) or HK$1.50 (upper deck), it's a real travel bargain. It's often said that this is one of the most picturesque public transport journeys in the world. The schedule for all three ferries is as follows:

Tsimshatsui – Central (Edinburgh Place), every five to 10 minutes from 6.30 am until 11.30 pm
Tsimshatsui – Wanchai, every 10 to 20 minutes from 7.30am to 10.50 pm
Hunghom – Central (Edinburgh Place), every 12 to 20 minutes from 7 am to 7.20 pm (every 20 minutes on Sunday & holidays)

Hoverferries

These are most useful for getting to the New Territories, but you may have to queue during rush hours. The schedule is as follows:

Tsimshatsui East – Central (Queen's Pier), every 20 minutes from 8 am to 8 pm
Tsuen Wan – Central (Government Pier), every 20 minutes from 7.20 am to 5.20 pm
Tuen Mun – Central (Central Harbour Services Pier), every 10 to 20 minutes from 6.45 am to 7.40 pm

Kaidos

A kaido is a small to medium-sized ferry which can make short runs on the open sea.

Few kaido routes operate on regular schedules, preferring to adjust supply according to demand. There is sort of a schedule on popular runs, such as the trip between Aberdeen and Lamma Island. Kaidos run most frequently on weekends and holidays when everyone tries to 'get away from it all'.

A sampan is a motorised launch which can only accommodate a few people. A sampan is too small to be considered seaworthy, but can safely zip you around typhoon shelters like Aberdeen Harbour.

Bigger than a sampan, but smaller than a kaido, is a walla walla. These operate as water taxis on Victoria Harbour. Most of the customers are sailors living on ships anchored in the harbour.

Outlying Island Ferries

The HKTA can supply you with schedules for these ferries. Fares are higher on weekends and holidays, and the boats can get crowded. From Central, most ferries go from the Outlying Island piers between the Star Ferry and Macau Ferry terminals. Major island destinations from Central are as follows:

Cheung Chau
    21 ferries daily from 6.25 am to 12.30 am, five hoverferries Monday to Friday only between 9 am and 4 pm
Lamma Island
    Two destinations, Yung Shue Wan (14 ferries between 6.50 am and 12.30 am) and Sok Kwu Wan (seven ferries between 8 am and 11 pm), plus kaido service between Sok Kwu Wan and Aberdeen
Lantau Island
    To the port of Mui Wo (Silvermine Bay), 20 ferries daily between 6.10 am and 12.20 am, four of which stop at Peng Chau en route; also four hoverferries daily between 9.40 am and 4.25 pm, all of which stop in Peng Chau
Peng Chau
    18 ferries daily between 7 am and 12.20 am, plus an inter-island ferry to Cheung Chau and Lantau Island

TOURS

There are dozens of these, including boat tours. All can be booked through the HKTA, travel agents, large tourist hotels or directly from the tour company.

Around the Country

KOWLOON 九龍

Kowloon, the peninsula pointing out towards Hong Kong Island, is packed with shops, hotels, bars, restaurants, nightclubs and tourists. Nathan Rd, the main drag of Kowloon, has plenty of all. Some of the ritziest shops are in the Ocean Terminal beside the Star Ferry. There always seems to be one ocean liner moored here which is full of elderly millionaires.

Things to See

The tip of the peninsula, the area most popular with tourists, is known as Tsimshatsui. If you continue north along Nathan Rd you come into the tightly packed Chinese residential and business districts of Yaumatei and Mongkok.

Start your exploration from Kowloon's southern tip. Adjacent to the Star Ferry Terminal is the **Hong Kong Cultural Centre**. Just next door is the **Museum of Art**. Both are closed on Thursday, otherwise operating hours are weekdays (including Saturday) from 10 am to 6 pm, and Sunday and holidays from 1 to 6 pm.

Adjacent to the Hong Kong Cultural Centre is the **Space Museum**, which has several exhibition halls and a **Space Theatre** (planetarium). Opening times for the exhibition halls are weekdays (except Tuesday) from 1 to 9 pm, and from 10 am to 9 pm on weekends and holidays. The Space Theatre screens about seven shows each day (except Tuesday), some in English and some in Cantonese, but headphone translations are available for all shows. Check times with the museum.

Hidden behind Yue Hwa's Park Lane Store on Nathan Rd is **Kowloon Park**, which seems to become less of a park and more like an amusement park every year. The swim-

ming pool is perhaps the park's finest attribute – it's even equipped with waterfalls.

The **Hong Kong Museum of History** is in Kowloon Park near the Haiphong Rd entrance. It covers all of Hong Kong's existence from prehistoric times (about 6000 years ago) to the present, and contains a large collection of old photographs. The museum is open Monday to Thursday and Saturday from 10 am to 6 pm, and Sunday and public holidays from 1 to 6 pm. It is closed on Friday. Admission costs HK$10.

The **Kowloon Mosque** stands on Nathan Rd at the corner of Kowloon Park. It was opened in 1984 on the site of an earlier mosque constructed in 1896. Unless you are Muslim, you must obtain permission to go inside. For enquiries call (☎ 7240095).

The **Hong Kong Science Museum** is in Tsimshatsui East on the corner of Chatham and Granville Rds. This multilevel complex houses over 500 exhibits. Admission costs HK$25 for adults and HK$15 for students and seniors. Operating hours are from 1 to 9 pm Tuesday to Friday, and 10 am to 9 pm on weekends and holidays. The museum is closed Monday.

The most exotic sight in the Mongkok district is the **Bird Market**. It's on Hong Lok St, an obscure alley on the south side of Argyle St, two blocks west of Nathan Rd.

The **Wong Tai Sin Temple** is a very large and active Taoist temple built in 1973. It's right near the Wong Tai Sin MTR station. Adjacent to the temple is an arcade filled with about 150 booths operated by fortune tellers. Some of them speak good English, so if you really want to know what fate has in store for you, this is your chance to find out. The temple is open daily from 7 am to 5 pm.

In the middle of a high-rise housing estate is the *Whampoa*, a full-sized concrete model of a luxury cruiser. While not very seaworthy, the 'ship' is impressive, it's 100 metres long and four decks tall. The whole thing is actually a fancy shopping mall called **Whampoa Gardens**. Adjacent to it are more shopping areas such as Bauhinia Plaza, Whampoa Plaza and Hong Kong Place. Hong Kong Place is notable for housing one

HONG KONG

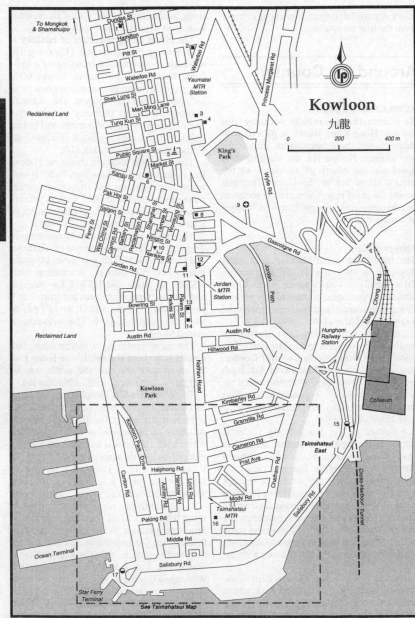

Kowloon
九龍

To Mongkok
& Shamshuipo

Dundas St

Hamilton

Pitt St

Waterloo Rd

Shek Lung St

Man Ming Lane

Tung Kun St

Reclaimed Land

Public Square St

Market St

Kansu St

Pak Hoi St

Saigon St

Ferry St

Wai Ching St

Canton Rd

Battery St

Reclamation St

Shanghai St

Temple St

Ningpo St

Nanking St

Jordan Rd

Bowring St

Parkes St

Pilkem St

Austin Rd

Reclaimed Land

Kowloon
Park

Kowloon Park Drive

Canton Rd

Haiphong Rd

Ashley Rd

Hankow Rd

Lock Rd

Peking Rd

Middle Rd

Ocean Terminal

Salisbury Rd

Star Ferry
Terminal

See Tsimshatsui Map

Waterloo Rd

Yaumatei
MTR
Station

King's
Park

Princess Margaret Rd

Wylie Rd

Gascoigne Rd

Jordan
Path

Jordan
MTR
Station

Austin Rd

Hillwood Rd

Nathan Road

Kimberley Rd

Granville Rd

Cameron Rd

Prat Ave

Chatham Rd

Mody Rd

Tsimshatsui
MTR

Hunghom
Railway
Station

Hong Chong Rd

Coliseum

Tsimshatsui
East

Cross-Harbour Tunnel

0   200   400 m

2

3
4

5
6

7
8

9

10

12

11

13
14

15

16

17

HONG KONG

PLACES TO STAY

1   STB Hostel
2   YMCA International House
3   Booth Lodge
4   Caritas Bianchi Lodge
7   Fortuna Hotel
8   Nathan Hotel
12 New Lucky Mansions
13 Shamrock Hotel
14 Bangkok Royal Hotel
16 Chungking Mansions

PLACES TO EAT

10 Temple St Night Market

OTHER

5   Tin Hau Temple
6   Jade Market
9   Queen Elizabeth Hospital
11 Yue Hwa Chinese Products
15 Cross-Harbour Bus Stop
17 Star Ferry Bus Terminal

---

of the three 'music fountains' in Hong Kong (the other two are at Shatin and Tsuen Wan in the New Territories). You can get to Whampoa Gardens from Tsimshatsui by taking a green minibus No 6 from Hankow Rd (south side of Peking Rd). There is also a Star Ferry to Hunghom which docks at the waterfront a couple of blocks away from the Whampoa.

The **Laichikok Amusement Park** has standard dodgem cars, shooting galleries and balloons for the kiddies, but the ice-skating rink may be of interest for the sports minded. There is a theatre within the park's grounds which has Chinese opera performances. Operating hours for the park are Monday to Friday from noon to 9.30 pm, and from 10 am to 9.30 pm on weekends and holidays. From the Kowloon Star Ferry bus terminal take bus No 6A, which terminates near the park. Otherwise, it's a 15-minute walk from the Mei Foo MTR station. Admission is HK$15.

Adjacent to the Laichikok Amusement Park is the **Sung Dynasty Village**, which is hyped up as an authentic re-creation of a Chinese village from 10 centuries ago. The village is open from 10 am to 8.30 pm daily. Admission costs HK$120. It drops to HK$80 on weekends and public holidays between 12.30 and 5 pm.

HONG KONG ISLAND (NORTH SIDE)

The north and south sides of the island have very different characters. The north side is an urban jungle, while much of the south is still surprisingly rural (but developing fast). The central part of the island is incredibly mountainous and protected from development by a country park.

Things to See

Central is the bustling business centre of Hong Kong. A free shuttle bus from the Star Ferry Pier brings you to the lower station of the famous Peak Tram on Garden Rd. The tram terminates at the top of **Victoria Peak**. It's worth repeating the peak trip at night as the illuminated view is something else if the weather cooperates. Don't just admire the view from the top, wander up Mt Austin Rd to **Victoria Peak Garden** or take the more leisurely stroll around Lugard and Harlech Rds – together they make a complete circuit of the peak. You can walk right down to Aberdeen on the south side of the island or you can try Old Peak Rd for a few km return to Central. The more energetic may want to walk the **Hong Kong Trail** which runs along the top of the mountainous spine of Hong Kong Island from the Peak to Big Wave Bay.

There are many pleasant walks and views in the **Zoological & Botanical Gardens** on Robinson Rd overlooking Central. There's free entry to the **Fung Ping Shan Museum** in Hong Kong University (closed Sunday).

Hong Kong Park is just behind the city's second tallest skyscraper, the Bank of China. It's an unusual park, not at all natural but beautiful in its own weird way. Within the park is the **Flagstaff House Museum**, the oldest Western-style building still standing in Hong Kong. Inside, you'll find a Chinese tea-service collection. Admission is free.

Between the skyscrapers of Central you'll

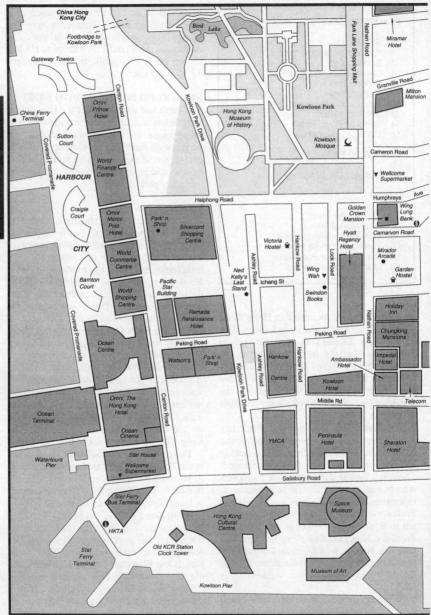

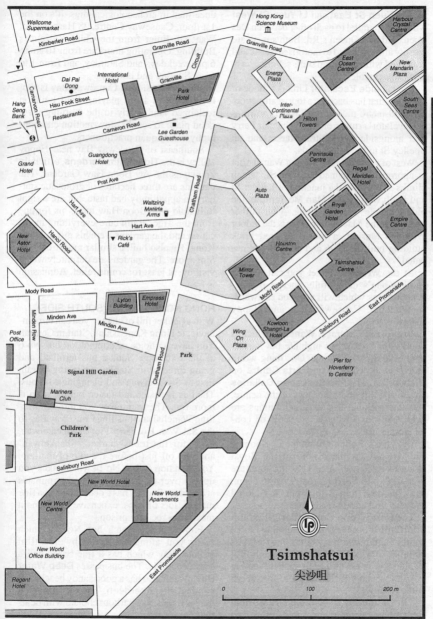

HONG KONG

Wellcome
Supermarket

Kimberley Road

Granville Road

Hong Kong
Science Museum

Granville Road

Harbour
Crystal
Centre

Dai Pai
Dong

International
Hotel

Granville
Circuit

Granville

Park
Hotel

Energy
Plaza

East
Ocean
Centre

New
Mandarin
Plaza

Camarvon Road

Hau Fook Street

Hang
Seng
Bank

Restaurants

Cameron Road

Lee Garden
Guesthouse

Inter-
Continental
Plaza

Hilton
Towers

Peninsula
Centre

South
Seas
Centre

Grand
Hotel

Guangdong
Hotel

Prat Ave

Chatham Road

Auto
Plaza

Regal
Meridien
Hotel

Hart Ave

Waltzing
Matilda
Arms

Royal
Garden
Hotel

Empire
Centre

Hanoi Road

Hart Ave

Rick's
Café

New
Astor
Hotel

Houston
Centre

Tsimshatsui
Centre

Mody Road

Lyton
Building

Empress
Hotel

Mirror
Tower

Mody Road

East Promenade

Minden Row

Minden Ave

Minden Ave

Salisbury Road

Post
Office

Wing
On
Plaza

Kowloon
Shangri-La
Hotel

Chatham Road

Park

Pier for
Hoverferry
to Central

Signal Hill Garden

Mariners
Club

Children's
Park

Salisbury Road

New World Hotel

New World
Apartments

New World
Centre

New World
Office Building

Regent
Hotel

East Promenade

Tsimshatsui

尖沙咀

0   100   200 m

find **Li Yuen St East** and **Li Yuen St West** which run parallel to each other between Des Voeux Rd and Queen's Rd. Both streets are narrow alleys, closed to motorised traffic and crammed with shops and stalls selling everything imaginable.

The **Hillside Escalator Link** is a mode of transport that has become a tourist attraction. The 800-metre moving walkway (known as a 'travelator') runs from the Vehicular Ferry Pier alongside the Central Market and up Shelley St to the Mid-Levels.

West of Central in the Sheung Wan district is appropriately named **Ladder St**, which climbs steeply. At the junction of Ladder St and Hollywood Rd is **Man Mo Temple**, the oldest temple in Hong Kong. A bit farther north near the Macau Ferry Pier is the indoor **Western Market**, a four-storey red brick building built in 1906 and now fully renovated.

At the Western Market you can hop on Hong Kong's delightfully ancient double-decker trams which will take you eastwards to Wanchai, Causeway Bay and Happy Valley.

Just east of Central is **Wanchai**, which is known for its raucous nightlife but is relatively dull in the daytime. One thing worth seeing is the **Hong Kong Arts Centre** on Harbour Rd. The **Pao Sui Loong Galleries** are on the 4th and 5th floors of the centre, and international and local exhibitions are held year-round with the emphasis on contemporary art.

Wanchai's **Police Museum**, 27 Coombe Rd, emphasizes the history of the Royal Hong Kong Police Force. Opening hours are Wednesday to Sunday from 9 am to 5 pm, and Tuesday from 2 to 5 pm. It's closed Monday and admission is free.

The **Hong Kong Convention & Exhibition Centre** is an enormous building on the harbour and boasts the world's largest 'glass curtain' – a window seven-storeys high. Just be glad you're not the one to wash it. You can ride the escalator to the 7th floor for a superb harbour view.

The **Museum of Chinese Historical Relics** houses cultural treasures from China unearthed in archaeological digs. It's on the 1st floor, Causeway Centre, 28 Harbour Rd, Wanchai. Enter from the China Resources Building. Operating hours are from 10 am to 6 pm weekdays and Saturday, and from 1 to 6 pm Sunday and holidays.

On the east side of Causeway Bay is **Victoria Park**, a large playing field built on reclaimed land. Early in the morning it's a good place to see the slow-motion choreography of taijiquan practitioners.

Southeast of Causeway Bay near Happy Valley is the **Tiger Balm Gardens**, officially known as the Aw Boon Haw Gardens. The gardens are three hectares of grotesque statuary in appallingly bad taste, but are a sight to behold. Aw Boon Haw made his fortune from the Tiger Balm cure-everything medication and the gardens were his gift to Hong Kong. He also built a similar monstrosity in Singapore. The gardens are definitely worth visiting, at least for comic relief. Admission is free.

HONG KONG ISLAND (SOUTH SIDE)

With a pocket full of change you can circumnavigate Hong Kong Island. Start in Central. You have a choice of hopping on bus No 6 at the Exchange Square bus terminal and going directly to Stanley, or taking a tram first to Shaukeiwan and changing to a bus. The bus is easier and faster, but the tram is more fun. The tram takes you through hustling Wanchai and bustling Causeway Bay to the Sai Wan Ho Ferry Pier at Shaukeiwan. Look for the trams marked 'Shaukeiwan' and hop off just before the end of the line. You then hop on bus No 14 which takes you up and over the central hills and terminates at **Stanley**. Stanley has a decent beach, a fine market, lots of pubs, expensive villas and a maximum security prison.

From Stanley, catch bus No 73 which takes you along the coast by beautiful **Repulse Bay** which has a fine beach and a seaside temple. The bus passes **Deep Water Bay**, which also has a good sandy beach, and continues to **Aberdeen**. The big attraction here is the fishing harbour choked with boats that are also part-time residences for Hong

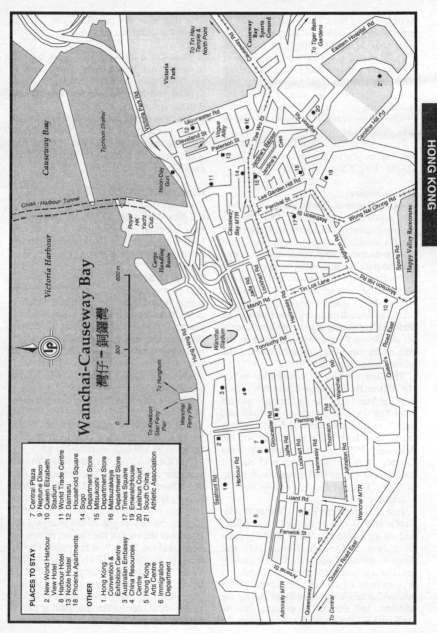

Wanchai-Causeway Bay
灣仔－銅鑼灣

PLACES TO STAY
2 New World Harbour View Hotel
8 Harbour Hotel
13 Noble Hostel
18 Phoenix Apartments

7 Central Plaza
9 Neptune Disco
10 Queen Elizabeth Stadium
11 World Trade Centre
12 Daimaru Household Square
14 Sogo Department Store
15 Mitsukoshi Department Store
16 Matsuzakaya Department Store
17 Times Square
19 EmeraldHouse
20 Leishun Court
21 South China Athletic Association

OTHER
1 Hong Kong Convention & Exhibition Centre
3 Australian Embassy
4 China Resources Centre
5 Hong Kong Arts Centre
6 Immigration Department

Kong's fishing fleet. There will generally be several sampans ready to take you on a half-hour tour of this floating city for about HK$35 per person (it's worth seeing), or bargain for a whole boat for a group (about HK$100). Floating regally amidst the confusion in Aberdeen are several palace-like restaurants, the largest being the Jumbo Floating Restaurant. This restaurant runs its own shuttle boat.

From Aberdeen, a final short ride on bus No 7 takes you back to your starting point via the Hong Kong University.

Things to See

Close to Aberdeen, **Ocean Park** is a spectacular aquarium and funfair. Don't try to include it on a tour to Aberdeen, Ocean Park itself is worth a full day of your time. Spread over two separate sites, connected by a cable car, the park includes what is reputed to be the world's largest aquarium, but the emphasis is on the funfair, with its roller coaster, space wheel, octopus, swinging ship and other astronaut-training machines. The **Middle Kingdom** is an ancient Chinese spin-off of Ocean Park and is included in the admission fee. The entrance fee for the whole complex is HK$130.

The cheapest way to Ocean Park is on bus No 70 from the Exchange Square bus station near the Star Ferry Pier in Central – get off at the first stop after the tunnel. Alternatively, there's an air-con Ocean Park Citybus which leaves from both Exchange Square and the Admiralty MTR station (underneath Bond Centre) every half-hour from 8.45 am and costs HK$9. Ocean Park is open from 10 am to 6 pm. Get there early because there is much to see.

Just next to Ocean Park is **Water World**, a collection of swimming pools, waterslides and diving platforms. Water World is open from June to October. During July and August, operating hours are from 9 am to 9 pm. During June, September and October it is open from 10 am to 6 pm. Admission for adults/children costs HK$60/30 during the daytime, but during the evening falls to HK$40/20. Take bus No 70 and get off at the first stop after the tunnel. If you take the Ocean Park Citybus, be sure to get off at the first stop.

Shek O, on the south-east coast, has one of the best beaches on Hong Kong Island. To get there, take the MTR or tram to Shaukeiwan, and from Shaukeiwan take bus No 9 to the last stop.

Big Wave Bay, another excellent beach, is two km north of Shek O, but there is no public transportation. It does make a nice walk, passing the Shek O Country Club and Golf Course along the way.

NEW TERRITORIES 新界

You can explore the most interesting parts of the New Territories by bus and train in one very busy day, assuming that you don't go hiking or swimming (both worthwhile and recommended activities).

Things to See

You start out by taking the MTR to the last stop at **Tsuen Wan**. The main attraction here is the **Yuen Yuen Institute**, a Taoist temple complex, and the adjacent Buddhist **Western Monastery**. You reach the institute by taking minibus No 81 from Shiu Wo St, which is two blocks south of the MTR station. Alternatively, take a taxi which is not expensive.

Chuk Lam Sim Yuen is another large monastery in the hills north of Tsuen Wan. The instructions for getting there are almost the same as for the Yuen Yuen Institute. Find Shiu Wo St and take maxicab No 85.

At Tsuen Wan you have an option. You can continue west to Tuen Mun, or north to **Tai Mo Shan** (elevation 957 metres), Hong Kong's highest peak. To reach Tai Mo Shan, take bus No 51 from the Tsuen Wan MTR station; the bus stop is on the overpass that goes over the roof of the station, or you can board it at the Tsuen Wan ferry pier. The bus heads up Route Twisk (Twisk is derived from Tsuen Wan into Shek Kong). Get off at the top of the pass, from where it's uphill on foot. You will walk along a road but it's unlikely you'll encounter traffic. The path is part of the **MacLehose Trail**, which is 100 km long.

The trail runs from Tuen Mun in the west to the Sai Kung Peninsula in the east and walking the entire length would take several days.

If you choose not to visit Tai Mo Shan, from Tsuen Wan take bus No 60M or 68M to the bustling town of **Tuen Mun**. Here you can visit Hong Kong's largest shopping mall, the Tuen Mun Town Centre. From here, hop on the Light Rail Transit (LRT) system to reach **Ching Chung Koon**, a temple complex on the north side of Tuen Mun.

You then get back on the LRT and head to Yuen Long. From here, take bus No 54, 64K or 74K to the nearby walled villages at **Kam Tin**. These villages with their single stout entrances are said to date from the 16th century. There are several walled villages at Kam Tin but most accessible is **Kat Hing Wai**. Drop about HK$5 into the donation box by the entrance and wander the narrow little lanes. The old Hakka women in traditional gear require payment before they can be photographed.

The town of Sheung Shui is about eight km north-east on bus No 77K. Here you can hop on the Kowloon-Canton Railway (KCR) and go one stop south to **Fanling**. The main attraction in this town is the **Fung Ying Sin Kwun Temple**, a Taoist temple for the dead.

At Fanling, get on the KCR and head to Tai Po Market station. From here, you can walk 10 to 15 minutes to the **Hong Kong Railway Museum**. You can get back on the KCR and go south to the Chinese University where there's the art gallery at the **Institute of Chinese Studies**. Admission is free.

Tai Po Kau is Hong Kong's most extensive woodlands and is a prime venue for birdwatching. This forest reserve between Tai Po KCR station and the Chinese University is a great place to get away from the crowds any time except Sunday. To get there, take bus No 72A, which runs from Tai Wai to Tai Po Industrial Estate and get off at the stop before Shatin. You can also take bus No 72 from Mongkok or a taxi (about HK$20) from Tai Po Market KCR station.

The KCR stops in Shatin, a lively, bustling city where you can visit the huge **Shatin**

Town Centre, one of Hong Kong's biggest shopping malls. Also, from here you begin the climb up to the **Temple of 10,000 Buddhas** (which actually has over 12,000).

All of the above will more than fill your day, but there are other places to visit in the New Territories. The **Sai Kung Peninsula** is one of the least spoilt areas in the New Territories and a prime destination for hikers. The best beaches in the New Territories are also found around the Sai Kung Peninsula. The only town of any significant size in the area is Sai Kung Town. To get there, take the MTR to the Choi Hung station. Exit the station where the sign says 'Clearwater Bay Road North'. Here you can catch bus No 92 to Sai Kung Town, or alternatively the No 1 maxicab which is more frequent. The ride from Choi Hung to Sai Kung Town takes about 30 minutes. Along the way, the bus passes **Hebe Haven**, the yachting centre of the New Territories.

Pak Tam Chung is the easternmost point you can reach by bus in the Sai Kung Peninsula. It's also the eastern terminus of the MacLehose Trail. You can get to Pak Tam Chung on bus No 94 from Sai Kung Town, but this bus runs only once an hour. On Sunday and holidays only there is the additional bus No 96R from Choi Hung which runs every 20 to 30 minutes. While in Pak Tam Chung, visit the **Sai Kung Country Parks Visitor Centre** which has excellent maps, photographs and displays of the area's geology, fauna and flora. The centre is open everyday from 9 am to 5 pm.

From Pak Tam Chung, it's a 25-minute walk south along a trail to find the **Sheung Yiu Folk Museum**, a restored Hakka village typical of those found in Hong Kong in the 19th century. The museum is open daily except Tuesday from 9 am to 4 pm. Admission is free. From Pak Tam Chung you can also walk to **High Island Reservoir**. If you want to explore the north shore of the Sai Kung Peninsula, bus No 94 continues from Pak Tam Chung to Wong Shek Pier in Tai Tan.

You can get from village to village on boats in **Tolo Harbour**. The Tolo Harbour

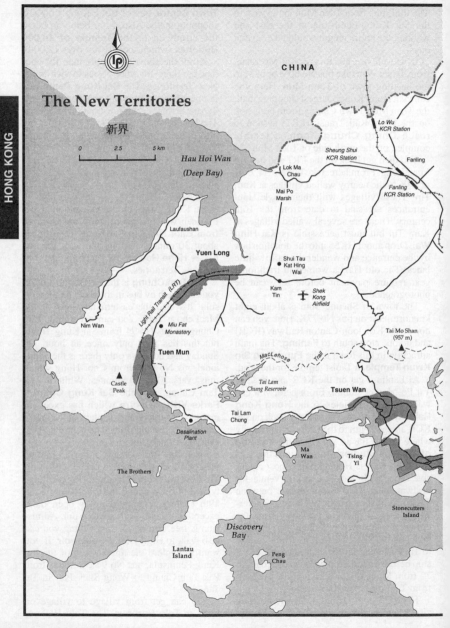

CHINA

The New Territories

新界

0   2.5   5 km

Hau Hoi Wan
(Deep Bay)

Lo Wu
KCR Station

Sheung Shui
KCR Station

Fanling

Lok Ma
Chau

Fanling
KCR Station

Mai Po
Marsh

Laufaushan

Yuen Long

Shui Tau
Kat Hing
Wai

Kam
Tin

Shek Kong
Airfield

Nim Wan

Light Rail Transit (LRT)

Miu Fat
Monastery

Tai Mo Shan
(957 m)

Tuen Mun

MacLehose
Trail

Castle
Peak

Tai Lam
Chung Reservoir

Tsuen Wan

Tai Lam
Chung

Desalination
Plant

Ma
Wan

Tsing
Yi

The Brothers

Stonecutters
Island

Discovery
Bay

Lantau
Island

Peng
Chau

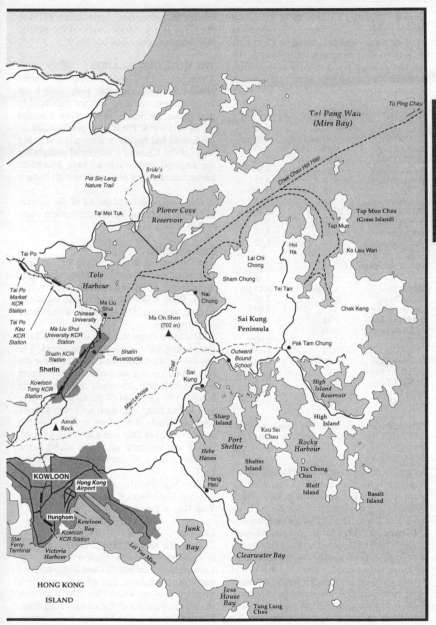

ferry is operated by the Polly Ferry Co (☎ 7711630). Ferries begin the journey at Ma Liu Shui, which is about a 15-minute walk from the University KCR station. The HKTA can supply you with the current ferry schedule, but at the time of writing it was as follows:

Mon – Sat

	1st	2nd
Ma Liu Shui	8.30 am	3.15 pm
Sham Chung	9.00	3.45
Lai Chi Chong	9.15	4.00
Tap Mun Chau	9.45	4.30
Ko Lau Wan	9.50	4.35
Tai Tan	10.05	5.00*
Chek Keng	10.20	4.45*
Tap Mun Chau	10.40	5.20
Lai Chi Chong	11.10	5.50
Sham Chung	11.15	6.05
Ma Liu Shui	11.55	6.35

Sun & Holidays

	1st	2nd
Ma Liu Shui	8.30 am	3.15 pm
Sham Chung	9.00	3.45
Lai Chi Chong	9.15	4.00
Tap Mun Chau	9.45	4.30
Ko Lau Wan	9.50	4.35
Tai Tan	10.05	5.00*
Chek Keng	10.20	4.45*
Tap Mun Chau	10.40 arr	5.20
Tap Mun Chau	1.45 pm depart	
Lai Chi Chong	2.15	5.50
Sham Chung	2.30	6.05
Ma Liu Shui	6.35	6.35

* The second boat arrives at Chek Keng before sailing to Tai Tan, which is the opposite order of the first boat

As an alternative to the Tolo Harbour ferry, an easy way to reach Tap Mun Chau is to take a kaido from Tai Tan (Wong Shek Pier), which is at the last stop of bus No 94 from Sai Kung Town. The kaidos run once hourly.

Clearwater Bay is in the south-east corner of the New Territories. There is a fine beach here, but Mediterranean-style villas sprouting along the coast are a reminder that this is not the wilderness. Another major development is the pricey Clearwater Bay Country Club, complete with golf course, squash and tennis courts, jacuzzi, badminton etc. To reach Clearwater Bay, first take the MTR to the Choi Hung station, walk to the nearby bus terminus and catch bus No 91.

THE OUTLYING ISLANDS 離島
There are 235 islands dotting the waters around Hong Kong, but only four have bedroom communities and are thus readily accessible by ferry. While very tranquil during the week, the islands get crowded on weekends and holidays. Eating is a very big deal for the Chinese – they head straight for the seafood restaurants or have beachside barbecues, leaving plenty of rubbish in their wake.

Cars are prohibited on all of the islands except Lantau, and even there vehicle ownership is very restricted.

Cheung Chau 長洲
This dumbbell-shaped island has a large community of Western residents who enjoy the slow pace of island life and relatively low rents. Were it not for the Chinese signs and people, you might think you were in a Greek island village.

The town sprawls across the narrow neck connecting the two ends of the island. The bay on the west side of the island (where the ferry lands) is an exotic collection of fishing boats much like Aberdeen on Hong Kong Island. The east side of the island is where you'll find Tung Wan Beach, Cheung Chau's longest beach. There are a few tiny but remote beaches that you can reach by foot, and at the southern tip of the island is the hideaway cave of notorious pirate Cheung Po Tsai.

The big gwailo nightlife spot is the *Garden Cafe/Pub* (☎ 9814610) at 84 Tung Wan Rd, in the centre of the island.

Lamma 南丫島
This is the second largest of the outlying islands and the one closest to the city. Lamma has good beaches and a very relaxed pace on weekdays, but on weekends it's mobbed like anywhere else. There are two main communities on the island, Yung Shue Wan in the north (the Western expat centre)

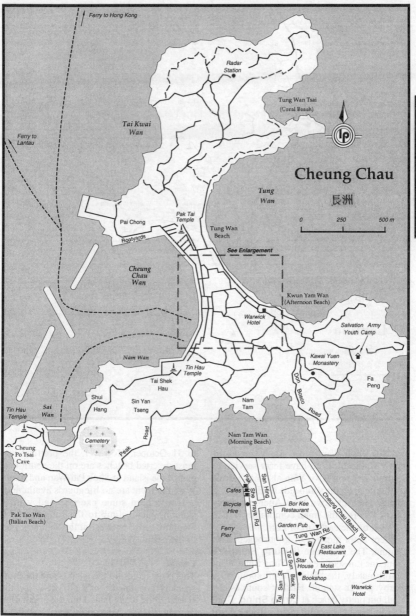

HONG KONG

Cheung Chau

長洲

0   250   500 m

Ferry to Hong Kong

Radar
Station

Tung Wan Tsai
(Coral Beach)

Tai Kwai
Wan

Tung
Wan

Ferry to
Lantau

Pak Tai
Temple

Pai Chong

Boatyards

Tung Wan
Beach

See Enlargement

Cheung
Chau
Wan

Kwun Yam Wan
(Afternoon Beach)

Warwick
Hotel

Salvation Army
Youth Camp

Kawai Yuen
Monastery

Fa
Peng

Nam Wan

Tin Hau
Temple

Tai Shek
Hau

Shui
Hang

Sin Yan
Tseng

Nam
Tam

Don Bosco Road

Tin Hau
Temple

Sai
Wan

Cemetery

Peak Road

Nam Tam Wan
(Morning Beach)

Cheung
Po Tsai
Cave

Pak Tso Wan
(Italian Beach)

Cafes

Bicycle
Hire

Ferry
Pier

She Praya Rd

Pak St

San Hing
St

Bor Kee
Restaurant

Garden Pub

Tung Wan Rd

East Lake
Restaurant

Star
House

Motel

Bookshop

Cheung Chau Beach Rd

Tai Sun St

Tai San Back St

Warwick
Hotel

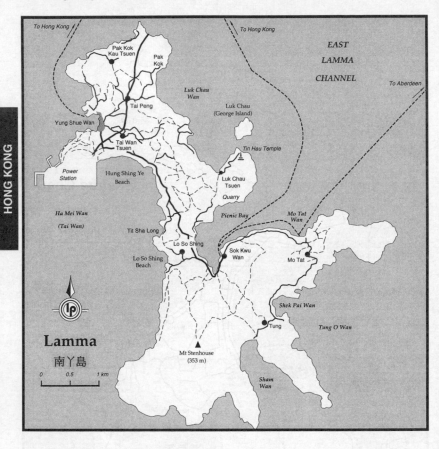

Lamma

南丫島

```
0      0.5      1 km
```

EAST
LAMMA
CHANNEL

To Hong Kong

To Hong Kong

To Aberdeen

Pak Kok
Kau Tsuen

Pak
Kok

Luk Chau
Wan

Luk Chau
(George Island)

Tai Peng

Yung Shue Wan

Tai Wan
Tsuen

Tin Hau Temple

Power
Station

Hung Shing Ye
Beach

Luk Chau
Tsuen

Quarry

Ha Mei Wan

(Tai Wan)

Picnic Bay

Mo Tat
Wan

Tit Sha Long

Lo So Shing

Sok Kwu
Wan

Mo Tat

Lo So Shing
Beach

Shek Pai Wan

Tung

Tung O Wan

Mt Stenhouse
(353 m)

Sham
Wan

and Sok Kwu Wan in the south (predominantly Chinese). Both have ferry service to
Central, and Sok Kwu Wan also has ferries
to Aberdeen on the south side of Hong Kong
Island. The Sok Kwu Wan-Aberdeen ferry
makes a stop at the small community of Mo
Tat Wan on the east part of Lamma.

There are a number of good beaches on
Lamma. The main one is **Hung Shing Ye**
about one km south-east of Yung Shue Wan.
Unfortunately, the view is a bit spoilt by a
nearby power station. Farther south is the
small but pretty beach at **Lo So Shing**. Both
of these beaches have lifeguards from 1 April

to 31 October. However, the prettiest and
most deserted beaches are on the south-east
part of the island at Shek Pai Wan and Sham
Wan, but there are no lifeguards available.

If you need some exercise and want a
stunning view, climb to the summit of Mt
Stenhouse (353 metres) at the southern part
of the island.

Lantau 大嶼山

This is the largest of the islands and the most
sparsely populated – it's almost twice the
size of Hong Kong Island but the population
is only 30,000. You could easily spend a

couple of days exploring the mountainous walking trails and enjoying uncrowded beaches.

Mui Wo (Silver Mine Bay) is the major arrival point for ferries. As you exit the ferry, to your right is the road leading to the beach. It passes several eateries and hotels along the way.

From Mui Wo, most visitors board bus No 2 to **Ngong Ping**, a plateau region 500 metres above sea level in the western part of the island. It's here that you'll find the impressive **Po Lin Monastery**. It's a relatively recent construction and almost as much a tourist attraction as a religious centre. Just outside the monastery is the world's largest outdoor Buddha statue. It's possible to have a vegetarian lunch at the monastery dining hall and you can spend the night here (see Places to Stay later in this section). The main reason to stay overnight is to launch a sunrise expedition to climb Lantau Peak (elevation 934 metres).

Another place to visit is Tai O, a village at the west end of the island accessible by bus No 1.

The two-km long **Cheung Sha Wan** on Lantau Island is Hong Kong's longest beach. You'll have it to yourself on weekdays, but forget it on weekends.

On Lantau's north shore is the farming region of **Tung Chung**, but the main visitors' attraction is the 19th-century **Tung Chung Fort** which still has its old cannon pointing out to sea. The bad news here is that just off the coast, construction is proceeding on Hong Kong's new airport. The project has run into opposition from China (the Chinese want to make sure the British pay for the whole thing), but work is continuing. When finished, Lantau will be connected to Kowloon with a bridge and the island's character will surely change for the worse.

To get a taste of abominations to come, you should probably visit **Discovery Bay** (affectionately known to locals as 'Disco Bay'). This is a very upscale housing development complete with high-rises, shopping mall, a McDonald's, yacht club, golf course and a fancy pub. The majority of the residents are well-heeled Westerners. Jet-powered ferries run from Discovery Bay to Central every 20 minutes, but there are no places to stay and tourism is actively discouraged. However, the beach is pretty and is one of the cleanest in Hong Kong. The main reason for visiting isn't to see Discovery Bay, but to walk for one hour southwards along the coastline to find the **Trappist Haven Monastery**. Walking about another 1½ hours from the monastery over a dangerously slippery trail brings you out to Mui Wo (Silvermine Bay), from where you can get ferries back to Central. There is a ferry connecting Discovery Bay to Peng Chau.

Peng Chau 坪洲
This is the smallest of the outlying islands that is readily accessible. It's also the most traditionally Chinese, with narrow alleys, an outdoor meat and vegetable market and a very tiny gwailo community.

The **Tin Hau Temple** was originally built in 1792. A climb to the top of **Finger Hill** (elevation 95 metres) will reward you with a view of the entire island and nearby Lantau. A walk out to the north-east corner of the island near the radio transmitting station is also pleasant.

South of the main ferry pier and right along the shoreline are the two best Western restaurants and pubs, the *Sea Breeze Club* and the adjacent *Forest Pub*. There are no places to stay in Peng Chau unless you can rent a holiday flat.

PLACES TO STAY
The cost of accommodation is the major expense in visiting Hong Kong. There are a number of youth hostels and similarly oriented places with dormitory accommodation – many travellers head straight for the guesthouses clustered in Tsimshatsui's Chungking Mansions.

The majority of cheap accommodation is on the Kowloon side. With a few exceptions, the places on Hong Kong Island are midrange to top-end hotels. Rentals are cheaper by the week, but stay one night first to make

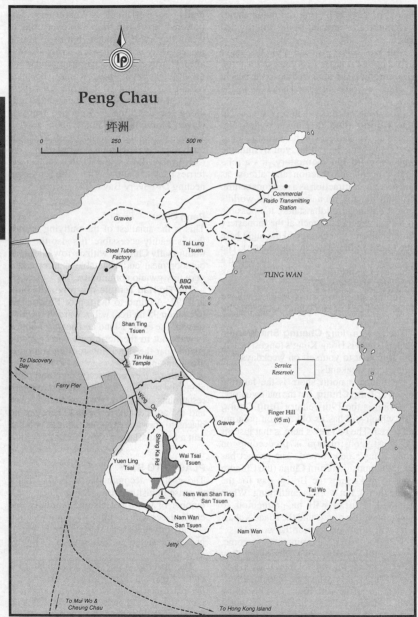

Peng Chau

坪洲

0   250   500 m

Graves

Commercial
Radio Transmitting
Station

Steel Tubes
Factory

Tai Lung
Tsuen

BBQ
Area

TUNG WAN

Shan Ting
Tsuen

Tin Hau
Temple

To Discovery
Bay

Ferry Pier

*Service
Reservoir*

Wing
On
St

Finger Hill
(95 m)

Graves

Shing
Ka
Rd

Yuen Ling
Tsai

Wai Tsai
Tsuen

Tai Wo

Nam Wan Shan Ting
San Tsuen

Nam Wan
San Tsuen

Nam Wan

Jetty

To Mui Wo &
Cheung Chau

To Hong Kong Island

sure it's acceptable. At the airport, there is a hotel reservation desk, dealing only with the more expensive hotels.

Kowloon

Dormitories One of the better dorms is *Victoria Hostel* (☎ 3760621), 1st floor, 33 Hankow Rd, Tsimshatsui. Beds cost HK$100 for the first day and HK$80 for subsequent days. If you pay by the week, it's HK$70 per day.

There is probably no other place in the world like Chungking Mansions, the bottom-end accommodation ghetto of Hong Kong. It's a huge high rise dump at 30 Nathan Rd in the heart of Tsimshatsui. It is divided into five blocks labelled A to E, each with its own lift. Each block of Chungking Mansions has numerous guesthouses, including a few dormitories.

On the 16th floor of A Block in Chungking Mansions is *Travellers' Hostel* (☎ 3687710), a Hong Kong landmark. You may have to queue for 20 minutes to get up in the lift, but when you finally arrive beds are just HK$60 *if* it's not full. Double rooms with/without attached bath cost HK$150/170. The management also operates a cheap beachside hostel at Ting Kau in the New Territories.

On the 12th floor of A Block is the friendly *Super Guest House*, where dormitory beds start at HK$60. On the 6th floor of A Block is *New World Hostel* (☎ 7236352). Dormitories are HK$60 and double rooms go for HK$180.

Friendship Travellers Hostel (☎ 311-0797, 3112523), B Block, 6th floor, has mixed dormitory accommodation. The first night costs HK$80, the second HK$70 and anything thereafter is HK$60.

Around the corner from Chungking Mansions is the *Garden Hostel* (☎ 7218567). It's in Mirador Arcade, 58 Nathan Rd, but it's easier to find if you enter from Mody Rd. Turn right as you come out of the main entrance to Chungking and then right at the first street (Mody Rd). On the left side of the street is an obvious sign. Follow the stairs to the 3rd floor. Beds cost HK$80 in the dorm,

but drop to HK$65 per night if paid by the week.

On the 13th floor of Mirador Arcade at 58 Nathan Rd, is the *Kowloon Hotel* (☎ 311-2523) and *New Garden Hotel* (same phone and same owner). Dormitories are HK$60. Singles with shared bath are HK$150, rising up to HK$200 for rooms with private bath. Ask about discounts if you want to rent long term.

The *Golden Crown Guest House* (☎ 369 1782), Golden Crown Mansion, 5th floor, 66-70 Nathan Rd, Tsimshatsui, has dormitory beds for HK$100, singles from HK$250 and doubles from HK$300.

Guesthouses The already mentioned Chungking Mansions has more than just dorms. There are approximately 60 licensed guesthouses plus a few illegals. The price range for a private room is roughly HK$150 to HK$250. Some of the better places to stay are as follows:

A Block: *Park Guest House* (☎ 3681689), 15th floor; *New Hawaii Guest House* (☎ 3666127), 14th floor; *Peking Guest House* (☎ 7238320), 12th floor; *New International Guest House* (☎ 3692613), 11th floor; *New Mandarin Guest House* (☎ 3661070), 8th floor; *Welcome Guest House* (☎ 7217793), 7th floor; and *London Guest House* (☎ 7245000) 6th floor.

B Block: *Astor Guest House*, 16th floor; *Carlton Guest House* (☎ 7210720), 15th floor; *New Washington Guest House* (☎ 3665798), 13th floor; *Grand Guest House* (☎ 3686520), 9th floor; *New York Guest House* (☎ 3395986), 7th floor; and *Dragon Inn*, 3rd floor.

C Block: *Tom's Guest House* (☎ 3679258), 16th floor; *New Grand Guest House* (☎ 3111702), 13th floor; *Marria Guest House*, 11th floor; *Garden Guest House* (☎ 3687414), 7th floor; *New Brother's Guest House* (☎ 7240135), 6th floor; and *Maharaja Guest House*, 4th floor.

D Block: *Four Seas Guest House* (☎ 3687469), 15th floor; *Guangzhou Guest House* (☎ 7241555), 13th floor; *China Town* (☎ 7213723), 10th floor; *Fortuna Guest House* (☎ 3664524), 8th floor; *Royal Plaza Inn* (☎ 3671424), 5th floor; and *Mt Everest Guest House*, 4th floor.

E Block: *Far East Guest House* (☎ 3681724), 14th floor; *Chungking Mansion Mandarin Guest House*, 13th floor; and *Regent Guest House* (☎ 7220833), 6th floor.

HONG KONG

HONG KONG

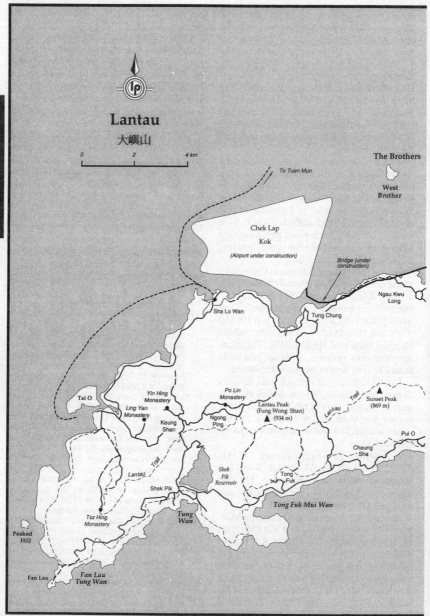

Lantau

大嶼山

0   2   4 km

To Tuen Mun

The Brothers

West Brother

Chek Lap Kok
(Airport under construction)

Bridge (under construction)

Ngau Kwu Long

Sha Lo Wan

Tung Chung

Tai O

Yin Hing Monastery

Po Lin Monastery

Sunset Peak (869 m)

Ling Yan Monastery

Keung Shan

Ngong Ping

Lantau Peak (Fung Wong Shan) (934 m)

Lantau Trail

Pui O

Cheung Sha

Lantau Trail

Shek Pik Reservoir

Tong Fuk

Shek Pik

Tsz Hing Monastery

Tung Wan

Tong Fuk Mui Wan

Peaked Hill

Fan Lau

Fan Lau Tung Wan

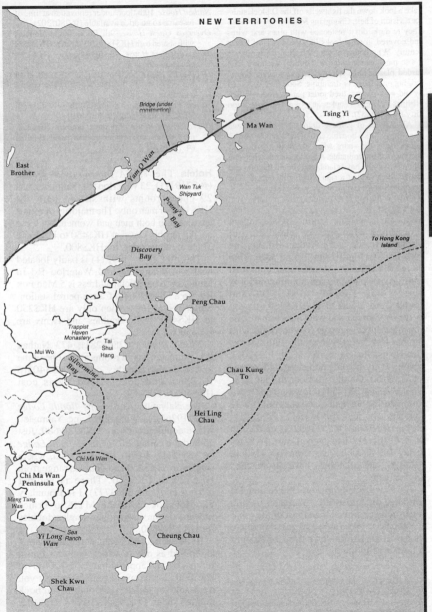

HONG KONG

NEW TERRITORIES

Tsing Yi

Ma Wan

Bridge (under construction)

East Brother

Yam O Wan

Wan Tuk Shipyard

Penny's Bay

Discovery Bay

To Hong Kong Island

Peng Chau

Trappist Haven Monastery

Tai Shui Hang

Mui Wo

Silvermine Bay

Chau Kung To

Hei Ling Chau

Chi Ma Wan

Chi Ma Wan Peninsula

Mong Tung Wan

Yi Long Wan

Sea Ranch

Cheung Chau

Shek Kwu Chau

Take a look down the lightwells off the D block stairs for a vision of hell, Chungking Mansions at its worst. They're dark, dirty, festooned with pipes and wires and covered in what looks like the debris of half a century. Why bother to put rubbish in the bin when it's so much easier to throw it out the window? Discarded plastic bags fall only halfway down before lodging on a ledge or drainpipe. Soon they're joined by old newspapers, used toilet paper, clothes fallen off lines, half-eaten apples, an expired rat (was it too dirty for him too?).

All manner of garbage drapes and hangs down from above. It's a horrible sight. Occasionally you're forced onto the stairs when the wait for the lift becomes too interminable. A buzzer sounds when one too many people have clambered aboard the lifts and in one lift I spotted a sign which announced, 'The Irresponsible for Accident due to Overloading'.

You can avoid the stigma of staying in Chungking Mansions by checking out Mirador Arcade at 58 Nathan Rd. On the 14th floor in Flat F2 you'll find *Man Hing Lung* (☎ 7220678). All rooms are equipped with private bath, air conditioning and TV. Singles cost HK$260 to HK$280 and doubles are HK$320 to HK$360. If you arrive by yourself and want a roommate, the management can arrange for you to stay with another traveller. Down on the 12th floor in Flat B5 is *Ajit Guest House* (☎ 3691201), which is very friendly and clean with rooms for HK$150. On the 7th floor in Flat F2 is *Mini Hotel* (☎ 3672551). It was under renovation during our visit, so no one could quote a price.

Tourists Home (☎ 3112622) is on the 6th floor, G Block, Champagne Court, 16 Kimberley Rd. Doubles are from HK$280 to HK$320, and all rooms have an attached private bath.

The *New Lucky Mansions*, 300 Nathan Rd (entrance on Jordan Rd), Yaumatei, is in a better neighbourhood than most of the other guesthouses. There are eight guesthouses to choose from. The rundown from top floor to bottom is as follows:

Great Wall Hotel, 14th floor, very posh doubles for HK$450 (☎ 3887645)
Ocean Guest House, 11th floor, singles/doubles HK$300/350 (☎ 3850125)

Nathan House, 10th floor, under renovation at time of research so no price available (☎ 7801302)
Overseas Guest House, 9th floor, singles/doubles with shared bath HK$180/190, clean and friendly
Tung Wo Guest House, 9th floor, singles HK$150, cheap but not so nice
Hoi Pun Uk House, 5th floor, doubles HK$280, good but currently no English sign, owner speaks Mandarin (☎ 7807317)
Hitton Inn, 3rd floor, double with private bath HK$230, good value (☎ 7704880)
Hakkas Guest House, 3rd floor, doubles HK$250, nice rooms and owner speaks good English (☎ 7701470)

Hotels The *YMCA International House* (☎ 7719111), 23 Waterloo Rd, Yaumatei, has 29 cheap rooms with shared bath for HK$150 for men only. The majority of rooms are rented to both men and women, but these are not terribly cheap at HK$450 to HK$660. There are some suites for HK$800.

The *YWCA* (☎ 7139211) is badly located near Pui Ching Rd and Waterloo Rd in Mongkok. The official address is 5 Man Fuk Rd, up a hill behind a Caltex petrol station. Single rooms for women only are HK$250 to HK$400, while doubles and twins are HK$500.

King's Hotel (☎ 7801281), 473 Nathan Rd, Yaumatei, has 72 rooms and is one of the better deals. Singles cost HK$340 to HK$360, and doubles and twins cost HK$400 to HK$430.

The Salvation Army runs *Booth Lodge* (☎ 7719266), 11 Wing Sing Lane, Yaumatei, where doubles/twins are HK$380/680. Just around the corner is *Caritas Bianchi Lodge* (☎ 3881111), 4 Cliff Rd, Yaumatei, where singles are HK$450 and doubles range from HK$520 to HK$640. There is another *Caritas Lodge* (☎ 3393777), 134 Boundary St, Mongkok (take the MTR to Prince Edward station), which has singles/doubles for HK$330/390.

By Kowloon standards, a mid-range hotel is defined as one in which you can find a room costing approximately HK$400 to HK$800. Some travel agencies can get you a sizeable (up to 50%) discount if you book through them. One such place is Traveller Services (☎ 3752222) but a few other agents do it as well. Some places in the mid-range category include:

Bangkok Royal, 2-12 Pilkem St, Yaumatei (Jordan MTR station), 70 rooms, singles HK$350 to HK$450, doubles and twins HK$460 to HK$580 (☎ 7359181)

Concourse, 22 Lai Chi Kok Rd, Mongkok (Prince Edward MTR station), 359 rooms, doubles and twins HK$780 to HK$1280, suites HK$1680 (☎ 3976683)

Eaton, 380 Nathan Rd, Yaumatei (Jordan MTR station), 392 rooms, doubles and twins HK$630 to HK$1250, suites HK$1450 (☎ 7821818)

Fortuna, 355 Nathan Rd, Yaumatei (Jordan MTR station), 187 rooms, singles HK$600 to HK$1000, doubles and twins HK$900 to HK$1100 (☎ 3851011)

Grand Tower, 627-641 Nathan Rd, Mongkok, 549 rooms, singles HK$760 to HK$1000, doubles and twins HK$830 to HK$1100 (☎ 7890011)

Guangdong, 18 Pratt Ave, Tsimshatsui, 245 rooms, doubles and twins HK$800 to HK$990 (☎ 7393311)

Imperial, 30-34 Nathan Rd, Tsimshatsui, 214 rooms, singles HK$720 to HK$920, doubles and twins HK$800 to HK$1000, suites HK$1400 to HK$1700 (☎ 3662201)

International, 33 Cameron Rd, Tsimshatsui, 89 rooms, singles HK$380 to HK$680, twins HK$500 to HK$880, suites HK$1100 to HK$1400 (☎ 3663381)

Metropole, 75 Waterloo Rd, Yaumatei, 487 rooms, doubles and twins HK$720 to HK$1250, suites HK$2200 to HK$4200 (☎ 7611711)

Nathan, 378 Nathan Rd, Yaumatei, 186 rooms, singles HK$550, doubles and twins HK$650 to HK$700, suites HK$850 (☎ 3885141)

New Astor, 11 Carnarvon Rd, Tsimshatsui, 151 rooms, doubles and twins HK$780 to HK$1080, suites HK$1500 to HK$2400 (☎ 3667261)

Newton, 58-66 Boundary St, Mongkok, 176 rooms, singles HK$700 to HK$950, doubles and twins HK$750 to HK$1000 (☎ 7872338)

Prudential, 222 Nathan Rd, Yaumatei (Jordan MTR station), 434 rooms, singles HK$480 to HK$1280, twins HK$550 to HK$1350, suites HK$1680 to HK$1800 (☎ 3118222)

Shamrock, 223 Nathan Rd, Yaumatei, 148 rooms, singles HK$380 to HK$650, doubles and twins HK$450 to HK$750, suites HK$800 to HK$850 (☎ 7352271)

YMCA, 41 Salisbury Rd, Tsimshatsui, singles HK$590, doubles and twins HK$690 to HK$860, suites HK$1150 to HK$1350 (☎ 3692211)

Hong Kong Island

Hostel *Ma Wui Hall* (☎ 8175715) on top of Mt Davis on Hong Kong Island offers stunning views and is the most accessible of the YHA hostels. The drawback is that it's 'centrally located' in the relative sense only. From the Star Ferry pier in Central it's still a good hour's journey.

Before embarking on the trek, ring up first to be sure a bed is available. To get there, take a No 5B bus to the end of the line, walk back 100 metres and look for the YHA sign. You've then got a 20 to 30-minute climb up the hill! There are 112 beds here and the nightly cost is HK$50. You need a YHA card to stay. The hostel is closed from 10 am to 4 pm and it's lights out by 11 pm.

Aside from the difficult transport situation, there have been many complaints that the hostel's wardens are uncooperative to the point of outright hostility. In one incident, travellers were left outside banging on the door during a severe typhoon – the warden wouldn't open the door because it wasn't yet 4 pm!

Dormitory *Benjamin's* (☎ 8519594; fax 8519501), 1st floor, 13 Graham St, Central, is the only privately run dormitory on Hong Kong Island. Due to the extreme popularity of this place, beds are only rented by the week or month. It costs HK$450 by the week or HK$1750 by the month. Entrance to the building is from Wellington St, just west of where it intersects with Graham St.

Guesthouses *Noble Hostel* (☎ 5766148) is surely one of the best guesthouses in Hong Kong, but is often full. Due to popular demand, the owner has expanded to five locations. There are two offices where you can check in: one at Flat C1, 7th floor, 37 Paterson St, Paterson Building, Causeway Bay. The other is nearby at Flat A3, 17th floor, 27 Paterson St. Singles with shared bath are HK$200 to HK$220; doubles with shared bath HK$260 to HK$280; and doubles with private bath are HK$330 to HK$350. If the guesthouse is full, the

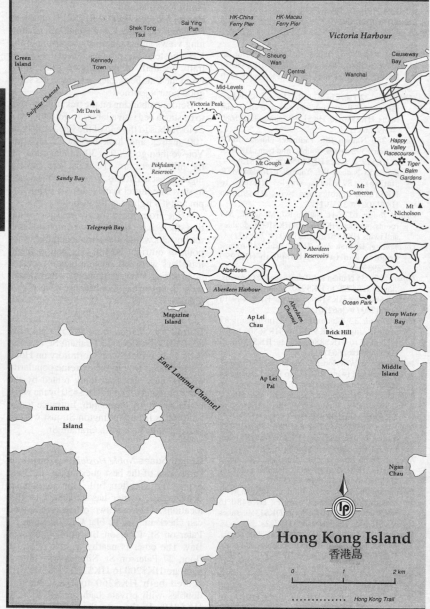

Hong Kong Island
香港島

0   1   2 km

.... Hong Kong Trail

HONG KONG

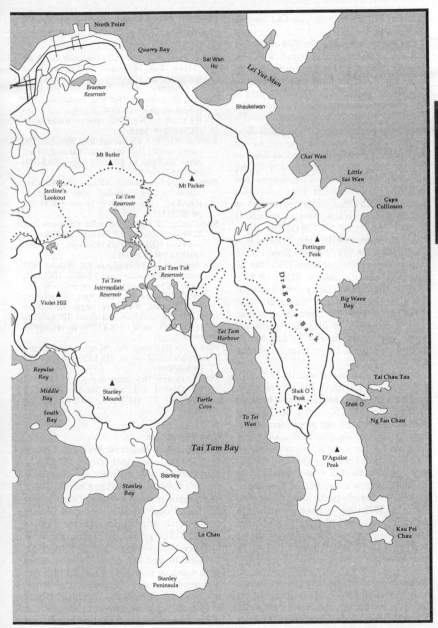

manager will try to help you find another place to stay.

The *Phoenix Apartments*, 70 Lee Garden Hill Rd, Causeway Bay, (look for New Phoenix Shopping Centre on the ground floor) has a number of elegant and reasonably priced guesthouses. The catch here is that most are short-time hotels where rooms are rented by the hour. One hotel proudly advertises 'Avoidance of Publicity & Reasonable Rates'. Nevertheless, rooms are available for overnighters, and as long as they've changed the sheets recently it's not a bad place to stay. The *Sunrise Inn* (☎ 5762419) on the 1st floor advertises rooms for HK$128 if you stay overnight or HK$58 for two hours. Another cheapie is *Garden House* (☎ 5777391), 2nd floor, which has rooms for HK$160. The *Hoi Wan Guest House* (☎ 5777970), 1st floor, Flat C, has plush rooms starting at HK$250. The 1st floor also has the *Baguio Motel* (☎ 576-1533), where very fancy rooms go for HK$400. The *Fulai Hotel* on the 5th floor also charges HK$400. There are numerous other guesthouses in Phoenix Apartments where you might be able to negotiate a cheaper rate for a longer term (or shorter term).

Nearby is *Emerald House* (☎ 5772368), 1st floor, 44 Leighton Rd, where clean doubles with private bath and round beds (no kidding) are HK$350. Enter the building from Leighton Lane just around the corner. Guesthouses are plentiful in this section of Leighton Rd, but some are pretty grotty.

Leishun Court at 116 Leighton Rd, Causeway Bay, is another cheap option. The building houses a number of low-priced guesthouses, mostly on the lower floors. *Fuji House* (☎ 5779406), 1st floor, is excellent at HK$250 for a room with private bath. On the same floor is the *Villa Lisboa Hotel* (☎ 5765421). On the 3rd floor is *Sam Yu Apartment*.

Hotels In terms of mid-range hotels, there's even less available on Hong Kong Island than in Kowloon; figure on at least HK$450. Again, check with Traveller Services

(☎ 3752222) or other travel agents for discounts. Some places to check out include:

China Merchants, 160-161 Connaught Rd West, Sheung Wan, 285 rooms, doubles and twins HK$650 to HK$950, suites HK$1800 (☎ 5596888)

Emerald, 152 Connaught Rd West, Sheung Wan, 316 rooms, singles HK$500, doubles and twins HK$600 to HK$800, suites HK$850 to HK$1200 (☎ 5468111)

Harbour, 116-122 Gloucester Rd, Wanchai, 200 rooms, singles HK$500 to HK$800, doubles and twins HK$680 to HK$950, suites HK$1400 (☎ 5118211)

Harbour View International, 4 Harbour Rd, Wanchai, 320 rooms, doubles and twins HK$620 to HK$850, suites HK$950 to HK$1050 (☎ 8021111)

New Cathay, 17 Tung Lo Wan Rd, Causeway Bay, 223 rooms, singles HK$550 to HK$800, doubles and twins HK$690 to HK$850, suites HK$1300 to HK$1500 (☎ 5778211)

New Harbour, 41-49 Hennessy Rd, Wanchai, 173 rooms, doubles and twins HK$680 to HK$1050, suites HK$1100 to HK$1400 (☎ 8611166)

Newton, 218 Electric Rd, North Point (Fortress Hill MTR station), 362 rooms, singles HK$700 to HK$1050, doubles and twins HK$750 to HK$1100, suites HK$1750 to HK$1800 (☎ 8072333)

Wesley, 22 Hennessy Rd, Wanchai, 251 rooms, doubles and twins HK$650 to HK$950 (☎ 8666688)

YWCA – Garden View International, 1 MacDonnell Rd, Central, 131 rooms, doubles and twins HK$480 to HK$580, suites HK$780 (☎ 8773737)

New Territories

The *Travellers' Hostel* (☎ 3687710), Chungking Mansions, 16th floor, A Block, Tsimshatsui, also operates the *Beachside Hostel* (☎ 4919179) at Ting Kau near Tsuen Wan, opposite Tsing Yi Island. Dorm beds at the hostel cost HK$80 a night. A private room with shared/private bath costs HK$150. You get there by taking the MTR to Tsuen Wan, then minibus No 96 or 96M. It's hard to find this place if you've never been there, so ring up first and the manager will send someone to meet you. Alternatively, enquire first at the Travellers' Hostel in Chungking Mansions.

The Hong Kong Youth Hostel Association

(HKYHA) operates several hostels in the New Territories. All are in fairly remote locations and it isn't practical to stay in these places and commute to the city. The only reason for staying there would be to enjoy the countryside and do a bit of exploring and hiking. For all of these places, you need a YHA card. You are also strongly advised to telephone first to make sure that a bed is available. The following three places are all YHA operated.

Sze Lok Yuen (☎ 4888188) is on Tai Mo Shan Rd. Beds cost HK$50 and camping is permitted. Take the No 51 bus (Tsuen Wan Ferry Pier-Kam Tin) at Tsuen Wan MTR station and alight at Tai Mo Shan Rd. Follow Tai Mo Shan Rd for about 45 minutes, then turn on to a small concrete path on the right-hand side which leads directly to the hostel. This is a good place from which to climb Tai Mo Shan, Hong Kong's highest peak. Because of the high elevation it can get amazingly cold at night, so be prepared.

Pak Sha O Hostel (☎ 3282327) charges HK$50 a bed and also permits camping. Take bus No 92 from the Choi Hung Estate bus terminal and get off at the Sai Kung terminal. From Sai Kung, take bus No 94 towards Wong Shek Pier, but get off at Ko Tong village. From there, find Hoi Ha Rd and a road sign 30 metres ahead showing the way to Pak Sha O.

Also on the Sai Kung Peninsula is *Bradbury Hall* (☎ 3282458) in Chek Keng. From Choi Hung Estate bus terminal, take bus No 92 to the Sai Kung terminal. From Sai Kung, take bus No 94 to Yellow Stone Pier, but get off at Pak Tam Au. There's a footpath at the side of the road leading to Chek Keng village. The hostel is right on the harbour just facing the Chek Keng Ferry pier. An alternative route is to take the ferry from Ma Liu Shui (adjacent to the Chinese University railway station) to Chek Keng pier.

Outlying Islands
Cheung Chau Cheung Chau has one upmarket hotel, the *Warwick Hotel* (☎ 9810081). Doubles cost HK$920 on a

weekday and HK$1050 on a weekend, plus a 10% service charge and 5% tax.

The *Star House Motel* (☎ 9812186) at 149 Tai Sun Bak St has double rooms starting at HK$200 on weekdays and between HK$600 and HK$700 a night on weekends.

There is a solid line-up of booths offering flats for rent opposite the ferry pier. Small flats for two persons cost HK$200 but easily double on weekends and holidays.

Lamma There are several places to stay in Yung Shue Wan. Right by the Yung Shue Wan ferry pier is the *Man Lai Wah Hotel* (☎ 9820220), where doubles cost HK$300 on weekdays, rising to HK$500 to HK$600 on weekends. *Lamma Vacation House* (☎ 9820427) is at 29 Main St and offers coffin-sized rooms for HK$120 or reasonably cushy flats for HK$200.

Lantau As you exit the ferry in Silvermine Bay, turn right and head towards the beach. Here you'll find several hotels with a sea view. Places to stay include the *Sea House* (☎ 9847757), which has rather dumpy-looking rooms starting from HK$200 on weekdays or HK$400 on weekends. One of the best deals around is the *Mui Wo Inn* (☎ 9841916), with doubles from HK$243 to HK$435 on weekdays, and HK$435 to HK$565 on weekends. Top of the line is the *Silvermine Beach Hotel* (☎ 9848295), which has doubles from HK$680 to HK$980 plus a 15% surcharge.

There are two places to stay in Ngong Ping. The *Po Lin Monastery* offers dormitory beds for HK$200 (price includes vegetarian meals), but it's not a friendly place. A better deal is the nearby *S G Davis Youth Hostel* which costs HK$50, but a YHA card is required.

PLACES TO EAT
Hong Kong has just about every dining choice you can think of from McDonald's to Mexican or Sichuan to spaghetti. It's not a fantastically cheap-food trip like Bali but you can still eat well at a reasonable price. If you're really economising, you might find

yourself eating more Big Macs than you might have expected.

Kowloon

Breakfast The window of the *Wing Wah Restaurant* (☎ 7212947) is always filled with great looking cakes and pastries. It's at 21A Lock Rd near Swindon's Bookstore and the Hyatt Regency. Either take away food or sit down with some coffee. Prices are very reasonable and this place has kept me alive for years. Inexpensive Chinese food is also served and, a rare treat for a Hong Kong budget Chinese cafe, there is an English menu.

A very similar cafe with cakes, coffee and other delicacies is the nearby *Kam Fat Restaurant* at 11 Ashley Rd. Prices here are slightly higher than Wing Wah but the atmosphere is better.

Deep in the bowels of *every* MTR station you can find *Maxim's Cake Shops*. The cakes and pastries look irresistible, but don't sink your teeth into the creamy delights until you're back on the street as it is prohibited to eat or drink anything in the MTR stations or on the trains, it will be a HK$1000 fine if you do.

There is a chain of bakeries around Hong Kong with the name *St Honore Cake Shop*, there's no English sign on their stores but you'll soon recognise their ideogram. You will find one at 221 Nathan Rd, Yaumatei, and a much smaller one at 8 Canton Rd, Tsimshatsui.

If you're up early before the aforementioned places open, *7 Eleven* operates 24 hours and serves good coffee, packaged breads and microwave cuisine.

American *Dan Ryan's Chicago Grill* (☎ 7356111), Shop 200, Ocean Terminal, Harbour City, Canton Rd, Tsimshatsui, is a trendy spot with prices to match.

Chinese – dim sum This is normally served from around 11 am to 3 pm, but a few places have it available for breakfast. Nothing in Hong Kong is dirt cheap, but the following places are chosen for their reasonable prices:

Canton Court, Guangdong Hotel, 18 Prat Ave, Tsimshatsui, dim sum served from 7 am to 4 pm (☎ 7393311)

Harbour View Seafood, 3rd floor, Tsimshatsui Centre, 66 Mody Rd, Tsimshatusi East, dim sum served from 11 am to 5 pm, restaurant closes at midnight (☎ 7225888)

New Home, 19-20 Hanoi Rd, Tsimshatsui, dim sum served from 7 am to 4.30 pm (☎ 3665876)

Orchard Court, 1st and 2nd floors, Ma's Mansion, 37 Hankow Rd, Tsimshatsui, dim sum served from 11 am to 5 pm (☎ 3175111)

Tai Woo, 14-16 Hillwood Rd, Yaumatei, dim sum served from 11 am to 4.30 pm (☎ 3699773)

Eastern Palace, 3rd floor, Omni, The Hongkong Hotel, Shopping Arcade, Harbour City, Canton Rd, Tsimshatsui, dim sum served from 11.30 am to 3 pm (☎ 7306011)

North China Peking Seafood, 2nd floor, Polly Commercial Building, 21-23 Prat Ave, Tsimshatsui, dim sum served from 11 am to 3 pm (☎ 3116689)

Chinese – street stalls The cheapest place to enjoy authentic Chinese cuisine is the *Temple St Night Market* in Yaumatei. It starts at about 8 pm and begins to fade at 11 pm. There are also plenty of mainstream indoor restaurants with variable prices.

Filipino The *Mabuhay* (☎ 3673762), 11 Minden Ave, Tsimshatsui, serves good Filipino and Spanish food, though it is not really cheap.

Indian The greatest concentration of cheap Indian restaurants is in Chungking Mansions on Nathan Rd. Despite the grotty appearance of the entrance to the Mansions, many of the restaurants are surprisingly plush inside. A meal of curried chicken and rice, or curry with chappatis and dahl, will cost around HK$30 per person.

Start your search for Indian food on the ground floor of the arcade. The bottom of the market belongs to *Kashmir Fast Food* and *Lahore Fast Food*. These open early, so you can have curry, chapatis and heartburn for breakfast. Neither offers any kind of cheery atmosphere, so it's no place to linger.

Upstairs in Chungking Mansions are many other places with better food and a more pleasant atmosphere. Prices are still low, with set meals from HK$35 or so. The following are presented in order from A to E blocks, from top floor to bottom, rather than by order of price and quality:

Nanak Mess, 11th floor, flat A-4, decent but not one of the top spots

Kashmir Club (☎ 3116308), 3rd floor, A Block, highly rated and even offers free home delivery

Centre Point Club (☎ 3661086), 6th floor, B Block, also highly recommended

Ashok Club, 5th floor, B Block, Nepali food, atmosphere could stand some improvement

Taj Mahal Club Mess (☎ 7225454), 3rd floor, B Block, excellent

Sher-I-Punjab Club Mess (☎ 3680859), 3rd floor, B Block, Nepali and Indian food

Mumtaj Mahal Club, (☎ 7215591), 12th floor, C Block, good if you're staying in this block

Islamabad Club (☎ 7215362), Indian and Pakistani halal food, looks decent

Delhi Club (☎ 3681682), 3rd floor, the best in C Block

New Madras Mess (☎ 3685021), 16th floor, Muslim and vegetarian halal food, grotty atmosphere

Royal Club Mess (☎ 3697680), 5th floor, D Block, Indian and vegetarian, offers free home delivery and is my personal favourite in Chungking Mansions

Karachi Mess (☎ 3681678), halal food, looks like you've stepped right into Pakistan

Khyber Pass Club Mess (☎ 7212786), 7th floor, E Block, looks decent

Indonesian The *Java Rijsttafel* (☎ 367 1230), Han Hing Mansion, 38 Hankow Rd, Tsimshatsui, is a good place to enjoy a 'rijsttafel', literally meaning a rice table. This place packs out with Dutch expats.

There is also the *Indonesian Restaurant* (☎ 3673287) at 66 Granville Rd, Tsimshatsui.

Italian *Mama Italia* (☎ 7233125), 2A Hart Ave, Tsimshatsui, offers mostly take-away Italian treats at very low prices. There are just a couple of stools if you want to eat the pizza and lasagna on the spot.

A great Italian restaurant is *Valentino* (☎ 7216449) at 16 Hanoi Rd, Tsimshatsui. Also highly rated is *La Taverna* (☎ 376-1945), Astoria Building, 36-38 Ashley Rd, Tsimshatsui.

Pizza World (☎ 3111285), ground floor, New World Centre, 22 Salisbury Rd, is

extremely popular and has the best salad bar in Hong Kong – the large sized salad for HK$30 is a meal in itself.

Korean There are several excellent and easily accessible Korean restaurants. A good one is *Seoul House* (☎ 3143174), 35 Hillwood Rd, Yaumatei.

Another place is *Manna*, a chain restaurant with outlets in Tsimshatsui at 83B Nathan Rd (☎ 7212159); Lyton Building, 32B Mody Rd (☎ 3674278); and 6A Humphrey's Rd (☎ 3682485).

Two other centrally located Korean restaurants are *Arirang* (☎ 7352281), ground floor, room 9, Sutton Court, Harbour City, Canton Rd, Tsimshatsui, and *Korea House* (☎ 3675674), Empire Centre, 68 Mody Rd, Tsimshatsui East.

Kosher The *Beverley Hills Deli* (☎ 369 8695), Level 2, Shop 55, New World Centre, Salisbury Rd, Tsimshatsui, is where you'll find gefilte fish and lox. It's good, but *not* cheap.

Malaysian *Singapore Restaurant* (☎ 376-1282) at 23 Ashley Rd, Tsimshatsui, is a great bargain. It's coffee-shop style, but forget the decor because the food is excellent and cheap. Excellent Malaysian, Chinese and Western food costs about HK$45 for a set dinner. It's open from 11 am until midnight.

Mexican *Someplace Else* (☎ 3691111 ext 5), Sheraton Hotel, 20 Nathan Rd, Tsimshatsui, is part bar and part Mexican restaurant. The Tex-Mex luncheons are worth trying, but in the evening it becomes very busy. Operating hours are from 11 am to 1 am.

Thai Thai food is devastatingly hot but excellent. A reasonably priced and good Thai restaurant is *Royal Pattaya* (☎ 3669919), 9 Minden Aven, Tsimshatsui. Also good is *Sawadee* (☎ 3763299), 6 Ichang St, Tsimshatsui.

Vegetarian The *Bodhi* (☎ 7392222), ground

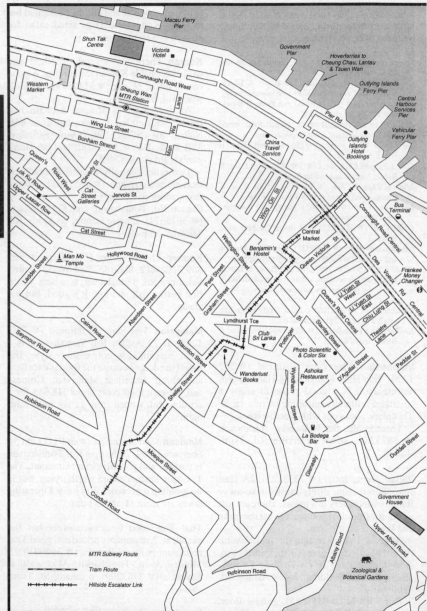

Macau Ferry Pier

Shun Tak Centre

Victoria Hotel

Government Pier

Hoverferries to Cheung Chau, Lantau & Tsuen Wan

Outlying Islands Ferry Pier

Central Harbour Services Pier

Connaught Road West

Western Market

Sheung Wan MTR Station

Wing Lok Street

Pier Rd

Vehicular Ferry Pier

Bonham Strand

Main St

Wa Lane

China Travel Service

Outlying Islands Hotel Bookings

Bus Terminal

Queen's Road West

Lok Ku Road

Cleverly St

Wing On St

Connaught Road Central

Upper Lascar Row

Cat Street Galleries

Jervois St

Central Market

Des Voeux Rd Central

Frankee Money Changer

Cat Street

Man Mo Temple

Hollywood Road

Wellington Street

Benjamin's Hostel

Queen Victoria St

Li Yuen St West

Li Yuen St East

Ladder Street

Aberdeen Street

Peel Street

Graham Street

Queen's Road Central

Stanley Street

Chiu Lung St

Theatre Lane

Caine Road

Lyndhurst Tce

Pottinger St

Photo Scientific & Color Six

D'Aguilar Street

Pedder St

Seymour Road

Staunton Street

Club Sri Lanka

Wanderlust Books

Wyndham Street

Ashoka Restaurant

Robinson Road

Shelley Street

La Bodega Bar

Duddell Street

Mosque Street

Glenealy

Government House

Conduit Road

Upper Albert Road

Albany Road

Robinson Road

Zoological & Botanical Gardens

—————— MTR Subway Route

┄┄┄┄┄┄ Tram Route

╫╫╫╫╫╫ Hillside Escalator Link

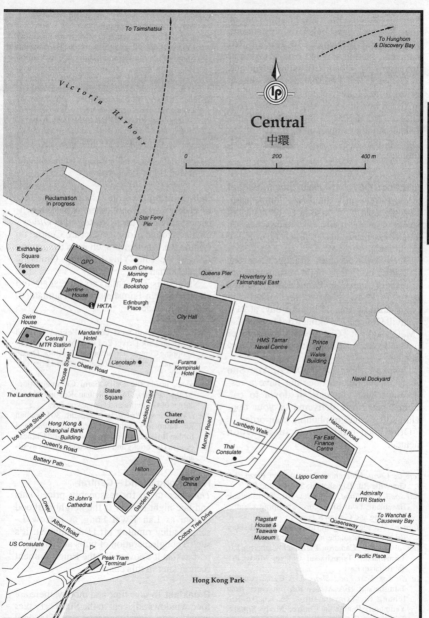

HONG KONG

To Tsimshatsui

To Hunghom & Discovery Bay

Victoria Harbour

Central
中環

0   200   400 m

Reclamation in progress

Star Ferry Pier

Exchange Square
Telecom

GPO

South China Morning Post Bookshop

Queens Pier

Hoverferry to Tsimshatsui East

Jardine House

HKTA

Edinburgh Place

City Hall

Swire House

Central MTR Station

Mandarin Hotel

Cenotaph

Furama Kempinski Hotel

HMS Tamar Naval Centre

Prince of Wales Building

Naval Dockyard

Ice House Street

Chater Road

The Landmark

Statue Square

Jackson Road

Chater Garden

Lambeth Walk

Harcourt Road

Ice House Street

Hong Kong & Shanghai Bank Building

Queen's Road

Battery Path

Murray Road

Thai Consulate

Far East Finance Centre

Hilton

Garden Road

Bank of China

Lippo Centre

Admiralty MTR Station

St John's Cathedral

Cotton Tree Drive

Flagstaff House & Teaware Museum

Queensway

To Wanchai & Causeway Bay

Lower Albert Road

US Consulate

Peak Tram Terminal

Pacific Place

Hong Kong Park

floor, 56 Cameron Rd, Tsimshatsui, is one of Hong Kong's biggest vegetarian restaurants with several branches: 36 Jordan Rd, Yaumatei; 1st floor, 32-34 Lock Rd (you can also enter at 81 Nathan Rd), Tsimshatsui; and 56 Cameron Rd, Tsimshatsui. Dim sum is served from 11 am to 5 pm.

Also excellent is *Pak Bo Vegetarian Kitchen* (☎ 3662732), 106 Austin Rd, Tsimshatsui. Another restaurant to try is *Fat Siu Lam* (☎ 3881308) at 2-3 Cheong Lok St, Yaumati.

Fast Food *Oliver's* is on the ground floor at Ocean Centre on Canton Rd, Tsimshatsui. It's a great place for breakfast – inexpensive bacon, eggs and toast. The sandwiches are equally excellent, though it gets crowded at lunchtime.

McDonald's occupies strategic locations in Tsimshatsui. Late-night restaurants are amazingly scarce in Hong Kong, so it's useful to know that two McDonald's in Tsimshatsui operate 24 hours a day: at 21A Granville Rd and 12 Peking Rd. There is also a McDonald's at 2 Cameron Rd, and another in Star House just opposite the Star Ferry pier.

Domino's Pizza (☎ 7650683), Yue Sun Mansion, Hunghom, does not have a restaurant where you can sit down to eat. Rather, pizzas are delivered to your door within 30 minutes of phoning your order.

Other fast-food outlets in Kowloon include:

Café de Coral, Mezzanine floor, Albion Plaza, 2-6 Granville Rd, Tsimshatsui; 54A Canton Rd
Fairwood Fast Food, 6 Ashley Rd, Tsimshatsui; Basement Two, Silvercord Shopping Centre, Haiphong and Canton Rds
Hardee's, Arcade of Regent Hotel, south of Salisbury Rd at the very southern tip of Tsimshatsui
Jack in the Box, Cameron Plaza, 21 Cameron Rd, Tsimshatsui; Tsimshatsui Centre, Mody Rd, Tsimshatsui East
Ka Ka Lok Fast Food Shop, 55A Carnarvon Rd, Tsimshatsui; 16A Ashley Rd, but enter from Ichang St, Tsimshatsui; 79A Austin Rd, Yaumatei; Peninsula Centre, Mody Square, Tsimshatsui East

Kentucky Fried Chicken, 2 Cameron Rd, Tsimshatsui; 241 Nathan Rd, Yaumatei
Pizza Hut, Lower Basement, Silvercord Shopping Centre, Haiphong and Canton Rds, Tsimshatsui; Shop 008, Ocean Terminal, Harbour City, Canton Rd, Tsimshatsui; 1st floor, Hanford House, 221C-D Nathan Rd, Yaumatei; Port A, Basement 1, Autoplaza, 65 Mody Rd, Tsimshatsui East
Spaghetti House, 3B Cameron Rd; 1st floor, 57 Peking Rd; Basement, 6-6A Hart Ave; 1st floor, 38 Haiphong Rd, Tsimshatsui; 1st floor, Imperial Hotel, 30-34 Nathan Rd, Tsimshatsui; 001-2, Phase I, Barton Court, Harbour City, Canton Rd, Tsimshatsui
Wendy's, Basement, Albion Plaza, 2-6 Granville Rd, just off Nathan Rd, Tsimshatsui

Self-Catering If you're looking for the best in cheese, bread and other imported delicacies, check out the delicatessen at *Oliver's* on the ground floor of Ocean Centre on Canton Rd. Another branch is on the ground floor of the Tung Ying Building, Granville Rd (at Nathan Rd).

Numerous supermarkets are scattered about. A few in Tsimshatsui and Yaumatei to look for include:

Park'n Shop, south-west corner, Peking Rd and Kowloon Park Drive; 2nd basement, Silvercord Shopping Centre, 30 Canton Rd; 3rd floor, Ocean Terminal, 3 Canton Rd (near the Star Ferry Terminal)
Wellcome, inside the Dairy Farm Creamery (ice-cream parlour), 74-78 Nathan Rd; north-west corner of Granville and Carnarvon Rds
Yue Hwa Chinese Products, basement, 301 Nathan Rd, Yaumatei (north-west corner of Nathan and Jordan Rds), both Western products and Chinese exotica (tea bricks and flattened chickens) available

Hong Kong Island – Central

The place to go for reasonably priced eats and late-night revelry is the neighbourhood known as Lan Kwai Fong, a narrow L-shaped alley running off D'Aguilar St. It's such a conglomeration of pubs and all-night parties that it's covered in the Entertainment section later in this chapter.

Breakfast To save time and money, there are food windows adjacent to the Star Ferry pier which open shortly after 6 am. Standard commuter breakfasts consisting of bread, rolls and coffee are served, with no place to sit except on the ferry itself. As you face the ferry entrance, a *Maxim's* fast-food outlet is off to the right, also with no seats.

If you'd prefer something better, *Jim's Eurodiner* (☎ 8686886), Paks Building, 5-11 Stanley St, serves outstanding morning meals between 8 and 10.30 am for around HK$20 to HK$30. From noon until 10 pm it's standard Western fare.

Chinese – dim sum All of the following places are in the middle to lower price range:

Tai Woo, 15-19 Wellington St, Central, dim sum served from 10 am to 5 pm (☎ 5245618)
Luk Yu Tea House, 26 Stanley St, Central, dim sum served from 7 am to 6 pm (☎ 5235464)
Zen Chinese Cuisine, LG 1, The Mall, Pacific Place Phase I, 88 Queensway, Central, dim sum served from 11.30 am to 3 pm (☎ 8454555)

French Wine, cheese, the best French bread and bouillabaisse can be found at *Papillon* (☎ 5265965), 8-13 Wo On Lane. This narrow lane intersects with D'Aguilar St (around No 17) and runs parallel to Wellington St.

Indian The ever-popular *Ashoka* (☎ 524 9623) is at 57 Wyndham St. Just next door in the basement at 57 Wyndham St is the excellent *Village Indian Restaurant* (☎ 5257410).

Greenlands (☎ 5226098), 64 Wellington St, is another superb Indian restaurant offering all-you-can-eat buffets for HK$68.

Club Sri Lanka (☎ 5266559), in the basement of 17 Hollywood Rd (almost at the Wyndham St end), serves great Sri Lankan curries. Their fixed price all-you-can-eat deal is a wonderful bargain – HK$66 for lunch and HK$75 for dinner.

Kosher The *Shalom Grill* (☎ 8516300), 2nd floor, Fortune House, 61 Connaught Rd, serves up kosher and Moroccan cuisine. If you're in the mood for a Jerusalem felafel or a Casablanca couscous, this is the place.

Malaysian If you like Malaysian food, try the *Malaya* (☎ 5251675), 15B Wellington St, Central. It serves Western food too, but it's considerably more expensive.

Vegetarian If you crave curry dishes of the Indian and Sri Lankan variety, check out the *Club Lanka II* (☎ 5451675) in the basement at 11 Lyndhurst Terrace, Central. The all-you-can-eat luncheon buffet costs HK$65 (free drinks), and dinner is HK$70 (includes one drink).

Fast Food *Domino's Pizza* (☎ 8109729), 9 Glenealy, Central, has no restaurant facilities but delivers to any address within a two km radius.

Famous fast-food chains have the following outlets in Central:

Café de Coral, 10 Stanley St; 18 Jubilee St; 88 Queen's Rd
Fairwood, Ananda Tower, 57-59 Connaught Rd
Hardee's, Grand Building, 15 Des Voeux Rd
Kentucky Fried Chicken, 6 D'Aguilar St; Pacific Place
Maxim's, Sun House, 90 Connaught Rd
McDonald's Hang Cheong Building, 5 Queen's Rd; Basement, Yu To Sang Building, 37 Queen's Rd; Sanwa Building, 30-32 Connaught Rd; Shop 124, Level 1, The Mall, Pacific Place, 88 Queensway
Pizza Hut B38, Basement 1, Edinburgh Tower, The Landmark, 17 Queen's Rd
Spaghetti House, lower ground floor, 10 Stanley St

Self-Catering A health-food store with great bread and sandwiches is Eden's Natural Synergy (☎ 5263062), 2nd floor, 226-227 Prince's Building, 10 Chater Rd, Central.

For imported delicacies, check out *Oliver's Super Sandwiches* with three locations: Shop 104, Exchange Square II, 8 Connaught Place; Shop 233-236, Prince's Building, 10 Chater Rd (on the corner of Ice House St); and Shop 8, Lower ground floor, The Mall, Pacific Place, 88 Queensway.

The largest stock of imported foods is found at the Seibu Department Store, Level LG1, Pacific Place, 88 Queensway (near Admiralty MTR station). Besides the imported cheeses, breads and chocolates,

HONG KO

tucked into one corner is the Pacific Wine Cellar. This is *the* place to get wine, and there are frequent sales of wine by the case. It's open from 11 am until 8 pm.

Of special interest to chocolate addicts is *See's Candies*, with two stores in Central: B66 Gloucester Tower, The Landmark, 11 Pedder St; and Shop 245, Pacific Place, Phase II, Queensway (near Admiralty MTR station).

Outlying Islands

Cheung Chau Restaurants around the ferry pier are ubiquitous, and you can take a free sampan (the one with the flag) to the *Floating Restaurant* in the typhoon shelter.

Two restaurants popular with expats are *Bor Kee* and *East Lake*, on Tung Wan Rd just east of the Garden Pub. During summer nights, outdoor tables are set up and the place takes on the atmosphere of an open-air party.

Lamma In Yung Shue Wan, the cheapest eats can be found at the *Man Kee Restaurant*. Just south of the Man Kee is the legendary *Deli Lamma* (☎ 9821582), which specialises in Italian food. The *Banyan Cafe* is strictly a gwailo hangout with 'healthy Western food' as the house speciality. Close to the ferry pier is the *Man Fung Seafood Restaurant* (☎ 9821112), which also serves morning dim sum from 6 to 11 am. A favourite of the expat community is the *Lung Wah Seafood Restaurant* (☎ 9820791) at 20 Main St, next to the Hong Kong Bank. *Lamcombe Restaurant* is the best in the mid-range, offering outstanding specialities like fried squid, sweet and sour pork and scallop broccoli garlic.

Sok Kwu Wan is lined with seafood restaurants which operate mostly in the evening, but they are not cheap and the view of a nearby quarry is not very aesthetic. The *Coral Seafood Restaurant* (☎ 9828328) at Mo Tat Wan does excellent seafood and is somewhat cheaper than Sok Kwu Wan's eateries.

Lantau As you exit the ferry in Mui Wo (Silvermine Bay), just to your right is the *Mui Wo Cooked Food Market* which harbours a large number of food stalls and relatively cheap restaurants. Farther down the beach is the *Seaview Restaurant*.

Peng Chau There are two popular pub-restaurant combinations that are a big hit with the gwailos. The larger of the two is the *Sea Breeze Club* (☎ 9838785), 38 Wing Hing St, known for its fine T-bone steak dinners. The food is so good and so reasonably priced that residents from nearby Discovery Bay take the ferry across just to eat there. It packs out on Sunday, especially in the afternoon.

The *Forest Pub* (☎ 9838837) is just next door at No 38C. It's a small but cosy place with good pub grub. It owes much of its ambience to the friendly owner, an expat New Zealander.

ENTERTAINMENT
Kowloon

Rick's Cafe (☎ 3672939), Basement, 4 Hart Ave, is popular with the backpacker set.

Jouster II (☎ 7230022), Shops A & B, Hart Ave Court, 19-23 Hart Ave, Tsimshatsui, is a fun multi-storey place with wild decor. Normal hours are from noon to 3 am, except Sunday when it's open from 6 pm to 2 am. Happy hour is any time before 9 pm.

Ned Kelly's Last Stand (☎ 3760562), 11A Ashley Rd, open from 11 am to 2 am, became famous as a real Australian pub complete with meat pies. Now it is known mainly for its Dixieland jazz and Aussie folk-music bands.

Amoeba Bar (☎ 3760389), 22 Ashley Rd, Tsimshatsui, has local new wave live music from around 9 pm, and the place doesn't close until about 6 am.

The *Red Lion* (☎ 3760243), 15 Ashley Rd, is just down the street from the Amoeba. A feature of this pub is that customers are invited to sing along with the band.

The *Kangaroo Pub* (☎ 3120083), 1st and 2nd floors, 35 Haiphong Rd, Tsimshatsui, is an Aussie pub in the true tradition. This place does a good Sunday brunch.

Mad Dog's Pub (☎ 3012222), Basement, 32 Nathan's Rd, is a popular Aussie-style pub. From Monday to Thursday it's open from 7 am until 2 am, but from Friday to Sunday it's 24-hour service.

The *Blacksmith's Arms* (☎ 3696696) at 16 Minden Ave, Tsimshatsui, is a British-style pub with darts and barstools.

Hong Kong Island

Lan Kwai Fong Running off of D'Aguilar St in Central is a narrow L-shaped alley closed to cars. This is Lan Kwai Fong, and along with neighbouring streets and alleys is Hong Kong's No 1 eating, drinking, dancing and partying venue. Prices range from economical to outrageous.

One place which plays a cat and mouse game with the safety inspector-type authorities is *Club 64* (☎ 5232801), 12-14 Wing Wah Lane, D'Aguilar St. The bureaucrats' complaint is also the pub's greatest asset – it's one of the few places in Hong Kong where you can sit outside while eating, drinking and chatting.

As you face the entrance of Club 64, off to your left are some stairs (outside the building, not inside). Follow the stairs up to a terrace to find *Le Jardin Club* (☎ 5262717), 10 Wing Wah Lane. This is an excellent place to drink, relax and socialise.

Facing Club 64 again, look to your right to find *Bon Appetit* (☎ 5253553), a Vietnamese restaurant serving up cheap but scrumptious meals.

Top Dog (☎ 8689195, 8689196), 1 Lan Kwai Fong, produces every kind of hot dog imaginable. It stays open late and the management's policy is to stay open 'until nobody is left in the street'.

As the name implies, late-night hours are kept at *Midnight Express* (☎ 5255010, 5234041), 3 Lan Kwai Fong. This place has a combination menu of Greek, Indian and Italian food, with deliveries available from Monday to Saturday. The kebabs are outstanding and cost around HK$35 to HK$45. Opening hours are 11.30 am to 3 am the next day, except on Sunday when it opens at 6 pm.

While 'glasnost' is already becoming yesterday's buzzword, you can still find it at *Yelt's Inn* (☎ 5247796), 42 D'Aguilar St.

This place boasts Russian vodka, a bubbly party atmosphere and extremely loud music.

If it's fine Lebanese food, beer and rock music you crave, where better to find it than at *Beirut* (☎ 8046611)? It's at 27 D'Aguilar St.

If you prefer Europe to the Middle East, visit *Berlin* (☎ 8778233), 19 Lan Kwai Fong. This place features loud disco music with members of the audience invited to sing along; think of it as disco karaoke.

Post 97 (☎ 8109333), 9 Lan Kwai Fong, is a very comfortable eating and drinking spot. During the daytime it's more of a coffee shop, and you can sit for hours to take advantage of the excellent selection in the rack of Western magazines and newspapers. It can pack out at night, and the lights are dimmed to discourage reading at that time.

Next door in the same building and under the same management is *1997* (☎ 8109333), known for really fine Mediterranean food. Prices are mid-range.

Graffiti (☎ 5212202), 17 Lan Kwai Fong, is a very posh and trendy restaurant and bar, but high drink prices don't seem to have hurt business.

It's raging revelry at the *Acropolis* (☎ 877-3668), on the ground floor of Corner II Tower, 21 D'Aguilar St. Shoulder to shoulder crowds, loud music and reasonably cheap drinks contribute to the party atmosphere.

The California Entertainment Building is on the corner of Lan Kwai Fong and D'Aguilar St. There are numerous places to eat here at varying price levels, but they tend to be upmarket. Note that the building has two blocks with two separate entrances, so if you don't find a place mentioned in this book be sure to check out the other block.

Top-flight food at high prices can be found at *Koh-I-Noor* (☎ 8779706), an Indian restaurant. *Il Mercato* (☎ 8683068) steals the show for Italian food. Both places are in the California Entertainment Building. Prices are mid-range.

The *California* (☎ 5211345), also in the California Entertainment Building, is perhaps the most expensive bar mentioned

HONG KONG

in this book. Open from noon to 1 am, it's a restaurant by day, but there's disco dancing and a cover charge Wednesday to Sunday nights from 5 pm onwards.

The American Pie (☎ 5213381) is *the* locale for desserts in Hong Kong. Not only pies, but all sorts of killer desserts like cakes, tarts, puddings and everything else containing sinful amounts of sugar, not to mention superb coffee and tea. If you're on a diet, don't even go near the place. Despite it's very upmarket appearance, prices are reasonable. This shop is on the 4th floor of the California Entertainment Building.

The *Jazz Club* (☎ 8458477), 2nd floor, California Entertainment Building, has a great atmosphere. Bands playing blues and reggae are a feature here, as well as friendly management and customers. Beer is reasonable at HK$40 a pint, but a cover charge is tacked on for special performances, sometimes up to HK$250 (half-price for members).

DD II (☎ 5235863) is short for 'disco disco'. This trendy place is in the California Entertainment Building, and is open from 9.30 pm until 3.30 am.

The *Cactus Club* (☎ 5256732), 13 Lan Kwai Fong, serves passable Mexican food. It seems like more of a pub than a restaurant, with top-grade beer and tequila imported from Mexico. Their Mescal, brewed from the peyote cactus, is pretty strong stuff – it tastes like it still has the needles in it.

Supatra's (☎ 5225073), 50 D'Aguilar St, is Lan Kwai Fong's top venue for Thai food.

Al's Diner (☎ 5218714), 39 D'Aguilar St, Lan Kwai Fong, is a Hong Kong institution. The place looks like it was lifted lock, stock, burgers and French fries from a New York diner of the 1930's. The food is fine but none of it comes cheaply.

Schnurrbart (☎ 5234700) in the Winner Building on D'Aguilar St, Lan Kwai Fong, is a Bavarian-style pub. There are a couple of other German pubs on either side.

Oscar's (☎ 8046561), 2 Lan Kwai Fong, is a very posh cafe and bar combination. Specialties include pizza, pasta and sandwiches on pita bread. Food is available from

noon until 11 pm and the place stays open until 2 am. Bring lots of money.

Other Central Pubs & Grub The *Fringe Club* (☎ 5217251), 2 Lower Albert Rd, is an excellent pub known for cheap beer and an avant-garde atmosphere. Live music is provided nightly by various local folk and rock musicians.

The *Mad Dogs Pub* (☎ 5252383), 33 Wyndham St, Central, is just off the trendy Lan Kwai Fong. It's a big two-floor Australian-style pub serving pub grub and drinks.

LA Cafe (☎ 5266863) on the ground floor, Shop 2, Lippo Centre, 89 Queensway (near Admiralty MTR station) has a large loyal following of late-night rowdies. The mostly Mexican luncheons are not to be discounted either – great guacamole, burritos and other Tex-Mex delights, but it isn't cheap.

La Bodega (☎ 8775472), 31 Wyndham St, is an unusual place. It's a comfortable bar with a Mediterranean flavour. Although moderately expensive, drinks are half-price on Friday until somebody goes to the toilet! A Spanish-style band (with Filipino musicians) provide the entertainment.

The *Bull & Bear* (☎ 5257436), ground floor, Hutchison House, 10 Harcourt Rd, Central, is British style and gets pretty lively in the evenings. It opens from 8 am to 10.30 am, and again from 11 am to midnight.

Portico (☎ 5238893), lower ground floor, Citibank Plaza, 3 Garden Rd, has fine live music every Saturday night from around 10 pm.

Wanchai Most of the action concentrates around the intersection of Luard and Jaffe Rds.

Joe Bananas (☎ 5291811), 23 Luard Rd, Wanchai, has become a trendy disco nightspot and has no admission charge, but you may have to queue to get in. Happy hour is from 11 am until 9 pm (except Sunday) and the place stays open until around 5 am.

Neptune Disco (☎ 5283808), basement of Hong Kong Computer Centre, 54-62 Lockhard Rd, is pure disco and heavy metal from 4 pm until 5 am. To say this place is popular is an understatement. To survive the night, spend the previous week doing aerobic exercises, bring your dancing shoes and earplugs.

To accommodate the spillover crowd, there is now *Neptune Disco II* (☎ 8652238), 98-108 Jaffe Rd. This place has live bands and a weekend cover charge of HK$70.

West World (☎ 8241066), also known as *The Manhattan*, is known for its fine late-night dancing music. Admission is free, except on Friday and Saturday when it costs HK$140 (one drink included). It's on the 4th floor of the New World Harbour View Hotel – ask at the front desk where to find the lift.

JJ's (☎ 5881234 ext 7323), Grand Hyatt Hotel, 1 Harbour Rd, Wanchai, is known for its rhythm & blues bands. There is a cover charge after 9 pm.

The Big Apple Pub & Disco (☎ 5293461), 20 Luard Rd, is thumping disco. There is a weekend cover charge of HK$60 for men and HK$40 for women. From Monday to Friday it operates from noon until 5 am, and on weekends and holidays it's open from 2 pm until 6 am.

Old Hat (☎ 8612300), 1st floor, 20 Luard Rd, keeps some of the latest hours around. It's open 24 hours on Friday and Saturday nights, so you can stay up all evening and have breakfast there. There are daily set lunches Monday to Friday from noon until 2.30 pm, happy hours, crazy hours, satellite TV, take-away burgers, French fries, pizza and satay.

Crossroads (☎ 5272347) at 42 Lockhart Rd, Wanchai, is a loud disco which attracts a young crowd. Dancing is from 9 pm to 4 am. There is a cover charge, but one drink is included.

At 54 Jaffe Rd just west of Fenwick Rd is the *Wanchai Folk Club* (☎ 5590058), better known as *The Wanch*. It stands in sharp contrast to the more usual Wanchai scene of hard rock and disco. This is a very pleasant little folk-music pub with beer and wine at low prices, but it can get packed out.

Outlying Islands

Cheung Chau There is only one real nightlife spot, the *Garden Cafe/Pub* (☎ 9814610), 84 Tung Wan Rd, just to the west of the Bor Kee Restaurant.

Lamma Yung Shue Wan has the island's only nightlife. Gwailos congregate at the *Waterfront Bar* and the *Island Bar*.

North Korea

Workers' paradise or totalitarian dictatorship – your image of North Korea may depend on your ideology. While other formerly hardline Communist countries are opening up to Western-style capitalism, North Korea remains devoutly Marxist.

This may not sound like a travellers' paradise. Indeed, it is entirely possible that North Korea hosts fewer foreign tourists than any other country on earth, and those who do manage a visit are restricted to seeing certain places and must be accompanied by a guide all the time. Visitors also find that they are subjected to nonstop propaganda – the 'US imperialist aggressors' and 'South Korean puppet stooges' are the favourite themes. And finally, all this costs plenty – North Korea is one of the most expensive countries in the world to visit.

So why go? Simply put, North Korea is

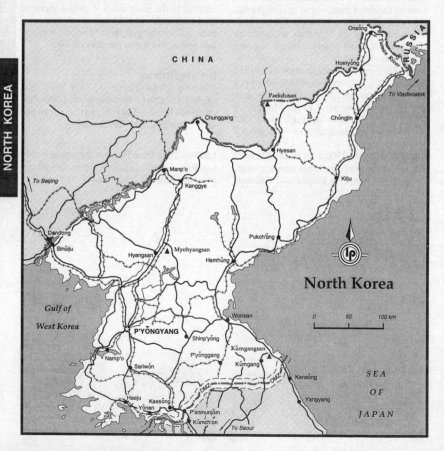

fascinating. Tourists are drawn to this country out of pure curiosity.

Some travellers come away from North Korea impressed by the cleanliness and orderliness of the society. Many come away horrified. But the big question is whether or not you'll be able to go at all.

North Korea periodically opens and closes its doors to foreign tourists, and at the time of this writing it was slammed shut once again. Yet that could all change tomorrow – the only thing predictable about North Korea is that it's unpredictable. The country is in desperate financial condition and badly needs every dollar of hard currency that tourists can bring. But at the same time, North Korea is the world's most xenophobic country. All foreign tourists are regarded as potential spies and saboteurs, capable of spreading dangerous ideas to the masses.

Facts about the Country

HISTORY

See the South Korea chapter of this book for Korean history prior to 1945.

North Korea's history as a separate political entity began from the end of WW II. The USA, the UK and the USSR had made a deal at the Yalta Conference in the closing days of the war – the USSR was temporarily to occupy Korea north of the 38th parallel to accept the Japanese surrender, while the USA would occupy the south. This 'temporary' partitioning was also done to Germany, with the same tragic result. In 1948, the uncompromising Kim Il-sung became head of North Korea, and the temporary division became permanent as neither side was willing to yield. Negotiations failed to resolve the problem, but the USA and USSR pulled most of their troops out of Korea by 1949. However, the Soviets gave Kim Il-sung massive military assistance, and on 25 June 1950, with US aid to the South on its way, North Korea invaded the South.

The Korean War

The North Koreans swiftly pushed the South Korean and US troops into a tiny enclave around Pusan. Under US prompting, the United Nations passed a resolution calling for other countries to send in troops to halt the aggression. The war effort took a dramatic turn when UN forces landed behind enemy lines at Inch'ŏn on 15 September 1950. Within a month, UN forces defeated the North Koreans, pushing them back to the Chinese border. Fortunes changed again when China's Mao Zedong decided to support the North Korean effort and sent in 180,000 Chinese 'volunteers'. UN forces were pushed back again to the 38th parallel. The war reached a stalemate while negotiations for a truce dragged on for two years. In 1953 the war ended with the Korean Peninsula split at the Demilitarised Zone (DMZ). The Korean War resulted in two million deaths and devastated the country's economy and infrastructure.

Postwar Standoff

Constant provocations by the North have kept relations between the two Koreas at the subzero level for more than 45 years. In the 1970s, it was discovered that the North was drilling invasion tunnels under the DMZ. In 1983, North Korean terrorists tried to murder South Korean President Chun while he was making an official visit to Burma – Chun survived the bomb blast but several of his fellow ministers were killed.

In 1987, two North Koreans posing as Japanese tourists boarded a South Korean civilian airliner and planted a bomb, causing 115 deaths. Both terrorists tried to commit suicide with cyanide, but one – Kim Hyun-hui – survived.

If the USA is North Korea's No 1 enemy, then Japan is certainly No 2. The North Korean book entitled *Kim Il-sung on the Five-Point Policy for National Reunification* has this to say:

The Japanese militarists, dancing to the tune of the US imperialists, have also hampered the north-south dialogue and taken many actions against the reunification of our country. The US imperialists and the Japanese militarists aim, in the final analysis, at keeping our country divided indefinitely, and making south Korea their permanent colony and commodity market.

Cold War Continues

In 1991, normalisation talks between Japan and North Korea ground to a halt when US military experts rolled out satellite photos showing that North Korea appears to be developing nuclear weapons at its reprocessing centre near Yŏngbyŏn, north of P'yŏngyang.

Optimists predicted a negotiated solution, but in the end it was the pessimists who proved correct. An inspection team from the International Atomic Energy Agency (IAEA) was denied access to North Korean nuclear facilities in January 1993. Further pressure from the IAEA caused P'yŏngyang to announce in March that it would withdraw from the Nuclear Non-Proliferation Treaty. Negotiations accomplished nothing, with P'yŏngyang demanding the total withdrawal of US military forces from the Korean Peninsula as the price of cooperation on the nuclear issue.

The nuclear issue remains unresolved. Kim Il-sung died suddenly of a heart attack in July 1994, and power theoretically passed to his son, Kim Jong-il. Since the death of Kim Il-sung, North Korea has become even more of an enigma – the country has virtually sealed itself off from the outside world.

GEOGRAPHY

North Korea occupies 55% of the land area on the Korean Peninsula. The northern and eastern regions are mostly rugged mountains and not well suited to agriculture. The official name is the Democratic People's Republic of Korea (DPRK).

A trip to North Korea makes an interesting comparison to the South. While South Korea suffers from some serious environmental problems, there is almost no pollution in the North, whether it be industrial waste or just pure trash. The one thing which strikes most visitors to North Korea is its squeaky clean appearance.

CLIMATE

The weather is similar to South Korea's, but colder and drier in winter. There are four distinct seasons. Autumn is the preferred time for a visit, with crisp, dry weather and a chance to see the leaves changing colour. Over 60% of the annual rainfall falls from June to September.

GOVERNMENT

From 1948 until 1994, Kim Il-sung was the government of North Korea. Window-dressing was, and still is, provided by the Korean Workers' Party. There is also a Politburo consisting mainly of geriatric generals who have been locked into office since the last Party Congress in 1980. All opposition to the government has been ruthlessly suppressed with a thoroughness that would have made Stalin or Hitler envious.

The death of Kim Il-sung, who was referred to by North Koreans as the 'Great Leader', 'His Excellency' and 'the Greatest Genius Mankind has Ever Known', has left the country in a state of confusion. If there was ever anyone who outdid Stalin or Mao Zedong in the cult of personality, then it was Kim Il-sung. He was virtually God in North Korea, and huge statues and portraits of him litter the North Korean countryside and cities. Everybody, young or old, at home or abroad, wears a small metal badge with the face of the 'Great Leader' on it.

This sort of cult following and passionate belief in every gem of wisdom which fell from the 'Great Leader's' lips was (and probably still is) a cornerstone of the education system and nobody escapes it. It even has its attraction for some university students in South Korea, who display the utmost naivety by uncritically espousing his totalitarian strictures on the evils of South Korea's political, economic and social policies, and his passionate anti-Western rhetoric. Of course, many things are far from perfect in the South, but it's true to say that few would prefer Kim's brand of utopia, given the choice.

The elder Kim cultivated Kim Jong-il (the 'Dear Leader') to inherit the throne, the first case of a communist dynastic succession (which is totally contrary to communist theory). Officially, the North Korean news media gives the impression that the Dear Leader, the 'Son of God', will step into his father's shoes. However, it may not be so simple. The younger Kim is said to lack his father's charisma. He's known to be an introvert, almost never gives speeches or makes public appearances and he even fails to show up for banquets held in his honour. At his father's elaborate funeral, he simply stood stonefaced while others did all the talking. But the big question is whether or not he can control his own military – younger rivals may not fancy the idea of living under his thumbs. Outsiders will just have to wait and see how the situation in P'yŏngyang unfolds.

It may seem incredible to a Western liberal accustomed to multiparty democracy that such totalitarianism could exist in the late 20th century, but it does. If any society comes close to the nightmare depicted in George Orwell's book *1984*, North Korea is it.

ECONOMY

Capitalism does not exist in North Korea, not even street vendors. The Marxist economy has been augmented with Kim Il-sung's ideology of *juche* (self-reliance) which has resulted in the country's spurning overseas aid and trade, especially with the West. The country has poured its resources into the military, heavy industries, monuments and statues of the Great Leader, all at the expense of agriculture and consumer goods.

North Korea is widely believed to be in a period of steep economic decline as subsidies from the former USSR ended in 1990.

As for exports, North Korea has little to sell, except weapons and ammunition which have found a ready market in Africa and the Middle East.

POPULATION & PEOPLE

The population is approximately 22 million – about half the population of the South. The government has encouraged population growth which is estimated at 2.1% annually.

You won't be seeing any minority groups; Korea is ethnically almost totally homogeneous.

ARTS

One thing you must say for Kim Il-sung, he indeed promoted traditional Korean arts and culture. His motives for doing so are a subject of debate. Kim was a fierce nationalist, and relentlessly emphasised the superiority of Korean culture. North Koreans were told they were culturally superior, their country was the best in the world and Kim Il-sung was the greatest man in the world. The focus on Korea's cultural superiority reinforced Kim's position as the greatest leader in the world and also helped divert attention from North Korea's genuinely serious problems.

Whatever his motives, tourists with an interest in traditional arts can benefit – visits to Korean song-and-dance performances can easily be arranged. Some even argue that in terms of traditional culture, the North is the 'real Korea'.

RELIGION

Although Buddhist temples do exist, and in some cases have been renovated, they no longer function. Buddhism is regarded as an expression of a so-called 'bourgeois mentality' and is therefore proscribed. Confucianism has been similarly suppressed. The traditional arts associated with such temples and shrines, on the other hand, have been harnessed to serve the greater glory of Kim Il-sung's 'vision'. Christians and showcase Christian churches do exist here though they're few in number and any belief in the holy trinity is likely to be expressed in the form of the Great Leader (Kim Il-sung), the Dear Leader (Kim Jong-il), and the holy spirit of Juche – the national ideology of self-reliance.

LANGUAGE

This is essentially the same as that of South Korea, but the North has developed a some-

NORTH KOREA

what different accent and vocabulary. Very few people speak English or any other foreign language.

Facts for the Visitor

VISAS & EMBASSIES

North Korea was opened up to Western group tourism in 1986 and to individual Western travellers in 1989, but at the moment tourist visas are frozen. Business visas are still possible – plutonium vendors take note.

Your best bet is to first approach the North Korean Visa Office in Macau. They are in the business of selling tours, and will normally respond much more favourably to travellers than the North Korean Embassy in Beijing. They offer several standard tours of varying lengths, or you may put together a specialised itinerary of your own. You fill out a visa application which they fax off to P'yŏngyang straight away. They can usually give you an approval or rejection within 10 minutes. The first question you will be asked is 'Are you a journalist?' If you really want to go to North Korea, you'd better say 'No'. They normally issue your visa as soon as you pay the full charge. Three photographs are required and there is a US$15 visa fee. If you're with a group of over 16 people, the 16th person visits free of charge.

The fee you pay only covers your tour within North Korea. You still must book your transport to and from P'yŏngyang. The normal starting point is Beijing, and you book at China International Travel Service (CITS) in the Beijing International Hotel. You must then inform the North Korean Visa Office in Macau. They will call ahead to make sure that your guide is there to meet you and that your hotels are booked and transport within Korea is arranged. You'd better also call or fax the Visa Office in Macau – the North Korean Embassy in Beijing has often proved to be unreliable.

Trying to book your tour directly with the North Korean Embassy in Beijing is much less certain. Some travellers have received a warm welcome at the embassy, while others have been told 'the person you need to see won't be back for two months'. Assuming they respond favourably, you may be issued the visa in anything between 10 minutes and three weeks. As in Macau, you must pay for the entire trip in advance in hard currency before your visa is issued, and then arrange your own transport for getting to/from North Korea.

There are no little tricks like entering on a transit visa and then extending after arrival. Don't even think about sneaking in to North Korea. This is one country where you dare not thumb your nose at the authorities.

Getting your visa extended is easy as long as you pay. Just how much your extended stay will cost is subject to negotiation, but include in your calculations your hotel bill, meals and a service charge for your guide. If you want a visa extension and can come up with the cash, your guide will make all the arrangements.

Even citizens of the USA have been allowed to visit, despite North Korea's vehemently anti-US stand. The same goes for Japanese nationals (enemy No 2). Only Israelis are officially prohibited entry. However, policies in North Korea change.

The visa is not stamped into your passport (which might prejudice future visits to the USA or South Korea) but onto a separate sheet of paper which will be retained by the immigration authorities when you leave North Korea.

If your time is limited and you want to arrange everything before arriving in Macau or China, there are a few travel agents (very few!) who deal with tours to North Korea. See under Tours in the Getting Around section later in this chapter for details.

Most likely, you'll be entering and returning through China. This means you should get a dual or multiple-entry visa for China. Otherwise, you can arrange a return visa at the Chinese Embassy in P'yŏngyang, but this will consume some of your scarce time and North Korea is an expensive place to hang around.

North Korea - Facts for the Visitor 289

Booking a tour through a travel agent usually requires a minimum wait of six weeks, two weeks of which are needed to process your visa application – you must part with your passport for these two weeks. In the UK, try Regent Holidays Ltd (☎ 0117 9-211711), 13 Small St, Bristol BS1 1DE. In Australia, try Passport/Red Bear Travel (☎ 03-8247183; fax 8223956), 320 Glenferrie Rd, Malvern; or Orbitours (☎ 02-2217322), 7th floor, Dymocks Building, 428 George St, Sydney 2000. In Hong Kong, the agent specialising in these trips is Wallem Travel (☎ 5286514), 46th floor, Hopewell Centre, 183 Queen's Rd East, Wanchai.

The China International Travel Service (CITS) office in Shenyang, Liaoning Province, has been known to book tours to North Korea. The Beijing CITS does not book these tours or help you obtain a visa, but they do arrange transport.

North Korean Visa Offices

Visas and information can be obtained from the following embassies overseas:

China
    Embassy of the Democratic People's Republic of Korea, Ritan Beilu, Jianguomenwai, Chaoyang District, Beijing (☎ 5321186)
Macau
    DPR Korea-Macau International Tourism Company, 23rd floor, Nam Van Commercial Centre, 57-9 Rua da Praia Grande (☎ 333355; fax 333939)
Russia
    Embassy of the Democratic People's Republic of Korea, PO Box ulitsa Mosfilmovskaya 72 (☎ 5787580; telex 413272 ZINGG SU)

Foreign Embassies in North Korea

There are about 25 embassies, but the only ones of significant size are the Chinese and Russian embassies. The rest are small offices staffed by one or two persons representing mostly Third World countries in Africa and the Middle East. The only Western country with a full-time representative is Sweden.

CUSTOMS

North Korean customs are surprisingly easy – we were not hassled at all. Besides the usual prohibitions against guns and narcotics, the government lists several other things which you may not bring in:

1) Telescopes and magnifiers with over six magnification
2) Wireless apparatus and their parts
3) Publications, video tapes, recording tapes, films, photos and other materials which are hostile to our socialist system or harmful to our political, economic and cultural development and disturb the maintenance of social order
4) Seeds of tobacco, leaf tobacco and other seeds

MONEY
Currency

The unit of currency is the won = 100 jon. There are bank notes for W1, W5, W10, W50 and W100, and coins for W1 and jon 1, 5, 10 and 50.

In addition, there are three types of North Korean currency. The first is coloured green (for won) or blue (for jon) if you're converting hard currency. The second is coloured red if you're exchanging 'non-convertible' currency (basically Communist bloc and Third World currency). The last is local currency for use by Koreans only. Local currency comes in both banknotes and coins whereas green/blue and red currency comes only in banknotes. As a foreigner, you must pay for hotels, restaurants and goods bought in stores in either green/blue or red banknotes and change will only be given in matching notes.

Red currency is North Korea's way of saying it doesn't particularly want roubles or the like. There are certain limits on consumer goods that can be bought with red currency. There are also two sets of prices for certain goods – a green price and a red price. The red price is often up to 10 times greater than the green price.

The only time you're likely to need local currency is if you use the Metro in P'yŏngyang since the escalator takes only coins. You'll also need coins if you want to make a call from a public pay phone.

Foreigners must exchange money at hotels. You are much better off changing cash rather than travellers' cheques since the

NORTH KOREA

hotels have a W3 service charge for cashing cheques. There's no black market but you can, with some people, swap green for red or local currency. Most Koreans would love to have the green currency since it can be used to buy rare imported goods.

Exchange Rates
The only convertible currencies you are able to exchange easily are the Deutschmark, French franc, British pounds, US dollars and Japanese yen. Exchange rates are as follows:

DM1	=	W1.32
FFr1	=	W0.38
UK£1	=	W3.30
US$1	=	W2.22
¥100	=	W2.13

There is also a highly punitive 'external exchange rate' of US$1 = W0.97. Usually, you will not have to worry about this, but some travellers have run into it when trying to buy air tickets from outside North Korea (see the Getting There & Away section later in this chapter).

Costs
All in all, it's going to be an expensive trip to North Korea, even more so than to Japan. You're looking at between US$70 and US$190 per day all-inclusive (not including transport to and from North Korea). You can save up to US$25 per day by choosing 'standard' accommodation rather than 'deluxe'. There are also four price levels depending on the number of persons in your group: one person, two to five persons, six to nine persons or 10 to 15 persons. A 16th person can go for free.

Prices quoted by the DPR Korea travel office in Macau for a single traveller are as follows: four days all-inclusive tour in deluxe/standard accommodation, US$646/544; five days, US$840/717; eight days, US$1487/1272; and 11 days, US$2130/1821.

Transport to/from P'yŏngyang costs extra. See the Getting There & Away section later in this chapter for details.

If it's any consolation, they do give very good service for your money.

WHAT TO BRING
There is a shortage of basic consumer items, so bring everything you think you'll need. Korean men smoke like chimneys and foreign cigarettes make good gifts – you can buy a carton of Dunhills at the hard currency shops for US$14, but if you have a cheaper source, bring them. Marlboro reds are especially valued since they are not available in North Korea. Postage stamps seem to be glueless, so a gluestick will prove valuable.

TOURIST OFFICES
Local Tourist Offices
Ryohaengsa (☎ 850-2-817201), the government tourist agency, is also known as the Korea International Tourist Bureau. You can reach them by telex (5998 RHS KP) or fax (850-2-817607). The mailing address is: Ryohaengsa, Central District, P'yŏngyang, Democratic People's Republic of Korea.

Overseas Reps
DPR Korea-Macau International Tourism Company (☎ 333355; fax 333939) is on the 23rd floor, Nam Van Commercial Centre, 57-9 Rua da Praia Grande, Macau. This is currently the easiest place to arrange a visa.

BUSINESS HOURS & HOLIDAYS
Official working hours are Monday to Saturday from 9 am to 6 pm. Public holidays include: New Year's Day, 1 January; Kim Jong-il's birthday, 16 February; Kim Il-sung's birthday, 15 April; Armed Forces Day, 25 April; May Day, 1 May; National Foundation Day, 9 September; and Korean Workers' Party Foundation Day, 10 October.

CULTURAL EVENTS
By all means try to be in P'yŏngyang during Kim Jong-il's birthday (16 February) or Kim Il-sung's birthday (15 April). Both events are huge extravaganzas with military-style parades and portraits of the Great and Dear Leaders being carried through the streets.

An interesting thing about the Dear

Leader's birthday is that it's been changed: he was born in 1942 but this was recently changed to 1941 and all previous North Korean history books had to be altered to reflect the new 'reality'. Just why Kim Jong-il was made one year older is subject to speculation, but the currently accepted theory is that the Great Leader liked even numbers and wanted his son to be exactly 30 years younger than him.

POST & TELECOMMUNICATIONS
Postal Rates
A postcard to Australia costs W1.30. To the USA it's W1.50.

Sending Mail
You needn't bother trying to track down the post office, since most major hotels offer postal service.

You're best off sending postcards since these give the authorities a chance to read what you've said without having to tear open your letters. Saying a few nice things about how clean and beautiful North Korea is will increase the chances of your mail getting through.

Receiving Mail
You can forget about the GPO and poste restante. Given the short time you're likely to be spending in North Korea, it's hardly worth bothering trying to receive any letters. However, if you want to try, the most likely place to receive your mail is at the P'yŏngyang Koryo Hotel, Tonghung-dong, Central District, P'yŏngyang; or care of the Korea International Tourist Bureau (Ryohaengsa), Central District, P'yŏngyang. There is a better than average chance that your letters will be opened and read.

Telephone
It's easy to book an overseas call from major hotels, and some even offer International Direct Dialling (IDD) right from your room. Phone calls usually go through without much trouble.

Public pay phones require 10 jon coins, which means you'll need some local money if you want to use them. Coin-operated phones are not very common even in P'yŏngyang, but you probably won't find too many people to call anyway.

If you are dialling direct to North Korea from abroad, the country code is 850. A number of Western countries do not have phone connections with North Korea, but making an IDD call from Beijing to P'yŏngyang is very easy.

Fax, Telex & Telegraph
Fax and telex services are readily available from major hotels like the Koryo in P'yŏngyang. Telegraph (cable) service does not seem to be available.

TIME
The time in Korea is Greenwich Mean Time plus nine hours. When it is noon in Korea it is 2 pm in Sydney or Melbourne, 3 am in London, 10 pm the previous day in New York and 7 pm the previous day in Los Angeles or San Francisco.

ELECTRICITY
Electric power is 220 V, 60 Hz, though luxury hotels often have an outlet for 110 V. If so, this will be clearly labelled. All outlets are of the US type with two flat prongs, but no ground (earth) wire.

BOOKS & MAPS
Literature about North Korea is rare, and tourist literature is even rarer. The easiest place to get travel brochures is from the DPR Korea-Macau International Tourism Company in Macau. These are printed in several languages – English, German, French, Japanese, Chinese etc, and give all the major sites open to foreign tourists, the hotels, an airline schedule and a breakdown of suggested itineraries ranging from three days to 16 days. The North Korean Embassy in Beijing has these brochures but does not give them to Westerners, though ethnic Koreans seem to be able to obtain them without difficulty.

Within North Korea, there are numerous propaganda books and pamphlets. Though

NORTH KOREA

these have scant useful information, they are rare gems for collectors.

As for getting a general feel for the place, what could be more relevant than George Orwell's *1984* or *Animal Farm*? Read these before or after you arrive, as it would not be wise to carry them through North Korean customs.

Perhaps more to the point is a report on human rights in North Korea published jointly by Asia Watch (Washington DC, USA) and the Minnesota Lawyers International Human Rights Committee. A brief summary of this report appeared in the Far Eastern Economic Review, 19 January 1989, which should be available from libraries in Hong Kong. North Korea has harshly denounced this report.

Maps of P'yŏngyang and Korea can be purchased at major tourist hotels.

MEDIA
Information about the rest of the world is hard to come by in North Korea. The press is rigidly controlled and prints only what the government tells it to print. Likewise, TV programmes are all designed to reinforce the reigning ideology. North Koreans cannot receive foreign news broadcasts because all radio and TVs are designed to only pick up the government broadcasting frequencies.

Newspapers & Magazines
There are no foreign publications available, so if you want to read *Time* or *Newsweek* you'll have to bring your own copies.

As for local publications in English, the selection is severely limited. There are free magazines everywhere in a variety of languages, especially the colourful *Democratic People's Republic of Korea* magazine. This is filled with the usual tirade against US imperialists and South Korean puppets, plus articles about the Great Leader and Dear Leader. You'll also learn that the Juche idea is a shining beacon of hope which has swept the world by storm. At the tourist hotels you can pick up a free weekly English-language newspaper, the *P'yŏngyang Times*, but every issue is practically the same.

Radio & TV
There are two AM radio stations and two regular TV stations. It is said that there is a third TV station which broadcasts cultural events on holidays only, but we haven't seen it. The two TV stations broadcast approximately from 6 to 11 pm. Like the rest of the mass media, the content is thoroughly politicised.

It's interesting to note that approximately one hour per week of North Korean TV is now shown in South Korea. When this was first permitted, the South Koreans were fascinated, but quickly grew bored with it. You can rest assured that no South Korean TV shows are shown in the North except for news clips of student protests and riots.

FILM & PHOTOGRAPHY
You can buy colour print film at reasonable prices from the hard currency gift shops, but everything else is expensive so bring what you need. There are photoprocessing facilities on the 2nd floor at the Koryo Hotel, but you'd probably be better off waiting until you return to China or Hong Kong for example. This same place can do visa photos in case you need some.

If you visit the International Friendship Exhibition (IFE) centre at Myohyangsan, you'd be wise to bring a tripod and cable release for time exposures because an electronic flash is not permitted. Since many of the exhibits are behind glass, a polarising filter would also come in handy.

You are surprisingly free to photograph what you like, but ask first before taking pictures of soldiers. In many cases, permission *will* be given.

HEALTH
There seems to be no problem with food and most Koreans drink their water unboiled. You won't have to worry about eating from dirty street stalls either, because there aren't any.

That having been said, North Korea is not a good place to get sick since there are shortages of basic Western medicines. On the other hand, you can try traditional Korean medicine which is similar to the Chinese variety.

WOMEN TRAVELLERS

We saw a few foreign women travelling in North Korea, but they were always part of a group that included men. This isn't to say that a single woman or group of women couldn't travel without male companions in North Korea, but it seems to be a very rare occurrence. Also, we never saw a female guide leading any of these tour groups, though Ryohaengsa claims that female guides are available. It's the opposite situation in South Korea, where most tour guides are women.

One thing we can say for sure – Korea is a very male-dominated society. While no North Korean woman holds any position of power (except possibly Kim Song-ae, Kim Il-sung's widow), there are two who are revered: the Great Leader's mother, Kang Ban-sok, sometimes referred to as the 'Mother of Korea', and Kim Jong-suk, mother of the Dear Leader.

DANGERS & ANNOYANCES

As far as we can tell, crime is not a problem. The North Korean penal system is an enigma, but we'd be willing to guess that thieves are dealt with harshly – possibly with the death penalty. This doesn't mean you should be careless with your valuables, but the chance of theft is probably lower than in most countries.

The one thing which will get you into serious trouble fast is to insult the Great Leader or the Dear Leader.

Male travellers should not even think about touching a North Korean woman regardless of how friendly, charming and receptive she might seem to be. Even something fairly innocent like shaking hands could be construed as an 'immoral act' and could result in serious punishment for both parties to this 'crime'. As for relations between North Korean men and foreign women, it's a big unknown. Most North Korean men would probably not dare touch a foreign woman, but given the fact that

Korea is a bastion of male chauvinism, it would probably be viewed less seriously than contact between a foreign man and a Korean woman.

Besides thinking about dangers to yourself, give some thought to the Koreans you meet. Giving them gifts like foreign coins or photos of yourself could have unpredictable consequences for them. What might seem like an innocent act for you might result in them spending time in a concentration camp.

The US Treasury Department has a list of regulations (available from US embassies) governing the economic conduct of US citizens abroad. One little-known rule is that US citizens may not use a credit card in North Korea – not for the purchase of goods or even to pay living expenses! Breaking this rule is a crime and the violator may be prosecuted.

ACCOMMODATION

You will have to stay at certain designated hotels everywhere you go. These are modern, multi-star hotels which have been built specifically for foreign tourists and, as you might expect, they're expensive, though there are several grades of them. And since you must stay in the large tourist hotels, this also limits where you can go.

FOOD

Despite continuous reports of food shortages, foreigners with dollars eat very well. Your guide orders your food, so if you have any special requests, make your wishes known early. The food is heavily based on meat, fish and poultry – vegetarians are liable to have a difficult time. There is a tendency to order Western food for Westerners, so if you want Korean food, ask for it.

DRINKS

Korean beer is not bad, but most hard liquor is imported. As for nonalcoholic beverages, North Korea produces mineral water and some pleasant-tasting carbonated fruit drinks. There are plenty of imported drinks, including Coca-Cola, available in the hotels and hard currency shops.

NORTH KOREA

Getting There & Away

AIR

There are flights between Beijing and P'yŏngyang by either the Chinese national airline, Air China, once weekly, or the North Korean airline, Korean Airways (also known as Chosonminhang), twice weekly. The flight takes less than two hours. We found the staff at the Air China office in P'yŏngyang to be very friendly – though they were much preoccupied with raising fish in the bathtub and vegetables on the terrace because they can't buy these things without hard currency.

The airfares are insane. The one-way Beijing-P'yŏngyang ticket costs US$120, but a one-way P'yŏngyang-Beijing flight is US$274 if the ticket is bought in China! If bought in P'yŏngyang, it's only US$120! This is because Air China calculates the fare using the absurd 'external exchange rate' of US$1 = W0.97. To make it more absurd, a round-trip Beijing-P'yŏngyang-Beijing air ticket bought in China costs US$220, or US$54 less than a one-way ticket.

There are flights between Khabarovsk and P'yŏngyang in either direction and between Moscow and P'yŏngyang by either Aeroflot or Korean Airways.

You're advised to book as far in advance as possible, though most aircraft fly nearly empty. Occasionally, delegations of diplomats descend on P'yŏngyang for some special event and seats suddenly become scarce.

Sunan International Airport is 30 km west of P'yŏngyang, about 20 minutes by car.

TRAIN

There are four trains per week in either direction between Beijing and P'yŏngyang via Tianjin, Tangshan, Jinxi, Dandong and Shinuiju. The Chinese trains leave on Monday and Thursday and the North Korean trains leave on Wednesday and Saturday. All these trains leave Beijing at 4.48 pm and arrive at P'yŏngyang the next day at 3.55 pm (about 23 hours). Going the other way, trains depart from P'yŏngyang at noon on Monday, Wednesday, Thursday and Saturday. The one-way fare is US$73 in hard sleeper (economy class) or US$99 in soft sleeper (1st class).

Chinese trains are more comfortable than the North Korean ones. North Korean trains don't have air-conditioning even in the soft-sleeper section, and the windows are locked so ventilation is nonexistent.

The North Korean train is actually just two carriages attached to the main Beijing-Dandong train, which are detached at Dandong (Chinese side) and then taken across the Yalu River bridge to Shinuiju (Korean side), where more carriages are added for local people. Non-Koreans remain in their original carriages.

Customs and immigration on both sides of the border are relatively casual and your passport will be taken away for stamping. The trains spend about four hours at the border for customs and immigration – two hours at Dandong and two hours at Shinuiju. You are permitted to wander around the stations but you should not attempt to go beyond the entrance gate.

Shinuiju Station will be your first introduction to North Korea and the contrasts with China will be quite marked. Everything is squeaky clean and there are no vendors plying their goods. A portrait of the Great Leader looks down from the top of this station, and at all other railway stations in North Korea. You may wander around the station and take photos. One of the buildings is a rest area for foreign passengers, and here you will encounter the first of many billboards with photos and captions in English: 'The US Aggression Troops Transferring Missiles'; 'South Korean Puppet Police'; 'US Imperialists and South Korean Stooges' etc.

Soon after departing Shinuiju, you will be presented with a menu (complete with colour photographs) of what's for dinner. The food is excellent and the service is fine. It's all very civilised. Make sure you have some small-denomination US dollar bills to pay for the meal, as this is not included as part of the package deal you paid for in advance. There are no facilities for changing money at Shinŭiju or on the train. The dining car is for the use of non-Koreans only.

Your guide will meet you on arrival at P'yŏngyang Railway Station and accompany you to your hotel. Likewise, when you leave North Korea, your guide will bid you farewell at P'yŏngyang Railway Station or the airport and you'll travel to China unaccompanied.

When leaving North Korea, you can link up with the Trans-Siberian train at Shinŭiju/Dandong in China. To make this connection you need to take the noon train from P'yŏngyang on Saturday which arrives in Moscow the following Friday. There's also the possibility of crossing directly from North Korea into Russia in the north-east via Hasan and then taking the Trans-Siberian to Moscow. This connection leaves P'yŏngyang on Monday and Wednesday at 5.30 pm. These trains arrive in Moscow on Monday and Wednesday respectively.

BOAT

A passenger ship, the *Sam Jiyon*, plies between Wonsan on the east coast of North Korea and Nagasaki (Japan) once a month. It's a North Korean ship and is primarily intended to enable Koreans living in Japan to visit their homeland – most of the Koreans living in Japan originally came from North Korea. It's popular with youth groups from Japan, who get VIP treatment on arrival in the North, and is a possible port of entry if you already have a visa for North Korea.

If you have limited time at your disposal, you'll need to know the departure dates of this ship. North Korean embassies *may* know the details but don't be surprised if they don't or won't tell you. Don't just think you can hop on this ship even if you have a North Korean visa – you'd better clear it with the North Korean Embassy first, and in any event, a guide must be informed that you're coming so you will be met on arrival.

You can get information about the ship by contacting the General Association of Korean Residents in Japan (Soren). Soren is P'yŏngyang's mouthpiece in Japan, with branches all over the country, and heavily guarded headquarters in Tokyo. Members of Soren run many of Japan's pachinko (slot machine) parlours, and a sizeable chunk of their cash goes to subsidise the North Korean economy.

LEAVING NORTH KOREA

You should make your reservations for departure before you arrive in North Korea. Ryohaengsa, the government tourist agency, can easily do this for you as long as you inform them in advance.

If you are departing by air, your guide will accompany you to the airline office so you can buy your ticket, or to reconfirm your outbound flight if you've already bought one. You must pay an airport departure tax of W13 at the time you reconfirm, rather than at the airport.

Money-changing facilities are available at the airport but not at the railway station.

Getting Around

Public transport isn't anywhere near as well developed in North Korea as in the South. However, you will have few opportunities to use it, usually only when accompanied by your guide.

One thing you'll notice is the distinct lack of traffic in the countryside. Most of the vehicles you'll see will be military transports.

AIR

There are no regularly scheduled domestic flights. There are occasional charters to Paekdusan for W2000 return, but these only fly if there are sufficient passengers, which is seldom the case.

BUS

There are hardly any public buses in the countryside or between major cities, a reflection of the fact that North Koreans are not allowed to move freely around their own country without permission. Most of the time, you'll be travelling by car accompanied by your driver and guide. If you're with a larger group, you'll ride in a specially arranged tourist bus.

TRAIN

You'll probably take the railway to visit some of the major tourist sites such as Kaesŏng and Myohyangsan. You'll be accompanied by your guide during these trips, and you'll ride in sleeper cars rather than the hard-seat carriages used by the masses.

BICYCLE

A major contrast with China is the distinct lack of bicycles. There are almost none in P'yŏngyang and very few elsewhere. Outside of P'yŏngyang, most people walk. Presumably, the absence of bicycles in P'yŏngyang indicates a ban on their use. Occasionally, you'll come across a few in a department store in P'yŏngyang, usually with no price tags on them. Certainly you cannot rent bikes anywhere.

Finally, even if you did have your own bike, you'd be hard-pressed to find your way around either in the cities or in the countryside because there are no street signs in the cities or direction signs in the countryside, and road maps are almost impossible to find. The only street map you'll find available is for P'yŏngyang.

TOURS

You must be accompanied at all times by a guide whose fees you will already have paid. In a few places you are allowed to walk around alone – basically in P'yŏngyang and a few of the beauty spots – though this is only reluctantly conceded. Guides who can speak English, French, German, Chinese, Japanese and Russian as well as a number of other languages are available.

Tours booked through a private travel agent are more expensive, but only slightly, than booking directly with Ryohaengsa. Presumably, the travel agents are shielding you from all the hassles of dealing with the North

Korean bureaucracy and China International Travel Service (CITS) in Beijing. For a five-day trip, Wallem Travel in Hong Kong charges US$880 for one person; US$683 each for two to five persons; US$502 each for six to nine persons; US$485 for 10 to 15 persons; and a 16th person can go for free. If booked in conjunction with a Trans-Siberian tour, these charges are reduced by US$153 per person.

There are a number of special interest tours. One is the 'Tour for Traditional Korean Medical Treatment', which involves acupuncture, moxibustion (suction using vacuum flasks) manipulative (chiropractic) treatment and physical therapy. Cure rates of 90% are claimed for most illnesses. The costs for these treatments vary, but don't expect them to be cheap.

P'yŏngyang 평양

Being the capital, P'yŏngyang is a superb example of the regime's determination to project its own image of progress, discipline and the wellbeing of its citizens. You won't find the hustle and bustle, the noise and smells of other cities in Asia here. Kim Il-sung's version of the model Communist capital city excludes people with disabilities (except the Great Leader, who had a large visible bulge on the back of his head from a benign brain tumour). Also excluded are the very old, bicycles, animals and street vendors. Even pregnant women were banned for a while. It's said that only those with proven records of unswerving loyalty to the country's leaders are allowed to live in P'yŏngyang.

Fascinating indicators of the mentality of the regime are the stores with big glass display windows, well-stocked with goods for all to see. The problem is that the doors are always locked and no one is inside.

Orientation

Like Seoul, P'yŏngyang is built on the banks of a major river, in this case the Taedong.

One of the most popular sights here are the two mid-river fountains which rise to a height of 150 metres. Your guide will proudly tell you they're the highest in the world, and this is probably true (Canberra's single jet reaches only 140 metres and the one in Geneva only 122 metres).

If walking around the city, beware of jaywalking even if there's not a car in sight! There are underground walkways or pedestrian crossings at all major intersections and *everyone*, without exception, uses them.

Things to See

Since P'yŏngyang is one of the few places where you'll be allowed to walk around unaccompanied (with a little gentle but persistent persuasion), it's a good idea to take this opportunity either before or after you've been chauffeured around the main sights. If you request it, you can, for instance, be dropped on the far side of the city at Liberation Tower and walk back from here to the city centre calling in at department stores along the way if you want.

Your first day out in P'yŏngyang will undoubtedly be a guided tour of the monuments by car. How many of them you will see depends on the time available and what preferences you express. It's a good idea to make your preferences known as early as possible after arrival in North Korea or even beforehand if you want to be sure of being taken to the ones of your choice.

One of the principal monuments is the **Tower of the Juche Idea**, a 170-metre phallic symbol which you can get to the top of by express lift for an unencumbered view of the city. The ride costs W5. In an alcove at the bottom are commemorative messages from various parts of the world hewn in stone and brick extolling the concept of Juche. As the plaques indicate, the Juche idea is also referred to as 'Kim Il-sungism'.

Other monuments include the **Arch of Triumph**, which marks the spot where Kim Il-sung made his rallying speech following the departure of the Japanese, and which is a full three metres higher than its counterpart in Paris, and the **Chollima Statue**, a bronze

Pegasus representing the high-speed progress of the socialist reconstruction of North Korea. On Munsu Hill, overlooking the Taedong River, is the **Grand Monument** itself. As you might expect, this is where an enormous and highly polished bronze statue of the Great Leader stands, flanked by carvings of oppressed but ultimately victorious workers.

Of a more traditional nature are the **Chilsong** and **Taedong Gates**, two of the old city's gates, the latter with a two-tiered roof similar to its counterpart in Seoul.

For an exposition of North Korea's version of the country's history there is the **Korean Central History Museum**. The counterpart to the South's Independence Hall outside Ch'ŏnan, the museum houses exhibits, artefacts and drawings tracing Korean history from prehistoric times right up to the revolution. Your guide will provide a running commentary.

If time permits, you may be taken to the **P'yŏngyang Maternity Hospital**. The most intriguing thing about this showcase hospital is that when the first foreign tour groups were herded through the maternity wards, all the 'patients' were beautiful, smiling young women who weren't pregnant.

Other institutes which may well be worth a visit include the **Students' & Children's Palace**, established in 1963 as a centre for after-school activities and where you can see students doing everything from ping-pong to dance, gymnastics and playing music, and the **P'yŏngyang Embroidery Institute**, where you can see an exhibition of very impressive embroidery as well as prototype designs which are then copied by manufacturers around the country.

The major site of interest is the outer district of **Mangyongdae** – the so-called 'Cradle of the Revolution'. This is where Kim Il-sung was born and spent his childhood. His old thatched house here, set in carefully tended gardens, has been turned into a shrine, and houses photographs of his family as well as a few everyday household utensils to indicate the humble background from which he came. The surrounding pine

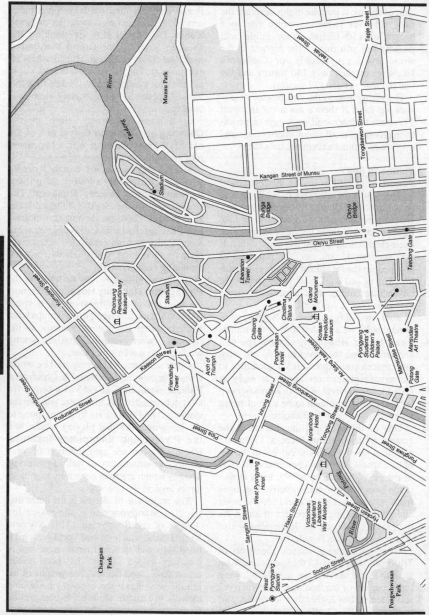

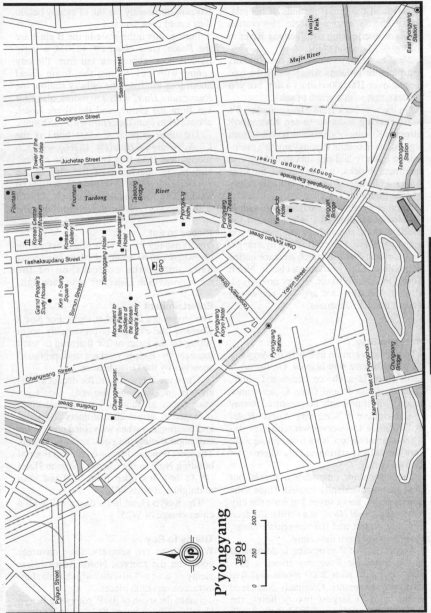

NORTH KOREA

P'yŏngyang
평양

0   250   500 m

woods hold the burial mounds of his relatives. There's also a marble observation platform overlooking the Taedong River at the top of Mangyong Hill.

Near to Mangyongdae are two funfairs and pleasure grounds which you'll be told receive over 100,000 visitors a day, but you can take that with a pinch of salt.

On the way back from Mangyongdae, it's worth making a detour to see **Kwangbok Street**, a Kowloonesque suburb visible from high points in central P'yŏngyang. It's essentially a linearly laid-out suburb of high-rise apartment blocks, which stretch for over three km on either side of the virtually empty 13-lane highway.

Another worthwhile excursion is a visit to the **Movie Studio**. This is not part of the standard tours, so you must request it if you want to go there. It is not difficult to arrange, but give your guide as much advance notice as possible. Like everything else in North Korea, the movie studio is very politicised. Most of the films are anti-US, anti-South Korean and anti-Japanese.

Places to Stay
Wherever you choose to stay in P'yŏngyang it's going to cost you heavily. On the one hand, there is a choice between Deluxe, Class A, Class B and Class C accommodation. You'll probably be pressured to stay at the deluxe *P'yŏngyang Koryo Hotel* (☎ 38106), a 45-storey tower with a revolving restaurant on top. It's a five-minute walk from the railway station and it's where most foreigners stay.

There are some other deluxe hotels, but most are inconveniently located. There's the *Tourist Hotel*, about seven km from the city centre; the *Angol Hotel*, at a similar distance from the centre; and the *Yanggakdo Hotel*, about four km from the centre.

The skyline of P'yŏngyang is dominated by the incredible *Ryugyong Hotel*, a 105-storey pyramid with 3000 rooms and five revolving restaurants. Originally conceived as the world's largest luxury hotel, the pyramid was erected in 1989 but the North Koreans apparently ran out of money before they could complete it.

Further down the scale in the B class are the *Potonggang Hotel* (☎ 48301), a fairly modest hotel about four km from the city centre with 161 rooms; the *Sosan Hotel* about four km from the railway station; the *Ryanggang Hotel* with 330 rooms, also four km from the centre; and the *Youth Hotel*, about 10 km from the centre with 465 rooms.

The most popular C class hotel is the *Changgwangsan Hotel* (☎ 48366), with 326 rooms, less than two km from the railway station. In the heart of the city is the *P'yŏngyang Hotel* (☎ 38161) with 170 rooms. The *Taedonggang Hotel* (☎ 38346) with 60 rooms is also in the centre of the city.

Places to Eat
You'll usually eat at your hotel, but eating elsewhere can be arranged. Many foreigners hang out at the coffee shop of the *Changgwangsan Hotel*, but prices are high.

Entertainment
The streets are deserted at night. For North Koreans, the evening is presumably spent sitting by the radio or TV listening to testimonials by happy workers and profound speeches by the Great Leader.

There are a few discos for decadent foreigners (no Koreans allowed). Don't get your hopes up though – the largest disco managed to attract 20 customers (19 males and one female) when we visited on a Saturday night during the peak summer season. The most popular disco is on the top floor of building No 2 in the Changgwangsan Hotel (☎ 48366). It's open from 9.30 pm until midnight and costs W2.

The Koryo Hotel has a dance hall with a cover charge of W25.

Things to Buy
While there are scarcely any consumer goods on the shelves, North Korea offers plenty of unique souvenirs which make fantastic conversation pieces.

Just to the south of the P'yŏngyang Koryo Hotel on Changgwang St is a place selling postage stamps (sign in English), and it's well worth your time to stop in here. One unique stamp shows a crowd of angry Koreans beating a US soldier to death while someone sticks a knife through his throat.

Many tourists have expressed an interest in purchasing the metal badge which every North Korean wears, with the Great Leader's picture printed on it. However, these are not for sale.

Ginseng is for sale in hotels, but prices are ridiculously high. You can buy it much more cheaply in the South. Aspiring acupuncturists can find acupuncture needles in the medicine shops at rock-bottom prices.

Getting Around

All public transport in P'yŏngyang costs 10 jon. It is paid in coins, so you'll need local money. As a general rule, foreigners are discouraged from using the public transport system except for the Metro (underground), which is something of a showcase.

Bus It's unlikely you'll ever use the urban bus network as the queues are phenomenally long and the buses crammed to bursting point, but if you do they run until 10 pm each day. Women with children form separate queues and have priority in boarding buses.

Underground You should definitely visit a Metro station if only to see the extravagance with which the stations have been constructed. Each station is designed differently, with varying bronze sculptures, murals, mosaics and chandeliers, and all the pillars, steps, corridors and platforms are fashioned in marble. The trains themselves are nowhere near as impressive, being dim and dingy, but each car contains a picture of His Excellency. There are 17 stations in all served by two lines covering a total length of 24 km, and the present system was completed in 1978. The cost of a ride on this system is a standard 10 jon and it's a very convenient way of quickly visiting different parts of the city.

Tram P'yŏngyang's tram began service in 1991. It's not a bad way of getting around, but it's often extremely crowded.

Taxi You won't find taxis plying the streets like in most major capital cities, but you can book a taxi from a tourist hotel. The word 'taxi' is not written on the car, nor will you see a meter, but the fare is based on distance. The fare is approximately W2 per km, depending on the type of vehicle (Mercedes are most expensive). The price also rises slightly late at night. In the rare event that you don't find a taxi waiting outside your hotel, you can call one (☎ 10507).

Around the Country

What you get to see outside P'yŏngyang depends on what sort of itinerary you request and how much time you have. It will also be limited to the places where tourist hotels are.

MYOHYANGSAN

A visit here from P'yŏngyang can be adequately covered in a day trip using the train as your means of transport. It's 160 km north-east of the capital.

The main centre of interest in Myohyangsan is the **International Friendship Exhibition (IFE)** centre, about three to four km from the railway station. It's another of those monuments to the greater glory of the Great Leader and, to a lesser extent, of the Dear Leader. It's a six-storey building in traditional Korean style which houses gifts given to Kim Il-sung and Kim Jong-il from all over the world and is magnificently set among densely wooded hills. You need to be on your best behaviour here, as the building is maintained as a hallowed shrine. The building is thermostatically temperature-controlled and is quite cold inside, so bring a jacket even in summer.

When you've seen the exhibition, it's possible to go for a three-km hike up the **Sangwon Valley**, via a clearly defined pathway, stone steps and a suspension footbridge to three sets of waterfalls (Kŭmgang,

Taeha and Sanju). Nearby, there's an observation platform from where you can view the surrounding countryside. A short hike above the falls is a Buddhist temple – Sangwonsa – which is in good order though no longer used.

There's also the Buddhist temple **Pohyonsa**, just a short walk from the IFE at the start of the hike up Sangwon Valley, which consists of several small pagodas and a large hall housing images of the Buddha, as well as a museum which sports a collection of wood-block Buddhist scriptures.

The village of Myohyangsan itself consists of just one main street lined by traditional Korean houses. The main tourist hotel in this vicinity is the *Hyangsan Hotel*, about halfway between the station and the IFE, rated as class A. There is also the class C *Chongbyong Hotel* and the class D *Chongchon Hotel* about one km from the railway station.

The train leaves P'yongyang daily at 6 am and arrives at Myohyangsan at 9 am. On the return journey, the train leaves Myohyangsan at 7 pm and arrives at P'yongyang at 10.20 pm. Breakfast is taken on the train in the foreigners-only dining car.

KAESŎNG

Kaesŏng (population 200,000) is one of the few North Korean towns where burial sites of the former kings and queens of Korea can be seen. You can see here the burial mounds along with associated statuary of King Kongmin (the 31st Koryo king who reigned between 1330 and 1374) and his queen, about 13 km from the centre of the city. It's a very secluded site and there are splendid views over the surrounding tree-covered hills from a number of vantage points. You'll need a car to get there.

In the city itself are a number of obligatory tourist sights. Included among them are the **Sonjuk Bridge**, a tiny clapper bridge built in 1216 and, opposite, the **Pyochung Stele**, similar to those at the shrines outside of Kyŏngju and elsewhere in South Korea. A short drive from town is the **Songgyungwan Confucian College** which was

originally built in 992 and rebuilt after fire in the 17th century. Today it's a museum of vases and other relics. The buildings surround a wide courtyard dotted with ancient trees.

Kaesŏng itself is a modern city of scant interest, though it does have an interesting old part consisting of traditional tile-roofed houses sandwiched between the river and the main street. There's also Nammun (South) Gate at the beginning of the main street which dates from the 14th century. From the main street, a wide driveway sweeps up to the summit of Chanamsan, where there's a massive bronze statue of – guess who?

If you stay in Kaesŏng, you'll be based at either the *Channamsan Hotel* or *Kaesŏng Minsok Hotel*. If you have a choice, definitely choose the latter, which is built in the traditional Korean yogwan style. Both hotels are rated class 'C'.

To get to Kaesŏng you can either take the train or a car, though a car is preferable if you want to see the towns en route. Driving time between P'yongyang and Kaesŏng is about 3¼ hours with a tea stop at a tourist halt built on a rocky outcrop overlooking the Sohung River along the way.

P'ANMUNJŎM

This is one of the most morbidly fascinating sights in Korea. Even if you've visited this 'Truce Village' from the South, the trip from the northern side is well worth the effort.

After viewing the Truce Village, the next stop on the agenda is the 'Wall'. According to the North, the Americans and South Koreans have built a concrete wall all the way across the peninsula (240 km) along the southern side of the DMZ. The wall is in fact an anti-tank barrier.

KŬMGANGSAN

South of Wonsan on the east coast, Kŭmgangsan (the Diamond Mountains) are the North Korean equivalent of the South's Sŏraksan and Odaesan mountains – an area of outstanding natural beauty.

Much like Sŏraksan in the South, Kŭmgangsan is divided into Inner, Outer and

Sea Kŭmgang, and the main activities here are hiking, mountaineering, boating and sightseeing. The area is peppered with former Buddhist temples and hermitages, waterfalls, mineral springs, a lake (Samil Lake) and museum. It's up to you how long you spend here and what you do, but maps of the area are provided to help you decide where you want to go.

Two of the most popular excursions are to **Kuryong Falls** and **Samil Lake**. The falls are a 15-minute drive from the hotel via Onjong-ri along an unsurfaced road through conifer forest to the *Mongran Restaurant*. The restaurant is hemmed in by steep rock faces and its balcony overlooks the waters of the river which flows down from the falls. It's a pleasant place to eat lunch. From the restaurant it's a 4.5 km walk along footpaths, over rocks and across suspension bridges to the falls.

Samil Lake is in an area of conifer forests and was once connected to the sea, and although you can see the ocean from here you're not permitted to go to the seashore at this point. Boats are available for hire at the lake, and for meals there's the *Danpung Restaurant* on the lake side.

PAEKDUSAN

The highest mountain in the whole of Korea at 2744 metres, Paekdusan (Mt Paekdu) is an old volcano sitting astride the Korean/Chinese border in the far north. It's a sacred spot to both South and North Koreans –

according to Korean mythology, this is where the Korean race began. It should be no mystery then why Kim Il-sung claimed that his son was born here, even though all sources outside North Korea maintain that Kim Jong-il was born in the Russian city of Khabarovsk. New North Korean mythology even claims that flying white horses were seen by witnesses after little Kim entered the world.

On top of the now-extinct volcano is a crater lake (Lake Chon) which is some 14 km in circumference and reaches a maximum depth of 380 metres. This makes it one of the deepest alpine lakes in the world.

Places to Stay

Hotels to stay at in this area include the *Hyesan Hotel*, in the town of the same name, the *Samjiyon Sin Hotel*, some 67 km from Hyesan, and the *Onsupyong Hotel*. The first two are 'B' class hotels whilst the latter is a 'C' class hotel.

Getting There & Away

Paekdusan is only accessible from around late June to mid-September. Access to the mountain is by air or train followed by car.

You can also visit the mountain and crater lake from the Chinese side – a trip that's now popular with South Korean tourists. Paekdusan is called Changbaishan in Chinese and the crater lake is named Tianchi (Lake of Heaven).

South Korea

Despite the nonstop efforts of the national tourist organisation, South Korea still remains very much off the beaten track. Some travellers get to the capital, Seoul, and a handful of intrepid individuals make it to Chejudo and Kyŏngju, but very few take the time to explore South Korea's numerous other attractions. This is a pity, since South Korea offers numerous opportunities for adventurous travellers. There are lovely national and provincial parks where you can hike among waterfalls, brilliant autumn leaves and craggy granite formations; beautifully crafted temples; tombs from Korea's ancient dynasties; the world's longest lava tube; one of the world's rare waterfalls that plunges directly into the sea; numerous rugged islands off the south and east coasts barely touched by foreign visitors; ski resorts and other modern sports facilities; Seoul with its bustling markets and nightlife; and the exotic (and fiery hot) cuisine.

South Korea is prosperous, clean, friendly and safe, which makes it very relaxing if you've recently been slugging it out in the backwaters of China or Mongolia. Despite the creature comforts, South Korea is significantly cheaper than Japan. Especially outside Seoul, you will find a culture that has maintained strong links with the past, striking a fine balance with the environment, thus preserving the best of South Korea for motivated travellers to discover.

Facts about the Country

HISTORY

Folk legends say that the first Korean was born in 2333 BC, but scientific research places it at around 30,000 BC, when migrating tribes from central and northern Asia arrived in the peninsula.

Constant wars with the Chinese made it necessary for an early alliance between the tribes of the northern Korean peninsula, which eventually led to the formation of the first Korean kingdom, Koguryo, around the 1st century AD. By the 3rd century AD two powerful kingdoms, Silla and Paekje, had emerged to dominate the southern half of the peninsula.

The Three Kingdoms, Silla, Paekje and Koguryo, were often at war, but in 668 AD Silla formed an alliance with the two others.

China heavily influenced Korean arts and religion, and the Koreans in turn influenced the Japanese. The unified Silla Kingdom presided over one of Korea's greatest eras of cultural development, and this is apparent in the countless tombs, temples, pagodas, palaces, pleasure gardens and other relics that dot the countryside in and around Kyŏngju, the Silla capital.

By the beginning of the 9th century, discontent, fostered by rival warlords, threatened to break the kingdom apart, and the last Silla king offered his kingdom to the ruler of Koguryo to avoid further destruction.

The capital was moved to Kaesong, north of Seoul, and the new dynasty was called Koryo. A Confucian bureaucracy became well established, and Buddhism reached new heights.

The Mongols laid waste to the country during the early 13th century, and as the Mongol Empire crumbled, the Yi Dynasty was born.

Sejong (1418-50) was one of Korea's most enlightened kings. He presided over the invention of a phonetic script (han'gŭl) for the Korean language, which led to a vast increase in literacy.

In 1592 the country was invaded by the Japanese. The Japanese conquest was an unprecedented disaster for Korea. The war dragged on for four years until Korean guerrilla resistance and Chinese intervention forced it to a conclusion. The next years saw further fighting against the Chinese, which the depleted kingdom could ill afford. Throwing in their lot with the Chinese Ming Dynasty, the Koreans were eventually invaded by the powerful Manchus. The Korean forces were disastrously defeated and severe restrictions were placed on their sovereignty.

After this series of unhappy events, Korea withdrew from the world for almost a century and became known as the 'Hermit Kingdom'. In 1905, Japan began to reoccupy Korea and formally annexed the country in 1910. For the next 35 years, Korea was harshly ruled by Japan, and Korean resentment of the Japanese remains strong to this day. When the Americans dropped the atomic bombs on Japan in 1945, most Koreans thought two bombs weren't enough.

After WW II, Korea was temporarily occupied by the Soviet Union in the north and the USA in the south. Negotiations to reunify the country floundered. Elections that were to decide the political future of all Korea were held only in the south. After the new South Korean government declared its independence, the Communists invaded the South in 1950. The Korean War dragged on for three years before a truce was called. About two million people died in the war, and the Korean nation remains divided to this day.

In the aftermath of the war, various governments were tested and rejected. South Korea was governed more or less progressively from 1961 by General Park Chung-hee, but he declared martial law in 1972 and his regime became increasingly tyrannical. This ended in 1979 when Park was assassinated by his own chief of the Korean Central Intelligence Agency.

There followed a brief period of political freedom, but in 1980 General Chun Doo-hwan declared martial law and took control of the country. In 1987, Chun announced his intention to step down from the presidency in February 1988. A former military classmate, Roh Tae-woo, was nominated to succeed him. After intense pressure from Korean citizens and the US government, it was decided that Roh should stand for election against the aspiring opposition. The two opposition leaders, Kim Dae-jung and Kim Young-sam, failed to form an alliance; they split the vote and Roh Tae-woo won the election with 37% of the total.

Korea was at the world's centre stage in 1988, when the summer Olympics were held in Seoul. Student protesters even laid low for the event to enhance the nation's image, but quickly resumed their activities after the games ended.

Despite heavy criticism of his military background, Roh Tae-woo continued the process of political liberalisation. Former opposition leader Kim Young-sam merged his party with the ruling Democratic Liberal Party in 1990. In 1992, Kim was elected president, and his regime has pursued a number of important reforms.

Like previous South Korean governments, the current regime is forced to spend heavily on the military because of constant threats from the unpredictable North. Ever the optimists, Koreans talk about 'peaceful reunification' of the divided peninsula as if it will happen next week. However, relations between the two Korea's were further eroded in 1993 with revelations of North Korea's secret nuclear weapon's programme. Negotiations on the nuclear issue started in 1994 after the death of North Korea's leader, Kim Il-sung.

GEOGRAPHY

The peninsula is divided roughly at the 38th parallel, with North Korea holding 55% of the land and the remainder going to South Korea. The dividing line is the ludicrously misnamed Demilitarised Zone (DMZ) – probably the most militarised border in the world. A favourite pastime of North Korean infiltrators is digging tunnels under the DMZ or trying to paddle around it in rubber rafts.

The Korean Peninsula borders on Manchuria and Russia in the north, and faces China across the Yellow Sea, and Japan across the East Sea (Sea of Japan) to the east and south-east. Its length from north to south is about 1000 km, while at its narrowest point

SOUTH KOREA

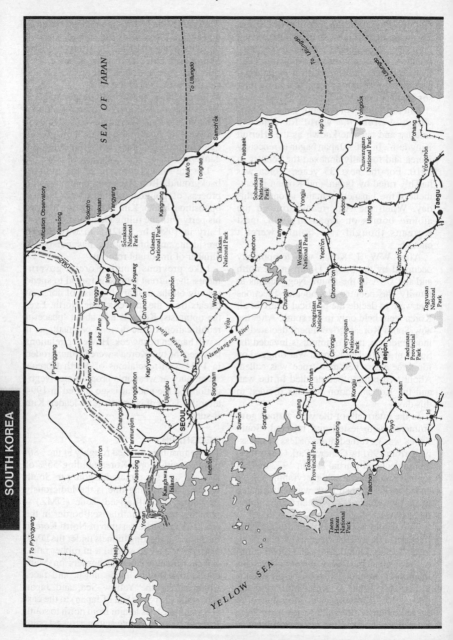

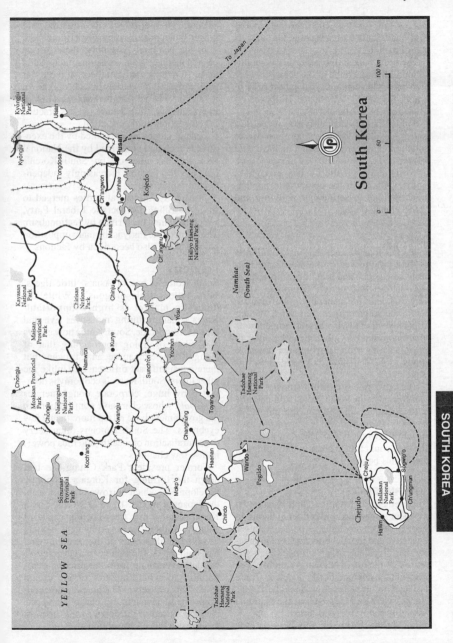

SOUTH KOREA

it is 216 km. Taken together, the land area of North and South Korea is about the same as that of the UK.

The great bulk of the peninsula is mountainous, although none of the peaks are very high by world standards. The tallest peak in South Korea is 1950-metre Hallasan on Chejudo (Cheju Island).

South Korea's early efforts at industrialisation resulted in heavy air and water pollution, but efforts to clean it up have paid off and today the country is mostly clean. Unfortunately, prosperity has brought a rapid explosion in the automobile population, resulting in serious air pollution and traffic in major cities.

CLIMATE

Korea has four distinct seasons. Autumn is the best time to visit – the forests are riotously colourful – and is at its most perfect in late October and early November. April, May and June are generally good months, before the summer monsoon rains. Winter, from November to March, sees temperatures hovering around 0°C, but it can be bitter in the mountains with temperatures down to minus 15°C. The snow, however, is picturesque.

Chejudo, off the south coast, is the warmest place in South Korea and also the wettest. Except for autumn, the climate is generally dreary and will leave you wondering why the whole island doesn't wash away. See the Seoul climate chart in the Appendix later in this book.

GOVERNMENT

Power emanates from the Blue House (the president's residence and office) in Seoul. In theory, the president shares power with the legislative and judicial branches, but in practice the president is far stronger than the entire 299-member National Assembly. The president is democratically elected. There has been no vice-president since the 1960s. The president and members of the National Assembly serve five-year terms.

The prime minister, the head of the cabinet, in theory wields considerable power, but in practice is mostly a figurehead.

In the National Assembly, there is one elected member from each constituency and up to 10 non-elected members 'at large' for each party. All the parties have been known to sell the 'at large' seats to the highest bidder as a means of raising money, but this practice is being increasingly criticised.

Federal judges are appointed by the executive branch and confirmed by the National Assembly. As time goes on, South Korea's judiciary has become increasingly independent of politicians.

In early 1990, several parties merged to form the ruling Democratic Liberal Party, which has since been riven by factionalism. The Democratic Party is the main opposition party, and has also been riven by factions.

ECONOMY

South Korea is one of Asia's 'little tigers' (also called 'little dragons'). While the domestic market is highly important, Korea's manufacturing industries live and die on foreign trade. South Korea now enjoys a standard of living approaching that of Hong Kong, Singapore and Taiwan, but there are significant differences. Unlike the other tigers, South Korea's economy is dominated by huge, corporate conglomerates (chaebol), whose charitable contributions to the government have raised more than a few eyebrows. The South Koreans often decry the centralisation of wealth (and thus power) into so few channels.

Former president Park Chung-hee laid down the formula for Korea's economic development, which borrowed heavily from the Japanese model. In other words, South Korea is *not* a true freewheeling capitalist country. Rather, the government is heavily involved in all sectors of the economy and has built up a formidable bureaucracy to regulate everything from the price of automobiles to what flavours of ice cream restaurants can serve. The bureaucratic controls extend through the chaebol and the banking system right down to the smallest enterprises. Indeed, the notion of 'Korea Inc' seems even more valid than the familiar 'Japan Inc', and as in Japan, the heavy-handed controls have proved to be a mixed blessing. Calls for reform have been resisted by the bureaucrats, but the Korean government has committed itself to follow the more liberal trading policies required by the General Agreement on Tariffs & Trade (GATT).

Rising labour costs have recently forced many South Korean companies to move manufacturing industries offshore to low-wage countries like China and Indonesia.

POPULATION & PEOPLE
The population of South Korea is 43.7 million, 25% of whom live in Seoul. The population is increasing 0.8% annually, which is one of the lowest rates of population growth in Asia.

Korea is one of the most ethnically homogeneous countries in the world. About 50,000 ethnic Chinese comprise the country's only minority group.

Over 20% of the population uses the surname 'Kim' and 15% are named 'Lee', though there are some variations in the romanised spellings. In traditional Confucian ideology, it is considered incest to marry someone with the same surname, which certainly limits marriage prospects among Koreans! Only in 1988 was the law changed to permit couples with the same surname to marry, causing a great protest from the Confucianists.

ARTS
Traditional Korean folk dances, drum dances (*sungmu*) and operas are well worth watching. There are performances at the Korean Folk Village near Suwon.

CULTURE
Koreans don't have the Japanese obsession with bowing, but a short nod or bow is considered respectful when greeting somebody or when you're departing.

Politeness is the key word to remember when dealing with Koreans. Koreans are a proud people, which basically means they have a short fuse. Avoid criticism – some polite bowing and smiling will smooth things over when you must complain about something or disagree on a topic of discussion.

If you're ever invited out for a meal or even just a drinking and dancing session with Korean friends, you'll find it difficult to pay for the bill yourself or even contribute to it. The same applies even if it's you that's doing the inviting. All manner of ruses will be used to beat you to the cashier even if it means that the person who pays is going to have to live on bread and water for the next week. The bill for a group is always paid by one person and one only. If you want to contribute then make these arrangements before you go out and square up after you leave. Never attempt to do it in front of the cashier or you will seriously embarrass your host. Indeed, by doing anything like this, you may embarrass them to such a degree that they'll never be able to return to that particular restaurant or club. If you're a man taking a woman out for the night, you pay.

RELIGION
Practicing Buddhists make up about a quarter of the total population. The majority of Buddhists also adhere to Confucianism, a conservative doctrine that permeates every aspect of the society. Shamanism is said to be largely a religion of the past, yet it still flourishes throughout the peninsula in many different guises, ranging from 'spirit posts' at the entrance to villages to strings of chillis, charcoal and pine needles over the front door of houses where a son has recently been born. Nevertheless, don't expect all Korean Buddhists to be vegetarians and ascetic – in Seoul, you may even get to see a monk eating a Big Mac at McDonald's.

Christianity has made major inroads in South Korea, and now equals Buddhism as a religious force.

LANGUAGE
The Korean language is a member of the Ural-Altaic group, which includes Mongolian, Turkish and Finnish. The spoken

language has been around for 5000 years, but it was only in the 15th century that the alphabet, known as han'gŭl, was invented. Han'gŭl is one of the most phonetic alphabets in the world and can be learned in one day, though it normally takes a few weeks to get proficient with it. However, maps, books and timetables published in South Korea are often partially or wholly in Chinese. This can be a source of frustration, but it doesn't compare with the confusion you're likely to experience initially with the chaotic romanising of the Korean language.

Officially, the McCune-Reischauer system is supported by the Korean government as the standard romanisation system, and it is used in this book. However, most Koreans have never studied this system and therefore use all kinds of mismatched transliterations. Many Koreans write their names in romanised spellings of their own fancy, so Mr Chae and Miss Choi might be brother and sister. There are also wide divergences in the spelling of place names. You might, for example, see Pusan spelled as Busan, or Poshingak as Bosingag. The thing to do is to stay on your toes and try to anticipate these discrepancies. Best of all, learn enough han'gŭl to be able to double check place names.

Korean contains several sounds not found in English so the following examples given should be considered only as close approximations. The best way to learn exact pronunciation is to listen to native speakers.

Vowels

ㅏ	a	like the 'a' in 'car'
ㅑ	ya	like the 'ya' in 'yard'
ㅓ	ŏ	like the 'o' in 'of'
ㅕ	yŏ	like the 'yo' in 'young'
ㅗ	o	like the 'o' in 'home'
ㅛ	yo	like the 'yo' in 'yoke'
ㅜ	u	like the 'u' in 'flute'
ㅠ	yu	like the word 'you'
ㅡ	ŭ	like the 'oo' in 'look'
ㅣ	i	like the 'ee' in 'beet'

Vowel Combinations

Vowels sometimes occur together in syllables but are usually pronounced separately. Thus 'oe' will sound something like the English word 'way'. On the other hand, 'ae' is a single sound.

ㅐ	ae	like the 'a' in 'hat'
ㅒ	yae	like the 'ya' in 'yam'
ㅔ	e	like the 'e' in 'ten'
ㅖ	ye	like the 'ye' in 'yes'
ㅚ	oe	like the 'wa' in 'way'
ㅟ	wi	like the word 'we'
ㅢ	ŭi	'u' plus 'i'
ㅘ	wa	like the 'wa' in 'waffle'
ㅝ	wŏ	like the 'wo' in 'won'
ㅙ	wae	like the 'wa' in 'wax'
ㅞ	we	like the 'we' in 'wet'

Consonants

Korean consonants can assume different sounds according to their position in the word. For example, the Korean letter ㄱ can sound like an English 'k' if it appears at the beginning of a word but sounds more like 'g' if it appears between vowels.

Aspirated consonants have an apostrophe after the romanised letter and should be pronounced with extra breath.

Korean Letters	Initial Position	Medial Position	Final Position
ㄱ	k	g	k
ㄴ	n	n	n
ㄷ	t	d	t
ㄹ	r	r/n	l
ㅁ	m	m	m
ㅂ	p	b	p
ㅅ	s/sh	s	t
ㅇ	ng (silent)	ng	ng
ㅈ	ch	j	t
ㅊ	ch'	ch'	t
ㅋ	k'	k'	k
ㅌ	t'	t'	t
ㅍ	p'	p'	p
ㅎ	h	h	ng

ㅅ is pronounced *sh* if followed by the vowel ㅣ + *(i)*.

Medial ㄹ is pronounced *n* when it follows ㅇ +*(ng)*.

Double Consonants

Double consonants are said with more stress than single consonants.

Korean Letters	Initial Position	Medial Position	Final Position
ㄲ	kk	gg	k
ㄸ	tt	dd	–
ㅃ	pp	bb	–
ㅆ	ss	ss	t
ㅉ	jj	jj	–

Complex Consonants

These occur only in a medial or final position in a word.

Korean Letters	Initial Position	Medial Position	Final Position
ㄱㅅ	–	ks	k
ㄴㅈ	–	nj	n
ㄴㅎ	–	nh	n
ㄹㄱ	–	lg	k
ㄹㅁ	–	lm	m
ㄹㅂ	–	lb	p
ㄹㅅ	–	ls	l
ㄹㅌ	–	lt'	l
ㄹㅍ	–	lp'	p
ㄹㅎ	–	lh	l
ㅂㅅ	–	ps	p

Greeting & Civilities

Hello.
 Annyŏng hashimnika. (formal)
 안녕하십니까
 Annyŏng haseyo. (less formal)
 안녕하세요
Goodbye. (to person leaving)
 Annyŏnghi kaseyo.
 안녕히가세요
Goodbye. (to person staying)
 Annyŏnghi kyeseyo.
 안녕히계세요
Please.
 Put'ak hamnida.
 부탁합니다
Thank you.
 Kamsa hamnida.
 감사합니다

Yes.
 Ye/ne.
 예 / 네
No.
 Anyo.
 아니요
Excuse me.
 Shillye hamnida.
 실례합니다

Getting Around

I want to go to...
 ...e kago shipsŭmnida.
 …에 가고싶습니다
What time does it leave?
 Myŏtshi e ch'ulbal hamnigga?
 몇시에 출발합니까?
What time does it arrive?
 Myŏtshi e toch'ak hamnigga?
 몇시에 도착합니까?
Does this train stop at...?
 I yŏlchanŭn...e sŏmnigga?
 이 열차는 …에 섭니까?
Where can I catch the bus to...?
 ...haeng bŏsŭnŭn ŏti e sŏ tapnigga?
 …행 버스는 어디에서 탑니까?
I want to get off here.
 Yŏgiyae naeryŏ chuseyo.
 여기에 내려 주세요

airport
 konghang
 공항
Asiana Airlines ticket office
 ashiana hangkong mepyoso
 아시아나항공 매표소
Korean Air ticket office
 taehan hangkong mepyoso
 대한항공 매표소
bus
 bŏsŭ
 버스
airport bus
 konghang bŏsŭ
 공항버스
taxi
 t'aekshi
 택시

long-distance (bullet) taxi
ch'ong'al t'aekshi
총알택시

train
kich'a
기차

1st-class train
saemaul ho
새마을호

2nd-class train
mugunghwa ho
무궁화호

3rd-class train
tong'il ho
통일호

4th-class train
pidulgi ho
비둘기호

boat
pae
배

bus stop
bŏsŭ chŏngnyujang
버스 정류장

express bus terminal
kosok bŏsŭ t'ŏminŏl
고속버스터미널

ferry pier
pudutga
부둣가

inter-city bus terminal
shi'oe bŏsŭ t'ŏminŏl
시외버스터미널

lockers
lakk'a
락카

lost & found office
punshilmulpo kwansaenta
분실물보관센타

luggage-storage room
mulpumbo gwanch'anggo
물품보관창고

one-way (ticket)
p'yŏndo
편도

open/closed
yŏngŏpchung/hyuil
영업중 / 휴일

railway station
kich'a yok
기차역

refund a ticket
hwanbul
환불

return (ticket)
wangbok
왕복

ticket
p'yo
표

ticket office
maep'yoso
매표소

Around Town
Where is the...?
...ŭn ŏdi'imnigga?
...은 어디입니까?

bank
ŭnhaeng
은행

Bank of Korea
hanguk ŭnhaeng
한국은행

Chohung Bank
chohŭng ŭnhaeng
조흥은행

Hanil Bank
hanil ŭnhaeng
한일은행

Korea Exchange Bank
oehwan ŭnhaeng
외환은행

Korea First Bank
cheil ŭnhaeng
제일은행

immigration office
chul'ibkuk kwali so
출입국관리소

private language school
hagwon
학원

tourist information office
kwangwang annaeso
관광안내소

Map Reading

beach
  hesuyokjang
  해수욕장

big (great)
  dae
  대

cave
  donggul
  동굴

city
  shi
  시

county
  do
  도

east
  tong
  동

fortress
  sŏng
  성

gate
  mun
  문

hall
  jong
  정

hermitage
  am
  암

hot springs
  wonch'ŏn
  온천

island
  do
  도

lake
  ho
  호

mountain
  san
  산

north
  puk
  북

park
  kongwon
  공원

pavilion
  gak
  각

province
  do
  도

river
  gang
  강

road
  no, ro
  로

sea
  hae
  해

section
  ga
  가

shrine
  myo, tae
  묘, 대

south
  nam
  남

street
  gil
  길

temple
  sa
  사

tomb
  nŭng, rŭng
  릉

township
  myŏn, ŭp
  면, 읍

village
  ri
  리

west
  sŏ
  서

waterfall
  p'okp'o
  폭포

Accommodation

campground
  yayŏngji
  야영지

home stay
minbak
민박

cheap hotel
yŏgwan
여관

cheapest hotel
yŏinsuk
여인숙

hotel
hot'el
호텔

youth hostel
yusu hosutel
유스호스텔

What is the address?
Chuso ga ŏdi imnigga?
주소가 어디입니까?

Please write it down.
Ssŏ chuseyo.
써주세요

single room
singgul lum
싱글룸

double room
tobul lum
더블룸

with shared bath
yokshil omnun pang chuseyo
욕실 없는 방 주세요

with private bath
yokshil innun pang chuseyo
욕실 있는 방 주세요

May I see the room?
Pang'ŭl polsu issŏyo?
방을 볼 수 있어요?

Do you have anything cheaper?
Tŏ ssan kot sun ŏpsŭmnigga?
더 싼 것은 없습니까?

Can you have my clothes washed?
Setak ssobisŭ taemnikka?
세탁 써비스 됩니까?

bathhouse
mo gyok tang
목욕탕

hotel name card
myongham
명함

towel
sugŏn
수건

Post & Telecommunications

aerogramme
hanggong sŏ gan
항공서간

International Express Mail (EMS)
kokje t'ŭkgŭ pop'yŏn
국제특급우편

post office
uch'eguk
우체국

stamp
u'pyo
우표

telephone card
chŏnhwa kadŭ
전화카드

telephone office
chŏnhwa kuk
전화국

Necessities

anti-diarrheal drug
susa yak
설사약

condoms
kondom
콘돔

laxative
pyunbi yak
변비약

pain killer/Tylenol
chintongche/tailenol
진통제 / 타이레놀

pharmacy (medicine)
yak
약

sanitary pads
saengnidae
생리대

tampons
tempo
템포

toilet
hwajangshil
화장실

toilet paper
hwajangji
화장지

Money

May I have change please?
Chandonŭro pakkwŏ chuseyo?
잔돈으로 바꿔 주세요
How much does it cost?
Ŏlmayeyo?
얼마예요?
Too expensive.
Nŏmu pissayo.
너무 비싸요
Can I have a discount?
Chom ssage hae juseyo?
좀 씨게 해 주세요

Time

When?
Ŏnje imnigga?
언제 입니까?
today
onŭl
오늘
tomorrow
naeil
내일
in the morning
ochŏne
오전에
in the afternoon
ohu'e
오후에

Numbers

Korean has two counting systems. One is of Chinese origin and the other a native Korean system. Korean numbers only go up to 99 and are used to count days, minutes and mileage (as long as the total doesn't exceed 99). The Chinese system is used to count money, not surprising since the smallest Korean banknote is W1000.

Number	Chinese		Korean	
0			*yŏng*	영
1	*il*	일	*hana*	하나
2	*i*	이	*tul*	둘
3	*sam*	삼	*set*	셋
4	*sa*	사	*net*	넷
5	*o*	오	*tasŏt*	다섯
6	*yuk*	육	*yŏsŏt*	여섯
7	*ch'il*	칠	*ilgop*	일곱
8	*p'al*	팔	*yŏdŏ*	여덟
9	*ku*	구	*ahop*	아홉
10	*ship*	십	*yŏ*	열

Number	Combination	
11	*ship'il*	십일
20	*i'ship*	이십
30	*sam'ip*	삼십
40	*sa'ip*	사십
48	*sa'shippal*	사십팔
50	*o'ship*	오십
100	*paek*	백
200	*i'paek*	이백
300	*sampaek*	삼백
846	*p'alpaek saship'yuk*	팔백사십육
1000	*ch'ŏn*	천
2000	*i'ch'ŏn*	이천
10,000	*man*	만

Emergencies

Help!
Saram sallyŏ!
사람살려!
Thief!
Todduk iya!
도둑이야!
Fire!
Pul'iya!
불이야!
Call a doctor!
Ŭisarul pulŏ chuseyo!
의사를 불러 주세요!
Call the police!
Kyŏngch'alŭl pulŏ chuseyo!
경찰을 불러주세요!
hospital
pyŏngwon
병원
I'm allergic to penicillin.
Penishillin allerugiga issŏyo.
페니실린 알레르기가 있어요
I'm allergic to antibiotics.
Hangsaengche allerugiga issŏyo.
항생제 알레르기가 있어요

SOUTH KOREA

I'm diabetic.
Tangnyopyŏngi issŏyo.
당뇨병이 있어요

Facts for the Visitor

VISAS & EMBASSIES

With an onward ticket, visitors from almost anywhere, except the Philippines, eastern Europe and countries with governments not recognised by South Korea (eg, Cuba, Laos and Cambodia), will be granted a stay of up to 15 days without a visa, but this is *not* extendable. In addition, South Korea grants visa exemptions to nationals of any west European nation except Ireland. If you fall into this category you'll be given a 90-day or three-month permit; 60 days in the cases of Italy and Portugal.

Nationals of all other countries, including Australia, Canada, New Zealand and the USA, require visas for stays over 15 days. Tourist visas are usually issued for a stay of 90 days. If you apply for a visa in your own country, you might get a multiple-entry visa – you usually *cannot* get this if you apply at a South Korean embassy in a nearby Asian country. Onward tickets and/or proof of 'adequate funds' are not normally required.

Many South Korean embassies are notoriously slow when it comes to processing visa applications. Figure on three working days no matter what the staff tell you over the telephone.

South Korean Embassies

Visas and information can be obtained at the following South Korean embassies overseas:

Australia
    113 Empire Circuit, Yarralumla, Canberra ACT 2600 (☎ 06-273 3044)
    Sydney Consulate (☎ 02-221 3866)
Austria
    Prater Str 31, 1020 Vienna (☎ 0222-216 3441)
Belgium
    Avenue Hamoir 3, 1180 Bruxelles (☎ 02-375.39.80)

Canada
    151 Slater St, 5th floor, Ottawa, Ontario K1P 5H3 (☎ 613-232 1715)
    Toronto Consulate (☎ 416-920 3809)
    Vancouver Consulate (☎ 6049-681 9581/2)
China
    China World Trade Centre, 1 Jianguomenwai Dajie, Beijing (☎ 505 2608)
    Shanghai Consulate (☎ 021-219 6917)
Denmark
    Svanemollevej 104, 2900 Hellerup (☎ 45-39 401233)
France
    125 Rue De Grenelle, 75007 Paris (☎ 01-47.75.01.01)
Germany
    Adenauerallee 124, 5300 Bonn 1 (☎ 0228-267960)
    Berlin Consulate (☎ 30-885 9550)
    Frankfurt Consulate (☎ 069-563051/3)
Greece
    1 Eratosthenous Str, 6th floor, GR-116 35, Athens (☎ 01-701 2122)
Hong Kong
    5th floor, Far East Finance Centre, 16 Harcourt Rd, Central (☎ 529 4141)
Indonesia
    57 Jalan Gatot Subroto, Jakarta (☎ 520 1915)
Ireland
    20 Clyde Rd, Ballsbridge, Dublin 4 (☎ 01-608800)
Japan
    205 Minami-Azabu, 1-Chome, Minato-Ku, Tokyo 106 (☎ 03-3452 7611/8)
    Fukuoka Consulate (☎ 092-771 0461)
    Kōbe Consulate (☎ 078-221 4853/5)
    Nagoya Consulate (☎ 052-935 4221)
    Naha, Okinawa Consulate (☎ 0988-676940/1)
    Niigata Consulate (☎ 025-230 3400)
    Osaka Consulate (☎ 06-213 1401)
    Sapporo Consulate (☎ 011-621 0288/9)
    Sendai Consulate (☎ 022-221 2751)
    Shimonoseki Consulate (☎ 0832-665341/4)
    Yokohama Consulate (☎ 045-621 4531)
Malaysia
    22nd floor, Wisma Mca No 163, Jalan Ampang 50450, Kuala Lumpur (☎ 03-262 2377)
Mongolia
    Baga Toyruu St 37, Ulaanbaatar (☎ 23541)
New Zealand
    Level 6, Digital House, 86 Victoria St, 6th Elders, Wellington (☎ 04-473 9073/4)
Netherlands
    Verlengde Tolweg 8, 2517 JV, The Hague (☎ 070-352 0621)
Norway
    Inkognitogaten 3, 0224, Oslo 2 (☎ 02-2255 2018/9)
Philippines
    Alpap 1 building, 140 Alfaro St, Salcedo Village, Makati, Manila (☎ 02-817 5827)

Poland
   I Krasickiego 25, 02-611, Warsaw (☎ 483337)
Portugal
   Av Miguel Bombarda, 36-7 1000, Lisbon (☎ 01-793 7200/3)
Russia
   Ul Alexeya, Tolstova 14, Moscow (☎ 203 3850)
   Vladivostok Consulate (☎ 4332-227729)
Singapore
   101 Thomson Rd, United Square, 10-02/04, 13-05, Singapore 1130 (☎ 256-1188)
Spain
   Miguel Angel 23, 28010, Madrid (☎ 310 0053)
Sri Lanka
   98 Dharmapala Mawatha, Colombo 7 (☎ 01-699036)
Sweden
   Sveavagen 90, Stockholm (☎ 08-160 480)
Switzerland
   Kacheggweg 38, 3006 Bern (☎ 031-431 081)
Thailand
   23 Thirmruammit Rd, Ratchadpisek, Huay Kwang, Bangkok 10310 (☎ 02-247 7537)
UK
   4 Palace Gate, London W8 5NF (☎ 0171-581 0247)
USA
   2450 Massachusetts Ave, NW, Washington DC (☎ 202-939 5600)
   Guam Consulate (☎ 671-472 6488)
   Anchorage Consulate (☎ 907-561 5488)
   Atlanta Consulate (☎ 404-522 1611/3)
   Boston Consulate (☎ 617-348 3660)
   Chicago Consulate (☎ 312-822 9485/8)
   Honolulu Consulate (☎ 808-595 6109)
   Houston Consulate (☎ 713-961 0186)
   Los Angeles Consulate (☎ 213-385 9300)
   Miami Consulate (☎ 305-372 1555)
   New York Consulate (☎ 212-752 1700)
   San Francisco Consulate (☎ 415-921 2251)
   Seattle Consulate (☎ 206-441 1011)
Vietnam
   3rd floor, Boss Hotel, 60-62 Nguyen Du St, Hanoi (☎ 04-269160)

Visa Extensions

As a general rule, tourist visas cannot be extended. About the only exceptions are for emergencies, such as accidents or illness, cancelled flights, loss of a passport etc. You are supposed to apply for this extension at least one day before the visa expires, and overstaying your visa can result in a stiff fine.

Working visas are valid for one year and are extendable for a further year. For a second extension you will need to leave the country for about two weeks.

Re-Entry Visas

If you don't want to forfeit your working visa you should apply for a multiple re-entry visa before making any trips out of the country. This must be done at the immigration office of whichever county you happen to be living in.

DOCUMENTS
Resident Certificate

If you are working or studying in South Korea on a long-term visa it is necessary to apply for a residence certificate within 90 days of arrival. This must be done at the immigration office for your county of residence, which is not necessarily the closest immigration office to where you live.

CUSTOMS

For visiting foreigners, customs are very easy. It is required that you declare foreign currency worth over US$10,000 (and this includes travellers' cheques). By not doing so you could risk having the balance confiscated when you try to leave with it.

There is a duty-free allowance of 200 cigarettes (or 50 cigars), 60 grams of perfume and one bottle of spirits (not exceeding a total of one litre). It's prohibited to bring in two-way radios (walkie-talkies) or any literature, cassette tapes or motion pictures that are deemed 'subversive to national security or harmful to public interests'. You can leave any prohibited items in bonded baggage for about US$2 per day.

MONEY
Currency

The US dollar is the most acceptable foreign currency, but you won't have trouble exchanging other major currencies. The South Korean unit of currency is the won (W) with coins of W1, W5, W10, W50, W100 and W500. The W1 coins are rarely seen outside banks. Notes come in denominations of W1000, W5000 and W10,000.

Up to US$500 can be reconverted into

hard currency on departure without exchange receipts, but if you save your receipts you can reconvert within 90 days.

Exchange Rates

Australia	A$1	=	W599
Canada	C$1	=	W603
China	Y1	=	W95
France	Ffr1	=	W144
Germany	DM1	=	W495
Hong Kong	HK$1	=	W107
Japan	¥1	=	W7.98
New Zealand	NZ$1	=	W483
Singapore	S$1	=	W533
Switzerland	Sfr1	=	W600
Taiwan	NT$1	=	W31
UK	UK£1	=	W1236
USA	US$1	=	W830

Costs

It's possible to live on as little as US$20 a day if you stay in the cheapest hotels and don't do much shopping or travelling around. Korea is much more pleasant if you have about US$30 to US$40 a day to spend.

To save money on haircuts, men should go to a women's beauty shop – barbershops do manicures and massage, and some are fronts for prostitution. A haircut costs around W3000 in a beauty shop while a barbershop charges about W10,000.

Tipping

South Korea is one of those marvellous countries where tipping isn't necessary or expected. A 10% service charge is added to the bill at tourist hotels so tipping isn't required there either.

Bargaining

There is some latitude for bargaining in cheaper hotels, in street markets and with taxi drivers. Remember that Koreans are very proud people, and they get hot under the collar fast if they think you're looking down at them. Bargaining should be polite and done with a smile.

Consumer Taxes

Most items purchased in South Korea are subject to a 10% Value Added Tax (VAT) which is included in the selling price. At upmarket hotels, there is also a 10% VAT, but you escape this at the bottom-end hotels.

WHEN TO GO

The best times to visit Korea are April, May and June before the monsoon, and September, October and early November after the rains. Summer not only suffers from hot and rainy weather, but also massive crowds of domestic tourists at all scenic spots.

WHAT TO BRING

As a general rule, things made in Korea are cheap, while imported goods can be difficult to find or ridiculously expensive. This includes certain pharmaceutical items such as dental floss, mosquito repellent, sunblock (UV) lotion, shaving cream, deodorant and imported vitamins or medicines. If you run out of deodorant, try looking in big tourist hotels like the Lotte Hotel Pharmacy in Seoul. Tampons *(tempo)* are generally available from supermarkets and some pharmacies. It's totally impossible to buy an electric immersion heater for making hot water in a teacup.

TOURIST OFFICES
Local Tourist Offices

The Korean National Tourism Corporation (KNTC) produces an extensive range of well-illustrated booklets and maps. You can pick them up at the three international airports: Kimp'o Airport (☎ 02-665 0088) near Seoul; Kimhae Airport (☎ 051-973100) at Pusan; and Cheju Airport (☎ 064-420032).

Almost every city has a tourist information office in the city hall. In large cities these offices have English-speaking staff and are well-equipped with maps, but in remote places the staff might only speak Korean and have scant literature to offer you. Not surprisingly, Seoul has the biggest and best of these information offices, with Pusan in second place.

In some large cities, there are also information booths with English speakers in crucial spots such as tourist sites and some railway or bus stations. Again, these information booths are concentrated in Seoul, but can be found elsewhere – the one in Kyŏngju may be particularly useful.

KNTC Overseas Tourist Offices

Overseas offices of the KNTC include:

Australia
17th floor, Tower Building, Australia Square, George St, Sydney 2000 (☎ 02-252 4147; fax 251 2104)
Canada
Suite 406, 480 University Ave, Toronto, Ontario M5G 1V2 (☎ 416-348 9056; fax 348 9058)
France
Tour Maine Montparnesse, 33 Avenue de Maine, Paris (☎ 01-45.38.71. 23; fax 45.38.74.71)
Germany
Mainzer Land Strasse 71, 60329 Frankfurt am Main 1 (☎ 069-233226; fax 253519)
Hong Kong
Suite 3203, 32nd floor, Citibank Tower, 3 Garden Rd, Central (☎ 523 8065; fax 845 0765)
Japan
Room 124, Sanshin building, 4-1 1-chome, Yuraku-cho, Chiyoda-ku, Tokyo (☎ 03-3580 3941; fax 3591 4601). There are branch offices in Fukuoka (☎ 092-471 7174), Osaka (☎ 06-266 0847) and Sapporo (☎ 011-210 8081).
Singapore
24 Raffles Place, 20-03 Clifford Centre, Singapore 0104 (☎ 533 0441; fax 845 0765)
Switzerland
PO Box 343, CH-8126, Zumikon (☎ 01-918 0882)
Taiwan
Room 1813, International Trade Centre Building, 333 Keelung Rd, Section 1, Taipei (☎ 02-720 8049; fax 757 6514)
Thailand
15th floor, Silom Complex, 191 Silom Rd, Bangkok 10500 (☎ 231 3895; fax 231 3897)
UK
2nd floor, Vogue House, 1 Hanover Square, London W1R 9RD (☎ 0171-409 2100; fax 491 2302)
USA
3435 Wilshire Blvd, suite 350, Los Angeles, CA 90010 (☎ 213-382 3435; fax 480 0483)
205 North Michigan Ave, suite 2212, Chicago, IL 60601 (☎ 312-819 2560; fax 819 2563)
2 Executive Drive, 7th floor, Fort Lee, NJ 07024 (☎ 201-585 0909; fax 585-9041)

USEFUL ORGANISATIONS

If you have problems with transport, food, shopping or accommodation, there is a KNTC Tourist Complaint Centre (☎ 02-735 0101) at 10 Ta-dong, Chung-gu, Seoul 100-180. For complaints about taxis and other transport, you can also try the Transportation Complaint Centre (☎ 02-392 4745), 122 Pongnae-dong 2-ga, Chung-gu, Seoul 100-162.

Outside Seoul, the provincial governments have offices to assist travellers experiencing difficulties: Taegu (☎ 053-422 5611); Ch'ŏngju (☎ 0431-520202); and in all other cities, dial the area code followed by 0101.

BUSINESS HOURS & HOLIDAYS

For most government offices, business hours are from 9 am to 6 pm Monday to Friday, and until 1 pm on Saturday. From November to February, government offices close at 5 pm.

Private businesses normally operate from 8.30 am until 7 pm on weekdays, and until 2 pm on Saturday. Department stores are open from 10.30 am to 7.30 pm daily, while small shops may stay open from dawn until late at night.

Banking hours are from 9.30 am to 4.30 pm weekdays, and until 1.30 pm on Saturday.

There are two types of public holidays – those that go according to the solar calendar and those that follow the lunar calendar. Solar holidays include: New Year's Day, 1 & 2 January; Independence Movement Day, 1 March; Arbour Day, 5 April; Children's Day, 5 May; Memorial Day, 6 June; Constitution Day, 17 July; Liberation Day, 15 August; Armed Forces Day, 1 October; National Foundation Day, 3 October; and Christmas, 25 December.

Lunar holidays will of course fall on different solar calendar dates every year. The Lunar New Year, 1st day of the 1st moon, falls somewhere between mid-January and late February; see the introductory Facts for the Visitor chapter earlier in this book for dates. Buddha's Birthday (Feast of the Lanterns) is the 8th day of the 4th moon. The Harvest Moon Festival (Chusŏk) is the 15th day of the 8th moon.

SOUTH KOREA

CULTURAL EVENTS

A fascinating ceremony called Sŏkchŏnje is held twice a year according to the lunar calendar (1st day of the 2nd moon, and 1st day of the 8th moon). The ceremony is held in the courtyard of the Confucius Shrine at Sungkyunkwan University in the north of Seoul. The nearest subway stop is Hyehwa.

If you're in Seoul on Buddha's Birthday, there is an evening lantern parade from Yŏŭido Plaza to Chogyesa Temple, starting around 6.30 pm. On the same evening, there is a similar lantern parade at Popchusa Temple in Songnisan National Park in the central part of the country.

The Tano Festival is held throughout South Korea on the 5th day of the 5th lunar month (around June). The festival features processions of Shamans and mask dance dramas.

There is a week-long cherry blossom festival held in the southern city of Chinhae, which usually occurs in the first half of April.

POST & TELECOMMUNICATIONS
Postal Rates

Domestic rates are W110 for up to 50 grams and postcards cost W80. International rates vary according to region. The Korean postal service divides the world into four zones: Zone 1 is Japan, Taiwan, Hong Kong and Macau; Zone 2 is China and South-East Asia; Zone 3 is Australia, New Zealand, the USA, the Middle East and Western Europe; and Zone 4 is Latin America, Africa, Eastern Europe and the Pacific Islands. (See the Postal Rates table below.)

Sending Mail

Post offices are open from 9 am to 6 pm Monday to Friday (until 5 pm during winter) and until noon on Saturday. Public mail boxes are always coloured red. Domestic mail can be delivered in about two days if it bears an address in Korean characters – if written in English, figure on it taking a week.

Receiving Mail

Poste restante is available at all main city post offices, but only in Seoul and Pusan will you find a counter exclusively for poste restante. Elsewhere such letters may go astray because few postal workers speak English.

Telephone

There is a 30% discount on calls made from 9 pm to 8 am daily, and for 24 hours on Sunday and public holidays.

Pay phones accept three types of coins, W10, W50 and W100 (but *not* W500). Pay phones can be used for local and long-distance calls, and there is no time limit as long as you keep feeding money into the machine. The cost for local calls is W30 for three minutes. The machines do not give change, but you can make a follow-on call by pressing the green button on the phone and dialling.

There are also card telephones, and these can be used for local, long-distance and international calls. The telephone cards (*chŏnhwa kadŭ*) come in denominations of W3000, W5000 and W10,000, but you get a discount and only have to pay W2900,

Postal Rates

	Zone 1	Zone 2	Zone 3	Zone 4
aerograms	W350	W350	W350	W350
postcards	W300	W300	W300	W300
letters (10 grams)	W370	W400	W440	W470
letters (20 grams)	W400	W460	W540	W600
registered letter (10 grams)	W1170	W1200	W1240	W1270
printed matter (20 grams)	W200	W220	W250	W300

W4800 and W9500 respectively. The cards can be bought from banks, shops and convenience stores near the card telephones. It's wise to buy the cheapest denomination (W3000) because the cards tend to become defective quickly, though you get a larger discount on the big denominations. You can return defective cards to the phone company for credit, but this is a hassle best avoided.

To dial an international call direct, first dial 001, then the country code, area code (minus the initial zero if it has one) and then the number you want to reach. You can place an international reverse charge call with an operator by dialling 007.

The country code for dialling South Korea is 82.

Fax, Telex & Telegraph

Every major city has a main telephone office, usually near the Central Post Office (CPO). From these offices you can make international calls and send fax messages, telexes and telegrams. Telegrams are of two types: ordinary (ORD) which take 12 hours, and letters and telegrams (LT) which take 24 hours.

TIME

The time in South Korea is GMT/UTC plus nine hours. When it is noon in South Korea it is 2 pm in Sydney, 3 am in London, 10 pm the previous day in New York and 7 pm the previous day in Los Angeles or San Francisco.

LAUNDRY

Most hotels, including cheap ones, can do laundry if you prefer not to do it yourself. Charges for this service are usually reasonable.

WEIGHTS & MEASURES

South Korea uses the international metric system.

ELECTRICITY

Both 110 V and 220 V are in common use. The way to tell the difference is from the design of the electrical outlets: two flat pins is 110 V and two round pins is 220 V. There is no third wire for earth (ground).

BOOKS & MAPS

Discovering Seoul by Donald Clark & James Grayson is available from the Royal Asiatic Society in Seoul and covers everything you ever wanted to know about this city. *Living in Korea* by the American Chamber of Commerce is, as the title implies, geared for those who plan to live here.

Those interested in South Korea's economy should pick up a copy of *The Chaebol* by Steers, Shin & Ungson (Harper & Row, New York, 1989)

Lonely Planet publishes the following comprehensive guides, *Korea – a travel survival kit*, *Seoul City Guide* and the pocket-sized *Korean Phrasebook*.

For detailed hiking maps, the largest collection is available at the Chung-ang Atlas Map Service (☎ 02-720 9191/3) at 125-1 Gongpyŏng-dong, Chongno-gu, Seoul. Bookshops sell excellent atlases covering the whole country in detail. Maps of specific cities are also available from the city halls throughout the country.

MEDIA

Newspapers & Magazines

There are two English-language newspapers published in South Korea, the *Korea Times* and *Korea Herald*. These papers are printed daily except Monday.

You'd probably enjoy the newspapers more if you could read Korean – in them you'll find xenophobic diatribes against foreigners committing heinous crimes against the Korean people, like trying to force open South Korea's closed markets.

Some local monthly magazines include the *Korea Economic Report*, *Korea Post* and *Business Korea*. Large bookshops and hotel gift shops in Seoul and Pusan sell imported publications such as the *International Herald Tribune*, the *Asian Wall Street Journal*, *Time*, *Newsweek* and the *Economist*.

SOUTH KOREA

Radio & TV

There are four Korean-language TV networks: KBS, MBC, SBS and EBS. A few programmes are bilingual, but a special TV is needed to switch between Korean and English. AFKN is an English-language station run by the US military and features typical US shows, but without commercial advertising. However, you do have to listen to some military advertisements and safety tips like 'Study the Uniform Code of Military Justice' and 'Driving and alcohol don't mix'.

AFKN radio broadcasts in English on AM (549 kHz) and FM (102.7 mHz). A complete schedule of TV and radio programmes is listed in the daily English-language newspapers.

FILM & PHOTOGRAPHY

Fuji and Kodak film are readily available, along with some Korean brands. Slide film is harder to find – look for it in big cities. Kodachrome is not available nor can it be processed in South Korea. Photo processing facilities are of a high standard and the cost of processing is moderate.

Cameras and camera accessories are mostly imported and absurdly expensive in South Korea. Korean-made cameras are also not particularly cheap unless you buy them outside South Korea.

. During winter, the traditional Korean form of underfloor heating can cook your film if you leave your camera or bags on the floor.

Photography is prohibited around military installations. Monks usually do not like their photographs taken, and it is wise to respect their wishes. Student rioters are not particularly fond of being photographed either.

HEALTH

South Korea is a very safe country to travel in as far as health goes and you are unlikely to encounter any of the things that might have you running for the nearest pharmacy in Thailand, the Philippines or Indonesia.

Most South Koreans drink water straight from the tap without boiling it. If you have

some trouble with travellers' diarrhoea, you might consider boiling the water until your body adjusts to the local microbes, but there is little chance of contracting dysentery or other serious intestinal infections.

Korea has two systems of medicine: Western and traditional. The traditional system, known as *hanyak*, is based on Chinese herbal remedies and acupuncture.

Emergency medical care in hospitals is excellent and reasonably cheap, but normal outpatient care leaves much to be desired. Westerners are liable to become very frustrated with Korean doctors because most will not answer questions from patients regarding illness, laboratory tests or the treatment being given. Questions are regarded as insults to the doctor's competence, thus causing a loss of face. Doctors who have studied and worked abroad may be more used to Western ways.

WOMEN TRAVELLERS

Confucius could be regarded as the world's most celebrated male chauvinist, and South Korea is still a Confucian society, though things are now changing. By watching South Korean-made movies, it's easy to get the impression that rape and wife beating are national sports. As for foreign women, the chance of being physically attacked is small, but sexual harassment can be a problem. There are more than a few drunken men wandering around Seoul at night and they can be obnoxious. Groping on crowded buses and trains is not uncommon – South Korean women sometimes carry sharp pins to fend off unwelcome probing hands. Wearing miniskirts or shorts will invite stares and rude comments.

DANGERS & ANNOYANCES

South Korea is one of the safest countries in Asia, but there are problems. South Korea has very strict gun control laws, and almost no drug addicts, both of these factors undoubtedly keep crime rates down. Unfortunately, South Korea is no longer the crime-free country it once was. In Seoul, burglaries have become common while muggings and rapes are on the rise. It's still much safer than cities like Manila or New York, but you should keep your valuables secure. The back alleys of It'aewon should be avoided late at night, but you can walk major streets after dark without fear. However, pickpockets may be encountered in any crowded area.

Student rioting is a seasonal sport most common in late spring or early summer. Although fatalities are rare, injuries are common. It's best to avoid riots unless your idea of a good time is getting clubbed or tear-gassed (by police), or firebombed (by students) or stoned (with rocks).

In winter, Koreans use a form of heating known as *ondol* in which the floor is heated, turning into a giant radiator. In traditionally constructed houses, coal is burned in an oven right under the floor and there is a danger of carbon monoxide poisoning if the floor develops any cracks. Concrete floors are usually safe, but older buildings usually have a floor made of stone or clay with a wood surface, and these are prone to leaking carbon monoxide. Modern houses use a safer system – hot water is pumped through pipes in the floor. In the older buildings, it would be prudent to leave a window partially open at night.

Air-raid drills are held once a month at unannounced times – when you hear the sirens you must get off the streets and keep away from doors and windows. If you're on a bus during an air raid, the bus will stop and you'll have to get off and seek shelter. After the all-clear signal is given, you are permitted to get back on the bus again without paying an additional fare; some people take advantage of this to get a free ride.

Because of the threat of North Korean infiltrators, there is a dusk-to-dawn curfew applying to most beaches.

WORK

Employment is not permitted on a transit or tourist visa and the immigration authorities have become very strict. There are now stiff fines and deportations of travellers working illegally, and those who can't pay the fine are usually imprisoned.

It is still possible to get a job teaching English and other European languages, but to do it legally you must first line up the job, then leave South Korea and apply for the work visa while outside the country. Most travellers do this from Japan or Taiwan. If a work visa is issued, it is only valid for one job only – if you want to change jobs, you must first get another work visa. You are not permitted to work a second job on the same visa without government approval. When your employment contract ends, or if you quit or get fired, you must leave the country within three days. Check with the immigration authorities in Seoul for the latest requirements. Documentation is needed, usually in the form of a formal letter of invitation for employment. Don't sign any contracts until *after* you receive the work visa.

Many travellers have complained of 'misunderstandings' (outright cheating) on wages, so be sure to get everything written down airtight. More and more schools are requiring academic credentials. Many private schools now want a bachelor's degree and university teaching positions usually require a master's degree.

One unusual method of fund raising is to turn in a North Korean spy – the government pays from W1,000,000 to W5,000,000 for each one you report. The telephone number for the spy hotline is ☎ 113.

ACTIVITIES
Courses

It is very important that you obtain a student visa *before* enrolling in any kind of course – the schools will not tell you this! Even if you already have a work visa, you cannot legally enrol in a school without first getting a student visa. The fine for breaking this rule is at least W100,000.

Hiking

Every province of Korea offers outstanding opportunities for hiking. Indeed, you'll find

SOUTH KOREA

many challenging walking and climbing areas right in the suburban areas of Seoul.

Mountain Biking

The Korean Mountain Biking Association – KMTBA (☎ 02-967 9287) is a friendly organisation based in Seoul that arranges outings. If you don't already have a mountain bike, the KMTBA can direct you to a shop that rents bikes. This organisation is very 'foreigner friendly', though you might want to have a Korean ring up to avoid any language problems.

Skating

Both roller skating and ice skating are popular pastimes. A few large cities have good indoor ice-skating rinks, but in most other areas skating is outdoors and therefore strictly a winter sport.

Skiing

Although Korea's mountains don't compare with the Swiss Alps, there are some good places where you can practise the art of sliding downhill. The ski season is from about early December to mid-March. Facilities include hotels, artificial snow and equipment hire. These places can be crowded at weekends, so get there early if you need to hire equipment. Since ski resorts are on remote mountaintops, some of them don't have a regular bus service, but numerous travel agencies run tour buses up to these places as part of a package tour. Otherwise, hire a taxi for the last leg of the journey, or hitchhike.

The United Service Organisation, commonly known as the USO (☎ 02-792 3028/3063), runs inexpensive weekend ski trips to Bear's Town, Alps and Yongpyŏng resorts. It also sells tickets for the daily shuttle bus to Bear's Town and Yongpyŏng. For a higher price, Korea Travel Bureau – KTB (☎ 02-778 0150) organises day trips to the Bear's Town resort, which includes transport from Seoul, equipment, lift tickets and lunch. KTB is on the 3rd floor of the Lotte Hotel.

All ski resorts have a representative office in Seoul that you can call for information. The seven resorts are as follows:

Yongpyŏng (Dragon Valley), 16 slopes, just south of Odaesan National Park on the east coast about 3½ hours from Seoul. This is South Korea's premier resort – the slopes are equipped with lighting for night skiing. There is a youth hostel here that charges W5500 for a dormitory bed, while double rooms cost W66,000 (☎ 02-548 2251).

Alps Ski Resort, eight slopes, about 45 minutes northwest of Sokch'o and just north of Sŏraksan National Park. This area gets the most snow and has the longest season (☎ 02-756 5481).

Bear's Town, seven slopes, about 40 minutes northeast of Seoul (☎ 02-546 7210)

Ch'ŏnmasan, six slopes, about 50 minutes north-east of Seoul (☎ 02-744 6019)

Yangji, seven slopes, near the Korean Folk Village in Suwon, about one hour from Seoul (☎ 02-511 3033)

Suanbo Aurora Valley, seven slopes, near Suanbo Hot Springs about three hours south-east of Seoul near Woraksan National Park (☎ 02-546 5171)

Muju, three slopes (more planned), 3½ hours from Seoul near Tŏgyusan National Park, south-east of Taejŏn (☎ 02-515 5500)

Taekwondo

An effective form of self-defence, *taekwondo*, was developed in Korea. If you're interested in either observing or studying, call the Korea Taekwondo Association (☎ 02-420 4271).

HIGHLIGHTS

In terms of culture and history, South Korea's top attractions include Kyongbok Palace in Seoul and Kyŏngju in south-east Korea.

Perhaps the most outstanding natural beauty spot is Sŏraksan National Park on the east coast. Chejudo off the south coast is worthwhile for the chance to climb South Korea's highest peak, Hallasan. Both of these areas are best visited in autumn.

The southern coast of Korea is dramatic and much of it can be explored by boat and on foot. Ditto for the island of Ullŭngdo off the east coast.

ACCOMMODATION
Camping

At least when the weather cooperates, Korea is a paradise for campers. Every national park has campgrounds and most are free. When a fee is charged, it's usually no more than W2000 and this buys you access to fine facilities like hot showers and flushing toilets. There are a few private campgrounds, but most are government run.

Hostels

There are 10 youth hostels scattered around the country. Unlike their counterparts in Europe, the USA and Australia, South Korean hostels are generally huge, luxurious places with incredible facilities and some private rooms. The problem is that there simply aren't very many hostels, and none at all in places where you'd expect to find them (eg, Chejudo and Kyŏngju). Dorm beds vary between W5000 and W9000, but private rooms cost as much as W30,000. All the hostels have their own restaurants with meals at very reasonable prices.

For more information and reservations contact the Korean Youth Hostel Association (☎ 02-725 3031; fax 725 3113), room 409, Chŏksŏn Hyŏndae Building, Chŏksŏn-dong, Chongno-gu, Seoul, 110-052.

Guesthouses

Yŏgwan & Yŏinsuk Western-style accommodation in the major centres is generally very expensive, so budget travellers usually head for the traditional Korean inns known as *yŏgwan* or *yŏinsuk*. The more upmarket yŏgwan are called *jang yŏgwan* (sometimes just abbreviated to *jang*). The jang yŏgwan are becoming more popular and are pushing out the other two categories.

The name gives an indication of what facilities you can expect. Yŏgwan usually have at least some rooms with private bath, while yŏinsuk almost never do. Rooms in the jang yŏgwan all have private baths.

Doubles and singles are usually the same price, though a third person might be charged extra. The proprietors are highly unlikely to speak English, but they'll expect you to want to see the room and bathroom facilities before you decide to stay.

Basic yŏinsuk rooms, with communal washing facilities, generally cost no more than W15,000 and sometimes as low as W7000. Prices in yŏgwan start around W15,000, but W20,000 or more isn't unusual. Prices in Seoul are slightly higher than elsewhere.

Yŏgwan and yŏinsuk are usually clustered around bus and railway stations. Most yŏgwan are run by married women and you should refer to them by the title of *ajimah*.

Minbak Another form of traditional accommodation is *minbak*, which could be translated as 'home stay'. Essentially, it's a room in a private house. Bathing and cooking facilities are shared with the family, although occasionally you may find separate facilities for guests. Some of these places will be signposted but many are not. Souvenier shops, teashops and small restaurants can usually point you in the right direction, and may actually be minbak themselves. In many rural areas, minbak may be the only form of accommodation available. Prices are always on a 'per room' basis and should cost roughly W10,000, except in Seoul where they charge around W12,000. Meals can generally be provided on request. Minbak offer considerable discounts if you plan to stay for a month or more.

Hotels

If you've got more cash to burn, Korea can accommodate you in style. Hotels start at the W20,000 level and easily accelerate to over W150,000 for deluxe rooms in Seoul. For the purposes of this book, we'll consider anything up to W25,000 as 'bottom-end', while 'mid-range' is defined as W26,000 to W75,000. Anything above W75,000 qualifies as 'top-end'. In addition to this, top-end places will charge an extra 10% tax plus another 10% service charge.

FOOD
Korean

Traditional Korean food is heavily based on

vegetables, often pickled and preserved with hot chilli pepper to last through the cold winters without refrigeration.

The basic Korean meal is known as *pekpan*, which consists of rice, soup and vegetable dishes that vary in type and number from restaurant to restaurant. They can number a dozen or more but will always include *kimch'i* – a fiery hot fermented cabbage which makes a reasonable substitute for tear gas. A basic pekpan meal will cost around W2500, but if you want something more substantial with meat or fish, the main possibility is the national dish, *pulgogi*. In descending order of cost this will be thinly sliced marinated beef, marinated ribs, unmarinated sliced beef or unmarinated sliced pork. Pulgogi is cooked at your table, so if that's what you plan to have make sure you sit down at a properly equipped table. For pulgogi or *kalbi*, marinated beef or pork short ribs, grilled over charcoal, you can expect to pay around W10,000.

An inexpensive dish is an *omŭ raisŭ* (omelette with rice), which you can safely call 'om rice' and be understood. The Koreans also love *kimbap* (sushi), which as far as they're concerned isn't Japanese food. A typical sushi/kimbap meal costs around W2000 in a Korean restaurant, and this often includes a bowl of soup and pickled radishes.

A good meal can be made from *mandu* (steamed dumplings), which are cheap and on sale everywhere.

With such an extensive coastline it is not surprising that Koreans also have plenty of seafood. Many restaurants, especially in coastal towns and cities, serve nothing else. Seafood is always expensive, but it costs several times more for raw fish. Cooking it brings down the price considerably (figure that out).

Chinese

Chinese restaurants are very popular, usually cheap and offer the opportunity to eat something besides spicy hot cuisine. If the owners are ethnic Chinese (many are), then Chinese characters will be displayed above the entrance. Ethnic Koreans also operate Chinese restaurants, but these are less obvious since Chinese characters are not normally displayed. The cheapest dishes are usually *jjajang myŏn* (noodles with sauce), *kun mandu* (fried dumplings), *poggŭm bap* and *chapch'ae bap* (fried rice). More expensive meat dishes include *t'angsu yuk* (sweet and sour pork).

Japanese

Japanese restaurants are nowhere near as common as Korean and Chinese ones, and tend to be expensive. Here you'll find tempura and other Japanese dishes. Sushi is very cheap if you buy it from a Korean restaurant, but the price doubles as soon as it's officially labelled 'Japanese'.

Western

Western-style fast-food restaurants are catching on, especially in Seoul. Fried chicken is available in many Korean restaurants as well. High-class Western restaurants are found in either expensive hotels or the top floors of big department stores. Much cheaper are the familiar fast-food chains like Kentucky Fried Chicken, McDonald's and Wendy's.

Self-Catering

Given the expense of eating out, self-catering is not a bad idea at all. One great feature of Korea is the existence of little hole-in-the-wall grocery shops open from early morning until late at night. The biggest problem with self-catering is simply finding cooking facilities. Some yŏgwan will allow you access to the kitchen or at least have hot water available, but you can seldom count on this.

In large cities such as Seoul, your salvation may be convenience stores. You can find 24-hour chains such as 7 Eleven, Family Mart, Circle K, Lucky-Goldstar (LG-25) etc, and these stores always have microwave ovens, hot water and even a table where you can stand (but not sit) while eating. Everything you need is included: a styrofoam bowl, plastic spoon and chopsticks. However, these types of shops are not easily found in the countryside.

An alternative is to carry a small electric heating coil or electric teapot for boiling water. One complication is the existence of two voltages (see Electricity earlier in this section).

DRINKS

Koreans love their booze and there is no shortage of drinking establishments. The traditional drink is *makkoli*, a kind of white-coloured rice brew which is cheap but, like kimch'i, is an acquired taste. It's sold in raucous beverage halls known as *makkoli jip*.

Soju is the local firewater, it's potent stuff similar to bad vodka. Makkoli and soju are often drunk with various snacks known as *unju*. They include fresh oysters, dried squid, salted peanuts and *kim* (seaweed).

Korea's best wine is Kyŏngju Beobjoo. Beer *(maekju)* comes in two brands: OB and Crown. If you drink in a beerhall, the management expects you to buy some snacks (peanuts etc) along with it.

Tea/coffee rooms *(tabang)* are great social centres. No food is served (by government edict), but it is possible to take sandwiches in.

Korea produces some fine herb teas. Ginseng tea *(insam ch'a)* is the most famous, but also check out spicy herbal tea *(ssanghwa ch'a)* made from three different roots and often served with an egg yolk or pine nuts floating in it. Ginger tea *(saengkang ch'a)* is also excellent. But the thumbs-down award goes to mugwort tea *(ssuk ch'a)*, which is definitely an acquired taste. There are lots of instant herbal teas available from supermarkets.

ENTERTAINMENT

Korea's nightlife is significantly dampened by government-imposed midnight closing hours. This restriction has its roots in a curfew which was enforced back in the days when Korea was a military dictatorship. The dictatorship is gone, but the government feels the need to shut down bars at midnight to protect the morals of the nation. In some pubs, you will be allowed to remain after midnight if you are already inside when they lock the doors, but the door will not be opened to admit new customers.

Billiards & Bowling

The Koreans are keen on bowling and even keener on billiards. Billiard halls are to be found everywhere; an unmistakable sign identifies these places. Koreans can advise you on the location of bowling alleys, though they are not difficult to find. Operating hours are approximately from 10 am until midnight.

Cinemas

Young Koreans are certainly fond of movies, and the *yŏnghwa gwan* or *kukjang* (cinemas) tend to pack out on weekends and holidays. Indeed, you might even have to buy a 'black market' ticket from scalpers who hang around the cinemas on Sunday. However, there are few problems on weekdays.

Drinking

Pubs are also known as hofs *(hop'ŭ)* or soju parlours *(soju bang)*. One Korean innovation with a long history are soju tents. These are usually set up in the evening alongside the bank of a river, and serve inexpensive drinks and snacks. The government frowns on these places, believing that they are a relic from the poverty-stricken past which have no place in modern Korea. They are also extremely popular! However, soju tents are now banned in Seoul, though they can still be found in most other cities and towns. If the government ever gets really serious about cracking down, soju tents will become a thing of the past.

Video Parlours

These are supposedly illegal, and so they try to maintain a low profile. Video parlours *(pidio bang)* are no different from video rental shops except that you watch the movies on their equipment. There is no reason why they should be illegal, but movie producers fear that these places compete against large-screen cinemas. Legal or not, you can find these places easily enough if you ask a Korean to assist you.

SOUTH KOREA

THINGS TO BUY

Traditional craftwork and the arts are alive and well in Korea, and even the impecunious traveller will have a wide range of things to choose from. Many visitors take a liking to the lacquerware boxes inlaid with mother-of-pearl. Ceramics and carved wooden masks are other traditional items. Koreans produce their own versions of Chinese-style brush pens (for calligraphy) and name seals. If you get a name seal carved, have a friend help you choose a Korean name.

If you're not an art or jewellery collector, South Korea does produce a wide range of practical consumer goods such as home appliances, Reebok shoes (both real and fake), unreliable fake Rolex watches, luggage, handbags, cookware and clothing.

One of Korea's main exports is sporting equipment. There are good deals to be had on tents, sleeping bags, hiking boots, backpacks, rock-climbing equipment, tennis rackets and other such items. Indoor sports enthusiasts will find various sorts of springs, weights, trampolines and other contortionist devices.

Ginseng is one of Korea's major exports; its sale is controlled by a government monopoly but you won't find it cheaper or better anywhere in the world.

Getting There & Away

AIR

Most travellers arrive in South Korea at Kimp'o International Airport in Seoul. There are also international airports in Pusan and Chejudo, but the only international flights available to these airports are from Japan.

You can get pretty good deals on air tickets purchased in South Korea, though Hong Kong still offers the cheapest in the region. Quoted prices on one way/return economy tickets bought in Seoul are as follows: Bangkok, US$400/550; Guam, US$300/360; Hong Kong, US$240/320; Jakarta, US$544/720; London, US$1000/1300; Los Angeles, US$500/750; Manila, US$215/369; New York, US$870/1050; Saigon, US$665/725; Shanghai US$250/500; Singapore, US$407/680; Sydney, US$700/950; Taipei, US$220/398; Tokyo, US$176/372; and Vancouver, US$870/1100.

SEA

There are a number of ferries connecting Japan and South Korea. Most popular is the Pusan-Shimonoseki ferry. There is a ferry between the Korean port of Pusan and the Japanese ports of Kōbe, Osaka and Hakata (Fukuoka). For details, see the introductory Getting Around chapter earlier in this book.

The Korean port of Inch'ŏn also has ferries to the Chinese ports of Tianjin, Qingdao and Weihai. See the introductory Getting Around chapter.

LEAVING KOREA

Airport departure tax on international flights is W8000. If you're departing by ship it's W2000.

Getting Around

Koreans are very helpful to lost-looking foreigners, so if you stand around looking bewildered with a map in your hands, someone will probably offer to assist you.

AIR

Given the small distances, you won't have to take to the air often, although you may prefer to fly rather than take a ferry to the island of Chejudo. The two domestic carriers, Korean Air and Asiana Airlines, have a good network connecting all the main cities, and both charge the same fares which are reasonable. You can carry a camera on board domestic flights, but don't take photographs of the airports or out the windows of a flying aircraft.

The following are the routes and airfares

available, and you must add a domestic departure tax of W2000:

Route	Fare	Airline
Seoul-Cheju	W46,300	(A, K)
Seoul-Chinju	W37,200	(A, K)
Seoul-Kunsan	W19,300	(K)
Seoul-Kwangju	W28,300	(A, K)
Seoul-Mokp'o	W32,800	(A, K)
Seoul-P'ohang	W29,400	(A, K)
Seoul-Pusan	W36,200	(A, K)
Seoul-Sokch'o	W24,600	(K)
Seoul-Taegu	W27,000	(A, K)
Seoul-Ulsan	W32,500	(A, K)
Seoul-Yech'ŏn	W16,900	(A)
Seoul-Yŏsu	W36,700	(A, K)
Cheju-Chinju	W26,300	(K)

Cheju-Kunsan	W27,000	(K)
Cheju-Kwangju	W17,800	(A, K)
Cheju-Mokp'o	W14,700	(K)
Cheju-P'ohang	W39,100	(A)
Cheju-Pusan	W29,500	(A, K)
Cheju-Taegu	W36,500	(A, K)
Cheju-Ulsan	W35,000	(A, K)
Cheju-Yŏsu	W21,000	(K)
Pusan-Kwangju	W18,900	(A)
Sokch'o-Kwangju	W49,200	(K)
Sokch'o-Taegu	W46,100	(K)

A = Asiana Airlines
K = Korean Air

The Sokch'o-Kwangju and Sokch'o-Taegu flights are via Seoul.

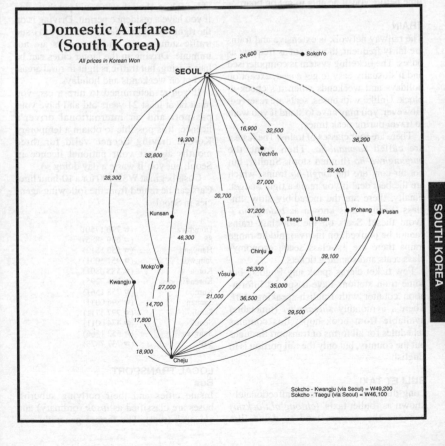

Domestic Airfares (South Korea)

All prices in Korean Won

SEOUL

Sokch'o   24,600

19,300   16,900   32,500   36,200

32,800   Yech'ŏn   29,400

28,300   27,000

36,700   37,200   P'ohang   Pusan

Kunsan   Taegu   Ulsan

46,300   Chinju   39,100

Mokp'o   Yŏsu   35,000

27,000   26,300   36,500

Kwangju   21,000   29,500

14,700

17,800

18,900   Cheju

Sokcho - Kwangju (via Seoul) = W49,200
Sokcho - Taegu (via Seoul) = W46,100

SOUTH KOREA

BUS

South Korean bus travel is a dream come true; it's fast, frequent, safe and on time. On major routes, there are two classes: *kosok* (express) and *chikheng* (ordinary). In real backwaters you may encounter the very slow *wanheng* (local) buses which stop everywhere. Express buses costs about 50% more than the ordinary buses, and usually operate out of separate terminals.

Seats are not reserved and you are not even committed to depart at any particular time, so just hop on any bus that matches the class of the ticket you bought. On weekends and holidays, you might have to queue a long time before you'll be able to get on board.

TRAIN

The railway network is extensive and trains are fairly frequent, though not as frequent as buses. The ticketing system is computerised and it's usually easy to get a seat, except on holidays and weekends when it's chock-a-block. Unlike with buses, seats are reserved. However, you may have to stand if you want to travel during peak times.

There are four classes of trains. The fastest are called *saemaul-ho*. Then come the *mugunghwa-ho* (limited stop). Similar, but not air-con, are the *tongil-ho* trains, which are the best deal if you're on a tight budget. Finally, there are the incredibly slow 4th-class (local) trains known as *bidulgi-ho* – avoid these! Seats on the 4th-class trains cannot be booked; on the two middle-range trains there are 1st-class seats, economy-class seats and standing tickets.

Few ticket clerks speak any English, but some train stations have a special information counter with English-speaking staff. There's a monthly *shigakp'yo* (timetable) available from bookshops; this contains schedules for all forms of transport throughout the country, but only the rail portion is in English.

BULLET TAXI

Long-distance share taxis are affectionately known as 'bullet taxis' (*ch'ong'al t'aekshi*) because the drivers tend to drive like maniacs. These taxis can be found at two places: at some major tourist sites and at bus or train stations. For example, they often meet incoming ferries such as the boat on Lake Soyangho near Ch'unch'ŏn. You can also find them around the Seoul Express Bus Terminal at night when the regular buses stop running.

Meters are not used, so you must negotiate the fare in advance.

CAR & MOTORBIKE

It makes no sense to rent a car in South Korea as the cost is outrageous and public transport is excellent. Motorbikes are seldom available for hire, though you could purchase one if you have a residence permit. Driving is on the right side of the road. Police love to issue traffic summonses, and foreigners are not immune. Driving in the larger cities can be hair-raising, but traffic is light in rural areas, except on weekends and holidays.

If you're determined to hire a car, you must be at least 21 years old and have your passport and an international driver's licence. It is possible to obtain a temporary Korean driving licence valid for three months against your national licence in Seoul, but you'll waste a day doing so.

Costs begin at W32,000 for a 10-hour hire. Cars can be rented from the following agencies in Seoul:

Donghwa	(☎ 790 1750)
88	(☎ 699 3885)
Hanyang	(☎ 553 5812)
Jangwon	(☎ 951 5001)
Korea	(☎ 585 0801)
Korea Express	(☎ 719 7295)
Kumho	(☎ 758 1561)
Saehan	(☎ 896 0031)
Sambo	(☎ 797 5711)
Seoul	(☎ 474 0011)
Sungsan	(☎ 552 1566)
VIP	(☎ 737 7878)

LOCAL TRANSPORT
Bus

Inside cities and their outlying suburbs, buses are classified as *ipsŏk* (ordinary) and *chwasŏk* (seat). The former generally cost

W300 regardless of distance (or W290 if you buy tokens from a booth beforehand), but they get incredibly crowded at rush hours. A chwasŏk bus over the same route will cost W600. All city buses display a route number and a destination on the front and the sides of the bus. Bus stops, likewise, display panels indicating the route served. None of these will be in English so you need to be able to recognise the name of your destination in Korean.

Underground

Seoul and Pusan have underground railways, which are a very convenient and cheap way of getting around. All signs for both the trains and the stations are in Korean and English. Tickets are bought at vending machines or at ticket windows.

Taxi

There are two types of taxis, 'ordinary' and 'deluxe'. 'Deluxe' not only means that the taxi is very pleasant inside, but also that it functions the way you expect a taxi to work. That is, you flag down a taxi, get inside and say where you want to go. A *mobŏm t'aekshi* (deluxe taxi) is black with a yellow sign on the roof and the words 'Deluxe Taxi' written on the sides. Deluxe taxis are only supposed to pick up passengers from designated stands at hotels, bus terminals, train stations and certain major streets.

It is a very different situation with the ordinary taxis, which are (unfortunately) the vast majority of taxis on the road. The way these work is that you stand by the roadside and shout out your destination. Usually the taxi will slow down long enough to hear your call, and in nine cases out of 10 will then shoot off again.

The other factor in these unique arrangements is that the ordinary taxis basically operate as minibuses. Once the driver is on a certain route he will continue to slow down to listen out for the calls of other hopefuls as long as there is spare seating in the taxi. This won't make your fare any cheaper, although it does make sorting out exactly how much it should be a bit more complicated as, if

there are already passengers in the taxi, the meter will be running when you get in. To protect yourself, you must look at the meter when you get into the taxi, note the fare, and subtract it from what the meter says when you get out. If two or more of you get in the taxi at the same time for the same destination, you should pay a single fare, not the same fare multiplied two or more times.

The basic charges for ordinary taxis is W1000 for the first two km and an additional W100 for every 381 metres. From midnight there is a 20% surcharge. When caught in traffic and going slower than 15 km/h, there is a surcharge of W100 for every 92 seconds. Fares are 20% higher from midnight to 4 am.

The deluxe taxis cost considerably more, and a receipt will be issued. Flagfall is W3000 which takes you three km, then W200 for each additional 250 metres or each 60 seconds when the speed drops below 15 km per hour. On the other hand, there is *no* late-night surcharge for the deluxe taxis.

In the countryside, few taxis are metered so you'll have to negotiate the fare before you set off.

TOURS

The Royal Asiatic Society – RAS (☎ 02-763 9483; fax 766 3796) in Seoul operates tours every weekend. The day tours are reasonably priced, but overnight trips are somewhat expensive because accommodation is in good hotels rather than cheap yŏgwan. The RAS is in room 611 of the Korean Christian Building (also called the CBS Building) on Taehangno. Office hours are from 10 am to 5 pm, Monday to Friday. Take subway line 1 to the Chongno 5-ga station.

The Korean Travel Bureau (☎ 02-585 1191) runs commercial tours of Seoul, P'anmunjŏm, Korean Folk Village, Kyŏngju, Pusan, Chejudo island and Sŏraksan. You can also contact their office on the 3rd floor of the Hotel Lotte (☎ 02-778 0150) in Seoul for more information.

The USO (☎ 02-795 3063, 795 3028) runs tours at bargain prices and you don't have to be a member of the US military to join. The Seoul office is opposite Gate 21 of the

SOUTH KOREA

Yongsan military compound. There is also a USO in Pusan (☎ 051-462 3732).

Seoul 서울

Seoul is a city of incredible contrasts. It was flattened during the Korean War but has risen from the ashes to become a modern metropolis with a population of more than 10 million. Although the city now boasts high-rise buildings, 12-lane boulevards and urban problems to match, the centuries-old royal palaces, temples, pagodas and imposing stone gateways remain timeless and elegant.

Seoul dates from the establishment in 1392 of the Yi Dynasty, which ruled Korea until 1910. During this time, when Korea was largely closed to the outside world, the shrines, palaces and fortresses that still stand today were built. Government funding for the repair and restoration of historic sites is outstanding in South Korea and is the reason the very new and the ancient continue to exist side by side.

Seoul is the cultural hub of the country, catering for every taste. It's a magnet for foreigners, and it has excellent public transport and cheap accommodation, even right in the city centre. It's certainly worth spending a week in Seoul, but do make the effort to get out of town and see the rest of South Korea. Many travellers never do.

Orientation

Locating addresses in Seoul is much like in Tokyo – chaos reigns supreme! Very few roads are signposted, and most smaller streets and alleys have no name at all. But there is a decrepit system of sorts, and it helps if you learn it.

A *gu* is an urban district only found in large cities like Seoul and Pusan. A *dong* is a neighbourhood smaller than a gu. Seoul presently has 22 gu and 494 dong. Thus, an address like 104 It'aewon-dong, Yongsan-gu, means building No 104 in the It'aewon neighbourhood of the Yongsan district.

Buildings have names, and the name is crucial to finding the correct address.

The word for a large street or boulevard is *no* or *ro*. So Chongno means Chong St, Ŭlchiro is Ulchi St etc. Also worth knowing is that large boulevards are divided into sections called *ga*. Thus, you'll see on the Seoul subway map that there is a station for Ŭlchiro 3-ga and Ŭlchiro 4-ga; these are just different sections of a street named Ŭlchi St. A *gil* is a smaller street than a no/ro, Sambonggil is an example.

Chung-gu is the central district around the city hall area north of Namsan Park. Chongno-gu is from Chongno (Chong St) northwards to the Kyŏngbok Palace area. This district has most of the budget hotels and the city's best sights. It'aewon-dong is a neighbourhood on the south side of Namsan Park famous for its shopping, bars and nightlife.

Kangnam-gu is the district on the south side of the Han River and includes two of Seoul's most high-class neighbourhoods, Yong-dong and Chamshil-dong.

If you can't find a certain address, try the police boxes which are in every neighbourhood. A surprisingly large number of police officers speak English, though it still helps considerably if you have your destination written in Korean script.

Information

The Korean National Tourism Corporation (KNTC) Tourist Information Centre (☎ 757 0086) is in the basement of the KNTC Building, 10 Ta-dong, Chung-gu. KNTC is open daily from 9 am until 6 pm (until 5 pm from November to February).

Another good source of information is the Seoul City Tourist Information Centre (☎ 731 6337, 735 8688) inside City Hall. It's open every day from 9 am to 6 pm, but closes from noon to 1 pm. There are also tourist information kiosks at various points in the city.

The RAS (☎ 763 9483; fax 766 3796) is in room 611 of the Korean Christian Building on Taehangno. The RAS is a gold mine of information for people who want to dig deep into Korea's culture, history, economy and geography. The society sells books, sponsors free lectures and runs weekend trips. Take subway line No 1 to the Chongno 5-ga station. Office hours are from 10 am to 5 pm Monday to Friday. The mailing address is CPO Box 255, Seoul.

Post & Telecommunications Poste Restante is on the 3rd floor of the Central Post Office (CPO). All incoming letters are entered into a logbook which you have to sign when you pick up a letter or package. Look over this logbook carefully for your name because staff often misfile letters.

The telecommunications building is just behind the CPO; fax, telephone and telex service is available.

Foreign Embassies The addresses of foreign embassies in Seoul include the following:

Australia
    11th floor, Kyobo Building, 1-1, Chongno 1-ga, Chongno-gu (☎ 730 6490/5)
Austria
    1, Chongno 1-ga, Chongno-gu (☎ 732 9071/2)
Belgium
    1-65, Tongbinggo-dong, Yongsan-gu (☎ 749 0381/6)
Canada
    10th floor, Kolon Building, 45, Mugyo-dong, Chung-gu (☎ 753 2605/8)
China
    83, Myŏng-dong 2-ga, Chung-gu (☎ 773 0214)
Denmark
    Suite 701, Namsong Building, 260-199, It'aewon-dong, Yongsan-gu (☎ 795 4187/9)
Finland
    1, Chongno 1-ga, Chongno-gu (☎ 732 6737)
France
    30, Hap-dong, Sŏdaemun-gu (☎ 312 3272)
Germany
    4th floor, Daehan Fire & Marine Insurance Building, 51-1, Namch'ang-dong, Chung-gu (☎ 726 7114)
Ireland
    Daehan Fire & Marine Insurance building, 51-1, Namch'ang-dong, Chung-gu (☎ 774 6455)
Israel
    823-21, Yŏksam-dong, Kangnam-gu (☎ 564 3448)
Italy
    1-398, Hannam-dong, Yongsan-gu (☎ 796 0491)

Japan
    18-11, Chunghak-dong, Chongno-gu (☎ 733 5626)
Netherlands
    14th floor, Kyobo Building, 1-1, Chongno 1-ga, Chongno-gu (☎ 737 9514/6)
New Zealand
    18th floor, Kyobo Building, 1-1, Chongno 1-ga, Chongno-gu (☎ 730 7794)
Norway
    124-12, It'aewon-dong, Yongsan-gu (☎ 795 6850/1)
Philippines
    559-510, Yŏksam-dong, Kangnam-gu (☎ 568 9434)
Russia
    1001-13, Taech'i-dong, Kangnam-gu (☎ 552 7094/8)
South Africa
    Office 230, Hotel Westin Chosun (☎ 317 0466)
Sweden
    8th floor, Boyung Building, 108-2, P'yŏng-dong, Chongno-gu (☎ 738 1149, 738 0846)
Switzerland
    32-10, Songwol-dong, Chongno-gu (☎ 739 9511/4)
Taiwan
    6th floor, Kwanghwamun Building, Chung-gu (☎ 399 2767)
Thailand
    653-7, Hannam-dong, Yongsan-gu (☎ 795 3098)
UK
    4, Chŏng-dong, Chung-gu (☎ 735 7341/3)
USA
    82, Sejongno, Chongno-gu (☎ 738 7118, 393 4114)
Vietnam
    33-1, Hannam-dong, Yongsan-gu (☎ 741 0036)

Cultural Centres The Seoul Arts Centre (☎ 585 3151), 700 Socho-dong, Socho-gu, is the best place to see folk dances, court dances and other traditional performances. Admission costs only W3000 and there are performances every Saturday. Take subway line No 3 to the Cargo Truck Terminal at the south end of town.

Korea House (☎ 266 9101) has similar performances to those of the Seoul Arts Centre, but these are performed every evening at 7.20 and 8.40 pm. Unfortunately, these shows are expensive at W14,300. It's on the north side of Namsan Park; take subway line No 3 or 4 to the Ch'ungmuro station.

SOUTH KOREA

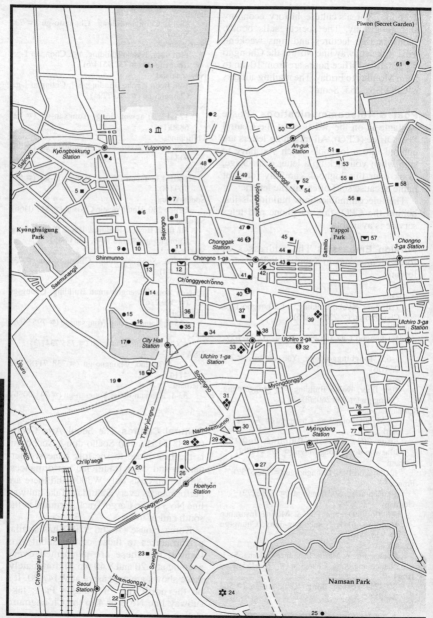

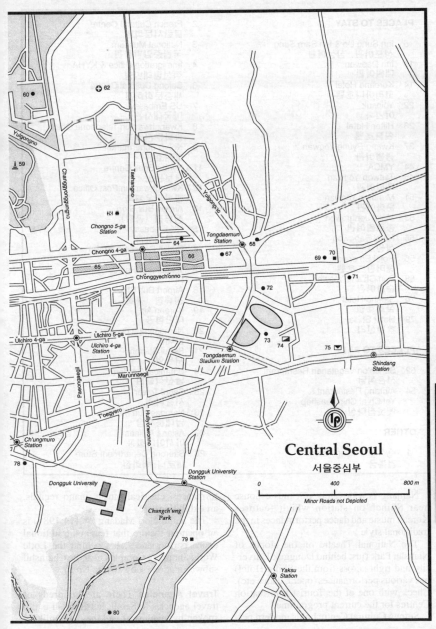

Central Seoul
서울중심부

0   400   800 m

Minor Roads not Depicted

SOUTH KOREA

PLACES TO STAY

5 Inn Sung Do & Inn Sam Sung
   성도여관, 삼성여관
10 Inn Daewon
   대원여관
14 Koreana Hotel
   코리아나호텔
22 Yŏinsuk
   여인숙
23 Hilton Hotel
   힐튼호텔
37 Kwang Pyung Yŏgwan
   광평여관
44 YMCA
45 Taewon Yŏgwan
   대원여관
51 Munhwa Yŏgwan
   문화여관
53 Motel Jongrowon
   종로원여관
55 Hotel Sangwon
   상원호텔
56 Hotel Emerald
   애머랄드호텔
58 Sun Ch'ang Yŏgwan
   순창여관
70 Samho Hotel
   삼호호텔
79 Hotel Shilla
   호텔신라

PLACES TO EAT

52 Sanch'on Vegetarian Restaurant
   산촌식당
54 Airirang Restaurant &
   Yet Ch'at Chip Teashop
   옛찻집다실

OTHER

1 Kyŏngbokkung Palace
   경복궁
2 French Cultural Centre
   불란서문화원
3 National Museum
   국립중앙박물관
4 Immigration Office & KYHA
   적선현대빌딩
6 Sejong Cultural Centre
   세종문화회관
7 US Embassy
   미국대사관
8 Kwanghwamun Telephone Office
   광화문전화국
9 Koryŏ Supermarket
   고려쇼핑
11 Kyobo Book Centre
   교보문고
12 Kwanghwamun Post Office
   광화문우체국
13 Airport Bus Stop
   정류장 (공항)
15 UK Embassy
   영국대사관
16 British Council (Library)
   영국문화원
17 Tŏksukung Palace
   덕수궁
18 Airport Bus Stop
   정류장 (공항)
19 Korean Air
   대한항공
20 Namdaemun Gate
   남대문
21 Seoul Station
   서울역
24 Botanical Garden
   남산식물원
25 Seoul Tower
   서울타워
26 Namdaemun Market
   남대문시장
27 Asiana Airlines
   아시아나항공
28 Saerona Department Store
   새로나 백화점

Nanjang is a privately run music house near Shinch'on station which features Korean music and dance performances in the traditional style.

The National Theatre on the slopes of Namsan Park (just behind Dongguk University and right across from the Shilla Hotel) has various performances (opera, dance etc). Check with one of the Tourist Information Centres for the current programme.

Sejong Cultural Centre holds modern per-formances, classical music, piano recitals, art exhibitions etc.

The Seoul Nori Madang (☎ 414 1985) is an open-air theatre that features traditional dance performances. It's behind the Lotte World Shopping Complex near the Chamshil subway station (subway line No 2).

Travel Agencies There are hundreds of travel agencies in Seoul, but English is not spoken by many staff and they are unlikely

29	Shinsegae Department Store 신세계 백화점	59	Chongmyo (Royal Shrine) 종묘
30	Central Post & Telephone Office (CPO) 중앙우체국. 중앙전화국	60	Ch'anggyŏnggung Palace 창경궁
31	Midopa Department Store 미도파 백화점	61	Ch'angdŏkkung Palace 창덕궁
32	Korea Exchange Bank 외환은행	62	Seoul National University Hospital 서울대학교병원
33	Lotte Department Store 롯데백화점	63	Royal Asiatic Society (RAS) 로얄아시아협회
34	USIS 미국문화원	64	Herbal Medicine Arcade 한약상가
35	City Hall 시청	65	Kwangjang Market 광장시장
36	Joy Travel Service 죠이항공	66	Tongdaemun Market 동대문시장
38	Ŭlchi Book Centre 을지서적	67	Tongdaemun Chain Store 동대문종합시장
39	Printemps Department Store 쁘렝땅 백화점	68	Tongdaemun Gate 동대문
40	KNTC 한국관광공사	69	Shoe Shops 신발류도매시장
41	Youngpoong Bookshop 영풍문고	71	Hwanghak-dong Flea Market 황학동시장
42	Poshingak (Belfry) 보신각	72	Hŭng'in Market 흥인시장
43	Chongno Book Centre 종로서적	73	Tongdaemun Stadium 동대문운동장
46	Korea First Bank 제일은행	74	Swimming Pool 수영장
47	Chung'ang Map & Atlas 중앙지도	75	Hŭng'in-dong Post Office 흥인동우체국
48	Japan Embassy 일본대사관	76	Kodak Photo Shop 코닥양행
49	Chogyesa (Temple) 조계사	77	Fujicolor Plaza 후지칼라 프라자
50	Anguk Post Office 안국우체국	78	Korea House 한국의집
57	T'apkol Post Office 탑골우체국	80	National Theatre 국립극장

to be accustomed to Westerners' preoccupation with getting the cheapest price. Highest recommendations go to Joy Travel Service (☎ 776 9871; fax 756 5342), 10th floor, 24-2 Mukyo-dong, Chung-gu, Seoul, which is directly behind City Hall. You'll also find two good discounters on the 5th floor of the YMCA building on Chongno 2-ga (next to Chonggak subway station): Korean International Student Exchange Society (KISES) (☎ 733 9494; fax 732 9568) in room 505;

and Top Travel (☎ 739 5231; fax 736 9078) in room 506.

Bookshops The best place is the Ŭlchi Book Centre (☎ 757 8991) in the north-east section of the underground arcade at the Ulchiro 1-ga subway station (intersection of Namdaemunno & Ŭlchiro). This is *not* Seoul's largest bookshop, but it's got a great selection, the manager speaks English and you can even specially order books here

SOUTH KOREA

(the other bookshops will never do that for you).

Seoul's largest bookshop is the Kyobo Book Centre in the basement of the Kyobo Building on the north-east corner of Sejongno and Chongno; you can enter through the pedestrian subway.

Libraries There are two good libraries with English-language books. The largest is at USIS, just east of City Hall. The other is the British Council, just north of Toksukung and east of the British Embassy.

Emergency Asia Emergency Assistance (☎ 353 6475/6) has English speaking staff on duty 24 hours daily. This organisation will relay your request for help to the proper authorities. However, a fee is charged for this service.

During office hours, you might be able to get a call for help relayed through the Seoul City Tourist Information Centre (☎ 735 8688) or KNTC (☎ 757 0086). However, don't count on it if your life (or someone else's) is in danger.

If you want to try your luck with someone who probably won't speak English, the emergency telephone number for police is ☎ 112; for an ambulance or fire it's ☎ 119.

Seoul has a number of good hospitals with English-speaking doctors, but most are horribly overcrowded. For emergencies, the biggest, best and jam-packed is Seoul National University Hospital (☎ 762 5171). For normal outpatient treatment, the best place to go is the Foreigners' Clinic at Severance Hospital (☎ 392 0161), which is attached to the Yonsei University Medical School – several US doctors work here. Other hospitals with English-speaking doctors include Cheil (☎ 269 2151), Ewha (☎ 762 5061), Soonchunhyang (☎ 794 7191) and St Mary's (☎ 789 1114).

Lost & Found If you leave something in a taxi or on public transport, there is a chance of recovering it from the Lost & Found at the Korean Broadcasting System (KBS) Building (☎ 781 1325) on the island of Yŏŭido.

However, first try calling the Citizen's Room of the Seoul Metropolitan Police Bureau (☎ 725 4401). There is also a subway Lost & Found (☎ 753 2408).

Things to See

The **Kyŏngbokkung Palace**, at the back of the former Capitol Building at the north end of Sejongno, is a magnificent palace first built in 1392 by the founder of the Yi Dynasty, King Taejo. It was burnt down during the Japanese invasion of 1592 and left in ruins until it was rebuilt in 1867, when it became the residence of the 26th ruler. The walled grounds contain some exceptionally beautiful buildings and a collection of old stone pagodas from other parts of the country, many of them moved there by the Japanese during their occupation of Korea.

The palace is open daily from 9.15 am to 6.30 pm from April to October, and from 9.30 am to 5.30 pm from November to March. Entry costs W550.

Also in the grounds are the **National Folk Museum** and the **National Museum**. The National Folk Museum (closed Tuesday) has lifelike recreations of traditional houses, festivals and clothing styles, and a display of moveable metal type that was invented and used in Korea around 1234 (200 years before Gutenberg's invention of moveable type printing in Europe). Entry costs W110.

The National Museum (closed Monday) has displays of ancient pottery and a collection of stone and brass buddhas and bodhisattvas. It may be permanently closed by the time you read this as there are plans to tear it down and move it elsewhere.

Chongmyo Royal Ancestral Shrines is a forested park east of the Kyŏngbokkung Palace. It contains a collection of beautiful traditional Korean temples that house the ancestral tablets of the 27 Yi Dynasty kings and queens. The two main shrines are only open to the public on certain ceremonial days. One of these is the first Sunday of May each year when the descendants of the royal family come to honour the spirits of their ancestors in a very colourful Confucian ceremony. Don't miss it if you happen to be in

Seoul at the time. Entry costs W1000, and the park is open daily between 9 am and 6 pm.

The best preserved of Seoul's five palaces is **Ch'angdŏkkung**, once the residence of Korea's royal family. It was originally built in 1405 and rebuilt in 1611. It is also the site of the enchanting **Piwon** (Secret Garden), a landscaped wooded retreat covering 32 hectares and incorporating over 40 pleasure pavilions, as well as many ponds and stone bridges. The garden was originally reserved for members of the royal family and the king's concubines. The palace and Piwon are open daily, but to see them you must join a tour group. Each tour lasts about 1½ hours and costs W1800, which includes the admission price. The tour guides speak English.

Tŏksukung is an attractive palace opposite the city hall. The palace grounds contain the **Museum of Modern Art**. It's open from 9.15 am to 6.30 pm April to October, and from 9.30 am to 5.30 pm November to March. Entry costs W550.

In the centre of the city you will find **Pagoda Park**, famous for its 10-storey Koryŏ pagoda. **Poshingak**, near the Chonggak subway station, houses Seoul's city bell.

For superb views over the city (smog permitting), go to **Seoul Tower**, which is perched on top of Namsan (South Mountain), between central Seoul and It'aewon. You have a choice of ascending the mountain by cable car or doing a 20-minute walk up from the Namsan Public Library. For a different perspective, go up at night. Operating hours are from 10 am to 9.30 pm (until 10.30 pm in summer).

One sight often overlooked by visitors is the **Subterranean City**, the name for the underground shopping arcades and interconnecting passages. There is a maze of these arcades twisting and winding under the city; the tourist bureau maps show only part. Longest is the Ŭlchiro Underground Arcade running from City Hall to the Ŭlchiro 7-ga subway station; about 2.8 km. More interesting is the Sogong Arcade (near the Seoul Plaza Hotel) which connects to the Myŏng-dong Arcade (near the CPO) and the basement of the Lotte department store. This is a good walk with plenty to see.

Lotte World is an interesting though bizarre place to visit – it's a huge mass of shops, restaurants and movie theatres, with a monorail, indoor swimming pool, ice-skating rink and laser light show thrown in for good measure. Just behind Lotte World is **Magic Island**, South Korea's answer to Disneyland. Take subway line No 2 to the Chamshil station.

The enormous **Olympic Stadium** on the south bank of the Han River accommodates around 100,000 spectators, and the surrounding sports complex covers almost three sq km. The stadium and sports complex are open to the public.

Yŏŭido (*do* means island) is in the Han River and is Seoul's answer to Manhattan. It's certainly got Seoul's densest collection of high-rises, one of which is a luxury hotel called the Manhattan. Yŏŭido is home to the ugly National Assembly Building, the stock exchange and South Korea's tallest structure, the DLI 63 Building. You can visit the observation platform in DLI 63, though the view is nowhere near as good as from Seoul Tower. The building also contains an aquarium and the IMAX Theatre, the latter offers a viewing screen 10 times larger than the average cinema and an excellent sound system. Yŏŭido also boasts an outdoor collection of warplanes and tanks at the **Korean War Museum**. The best sight on the island is **Riverside Park**. Overall, Yŏŭido is somewhat overrated as a tourist attraction.

Activities

River Cruise During the summer months there are six different cruises on the Han River. There are less frequent cruises in spring and autumn, but you can forget them in winter unless you want to hire an icebreaker.

There are several routes, the longest being 15 km (Yŏŭido-Chamshil). The cruises are operated by Semo Corporation, which you can contact for reservations and information (Main Office ☎ 499 6262/3; Yŏŭido ☎ 785 5522; Chamshil ☎ 416 8615; Ttuksŏm

River Cruises

Route	Duration	Fare
Yŏŭido-Chamshil	70 min	W4000
Chamshil-Yŏŭido	70 min	W4000
Ttuksŏm-Yŏŭido	60 min	W3400
Yŏŭido-Ttuksŏm	60 min	W3400
Yŏŭido-Tongjak Bridge-Yŏŭido	60 min	W3400
Chamshil-Tongho Bridge-Chamshil	60 min	W3400
Ttuksŏm-Tongho Bridge-Ttuksŏm	60 min	W3400
Ttuksŏm-Chamshil	10 min	W650
Chamshil-Ttuksŏm	10 min	W650

☎ 469 4459). In the peak season (summer), boats run from 10 am until 9.10 pm. For information on the duration and cost of the river cruises see the table below.

Swimming Thanks to the 1988 Olympics, there are several indoor Olympic-sized swimming pools. One is in the Seoul Sports Complex and another is in Olympic Park. Lotte World also has a pool.

Language Courses There are several large government-run language schools such as the Yonsei University Foreign Language Institute (FLI) and Ehwa Women's University in Seoul. The Language Research Teaching Centre (LRTC) in Seoul is a well-known private language school. Other language schools advertise in the *Korea Times* and *Korea Herald*. Remember that you *must* obtain a student visa *before* enrolling.

Places to Stay – bottom end
The cheapest place where you can have your own private room is just to the south-east of Seoul station (see the Central Seoul map). There are three alleys here harbouring eight yŏinsuk, though every one of them is a grim, windowless hovel. Don't bother asking the ajimah to change the sheets, and look at the closet-sized rooms first before you pay the W7000. On the north alley you'll find *Hanwon Yŏinsuk* and *Sŏjŏng Yŏinsuk*. The tiny east alley has just one place, the *Kwangshil Yŏinsuk*. The south alley has five yŏinsuk: the *Kyŏnggi*, *Songning*, *Myŏngshil*, *Sŏngnam* and *Hyŏndae*.

If you're feeling lonely, you may want to stay at the *Inn Daewon* (☎ 735 7891), 26 Tangju-dong, Chongno-gu. Many budget travellers wind up here largely because its central, it's also cheap and nearby competing yŏgwan have sold out to high-rise developers. A dormitory bed in this firetrap costs W6000 and double rooms cost W10,000. All share one grotty washroom with barely functional plumbing. There have been rumours for years that this place will be sold and demolished (it should be), but so far the building has managed to survive. If it isn't torn down soon, it might just fall down by itself.

The second most popular place with budget travellers is the *Inn Sung Do* (☎ 737 1056, 738 8226), 120 Naesu-dong, Chongno-gu. This place belongs to the same family that owns Inn Daewon, but there is a difference, it's liveable. In fact, rooms are pretty decent and it's often full with long termers. Doubles with shared bath cost W10,000, and a double with private bath costs W15,000. This yŏgwan has a sign in English.

Just next door to the Inn Sung Do is *Inn Sam Sung* (☎ 737 2177). Rates are exactly the same as its neighbour.

Highly recommended is *Munhwa Yŏgwan* (☎ 765 4659), 69 Unni-dong, Chongno-gu, where beautiful double rooms with shared bath cost W8000. With private bath it's W12,000. This place is very close to Duksung Women's University, a few blocks north of T'apkol Park. The English sign is yellow with blue letters and only says 'Hotel'.

Just a few doors south of the Munhwa Yŏgwan is the *Motel Jongrowon* (☎ 745 6876). This is a relatively upmarket yŏgwan with beautiful rooms for W18,000.

A little north of the Chongno 3-ga subway station and just west of Chongmyo (Royal Shrine) is an alley where you'll find *Sun Ch'ang Yŏgwan* (☎ 765 0701). At W10,000, it's reasonable though the rooms are small. There is a small courtyard and the ajimah is very nice.

As you face the YMCA, on the right side of the building you'll find an alley. If you head up this alley, you'll find a sign in English saying 'Hotel'. This is the *Taewon Yŏgwan* (☎ 735 1588), where doubles with shared bath cost W8000.

Another popular yŏgwan in the same price bracket is over near the Lotte Hotel. The *Kwang Pyung Yŏgwan* (☎ 778 0104), 123-1, Ta-dong, has rooms arranged around a traditional courtyard for W15,000. To find it, look for the lane with the Mirim Tailor store and then look out for the sign advertising the yŏgwan.

If you're prepared to spend a little more for your creature comforts, check out Insadonggil, the antiques street. As you walk up the road you will see bathhouse symbols on almost every one of the side alleys. Most of these places are of a similar standard and charge similar prices. Most travellers head for the Anguk subway-station end of Insadonggil because that's easiest for transport. One of the many offerings in this area is the *Hanhung-jang Yŏgwan* (☎ 734 4265), 99, Kwanhun-dong, where a double room with attached bath costs W20,000. Farther down the alley is the *Kwanhun-jang Yŏgwan* with the same deal. No English is spoken but the staff are very friendly. At the end of this alley is the *Shingung-jang Yŏgwan* (☎ 732 1682), which offers the same deal as its neighbors.

Places To Stay – Middle

There are no shortage of places to stay in this category, it just depends where you want to base yourself. All of the places listed here are in the central area, as that's where most

foreigners want to say. In many respects, the lower end of the mid-range accommodation represents less of a bargain than Seoul's yŏgwan. But there are benefits: English-speaking staff and (sometimes) business facilities like fax and international phone call service.

An old reliable standby is the *YMCA* (☎ 732 8261) on Chongno 2-ga. It's on the north side of the street just west of T'apkol Park. Singles/doubles cost W26,400/34,100.

In an alley just to the north of T'apkol Park by the Nagwan elevated arcade is the *Hotel Emerald* (☎ 743 2001), 75 Nagwon-dong, Chongno-gu. A comfortable double with private bath is W20,000. In another alley just slightly to the north is the relatively luxurious *Hotel Sangwon* (☎ 765 0441) at 33 Nagwon-dong, Chongno-gu. Doubles are W32,000.

In an alley right by the south-east corner of Ŭlchiro and Tonhwamunno is the *Eulji Hotel* (☎ 278 5000) at 291-45 Ŭlchiro 3-ga, Chung-gu. Korean-style doubles are W22,000 and Western-style are W25,000.

Some budget travellers head over to It'aewon, though this is a much less popular area than Insadong. The *Sungji Hotel* (☎ 795 1691), 211-30, It'aewon 2-dong, is a popular option, with rooms with an attached bathroom going for W18,000. Right in the heart of the action, at the top of that infamous stretch of alleyway known by locals as 'hooker hill', is the *Hilltop Motel*, with singles/doubles with attached bathroom, colour TV and air-con for W18,000. The sign is in English and some English is spoken by the staff too. This place probably gets pretty rowdy at night. Back down the hill on the left-hand side is a sign simply saying 'motel'. Rooms here are also W18,000. Finally, back on the main drag is the *Mido Hotel*, where a single room with attached bathroom costs W18,000.

Other places to consider in the hotel battlefield include:

Astoria Hotel, 13-2, Namhak-dong, Chung-gu (five-minute walk from Ch'ungmuro station on Subway line 3 or line 4); doubles W34,686, twins W36,668; plus 20% tax and surcharge (☎ 268 7111; fax 274 3187)

SOUTH KOREA

Chonji Hotel, 133-1, Ŭlchiro 5-ga, Chung-gu (five-minute walk from Tongdaemun Stadium station on subway line 2); doubles W24,200, twins W30,000; plus 20% tax and surcharge (☎ 265 6131; fax 279 1184)

Daehwa Hotel, 18-21, Ŭlchiro 6-ga, Chung-gu (five-minute walk from Tongdaemun Stadium station on subway line 2 or line 4); singles and twins W30,000, suites W35,000; plus 20% tax and surcharge (☎ 265 9181/9; fax 277 9820)

Metro Hotel, 199-33, Ŭlchiro 2-ga, Chung-gu (two-minute walk from Ulchi 1-ga station on subway line 2); singles W33,000, doubles W36,300, twins W41,800, suites W90,000; plus 20% tax and surcharge (☎ 752 1112; fax 757 4411)

New Oriental Hotel, 10, Hoehyon-dong 3-ga, Chung-gu (three-minute walk from Myŏngdong station on subway line 4); singles W30,580, doubles W36,300, twins W41,800, suites W62,700; plus 20% tax and surcharge (☎ 753 07016; fax 755 9346)

Poongjun Hotel, 73-1, Inhyon-dong 2-ga, Chung-gu (two-minute walk from Ŭlchiro 4-ga station on subway line 2); singles W47,900, doubles W60,000, twins W68,500, suites W120,000; plus 20% tax and surcharge (☎ 266 21519; fax 274 5732)

Rio Tourist Hotel, 72-7, Kwanghui-dong 1-ga, Chung-gu (five-minute walk from Tongdaemun Stadium subway station on line 2 and line 4); singles W25,000, doubles W35,000, twins W38,000; plus 20% tax and surcharge (☎ 278 57009; fax 275 7207)

Savoy Hotel, 23-1, Ch'ungmuro 1-ga, Chung-gu (two-minute walk from Myŏngdong station on subway line 4); singles W33,000, doubles W38,500, twins W41,800, suites W66,300 to W101,200; plus 20% tax and surcharge (☎ 776 2641; fax 755 7669)

Seoul Prince Hotel, 1-1, Namsan-dong 2-ga, Chung-gu (two-minute walk from Myŏngdong station on subway line 4); singles W27,000, doubles W33,000, twins W38,000, suites W65,000; plus 20% tax and surcharge (☎ 752 71118; fax 752 7119)

Places to Eat

The only problem finding food is deciding where to start looking as the supply is limitless. If you're on a tight budget, the best bargains are found in the basements of large department stores, where you can often find supermarkets and lunch counters. The Saerona department store is a personal favourite, mainly because it's relatively uncrowded. The Shinsegae department store has some cheap lunch counters in the basement, though selection is limited. The Printemps department store has excellent restaurants in the basement and on the 7th floor. The Lotte department store is the largest but is very crowded.

If you're in the area of the Inn Daewon or the Kyobo Book Centre, a place you should definitely check out is *Koryŏ Supermarket* (no English sign). The lunch counters are hidden in the back and to your right, and you can eat well for around W1500. The supermarket itself is one of the cheapest and has sustained many a budget traveller in Seoul.

The Lotte department store is one place to get a broad overview of what Korean food is all about. The 9th floor is restaurant city, and for the most part it is given over to Korean food. The restaurants have no English names, but as they each specialise in a few dishes there's no problem sorting out which is which. Best of all, most of the restaurants have plastic imitations of the meals they serve on display with English labelling.

Yet another place to look is in the large subway stations and underground shopping malls, where sushi with soup and pickled vegetables should go for around W2000.

Uncle Joe's Hamburgers not only has good hamburgers but also the best ice cream in Korea. There are 45 branches around Seoul, though mostly *not* in the city centre because of sky-high rents. The one branch in the city centre is very tiny, but popular with foreigners; it's just east of Kyobo Book Centre. There is another (much larger) branch in the trendy Taehangno entertainment district near the Hyehwa subway station (line 4).

Coco Fried Rice is another chain store, with about 30 branches in Seoul. Specialities are a sort of Korean-Chinese fast food, which isn't bad at all. One of the more accessible branches is in the Taehangno district near the Hyehwa subway station on line 4.

Sapporo Pub & Restaurant is opposite Sejong Cultural Centre on the south side of the street. The Japanese food here is very reasonably priced (a rare find). You can have dessert and coffee just next door at *Paris*

Baguete, or walk just one door to the west to sample the delights at *Pizza Inn*.

The area around the Chinese Embassy in Myŏng-dong is the place to look for Chinese restaurants. This small collection of restaurants and one or two bookshops is about as close as Seoul gets to a Chinatown. On the north side of the CPO is an obvious Chinese restaurant with an English sign that simply says 'Chinese Restaurant'. Most of the others bear the same name.

The Insadong area is good for upmarket, traditional-style Korean restaurants. The best known of these restaurants is *Sanch'on* (☎ 735 0312), which specialises in Buddhist temple cuisine (vegetarian). The W17,000 special full course allows you to sample 15 courses that include such oddities as acorn jelly and wild sesame gruel. Seating is cushions on the floor, and there are traditional dance performances every evening from 8 to 9 pm to the twingings and twangings of Korean stringed instruments. Sanch'on is down a small alley off Insadonggil, but it's easy to find because of the English sign out on the street.

Not surprisingly, It'aewon has a number of restaurants offering non-Korean food and English-speaking waiters. Some places catering to foreign tastes include:

Ashoka (☎ 794 1171), Indian food
Chalet Swiss (☎ 795 1723), Swiss food
La Cucina (☎ 798 1631), Italian food
Moghul (☎ 796 5501/2), Pakistani food
Shakey's Pizza (☎ 793 3122/3), fast food
Sebastian (☎ 796 2384), Western food

Entertainment

Taehangno Taehangno literally means 'University St' because it was the former campus of Seoul National University. The university has long since moved, but the area has evolved into Seoul's trendiest cafe, pub, video parlour, karaoke and theatre district. On weekends the street, near line 4 Hyehwa subway station, is usually closed to traffic. Street theatre is frequently held here, though only Korean is spoken. Your best chances of seeing street theatre are on Saturday or Sunday afternoons, especially if the weather is fine. The street should be closed from 6 to 10 pm on Saturday and noon to 10 pm on Sunday.

It'aewon Officially called It'aewon-dong, It'aewon is on the south side of Namsan Park near the US military base. It's an area of bars, music and dancing clubs, restaurants, brothels and more. The area used to cater solely to US soldiers, but it's becoming more and more Koreanised. One place which has become a legend in It'aewon is the *King Club*, which features disco music, a dance floor and no cover charge, though you're expected to buy drinks. Just across the street is another lively place, *Heavy Metal*. Also in the neighbourhood is *All That Jazz*. *Nashville* is reputed to have good hamburgers, and boasts big screen movies and dart games along with the drinks.

From directly in front of the YMCA, you can catch bus No 23 which goes to It'aewon. You can also catch this bus from in front of the Samsung Building.

Myŏng-dong Besides It'aewon, the other part of Seoul that has numerous discos is in Myŏng-dong, east of the CPO. It's a very exclusive neighbourhood featuring high prices.

Chonggak & Chongno 3-ga The area south the YMCA (around Chonggak subway station on line 1) is a good nightlife area. A little farther east near the Chongno 3-ga subway station is the big movie district, but it's best avoided on weekends when the cinemas are packed out. Movies are sometimes advertised in the English newspapers, but you'll need to get a Korean paper to find out screening times. Tickets cost around W4000 unless you buy them from scalpers.

Things to Buy

The open-air markets are said to have the best deals. Close to the CPO is Namdaemun (south gate) Market. In Namdaemun, look for camping gear on the south side of the market (facing the Hoehyŏn subway station on line 4). Also within Namdaemun is Namraemun, which is two floors (underground) where black-market goods (smuggled from US military bases) are sold. It's one of the few places in Seoul where you can buy deodorant, but prices are not cheap. Namdaemun is closed on Sunday.

Right near the Chongno 5-ga subway station on line 1 is Tongdaemun Market. This place has the best selection of camping shops where you can buy very cheap rucksacks, tents etc. It's also a good place to pick up more fancy travel bags and suitcases. Tongdaemun is closed on the first and third Sunday of each month.

Hwanghak-dong Flea Market is perhaps the most important shopping area for newly arrived shoestring travellers interested to set up in Seoul. Everything from second-hand furniture to used refrigerators can be bought here. The market is east of Tongdaemun. Take the line 2 subway to the Shindang station and walk north. You will first encounter the Chung-ang Market, which basically sells food (even live chickens and dogs). Continue north for another block and you'll find the flea market; if you've passed the elevated roadway then you've gone too far.

It'aewon is the cheapest and best shopping district for clothes, shoes and leathercraft. Insadonggil is a shopping street north of the YMCA which is a popular area for buying antiques, arts and crafts.

The Yongsan Electronics Market is to the west of It'aewon and is a good place to look for all manner of appliances: computers (including software), tape players, Nintendo games etc. You can reach the market by taking the Suwon train on subway line No 1 and getting off at Yongsan station; from there follow the elevated walkway over the tracks. Part of the electronics market is in one enormous building (a former bus terminal), but the market now spills out into many side streets as well.

Getting There & Away

Air Seoul's Kimp'o Airport is the main international arrival point in South Korea, and it's also the hub for domestic flights. The Getting

There & Away and Getting Around sections in this chapter give a rundown on the flights available and prices.

If you've arrived in Korea with an onward ticket, you need to reconfirm your reservation at least 72 hours before departure. The current list of airline offices in Seoul includes:

Airline	Code	Telephone
Aeroflot Soviet Airlines	SU	551 0321/4
Air China	CA	518 0330
Air France	AF	773 3151
Air New Zealand	NZ	777 6626
Alitalia Airlines	AZ	779 1676
All Nippon Airways	NH	752 5500
Asiana Airlines	OZ	774 4000
British Airways	BA	774 5511
Cathay Pacific Airways	CX	773 0321
China Eastern Airlines	MU	518 0330
Continental Airlines	CO	773 0100
Delta Airlines	DL	754 1921/3
Garuda Indonesia Airways	GA	773 2092/3
Japan Airlines	JL	757 1720
Japan Air System	JD	752 9090/1
KLM Royal Dutch Airlines	KL	753 1093
Korean Air	KE	756 2000
Lufthansa German Airlines	LH	538 8141
Malaysia Airlines	MH	777 7761/2
Northwest Airlines	NW	734 7800
Philippine Airlines	PR	774 3581
Qantas Airways	QF	777 6871/3
Singapore Airlines	SQ	755 1226
Swiss Air	SR	757 8901/8
Thai Airways Int'l	TG	754 9960/5
United Airlines	UA	757 1691
VASP Brazilian Airlines	VP	779 5651
Vietnam Airlines	VN	775 5477/8

Bus The main bus station is the Seoul Express Bus Terminal on the south side of the Han River; take subway line No 3 and leave at the Express Bus Terminal station. The terminal is very well organised, with signs in English and Korean over all the ticket offices and bus bays, so you can't go wrong as long as you don't confuse places like Kongju, Kwangju and Kyŏngju.

In addition to this terminal there are a farther six long-distance bus terminals. The Tong-Seoul (east Seoul) bus terminal is also useful, especially for getting to places on the east coast and some tourist spots such as Yong-in Farmland, Ch'ungju, Suanbo Hot

Springs, Onyang, Andong, and Songnisan and Chuwangsan national parks. You can reach Tong-Seoul bus terminal by taking subway line 2 to the Kangbyŏn station.

Sangbong bus terminal, in the eastern suburbs, is useful for people heading east. It's the terminal for buses to and from Ch'unch'on, Sokch'o, Kangnŭng, Wonju, Tongduch'on, Soyosan, Ŭijŏngbu and Yŏju. Sangbong bus terminal is connected by bus with Ch'ŏngnyangni railway station (the terminus of subway line No 1). It takes 15 minutes from Ch'ŏngnyangni to reach Sangbong on bus Nos 38-2, 165, 165-2, 166 and 522-1; or 50 minutes by bus from Chongno 1-ga on bus Nos 131 and 131-1.

Train Most long-distance trains departing from Seoul leave from Seoul station. The one important exception is the train heading east towards Ch'unch'ŏn. For this, go to Ch'ŏngnyangni railway station, which you reach by taking subway line No 1 to its terminus.

Getting Around

To/From the Airport Kimp'o Airport is 18 km west of the city centre, and handles both domestic and international flights. Construction is proceeding apace on the subway connection between the airport and central Seoul. This will undoubtedly be the most convenient transport option when it begins operating. Completion is scheduled for late 1995.

When the subway gets running, it will no doubt cause major changes to the bus routes. No information is yet available on these changes, but what follows was current at the time of this writing.

At present, there are different kinds of buses going to and from the airport, charging different prices. Some buses are express and some are not, but it makes little difference – traffic jams are the key factor in determining how long the journey takes. However, the fancier buses do offer fancier facilities and extra room to store luggage.

The best deal is bus No 600 or No 601, both of which are express buses and guaran-

tee a seat for all passengers. The No 601 bus goes into central Seoul, stopping at Shinch'on subway station, the Koreana Hotel, Tŏksugung, Seoul station, Nandaemun, Chongno 3-ga, Chongno 6-ga, Tongdaemun Gate and on to the Sheraton Walker Hill Hotel. The No 600 bus goes from Kimp'o into the areas south of the Han river, stopping at the National Cemetery, Palace Hotel, Seoul Express Bus Terminal, Yŏngdong market, Nam Seoul Hotel, KOEX, the Seoul Sports Complex and Chamshil subway station. There is also a bus No 600-2, which follows the same route as the 600 but terminates at the Seoul Express Bus Terminal. These buses leave every seven minutes from 5.40 am to 10 pm. The cost is W700.

Alternatively, there are local buses. These are more frequent than express buses and cost W600. The No 63 bus stops next to Tŏksugung and just north of the Koreana Hotel at the Donghwa Duty-Free Shop. The No 68 bus also stops close to City Hall and Midopa department store. The disadvantage of both these buses is that they will allow standing passengers and there is very little room for baggage.

Noticeably more upmarket is bus No 1002, which costs W1300. It follows much the same route as the No 63 and stops at the same spots in the city centre.

Bus City buses run from approximately 5.30 am until midnight. The ordinary buses are colour-coded purple and white or blue and white, and cost W300 (exact change please) or W290 with a token (same word in Korean) bought from one of the bus-token booths found at most major bus stops. The green and white chwasŏk buses (the ones with seats) cost W600 and no tokens are available. The token booths sell a *Bus Route Guide (Bŏsŭ Nosŏn Onnae)* for W700, but it's written entirely in Korean, even though some editions have had an English title on the cover.

Minibuses are privately owned and operate illegally, but are tolerated by the government because they provide services to

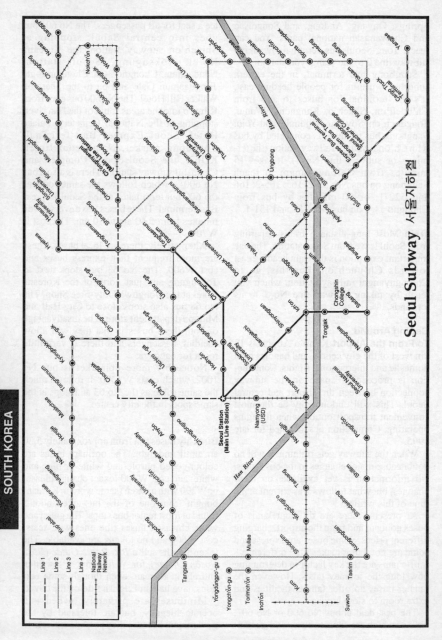

Seoul Subway 서울지하철

Line 1
Line 2
Line 3
Line 4
National
Railway
Network

areas not reached by public transport. The fare depends on the distance travelled.

Underground The Seoul subway system is modern, fast and cheap, but can be so crowded that if you drop dead, you'll never hit the ground. There are four lines in total, all of them colour coded. The system is very user friendly, and finding your way around should be no trouble. Trains run at least every six minutes from 5 am until midnight.

The basic charge is W350 for Zone 1, which includes most of the city. The fare increases to W400 if you cross into Zone 2. The machines where you buy tickets have a self-explanatory fare map, but you'll rarely need to go outside Zone 1. There are additional charges for suburban lines like the one to Suwon – buy these tickets from the ticket windows.

The subway system is still expanding. By 1997, the city hopes to have completed four new lines, thus doubling capacity. Most useful will be line No 5 which will extend all the way out to Kimp'o International Airport via Yŏŭido.

Taxi Demand is so much greater than supply that you practically have to throw yourself in front of a taxi to get the driver's attention. However, drivers of the deluxe (expensive) taxis are often on the prowl for foreigners. If you don't mind paying for this luxury, you'll have some tactical advantage over the locals.

As for the ordinary taxis, you'll have to fight it out (literally) with the Koreans. Remember as the taxi goes sailing past that you must look confident and shout loudly. There is no room for the meek when it comes to trying to catch a taxi in Seoul.

Around Seoul

PUK'ANSAN 북한산
Just to the north of Seoul is Puk'ansan National Park, a popular area for hiking, rock climbing and photography. The summit of Puk'ansan is 836 metres high and offers the best views of Seoul if the smog doesn't get in the way. The rugged landscape of granite peaks and cliffs offers stunning scenery. Within the park is Puk'ansansong (North Mountain Fortress).

Getting There & Away
Take bus No 156 from the Sejong Cultural Centre to the Puk'ansan entrance (Puk'ansan ipku).

P'ANMUNJŎM 판문점
This is a good place to visit for a sobering dose of reality. Situated 56 km north of Seoul, P'anmunjŏm is the truce village on the ceasefire line established at the end of the Korean War in 1953. It's in a building here that the interminable 'peace' discussions continue.

Tours are run by Korea Travel Bureau (☎ 02-585 1191), which has an office on the 3rd floor of the Hotel Lotte. Tours cost W45,000, and, if it helps any, lunch is thrown in free. The tour includes a visit to the third invasion tunnel which North Korea dug under the DMZ, which was discovered in 1978. The trip takes seven hours and runs daily except weekends.

The USO (☎ 03-795 3063, 795 3028) also arranges tours at the bargain price of US$21 or the equivalent in Korean won, but without lunch or a tour of the invasion tunnel. You *do not* have to be a US citizen or military personnel to attend, but USO tours are extremely popular so book in advance.

While you are permitted to take photos and use binoculars, there are a number of restrictions that visitors must adhere to. You must bring your passport; children under 10 years of age are not allowed; Korean nationals are not allowed; and there is strict dress code which civilians must follow. Many travellers run afoul of this rule! The military lists the following as examples of inappropriate clothing for this formal occasion:

1) Shirts (top) without sleeves, T-shirts, tank tops and shirts of similar design.
2) Dungarees or blue jeans of any kind, including 'designer jeans'.

SOUTH KOREA

3) Shorts of any style, including hiking, bermuda, cut offs, or 'short shorts'.
4) Miniskirts, halter tops, backless dresses and other abbreviated items of similar design.
5) Any item of outer clothing of the sheer variety.
6) Shower shoes, thongs or 'flip-flops'.
7) Items of military clothing not worn as an integral part of a prescribed uniform.
8) Any form-fitting clothing, including tight-knit tops, tight-knit pants and stretch pants.

SUWON 수원

Suwon is an ancient fortress city 48 km south of Seoul. The walls were constructed in the later part of the 18th century by King Kongjo in an unsuccessful attempt to make Suwon the nation's capital. The walls, gates, a number of pavilions and an unusual water gate have all been reconstructed along original lines.

To get there take subway line No 1 heading south all the way to the last stop, making sure the train is marked Suwon. The journey takes about 45 minutes.

KOREAN FOLK VILLAGE 한국민속촌

This major attraction *(min sok ch'on)* is as near to being authentic as throngs of tourists will allow. The village has examples of the traditional peasants', farmers' and civil officials' housing styles from all over the country, as well as craft workshops, a brewery, Confucian school, Buddhist temple and a market place.

To get there, go to Suwon by subway and cross the road to find the office of the Folk Village. You can catch a free bus from there. Admission to the Folk Village costs W3600 and opening hours are from 9 am to 5 pm.

YŎJU 여주

About two km to the east of Yŏju is **Shiluksa**, a magnificent temple built around 580 AD. The temple is open from 8 am to 4 pm.

A short bus ride to the west of Yŏju is Yongnung, where you can find the **Tomb of King Sejong**. Sejong, whose face adorns the W10,000 bill, invented the modern Korean script (han'gŭl) and is considered the greatest of Korea's kings. The tomb site is open

from 8.30 am to 6 pm, and there is a small museum on the grounds.

Getting There & Away

Yŏju is to the south-east of Seoul. You can get there by bus from Seoul's Sangbong bus terminal.

North-East Korea

CH'UNCH'ŎN 춘천

This is the provincial capital of Kangwon-do (Kangwon Province) and the urban centre of South Korea's northern lake district, which includes lakes Soyang and Paro. The main attraction is a boat trip on the lakes. Set in a beautiful mountainous area, Ch'unch'ŏn makes a good stopover en route to the Sŏraksan and Odaesan national parks.

Places to Stay

The main places for cheap yŏinsuk (about W8000) is just to the north-east of the bus terminal on the way towards the post office. There are plenty of more expensive yŏgwan (W18,000) near the bus terminal itself. Some good places include the *Ch'ŏnghwa-jang Yŏgwan* and *Yŏŭn-jang Yŏgwan*.

Getting There & Away

Bus Buses to Ch'unch'ŏn depart from Seoul's Sangbong bus terminal, but the train is certainly more convenient. The same bus continues on from Ch'unch'ŏn to Sokch'o on the east coast.

Train Trains to Ch'unch'ŏn depart from Seoul's Ch'ŏngnyangni railway station at the terminus of subway line No 1. The one-way trip takes a little over 1½ hours. Unfortunately, the two railway stations in town are both equally far from the bus terminal, so you'll need to deal with the city buses, take a taxi or walk about 1.5 km.

Boat Trips

There are two excellent boat trips on Lake Soyang. A popular short trip is the one from

Ch'unch'ŏn to Chongpyongsa, a Buddhist temple up in the hills north of the lake. The boats run daily every half-hour or so depending on sufficient numbers. The trip takes about 10 minutes.

It's much more interesting to travel by a combination of boat and bus or taxi to Sŏraksan National Park via the town of Inje. The boat follows Lake Soyang from Ch'unch'ŏn to just outside Inje where you catch a bus or share-taxi into town. Many of these share-taxis will take you all the way to Paektamsa at Inner Sŏrak, the least crowded part of Sŏraksan National Park. Negotiate the fare before heading out.

SŎRAKSAN NATIONAL PARK
설악산국립공원
This is the most scenically beautiful area in South Korea, with high craggy peaks, forests, tremendous waterfalls, crystal-clear water, old temples and hermitages. Though most of the trails are well marked, you'll need a map if you intend to go out into the real wilderness. Sŏraksan is an excellent place to go walking for a few days or even longer if you have camping equipment with you. Entry to the national park costs W1600.

Unfortunately, during the summer peak season, Sŏraksan gets so crowded it's a wonder the whole mountain doesn't collapse. Your best chance of avoiding the stampede is to head for Inner Sŏrak at the west end of the park. The spring season is relatively uncrowded, but the hiking trails may be closed at that time due to fire hazard.

Places to Stay
The main entrance to the park is on the east side of the tourist village of Sŏrak-dong. Unfortunately, accommodation tends to be expensive here. In the peak season, it could easily cost up to W30,000 if you can find anything at all! Your best bet is probably to stay in the nearby city of Sokch'o or the youth hostel in Naksan.

Getting There & Away
You get to Sŏraksan and the trails into the mountains via Sŏrak-dong, which is at the end of the road that branches off from the coast road about halfway between Naksan and Sokch'o. There are frequent buses both from Yangyang, a few km south of Naksan, and from Sokch'o every 10 to 15 minutes from around dawn to 9.30 pm. In Sokch'o, take bus No 7 (W300).

SOKCH'O 속초
This small city on the north-east coast is mainly of interest to travellers as a staging area for visiting Sŏraksan National Park. Other nearby attractions are the beaches on the south side of town and a temple at Naksan.

Places to Stay
Most of the cheap yŏinsuk are clustered around the long-distance bus station in the centre of town. Places to try include *Hyŏndae Yŏinsuk* and *Ŭngwang Yŏinsuk*. Also around this station are the *Yŏngho-jang Yŏgwan* and the *Yugwang-jang Yŏgwan*.

The express bus terminal is five km farther south. You may actually find it more convenient to stay in this area as it's closer to Sŏraksan and the beaches. Here you'll find the *Myŏshi Yŏinsuk* plus several more expensive yŏgwan.

Getting There & Away
Korean Air offers flights on the Seoul-Sokch'o route.

From the Seoul Express bus terminal there are departures for Sokch'o once every 40 minutes between 6.30 am and 6.40 pm. From Tong-Seoul bus terminal, departures are once every 1½ hours. The journey takes about five hours.

NAKSAN 낙산
Naksan is famous for its temple, Naksansa, which dates from 671 AD, and its huge white statue of Avalokitesvara (completed in 1977), which looks out to sea from on top of a small pine-covered rocky outcrop. Below the temple is Naksan beach.

Places to Stay
There are several yŏgwan and yŏinsuk on the beach side of the coast road, where meals can

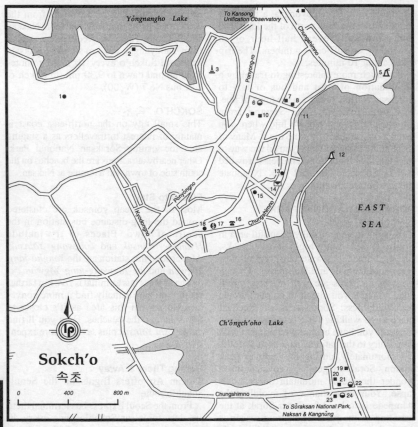

Sokch'o

속초

Yǒngnangho Lake

To Kansong
Unification Observatory

*EAST
SEA*

Ch'ǒngch'oho Lake

To Sǒraksan National Park,
Naksan & Kangnǔng

0   400   800 m

also be arranged. But the most popular place for budget travellers is *Naksan Youth Hostel* (☎ 0396-672 3416) near the temple. It's a huge, plush place with English-speaking staff, hot and cold running water, and its own restaurant and coffee shop. At W5000 it's good value and the cheapest place to use as a base for Sǒraksan.

Getting There & Away

All the local buses plying between Sokch'o and Yangyang pass Naksan, and there will be a bus every 10 to 15 minutes. Buses from either place to Naksan cost W300 and take about 25 minutes.

ODAESAN NATIONAL PARK
오대산국립공원

Like Sǒraksan, Odaesan is a mountain massif where nature reigns supreme. There are excellent hiking possibilities and superb views. Deep inside the western section of the park are two of the most famous Buddhist temples in Korea: Wolchǒngsa and Sangwonsa. Entry to the park costs W1600.

Hikers may want to challenge Pirobong, the park's highest peak at 1563 metres. Other

1	Sokch'o Country Club 속초컨트리클럽	13	City Hall 시청
2	Condominium 콘도미니엄	14	Post Office 우체국
3	Pogwangsa (Temple) 보광사	15	Chung'ang Market 중앙시장
4	Sŏrak Beach Hotel 설악비치리조텔	16	Telephone Company 전화국
5	Lighthouse 등대	17	Chohŭng Bank 조흥은행
6	Inter-City Bus Terminal 시외버스터미널	18	Korean Air 대한항공 매표소
7	Yugwang-jang Yŏgwan 유관장여관	19	Usŏng-jang Yŏgwan 우성장여관
8	Petel-jang Yŏgwan 벤엘장여관	20	Royal-jang Yŏgwan 로얄장여관
9	Yŏngho-jang Yŏgwan 영호장여관	21	Myŏshi Yŏinsuk 며시여인숙
10	Hyŏndae & Ŭngwang Yŏinsuk 현대여인숙, 은광여인숙	22	Express Bus Terminal 고속버스터미널
11	Pagoda Park 탑공원	23	Tongsŏ-jang Yŏgwan 동서장여관
12	Lighthouse 등대	24	Bus Stop (To Soraksan & Naksan) 정류장 (설악산, 낙산)

notable peaks include Horyongbong, Sangwangbong, Tongdaesan and Turobong.

Back-country cooking and camping is currently prohibited.

Getting There & Away

A trip to Odaesan National Park starts in Kangnŭng, and there's a choice of direct bus or local buses that involve a change at Jinbu, just off the expressway.

There are four direct buses per day from Kangnŭng to Wolchŏngsa temple, the first at 9.10 am and the last at 4.05 pm. The fare is W900 and the journey takes about 1½ hours. These buses will have Wochŏngsa on their destination indicator.

East-Central Korea

KYŎNGJU 경주

For almost a thousand years Kyŏngju was the capital of the Silla Dynasty and for nearly 300 years of that period it was the capital of the whole peninsula. Its origins date back to

57 BC, and it survived right through to the 10th century AD, when it fell victim to division from within and invasion from outside. After its conquest by the Koryo Dynasty, the capital of Korea was moved far to the north and Kyŏngju fell into decline.

A small, provincial town with easy-going people, Kyŏngju is an open-air museum. Temples, tombs, shrines, the remains of palaces, pleasure gardens and castles survive as fine examples of Silla artistry.

Things to See

Right in the centre of Kyŏngju city is **Tumuli Park**, a huge walled area with 20 royal tombs. One huge tomb, the Chonmachong (Heavenly Horse Tomb), is open in cross section to show the method of construction. Facsimiles of the golden crown, bracelets, jade ornaments, weapons and pottery found here are displayed in glass cases.

A few hundred metres away is the stone observatory of **Chomsongdae**, and a little farther on is the **Castle of the Crescent Moon**, or Panwolsong. This was once the royal castle and the site of a fabled palace,

SOUTH KOREA

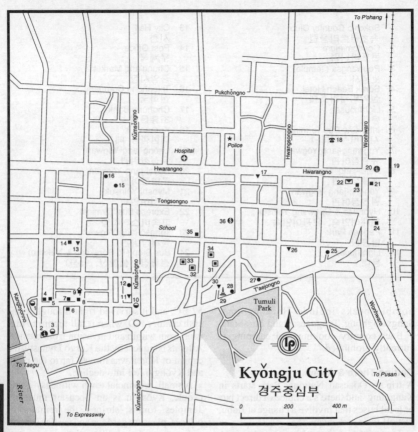

Kyŏngju City
경주중심부

0   200   400 m

which dominated the whole area. Little is left of this fortress but thousands of relics were dredged up from the pond when it was drained in 1975.

Also on this circuit is the **Punhwangsa Pagoda**, the oldest datable pagoda in Korea. Only three of the original nine storeys are left.

Just a little to the south on the road to Pulguksa is the superb **Kyŏngju National Museum**, one of Korea's best. The museum is closed on Monday.

Crossing the river bridge south of the city brings you to the **Onŭng Tombs**, five of the most ancient tomb mounds in the area. A long walk farther on is the beautiful Posokjong Bower, elegant gardens from the Silla Dynasty. Less than a km down the road are the mysterious **Triple Buddhas**, which were only discovered in 1923. Last on this circuit are the four **Samnŭng Tombs**, nearly 1000 years younger than the tombs in the Onŭng compound.

In the western area are the **Muyol Tombs**. The main tomb is that of King Muyol who, in the mid-7th century, paved the way for the unification of Korea by conquering the rival Paekje Kingdom.

PLACES TO STAY

4   Buhojang Hotel
    부호장여관
6   Hotel Kirin
    기린장여관
7   Hotel Seorimjang
    시림장여관
8   Oksan-jang Yŏgwan
    옥산장여관
9   Hanjin Hostel
    한진장여관
14 Hyopsong Tourist Hotel
    협성관광호텔
21 Cheil Yŏinsuk
    제일여인숙
23 Myŏngji Yŏgwan
    명지여관
24 Sŏnin-jang Yŏgwan
    선인장여관
35 Ch'onil Hotel
    천일호텔

PLACES TO EAT

11 Sŏrabŏl Panjŏm Chinese
    Restaurant
    서라벌 (중국집)
13 Grand Restaurant
    그랜드식당
17 Americana Hamburger
    아메리카나
26 Shiga Restaurant & Bar
    시가식당
30 Sarangch'ae Restaurant
    사랑채식당

OTHER

1   Inter-City Bus Terminal
    시외버스터미널

2   Tourist Information Kiosk
    관광안내소
3   Express Bus Terminal
    고속버스터미널
5   Korean Air
    대한항공
10 Bus Stop for Pulguksa
    정류장 (불국사)
12 Taesong Shikdang
    대성식당
15 Chung'ang Market
    중앙시장
16 Fruit & Vegetable Market
    청과물시장
18 Telephone Office
    전화국
19 Railway Station
    경주역
20 Tourist Information Kiosk
    관광안내소
22 Post Office
    우체국
25 Yurim Teahouse
    유림
27 City Hall
    시청
28 Bicycle Rental
    자전거대여
29 Pŏpchangsa Temple
    법장사
31 Kumnyongch'ong (Tomb)
    금령총
32 Kumgwanch'ong (Tomb)
    금관총
33 So Bongch'ong (Tomb)
    서봉총
34 Ponghwadae (Tomb)
    봉화대
36 Korea Exchange Bank
    외환은행

To the south-east is the crowning glory of Silla temple architecture, **Pulguksa**, built on a series of stone terraces about 16 km from Kyŏngju. It's Korea's most famous temple and is simply magnificent. Take bus No 11 from the city to Pulguksa.

High above Pulguksa, reached by a long, winding sealed road, is the famous **Sŏkkuram Grotto**, where a seated buddha figure looks out over the spectacular landscape towards the distant sea. To get to the grotto from Pulguksa, take one of the fre-

quent minibuses that leave from the tourist information pavilion in the car park below the temple.

Places to Stay

The *Hanjin Hostel* (☎ 0561-771 4097) is two blocks north-east of the bus terminal and easily identified by a large English sign on the roof. The owner, Mr Kwon Young-joung, speaks good English, hands out free maps and is very knowledgeable about local sights. This place has become a sort of

backpackers' unofficial travel and information centre for Kyŏngju. Prices here for
singles start at W14,000, and doubles are
from W18,000 to W20,000.

There are heaps of other yŏgwan near the
bus terminal, all charging similar or higher
prices. Some worth checking out include the
Hotel Kirin and *Hotel Seorimjang*.

Getting There & Away
Bus The two bus stations, express and long
distance, are adjacent to each other. Direct
buses to Seoul, Pusan, Taegu etc are frequent.

Train There are only two direct trains connecting Seoul to Kyŏngju (three on Sunday),
and these are high-priced saemaul-ho trains.
You can do the trip for much less by taking
one of the cheaper trains from Seoul to
Tongdaegu (east Taegu station) and then
changing to the Taegu-Kyŏngju express bus.
The express bus station at Tongdaegu is
called the *kosok t'ŏminŏl*.

TAEGU 대구
This is South Korea's third largest city.
Although you'll hardly want to go to Taegu
just to say you've been there, it's another one
of those vital crossroads.

Places to Stay & Eat
There are plenty yŏgwan around the Express
bus terminal and the Tongdaegu railway
station, such as the *Shinra-jang Yŏgwan* and
Tongdaegu-jang Yŏgwan.

Getting There & Away
Taegu station in the town centre is for local
trains only, and unless you're staying in
Taegu, don't get off the train here! The
Tongdaegu station on the east side of the city
is where express trains stop, and this is where
you should get off if you're continuing on to
Kyŏngju by bus. Taegu has five bus terminals: one express plus north, south, east and
west long-distance stations.

KAYASAN NATIONAL PARK
가야산국립공원
High up on the steep, forested slopes of
Kayasan National Park is Haeinsa. This
temple is the repository of the 80,000 carved
wooden blocks that make up the *Tripitaka
Koreana*. If you don't manage to get into the
library to see these Buddhist scriptures (ask
a monk), there's plenty of interest in other
buildings. The original set, completed in
1251, was destroyed during a 14th-century
Mongol invasion. The current replacement
set dates from that time.

You can take a day trip from Taegu or stay
near the temple. Buses to the park run from
Taegu's West inter-city bus terminal (*sŏbu
shi-oe t'ŏminŏl*) once every 20 minutes from
6.30 am until 8 pm.

ULLŬNGDO 울릉도
Isolated out in the storm-lashed Sea of Japan
(which the Koreans call the East Sea), this
rugged island is one of Korea's most unusual
hidden treasures.

Most of the people live in small villages
along the coast, making their living from the
sea. There are virtually no roads and only
two buses; people get around on foot or in
fishing boats. Todong is the largest town,
almost hidden away like a pirate outpost in a
valley between two craggy, forested mountains with a very narrow harbour front. It was
only settled in the late 19th century, but what
it lacks in the way of nightlife it makes up
for in friendliness.

Places to Stay
The cheapest places to stay are in minbak.
The usual price is W10,000 per room. There
are fancier yŏgwan, and for campers (with
their own tents) there's a landscaped site just
below the mineral springs that costs W3000
per tent.

Getting There & Away
You can get to Ullŭngdo by ferry from
P'ohang (217 km, 7½ hours), Hup'o (156
km, 2½ to 3½ hours) and Tonghae (137 km,
2½ hours). Be aware that boats are fre-

quently cancelled due to rough seas. The above table lists the official schedule.

South-East Korea

PUSAN 부산

Pusan is the second largest city and principal port of South Korea. It is superbly located between several mountain peaks, though the city itself has that gone-to-seed appearance common in major seaports. Many people regard Pusan as a concrete jungle to be avoided, so they come here only to take the ferries to Yŏsu, Chejudo or Japan.

Information

Tourist Office The tourist information office (☎ 462 9734) is in the City Hall. There are also tourist information kiosks at Kimhae Airport (☎ 973 1100), outside Pusan railway station (☎ 463 4938) and at the Kukche ferry terminal (☎ 460 3331 ext 5450) where you catch the international Pukwan ferry to Japan.

Foreign Embassies The addresses of

Ferry Fares to Ullŭngdo

P'ohang-Ullŭngdo

Period	P'ohang	Ullŭngdo	Frequency	Travel Time	Ship's Name
6 Aug-15 Jul	noon	10am	every 2 days	7½ hours	Daea Express
22 Jul-16Aug	noon	11.30 pm	daily	7½ hours	Daea Express
16 Aug-25 Jul	10 am	3 pm	daily	3½ hours	Sea Flower
26 Jul-15 Aug	10 am	4.30 pm	daily	3½ hours	Sea Flower

Hup'o-Ullŭngdo

Period	Hup'o	Ullŭngdo	Frequency	Travel Time	Ship's Name
1 Jun-19 Jul	noon	4 pm	daily	2½ hours	Ocean Flower
21 Aug-30 Oct	noon	4 pm	daily	2½ hours	Ocean Flower
21 Jul-20 Aug	10 am & 6 pm	5 am & 2pm	2 daily	2½ hours	Ocean Flower
24 Jul-10 Aug	7 pm	3 pm	daily	2½ hours	Sea Flower

Sokch'o-Ullŭngdo

Period	Sokch'o	Ullŭngdo	Frequency	Travel time
1 Mar-20 Jul	2 pm	9 am	daily	4 hours
21 Jul-20 Aug	9 am	4 am	daily	4 hours
21 Aug-31 Oct	2 pm	9 am	daily	4 hours

Tonghae (Muk'o)-Ullŭngdo

Period	Tonghae	Ullŭngdo	Frequency	Travel Time
16 Jul-20 Aug	9.30 am & 5 pm	5.30 am & 1.30 pm	2 daily	2½ hours
21 Mar-15 Jul	1 pm	8.30 am	daily	2½ hours
21 Aug-31 Oct	1 pm	8.30 am	daily	2½ hours
1 Nov-20 Mar	1 pm	10.30 am	Tue & Fri	2½ hours

Fares to Ullŭngdo

Route	Ship's Name	berth	deluxe	1st class	2nd class
Hup'o	Ocean Flower				W25,250
P'ohang	Daea Express	W33,470		W22,310	
P'ohang	Sea Flower		W36,000	W32,800	
Sokch'o	Taewon Catamaran			W32,500	
Tonghae	Taewon Catamaran			W21,800	

Central Pusan
부산중심부

foreign embassies in Pusan include the following:

Japan
1147-11, Ch'oryang-dong, Tong-gu (☎ 051-465 5101/5)

Russia
10th floor, Korea Exchange Bank, 89-1, Chung'ang-dong 4-ga, Chung-gu (☎ 051-441 9904)

USA
American Consulate Building, 24, Taech'ŏng-dong 2-ga, Chung-gu (☎ 051-246 7791)

Things to See

Take the lift to the top of **Pusan Tower** for incredible views over the city. At night, foreigners head to **Texas St**, opposite the railway station, which is a colourful area with music clubs, bars and pick-up joints. At **Chagalch'i Fish Market** you can watch catches being unloaded from the boats and buyers haggling over prices.

Places to Stay

There are no yŏinsuk around the bus terminals, but there are heaps of yŏgwan costing around W16,000 to W18,000. Staying by the East inter-city bus terminal

PLACES TO STAY

5 Arirang Hotel
아리랑호텔
6 Plaza Hotel
프라쟈호텔
9 Commodore Hotel
코모도호텔
12 Kŭmhwa Yŏgwan
금화여관
15 Ch'ŏnch'o-jang Yŏgwan
천초장여관
16 Ferry Hotel
훼라호텔
17 Bando Hotel
반도호텔
23 Hyundae Yŏinsuk
휸대여인숙
25 Sorabol Hotel
서라벌호텔
30 Tower Hotel
타워호텔
31 Pusan Hotel
부산호텔
35 Tongyang Tourist Hotel
동양관광호텔
36 Royal Hotel
로얄호텔
38 Phoenix Hotel
피닉스호텔

PLACES TO EAT

22 Roast Chicken & Duck Restaurant
부로이라

OTHER

1 Foreigners' Arcade
외인전용상가
2 Pusan Station
부산역
3 Tourist Information Kiosk
관광안내소
4 Pusan Railway Station
부산역

7 Telephone Office
전화국
8 Korean Air
대한항공
10 Maryknoll Hospital
메리놀병원
11 Chung'ang-dong Station
중앙동
13 Korea Exchange Bank
외한은행
14 Asiana Airlines
아시아나항공
18 Customs Office
부산세관
19 Immigration Office
출입국관리사무소
20 International Ferry Terminal
부관훼리터미널
21 Central Post Office (CPO)
중앙우체국
24 Korea First Bank
제일은행
26 USIS
미국문화원
27 Bank of Korea
한국은행
28 Yuna Department Store
유나백화점
29 Pusan Tower
부산타위
32 Domestic Ferry Terminal
연안여객선터미널
33 City Hall & Tourist Information
시청
34 Namp'o-dong Station
남포동
37 Mihwadang Department Store
미화당백화점
39 Chagalch'i Station
지갈치
40 Shinch'ŏnji Department Store
신천지백화점
41 Chagalch'i Fish Market
자갈치시장

SOUTH KOREA

is reasonably convenient because it's near a subway station.

The cheapest places near the city centre are the yŏinsuk on the south side of the Pusan railway station.

Getting There & Away

Air There are international flights to Fukuoka and Sendai in Japan. There are domestic flights to Seoul, Cheju on Chejudo and Kwangju.

Bus The Express bus terminal (kosok t'ŏminŏl) and the East local bus terminal (tongbu shi-oe t'ŏminŏl) are a long way from the city centre out in the suburb of Tongnae.

The East inter-city bus terminal is more convenient, being right next to Myŏngnyun-dong subway station. The Express bus terminal is about one km from the Tongnae subway station.

Train Pusan is the southern terminus of the Seoul-Pusan railway. Pusan's main railway station is right in the city centre.

Boat The journey between Pusan and Yŏsu via the Hallyo Waterway National Park on the *Angel* hydrofoil should be one of your high priorities – the views are great. The only downer is that the ferries are completely enclosed by glass windows. There are no open decks and you must occupy a seat, which may face backwards. The ferry makes five stops along the way. There's no need to book in advance if you avoid holidays and weekends. See the *Angel* hydrofoil time table below for the summer-season schedule.

Getting Around
To/From the Airport There are two airport terminal shuttle buses which connect Kimhae Airport with the city. Bus No 201 runs from the airport terminal to Chung-gu (the city centre) via Pusan station and City Hall. Bus No 307 runs from the airport terminal to Haeundae Beach and the Express bus terminal.

Subway Pusan has a subway system connecting such vital places as the East inter-city bus terminal with the city centre and the ferry piers.

AROUND PUSAN
The **Tongdosa** temple, one of the largest and most famous in Korea, sits amidst beautiful forested mountains and crystal-clear streams. There are 65 buildings, including 13 hermitages behind the main temple complex.

You can visit it on the way from Pusan to Kyŏngju by taking a Pusan-Taegu long-distance bus. It's less than a one-km walk to Tongdo village from where the bus drops you. From the village you can take a taxi the final 1.5 km to the temple or walk. There's also a direct bus to Tongdo village from the East inter-city bus terminal in Pusan – this way means you won't have to walk from the freeway to Tongdo village.

South-West Korea

YŎSU 여수
Yŏsu lies halfway along the mountainous and deeply indented southern coast of Korea. An impressive area of islands and peninsulas, a large section now makes up the Hallyŏ

Angel Hydrofoil Time Table

Pusan	Sŏngp'o	Ch'ungmu	Saryangdo	Samch'ŏnp	Namhae	Yŏsu
7 am	8.20 am	8.40 am	9.10 am	9.35 am	10.10 am	10.40 am
9.10 am	10.30 am					
11.15 am	12.35 am	12.55 am	1.25 pm	1.50 pm	2.15 pm	2.45 pm
1.10 pm	2.30 pm					
3.10 pm	4.30 pm	4.50 pm	5.20 pm	5.45 pm	6.20 pm	6.50 pm
5.10 pm	6.30 pm					

Yŏsu	Namhae	Samch'ŏnp'o	Saryangdo	Ch'ungmu	Sŏngp'o	Pusan
7 am	7.20 am	8.40 am				
7 am	7.45 am	8.20 am	8.45 am	9.15 am	9.35 am	10.55 am
11.05 am	11.25 am	12.45 pm				
11.15 am	11.50 am	12.15 pm	12.40 pm	1.10 pm	1.30 pm	2.50 pm
3.20 pm	3.40 pm	5 pm				
3.10 pm	3.55 pm	4.30 pm	4.55 pm	5.25 pm	5.45 pm	7.05 pm

Pusan Subway

- Nop'o-dong 노포동
- Pŏmŏsa 범어사
- Namsan-dong 남산동
- Tushil 두실
- Kusŏ-dong 구서동
- Changjŏn-dong 장전동
- Pusan University 부산대학교
- Onch'ŏnjang 온천장
- East Inter-City Bus Terminal — Myŏngnyun-dong 명륜동
- Express Bus Terminal — Tongnae 동래
- Teachers' College 교육대학
- Yŏnsan-dong 연산동
- Yŏnje 여제
- Yangjŏng 양정
- Pujŏn 부전
- Sŏmyŏn 서면
- Pŏmnaegol 범내골
- Pŏmil-dong 범일동
- Chwach'ŏn-dong 좌천동
- Pusanjin 부산진
- Ch'oryang 초량
- Pusan Station 부산역
- Ferryboat Terminals & Central — Chung'ang-dong 중앙동
- Namp'o-dong 남포동
- Fish Market — Chagalch'i 자갈치
- T'osŏng-dong 토성동
- Tongdaeshin-dong 동대신동
- Sŏdaeshin-dong 서대신동

Haesang National Park. The hydrofoil trip from Yŏsu to Pusan via Sŏngp'o, Ch'ungmu, Saryangdo, Samch'ŏnp'o and Namhae is extremely popular. See under Pusan in the previous South-East Korea section for details.

Admiral Yi's Turtle Ship
Yŏsu's historical claim to fame is in connection with Admiral Yi, who routed the Japanese navy on several occasions during the 16th century. On display in Yŏsu is a full-size re-creation of one of the admiral's famous iron-clad war vessels, known as turtle ships.

The ship can be found on the island of Tolsando, which is south of town and connected to the mainland by an enormous suspension bridge. From the bridge you can see dozens of souvenir stalls, and maybe even the ship itself; it's moored in the water and you can go inside.

Places to Stay
The cheapest yŏinsuk are around the railway station, which is almost a km north-east of the town centre. There are plenty of yŏgwan around the bus terminal, but that's almost three km north-west out of town.

Getting There & Away
There are direct flights between Yŏsu and Seoul, and also Yŏsu and Cheju.

The express and inter-city bus terminals are near each other on the north-west side of town, on the road to Sunchŏn and the airport. Many city buses can drop you off there.

Departing or arriving by hydrofoil is the most fun. The ferry terminal is right near the town centre and is easy to find. For the hydrofoil schedule, see Getting There & Away under Pusan in the previous South-East Korea section.

MOAKSAN PROVINCIAL PARK
모악산도립공원
The area has nice views from Moaksan (elevation 794 metres), but the big attraction here is the temple of Kumsansa. This was built in 599 AD. There are a number of

SOUTH KOREA

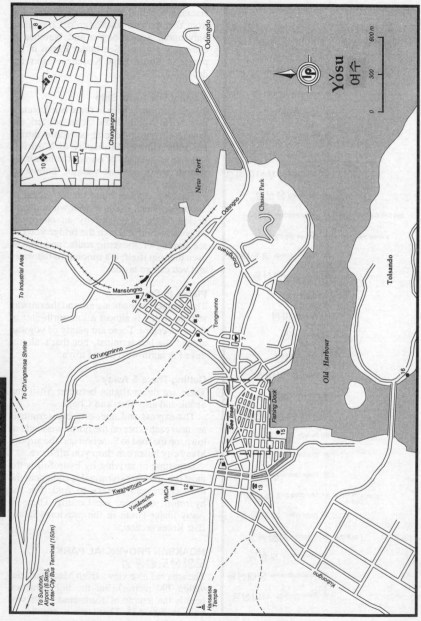

1 Railway Station
   여수역
2 Osŏng & Taedong yŏinsuk
   오성여인숙. 대동여인숙
3 Kungsil & Kwangsŏng-jang yŏgwan
   궁실장여관. 광성장여관
4 Yŏsu Hotel
   여수호텔
5 Sejong Hotel
   세종관광호텔
6 Yŏsu Park Hostel
   여수파크호텔
7 Yŏsu Post Office
   여수우체국
8 Chinnamgwan Pavilion
   진남관
9 Samoa Department Store
   사모아백화점
10 Citizens Department Store
   시민백화점
11 Yŏsu Beach Hotel
   여수비치호텔
12 Korean Air
   대한항공 매표소
13 Telephone Company
   전화국
14 Kyodong Post Office
   교동우체국
15 Ferry Terminal
   여객선터미널
16 Turtle Ship
   거북선

unusual buildings on the temple grounds, including the unusually shaped pagoda in front of the main hall.

Transport is most convenient from the city of Chŏnju, from where you can get buses every 30 minutes between 6.20 am and 8.45 pm.

MAISAN PROVINCIAL PARK
마이산도립공원

Maisan (elevation 685 metres) means 'horse ears mountain', which roughly describes the shape of the two rocky outcrops which make up the twin peaks.

T'apsa (Pagoda Temple) is stuck right between the two 'horse ears'. It's a temple of unique design, decorated by hundreds of stone formations created by stacking rocks on top of one another.

For the best views, climb up the small path to the left of the souvenir stands coming down from the main temple. You'll pass a camping area and a small hermitage. The trail leads up to the top of yet another monolith – the views are incredible.

There is another temple on the mountain called Kumdangsa and a cave called Hwaamgul.

Getting There & Away
Bus transport is via the tiny town of Chinan at the park's entrance. First take a bus from Chŏnju (every 10 minutes from 6.30 am until 9.30 pm) to Chinan. The journey takes 50 minutes. From Chinan, buses to the temple leave every 30 minutes between 8 am and 6.20 pm, and the ride takes 10 minutes.

NAEJANGSAN NATIONAL PARK
내장산국립공원

Yet another beautiful park, the landscape is arranged like an amphitheatre. Once you've climbed to the rim, you can walk all the way to the other side, though it's strenuous. There are ladders to help hikers master the cliffs, and the views are just amazing all around. It takes at least three hours to walk the circuit, but try to allow more time.

Temples in the park include Naejangsa and Paegyangsa. Other sights spread out all over this large park include Todogam Hermitage, the Kumson and Wonjok valleys, Todok Waterfall and Yonggul Cave.

Getting There & Away
You can reach Naejangsan from Chŏngju (not to be confused with Chŏnju which is farther north). The bus drops you off in a tourist village, from where you have a 30-minute walk to Naejangsa Temple and the start of the climb.

SŎNUNSAN PROVINCIAL PARK
선운산도립공원

Sŏnunsan is a gorgeous place which boasts a temple called Sŏnunsa and small sub-

SOUTH KOREA

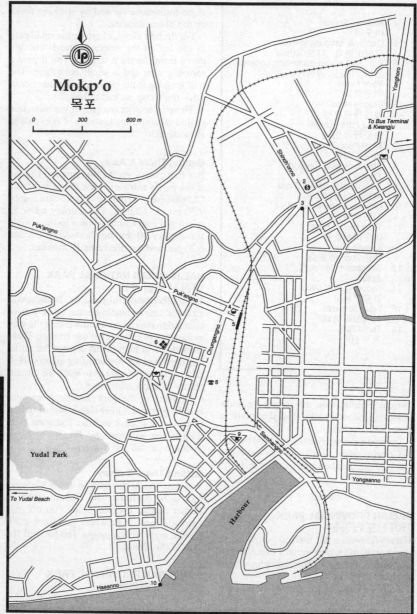

1 Mokp'o Post Office
   목포우체국
2 Korea Exchange Bank
   외환은행
3 Kukto Cinema
   국도극장
4 Bus No 1 Bus Stop
   정류장 (시외터미널)
5 Railway Station
   목포역
6 Cheil Department Store
   제일백화점
7 Ch'angp'yŏng Post Office
   창평우체국
8 Telephone Office
   전화국
9 Main Yŏgwan Area
10 Ferry Terminal
   목포한여개터미널

temples perched all around a gorge near the sea. One traveller wrote that this place is 'possibly the most beautiful spot in all Korea, if not the world'.

Getting There & Away

There are only five buses daily direct from Chŏngju to the park. Failing that, get a bus from Chŏngju to Koch'ang. These run every 10 minutes from 6.15 am until 9 pm, and the ride takes 40 minutes. From Koch'ang, buses leave for the temple every 45 minutes from 7 am until 8.20 pm. Do not confuse Koch'ang with Kŏch'ang, which is southwest of Taegu near Kayasan National Park.

KWANGJU 광주

There is nothing to see in this city of concrete, but it's a major transport hub and you are likely to pass this way.

Places to Stay

The bus terminal has moved way out to the west of town, which is inconvenient in terms of finding yŏgwan. Currently there are three yŏgwan to the north-east of the bus terminal, all charging at least W18,000: *Paekrim-jang Yŏgwan*, *Royal-jang Yŏgwan* and *Kwangch'ŏn-jang Yŏgwan*. The alleys opposite the

railway station have relatively cheap yŏinsuk plus a number of yŏgwan.

MOKP'O 목포

The fishing port of Mokp'o is at the end of the railway line near the south-western tip of mainland Korea. Mokp'o is the departure point for the cheapest ferries to the island of Chejudo.

Offshore Islands

There are scores of local ferries from Mokp'o to the small islands west and south of the town. A beautiful island is **Hongdo**, which is one of the most westerly islands and is part of the Tadohae Haesang National Park. To the south is **Wando**, connected by a bridge to the mainland and therefore reachable by bus. Wando even has ferry service direct to Chejudo.

Places to Stay & Eat

The cheapest yŏinsuk are in the streets on the south side of the railway station. The line-up here includes *Wando Yŏinsuk*, *Oddugi Yŏinsuk* and *Kwangju Yŏinsuk*. More expensive yŏgwan are also ubiquitous.

Getting There & Away

The bus terminal is a considerable distance to the north-east of the town centre, but is served by local bus No 1.

The boat terminal at Mokp'o handles all ferry departures and arrivals. Advance booking isn't necessary, just get to the boat terminal about two hours before departure time. There are two ferries daily to Chejudo, at 9 am and 4 pm, which take 5½ hours.

Chejudo 제주도

Chejudo (Cheju Island) lies 85 km off the southern tip of the peninsula. Centuries of isolation have resulted in the island acquiring its own history, cultural traditions, dress, architecture and even language.

The island landscape is dominated by the volcano of Hallasan, the highest mountain in

SOUTH KOREA

South Korea, and at Sŏgwip'o on the south coast, where the impressive Chongbang Falls cascade directly into the sea. There is also the enigma of the *harubang*, or grandfather stones, carved from lava rock. Their purpose is still debated by anthropologists, but they may have represented legendary guardians of the gates of Cheju's ancient towns.

Since the government realised the island's tourist potential, Cheju's atmosphere has changed significantly. The island's supposed matriarchal society, exemplified by the skin-diving women who are the subject of folk songs, trinkets and photographs in tourist literature, is on the wane. Commercialisation has arrived, and activities include power boating, scuba diving, golfing, and helicopter and submarine rides. Nevertheless, Cheju retains much of its charm and is a favourite venue for Korean couples on their honeymoon.

Chejudo's only real problem is the weather, which can put a dampener on your travel plans. Although Chejudo's winters are noticeably warmer than on the mainland, this island is the rainiest spot in Korea. You are most likely to encounter blue skies during autumn.

CHEJU CITY 제주

The island's capital is easy-going and compact. There is a whole new suburb to the south-west called Shincheju, which is a land of expensive hotels designed to milk the tourist market. Most budget travellers keep to the original part of the city.

Right in the city centre is Cheju's oldest building, the 15th-century **Kwandŏkjong Pavilion** complete with grandfather stone. Also worth seeing are the **Samsŏnghyŏl Shrine** and the **Yongduam**, or Dragon's Head Rock, on the shore between the city centre and the airport.

Places to Stay

Only a short distance away from the boat terminal on Sanjiro are several yŏinsuk which all charge W7000. These include *Yangsando*, *Hanil*, *Yonan*, *Namyang* and *Yongjin*.

You'll find more creature comforts around the corner for W16,000 at the *Kŭmsan-jang Yŏgwan*. A place to avoid is *Mankyŏng-jang Yŏgwan* which is overpriced and depressing.

Places to Eat

Not surprisingly, seafood is a speciality here but check prices as certain kinds of fish are amazingly expensive.

Getting There & Away

Air Domestic flights connect Cheju to Seoul, Chinju, Kunsan, Kwangju, Mokp'o, P'ohang, Pusan, Taegu, Ulsan and Yŏsu. There are international flights to Fukuoka and Sendai in Japan.

Boat There are boats from Pusan, Mokp'o and Wando. The boats to Pusan are relatively expensive as the journey is much farther. The fastest boats are from Wando.

Cheju-Pusan
> Car Ferry Queen takes 12 hours and departs from Pusan on Tuesday, Thursday and Sunday at 7 pm and from Cheju City on Monday, Wednesday and Saturday at 7.30 pm. Tong Yang Car Ferry No 5 sails daily except Sunday at 7.30 pm from either end. For all ferries, fares are from W12,580 to W88,300.

Mokp'o-Cheju
> Tongyang Car Ferry No 2 departs from Mokp'o daily except Sunday at 4 pm. Departures from Cheju are daily except Monday at 5 pm. The journey takes 5½ hours and costs from W8380 to W23,190.

Wando-Cheju
> Hanil Car Ferry No 1 sails from Wando daily except the 1st and 3rd Thursday of each month at 7.20 am; it departs from Cheju at 4 pm daily except the 2nd and 4th Friday. Hanil Car Ferry No 2 departs from Wando at 9.20 am daily except on the 2nd and 4th Thursday of every month; it departs from Cheju at 5 pm daily except the 2nd and 4th Friday. On either boat, the journey takes three hours and fares range from W8020 to W10,310. The schedule is cut back in winter.

Getting Around

To/From the Airport Bus No 100 connects the airport and the budget hotel area on Sanjiro. The fare costs W400 and the journey takes 35 minutes.

Bus Taking buses to the inter-city bus terminal *(shi-oe t'ŏminŏl)* is a little tricky since most of them are not numbered. You can find them at the bottom of the hill in the city centre on Chungangno – just ask the conductors and the other people waiting at the stop. The alternative is to take bus No 3 to the big junction past the KAL Hotel and then take another bus along Sogwangno where the terminal is. There are plenty of buses from the terminal to most places of interest around the island.

There are only four main roads out of Cheju city, all of which eventually lead to Sŏgwip'o on the southern coast. There are four or five buses an hour along these roads. Going west you will reach the best selection of beaches. Going east you will get to Manjanggul, around to Cheju Folk Village and then to Sŏgwip'o. The two cross-island highways skirt Hallasan and are the ones you will need if you are going to climb the mountain.

AROUND THE ISLAND

At Sŏgwip'o the main attraction is the 23-metre-high waterfall, **Chongbang**, 10 to 15 minutes' walk from the centre of town. The falls are an impressive sight, and are among the few in the world where the water plunges directly into the sea. **Chonjiyon** is another waterfall on the other side of town, about 20 minutes' walk from the centre.

Ch'ungmun Beach is near the small village of Ch'ungmun, west of Sŏgwip'o at the junction of the coast road and the second cross-island highway. This is probably the best and longest beach on the island, but it has developed into a tourist resort with all the trimmings.

A short bus ride north of Pyoson is **Sŏng-ŭp**, Cheju's ancient capital, which dates from the early 15th century and is now designated as a folk village. The whole village has been preserved in the traditional style and there are plenty of well-illustrated billboards in Korean and English pointing out the history and the main features of the most important sites.

East of Cheju City and about 2.5 km off the coast road from Kimnyong is the **Manjanggul**, considered the longest lava tube in the world with a length of seven km. It is well lit but damp and cool so take appropriate clothing. Direct buses from Cheju City take about 45 minutes.

Just south of Hallim on the north-western side of the island is **Hyŏpchaegul**, another lava-tube cave complete with stalagmites and stalactites. This one is actually a system of two interconnected caves, the larger of which is the spectacular Sŏch'ongul, with a length of 2500 metres. Due to an abundance of subtropical vegetation its two entrances resemble huge subterranean botanical gardens.

At **Sŏngsan** you can watch women diving for seaweed, shellfish and sea urchins. This is the town at the extreme eastern tip of Chejudo, nestled at the foot of the spectacular volcanic cone of **Songsan-ilch'ubong** (Sunrise Peak), whose sides plunge straight down into the surf. Unlike Hallasan, there's no longer any crater lake on the summit and the area below the jagged outer edges of the peak is continuously harvested for cattle fodder. It is one of Chejudo's most beautiful spots. There are ferries from here heading north-east to the island of Udo, which is very rural and free from motor cars.

Sanbanggulsa temple is carved into the side of a volcanic cone overlooking the sea and the Andok valley in the south-western part of the island. Take a bus from Sŏgwip'o to get there.

Walking up **Hallasan** is one of the highlights of a visit to the island. Be sure to get off to an early start as the summit is often shrouded in cloud by late afternoon. Don't let the warm sunny weather fool you, it can turn cold and wet as you approach the top. Entry to the area, which is a national park, is W600, and detailed trail maps are available free at the ticket offices at the beginning of the five trails. Ascending from the western side is easiest, but make local enquiries because some routes are frequently closed by rock slides.

As silly as it might sound to hardcore budget travellers, taking a tour of Chejudo

SOUTH KOREA

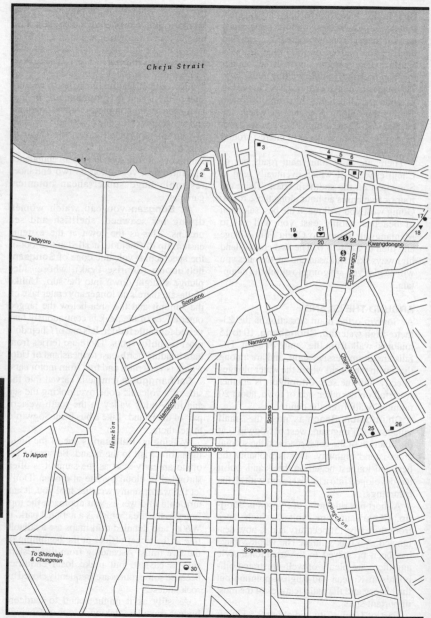

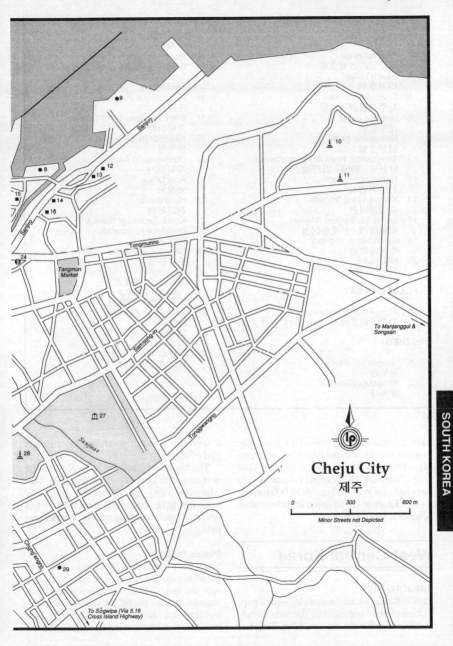

Cheju City

제주

0   300   600 m

Minor Streets not Depicted

To Manjanggul &
Songsan

To Sŏgwipa (Via 5.16
Cross Island Highway)

Tangmun
Market

SOUTH KOREA

PLACES TO STAY

3 Oriental Hotel
제주오리엔탈호텔
4 Beach Hotel
비치호텔
5 Cheju Seoul Hotel
제주서울관광호텔
6 Seaside Hotel
해상호텔
7 Namgyŏng Hotel
남경호텔
12 Yangsando, Hanil & Yonan Yŏinsuk
양산도. 한일. 연안여인숙
13 Namyang Yŏinsuk
남양여인숙
14 Kŭmsan-jang Yŏgwan
금산장여관
15 Seil & Sansu-jang Yŏgwan
세일여관. 산수장여관
16 Sujŏng-jang Yŏgwan
수정장여관
26 KAL Hotel
KAL 호텔

PLACES TO EAT

18 Atom Plaza (Restaurant)
가자아톰플라자

OTHER

1 Yongdu'am (Rock)
용두암
2 Yongaksa (Temple)
용악사
8 Fish Market
어시장
9 Ferry Terminal
여객선터미널
10 Sarasa (Temple)
사라사
11 Moch'ungsa (Shrine)
모충사
17 Waybang Travel (Air Tickets)
외방여행사
19 Kwandŏkjong Pavilion
관덕정
20 Underground Arcade
지하상가
21 Post Office
우체국
22 Hanil Bank
한일은행
23 Korea Exchange Bank &
Don Jose Restaurant
외환은행
24 Chohŭng Bank
조흥은행
25 Korean Air
대한항공 매표소
27 Folkcraft & Natural History Museum
민속자연사박물관
28 Samsŏnghyŏl Shrine
삼성혈
29 City Hall
시청
30 Inter-City Bus Terminal
시외버스터미널

isn't as absurd as it seems – it's a good way to get an overview of the island before deciding where you want to spend most of your time. Tours can be arranged for one or two days and cost W21,000 and W37,000 respectively. Enquire at the airport information counter if you're interested.

West-Central Korea

TAEJŎN 대전

This is Korea's sixth largest city with a population close to one million. You aren't likely to come here for the city itself, but Taejŏn is

a very useful transit point for places in this part of Korea.

The one interesting spot in Taejŏn is at the northern edge of the city, the Expo '93 Site. Although 1993 has come and gone, the buildings have been retained and the area is operated as something of an amusement park.

Places to Stay

Since the main reason for coming here is to get to someplace else, you'll do best to stay near the bus station. There are several bus stations, but the useful ones are the Express bus terminal (*kosok t'ŏminŏl*) and the East inter-city bus terminal (*tongbu shi-oe t'ŏminŏl).* These two terminals are next to one another, a rare convenience in Korea. Yŏgwan in this area are not the cheapest – figure around W18,000 for a double. Some options include *Yaksu-jang P'ak'ŭ Yŏgwan, Pugok P'akŭ Yŏgwan* and *Honey Park Hotel.*

Places to Eat
You'll probably have to eat near the bus station if you're staying around there, but the city centre does have much more to offer. The area just south-west of the railway station by the river is Chung-ang Market, which really comes alive at night. There are lots of cheap street stalls and more perma nent-looking restaurants. Soju tents are set up alongside the river at night, offering simple food and plenty of alcohol to wash it down.

Getting There & Away
Taejŏn is a major crossroads and can be approached by air, rail and bus. As usual, weekend travel is best avoided.

TAEDUNSAN PROVINCIAL PARK
대둔산도립공원
This is small and compact as parks go, but the scenery is breathtaking. It's noted for granite spires, cliffs and steep trails – definitely no place for acrophobes! The ascent involves crossing a hair-raising steel rope bridge stretched precariously between two rock pinnacles, then climbing an extremely steep and long steel stairway.

Taedunsan is south of Taejŏn. You can catch buses from Taejŏn's East inter-city bus terminal or the neighbouring express-bus terminal. There are buses every hour from 7.30 am to 6.20 pm, and the journey takes about one hour.

SONGNISAN NATIONAL PARK
속리산국립공원
The luxuriously forested mountains of the Songnisan National Park beckon with many well-marked hiking trails. There are several hermitages in the forest, all clearly signposted in English.

The natural beauty of Songnisan should be enough to entice you, but this park also is home to one of Korea's finest temples, **Popchusa**. Here you can see one of the largest statues of Buddha in the world, it's 33 metres high and made out of 160 tonnes of brass.

Popchusa is the scene of one of Korea's most colourful night-time lantern festivals, which is held on Buddha's birthday. This national holiday occurs according to the lunar calendar on the 8th day of the 4th moon (around May).

Places to Stay
Songni-dong, the village before the temple where the buses terminate, is quite large and there's a good selection of minbak and yŏgwan. You probably won't have to look very hard, touts come to the bus terminal looking for customers unless the hotels are already full. Expect to pay W10,000 for a room in a minbak and W20,000 in a yŏgwan. Some polite bargaining during off-peak times is possible.

Getting There & Away
Direct buses to Popchusa from Taejŏn depart from the East inter-city bus terminal about every 20 minutes. You can also get buses from the inter-city bus terminal in Ch'ŏngju. This is a better option since traffic will be less severe and the route is shorter.

KONGJU 공주
This second capital of the Paekje kingdom was established in 475 AD, and the tombs of many of the Paekje kings are here. Over the centuries most of the tombs were looted of their treasures, but in 1971 archaeologists came across the undisturbed tomb of King Mynyŏng (501-23 AD). The find was one of 20th-century Korea's greatest discoveries and the hundreds of priceless artefacts uncovered now form the basis of the Kongju National Museum.

Things to See
Opened in 1972, **Kongju National Museum** was built to resemble the inside of King Mynyŏng's tomb. It houses the finest collec-

SOUTH KOREA

tion of Paekje artefacts in Korea. The museum is open daily, except Monday, from 9 am to 6 pm during summer and until 5 pm during winter. Admission is W110.

The **Royal Paekje tombs** are clustered together on Songsan-ri Hill, a 20-minute walk from the centre of town. Three of the chambers of King Munyŏng's tomb are open for viewing from 9 am to 6 pm.

Kongsansong (Kongju Mountain Fortress) was once the site of the Paekje Royal Palace. Now it's a park with pavilions and a temple. The castle walls, though they originated in Paekje times, are the remains of a 17th-century reconstruction.

Places to Stay & Eat

The two bus terminals both recently moved,

and so far there is only one yŏgwan in the neighbourhood, the *Kumgangpak'ŭ Yŏgwan.* Undoubtedly, more will be built as time goes on. The bus terminal itself is a good place to eat, with a cheap Chinese restaurant upstairs.

Across the river in the town are many other reasonable places to stay. The selection includes *Samwon Yŏinsuk, Kongwan-jang Yŏgwan* and *Kŭmho-jang Yŏgwan.*

Getting There & Away

Both the express and inter-city bus terminals are on the north side of the river, opposite the town. You'll have to take a bus or taxi, or else walk about 1.5 km to commute between the terminal and the town.

Macau

Sixty km west of Hong Kong, on the other side of the Pearl River's mouth, is the oldest European settlement in the East – the tiny Portuguese territory of Macau. The lure of Macau's casino gaming tables has been so actively promoted that its other attractions are almost forgotten.

Macau is a fascinating blend, steeped in history and Old World elegance, but prosperous and changing fast. It has a very different look and feel from Hong Kong, and is well worth the one-hour boat trip to get there. Better yet, spend at least one night – this is a place to enjoy and relax.

Facts about the Country

HISTORY

Portuguese galleons visited Macau in the early 1500s, and in 1557, as a reward for clearing out a few pirates, China ceded the tiny enclave to the Portuguese.

For centuries, it was the principal meeting point for trade with China. In the 19th century, European and American traders could operate in Guangzhou (just up the Pearl River) only during the trading season. They would then retreat to Macau during the off season.

When the Opium Wars erupted between the Chinese and the British, the Portuguese stood diplomatically to one side and Macau soon found itself the poor relation of more dynamic Hong Kong.

Macau's current prosperity is given a big boost from the Chinese gambling urge, which every weekend sends hordes of Hong Kongers shuttling off to the casinos. In recent years, Macau's economy has been helped by the high wages and rents in Hong Kong, which has caused a migration of light manufacturing industries to Macau.

Macau is slated to be handed back to

China in 1999, two years after Hong Kong. It's said that the Portuguese wanted to last out 500 years, which would have taken them well into the next century. They finally settled for any date which put them one up on Hong Kong.

GEOGRAPHY

Macau's 16 sq km consists of the city itself, which is part of the Chinese mainland, and the islands of Taipa and Coloane, which are joined together by a causeway and linked to Macau city by two bridges.

CLIMATE

The weather is almost identical to that of Hong Kong, with short, occasionally chilly winters, and long, hot and humid summers. November is usually the best month, with mild temperatures and dry weather. Typhoons are most common from June to October. See the Macau climate chart in the Appendix later in this book.

GOVERNMENT

Officially, Macau is not considered a colony. Instead, the Portuguese government regards Macau as a piece of Chinese territory under Portuguese administration. The colony/Chinese territory has a governor who is appointed by Portugal's president, but in theory the main governing body is the 23-member Legislative Assembly of which eight members are elected by direct vote, while the remainder are appointed by the governor and 'economic interest groups'.

ECONOMY

The spin of the wheel and the toss of the dice still play an important part in Macau's economy, but there's also a variety of local industries, including textiles and toy manufacturing. Trade with China is giving the economy an extra boost, and the new airport

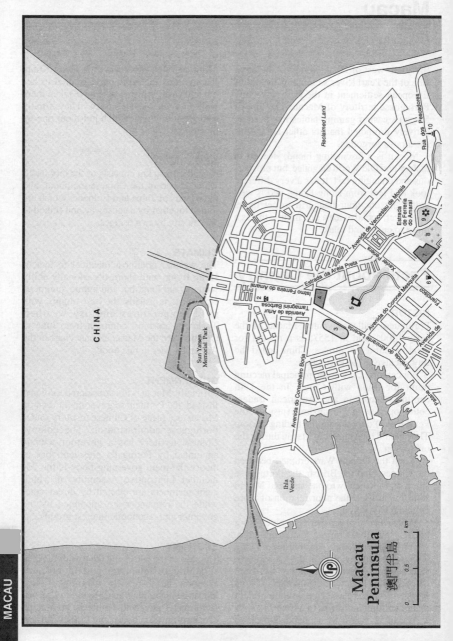

CHINA

Reclaimed Land

Rua dos Pescadores

Avenida de Venceslau de Morais

Estrada de Ferreira do Amaral

Xavier Pereira

Estrada da Areia Preta

Istmo Ferreira do Amaral

Avenida do Coronel Mesquita

Avenida de Artur Tamagnini Barbosa

Avenida da Amizade Lacerda

Sun Yatsen Memorial Park

Avenida do Conselheiro Borja

Ilha Verde

Avenida de

Francisco

Macau
Peninsula
澳門半島

0   0.5   1 km

MACAU

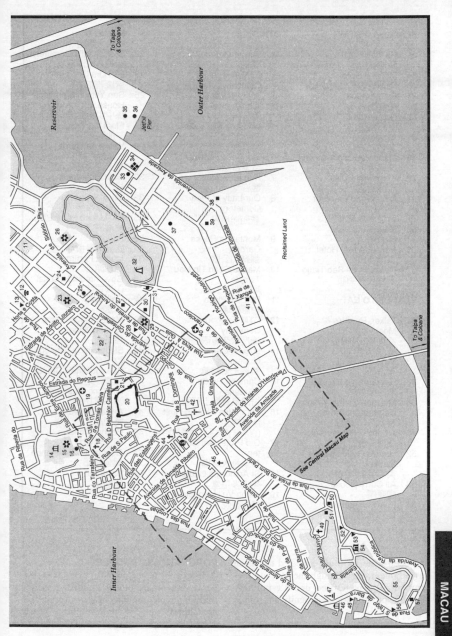

PLACES TO STAY

21 Holiday Hotel
   假期酒店
24 Mondial Hotel
   環球酒店
27 Estoril Hotel
   愛都酒店
30 Royal Hotel
   皇都酒店
31 Guia Hotel
   東望洋酒店
38 Mandarin Oriental Hotel
   文華東方酒店
39 Kingsway Hotel
   金域酒店
41 New World Emperor
   Hotel
   新世界帝濠酒店
50 Hotel Bela Vista
   峰京酒店
51 Pousada Ritz Hotel
   豪璟酒店
57 Pousada de Sao Tiago
   聖地牙哥酒店

PLACES TO EAT

6   Talker, Pyretu's &
   Moonwalk Pubs
   高地烏街104號
   (觀音堂對面)
13 McDonald's III
   麥當勞
28 Restaurante Violeta
   紫晶閣餐廳
34 McDonald's II & Yaohan
   Department Store
   麥當勞/八佰伴
48 A Lorcha Restaurant
   船屋餐廳
52 Henri's Galley & Café
   Marisol
   美心餐廳/咖喱屋
53 Ali Curry House
   咖喱屋
56 Pele Restaurant
   比利餐廳

OTHER

1   Barrier Gate
   關閘
2   CTM Telephone
   Company
   澳門電訊有限公司
3   'Canidrome'
   跑狗場
4   Lin Fong Miu Lotus
   Temple
   蓮峰廟
5   Mong-Ha Fortress
   望廈古堡
7   Kun Iam Temple
   觀音堂
8   Our Lady of Piety
   Cemetery
   新西洋境場
9   Montanha Russa
   Garden
   螺絲山公園
10 Macau-Seac Tin Hau
   Temple
   馬交石天后廟
11 Pak Vai Plaza
   柏蕙廣場
12 CTM Telephone
   Company
   澳門電訊有限公司
14 Luis de Camoes
   Museum
   賈梅士博物館
15 Camoes Grotto &
   Gardens
   白鴿巢賈梅士花園
16 Future Ice Skating Rink
   佳景樂園
   (白鴿巢賈梅士花園對面)
17 Old Protestant Ceme-
   tery
   舊基督教墳場
18 St Anthony's Church
   聖安多尼堂
19 Kiang Vu Hospital
   鏡湖醫院

20 Monte Fort
   中央大炮台
22 St Michael's Cemetery
   聖美基西洋境場
23 Lou Lim Ieoc Garden
   盧廉若花園
25 Sun Yatsen Memorial
   House
   孫中山紀念館
26 Flora Garden
   二龍喉花園
29 Vasco da Gama
   Garden
   華士占達嘉馬花園
32 Guia Lighthouse
   松山燈塔
33 Jai-Alai Casino
   回力球娛樂場
35 HK-Macau Ferry Pier
   澳港碼頭
36 Heliport
   直昇機停機坪
37 Macau Forum
   綜藝館
40 Government Hospital
   山頂醫院
42 Cathedral
   大堂
43 Macau Government
   Tourist Office
   旅遊司
44 St Dominic's Church
   玫瑰堂
45 St Augustine's Church
   聖奧斯定堂
46 Maritime Museum
   海事博物館
47 A-Ma Temple
   媽閣廟
49 Penha Church
   西望洋聖堂
54 Governor's Residence
   總督私邸
55 Barra Hill
   媽閣山

and deep-water port are expected to hasten development. And though the Macau Government Tourist Office doesn't publicly admit it, prostitution is a significant source of revenue.

POPULATION & PEOPLE

A 1992 census accounted for 354,000 residents, but other sources claim that half a million people populate Macau. About 95% are Chinese, and 3% are Portuguese. Nearly 1% of the population is from Thailand and the Philippines, mostly female and employed in what is loosely called the 'entertainment industry'.

ARTS
Chinese art is covered in the Hong Kong and China sections of this book. As for the Portuguese, their art is most visible in the old churches and cathedrals which grace Macau's skyline and contain some fine examples of painting, stained-glass windows and sculpture.

CULTURE
The Chinese population is indistinguishable culturally from that of Hong Kong, except a higher percentage can speak Mandarin (as opposed to Cantonese). Of course, the Portuguese minority has a vastly different culture, which they have kept largely intact. Although mixed marriages are not uncommon in Macau, there has been little cultural assimilation between the two ethnic groups – most Portuguese people cannot speak Chinese and vice versa.

RELIGION
For the Chinese majority, Buddhism and Taoism are the dominant religions, but Portuguese influence has definitely had an impact and Catholicism is very strong in Macau. Many Chinese have been converted and you are likely to see Chinese nuns.

LANGUAGE
Portuguese may be the official language but Cantonese is the one most used. Mandarin Chinese (putonghua) is spoken by about half the population. See the Hong Kong chapter earlier in this book for a few Cantonese phrases.

The level of spoken English is lower in Macau than in Hong Kong. All major hotels employ English speakers, but communicating in the real budget guesthouses can be problematic.

On the other hand, virtually all Portuguese people in Macau can speak English well.

There is no real need to learn Portuguese, but it can be helpful (and fun) to know a few words for reading maps and street signs. The following phrases should come in handy:

alley
beco
avenue
avenida
bay
baía
beach
praia
big
grande
bridge
ponte
building
edifício
bus stop
paragem
cathedral
sé
church
igreja
courtyard
pátio
district
bairro
fortress
fortaleza
friendship
amizade
garden
jardim
guesthouse
hospedaria or *vila*
guide
guia
hill
alto or *monte*
hotel
pousada
island
ilha
lane
travessa
lighthouse
farol

lookout point
 miradouro
market
 mercado
moneychanger
 casa de cambio
museum
 museu
of
 da, do
pawnshop
 casa de penhores
pier
 ponte-cais
police station
 esquadra da polícia
post office
 correios
restaurant (small)
 casa de pasto
path
 caminho
road
 estrada
rock, crag
 penha
school
 escola
small hill
 colina
square
 praça
square (small)
 largo
steep street
 calçada
street
 rua

Facts for the Visitor

VISAS & EMBASSIES
For most visitors, all that's needed to enter Macau is a passport. Everyone gets a 20-day stay on arrival. Visas are not required for citizens of the following nations: Australia, Austria, Belgium, Brazil, Canada, Denmark, Finland, France, Germany, Greece, Hong Kong, India, Ireland, Italy, Japan, Luxembourg, Malaysia, the Netherlands, New Zealand, Norway, Philippines, Singapore, South Africa, South Korea, Spain, Sweden, Switzerland, Thailand, the UK and USA.

All other nationalities must have a visa, which can be obtained on arrival in Macau. Visas cost M$175 for individuals, M$350 for married couples and families and M$88 per person in a bona fide tour group (usually 10 persons minimum). People holding passports from countries which do not have diplomatic relations with Portugal must obtain visas from an overseas Portuguese consulate before entering Macau. An exception is made for Taiwanese people, who can get visas on arrival despite their lack of diplomatic relations. The Portuguese consulate (☎ 5225488) in Hong Kong is on the 10th floor, Tower Two, Exchange Square, Central.

MONEY
Currency
The pataca is divided into 100 avos and is worth about 4% less than the HK$. HK$ are accepted everywhere, which is just as well because there's nowhere to change currency on arrival. So make sure you have some HK$ or you'll have difficulty getting from the Jetfoil pier into town!

Although Hong Kong coins are accepted in Macau, you'll need pataca coins to make calls at public telephones. Get rid of your patacas before departing from Macau as they are hard to get dispose of in Hong Kong, though you can change them at the Hang Seng Bank.

Exchange Rates

Australia	A$1	=	M$5.49
Canada	C$1	=	M$6.08
China	Y1	=	M$0.93
France	Ffr1	=	M$1.35
Germany	DM1	=	M$4.59
Hong Kong	HK$1	=	M$1.04
Japan	¥100	=	M$7.72
New Zealand	NZ$1	=	M$4.48
Switzerland	Sfr1	=	M$5.41
Taiwan	NT$	=	M$0.30

MACAU

UK	UK£1	=	M$11.88
USA	US$1	=	M$8.03

Costs

As long as you don't go crazy at the roulette wheel or slot machines, Macau is cheaper than Hong Kong. To help keep costs down, avoid visiting during weekends.

Tipping

Classy hotels and restaurants automatically hit you with a 10% service charge, a mandatory tip. Just how much of this money actually goes to the employees is a matter for speculation.

You can follow your own conscience, but tipping is not customary among the Chinese. Of course, porters at expensive hotels have become accustomed to hand-outs from well-heeled tourists.

Bargaining

Most stores have fixed prices, but if you buy clothing, trinkets and other tourist junk from the street markets, there is some scope for bargaining. On the other hand, if you buy from the pawnshops, bargain ruthlessly. Pawnbrokers are more than happy to charge whatever they can get away with – charging five times the going price for second-hand cameras and other goods is not unusual!

TOURIST OFFICES
Local Tourist Offices

The Macau Government Tourist Office – MGTO (☎ 315566) is well-organised and extremely helpful. It's at Largo do Senado, Edificio Ritz No 9, next to the Leal Senado building in the square in the centre of Macau.

Overseas Reps

On Hong Kong Island there's a useful branch of the MGTO (☎ 5408180) at room 3704, Shun Tak Centre, 200 Connaught Rd, at the Macau Ferry pier. The MGTO is closed for lunch from 1 to 2 pm. Macau also maintains overseas tourist representative offices as follows:

Australia
    Macau Tourist Information Bureau, 449 Darling St, Balmain, Sydney, NSW 2041 (☎ 02-555 7548; fax 555 7559)
Canada
    Macau Tourist Information Bureau, suite 157, 10551 Shellbridge Way, Richmond, BC V6X 2W9 (☎ 604-231 9040; fax 231 9031)
    13 Mountalan Ave, Toronto, Ontario M4J 1H3 (☎ 416-466 6552)
France
    Portuguese National Tourist Office, 7 Rue Scribe, 75009 Paris (☎ 745557)
Germany
    Portuguese National Tourist Office, Kaiserstrasse 66-IV, 6000 Frankfurt/Main (☎ 0611-234097; fax 231433)
Japan
    Macau Tourist Information Bureau, 4th floor, Toho Twin Tower Building, 5-2 Yurakucho 1-chome, Chiyoda-ku, Tokyo 100 (☎ 03-35015022; fax 35021248)
Malaysia
    Macau Tourist Information Bureau, c/o Discover the World Marketing Sdn Bhd, 10.03 Amoda, 22 Jalan Imbi, 55100, Kuala Lumpur (☎ 2451418; fax 248 6851)
Portugal
    Macau Tourist Representative, Avenida 5 de Outubro 115, 5th floor, 1000 Lisbon (☎ 769964)
Singapore
    Macau Tourist Information Bureau, 11-01A PIL Building, 140 Cecil St, Singapore 0106 (☎ 225 0022; fax 223 8585)
Thailand
    Macau Tourist Information Bureau, 150/5 Sukhumvit 20, Bangkok 10110, or GPO Box 1534, Bangkok 10501 (☎ 258 1975)
UK
    Macau Tourist Information Bureau, 6 Sherlock Mews, Paddington St, London W1M 3RH (☎ 0171-224 3390; fax 224 0601)
USA
    Macau Tourist Information Bureau, 3133 Lake Hollywood Drive, Los Angeles, CA, or PO Box 1860, Los Angeles, CA 90078 (☎ 213-851 3402, 800-331 7150; fax 851 3684)
    Suite 2R, 77 Seventh Ave, New York, NY 10011 (☎ 212-206 6828; fax 924 0882)
    630 Green Bay Rd, PO Box 350, Kenilworth, IL 60043-0350 (☎ 708-251 6421; fax 256 5601)
    PO Box 2218, Honolulu, HI 96922 (☎ 808-538 7613)

BUSINESS HOURS & HOLIDAYS

The operating hours for most government offices in Macau are weekdays from 8.40 am to 1 pm and 3 to 5 pm, and until 1 pm on

MACAU

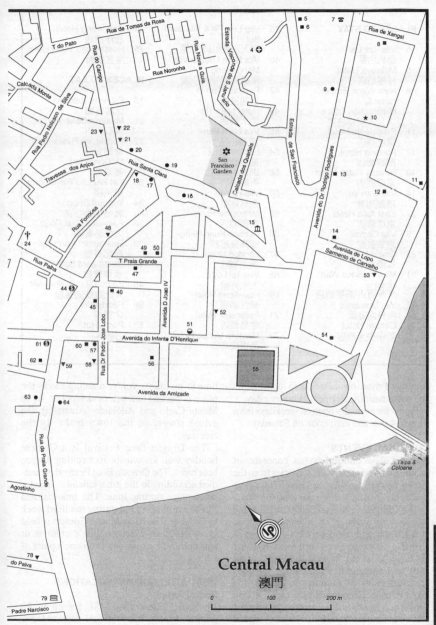

Rua de Tomas da Rosa
T do Pato
Rua do Campo
Rua Nova a Guia
Rua Noronha
Rua de Xangai
Estrada Visconde de S Januario
Calcada Monte
Rua Pedro Nolasco da Silva
23 ▼ 22 ▼
21 ▼
20 ●
Travessa dos Anjos
Rua Santa Clara 19 ●
Rua Formosa
18 ● 17 ●
16 ●
Estrada da Sao Francisco
San Francisco Garden
Calcada dos Quartais
Avenida do Dr Rodrigo Rodrigues
24 †
48 ▼
49 ■ 50 ■
T Praia Grande
47 ●
Rua Palha
44 ●
45 ■
40 ■
Avenida D Joao IV
51 ●
52 ▼
Avenida do Infante D'Henrique
Rua Dr Padre Jose Lobo
61 ●
60 ■ 57 ■
62 ■ 59 ▼ 58 ▼
56 ●
55
Avenida da Amizade
63 ●
64 ●
Rua da Praia Grande
Agostinho
do Paiva
78 ▼
79 ▣
Padre Narcisco

5 ■
6 ■
7 ☎
4 ⊕
8 ■
9 ●
★ 10
13 ■
11 ■
12 ■
14 ■
Avenida de Lopo Sarmento de Carvalho
53 ▼
54 ●
15 🏛

Taipa & Coloane

Central Macau
澳門

0   100   200 m

MACAU

PLACES TO STAY

5 Vila Tak Lei
   德利別墅
6 Matsuya Hotel
   松屋酒店
8 New World Emperor
   Hotel &
   Immigration Office
   人民入境事務處
11 Presidente Hotel
    總統酒店
12 Fortuna Hotel
    財神酒店
13 Beverly Plaza Hotel
    富豪酒店
14 Vila San Vu
    珊瑚別墅
27 East Asia Hotel
    東亞酒店
28 Vila Capital
    京華賓館
29 Grand Hotel
    國際酒店
31 Man Va & Ko Wah
    Hotel
    文華酒店/高華酒店
32 Vila Universal
    世界迎賓館
38 Central Hotel
    新中央大酒店

45 Vila Loc Tin & Vila Sam
    Sui
    樂天別墅/山水別墅
46 Vila Nam Loon & Vila
    Meng Meng
    南龍別墅/明明別墅
47 Pensao Nam In
    南苑賓館
49 Hotel Nam Tin
    南天酒店
50 Vila Nam Pan
    南濱小築
54 Lisboa Hotel
    葡京酒店
56 Sintra Hotel
    新麗酒店
60 Vila Kimbo
    金賓別墅
62 Metropole Hotel
    京都酒店
66 Pensao Kuan Heng
    群興賓館群
67 London Hotel
    英京酒店
68 Vila Tai Loy
    大來賓館
69 Hou Kong Hotel
    濠江酒店
71 Peninsula Hotel
    半島酒店
73 Masters Macau Hotel
    萬事發酒店

74 Ung Ieong Hotel
    五洋酒店
75 Hospedaria Vong Hong
    皇宮旅館

PLACES TO EAT

18 Pizzeria Toscana
    比薩餐廳
21 Maxim's Bakery
    美心西餅
22 Portugués Restaurant
    葡國餐廳
23 McDonald's I
    麥當勞
33 Fat Siu Lau Restaurant
    佛笑樓
34 Yoghurt Shop
    義順牛奶公司
36 Fairwood Fast Food
    大快活餐廳
39 Restaurant Long Kei
    龍記餐廳
40 Restaurant Safari
    金池餐廳
48 Ze do Pipo Restaurant
    八比龍葡國餐廳
52 Foodstalls
    大排檔
53 Pizza Hut
    必勝客

Saturday. Private businesses keep longer hours and some casinos are open 24 hours a day.

Banks are normally open on weekdays from 9 am to 4 pm, and until noon on Saturday.

CULTURAL EVENTS

Find out about cultural events, concerts, art exhibitions and other such activities from the tourist newspaper *Macau Travel Talk*. Free copies are available from the tourist office.

The Chinese in Macau celebrate the same religious festivals as their counterparts in Hong Kong, but there are also a number of Catholic festivals and Portuguese national holidays. Most important is the Feast of Our Lady of Fatima, when the Fatima image is removed from St Dominic's Church and taken in procession around the city.

Macau's main festival time is November when the Grand Prix is held – it's not a good time to go unless you're a racing fan as the place is packed and prices skyrocket. As in Monte Carlo and Adelaide (Australia), the actual streets of the town make up the raceway.

The Dragon Boat Festival is a Chinese holiday well known for its exciting dragon boat races. The Dragon Boat Festival, scheduled according to the lunar calendar, usually takes place during June. The International Music Festival is held during the third week of October. The Miss Macau Contest is held every August. Whether this a cultural or anti-cultural event depends on one's point of view.

POST & TELECOMMUNICATIONS
Postal Rates

Domestic letters cost M$1 for up to 20 grams. As for international mail, Macau

MACAU

58	New Ocean Restaurant 新海洋大酒樓	19	Cineteatro Macau 澳門大會堂	55	Bank of China 中國銀行
59	Solmar Restaurant 沙利文餐廳	20	Watson's Drugstore 屈臣氏	57	Foto Princesa 照相館
78	Estrela do Mar 海星餐廳	23	Capitol Theatre 京华戏院	61	Bank of China 中國銀行
		24	Cathedral 大堂	63	Days & Days Super-market 大利時超級市場
OTHER		25	Livraria Portuguesa (Portuguese Book-shop) 葡文書局	64	Jorge Alvares Statue 歐維士石像
1	St Anthony's Church 聖安多尼堂				
2	Ruins of St Paul 大三巴牌坊	26	St Dominic's Church 玫瑰堂	65	St Augustine Church 聖奧斯定堂
3	Monte Fort 大炮台	30	Casino Kam Pek 金碧娛樂場	70	Kee Kwan Motors (Buses to Guangzhou) 往廣州公共汽車
4	Government Hospital 山頂醫院	35	St Dominic's Market 營地街市場		
7	CTM Telephone Company 澳門電訊有限公司	37	Macau Government Tourist Office 旅遊司	72	Floating Casino (Macau Palace) 皇宮娛樂場
9	Macau Exhibition Centre 澳門展覽中心	41	Leal Senado 市政廳	76	Park 'n Shop 百佳超級市場
10	Main Police Station 總警署	42	GPO 郵政局	77	St Lazarus Church 聖老楞佐堂
15	Military Museum 軍事博物館	43	CTM Telephone Office 澳門電訊有限公司	79	Government House 澳督府
16	Chinese Library 八角亭	44	Hongkong Bank 匯豐銀行		
17	Livraria Sao Paulo (bookshop) 聖保祿書局	51	Bus Stop to Taipa & Coloane 往路環車站		

divides the world into zones: Zone 1 is east Asia, including Korea, Taiwan etc; and Zone 2 is everything else. There are special rates for China and Portugal. The rates for airmail letters, postcards and aerogrammes are as follows:

Grams	China	Portugal	Zone 1	Zone 2
10	2.00	3.00	3.50	4.50
20	3.00	4.50	4.50	6.00
30	4.00	6.00	5.50	7.50
40	5.00	7.50	6.50	9.00
50	6.00	9.00	7.50	10.50

Printed matter receives a discount of about 30% off the above rates. Registration costs an extra M$12.

Sending & Receiving Mail

The GPO on Leal Senado is open from 9 am

to 8 pm, Monday to Saturday. Large hotels, like the Lisboa, also sell stamps and post-cards and can post letters for you. Scattered around Macau are several red-coloured 'mini-post offices', which are basically machines that sell stamps. The current postal rates are marked clearly on the machines.

Telephone

Companhia de Telecomunicacoes (CTM) runs the Macau telephone system, and for the most part the service is good. However, public pay phones can be hard to find, being mostly concentrated around the Leal Senado. Most large hotels have a payphone in the lobby, but demand is often great and you may have to stand in line to use it.

Local calls are free from a private or hotel telephone. At a public pay phone, local calls cost M$1 for five minutes.

MACAU

All pay phones permit International Direct Dialling (IDD). The procedure for dialling to Hong Kong is totally different to all other countries. You first dial 01 and then the number you want to call, you must *not* dial the country code. The international access code for every country *except* Hong Kong is 00. To call into Macau from abroad, the country code is 853.

Telephone cards from CTM are sold in denominations of 50, 100 and 200 patacas. A lot of phones which accept these cards are found around Leal Senado, the Jetfoil Pier and at a few large hotels. You can also make a call from the telephone office on Largo do Senado, next to the GPO. Leave a deposit with a clerk and they will dial the number for you. When your call is completed, the clerk deducts the cost from the deposit and refunds the balance. The office is open from 8 am until midnight Monday to Saturday, and from 9 am until midnight on Sunday.

Useful Phone Numbers

Some useful telephone numbers follow:

Emergency	☎ 999
Police	☎ 573333
Directory Assistance (Macau)	☎ 181
Directory Assistance (Hong Kong)	☎ 101
Time	☎ 140

Fax, Telex & Telegraph

Unless you're staying at a hotel that has its own fax, the easiest way to send and receive a fax is at the GPO (not the telephone office) on Leal Senado. The number for receiving faxes at this office is (853) 550117, but check because the number can change. The person sending the fax must put your name and hotel telephone number on top of the message so the postal workers can find you. The cost for receiving a fax is M$7.50 regardless of the number of pages.

Telex messages are sent from the telephone office next to the GPO. The telephone office also handles cables (telegrams).

TIME

Like Hong Kong, Macau is eight hours ahead of GMT/UTC and does not observe daylight-saving time.

When it is noon in Macau, it is also noon in Singapore, Hong Kong and Perth; 2 pm in Sydney; 8 pm the previous day in Los Angeles; 11 pm the previous day in New York; and 4 am in London.

BOOKS & MAPS

Lonely Planet's *Hong Kong, Macau & Guangzhou – a travel survival kit* has a section on Macau with much more detailed information. There are various books about Macau which are available in Hong Kong or the MGTO on Largo do Senado in Macau.

Bookshops

Macau's best bookshop for English-language publications is Livraria Sao Paulo (☎ 323957) on Rua do Campo (near McDonald's). For Portuguese-language publications, check out Livraria Portuguesa (☎ 566442), 18-20 Rua de Sao Domingos.

MEDIA
Newspapers & Magazines

Other than the monthly tourist newspaper *Macau Travel Talk*, there is no English-language newspaper published in Macau. However, the *South China Morning Post*, *Hong Kong Standard* and *Eastern Express* are readily available. It's also easy to buy foreign news magazines.

Radio & TV

Macau has three radio stations, two of which broadcast in Cantonese and one in Portuguese. There are no local English-language radio stations, but you should be able to pick up Hong Kong stations.

Teledifusao de Macau (TdM) is a government-run station which broadcasts on two channels. The shows are mainly in English and Portuguese, but some Cantonese programmes are televised. It's easy to pick up Hong Kong stations in Macau (but not vice versa) and you can also receive stations from China. Hong Kong newspapers list Macau TV programmes.

Hong Kong's famous satellite TV system,

STAR TV, is readily available in Macau at any hotel with a cable or satellite dish hookup.

FILM & PHOTOGRAPHY
You can find most types of film, cameras and accessories in Macau, and photo processing is of a high standard. The best store in town for all photographic services is the Foto Princesa (☎ 555959) at 55-59 Avenida Infante D'Henrique, one block east of Rua da Praia Grande. This is also the best place to get visa photos taken and processed.

HEALTH
The water, purified and chlorinated, is OK to drink. Nevertheless, the Chinese always boil it (more out of custom than necessity). Hotel rooms are always supplied with a thermos filled with hot water.

Medical treatment is available at the Government Hospital (☎ 514499, 313731).

WOMEN TRAVELLERS
Wearing a skimpy bikini at the beach will elicit some stares, but travel in Macau is as safe for women as in any Western country.

DANGERS & ANNOYANCES
In terms of violent crime, Macau is pretty safe, though not as safe as it used to be. Residential burglaries and pickpocketing are problems. Most hotels are well guarded, and if you take reasonable care with your valuables you should have no trouble. Security at casinos is particularly heavy.

Traffic is congested and quite a few tourists have been hit while jaywalking. Cars are supposed to stop for pedestrians at crosswalks, but you can rest assured that they won't stop for pedestrians anywhere else. Macau police are tough with traffic violators and foreigners also get fined for jaywalking.

Cheating at gambling is a serious criminal offence, so don't even think about it.

WORK
Unless you hold a Portuguese passport, you can pretty much forget about working in Macau. Most Portuguese people speak excellent English, so there is little need to import foreign English teachers. Most of the foreigners employed in Macau are Thai prostitutes, Filipina waitresses and Filipino musicians. Unskilled labour is supplied by workers from nearby China, who are paid a pittance.

ACTIVITIES
Future Ice Skating Rink (☎ 9892310) is on Praca Luis de Camoes, just on the south side of Camoes Grotto & Gardens.

Up around the Guía Lighthouse is the best track for jogging. It's also the venue for early morning taiji exercises.

There are two good swimming beaches on Coloane, Hac Sa and Cheoc Van. Cheoc Van Beach has a yacht club, and Hac Sa has a horse-riding stable. Hac Sa Beach also has a number of sea toys for rent, including windsurfers and water scooters. In the hills of Coloane is a hiking trail over eight km in total length. Bicycles are available for hire on both islands, but not on the Macau Peninsula. Coloane also boasts a golf course.

HIGHLIGHTS
Although gambling is what draws most people to Macau, the fine colonial architecture is what makes this place unique. Highlights include the Ruins of St Paul, Monte Fort, Guía Fortress, Leal Senado and the Penha Church. St Michael's Cemetery is a fascinating place to walk through, and many visitors are impressed by A-Ma Temple. Taipa Village on Taipa Island is unique, and there is no better way to round off a trip to Macau than having a fine meal at a Portuguese restaurant.

ACCOMMODATION
There's good and bad news about accommodation in Macau. The bad news is that hotel prices continue to rise – the old dumps are being torn down and replaced with comfortable hotels, which usually charge uncomfortable prices. Nor are there Hong Kong-style dormitories catering for the budget backpacker market.

MACAU

But there is good news. Hotels in Macau are cheaper than those in Hong Kong. For the same price that you'd pay in Hong Kong for a dormitory bed, you'll be able to find a private room (without private bath) in Macau. For about the same that you'd pay for a dumpy room in Hong Kong, you can get a comfortable room in Macau with air-conditioning, private bath, TV and fancy carpeting. In other words, staying in Macau will probably wind up costing you the same as in Hong Kong – you won't live cheaply, but you'll live better.

Just remember to avoid visiting during weekends and holidays, when room prices double and accommodation of any kind is difficult to get. For definition purposes, 'weekend' means both Saturday and Sunday nights. Friday night is usually not a problem unless it's also a holiday. Also, during special events, like the Macau Grand Prix, rooms can be impossible to obtain.

Another way to save money is to avoid visiting during the peak season (summer).

FOOD

Given Macau's cosmopolitan past, it's not surprising that the food is an exotic mixture of Portuguese and Chinese cuisine. There is also a little influence from other European countries and Africa. The English-speaking waitresses are invariably from the Philippines.

The most famous local speciality is African chicken baked with peppers and chillis. Other specialties include *bacalhau*, which is cod, served baked, grilled, stewed or boiled. The cod is imported and rather salty. Sole, a tongue-shaped flatfish, is another Macanese delicacy. There's also ox tail and ox breast, rabbit prepared in various ways and soups, like *caldo verde* and *sopa a alentejana,* made with vegetables, meat and olive oil. The Brazilian contribution is *feijoadas* – a stew made of beans, pork, potatoes, cabbage and spicy sausages. The contribution from the former Portuguese enclave of Goa on the west coast of India is spicy prawns.

DRINKS

The Portuguese influence is most visible in the many fine imported Portuguese red and white wines, port and brandy. Wines are cheap. Mateus Rosé is the most famous, but even cheaper are bottles of red or white wine.

Spirits and beer are cheaper in Macau than in Hong Kong, and even cheaper than at duty-free stores. Wine prices vary in the restaurants but are usually not too expensive. Many people leave the place with a bottle of Mateus tucked under their arm.

THINGS TO BUY

Pawnshops are ubiquitous in Macau, and it is possible to get good deals on cameras, watches and jewellery, but you must be prepared to bargain without mercy.

The MGTO has T-shirts for sale at the bargain prices. Ditto for posters, postcards and other tourist paraphernalia.

If you've got the habit, Macau is a bargain place for tobacco, including cigars and pipe tobacco.

Getting There & Away

AIR

Macau's new airport is planned for completion in 1995. When it finally opens, expect major changes, not only to transport, but to Macau's character. There is currently outrageously expensive helicopter service between Hong Kong and Macau, see the introductory Getting Around chapter for details.

LAND

Macau is an important gateway into China. You simply take a bus to the border and walk across. Bus No 3 runs between the Jetfoil Pier and the Barrier Gate at the Macau-China border. You can also catch a bus directly from Macau to Guangzhou. Tickets are sold at Kee Kwan Motors, across the street from the Floating Casino.

SEA

The journey between Hong Kong and Macau only takes around an hour by sea. The vast majority of travellers enter and exit Macau this way. For details, see the Getting Around chapter at the beginning of this book.

There is also a Macau-Taiwan ferry, though it is unreliable. See the introductory Getting Around chapter.

Getting Around

Macau is fairly compact and it's relatively easy to walk almost everywhere, but you'll definitely need motorised transport to visit the islands of Taipa and Coloane. The pedicabs are essentially for touristy sightseeing. They have to be bargained for and it's hardly worth the effort, and if there are two of you make sure the fare covers both people.

BUS

There are minibuses and large buses, and both offer air-conditioning and frequent service. They operate from 7 am until midnight.

You'll find it easier to deal with the bus system if you buy a good map of Macau showing all the routes.

Buses on the Macau Peninsula cost M$1.80. The major routes are as follows:

No 3 Jetfoil Pier, Beverly Plaza Hotel, Lisboa Hotel, San Francisco Garden, Avenida de Almeida Ribeiro, GPO, Grand Hotel, Avenida do Almirante Lacerda, Lin Fong Miu (Lotus Temple), Barrier Gate
No 3A Jetfoil Pier, Beverly Plaza Hotel, Lisboa Hotel, San Francisco Garden, Avenida de Almeida Ribeiro, GPO, Floating Casino, Praca Ponte e Horta
No 9 (loop route) Barra Fortress, A-Ma Temple, Floating Casino, GPO, Rua do Campo, Lou Lim Ieoc Garden, Avenida Horta e Costa, Barrier Gate, Lin Fong Miu (Lotus Temple), Canidrome, Avenida do Almirante Lacerda, Avenida do Ouvidor Arriaga, Flora Garden, Sun Yat-sen Memorial Home, St Dominic's Church, GPO, Avenida de Almeida Ribeiro, Rua da Praia Grande, Government House, Avenida da República, Barra Fortress

No 10 Barra Fortress, Floating Casino, Grand Hotel, Avenida de Almeida Ribeiro, GPO, Metropole Hotel, Sintra Hotel, Lisboa Hotel, Presidente Hotel, Macau Forum, Outer Harbour, Barrier Gate
No 12 Jetfoil Pier, Beverly Plaza Hotel, Lisboa Hotel, Rua do Campo, Lou Lim Ieoc Garden, Mondial Hotel, Avenida Horta e Costa, Avenida Coronel Mesquita, Kun Iam Temple, Bairro da Areia Preta
No 18 Barra Fortress, Floating Casino, Avenida de Almeida Ribeiro, Camoes Gardens, Rua da Barca, Rua Francisco Xavier Pereira, Avenida Coronel Mesquita, Montanha Russa Garden, Areia Preta, Avenida Coronel Mesquita, Jun Iam Temple, Lou Lim Ieoc Gardens, Avenida Sidonio Pais, Rua do Campo, Government House, St Lazarus Church, Barra Fortress
No 28C Jetfoil Pier, Beverly Plaza Hotel, Lisboa Hotel, Estrada de Sao Francisco, Matsuya Hotel, Guia Hotel, Royal Hotel, Lou Lim Ieoc Garden, Mondial Hotel, Avenida Horta e Costa, Avenida Coronel Mesquita, Kun Iam Temple, Bairro da Areia Preta, Barrier Gate

Buses to the island of Taipa cost M$2.30, while buses to Coloane are M$3.30. The complete bus routes to the islands are as follows:

No 11 Barra Fortress, Floating Casino, Avenida de Almeida Ribeiro, GPO, Lisboa Hotel, bridge, Hyatt Regency Hotel (Taipa), University of Macau, Taipa Village, Macau Jockey Club
No 14 Taipa Village, Causeway, Coloane Park, Coloane Village, Pousada de Coloane, Hac Sa Beach
No 15 Coloane Village, Ka Ho
No 21 Barra Fortress, Praca Ponte e Horta, Floating Casino, Avenida de Almeida Ribeiro, GPO, Lisboa Hotel, bridge, Hyatt Regency Hotel (Taipa), Coloane Park, Coloane Village
No 21A Barra Fortress, Praca Ponte e Horta, Floating Casino, Avenida de Almeida Ribeiro, GPO, Lisboa Hotel, bridge, Hyatt Regency Hotel (Taipa), Taipa Village, Coloane Park, Coloane Village, Cheoc Van Beach, Hac Sa Beach
No 28A Jetfoil Pier, Beverly Plaza Hotel, Lisboa Hotel, bridge, Hyatt Regency Hotel (Taipa), Macau University, Taipa Village
No 33 Fai Chi Kei, Lin Fong Miu (Lotus Temple), Avenida de Almeida Ribeiro, Lisboa Hotel, Hyatt Regency Hotel (Taipa), Macau University, Taipa Village, Macau Jockey Club
No 38 Special bus running from the city centre to the Macau Jockey Club one hour before the races

MACAU

TAXI

Macau taxis are black with cream roofs. They all have meters and drivers are required to use them. Flagfall is M$6.50 for the first 1.5 km, thereafter it's 80 avos every 250 metres. There is a M$5 surcharge to go to Taipa and M$10 to go to Coloane, but there is no surcharge if you're heading the other way back to Macau. There is also an additional M$1 service charge for each piece of luggage carried in the boot (trunk). Taxis can be dispatched by radio if you telephone (☎ 519519). Not many taxi drivers speak English, so it would be helpful to have a map with both Chinese and English or Portuguese labels.

CAR

The mere thought of renting a car in Hong Kong is ridiculous but sharing the cost between a group might make sense for exploring the islands of Taipa and Coloane. On Macau Peninsula, horrendous traffic and the lack of parking space makes driving more of a burden than a pleasure.

As in Hong Kong, driving is on the left-hand side of the road. Another local driving rule is that motor vehicles must always stop for pedestrians at a crosswalk if there is no traffic light. It's illegal to beep the horn.

Macau Mokes (☎ 378851) is Macau's rent-a-car pioneer. It is on Avenida Marciano Baptist, just across from the Jetfoil Pier in Macau. There is a Hong Kong office (☎ 5434190) at 806 Kai Tak Commercial Building, 317-321 Des Voeux Rd, Sheung Wan, near Macau Ferry Terminal on Hong Kong Island. A moke costs 280 patacas on weekdays and 310 patacas on weekends and holidays.

You can also rent mokes from Avis (☎ 336789, 567888 ext 3004) at the Mandarin Oriental Hotel. You can book in advance at the Avis Hong Kong office (☎ 5412011) – probably not necessary on weekdays.

BICYCLE

You can hire bicycles out on the islands of Taipa and Coloane. On the peninsula, there are no places to hire bikes, and it wouldn't

be pleasant riding anyway with the insane traffic.

TOURS

A typical city tour (booked in Macau) of the peninsula takes three to four hours and costs about M$100 per person, often including lunch. Bus tours out to the islands start from about M$50 per person. You can also book a one-day bus tour across the border into Zhuhai in China, which usually includes a trip to the former home of Dr Sun Yat-sen in Zhongshan County. There are large numbers of tour operators.

Around Macau

THINGS TO SEE
Macau Peninsula

There's far more of historical interest to be seen in Macau than Hong Kong. Simply wandering around is a delight – the streets are winding and always full of interest. Old hands say Macau's now getting speedy like Hong Kong but it has a way to go.

The **Ruins of St Paul** are the symbol of Macau, and the facade and majestic stairway are all that remain of this old church. It was designed by an Italian Jesuit and built in 1602 by Japanese refugees who had fled anti-Christian persecution in Nagasaki. In 1853 the church was totally burned down during a catastrophic typhoon.

The **Monte Fort** overlooks the Ruins of St Paul and almost all of Macau from its high and central position. It was built by the Jesuits. In 1622, a cannonball fired from the fort conveniently landed in a Dutch gunpowder carrier during an attempted Dutch invasion, demolishing most of their fleet.

The **Kun Iam Temple** is the city's most historic. In the temple study 18 wise men are displayed in a glass case – the one with the big nose is said to be Marco Polo. The 400-year-old temple is dedicated to Kun Iam, the queen of heaven and goddess of mercy.

The **Old Protestant Cemetery** is a fascinating place to wander around. Lord

Churchill (one of Winston's ancestors) and the English artist George Chinnery are buried here, but far more interesting are the varied graves of missionaries and their families, traders, seamen and the often detailed accounts of their lives and deaths. One American ship seems to have had half its crew 'fall from aloft' while in port.

Next door to the cemetery is the fine little **Luis de Camoes Museum**, which has items from China and a fine collection of paintings, prints and engravings showing Macau in the last two centuries.

The **Barrier Gate** used to be of interest because you could stand 100 metres from it and claim that you'd seen into China. Now you can stand on the other side and claim you've seen Macau.

The **Leal Senado** (Loyal Senate) looks out over the main town square and is the main administrative body for municipal affairs. At one time it was offered (and turned down) a total monopoly on all Chinese trade! The building also houses the **National Library**.

The highest point in Macau is the **Guía Fortress**, with a 17th-century chapel and lighthouse built on it. The lighthouse is the oldest (first lit up in 1865) on the Chinese coast.

One of the most beautiful churches in Macau is **St Dominic's Church**, a 17th-century building which has an impressive tiered altar. There is a small museum at the back, full of church regalia, images and paintings.

The peaceful **Lou Lim leoc Garden**, with it's ornate mansion (now the Pui Ching School), reflects a mixture of Chinese and European influences with huge shady trees, lotus ponds, pavilions, bamboo groves, grottoes and odd-shaped doorways.

Macau means the 'City of God' and takes its name from A-Ma-Gau, the Bay of A-Ma. The **A-Ma Temple** (Ma Kok Miu), which dates from the Ming Dynasty, stands at the base of Penha Hill on Barra Point. According to legend, A-Ma, goddess of seafarers, was supposed to have been a beautiful young woman whose presence on a Guangzhou-bound ship saved it from disaster. All the other ships of the fleet, whose rich owners had refused to give her passage, were destroyed in a storm. The boat people of Macau come here on a pilgrimage each year in April or May.

A restored colonial-style building beside the A-Ma Temple houses the **Macau Maritime Museum**. Across the road on the waterfront are a number of boats, including a tug, a dragon boat and a *lorcha*, a type of sailing cargo-vessel used on the Pearl River.

Macau Islands

Directly south of the mainland peninsula are the islands of Taipa and Coloane. A bridge connects Taipa Island to the mainland, and a causeway connects Taipa and Coloane.

Taipa This island seems to have become one big construction site with the Hyatt Regency hotel and Macau University just the first of a number of projects. Taipa village is pleasant and there are some fine little restaurants to sample. There's an old church, a couple of temples and the **Taipa House Museum**. You can rent a bicycle to explore the village and farther afield.

Coloane This island also has a pretty village where you can see junks under construction. Situated in a muddy river mouth, Macau is hardly likely to be blessed with wonderful beaches but Coloane has a couple that are really not bad. **Hac Sa Beach** is a long but not particularly inspiring stretch of sand, while tiny **Cheoc Van Beach** is really quite pretty. Bicycles can also be rented there.

PLACES TO STAY

Weekends are a bad time to visit Macau; try to make your trip on a weekday. During the quieter mid-week time, it's worth bargaining a little.

Places to Stay – bottom end

The street in front of the Floating Casino is Rua das Lorchas, and one block east is an alley called Rua do Bocage. At No 17 you'll find *Ung Ieong Hotel* (☎ 573814), though a

MACAU

sign on the door says 'Restaurante Ung Ieong'. The rooms are so huge you could fit an army in there! Auditorium-sized doubles go for M$52 and some have attached bath. Before you pay, go upstairs and take a look – it's very rundown.

Two blocks to the south of the Floating Casino, on Rua das Lorchas, is a large square called Praca Ponte e Horta. There are several villas around the square. On the east end of the square is *Pensao Kuan Heng* (☎ 573629, 937624), 2nd floor, Block C, Rua Ponte e Horta. Singles/doubles are M$150/250, and it's very clean and well-managed.

The *Vila Tai Loy* (☎ 937811) is on the corner of Travessa das Virtudes and Travessa Auto Novo. At M$200 it's barely in the budget class, but the rooms are attractive and the manager is friendly.

Moving to the east side of the peninsula, the area between the Lisboa Hotel and Rua da Praia Grande has some budget accommodation. Intersecting with Rua da Praia Grande is a small street called Rua Dr Pedro Jose Lobo where there's a dense cluster of guesthouses, including *Vila Meng Meng* (☎ 710064) on the 3rd floor at No 24. If you don't mind a shared bathroom, this is one of the best deals in town – air-conditioned rooms are M$130. Next door is the *Vila Nam Loon*. It's possibly a cheapie but it was being renovated at the time of writing and the new prices are unknown.

Just above Foto Princesa (the camera shop) at Avenida do Infante D' Henrique 55-59 is *Vila Kimbo* (☎ 710010), where singles go for M$130 and up.

On Rua Dr Pedro Jose Lobo, the *Vila Sam Sui* (☎ 572256) seems very nice and just barely qualifies as budget with rooms for M$200. Its neighbour, *Vila Loc Tin* has moved upmarket and rooms are M$250.

Running off Avenida D Joao IV is an alley called Travessa da Praia Grande. At No 3 you'll find *Pensao Nam In* (☎ 710024), where singles with shared bath are M$110 or it's M$230 for a pleasant double with private bath. On the opposite side of the alley is the *Vila Nam Tin* (☎ 711212), which looks cheap but isn't, singles are M$330! The *Vila Nam*

Pan (☎ 572289) on the corner has also gotten too pricey with singles for M$250, but try polite bargaining.

Behind the Lisboa Hotel on Avenida de Lopo Sarmento de Carvalho is a row of pawnshops and a couple of guesthouses. The *Vila San Vu* is friendly and has good rooms for M$200.

Places to Stay – middle

An excellent place to stay in Macau is the *East Asia Hotel* (☎ 922433), Rua da Madeira 1-A. Spotlessly clean singles are M$230 with private bath and fierce air-conditioning. The dim sum restaurant on the 2nd floor has outstanding breakfasts for about M$20.

Almost next door to the East Asia Hotel is the *Vila Capital* (☎ 920154) at Rua Constantino Brito 3. Singles/doubles are M$230/280.

1	Rasa Sayang Restaurant 莎洋餐廳
2	Ocean Garden Luxury Flats 海洋花園
3	Restaurant Bee Vee 葡國餐廳
4	Pou Tai Un Temple 菩提園
5	Hyatt Regency Hotel 凱悅酒店
6	New Century Hotel 新世紀酒店
7	Kun Iam Temple 觀音岩
8	Macau University 澳門大學
9	United Chinese Cemetery 孝思墳場
10	Police Station 警察局
11	Petrol Station 加油站
12	Macau Jockey Club 澳門賽馬會
13	Four-Faced Buddha 四面佛
14	Horse Racetrack 賽馬場
15	Kartodrome 小型賽車場

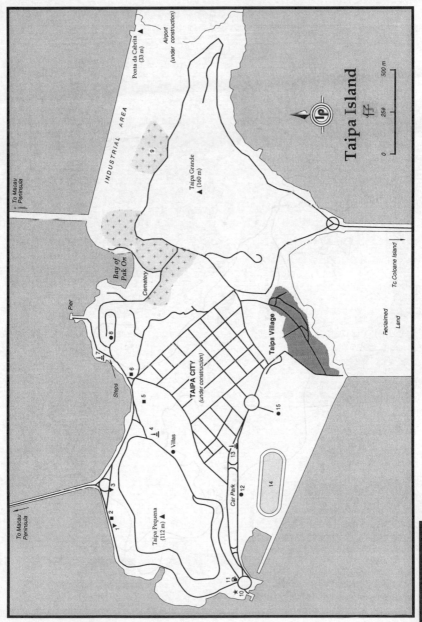

To Macau Peninsula

Ponta da Cabrita (33 m) ▲

Airport (under construction)

INDUSTRIAL AREA

9

Taipa Grande ▲ (160 m)

Taipa Island 仔

0   250   500 m

Bay of Pak On

Cemetery

Pier

8 ●

7

Steps

6 ■

5 ■

4

Villas ●

TAIPA CITY (under construction)

Taipa Village

To Coloane Island

Reclaimed Land

15 ●

13

Car Park

12 ●

14

To Macau Peninsula

3

1 ▼ 2 ■

Taipa Pequena ▲ (112 m)

11

10 ★

MACAU

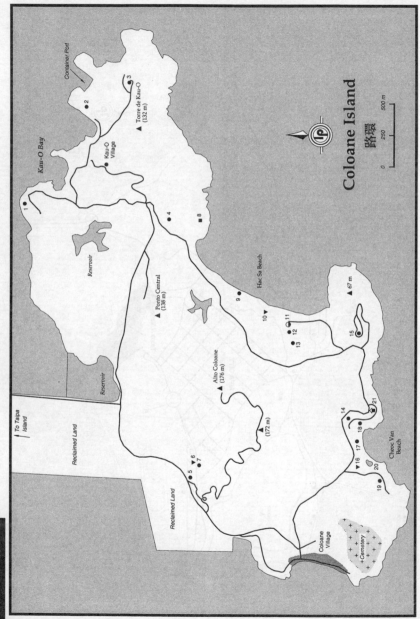

Coloane Island 路環

1	Power Plant	發電所
2	Macau Cement Plant	水泥場
3	Catholic School Centre	天主教堂
4	Golf Course	高爾夫球俱樂部
5	Coloane Park	路環郊野公園
6	Dalichao Restaurant	金龍餐廳
7	Aviary	鳥舍
8	Westin Hotel	威斯汀酒店
9	Waterscooter & Windsurfer Rentals	水上電單車出租
10	Fernando's Restaurant	法蘭度餐廳
11	Bus Stop	黑沙車站
12	Swimming Pool & Tennis Courts	游泳池/網球場
13	Horse-riding Ranch	騎術訓練中心
14	Pousada de Coloane	竹灣酒店
15	Satellite Station	天線
16	La Torre Italian Restaurant	斜塔餐廳
17	Snack Bar & Changing Rooms	小吃部
18	Yacht Club	帆船俱樂部
19	Villas	別墅
20	Swimming Pool	竹灣游泳池
21	Youth Hostel	青年會

The *Central Hotel* (☎ 373838) is centrally located at Avenida de Almeida Ribeiro 26-28, a short hop west of the GPO. The hotel looks better on the outside than it does on the inside – look at the rooms before you decide to stay. Singles/doubles with private bath cost from M$207/238.

The *London Hotel* (☎ 937761) on a large square called Praca Ponte e Horta (two blocks south of the Floating Casino) has

singles for M$230. Rooms are comfortable and clean.

A few doors to the south of the Floating Casino you'll find an alley called Travessa das Virtudes. On your left as you enter the alley is the *Hou Kong Hotel* (☎ 937555), which has singles/doubles for M$230/322. Its official address is Rua das Lorchas 1.

One block to the north of the Floating Casino is the *Grand Hotel* (☎ 922418) at Avenida de Almeida Ribeiro 146, where singles/doubles cost M$262/386.

One block to the east of the Floating Casino is a street called Travessa Caldeira, where you'll find the *Man Va Hotel* (☎ 388655), Rua da Caldeira 32, with doubles at M$340. Nearby at Rua de Felicidade 71, close to Travessa Auto Novo, is *Ko Wah Hotel* (☎ 375599) which has doubles for M$250.

Just on the north side of the Floating Casino on Rua das Lorchas is the *Peninsula Hotel*) (☎ 318899). Singles/twins are M$300/350. This hotel is large, clean and popular.

One more place to look around is the area north of the Lisboa Hotel on a street called Estrada de Sao Francisco. You have to climb a steep hill to get up this street. Here you'll find the fancy *Matsuya Hotel* (☎ 577000; fax 568080), where doubles/twins cost M$330/390 and suites are M$650.

Next to the Matsuya Hotel at Estrada de Sao Francisco 2A is *Vila Tak Lei* (☎ 577484), where doubles go for M$300. However, bargaining is possible in this place.

PLACES TO EAT
One of the most conveniently located street markets serving cheap food is Rua da Escola Commercial, a tiny lane one block west of the Lisboa Hotel, just next to a sports field. For economy snacks, try the *Yoghurt Shop* at 65 Avenida de Almeida Ribeiro, where yoghurt is served Chinese style in a rice bowl.

A long, lazy Portuguese meal with a carafe of red to wash it down is one of the most pleasant parts of a Macau visit. The menus are often in Portuguese, so a few useful words are cozido (stew), cabrito (kid), cordeiro (lamb), carreiro (mutton), galinha (chicken), caraguejos (crabs), carne de vaca (beef) and peixe (fish). Apart from carafe wine you can also get Mateus Rosé.

Another Macau pleasure is to sit back in one of the many little cake shops (pastelarias) with a glass of cha de limao (lemon tea) and a plate of cakes – very genteel! These places are good for a cheap breakfast. People eat early in Macau, and you can find the chairs being put away and that the chef has gone home at around 9 pm.

Henri's Galley (☎ 556251) is on the waterfront at 4 Avenida da República, on the south end of the Macau Peninsula. Also known as Maxims (not the Hong Kong fast-food chain), Henri's Galley is known for its African chicken, spicy prawns, prawn fondue and Chinese food.

Next door is the excellent *Café Marisol*. Staff set up outdoor tables so you can take in the view across to the islands. Adjacent to Henri's Galley is the *Ali Curry House*, which also has outdoor tables and a diverse menu consisting of curry dishes and steaks with a Portuguese flavour.

For Portuguese and Macanese food which is both good and cheap, the *Estrela do Mar* (☎ 81270) at 11 Travessa do Paiva, off the Rua da Praia Grande, is the place to go. So is the *Solmar* (☎ 74391) at 11 Rua da Praia Grande. Both places are famous for African chicken and seafood.

Fat Siu Lau (☎ 73580) serves Portuguese and Chinese food. It's at 64 Rua de Felicid-ade, once the old red-light Street of Happiness. The speciality is roast pigeon.

Another place known for good Portuguese food is *Portugués* (☎ 75445) at 16 Rua do Campo. For good food and fine Spanish decor visit *Algarve Sol* (☎ 89007) at 41-43 Rua Comandante Mata e Oliveira, two blocks west of the Lisboa Hotel between Rua da Praia Grande and Avenida D Joao IV.

An excellent place is *Restaurant Safari* (☎ 574313) at 14 Pateo do Cotovelo, a tiny square off Avenida de Almeida Ribeiro across from the Central Hotel. It has good coffee-shop dishes as well as spicy chicken,

steak and fried noodles. For a good pizza, try *Pizzeria Toscana*, Rua Formosa 28B.

Lots of people hop over to Taipa village for its excellent restaurants, but they're no longer cheap. One place to try is *Pinocchio's*. Other popular Taipa village restaurants include the very Portuguese *Restaurante Panda*, the Italian (despite the name) *Restaurante Leong Un*, the cheaper *Casa de Pasto Tai Tung*, the *Kung Kai, Cozinha Ricardo's Kitchen* and the pleasant sidewalk-cafe-like *Cafe Tai Lei Lai Kei*, opposite the Tin Hau Temple.

At Hac Sa Beach on Coloane Island, *Fernando's* deserves honourable mention for some of the best food in Macau. Fernando recommends the clams.

For economy-minded wine lovers, Macau offers some of the best bargains around. You can bring a litre of wine or spirits back to Hong Kong, where it's more expensive.

ENTERTAINMENT
Gambling
Even if gambling holds no interest for you, it's entertaining to wander the casinos at night. The largest and most fun arena for losing money is the Lisboa Hotel.

For 200 patacas, you can watch about 10 graduates of the Crazy Horse in Paris cavort around the stage of the Lisboa Hotel attired in outfits ranging from very little to nothing at all. It's called the Crazy Paris Show.

There's also horse racing on Taipa Island and dog racing at the 'Canidrome' (yes, they really call it that).

Pubs
There are three pubs in a row that can claim to be the centre of Macau's nightlife. All are near the Kun Iam Temple on the same street, Rua de Pedro Coutinho. At No 104 is *Talker Pub* (☎ 550153, 528975), just next door at No 106 is *Pyretu's Bar* (☎ 581063), and at No 114 is *Moonwalk Pub* (☎ 529201). All of these places open around 8 pm but don't get moving until after 9 pm. Portuguese and other Westerners make up the majority of the customers here.

THINGS TO BUY

Pawnshops are ubiquitous in Macau, and it is possible to get good deals on cameras, watches and jewellery, but you must be prepared to bargain without mercy. In Macau at least, the nasty reputation of pawnbrokers is well-deserved!

The MGTO has a number of good souvenir items for sale at bargain prices. Some of the items to consider are Macau T-shirts, poster-size 'antigue maps of Macau', sets of postcards, umbrellas and raincoats.

St Dominic Market, in the alley behind the Central Hotel, is a good place to pick up cheap clothing.

Mongolia

The name 'Mongolia' has always stirred up visions of the exotic – Genghis Khan, the Gobi Desert, wild horses galloping across the Siberian steppes. Even today, Mongolia seems like the end of the earth – outside of the few major cities, you begin to wonder if you haven't stepped into another century rather than another country.

Paradoxically, many Western travellers visit Mongolia yet never set foot on it. The Trans-Siberian Railway runs right through the centre of the country, but most foreigners are only issued transit visas. As a result, few Westerners get to see more than the view from the train's window. There are numerous bureaucratic hurdles to clear before getting a tourist visa, and few want to waste the time and money just to see a tiny slice of Mongolia.

This is a pity, because this country has much to offer. A land of vast deserts, rolling grasslands, high mountains, forests and crystal clear lakes: Mongolia's environment is the most pristine in Asia. This is largely due to the harsh climate, which has always made human existence a precarious proposition in this part of the planet. Not surprisingly, the Mongols are a tough people – indeed, in the 13th century they conquered half the world.

The unique culture of the Mongols has fascinated Western travellers since the time of Marco Polo, but the door slammed shut in 1921 with a Marxist revolution. Now that the Cold War has been banished, Mongolia is cautiously opening up. With neighbouring China rapidly modernising, Mongolia is sure to follow. The country is desperate for foreign exchange, and the most likely way to earn it is to open up to Western tourism. Perhaps in another decade we'll be seeing Genghis Khan Burger chain restaurants in the Gobi Desert, but for now Mongolia remains a barely explored traveller's destination. If you hurry up, you may be among the first.

Facts about the Country

HISTORY

Early Chinese manuscripts refer to 'Turkic-speaking peoples' living in what we now call Mongolia as early as the 4th or 5th century BC. The name 'Mongol' was first recorded during China's Tang Dynasty (618-907 AD). The Mongols at this time were scattered nomadic tribes, barely noticed by the outside world.

All this was to change dramatically in the 13th century. A Mongol by the name of Temüjin was born in 1162. He united the Mongols after 20 years of internal warfare, and in 1206 he was given the honorary name Genghis Khan (universal ruler). His swift troops on horseback launched themselves against Russia and China. By the time of his death in 1248, the empire already extended from Beijing to the Caspian Sea.

It was Genghis Khan's grandson, Kublai Khan, who completed the subjugation of China. He set himself up in Beijing as the emperor of the Yuan Dynasty. This was the height of glory for the Mongol Empire, which stretched from Vietnam to Hungary – the largest nation the world has ever known. The Mongols improved the road system linking China with Russia and promoted trade throughout the empire and with Europe. They instituted a famine relief scheme and expanded the canal system which brought food from the countryside to the cities. They were the first society to make paper money the sole form of currency. It was the China of the Mongols that Marco Polo and other Westerners visited, and their books described the empire to an amazed Europe.

The splendour of the Mongol Empire didn't last for long. Kublai Khan died in 1294 and the Mongols became increasingly corrupted by the empire they ruled. They

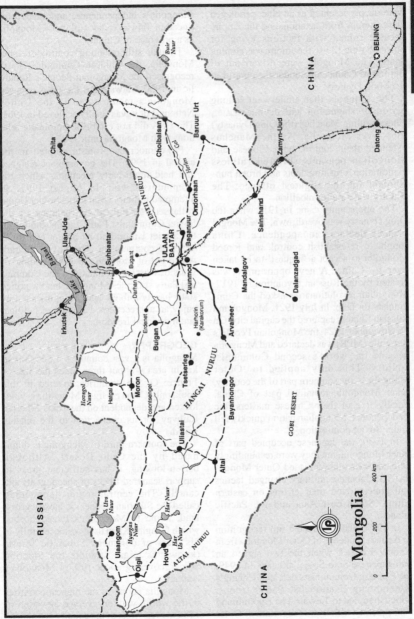

Mongolia

were deeply resented as an elite, privileged class exempt from taxation, and the empire became ridden with factions vying for power. By the 1350s, the empire was coming apart. The Mongols were driven out of Beijing as China came under the control of the Ming Dynasty.

The Mongols then underwent a long period of stagnation and decline. Later, China's ruling Manchus (the Qing Dynasty) took over Mongolia. As the Manchus extended their control, both Chinese and Mongolian peasants suffered ruthless exploitation, crushing debts and brutal punishment for the slightest offence. The country was ripe for rebellion.

The opportunity came in 1911 when the Qing Dynasty was overthrown. The Mongol princes declared independence. China sought to re-establish control, and forced Mongolia to accept a 'request' to be taken over by China. A new opportunity was created by the Russian revolution of 1917. Mongolian revolutionaries asked the Communists for help. In July 1921, Mongol and Russian fighters captured the capital city. On 26 November 1924, the Mongolian People's Republic (MPR) was declared and Mongolia became the world's second Communist country. This only applied to 'Outer Mongolia' – the southern part of the country, Inner Mongolia, remained part of China. Finally free of their Chinese masters, the 'independent' Mongolian nation quickly fell under Soviet domination.

In 1939, the Japanese occupied part of Inner Mongolia, but they were resoundingly defeated when they invaded Outer Mongolia. The Japanese military changed tactics and concentrated their efforts on eastern China, South-East Asia and the Pacific islands.

In 1945, Stalin extracted full recognition of the independence of Outer Mongolia from Chiang Kaishek when the two signed an anti-Japanese Sino-Soviet alliance. In 1949, the Chinese Communists defeated Chiang's Kuomintang (Nationalist Party) troops, which then fled to Taiwan. The Kuomintang subsequently withdrew recognition of Outer Mongolia's independence, and maps produced in Taiwan today still show Mongolia as a province of China.

Though still retaining control of Inner Mongolia, the Chinese Communist Party recognised the Mongolian People's Republic in 1950. Taiwan and the USA opposed Mongolia's membership in the United Nations, but it was finally achieved in 1961. The USA did not establish diplomatic relations with Mongolia until 1987.

Pro-democracy protests erupted in the capital in 1990. The government resigned and held multi-party elections, which the Communists won. In August 1991, an attempted military coup in the Soviet Union collapsed, leading to the banning of the Soviet Communist Party, the dissolution of the Soviet Union and an abrupt end to 72 years of communism. The Soviet military pulled out of Mongolia in 1992, ending 71 years of Russian domination. The Communist Party still rules Mongolia, but the police state has crumbled and Mongolians now enjoy an unprecedented amount of political and individual freedom.

GEOGRAPHY

Mongolia is a vast country – 1,566,000 sq km in area – about three times the size of France. Of the countries covered in this book, only China is larger. Mongolia is landlocked and dependent on the Trans-Siberian Railway for its connection to the outside world.

The southern third of Mongolia is dominated by the Gobi Desert. Although barren-looking, it has sufficient grass to support scattered flocks of sheep, goats and camels. The central region (commonly called the Siberian steppes) is mostly grassland, home to Mongolia's famed horses, which Genghis Khan used so successfully in his wars of conquest. Subarctic forests (known as taiga) straddle the Siberian border, covering about 10% of Mongolia's land area.

Mongolia is one of the highest countries in the world, with an average elevation of 1580 metres. Most of the country is a plateau with flat plains, rolling hills and a few dramatic peaks. The tallest mountain is 4374-metre Tavanbogd (Five Saints), at the very westernmost tip of Mongolia in the Altai range. The summit straddles the border with China and Russia, and is therefore also called Nairamdal (Friendship Peak). The lowest point is in eastern Mongolia at Hoh Nuur (blue lake) with an elevation of 560 metres.

Near the centre of the country is the Hangai range, with peaks over 3900 metres. On the north slope of these mountains is the Selenge River, Mongolia's largest, which flows northward into Lake Baikal in Siberia. The Hentii Nuruu is the beautiful range of forested mountains north-east of the capital city.

The capital and largest city is Ulaan Baatar. Some 200 km to the north is the second largest city, Darhan, and to the northwest is the third largest city, Erdenet. These three cities are autonomous municipalities. The rest of the country is divided into 18 provinces known as *aimags*.

CLIMATE

Mongolia is a land of extremes. Although much of the country is desert, Siberian-style winters are the norm. The Gobi Desert of the south is Mongolia's banana belt – summer temperatures hit 40°C, but winter winds often send the mercury plummeting to minus 30°C or lower. Humidity is zilch and sunshine is intense, with over 260 sunny days a year.

The Siberian steppes are chilly even in summer – the July average is only 10°C. Winter is no joke, minus 50°C is not unknown.

Even spring and autumn are frosty – July is ideal. There is a short rainy season from

mid-July to September, but the showers tend to be brief. Because of the high altitude, evenings are cool even in summer. Mongolia is a windy place, especially in spring.

GOVERNMENT

The political landscape is changing rapidly. For years, the country stagnated under the fossilised rule of the Communist Party, also known as the Mongolian People's Revolutionary Party (MPRP). All other political parties were banned. A political earthquake came in March 1990, when the government resigned after massive street protests. Multiparty elections were held in July, still leaving the MPRP in control. Another election in 1992 brought victory to the MPRP, but with widespread accusations of ballot rigging. The next election is scheduled for 1996. Despite its Communist heritage, the MPRP is pursuing gradual free-market economic reforms.

ECONOMY

Even before the days of Genghis Khan, Mongolia's economy rode on the backs of sheep, goats, cattle, horses, yaks and camels. There are 25½ million head of livestock in Mongolia, which is more than 10 times the human population. Less than 1% of the land is under cultivation, and this is mostly used to grow wheat and potatoes. The main manufacturing industries are the production of leather and wool, plus a few finished products like boots and clothing.

Subsidies from the former USSR kept Mongolia's economy relatively prosperous for years. The bubble burst in 1991 when the subsidies abruptly ended. By 1992, the country was faced with famine and only emergency food aid from Western countries

| Ulaan Baatar Temperatures & Rainfall | | | | | | | | | | | |
	Jan	Feb	Mar	Apr	May	Jun	Jul	Aug	Sep	Oct	Nov	Dec
Temp (°C)	-26	-21	-11	0	8	15	17	15	8	-2	-14	-24
Rain (mm)	1	2	3	7	15	48	72	48	24	6	4	2

MONGOLIA

prevented disaster. Shortages of fuel, machinery, spare parts and consumer goods still plague the economy. Rural families (about half the population) are nearly self-sufficient, and have weathered the economic storm by feeding themselves. However, urban residents produce little and have been hard hit by inflation. Unemployment is the norm in urban areas, but some Mongolians have started their own businesses and are doing well. Mongolia has withdrawn ration coupons and food supplies are improving, but the road to a free-market economy appears to be a long and difficult one.

POPULATION & PEOPLE

The population stands at 2.3 million, with more than 25% living in the capital, Ulaan Baatar. With an average population density of about 1.4 persons per sq km, Mongolia is one of the most sparsely inhabited countries on earth. Following Marxist theories that more people meant more production, the government actively encouraged a high birth rate. The distribution of contraceptives was made illegal, as was abortion. This policy has only recently been reversed, but Mongolia still has no organised family-planning facilities. Population growth now stands at 2.8% annually, the highest in North-East Asia.

In the past, the government also encouraged migration to urban areas in the belief that this would increase industrialisation – the result has been a labour shortage in agriculture and an excess of unemployed youths in the cities. This policy has also been cancelled.

The Mongols are not a single ethnic group. Halhs make up 80% of the population. The most important minorities are: Kazakh (5.3% of the population); Dorvod (2.8%); Bayad (1.9%); Buriad (1.8%); Dariganga (1.5%); Zahchin (1.3%); Urianhai (1.2%); Oold (0.6%); and Torguud (0.6%).

ARTS

Mongolia has a mixture of local traditional arts and imports from Russia and the West. The government promotes operas, plays, folk music, folk dancing, ballet and circuses.

Traditional Mongolian folk dancing is performed in brightly coloured costumes to the accompaniment of loud instruments (such as drums, cymbals, horns etc).

More recent artistic expression comes from the West. Disco is the rage, and so is US-style rap dancing. Scantily clad dancers perform erotic dance on stage – it's enough to make Genghis fall off his horse.

Mongolia has produced a few home-grown rock groups, among them Soyol Erdene (known abroad as Genghis Khan), which took seventh place at the World Pop Festival held in Tokyo in 1991.

CULTURE

The Soyombo is the national symbol of Mongolia and dates back at least to the 17th century. You'll most likely first see it on the covers of Mongolian passports and also on the Mongolian flag. It signifies freedom and independence.

Some aspects of Chinese culture have deeply influenced the Mongolians. You will often see Mongolian cashiers use a Chinese abacus to count up the bill. The Mongolians also use the Chinese zodiac with its 12 animal signs.

RELIGION

Under the Communists, religion was suppressed and nearly disappeared. Since the liberalisation of 1990, there has been a phenomenal religious revival. Monasteries have reopened all over the country.

The main religion is Lamaism (Tibetan or Tantric Buddhism). Muslims account for about 5% of the population.

LANGUAGE

The national language is Mongolian, a member of the Ural-Altaic family of languages which includes Finnish, Turkish, Kazakh, Uzbek and Korean. Since 1944, a modified version of the Russian Cyrillic alphabet has been used to write Mongolian. Russian Cyrillic has 33 letters, but the Mongolians have added two more.

The traditional Mongolian script was borrowed from China's Uigurs, who brought it from the Middle East. The traditional script is composed of 26 letters, written in a fashion that forms beautiful characters. The script is written downwards, starting from the top-left corner of the page. In 1994, the traditional Mongolian script was resurrected and made the official writing system, even though few Mongolians can read it. At least for now, you'll find it easier getting around if you can learn to read and write Cyrillic.

As for Romanisation, there was a spelling reform in 1987, so the capital city, previously written as Ulan Bator, is now Ulaan Baatar.

The most common foreign language is Russian, but English is rapidly gaining popularity. A few Mongolians speak German.

Greetings & Civilities
Hello.
Sain baina uu.
САЙН БАЙНА УУ?
Goodbye.
Bayartai.
БАЯРТАЙ
Thank you.
Bayarllaa.
БАЯРЛАЛАА
You're welcome.
Zugeer.
ЗҮГЭЭР
I'm sorry.
Uuchlaarai.
УУЧЛААРАЙ
I don't understand.
Bi oilgohgui baina.
БИ ОЙЛГОХГҮЙ БАЙНА
I do understand.
Bi oilgoj baina.
БИ ОЙЛГОЖ БАЙНА

Getting Around
Where is the...?
...haana baina ve?
...ХААНА БАЙНА ВЭ?
airport
nisih ongotsny buudal
НИСЭХ ОНГОЦНЫ БУУДАЛ
big temple
huree
ХҮРЭЭ

bus station
avtobusny zogsool
АВТОБУСНЫ ЗОГСООЛ
MIAT ticket office
MIAT-yn bilyetyn gazar
МИАТ-ЫН БИЛЕТЫН ГАЗАР
monastery
hiid
ХИЙД
museum
muzei, uzesgelen
МУЗЕЙ, ҮЗЭСГЭЛЭН
petrol
bensin
БЕНЗИН
petrol station
shathuun tugeeh gazar
ШАТАХУУН ТҮГЭЭХ ГАЗАР
temple
sum
СҮМ
train station
galt teregnii buudal
ГАЛТ ТЭРЭГНИЙ БУУДАЛ
I'm lost.
Bi toorchihloo.
БИ ТӨӨРЧИХЛӨӨ

go straight
shuluun yavaarai
ШУЛУУН ЯВААРАЙ
stop here
end zogsooroi
turn around
toirooroi
ТОЙРООРОЙ
turn left
zuun tiish ergeerei
ЗҮҮН ТИЙШ ЭРГЭЭРЭЙ
turn right
baruun tiish ergeerei
БАРУУН ТИЙШ ЭРГЭЭРЭЙ
map
gazryn zurag
ГАЗРЫН ЗУРАГ

Accommodation
hotel
zochid buudal
ЗОЧИД БУУДАЛ

room
oroo
ӨРӨӨ

room with shared bath
ugaalgyn oroogui oroo
УГААЛГЫН ӨРӨӨГҮЙ ӨРӨӨ

room with private bath
ugaalgyn orootei oroo
УГААЛГЫН ӨРӨӨТЭЙ ӨРӨӨ

single room
neg hunii oroo
НЭГ ХҮНИЙ ӨРӨӨ

double room
hoyor hunii oroo
ХОЁР ХҮНИЙ ӨРӨӨ

cheap room
hyamd oroo
ХЯМД ӨРӨӨ

room key
oroonii tulhuur
ӨРӨӨНИЙ ТҮЛХҮҮР

Necessities

sanitary pads (Kotex)
ariun tsevriin hereglel
АРИУН ЦЭВРИЙН ХЭРЭГЛЭЛ

toilet
biye zasah gazar jorlon
ЖОРЛОН

toilet paper
ariun tsevriin tsaas
ЖОРЛОНГИЙН ЦААС

How much does it cost?
Ene yamar unetei ve?
ЭНЭ ЯМАР ҮНЭТЭЙ ВЭ?

Too expensive.
Heterhii untei yum.
ХЭТЭРХИЙ ҮНЭТЭЙ ЮМ

Post & Telecommunications

fax
fax
ФАКС

postcard
il zahidal
ИЛ ЗАХИДАЛ

post office
shuudan
ШУУДАН

poste restante
ooroo huleen avah
ӨӨРӨӨ ХҮЛЭЭН АВАХ

registered mail
batalgaatai zahia
БАТАЛГААТАЙ ЗАХИА

stamps
mark
МАРК

telegram
tsahilgaan utas
ЦАХИЛГААН УТАС

telephone
utas
УТАС

telex
telex
ТЕЛЕКС

I want to book a call to...
...utasnii zahialga ogmoor baina.
БИ ... УТАСНЫ ЗАХИАЛГА ӨГМӨӨР БАЙНА

I want to send a...
...ilgeemeer baina.
БИ...ИЛГЭЭМЭЭР БАЙНА

Time

When?
Hezee?
ХЭЗЭЭ?

What time is it?
Tsag hed bolj baina ve?
ЦАГ ХЭД БОЛЖ БАЙНА ВЭ?
...o'clock
...tsag bolj baina
...ЦАГ БОЛЖ БАЙНА

yesterday
ochigdor
ӨЧИГДӨР

today
onoodor
ӨНӨӨДӨР

tomorrow
margaash
МАРГААШ

in the morning
ogloonii
ӨГЛӨӨНИЙ

in the afternoon
odriin
ӨДРИЙН
in the evening
oroiny
ОРОЙНЫ

Numbers

1 *neg*
2 *hoyor*
3 *gurav*
4 *dorov*
5 *tav*
6 *zurgaa*
7 *doloo*
8 *naim*
9 *yes*

Emergency

Help!
Tuslaarai!
ТУСЛААРАЙ
Thief!
Hulgaich!
ХУЛГАЙЧ!
Fire!
Gal!
ГАЛ!
Call the police.
Tsagdaa duudaarai.
ЦАГДАА ДУУДААРАЙ
I'm injured.
Bi bertsen.
БИ БЭРТСЭН
I'm sick.
Bi ovchtei baina.
БИ ӨВЧТЭЙ БАЙНА
I've been bitten by a snake.
Bi mogoind hatguulchihlaa.
БИ МОГОЙНД ХАТГУУЛЧИХЛАА
I've been stung by a scorpion.
Bi hilentset horhoind hazuulchihlaa.
БИ ХИЛЭНЦЭТ ХОРХОЙНД
ХАЗУУЛЧИХЛАА
Please take me to the hospital.
Namaig emnelegt hurgej ogno uu.
НАМАЙГ ЭМНЭЛЭГТ ХҮРГЭЖ
ӨГНӨ ҮҮ

aspirin
aspirin
АСПИРИН

Facts for the Visitor

VISAS & EMBASSIES

There are two kinds of visas: 'transit' and 'tourist'. Most travellers taking the Trans-Siberian get a transit visa, which means they cannot go beyond the train platform in the Ulaan Baatar station. In other words, they only get to watch Mongolia roll by from the train window. Some travellers have reckoned that they could arrive on a transit visa, get off and 'miss' their train. Unfortunately, this deception will easily be discovered on exiting the country and a huge fine will have to be paid. Getting a transit visa extended seems to be impossible, so most visitors will want to get a tourist visa.

A tourist visa will allow you to visit almost anywhere in the country, but there is a catch. For most Western nationalities, you can only be issued a tourist visa if you're invited. To be invited, you must make all bookings for hotels and transport and pay for everything in advance. After this, your host will send a wire to the Mongolian embassy inviting you to visit the country. Only then will the visa watchdog let you pass.

The tail that wags this dog is Juulchin (also spelled 'Zhuulchin'), Mongolia's national tourist organisation. Juulchin means 'tourist', though some say it means 'sucker'. Juulchin was created in the image of the old Soviet tourist bureau, Intourist, with the same philosophy – milk the capitalists for every cent they have. Juulchin can book your hotel rooms, arrange transport within Mongolia, provide guides and extend the invitation that you need to get a tourist visa. Unfortunately, service is shoddy and expensive.

The arrival of the free market has created an explosion of private tour operators in Mongolia. This free-market competition has forced prices down (somewhat), but none of

MONGOLIA

these tours are really cheap. Furthermore, many of the fledgling private companies are pretty shaky operations (for further information see under Tours in the Getting Around section later in this chapter).

At least in theory, any individual Mongolian can issue the requisite invitation. In practice, embassy staff are loath to issue visas if you haven't booked a tour. Indeed, some of the embassy employees have close relatives who have gone into the tour business, which means that freely issuing visas would hurt their own financial interests. Most travellers will either need to book a tour or befriend a well-placed Mongolian government official to secure a valid invitation. However, some embassies are inexplicably more liberal than others, so you might get lucky by shopping around for visas.

The Mongolian Embassy in Beijing, China, is open all day, but the visa section keeps short hours – only on Monday, Tuesday, Thursday and Friday from 8.30 to 11.30 am. It is closed for all Mongolian holidays, and is shut down completely for the entire week of National Day (Naadam), which officially falls on 11-13 July. Transit visas cost US$20 if picked up the third day or US$25 for same-day delivery. Tourist visas cost US$25 if processed in three days or US$30 for same-day delivery, but some nationalities (India, Finland etc) are charged nothing. Two photos are required, and visas *must* be paid for in US$ cash.

Visas are for a single entry. Multiple-entry visas exist, but are usually only issued to diplomats and consultants.

Mongolian Embassies

Belgium
593, Chausee De Wavre, 1040 Bruxelles (☎ 2-64680)

Bulgaria
Frederic St, 113 Sofia (☎ 659431, 659291)

China
2 Xiushui Beilu, Jianguomenwai, Beijing (☎ 5321203)

Cuba
Calle 66, No 505, Esguina a 5 ta-A, Miramar, Havana (☎ 332713)

Czech
Koriska 5, Prague (☎ 32 8992, 32 9067)

Egypt
3 Midan el Nasr, Gameatdowai el Arabie St (☎ 346 0670)

France
5 Ave Robert Schumann 92, Boulogne, Billancourt (☎ 46.05.28.12, 46.05.23.18)

Germany
Botschaft der MVR, 1157 Berlin Karlshorst Fritz Schmenkel Strasse 81, Berlin (☎ 5098954)
Bonn office (☎ 02241-402727)

Hungary
X 11 Istenhedyi UT-59-61, Budapest (☎ 55 6219)

India
34 Archbisop Makarios Marg, New Delhi 11003 (☎ 461 7989)

Japan
Shoto Pinecrest Mansion, 21-4 Kamiyamacho Shibuya-ku, Tokyo 150 (☎ 03-3469 2088, 3469 2092)

Kazakhstan
Markovo Ulitsa 47a, Flat 33, Alma-Ata 48000 (☎ 327612)

Korea (North)
Mansu-dong, Pyongyang (☎ 2-817322)

Korea (South)
A-302 Namsan Village, San, 1-139 Itaewon-dong, Yongsan-gu, Seoul (☎ 02-793 5611 ext 2911 or 2302)

Laos
Route Tha Deau Km 2, BT-370, Vientiane (☎ 3666)

Poland
Warszawa al Ulazdowskie 12, Warsaw (☎ 28 9765, 28 1651)

Romania
Bucuresti Strada Fagaras 6, Ambassade Mongolie, Bucharest (☎ 49 6340, 56 0040)

Russia
Spas Peskovskii per 1/7, Moscow (☎ 229 6765; telex 41-4486)
Buryat Republic, Hotel Baikal, Erbanova Ulitsa, 12, Ulan Ude (☎ 20507, 22934)
Irkutsk Consulate, ulitsa Lapina 11, Irkutsk (☎ 42370, 42260)

Switzerland
(for Swiss citizens only) 4 Chemin des Mollies, 1293 Bellevue, Geneva (☎ 74 1974, 74 1975)

Ukraine
Kotsubinskii Ulitsa 3, Kiev (☎ 216 8891)

UK
7 Kensington Court, London W8 5DL (☎ 0171-937 0150, 937 5235)

USA
10201 Iron Gate Rd, Potomac, MD 20854 (☎ 301-983 1962)

Uzbekistan
    Gogol Ulitsa 57, Tashkent 70000 (☎ 332551, 338313)

Visa Extensions

The Ministry of Foreign Affairs in Ulaan Baatar is the only place in Mongolia where you can have your visa extended. Although it is not possible to extend a transit visa, a tourist visa can be extended but it will cost you. The ministry requires that you get some sort of official document from whoever sponsored you for the original visa. In most cases, this means Juulchin. In order to get Juulchin to come up with the papers, you'll have to pay through the nose.

The cost of a tourist visa extension is US$15 for 30 days and one photo is required. Processing the paperwork usually takes one or two days, and you'll need to leave your passport.

Exit & Re-Entry Visas

Tourists needn't worry about this, but those coming to work in Mongolia are usually issued a single-entry visa without an expiry date and valid for entry only. For such people, another visa is required to leave the country. These visas are available from the Ministry of Foreign Affairs in Ulaan Baatar at a cost of US$20. Another visa is required for re-entry. Again, see the Ministry of Foreign Affairs in Ulaan Baatar or a Mongolian embassy abroad.

CUSTOMS

Baggage searches tend to be light to non-existent for foreigners, but it's a different story for Mongolians, who have become skilled smugglers. Chinese and Mongolian people on the train carry tremendous amounts of luggage and may ask you to carry it for them – in most cases this is not a good idea.

Other than that, there are few problems. For electronic goods (Walkmans etc), you can usually bring one of each item duty-free, but you must pay 100% import duty on each additional one.

MONEY
Currency

The unit of currency is the *togrog*. Bills are issued in denominations of 1, 3, 5, 10, 20, 50, 100 and 500 togrogs. The US$ is the unofficial currency of Mongolia, demanded by many hotels and some shops which sell imported goods.

It would be wise to bring lots of cash US$, preferably in denominations no larger than US$20. Most imported items are only available if you pay in US$. US coins could prove helpful as the shops frequently run out and therefore cannot give any change smaller than US$1. It's not unusual to receive change in chewing gum, candy and even condoms.

Some hotels and shops accept American Express, JCB, MasterCard and Visa credit cards. Getting a cash advance on a credit card is not impossible, but difficult.

Black market money changers certainly do exist, but there is little benefit in using their services unless you simply cannot get to a bank. The chances of getting ripped off by black marketeers should not be taken lightly.

Finding *legal* places to change money outside of Ulaan Baatar is next to impossible. When cashing travellers' cheques, a 2% commission is charged if you want to be paid in US$. There is no commission if you accept togrogs. Keep your exchange receipts for changing money back on departure.

Exchange Rates

The best exchange rates are offered for US$. The actual buy and sell rates offered by Mongolian banks are significantly worse than the official exchange rates, particularly for currencies the Mongolians don't want (like Hong Kong dollars). Many hard currencies (such as Australian and New Zealand dollars) cannot currently be exchanged in Mongolia. On the other hand, some unusual currencies are acceptable (Italian lira and Austrian shillings). Furthermore, some currencies are sold by Mongolian banks but will not be bought, while others can be bought but not sold. Confused? You should be. It could all change next week, but this is the current foreign exchange battleground:

Country	Unit	Rate	Buy	Sell
Austria	S1	T34		T36
Canada	C$1	T297		T305
China	Y1	T47	T30	
France	Ffr1	T71	T66	T73
Germany	DM1	T244	T226	T250
Hong Kong	HK$1	T53	T30	
Italy	L1	T0.25		T0.26
Japan	¥100	T3.97	T3.69	T4.07
Switzerland	Sfr1	T288	T267	T296
UK	UK£1	T606	T562	T622
USA	US$1	T409	T407	T420

Costs

Mongolia is either dirt cheap or very expensive, depending on your ability to circumvent the official system for ripping off tourists. At the official rates, Mongolia is bad value – high prices for poor service. A Mongolian tourist could easily live for under US$5 per day, but foreigners are customarily charged five to 10 times the local price.

Typically, the combined cost of bottom-end accommodation and food (for foreigners) in Ulaan Baatar will start at US$20 per day, but could be two or three times that at an upmarket hotel. Costs are generally much lower outside the capital city, but transport expenses (especially jeep rentals) can easily eat up savings. Given the difficulties of arranging visas, food and transport, an organised tour might be worthwhile. Tour prices can range from US$50 to US$200 per day. See under Tours in the Getting Around section later in this chapter for more information.

Tipping

In general, tipping is not a Mongolian custom, so don't make it one. There is an exception at restaurants in Ulaan Baatar where waiters expect a tip, especially from foreigners.

Bargaining

Bargaining is definitely catching on. At hotels, bargaining can often knock down prices to less than half (sometimes much less) of what was originally asked.

WHEN TO GO

For most travellers, summer (July and August) is the only feasible time to visit. Hotels can pack out during the Naadam festival in mid-July.

WHAT TO BRING

Shortages of basic consumer goods are the norm, but the situation is steadily improving in Ulaan Baatar. Outside of the capital, the shelves are bare and you must bring whatever you need. Don't take this warning lightly – everything from fuel to food are nearly impossible to buy. There is an acute shortage of toilet paper, but if you run out you can always use togrogs. It's also recommended that you bring toothpaste, shampoo, soap, razor blades, tampons, condoms, tea or coffee and a cup. Hot water for making tea or coffee is seldom available, so an electrical immersion coil is worth its weight in gold. However, electricity is often not available, so don't count on cooking with an immersion coil. A few jars of peanut butter, meat in tins and biscuits are crucial survival rations. Plastic bags and twist ties are hard to come by, but will prove valuable for storing bread. Warm clothes will be needed for any time of year, even summer evenings can be chilly. UV (sunblock) lotion and sunglasses are essential.

TOURIST OFFICES
Local Tourist Offices

See the Ulaan Baatar section later in this chapter for the address of Juulchin's head office.

Overseas Reps

China
    c/o MIAT, Jing Guang Centre, 8th floor, room 06, Hujia Lou, Chaoyang Qu, Beijing 100020 (☎ 5014544; fax 5077397)
Germany
    Arnold Zweigstr 2.3R 13187, Berlin (☎ 030-471 8833)

Japan
> MJT, 8th floor, JBP Shibuya East 11, 16-9, Higashi 2-chome, Shibuya Ku, Tokyo 150 (☎ 03-3486 7351; fax 3486 7440)

USA
> MTCA, 37th floor, 666 5th Ave, New York, NY 10103 (☎ 212-5863088; fax 5868360)

BUSINESS HOURS & HOLIDAYS

Only in Mongolia could a restaurant be 'closed for lunch'. At any government-run office, 'lunch' is around 11 am to 3 pm. Nevertheless, there are at least theoretical business hours. Government offices are open from 9 am to 5 pm on weekdays, and until noon on Saturday. Banks stay open from 9 am to 12.30 pm weekdays, and until 11 am on Saturday. Most offices are closed on Sunday.

Private businesses and state shops open from about 10 am and close sometime between 5 and 8 pm. Most restaurants open at noon, but the few that serve breakfast open around 7.30 am.

The following are public holidays: 1 January, New Year's Day; Lunar New Year (Tsagaan Sar, meaning 'White Month', a three-day holiday); 8 March, Women's Day; 11-13 July, National Day (Naadam, anniversary of the 1921 Mongolian revolution); and 26 November, Mongolian Republic Day. The Lunar New Year is celebrated some time in late January or early February.

CULTURAL EVENTS

The biggest event of the year, which attracts foreigners and locals alike, is Naadam, held on National Day (11 to 13 July) in Ulaan Baatar. Outside the capital, Naadam festivities might be held the week before or the week after National Day. Naadam is a fair featuring traditional Mongolian summer sports such as horse riding, wrestling and archery, and offers prizes for the winners.

POST & TELECOMMUNICATIONS
Postal Rates

International postcards cost T18. International letters up to 20 grams cost T22 if unregistered, or T44 if registered. Domestic letters cost T10.

You can send parcels from the post office at low cost, but if you need air freight service and are willing to pay a minimum of US$35, the privately run carrier DHL (☎ 23722) can be contacted at the Ministry of Communications, Suhbaatar Square-9, Ulaan Baatar 210611.

Sending Mail

There is no such thing as airmail. Letters sent abroad can take from two weeks to three months to be delivered. Foreign residents of Ulaan Baatar find it much faster to give letters (and cash to buy stamps) to other foreigners who are departing.

You won't find letter boxes on the streets. In most cases, you will have to post your letters from the post office.

If you need stamps, buy them in Ulaan Baatar. Elsewhere, stamp supplies are irregular.

Receiving Mail

Poste restante at the central post office in Ulaan Baatar seems to work quite well. Again, expect delays of up to three months.

Telephone

International Direct Dialling (IDD) is available in Ulaan Baatar but nowhere else. International hotels and the central post office are where you find this service.

You cannot dial long-distance domestic calls direct; they must be booked. This is done from the post office, assuming the town you are in has a post office. You pay in advance for the number of minutes you want to talk, and when the time is up you'll automatically be cut off. If you are staying in a hotel room that has a phone, you can ask the operator at the post office to call you at a specified time and then you'll be connected. There are not enough phone lines, so making a long-distance call during the daytime can take many hours, but service is faster at night.

Public payphones are virtually nonexistent. However, you can make free local calls from the reception desks of most hotels. The phone system is in decrepit condition and you'll often have to dial many times before you finally get connected. Lines are faint and noisy.

The international country code for Mongolia is 976. Ulaan Baatar's area code is 1, but it's only used if you dial from outside the country.

Fax, Telex & Telegraph

It's close to impossible to send international fax, telex and telegraph messages once you get outside of the capital city. The cheapest rates for fax and telex are offered by the Ulaan Baatar Hotel, not by the government-owned telecommunications service. The Ulaan Baatar Hotel's rates (per minute) are as follows:

Country	Fax	Telex
Australia	US$8.40	US$10
China	US$6	US$5.50
Europe	US$8.40	US$6.40
Japan	US$6	US$8.40
USA	US$8.40	US$11

TIME

Mongolia is divided into two time zones: the three western provinces of Bayan-Olgii, Uvs and Hovd are one hour earlier than Ulaan Baatar, and the rest of the country follows Ulaan Baatar's time.

The standard time in Ulaan Baatar is GMT/UTC plus eight hours. When it is noon in Ulaan Baatar it is also noon in Beijing, Hong Kong, Singapore and Perth; 2 pm in Sydney; 8 pm the previous day in Los Angeles; 11 pm the previous day in New York; and 4 am in London.

Mongolia observes daylight-saving time from the last Sunday in March until the last Sunday in September.

There is another form of 'Mongolian standard time' – add two hours to any appointments you make. Perhaps you should adjust your watch to compensate for the difference.

LAUNDRY

Some hotels offer cheap laundry service, but travellers have complained of clothes being worn out after just two or three washings! It's best to bring some laundry detergent and wash your clothes by hand.

WEIGHTS & MEASURES

Mongolia uses the international metric system.

ELECTRICITY

Electric power is 220 V, 50 Hz. The sockets are designed to accommodate two round prongs in the European style, but there is no third prong for earth (ground). Blackouts and brownouts are common, and voltage surges can damage sensitive electrical equipment.

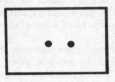

BOOKS & MAPS

One of the best recent books about Mongolia is *The Lost Country; Mongolia Revealed* by Jasper Becker (Sceptre 1993). *In Search of Genghis Khan* by Tim Severin (Century-Hutchinson, London) is a popular travelogue.

For a more in-depth view of the country, see Lonely Planet's *Mongolia – a travel survival kit*.

Indiana University Publications (☎ 317-274 5555), 620 Union Drive, Indianapolis, IN 46202, USA, leads the field in scholarly books about Mongolia. You might try contacting the office and asking what it currently has in print. One book from this source is *A Modern Mongolian-English Dictionary* by Gombojab Hangin (1986, Indiana University, Research Institute for Inner Asian Studies). It costs US$115 with a language tape included. However, you can buy a decent English-Mongolian dictionary in Mongolia for US$8, though it does not include a tape.

The best maps of Mongolia available outside the country are the 'operational navigation charts' produced in the USA for air navigation purposes. You can order navigation charts from better map shops (ask any private pilot), or contact the Defense Mapping Agency Center, 3200 South 2nd St, St Louis, MS 63118-3399, USA. In the UK, try Stanford's (☎ 0171-8361321), 12 Long Acre, London WC2E 9LP.

Within Mongolia, maps are scarce and all will be written in Cyrillic script.

MEDIA
Newspapers & Magazines
There is one English-language newspaper, the weekly *Mongol Messenger*, available from the post office and major hotels. Everything else is published in Mongolian.

Radio & TV
Mongolian radios use the exotic Russian system: rather than broadcasting radio waves through the air, the programmes are transmitted via cable. The cable also carries the electricity which powers the radio.

When you plug a Soviet-built radio into the wall, you must choose the special radio socket, which, unfortunately, is almost identical to a regular 220-volt electrical socket. The only way to identify a radio socket is that the word 'radio', written in Russian (радио), should be somewhere on the socket cover, but it's not at all conspicuous. If you plug a Mongolian radio into a 220-volt socket, it will blow up, and the hotel management will not be happy with you at all.

Broadcast radio does exist, mostly for the benefit of people riding in vehicles. There is one AM and one FM station, both broadcasting the same programmes nationwide.

There are two TV stations carrying both Mongolian and Russian programmes. Satellite TV is available at several hotels, a boon to English speakers.

FILM & PHOTOGRAPHY
Kodak and Fuji colour print film is available from dollar shops, but prices tend to be high and you should check the expiry date on the box. You can get colour print film processed in one hour at the Agfa Photoprocessing Centre on the west side of Suhbaatar Square, just north of the Ulaan Baatar Stock Exchange.

Slide film is rare, so bring what you need and get it developed elsewhere.

Photography is prohibited in temples and most museums, but you can sometimes obtain special permission to take photographs in exchange for a cash contribution.

Mongolians are not especially enthusiastic about having their photos taken. Many Westerners don't seem to care what the locals think, and poke camera lenses into the face of whoever looks interesting. This has led to arguments and even fist fights. Try to be an ambassador of good will – your dental work may depend upon it.

HEALTH
Except for getting frostbite in winter, Mongolia is generally a healthy country to travel in. Mongolians insist that the tap water is safe to drink in Ulaan Baatar, and in any event you'll have a hard time finding boiled water unless you boil it yourself. Care should be taken drinking water in areas where it could be contaminated by livestock. In the countryside, there have been reports of rabies; marmots are the main source, so leave the critters alone.

Mongolia is a high-risk area for brucellosis. This is a disease of cattle, yaks, camels and sheep, but it can also infect humans. The most likely way for humans to contract this disease is by drinking unboiled milk or eating home-made cheese. Another way is for humans with open cuts on their hands to handle freshly killed meat. Cow dung (which the Mongolians use for building fires) is another possible source of infection.

DANGERS & ANNOYANCES
Theft is becoming increasingly common. The locals say that walking around at night in Ulaan Baatar is not safe, especially in poorly lit areas on the outskirts of town. Caution with your valuables is advised, even hotel staff should not be trusted. Pickpockets do a brisk business on buses and in other crowded areas.

Perhaps the biggest annoyance is the presence of drunken men who wander the streets and occasionally become very aggressive.

Your chances of getting into a fight are greatly increased if you're mistaken for a Russian, apparently the locals don't like them. Probably your best protection against trouble of all kinds is to stay in a group with a couple of other foreigners or Mongolian friends, at least when walking around in the evening.

WORK

The good news is that there are now plenty of opportunities to get English-teaching jobs in Mongolia. The bad news is that pay is next to nothing. Still, working in Mongolia is one way to experience the country.

A good organisation in Mongolia which can help you find such jobs is the Federation of Mongolian Peace & Friendship Organisations (☎ 26981; telex 79316 FPFO MH), Mongolian Peace & Friendship House, room 21, 3rd floor, Ulaan Baatar 210644.

In the USA, one place that arranges these jobs is the US Information Agency, English Teaching Fellow Program (E/CM), room 304, 301 4th St SW, Washington DC 20547. You can also try contacting the US Peace Corps. The UK has an equivalent organisation, called Voluntary Service Overseas (VSO). The British Council also has staff working in Mongolia.

ACTIVITIES

Mongolia has some splendid places for hiking, but the biggest problem will be arranging transport to the countryside. Mongolia is also a fine place for cross-country skiing, but bring your own equipment.

Ice skating is popular. In January you won't have to worry about falling through the ice, as many lakes and rivers freeze right down to the bottom.

Horse and camel riding can be arranged by tour agencies. Rafting is feasible on the Hovd River in the far west, for a price.

HIGHLIGHTS

For outstanding natural beauty, you would be hard pressed to find a lovelier spot than Hovsgol Nuur (Lake Hovsgol) near the Si-

berian border. Wildlife enthusiasts will be delighted with the regions around Har Us Nuur (Black Water Lake) in Mongolia's far west.

Many travellers seem to like the Gobi Desert, but we suggest you avoid it during summer; extremely hot and dry weather can be uncomfortable and sometimes dangerous. More accessible places to enjoy nature are Terelj (north-east of Ulaan Baatar) and Tsetseegun (south of Ulaan Baatar).

Not all of Mongolia's incredible sights are natural. Erdenezuu Hiid (Erdenezuu Monastery) in Harhorin is one of the greatest monuments to Tibetan Buddhism. Closer to the capital is Manzshir Hiid.

ACCOMMODATION
Camping

A *ger*, commonly known in the outside world as a *yurt*, is a circular-shaped Mongolian dwelling made of felt draped on a wooden frame. Gers were meant to be mobile, making them suitable for the traditional nomadic lifestyle of Mongolian shepherds and herders. Although most Mongolians are no longer nomads, gers are still immensely popular. Indeed, 'ger suburbs' surround every Mongolian city. The more cushy gers come complete with carpeting, wood stoves and (sometimes) electricity, but toilets and showers are always outside. Staying in a ger is part of the Mongolian experience, and Juulchin caters to this market with stylish gers located in premium-priced 'tourist camps'.

If you want to camp in a Western-style tent, you'll have to bring your own. Many Mongolians have commented that 'Western gers' look vastly inferior to Mongolian ones, though they usually admit that the foreign designs are easier to move. The biggest problem with camping is simply getting to the countryside, as transport is difficult to arrange.

Hotels

The Russians constructed many small but beautiful hotels throughout the country, fea-

turing high ceilings, chandeliers, wood pan-
eling and other displays of 1950s elegance.
Much of this fine handicraft is falling apart,
but a few hotels are being restored (often in
appallingly bad taste). Foreigners typically
pay 10 times the Mongolian price, but
incredible accommodation bargains can still
be found in the backwaters.

FOOD

There are serious shortages of food in Mongolia, though the problem is now under
control in Ulaan Baatar. Once you venture
far from the capital, don't expect to find any
food on the shelves.

There are basically two types of restaurants: those which serve Western food and
those which serve Mongolian cuisine. The
true Mongolian restaurants are cheaper, but
the food generally gets the thumbs down
from foreigners.

The most common dish is mutton, served
in numerous styles. It's at its best in the form
of *shorlog* (Mongolian barbecue, or shish
kebab). Another delicacy is *horhog*, an entire
goat or sheep carcass slowly roasted from the
inside out by placing hot rocks inside the
carcass. Steamed *buuz* (buns) with mutton
filling resemble the Chinese variety, but the
Mongolians use more meat, plenty of fat and
less flour. There are also smaller boiled
bansh (dumplings). Out in the gers you can
sample *guriltai shol* (mutton noodle soup).
Another delicacy is a *huushuur* (pancake
made with flour and mutton) – so greasy it
sits in your stomach like a brick.

The problem is that most Mongolians
prefer their mutton boiled, a cooking method
which puts out a nauseating odour that sends
most foreigners scurrying for the toilet. If
you don't believe this, just walk into the
Ulaan Baatar railway station restaurant and
take a whiff of the air! The odour permeates
everything – even Mongolian biscuits and
butter smell like boiled mutton, and when
you try to wash off the odour, you may find
the soap smells like mutton too. Even the
paper money soon develops that mutton fra-
grance.

Food Vocabulary

barbecue		
shorlog	ШОРЛОГ	
beef		
uhriin mah	ҮХРИЙН МАХ	
boiled dumplings		
bansh	БАНШ	
bread		
talh	ТАЛХ	
butter		
maslo	МАСЛО	
cabbage		
baitsaa	БАЙЦАА	
cake		
byaluu	БЯЛУУ	
carrot		
luuvan	ЛУУВАН	
cheese		
byaslag	БЯСЛАГ	
cucumber		
orgost hemh	ӨРГӨСТ ХЭМХ	
egg		
ondog	ӨНДӨГ	
mutton		
honiny mah	ХОНИНЫ МАХ	
mutton noodle soup		
guriltai shol	ГУРИЛТАЙ ШӨЛ	
mutton pancake		
huushuur	ХУУШУУР	
noodles		
goimon	ГОЙМОН	
onion		
songino	СОНГИНО	
pepper		
haluun nogoo, perets		
ХАЛУУН НОГОО, ПЕРЕЦ		
pork		
gahainy mah	ГАХАЙНЫ МАХ	
potato		
toms	ТӨМС	
rice		
budaa	БУДАА	
roasted goat carcass		
horhog	ХОРХОГ	
salt		
davs	ДАВС	
soup		
shol	ШӨЛ	
steamed meat buns		
buuz	БУУЗ	

MONGOLIA

tomato
   ulaan lool'   УЛААН ЛООЛЬ
yoghurt
   tarag   ТАРАГ

Useful Terms
I'll eat whatever you have.
   Bi tanaid baigaa hoolyg idmeer baina.
   БИ ЯМАР ХООЛ БАЙГААГ
   ИДМЭЭР БАЙНА
menu
   hoolny tses   ХООЛНЫ ЦЭС
bill
   tootsoony tsaas   ТООЦООНЫ ЦААС

DRINKS
Nonalcoholic Drinks
The Mongolians prepare tea like no one else. A classic Mongolian drink is salty tea, either with or without milk and sugar. Some foreigners find it revolting, but many learn to tolerate it.

Better restaurants offer coffee and soft drinks. There is also a sweet, sticky drink called *sirop*, which is appropriately named since it tastes like cough syrup.

Alcohol
Mongolians can drink you under the table if you challenge them. Herders make their own unique home brew, *airag (koumis* in Russian), which is fermented horse's milk with an alcohol content of about 3%. Many foreigners have reported that airag causes diarrhoea. Although you aren't likely to get drunk from airag alone, many Mongolians distil this drink further to produce *shimiin arhi* which boosts the alcohol content to around 12%.

Drinks Vocabulary
beer
   piiv   ПИВО
coffee
   kofe   КОФЕ
fermented horse's milk
   airag   АЙРАГ
hot water
   haluun us   ХАЛУУН УС

milk
   suu   СҮҮ
salty milky tea
   suutei tsai   СҮҮТЭЙ ЦАЙ
soft drink
   shuus, undaa   ШҮҮС, УНДАА
sweet sticky drink
   sirop   СИРОП
tea
   tsai   ЦАЙ
vodka
   arhi   АРХИ
without milk
   suugui   СҮҮГҮЙ
without salt
   davsgui   ДАВСГҮЙ

ENTERTAINMENT
Cinemas can be found in Ulaan Baatar and all the provincial capitals. Most foreign films have no dubbing. Except for the Russian movies, the audience doesn't have a clue what's being said – they come to see the action, which means you can expect movies to concentrate on guns, fights, car chases and soft porn.

Drinking is a national obsession and most nightlife is concentrated in bars. Watching drunken fist fights and people vomiting might provide some entertainment value, but most travellers would be wise to give this scene a miss.

THINGS TO BUY
Many foreigners like to pick up a traditional Mongolian *deel* (robe) and *bus* (cloth waistbelt) to go with it. Other traditional clothing includes a *janjin malgai* (pointed hat) and *Mongol gutal* (Mongolian boots with upturned toes).

Cashmere jumpers (sweaters) and leather coats with a sheepskin lining are important export items. Almost everything else you find in the stores is imported from China, and none of it is cheap.

The widest selection of goods can be found in 'dollar shops', which are just what the name implies. Mongolian togrogs are either not accepted in these places or exchanged at a bad rate.

Getting There & Away

AIR

Only three airlines fly into Mongolia: the Mongolian state airline, MIAT, the Chinese airline CAAC and the Soviet airline Aeroflot. See the Beijing section of the China chapter earlier in this book for the Beijing addresses of Aeroflot, CAAC and MIAT.

MIAT runs three flights weekly between Beijing and Ulaan Baatar for US$150 one way. CAAC flies the route twice weekly and charges the same fare. CAAC also offers flights between Hohhot, China and Ulaan Baatar.

Between Moscow and Ulaan Baatar, there are flights with MIAT (twice weekly) and Aeroflot (once weekly) for US$320. There are also flights between Ulaan Baatar and Irkutsk that cost US$99.

Getting to Mongolia is only half the battle. Getting away can be a real problem during the summer peak season. Buy your onward or return ticket in advance. If you can't get a ticket, try flying standby – there are often seats available on MIAT even when a flight is 'all full'.

LAND

The Trans-Siberian from Beijing takes 1½ days to reach Ulaan Baatar. Moscow to Ulaan Baatar is four days. There are major delays at the China-Mongolia border while customs agents rip through the mountains of baggage carried by Mongolian passengers.

The official prices (you'll probably pay more) for Beijing-Ulaan Baatar tickets are US$88 to US$154 depending on class.

If you enter Mongolia on the Trans-Siberian, arrange your onward ticket to Beijing or Moscow in advance. Otherwise, you'll be scrambling for tickets in Ulaan Baatar, and these can be very difficult to get.

LEAVING MONGOLIA

Airport departure tax is US$8. If you're insistent enough they'll accept togrogs but will charge you double. There is no departure tax if you're flying to Moscow.

Getting Around

AIR

Mongolia is a vast, sparsely inhabited country, and flying is the most practical way to get around if you're going far afield from Ulaan Baatar. The state airline, MIAT (Maybe I Arrive Today), is known for poor safety, cancelled flights and chronic overloading of ancient, Soviet-built aircraft. Except for international service, MIAT has been known to shut down for months due to fuel shortages. This has often been done with no advance notice whatsoever, leaving thousands of passengers stranded in the countryside!

Foreigners must pay for domestic flights in US$, and this works out to roughly 10 times what Mongolians pay. Foreigners living and working in Mongolia (and with credentials to prove it) can pay Mongolian prices. Children aged five to 11 pay half fare, and those under five are carried free.

Fuel permitting, MIAT flies several times weekly from Ulaan Baatar to the following cities:

Altai (US$86), Arvaiheer (US$44), Baruun Urt (US$60), Bayanhongor (US$60), Bulgan (US$32), Choibalsan (US$64), Dadal (US$60), Dalanzadgad (US$60), Erdenet (US$30), Harhorin (US$38), Hatgal (US$76), Hovd (US$104), Hujirt (US$38), Mandalgov' (US$30), Moron (US$60), Olgii (US$112), Ondorhaan (US$38), Tosontsengel (US$72), Tsetserleg (US$48), Ulaangom (US$102) and Uliastai (US$90)

BUS

There are buses connecting Ulaan Baatar with Darhan. Other than that, there are no long-distance buses. There are buses to the suburban regions around Ulaan Baatar.

TRAIN

More than 90% of Mongolia's railway tracks consist of a single line running from Siberia

MONGOLIA

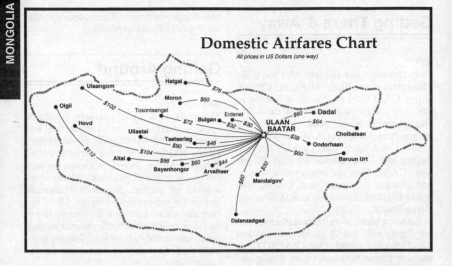

Domestic Airfares Chart

All prices in US Dollars (one way)

Ulaangom
Hatgal
$76
Olgii
Moron $60
Tosontsengel
$102
Hovd $72 Erdenet $60 Dadal
Bulgan $32 $30 ULAAN $64
Uliastai $30 BAATAR
Tsetserleg $39 Choibalsan
$90 $48 Ondorhaan
$112 $104 $60 Baruun Urt
Altai $86 $60 $44
Bayanhongor Arvaiheer
$30
$60 Mandalgov'

Dalanzadgad

to China via Ulaan Baatar. There are two small spur lines running to Erdenet and Baganuur, which are both mining centres. An obscure railway connects Choibalsan in north-east Mongolia to the Trans-Siberian system.

Most foreigners have little use for the domestic railway system, though the international trains are a good way to enter or exit Mongolia.

JEEP
A long-distance journey across Mongolia by jeep is the best way to get a close look at the countryside. However, such trips can be expensive and dangerous. The biggest danger is a vehicle breakdown – death is a fairly easy thing to come by if you get stranded for a day or two in the wilderness.

There is no particular place where you can go to rent a jeep, except maybe for travel agencies like Juulchin (read 'expensive'). To find a sturdy vehicle and competent driver, make local enquiries.

BICYCLE
The fierce climate, wide open spaces and bad roads discourage long-distance biking. Nev-

ertheless, a few hardy souls have cycled all across Mongolia and survived, but this is not for the faint-hearted. Sweltering deserts, frigid mountain passes and washboard roads are obstacles which should not be taken lightly. The lack of food, water and shelter can have fatal consequences. You will also need to be very self-sufficient in terms of tools and spare parts.

Within the urban confines of Ulaan Baatar, cycling is a more realistic proposition. Bike rentals are not available, so you'll have to bring your own wheels. Bikes are much in demand, so keep yours securely locked.

LOCAL TRANSPORT
Bus
A few cities (Ulaan Baatar, Darhan and Choibalsan) all have a somewhat broken-down bus system, but it beats walking. In other cities, transport is by foot.

Taxi
There are very few genuine taxis anywhere, even in Ulaan Baatar. But this hardly matters because *any* car or truck is a potential taxi. Just flag down any passing vehicle (we've

even used ambulances!), negotiate a price with the driver and you'll be on your way. At least this works well within urban areas.

The fare is currently a standard T100 per km (subject to inflation). Be sure to write down the odometer reading when you enter the vehicle; the driver will expect you to do this.

TOURS

Mongolia's official state-run tour agency is Juulchin. In general, Juulchin's services are overpriced and many of the guides (especially older ones) are abysmal, having obtained their jobs through political connections rather than ability. However, with luck you might get one of the new, younger guides who hasn't yet been thoroughly corrupted. Juulchin makes all travel arrangements (food, transport, accommodation etc), for which you can expect to pay something like US$100 per day. Juulchin has precious few offices either inside or outside Mongolia, but you'll need to track them down and make all arrangements before you arrive.

Juulchin needs to know: your nationality, purpose of tour, itinerary, and means of transport (air or train) for arrival and departure. You have to make these international transport arrangements yourself, though once you are in the country, a Juulchin guide will meet you at the railway station or airport and arrange transport around the country. Juulchin can organise special interest tours such as trekking, hunting, bird-watching etc.

Some Western tour agencies can make the bookings for you. This is not terribly cheap, but usually cheaper and more reliable than any deal you can get directly from Juulchin. One of the less expensive agencies specialising in Mongolia tours is Moonsky Star (also known as Monkey Business), which has an office in Hong Kong and one in Beijing. The Hong Kong office (☎ 723 1376; fax 723 6653) is on the 4th floor, E-Block, Flat 6, Chungking Mansions, 36-44 Nathan Rd, Tsimshatsui, Kowloon. The Beijing office (☎ 3012244 ext 716) is in room 716 of the Qiaoyuan Hotel. The tour can be booked starting from either Beijing or Moscow. An 11-day package tour (seven days in Mongolia and four days on the train) starting from Beijing costs US$625. Additional days can be added at US$30 per day.

In the UK, we've had good reports about Regent Holidays Ltd (☎ 0117 9-211711), 13 Small St, Bristol BS1 1DE.

A German travel agency called Mongolia Tourist Information Service (MTIS) also does tours. The company is also called Lernidee-Reisen (☎ 030-784 8057) and can be found at Postfach 62 05 29, D-1000 Berlin 62.

In Australia, try Access Travel (☎ 02-241 1128), 5th floor, 58 Pitt St, Sydney.

US residents might be interested in the occasional expeditions to Mongolia offered by Boojum Expeditions (☎ 406-587 0125), 14543 Kelly Canyon Rd, Bozeman, MT 59715.

Ulaan Baatar

Ulaan Baatar is the sprawling capital city of Mongolia with a population of over 600,000. There's plenty of open space – wide boulcvards, squares, parks, monuments and very little traffic. There are a few high-rise apartments in the city centre, but much of the population lives in ger suburbs on the outskirts of town. These are enclosed by fences which provide protection from the fierce winds.

Ulaan Baatar has the look and feel of a 1950s Soviet city, from the columned buildings to the vintage Russian-built cars. The city has changed names many times. The present name, Ulaan Baatar, was given in 1924 and means 'Red Hero'.

Orientation

Street signs don't exist and most buildings have no numbers, but theoretical addresses do exist. It must be a real nightmare for Mongolian postal workers, which probably explains why mail delivery takes months and post office boxes are so popular.

MONGOLIA

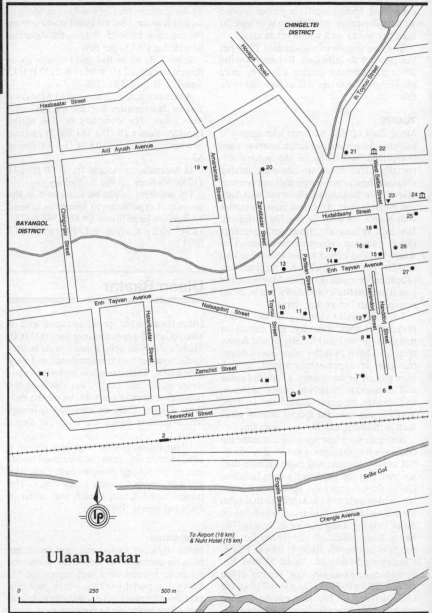

CHINGELTEI
DISTRICT

BAYANGOL
DISTRICT

Horool Road

Ih Toyruu St

West Selbe Street

Hasbaatar Street

Ard Ayush Avenue

Amarsanaa Street

Chingunjav Street

Zambazar Street

Partisan Street

Hudaldaany Street

Enh Tayvan Avenue

Tserendorj Street

Handorj Street

Enh Tayvan Avenue

Hatanbaatar Street

Natsagdorj Street

Ih Toyruu Street

Zamchid Street

Teeverchid Street

Selbe Gol

Engels Street

Chengis Avenue

To Airport (16 km)
& Nuht Hotel (15 km)

21 • 22 🏛
20 •
23 ▼ 24 🏛
19 ▼
25 •
18 ■
17 ▼ 16 ■ 26 •
14 ■ 15 ■
13 • 27 •
10 ■ 11 •
12 ▼
9 ▼ 8 ■
4 ■ 7 •
5 ⊙ 6 •
1 ■
2 ▬

Ulaan Baatar

0   250   500 m

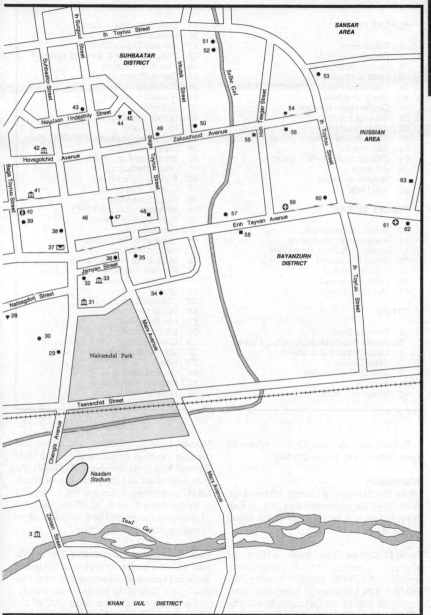

PLACES TO STAY

1 Baigal Hotel
4 Golden Star Hotel
8 Hangai Hotel (closed)
10 Bambai Hotel
14 Mongolian Peace & Friendship House
16 Mandukhai Hotel
18 Gegee Hotel-Apartments
29 Bayangol Hotel
45 Zaluuchuud Hotel
48 Ulaan Baatar Hotel
54 Altai Hotel
55 Chingis Khaan Hotel (closed)
56 Zul Hotel
58 Negdelchin Hotel
63 Star Hotel

PLACES TO EAT

9 Solongo Restaurant
12 Bogd Hangai Restaurant
17 Green Club Bar & Restaurant
19 Praha Restaurant
23 Tuul Restaurant
28 Pizza Restaurant
44 Ider Restaurant

OTHER

2 Railway Station
3 Winter Palace Museum of Bogd Haan
5 Long-Distance Bus Station
6 State Circus
7 Zinchin Supermarket
11 Aeroflot
13 Diplomatic Store
15 State Department Store
20 Gandan Monastery
21 Railway Ticket Office
22 Cultural Centre & Geology Museum
24 Fine Arts Museum
25 Canon Photocopy Store
26 Bookshop
27 Russian Embassy
30 Juulchin
31 Natsagdorj Museum
32 Indoor Bazaar
33 Monastery-Museum of Choijin Lama
34 Japanese Embassy
35 Ministry of Foreign Affairs (visa extensions)
36 Ballet & Opera Hall
37 Central Post Office
38 Stock Exchange
39 Mongolian Airlines (MIAT)
40 State Bank of Mongolia International
41 Museum of Mongolian National History
42 Museum of Natural History
43 German Embassy
46 Suhbaatar Square
47 Drama Theatre
49 Chinese Embassy
50 Polish Embassy
51 Lao Embassy
52 US Embassy
53 Chinese Shop
57 Vietnamese Embassy
59 Hospital No 2
60 UK Embassy
61 Russian Polyclinic
62 Russian Dollar Shop

The city is divided into districts. Within all these districts are 'micro-districts'.

Information

Visas The Ministry of Foreign Affairs is the place to go for visa extensions. It's on Enh Tayvan Ave, one block south of the Ulaan Baatar Hotel.

Tourist Office The head office of Mongolia's national tourist organisation, Juulchin (☎ 328428; fax 320246; telex 232, 79318 JULN MH), can be found in a building at the rear of the Bayangol Hotel. The official address is Chengis Ave 5B.

Money Foreign currency and travellers' cheques can only be exchanged at the State Bank of Mongolia International (SBMI), the Bayangol Hotel and the Ulaan Baatar Hotel. SBMI's operating hours are brief: Monday to Friday from 9 am to 12.30 pm and until 11.30 am on Saturday. There are no facilities to change money at the airport.

Post & Telecommunications The central post office is on the west side of Suhbaatar Square. There is also a convenient letter box just by the door of the Ulaan Baatar Hotel.

The business centre in room 202 of the Ulaan Baatar Hotel is the cheapest for international fax and telex. This office is open from 9 am to 10 pm. Fax, telex and telegram services are also available at the central post office, but the rates charged are about double what you'll pay at the Ulaan Baatar Hotel.

Foreign Embassies Ulaan Baatar has an unusual collection of embassies, as follows:

Afghanistan
    Enh Tayvan Ave 68 (☎ 53958, 53876)
Bulgaria
    Marx St 8 (☎ 21119, 29721)
China
    Zaluuchuud Ave 5 (☎ 20955, 23940)
Cuba
    Marx St 8/2 (☎ 27709)
Czech & Slovakia
    Marx St 8/1 (☎ 21886, 25542)
Germany
    Negdsen Undestniy St 5 (☎ 23325)
Hungary
    Enh Tayvan Ave 3 (☎ 27328, 20978)
India
    Enh Tayvan Ave 26A (☎ 50772)
Japan
    Hovsgolchid Ave 5 (☎ 28019, 28112)
Laos
    Ih Toyruu St 59 (☎ 26440, 26418)
North Korea
    Negdsen Undestniy St 7 (☎ 22795, 23458)
Poland
    Zaluuchuud Ave 10 (☎ 23365)
Romania
    Enh Tayvan Ave 5 (☎ 22925)
Russia
    Enh Tayvan Ave 4 (☎ 72851, 26836)
South Korea
    Baga Toyruu St 37 (☎ 23541)
UK
    Enh Tayvan Ave 30A (☎ 51034)
USA
    Ih Toyruu St 59/1 (☎ 29095)
Vietnam
    Enh Tayvan Ave 18/A (☎ 50465, 50547)
Yugoslavia
    Enh Tayvan Ave 9A (☎ 22380)

Cultural Centres Venues for cultural events include the Drama Theatre at Suhbaatar Square and the State Circus south of Natsagdorj St.

Bookshops The dollar shop behind the Bayangol Hotel (same building as Juulchin)

has English-language books and maps. The dollar shop in the Ulaan Baatar Hotel sells city maps in English.

Emergency There are emergency numbers for fire ☎ 01, police ☎ 02 and ambulance ☎ 03, but don't expect anyone to speak English. Two hospitals in Ulaan Baatar cater to foreigners: Hospital No 2 and the Russian Polyclinic. Payment is in US$.

Things to See
The **Museum of Natural History** is well worth a visit. The most astonishing sight is the two complete dinosaur skeletons which were found in the south Gobi Desert. This museum and most others are closed on Tuesday.

The **Gandan Monastery** (Gandanteg-chinlen) was nearly deserted during the years of Communist domination, but is now experiencing an amazing revival. You can take photographs outside, but not inside, the temple.

The **Winter Palace Museum of Bogd Haan** is where the last Mongolian king (1869-1924) lived. You can enter his house which is stocked full of fascinating artefacts. The temple grounds are adjacent to the house. Photography is prohibited.

The **Monastery-Museum of Choijin Lama** is also known as the Museum of Religion. Construction of the monastery was completed in 1908. It was built to be an active monastery, and to honour Luvsanhaidavt, a monk and brother of one of the Mongolian kings. The name 'Choijin' is an honorary title given to some monks.

Originally, the **Museum of Mongolian National History** was called the Revolutionary Museum and was devoted to the glories of the communist revolution. These days much of it is devoted to the glories of Genghis Khan.

The 1st floor of the **Fine Arts Museum** is devoted to paintings, including modern works (which are for sale) and reproductions of European art. The 2nd floor has a rare collection of religious art and artefacts.

Dashdorjiin Natsagdorj (1906-37) is the

MONGOLIA

best known Mongolian writer and poet. The small but interesting **Natsagdorj Museum** tells his life story.

The old Lenin Museum has now become the **Cultural Centre & Geology Museum**. Downstairs is a bar and in the back is a dollar shop. Perhaps the giant bust of Lenin is for sale?

On the south side of town is **Nairamdal Park**, which has Mongolia's only ferris wheel, among other things.

The **State Circus** is well worth visiting if it's in town. Unfortunately, the troupe is often overseas, because of the dire need for foreign currency.

Places to Stay – bottom-end & middle

The *Altai Hotel* (☎ 50110) gets most of the budget travellers. A basic single room with shared bath goes for US$6, and very pleasant doubles with private bath cost US$21. The Altai is in the eastern end of town. To get there, face the steps of the Ulaan Baatar Hotel, turn to the right and walk to the No 9 bus stop and take this bus to the end of the line. It lets you off at a culvert; from there, walk up the steps and you'll see the enormous neon sign (usually unlit) designating the Altai Hotel.

Probably the best deal in town is the *Zul Hotel* (☎ 51438). The rooms are converted flats, so you get a kitchen (but no stove), living room, bedroom and private bath for US$20. Bargaining can produce lower rates in the off season. The Zul is directly opposite the Altai. There is no sign on the outside of the building, but it's building No 9.

The *Mandukhai Hotel* (☎ 322204) looks much better on the outside than it is on the inside. Rooms run from coffin-sized to luxurious, and cost US$10 to US$40.

The *Baigal Hotel* (☎ 366881), west of the railway station, is an old apartment block now converted into a hotel. It's a fine old building, but the neighbourhood is depressing. Rooms go for US$3 to US$25. The top-end rooms even have a kitchen.

The *Zaluuchuud Hotel* (☎ 324594) is pleasant enough, but it's usually full of visiting Russians. Room prices start at US$10.

Near the bus station is the *Golden Star Hotel* (☎ 714549; fax 312071). The rooms look fine but there is one serious flaw – no private bath! Perhaps this would not matter, except that room prices range from US$30 to US$60. Try bargaining.

The *Bambai Hotel* (☎ 326017), just west of the Aeroflot office, looks awful on the outside but has a few fine rooms on the top floor. Grotty rooms with no bath cost US$3, and deluxe accommodation is a very reasonable US$10. The hotel does not have a sign on the outside and the management seems indifferent.

The *Gegee Hotel-Apartments* (☎ 312027) is near the State Department Store and is identified by a sign saying 'Serving Foreigners Company'. Short-term rentals are US$20 to US$30, but substantial discounts can be negotiated for long-term stays.

The *Negdelchin Hotel* (☎ 53230) has rooms with shared bath for US$5 to US$15 and deluxe rooms with private bath for US$20.

Places to Stay – top end

The *Ulaan Baatar Hotel* (☎ 320237; fax 324485) is an old favourite. Room prices range from US$32 (shared bath) to US$102 (private bath, deluxe).

The recently renovated *Bayangol Hotel* (☎ 328632; fax 329068) is arguably the best hotel in town. Singles/doubles range from US$60/81 to US$92/122. If it's any consolation, breakfast is thrown in for free.

The *Star Hotel* (☎ 358137; fax 358103) looks small and tattered on the outside, but is luxurious on the inside and definitely recommended to those who can afford it. Rooms range from US$60 to US$100. The hotel is in the Russian area on the eastern edge of town.

The *Ih Tenger Guest House* is a country resort where rooms come with a US$120 per day price tag. The hotel is about five km south of the centre, close to the mountains.

Another place, which is not quite as good, is the *Nuht Hotel*, 15 km south-west of the city near the airport. Prices range from

US$25 to US$90 per person with meals included.

Places to Eat
The most popular restaurant with foreigners is inside the *Ulaan Baatar Hotel*. There are two restaurants here: the one on the ground floor is cheap and good, but service can be indifferent. The upstairs restaurant is smaller and demands US$, but the service is faster.

The *Bayangol Hotel* has a good restaurant, but get the price straightened out when you order. How much you pay seems to depend on what you look like.

The best Chinese restaurant is on the 3rd floor of the *Mandukhai Hotel*. *Bogd Hangai* is the only other Chinese restaurant in the country, but is best avoided as chronic overcharging seems to be a serious problem.

The Green Club (☎ 311447) is hidden behind the Mongolian Peace & Friendship House. This place boasts vegetarian food, but meat dishes are also available. It's open from noon to 3 am, and tends to become more like a bar than a restaurant as the evening wears on.

The *Pizza Restaurant* is on Natsagdorj St, a little way to the west of the Bayangol Hotel. Spaghetti and salad are on the menu.

Praha Restaurant was a Mongolian-Czechoslovak joint venture, but the Czechs have pulled out and the service has taken a dive. Still, it's a reasonable place to eat.

There are some cheap restaurants in the city centre serving mostly Mongolian food. Two notable ones are *Tuul* on Hudaldaany St, and *Ider* next to the Zaluuchuud Hotel. In the same category is the *Solongo Restaurant,* opposite the Aeroflot office.

Self-caterers should check out the *Zinchin Supermarket* west of the State Circus. The *Russian Dollar Shop* near the Russian Polyclinic has a good selection of imported tinned fish, caviar etc. The *Diplomatic Dollar Shop* has a reasonable selection of imported goodies.

Entertainment
Ulaan Baatar is not Bangkok – nightlife is definitely tame. Locals either get plastered on vodka or visit the cinemas. For foreigners, nightlife consists of the bars in the big hotels.

Getting There & Away
Air MIAT has two offices in town, both adjacent to one another on Baga Toyruu St. One office books domestic flights and the other does international tickets. Although it's possible to purchase tickets at the airport, this often doesn't work well and it's a hassle best avoided.

Air China (☎ 28838) has an office in room 201, building B of the Bayangol Hotel. Not surprisingly, the staff speak excellent Chinese, but they can manage some English too.

The Aeroflot office is on Natsagdorj St, near the intersection with Partisan St.

Bus There are buses to Darhan, Zuunmod and the suburbs surrounding Ulaan Baatar. The long-distance bus station is at the southern end of Ih Toyruu St.

Train Domestic tickets are sold at the railway station, but for international train tickets you must go to the Railway Ticket Office next to the Dayan Derh dollar shop. Hours of operation are Monday to Saturday from 9 am to 2 pm. On Tuesday, there are additional afternoon hours from 3 to 5 pm. You can, theoretically at least, buy train tickets from Juulchin.

Getting Around
To/From the Airport Buyant Uha Airport is 18 km south-west of the city, but with suicidal driving the journey takes less than 15 minutes by car. Bus Nos 8 and 11 both go to the airport, and you can catch them from the square right in front of the Fine Arts Museum. 'Taxis' (any vehicle you can stop) are available and drivers expect around US$10 for the journey.

Bus There is a skeletal network of electric trolleys and buses, but they can be packed to the roof and beyond. All buses charge T10.

MONGOLIA

Around the Country

ULAAN BAATAR ENVIRONS

The **Terelj Tourist Camp**, 80 km north-east of Ulaan Baatar, is usually included on most tours. At 1600 metres altitude, the area is cool, forested and alpine. The scenery is magnificent, and there are opportunities for hiking, swimming (in icy water!), Mongolian barbecues and horse riding. On the way going up there, you pass grazing sheep, cattle, horses and yaks. The place has some nightlife too; a disco operates from 8.30 pm until midnight during the summer months. There is a touristy ger-style hotel.

Unfortunately, getting to Terelj poses logistical problems. There is no public transport, and access is mostly by tour bus. Hitchhiking is one possibility, though the only vehicles going up there are usually trucks and tour buses. A mountain bike

would be fine if you don't mind 80 km of uphill riding. Long-distance taxi is another possibility, but it will cost you. Once you do get to Terelj, hitching a ride back to Ulaan Baatar is relatively easy. Almost all tour groups, even the budget ones, usually include a trip to Terelj.

Nestled in a valley 43 km south of Ulaan Baatar is **Zuunmod**, the laid-back capital of Tov Province. The city boasts a decent museum, and the main attraction in the area is **Manzshir Hiid**, a monastery five km north of town. Equipped with a compass, it's possible to hike six km north of Manzshir Hiid to reach the summit of **Tsetseegun**. There are buses to Zuunmod from Ulaan Baatar, but you'll have to walk, hitch or find a taxi to reach Manzshir Hiid.

HARHORIN

About 400 km south-west of Ulaan Baatar is Harhorin (formerly Karakorum), the ancient

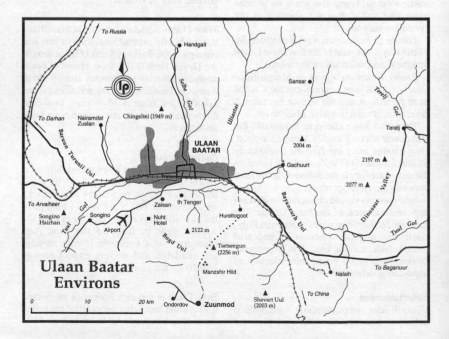

Ulaan Baatar Environs

capital of the Mongolian Empire before Kublai Khan moved it to Beijing. Modern-day Harhorin is just a small town in the grasslands, while the ruins of the ancient capital are about two km away. There isn't much left of the ruins because many of the stones were hauled away to build the nearby **Erdenezuu Monastery**, which was constructed in 1586, and was the first Buddhist centre in Mongolia. This impressive monastery is enclosed in an immense walled compound decorated with 108 stupas, and inside is the Lavran Sum (Lavran Temple).

About 54 km south-west of Harhorin by road is **Hujirt**, a Juulchin-promoted tourist camp noted for its hot springs. Soaking your body in these is claimed to cure everything from arthritis to nappy rash. After you've been properly soaked, you can also arrange a jeep excursion to **Orhon Hurhree** (Orhon Waterfall), 82 km west of Hujirt.

Places to Stay & Eat
Right in the centre of Harhorin on the city square is *Hangbayin Hotel*, which also has a restaurant. The other place to stay is the *Orhon Hotel*, about two km west of town, right by the mountains and a river. It's a lovely place, built in log-cabin style, and they set up fancy gers during the summer.

Getting There & Away
Fuel permitting, MIAT runs helicopter flights from Ulaan Baatar to Harhorin. There are also flights to Hujirt.

SOUTH GOBI
The capital of the Omnogov' Province, **Dalanzadgad**, is a good base to explore what the region has to offer. West of town is the **South Gobi Tourist Camp**, a Juulchin-inspired resort complete with hotels, gers, camel rides and opportunities to dress up like Genghis Khan. Tourists are usually herded through **Yolyn Am** (Vulture's Mouth), an attractive canyon noted for its wildlife. Nearby **Bayanzag** is a colourful desert region where dinosaur bones and dinosaur eggs are frequently found. A visit to the local sand dunes is also requisite.

Places to Stay & Eat
There are two hotels in Dalanzadgad. The *South Gobi Tourist Camp* is 35 km north-west of Dalanzadgad. There is a small tourist camp (15 gers), 7.5 km away from the big camp (50 gers). The smaller camp is more attractive.

Getting There & Away
There are direct flights between Ulaan Baatar and Dalanzadgad. However, some of these flights fly directly from the South Gobi Tourist Camp and don't stop in Dalanzadgad – you need to check at the tourist camp before departure. The aircraft land at the large tourist camp, not the small one. Unfortunately, there is competition between the two camps and the big one will not pass information to the smaller one.

HOVSGOL NUUR
Near the Russian border is Hovsgol Nuur (Lake Hovsgol), one of Mongolia's most spectacular sights. The lake is surrounded by pine forests, lush meadows and numerous caves.

To get there, first fly from Ulaan Baatar to the provincial capital of Moron. From there, you can travel by a chartered bus or jeep. There are also occasional flights directly to Hatgal on the southern shore of the lake.

HOVD
The far western part of Mongolia has a totally different character from the rest of the country. It's a land of snow-capped mountains amid barren deserts.

The small provincial capital of Hovd is a good place to start your exploration of this region. About 30 km to the east of Hovd is **Har Us Nuur** (Black Water Lake), the second-largest freshwater lake in Mongolia (after Hovsgol Nuur). A river flows into this lake, creating a giant delta that is the perfect habitat for wild duck, geese, wood grouse, partridges and numerous other birds. Har Us Nuur supports a population of seagulls, including the rare relict gull and common herring gull. If you're able to endure temperatures of minus 30°C, then you can try ice fishing in winter, but you'll need a good drill because the ice is over one metre thick in January.

Hovd has a couple of odd hotels and restaurants, and the city can be reached by direct flights from Ulaan Baatar.

Taiwan

A subtropical island – and officially a province of China – Taiwan is still the focus of a political tug of war between the mainland Chinese Communist Party and Taiwan's ruling Kuomintang, both of which claim to represent all of China. Like Hong Kong, Taiwan has been an embarrassment to the Communists; although the mainland has over 50 times the population and 265 times the area, Taiwan's per capita income is about 20 times higher. Both sides continue to exchange verbal abuse (they used to exchange artillery shells), but these days Taiwanese tourists flock to the mainland in droves. Mainlanders also flock to Taiwan – illegally, on fishing boats and even hijacked aircraft.

Politics aside, Taiwan has much to offer the foreign traveller. There are unsurpassed mountains, gorges, beaches, forests, Taoist and Buddhist temples, and small offshore islands harbouring a fascinating aboriginal culture. Taiwan also preserves the finest of Chinese art, much of which was destroyed on the mainland during the Cultural Revolution. Taipei's National Palace Museum holds the world's richest collection of ancient Chinese art and is rated as one of the world's top museums.

Taiwan is one of the world's most densely populated regions, yet over half of the island is mountainous and almost uninhabited. The spectacularly beautiful mountain regions offer numerous opportunities for outdoor recreation.

Facts about the Country

HISTORY

Little is known of Taiwan's earliest history, but it is thought that people have inhabited the island for at least 10,000 years. The first known inhabitants were not Chinese at all, but probably migrants from the Pacific islands.

Taiwan may have had contact with mainland China as early as the Sui Dynasty (581 to 618 AD) but there was no significant migration until the 15th century. Starting in the 1400s, large numbers of Chinese from Fujian Province started migrating to Taiwan.

In 1517 the first Europeans – Portuguese sailors – landed on Taiwan's shores and were so impressed by the scenery that they named it Ihla Formosa, which means 'Island Beautiful'. The name Formosa has been used right up to the present. The Dutch invaded Taiwan in 1624 and established the island's first capital at Tainan. In 1626, the Spanish grabbed control of north Taiwan, but were expelled by the Dutch in 1641.

Soon thereafter, Ming-Dynasty loyalist Cheng Chengkung (also known as Koxinga) arrived with 35,000 Chinese troops, fleeing the invading Manchus. In 1661, Koxinga expelled the Dutch, but by 1682 the Manchus had captured Taiwan. For the next 200 years, there was steady migration from the mainland. Taiwan remained a county of Fujian Province until 1887.

In 1895 the Japanese occupied the island and held it for the next 50 years. Under the Yalta Agreement (1945), China regained sovereignty over Taiwan following Japan's defeat in WW II. In 1949 the Communists took control of the mainland, and the Kuomintang (Nationalist Party) led by Chiang Kaishek fled to Taiwan. The Kuomintang has vowed ever since to retake the mainland – it hasn't happened yet.

In October 1971, the Kuomintang lost the Chinese UN seat. A further blow came in January 1979 when the USA withdrew recognition of the Republic of China (ROC) and established diplomatic relations with the Communists on the mainland. Recognition of two Chinas was impossible – the Kuomintang and the Communists agree on little else, but both sides insist that Taiwan is a province of China.

In 1975 Chiang Kaishek died, and in 1978

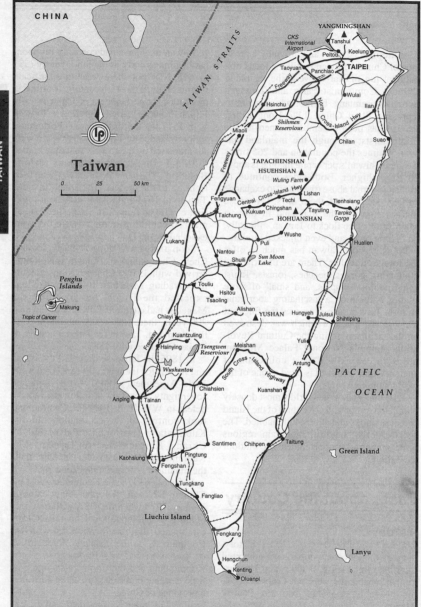

CHINA

TAIWAN STRAITS

YANGMINGSHAN

CKS International Airport

Tanshui
Peitou
Keelung
Taoyuan
Panchiao
TAIPEI
Freeway
Hsinchu
Wulai
North Cross-Island Hwy
Ilan
Shihmen Reserviour
Miaoli
Chilan
Suao

Taiwan

0   25   50 km

TAPACHIENSHAN
HSUEHSHAN
Wuling Farm
Lishan
Tienhsiang
Central Cross-Island Hwy
Techi
Chingshan
Tayuling
Taroko Gorge
Fengyuan
Kukuan
HOHUANSHAN
Taichung
Changhua
Wushe
Lukang
Puli
Hualien
Nantou
Sun Moon Lake
Shuili
Touliu
Hsitou
Tsaoling
Alishan
Chiayi
YUSHAN
Hungyeh
Juisui
Shihtiping

Penghu Islands

Makung

Tropic of Cancer

Yuli

Kuantzuling
Hsinying
Tsengwen Reserviour
Meishan
Antung
Wushantou
South Cross-Island Highway
PACIFIC
Chiahsien
Kuanshan
OCEAN
Anping
Tainan
Santimen
Chihpen
Taitung
Green Island
Kaohsiung
Pingtung
Fengshan
Tungkang
Fangliao

Liuchiu Island

Fengkang

Hengchun
Kenting
Oluanpi

Lanyu

his son, Chiang Chingkuo, became president. Criticism arose over the Kuomintang's one-party rule and the establishment of a 'Chiang Dynasty'. Opposition candidates formed the Democratic Progressive Party in 1986 and were permitted seats in the legislature. In 1987, 38 years of martial law ended. In 1988, Chiang Chingkuo died and was succeeded by his vice president, Lee Tenghui, the first native-born Taiwanese to assume the presidency.

Although tensions with mainland China have eased somewhat, relations between the 'two Chinas' remain icy.

GEOGRAPHY

Shaped roughly like a leaf, Taiwan is an island just a mere 160 km from the Chinese mainland. The island's maximum length is 395 km and its maximum width is 144 km. A narrow plain on the west coast is where 90% of the population lives – it's overcrowded, industrialised and badly polluted. Fortunately, the rest of the island is extremely mountainous and mostly unspoilt. Taiwan's highest peak is Yushan – at 3952 metres, it's the highest peak in North-East Asia outside of the Tibetan plateau.

In addition to Taiwan itself, there are a number of smaller offshore islands, including the Penghu group, Lanyu, Green Island and Liuchiu Island. The ROC also controls Kinmen, Matsu and Wuchiu, three islands within sight of mainland China.

Taipei is the largest city and the seat of government. Other prominent cities are all on the west side of the island, including Kaohsiung, Taichung and Tainan.

CLIMATE

The island is subtropical, but the mountains can be chilly in summer and experience snow during winter. The north-east coast gets almost continuous rain in winter, while the south-west is noticeably warmer and drier. However, summer is uniformly hot and sticky at low elevations, and mountain areas get the heaviest summer rains. The typhoon season can run from June until the end of October, but is unpredictable. See the Taipei climate chart in the Appendix later in this book.

GOVERNMENT

The Kuomintang (KMT) has held power continuously since 1945. The Democratic Progressive Party (DPP) is by far the largest opposition party, often winning over 35% of the popular vote against the KMT's 60%. The DPP's major policy platform is independence for Taiwan, while the KMT at least officially supports reunification with mainland China 'when the time is right'. In the meantime, DPP and KMT legislators entertain themselves (and the public) by getting into fist fights with one another on the floor of the National Assembly. However, they also take time out for fighting among themselves. In 1993 the New Party was founded, a spin-off of KMT legislators, whose policy is to clean up corruption.

Power is distributed among five major branches of government which are called Yuan – the Legislative, Executive, Judicial, Examination and Control Yuan. The first three are self-explanatory. The Examination Yuan oversees Taiwan's formidable system of exams, which determines one's access to education, jobs, business licences etc. The Control Yuan is a watchdog agency that tries to keep things honest.

ECONOMY

Starting from an economy shattered by WW II, the island has experienced rapid economic growth. Taiwan is now called a 'Newly Industrialised Economy' (NIE). It was formerly known as a 'Newly Industrialised Country' (NIC) until mainland China threw a tantrum, pointing out that Taiwan is not a country, but a province of China.

Taiwan lives on foreign trade. Even trade with the 'communist enemy' is a multi-billion dollar business, though it moves via Hong Kong. Rapidly escalating wages have forced Taiwanese companies to move upmarket into the production of high-tech goods like computers while abandoning labour-intensive industries like shoemaking. However, many Taiwanese companies have survived by moving production overseas to low wage countries like Vietnam.

POPULATION & PEOPLE

Except for some 300,000 aborigines, the population of 21 million is mostly of Chinese descent. While the population growth rate has slowed to around 1.4%, the average of 573 persons per sq km makes Taiwan one of the most crowded places in the world. On the other hand, the population is heavily concentrated in the north and west coastal areas, leaving the centre and east coast with a rural character.

ARTS

Traditional arts are basically the same as in mainland China. See the China chapter earlier in this book for details. The main difference is that Taiwan is much more open to the outside world. Consequently, there is a good deal of Western influence in music, movies and other arts.

CULTURE

There are many similarities with mainland China, but the Taiwanese are far more friendly and much less interested in ripping off foreigners. Xenophobia is perhaps less of a problem in Taiwan than in any other country covered in this book. Indeed, marriages between Taiwanese and Westerners are common.

Death is a totally taboo topic of conversation. The number four sounds just like the Chinese word for death – hospitals never put patients on the 4th floor. The most popular brand of cigarettes in Taiwan is named 'Long Life'.

RELIGION

Depending on who's counting, about 2% to 5% of the population are Christian. The vast majority of people in Taiwan today consider themselves Buddhist or Taoist with Confucian influence. Taiwan has the most comprehensive collection of Chinese temples in the world. Taiwan's aborigines have mostly adopted Christianity.

LANGUAGE

Mandarin Chinese is the official language, taught in the schools and used for all formal purposes. Taiwanese – almost identical to the Fujian dialect on the mainland – is popular but has no written script.

Unfortunately, there are three competing romanisation systems for Chinese in common use. In mainland China, pinyin is used; on Taiwan you'll find Wade-Giles – the oldest system – in use for street signs, maps, books, newspapers and name cards; and to add more confusion, the Yale system (now abandoned by Yale University in favour of pinyin) appears in many outdated textbooks published in Taiwan. Romanisation is unfortunately not taught in Taiwan's schools, so the locals are usually unfamiliar with it and mistakes are common. Most Taiwanese cannot even romanise their own names.

See the China chapter for an explanation of pronunciation and pinyin romanisation.

Taiwan's writing system also differs from mainland China's. China uses simplified characters, while Taiwan sticks to the traditional form (as do Hong Kong and Macau). Some vocabulary to get you started follows.

Greetings & Civilities

Hello.
Nǐ hǎo.
你好

name card
míng piàn
名片

Goodbye.
Zài jiàn.
再見

Thank you.
Xiè xie.
謝謝

Thank you very much.
Duō xie.
多謝

You're welcome.
Bú kè qì.
不客氣

Yes/Have.
Yǒu.
有

No/Don't have.
Méi yǒu.
沒有

Maybe (it's possible).
Yǒu kě néng.
有可能

I'm sorry (excuse me).
Duì bù qǐ.
對不起

Useful Expressions

Do you speak English?
Nǐ huì jiǎng yīng wén mā?
你會講英文嗎

Does anyone speak English?
Yǒu méi yǒu rén huì jiǎng yīng wén?
有沒有人會講英文

I don't understand.
Wǒ tīng bù dǒng.
我聽不懂

Just a moment.
Děng yī xià.
等一下

Please write it down.
Qǐng nǐ xiě xià lái.
請你寫下來

How much is it?
Duō shǎo qián?
多少錢

I want to change money.
Wǒ yào huàn qián.
我要換錢

Directions

Where is the toilet?
Cè suǒ zài nǎ lǐ?
廁所在哪裡

I'm lost.
Wǒ mí lù.
我迷路

I want to buy a map.
Wǒ yào mǎi dì tú.
我要買地圖

I want to go to...
Wǒ yào qù...
我要去...

　　Bank of Taiwan
　　tái wān yín háng
　　台灣銀行

International Commercial Bank of China
guó jì shāng yè yín háng
國際商業銀行

tourist information office
guān guāng jú
觀光局

Please show me where we are on the map
*Wǒ mèn xiàn zài de wèi zhì zài dì tú shàng
de nǎ lǐ.*
我們現在的位置在地圖上的哪裡

Turn right.
Yòu zhuǎn.
右轉

Turn left.
Zuǒ zhuǎn.
左轉

Go straight.
Yì zhí zǒu.
一直走

Turn around.
Zhuǎn ge wān.
轉個彎

far
yuǎn
遠

near
jìn
近

Air Transport

airport
fēi jī chǎng
飛機場

reserve a seat
dìng wèi zǐ
定位子

cancel
qǔ xiāo
取消

ticket
piào
票

one-way (ticket)
dān chéng piào
單程票

return (ticket)
lái huí piào
來回票

buy a ticket
mǎi piào
買票
refund a ticket
tuì piào
退票
reconfirm (air ticket)
què rèn
確認
boarding pass
dēng jì zhèng
登記證

Rail Transport

train
huǒ chē
火車
timetable
shí kè biǎo
時刻表
1st-class train
zì qiáng hào
自強號
2nd-class train
jǔ guang hào
莒光號
3rd-class train
fù xīng hào
復興號
slow local train
pǔ tōng chē
普通車
railway station
huǒ chē zhàn
火車站
Which platform?
Dì jǐ yuè tái?
第幾月台
upgrade ticket (on train)
bǔ piào
補票
luggage storage room
xíng lǐ shì
行李室
lockers
bǎo xiǎn xiāng
保險箱

Other Public Transport

What time is the...?
...jǐ diǎn zhōng?
⋯幾點鐘
　first
　dì yī ge
　第一個
　last
　zuì hòu
　最後
　next
　xià yī ge
　下一個
bus (local, long-distance)
gōng chē, bā shì
公車/巴士
bus station
bā shì zhàn
巴士站
boat
chuán
船
pier
mǎ tóu
碼頭
taxi
jì chéng chē
計程車
I want to get off (bus/taxi).
Xià chē.
下車

Car & Motorbike

motorbike hire
jī chē chū zū
機車出租
petrol station
jiā yóu zhàn
加油站
Fill it up.
Jiā mǎn.
加滿

Accommodation

campground
lù yíng qū
露營區
hotel
lǚ guǎn
旅館

guesthouse
lü shè
旅社

youth hostel
qīng nián huó dòng zhōng xīn
青年活動中心

room
fáng jiān
房間

dormitory
tuán tǐ fáng, duō rén fáng
團體房/多人房

private room
ge rén fáng
個人房

cheap room with shared bath
pǔ tōng fáng
普通房

small room with private bath
tào fáng
套房

single room
dān rén fáng
單人房

double room (twin beds)
shuāng rén fáng
雙人房

How much per person?
Yī ge rén duō shǎo qián?
一個人多少錢

How much for a room?
Yī jiān fáng jiān duō shǎo qián?
一間房間多少錢

Can I see the room first please?
Qǐng xiān gěi wǒ kàn fáng jiān?
請先給我看房間

May I have a name card for this hotel?
Qǐng gěi wǒ lü guǎn de míng piàn?
請給我旅館的名片

Necessities
bathroom (washroom)
xǐ shǒu jiān
洗手間

laundromat (laundry service)
xǐ yī zhōng xīn
洗衣中心

mosquito incense coils
wén xiāng
蚊香

mosquito mats
diàn wén xiāng
電蚊香

sanitary pads (Kotex)
wèi shēng mián
衛生棉

sunscreen (UV) lotion
fáng shài yóu
防曬油

tampons
wèi shēng mián tiáo
衛生棉條

tissue paper
miàn zhǐ
面紙

toilet paper
wèi shēng zhǐ
衛生紙

Post
aerogramme
yóu jiǎn
郵簡

airmail
háng kōng xìn
航空信

domestic 'prompt delivery' mail
xiàn shí zhuān sòng
限時專送

domestic super-express mail
guó nèi kuài dì
國內快遞

GPO
yóu zhèng zǒng jú
郵政總局

International Express Mail (EMS)
guó jì kuài jié
國際快捷

poste restante
cún jú hòu lǐng
存局候領

post office
yóu jú
郵局

printed matter
yìn shuā pǐn
印刷品

registered mail
guà hào
掛號

seamail
hǎi yùn
海運

stamp
yóu piào
郵票

telegram
diàn bào
電報

Telecommunications

direct dial
zhí bō diàn huà
直撥電話

fax
chuán zhēn
傳眞

international call
guó jì diàn huà
國際電話

reverse-charge call
duì fāng fù qián
對方付錢

telephone
diàn huà
電話

telephone card
diàn huà kǎ
電話卡

telephone office
diàn xìn jú
電信局

telex
diàn chuán
電傳

Emergencies

I'm sick.
Wǒ shēng bìng le.
我生病了

I'm injured.
Wǒ shòu shāng le.
我受傷了

I want to see a doctor.
Wǒ yào kàn yī shēng.
我要看醫生

I want to go to the hospital.
Wǒ yào qù yī yuàn.
我要去醫院

Please call an ambulance.
Qǐng nǐ dǎ diàn huà zhǎo jiù hù chē.
請你打電話找救護車

I'm allergic to...
Wǒ duì...hěn guò mǐn.
我對…很過敏

  penicillin
  jīn méi sù
  金黴素

  antibiotics
  kàng jūn sù
  抗菌素

I'm a diabetic.
Wǒ yǒu táng niào bìng.
我有糖尿病

Please call the police.
Qǐng nǐ zhǎo jǐng chá.
請你找警察

Fire!
Huǒ zāi!
火災

Help!
Jiù mìng a!
救命啊

Thief!
Xiǎo tōu!
小偷

emergency room
jí zhěn
急診

foreign affairs police
wài shì jǐng chá
外事警察

pickpocket
pá shǒu
扒手

rapist
qiáng jiān zhě
強姦者

Time

When?
Shén me shí hòu?
甚麼時候

What is the time now?
Xiàn zài jǐ diǎn zhōng?
現在幾點鐘

What time does it open?
Jǐ diǎn kāi shǐ yíng yè?
幾點開始營業
What time does it close today?
Jīn tiān yíng yè dào jǐ diǎn?
今天營業到幾點
7.15 am
zǎo shàng 7 diǎn 15 fēn
早上7點15分
7.15 pm
wǎn shàng 7 diǎn 15 fēn
晚上7點15分

now
xiàn zài
現在
today
jīn tiān
今天
tomorrow
míng tiān
明天

Sunday
Xīng qī tiān
星期天
Monday
Xīng qī yī
星期一
Tuesday
Xīng qī èr
星期二
Wednesday
Xīng qī sān
星期三
Thursday
Xīng qī sì
星期四
Friday
Xīng qī wǔ
星期五
Saturday
Xīng qī liù
星期六

Numbers

0	*líng*	零
1	*yī*	一
2	*èr, liǎng*	二, 兩
3	*sān*	三
4	*sì*	四
5	*wǔ*	五
6	*liù*	六
7	*qī*	七
8	*bā*	八
9	*jiǔ*	九
10	*shí*	十
11	*shí yī*	十一
12	*shí èr*	十二
20	*èr shí*	二十
21	*èr shíyī*	二十一
100	*yì bǎi*	一百
200	*liǎng bǎi*	兩百
1000	*yì qiān*	一千
2000	*liǎng qiān*	兩千
10,000	*yí wàn*	一萬
20,000	*liǎng wàn*	兩萬
100,000	*shí wàn*	十萬
200,000	*èr shí wàn*	二十萬

Facts for the Visitor

VISAS & EMBASSIES

There are 12 nationalities for which visa-free entry is permitted, but you only get to stay a big five days and this *cannot* be extended. The honoured 12 nations are Australia, Belgium, Canada, France, Germany, Italy, Japan, Luxembourg, the Netherlands, New Zealand, the UK and the USA. Visa-free entry also requires that you have a ticket out.

Most travellers will need a visa. There are two types, single entry and multiple entry. Single-entry visas are easily obtained, but a multiple-entry visitor visa is usually only issued in your home country and not every nationality qualifies. Both of these permit a stay of 60 days.

The official name for Taiwan's government, the Republic of China (ROC), is recognised by very few countries. This means you won't find many ROC embassies in the world. Nevertheless, you can easily obtain a visa from Taiwan's various pseudo-embassies, commonly known as 'trade offices', 'travel services' and 'friendship associations'.

TAIWAN

Taiwan Visa Offices

You can get a visa for Taiwan at any of the following offices:

Australia
Taipei Economic & Cultural Office, Unit 8, Tourism House, 40 Blackall St, Barton, ACT 2600 (☎ 06-273 3344)
D401, International House (PO Box 148), World Trade Centre, cnr Flinders & Spencer Sts, Melbourne (☎ 03-611 2988)
Suite 1902, 9th floor, MLC Centre, King St, Sydney (☎ 02-223 3207)
Canada
Taipei Economic & Cultural Office, Island Park Drive, Ottawa, Ontario (☎ 613-722 6960)
Suite 1202, 151 Yonge St, Toronto, Ontario M5C 2W7 (☎ 416-369 9030)
No 2008, Cathedral Place, 925 W Georgia St, Vancouver, BC V6C 3L2 (☎ 604-689 4111)
Germany
Taipei Wirtschafts und Kulturburo, Dahlmannstr 23, 1000 Berlin 12 (☎ 030-323 6010)
Villichgasse 17, IV, OG, 5300 Bonn 2 (☎ 364014)
Mittelweg 144, 2000 Hamburg 13 (☎ 040-447 788)
Grassistrasse 12, 0-7010 Leipzip (☎ 041-717 0563)
Tengstrasse 38, 8000 Munich 40 (☎ 089-271 6061)
Hong Kong
Chung Hwa Travel Service, 4th floor, Lippo Centre, No 89, Queensway, Central (☎ 525 8315)
Indonesia
Taipei Economic & Trade Office, 7th floor, Wisma Dharmala, Sakti, Jalan Jend Sudirman 32, Jakarta 10220 (☎ 570 3047)
Japan
Taipei Economic & Cultural Representative, 20-2 Shironganedai 5-Chome, Minato-Ku, Tokyo 108 (☎ 3280-7811)
3rd floor, Sun Life Building III, 5-19, 2-Chome, Hakataeki, Higashi Hakata-Ku, Fukuoka (☎ 092-473 6655)
Malaysia
Taipei Economic & Cultural Centre, 9th floor, Amoda Building, 22 Jalan Imbi 55100, Kuala Lumpur (☎ 241 0015, 242 5549)
New Zealand
Taipei Economic & Cultural Office, Level 21, Marac House, 105-109 The Terrace, Wellington (☎ 04-473 6474)
4th floor, Norwich Union Building, cnr Durhan & Queen Sts, Auckland (☎ 09-303 3903)

Philippines
Taipei Economic & Cultural Office, 28th floor, Pacific Star Building, Sen Gil J Puyat Ave (PO Box 1097), Makati Central Post Office, cnr Makati Ave, Makati, Metro Manila (☎ 881381)
Singapore
Taipei Trade Representative, 460 Alexandra Rd, 23-00 PSA Building, Singapore 0511 (☎ 278 6511)
Thailand
Taipei Economic & Trade Office, 10th floor, Kian Gwan Building, 140 Wit Thayu Rd, Bangkok (☎ 251 9274, 251 9393)
UK
Taipei Representative Office, South Grosvenor Gardens, London, SW1W 0EB (☎ 0171-396 9152; fax 396 9151)
USA
Head Office, 4201 Wisconsin Ave NW, Washington, DC 20016-2137 (☎ 202-895 1800)
Atlanta, GA (☎ 404-872 0123)
Boston, MA (☎ 617-737 2050)
Chicago, IL (☎ 312-616 0100)
Agana, Guam (☎ 671-472 5865)
Honolulu, HI (☎ 808-595 6347)
Houston, TX (☎ 713-626 7445)
Kansas City, MO (☎ 816-513 1298)
Los Angeles, CA (☎ 213-389 1215)
Coral Gables, FL (☎ 305-443 8917)
New York, NY (☎ 212-697 1250)
San Francisco, CA (☎ 415-362 7680)
Seattle, WA (☎ 206-441 4586)
Vietnam
Taipei Economic & Cultural Office, Building No 2D, Khu Ngoai Giao, Doan Van Phue, Badinh District, Hanoi (GPO Box 104) (☎ 4-234403)
No 68 Tran Quoc Thao St, District 3, Ho Chi Minh City (☎ 8-299343)

Pseudo-Embassies in Taiwan

Taiwan has diplomatic relations with fewer than 30 countries, all major world powers like Guatemala and Niger. In order to keep mainland China happy, most other countries don't have embassies in Taiwan but maintain 'trade offices', which also issue visas and replace lost passports. Some of these pseudo-embassies are slow because they must process the paperwork through Hong Kong or some other location where they have a 'real embassy'.

American Institute in Taiwan (AIT)
7 Lane 134, Hsinyi Rd, Section 3 (☎ 7092000)

Australian Commerce & Industry Office
    Room 2605, 26th floor, International Trade Building, 333 Keelung Rd, Section 1 (☎ 7202833)
Austrian Trade Delegation
    Suite 608, Bank Tower, 205 Tunhua N Rd (☎ 7155221)
Belgian Trade Association
    Suite 901, 131 Minsheng E Rd (☎ 7151215)
British Trade & Cultural Office
    9th floor, 99 Jenai Rd, Section 2 (☎ 3224242)
Canadian Trade Office
    13th floor, 365 Fuhsing N Rd (☎ 7137268)
Euro-Asia Trade Organisation
    4th floor, 1 Hsuchou Rd (☎ 3932115)
French Institute, 10th & 13th floors
    Bank Tower, 205 Tunhua N Rd (☎ 5456061)
German Trade Office
    4th floor, 4 Minsheng E Rd, Section 3 (☎ 5069028)
Indonesian Chamber of Commerce
    3rd floor, 46-1 Chungcheng Rd, Section 2, Tienmu, Shihlin District (☎ 8310451)
Ireland Institute of Trade & Investment
    7B-09, TWTC Building, 5 Hsinyi Rd, Section 5 (☎ 7251691)
Italian Trade Promotion Office
    Suite 1807, International Trade Building, 333 Keelung Rd, Section 1 (☎ 7251542)
Japan Interchange Association
    43 Chinan Rd, Section 2 (☎ 3517250)
Korea National Tourism Centre
    18th floor, 333 Keelung Rd, Section 1 (☎ 7208281)
Malaysian Friendship & Trade Centre
    8th floor, 102 Tunhua N Rd (☎ 7132626)
Netherlands Trade & Investment Office
    Room B, 5th floor, 133 Minsheng E Rd, Section 3 (☎ 7135760)
New Zealand Commerce & Industry Office
    Room 2501, 25th floor, CETRA Tower, 333 Keelung Rd, Section 1 (☎ 7577060)
Norwegian Trade Office
    11th floor, 148 Sungchiang Rd (☎ 5435484)
Philippines
    Manila Economic & Cultural Office, 4th floor, 107 Chunghsiao E Rd, Section 4 (☎ 7786511)
Singapore Trade Office
    9th floor, 85 Jenai Rd, Section 4 (☎ 7721940)
    Singapore Tourist Promotion, Unit H, 6th floor, 168 Tunhua N Rd
South African Embassy
    13th floor, 205 Tunhua N Rd (☎ 7153250)
Spanish Chamber of Commerce
    7th floor, 60 Tunhua S Rd, Section 2 (☎ 3256234)
Swedish Trade Council
    Room 812, 8th floor, 333 Keelung Rd, Section 1 (☎ 7576573)
Swiss Industries Trade Office
    Room 3101, 31st floor, 333 Keelung Rd, Section 1 (☎ 7201001)

Thai Airways International Ltd
    6th floor, 150 Fuhsing N Rd (☎ 7121882)

Visa Extensions

It is possible to extend a visitor visa twice for a total stay of 180 days, but you will need some valid reason such as studying in a government-approved language school. The people to contact are the Foreign Affairs Police, who speak English and have a regional office in each of Taiwan's county seats (☎ 3817475 in Taipei).

DOCUMENTS
Mountain Permits

Permits are required to climb some of Taiwan's most spectacular peaks such as Yushan and Tapachienshan.

There are two basic types of mountain permit, one which is easy to obtain and another which is difficult. The difficult one is called a class A pass and the easy one is a class B pass.

Class B permits can usually be obtained right at the roadside entrance or trail head in a few minutes, after you've filled out a simple form. You can also get them in Taipei from the Foreign Affairs Office, Taiwan Provincial Police Administration, 7 Chunghsiao E Rd, Section 1, Taipei, which is directly across the street from the Lai Lai Sheraton Hotel.

A class A pass is big trouble – usually you have to be accompanied by a group and licensed guide. If you go with a mountain club, they will need photocopies of your passport and alien resident certificate (if you have one) at least a week in advance. The club will apply for the permit and make all the arrangements. The best club for arranging this is the ROC Alpine Association (☎ 5942108), 10th floor, 185 Chungshan N Rd, Section 2, Taipei.

CUSTOMS

Unless you're carrying guns and drugs, you aren't likely to have much trouble with customs. Travellers entering the country are permitted a duty-free allowance of US$5000 worth of goods.

Any amount of foreign currency can be brought in but must be declared on arrival. Otherwise, only US$5000 in cash or the equivalent amount in another foreign currency can be taken out on departure. No more than NT$40,000 can be brought in or taken out. Travellers' cheques and personal cheques are not considered cash and do not have to be declared.

Any gold or silver brought in must be declared on arrival or else it can be confiscated.

Everyone aged 20 and over can bring in a litre of liquor and either 200 cigarettes, 25 cigars or 500 grams of tobacco duty-free.

MONEY
Currency
The official unit of currency is the New Taiwan dollar (NT$), which totals 100 cents. Coins in circulation come in denominations of 50 cents, NT$1, NT$5, NT$10 and NT$50; notes come in denominations of NT$50, NT$100, NT$500 and NT$1000.

The easiest places to change money are at the airport, Bank of Taiwan and International Commercial Bank of China (ICBC). All these places give you the official rate. Money is easy to change in major cities, but banks in rural areas either don't change money at all or charge very high commissions. When you change money, it is essential to save your receipts if you wish to reconvert excessive NT$ when you depart.

Exchange Rates

Australia	A$1	=	NT$18
Canada	C$1	=	NT$20
China	Y1	=	NT$3
Germany	DM1	=	NT$15
France	Ffr1	=	NT$4.5
Hong Kong	HK$1	=	NT$3.5
Japan	¥1	=	NT$0.24
New Zealand	NZ$1	=	NT$15
Singapore	S$1	=	NT$17
Switzerland	Sfr1	=	NT$18
Thailand	B1	=	NT$1
UK	UK£1	=	NT$40
USA	US$1	=	NT$27

Costs
Prices have risen almost to European levels. Taiwan is still much cheaper than Japan, but almost every country is. Excluding airfares, you could possibly manage on NT$500 a day if you stay in youth hostels, eat noodles and don't travel around much.

Tipping
Fortunately, tipping is not a custom in Taiwan.

Bargaining
There's some latitude for bargaining in street markets, but not much hope elsewhere. Some small shops can be persuaded to give a discount on clothing, cameras and a few big-ticket items, but don't expect to knock off more than 10%, or even that.

Consumer Taxes
Taxes are high for some consumer goods but are already added to the price tags. Expensive hotels add a 10% service charge plus a 5% Value Added Tax (VAT) to the bill, but cheaper hotels include all taxes in the quoted price.

WHEN TO GO
The best time for a visit is during October and November.

WHAT TO BRING
Most needs can be catered for, though pharmaceutical items and clothing tend to be overpriced.

It's impossible to find an electric immersion heater for making hot water in a teacup, but you can buy electric teapots (bulky for travelling though) at supermarkets and hardware stores.

TOURIST OFFICES
Local Tourist Offices
Just beyond customs at CKS International Airport is a very helpful tourist information counter.

There is a Tourist Information Hot Line in Taipei (☎ 7173737, or toll-free 080-211734) which accepts calls from 8 am to 8 pm, every day of the year. You can call for emergencies (police, fire, ambulance) and the message will be relayed to the appropriate authorities.

The head office of the ROC Tourism Bureau is in Taipei. See the Taipei section later in this chapter for details.

Overseas Reps
Taiwan's visa-issuing pseudo-embassies also dispense tourist information. See the Visas & Embassies section in this chapter.

BUSINESS HOURS & HOLIDAYS
Business hours are almost the same as in Western countries – weekdays from 8 or 8.30 am to 5 or 5.30 pm. On Saturday, most people work a half-day until noon. Many offices shut down for lunch from noon until 1.30 pm. Department stores are usually open daily from 11 am to 10 pm. Small shops keep long hours, typically from 6 am to 11 pm. Banks are open from 9 am to 3.30 pm Monday to Friday and until noon on Saturday.

There are two types of public holidays – those that go according to the solar calendar and those that follow the lunar calendar. Solar holidays include Founding Day, 1 January (few work on 2 January); Youth Day, 29 March; Tomb Sweep Day, 5 April, or 4 April in leap years; Teacher's Day, 28 September; National Day, 10 October; Restoration Day, 25 October; Chiang Kaishek's Birthday, 31 October; Sun Yatsen's Birthday, 12 November; and Constitution Day, 25 December.

There are only three lunar public holidays: the Chinese lunar new year, first day of first moon (see the introductory Facts for the Visitor chapter for dates); the Dragon Boat Festival, fifth day of fifth moon; and the Mid-Autumn Festival, 15th day of eighth moon.

CULTURAL EVENTS
National Day (10 October) is a good time for visiting Taipei – there are fireworks over the Tanshui River starting around 7 pm, a light show around the Presidential Building and special exhibits and discounts at the National Palace Museum.

Taoist temples are at their most active during Kuanyin's Birthday (19th day of 2nd moon) and Matsu's Birthday (23rd day of 3rd moon). Ditto for the first and 15th days of the 7th lunar month – the 'Ghost Month'.

The Chinese lunar new year is a cultural event that travellers should avoid! It's a family holiday – businesses shut down while hotels and transport fill to overflowing.

POST & TELECOMMUNICATIONS
Post offices are open from 8 am to 5 pm Monday to Saturday.

Postal Rates
Domestic express letters arrive within 24 hours. Rates are NT$5 for letters and NT$10 for 'prompt delivery' *(xiàn shí zhuān sòng)*. There is also a super-express mail *(kuài dì)*, which is very expensive, but your letter will be delivered in just a few hours. International Express Mail Service (EMS) is available – count on NT$350 minimum. Another service you might use is registered mail *(guà hào)*, available for both domestic and international mail for NT$24.

Postal Rates

Destination	Airmail	Aerogramme	Postcard
Hong Kong, Macau & China	NT$9	NT$8	NT$6
Asia & Australia	NT$13	NT$11	NT$10
South America	NT$17	NT$14	NT$12
Europe & Africa	NT$17	NT$14	NT$12
USA & Canada	NT$15	NT$12	NT$11

The rates for aerogrammes and international letters vary according to destination. See the table on page 435 for prices.

Sending Mail

When mailing a letter overseas, use the red mailboxes. The left slot on the box is for international airmail and the right slot is for domestic express. Green mailboxes are for domestic surface mail; the right slot is for local letters and the left slot is for 'out of town'. Should you mistakenly put the letter in the wrong box or slot, don't panic. It will be delivered but may be delayed a couple of days at the most.

Receiving Mail

Poste restante is available at all main city post offices. At the Taipei office there is a separate window for poste restante – in other cities, check at the information desk.

Telephone

Local calls cost NT$1 for three minutes. Public phones work as expected, but privately owned pay phones found in some hotels and youth hostels are for local calls only. You must pick up the receiver before inserting the coin or else you will lose the call. Furthermore, after you are connected you must push a button on the phone so the money goes down. If you fail to push the button, you will be able to hear the other party but they will not be able to hear you.

Most convenient are telephone cards which can be purchased for NT$100 at 7 Eleven and other stores near where the phones are located. If the phone card runs out of money before you're finished talking, you can insert a new one if you first push the button to the left of the keypad. If a card phone is labelled International Subscriber Dialling (ISD) you can dial direct overseas. ISD card phones are most common around major bus and railway stations, or at the telephone company. There are significant discounts on domestic calls from 7 pm until 7 am. Discounts on international calls are from midnight to 7 am.

Some other useful phone numbers and prefixes include the following:

Chinese local directory assistance	☎ 104
Chinese long-distance directory assistance	☎ 105
English directory assistance	☎ 02-3116796
Fire (Chinese-speaking)	☎ 119
ISD prefix	☎ 002
Overseas dialling information	☎ 02-3212535
Overseas operator	☎ 100
Police (Chinese-speaking)	☎ 110
Reverse charges	☎ 108
Taipei foreign affairs police	☎ 02-3818341
Taiwan's country code	☎ 886
Telephone repair	☎ 112
Time	☎ 117
Weather	☎ 166

Area Codes Taiwan's area codes all start with a '0'. The area codes depend on what county you're calling – in alphabetical order, these are as follows:

Changhua	(04)
Chiayi	(05)
Hsinchu	(035)
Hualien	(038)
Ilan	(039)
Kaohsiung	(07)
Kinmen	(0823)
Matsu	(0836)
Miaoli	(037)
Nantou	(049)
Penghu	(06)
Pingtung	(08)
Taichung	(04)
Tainan	(06)
Taipei	(02)
Taitung	(089)
Taoyuan	(03)
Wuchiu	(0826)
Yunlin	(05)

Fax, Telex & Telegraph

Fax, telex and telegraph services are available at the main branches of the telephone company. The cost for international faxes is NT$200 per page, while hotels typically charge NT$500 per page for the same service.

TIME

The time in Taiwan is GMT/UTC plus eight hours. When it is noon in Taiwan it is also noon in Singapore, Hong Kong and Perth; 2 pm in Sydney; 8 pm the previous day in Los Angeles; 11 pm the previous day in New York; and 4 am in London. Daylight-saving time is not observed.

LAUNDRY

Some of the youth hostels offer laundry service and others have a machine (often broken) for your use. There are plenty of laundry services in Taiwan, but most are slow, expensive and geared towards ironing and dry cleaning. Fortunately, there are fast and cheap laundry services around the universities catering to the student population. They charge by the weight of the clothes and some have a four kg minimum.

WEIGHTS & MEASURES

Taiwan uses the international metric system, but ancient Chinese weights and measures still persist. One catty *(jīn)* is 0.6 kg (1.32 pounds). There are 16 taels *(liǎng)* to the catty, so one tael is 37.5 grams (1.32 ounces). Most fruits and vegetables in Taiwan are sold by the catty, while tea and herbal medicine are sold by the tael.

ELECTRICITY

Taiwan uses AC 60 cycles, 110 V, with two flat pins and no ground (earth). That having been said, most new apartments have at least one 220 V outlet available solely for the use of air-conditioners – a few travellers have managed to blow up their appliances by plugging into it. To prevent this from happening to you, look at the following diagram:

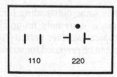

BOOKS & MAPS

Most good books about Taiwan are only available within Taiwan itself. One exception is Lonely Planet's comprehensive *Taiwan – a travel survival kit.*

The Island of Formosa, Past and Present by James W Davidson, is a monumental work first published in 1903. It's now available for sale at some Taiwan bookshops (try Caves Books) or from SMC Publishing Co (☎ 3620190), PO Box 13-342, Taipei 10764. *Taipei*, a Times edition, has good photos, interesting text and historical information.

The *Insight Guide to Taiwan* (APA Productions, Singapore) has some practical but very out-of-date tour information. The cultural stuff is interesting and illustrations and photographs are excellent.

It doesn't require much explanation to understand the main topic of *The 100 Best Bars in Taipei* by Jim Ehrhart & Anthony Watts.

The *Directory of Taiwan* is published annually by the China News, one of Taiwan's English-language newspapers. The book is basically a laundry list of names, addresses and phone numbers of organisations and businesses in Taiwan.

Every bookshop in Taiwan sells maps and atlases, but most are exclusively in Chinese characters. The Tourism Bureau has a collection of maps, which all have the great advantage of being free.

If you're willing to fork out NT$120, there is an excellent bilingual map of Taiwan available from some of the English-language bookshops. It's simply called *Taiwan Map*, published by International Travel Press. The Universal Map Company of Hong Kong publishes a decent map in English of Taipei.

MEDIA
Newspapers & Magazines

Taiwan produces two English-language newspapers, the *China Post* and the *China News*. Both are known for scanty coverage.

A few bookshops and some tourist hotels in the main cities sell imported magazines and newspapers.

Radio & TV

International Community Radio Taipei (ICRT) broadcasts in English 24 hours a day on AM at 576 mHz and FM at 100 mHz. There are no local English-language TV stations, but some shows shown late at night are in English with Chinese subtitles. The English-language newspapers carry the daily TV programming schedule. Satellite TV is widely available, offering many programmes in English and Japanese.

FILM & PHOTOGRAPHY

Photographic equipment is slightly more expensive in Taiwan than in Hong Kong, but not by much. Film is cheap, but Kodachrome is not available. Slide film is readily available in big cities, but scarce in rural areas. Kodak's photoprocessing standards in Taiwan seem to be higher than those offered by the Japanese competition.

Photography is prohibited around military installations.

HEALTH

Food and water are safe, though some travellers get diarrhoea from drinking unboiled tap water. Taiwan's medical care is of a very high standard and surprisingly cheap, but it's best to go to a public hospital rather than a private doctor if you need medical tests.

Taiwan is possibly the best place in Asia to get your teeth fixed.

WOMEN TRAVELLERS

There was a spate of rapes and robberies committed by taxi drivers around 1990, though this has declined as a result of crackdowns on licensing requirements. While excessive paranoia is not called for, you can protect yourself by calling a radio dispatch taxi. There is an English-speaking dispatcher in Taipei (☎ 2821166).

Another precaution is to have a friend write down the taxi's licence plate number before you enter the vehicle and note the time and location. It should be made clear to the driver that this is being done – they are not likely to take you for a special ride if they know their number has been recorded by someone else. This has become a common practice and drivers are used to it. The licence plate number is displayed on the rear window and should be highly visible. Never

get into a taxi if the licence plate number appears to have been obscured.

DANGERS & ANNOYANCES

Violent crime is not common, but residential burglaries are a problem in large cities. Shiny new motorcycles and cars also attract thieves, but they are not interested in old rust buckets.

By far the greatest danger and annoyance is the traffic. The Taiwanese are perhaps the worst drivers in the world, and some cynics say this is the real reason why the population growth rate is falling as living standards rise. The highway carnage is mostly an urban problem, but mountain resorts also experience 'rush hour traffic' during weekends and holidays.

WORK

Many foreigners find employment teaching English in Taiwan, and salaries are not bad. The big hurdle is immigration authorities. Crackdowns on illegal teachers have become common, so you need a work visa to avoid trouble. Getting such a visa usually requires signing a one-year contract, paying taxes and waiting several months for the bureaucratic wheels to turn. Breaking your contract early could cause you to forfeit a large amount of prepaid taxes.

If you're interested, ask around Taipei's youth hostels and language schools. The English-language newspapers also carry advertisements for teachers.

ACTIVITIES
Hiking

Taiwan has some outstanding hiking areas. The terrain is extremely mountainous and the subtropical weather permits year-round activities, but be prepared for sudden storms.

Surfing

The west coast is a dead loss as the water is far too calm. The best surfing spots are on the east coast, extreme north and extreme southern tips of Taiwan.

Feitsuiwan (Green Bay) is a small stretch of sandy beach west of Keelung and is the closest surfing spot to Taipei. Fulung Beach and Miyuewan (Honeymoon Bay) east of Taipei are even better. At the very southern tip of Taiwan is the warmest surfing beach at Kenting.

Whitewater Rafting

The Hsiukuluan River south of Hualien on Taiwan's east coast is the venue for this activity. See the Hualien section later in this chapter for details.

Windsurfing

Windsurfing equipment is available for rent at Kenting National Park and the beach resort at Chipei Island in the Penghu Archipelago.

HIGHLIGHTS

If you have a passion for ancient Chinese art, the National Palace Museum in Taipei is unmatched. Taipei also has a rich collection of temples.

Taroko Gorge on the east coast is Taiwan's most famous natural attraction. Alishan offers fine mountain scenery for both hikers and low-energy tourists. So does the Central Cross-Island Highway. Hohuanshan is a fairly easy mountain to climb; more challenging is Yushan, Taiwan's highest peak. Lanyu – an island off the south-east coast – offers a chance to view a unique aboriginal culture and fine scenery.

ACCOMMODATION
Camping

Many of the established campgrounds are adjacent to government-run youth hostels, providing a means of accommodating the masses when the hostels fill up. At the better hostels, tents are usually already set up so you needn't bring your own. Unfortunately, the trend of recent years has been to require campers to bring their own tents and other equipment. A camping fee of about NT$50 to NT$250 is charged. Some of the hostels in mountain areas will allow you to set up your own tent next to the hostel for free, but always ask first. In open country areas, there is usually no objection to setting up a tent just about anywhere.

Hostels

There are basically two types of youth hostels in Taiwan – private and public. The private ones are definitely in the minority, currently found only in two cities, Taipei and Kaohsiung. Private hostels rent dorm beds for NT$180 per night, with discounts if you rent by the week.

Taiwan's government-run youth hostels are operated by various branches of the bureaucracy. The majority are operated by the China Youth Corps (CYC). This organisation is not connected with Hostelling International (HI) and therefore you do not need an HI card. In addition to CYC hostels, there are urban hostels in Keelung, Taipei, Tainan and Kaohsiung called Labourers' Recreation Centres. There are also Teachers' Hostels in some places – the ones in Hualien and Penghu are bargains at NT$150, but others (like the one at Sun Moon Lake) are absurdly expensive. There are also the so-called 'Public Hostels' – these are nothing more than expensive government-owned hotels. During school holidays, government-run hostels tend to be full.

Hotels

Older hotels sometimes have cheap Japanese-style *tatami* (straw mat floor) rooms. In resort areas, you can sometimes find a dormitory. These are usually meant for large groups, but sometimes you can attach yourself to a group of students. Prices can be as low as NT$100.

Next up the scale is a room with shared bath – prices start at NT$400. Rooms with private bath start at about NT$500. All resort areas have discounts from Monday to Friday, excluding holidays.

Your best bet for saving money is to travel with a friend as double rooms are usually the same price as singles.

FOOD

Taiwan's food is nothing short of outstanding, but English menus are scarce. Prices vary from bargain basement to outrageous, and seafood is especially dear. Your best bet for keeping costs down is to eat at inexpensive stalls and noodle shops. Cafeterias *(zì zù cān)* offer cheap meals for lunch and dinner. The traditional Chinese breakfast of steamed buns and soybean milk is inexpensive and nutritious. Western food is considered something of a delicacy by the Taiwanese and is usually expensive.

Self-Catering

Convenience stores (7 Eleven, Nikomart and so on) all offer microwave rice and noodle dishes, hot dogs, steamed buns, boiled 'tea eggs' and other instant cuisine. Many of these stores are open 24 hours a day.

The following list gives standard dishes in Chinese script with a transliterated pronunciation guide, and an English translation and description.

Rice

plain white rice
bái fàn 白飯
white rice & assorted meats
sān bǎo fàn 三寶飯
fried rice (assorted)
shí jǐn chǎo fàn 什錦炒飯
beef with white rice
niú ròu fàn 牛肉飯

Noodles

soupy noodles
tāng miàn 湯麵
noodles (not soupy)
gān miàn 乾麵
fried noodles
chǎo miàn 炒麵
simple & cheap noodles
yáng chūn miàn, yì miàn 陽春麵/意麵
sesame paste noodles
má jiàng miàn 麻醬麵
bean & meat noodles
zá jiàng miàn 雜醬麵
wanton & noodles
hún dùn miàn 餛飩麵
seafood noodles
wū lóng miàn, guō shāo miàn
烏龍麵/鍋燒麵

fried noodles with beef
niú ròu chǎo miàn 牛肉炒麵
fried rice with beef
niú ròu sī chǎo fàn 牛肉絲炒飯
noodles with beef (soupy)
niú ròu tāng miàn 牛肉湯麵
noodles with beef (no soup)
niú ròu gān miàn 牛肉干麵
fried noodles with chicken
jī sī chǎo miàn 雞絲炒麵
noodles with chicken
jīsī tāng miàn 雞絲湯麵
duck with noodles
yā ròu miàn 鴨肉麵
noodles, pork & mustard greens
zhà cài ròu sī miàn 榨菜肉絲麵
fried noodles with shrimp
xiā rén chǎo miàn 蝦仁炒麵
flat noodles
bǎn tiáo, kē zǎi tiáo 板條/粿仔條
sliced noodles
dāo shāo miàn 刀削麵

Bread, Buns & Dumplings

boiled dumplings
shuǐ jiǎo 水餃
fried leek dumplings
jiǔ cài hé zi 韭菜盒子
fried meat dumplings
guō tiē 鍋貼
fried vegetable dumplings
shuǐ jiān bāo 水煎包
steamed buns
mán tóu 饅頭
steamed dumplings
zhēng jiǎo 蒸餃
steamed meat buns
bāo zi 包子
steamed vegetable buns
cài bāo 菜包

Vegetable Dishes

Chinese salad
jiā cháng liáng cài 家常涼菜
assorted vegetarian food
sù shí jǐn 素什錦
bean curd & mushrooms
mó gū dòu fǔ 磨菇豆腐
bean curd casserole
shā guō dòu fǔ 沙鍋豆腐

dried tofu
dòu fǔ gān 豆腐乾
fried beansprouts
sù chǎo dòu yá 素炒豆芽
fried cauliflower & tomato
fān qié cài huā 蕃茄菜花
fried eggplant
sù shāo qié zi 素燒茄子
fried peanuts
yóu zhà huā shēng mǐ 油炸花生米
spicy hot bean curd
má pó dòu fǔ 麻婆豆腐
spicy peanuts
wǔ xiāng huā shēng mǐ 五香花生米

Egg Dishes

egg & flour omelette
dàn bǐng 蛋餅
fried rice with egg
jī dàn chǎo fàn 雞蛋炒飯
fried tomatoes & eggs
xī hóng shì chǎo jī dàn 西紅柿炒雞蛋

Chicken Dishes

angelica chicken
dāng guī jī 當歸雞
chicken braised in soy sauce
hóng shāo jī kuài 紅燒雞塊
chicken curry
gā lǐ jī ròu 咖哩雞肉
chicken leg with white rice
jī tuǐ fàn 雞腿飯
drunken chicken
suān jī 酸雞
fried rice with chicken
jī sī chǎo fàn 雞絲炒飯
roast chicken
shǒu pá jī 手扒雞
sliced chicken with crispy rice
jī piàn guō bā 雞片鍋巴
spicy hot chicken & peanuts
gōng bào jī dīng 宮爆雞丁
sweet & sour chicken
téng cù jī dīng 糖醋雞丁

Duck Dishes

angelica duck
dāng guī yā 當歸鴨
duck with white rice
yā ròu fàn 鴨肉飯

duck's blood & rice popsicle
yā mǐ xiě 鴨米血
Peking duck
běi píng kǎo yā 北平烤鴨

Pork Dishes

fried rice with pork
ròu sī chǎo fàn 肉絲炒飯
pork chop with white rice
pái gǔ fàn 排骨飯
pork with crispy rice
ròu piàn guō bā 肉片鍋巴
shredded pork & green peppers
qīng jiāo ròu sī 青椒肉絲
sweet & sour pork slices
táng cù zhū ròu piàn 糖醋豬肉片

Seafood Dishes

clams
gé lì 蛤蠣
crab
páng xiè 螃蟹
deep-fried shrimp
zhà xiā rén 炸蝦仁
diced shrimp with peanuts
gōng bào xiā rén 宮爆蝦仁
fish
yú 魚
fried rice with shrimp
xiā rén chǎo fàn 蝦仁炒飯
lobster
lóng xiā 龍蝦
oyster
mǔ lì 牡蠣
squid
yóu yú 魷魚

Soup

soup
tāng 湯
thick soup
gēng 羹
bean curd & vegetable soup
dòu fǔ cài tāng 豆腐菜湯
clear soup
qīng tāng 清湯
egg & vegetable soup
dàn huā tāng 蛋花湯
fish ball soup
yú wán tāng 魚丸湯

TAIWAN

pork ball soup
    gòng wán tāng 貢丸湯
seaweed soup
    zǐ cài tāng 紫菜湯
sweet & sour soup
    suān là tāng 酸辣湯
vegetable soup
    shū cài tāng 蔬菜湯
wanton soup
    hún dùn tāng 餛飩湯

Condiments

black pepper
    hú jiāo 胡椒
hot sauce
    là jiāo jiàng 辣椒醬
salt
    yán 鹽
soy sauce
    jiàng yóu 醬油
sugar
    táng 糖

Food Restrictions

I'm a vegetarian.
    Wǒ chī sù. 我吃素
I don't eat meat.
    Wǒ bù chī ròu. 我不吃肉
I don't eat pork.
    Wǒ bù chī zhū ròu. 我不吃豬肉
I cannot eat spicy food.
    Wǒ bù néng chī là. 我不能吃辣
I cannot eat MSG.
    Wǒ bù néng chī wèi jīng. 我不能吃味精
I cannot eat salt.
    Wǒ bù néng chī yán. 我不能吃鹽
I cannot eat sugar.
    Wǒ bù néng chī táng. 我不能吃糖

DRINKS

Taiwan produces top-grade tea, the best being oolong and green teas. These are both heavy in caffeine and will get your heart pumping (or maybe stop it completely if you drink too much). Chinese tea is never served with milk. Sugar is never put in hot tea, but iced tea will normally be very sweet.

Taiwan's home-brewed beer is called, appropriately, Taiwan Beer. It gets mixed reviews from foreigners but is the cheapest one available. Taiwanese liquor tastes similar to rocket fuel, especially Kaoliang, which is distilled from sorghum and contains a mere 65% alcohol.

Drinks Vocabulary

hot
    rè de 熱的
ice cold
    bīng de 冰的
ice cubes
    bīng kuài 冰塊

Common Drinks

Coca-Cola
    kě kǒu kě lè 可口可樂
carrot juice
    hóng luó bó zhī 紅蘿蔔汁
fizzy drink (soda)
    qì shuǐ 汽水
grass jelly
    xiàn cǎo 現草
lemon soda
    níng méng qì shuǐ 檸檬氣水
mineral water
    kuàng quán shuǐ 礦泉水
orange juice
    liǔ chéng zhī 柳橙汁
papaya milkshake
    mù guā niú nǎi 木瓜牛奶
passionfruit juice
    bǎi xiāng guǒ zhī 百香果汁
pineapple milkshake
    fèng lí niú nǎi 鳳梨牛奶
soybean milk
    dòu jiāng 豆漿
starfruit juice
    yáng táo zhī 楊桃汁
sugar cane juice
    gān zhè zhī 甘蔗汁
water
    kāi shuǐ 開水
watermelon milkshake
    xī guā niú nǎi 西瓜牛奶

Tea & Coffee

black tea
    hóng chá 紅茶

coffee
kā fēi 咖啡
green tea
lü chá 綠茶
jasmine tea
mò lì huā chá 茉莉花茶
oolong tea
wū lóng chá 烏龍茶
tea
chá 茶

Alcohol

beer
pí jiǔ 啤酒
Kaoliang (sorghum liquor)
gāo liáng jiǔ 高粱酒
red-grape wine
hóng pú táo jiǔ 紅葡萄酒
rum
lán mǔ jiǔ 蘭姆酒
vodka
fú tè jiā jiǔ 伏特加酒
whisky
wēi shì jì jiǔ 威士忌酒
white-grape wine
bái pú táo jiǔ 白葡萄酒

ENTERTAINMENT

Large cities (especially Taipei) have a well-established pub and disco scene catering to foreigners. MTV clubs offer video tapes which you can view in private cubicles, but most of these places have been forced to close because of stringent government regulations on fire safety and copyright infringement.

Among the Chinese, karaoke dominates the scene. Look for the 'KTV' signs.

THINGS TO BUY

Overall, there are few bargains in Taiwan. The only exceptionally cheap items are motorcycle accessories (rain gear, safety helmets etc) and computers.

Taiwan does produce some beautiful arts and crafts, but these don't come cheaply. Things to look for include tea sets (check the department stores), lacquerware, scroll paintings, calligraphy brushes, incense burners and wood carvings. Some travellers

like to get a Chinese name chop (seal) carved.

Getting There & Away

AIR

Most travellers arrive at CKS International Airport at Taoyuan, near Taipei. There is another international airport at Kaohsiung in the south of the island. Taiwan is well connected to most countries in the region, but there are no direct flights to mainland China.

As elsewhere, Taiwan's travel agents give better deals than buying directly from the airlines. Some sample airfares follow:

Airfares from Taipei

	One-Way	Return
Auckland	NT$19,200	NT$31,400
Bangkok	NT$4600	NT$9000
Frankfurt	NT$13,700	NT$21,500
Guam	NT$8200	NT$9700
Hanoi	NT$9400	NT$15,300
Ho Chi Minh City	NT$9400	NT$15,300
Hong Kong	NT$3500	NT$5500
Honolulu	NT$11,100	NT$17,000
Jakarta	NT$7500	NT$14,500
Laoag		NT$7000
London	NT$13,700	NT$21,500
Los Angeles	NT$11,500	NT$17,700
Manila	NT$5200	NT$9800
New York City	NT$15,200	NT$27,800
Okinawa	NT$3375	NT$6750
Seoul	NT$4300	NT$7600
Singapore	NT$7800	NT$10,700
Sydney	NT$15,200	NT$26,400
Tokyo	NT$5700	NT$8800
Vancouver	NT$13,900	NT$22,700

Sample airfares from Kaohsiung to the Philippines include:

	One-Way	Return
Manila	NT$5200	NT$9800
Cebu	NT$6900	NT$13,000
Laoag		NT$6000

SEA

There are ferries between the Japanese island of Okinawa and the two Taiwanese ports of Keelung and Kaohsiung. There are also boats at least once weekly between Kaohsiung and Macau. See the introductory Getting Around chapter earlier in this book for details.

LEAVING TAIWAN
Departure tax on international flights and boats is NT$300.

Getting Around

Taiwan's public transport is ubiquitous, but buses and taxis move slowly during the rush hour. There are frequent accidents on the North-South Freeway which can result in long delays.

AIR
Given Taiwan's small size there is little need to fly unless you want to visit some of the smaller islands around Taiwan, like Penghu or Lanyu. For all flights you must carry your passport and arrive at the airport about an hour before departure time. This is especially true during the holidays, when they are quite likely to give away your seat if they need the space.

Buy domestic air tickets directly from the airlines because it will be much easier to obtain a refund. Travel agents give discounts only on international tickets.

BUS
There are two basic kinds of buses – government-owned and private. The private bus companies are known as 'wild chickens'. The wild chickens are slightly cheaper, sometimes faster and often more dangerous. They also allow passengers to smoke, which is supposedly against the rules.

When travelling on buses you must save your ticket stub. You should return it in to the driver or conductor when you get off the bus or you will have to pay the full fare again.

TRAIN
The railway circumnavigates the island and service is good. The west coast trains run

about once every 20 minutes from 6 am to midnight, while east coast trains run about once every hour. There are a few spur routes like the one to Alishan. Timetables cost NT$20 but are entirely in Chinese.

There are four classes – the first three are fast, have air-con, reserved seats and cost more than buses. Fourth class is cheaper than the bus but lacks air-con, reserved seats and is very slow.

In all classes, you are permitted to board even if all seats are full but you'll have to stand. Save your ticket as you must turn it in when you get off. If you want to change your destination after boarding, find the conductor and upgrade your ticket.

Tickets can be purchased up to four days in advance (seven days before major holidays). You can receive a 15% discount on return tickets, but the ticket must be used within 15 days of purchase. If necessary, you can get a refund for the unused return trip.

TAXI
Rural long-distance share taxis are best avoided. They are expensive and many of the drivers are thugs. If you must take one, write down the taxi's licence plate number before you get in, just in case you have to file a complaint later. Always agree on the fare in advance and don't pay until you arrive at your destination.

CAR & MOTORBIKE
An International Driving Permit is necessary in Taiwan unless you obtain a Taiwanese driver's licence. If you wish to obtain a local driver's licence be sure to bring along your home country's licence because you can use it to get a Taiwanese licence without taking a written exam or driving test.

Motorbikes can be hired around tourist resorts like Hualien, Lanyu and Penghu. In cities they are very hard to hire. Nor can foreigners buy a motorbike unless they have a residence permit.

Overall, Taiwanese drivers are insane. The traffic rules are also insane and it's often hard to know what is or isn't legal. In Taipei, the police use hidden cameras to catch traffic

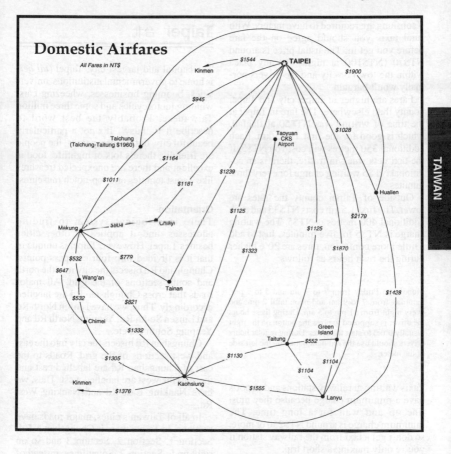

Domestic Airfares

All Fares in NT$

TAIPEI

Kinmen — $1544

$1900

$945

$1028

Taoyuan
CKS
Airport

Taichung
(Taichung-Taitung $1960)

$1164

$1239

$1011

$1181

Hualien

$1125

Makung

$804

Chiayi

$1125

$2179

$1125

$1870

$532

$779

$1323

$647

Wang'an

$532

$821

Tainan

$1428

Chimei

$1332

Green
Island

$1305

Taitung — $552

$1130

$1104

Kinmen — $1376

Kaohsiung — $1555

$1104

Lanyu

violators, which means the owner of the vehicle gets the citation, not necessarily the driver. Many car rental agencies are upset about this and will often demand you put up a deposit or sign a blank cheque to cover the possibility of them receiving a citation after you've departed the country. In general, driving is a big headache in Taiwan, but if you're determined, get a safety helmet (for motorbikes) and have your will updated.

LOCAL TRANSPORT
Bus
Bus service is good in Taipei and reasonably

OK in Taichung and Kaohsiung, but elsewhere inner city buses are scarce. Cost varies from NT$10 to NT$15.

Metropolitan Rapid Transit (MRT)
Taipei is building a rail mass transit system, part of which is elevated above the streets and part of which is underground. At present the whole city is a big mess from the construction. Outside Taipei, no other city in Taiwan has an underground railway.

Taxi
The taxis in Taipei, Taichung, Tainan and

Kaohsiung are required to have meters. With rural taxis you should agree on the fare before you get in. The usual price is around NT$70 (NT$100 at night) for any place within the town or city and the drivers normally won't bargain.

Fares are higher in Taipei city and Taipei county than elsewhere. The fare in Taipei at the time of writing was NT$50 at flagfall, which is good for the first 1.375 km. Each additional 350 metres will cost you NT$5. If the taxi gets stuck in traffic, there is an additional NT$5 waiting charge for every three minutes.

Outside of Taipei county the rates are lower. The first 1.5 km costs NT$35 and each additional 400 metres is NT$5. The waiting charge is NT$5 for five minutes. Just to add a little more confusion, fares are 20% higher during the rush hours as follows:

Monday to Friday from 7 to 9 am and 5 to 7 pm; Saturday from 7 to 9 am and noon until 2 pm; and every night from 11 pm to 5 am. During these hours the driver is supposed to press the button on the right (usually blue) to start the meter. During regular hours drivers should use the red light button on the left side of the meter.

Taxis waiting at railway stations and airports have a minimum charge because they must line up and wait for a long time. The minimum charge is around NT$250 or more, so don't get a taxi from the railway station if you're only making a short trip.

TOURS

There are a number of agencies offering guided tours and English-speaking tour guides. Tour agencies in Taipei include:

Edison Travel Service
    4th floor, 190 Sungchiang Rd (☎ 5635313)
Grayline
    China Express Transportation, 70 Chungshan N Rd, Section 2 (☎ 5416466)
Huei-Fong Travel Service
    4th floor, 50 Nanking E Rd, Section 2 (☎ 5515805)

Taipei 台北

The capital and largest city, Taipei *(tái běi)* is home to governmental institutions, universities, booming businesses, wheezing cars, whining motorcycles and some three million Taiwanese. Probably the best word to describe it is 'busy'. It's not a particularly beautiful city, but it's prosperous, the people are friendly, there's lots of nightlife, food is excellent and there are unexpected treasures like Taoist temples and top-notch museums.

Orientation

There is a logical system to finding addresses, and it applies to other cities besides Taipei. However, Taipei is unique in that it is divided into four compass points. Chunghsiao Rd bisects the city into the north and south sections of the grid. All major roads that cross Chunghsiao Rd are labelled accordingly. Thus, we have Linsen North Rd and Linsen South Rd, Yenping North Rd and Yenping South Rd etc.

Chungshan Rd bisects the city into the east and west sections of the grid. Roads to the east of Chungshan Rd are labelled east and those to the west are labelled west. Thus, we have Nanking East Rd and Nanking West Rd.

In all of Taiwan's cities, major roads have sections. In Taipei there is Chungshan N Rd, Section 1, Section 2, Section 3 and so on right up to Section 7. Sometimes, instead of writing 'Wufu Rd, Section 3', they might write 'Wufu 3rd Rd', but the meaning is the same. A section is normally about three blocks long. When finding an address you really have to pay attention to which section you are in.

All of Taiwan's cities have lanes. Lanes, as the name implies, are small side streets and never have names, just numbers. A typical address might read: 16 Lane 20, Chungshan N Rd, Section 2. The 16 simply refers to the house number and Lane 20 is the name of the lane which intersects with Section 2 of Chungshan N Rd. That's not too difficult, but is there an easy way to locate Lane 20? Fortunately, there is. As you walk along Chungshan N Rd, Section 2, keep your eye on the house numbers. Lane 20 should intersect with Chungshan N Rd just near a building bearing the street address number 20. Once you understand this system, it becomes very easy to find the lane you are looking for.

Occasionally, you'll have to find an alley. An alley is a lane which runs off a lane. Again, the same system is used. Alley 25 will intersect with a lane, and the house at the corner of this intersection should be number 25. A typical address could be 132 Alley 25, Lane 20, Chungshan N Rd, Section 2, Taipei. It may look complicated, but it's very systematic.

Information

Tourist Offices A plentiful supply of maps, pamphlets and general information can be obtained from the ROC Tourism Bureau (☎ 3491500), 9th floor, 280 Chunghsiao E Rd, Section 4. Less useful is the Travel Information Service Centre (☎ 7121212, ext 471) at Sungshan Domestic Airport.

Money The bank at CKS Airport is supposed to remain open whenever international flights are arriving or departing. In Taipei, the International Bank of China (ICBC) is the best place to change money. Branches can be found at the following addresses:

Chungshan District, 15 Chungshan N Rd, Section 2 (☎ 5119231)
Ta'an Branch, 233 Chunghsiao E Rd, Section 4 (☎ 7711877)
Shihlin District, 126 Chungshan N Rd, Section 6 (☎ 8345225)

The other most likely place to change money is at the Bank of Taiwan:

Chungshan District, 150 Chungshan N Rd, Section 1 (☎ 5423434)
Ta'an District, 560 Chunghsiao E Rd, Section 4 (☎ 7073111)
Shihlin District, 248 Chungshan N Rd, Section 6 (☎ 8367080)

Post & Telecommunications The GPO in Taipei is on Chunghsiao W Rd, close to the railway station, and is called the North Gate Post Office. There is a separate window for poste restante.

You can make overseas calls and send fax messages, telegrams and telexes from the main telephone company (ITA) office (☎ 3443781) at 28 Hangchou S Rd, Section 1, which is open 24 hours a day. With a telephone card, you can make international direct-dial phone calls from the Taipei railway station.

Cultural Centres Within the grounds of the Chiang Kaishek Memorial are two cultural centres: the National Theater (☎ 3925091) and National Concert Hall (☎ 3924954). A schedule of events is published monthly and is available from the Tourism Bureau. Tickets for performances can be bought at Caves Books and New Schoolmate Books (see Bookshops for addresses).

Bookshops Caves Books (☎ 5371666), 103 Chungshan N Rd, Section 2, has one of the largest selections of English-language titles, but don't confuse it with the nearby branch at 81 Chungshan N Rd, Section 2, which has Chinese titles only. Other good bookshops include: New Schoolmate Books (☎ 700-7000), 259 Tunhua S Rd, Section 1 at Jenai Rd; Lucky Bookshop (☎ 3927111), 129-1 Hoping E Rd, Section 1; and Sung Kang Computer Book Company (☎ 7082125), 3rd floor, 337 Tunhua S Rd, Section 1 at Hsinyi Rd.

Libraries The American Cultural Centre (☎ 3327981), 54 Nanhai Rd (opposite the Botanical Gardens), is a library maintained by the American Institute in Taiwan. Library hours are 10 am until 5 pm Monday to Friday.

The National Central Library (☎ 361-9132) at 20 Chungshan S Rd is Taiwan's largest and the facilities are stunning. The library is adjacent to the Chiang Kaishek Memorial Hall.

TAIWAN

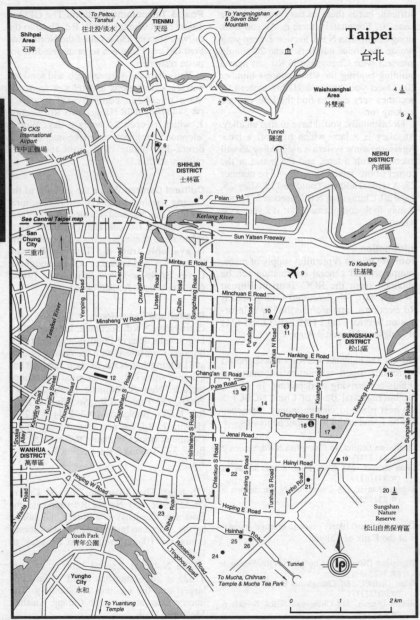

Taipei
台北

Shihpai Area
石牌

To Peitou, Tanshui
往北投/淡水

TIENMU
天母

To Yangmingshan & Seven Star Mountain

1

Waishuangshi Area
外雙溪

4

5

To CKS International Airport
往中正機場

Chungcheng

Road

2

3

6

Tunnel
隧道

SHIHLIN DISTRICT
士林區

NEIHU DISTRICT
內湖區

7

8   Peian Rd

Keelung River

See Central Taipei map

San Chung City
三重市

Sun Yatsen Freeway

Mintsu E Road

To Keelung
往基隆

Tanshui River

Chengtu Road

Chungshan N Road

Linsen Road

Chilin Road

Sungchiang Road

Yenping Road

Minsheng W Road

Minchuan E Road

9

Minchuan E Road

Fuhsing N Road

Tunhua N Road

10

11

Nanking E Road

SUNGSHAN DISTRICT
松山區

Chunghua Road

Chungshan S Road

12

Kunming Street

Kending Road

Chang'an E Road

Pate Road

13

14

Kuangfu Road

Keelung Road

15   16

Hsinsheng S Road

Chunghsiao E Road

18

17

Sungshan Road

Snake Alley

WANHUA DISTRICT
萬華區

Chienkuo S Road

Jenai Road

Fuhsing S Road

Hsinyi Road

Tunhua S Road

19

20

Wanta Road

Hoping W Road

22

Anho Road

21

Sungshan Nature Reserve
松山自然保育區

23

Shihta Road

Hoping E Road

Youth Park
青年公園

25   26

Hsinhai

Road

Roosevelt Road

24

Tingchou Road

Tunnel

Yungho City
永和

To Mucha, Chihnan Temple & Mucha Tea Park

To Yuantung Temple

0   1   2 km

1	National Palace Museum 故宮博物館	15	Jaoho Night Market 饒河街夜市
2	Movie Studio 電影文化城	16	Sungshan Railway Station 松山火車站
3	Soochow University 東吳大學	17	Sun Yatsen Memorial 國父紀念館
4	Pishan Temple 碧山寺/碧山巖開漳聖廟	18	ROC Tourism Bureau 觀光局
5	Pishan Camping Ground 碧山露營場	19	World Trade Centre 世貿中心
6	Shihlin Night Market 士林夜市	20	Sheng'en Temple 聖恩宮
7	Grand Hotel 圓山大飯店	21	Tunghua Night Market 通化街夜市
8	Martyrs' Shrine 忠烈祠	22	American Institute in Taiwan (AIT) 美國在台協會
9	Sungshan Domestic Airport 松山機場	23	Taiwan Normal University 師大
10	American Express 美國運通銀行	24	National Taiwan University 台大
11	Citibank 花旗銀行	25	Language Training Centre 財團法人語信訓練測驗中心
12	Taipei Railway Station 台北車站	26	Taipei International Youth Activity Centre 國際青年活動中心
13	Chunglun Bus Station 中崙站		
14	Dinghao Market 頂好市場		

Emergency The Adventist Hospital has English-speaking doctors and caters to foreigners, but is very expensive – if you have health insurance you might be covered. Other hospitals are government-run and of a high standard, but can be very crowded. Some hospitals in Taipei include:

Adventist Hospital (*táiān yī yuàn*), 424 Pate Rd, Section 2 (☎ 7718151)

Chang Gung Memorial Hospital (*cháng gēng yī yuàn*), 199 Tunhua N Rd (☎ 7135211)

Mackay Memorial Hospital (*mǎ jiē yī yuàn*), Chungshan N Rd, Section 2 (☎ 5433535)

National Taiwan University Hospital (*táidà yīyuàn*), 7 Chungshan S Rd (☎ 3970800)

Taipei Medical College Hospital (*táiběi yīxué yuàn*), 252 Wuhsing St (☎ 7372181)

Tri-Service General Hospital (*sān jūn zhōng yī yuàn*), 226 Tingchow St (☎ 3117001)

Veterans General Hospital (*róng mín zhōng yī yuàn*), 201 Shihpai Rd, Section 2 (☎ 8712121, English ext 3530)

English-speaking police can be contacted at the city centre office by calling ☎ 3119940, or ☎ 3119816, ext 264; in the Chungshan area, call ☎ 5119564; and in Tienmu, call ☎ 8714110, 8714440. As elsewhere in Taiwan, the Chinese-speaking emergency numbers are ☎ 110 for police and ☎ 119 for fire.

For an ambulance, call ☎ 7216315. If this doesn't work, call the Tourist Information Hot Line (☎ 7173737).

Things to See

The **National Palace Museum** (*gù gōng bó wù yuàn*) holds the world's largest collection of Chinese artefacts, about 700,000 items in all. There are so many that they cannot be displayed all at once, so the display is rotated. There are good English tours of the museum twice daily at 10 am and 3 pm, and the museum is open from 9 am to 5 pm every day of the year. Admission is NT$40. Buses which go to the museum are Nos 213, 255 and 304, and minibus No 18. If you take No

TAIWAN

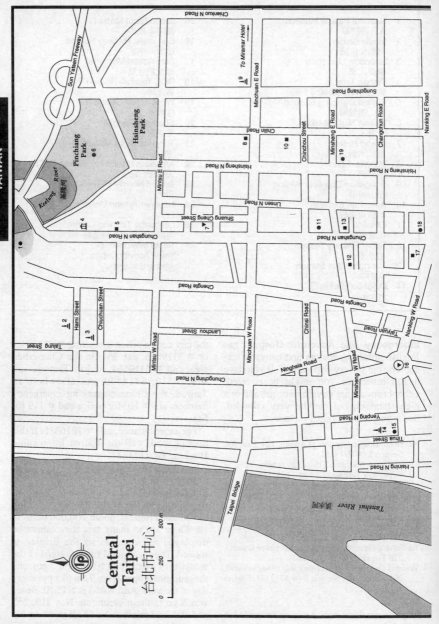

TAIWAN

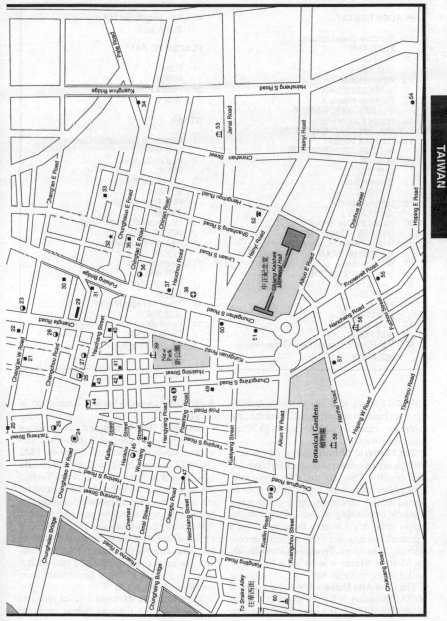

PLACES TO STAY

5   Rainbow Guest House
    彩虹招待所
8   Ritz Hotel
    亞都大飯店
10 Amigo Hostel
    吉林路286號3/4樓
12 Formosa Hostel II
    中山北路二段62巷5號2樓
13 Happy Family Hostel IV
    中山北路二段77巷12-5號5樓
17 Formosa Hostel I
    中山北路二段20巷16號3樓
20 Hotel 6F
    銀寶賓館
21 Queen Hotel
    皇后賓館
22 Senator Hotel
    信州大飯店
30 Happy Family Hostel II
    中山北路一段56巷2號2/3樓
31 Happy Family Hostel I
    北平西路16-1號4樓
33 Taipei Hostel
    林森北路5號11號6樓
35 Lai Lai Sheraton Hotel
    來來大飯店
40 YMCA
    基督教青年會
41 Paradise Hotel
    南國大飯店
42 Yon Hong & Chuan Chia Huam Hotels
    懷寧街10號

43 New Mayflower Hotel
    華美大飯店

PLACES TO EAT

7   Pubs
    啤酒屋
16 Food Circle
    圓環

OTHER

1   Children's Recreation Centre
    兒童育樂中心
2   Pao'an Temple
    保安寺
3   Confucius Temple
    孔子廟
4   Fine Arts Museum
    美術館
6   Lin Antai Old Homestead
    林安泰古厝簡介
9   Hsingtien Temple
    行天宮
11 Caves Books
    敦煌書局
14 Chenghuang Temple
    城隍廟
15 Tihua St Night Market
    迪化街夜市
18 International Commercial Bank of
    China (ICBC)
    中國國際商業銀行

304, you can get off at the terminus, but for the other buses you have to ask. From the city centre you must pay double fare (NT$20) as it is a long way out.

The **Martyrs' Shrine** *(zhōng liè cí)* was built to honour those who died fighting for their country. There are two rifle-toting military police who stand guard at the gate in formal dress – absolutely rigid, not moving a muscle or blinking an eye – while tourists harass them. It's a wonder these guys don't run amok and bayonet a few of their camera-clicking tormentors. From the Grand Hotel, the Martyrs' Shrine is less than a 10-minute walk east along Peian Rd.

The **Fine Arts Museum** *(měi shù guǎn)* is at 181 Chungshan N Rd, Section 3, just south of the Grand Hotel. It's open from 10 am to 6 pm daily, closed Monday. Admission is NT$10.

Lin Antai Old Homestead *(lín ān tài gǔ cuò jiǎn jiè)* is a remarkable traditional Taiwanese structure first built between 1822 and 1827 in Taipei's Ta'an District. It would have been demolished in 1978 when Tunhua Rd was being widened, but a successful effort was mounted to relocate it. This graceful building now stands on peaceful grounds in Pinchiang Park *(bīn jiāng gōng yuán)* east of Hsinsheng N Rd and north of Mintsu E Rd. Admission is free. Bus No 222 is probably the most convenient – you can catch it on Chungshan S Rd. You could walk from the Fine Arts Museum.

The **Botanical Gardens** *(zhí wù yuán)* on Nanhai Rd are a pleasant retreat from the

19	Taipei Labourer's Recreation Centre 新生北路二段101巷2號	46	Foreign Affairs Police (Visa Extensions) 警察局外事課
23	Tonglien Bus Company 統聯客運	47	Tower Records 淘兒唱片行
24	North Gate 北門	48	Bank of Taiwan 台灣銀行
25	Buses to Tanshui 往淡水公車站	49	Presidential Building 總統府
26	West Bus Station 台汽西站	50	Foreign Affairs Ministry (VISA Changes) 外交部
27	East Bus Station 台汽東站	51	National Central Library 中央圖書館
28	North Bus Station 台汽北站	52	Telephone Company (ITA) Main Office 電信局
29	Taipei Railway Station 台北車站	53	Chang Foundation Museum 鴻禧美術館
32	Provincial Police (Mountain & Re-Entry Permits) 警政署	54	Lucky Bookshop 師大書苑
34	Kuanghua Computer Market 光華商場	55	Mandarin Daily News 國語日報
36	Buses to Wulai 往烏來公車站	56	Postal Museum 郵政博物館
37	Chinese Handicraft Centre 中華工藝館	57	American Cultural Centre (Library) 美國文化中心
38	Taiwan University Hospital 台大醫院	58	National Museum of History 歷史博物館
39	Taiwan Provincial Museum 台灣省博物館	59	Little South Gate 小南門
44	GPO 郵政總局	60	Lungshan Temple 龍山寺
45	Buses to Sanhsia 往三峽公車站		

TAIWAN

noisy city. There is a beautiful lotus pond in the gardens, next to the National Museum of History, National Science Hall and National Arts Hall – all worth a look. The National Museum of History is open daily from 9 am to 5 pm; admission is NT$10. You can get there on bus No 1, 204, 242 or 259.

The **Chiang Kaishek Memorial** (*zhōng zhèng jì niàn táng*) is an enormous piece of architecture surrounded by a lush garden. You'll find it on Hsinyi Rd, Section 1.

Lungshan Temple (*lóng shān sì*) is an extremely colourful temple and is packed with worshippers most of the time; the air is heavy with smoke from burning incense and 'ghost money'. Adjacent to the temple is an active market and two blocks away is the famous Snake Alley.

Snake Alley (*húa xī jīe*) is an unusual night market where you can see snake vendors taunt live cobras before serving them up on your dinner plate (boiled, fried or pickled). Prices are high. It's in the Wanhua area between Chunghua Rd and the river.

Pao'an Temple (*bǎo ān gōng*) is a lovely old Taoist structure a short walk from the Confucius Temple. The address is 16 Hami St, not far from the Grand Hotel.

Pishan Temple (*bì shān sì*) is a magnificent place perched on the side of a mountain with a breathtaking view of Taipei. It's in the Neihu District in the high-class north-east part of Taipei. From the Hilton Hotel area (near the railway station) take bus No 247 and tell the driver you want to get off at the

Golden Dragon Temple *(jīn lóng sì)*. From this temple you must walk uphill farther into the mountains to reach Pishan Temple.

Shihlin Night Market *(shì lín yè shì)* is one of the largest in Taipei. It's to the north-west of the Grand Hotel, just to the west of Wenlin Rd and starts from the south side of Chungcheng Rd. This market is open in the daytime, but really comes alive at night. It normally shuts down around 10 to 11 pm but hours are longer on weekends.

A pleasant mountain park north of Taipei, **Yangmingshan** *(yáng míng shān)* has hot springs, peaks to climb and something else that Taipei lacks – breathable air. Here you'll find **Seven Star Mountain** *(qī xīng shān)*, the highest point in Taipei with an elevation of 1120 metres. A path leads to the summit, but be equipped for changeable weather if you want to climb it. From the centre you can get to Yangmingshan on bus No 301 or 260, which run along Chungshan N Rd. Minibus No 9 also goes to the park.

The **Taipei-Mucha Zoo** *(mù zhà dòng wù yuán)* is in the south-east section of Taipei. This area is officially called the Wenshan District, but it was formerly Mucha (Wooden Fence) and that's the name still usually applied to the zoo. Bus Nos 236, 237, 258, 282, 294 and 295 go there. If the MRT ever gets finished, the brown line will terminate at the zoo. Opening hours are from 8.30 am to 4.30 pm daily.

Chihnan Temple *(zhǐ nán gōng)* is one of the largest temples in north Taiwan. It's 19 km south-east of the centre in Taipei's Wenshan District. There are several routes used for getting there. You can take bus No 236 or 237 to Chengchih University in the Wenshan District, then walk uphill to the temple. Alternatively, you can get there from the city centre by taking a bus operated by the Chihnan (CN) Bus Company *(zhǐ nán kè yùn)*. CN bus No 1 runs along Nanking E Rd, then Sungchiang Rd, Hsinsheng S Rd, Roosevelt Rd and on out to Mucha, ending at the Chihnan Temple. CN bus No 2 runs down Chunghua Rd, Aikuo Rd, Roosevelt Rd and finally terminates in the Wenshan District. Be sure to tell the driver your destination –

some of the buses take a different route and terminate at the zoo rather than the temple. No matter which bus you take, from where the bus drops you off you cannot see the temple. Follow the steep steps up and up until you reach a small Taoist temple. The main temple is to your right; to the left are some picnic grounds.

The hilly **Mucha Tea Park** *(mù zhà guān guāng cháyuán)* is a good area for walking. There are over 60 teahouses here and numerous tea plantations. The park is in the Wenshan District at the southernmost tip of Taipei city proper. Minibus Nos 10 and 11 go to the park from Chengchih University. These buses only run about once every 30 minutes and do not run late in the evening. To reach Chengchih University, you can take bus No 236 or 237.

Activities
Bungee Jumping You can contact Bungee International (☎ 3325523), 9th floor, Room 1, 180 Chungching S Rd, Section 3.

Language Courses You can contact the following schools in Taipei for further information:

Cathay Language Centre	(☎ 8729165)
China Language Institute	(☎ 7087157)
Chinese Cultural University	(☎ 3567356)
Mandarin Daily News	(☎ 3915134)
My Language School	(☎ 3945400)
Perfect Language Institute	(☎ 3120632)
Pioneer Language Institute	(☎ 3410111)
Taipei Language Institute	(☎ 3410022)
Taiwan Normal University	(☎ 3639123)
Tamkang University Language Centre	(☎ 3567356)

Places to Stay
Hostels There are a number of privately operated hostels in Taipei, and all charge nearly the same price. For dormitories, it's NT$180 per night or NT$1050 per week. Several of these hostels even have single rooms for only slightly more.

The *Happy Family Hostel I* (☎ 3753443) is on the 4th floor, 16-1 Peiping W Rd, about a stone's throw from the railway station.

Under the same management is the *Happy*

Family II (☎ 5810716), 2nd & 3rd floors, 2 Lane 56, Chungshan N Rd, Section 1; it's a short walk away from the railway station. Call first because it's often full.

Happy Family IV (☎ 5633341) is on the 5th floor, 12-5 Lane 77, Chungshan N Rd, Section 2. This is one of the newest and best hostels in Taipei, with air-conditioning, kitchen, washing machine, TV, video and good hot showers.

Amigo Hostel (☎ 5420292, 5710612), 3rd & 4th floors, 286 Chilin Rd, is also a good deal. From the railway station take bus No 502 and get off at the corner of Minchuan E and Chilin Rds, opposite the Ritz Hotel *(yǎ dū dà fàn diàn)*. Bus No 49 also stops nearby. Better yet, if you're coming from the airport (and you've phoned ahead to reserve a bed), take the airport bus going to Sungshan Airport *(not* the railway station) and get off at the stop for the Miramar Hotel *(měi lì hu dà fàn diàn)*. The Miramar is on Minchuan Rd, two blocks east of the hostel.

Another excellent clean and well-managed hostel is *Formosa Hostel II* (☎ 5116744). The hostel is on the 2nd floor, 5 Lane 62, Chungshan N Rd, Section 2. The nearby *Formosa Hostel I* (☎ 5622035), 3rd floor, 16 Lane 20, Section 2, Chungshan N Rd, is under the same management. Facilities include a kitchen and washing machine.

The *Taipei Hostel* (☎ 3952950), 6th floor, 11 Lane 5, Linsen N Rd, features enormous dorms. Double rooms are available here for NT$400 per day or NT$2450 per week. The location is very central near the Lai Lai Sheraton Hotel.

Hotels Huaining St *(huái níng jiē)* is just south of the railway station and is a happy hunting ground for relatively cheap hotels. One of the best bargains on this street is the *Paradise Hotel* (☎ 3313311) *(nán guó dà fàn diàn)*, 7 Huaining St, where doubles cost NT$600 to NT$700. Just across the street is the *Yon Hong Hotel* (☎ 3611906) *(yǒng fēng bīn guǎn)*, 10 Huaining St, where doubles are NT$650. Also nearby is the plush-looking *Chuan Chia Huam Hotel* (☎ 3814755)

(quán jiā huān bīn guǎn), 4th floor, 6 Huaining St, where doubles cost NT$900.

One block to the west is Chungching S Rd, which has a few places worth checking out. The *New Mayflower Hotel* (☎ 3617581) *(huáměi dà fàn diàn)*, 1 Chungking S Rd, Section 1, has doubles for NT$800.

Chang'an W Rd, one block north of the railway station, is another place to look for cheapish hotels. An excellent bargain is the *Queen Hotel* (☎ 5590489) *(huáng hòu bīn guǎn)* on the 2nd floor at No 226. Doubles are NT$500 to NT$600. Unfortunately, there is no English sign, so look for the street number.

Also in the vicinity is the *Senator Hotel* (☎ 5586511) *(xìn zhōu dà fàn diàn)*, 839 Chang'an W Rd, where doubles cost NT$830 to NT$930. The same management runs the *Hotel 6F* (☎ 5551130) *(yín bǎo bīn guǎn)*, on the 6th floor at 251 Chang'an W Rd, where doubles are NT$830 to NT$930.

Places to Eat
Budget eats are found in back alleys or from street vendors.

There is a large collection of cheap restaurants in a place called the *Food Circle (yuán huán)* at the intersection of Chungching N and Nanking W Rds. In addition to the Food Circle itself, street vendors appear at night in all the side streets adjoining the circle.

Where you find students, you find cheap restaurants. Just south of the railway station is Wuchang St, the home of numerous 'cram schools' that train students to pass Taiwan's rigid university entrance exams. The high concentration of schools and students guarantees an infinite choice of cheap eating places in this area.

Cheap restaurants also surround Taiwan University and Taiwan Normal University. Don't forget the universities themselves – no student ID is needed to eat in the student cafeterias. In the basement of the dormitory (south side of Hoping Rd) across the street from the Mandarin Training Centre (Taiwan Normal University) is a superb cafeteria – it costs NT$35 for a mountain of rice and three dishes that would cost twice this much elsewhere. If you eat in the university cafeterias, you have to be on time – lunch is from 11.30 am to 12.30 pm, and dinner from 5.30 to 6.30 pm.

A great place to sample Taiwan's famous dumplings is at the row of restaurants on the north-west corner of Linsen N and Nanking E Rds. These places charge NT$2 for each dumpling.

The 2nd floor of the Taipei railway station has a collection of moderately priced restaurants.

Entertainment

Chinese Opera *(píng jù)* Operas are performed almost every night at 7 pm in the Armed Forces Cultural Activity Centre (☎ 3114228) *(guó jūn wén yì zhōng xīn)*, 69 Chunghua Rd, Section 1. However, performances here tend to be by amateur groups and are often not of a high standard.

MTV One of the few remaining MTV clubs in Taipei is *Barcelona* (☎ 7012174), 175 Hsinyi Rd, Section 4.

Pubs & Discos One of the longest-running pubs in Taipei is *Roxy* (☎ 3635967) at 22 Hoping E Rd, Section 1. There is no cover charge, but minimum expenditure on food or drinks is NT$70. It's open from noon until 4 am.

High recommendations go to the *Pig & Whistle* (☎ 8731380) at 78 Tienmu E Rd. Dancing and loud music feature at *Spin* (☎ 3569288), in the basement at 91 Hoping E Rd, Section 1. The cover charge is NT$100.

Another place getting rave reviews from travellers is *Whiskey A-Go-Go* (☎ 7375773, 7354715), 65 Hsinhai Rd, Section 3, near National Taiwan University. There's a large dance floor, flashing strobes, the whole lot.

Enjoy (☎ 3629257), 10 Lane 104, Hoping E Rd, Section 1, has drinks and decent food. The environment is European-style, right down to French and British newspapers. Also on Lane 104 is *Fuba*, a quiet but romantic place good for drinking, watching cable TV, chatting and playing checkers.

Cheers Pub (☎ 3638194), in the basement at 128-1 Shihta Rd, is an excellent place. Or go up to the 4th floor of the same building to find *Blue Note*, a jazz bar which sometimes has loud music.

Lane 86 (☎ 3671523) is at 7 Lane 86, Hsinsheng Rd, Section 3. This is a student district so it's not expensive. There's a DJ and a big selection of CDs. During the day, it's a reasonably quiet Chinese coffee shop, but it really gets hopping at night.

One of the most interesting places to visit in Taipei is *Indian* (☎ 7410550), 196 Pate Rd, Section 2. It's a pub and restaurant, but distinguishes itself with dinosaur bones sticking out of the walls. The waiters and waitresses wear dinosaur bone shirts.

There's thumping music at *Gorgon Discoland* (☎ 7534992), 47 Kuangfu S Rd. This place has an incredible decor – strobe lights, monsters hanging out of the walls and a moving Medusa head.

Things to Buy

The place to go for backpacking gear is Taipei Shanshui, 12 Chungshan N Rd, Section 1. Just a few doors up the street is another good shop, Deng Shan You, 18 Chungshan N Rd, Section 1.

The Taiwan Crafts Centre (☎ 3315701), 7th floor, 110 Yenping S Rd, has a self-explanatory name. Even if you don't buy, there are interesting arts and crafts displays here. It's open from 10 am until 6 pm daily, except Monday and public holidays.

The widest selection of music tapes and CDs can be found at Tower Records (☎ 3892025), 12 Chengtu Rd. It's right on the huge roundabout at the corner of Chengtu and Chunghua Rds.

The Holiday Flower Market *(jià rì huā shì)* is held on Saturday (when there are relatively few customers) but expands enormously on Sunday and holidays. The market is under an overpass on Chienkuo N Rd, between Jenai and Hsinyi Rds. Buses which stop nearby include Nos 36, 37, 48, 65, 263,

270, 275, 298, Hsinyi Rd Line and Jenai Rd Line. Operating hours are roughly from 10 am until 8 pm.

The Holiday Jade Market (*jià rì yù shì*) is underneath the overpass at the intersection of Pate and Hsinsheng S Rds. Even if you don't want to buy flowers or jade, it's interesting to come here and look.

Getting There & Away

Air CKS International Airport is 40 km from Taipei near the city of Taoyuan. Airline offices in Taipei include:

Air New Zealand, 6th floor, 98 Nanking E Rd, Section 2 (☎ 5313980)
Asiana, 5th floor, 65 Chienkuo N Rd, Section 2 (☎ 5081114)
Australia Asia, 3rd floor, 101 Nanking E Rd, Section 2 (☎ 5221001)
Canadian International, 4th floor, 90 Chienkuo N Rd, Section 2 (☎ 5034111)
Cathay Pacific, 12th floor, 129 Minsheng E Rd, Section 3 (☎ 7152333)
China Airlines, 131 Nanking E Rd, Section 3 (☎ 7151212 – 24 hours a day)
Continental, 2nd floor, 150 Fuhsing N Rd (☎ 7152766)
Delta Airlines, 50 Nanking E Rd, Section 2 (☎ 5513656)
EVA Airways, 166 Minsheng E Rd, Section 2 (☎ 5011999)
Garuda Indonesia, 66 Sungchiang Rd (☎ 5612311)
Japan Asia, 2 Tunhua S Rd, Section 1 (☎ 7765151)
KLM, 1 Nanking E Rd, Section 4 (☎ 7171000)
Korean Air, 53 Nanking E Rd, Section 2 (☎ 5214242)
Lauda Air, 7th floor, 18 Chang'an E Rd, Section 1 (☎ 5435083)
Malaysian Airlines, 102 Tunhua N Rd (☎ 7168384)
Mandarin, 13th floor, 134 Minsheng E Rd, Section 3 (☎ 7171230, 7171188)
Northwest, 7th floor, 168-170 Tunhua N Rd (☎ 7161555)
Philippine Airlines, 2nd floor, 90 Chienkuo N Rd, Section 2 (☎ 5051255)
Royal Brunei, 11th floor, 9 Nanking E Rd, Section 3 (☎ 5312884)
Sempati, 174 Chunghsiao E Rd, Section 1 (☎ 3966934, 3966910)
Singapore Airlines, 148 Sungchiang Rd (☎ 5516655)
South African Airways, 12th floor, 205 Tunhua N Rd (☎ 7136363)
Thai Airways, 2nd floor, 150 Fuhsing N Rd (☎ 7175299, 7175200)
United Airlines, 12th floor, 2 Jenai Rd, Section 4 (☎ 3258868)

Every domestic carrier has an office in Taipei or a counter at Sungshan Airport (which is right in the city). The domestic airlines are:

China Airlines, 131 Nanking E Rd, Section 3 (☎ 7151122)
Far Eastern Airlines, 36 Kuanchien Rd (☎ 3615431)
Formosa Airlines, Sungshan Airport (☎ 5149636)
Great China Airlines, 38 Jenai Rd, Section 1 (☎ 3568000)
Makung Airlines, Sungshan Airport (☎ 5148188)
Taiwan Airlines, Sungshan Airport (☎ 5142881)
Trans-Asia Airways, 8th floor, 139 Chengchou Rd (☎ 5579000)

Bus There are four important bus terminals near the railway station and another about two km to the east. Probably most important is the West Bus Station, where you get government-operated (Taiwan Bus Company) highway buses to major west coast cities, including Taichung, Chiayi, Tainan and Kaohsiung. There are also buses from here to a few major resort areas like Kenting and Alishan. The West Bus Station is on Chunghsiao W Rd, a three-minute walk west of the railway station.

The East Bus Station is almost right in front of the railway station. From here you get buses to CKS Airport and Keelung.

The North Bus Station is on the north side of the railway station. Here you can get buses to Changhua, Hsinchu, Hualien (transfer in Suao), Keelung, Puli, Suao, Sun Moon Lake and Taoyuan.

One block north of the North Bus Station at the north-east corner of Chengte and Chang'an Rds is the Tonglien Bus Station. This company is Taiwan's leading wild chicken bus company. Departures for all major west coast cities are frequent.

The Chunglun Bus Station is on the southwest corner of Pate and Fuhsing Rds, over two km east of the railway station. You can get there from the Taipei railway station area (Chunghsiao E Rd in front of Asiaworld department store) by taking city buses Nos 57, 205 and 276. Important departures from Chunglun Station include buses to Chinshan Beach, Keelung, Yehliu and Fengyuan.

TAIWAN

Travel Agencies

If you qualify as a student (studying Chinese at a Taiwanese university will do) or if you're under the age of 27, you can get a special discount on international air tickets from Youth Travel International (☎ 7211978; fax 7212784), suite 502, 142 Chunghsiao E Rd, Section 4. With proper credentials (student ID card or acceptance letter from a university), you can purchase an ISIC card here for NT$150. You can also get an STA Travel Youth Card for NT$250 if you're aged 13 to 26, even if you're not a student. This place also sells the Hostelling International (HI) Guidebook.

An organisation to *avoid* is the Chinese Taipei Youth Hostel Association. For years they have been masquerading as an HI representative – in fact they are not, and have been charging an NT$1000 membership fee to use their services.

Other travel agents advertise in the English-language newspapers and most seem to be reliable. Some agencies in Taipei that we've found to be OK include:

Jenny Su Travel, 10th floor, 27 Chungshan N Rd, Section 3 (☎ 5947733, 5962263; fax 5920068)
Southeast Travel, 60 Chungshan N Rd, Section 2 (☎ 5713001)
Wing On Travel, 73-79 Jenai Rd, Section 4 (☎ 7722998)

Getting Around

To/From CKS Airport

It takes nearly an hour to travel between CKS Airport and central Taipei, and even longer during the rush hour.

Limousine buses run every 15 minutes, beginning at 6.30 am and ending at 10.30 pm. There are two limousine buses – the more popular one with travellers goes to the Taipei railway station right in the city centre. The other limousine bus goes to Sungshan Domestic Airport in the north-east part of the city. Both buses cost NT$85.

When heading to the airport from Taipei, you can catch the limousine bus from two locations; the East Bus Station at 173 Chunghsiao W Rd (in front of the Taipei railway station), or from the bus terminal on the western end of Sungshan Domestic Airport. Bus No 502 connects Sungshan Airport to the Taipei railway station.

Bus There is a reasonably good English bus guide available from Caves Books and Lucky Bookstore for NT$100, but it's getting out of date. On the cash box next to the driver should be a sign in Chinese or a red light telling you to pay when you get on *(shàng)* or when you get off *(xià)*. You may have to pay both when getting on *and* when getting off if the bus crosses into another fare zone.

MRT This should be nice, if they ever finish building it. The Fuhsing line should be open by the time you read this.

Car Driving is not recommended for the city, but a car could be of some use in the country-side. Taipei has several agencies that can put you in the driver's seat:

Taipei Budget Rent-A-Car (☎ 8312906)
Central Auto Rental (☎ 8821000)
International Auto Service (☎ 8331225)
VIP Car Rental (☎ 7131111)

Around the Country

CENTRAL CROSS-ISLAND HIGHWAY
中部橫貫公路

This spectacular highway connects Taroko Gorge on the east side of Taiwan with the city of Taichung on the west, a distance of 195 km. Virtually every km of this highway offers a stunning view of lush forests and towering mountain peaks. The road is occasionally closed because of landslides, especially after a typhoon.

Getting There & Away

Buses to Taichung depart from Hualien at 7.35, 9.35 and 11.05 am. Tickets cost NT$459. Another bus leaves Hualien at 11.50 am which only goes as far as Lishan, half way to Taichung along the same route. Coming the other way, buses depart from Taichung at 7, 8 and 9.30 am. You can also catch any of these buses in Tienhsiang. Although the trip can be done in one day (eight hours), three days would be more reasonable to allow for side trips to Wuling Farm and Hohuanshan.

If you're not headed to south Taiwan, then Fengyuan is an important transit point at the western end of the highway. It's about an hour north of Taichung. You can get a train from Taipei to Fengyuan and bypass Taichung completely. This saves nearly two hours on a trip from Taipei to the Central Cross-Island Highway.

TAICHUNG
(tái zhōng) 台中
Taiwan's third-largest city, Taichung is a major transport hub on the western end of the Central Cross-Island Highway. Although the city has a few museums, temples and other places of interest, for most travellers it will just be an overnight stop on the way to somewhere else.

Places to Stay
Best in the budget class is the *First Hotel* (☎ 2222205) *(dì yī lǚ shè)*, 51 Chikuang Rd *(jì guāng jiē)*, where singles start at NT$300 with private bath.

If you're willing to stay in a closet-sized room and use a shared bath, one of the cheapest places in town is *Zhongzhou Hotel* (☎ 2222711) *(zhōng zhōu lǚ shè)*, 2nd floor, 129 Chienkuo Rd, where singles/doubles cost NT$200/250. It's on the circle just opposite the railway station behind the bus stop, between Chungcheng and Chungshan Rds. Just to the left of this place is a narrow alley called Lane 125 – here you'll find *Jiancheng Hotel* (☎ 2222497) *(jiàn chéng lǚ shè)*, 10 Lane 125, Chienkuo Rd. Singles/doubles are NT$200/250 with shared bath or NT$350 with private bath. The *Dongcheng Hotel* (☎ 2225001) *(dōng chéng dà lǚ shè)*, 14 Chungshan Rd, has doubles starting at NT$250 with shared bath, NT$350 with private bath.

Getting There & Away
It's 105 km south of Taipei on the major north-south freeway and railway line, so you won't have trouble getting to Taichung. There are also buses coming over the mountains from Hualien on the east coast, via the scenic Central Cross-Island Highway. There are direct buses to many scenic areas in central Taiwan, such as Sun Moon Lake.

There are three major bus terminals in Taichung. The one in front of the railway station is for buses heading for Taipei and other places in the north. The one behind the railway station is for southbound buses. For eastbound buses (Sun Moon Lake, Kukuan, Lishan, Hualien) go to the Gancheng bus terminal *(gān chéng chē zhàn)*, two blocks north-east of the railway station (see the corresponding Taichung map). There is also a bus stop (not really a station) on the roundabout in front of the railway station where you can catch buses to Kukuan.

KUKUAN
(gǔ guān) 谷關
Kukuan is a small town and hot spring resort towards the western end of the Central Cross-Island Highway, about 1½ hours by bus from Taichung. Kukuan has an elevation of 750 metres.

The hot springs are piped into hotel baths; unfortunately, there are no outdoor pools. In addition to the hot springs, another attraction is the hike up to Dragon Valley Waterfall *(lóng gǔ pù bù)*, which also contains a zoo and botanical gardens. It's an easy 3.3 km (round-trip) hike to the falls, but there is an admission charge of NT$100. To find it, cross the footbridge near the Dragon Valley Hotel and just follow the trail.

Places to Stay
Cross the footbridge to the north bank to find the *Kukuan Hot Springs Hotel* (☎ 5951126) *(gǔ guān wēn quán shān zhuāng)*. It's the only place which has cheapish tatami rooms.

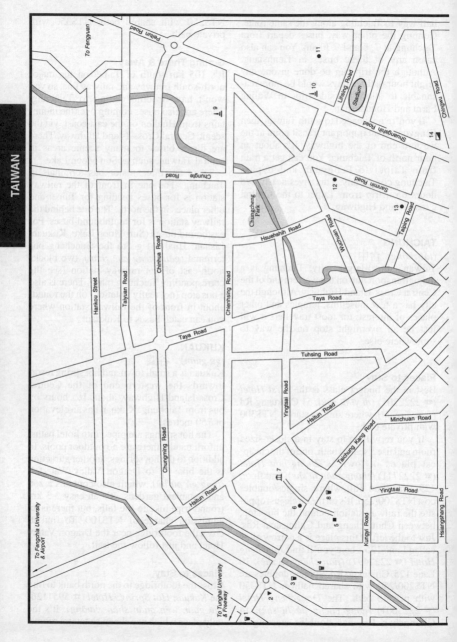

TAIWAN

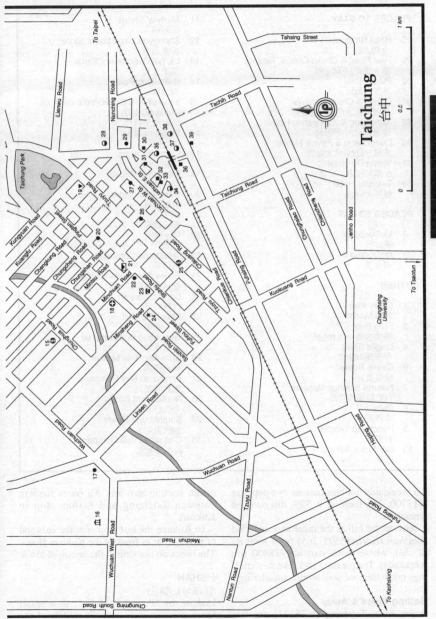

Taichung
台中

PLACES TO STAY

5   Hotel National
    全國大飯店
26 First Hotel & Chaku Chugui Teashop
    第一旅社/茶窟出軌
30 Plaza Hotel
    達欣大飯店
31 Crown & Chance Hotels
    王冠大飯店/巧合大飯店
32 Jiancheng & Zhongzhou Hotels
    建城旅社/中洲旅社
33 Dongcheng & Palace Hotels
    東城旅社/華宮大飯店
36 Yeong Du Hotel
    永都大飯店
39 Twinstar Hotel
    雙星大飯店

PLACES TO EAT

2   McDonald's
    麥當勞
19 McDonald's
    麥當勞

OTHER

1   Crazy Pub
    精誠路16號
3   Frog Pub
    華美西街一段105號
4   Luigi's (Pub)
    華美街392號
6   Caves Books
    敦煌書局
7   Natural Science Museum
    自然科學博物館
8   Pubs
    啤酒屋
9   Paochueh Temple
    寶覺寺
10 Confucius Temple
    孔廟
11 Martyrs' Shrine
    忠烈祠
12 Zhongyou Department Store
    中友百貨
13 Lai Lai Department Store
    來來百貨
14 Swimming Pool
    游泳池
15 International Commercial Bank of
    China (ICBC)
    國際商業銀行
16 Museum of Art
    美術館
17 Cultural Centre
    文化中心
18 Taichung Hospital
    台中醫院
20 Central Bookstore
    中央書局
21 GPO
    郵政總局
22 City Hall
    市政府
23 Telephone Company
    電信局
24 Police (Visa Extensions)
    警察局外事課
25 Bank of Taiwan
    台灣銀行
27 Shopping Mall
    第一廣場
28 Gancheng Bus Terminal
    干城車站
29 Chienkuo Tool Market
    建國市場
34 Fengyuan Bus Company
    豐原客運站
35 Northbound Buses
    台汽台中站
37 Southbound Buses
    台汽南站
38 Changhua Bus Company
    彰化客運站

On weekends doubles cost an eye-popping NT$700, but there is a 50% discount on weekdays.

Just up the hill is the quiet and secluded *Wenshan Hotel* (☎ 5951265) *(wèn shān dà lü shè)*, where twins start at NT$800 (on weekends). The pleasant park-like surroundings make this one well worth considering.

Getting There & Away

Buses from Taichung (NT$121) are frequent, starting at 6 am. All buses running between Taichung and Lishan stop in Kukuan.

In Kukuan the bus stop is at the east end of town, right in front of the Kukuan Hotel. The buses do not stop in the centre of town.

LISHAN

(lí shān) 梨山

Lishan, or 'Pear Mountain', is a small farming community near the middle of the

Central Cross-Island Highway. Some 1900 metres above sea level, the area is famous for growing cold-weather fruits which cannot grow in the subtropical lowlands. Lishan is also a weekend tourist resort – especially during summer – and is also a useful transit point for trips to Wuling Farm, Hsuehshan and Hohuanshan.

Hiking opportunities are limited in Lishan because most of the land is occupied by orchards. However, there is a mountain road you can hike or hitch along to three scenic spots: Lishan Culture Museum (*lí shān wén wù guǎn*), 1.5 km from Lishan; Lucky Life Mountain Farm (*fú shòu shān nóng chǎng*), five km from Lishan; and Heaven's Pool (*tiān chí*), 12 km from Lishan. Heaven's Pool is at 2590 metres, and next to the pool is a summer villa once occupied by Chiang Kaishek. To find the road leading up there, walk out of town on the highway going east (towards Hualien). Less than a km of walking brings you to a church on the left side of the road. On the right side is the road you want. The road passes the elementary school (a useful landmark) and then climbs steeply.

Places to Stay

So many tour buses arrive in Lishan at weekends and on holidays that it's a wonder the mountain doesn't collapse. Accommodation is very tight at these times, so you're definitely better off arriving on a weekday.

Cheapest in town is the *Guocheng Hotel* (☎ 5989279) (*guó chéng dà lü she*) at 54 Chungcheng Rd. Doubles without/with private bath are NT$500/700, but you can bargain that down by at least NT$100 on weekdays, even during summer.

Chungcheng Rd is the main road in town and part of the Cross-Island Highway. It's mostly lined with restaurants, but there are a few hotels, including the tattered-looking *Lishan Hotel* (☎ 5989261) (*lí shān lü shè*), which charges NT$500/800 for doubles without/with attached bath.

One block south of Chungcheng Rd and running parallel to it is Mintsu Rd, which is where most of the hotels are. Three hotels here charge NT$800 for a double with private bath: the *Guangda Hotel* (☎ 598-9216) (*guǎng dá dà lü shè*), 21 Mintsu Rd (next to the fire station)) (*Yanhualou Hotel* (☎ 5989615, 5989511) (*yàn huálóu dà lü shè*), 22 Mintsu Rd; and the *Shengxin Hotel* (☎ 5989577) (*shèng xīn dà fàn diàn*).

Getting There & Away

Lishan is easily reached by any bus going along the Cross-Island Highway between Hualien and Taichung.

From Taichung there are 13 buses daily, the first departing at 6 am and the last leaving at 2.30 pm. Most of the buses from Taichung terminate the trip in Lishan but a few continue to Hualien. The trip takes 3½ hours and costs NT$214. From Hualien, the buses cost NT$246 and leave at 7.35, 9.35, 11.05 and 11.50 am, taking 4½ hours to reach Lishan. You pay just NT$186 and save an hour if you board the bus at Fengyuan rather than Taichung.

There are three buses daily going to Lishan from the north-east coast cities of Ilan (NT$212) and Lotung (NT$213). There are also buses to Wuling Farm.

WULING FARM

(*wǔ líng nóng chǎng*) 武陵農場

Wuling Farm is a fruit-growing area, but its main attraction is to hikers who want to challenge Taiwan's second-highest peak, Hsuehshan (*xuěshān*), or 'Snow Mountain', which is 3884 metres in elevation.

Hikes

A mountain permit is supposedly required for Hsuehshan, but there is no one around to check it. It's a 10 to 12-hour climb to the summit. There are two huts along the way where you can spend the night. The first one, Chika Hut (*qī kǎ shān zhuāng*), is a two-hour hike from the trailhead and has water. The second one, Three Six Nine Hut (*sān liù jiǔ shān zhuāng*), is an additional six-hour climb and has no water. There are no facilities at the huts, so you'll need a sleeping bag, food,

stove and all the other backpacking paraphernalia.

A much easier hike would be to Yensheng
Waterfall *(yān shēng pù bù)*. It's at the top
end of the valley past the Youth Activity
Center. From there you could also climb
Peach Mountain *(táo shān)*, which has an
elevation of 3324 metres.

Places to Stay

There are three places to stay in Wuling. The
Wuling Guest House (☎ 5901183) *(wǔ líng
guó mín bīn guǎn)* is the classiest, with twins/
triples at NT$1600/1800.

The *Wuling Farm Travel Service Centre*
(☎ 5901259) *(wǔ líng nóng chǎng lü yóu fú
wù zhōng xīn)* is notably cheaper and is right
near the bus stop. Rooms cost NT$750 to
NT$1000.

Enquire at the Service Centre if you want
to stay in the campground. No equipment is
supplied so you need to bring your own.

Aside from camping, the cheapest place is
the *Wuling Mountain Hostel* (☎ 5901020)
(wǔ líng shān zhuāng), but it's a five-km hike
up the valley road from the last bus stop. The
dormitory costs NT$195 and doubles are
NT$1350.

All hotels can be full, even on weekdays,
during the summer months. On weekdays
when the kids are back in school you
shouldn't have any trouble. Weekends and
holidays are always problematic unless a
convenient typhoon blows the tour buses
away.

Places to Eat

While the *Wuling Guest House* can dish up
pricey meals, the best bet for budget travellers are the instant noodles (hot water
supplied) from the shop inside the *Wuling
Farm Travel Service Centre*.

Getting There & Away

Wuling Farm is 25 km north-east of Lishan,
just off the branch highway leading down to
the coast at Ilan. It's most easily reached by
bus from Lishan. There are six buses daily,
departing from Lishan at 8.30 and 9 am,
noon, and 1, 2 and 4.50 pm. This schedule

includes the buses going from Lishan to Ilan
and Lotung, all of which also stop at Wuling
Farm. Buses between Lishan and Wuling
Farm cost NT$47.

HOHUANSHAN

(hé huān shān) 合歡山

Hohuanshan reaches an elevation of 3416
metres and the summit is above the tree line.
The mountain lies within Taroko National
Park and is popular with students during the
summer holidays. In the morning, you can
usually witness that beautiful Taiwanese
phenomenon, the 'sea of clouds'. Climbing
parties come here to challenge nearby
Chilaishan, one of Taiwan's most dangerous
peaks.

For such a high mountain, it's unusually
accessible. Taiwan's highest road reaches the
summit. At this height it is cool even in
summer, but in winter the night temperatures
can dip well below freezing and snow is
possible. Most Taiwanese have few opportunities to see snow, so when the white stuff
falls everyone converges on the mountain. At
such times, safety becomes an issue – the icy
road is dangerous in winter and most Taiwanese drivers do not own tyre chains.

Places to Stay

There is a youth hostel (NT$200 per bed)
near where the bus drops you off in Tayuling.
Take the switchback trail up the hill to reach
the hostel. Otherwise, you'll have to walk up
a long dirt driveway. Reservations for this
hostel are usually made from the Tienhsiang
Youth Hostel (☎ 038-691111/3). The local
hostel is called *Tayuling Youth Hostel (dà yǔ
lǐng shān zhuāng)*.

An alternative is the small and obscure
Luoyin Hostel (luò yīn shān zhuāng), slightly
uphill from Tayuling on the road leading to
Hohuanshan. Tatami singles cost NT$120.

At Hohuanshan itself there is only one
place to stay, *Pine Snow Hostel* (☎ 802732)
(sōng xuě lóu). The dormitory costs NT$200
per bed and twins are NT$1200 to NT$2200.
There are no stores in or near the hostel, so

bring food, film, toilet paper, a flashlight and plenty of warm clothes.

Places to Eat

Pine Snow Hostel is the only place that has food or anything else. Prepared meals are available but only if you make a reservation in advance. You are therefore strongly advised to bring extra food unless you want to forage for nuts and berries.

Getting There & Away

Hohuanshan is reached by a side road running off the Central Cross-Island Highway. This narrow road runs between Tayuling and Wushe. One major tactical problem with visiting the peak is that there is no bus service all the way to the summit, other than tour buses. Aside from guided tours, walking, hitching or driving your own vehicle are the only options. Opportunities for hitching are good in summer, poor in winter and risky during snowstorms.

North Side Tayuling is right on the Central Cross-Island Highway, and this is the nearest bus stop for Hohuanshan. From Tayuling it's a steep nine-km walk, four hours uphill or three hours downhill.

South Side From Puli, you can get a bus to Tsuifeng (*cùi fēng*; elevation 2375 metres) and from there it's 15 km, or about 6½ hours of walking. The bus leaves Puli from the Nantou Bus Company Station (*nán tóu kè yùn zhàn*). There are no taxis in Tsuifeng, nor is there a place to stay unless you camp out. The nearest place that has accommodation is Chingching Farm, but Wushe has a youth hostel and is a better option for budget travellers. The bus from Puli passes through Wushe and Chingching Farm, and terminates in Tsuifeng. Start early because the weather is usually clearest in the morning.

TIENHSIANG
(*tiān xiáng*) 天祥

Tienhsiang is a resort town nestled between towering cliffs at the upper end of Taroko

Gorge, Taiwan's top scenic drawcard. The gorge is 19 km long with a rushing white-water river surrounded by sheer cliffs. The road – which is the eastern end of the Central Cross-Island Highway – was carved out of the cliffs at a cost of US$11 million and some 450 lives.

Things to See
Taroko Gorge (*tài lǔ gé*) The best way to see the gorge is to walk down from Tienhsiang to the Eternal Spring Shrine at the bottom of the gorge. The walk takes about four hours and it's best to hike in the morning when rain is least likely. There are no stores in the gorge, so be prepared to be self-sufficient. It's best not to go on Sunday or holidays, since the number of cars on the road will be much greater at those times.

Eternal Spring Shrine (*cháng chūn cí*) A short distance inside the entrance at the lower (eastern) end of the gorge is the Eternal Spring Shrine, which features a pavilion with a waterfall passing through it. The shrine is reached by hiking up a short hill from the highway. It was built in memory of those who lost their lives while constructing the highway.

Tunnel Hike If you walk exactly one km uphill from Tienhsiang on the main highway, on your left you will find a tunnel with a red gate. The gate is too small to permit motor vehicles to enter but a hiker can easily squeeze through. This is your gateway to a really interesting hike, but you'll need a torch, mosquito repellent and a plastic bag to protect your camera. A raincoat or umbrella wouldn't hurt either because you'll be walking through many tunnels with 'rain' inside. Just follow the road – you can't get lost – and walk for about six km. The destination is an impressive waterfall which cascades over the road.

Wenshan Hot Springs (*wén shān wēn quán*) About three km up the main highway is Wenshan Hot Springs at 575 metres above sea level. You can reach the springs by taking

TAIWAN

a bus or by hiking. The bus stops in front of a national park police station. Get off there and continue walking up the road for 400 metres. Before you enter the first tunnel up from Tienhsiang, there are some steps leading down to the river. Walk down, then cross the suspension bridge and go down a path on the other side to reach the hot springs.

Places to Stay

This resort is extremely popular, so hotel space can be a problem at times. It's best to ring up first.

The *Catholic Hostel* (☎ 691122) *(tiān zhǔ táng)*, on a hill just above the parking area, costs NT$100 in the dormitory and NT$800 for a double.

Continuing up the same hill just a little farther will bring you to a gleaming white building which is the *Tienhsiang Youth Activity Centre* (☎ 691111/3) *(tiān xiáng huó dòng zhōng xìn)*, a government-run place that has dormitory beds. Dorm beds/doubles are NT$200/800.

Getting There & Away

If you're coming from the west side of Taiwan over the Central Cross-Island Highway, you can stop in Tienhsiang.

The local bus between Hualien and Tienhsiang costs NT$68 one way. The bus schedule is a confused mess because there are two bus companies. The Hualien Bus Company officially only has buses to Tienhsiang at 6.50, 11.45 am and 1.15 pm. However, a number of long-distance buses operated by the Taiwan Bus Company pass through Tienhsiang. An important one is the 4.30 pm bus, your only hope of getting to the gorge in the late afternoon. The last bus returning to Hualien leaves Tienhsiang at 5 pm.

There are several tour buses from Hualien going to the gorge, all of which start out in the morning. They stop often so you can admire the scenery while the Chinese tourists take pictures of each other standing in front of the bus. There is a lunch stop before the tour concludes and then you will travel back to Hualien. The total cost is NT$500, lunch included.

Motorbikes can be rented near the Hualien railway station.

HUALIEN
(huā lián) 花蓮

The largest city on the east coast, Hualien is a pleasant place that sees a fair bit of tourist traffic. Actually, Hualien itself is not the main attraction in the area, but rather the nearby Taroko Gorge. You'll probably have to spend one night in Hualien if you're going to visit the gorge.

Activities

Whitewater rafting on the Hsiukuluan River south of Hualien is a popular pastime during summer. If you sign up for a tour, all transport, food and equipment is provided. For details, contact Hualien Travel Service (☎ 325108), 137 Chungshan Rd. Costs are around NT$1000.

Places to Stay

For budget travellers, the best bargain in town is the *Teachers' Hostel* (☎ 325880) *(jiào shī huì guǎn)*, 10 Kungcheng St, where dorm beds cost NT$150. Although theoretically just for teachers, others are welcome to stay.

Another cheap dormitory is the *Hualien Student Hostel* (☎ 324124) *(huā lián xué yuàn)* at 40-11 Kungyuan Rd. Beds are NT$150.

The *Daxin Hotel* (☎ 322125) *(dà xìn dà lü shè)* at 101 Chungshan Rd is one of my favourites because of the extremely friendly management. Rooms are clean and have air-con. Doubles with private bath cost NT$500 to NT$600.

Getting There & Away

Air Getting to Hualien by air takes 40 minutes from Taipei's Sungshan Domestic Airport. Flights are also available from Kaohsiung.

Bus There is no direct bus between Taipei

and Hualien. First you must get to the town of Suao and then take the bus down the spectacular Suao to Hualien Highway. From Suao to Hualien there is only one bus daily at 2.30 pm. Going in the opposite direction, the bus to Suao departs from Hualien at 6.30 am. The trip takes three hours and costs NT$137.

Buses to Taichung leave Hualien at 7.35, 9.35 and 11.05 am. From Taichung, buses to Hualien leave at 7, 8 and 9.30 am.

Buses between Taitung and Hualien run in both directions about once every hour from 6.30 am until 7 pm. Buses departing from Taitung at 7.30 am and 2.30 pm follow the coastal route. Going in the opposite direction, buses leaving Hualien at 8.10 am and 2.30 pm also follow the coastal road. The others all take the inland highway.

Train As the trip to Hualien is popular, it's best to book your train ticket a couple of days in advance. On this route, avoid the 4th class trains which don't have air-conditioning. The trains spend a lot of time going through tunnels, which makes them very noisy and dirty when the windows are open.

TAITUNG
(tái dōng) 台東
The last major population centre down the east coast, Taitung is the jumping-off point for the trip to Lanyu.

Things to See
Dragon Phoenix Temple *(lóng fèng fó gōng)* In Taitung itself, the main attraction is the Dragon Phoenix Temple, which is on a hill less than 10 minutes by foot from the main bus station.

Beaches About 10 minutes' walk from the centre is a beach at the end of Tatung Rd. It's pretty, but a little dangerous for swimming. The land seems to drop straight down here.

North of town there is an excellent beach, Shanyuan *(shān yuán hǎi shuǐ yù chǎng)*, which can be reached by bus or rented motorcycle. There is an NT$50 admission charge.

Hsiao Yehliu *(xiǎo yěliǔ)* is just north of Fukang harbour, about eight km by road north of Taitung. The scenery is great, but it's rocky and the surf is too rough to allow safe swimming.

Places to Stay
All the places listed here are within one block of the bus or train station in central Taitung.

Bottom of the barrel is the *Renai Hotel* (☎ 322423) *(rén ài lü shè)*, directly behind the bus station. All rooms are depressing boxes; singles are NT$180 with fan or NT$500 with air-conditioning. It's hardly worth the price.

The *Quan Cheng Hotel* (☎ 322611) *(quán chéng lü shè)* at 52 Hsinsheng Rd is NT$300/400 for singles/doubles. The *Dongbin Hotel* (☎ 322222) *(dōng bīn lü shè)* at 536 Chunghua Rd, Section 1, has doubles for NT$400. The *Hotel Jin An* (☎ 331168, 322368) *(jīn ān lü shè)*, 96 Hsinsheng Rd, has doubles for NT$500.

Getting There & Away
Air Flights connect Taitung to Green Island, Kaohsiung, Lanyu, Taichung and Taipei. The airline booking offices are as follows:

Far Eastern Airlines, 241 Hsinsheng Rd (☎ 326107)
Formosa Airlines, 380 Chungshan Rd (☎ 326677)
Makung Airlines, 268 Hsinsheng Rd (☎ 346422)
Taiwan Airlines, 86 Hsingsheng Rd (☎ 327061)

Bus It takes about four hours by express bus along the coastal highway to get from Hualien to Taitung.

There are plenty of buses connecting Taitung with Kaohsiung on the west coast, a four-hour journey. This same bus also stops at Fengkang, where you can change buses to go to Kenting.

Train From Taipei there is a frequent train service direct to Taitung via Hualien. The fastest trains take over five hours.

It takes about three hours to travel by rail between Taitung and Kaohsiung. Tickets cost NT$314 in 1st class, NT$253 in 2nd.

TAIWAN

TAIWAN

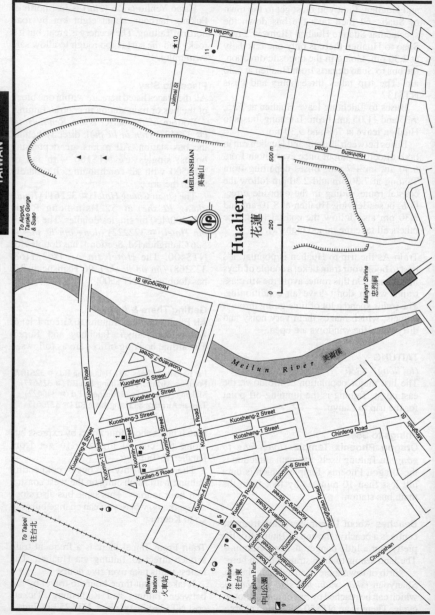

To Airport,
Taroko Gorge
& Suao

To Taipei
往台北

Railway
Station
火車站

To Taitung
往台東

Chungshan Park
中山公園

MEILUNSHAN
美崙山

Hualien
花蓮

Meilun River 美崙溪

Martyrs' Shrine
忠烈祠

Fuchien Rd

Jiahne St

Hsinhsing
Road

Hsiangchih St

Kuosheng-7 Street
Kuosheng-5 Street
Kuosheng-4 Street
Kuosheng-3 Street
Kuosheng-2 Street
Kuosheng-1 Street

Kuoshing Road
Kuomin-8 Street
Kuomin-9 Street
Kuomin-12 Street
Kuolien-4 Road
Kuolien-5 Road
Kuomin-6 Street

Kuolien-8 Street
Kuosheng-8 Street

Chinfeng Road

Meghan St

Shangsiao Road

Chungshan

Kuolien-5 St
Kuolien-3 Street
Kuolien-2 Street
Kuomin-5 St
Kuolien-3
Kuomin-3
Kuolien-1 Street
Kuomin-1 Street
Kuomin-2 Street
Kuolien-1 Road

500 m
250
0

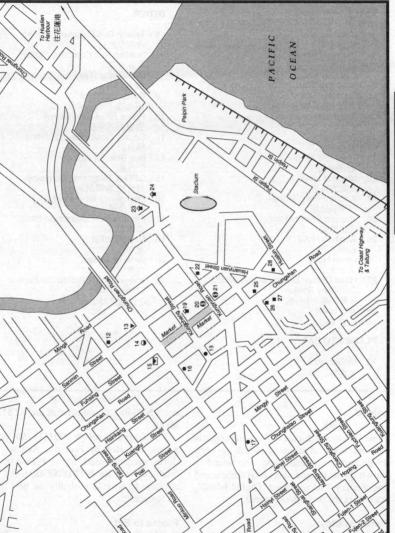

PLACES TO STAY

1 Hotel Royal
   老爺賓館
2 Dongjing Hotel
   東京賓館
3 Seaview Hotel
   海賓大飯店
5 Qingye Hotel
   青葉大飯店
8 Chan Tai Hotel
   仟台大飯店
12 Toyo Hotel
   東洋大飯店
19 Teachers' Hostel
   教師會館
22 Marshal Hotel
   統帥大飯店
23 Armed Forces Hostel
   國軍英雄館
24 Hualien Student Hostel
   花蓮學苑
25 Wuzhou Hotel
   五洲大旅社
26 Daxin Hotel
   大新大旅社
27 Hotel Golden Dragon & Hualien Bus
   Company Station
   花蓮客運中心站
28 Jinri Hotel
   今日大飯店

PLACES TO EAT

13 McDonald's
   麥當勞

OTHER

4 Taiwan Bus Company Station
   台汽客運站
6 Hualien Bus Company Station
   花蓮客運站
7 Motorcycle Hire
   機車出租
9 Swimming Pool
   游泳池
10 Police (Visa Extensions)
   警察局外事課
11 County Government Building
   縣政府
14 Bus Stop for Taitung
   往台東巴士
15 GPO & Telephone Company
   郵政總局/電信局
16 Zhongyuan Bookstore
   中原書局
17 Far Eastern Department Store
   遠東百貨
18 Night Market
   夜市
20 Bank of Taiwan
   台灣銀行
21 International Commercial Bank of
   China (ICBC)
   中國國際商業銀行

LANYU

(lán yǔ) 蘭嶼

Some 62 km south-east of Taiwan proper is the tropical island of Lanyu, which has been designated a national park. The island is known for its unique aboriginal culture and fine scenery. Lanyu means 'Orchid Island', but in fact the orchids are scarce.

Places to Stay

There are two hotels on the island, both charging high prices. Alternatively, you can sleep in a school, but ask first. Camping is another possibility.

The *Orchid Hotel* (☎ 325338) *(lán yǔ dà fàn diàn)* in Kaiyuan village is operated by Taiwan Airlines. Dormitory accommodation costs NT$400; doubles/twins are NT$1200/2000.

The *Lanyu Hotel* (☎ 732111) *(lán yǔ bié guǎn)*, operated by Formosa Airlines, has dorm accommodation for NT$400, and doubles/twins for NT$1800/3000. It's also adjacent to what is probably the best beach on the island.

Places to Eat

Food in Lanyu is available at the two hotels listed above but is expensive. There are a couple of cheaper noodle shops near the hotels and some closet-sized grocery stores.

Getting There & Away

Air Formosa Airlines and Taiwan Airlines fly

small aircraft between Taitung and Lanyu. Each airline also flies once daily between Lanyu and Kaohsiung. You can book these tickets at their offices right next to the Taitung bus station.

Boat It's possible to reach Lanyu by cargo ship from Taitung via Green Island, but this is slow, unreliable and not very comfortable. Enquire at the Lanyu Shipping Agency (☎ 310815) *(tái dōng xiàn lún chuán guǎn lǐ chù)*, 306 Po'ai Rd. The fare to Lanyu is NT$348. Departures are usually twice weekly, on Saturday and Tuesday, from Fukang at some indefinite time between 3 and 7 am. The ship is periodically taken out of service for maintenance. The journey to Lanyu takes five hours, and four hours to return to Taitung. You get a free stop off along the way at Green Island because the boat needs to unload cargo.

Getting Around

Walking is great for those who have the time and energy, but the island really is large and many travellers opt for motorised transport. Motorcycles are available for rent from the hotels for NT$500 per day.

A bus goes around the island four times daily, twice in a clockwise direction and twice anticlockwise. The last bus makes a run between 3.30 and 4.30 pm.

The two hotels occasionally run a touring minibus around the island if they can get enough passengers.

KENTING

(kěn dīng) 墾丁

Situated on a bay just a few km from Taiwan's southernmost tip, Kenting has the best beaches on the island. Although there is a chilly wind in winter, it is just warm enough for year-round bathing. It gets really crowded in summer – avoid Kenting on weekends when jet-ski gorillas take over the beaches. At other times, it's one of the most relaxing places in Taiwan.

Places to Stay

It's easy to find accommodation in Kenting, except at weekends and on holidays. If you arrive during the week you can book into a room, but be warned that some places will ask you to leave on Saturday because another group has booked and paid for all the rooms in advance. Weekend prices may double, if you can get a room at all. On weekends, you might be forced to stay in Hengchun, a less attractive town nine km to the north.

The *Kenting Youth Activity Centre* (☎ 8861221) *(qīng nián huó dòng zhōng xīn)* is a government-operated place that has dorms. However, it's expensive for what you get – dorm beds cost NT$300.

There are three cheap hotels right in a row in the central part of Kenting. One of these is the *Foremost Hotel* (☎ 8861007) *(fú lè bié guǎn)*, with singles/doubles for NT$400/600. As you face the Foremost, immediately to the right is the *Meixie Hotel* (☎ 8861176) *(měi xié bié guǎn)*, where prices are exactly the same. On the left side of the Foremost is the *Hongbin Hotel* (☎ 8861003) *(hóng bīn lü shè)*, where singles/doubles cost NT$500/600 during weekdays.

Just a little to the east of the Foremost, Meixie and Hongbin hotels is the *Herng Chang Hotel* (☎ 8861531) *(héng chāng bīn guǎn)*, a modern-looking hotel with doubles for NT$600.

Getting There & Away

Some buses go directly to Kenting, but if you can't catch one of these, then go to Hengchun, nine km north of Kenting. Shuttle buses connecting Hengchun with Kenting run about every 40 minutes between 8 am and 6 pm.

For travel to Taitung, Fengkang *(fēng gǎng)* is the crucial bus-transfer point. All buses on the Kaohsiung-Taitung or Kaohsiung-Hengchun route stop in Fengkang.

There are frequent buses from the Kaohsiung main bus station to Hengchun and/or Kenting.

Getting Around

There are plenty of bicycles for hire in

TAIWAN

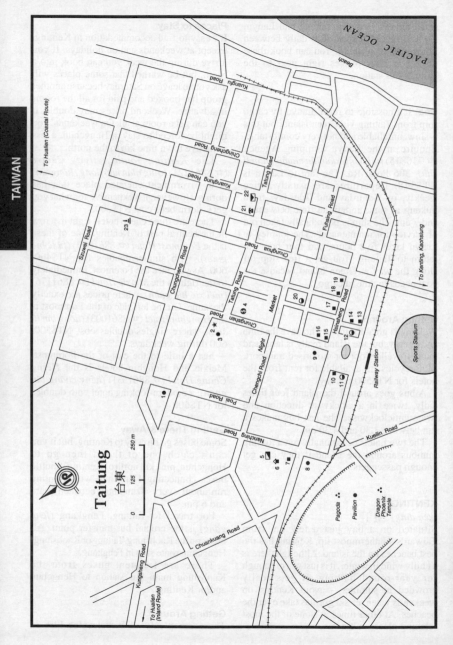

Taitung
台東

0   125   250 m

To Hualien (Inland Route)
To Hualien (Coastal Route)

Kungshang Road
Chuankuang Road
Kueilin Road
Nanching Road
Poai Road
Chengchi Road
Tatung Road
Market
Night
Chungshan Road
Chungcheng Road
Szuwei Road
Kwanghua Road
Kwangfung Road
Chingcheng Road
Kwangtu Road

Tatung Road
Fuhsing Road
Hsinsheng Road

Railway Station
Sports Stadium

To Kenting, Kaohsiung
To Hualien (Coastal Route)

PACIFIC OCEAN
Beach

Pagoda
Pavilion
Dragon
Phoenix
Temple

1
2
3
4
5
6
7
8
9
10
11
12
13
14
15
16
17
18
19
20
21
22
23

TAIWAN

PLACES TO STAY

6 Teachers' Hostel
    公教會館
7 Air Park Hotel & Makung Airlines
    馬公航空
10 Hotel Zeus & Far Eastern Airlines
    興東園大飯店
13 Lenya Hotel
    聯亞大飯店
14 Renai Hotel
    仁愛旅社
15 Hsin Hsin Hotel
    新新大旅社
16 Hotel Hsin-Fu-Chih
    新福治大旅社
17 Hotel Jin An & Taiwan Airlines
    金安旅社
18 Quan Cheng Hostel
    全成旅社
19 Dongbin Hotel
    東賓旅社

OTHER

1 Lanyu Shipping Office
    台東縣輪船管理處
2 Police (Visa Extensions)
    警察局外事課
3 City Hall
    市政府
4 Bank of Taiwan
    台灣銀行
5 Swimming Pool
    游泳池
8 Tungnung Supermarket
    東農超級市場
9 Formosa Airlines
    永興航空
11 Coastal Bus Station
    鼎東客運海線總站
12 Long-Distance Bus Station
    台汽客運站
20 Inland Bus Station
    (to Chihpen Hot Springs)
    鼎東客運山線總站
21 Telephone Company
    電信局
22 GPO
    郵政總局
23 Tienhou Temple
    天后宮

Kenting and you'll have no trouble finding a rental shop. A bike costs about NT$100 for eight hours.

If pedalling seems like too much work, you can hire motorcycles and 4WD jeeps all over Kenting. You won't have any trouble finding a rental place – you'll have to climb over the vehicles just to get into some of the restaurants and hotels. For a motorcycle, prices are NT$100 per hour, NT$300 for four hours, NT$500 for eight hours or NT$600 for 24 hours. Most of the bikes are 125 cc – if you don't have a Taiwanese or international licence, you might have to hire a 50 cc model (which requires no licence).

CHIAYI
(jiā yì) 嘉義
A small city in the centre of Taiwan, Chiayi is the departure point for journeys into Taiwan's high mountains, especially the trip to Alishan.

Places to Stay
The cheapest place in town is the *Penglai Hotel* (☎ 2272366) *(péng lái lǚ shè)*, 534 Jenai Rd, where dumpy/pleasant rooms cost NT$150/300.

Yongxing Hotel (☎ 2278246) *(yǒng xīng dà lǚ shè)*, 710 Chungcheng Rd, was second cheapest at NT$400, but try bargaining. I had the distinct impression that there was much discussion going on in Taiwanese about how much they should charge the foreign devil.

Jiaxin Hotel (☎ 2222280) *(jiā xīn dà fàn diàn)*, 687 Chungcheng Rd, is very nice and has doubles for NT$500 and NT$600. On the other side of the street is *Tongyi Hotel* (☎ 2252685) *(tǒng yī dà fàn diàn)*, 720 Chungcheng Rd, where doubles are NT$550 to NT$650.

The *Kowloon Hotel* (☎ 2254300) *(jiǔ lóng dà fàn diàn)*, 595 Kuangtsai St, is excellent value at NT$580/900 for doubles/twins.

Places to Eat
Eating places are ubiquitous, but an area that deserves special mention is the *night market* on Wenhua Rd, near the Chungshan Rd roundabout. The area is active in the daytime too, but at night it really comes to life.

The *Chetou Noodle Shop* at 542 Jenai Rd

TAIWAN

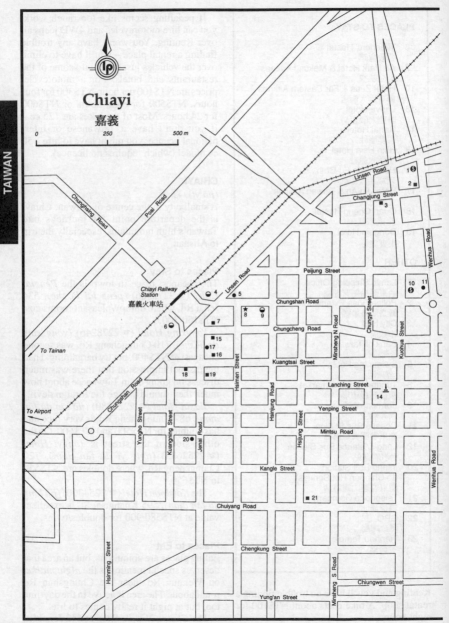

Chiayi
嘉義

0   250   500 m

TAIWAN

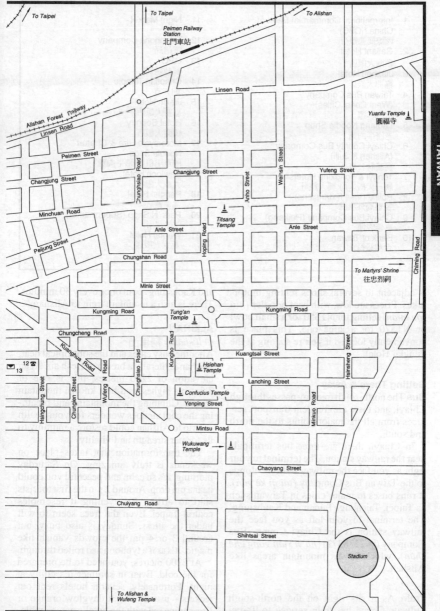

To Taipei

To Taipei

To Alishan

Peimen Railway Station
北門車站

Linsen Road

Yuanfu Temple
圓福寺

Alishan Forest Railway

Linsen Road

Peimen Street

Changjung Street

Changjung Street

Yufeng Street

Minchuan Road

Peijung Street

Chunghsiao Road

Anho Street

Weishin Street

Titsang Temple

Anle Street

Hoping Road

Anle Street

Chungshan Road

To Martyrs' Shrine
往忠烈祠

Chiming Road

Minie Street

Tung'an Temple

Kungming Road

Kungming Road

Chungcheng Road

Kuanghua Road

Wufeng N Road

Chunghsiao Road

Kungho Road

Kuangtsai Street

Hsinsheng Street

12 ☎
13

Hsingchung Street

Chungjen Street

Hsiehan Temple

Lanching Street

Confucius Temple

Minkuo Road

Yenping Street

Mintsu Road

Wukuwang Temple

Chaoyang Street

Chuiyang Road

Shihtsai Street

Stadium

To Alishan &
Wufeng Temple

TAIWAN

1	International Commercial Bank of China (ICBC) 國際商業銀行	11	Night Market 夜市
2	Gallant Hotel 嘉南大飯店	12	Telephone Company 電信局
3	Jiazhou Hotel 嘉洲大飯店	13	GPO 郵政總局
4	Taiwan Bus Company (West Coast Cities) 台汽客運	14	Chaotian Temple 朝天宮
5	Laotang Noodle Shop 老唐牛肉麵	15	Jiaxin Hotel 嘉新大飯店
6	Chiayi County Bus Company (Alishan & Juili) 嘉義縣公車站	16	Hotel Country 國園大飯店
7	Tongyi & Yongxing Hotels 統一大飯店/永興大旅社	17	Motorcycle Hire & Chetou Noodle Shop 機車出租/車頭牛肉麵
8	Police (Visa Extensions) 警察局外事課	18	Kowloon Hotel 九龍大飯店
9	Chiayi Bus Company (Peikang) 嘉義客運	19	Penglai Hotel 蓬萊旅社
10	Bank of Taiwan 台灣銀行	20	Park 'N Shop (Supermarket) 百佳超市
		21	Wantai Hotel 萬太大飯店

is adjacent to several shops renting motor-bikes. Prices are low, with beef noodles *(niú ròu miàn)* selling for NT$50 for a small bowl or NT$70 for a large one. This place is conveniently located if you're staying at the Penglai Hotel.

Getting There & Away

Bus The north-south freeway passes through Chiayi, and there are frequent transport services from all the major points to the north and south.

In Chiayi, there are three bus terminals near the railway station. The terminal to your right as you face the railway station belongs to the Taiwan Bus Company *(tái qì kè yùn)*. It runs buses to major cities in Taiwan such as Taipei, Taichung, Tainan and Kaohsiung. The terminal to your left as you face the railway station is the Chiayi County Bus Company (☎ 2238372) *(jiā yì xiàn gōng chē zhàn)*, which serves mountain areas like Alishan.

Train As it sits right on the north-south railway, Chiayi has train service to Taipei and Kaohsiung about once every 30 minutes. There is also a mountain train to Alishan.

ALISHAN
(ā lǐ shān) 阿里山

After the busy cities and the subtropical heat, Alishan is literally a breath of fresh air. At an elevation of 2200 metres, this is one of Taiwan's highest and best known mountain resorts. Climbing the mountains and breathing the cool air does wonders for your health – a trip to Alishan could restore a mummy to its former strength and vitality.

The transformation that takes place on weekends is truly amazing. On Saturday morning, it's so calm and peaceful you could hear a pin drop. Around 2 pm the first tourists start to arrive. By evening it resembles central Taipei. Even the trees seem to wilt under the stress. Sunday is also busy, but around 3 or 4 pm the crowds vanish like magic. It's as if a typhoon had rolled through.

At 2200 metres, you need to be prepared for the cold. Even in summer it's chilly at night. Fortunately, several hotels rent out jackets – usually bright dayglow orange or fire-engine red with the hotel's name emblazoned in big letters on the back. This is to ensure that you don't decide to take the jacket home.

There is a NT$90 charge to enter the Alishan Forest Recreation Area, but half-price for people shorter than 145 cm (no kidding).

Things to See & Do

Alishan Loop Hike The most popular hike is an easy walk going in a loop past the Two Sisters Pond, an elementary school, the Alishan Giant Tree and a museum. You can also stroll up to the summit of Chushan, which is very tranquil at any time other than the dawn rush hour.

Sunrise at Chushan The dawn trek to Chushan (Celebration Mountain) is religiously performed by virtually everybody who comes to Alishan. In fact, it's almost mandatory. Hotels typically wake up all their guests around 3 to 4 am so that they can stumble out of bed and begin the hour-long pilgrimage up the mountain. Bring warm clothes and a torch (flashlight). There are minibuses and a train for those who can't handle the hike. The minibuses depart from the main parking area and also from Alishan House. The train departs from the main Alishan station and also makes a stop at the Chaoping station near Alishan House. The departure time is about 45 minutes before sunrise – in summer, that's around 4.30 am. The one-way fare is NT$50 and the trip takes 30 minutes.

Monkey Rock After sunrise, the next event of the day is the train ride out to Monkey Rock *(shí hóu)*, eight km farther into the mountains. Monkey Rock itself is just a rock – it's the nine-km train ride out there on a steam locomotive that interests the tourists, and the views of the valleys below are impressive. The price is rather high for the short distance – NT$100 one way or NT$160 return, but there is a slight discount for students.

The train goes there twice a day, departing from Alishan at 9 am and 1.30 pm. Return from Monkey Rock is at 10.40 am and 3.10 pm.

Yushan At 3952 metres, Yushan (Jade Mountain) is Taiwan's highest peak. It's higher than Japan's Mt Fuji and not nearly as crowded. Unfortunately, a class A mountain permit is required to climb Yushan. This has to be arranged through a mountain club, such as the ROC Alpine Association (☎ 591-1498), 10th floor, 185 Chungshan N Rd, Section 2, Taipei.

Places to Stay

There seems to be no middle ground – either you camp out, stay in a tatami closet or pay through the nose for luxury. There is no official camping area but if you roll out a sleeping bag in the forest where it's not conspicuous, no one is likely to hassle you. It often rains at night.

Many travellers like the *Catholic Hostel* (☎ 2679602) *(tiān zhǔ jiào táng)*, which has dorm beds for NT$250 and doubles for NT$1200. It's at the lower end of the village, just past the entrance gate on the north side of the road.

The area just to the north of the bus station is home to Alishan's main cluster of hotels. *Kaofeng Hotel* (☎ 2679739) *(gāo fēng dà fàn diàn)* has tatami dormitories for NT$300 per person. The tatami rooms come in closet size for two people or larger four-person style. Double rooms with shared bath cost from NT$800 or NT$1200 with private bath. A sign in the lobby says 'Jocker for Rent' – could they mean 'Jacket'?

Near the Kaofeng Hotel is the *Shenmu Hotel* (☎ 2679666) *(shén mù bīn guǎn)*. The lowest-priced tatami with shared bath can be had for NT$300, but it's like pulling teeth – you have to negotiate. The upmarket rooms are the same as elsewhere in Alishan – NT$1200 and up.

Getting There & Away

Bus Chiayi to Alishan by road is 79 km and buses cost NT$139. The travelling time is 2½ hours going uphill, two hours coming down.

On weekdays, buses leave Chiayi at 7, 10 am and 1 pm; on weekends there are additional departures at 8.30 am and 3 pm. Buses depart from Alishan for Chiayi at 10 am and 2 and 4 pm on weekdays; weekends have additional buses at 8.30 am and noon.

From Taipei, there is one morning express bus to Alishan that departs at 8.30 am. Going the other way, the bus leaves Alishan at 9.30 am. The fare is NT$372. There are more buses on weekends and holidays, so ask.

From Kaohsiung there is a daily bus that stops in Tainan along the way. It departs from Kaohsiung at 7.20 am. From Alishan, a daily bus to Kaohsiung and Tainan leaves at 1.45 pm. One additional bus runs on weekends. The fare to Kaohsiung is NT$238, or NT$205 to Tainan.

From Taichung, daily departures are at 8 am. An additional bus departs at 11 am on holidays. From Alishan to Taichung, daily departures are at 1 pm, with an additional bus at 9.30 am on weekends. The bus makes a stop in Changhua. The Taichung-Alishan fare is NT$244; Changhua-Alishan costs NT$209.

Train The narrow-gauge railway is an interesting way to arrive or depart, but it's not cheap. The one-way fare is NT$367 for 1st class, NT$346 for 2nd class and NT$289 for 3rd class.

The 1st-class train *does not* stop at Chiayi station – you have to catch it at Peimen, a few km to the north (take a taxi). The 3rd-class train is a local and it stops at every station along the route. The train schedule at the time of writing was:

Uphill

	Chiayi	Peimen	Fenchihu	Alishan
1st class		9.30 am	11.21 am	12.35 pm
2nd class	12.30 pm	12.37 pm	2.28 pm	3.42 pm
3rd class	1.30 pm	1.37 pm	3.37 pm	4.55 pm

Downhill

	Alishan	Fenchihu	Peimen	Chiayi
1st class	9.25 am	10.41 am	12.30 pm	
3rd class	1.10 pm	2.30 pm	4.30 pm	4.35 pm

Japan

The cost of travelling in Japan makes it one of the few countries in Asia that sees very few budget travellers. This is a pity, as Japan remains one of the most interesting Asian experiences, and certainly shouldn't be written off as a Westernised theme park overrun with fast-food barns and hi-tech intelligent buildings. It's true that a combination of earthquakes, internal conflict, helter-skelter modernisation and the ravages of aerial bombing during WW II has taken its toll on Japan's historical legacy. But at the same time, the Japanese, more than other Asian people, have had the will and resources to restore much of what was destroyed. Age-old cultural traditions still have their place in contemporary Japan, its festivals are among the most colourful in all

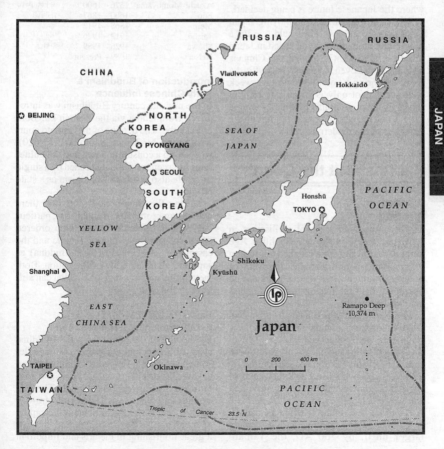

479

of Asia, and ritual visits to shrines and temples are still taken seriously.

To see something of traditional Japan, you will need to head out into the country. Check the Highlights entry of the Facts for the Visitor section later in this chapter, for ideas on everything from traditional architecture to Zen gardens. Japanese cities also have their place in any visit to Japan. The Japanese, of all Asian peoples, have been most successful at synthesising the modern world with their own traditional culture. The countryside may offer secluded pockets of history, but it is cities like Tokyo and Osaka where the Japanese future is being decided.

The final impediment to enjoying Japan is, of course, the cost. You could live for a month in China on what you spend in Japan in a week. The point is, though, that China is not Japan, and even if you can only afford a week exploring Kyoto, it would be a week well spent. Not only is Japan a rewarding travel experience, it also provides a unique insight into the whole Asian struggle with the demands of the modern world.

Facts about the Country

HISTORY
Prehistory
The first recorded signs of civilisation in Japan are found in the late Neolithic Age around 10,000 BC. This is called the Jōmon (Cord Mark) period after the discovery of pottery fragments with cord marks. The people at this time lived as fishers, hunters and food gatherers.

The Yayoi era, which dates from around 300 BC, is named after the site where pottery fragments were found near modern Tokyo. The period following the Yayoi era has been called the Kofun (Burial Mound) period by archaeologists who discovered thousands of grave mounds concentrated mostly in central and western Japan.

As more and more settlements banded together to defend their land, groups became larger until, by 300 AD, the Yamato

Kingdom had loosely unified the nation through conquest or alliance. The Yamato leaders claimed descent from the sun goddess, Amaterasu, and introduced the title of emperor (tennō) around the 5th century.

Historical Periods	Date	Kanji Script
Jōmon	10,000 – 300 BC	縄文時代
Yayoi	300 BC – 300 AD	弥生時代
Kofun	300 – 710	古墳時代
Nara	710 – 794	奈良時代
Heian	794 – 1185	平安時代
Kamakura	1185 – 1333	鎌倉時代
Muromachi	1333 – 1576	室町時代
Azuchi-Momoyama	1576 – 1600	安土桃山時代
Edo	1600 – 1867	江戸時代
Meiji	1868 – 1912	明治
Taishō	1912 – 1926	大正
Shōwa	1926 – 1989	昭和
Heisei	1989 – Present	平成

Introduction of Buddhism & Early Chinese Influence
In the mid-6th century Buddhism was introduced from China via the Korean kingdom of Paekche. The decline of the Yamato court was halted by Prince Shōtoku (573-620), who set up a constitution and laid the guidelines for a centralised state headed by a single ruler. He also instituted Buddhism as a state religion.

During the Nara period (710-794) there was strong promotion of Buddhism, particularly under Emperor Shōmu, who ordered construction of the Tōdai-ji Temple and the casting of its Daibutsu (Great Buddha) as supreme guardian deity of the nation. Both the temple and its image of Buddha can still be seen today in Nara.

Heian Period (794-1185) – Establishment of a Native Culture
By the end of the 8th century, the Buddhist clergy had become so politically meddlesome in Nara that Emperor Kammu decided to sever the ties between Buddhism and government by moving the capital. The site eventually chosen was Heian (modern-day Kyoto), and it was to continue as the capital of Japan until 1868. It was a period that saw a great flourishing in the arts and important

developments in religious thinking, as ideas and institutions imported from China adapted to the needs of their new homeland.

Kamakura Period (1185-1333) – Domination through Military Rule

After assuming the rank of *shōgun* (military leader), Minamoto Yoritomo set up his headquarters in Kamakura, while the emperor remained nominal ruler in Kyoto. It was the beginning of a long period of feudal rule by successive samurai families for Japan. In fact this feudal system was to effectively linger on until restoration of imperial power in 1868.

During this era, the popularity of Buddhism spread to all levels of society. From the late 12th century, Japanese monks returning from China introduced a new sect, Zen, the austerity of which offered a particular appeal to the samurai class.

The Mongols, under Kublai Khan, reached Korea in 1259 and sent envoys to Japan seeking Japanese submission. In response, the envoys were expelled and the Mongols reacted by sending an invasion fleet which arrived near present-day Fukuoka in 1274. This first attack was only just repulsed with a little help from a typhoon. A second invasion attempt in 1281 was thwarted by yet another typhoon. Ever since, this lucky typhoon has been known to the Japanese as the *kamikaze* (divine wind). In a vain attempt to repeat their luck, the Japanese tried using kamikaze pilots on suicide missions at the end of WW II.

Although the Kamakura government emerged victorious, it was unable to pay its soldiers and lost the support of the warrior class. Emperor Go-Daigo led an unsuccessful rebellion against the government and was exiled to the Oki Islands near Matsue, where he waited a year before trying again. The second attempt successfully toppled the government.

Muromachi Period (1336-1576) – Country at War

During this period Japan slipped steadily into civil war and chaos. Despite this, there was a flourishing of those arts now considered typically Japanese such as landscape painting, classical Nō drama, *ikebana* (flower arranging) and the *chanoyu* (tea ceremony). Many of Kyoto's famous gardens date from this period, as do such well-known monuments as the Kinkaku-ji (Golden Temple) and Ginkaku-ji (Silver Temple). Formal trade relations were reopened with Ming China and Korea, although Japanese piracy remained a bone of contention between both sides.

The Ōnin War, which broke out in 1467, developed into a full scale civil war. *Daimyō* (domain lords) and local leaders fought for power in bitter territorial disputes that were to last for a century.

Momoyama Period (1576-1600) – Return to Unity

In 1568 Oda Nobunaga, the son of a daimyō, seized power from the imperial court in Kyoto and used his military genius to initiate the process of pacification and unification in central Japan. His efforts were cut short when he was betrayed by one of his own generals, Akechi Mitsuhide, in 1582.

Nobunaga was succeeded by his ablest commander, Toyotomi Hideyoshi. Hideyoshi extended unification so that by 1590 the whole country was under his rule. He then became fascinated with grandiose schemes to invade China and Korea. The first invasion was repulsed in 1593 and the second was aborted on the death of Hideyoshi in 1598.

Edo or Tokugawa Period (1600-1867) – Peace & Seclusion

The supporters of Hideyoshi's young heir, Toyotomi Hideyori, were defeated in 1600 by his former ally, Tokugawa Ieyasu, at the battle of Sekigahara. Ieyasu set up his *bakufu* (field headquarters) at Edo, now Tokyo, and assumed the title of shōgun; the emperor and court continued to exercise purely nominal authority in Kyoto.

A strict political regime was introduced. The Tokugawa family, besides retaining large estates, also took control of major cities, ports and mines; the remainder of the country was allocated to autonomous daimyō. In descending order of importance, society consisted of the nobility, who had nominal power, the daimyō and their warriors (samurai), the farmers, and at the bottom of the list, artisans and merchants. To ensure political security the daimyō were required to make ceremonial visits to Edo every alternate year, and their wives and children were kept in permanent residence in Edo as virtual hostages of the government. This cost of the constant movement and the family ties in Edo made it difficult for the daimyō to remain anything but loyal.

Under Tokugawa rule, Japan entered a period of *sakoku* (national seclusion). Japanese were forbidden on pain of death to travel to or return from overseas or to trade abroad. However, by the turn of the 19th century, the Tokugawa government was facing stagnation and corruption. In 1853, Commodore Matthew Perry of the US Navy arrived with a squadron of 'black ships' to demand the opening of Japan to trade. Other countries moved in to demand the opening of treaty ports and relaxation of restrictions on trade barriers.

Imperial Restoration – Emergence from Isolation

The Meiji Restoration (1868-1912) marked the beginning of Japan's transition from an isolated feudal agricultural nation to one of the world's major powers. The economy underwent a crash course in Westernisation and industrialisation. An influx of Western experts was encouraged and Japanese students were sent abroad to acquire expertise in modern technologies. In 1889, Japan created a Western-style constitution.

The Taishō era (1912-26) and Emperor Hirohito's Shōwa era followed, with increased industrialisation and military confidence. Japan had been victorious over China in 1895 and Russia in 1905. During the 1930s the military increased their control and in 1937 invaded China. Then, following many years of strained relations with the USA, Japan entered WW II. The end result

of this particular venture was the tragic destruction of Hiroshima and Nagasaki by atomic weapons. It was also the first time in recorded history that Japan had been conquered. Occupation by foreign forces followed.

Post-War Reconstruction

At the end of the war the Japanese economy was in ruins and inflation rampant. A programme of recovery provided loans, restricted imports and encouraged capital investment and personal saving.

By the late '50s, trade was again flourishing and the economy continued to expand rapidly. From textiles and the manufacture of labour-intensive goods such as cameras, the Japanese 'economic miracle' has branched out into virtually every sector of economic activity. Economic recession and inflation surfaced in 1974 and again in 1980, mostly as a result of steep price hikes for imported oil on which Japan is dependent. In the early '90s, Japan, like other developed nations, underwent a period of protracted recession.

GEOGRAPHY

Japan consists of some 1000 small islands and four major ones: Honshū (slightly larger than Great Britain), Hokkaidō, Kyūshū and Shikoku. Okinawa, the largest and most significant of Japan's many smaller islands, is about halfway along an archipelago that runs almost all the way to Taiwan. It was far enough from the rest of Japan to have developed a culture that differs in many respects.

Some 85% of Japan is mountainous. Many of the mountains are volcanic, more than 40 of them presently active, blessing the islands with numerous hot springs and spectacular scenery, and at the same time bringing the danger of frequent eruptions and intense seismic activity. Indeed, Japan has the dubious distinction of being one of the most seismically active regions of the world. It is calculated that the country gets around 1000 earthquakes a year, most of them too small to notice without sophisticated seismic equipment. This seismic activity is particularly concentrated in the Kantō region, in which Tokyo is situated.

CLIMATE

The combination of Japan's mountainous territory and the length of the archipelago (covering 22° of latitude) makes for a complex climate. There are big climatic differences between Hokkaidō in the north, which has short summers and long winters with heavy snowfalls, and the southern Ryūkyū Islands, which enjoy a subtropical climate. Basically, you can expect hot, humid summer weather and very cold conditions in the winter. Typhoons and torrential rain are a problem from August to October. The best times to be in Japan are spring and autumn.

GOVERNMENT

Japan's government system is similar to the British parliamentary system rather than the American presidential one. Just as the British parliament has two houses so the Japanese Diet has the lower House of Representatives and the upper House of Councillors. The party that controls the majority of seats in the Diet is the party in power and has the right to appoint the prime minister, usually the party's president. The prime minister then appoints his cabinet, usually entirely constituted of Diet members.

In terms of the mechanics of political power, until very recently, from its formation in 1955, the Liberal Democratic Party (LDP), the conservative party in Japanese politics, had been continuously in power, shaking off scandal after scandal, apparently invincible. But by 1993, the scandals had become too much even for the Japanese, apparently the most forgiving voting public a corrupt political party could wish for. In 1994 the country was into its second coalition government, an unlikely union of the LDP and the Social Democratic Party of Japan (SDPJ). The two parties have little in common – except perhaps an entrenched conservation rooted in either end of the political spectrum – and can be expected to agree on not much at all. How long the coalition lasts is subject to much speculation.

ECONOMY

Japan is widely perceived as an economic powerhouse, utterly dominating world trade and with an enormous trade surplus being used to buy up industries and real estate in Western nations. Although that view has some truth, Japan's exports account for only 9% of its gross national product, a much smaller percentage than many European nations such as the UK (18%) or Germany (27%). Also, despite the huge Japanese investments overseas, these are still much smaller than the foreign investments of many other Western nations. Britain has far more industrial investment in the USA than Japan and the biggest foreign owners of real estate in the USA are not the Japanese but the Canadians.

The huge Japanese trade surpluses are chalked up not so much by massive exports as by a low level of imports. Japanese exports are highly visible – they're predominantly in consumer durables and their success in this field have made Japanese manufacturers (from Honda to Suzuki, Sony to Sanyo, Toshiba to National) familiar names throughout the world. The major Japanese imports are oil and energy resources, which are used frugally. Despite the limited land available for agricultural use, the Japanese manage to supply a large part of their food requirements by highly efficient and intensive land use.

This said, the Japanese economy is currently facing a recession largely due to speculative borrowing during the go-go days of the late '80s. There is also widespread dissatisfaction among ordinary Japanese that there has not been enough of a flow on effect of the success of their economy. Japanese face high consumer prices and generally enjoy a lower standard of living than their counterparts in comparably affluent countries. These tensions have led to significant political changes and numerous scandals in the early '90s.

JAPAN

POPULATION & PEOPLE

Japan has a population of around 123 million people (the seventh largest in the world) and, with 75% of it concentrated in urban centres, population density is extremely high.

A notable feature of Japan's population is its ethnic and cultural homogeneity. The Japanese have ensured that only a small number of foreigners settle in their country. Inhabitants of non-Japanese origin crept over the 1% mark for the first time in 1993. The vast majority of these are Koreans.

For outsiders, Koreans are an invisible minority. Indeed, even the Japanese themselves have no way of knowing that someone is of Korean descent if he or she adopts a Japanese name. Nevertheless, Japanese-born Koreans, in some cases speaking no language other than Japanese, were only very recently released from the obligation to carry thumb-printed ID cards at all times, and still face discrimination in the work place and other aspects of their daily lives.

Other ethnic groupings are the Chinese and a wide cross section of foreigners hitching a ride on the Japanese economic juggernaut. Groups such as the Ainu, the original inhabitants of Japan, have been reduced to very small numbers and are today found almost only in reservations on Hokkaidō.

ARTS

Here at the tail end of the 20th century, even the casual visitor to Japan has to reflect that one of the most remarkable qualities of the place is the way in which, more than any other non-European nation, it has adapted so successfully to the demands of the modern world. Unlike its huge continental neighbour, China, where modernity and tradition make for irascible bedfellows, Japan has taken the whole modern experience on board, synthesised it and made it uniquely Japanese.

Music

Gagaku is the 'elegant' music of the Japanese imperial court which was derived from Chinese models. It flourished between the 8th and 12th centuries, then declined for several centuries until it became part of a revival of interest in national traditions during the Meiji period. Those with an interest in traditional music should make enquiries at the Tokyo or Kyoto Tourist Information Centre (TIC) about performances or festivals that include performances.

On the contemporary music front, Japan has the second-largest domestic record market in the world. More than any other nation in Asia, the Japanese have taken to Western music and you can meet fans of everything and everybody from Bach fugues to acid Jazz, from Ry Cooder to Iggy Pop. Even if you don't speak any Japanese, you can at least sit around with young Japanese and swap the names of bands you like.

Painting

The techniques and materials used in the early stages of Japanese painting owed much to Chinese influence. Towards the end of the Heian period, however, after contacts between Japan and China had dwindled, the emphasis on religious themes painted according to Chinese conventions gave way to a purely Japanese style of painting. Known as *yamato-e*, this style covered indigenous subjects and was frequently used in scroll paintings and on screens.

Ink paintings (*suiboku* or *sumi-e*) by Chinese Zen artists were introduced to Japan during the Muromachi period and copied by Japanese artists who produced hanging pictures (*kakemono*), scrolls (*emaki*) and decorated screens and sliding doors.

Western techniques of painting, including the use of oils, were introduced during the 16th century by the Jesuits. Japanese painters who combined Western and Japanese styles sometimes produced interesting results: portraits of Westerners thoughtfully included an oriental incline to the eyes.

The Edo period gave birth to perhaps the most famous (at least in the West) of Japan's visual arts: the *ukiyo-e* (wood-block print). In the West, the vivid colours, novel composition and flowing lines of these prints caused great excitement, sparking a vogue which a French art critic dubbed 'Japonisme'. Ukiyo-e became a key influence on Impressionist (for example, Toulouse-Lautrec, Manet and Degas) and Post-Impressionist artists.

Japanese Theatre

The two most famous Japanese theatrical traditions are kabuki and Nō. Both are fascinating, though without a great deal of prior study, don't expect to understand much of the proceedings. This is not a major problem. Both forms work well on the level of spectacle. Even native Japanese speakers have difficulty understanding the archaic Japanese used in traditional theatre, so even if you've spent the last few years diligently working on your Japanese, it probably won't be much use to you. Fortunately, some theatres in Tokyo and Kyoto (the two places that you are most likely to see kabuki or Nō) have programmes with a synopsis of the play in English, and sometimes headphones are available for a commentary in English.

The best source for details of performances is the TIC in Tokyo or Kyoto. Some local publications such as *Tour Companion* in Kyoto and *Kansai Time Out* also publish theatre information.

Like kabuki, bunraku developed in the Edo period. It is Japan's professional puppet theatre, using puppets a half to two-thirds life size operated by three puppeteers. For bunraku, the main theatres are the National Theatre in Tokyo, Gion Corner in Kyoto and the Asahiza Theatre and National Bunraku Theatre, both in Osaka.

Art & Nature

Japanese gardens aim to imitate nature as opposed to the Western emphasis on reforming it. Although the real mecca for Japanese garden enthusiasts has to be Kyoto (which has dozens to choose from), Japan's three best gardens are said to be Okayama's Kōraku-en, Kanazawa's Kenroku-en and Mito's Kairaku-en. Other cities with renowned gardens are Tokyo, Yokohama,

Nagoya, Nara, Hiroshima, Takamatsu, Kumamoto and Kagoshima.

Bonsai is the artificial dwarfing of trees or the miniaturisation of nature. *Ikebana* is the art of flower arranging; its various schools claim millions of followers throughout Japan.

CULTURE
Traditional Lifestyle

Like all modern societies, Japan is undergoing a period of great change. Many of the old clichés regarding traditional codes of Japanese behaviour do not hold true when you are mixing with young Japanese. Nevertheless, when dealing with Japanese in formal circumstances – buying a train ticket, ordering in a restaurant, visiting a home, for example – it's worth bearing in mind that the Japanese are an extremely courteous people who are bound by strong codes of polite behaviour. You will be much more successful in your dealings with the Japanese if you are considerate of these rules.

Avoiding Offence

The first thing to remember is that as a foreigner you have far more room to make social blunders than a Japanese. Japanese are on the whole extremely tolerant of the social ineptitudes of visiting *gaijin* (as foreigners are known), and even expect you to be baffled by Japanese customs. That said, there are a few definite no-nos.

Always remove your shoes before entering a private house or any tatami-matted room. In Japanese-style accommodation, such as the ryokan, you should also remove your shoes and exchange them for slippers provided before entering. Slippers used for walking around a house or a ryokan should not be worn into the toilet – there are separate slippers for this.

The Japanese bath, or *ofuro*, is something of a cultural institution. It is meant for soaking not for washing. Wash yourself with soap at the tap or shower provided and rinse off before entering the bath. Japanese baths can be *very* hot, and it is not the done thing to add cold water.

JAPAN

Japanese avoid blowing their noses in public, and generally retire to a private place to do so. However, it is not uncommon to see men urinating in public, particularly at night after a few too many beers. As in most Asian cultures, eating on the street is not the done thing, though it's unlikely to seriously offend anyone – they'll simply see it as an odd gaijin custom.

Sport

Sumō is undoubtedly the most famous of Japan's indigenous sporting traditions. The rules of the game are deceptively simple: the *higashi* (east) wrestler tries to either push his *nishi* (west) opponent out of the ring or unbalance him so that some part of his body other than his feet touches the ground. The 4.55 metre diameter *dohyō* (ring) is on a raised platform, much like a boxing ring, but there the similarity ends. Sumō matches do not go 10 rounds, they are brief and often spectacular and the ritual and build up to the brief encounter is just as important as the clash itself.

Kendō, or the 'way of the sword', is the oldest of Japan's martial arts and was favoured by the samurai to acquire skills in using swords as well as develop mental poise. *Karate* (literally 'empty hands') is a martial art of Chinese/Okinawan origins and dates back to the 14th century. It only took hold in Japan in the first half of this century, and is not considered a traditional Japanese martial art. *Aikidō* and *Jūdō* are martial arts of local origin.

RELIGION

Shintō (the native 'religion' of Japan), Buddhism (a much-travelled foreign import originating in India), Confucianism (a Chinese import that is less a religion than a code of ethics) and even Christianity all play a role in contemporary Japanese social life, and are defining in some way of the Japanese world view.

Shintō is an indigenous religion that acquired its name, 'the way of the gods', to distinguish it from Buddhism, a later import. It seems to have grown out of an awe for manifestations of nature that included the sun, water, rock formations, trees and even sounds. All such manifestations were felt to have their *kami* (god), a belief that led to a complex pantheon of gods and a rich mythology. In particularly sacred spots, shrines were erected; important to Shintō is the concept of purification before entering such sacred domains.

Shintō is a religion without a founder, without a canon; indeed it is not a religion in the sense that you could convert to it. In a sense Shintō is an expression of the Japaneseness of the Japanese. It encompasses myths of the origin of Japan and the Japanese people, beliefs and practices in local communities and the highly structured rituals associated with the imperial family. Until 1945, Shintō belief dictated that the emperor was a kami, or divine.

The most famous Shintō shrines are the Meiji-jingū and Yasukuni-jinja in Tokyo, the Ise-jingū at Ise and the Izumo Taisha at Matsue. Shrines differ in architectural styles, but follow a defined pattern. At the entrance to the shrine is the *torii* (gateway) marking the boundary of the sacred precinct. *Shimenawa*, plaited ropes, decorated with strips of white paper *(gohei)* are strung across the top of the torii. They are also wrapped around sacred rocks or trees or above the actual shrine entrance. Flanking the main path are often pairs of stone lionlike creatures called *komainu*. Usually one has its mouth open in a roar and the other has its mouth closed.

Buddhism was introduced to Japan via Korea in the 6th century. It subsequently split into numerous sects, the most famous of which is Zen. There are Buddhist temples scattered throughout the length and breadth of Japan, but particularly important Buddhist centres can be found in Kyoto, Nara and Koya-san (all in the Kansai region), and in Kamakura (near Tokyo).

LANGUAGE

It is something of a cliché that Japanese spend years studying English at school and often at university or college without even being able to string a coherent English sentence together at the end of it all. It's not reasonable to assume, even in the big cities, that there's always going to be an English speaker around when you need one. So, it's a good idea to bring a Japanese phrasebook with you or pick one up when you arrive in Japan. Lonely Planet's *Japanese Phrasebook* should cover most of your daily travel needs. There is a host of Japanese language textbooks on the market. One of the best around (though it's a bit hefty to travel with) is *Modern Japanese*, published by the *Japan Times*.

One of the biggest problems for speakers of European languages in learning Japanese is word order. To the beginner it can seem as if the Japanese think back-to-front. Fortunately, it's not all bad news. Unlike other languages in the region (Chinese, Vietnamese and Thai among others) Japanese is not tonal and the pronunciation system is fairly easy to master. In fact, with a little effort, getting together a repertoire of traveller's phrases ('Would you like a jellybaby?' etc) should be no trouble – the only problem will be understanding what people say back to you.

Pronunciation

a	as the 'a' in 'apple'
e	as the 'e' in 'get'
i	as the 'i' in 'macaroni'
o	as the 'o' in 'lot' (British pronunciation)
u	as the 'u' in 'flu'

Vowels that have a bar (or macron) over them (*ā, ē, ō, ū*) are pronounced the same as standard vowels except that the sound is held twice as long.

Consonants are generally pronounced as in English, with the following exceptions:

f	this sound is produced by pursing the lips and blowing lightly
g	as the 'g' in 'goal' at the start of a word; as the 'ng' in 'sing' in the middle of a word
r	more like an 'l' than an 'r'

Greetings & Civilities

The all-purpose title *san* is used after a name as an honorific, the equivalent of Mr, Mrs, Ms and Miss.

Good morning.
  Ohayō gozaimasu.
  お早うございます
Good afternoon.
  Konnichiwa.
  こんにちは
Good evening.
  Kombanwa.
  こんばんは
How are you?
  O-genki desuka?
  お元気ですか？
Fine. (appropriate response)
  Okagesamade.
  ええ、おかげさまで
Goodbye.
  Sayōnara.
  さようなら
See you later.
  Ja mata.
  では、また.
Please (when offering something).
  Dōzo.
  どうぞ.
Please (when asking for something).
  Onegai shimasu.
  お願いします
Thank you.
  Arigatō gozaimasu.
  ありがとうございます
Yes.
  Hai.
  はい
No.
  Iie.
  いいえ
I'm sorry.
  Gomen nasai.
  ごめんなさい／すみません
Excuse me.
  Sumimasen.
  すみません

Getting Around

How much is the fare to ...?
... made ikura desuka?
..... まで、いくらですか？

Does this train go to ...?
Kono densha wa ... e ikimasuka?
これは..... へ行きますか？

Is the next station ...?
Tsugi no eki wa ... desuka?
次の駅は..... ですか？

Will you tell me when we get to ...?
... e wa tsuite oshiete kudasaimasuka?
...... に着いたら教えてください

Where is the ... exit?
... guchi wa doko desuka?
...... 出口はどこですか？
east/west/north/south
higashi/nishi/kita/minami
東／西／北／南

bus/tram
basu/romen densha
バス／トラム
train
densha
電車
boat/ferry
bōto/ferii
ボート／フェリーボート

one-way ticket
katamichi (kippu)
片道切符
return ticket
ōfuku (kippu)
往復切符
ticket office
kippu uriba
切符売場

Entrance
Iriguchi
入口
Exit
Deguchi
出口
Toilet
Oterai/toire
お手洗い

Around Town

Where is the/a...
...wa doko desuka?
...... はどこですか？
bank
ginkō
銀行
city centre
toshi no chūshin
都市の中心/市街地
post office
yūbinkyoku
郵便局
tourist information office
kankō annai-jo
観光案内所

Accommodation

hotel
hoteru
ホテル
inn
ryokan
旅館
I don't have a reservation.
Yoyaku shite imasen.
予約はしていません
Do you have any vacancies?
Aita heya wa arimasuka?
空いた部屋はありますか？
single room
shinguru rūmu
シングルルーム
double room
daburu rūmu
ダブルルーム
room with a bath
basu tsuki no heya
バス付きの部屋

Food

restaurant
restoran
レストラン
I am vegetarian.
Watashi wa bejitarian desu.
私は菜食主義です

Do you have an English menu?
Eigo no menü ga arimasuka?
英語のメニューはありますか？
What do you recommend?
O-susume wa nan desuka?
お勧めはなんですか？
How much is it?
Ikura desuka?
いくらですか？

Numbers

0	*zero/maru*	0
1	*ichi*	一
2	*ni*	二
3	*san*	三
4	*yon/shi*	四
5	*go*	五
6	*roku*	六
7	*nana/shichi*	七
8	*hachi*	八
9	*kyū/ku*	九
10	*jū*	十
11	*jūichi*	十一
12	*jūni*	十二
13	*jūsan*	十三
14	*jūyon*	十四
20	*nijū*	二十
21	*nijūichi*	二十一
30	*sanjū*	三十
100	*hyaku*	百
200	*nihyaku*	二百
223	*nihyaku nijūsan*	二百二十三
1000	*sen*	千
5000	*gosen*	五千
10,000	*ichiman*	一万
20,000	*niman*	二万
100,000	*jūman*	十万
1,000,000	*hyakuman*	百万

Emergencies
Help me!
Tasukete!
助けて！
Watch out!
Ki o tsukete!
気をつけて！
Call the police!
Keisatsu o yonde kudasai!
警察を呼んで下さい！

Call a doctor!
Isha o yonde kudasai!
医者を呼んで下さい！
I'm allergic to antibiotics/penicillin.
Kōsei busshitsu/penishirin ni arerugii desu.
抗生物質／ペニシリンにアレルギーです

Facts for the Visitor

VISAS & EMBASSIES
Many visitors who are not planning to
engage in any remunerative activities while
in Japan are exempt from obtaining visas.
Stays of up to six months are permitted for
citizens of Austria, Germany, Ireland,
Mexico, Switzerland and the UK. Stays of
up to three months are permitted for citizens
of Argentina, Belgium, Canada, Denmark,
Finland, France, Iceland, Israel, Italy,
Malaysia, the Netherlands, New Zealand,
Norway, Singapore, Spain, Sweden, the
USA and a number of other countries.

Visitors from Australia and South Africa
are among those nationals requiring a visa.
This is usually issued free, but passport
photographs are required and a return or
onward ticket must be shown.

Anyone, and this includes tourists, who
stays more than 90 days is required to obtain
an Alien Registration Card. The card can be
obtained at the municipal office of the city,
town or ward in which you're living, but
moving to another area requires that you
re-register within 14 days.

You must carry your Alien Registration
Card (or, if you are a tourist, your passport)
at all times as the police can stop you and ask
to see the card. If you don't have the card,
you will be taken back to the police station
and will have to wait there until someone
fetches it for you.

Embassies & Consulates
Australia
    112 Empire Circuit, Yarralumla, Canberra, ACT
    2600 (☎ 06-733 244); there are also consulates
    in Brisbane (☎ 07-221 5188), Melbourne (☎ 03-
    867 3244), Perth (☎ 09-321 3455) and Sydney
    (☎ 02-231 3455).

JAPAN

Canada
        255 Sussex Drive, Ottawa, Ontario K1N 9E6
        (☎ 236 8541); there are also consulates in
        Edmonton (☎ 422 3752), Montreal (☎ 866
        3429), Toronto (☎ 363 7038), Vancouver (☎ 684
        5868) and Winnipeg (☎ 943 5554).
France
        7 Ave Hoche, 75008-Paris (☎ 1-47.66.02.22)
Germany
        Bundeskanzlerplatz, Bonn-Center HI-701, D-
        5300 Bonn 1 (☎ 0228-5001)
Hong Kong
        25th Floor, Bank of America Tower, 12 Harcourt
        Rd, Central (☎ 522 1184-8)
Ireland
        22 Ailesbury Rd, Dublin 4 (☎ 69 40 33)
Israel
        Asia House, 4 Weizman St, 64 239 Tel-Aviv
        (☎ 03-257 292)
New Zealand
        7th Floor, Norwich Insurance House, 3-11
        Hunter St, Wellington 1 (☎ 731 540); there is also
        a consulate in Auckland (☎ 34 106)
Singapore
        16 Nassim Rd, Singapore 1025 (☎ 235 8855)
Thailand
        1674 New Petchburi Rd, Bangkok 10310 (☎ 252
        6151)
UK
        43-46 Grosvenor St, London W1X OBA
        (☎ 0171-493 6030)
USA
        2520 Massachusetts Ave, NW Washington DC
        20008-2869 (☎ 939 6800); there are also consul-
        ates in Anchorage (☎ 279 8428), Atlanta (☎ 892
        2700), Boston (☎ 973 9772), Chicago (☎ 280
        0400), Honolulu (☎ 536 2226), Houston (☎ 652
        2977), Kansas City (☎ 471 0111), Los Angeles
        (☎ 624 8305), New Orleans (☎ 529 2101), New
        York (☎ 371 8222), Portland (☎ 221 1811) and
        San Francisco (☎ 777 3533)

CUSTOMS

Customs allowances include the usual
tobacco products, three 760 ml bottles of
alcoholic beverages, 57 grams of perfume,
and gifts and souvenirs up to a value of
¥200,000 or its equivalent. Liquor is not
cheap in Japan, so it's worth bringing some
for personal consumption or as a gift; there
is no possibility of reselling it for profit. The
penalties for importing drugs are very
severe, and customs officials have become
very thorough in recent years – don't even
consider it.

There are no limits on the import of
foreign or Japanese currency. The export of
foreign currency is also unlimited but a ¥5
million limit exists for Japanese currency.

MONEY

The currency in Japan is the *yen* (¥) and
banknotes and coins are easily identifiable.
There are ¥1, ¥5, ¥10, ¥50, ¥100 and ¥500
coins, ¥1000, ¥5000 and ¥10,000 banknotes.
The ¥1 coin is an aluminium lightweight, and
the ¥5 and ¥50 coins have a hole in the middle.

You can change cash or travellers'
cheques at an 'Authorised Foreign Exchange
Bank' (signs will always be displayed in
English) or at some of the large hotels and
stores. US dollars, either in travellers'
cheques or in cash, is the preferred currency,
though major European currencies will
provide no problems. Exchanging Korean or
Taiwanese currency in Japan is a fruitless
task, so avoid bringing any if you're arriving
from those countries.

Banks are open Monday to Friday from 9
am to 3 pm and closed on Saturday, Sunday
and national holidays. If you're caught cash-
less outside regular banking hours, try a large
department store or major hotel.

If you are having money sent to a bank in
Japan, make sure you know *exactly* where
the funds are going: the bank, branch and
location. Telex or telegraphic transfers are
much faster, though more expensive, than
mail transfers. A credit card cash advance is
a worthwhile alternative; American Express
transfers require a trusty friend back home.
Credit cards are becoming more widespread
in Japan, but outside major cities, cash still
reigns supreme. American Express, Visa,
MasterCard and Diners Club are the most
widely accepted international cards.

Exchange Rates

A$1	=	¥73
C$1	=	¥73
DM1	=	¥64
HK$1	=	¥13
NZ$1	=	¥60
S$1	=	¥67
UK£1	=	¥156
US$1	=	¥99

Costs

Japan is probably the most expensive country in the world to travel in at the moment, thanks to the all-powerful yen. A skeleton daily budget, assuming you stay at the cheapest places (¥2200 per night in a hostel), eat modestly (¥1500) and spend ¥1500 on short-distance travel, would be ¥5000 (US$50). Add at least ¥1000 for extras like snacks, drinks, admission fees and entertainment. More expensive accommodation costs around ¥4200 to ¥5500 for a *minshuku* (Japanese-style B&B), cheap ryokan or business hotel.

Tipping & Tax

The total absence of tipping does reduce costs a little; nobody expects a tip so it's best to keep it that way.

Bargaining

Basically, bargaining is almost unheard of in Japan. The only time it applies is in discount electrical shops, and even here it is a kind of institutionalised bargaining. A polite request will lower the price by 10-15%.

WHEN TO GO

All things considered, the ideal trip to Japan would see you in Hokkaidō and Northern Honshū during the height of summer, in southern Honshū, Kyūshū and Shikoku from late summer to early autumn and in Central Honshū during autumn. Synchronising your trip with the cherry blossom season can be tricky. For one, the blossoms are notoriously fickle, blooming any time from early April to late April. Moreover, when the blossoms do come, their moment of glory is brief, lasting generally a mere week. Still, if you're going to be travelling in Japan during April, chances are you'll come across cherry blossoms somewhere.

The extremes of the Japanese climate make travelling in either summer or winter less pleasant than at other times. The Japan Sea side of Honshū and Hokkaidō receive huge winter snowfalls and, from December to February, very cold temperatures prevail.

On the other hand, summer (June to August) can be uncomfortably humid.

WHAT TO BRING

For the serious traveller, the number one rule in Japan is much the same as anywhere else – travel light. There's nothing so useful as more space in your bag. The advantages of travelling light are even more important for rail travellers, as trains usually have little space for storing bags.

Basically, if there's anything you've forgotten, you can relax in the knowledge that you will be able to pick it up it in Japan. Medication is expensive, and it would be wise to come prepared with anything you need on this front. Oral contraceptives are not as readily available as they are in the West, and many foreign men complain about the quality of Japanese-made condoms.

TOURIST OFFICES

The Japan National Tourist Organisation (JNTO), which has both Japanese and overseas offices, produces a great deal of literature.

JNTO operates three Tourist Information Centres (TIC); one at Narita International Airport (☎ 0476-32-8711), another in the Ginza in central Tokyo (☎ 03-3350-21461) and the third near the railway station in Kyoto (☎ 075-371-5649).

TIC offices have counters for making some hotel or ryokan reservations, but cannot make transport bookings; they will, however, direct you to agencies which can, such as the Japan Travel Bureau (JTB) or the Nippon Travel Agency (NTA). TIC's Tokyo (☎ 3503-2911) and Kyoto (☎ 361-2911) offices operate 'Teletourist', a round-the-clock taped information service on current events in town. JNTO also operate Goodwill Guides, a volunteer programme with over 30,000 members who wear a blue and white badge with a dove and globe logo.

JNTO operates a nationwide toll-free phone service available from 9 am to 5 pm; seven days a week. The main aim is to provide assistance for visitors unable to get to the TIC offices in Tokyo or Kyoto. To

JAPAN

contact an English-speaking travel expert, call ☎ 0120-22-2800 for information on eastern Japan; ☎ 0120-44-4800 for western Japan. You can also use this service to help with language problems when you're stuck in a hopeless linguistic muddle.

JNTO has recently set up a network of 75 information offices with English-speaking staff. They are scattered across the country from Naha to Sapporo, and information on them is provided throughout this book. For listings of their addresses, telephone numbers and opening hours, pick up a copy of JNTO's *Tourist Information Centers & "i" Tourist Information System* ❶ pamphlet.

JNTO Offices Overseas
JNTO representation includes the following overseas offices:

Australia
  115 Pitt St, Sydney, NSW 2000 (☎ 02-232 4522)
Canada
  165 University Ave, Toronto, Ontario M5H 3B8 (☎ 416-366 7140)
France
  4-8 Rue Sainte-Anne, 75001 Paris (☎ 01-42.96.20.29)
Germany
  Kaiserstrasse 11, 6000 Frankfurt am Main 1 (☎ 069-20353)
Hong Kong
  Suite 3606, Two Exchange Square, 8 Connaught Place, Central (☎ 5255295)
South Korea
  10 Da-Dong, Chung-Ku, Seoul (☎ 02-752 7968)
Switzerland
  13 Rue de Berne, 1201 Geneva (☎ 022-731 81 40)
Thailand
  Wall Street Tower Building, 33/61, Suriwong Rd, Bangkok 10500 (☎ 02-233 5108)
UK
  167 Regent St, London W1 (☎ 0171-734 9638)
USA
  Chicago: 401 North Michigan Ave, IL 60611 (☎ 312-222 0874)
  Dallas: 2121 San Jacinto St, suite 980, LB-53, TX 75201 (☎ 214-754 1820)
  Los Angeles: 624 South Grand Ave, suite 2640, CA 90017 (☎ 213-623 1952)
  New York: Rockefeller Plaza, 630 Fifth Ave, NY 10111 (☎ 212-757 5640)
  San Francisco: 360 Post St, suite 401, CA 94108 (☎ 415-989 7140)

BUSINESS HOURS & HOLIDAYS
Shops are typically open seven days a week from around 10 am to 8 pm. Department stores close slightly earlier, usually 6.30 or 7 pm, and also close one weekday each week. If a city has several major department stores, opening hours will probably be organised so that Mitsukoshi closes on Monday, Daimaru closes on Tuesday and so on. Large companies usually work a 9 am to 5 pm five-day week, some also operate on Saturday morning. (See the Money section for banking hours earlier in this chapter and the following Post & Telecommunications section for post office hours.)

Public holidays include: New Year's Day, 1 January; Adult's Day, 15 January; National Foundation Day, 11 February; Spring Equinox, 21 March (approximately); Green Day, 29 April; Constitution Day, 3 May; Children's Day, 5 May; Respect for the Aged Day, 15 September; Autumn Equinox, 23 September (approximately); Sports Day, 10 October; Culture Day, 3 November; Labour Thanksgiving Day, 23 November; and Emperor's Birthday, 23 December.

POST & TELECOMMUNICATIONS
Postal Rates
The airmail rate for postcards is ¥70 to any overseas destination; aerograms cost ¥80. Letters weighing less than 10 grams are ¥80 to other countries within Asia, ¥100 to North America or Oceania (including Australia and New Zealand) and ¥120 to Europe, Africa and South America. Sending parcels overseas from Japan often works out 30% cheaper with Surface Airlift (SAL) and only takes a week longer.

Sending Mail
District post offices (the main post office in a *ku* (ward), are normally open from 8 am to 7 pm on weekdays, until 3 pm on Saturday and 9 am to 12.30 pm on Sunday and public holidays. Local post offices are open from 9 am to 5 pm on weekdays and until 1 pm on Saturday. Main post offices in the larger

cities may have some counters open 24 hours a day.

Receiving Mail

Although any post office will hold mail for collection, the poste restante idea is not well known and can cause confusion in smaller places. It is probably better to have mail addressed to you at a larger central post office. Letters are usually only held for 30 days before being returned to sender. When enquiring about mail for collection ask for *kyoku dome yūbin*.

Telephone

The Japanese public telephone system is very well developed; there are a great many payphones and they work almost 100% of the time. Local calls cost ¥10 for three minutes; long-distance or overseas calls require a handful of coins which are used up as the call progresses and any unused coins are returned.

Most payphones will also accept prepaid phonecards. It's much easier to buy one of these, in ¥500 and ¥1000 denominations, rather than worry about having coins to hand. The cards (readily available from vending machines, telephone company card outlets and many shops) are magnetically encoded and, after each call, a small hole is punched to show how much value remains.

Japanese telephone numbers consist of an area code plus a local code and the number. You do not dial the area code when making a call within that area.

International payphones are becoming much more common on the streets of Japan. An overseas call (paid or operator-assisted) can be made from phones with a gold sign, from grey IDD phones and from credit card phones (blue with a chrome face).To place an international call through the operator, dial 0051 – international operators all seem to speak English. To make the call yourself, simply dial 001 (KDD), 0041 (ITJ) or 0061 (IDC) (rates between these three companies vary very little), then the international country code, the local code and the number.

Another option is to dial 0039 for home country direct which takes you straight through to a local operator in the country dialled. You can then make a reverse-charge (collect) call or a credit card call with a telephone credit card valid in that country.

Dialling codes include:

Country Direct	Dial Home	Country Direct
Australia	☎ 001-6	☎ 10039-611
Canada	☎ 001-1	☎ 0039-161
Hong Kong	☎ 001-852	☎ 0039-852
Netherlands	☎ 001-31	☎ 0039-311
New Zealand	☎ 001-64	☎ 0039-641
Singapore	☎ 001 65	☎ 0039-651
Taiwan	☎ 001-886	☎ 0039-886
UK	☎ 001-44	☎ 0039-441
USA	☎ 001-1	☎ 0039-111*

*for mainland USA you can also dial ☎ 0039-121, for Hawaii you can also dial ☎ 0039-181

TIME

Despite Japan's east-west distance, the country is all on the same time, nine hours ahead of GMT/UTC. So, when it is noon in Japan, it is 3 am in London, 11 am in Hong Kong, 1 pm in Sydney, 3 pm in Auckland, 10 pm the previous day in New York, 7 pm the previous day in San Francisco and 5 pm the previous day in Honolulu. Daylight-saving time is not used in Japan. Times are all expressed on a 24-hour clock.

LAUNDRY

Laundrettes are fairly common in suburban Japan, and the odd hostel also has a washing machine.

WEIGHTS & MEASURES

Japan uses the international metric system.

ELECTRICITY

The Japanese electric current is 100 V AC, an odd voltage found almost nowhere else in the world. Furthermore, Tokyo and eastern Japan are on 50 Hz, western Japan including Nagoya, Kyoto and Osaka is on 60 Hz. Most North American electrical items, designed to run on 117 V, will function reasonably well using Japanese currents. The plugs are flat two pin, identical to US and Canadian plugs.

BOOKS

A few recent releases make for interesting reading while you are in Japan. Jonathan Rauch's *Outnation – A Search for the Soul of Japan* (Littlebrown, 1992) is an intelligent and penetrating account of his six months in Japan. Pico Iyer's *The Lady and the Monk* is an unabashed romanticisation of Japan (mainly Kyoto), but it still makes for a good read, even if you might want to balance some of his reflections with the reality of modern Japan.

Inside Japan (Penguin, 1987) by Peter Tasker, is probably the best wide-ranging introduction to modern Japanese culture, society and the economy. Richard Storey's *A History of Modern Japan* (Penguin) is a concise and consistently interesting history of modern Japan.

The Enigma of Japanese Power by Karel van Wolferen is an attack on the Japanese 'system' and a book for the finger pointers and accusers who reckon Japan got to the top by playing dirty. The bad news keeps on coming with books like *Japan – The Coming Collapse* (Orion, 1992) by Brian Reading.

Other views on the growth of Japan as an economic superpower are found in *Trading Places: How America Allowed Japan to Take the Lead* (Charles E Tuttle) by Clyde V Prestowitz Jr and *The New Masters – Can the West Match Japan?* (Hutchinson Business Books, 1990) by Phillip Oppenheim. Ezra Vogel saw it coming more than 10 years ago in *Japan as Number One: Lessons for America* (Harvard University Press, 1979). Of course, Japan has hardly reached the top before someone is foreshadowing its descent – Bill Emmott describes it in *The Sun Also Sets*.

The Japanese Today (Belknap, 1988) by Edwin O Reischauer is a recently revised standard textbook on Japanese society and a must for those planning to spend time in Japan. Ian Buruma's *A Japanese Mirror*

(Penguin) provides an interesting examination of Japanese popular culture.

For more detailed travel information on Japan look for the Lonely Planet *Japan – travel survival kit*.

MAPS

For non-Japanese speakers, Japanese mapping is surprisingly unsatisfactory; most of the vast amount of mapping material available is in Japanese only. The JNTO's free *Tourist Map of Japan* is a reasonable 1:2,000,000 map of the whole country, which is quite adequate for general route planning. However, it's difficult to find larger-scale maps of single islands or parts of islands.

The *Japan Road Atlas* (Shobunsha, Tokyo, ¥2890) covers all of Japan at 1:250,000 except for Hokkaidō, which is covered at 1:600,000. Most towns are shown in *kanji* (Japanese script) as well as *romaji* (Roman script). However, mountains, passes, lakes, rivers and so on are only shown in romaji. Locating exactly where a small town or village is on the map is sometimes difficult and places are often left off.

The Lonely Planet *Japan travel atlas* is a handy traveller's atlas in book form designed for ease of use on the road.

MEDIA
Newspapers & Magazines

In the major urban centres at least, you won't have any problem finding English-language newspapers and magazines. However, since English publications are produced in Tokyo, the farther you get from the capital, the scarcer they become.

The *Japan Times*, with its good international news section and unbiased coverage of local Japanese news, is read by most newcomers looking for work because of its employment section – the Monday edition has the most extensive listings. The *Daily Yomiuri* rates alongside the *Japan Times* in its coverage of local and international news. Other English papers include the *Mainichi Daily News* and the *Asahi Evening News*.

As for magazines, the Tokyo-based *Tokyo*

Journal is the pick of the crowd with its comprehensive what's-on listings and informative, readable articles on local cultural and topical issues. Also based in Tokyo is the very similar *Tokyo Time Out*.

Kansai Time Out, produced in the Kansai region around Osaka, has excellent information about goings-on of interest to both foreign visitors and local residents. In the Nagoya area, *Eyes* is a useful what's-on magazine.

Radio & TV

The common consensus is that Japanese radio is pretty dismal, mainly because it places far more emphasis on DJ jive than it does on music. For English-language broadcasts, the possibilities are pretty much limited to the appallingly banal US armed services' Far East Network (FEN). Even the FM stations are fairly uninspiring, although J-WAVE in Tokyo has increased the music content and cut the talk. Bring a good supply of tapes and a Walkman if music is essential to your sanity.

Like radio, most television is inaccessible to the non-Japanese speaker and, even if you do speak the language, most programmes seem to be inane variety shows. It's worth watching a few hours as a window into the culture, but it won't take long to figure out what the programmes are all about.

FILM & PHOTOGRAPHY

The Japanese are a nation of photographers. This, combined with the fact that the Japanese are major producers of camera equipment and film, means there is no problem obtaining photographic equipment or film. Costs are expensive, however, and it's worth bringing your own film and processing it overseas when you leave.

HEALTH

Japan is the safest country to travel in Asia healthwise. Food and water are perfectly safe everywhere. Medical treatment is also reliable, though it is very expensive. Medical insurance is a good idea.

Emergency services in Japan will usually only react fast if you speak Japanese. Try the Tokyo English Lifeline (TELL) (☎ 3403-7106) for emergency assistance in English. The Japan Helpline (☎ 0120-461-997) is an emergency number which operates 24 hours a day, seven days a week. Don't clog the line unless you really do have an emergency.

WOMEN TRAVELLERS

The general crime rate is very low in Japan so the risk of rape or assault is minimal. Women should take normal precautions of course, but can travel by subway at night or wander the streets of the entertainment districts (dodging the reeling salary men) with little concern.

The major concern of women travellers in many countries – 'Will I be physically safe?' – is not a worry in Japan, though jam-packed rush-hour subways or buses can bring out the worst in the Japanese male. When movement is impossible, roving hands are frequently at work and women often put up with this interference because in Japan, it would simply be impolite or unseemly to make a fuss. There's no reason why you should put up with it, however. If possible grab the hand and hold it up; *te o dokete yo!* ('get your hands off me!') or *hentai-yo!* ('pervert!') are appropriate terms of abuse that will cause your assailant considerable embarrassment.

DANGERS & ANNOYANCES

The low incidence of theft and crime in Japan is frequently commented on, though of course, theft does exist and its rarity is no reason for carelessness.

WORK

In the current economic climate, forget it. In areas like English teaching and rewriting, traditional standbys for native English speakers looking to make a few yen, the work simply doesn't exist anymore. Even highly qualified teachers have been hard put to find work over the last couple of years.

Australians, Canadians and New Zealanders between the ages of 18 and 25 (it can be pushed up to 30) are eligible for a six-month working-holiday visa. The visa can be extended twice. Work is slightly easier to come by if you have this visa, simply because it saves your employer the trouble of getting you a working visa. Bear in mind that, unless you are very lucky, finding work will still take time and living costs are *extremely* high in Japan. The more cash you bring with you, the easier it will be to get established. Don't come with less than the A$2000 stipulated by the terms of the visa.

ACTIVITIES
Hiking

Japan is a good country for hiking, and this activity has the advantage of being free. Some hiking areas, like Mt Fuji, can be very crowded during the summer season. *Hiking in Japan* by Paul Hunt (Kodansha, 1988) is a useful guide.

Skiing

With more than 300 ski resorts scattered throughout the country, skiing is a major recreational pursuit in Japan. It is expensive though, and very few budget travellers end up skiing in Japan. The peak season is from December to March, and those interested should pick up a copy of JNTO's *Skiing in Japan*, which covers 20 resorts on Honshū and Hokkaidō.

Studying

Studying Japanese in Japan is expensive, particularly if you want a student visa. If you are on a tourist visa you can look into language exchanges (swapping English for Japanese), which is usually fairly easy to organise if you ask around.

The TIC leaflet *Japanese & Japanese Studies* lists government-accredited schools that belong to the Association of International Education. Figure on spending around ¥600,000 for a year of study in one of these schools.

The Japanese language is only one of the study options available in Japan of course. Alternatives range from Zen Buddhism to Ikebana. Again the TICs in Tokyo and Kyoto

are the best sources of information for courses in more offbeat areas of interest.

HIGHLIGHTS

Japan may have few obvious highlights (with the exception of Mt Fuji, which *everyone* has heard of), but it offers visitors a wealth of sights and experiences. For a real understanding of what the country is about, don't restrict yourself to the gardens, temples, shrines and castles. Try and take a look at the modern Japanese world too.

Probably the greatest original castle is Himeji-jō, the huge and impressive 'White Egret' Castle. It's an easy day trip from Kyoto. The contrasting black Matsumoto-jō is also well preserved and in very original condition.

On the garden front (Japanese love to rate things), the 'big three' in the garden category are the Kairaku-en (Mito), the Kenroku-en (Kanazawa) and the Kōraku-en (Okayama). Despite this, you're likely to find a random sampling of the gardens in Kyoto far more satisfying than a visit to any of the above three.

For a glimpse of Japan's rural past, Takayama, north of Nagoya, has many fine old buildings and a farmhouse village (Hida Folk Village). Kanazawa, in Central Honshū, and Kurashiki, in Western Honshū, also have some fine traditional buildings.

Kyoto and Nikkō are worthwhile destinations for checking out Japan's Shintō shrines. Meiji-jingū Shrine in Tokyo and Itsukushima-jinja, with its much photographed floating torii on Miya-jima Island, are also 'must-sees'. The three best destinations for Buddhist temples are Kyoto, Nara and Kamakura (an easy day trip from Tokyo).

Some of the most spectacular mountain scenery in Japan is found in Nagano-ken (Kamikōchi; Hakuba) and northern Gifu-ken (Takayama; Shōkawa Valley region). Of course, there is also Mt Fuji itself, a bashful peak that is best seen from Hakone or the Fuji Five Lakes area, both of which are within easy striking distance of Tokyo.

Hokkaidō, the second-largest but least

densely populated island, offers wonderful mountain scenery around Lake Mashu-ko in the Daisetsuzan National Park and around Tōya-ko and Shikotsu-ko lakes in the west. The Shiretoko-hantō and Shakotan-hantō peninsulas have fine coastal scenery.

Kyūshū has some wonderful volcanic scenery, particularly in the immense caldera of Mt Aso, the bleak, volcano-studded Kirishima National Park, and rumbling Sakurajima near Kagoshima.

ACCOMMODATION

Compared to the rest of Asia, Japanese budget places make a sizeable dent in the pocket. The average cost at a youth hostel is around ¥2200.

Camping

Camping is one of the cheapest forms of accommodation but official campgrounds are often only open during the Japanese 'camping season' (July to August), when you can expect an avalanche of students. Facilities range from bare essentials to deluxe. JNTO publishes Camping in Japan, a limited selection of campgrounds with details of prices and facilities.

In some restricted areas and national parks, camping outside designated areas is forbidden, but elsewhere, foreigners have reported consistent success. Even if there is no officially designated campground, campers are often directed to the nearest large patch of grass. Provided you set up camp late in the afternoon and leave early, nobody seems to mind, though it would be common courtesy to ask permission first (assuming you can find the person responsible). Public toilets, usually spotless, and water are very common, even in remote parts of Japan.

Youth Hostels

For anyone wanting to keep to a low budget, youth hostels are the best option and it is quite feasible to plan an entire itinerary using them. Bear in mind, however, that advance reservations are essential for the New Year holiday weeks, March, the late April/early May Golden Week, and July and August. You should state the arrival date and time, number of nights, number and sex of the people for whom beds are to be reserved and the meals required. When corresponding from abroad always include two International Reply Coupons.

By far the best source of information on hostels is the (Japan) Youth Hostel Handbook available for ¥580 from the Japan Youth Hostel Association – JYHA (☎ 3269-5831), Hoken Kaikan, 1-2 Sadohara, Ichigaya, Shinjuku-ku, Tokyo 162.

Branch offices in Tokyo which stock the handbook and can supply information are in the 2nd level basement of Sogo department store, Yūrakuchō (two minutes on foot from the TIC); the 4th floor of the Keiō department store, Shinjuku; and the 7th floor of the Seibu department store, Ikebukuro. Many hostels throughout Japan also sell the handbook.

The Youth Hostel Map of Japan (approximately ¥225) is a map with one-line entries for each hostel on the reverse. JNTO publishes Youth Hostels in Japan, a concise English-language listing of youth hostels.

Hostellers are expected to check in between 3 and 8 pm. Checkout is usually required before 10 am and dormitories are closed between 10 am and 3 pm. Bath time is usually between 5 and 9 pm, dinner time is between 6 and 7.30 pm and breakfast time is between 7 and 8 am.

Gaijin Houses

This is the cheapest category of accommodation, especially for long-term stays, but you should be prepared for basic dorms or shared tatami rooms and probably a communal kitchen. Per-person costs for the cheapest houses start around ¥1600 per night. Some places offer reductions for stays longer than a month.

Most of the gaijin houses are in Tokyo and Kyoto. You can find advertisements or listings of these places in publications such as Tokyo Journal, Kansai Time Out or Kyoto Visitor's Guide. TIC offices no longer provide information on gaijin houses, after they were told by authorities that most of them are illegal.

Cycling Terminals

Saikuringu tāminaru (cycling terminals) provide low-priced accommodation of the bunk-bed or tatami-mat variety and are usually found in scenic areas suited to cycling. If you don't have your own bike, you can rent one at the terminal.

At around ¥2500 per person per night or ¥4000 including two meals, terminal prices compare favourably with those of a youth hostel. For more information contact the Japan Bicycle Promotion Institute (☎ 03-3583-5444), Nihon Jitensha Kaikan Building, 1-9-3 Akasaka, Minato-ku, Tokyo.

Minshuku

A minshuku is usually a family-run private home, rather like a B&B in Europe or the USA. Minshuku can be found throughout Japan and offer one way to peep into daily Japanese life. The average price per person per night with two meals is around ¥5500. You are expected to lay out and put away your bedding and bring your own towel. JNTO publishes a booklet, *Minshukus in Japan*, which lists details of about 300 minshuku.

Ryokan

For a taste of traditional Japanese life, a stay at a ryokan is mandatory. Ryokan range from ultra-exclusive establishments (priced accordingly and available only to guests bearing a personal recommendation) to reasonably priced places with a homey atmosphere.

Prices start around ¥4200 (per person, per night) for a 'no-frills' ryokan without meals. The Japanese Inn Group (☎ 075-351-6748), c/o Hiraiwa Ryokan, 314 Hayao-chō, Kaminoguchi-agaru, Ninomiyacho-dōri, Shimogyo-ku, Kyoto 600, publishes an excellent listing of inexpensive ryokan, used to foreign guests, with full details on access, prices, facilities and mini-maps for each establishment.

Capsule Hotels

A uniquely Japanese concept, the capsule hotel is the masochistic claustrophobiac's dream. Your capsule measures two metres by one metre (about the size of a coffin), and inside is a bed, a TV, reading light, radio and alarm clock. Personal belongings are kept in a locker room.

Capsule hotels are common in the major cities and often cater to travellers who have partied too hard to make it home or have missed the last train. There are a few for women only, but the majority are only for men. Some capsule hotels have the added attraction of a sauna.

An average price is ¥3800 per night or ¥1400 for a three-hour stay, which is a lot of money to sleep in a box.

Business Hotels

Cheap single rooms in a business hotel can sometimes be found for ¥4500, though the average rate is around ¥6000; most business hotels also have twin rooms, though doubles are something of a rarity. Cheaper business hotels usually do not have a service charge, though places costing ¥7000 or more often add a 10% charge.

The Japan Business Hotel Association at 43 Kanda-Higashi, Matsusita-chō, Chiyoda-ku, Tokyo, publishes the *Business Hotel Guide*, a handy pamphlet which lists business hotels throughout Japan along with phone numbers, prices, addresses and access details.

Love Hotels

Love hotels are one of the wild cards in Japanese accommodation. Their primary function is to serve as a short-time base for couples to enjoy some privacy. Customers are not necessarily unmarrieds in search of sex; the hotels are also used by married couples who often lack space at home for relaxing together.

Charges on an hourly basis are at a peak during the day and early evening. Love hotels are of more interest to foreign visitors after 10 pm, when it's possible to stay the night for about ¥5000 per room (rather than per person), but you should check out early enough in the morning to avoid a return to peak-hour rates. Outside love hotels there will usually be a sign in Japanese (occasionally in English) announcing the rates for a 'rest' (usually two hours) or a 'stay' (overnight).

FOOD

For most budget travellers, the question is going to be less one of how to play the gourmet in Japan as of how to stay alive affordably. In the morning, the best deal around is provided by Japan's coffee shops (the country is swarming with them). *Māningu sābisu* are breakfast sets (generally one or two door-stop slices of toast, a boiled egg, salad and a cup of coffee) that are usually priced between ¥350 and ¥400. For lunch time and dinner, there is a wide variety of choices: *rāmen* (Chinese noodles) shops serve big bowls of noodles from ¥400 to ¥500; the fast-food chains are well established in Japan, and you can patch a junk meal together for around ¥500 easily; alternatively you can put together your own meal cheaply by shopping in a supermarket or a bakery.

English is seldom spoken in Japanese restaurants, particularly the cheaper varieties, and you can't expect English menus to be available. Fortunately, almost all restaurants in Japan have plastic replicas of the dishes they offer in their window displays – prices are usually indicated – and if it comes to the worst it's simply a matter of dragging one of the staff outside and pointing.

Popular Japanese dishes include *okonomiyaki*, an inexpensive Japanese dish, somewhat like a pancake or omelette with anything that's lying around in the kitchen thrown in. Rāmen has already been mentioned and is a Chinese noodle dish. The Japanese equivalents are *soba*, made with buckwheat noodles, and *udon*, similar, except that the noodles are white and thicker. *Sukiyaki* and *shabu-shabu* are both cooked in front of the diner – meat and vegetables are thrown into a simmering broth. *Sushi* and *sashimi* are probably the most famous elements in Japanese cuisine; sushi is raw fish served on a bed of rice, while sashimi is served on its own and dipped in soy sauce. *Tempura* is what fish & chips might have been – fluffy, non-greasy batter and delicate, melt-in-your mouth portions of fish, prawns and vegetables.

Any visit to Japan should include a visit to an *izakaya*. This is a drinking establishment that has a wide range of cooked snacks available. The most famous of the snacks is *yakitori* – chicken skewered on a stick and cooked over a charcoal fire.

DRINKS

By 11 pm in most major Japanese cities, it can seem that everyone on the streets is in various stages of inebriation. Fortunately, the Japanese are fairly good-natured drunks and it's extremely rare to see any trouble – though it does happen, especially in the hot summer months. A recent survey estimated that around 12% of the male population gets drunk every day, and nearly 70% get drunk once a week.

Introduced at the end of the last century, beer is now the favourite tipple of the Japanese. The quality is generally excellent and the most popular type is a light lager. The major brewers are Asahi, Suntory, Sapporo and Kirin. Beer is dispensed everywhere, from vending machines to beer halls and even in temple lodgings.

A standard can of beer from a vending machine is about ¥220; elsewhere the price of your beer starts around ¥500 and climbs upwards depending on the establishment. Draught beer *(nama biiru)* is widely available and imported beers are common.

Sake (rice wine) is a Japanese staple which has been brewed for centuries. Once restricted to imperial brewers, it was later produced at temples and shrines across the country. In recent years, consumption of beer has overtaken that of sake, but it's still a standard item in homes, in restaurants and in drinking dens.

Sake is usually served warm *(atsukan)* but may be served cold *(hiyazake)* or as a

JAPAN

summer drink with ice *(reishū)*. A different way to sample it cold, is in *masu* (little wooden boxes, traditionally used as measures) with a pinch of salt on the corner of the box. When served warm, sake enters the bloodstream extra fast – so don't underestimate its average alcohol content of 17%, which is slightly stronger than wine.

A variety of containers (ceramic pots, glass jars and bottles) are used for sake, but bars and restaurants favour the slim, clay flask *tokkuri*, holding 180 ml, which usually costs around ¥250 and provides several servings in miniature cups *(sakazuki)*.

ENTERTAINMENT
Bars
Most large urban centres have at least one inexpensive drinking establishment that has been appropriated by the local gaijin set. In some places, bars seek to attract gaijin by offering free admission or discounts on drinks, although this only occurs in more provincial centres. It's worth seeking some of these places out while you are in Japan. They normally have a good mix of local foreigners and Japanese, and provide an informal setting for getting to know locals. Drink prices normally range from ¥500, though happy-hour rates sometimes apply between 6 pm and 9 pm.

Cinemas
Foreign films are shown in their original language with Japanese subtitles, but Japanese cinemas are expensive. The average ticket price is ¥1800, though you can shave a couple of hundred yen off this by buying your tickets at advance ticket offices such as Saison – you can normally find these in central shopping districts.

Discos
Very few budget travellers venture into Japanese discos. Admission costs range from ¥3500 to ¥5000 (women generally get a discount of ¥1000), and although this usually includes a couple of drinks, it still makes for an expensive night out.

Karaoke
Not all that many foreigners venture into karaoke clubs. They tend to be expensive and the English songs on offer will be limited to a handful of 'classics' such as 'My Way' and 'Moon River'. A recent phenomenon in big cities like Osaka and Tokyo, however, are karaoke places that charge simply by the drinks you consume and offer a wide selection of contemporary Western music. Such places are popular with resident gaijin.

Nightclubs
Give them a miss. It's very unlikely anyone will attempt to entice you into one and, if you managed to get past the doorman squealing 'No foreigners!', you would be shocked by the prices anyway.

THINGS TO BUY
With the yen on a real roll, there are very few bargains to be had in Japan. If you are planning to do some shopping while you are in the country, come equipped with a knowledge of prices at home. The chances are they won't be any cheaper in Japan.

Cameras are more expensive in Japan than in the USA, Hong Kong or Singapore, though camera accessories can be reasonably priced. Second-hand cameras and lenses are a possible buy. Shinjuku and Ginza in Tokyo have the widest range of second-hand camera shops, and prices can be very reasonable.

Most of Japan's major urban centres have discount electrical goods areas. Akihabara in Tokyo and Nippombashi in Osaka are examples. Discounts of 10-15% are available and most of the bigger stores will have a floor for electronic goods aimed at foreign markets – useful as it saves the need for an adaptor for Japan's unique 100 V electricity supply.

If you are passing through Hong Kong or Singapore on your way to Japan, it's a good idea while there to pick up any clothes you need. It's not impossible to pick up clothing bargains in Japan, but you will need to shop around.

The *omiyage* (souvenir) market is huge in

Japan and it is possible to pick up interesting traditional arts & crafts all over Japan. Anything from carp banners to kimono can make good souvenirs for the converted Japanophile.

Getting There & Away

Flying into Tokyo is only one of a diverse range of ways of getting to Japan. There are many other airports in Japan, some of which make better entry points than Tokyo's inconvenient Narita International Airport. It's also possible to arrive in Japan by sea from a number of nearby countries, particularly South Korea. Japan also serves as a possible starting or finishing point for the popular Trans-Siberian Express trip across Russia.

AIR

Almost all international flights to Tokyo land at Narita Airport. China Airlines (of Taiwan) uses the much more convenient Haneda Airport, which also handles Tokyo's domestic flights.

Narita is one of the world's most inconvenient international airports. It is located 60 km from central Tokyo, and transport connections between the airport and the city are expensive and time consuming. A good way to avoid Narita (apart from flying China Airlines) is to use one of the other international airports: Niigata, Nagoya, Osaka (either Osaka Airport or Kansai International Airport), Fukuoka, Kumamoto, Kagoshima or Naha. Osaka Airport or Kansai International Airport are probably the best choices as you'll arrive in Kansai with its attractions of Kyoto and Nara.

To/From North America

Seven-day advance purchase return fares are US$910 to US$1125 from the west coast (depending on the season) and US$1156 to US$1370 from the east. Regular economy fares are much higher – US$874 to US$935 (one way) from the west coast, US$1195 to US$1279 from the east coast.

Better deals are available if you shop around. From the east coast, return fares as low as US$759 to US$879 and one-way fares of US$749 are possible. From the west coast fares can drop to US$559 and US$689 with Korean Airlines. There are also good deals available via Vancouver with Canadian Airlines International. From San Francisco or Los Angeles, fares to Tokyo range from US$629 to US$769 or to Nagoya from US$579 to US$779. Check the Sunday travel sections of papers like the *Los Angeles Times* or the *New York Times* for travel bargains. Council Travel and STA Travel are two good discount operations specialising in student fares and other cheap deals. They have offices all across North America.

Fares from Canada are similar to those from the USA. Canadian Airlines International, which operates out of Vancouver, often matches or beats the best fares available from the USA. Travel Cuts, the Canadian student travel organisation, offers one-way Vancouver-Tokyo flights from C$800 and returns from C$1000 or more depending on the season.

To/From Australasia

Japan Airlines (JAL), All Nippon Airways (ANA) and Qantas Airways all have direct flights between Australia and Japan. You can fly from most Australia state capitals to Tokyo, Osaka, Nagoya and Fukuoka. There's only a one hour time change between Australia and Japan, and a direct Sydney-Tokyo flight takes about nine hours.

A return excursion Sydney-Tokyo fare is around A$1500. Discount deals will involve round-about routes via other Asian capitals like Kuala Lumpur or Manila. If you shop around, you can find one-way flights from Sydney or Melbourne for around A$750, return flights for A$1100. STA Travel offices or the numerous Flight Centres International are good places to look for discount ticket deals.

From New Zealand, Auckland-Tokyo return excursion fares are around NZ$1900 in the off season rising to NZ$2500 in the high.

JAPAN

To/From Europe

Most direct flights between Europe and Japan fly into Tokyo but some continue to Osaka. Flight times vary widely depending on the route taken. The most direct route is across Scandinavia and Russia. Since Russia became hard up for cash, there have been far more flights taking this route as the Russians have opened their airspace in return for hefty fees.

The fastest nonstop London-Tokyo flights on the Russian route take just under 12 hours. Flights that stop in Moscow take an extra 2½ hours. Finnair's Helsinki-Tokyo flight over the North Pole and the Bering Strait takes 13½ hours. Before the Russians opened their skies, the popular route was via Anchorage, Alaska. Some flights still operate that way and take about 17 hours, including the Anchorage stopover. Finally, there are the old trans-Asian routes across the Middle East and South Asia, which take anything from 18 to 30 hours depending on the number of stops en route.

London remains one of the best places in Europe to purchase keenly priced airline tickets, although Amsterdam is also very good.

Return economy air fares between London and Tokyo are around UK£1000 and are valid for 14 days to three months. A ticket valid for a year costs about UK£1300. Although a wide variety of cheaper deals are available, generally, the lower the price, the less convenient the route. Expect to pay around UK£900 to UK£1000 for a one-year valid return ticket with a good airline via a fast route. For a less convenient trans-Asian route, count on UK£700 or lower and about half that for one-way tickets.

In London, STA Travel (☎ 0171-937 9962) at 74 Old Brompton Rd, London SW7 or 117 Euston Rd, London NW1; Trailfinders (☎ 0171-938 3366) at 46 Earls Court Rd and at 194 Kensington High St, London W8 7RG (☎ 0171-938 3444); and Travel Bug (☎ 0161-721 4000) all offer rock-bottom return flights to Tokyo and can also put together interesting round-the-world routes incorporating Tokyo on the itinerary. The weekly 'what's on' magazine *Time Out* or the various giveaway papers are good to look for travel bargains but take care with shonky bucket shops and prices that seem too low to believe. The really cheap fares will probably involve cash-strapped Eastern European or Middle Eastern airlines and may involve complicated transfers and long waits along the way.

The Far East Travel Centre (FETC) (☎ (0171) 734-9318) at 3 Lower John St, London W1A 4XE, specialises in Korean Airline ticketing and can fly you from London Gatwick via Seoul to your choice of Nagasaki, Nagoya, Osaka, Sapporo or Tokyo. This is a good option for visitors who don't want to take the conventional Tokyo route.

The Japan Centre (☎ (0171) 437-6445), 66-68 Brewer St, London W1R 3PJ, handles all sorts of ticket permutations. Its basement has a shop section (☎ (0171) 439-8035) with books and assorted Japanese paraphernalia as well as a Japanese restaurant with reasonable prices. It's worth a visit for a taste of Japan.

An alternative route to Japan from Europe is to fly to Hong Kong and buy an onward ticket from one of Hong Kong's very competitive travel agencies. London-Hong Kong flights are much more competitively priced than London-Tokyo ones. If you have to go to Hong Kong en route to Tokyo, a London-Hong Kong-London ticket plus a Hong Kong-Tokyo-Hong Kong ticket can work out much cheaper than a London-Hong Kong-Tokyo-London ticket.

To/From Asia

There are regular flights between Japan and other major centres like Manila, Bangkok, Kuala Lumpur, Singapore and Jakarta. Some of the cheapest deals between Europe and Japan will be via south Asia – Bangladesh Biman will fly you from London to Tokyo via Dhaka at about the lowest price going.

SEA

For travellers intending to take the Trans-

Siberian Railway to Moscow, the following ferry services are available:

Shimonoseki-Pusan
    Daily; US$65 students, US$85 economy
Osaka-Pusan
    Four times weekly; US$80 students, US$100 economy
Fukuoka-Pusan
    Three-hour hydrofoil service daily; US$120 one way, US$210 return
    Ferry service daily; US$85 one way, US$120 return
Kōbe/Osaka-Shanghai (ferries stop both in Kōbe and Osaka)
    Once weekly (approx); US$230 one way
Naha (Okinawa)-Taiwan
    Once weekly, alternating between Kaohsiung and Keelung for Taiwan arrivals and departures; US$110 economy

LEAVING JAPAN
Airport tax at Narita is ¥2000 for adults and ¥1000 for children aged two to 12 years. Other Japanese airports do not have a departure tax, though it is to be expected that the new Kansai International Airport will charge you to leave the country.

Getting Around

AIR
Japan Air Lines (JAL) is the major international carrier and also has a domestic network linking the major cities. All Nippon Airways (ANA) is the second-largest international carrier and operates a more extensive domestic system. Japan Air Systems (JAS) only does a couple of overseas routes but flies to many destinations in Japan. Air Nippon Koku (ANK) and South-West Airlines (SWAL) are smaller domestic carriers. ANK links many smaller towns all over Japan while SWAL is particularly good for connections through Okinawa and the other South-West Islands.

There's a 10% discount on return fares if the return flight is made within seven to 10 days. Some sample one-way fares (return fares are 10% less than two one-way fares) include:

Tokyo-Sapporo	¥23,850
Tokyo-Osaka	¥14,600
Tokyo-Naha	¥34,900
Osaka-Naha	¥29,100
Naha-Kagoshima	¥21,050

BUS
In addition to its local city bus services, Japan also has a comprehensive network of long-distance buses. These 'highway buses' are nowhere near as fast as the *shinkansen* (bullet trains) and heavy traffic can delay them even further, but the fares are comparable with those of the *futsū* (local train) without any reservation or express surcharges.

An option that is becoming increasingly popular among travellers is the network of night buses. They are relatively cheap, spacious (allowing room to stretch out and get some sleep) and save on a night's accommodation. They typically leave at around 10 or 11 pm and arrive the following morning at around 6 or 7 am. Some typical prices out of Tokyo include:

Destination	One-way Fare
Aomori	¥10,000
Sendai	¥7700
Niigata	¥5150
Nagoya	¥6300
Kyoto	¥8030
Osaka	¥8450
Hiroshima	¥11,840
Hakata	¥15,000

TRAIN
Japanese rail travel is usually fast, frequent, clean, comfortable and often very expensive. The services range from small local lines to the shinkansen super-expresses which have become a symbol of modern Japan.

Japan Railways (JR) is actually a number of separate private railway systems which provide one linked service. Together the system covers the country from one end to the other and also provides local services around major cities like Tokyo and Osaka. The private railway lines, on the other hand, usually operate over short routes, often no more than 100 km in length.

The fastest and best known train services in Japan are the 'bullet trains'. Nobody

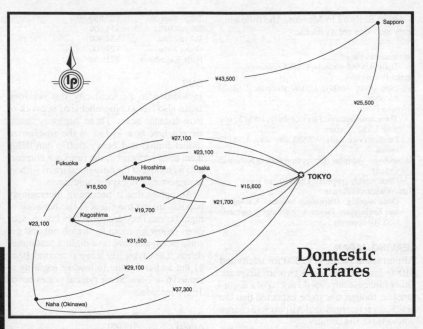

¥43,500

¥25,500

¥27,100

¥23,100

Fukuoka

Hiroshima

Matsuyama

Osaka

TOKYO

¥15,600

¥18,500

¥21,700

Kagoshima

¥19,700

¥23,100

¥31,500

Domestic Airfares

¥29,100

¥37,300

Naha (Okinawa)

knows them by that name in Japan, they're simply the shinkansen or super-expresses. There are three shinkansen routes, all starting from Tokyo. One runs via Nagoya, Kyoto, Osaka (Tōkaidō line) and Hiroshima to Shimonoseki at the western end of Honshū and on to Fukuoka/Hakata on the northern coast of Kyūshū (Sanyō line). Another runs via Sendai to Morioka (Tōhoku line), almost at the north-eastern end of Honshū. The third line runs north from Tokyo to Niigata (Jōetsu line) on the north coast of central Honshū.

Unless you come equipped with a rail pass, the shinkansen is probably going to be too expensive to use. Fortunately, most of Japan is well serviced with slower but cheaper lines. The slowest trains stopping at all stations are called *futsū*. A step up from this is the *kyūkō* (ordinary express) which stops at only a limited number of stations. A variation on the kyūkō trains is the *kaisoku* (rapid) services. Finally, the fastest regular (non-shinkansen) trains are the *tokkyū* (limited express) services. As the speed of

the train increases, the express surcharges mount up, and those looking at saving money will have to put up with long train journeys that involve stops every five minutes.

Tokyo or Ueno to	Distance (km)	Futsū	Shinkansen
Nagoya	366	¥5970	¥10,380
Kyoto	514	¥7830	¥12,970
Osaka	553	¥8340	¥13,480
Okayama	733	¥9990	¥16,050
Hiroshima	895	¥11,120	¥17,700
Shimonoseki	1089	¥12,570	¥20,690
Hakata	1177	¥13,180	¥21,300
Fukushima	273	¥4530	¥8330
Sendai	352	¥5670	¥10,190
Morioka	535	¥8030	¥15,370
Niigata	334	¥5360	¥9880

One of Japan's few travel bargains is the unlimited travel Japan Rail Pass. The pass lets you use any JR services for seven days for ¥27,800, 14 days for ¥44,200 or 21 days for ¥56,600. Green Car (1st class) passes are

¥37,000, ¥60,000 and ¥78,000 respectively. Children aged between six to 11 years get a 50% discount. The pass cannot be used for the new super-express Nozomi shinkansen service, but is OK for everything else. The only additional surcharge levied on the Japan Rail Pass is for overnight sleepers. Since a reserved seat Tokyo-Kyoto shinkansen ticket costs ¥12,970, you only have to travel Tokyo-Kyoto-Tokyo to make a seven day pass come close to paying off.

The pass can only be bought overseas and cannot be used by foreign residents in Japan. The clock starts to tick on the pass as soon as you validate it, which can be done at certain major railway stations or even at the JR counter at Narita Airport if you're intending to jump on a JR train immediately. Don't validate it if you're just going into Tokyo and intend to hang around the city for a few days. The pass is valid *only* on JR services, you will still have to pay for private railway services.

CAR & MOTORBIKE

Driving is on the left side of the road. To drive in Japan you need your driver's licence and an international driving permit. Be certain you're sober before getting behind the wheel as there are draconian penalties for drinking and driving.

Rental

Rental costs are generally a flat rate including unlimited km. Typical rental rates for a small car (a Toyota Starlet or Mazda 121 – one step up from the Japanese microcars) is ¥8000 to ¥9000 for the first day and ¥5500 to ¥7000 per day thereafter. Move up a bracket (a Mazda 323 or Toyota Corolla) and you're looking at ¥10,000 to ¥13,500 for the first day and ¥8000 to ¥9000 thereafter. On top of the rental charge there's a ¥1000 per day insurance cost. It's also worth bearing in mind that rental costs go up during peak seasons: 28 April to 6 May, 20 July to 31 August, 28 December to 5 January. The increase can make quite a difference to costs. A car that is costing ¥8800 a day usually will

go up to ¥9700 during any of the peak seasons.

Motorbike

As with driving a car, your driver's licence and international driving permit are all you need to ride a motorbike in Japan.

The 400 cc machines are the most popular large motorbikes in Japan but, for general touring, a 250 cc machine is probably the best bet. Apart from being quite large enough for a compact country like Japan, machines up to 250 cc are also exempt from the expensive *shaken* (inspections). Smaller machines are banned from expressways and are generally less suitable for long-distance touring but people have ridden from one end of Japan to another on little 50 cc 'step-thrus'. An advantage of these is that you can ride them with just a driving licence, and don't need to get a motorbike licence.

BICYCLE

A bicycle can be a practical proposition for touring. It is possible to bring your own as part of your luggage on most airlines, or you can rent one in Japan, although tall people may have trouble finding a frame big enough. Also, most Japanese bikes are one-speed clunkers. Bringing your own touring bike is best.

Many youth hostels have bicycles to rent – there's a symbol identifying them in the (Japan) *Youth Hostel Handbook*. The *saikuringu tāminaru* (cycling terminals) found in various locations around the country (see under Accommodation in the Facts for the Visitor section earlier in this chapter for details) also rent bicycles.

The Japan Bicycle Promotion Institute (Nihon Jitensha Kaikon Biru) (☎ 03-3583-5444) is also known as the Bicycle Cultural Centre and is across from the US Embassy at 1-9-3 Akasaka, Minato-ku, Tokyo. The institute has a museum and is a useful source of information regarding cycling terminals, maps, routes and types of bicycles suitable for foreign dimensions.

JAPAN

HITCHING

Japan can be an excellent country for hitch-hiking, partly because so few Japanese hitchhike and gaijin with their thumbs out are a very rare sight. There are many hitchhikers' tales of extraordinary kindness from motorists who have picked them up, but there are equally numerous tales of motorists who think the hitchhiker has simply lost his or her way to the nearest railway station, and accordingly takes them there!

The rules for hitchhiking are similar to anywhere else in the world. Make it clear where you want to go – carry cardboard and a marker pen to write in kanji the name of your desired destination. Write it in romaji as well, as a car-driving gaijin may just be coming by. Look for a good place to hitch: it's no good starting from the middle of town, though unfortunately, in Japan, many towns only seem to end as they merge into the next one. Expressway entrance roads are probably your best bet. A woman should never hitch alone, even in Japan.

Truck drivers are particularly good bets for long-distance travel as they often head out on the expressways at night. If a driver is exiting before your intended destination, try and get dropped off at one of the expressway service centres. The Service Area Parking Area (SAPA) guide maps (☎ 03-3403-9111 in Tokyo) are excellent for hitchers. They're available free from expressway service areas and show full details of each Interchange (IC) and rest stop – important orientation points if you have a limited knowledge of Japanese.

BOAT

Japan is an island nation and there are a great many ferry services both between islands and between ports on the same island. The routes vary widely from two-hour services between adjacent islands to 1½-day trips in what are really small ocean liners. The cheapest fares on the longer trips are in tatami-mat rooms where you simply unroll your futon on the floor. In this basic class, fares will usually be lower than equivalent land travel but there are also more expensive private cabins. Bicycles can always be brought along and most ferries also carry cars and motorbikes.

Information on ferry routes, schedules and fares can be obtained from information sheets available in TIC offices. Ask for a copy of the Japan Long Distance Ferry Association's excellent English-language brochure. Some ferry services and their lowest fares include:

Hokkaidō to Honshū

Muroran to Oarai	¥9570
Otaru to Maizuru	¥6590
Otaru to Niigata	¥5150
Otaru to Tsuruga	¥6590
Tomakomai to Nagoya	¥15,450
Tomakomai to Oarai	¥9570
Tomakomai to Sendai	¥8850

Routes from Tokyo

to Kōchi (Shikoku)	¥13,910
to Kokura (Kyūshū)	¥12,000
to Kushiro (Hokkaidō)	¥14,420
to Nachi-Katsuura (Honshū)	¥9060
to Naha (Okinawa)	¥19,670
to Tokushima (Shikoku)	¥8200
to Tomakomai (Hokkaidō)	¥11,840

Routes from Osaka

to Beppu (Kyūshū)	¥6900
to Imabari (Shikoku)	¥4500
to Kagoshima (Kyūshū)	¥10,300
to Kōchi (Shikoku)	¥4530
to Matsuyama (Shikoku)	¥4430
to Naha (Okinawa)	¥15,450
to Shin-Moji (Kyūshū)	¥4840
to Takamatsu (Shikoku)	¥2780

Other Routes from Honshū

Hiroshima to Beppu (Kyūshū)	¥3600
Kawasaki to Hyuga (Kyūshū)	¥17,720
Kōbe to Hyuga (Kyūshū)	¥7620
Kōbe to Kokura (Kyūshū)	¥4840
Kōbe to Matsuyama (Shikoku)	¥3500
Kōbe to Naha (Okinawa)	¥15,450
Kōbe to Oita (Kyūshū)	¥5050
Nagoya to Sendai (Honshū)	¥9580

Other Routes from Kyūshū

Hakata to Naha (Okinawa)	¥12,970
Kagoshima to Naha (Okinawa)	¥11,840
Kokura to Matsuyama (Shikoku)	¥3500

LOCAL TRANSPORT
Bus
Almost every Japanese city will have a bus service but it's usually the most difficult public transport system for gaijin to use. The destination names will almost inevitably be in kanji (the popular tourist town of Nikkō is a rare exception) and often there are not even numbers to identify which bus you want. Buses are also subject to the usual traffic delays.

Train
Several cities, in particular Osaka and Tokyo, have mass transit rail systems comprising a loop line around the city centre and radial lines into the central stations. Subway systems operate in Fukuoka, Kōbe, Kyoto, Nagoya, Osaka, Sapporo, Sendai, Tokyo and Yokohama. They are usually the fastest and most convenient ways of getting around the city. There is usually easily obtainable information in English for using the system.

Taxi
Taxis are convenient but expensive and are found in even quite small towns; the railway station is the best place to start looking. Fares vary very little throughout the country – flagfall (posted on the nearside windows) is ¥600 for the first two km, after which it's ¥90 for each 347 metres (slightly farther outside Tokyo). There's also a time charge if the speed drops below 10 km/h. A red light means the taxi is available, a green light means there's an additional night time surcharge and a yellow light means the cab is on a call.

Taxi drivers have just as much trouble finding Japanese addresses as anyone else. Just because you've gone round the block five times does not necessarily mean your driver is a country boy fresh in from the sticks. Asking directions and stopping at police boxes for help is standard practice.

Tokyo 東京

Tokyo is one of the most populous cities on the planet and one of Asia's metropolitan

highlights. Intensive aerial bombing towards the end of WW II and the occasional major earth movement has lightened the city of much of its historical legacy, but modern reconstructions of the Imperial Palace, Meiji-jingū Shrine and Sensō-ji Temple in Asakusa are all worth checking out.

Information
Tourist Office Practically on top of Hibiya subway station on the Hibiya, Chiyoda and TOEI Mita lines is the TIC (☎ 3502-1461), the single best source of information about Tokyo and the rest of Japan available in Tokyo. To get there take the A2 exit of Hibiya subway station – the centre, distinguishable by a large red question mark and a sign reading 'Tourist Information Office', is directly opposite, on the other side of the road running towards Hibiya-kōen Park.

The centre is open Monday to Friday from 9 am to 5 pm and on Saturday until noon. It is closed on Sunday and public holidays.

Post & Telecommunications Look for the red and white T with a bar across the top. Post boxes have two slots: the red-lettered slot is for Tokyo mail and the blue-lettered one is for all other mail. The Tokyo central post office (☎ 3284-9527) is next to Tokyo station in the Tokyo station plaza, Chiyoda-ku. Poste restante mail will be held there for 30 days; it should be addressed to Poste Restante, Central Post Office, Tokyo, Japan. International parcels and registered mail can be sent from the Tokyo international post office (☎ 3241-4891) next to Ōtemachi subway station.

Immigration Office The Tokyo Regional Immigration Bureau is best reached from Ōtemachi subway station on the Chiyoda line. Take the C2 exit, cross the street at the corner and turn left. Walk past the Japan Development building; the immigration bureau is the next building on your right.

Cultural Centres The library at the American Center (☎ 3436-0901) has books and magazines concerning the USA. It's close to

JAPAN

JAPAN

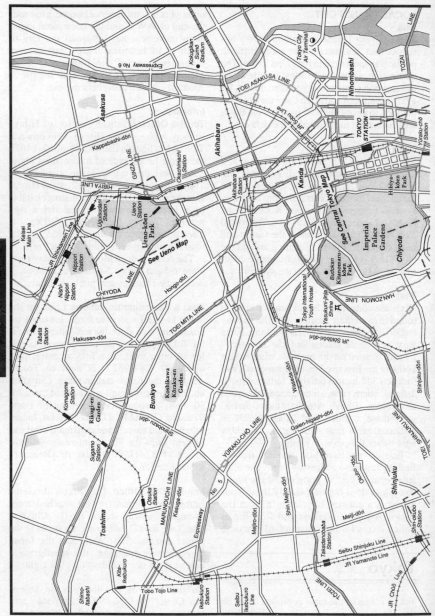

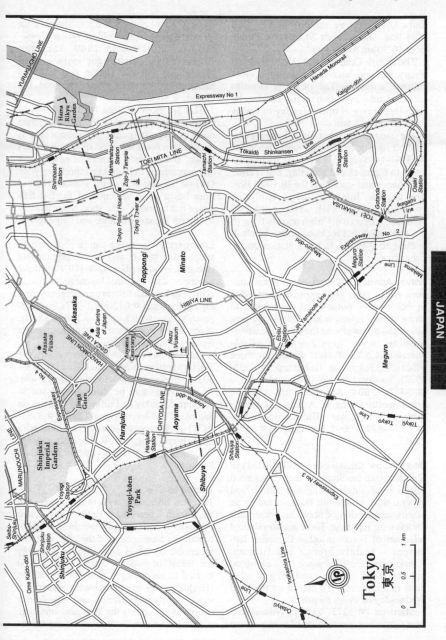

Tokyo 東京

JAPAN

Shiba-kōen subway station on the TOEI Mita line, and is open Monday to Friday from 10.30 am to 6.30 pm.

The British Council (☎ 3235-8031) has a library, and you can also enquire about other cultural activities. The office is close to Iidabashi subway station on the Yūraku-chō line. The library is open Monday to Friday from 10 am to 8 pm.

For languages other than English, the Bibliotheque de la Maison Franco-Japonaise (☎ 3291-1144) is open from 10 am to noon and 1 to 6 pm, closed Saturday, and is close to Ochanomizu station on the JR Chūō line. The Goethe Institute Tokyo Bibliotek (☎ 3583-7280), with around 15,000 volumes, is open daily from noon to 6 pm (8 pm on Friday), but is closed on weekends. It is close to Aoyama Itchōme station on the Ginza line.

Travel Agencies The discount ticket situation out of Tokyo has improved somewhat in recent years, but it's still much better to arrive with a return ticket. One of the best places to look is among the classified advertisements in the *Tokyo Journal*. A reliable operator is STA Travel, which has three offices in Tokyo, in Ikebukuro (☎ 5391-2922), Yotsuya (☎ 5269-0751) and Shibuya (☎ 5485-8380). Another long-standing agent worth trying is Across Traveller's Bureau, which has offices in Shinjuku (☎ 3374-8721) and Ikebukuro (☎ 5391-2871).

Bookshops Kinokuniya (☎ 3354-0131) in Shinjuku (see the Shinjuku map) has a good selection of English-language fiction and general titles on the 6th floor, including an extensive selection of books and other aids for learning Japanese. There is also a limited selection of books in other European languages – mainly French and German. Kinokuniya is a good place to stock up on guidebooks if you are continuing to other parts of the world. It's closed on the third Wednesday of every month.

Maruzen (☎ 3272-7211) in Nihombashi near Ginza has a collection of books almost equal to Kinokuniya's and it is always a lot quieter. This is Japan's oldest Western bookshop, established in 1869. Take the Takashimaya department store exit at Nihombashi subway station and look for Maruzen on the other side of the road. It's closed on Sunday.

The 3rd floor of Jena (☎ 3571-2980) in Ginza doesn't have quite the range of some other foreign-language bookshops but it does have a good selection of fiction and art books, and stocks a number of newspapers and magazines. In Ikebukuro check out Wise Owl on the east side of the station. The top floor has a good selection of English-language publications – the shop is particularly strong on Japanese culture and language.

Emergency The police can be contacted by telephoning ☎ 110, and the fire brigade and ambulance by telephoning ☎ 119. Both these numbers will require Japanese language skills. For English help in an emergency, ring Japan Helpline (☎ 0120-461-997), an emergency service which operates 24 hours a day, seven days a week. Don't bother them unless it really is an emergency.

For a clinic with foreign doctors, try the Tokyo Medical & Surgical Clinic (☎ 3436-3028) in Kamiya-chō on the Hibiya line. Appointments can be made from 9 am to 4.45 pm Monday to Friday and to 1 pm on Saturday. The International Clinic (☎ 3583-7831) in Roppongi is another clinic with English-speaking staff. It is open from 9 am to 5 pm Monday to Friday and until noon on Saturday.

Things to See
Tokyo is brimming with things to see, but apart from a few major sights many Tokyo excursions will simply be an excuse to savour the atmosphere of the city. With the exception of Meiji-jingū Shrine, arguably the finest of Japan's Shintō shrines and located in surprisingly peaceful grounds in Harajuku, you might consider skipping a strict sightseeing agenda and spending a couple of days doing the Yamanote line loop. All of Tokyo's main 'sub-cities' are on the

loop and all have something different to say about Tokyo itself.

Starting at Yūraku-chō station, about midway down the eastern side of the loop, you can visit the **Imperial Palace** and **Ginza**. The Imperial Palace is the home of Japan's emperor and imperial family, but there's very little to see. The palace itself is closed to the public for all but two days of the year: 2 January (New Year's) and 23 December (the emperor's birthday). Still, it is possible to wander around its outskirts and visit the gardens, where you can at least get a view of the palace with the **Nijū-bashi Bridge** in the foreground.

Ginza is home to some of the world's most expensive real estate and pricey department stores. Browsing is free, however, and there is also a multitude of free galleries and a sprinkling of hi-tech **showrooms** in the area that are worth checking out. The Sony Showroom (☎ 3573-2371) has fascinating displays of Sony's many products and Toshiba Ginza Seven (☎ 3571-5971) has Toshiba products.

Continuing northwards, Ueno station is worth a stop to visit **Ueno-kōen Park**, home to the best of Tokyo's galleries and museums. Undoubtedly the pick of the bunch is the **Tokyo National Museum**. It's Japan's largest museum, housing some 87,000 items, and also has the world's largest collection of Japanese art. Admission is ¥400, and it is open from 9 am to 4 pm, closed on Monday. The **National Museum of Western Art** has an impressive permanent collection; admission is ¥400, and it is open from 9.30 am to 4.30 pm, closed on Monday. Other attractions in the park include the **Tokyo Metropolitan Museum of Art** and the **National Science Museum**, but the **Shitamachi History Museum** is likely to be of most interest. It re-creates life in Edo's Shitamachi, the plebeian downtown quarters of old Tokyo. Admission is ¥200, and it is open from 9.30 am to 4 pm, closed on Monday.

Also worth a look in Ueno is **Ameyoko-chō Arcade**. This area, opposite Ueno station, was famous as a black-market district after the war and is still a lively shopping area where many bargains can be found.

Just three stops out from Ueno on the Asakusa subway line is **Asakusa**, one of the few areas remaining that retain something of the atmosphere of old Tokyo. The main attraction is **Sensō-ji Temple**, also known as the Asakusa Kannon Temple. The temple itself is a modern reconstruction, but this hardly matters as the bustling temple precincts are enough to make up for any architectural disappointments. Entry is free.

The northern arch of the Yamanote loop holds little of interest and there's not even any pressing need to stop in Ikebukuro, although there are a couple of worthwhile sights if your itinerary isn't too hurried. On the east side of the station is **Toyota Amlux**, which, even if you are not an auto buff, has to be seen to be believed. There are auto display areas, features on auto production and historical exhibitions, but best of all is the building itself, with its subterranean lighting and ambient sound effects. Entry is free, and it is open from 11 am to 8 pm weekdays, 10 am to 7 pm weekends and closed on Monday. While you are on Ikebukuro's west side, check out the **Seibu department store**, which until recently was the largest department store in the world, and still arguably the ultimate department store experience – just get lost in the place for a while.

South of Ikebukuro on the Yamanote line is **Shinjuku**, a city in itself and without doubt the most lively part of Tokyo. If you had only a day in Tokyo and wanted to see the modern Japanese phenomenon in action, Shinjuku would be the place to go. It's an incredible combination of high-class department stores, discount shopping arcades, flashing neon, government offices, stand-up drinking bars, hostess clubs and sleazy strip bars. The west side of the station is home to Tokyo's highest concentration of skyscrapers, several of which have fascinating hi-tech interiors. In particular look out for the **Tokyo Metropolitan Government Offices**. The east side, however, is altogether a more animated affair. **Kabuki-chō**, Tokyo's largest and

JAPAN

JAPAN

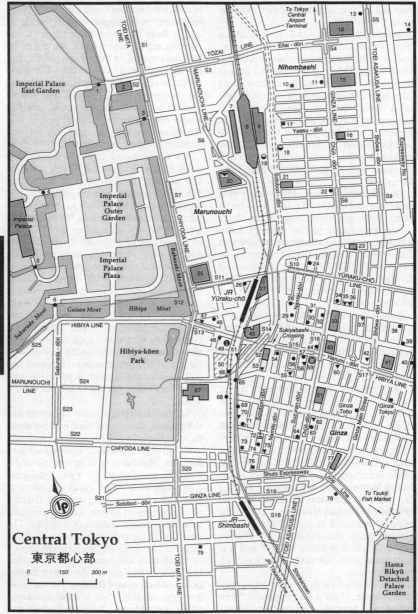

Central Tokyo
東京都心部

0   150   300 m

PLACES TO STAY

2 Palace Hotel
パレス　ホテル
7 Tokyo Station Hotel
東京ステーションホテル
10 Yaesu Terminal Hotel
八重洲ターミナルホテル
17 Business Hotel Heimat
ビジネスホテル　ハイマート
23 Hotel Seiyo Ginza
ホテル西洋銀座
38 Hotel Ginza Dai-ei
ホテル銀座ダイエー
40 Hotel Atami-so
ホテル熱海荘
67 Imperial Hotel
帝国ホテル
73 Ginza Nikkō Hotel
銀座日航ホテル
76 Ginza International Hotel
銀座国際ホテル
77 Ginza Dai-Ichi Hotel
銀座第一ホテル
79 Sun Hotel Shimbashi
サンホテル新橋

PLACES TO EAT

31 Kawa Restaurant
かわレストラン
35 Kalten-zushi Sushi
回転寿司
36 Volks Restaurant
フォルクス　レストラン
37 Tenya Restaurant
天屋レストラン
42 Nair's Indian Restaurant
ナイル　インド　レストラン
47 Saigon Restaurant
サイゴン
48 Dondo Restaurant
どんど
51 Yakitoris
焼き鳥屋
53 Ginza Palmy Building
銀座パーミイビル
55 New Torigin Restaurant
ニュー鳥ぎん
58 Munchen Beer Hall
ミュンヘン　ビアホール
60 Sapporo Maharaja Indian Restaurant
札幌マハラジャ　インドレストラン
62 Lion Beer Hall
ライオン　ビアホール
70 Sapporo Restaurant Indonesia
インドネシア

75 Kyubei Restaurant
久兵衛

OTHER

1 Ōte-mon Gate
大手門
3 Wadakura-mon Gate
和田倉門
4 Sakashita-mon Gate
坂下門
5 Nijū-bashi Bridge
二重橋
6 Sakurada-mon Gate
桜田門
8 JR Tokyo Station
ＪＲ東京駅
9 Daimaru Department Store
大丸百貨店
11 Maruzen Bookshop
丸善書店
12 Tokyū Department Store
東急百貨店
13 Kite Museum
凧の博物館
14 Yamatane Museum of Art
山種美術館
15 Takashimaya Department Store
高島屋
16 Bridgestone Museum of Art
ブリジストン美術館
18 Airport Limousine Bus Stop
空港リムジンバス
19 JR Highway Bus Terminal
ＪＲハイウエイバス
20 Central Post Office
中央郵便局
21 Yaesu Bookshop
八重洲書店
22 Meidi-ya Internationa
Bookshop
明治屋
24 American Express
アメリカンエクスプレス
25 Imperial Theatre & Idemitsu Art
Museum
帝国劇場／出光美術館
26 Sogo Department Store
そごう百貨店
27 Kōtsū Building
交通会館
28 Printemps Department Store
プランタン
29 Kodak Imagica
コダック　イマジカ
30 Kirin City
キリン　シティ

JAPAN

32 Nikon Gallery
ニコン　ギャラリー
33 Matsuya Department Store
松屋百貨店
34 Ito-ya Stationery Shop
伊東屋
39 World Magazine Gallery
ワールド　マガジンギャラリー
41 Kabuki-za Theatre
歌舞伎座
43 Mitsukoshi Department Store
三越百貨店
44 Wakō Department Store
服部和光
45 Hanky & Seibu Department Stores
阪急／西武百貨店
46 American Pharmacy
アメリカン　ファーマシー
49 TIC
旅行案内所
50 Hibiya Chanter (Cinema District)
日比谷シャンテ
52 Hankyū Department Store
阪急百貨店
54 Sony Showroom
ソニービル
56 Yoseido Gallery
三笠会館
57 Jena Bookshop
イエナ洋書店
59 Mitsubishi Building
三菱ビル
61 Matsuzakaya Department Store
松坂屋
63 Toshiba Ginza Seven
東芝銀座セブン
64 Hakuhinkan Toy Park
博品館トイパーク
65 Riccar Art Museum
リッカー美術館
66 Nishiginza Electric Centre
西銀座電力センター
68 International Arcade
インターナショナル　アーケード
69 Taikō Festival Shop
タイコー　フェスティバル
71 Henry Africa
ヘンリー　アフリカ
72 Hachikan-jinja Shrine
八幡神社
74 Takumi Souvenirs
たくみ土産物店
78 Tokyo P/N (National Panasonic
Showroom)
東京Ｐ／Ｎ
（ナショナル　パナソニック）

SUBWAY STATIONS

S1 Ōtemachi (Chiyoda Line)
大手町（千代田線）
S2 Ōtemachi (TOEI Mita Line)
大手町（都営三田線）
S3 Ōtemachi (Tōzai Line)
大手町（東西線）
S4 Nihombashi
日本橋
S5 Edobashi
江戸橋
S6 Tokyo-Ōtemachi
東京／大手町
S7 Nijūashi-mae (Chiyoda Line)
二重橋前（千代田線）
S8 Kyobashi
京橋
S9 Takara-chō
宝町
S10 Ginza-Itchōme
銀座一丁目
S11 Yūaku-chō
有楽町
S12 Hibiya (TOEI Mita Line)
日比谷（都営三田線）
S13 Hibiya (Hibiya & Chiyoda Lines)
日比谷（日比谷線／千代田線）
S14 Ginza (Marunouchi Line)
銀座（丸の内線）
S15 Ginza (Hibiya Line)
銀座（日比谷線）
S16 Ginza (Ginza Line)
銀座（銀座線）
S17 Higashi-Ginza
東銀座
S18 Shimbashi (TOEI Asakusa Line)
新橋（都営浅草線）
S19 Shimbashi (Ginza Line)
新橋（銀座線）
S20 Uchisaiwai-chō
内幸町
S21 Toranomon
虎ノ門
S22 Kasumigaseki (Chiyoda Line)
霞ケ関（千代田線）
S23 Kasumigaseki (Hibiya Line)
霞ケ関（日比谷線）
S24 Kasumigaseki (Marunouchi Line)
霞ケ関（丸の内線）
S25 Sakuradamon
桜田門

most notorious red light area, can be found here. It is safe to explore.

South of Shinjuku, **Harajuku** is probably the trendiest stop on the Yamanote loop. The best day to visit is Sunday, when Tokyo's subcultures put themselves on public display in the nearby **Yoyogi-kōen Park**, performing everything from avant-garde theatre to Sex Pistols-style punk. The activity starts at 1 pm and continues through to around 5 or 6 pm. For most visitors, Harajuku's main attraction is **Meiji-jingū Shrine**, built in memory of Emperor Meiji and Empress Shōken. It's a reconstruction of the 1920 original, but the reconstruction work has been reverently undertaken and the result is superb.

One stop south of Harajuku is **Shibuya**, a youth oriented version of Ginza. It has no outstanding sights as such, but is one of the best areas to take a peek at Tokyo's vision of the 21st century. Department stores such as Parco (I, II & III), Loft (youth paraphernalia), Tōkyū Hands (do-it-yourself) and Wave (CDs) all make for fascinating browsing, and there are some great photo opportunities on the streets.

Activities

On the club and association front there is something for everyone in Tokyo. The following is just a sprinkling of what's available. Those with more specialised interests should check with the TIC or the classifieds pages of *Tokyo Journal*.

Buddhist English Academy has lectures every Friday at 7 pm for ¥500 in Shinjuku (☎ 3342-6605)
Corn Popper Club is very much an American affair, but if you're from the USA and into popcorn, coffee, tea, billiards and the occasional party, this could be just the club for you (☎ 3715-4473)
International Adventure Club monthly meeting at Tokyo British Club (☎ 3403-7595)
International Feminists of Japan meets twice monthly; ring Makiko (☎ 0423-97-5609)
International House of Japan is a prestigious association that runs academic seminars and is able to provide accommodation to its members at reasonable rates, although membership is expensive (¥200,000) and requires two nominations from members (☎ 3470-4611)

Japan Association of Translators meets third Saturday of every month (fax 3385-5180)
Japan Foundation has, among other things, library classes and free screenings of Japanese films with English subtitles – a real rarity in Japan (☎ 3263-4503)
Will House International Club cultural exchange through sports, camps, music, seminars etc (☎ 3380-8000)

Places To Stay

Tokyo is probably one of the most expensive cities in the world when it comes to finding somewhere to sleep. There are two youth hostels in Tokyo itself, but you might want to consider being based outside Tokyo. There are youth hostels in Yokohama, Kamakura and Nikko; see the Around Tokyo section later in this chapter for more information.

Hostels The *Tokyo International Youth Hostel* (Iidabashi) (☎ 3235-1107) doesn't require that you be a member but does ask that you book ahead and provide some identification (a passport will do) when you arrive. To get there, exit from Iidabashi station (either JR or subway) and look for the tallest building in sight (it's long, thin and glass fronted). There is a basic charge of ¥2650 per person per night, and a sleeping sheet costs ¥150 for three nights. The Narita Airport TIC has a step-by-step instruction sheet on how to get to the hostel from the airport most cheaply.

The *Yoyogi Youth Hostel* (☎ 3467-9163) requires that you be a youth hostel member to stay and charges ¥2100. There are no meals available, but there are cooking facilities. To get there, take the Ōdakyū line to Sangubashi station and walk towards the Meiji-jingū Shrine gardens. The hostel is enclosed in a fenced compound, not a former prison camp but the National Olympics Memorial Youth Centre, in building No 14. Staff may let you exceed the three night limit if it is not crowded.

Private Accommodation The *Kimi Ryokan* (☎ 3971-3766) has been popular with travellers for many years, has clean tatami-style rooms, a meeting room and is relaxed about the hours you keep. It's on the west side of Ikebukuro station and prices range from ¥3500 (there are only a couple of these and they're rarely free) to ¥4300 for singles, from ¥7000 to ¥8000 for doubles and from ¥7500 for twins.

The *Asia Centre of Japan* (☎ 3402-6111), near Aoyama-Itchōme subway station on the Ginza line, is a popular option in the upper-budget category. This is another place that attracts many long-term stayers, and even though it's a lot bigger than the Kimi, it's still often fully booked. The station is under the easily recognisable Aoyama Twin Tower building on Aoyama-dōri. Walk past the building towards Akasaka-Mitsuke, turn right (towards Roppongi) and the Asia Centre is a short walk up the third street on the left. Rooms have pay TVs, and singles cost from ¥4900, twins/doubles from ¥6400. Rooms with bathrooms are significantly more expensive.

An easy place to get to from Narita Airport is the *Suzuki Ryokan* (☎ 3821-4944) in Nippori. Some of the rooms have private bathrooms and all include TVs. Take the Keisei line from Narita and get off at Nippori station, the last stop before Ueno station. Walking in the direction of Ueno, go to the end of the station and turn right. After you've crossed the tracks straight ahead, there's a flight of stairs that takes you up to a road. The Suzuki Ryokan is a few doors down on the right, just look for the English sign. Rooms cost ¥4200 per person, or ¥5000 with private bathrooms.

Close to the JR Gotanda station on the Yamanote line is the *Ryokan Sansui-sō* (☎ 3441-7475). This is not the greatest of locations, but it's only a few stops from Shibuya, the nearest main railway terminus. Take the exit farthest away from Shibuya and exit on the left-hand side. Turn right, take the first right after the big Tōkyū department store and then the first left. Turn left and then right, walk past the bowling centre and look for the sign on the right directing you down the side road to the ryokan. Prices for singles/doubles without bath are ¥4700/8000, with

bath ¥5000/8400; triples without bath cost ¥11,000.

In Ueno, which is a good place to be based for sightseeing, even if it is a bit of a trek from the bright lights, there are several budget ryokan. The *Sawanoya Ryokan* (☎ 3822-2251) is within walking distance of Nezu subway station on the Chiyoda line (see the Ueno map). If you're coming from Narita International Airport, it would probably be easier and just as cheap if there are more than one of you to catch a taxi from Ueno station. Singles cost ¥4300 to ¥4600, doubles cost ¥8000 without bath and ¥8600 with, and triples cost ¥10,800 without bath and 12,300 with.

A bit closer to Ueno station is *Ryokan Katsutarō* (☎ 3821-9808). If you follow the road that runs alongside Shinobazu Pond for about 10 minutes, you'll see the ryokan on the right. Singles/doubles/triples cost ¥4200/7800/10,500 without bath and doubles/triples with bath cost ¥8400/12,600. On the left, before you get to Ryokan Katsutaro, is the larger *Suigetsu Hotel* (☎ 3822-9611), which has a laundrette and rooms with private bathrooms. You can also change money there. Singles/doubles cost ¥6500/11,400 and triples cost ¥14,400. This is one hotel where you really pay through the nose for a Japanese-style room with your own bath – ¥17,820 for a single! Western-style singles/doubles with bath cost ¥7300/12,300.

One stop away from Ueno on the JR Yamanote line (Uguisudani station) is the *Sakura Ryokan* (☎ 3876-8118). Take the southern exit and turn left. Pass the Iriya subway station exits on the left; the Sakura Ryokan is on the right-hand side of the second street on your left. If you're exiting from Iriya subway station on the Hibiya line, take the No 1 exit and turn left. Singles/doubles without bath cost ¥5000/9000; triples cost from ¥12,000 to ¥13,500. There are also Western-style rooms available with bath from ¥6000 for a single.

Three stops away from Ueno on the Ginza line is Asakusa, which also has a few reasonably priced ryokan. *Ryokan Mikawaya*

Bekkan (☎ 3843-2345) is just around the corner from the Sensō-ji Temple in an interesting area. It's on a side street off the shop-lined street leading into the temple. From the Kaminari-mon Gate, the street is a few streets up on the left – there's a toy shop and a shoe shop on the corner. The ryokan is on the left-hand side of the road. Singles/doubles without bath cost ¥5700/10,400.

In Nishi Asakusa (near Tawaramachi subway station, which is one stop away on the Ginza line from Asakusa station) is the *Kikuya Ryokan* (☎ 3841-6404/4051). It's just off Kappabashi-dōri dōri. Prices are ¥4500/7800 for singles/doubles and ¥11,000 for triples. It gets good reports as a quiet and friendly place to stay.

There are several other budget alternatives worth checking out, although they are popular with long-term visitors and often full. In Ikebukuro, the *House Ikebukuro* (☎ 3984-3399) has singles/doubles/triples for ¥4000/6000/7700. Near Kotake-Mukaihara subway station, a few stops out of Ikebukuro on the Yūraku-chō line, is the *Rikkō Kaikan Guest Room*, with singles/doubles from ¥4000/8000.

The *YMCA Asia Youth Centre* (☎ 3233-0611) takes both men and women but is pretty expensive for what it offers. It's halfway between Suidobashi and Jimbō-chō subway stations. Rooms with bathroom cost ¥7000/13,000 for singles/doubles and triples cost ¥16,800. The *Tokyo YWCA Sadohara Hostel* (☎ 3268-4451), near the Ichigaya exit of Ichigaya subway station, accepts couples and is cheaper. Singles/doubles with toilet cost from ¥6180/14,420.

A place that verges on belonging to the gaijin house category is *Apple House* (☎ 0422-51-2277). The advantage of this place is that it is big and has three branches all close to each other. Rates can be paid on a night-by-night basis (which is not possible in most gaijin houses), and the guesthouse has good facilities (kitchen, laundry, fax, satellite TV etc). Singles are ¥2800 to ¥3400 nightly, ¥18,000 to ¥20,000 per person weekly and ¥65,000 to ¥73,000 monthly; share twins are ¥2200 to ¥2800 nightly,

¥18,000 to ¥20,000 weekly and ¥36,000 to ¥39,000 monthly. Cheaper rates are available for four-bed dormitory style accommodation (¥2000 per person per night).

To get to Apple House take the Chūō line from Shinjuku station (platform No 10) to Higashi Koganei station and ring the guesthouse. Somebody will come to the station and meet you. It's also a good idea to make sure it actually has a vacancy before you travel all the way out there.

Capsule Hotels Capsule hotels are a strictly male domain and you find them wherever there are large numbers of salary men, bars, hostess clubs and other drains for company expense accounts. Close to the western exit of Ikebukuro station is the *Ikebukuro Plaza* (☎ 3590-7770), which costs ¥3800 per night. An even cheaper option is the *Capsule Kimeya Hotel* (☎ 3971-8751), where capsules cost ¥3200. It's over on the east side of Ikebukuro, not far from Sunshine City.

In the heart of Kabuki-chō, Shinjuku's infamous red-light district, is the *Shinjuku-ku Capsule Hotel* (☎ 3232-1110). It's open from 5 pm to 10 am and costs ¥4100. See the Shinjuku map for a couple of other capsule hotels with similar prices.

Gaijin Houses Gaijin houses are generally for foreigners who are looking for long-term accommodation and can't afford to set up house in Tokyo. Some of them, however, also offer nightly rates these days, though this is a rarity as weekly and or monthly rates are more the norm. The following places have daily or weekly rates. Ring them before you head out to the area. Most gaijin houses have a pick-up service from the nearest station.

1A House, share rooms ¥30,000 per month, ¥7000 per week, ¥1000 per night; 20 minutes from Shinjuku (☎ 0422-51-2277)

Friendship House, share ¥9200 to ¥10,400 per week, singles ¥16,750 per week; five locations including Higashi-Kōenji (Marunouchi line) and Kichijōji (JR) (☎ 3327-3179)

JAPAN

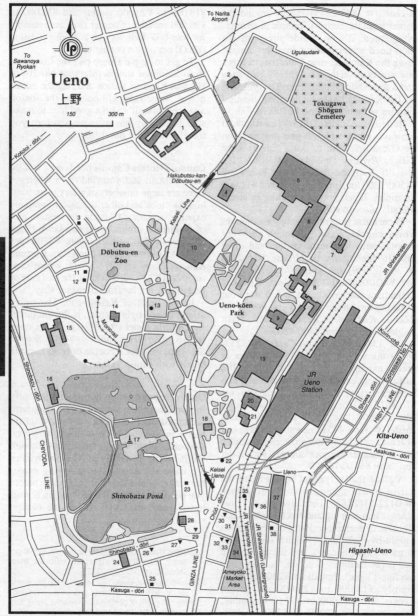

Ueno
上野

0   150   300 m

To Sawanoya
Ryokan

To Narita
Airport

Uguisudani

Tokugawa
Shōgun
Cemetery

Kottoi - dōri

Hakubutsu-kan-
Dōbutsu-en

Keisei Line

Ueno
Dōbutsu-en
Zoo

Ueno-kōen
Park

JR Shinkansen

Monorail

Shinobazu - dōri

CHIYODA LINE

Shinobazu Pond

JR
Ueno
Station

Konin-chō

Showa - dōri

Expressway No.1

HIBIYA LINE

Kita-Ueno

Asakusa - dōri

Keisei
Ueno

Chūō - dōri

Keisei
Ueno

Ueno

JR Yamanote Line

JR Shinkansen (Underground)

Higashi-Ueno

Shinobazu - dōri

GINZA LINE

Ameyoko
Market
Area

Kasuga - dōri

Kasuga - dōri

PLACES TO STAY

3　Ryokan Katsutarō
　旅館勝太郎
11　Hotel Ohgasio
　鴎外荘
12　Suigetsu Hotel
　酔月ホテル
23　Kinuya Hotel
　キメヤ　ホテル
24　Hotel Parkside
　ホテル　パークサイド
25　Hotel Pine Hill Ueno
　ホテル　パインヒル上野
38　Ueno Capsule Kimeya Hotel
　上野カプセル　きめやホテル

PLACES TO EAT

26　Yoshibei Restaurant
　芳兵衛
27　Izu-ei Restaurant
　伊豆栄
29　McDonald's
　マクドナルド
30　Kappazushi Restaurant
　かっぱ寿司
31　Maharaja Restaurant
　マハラジャ
32　Samrat Indian Restaurant
　サムラート　インドレストラン
33　Spaghetti House
　スパゲティ　ハウス
36　Irohazushi Restaurant
　いろは寿司

OTHER

1　Tokyo University of Fine Arts
　東京芸大
2　Kanei-ji Temple
　寛永寺

4　Gallery of Hōryūji Treasures
　法隆寺宝物館
5　Tokyo National Museum
　国立博物館
6　Gallery of Eastern Antiquities
　東洋アンティーク　ギャラリー
7　Rinno-ji Temple
　輪王寺
8　National Science Museum
　科学博物館
9　National Museum of Western Art
　西洋美術館
10　Tokyo Metropolitan Museum of Art
　東京都美術館
13　Five Storeyed Pagoda
　五重塔
14　Tōshō-gū Shrine
　東照宮
15　Ueno Zoo
　上野動物園
16　Aquarium
　水族館
17　Benzaiten Temple
　弁財天
18　Kiyomizu Kannon-dō Temple
　清水観音堂
19　Tokyo Metropolitan Festival Hall
　東京文化会館
20　Japan Art Academy
　芸術院会館
21　Ueno-no Mori Art Museum
　上野の森美術館
22　Saigō Takamori Statue
　西郷隆盛銅像
28　Shitamachi History Museum
　下町風俗資料館
34　Ameyoko Centre Building
　アメ横センタービル
35　Ameyoko-chō Arcade
　飴屋横町アーケード
37　Marui Department Store
　丸井百貨店

JAPAN

Liberty House, share weekly from ¥9000, monthly from ¥29,000; seven minutes from Ikebukuro and Shinjuku (☎ 5272-7238)

Maharaja Palace (somewhat infamous gaijin house), share weekly from ¥9000, singles/doubles monthly ¥59,000/70,000; 15 minutes from Gotanda, 30 minutes from Shibuya (☎ 3728-7061/5499-3779)

Marui House, daily singles/doubles ¥2600/3800, cheaper monthly rates available; good location in Ikebukuro, close to Kimi Ryokan (☎ 3962-4979)

Tokyo English Centre, share ¥2000 daily, ¥52,000 monthly; Fujimigaoka station (Keio-Inokashira line) (☎ 5370-8440)

Tokyo English House, ¥2900 a day, ¥18,000 a week ¥60,00 a month; share rooms also available at cheaper rates; three minutes' walk from Horikiri Shōbu-en station on the Keisei line (☎ 3335-0572/3693-4300)

Places to Eat

The great boon to cash-strapped foreign visitors to Tokyo (and indeed the rest of Japan) are the plastic food displays in restaurant windows. Prices are indicated and the displays give a fairly accurate idea of the dishes.

The fast-food barns are well represented in Tokyo. The McDonald's phenomenon has even spawned some Japanese variations on the same theme: *Mos Burger*, *Lotteria* and *Love Burger*, to name a few. Also worth seeking out are the Japanese food chains like *Yoshinoya* (with gyūdon – beef and rice – dishes) and *Tenya* (with tendon – tempura and rice – dishes). Some of the chains offer pretty good lunch-time specials – ¥650 for all the Shakey's pizza you can eat is an example.

The budget-priced coffee shop, of which there is an ever-increasing number, is another good fast-food option. The major chain is *Doutor* (look for the big yellow and brown signs). Doutor sells coffee for ¥190 and German hotdogs for ¥190. You can put together a good lunch, including a ¥150 piece of cake, for around ¥550, which is not bad in Tokyo. *Pronto* is another chain that specialises in inexpensive coffee, and in the evenings they become shot bars with beers from ¥330. The *Mr Donut* places are good for an economical donut, orange juice and coffee breakfast.

During the day, the best eating areas are the big shopping districts like Shibuya, Shinjuku, Harajuku and Ginza. Shinjuku could well take the prize as Tokyo's best daytime gourmet experience, with rows of restaurants in the big department stores and, at street level, an endless selection of reasonably priced restaurants and the best affordable Chinese food in Tokyo. Shinjuku is the busiest commuter junction in Tokyo, and there are a vast number of restaurants around the station and in the frenetic entertainment area. There are also many restaurants underground, along the 1.5 km of shopping streets which run from around the station.

The Ginza area is, as you might expect, a fairly bad area to seek out affordable eats, but it does have a selection of fast-food barns. You won't have any trouble finding them. An interesting alternative to these is *Nair's*, a small place with good Indian curries at affordable prices. Check out the restaurant floors of department stores: *Restaurant City*

on the 8th floor of the Matsuya department store; the 2nd basement level of the Matsuzakaya department store; and the basement of the Ginza Palmy building.

Ueno and Asakusa feature mainly Japanese restaurants, although both areas have a large number of standbys like *McDonald's* and *Kentucky Fried Chicken*. The best places to seek out reasonably priced Japanese fare in Ueno are the Ameyoko-chō arcade and Ueno station itself; look out for the restaurants serving monster-size bowls of rāmen from around ¥500.

In Asakusa, the area between Sensō-ji Temple and Kaminarimon-dōri is the best place for Japanese food. On Kaminarimon-dōri itself, *Tenya*, a tiny mod-con tendon shop, has tempura and rice dishes from ¥490, which is a bargain. To the right of the entrance to Sensō-ji Temple is *Tonkyu*, a small, family-run (tonkatsu) establishment, where you can eat well from ¥700. It's closed Thursday. To the left is a branch of *Yoshinoya*, a chain that can be found all over Tokyo, specialising in very inexpensive gyūdon.

In Ikebukuro, the east side of the station is the best area for meals. A short wander will turn up everything from the familiar fast-food options to economical noodle shops and revolving sushi shops.

Shinjuku, particularly the east side of the station, has some of the best dining out opportunities in Tokyo. It's a good place to splash out on an izakaya-style (beer and snacks) meal. Two good places to do this are *Daikokuya*, a popular student hangout with all-you-can-eat deals (yaki-niku ¥1700, shabu-shabu and sukiyaki ¥2300, add ¥1000 and it's all you can drink too), and *Iron-ohanihoheto* (what a mouthful), an affordable place with illustrated menus.

At the end of the day, however, the best advice for Shinjuku is just to strike off and see what you come up with. Look out for one of the numerous *kaiten-zushi*, or 'revolving sushi' restaurants (there are two indicated on the Shinjuku map) or take an escalator to the top floors of one of the department stores. The back lanes of Kabuki-chō are also packed with Japanese restaurants (among other things).

The Harajuku and Shibuya areas offer more in the way of pizzerias, ethnic bars and coffee shops than Japanese cuisine. Most of these are fairly expensive. In Harajuku look out for *Genroku* on Omote-sandō. It's a revolving sushi shop in a league of its own, with sushi from ¥130 a plate. Apart from the fast-food barns, the best bet in Shibuya is to head up to the upper floors of the department stores, but as Shibuya is a very fashionable area don't expect to find any real bargains.

Entertainment

Entertainment in Tokyo is expensive. If it's just some straight carousing you want, there are always a few bars that you can drop into and nurse a beer without having to negotiate a hefty door charge first, but discos and the like will probably cost upwards of ¥4000 entry (usually this includes a few drink vouchers).

Traditional Probably the top traditional entertainment attraction in Tokyo is kabuki at the *Kabuki-za Theatre* (☎ 3541-3131) in Ginza. It's a good idea to check with the TIC or with the theatre directly for programme information. Prices for tickets range from ¥2000 to ¥14,000, depending on how keen you are to see the stage, and 'earphone guides' with English explanations of the proceedings are ¥600. Bear in mind that 4th-floor tickets are available for less than ¥1000; you only get to watch part of the show (kabuki performances last forever) and earphone guides are not available in these seats. Fourth-floor tickets can be bought on the day of the performance. There are generally two performances daily, starting at around 11 am and 4 pm.

Nō performances are held at various locations around Tokyo. Tickets will cost between ¥3000 and ¥10,000, and it's best to get them at the theatre itself. Check with the TIC for the dates of performances and the location of theatres.

A fascinating alternative to kabuki and Nō is a sumō match. Sumō tournaments at Tokyo's *Ryōgoku Kokugikan Stadium* (☎ 3866-8700) in Ryōgoku take place in January, May and September, and last 15 days. Seats are expensive, but bench seats at the back cost about ¥1000. If you don't mind standing, you can get in for around ¥500. The cheaper tickets can be purchased on the day. The stadium is adjacent to Ryōgoku station on the northern side of the railway tracks.

Finally, on the traditional entertainment front, a few hotels in Tokyo hold tea ceremonies which you can observe and occasionally participate in for a fee of about ¥1000. The *Hotel New Otani* (☎ 3265-1111) has ceremonies on its 7th floor on Thursday, Friday and Saturday from 11 am to noon and 1 to 4 pm. Ring them before you go to make sure the show hasn't been booked out. The *Hotel Okura* (☎ 3582-0111) and the *Imperial Hotel* (☎ 3504-1111) also hold daily tea ceremonies.

Nightlife Travellers on a budget will be restricted to straight drinking bars when it comes to nightlife. Clubs with live entertainment or dancing tend to have prohibitively expensive entry charges. This doesn't mean that you have to shun the bright lights altogether. It's worth spending at least one night out on the town in Tokyo, and even areas like Roppongi, the nightlife capital of Tokyo, have a few places that you can walk into and spend no more than ¥500 on a beer.

Roppongi bars include *Henry Africa* (☎ 3405-9868), *Déjà Vu* (☎ 3403-8777) and *Motown* – all popular places to hang out and knock back a couple of beers. Déjà Vu is the cheapest of the three, with beers at ¥500. Close by Déjà Vu is *Gas Panic*, a place that's worth a look and then best avoided; the occasional knifing doesn't seem to do anything to lessen its popularity. Quieter and somehow a little more civilised (despite the name) is *Gaijin Zone*, a bar with dancing and cheap beer.

Those based in the Ikebukuro area have a few reasonably priced entertainment options to choose from. *One Lucky* (☎ 3985-0069) is a favourite among foreign residents and guests of the nearby Kimi Ryokan. It's a

JAPAN

JAPAN

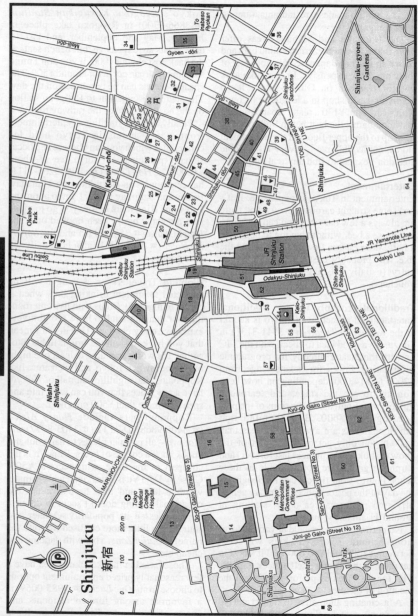

To
Inabaso
Ryokan

Shinjuku-gyoen
Gardens

Meiji-dōri

34

35

Gyoen - dōri

33

32

31

30

29

28

27

26

25

24

23

22

21

20

19

18

17

16

15

14

13

12

11

10

9

8

7

6

5

4

3

2

1

36

37

Shinjuku-
Sanchōme

38

40

41

39

42

43

44

45

46

47

48

49

50

51

52

53

54

55

56

57

58

59

60

61

62

63

64

Yasukuni - dōri

Shinjuku - dōri

Meiji - dōri

Shinjuku

Kabuki-chō

Okubo
Park

Seibu Line

Seibu
Shinjuku
Station

JR
Shinjuku
Station

Odakyū-Shinjuku

Keiō-
Shinjuku

JR Yamanote Line

Ōdakyū Line

Shin-sen
Shinjuku

TOEI SHINJUKU LINE

KEIŌ TEITO LINE

KEIŌ SHIN-SEN LINE

Kōshū-kaidō

Nishi-
Shinjuku

Ōme-kaidō

MARUNOUCHI LINE

✚ Tokyo
Medical
College
Hospital

Kyū-gō Gairo (Street No 9)

Go-gō Gairo (Street No 5)

Shichi-gō Gairo (Street No 3)

Jūni-gō Gairo (Street No 12)

Tokyo
Metropolitan
Government
Offices

Central

Park

Shinjuku

新宿

Shinjuku

200 m

100

0

LP

PLACES TO STAY

3　Green Plaza Shinjuku
　(capsule hotel)
　グリーンプラザ新宿
9　Shinjuku Prince Hotel
　新宿プリンスホテル
10　Star Hotel Tokyo
　スターホテル東京
13　Tokyo Hilton
　International
　東京ヒルトンホテル
14　Century Hyatt Hotel
　センチュリーハイヤット
27　Shinjuku-ku Capsule
　Hotel
　新宿区カプセルホテル
34　Hotel Sun Lite Shinjuka
　ホテル　サンライト新宿
36　Winning Inn Shinjuku
　(capsule hotel)
　ウィニング　イン新宿
47　Central Hotel
　セントラル　ホテル
58　Keio Plaza Inter
　Continental Hotel
　京王プラザ
　インターコンチネンタル
59　Shinjuku New City
　Hotel
　新宿ニューシティ　ホテル
61　Shinjuku Washington
　Hotel
　新宿ワシントンホテル
64　Shinjuku Park Hotel
　新宿パークホテル

PLACES TO EAT

1　Pekin Chinese
　Restaurant
　北京飯店
2　Tainan Taami Taiwan-
　ese Restaurant
　台南　台湾レストラン
4　Tokyo Kaisen Ichiba
　Chinese Restaurant
　東京海鮮市場
6　Kaiten-zushi Revolving
　Sushi Restaurant
　回転寿司
7　Ban Thai Restaurant
　バン・タイ　レストラン
8　Yōrōnotaki Restaurant
　養老の滝
20　Ibuki Restaurant
　伊吹レストラン

24　Champer Thai
　Restaurant
　チャンパー　タイ
25　Tōkaien Korean
　Restaurant
　東海苑　韓国レストラン
26　Yatai Mura (Kao Keng &
　Other Restaurants)
　屋台村
28　Hofbräuhaus Beer Hall
　ホーフブロイハウス
　ビアホール
31　Tokyo Dai Hanten
　Chinese Restaurant
　東京大飯店
39　Daikokuya Restaurant
　大黒屋
41　Tsunahachi Restaurant
　つな八
42　Irohanihoheto
　Restaurant
　いろはにほへと
43　El Borracho Mexican
　Restaurant
　エル　ボラッチョ
　メキシカン
46　Tatsukichi Restaurant
　たつ吉
48　Kaiten-zushi Revolving
　Sushi Restaurant
　回転寿司
49　Suehiro Restaurant
　スエヒロ
63　Rose de Sahara
　Restaurant
　ローズ　ド　サハラ

OTHER

5　Koma Theatre
　コマ劇場
11　Kaisai Kaijo Building
　海上ビル
12　Shinjuku Nomura
　Building
　新宿野村ビル
15　Shinjuku Sumitomo
　Building
　新宿住友ビル
16　Shinjuku Mitsui Building
　新宿三井ビル
17　Shinjuku Centre
　Building
　新宿センタービル
18　Odakyū Department
　Store
　小田急デパート

19　Charlie's Not Here
　チャーリーズ
　ノット　ヒア
21　Studio Alta Building
　スタジオ　アルタ　ビル
22　Konika Plaza
　コニカ　プラザ
23　Kirin City
　キリン　シティ
29　Golden Gai-jinja
　ゴールデン街
30　Hanazono-jinja Shrine
　花園神社
32　Milo's Garage
　ミロズ　ガレージ
33　Marui Men's
　Department Store
　丸井紳士服デパート
35　Isetan Park City
　伊勢丹パークシティ
37　Rolling Stone
　ローリング　ストン
38　Isetan Department
　Store
　伊勢丹
40　Mitsukoshi Department
　Store
　新宿三越
44　Kinokuniya Bookshop
　紀伊国屋書店
45　Marui Department
　Store &
　Virgin Megastore
　丸井デパート
50　My City Department
　Store
　マイ　シティ
51　Odaky Department
　Store
　小田急百貨店
52　Keio Department Store
　京王百貨店
53　Airport Limousine Bus
　Stop
　空港リムジンバス
54　Highway Bus Terminal
　ハイウェイ　バス
55　Yodobashi Camera
　淀橋カメラ
56　Sakuraya Camera
　カメラのサクラヤ
57　Post Office
　新宿郵便局
60　Shinjuku NS Building
　新宿ＮＳビル
62　KDD Building
　ＫＤＤビル

JAPAN

one-man show where the master-san prepares all the food (a delicious set-menu dinner for ¥700), pours the drinks (a beer is ¥500) and, most importantly, takes a photograph of everyone who visits. It's closed on Monday.

Shinjuku's nightlife opportunities are underrated by many of Tokyo's residents. The *Rolling Stone* is a long-running Tokyo institution and is an interesting alternative to the Roppongi scene. It's fairly quiet on weeknights, but gets packed out on Friday or Saturday nights – lots of heavy-metal kids. There's a ¥200 cover charge and beers cost ¥800 per bottle. Down on the other side of Yasukuni-dōri, actually inside the entrance to Hanazono-jinja Shrine (what a great place for a club), is *Milo's Garage*, a dance club with different 'happenings' every night of the week. Entry ranges from ¥1500 to ¥2000, but this usually includes a couple of drinks. It's a good place to go with a group of friends for a dance as it rarely gets crowded and hasn't really been discovered by the gaijin set.

Things to Buy

It won't take you long to realise that Tokyo is hardly one of Asia's premiere destinations when it comes to shopping. The rising yen has simply made retail prices too high. Department store sales can turn up some bargains, but generally you'll be better off checking out one of Tokyo's flea markets for your souvenirs. The following is a selection of the larger ones:

Tōgō-jinja Shrine, 4 am to 4 pm on the first and fourth Sunday of each month; Harajuku station, turn left and take the next right after Takeshita-dōri
Nogi-jinja Shrine, dawn to dusk on the second Sunday of each month; from Nogi-zaka subway station on the Chiyoda line, the shrine is on the other side of Gaien-higashi-dōri
Hanazono-jinja Shrine, 7 am to 5 pm on the second and third Sunday of every month; close to Isetan department store on the east side of Shinjuku station
Roppongi, 8 am to 8 pm on the fourth Thursday and Friday of every month; in front of the Roy building, close to Roppongi subway station

Iidabashi Antique Market, 6 am to 6 pm on the first Saturday of every month; Central Plaza, Ramura building close to Iidabashi JR and subway stations
Sunshine City Ikebukuro, 8 am to 10 pm on the third Saturday and Sunday of every month; Alpa shopping arcade

If your trip doesn't coincide with any markets, some other shopping suggestions include the 1st floor of the Satomi building (close to the east exit of Ikebukuro station), where there are more than 30 antique dealers open from 10 am to 7 pm, closed Thursday, and the Oriental Bazaar in Harajuku. The latter has a good range of souvenirs, some of them quite affordable.

Getting There & Away

Air With the exception of China Airlines, all international airlines touch down at Narita Airport rather than at the more conveniently located Haneda Airport. The former is probably one of the least friendly airports to arrive in Asia, and backpackers arriving from countries where drugs are available should expect long delays while customs officials test your toothpaste and so on, so don't even think about bringing anything you shouldn't. Bear in mind that Narita has a ¥2000 departure tax.

Train Arriving in Tokyo by train is a simple affair. Most of the major train lines terminate at either Tokyo or Ueno stations, both of which are on the JR Yamanote line. As a general rule of thumb, trains for the north and north-east start at either Ueno or Tokyo station and southbound trains start at Tokyo station. For day trips to areas such as Kamakura, Nikkō, Hakone and Yokohama, the most convenient means of transport is usually one of the private lines. With the exception of the Tōbu Nikkō line, which starts in Asakusa, all of them start from somewhere on the Yamanote line.

There are three shinkansen lines that connect Tokyo with the rest of Japan: the Tōkaidō line passes through Central Honshū, changing name along the way to the San-yō line before terminating at Hakata in

Northern Kyūshū; the Tōhoku line runs north-east via Utsunomiya and Sendai as far as Morioka; and the Jōetsu line runs north to Niigata. Of these lines, the one most likely to be used by visitors to Japan is the Tōkaidō line, as it passes through Kyoto and Osaka in the Kansai region. All three shinkansen lines start at Tokyo station, though the Tōhoku and Jōetsu lines make a stop at Ueno station.

Bus Most interesting for budget travellers are the night express services. They tend to work out slightly cheaper than travelling by train, are comfortable and save on a night's accommodation. For Kyoto and Osaka, overnight buses leave at 10 pm from Tokyo station and arrive between 6 and 7 am the following morning. They cost from ¥8000 to ¥8500. The buses are a JR service and can be booked at one of the Green Windows in a JR station. Direct buses also run from Tokyo station to Nara and Kōbe. And from Shinjuku station there are buses running to the Fuji and Hakone regions, including, for Mt Fuji climbers, direct services to the 'fifth stations', from where you have to walk.

Boat A ferry journey can be a great way to get from Tokyo to other parts of the country. Fares are not too expensive (by Japanese standards anyway) and there is the advantage that you save the expense of a night or two's accommodation.

From Tokyo, there are long-distance ferry services to Kushiro (☎ 5400-6080) and Tomakomai (☎ 3578-1127) in Hokkaidō (2nd class ¥14,420 and ¥11,840 respectively), to Kōchi (☎ 3578-1127) (2nd class ¥13,910) and Tokushima (☎ 3567-0971) (2nd class ¥8200) in Shikoku, to Kokura (☎ 3567-0971) in Northern Kyūshū (2nd class ¥12,000) and to Naha (☎ 3273-8911 or 3281-1831) in Okinawa (☎ ¥19,670).

Departures may not always be frequent (usually once every two or three days for long-distance services) and ferries are sometimes fully booked well in advance, so it pays to make enquiries early. The numbers given previously for ferry companies will require some Japanese-language skills or the assistance of a Japanese speaker. If you have problems, contact the TIC at Narita or in Tokyo.

Getting Around

Tokyo has an excellent public transport system. There are very few worthwhile spots around town that aren't conveniently close to a subway or JR station. When the rail network lets you down, there are generally bus services, though these are harder to use if you can't read kanji.

To/From Narita Airport Narita International Airport is used by almost all the international airlines but only by a small number of domestic operators. The airport is 66 km from central Tokyo, which means that getting into town is going to take from 50 minutes to 1½ hours, depending on your mode of transport.

All things considered, rail is the best mode of transport between Narita and Tokyo. For one, you are not going to get snarled up in the traffic and, two, if you don't mind taking a bit longer getting into town (80 minutes by rapid as opposed to 50 minutes by express), train can be cheaper (depending on how you do it).

There are three rail services between Narita International Airport and Tokyo: the private Keisei line, the JR Narita Express (N'EX) and Airport Narita services. From the airport, unless you plan to be based in Ueno or Asakusa, the N'EX service is probably the most convenient as it runs directly into Tokyo, Shinjuku and (less frequently) Ikebukuro stations. Those heading out to the airport should bear in mind that it is important to note which terminal (No 1 or 2) to alight at. The N'EX platforms in Tokyo, Shinjuku and Ikebukuro stations will have a list of the airline companies that operate from each of the terminals.

The N'EX services are fast, extremely comfortable and include services like drink dispensing machines and telephones, but they don't come all that cheap. If you don't mind standing, tickets are ¥500 cheaper. The trip to Tokyo station takes 53 minutes and costs ¥2890; to Shinjuku station takes 80 minutes and costs ¥3050; to Ikebukuro station takes 90 minutes and costs ¥3050; and to Yokohama station takes 90 minutes and costs ¥4100. JR also has Airport Narita rapid trains that take 90 minutes and cost ¥1260 to Tokyo central, ¥1850 to Yokohama and don't stop at Shinjuku or Ikebukuro. The latter service is also less frequent, running only once an hour between 7 am and 10 pm. N'EX services run approximately half hourly between the same hours, but Ikebukuro services are very infrequent and in most cases you will be better off heading to Shinjuku and taking the JR Yamanote line from there.

On the private Keisei line, there are two trains running between Narita International Airport and Ueno stations: the Skyliner, which runs nonstop and takes one hour (¥1740) and the limited express (tokkyū) service, which takes 70 minutes (¥940). You can buy tickets at the Keisei ticket office in the northern wing of the arrival lounge at Narita International Airport or at the station. Ueno is the final destination of the train and is connected to the rest of Tokyo by the JR Yamanote line and the Hibiya and Ginza subway lines.

The only affordable alternative to taking a train is a limousine bus. The buses take 1½ to two hours (depending on the traffic) to travel between Narita International Airport and a number of major hotels around Tokyo. Check departure times before buying your ticket, as services are not all that frequent. The fare to hotels in eastern Tokyo is ¥2800, while to Ikebukuro, Akasaka, Ginza, Shiba, Shinagawa, Shinjuku or Haneda Airport it is ¥2900. There is also a bus service straight to Yokohama, which costs ¥3300. The trip to Yokohama City Air Terminal (YCAT) takes at least two hours.

To/From Haneda Airport Most domestic flights and China Airlines (Taiwan) flights use the Haneda Airport.

Getting from Haneda Airport to Tokyo is a simple matter of taking the monorail to Hamamatsu-chō station on the JR Yamanote

line. The trip takes just under 20 minutes; trains leave every 10 minutes and cost ¥270.

Train Most visitors to Tokyo find themselves using the railway system far more than any other means of transport. In fact, the only real drawback with the Tokyo railway network is that it shuts down somewhere between midnight and 1 am and doesn't start up again until 5 or 6 am. Subway trains have a habit of stopping halfway along their route when closing time arrives. People who get stranded face the prospect of an expensive taxi ride home or of waiting the rest of the night for the first morning train.

Undoubtedly, the most useful line in Tokyo is the JR Yamanote line, which does a loop around the city, taking in most of the important areas. You can do the whole circuit in an hour for the ¥120 minimum fare, which is a great introduction to the city. Another useful above-ground JR route is the Chūo line, which cuts across the centre of town between Shinjuku and Akihabara.

The subway system can be a bit daunting at first, but you soon get the hang of it. All the subway lines are colour coded, so even if you can't read a thing you soon learn that the Ginza line is orange. For all local journeys, tickets are sold by vending machines called jidō kippu uriba. Above the vending machines you will find a rail map with fares indicated next to the station names. Unfortunately, the names are almost always in kanji only. Probably the best way around this problem is to put your money in the machine and push the lowest fare button (usually ¥120). This will get you on the train and when you get to your destination you can correct the fare at the fare adjustment office.

If you get tired of fumbling for change every time you buy a ticket, the JR system offers the option of 'orange cards'. The cards are available in denominations of ¥1000, ¥3000 and ¥5000. Fares are automatically deducted from the cards when you use them in the orange-card vending machines.

Bus Many Tokyo residents and visitors spend a considerable amount of time in the city without ever using the bus network. This is partly because the train services are so good and partly because the buses are much more difficult to use. In addition, buses are at the mercy of Tokyo's sluggish traffic flow. Services also tend to finish fairly early in the evening, making buses a pretty poor alternative all round.

Taxi Taxis are so expensive that you should only use them when there is no alternative. Rates start at ¥600, which gives you two km (after 11 pm 1.5 km), after which the meter starts to click an additional ¥90 for every 340 metres; you also click up ¥90 for every two minutes you sit idly gazing at the scenery in a typical Tokyo traffic jam.

Tours Guided tours of Tokyo are a very expensive way of seeing places that you could see more cheaply on your own. If you simply *must* join a tour, first stop should be the TIC, which has comprehensive listings of what's available.

Around Tokyo 東京の附近

Some of Japan's foremost attractions are clustered around Tokyo. If you've wrangled some cheap accommodation in the big city, some of them will make good day trips. Otherwise you might consider overnighting; Nikkō, Kamakura and Hakone are particularly good areas to do this.

IZU-HANTŌ PENINSULA 伊豆半島

Izu is of more interest to residents of Tokyo than to visitors with a hurried schedule. It makes a pleasant get away from the city, but is otherwise of limited interest.

Atami 熱海

Atami is a hot-spring town with expensive accommodation. You'll need to travel farther out onto the peninsula if you are looking for somewhere cheap to stay.

Getting There & Away An ordinary Tōkaidō line train from Tokyo station will get you to Atami in one hour 45 minutes for ¥1850.

Shimoda 下田

If you only have time for one town on the peninsula, make it Shimoda, the most pleasant of the hot-springs resorts (*onsen*). It's a peaceful place with a few historical sights as well as the usual touristy stuff.

About a 25-minute walk from Shimoda station is **Ryōsen-ji Temple**, famous as the site of a treaty, supplementary to the Treaty of Kanagawa, and signed by Commodore Perry and representatives of the Tokugawa Shogunate. Today the temple is less interesting than its next-door neighbour, **Chōraku-ji Temple**, which has a collection of erotic knick-knacks – pickled turnips with suggestive shapes and stones with vagina-like orifices in them. This odd museum is open from 8.30 am to 5 pm daily, and admission is ¥500.

Getting There & Away Shimoda is as far as you can go by train on the Izu-hantō Peninsula; the limited express from Tokyo station takes two hours 45 minutes and costs ¥5850. Alternatively, take an Izu Kyūkō line train from Itō station for ¥1340; the trip takes about an hour. There are a few express services each day from Atami station, but the express surcharges make them expensive.

Bus platform No 5 in front of the station is for buses going to Dogashima, while platform No 7 is for those bound for Shuzenji.

Cape Irō-zaki 石廊崎

Cape Irō-zaki, the southernmost point of the peninsula, is noted for its cliffs and lighthouse. It also has a jungle park, a tropical garden and some fairly good beaches. Buses from Shimoda to the Irō-zaki lighthouse take around 55 minutes and cost ¥840.

HAKONE 箱根

If the weather cooperates and Mt Fuji is clearly visible, the Hakone region can make a wonderful day trip out of Tokyo. You can enjoy cable-car rides, visit an open-air museum, poke around smelly volcanic hot-

JAPAN

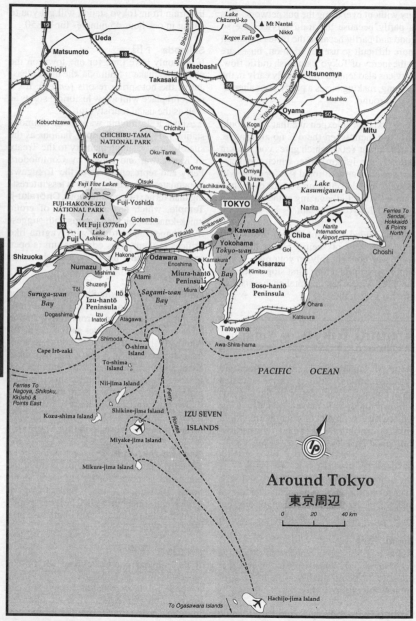

Lake
Chūzenji-ko   ▲ Mt Nantai

Kegon Falls   Nikkō

Ueda

Matsumoto

Shiojiri

Maebashi

Takasaki

Utsunomya

Mashiko

Oyama

Koga

Mitu

Kobuchizawa

Chichibu

Kawagoe

CHICHIBU-TAMA
NATIONAL PARK

Kōfu   Oku-Tama

Ōme

Tachikawa   Omiya
Urawa

Lake
Kasumigaura

Fuji Five Lakes   Ōtsuki

Narita
Ferries To
Sendai,
Hokkaidō
& Points
North

Fuji-Yoshida   TOKYO

FUJI-HAKONE-IZU
NATIONAL PARK

Mt Fuji (3776m)   Kawasaki

Gotemba   Narita
International
Airport

Fuji   Yokohama
Lake
Ashino-ko   Chiba

Shizuoka   Odawara   Goi   Choshi

Numazu   Enoshima
Mishima   Kamakura

Tōkaidō Shinkansen   Tokyo-wan

Tōi   Atami   Miura-hantō   Kisarazu
Shuzenji   Peninsula   Kimitsu

Izu-hantō   Itō   Bay
Peninsula   Sagami-wan   Boso-hantō
Izu   Bay   Peninsula
Suruga-wan   Inatori
Bay   Atagawa   Miura

Dogashima

Shimoda   Ōhara

Cape Irō-zaki   Ō-shima   Katsuura
Island

To-shima   Tateyama
Island

Awa-Shira-hama

Nii-jima Island   PACIFIC   OCEAN

Ferries To
Nagoya, Shikoku,
Kkūshū &
Points East

Ferry

Kozu-shima Island   Shikine-jima Island
Routes   IZU SEVEN

Miyake-jima Island   ISLANDS

Mikura-jima Island

Around Tokyo

東京周辺

0   20   40 km

Hachijo-jima Island

To Ogasawara Islands

JAPAN

water springs and cruise Lake Ashino-ko. Visibility permitting, a one-day circuit of the region offers some of the best opportunities for a glimpse of Japan's most famous mountain.

Things to See

An interesting loop through the region takes you from Tokyo by train (to Odawara) and toy train to **Gōra**; then by funicular and cable car up **Mt Soun-zan** and down to **Lake Ashino-ko**; by boat around the lake to **Moto-Hakone**, where you can walk a short stretch of the Edo era **Tōkaidō Highway**; and from there by bus back to **Odawara**, where you catch the train to Tokyo. (If you're feeling energetic, you can spend 3½ hours walking the old highway back to Hakone-Yumoto, which is on the Tokyo line.)

It's best to skip Odawara's attractions and head straight on to Gōra by way of the switchback railway. En-route you will pass **Chōkoku-no-Mori**, where an open-air museum contains a large number of sculptures. It's an interesting diversion, but entry is expensive at ¥1500.

Places to Stay

Hakone Soun-zan Youth Hostel (☎ 0460-2-3827) costs the standard ¥2300. To get there, you need to take the funicular from Gōra to Soun-zan, turn right, then left and then look out for the hostel which is around 100 metres up on your left.

The Japanese Inn Group have a couple of guesthouses in Hakone. The *Fuji Hakone Guest House* (☎ 0460-4-6577) is over in the Sengokuhara area, north of Lake Ashino-ko, and has singles from ¥5000 to ¥6000 and twins from ¥10,000 to ¥12,000. It's a 45-minute bus journey from stop No 4 at Odawara to the Senkyoro-mae bus stop. The guesthouse is close to the Porsche Museum and a swimming pool; give them a ring if you have trouble finding it. The other Inn Group Hotel, *Moto Hakone Guesthouse* (☎ 0460-3-7880), is in a better location in Moto-Hakone, and has rates of ¥5000 per person. To get there, walk away from the lake starting at the bus stop closest to the harbour; the

guesthouse is up a road to the right just before the next bus stop (Ashino-ko-mae).

Getting There & Away

Bus The Odakyū express bus service has the advantage of running directly into the Hakone region, to Lake Ashino-ko and to Hakone-machi for ¥1830. The disadvantage is that the bus trip is much less interesting than the combination of Romance Car, toy train (Hakone-Tōzan line), funicular, cable car (ropeway) and ferry. Buses run from the west exit of Shinjuku station 11 times daily and take around two hours.

Train JR trains run on the Tōkaidō line between Tokyo station and Odawara. Ordinary trains take 1½ hours, cost ¥1420 and run every 15 minutes or so. Limited express trains take one hour 10 minutes and the express surcharge is ¥1430. Shinkansen do the journey in 42 minutes, cost ¥3570 and leave Tokyo station every 20 minutes.

Trains also service Odawara from Shinjuku station on the private Odakyū line. Quickest and most comfortable is the Romance Car, which takes one hour 25 minutes, costs ¥1780 and leaves every half hour. There's also an express service, taking one hour 35 minutes, which at ¥990 is by far the cheapest way of reaching Odawara.

At Odawara, it is possible to change to the Hakone-Tōzan line, which takes you to Gōra. Alternatively, if you are already on the Odakyū line, you can continue on to Hakone-Yumoto and change to the Hakone-Tōzan line simply by walking across the platform. The latter is the most sensible course of action.

Getting Around

The Hakone Tōzan bus company and Izu Hakone bus company service the Hakone area, and between them they manage to link up most of the sights. If you finish up in Hakone-machi, Hakone Tōzan buses run between there and Odawara for ¥1000.

The Odakyū line offers an Hakone *furii pasu* (free pass), which costs ¥4850 in Shinjuku or ¥3500 in Odawara (which is the place to buy it if you are travelling on a JR rail pass), and allows you to use any mode of transport within the Hakone region for four days. The fare between Shinjuku and Hakone-Yumoto is also included in the pass, although you will have to pay a ¥620 surcharge if you want to take the Romance Car. This is a good deal for a Hakone circuit, as the pass will save you at least ¥1000 even on a one-day visit to the region.

You can get to Gōra from Odawara or Hakone-Yumoto stations on the Hakone-Tōzan line. The ride itself is very enjoyable, involving several switchbacks in a small train that heaves and puffs against the steep gradient. The journey takes around an hour from Odawara (¥520) or 40 minutes from Hakone-Yumoto (¥340).

Ferry services crisscross Lake Ashino-ko, running between Togendai, Hakone-machi and Moto-Hakone for ¥950 every 30 minutes or so. The new 'Pirate Ship' has to be seen to be believed, it's tourist kitsch at its worst, but fun all the same.

MT FUJI 富士山

Celebrated symbol of Japan, Mt Fuji is a bashful peak, and you will need fine weather to get a peek at it.

Climbing Mt Fuji

Officially the climbing season on Fuji is July and August, and the Japanese, who love to do things 'right', pack in during those busy months. The climbing may be just as good either side of the official season but transport services to and from the mountain are less frequent then and many of the mountain huts are closed. You can actually climb Mt Fuji at any time of year, but a mid-winter ascent is strictly for experienced mountaineers.

Although everybody, from small children to grandparents, makes the ascent in season, this is a real mountain and not to be trifled with. It's just high enough for altitude sickness symptoms to be experienced, and, as on any mountain, the weather on Mt Fuji can be viciously changeable. On the summit it can quickly go from clear but cold to cloudy, wet, windy, freezing cold and not just miserable

but downright dangerous. Don't climb Mt Fuji without adequate clothing for cold and wet weather; even on a good day at the height of summer, the temperature on top is likely to be close to freezing.

The mountain is divided into 10 'stations' from base to summit but these days most climbers start from one of the four 'fifth stations', which you can reach by road. From the end of the road, it takes about 4½ hours to climb the mountain and about 2½ hours to descend. Once you're on the top, it takes about an hour to make a circuit of the crater. The Mt Fuji Weather Station on the south-western edge of the crater is on the actual summit of the mountain.

You should aim to reach the top at dawn – both to see the *goraiko* (sunrise) and because early morning is the time when the mountain is least likely to be shrouded in cloud. Sometimes it takes an hour or two to burn the morning mist off, however. To time your arrival for dawn you can either start during the afternoon, stay overnight in a mountain hut and continue early in the morning, or climb the whole way at night. You do not want to arrive on the top too long before dawn, as it's likely to be very cold and windy, and if you've worked up a sweat during the climb, you'll be very uncomfortable.

Although nearly all climbers start from the fifth stations, it is possible to climb all the way up from a lower level. These low-level trails are now mainly used as short hiking routes around the base of the mountain, but gluttons for punishment could climb all the way on the Yoshida route from Fuji-Yoshida or on the Shoji route from near Lake Shoji-ko.

There are alternative sand trails on the Kawaguchi-ko (Yoshida), Subashiri and Gotemba routes which you can descend very rapidly by running and *sunabashiri* (sliding), pausing from time to time to get the sand out of your shoes.

There are four fifth stations around Fuji, and it's quite feasible to climb from one and descend to another. On the northern side of Fuji is the Kawaguchi-ko Fifth Station, at 2305 metres, which is reached from the town

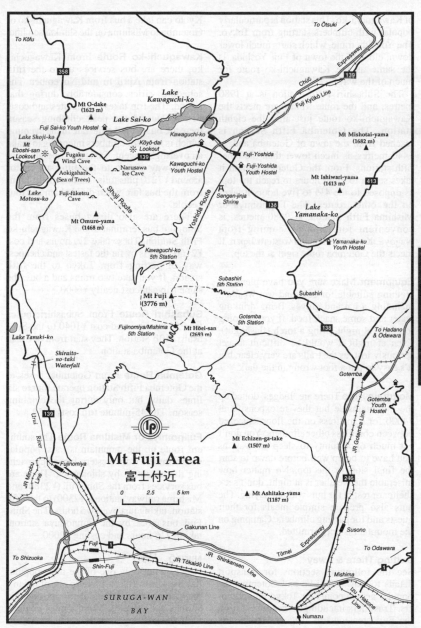

JAPAN

Mt Fuji Area
富士付近

0   5 km

of Kawaguchi-ko. This station is particularly popular with climbers starting from Tokyo. The Yoshida route, which starts much lower down, close to the town of Fuji-Yoshida, is the same as the Kawaguchi-ko route for much of the way.

The Subashiri Fifth Station is at 1980 metres, and the route from there meets the Kawaguchi-ko route just after the eighth station. The Gotemba Fifth Station is reached from the town of Gotemba and, at 1440 metres, is much lower than the other fifth stations. From the Gotemba station it takes seven to eight hours to reach the top, as opposed to the 4½ to five hours it takes on the other routes. The Fujinomiya or Mishima Fifth Station, at 2380 metres, is convenient for climbers coming from Nagoya, Kyoto, Osaka and western Japan. It meets the Gotemba route right at the top.

Equipment Make sure you have plenty of clothing suitable for cold and wet weather, including a hat and gloves. Bring drinking water and some snack food. If you're going to climb at night, bring a torch (flashlight). Even at night it would be difficult to get seriously lost, as the trails are very clear, but it's easy to put a foot wrong in the dark.

Mountain Huts There are 'lodges' dotted up the mountainside but they're expensive at ¥4000 for a mattress on the floor squeezed between countless other climbers. You don't get much opportunity to sleep anyway, as you have to be up well before dawn to start the final slog to the top. No matter how miserable the weather is at night, don't seek shelter or rest in the huts without paying. The huts also prepare simple meals for their guests and for passing climbers. Camping on the mountain is not permitted.

Getting There & Away
See the following sections for transport details to Kawaguchi-ko and Gotemba, the popular arrival points for Tokyo Fuji climbers. Travellers intending to head west from the Fuji area towards Nagoya, Osaka and

Kyoto can take a bus from Kawaguchi-ko or Gotemba to Mishima on the shinkansen line.

Kawaguchi-ko Route From Kawaguchi-ko, there are bus services up to the fifth station from April to mid-November. The schedule varies considerably during that period. The trip takes 55 minutes and costs ¥1610. During the peak climbing season there are buses until quite late in the evening, which is ideal for climbers intending to make an overnight ascent. Taxis also operate from the railway station to the fifth station for around ¥7210 plus tolls – not much different from the bus fare when divided among four people.

There are also direct buses from the Shinjuku bus terminal to the Kawaguchi-ko Fifth Station. These take 2½ hours and cost ¥2160. This is by far the fastest and cheapest way of getting from Tokyo to the fifth station. If you take two trains and a bus, the same trip can cost nearly ¥6000.

Subashiri Route From Subashiri, buses take 55 minutes and cost ¥1040 to the Subashiri Fifth Station. They start from or finish at the Gotemba station.

Gotemba Route From Gotemba, buses to the Gotemba Fifth Station operate four to six times daily, but only during the climbing season. The 45-minute trip costs ¥950.

Fujinomiya or Mishima Route The southern route up the mountain is most popular with climbers from western Japan approaching the mountain by shinkansen. There are bus services from the Shin-Fuji (¥2380) and Mishima railway stations (¥2300) to the fifth station, taking just over two hours. The Shin-Fuji bus goes by the Fujinomiya station, taking 1½ hours and costing ¥2000.

NIKKŌ 日光
Nikkō is not only one of the most popular day trips from Tokyo, it is also one of Japan's major tourist attractions due to its splendid shrines and temples. Visitors must contend with the jostling crowds found at any of

Japan's big-name attractions, but on weekdays they rarely reach the Yamanote-line proportions that you find in Kyoto. All things considered, it's worth trying to slot Nikkō into even the most whirlwind tour of Japan.

Information

First stop in Nikkō should be the Kyōdo Centre, with its excellent tourist information office (☎ 0288-53-3795), on the road up to Tōshō-gū Shrine. The office has a wealth of useful pamphlets and maps. There is another tourist information office in the Tōbu-Nikkō station.

Tickets Ticketing arrangements for the sights in Nikkō have become a bit more organised in recent years, though there's still room for confusion. Basically it works like this: Futara-san-jinja Shrine costs ¥200; Rinnō-ji Temple costs ¥710; and Tōshō-gū Shrine costs ¥1030. To save a few yen, the best idea is to buy a *nisha-ichiji-kōtsū-baikan-ken* (two-shrines-one-temple) ticket for ¥750. This covers all three of the above sights, with the one exception that it doesn't include entry to the Nemuri-Neko (Sleeping Cat) in Tōshō-gū Shrine, a sight that will set you back ¥430. Even if you do visit the Nemuri-Neko, though, you are still making a considerable saving on buying each of the tickets separately

Things to See

The foremost of Nikkō's attractions is **Tōshō-gū Shrine**. It comes in for some criticism from the cultural elite for its gaudiness, but it's easy to spend a couple of hours exploring the place. On your way to the shrine, you'll pass the **Shin-kyō Bridge**, an elegant structure that can be crossed on foot for ¥300. **Rinnō-ji Temple** has a 1200-year historical legacy, and the *senjū* (1000-armed Buddha) in the temple's Sambutsu-dō (Three Buddha Hall) is particularly impressive. Of less interest are **Futara-san-jinja Shrine** and **Taijūin-byō**. Those with time should consider a trip up to **Lake Chūzenji-ko**, a scenic area with an impressive waterfall. The 50-minute trip from Tōbu Nikkō station to Lake Chuzenji-ko costs ¥1050.

Places to Stay

The *Nikkō Daiyagawa Youth Hostel* (☎ 0288-54-1974) is the more popular of the town's two hostels. It costs ¥2300 per night and is behind the post office on a side road that runs parallel to the main street. A 10-minute walk away, on the other side of the Daiya-gawa River, is the *Nikkō Youth Hostel* (☎ 0288-54-1013), where beds are ¥2450 or ¥2650, depending on the time of year.

One of the more popular pensions in Nikkō is the *Turtle Inn Nikkō* (☎ 0288-53-3168), with rooms from ¥3900 per person without bath and from ¥5500 with. Meals are also available at ¥1000 for breakfast and ¥2000 for dinner. It's by the river, beyond the shrine area. It's quite a walk from the stations, so you'd be better off taking a bus to the sōgō-kaikan-mae bus stop, backtracking from there approximately 50 metres to the fork in the road and following the river for around five minutes.

Also popular is the *Logette St Bois* (☎ 0288-53-3399), which has both Western and Japanese-style singles/doubles starting at ¥5500/11,000 for rooms without baths. It's across the river, about a km north of the station.

The *Humpty Dumpty* (☎ 0288-53-4365) is another pension with similar rates. Very close to Humpty Dumpty are a couple of inexpensive minshuku: *Narusawa Lodge* (☎ 0288-54-1630) and *Ringo-no-Ie* (☎ 02.88-53-0131), which both have rates of ¥4500 per person or ¥6000 with two meals.

Getting There & Away

The best way to visit Nikkō is via the Tōbu-Nikkō line from Asakusa station in Tokyo. The station, which is separate from Asakusa subway station, is in the basement of the Tōbu department store, but is well signposted and easy to find from the subway. Limited express trains cost ¥2530 and take one hour 45 minutes. These trains require a reservation (on a quiet day you'll probably be able to organise this before boarding the

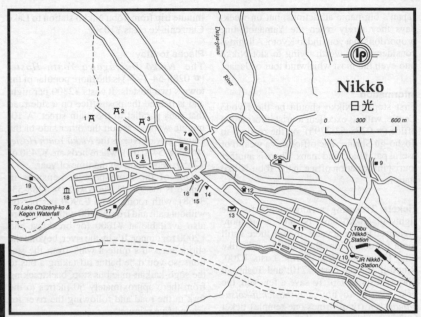

PLACES TO STAY

4 Nikkō Pension Green Age Inn
日光ペンション・グリーンエイジINN
6 Hotel Seikoen
ホテル清晃苑
8 Nikkō Youth Hostel
日光ユースホステル
9 Logette St Bois
ロジェチサンボワ
12 Nikkō Daiyagawa Youth Hostel
日光大谷川ユースホステル
15 Nikkō Kanaya Hotel
日光金谷ホテル
17 Turtle Inn Nikkō
タートルイン日光
19 Nikkō Green Hotel
日光グリーンホテル

PLACES TO EAT

11 Yōrō-no-taki Restaurant
養老の滝

14 Yakitori Restaurant
焼き鳥屋

OTHER

1 Taijūin-byō Shrine
家光大猷院廟
2 Futara-san-jinja Shrine
二荒山神社
3 Tōshō-gū Shrine
東照宮
5 Rinnō-ji Temple
輪王寺
7 Nikkō Tōkan-sō Ryokan
日光東観荘
10 Bus Terminal
バスターミナル
13 Post Office
郵便局
16 Shin-kyō Bridge
神橋
18 Nikkō Museum
日光博物館

train) and run every 30 minutes or so from 7.30 to 10 am; after 10 am they run hourly.

Rapid trains require no reservation, take 15 minutes longer than the limited express and cost ¥1270. They run once an hour from 6.20 am to 4.30 pm. Tickets for these are purchased from the automatic vending machine.

As usual, travelling by JR trains works out to be more time consuming, more expensive and only really of interest to those on a Japan Rail Pass. The quickest way to do it would be to take the shinkansen from Ueno to Utsunomiya (¥4510, 50 minutes) and change there for an ordinary train (no other options) for the 45-minute, ¥720 journey to Nikkō. The trains from Utsunomiya to Nikkō leave on average once every half hour. Not all Nikkō-line trains run the full distance to Nikkō; you may have to get off at an intermediate station and wait for the next Nikkō-bound train.

A limited express service taking 1½ hours (¥3690) and an ordinary service taking one hour 50 minutes (¥1850) also run between Ueno and Utsunomiya.

YOKOHAMA 横浜

Yokohama (population three million) is a bit of a dull extension of Tokyo and shouldn't really be included on a busy itinerary. It has a few points of interest, including a lively Chinatown, but generally lacks the pulling power of other attractions around Tokyo.

Things to See

Yokohama's main attractions are its **Chinatown**, **Sankei-en Garden** and the **Minato Mirai 21** complex. The latter is a recent addition to the Yokohama skyline, and is one of those characteristic Japanese visions of the 21st century: it features the Landmark Tower, currently the tallest building in Japan, an amusement park and various other attractions. Yokohama's Chinatown is basically a place to eat – the length of the queue outside a given restaurant is the best indicator of the quality of the fare inside; plastic food displays have prices indicated. The Sankei-en Garden is one of Japan's finest. There are two separate entry fees (for the outer and inner gardens) of ¥300. Take a No 8 bus from the road that runs parallel to the harbour behind the Marine Tower.

Places to Stay

The *Kanagawa Youth Hostel* (☎ 045-241-6503) costs ¥2300. From Sakuragi-chō station, exit on the opposite side to the harbour, turn right and follow the road along the railway tracks (look for the graffiti on the right). Cross the main road, turn left into the steep street with a bridge and a cobblestoned section, and the youth hostel is up the road on the right.

Getting There & Away

There are numerous trains from Tokyo, the cheapest being the Tōkyū Tōyoko line from Shibuya station to Sakuragi-chō station for ¥260. The trip takes 44 minutes by ordinary train and 35 minutes by limited express (same price). Trains also stop at Yokohama station on the way to Sakuragi-chō station.

The Keihin Tōhoku line from Tokyo station is a bit more convenient, passing through Kannai station, but at ¥610 it's considerably more expensive. To Yokohama station costs ¥440. The Tōkaidō line from Tokyo or Shinagawa stations also runs to Yokohama station, taking around 30 minutes and costing ¥470.

It is convenient to continue on to Kamakura on the Yokosuka line from Yokohama station. The Tōkaidō shinkansen stops at Shin-Yokohama station, a fair way to the north-west of town, on its way into the Kansai region. If you enter or leave Yokohama this way, Shin-Yokohama station is connected with Yokohama, Sakuragi-chō and Kannai stations via the Yokohama line.

KAMAKURA 鎌倉

Kamakura may not have as much to offer historically as Kyoto or Nara but a wealth of notable Buddhist temples and Shintō shrines make this one of Tokyo's most interesting day trips. The town has some relaxing walks and a peacefulness that is hard to come by in, say, Kyoto.

Things to See

The sights in Kamakura are spread over a fairly wide area and, although most of them can be seen on foot, there are times when it is necessary to catch a bus. You can either start at Kamakura station and work your way around the area in a circle or start north of Kamakura at Kita-Kamakura station and visit the temples between there and Kamakura on foot. The latter route is probably the best of the two.

Engaku-ji Temple is on the left as you exit Kita-Kamakura station and is one of the five main Rinzai Zen temples in Kamakura; entry is ¥200. Across the railway tracks from Engaku-ji is **Tōkei-ji Temple**, notable for its peaceful grounds; entry is ¥50. A couple of minutes farther on from Tōkei-ji Temple is **Jōchi-ji Temple**, considered one of Kamakura's five great Zen temples; entry is ¥100. **Kenchō-ji Temple** is not only Kamakura's most important Zen temple but something of a showcase generally. It's about 10 minutes' walk from Jōchi-ji Temple and entry is ¥200. A little farther on is **Hachi-man-gū Shrine**, an extensive Shintō shrine. The **National Treasure museum** on the grounds of the shrine is recommended, as it provides your only opportunity to see Kamakuran art, most of which is hidden away in the temples. The museum is open from 9 am to 4 pm, closed Monday, and admission is ¥150.

A short bus ride from Kamakura station is Kamakura's major attraction, the **Great Buddha** or the Daibutsu as it is known in Japanese. Cast in 1252, the buddha is 11.4 metres tall and is commonly considered to be artistically superior to its larger rival in Nara. To get to the Great Buddha, take a bus from the No 2, 7 or 10 bus stops in front of Kamakura station and get off at the Daibutsu-mae bus stop. The Great Buddha can be seen daily from 7 am to 5.30 pm, and admission is ¥150.

It's worth combining a visit to the Great Buddha with a brief look around **Hase-dera Temple**, also known as Hase Kannon Temple. The pleasant grounds have a garden and an interesting collection of statues of Jizō, the patron saint of travellers and souls of departed children. The main point of interest in the grounds, however, is the **Kannon statue**.

Places to Stay

The *Kamakura Kagetsuen Youth Hostel* (☎ 0467-25-1238) has beds for ¥2500. You can walk to the hostel from Hase-dera Temple by continuing to walk away from the Great Buddha along the road that runs in front of the temple. When you reach the T-junction, turn right and look for the hostel on the corner of the next road on the left. Hase station is also a five-minute walk away in the direction of Hase-dera Temple.

Getting There & Away

Trains on the Yokosuka line operate from Tokyo, Shimbashi and Shinagawa stations, just take your pick. The trip takes about 55 minutes and fares are ¥930 from Tokyo and Shimbashi and ¥880 from Shinagawa. It is also possible to catch a train from Yokohama on the Yokosuka line. If you're planning to get off at Kita-Kamakura station, it is the stop after Ofuna.

A cheaper but more complicated option begins with a one hour 15 minute ride on the Odakyū line from Shinjuku in Tokyo to Katase-Enoshima station for ¥530 by express. When you leave the station, cross the river and turn left. Enoshima station is a 10-minute walk away, and there you can catch the Enoden line to Kamakura for ¥220 (24 minutes). This is not a bad way to get to Kamakura if you were planning to take in Enoshima anyway.

Central Honshū
本州の中央部

Central Japan, known in Japanese as *chūbu*, extends across the area sandwiched between Tokyo and Kyoto. It divides into three geographical areas with marked differences in topography, climate and scenery. To the north, the coastal area along the Sea of Japan features rugged seascapes. The central area inland encompasses the spectacular mountain ranges and highlands of the Japan Alps, while the southern Pacific coast area is heavily industrialised, urbanised and densely populated.

NAGOYA 名古屋

Nagoya (population 2,154,000) is Japan's fourth-largest city. It's mainly a commercial and industrial city with little to offer the traveller, though many people pass through on their way to other places.

Information

If you need information on Nagoya or other areas in Central Honshū, the Nagoya International Centre (☎ 052-581-5678, ext 24/25) is on the 3rd floor of the International Centre (Kokusai Centre); a 10-minute walk east along Sakura-dori. It's open daily from 9 am to 8.30 pm and is staffed by English-speaking Japanese.

Things to See

The **Nagoya-jō Castle** is a 1959 ferroconcrete replica. Admission costs ¥400 and it's open from 9.30 am to 4.30 pm. The castle is a five-minute walk from Shiyakusho station on the Meijo subway line.

Atsuta-jingū Shrine, one of the most important shrines in Japan, dates from the 3rd century. From Shiyakusho subway station (close to the castle), take the Meijo line south to Jingū-nishi station (seven stops). To reach the shrine from Nagoya station, take the Meitetsu Nagoya Honsen line to Jingū-mae (four stops) and then walk for five minutes. The shrine is open from 9 am to 4 pm and is closed the last Wednesday and Thursday of every month; entry is ¥300.

Places to Stay

The *Aichi-ken Seinen-Kaikan Youth Hostel* (☎ 052-221-6001) is in a good location close to Nagoya station. As a result, it's the first budget place to be booked out, so reserve in advance if you want to be sure of a bed. The hostel charges ¥2500 per night. Japanese-style family rooms and guest rooms are available from ¥4100 per night. From Nagoya station (eastern exit), the hostel is a 20-minute walk south-east. Alternatively, you can take bus No 20 from the stop in front of the Toyota building and get off at the Nayabashi stop. From there, it's three minutes south on foot.

The *Nagoya Youth Hostel* (☎ 052-781-9845) is farther out to the east of town near Higashiyama-kōen Park. The charge is ¥1980 per night. From Nagoya station, take the subway on the Higashiyama line to Higashiyama-kōen station. From there, it's eight minutes on foot to the hostel.

The *Ryokan Meiryu* (☎ 052-331-8686) is a member of the Japanese Inn Group and charges ¥4500/8000 for singles/doubles. It's centrally located, and three minutes on foot from Kamimaezu subway station on the Meijo line.

Getting There & Away

Air Nagoya is served with domestic flights by All Nippon Airways (ANA), Japan Airlines (JAL) and Japan Air Systems (JAS) for cities such as Tokyo (Narita), Sapporo, Sendai, Fukuoka and Naha. As the bus takes 45 minutes from Nagoya's Komaki Airport to the city centre, the shinkansen from Tokyo is much quicker.

Bus A JR bus operates between Tokyo and Osaka with stops in Nagoya and Kyoto. The approximate times and prices to Nagoya are as follows: from Tokyo (six hours, ¥4500); from Kyoto (2¾ hours, ¥2000); and from Osaka (3½ hours, ¥2400). The Nagoya International Centre will have up-to-date details.

Train The JR shinkansen is the fastest rail service for Nagoya. The journey on the Hikari shinkansen takes one hour and 52 minutes from Tokyo (¥10,380), one hour and 2 minutes from Shin-Osaka station (¥6060) and 50 minutes from Kyoto (¥5340).

Nara is connected with Nagoya on the Kintetsu line. Nagoya to Nara takes two hours and 16 minutes.

For the Japan Alps and related side trips, you can take the JR Chūō line to Nagano via Matsumoto. To reach Takayama from Nagoya, you should take the Meitetsu

Inuyama line to Inuyama (Unuma station) and then change to the JR Takayama line.

Inuyama is connected with Nagoya station on the Meitetsu Inuyama line. The trip takes about 30 minutes. Gifu is connected with Nagoya station on the JR Tōkaidō Honsen line. The trip takes about 30 minutes.

Ferry The Taiheiyo Ferry (☎ 03-661-7007) runs between Nagoya and Tomakomai (Hokkaidō) via Sendai. Ferries depart from Nagoya-futō pier which is 40 minutes by bus from the Meitetsu bus centre or you can take

the Meijo subway south to its terminus at Nagoya-ko station.

The passenger fare from Nagoya to Sendai is ¥9580 and the trip takes 21 hours. There are evening departures every second day. The fare from Nagoya to Tomakomai is ¥15,450 and the full trip takes about 40 hours.

Hitching To hitch east from Nagoya to Tokyo, or west to Kyoto or Osaka, your best bet is the Nagoya Interchange on the Tomei Expressway. Take the subway on the

Higashiyama line from Nagoya station to Hongo station (13 stops), which is one stop before the terminus at Fujigaoka. The interchange is a short walk east of the station.

Getting Around
Express bus services run between the airport and the Meitetsu bus centre (3rd floor, stop No 5). The trip takes 45 minutes and the one-way fare is ¥640. Taxis take about 10 minutes less and cost around ¥3000.

Nagoya's excellent subway system is a much better way of getting around town than the buses. There are four lines, all clearly signposted in English and Japanese. The most useful lines for visitors are probably the Meijo line, Higashiyama line and the new Sakura-dōri line. The last two run via Nagoya station.

TAKAYAMA 高山
Takayama (population 65,000) lies in the ancient Hida district tucked away between the mountains of the Japan Alps. With its traditional inns, shops and sake breweries, Takayama is a rarity; a Japanese city (admittedly a small one) that has managed to retain something of its traditional charm.

Information
The Hida tourist information office (☎ 0577-32-5328), directly in front of JR Takayama station, is an excellent source of information on Takayama. There's even a video machine if you want a preview of the sights. The office is open from 8.30 am to 6.30 pm between 1 April and 31 October. During the rest of the year it closes at 5 pm.

Things to See
The centre of the old town is **Sanmachi Suji** and consists of three streets (Ichi-no-machi, Ni-no-machi and San-no-machi) lined with traditional shops, breweries, restaurants, museums and private homes. The **sake breweries** are easily recognised by the round basket of cedar fronds hanging above the entrance. **Hida Archaeology Museum** displays craft items and archaeological objects in a traditional house. Admission costs ¥300 and it's open from 8 am to 5 pm.

The **Fujii Folkcraft Museum** is close to the archaeology museum and displays folkcraft from Japan, China and Korea. Admission costs ¥300 and opening hours are from 9 am to 5 pm. The **Hirata Folk Art Museum** is a merchant's house dating from the turn of the century. Admission costs ¥200 and it's open from 9 am to 5 pm. The **Gallery of Traditional Japanese Toys** has an exhibition of some 2000 dolls and folk toys from the 17th century to the present day. The gallery is open from 8.30 am to 5 pm and entry costs ¥200.

The **Takayama Local History Museum** is devoted to the crafts and traditions of the region. Admission costs ¥300. It's open from 8.30 am to 5 pm, closed on Monday, with the exception of the high-season summer months, when it's open daily.

There are also a couple of well-preserved merchants' houses that are worth checking out. The **Kusakabe Heritage House** is fitted out as it would have been if you'd walked in to talk business in the late 1890s. Admission costs ¥500. It's open from 9 am to 5 pm, but closes half an hour earlier from December to March. **Yoshijima-ke House** is on the same street and is also a merchant's house. The house is open daily from 9 am to 4.30 pm, except from December to February, when it closes on Tuesday; admission costs ¥300.

If your visit to Takayama doesn't coincide with one of the big festivals, you can still see four of the *yatai* (festival floats) which are displayed in the **Takayama Festival Floats Hall** in seasonal rotation. Admission to the hall costs ¥460, and it's open from 9 am to 4.30 pm. Close by is the **Lion Mask Exhibition Hall**, which has a display of over 800 lion masks and musical instruments connected with lion dances commonly performed at festivals in central and northern Japan. Admission costs ¥600 and this includes the mechanical puppet show (displays every 15 minutes). The hall is open from 8.30 am to 5 pm.

There's a walking trail from the station that links the **Teramachi** and **Shiroyama-**

JAPAN

kōen Park areas. The information office in front of the station has a booklet (*Temples & Shrines in the Higashiyama Preserved Area*) which provides details on many of the temples in the area. Teramachi (literally 'Temple District') has over a dozen temples, and the youth hostel is in one of them – Tenshō-ji Temple. Various trails lead through the park and up the mountainside to the ruins of **Takayama-jō Castle**. As you descend, you can take a look at **Shōren-ji Temple**, which was transferred to this site from the Shirakawa Valley when a dam was built there in 1960. Admission to the main hall costs ¥200.

Arguably Takayama's foremost attraction is the **Hida Minzoku-mura** (Hida Folk Village), a large open-air museum with dozens of traditional houses which once belonged to craftspeople and farmers in the Takayama region. The houses were dismantled at their original sites and rebuilt here. The admission charge (¥700) admits you to both the eastern and western sections of the village, which are connected part of the way by a pleasant walk through fields. Allow at least two hours if you want to explore the village on foot at a leisurely pace. On a fine day, there are good views across the town to the peaks of the Japan Alps. The village is open from 8.30 am to 5 pm.

Festivals

Takayama is famed all over Japan for two major festivals which attract over half a million visitors. Book your accommodation well in advance.

The Sannō Matsuri Festival takes place on 14 and 15 April. The starting point for the festival parade is Hie-jinja Shrine. The Hachiman Matsuri Festival, which takes place on 9 and 10 October, is a slightly smaller version of Sannō Matsuri.

Places to Stay

If you are going to stay in Takayama for the big festivals in April or October, you must book months in advance and expect to pay up to 20% more than you would at any other time. Alternatively, you could stay elsewhere

in the region and commute to Takayama for the festival.

The *Hida Takayama Tenchō-ji Youth Hostel* (☎ 0577-32-6345) is a temple in the pleasant surroundings of Teramachi, but hostellers should be prepared to stick to a rigid routine. To get there from the station, it takes about 20 minutes to walk across town. A bed for the night costs ¥2100.

Other accommodation options in Takayama are expensive. Most of Takayama's ryokan have rates of between ¥8000 to ¥15,000 per person with two meals, and in most cases you will need to speak some Japanese in order to make the proprietors happy about taking you. Possibilities (there are seemingly millions of them) include the *Daimaru Ryokan* (☎ 0577-32-0630), which is close to the station and has rates from ¥9000. It's in a rather unryokan-looking white building; there's no English sign. *Hachibei* (☎ 0577-33-0573) is a pleasantly faded, rambling minshuku close to Hida No Sato Village and is slightly cheaper at ¥7000 with two meals. Take a bus to the Hida No Sato bus stop; from there it's an eight-minute walk to the north.

The cheapest alternative to youth hostel accommodation is the *New Alps Hotel* (☎ 0577-32-2888), just a minute's walk from the station. Singles/doubles start at ¥4500/9000, and are very good value. Over by the river, the *Hotel Alpha One* (☎ 0577-32-2211) is another reasonably inexpensive place, with singles from ¥5100 and twins/doubles for ¥10,400/9300. The sign outside has the Greek for *alpha* and a '1'. Around 10 minutes' walk from the station is the *Takayama Central Hotel* (☎ 0577-35-1881), where singles are ¥5500 and twins range from ¥10,000.

Places to Eat

Close to Takayama station is *Nama-Soba*, a soba restaurant where you can try Hida-soba, a local speciality. The restaurant also serves tempura and katsudon sets from around ¥800. There are numerous restaurants and teahouses in the Sanmachi Suji area, which serve the constant flow of tourists but these have slightly elevated prices.

Nomeya Utaeya is part of an izakaya chain, has a great atmosphere, reasonable food and drink prices and an illustrated menu for easy ordering. There's no English sign but you can look out for the red lanterns on the last alley before the bridge off the main shopping street leading from the station. For reasonable Italian fare, *Hole in the Wall* has pasta dishes from around ¥650. It's very close to the station.

Getting There & Away
Bus Many roads in this region close during winter. This means that bus schedules usually only start from early May and finish in late October. A bus service connects Takayama with Hirayu Onsen (one hour) and takes another hour to reach Kamikōchi. Direct buses run from Takayama via Hirayu Onsen to Shin-Hotaka Onsen and the nearby cable car (ropeway).

Another bus route runs on the spectacular Norikura Skyline Road connecting Norikura with Takayama in 1¾ hours.

The bus service between Kanazawa and Nagoya runs via Takayama and Shirakawa-gō, but only operates midsummer.

Train Takayama is connected with Nagoya on the JR Takayama line. The fastest limited express (tokkyū) takes two hours and 16 minutes.

Express trains run from Osaka and Kyoto to Gifu or Nagoya, and continue on the JR Takayama line to Takayama. The trip takes about five hours from Osaka and half an hour less from Kyoto. If you are travelling on a rail pass, the best course of action would be to take a shinkansen to Nagoya and change there to the Takayama line. Limited express trains from Nagoya to Takayama are not particularly frequent.

Toyama is connected with Takayama on the JR Takayama line. The fastest express from Toyama takes around 1½ hours whereas the local train (*futsū*) rambles to Takayama in just under three hours.

A bus/train combination runs from Takayama via Kamikōchi to Matsumoto. You take a bus from Takayama to Kamikōchi then change to another bus for Shin-Shimashima station on the Matsumoto Dentetsu line and continue by rail to Matsumoto.

Hitching Providing you are equipped for mountain conditions, hitching is quite feasible in the Japan Alps between May and late September.

Getting Around
With the exception of Hida Folk Village, the sights in Takayama can be easily covered on foot. You can amble from the station across to Higashiyama on the other side of town in 25 minutes.

The bus station is on your left as you exit the station. There is a circular bus route around the town and bus passes are available for one day (¥890) or two days (¥1350).

There are several bicycle rental places near the station and in town. Rates are high at ¥250 for the first hour, ¥200 for each additional hour and ¥1250 for the day. The youth hostel charges ¥100 per hour or ¥700 for the day and is probably the best deal available.

SHŌKAWA VALLEY 荘川
Both **Shirakawa-gō** and **Ogimachi** consist of traditional villages stretching for several km in the Shōkawa valley. Ogimachi is the most convenient place for bus connections, tourist information and orientation. When arriving by bus, ask to be dropped off at the Gasshō-shuraku bus stop.

Places to Stay
It's possible to stay in traditional *gasshō-zukuri* (the name means literally 'hands folded in prayer', which refers to the steep incline of the sloping roof) accommodation but costs are high. The tourist information office make reservations but expect to pay around ¥7500 per head. The *Etchū Gokayama Youth Hostel* is a gasshō-zukuri structure and is about two km from the bus

JAPAN

stop on the main road in the direction of Gokayama.

Getting There & Away

From 28 April to 10 May, 20 July to 31 August, 10 October to 3 November and 28 December to 15 January there are direct JR buses between Nagoya and Ogimachi. The trip takes around 5½ hours and costs ¥4500.

The simplest way to get to Ogimachi is from Takayama. Buses run four times daily and do the trip in two stages. The Nohi bus company runs to Makido. The trip takes just over an hour and costs ¥1800. At Makido change to a connecting JR bus to Ogimachi. The one-hour trip costs ¥1200.

KISO VALLEY REGION 木曽川

A visit to this region is highly recommended if you want to see several small towns with architecture carefully preserved from the Edo period.

Things to See

The old post road between Magome and Tsumago is now a popular hike. **Magome** itself is a small post town with rows of traditional houses and post inns (and souvenir shops, of course) lining a steep street. The tourist information office (☎ 0264-59-2336) is a short way up, on the right-hand side of the street. The office is open from 8.30 am to 5 pm, and dispenses tourist literature as well as reserving accommodation.

To walk from Magome to Tsumago, continue toiling up the street until the houses eventually give way to a forest path which winds down to the road leading up a steep hill to Magome-kōge Pass. This initial walk from Magome to the pass takes about 45 minutes and is not particularly appealing because you spend most of your time on the road. You can cut out this first section by taking the bus between Magome and Tsumago and getting off after about 12 minutes at the pass.

There's a small shop-cum-teahouse at the top of the pass where the trail leaves the road and takes you down to the right along a pleasant route through the forest. From the teahouse to Tsumago takes just under two hours.

Tsumago is so geared to tourism and so well preserved, it feels like an open-air museum. Designated by the government as a protected area for the preservation of traditional buildings, no modern developments such as TV aerials or telephone poles are allowed to mar the picture. The tourist information office (☎ 0264-57-3123), open from 8.30 am to 5 pm, is halfway down the main street. Tourist literature on Tsumago and maps are available, and the staff are happy to make reservations for accommodation.

As a special service for walkers on the trail between Magome and Tsumago, the tourist offices in both villages provide a baggage-forwarding service. For a nominal fee of ¥500 per piece of luggage, you can have your gear forwarded. The deadline for the morning delivery is 9 am and for the afternoon delivery it's 1 pm. The service operates daily from 20 July to 31 August, but is restricted to Saturday, Sunday and national holidays between 1 April and 19 July and throughout September and November.

Places to Stay & Eat

Both tourist information offices specialise in helping visitors find accommodation; telephone enquiries can only be dealt with in Japanese. There are many ryokan and minshuku. Prices for a room and two meals at a ryokan start around ¥9000 while minshuku prices for a similar deal start around ¥6500.

Minshuku Daikichi (☎ 0264-57-2595) is a friendly place just four minutes on foot from the bus terminal. It has per-person rates of ¥6700.

Magome and Tsumago have several restaurants on their main streets. The local specialities include gohei-mochi (a rice dumpling on a stick coated with nut sauce) and sansai (mountain greens), which can be ordered as a set meal (sansai teishoku) for about ¥800.

Getting There & Away

Train The main railway stations on the JR

Chūō line which provide access to Magome and Tsumago are Nakatsugawa station and Nagiso station respectively. Some services do not stop at these stations, which are about 12 minutes apart by limited express, so check the timetable. By limited express, the trip between Nagoya and Nakatsugawa takes 55 minutes (¥2980); between Nakatsugawa and Matsumoto it takes 85 minutes. Direct buses also operate between Nagoya and Magome, and the trip takes just under two hours.

Bus Buses leave every hour from outside Nakatsugawa station for Magome (30 minutes, ¥500). There's also an infrequent bus service between Magome and Tsumago (30 minutes, ¥580). If you decide to start your walk from the Magome-kōge Pass, take this bus and get off at the bus stop at the top of the pass.

From Tsumago, either take the bus (nine minutes) or walk to Nagiso station (1½ hours).

NAGANO 長野
Nagano (population 347,000) has been around since the Kamakura period (1185-1333), when it was a temple town centred around **Zenkō-ji Temple**. Today Zenkō-ji Temple is still Nagano's main attraction, drawing in more than four million visitors every year.

Places to Stay
Zenkō-ji Kyōju-in Youth Hostel (☎ 0262-32-2768) is a temple on a side street a couple of minutes on foot, east of Zenkō-ji Temple. Be sure to make an advance reservation. A bed for the night is ¥2500.

Shukubō (temple lodgings) are available around Zenkō-ji Temple (☎ 0262-34-3591). Either call direct and make reservations in Japanese, or ask the tourist office to help.

Getting There & Away
Trains from Ueno station in Tokyo via the JR Shin-etsu Honsen line take three hours and cost ¥3810, plus a ¥2770 limited express surcharge. The JR Shinonoi line connects Nagano with Matsumoto in 55 minutes. To

Nagoya it takes three hours and costs ¥4420 plus a ¥2770 limited express surcharge.

HAKUBA 白馬
The town of Hakuba is used as a staging point for access to outdoor activities in the nearby mountains. Skiing in the winter and hiking or mountaineering in the summer attract large numbers of visitors. The hiking trails tend to be less clogged during September and October. Even in midsummer you should be properly prepared for hiking over snow-covered terrain. For information in English about Hakuba and the surrounding region, contact the tourist information office in Matsumoto.

Things to See & Do
The ascent of **Mt Shirouma-dake** is a popular hike, but you should be properly prepared. There are several mountain huts which provide meals and basic accommodation along the trails.

From Hakuba station there are buses which take 40 minutes to reach Sarakura-sō (Sarakura Mountain Hut) which is the trail head. From here, you can head west to climb the peak in about six hours; note that there are two huts on this route. If you don't feel like climbing to the peak, you can follow the trail for about 1¾ hours as far as the Daisekkei (Snowy Gorge).

Tsugaike Natural Park (Tsugaike Shizen-en) lies below Mt Norikura-dake in an alpine marshland. A three-hour hiking trail takes in most of the park which is renowned for its alpine flora.

Happō-one Ski Resort is a busy ski resort in the winter and a popular hiking area in the summer. From Hakuba station, a five-minute bus ride takes you to Happō; from there it's an eight-minute walk to the cable-car base station. From the top station of the cable car you can use two more chair lifts, and then hike along a trail for an hour or so to **Happō-ike Pond** on a ridge below Mt Karamatsu-dake (2696 metres). From this pond you can follow a trail leading to Mt Maru-yama (one hour), continue for 1½ hours to the Karamatsu-dake San-sō (mountain hut) and then climb to the peak of **Mt Karamatsu-dake** in about 30 minutes.

Getting There & Away

Hakuba is on the JR Ōito line. From Matsumoto the trip takes about 1½ hours. From Shinano-ōmachi station allow 35 minutes.

If you continue north, the Ōito line eventually connects with the JR Hokuriku Honsen line at Itoigawa, which offers the options of heading north-east towards Niigata or south-west to Toyama and Kanazawa.

MATSUMOTO 松本

Matsumoto (population 200,000) is worth a visit for its superb castle, and is a convenient base for exploration of the Japan Alps.

Information

Matsumoto city tourist information office (☎ 0263-32-2814) is on your right at the bottom of the steps leading from Matsumoto station's eastern exit. The English-speaking staff can provide maps and leaflets, help with accommodation and give plenty of other travel information. The office is open daily from 9.30 am to 6 pm, and 9 am to 5.30 pm during winter.

The castle and the city centre are easily covered on foot.

Things to See

Even if you only spend a couple of hours in Matsumoto, make sure you see **Matsumoto-jō Castle**. Its main attraction is the original three turreted castle keep (donjon), built circa 1595, in contrasting black and white. Steep steps and ladders lead you up through six storeys. Opening hours are from 8.30 am to 4.30 pm daily, but it is closed from 29 December to 3 January. Admission costs ¥500 and is valid also for the **Japan Folklore Museum**. The castle is 15 minutes on foot from the station, or if you take a bus, the stop for the castle is Shiyakusho-mae.

Places to Stay

The tourist information office at the station

has lists of accommodation and can help with reservations. *Asama Onsen Youth Hostel* (☎ 0263-46-1335) is a bit distant, regimented and drab, and it charges the standard youth hostel rate of ¥2500. It closes at 9 pm and lights go out punctually at 10 pm. The hostel is closed from 28 December to 3 January.

To reach Asama Onsen by bus from the Matsumoto bus terminal, there are two options: either take bus No 6 to Shita-Asama or bus No 7 to Dai-ichi Koko-mae. The bus ride takes 20 minutes, and the hostel is then five minutes on foot.

Utsukushigahara Sanjiro Youth Hostel (☎ 0263-31-2021) is on an alpine plateau, nearly an hour's bus ride from Matsumoto. A bed for the night is ¥2300. It's closed from December to April. Take the bus bound for Utsukushigahara Bijitsukan and get off after 50 minutes at the Sanjiro bus stop. The hostel is two minutes on foot from there.

The *Enjyoh Bekkan* (☎ 0263-33-7233) is a member of the Japanese Inn Group. Prices at this ryokan start at ¥4800/9000 for singles/doubles, excluding meals. The hot-spring facilities are available day and night. A Western-style breakfast is available for ¥800. From Matsumoto, take the 20-minute bus ride to Utsukushigahara Onsen and get off at the terminal. From there it's 300 metres to the ryokan.

For a very reasonably priced ryokan close to the station, the best bet is *Nishiya* (☎ 0263-33-4332). Some English is spoken here and per-person costs are ¥3600 without meals.

Getting There & Away

Bus & Train From Tokyo (Shinjuku station), there are Azusa limited express services which reach Matsumoto in two hours 39 minutes and cost ¥3810 with a ¥2770 limited express surcharge. The fastest services on the JR Chūō Honsen line from Nagoya take 2½ hours. From Osaka, the fastest trip takes 3½ hours and requires a change of trains at Nagoya. The JR Shinonoi line connects Matsumoto with Nagano in 55 minutes. The trip from Matsumoto to Hakuba on the JR Ōito line takes about 1½ hours.

Both train and bus travel have to be combined for the connection between Matsumoto and Kamikōchi. From Matsumoto, take the Matsumoto Dentetsu line to Shin-Shimashima station – don't confuse this with the station called Shimojima. The trip takes 30 minutes and the fare is ¥670. From Shin-Shimashima station take the bus via Nakanoyu to Kamikōchi (¥2000, 75 minutes), though this service does not operate from mid-October to April. From Kamikōchi you can continue by bus via Hirayu Onsen to Takayama.

There are regular buses from Tokyo (3¼ hours), Osaka (5½ hours) and Nagoya (3½ hours).

Matsumoto bus terminal is diagonally across the main street to the right as you leave the station's east exit. The terminal is part of a large department store and this means you have to negotiate your way down to the basement before choosing your exit door, climbing the steps and finding the bus stop back at ground level.

KAMIKŌCHI 上高地

Kamikōchi lies in the centre of the northern Japan Alps and has some of the most spectacular scenery in Japan. It's a popular destination, but despite the thousands of visitors, Kamikōchi has so far resisted the temptation to go commercial. The best advice is probably to get there quick before the locals change their minds.

If you want to avoid immense crowds, don't plan to visit between late July and late August, or during the first three weeks in October. Between June and mid-July, there's a rainy season which makes outdoor pursuits depressingly soggy.

Information

Tourist Office At the bus terminal, there is an information office (☎ 0263-95-2405) which is open from late April to mid-November only. It's geared mostly to booking accommodation, but also has leaflets and maps. It's preferable to make prior use of the tourist information offices in Takayama or Matsumoto, which have English-speaking staff.

Books & Maps JNTO publishes a leaflet entitled *Matsumoto & Kamikochi* which has brief details and a map for Kamikōchi. The tourist offices also have several large maps (covering Kamikōchi, Shirahone Onsen and Norikura Kōgen Plateau) which show mountain trails, average hiking times, mountain huts and lists of tourist facilities. However, they are all in Japanese. *Hiking in Japan* by Paul Hunt covers some trails in the area.

Things to See

It's feasible to visit Kamikōchi as a day trip from Takayama or Matsumoto, but you'll miss out on a stay in the mountains and the possibility of early morning or late evening walks free of mobs of tourists.

If you want to do level walking for short distances, without any climbing, then you should stick to the river valley. A sample three-hour walk (round trip) of this kind would proceed east from **Kappa-bashi Bridge** along the right-hand side of the river to **Myōjin-bashi Bridge** (45 minutes) and then continue to **Tokusawa** (45 minutes) before returning. For variety, you could cross to the other side of the river at Myōjin-bashi Bridge.

West of Kappa-bashi Bridge, you can amble along the right-hand side of the river to the **Weston Monument** (15 minutes) or keep to the left-hand side of the river and walk to **Taishō-ike Pond** (20 minutes). A bridge across the river between Weston Monument and Taishō-ike Pond provides variation for the walk.

Places to Stay

Accommodation is relatively expensive, advance reservations are essential during the peak season, and the whole place shuts down from November to May. You'd be well advised to make reservations before arriving in Kamikōchi; the tourist information offices at Takayama and Matsumoto are convenient since they have English-speaking staff.

JAPAN

There is a handful of hotels, mostly around Kappa-bashi Bridge, which is a short walk from the bus terminal. Most of them will be well be too expensive for budget travellers. The *Gosenjaku Lodge* (☎ 0263-95-2221), for example, provides a bed and two meals from ¥10,000. For a bed only, the price should be ¥6500.

Dotted along the trails and around the mountains are dozens of mountain cottages or mountain huts *(san-sō* or *yama-goya)* which provide two meals and a bed for an average cost of around ¥6500. Given the usually lower standards of the food and lodging in such mountain accommodation, these prices are expensive. However, the proprietors have to contend with a short season and difficult access, and most hikers are prepared to pay the premium for somewhere out of the cold.

Campgrounds are available at the *Kamikōchi Konashidaira Kampu-jō*, which is next to the Visitor's Centre about 10 minutes' walk beyond Kappa-bashi Bridge, and at the *Tokusawa Kampu-jō*, which is about three km north-east of Kappa-bashi Bridge. Costs for tent hire tend to be rather high (¥3000 for a six person tent at Tokusawa).

The closest *youth hostels* are at Shirahone Onsen and on Norikura-kōgen Plateau, both within easy reach of Kamikōchi.

Getting There & Away

Bus services for Kamikōchi cease from mid-November to late April and the exact dates can vary. If you plan to travel at the beginning or end of this period, check first with a tourist office or call Japan Travel-Phone (☎ 0120-222800, toll free).

The connection between Kamikōchi and Matsumoto involves travel by train and bus. For more details, see the Getting There & Away section for Matsumoto.

Between Takayama and Kamikōchi there are frequent bus connections but *only* from April to October. The bus runs via Nakanoyu and you have to change to another bus at Hirayu Onsen. From Takayama to Hirayu Onsen takes around an hour and costs ¥1360,

and from Hirayu Onsen to Kamikōchi is around another hour of travel and costs ¥1400.

Between Norikura and Kamikōchi there are buses running via Hirayu Onsen approximately three times a day (two hours). The Norikura Skyline Road is *only* open from 15 May to 31 October. The whole trip takes around two hours and costs ¥2800.

There is also a relatively infrequent bus service between Kamikōchi and Shirahone Onsen. It takes one hour 15 minutes and costs ¥2000.

KANAZAWA 金沢

Kanazawa (population 442,000) on the northern Japan Sea coast of central Honshū is a major cultural attraction in the area. The most famous of the city's attractions is Kenroku-en Garden, one of Japan's 'big three'. The main sights can be seen in a day or so but a side trip to the Noto-hantō Peninsula is highly recommended.

Information

Ignore the small information office indicated with a '?' sign next door to the ticket turnstiles inside JR Kanazawa station and head over to the JR ticket sales office also in the station. At the back of the office is the excellent Kanazawa tourist information office (☎ 0762-32-6200). The office has English-speaking staff and is open daily from 10 am to 6 pm.

Things to See

The **Kenroku-en Garden** is Kanazawa's most famous attraction, ranked by Japanese as one of their three top gardens – the other two are Kairaku-en in Mito and Kōraku-en in Okayama. Admission costs ¥300 and it's open daily from 6.30 am to 6 pm. From 16 October to 15 March opening hours are from 8 am to 4.30 pm.

Seison-kaku Villa, on the south-eastern edge of Kenroku-en Garden, was built in 1863. Admission costs ¥500 and includes a detailed explanatory leaflet in English. It's open daily from 8.30 am to 4.30 pm, closed Wednesday.

Other worthwhile sights around Kanazawa include the **Nagamachi District**. Once a samurai quarter, it has retained a few of its winding streets and tile-roofed mud walls. Nomura Samurai House, though partly transplanted from outside Kanazawa, is worth a visit for its decorative garden. Admission costs ¥400 and it's open from 8.30 am to 5 pm.

If you follow the main road north from Terajima Samurai House and cross the Asano-gawa River, you reach the **Eastern Pleasure District**, which was established early in the last century as a centre for geisha to entertain wealthy patrons. There are several streets still preserved with the slatted, wooden façades of the geisha houses.

The **Teramachi District** stretches beside the Sai-gawa River, just south of the city centre. This old neighbourhood still contains dozens of temples and narrow backstreets: a good place for a peaceful stroll. One of the more interesting temples is the **Ninja-dera Temple**, also known as Myōryū-ji Temple. The popular name of Ninja-dera refers to the temple's connection with *ninjutsu* (the art of stealth) and the *ninja* (practitioners of the art). Admission costs ¥500 and is by reservation (☎ 0762-41-2877) only. It's open from 9 am to 4.30 pm but closes half an hour earlier between December and February.

Places to Stay
The tourist information office in the station can help with reservations for accommodation.

The *Matsui Youth Hostel* (☎ 0762-21-0275) is small and relaxed, but closes at 10 pm. Nightly costs are ¥2400. Note that the hostel is closed from 31 December to 2 January. From the station, take a bus from terminal No 7, 8 or 9 for the 14-minute ride to the city and get off at the Katamachi bus stop. Walk a few metres back up the street to a large intersection. Turn right here then take the second side street on your right. The hostel is halfway down this street.

Murataya Ryokan (☎ 0762-63-0455) is a member of the Japanese Inn Group. Prices for singles/doubles start at ¥4200/8000;

triples cost from ¥10,500. To find this ryokan, follow the directions for Matsui Youth Hostel. After turning right at the large intersection, take the first side street on your left and continue about 20 metres until you see the ryokan sign on your left.

The *Kanazawa Youth Hostel* (☎ 0762-52-3414) is way up in the hills to the east of the city and commands a superb position. Unfortunately, this also means that access to the hostel is mighty inconvenient, unless you have your own transport as bus services are infrequent. A dorm bed costs ¥2500, but foreign hostellers are given a ¥200 discount. Private rooms are a good deal at ¥3500 per person. The doors close at 10 pm and loudspeakers marshal the slumbering troops for reveille in the morning. To reach the hostel from the station, take bus No 90 for Utatsuyama-kōen Park and get off after about 25 minutes at the Suizokukan-mae bus stop, which is virtually opposite the hostel.

Getting There & Away
Bus There are regular bus services between Kanazawa and Tokyo (Ikebukuro, 7½ hours, ¥7700), Kyoto (four hours, ¥3990) and Nagoya (four hours, ¥3990). The Meitetsu bus service between Kanazawa and Nagoya operates from July to early November via Gokayama and Shirakawa-gō.

Train Kanazawa is linked to south-western destinations by the JR Hokuriku line: Fukui (55 minutes), Kyoto (2½ hours, ¥6580) and Osaka (3 hours, ¥7300). The same line runs north-east to Takaoka (45 minutes), Toyama (one hour), Naoetsu (2¼ hours) and Niigata (3¾ hours). To travel to Takayama (2½ hours), you need to change to the JR Takayama line at Toyama. The quickest way to travel between Tokyo and Kanazawa is by taking the Jōetsu shinkansen from Tokyo station to Nagaoka (one hour 40 minutes), and then travelling onwards by limited express to Kanazawa (three hours). The whole trip costs ¥13,210. There are two daily departures of the limited express Hakusan service from Ueno to Kanazawa. The journey takes just over six hours and costs ¥10,490.

The JR Nanao line connects Kanazawa with Wajima (Noto-hantō Peninsula) in 2¼ hours.

Getting Around

Bus Kanazawa's bus network is extensive and fares start at ¥170. From the station, bus Nos 10 and 11 will take you to the Kenroku-en-shita bus stop, a useful point if you just want to visit the main sights around Kenroku-en Garden. To ride from the station to the city centre, you can choose from several buses, including bus Nos 20, 21 and 30, and get off at the Kōrimbō bus stop.

Bicycle Bicycle rental is available (¥1000 for the day or ¥600 for four hours) at the station, but the hills and the urban traffic snarls aren't particularly inviting. The Kanazawa Youth Hostel also has bicycles for rent (cheaper prices), but it's quite a puff returning up the hill. The tourist information office in the station has details of bicycle rental places in the city centre.

Kansai Region
関西地方

The term Kansai ('west of the barrier') is loosely used to describe the area encompassed by Osaka, Kyoto, Kōbe and Nara. Historically the centre of the Japanese world, the Kansai region is the richest part of Japan in terms of cultural sights. Kansai's major drawcards are, of course, Kyoto and Nara, but the cities of Osaka and Kōbe are also vibrant and increasingly cosmopolitan urban centres.

KYOTO 京都

If there are two cities in Japan that *have* to be included on anyone's itinerary, they are Tokyo and Kyoto (population 1.4 million). Kyoto is a city that, like the other cities of Japan, has it's eyes far more firmly on the future than on the past. But, happily, it is still a city where the past lingers on: it has more than 2000 temples and shrines, a trio of palaces, and dozens of gardens and museums. Months or even years could be spent exploring Kyoto without running out of surprises.

Information

The best source of information on Kyoto and the Kansai region is the TIC (☎ 075-371-5649); it's four minutes on foot north of Kyoto station. Opening hours are from 9 am to 5 pm on weekdays and until noon on Saturday; it's closed on Sunday and holidays. The staff here have maps, literature and an amazing amount of information on Kyoto at their capable fingertips.

Things to See

Central Kyoto Although Central Kyoto looks much like any other Japanese city, there are a few major sights in the area. Foremost of central Kyoto's sights is the **Kyoto Imperial Palace**. Unfortunately, the palace can only be visited on a tour and you will need to reserve a place. This is organised by the Imperial Household Agency (Kunaichō) (☎ 075-211-1215), which is a short walk from Imadegawa subway station. You will have to fill out an application form and show your passport; children should be accompanied by adults over 20 years of age. Permission to tour the imperial palace is usually granted for the same day. English guided tours are given at 10 am and 2 pm; you should arrive no later than 20 minutes beforehand at the Seisho-mon Gate. Admission is free.

Not far from the Imperial Palace is **Nijō-jō Castle**. Entry to the inner palace and garden is ¥500, and it's open daily from 8.45 am until last admission at 4 pm (gates close at 5 pm). Also, it's closed from 26 December to 4 January. Bus Nos 9, 12, 50, 52, 61 and 67 go to the Nijō-jō-mae bus stop, in front of the castle. Alternatively, you can take the subway to Oike and then walk for 12 minutes.

Kansai Region
関西地方

0   30   60 km

Prefectural Boundary

Farther south, in the station area, **Higashi Hongan-ji Temple** is monumental in its proportions. Admission is free and the temple is open from 9 am to 4 pm. It's a five-minute walk north of Kyoto station.

Just south-west of Kyoto station is **Tō-ji Temple**, which was established in 794 by imperial decree to protect the city. Most of the buildings that remain today date from the 17th century. Admission to the temple costs ¥500; and it's open from 9 am to 4 pm.

Eastern Kyoto The eastern part of Kyoto, notably the Higashiyama (Eastern Mountains) district, merits top priority for a visit to its fine temples, peaceful walks and traditional night entertainment in Gion.

Sanjūsangen-dō Temple derives its name from the 33 *sanjūsan* (bays) between the pillars of this long, narrow building which houses 1001 statues of the Thousand-Armed Kannon (the Buddhist goddess of mercy). The temple is open from 8 am to 5 pm (16 March to 31 October) and 8 am to 4 pm (1 November to 15 March). Admission is ¥400. The temple is a 15-minute walk east of Kyoto station, or you can take bus No 206 or 208 and get off at the Sanjūsangen-dō-mae stop.

The **Kyoto National Museum** is housed

JAPAN

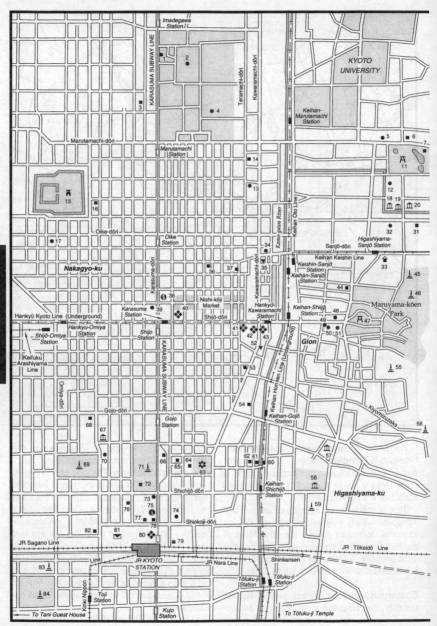

Imadegawa
Station

KARASUMA SUBWAY LINE

1
2

KYOTO
UNIVERSITY

3

Teramachi-dōri

Kawaramachi-dōri

4

Keihan-
Marutamachi
Station

Marutamachi-dōri

5   6
7

11

Marutamachi
Station

14

12

15

13

18 19
20
16

Kamo-gawa River

Keihan Oto Line

32   31

Oike-dōri

Oike
Station

17

34

Higashiyama-
Sanjō Station

Nakagyo-ku

Sanjō-dōri

Keihan Keishin Line

33   45

Karasuma-dōri

36   37

35

Kawaramachi-dōri

Keishin-Sanjō
Station
Keihan-Sanjō
Station

38

44

46

Karasuma
Station

39

40

Nishi-kōji
Market
Shijō-dōri

Hankyū-
Kawaramachi
Station

Keihan-Shijō
Station

Maruyama-kōen
Park

47

Hankyū Kyoto Line (Underground)

Shijō
Station

41
42   43
52

48
49
50 51

Shijō-Omiya
Station

Hankyu-Omiya
Station

KARASUMA SUBWAY LINE

Gion

Keifuku
Arashiyama
Line

53

Keihan Honsen Line (Underground)

55

Kiyomizuzaka

Omiya-dōri

Gojo-dōri

Gojo
Station

54

Keihan-Gojō
Station

56

68

67

57

69

70

71

66

65 64

62 61

60

58

Higashiyama-ku

72

63

Keihan-
Shichijō
Station

59

73
75

Shichijō-dōri

76   77

74

Shiokoji-dōri

78

82   81
80

79

JR Sagano Line

JR Tōkaidō Line

83

84

Line

Kinki Nippon

JR KYOTO
STATION

JR Nara Line

Shinkansen

Toji
Station

Tōfuku-ji
Station

Tōfuku-ji
Station

To Tani Guest House

Kujo
Station

To Tōfuku-ji Temple

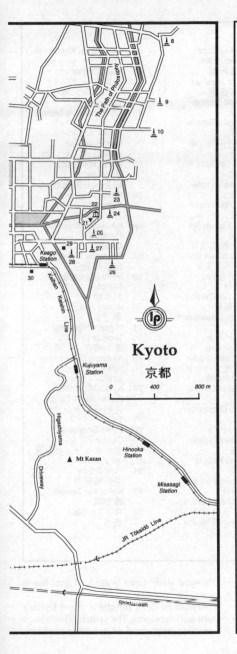

PLACES TO STAY

3 YWCA
6 YWCA
7 Three Sisters Inn
   洛東荘
14 Uno House
   宇野ハウス
10 International Hotel Kyoto
   京都国際ホテル
29 Yachiyo Ryokan
   八千代旅館
30 Miyako Hotel
   都ホテル
31 Kyoto Travellers Inn
   京都トラベラーズイン
33 Higashiyama Youth Hostel
   東山ユースホステル
36 YMCA
37 Tani House Annex
   谷ハウスアネクス
44 Iwanami Ryokan
53 Ryokan Hinomoto
   旅館ひのもと
54 Hotel Rich II
   ホテルリッチⅡ
60 Riverside Takase & Annexe
   Kyōka
   リバーサイド高瀬
   アネクス
61 Ryokan Hiraiwa
   平岩旅館
62 Yuhara Ryokan
   ゆはら旅館
64 Ryokan Murakamiya
   旅館村上家
65 Ryokan Kyōka
   旅館京花
66 Matsubaya Ryokan
   松葉屋旅館
68 Kyoto Tōkyū Hotel
   京都東急ホテル
72 Pension Station Kyoto
76 Kyoto Dai-San Hotel
   京都第3ホテル
77 Hokke Club Kyoto/
   Kyoto New Hankyū Hotel
   法華クラブ京都
   京都ニュー阪急ホテ
78 Kyoto Tower Hotel
   京都タワーホテル
79 Kyoto Century Hotel
   京都センチュリーホテル

JAPAN

82 Kyoto Grand Hotel
京都グランドホテル

PLACES TO EAT

21 Okutan Restaurant
奥丹
35 Capricciosa Restaurant
カピチオサ
52 Chikyuya Restaurant
ちきゅうや／地球屋

OTHER

1 Imperial Household
Agency
京都御所
2 Imperial Palace
京都皇居
4 Sentō Gosho Palace
仙洞御所
5 Kyoto Handicraft
Centre
京都ハンティクラフト
センター
8 Ginkaku-ji Temple
銀閣寺
9 Hōnen-in Temple
法然院
10 Anraku-ji Temple
安楽寺
11 Heian-jingū Shrine &
Time Paradox Eatery
タイムパラドクス
12 Kyoto Kaikan Hall
13 Ippō-dō Teashop
一保堂
15 Nijō-jō Castle
二条城
17 Nijō-jinya
二条陣屋
18 Museum of Traditional
Industry
伝統産業会館
19 National Museum of
Modern Art
国立近代美術館

20 Kyoto Municipal
Museum of Art
市立美術館
22 Nomura Museum
野村美術館
23 Eikan-dō Temple
永観堂
24 Chōshō-in Temple
聴松院
25 Nanzen-ji Temple
南善寺
26 Nanzen-in Temple
南善院
27 Tenju-an Temple
天授庵
28 Konchi-in Temple
金地院
32 Kanze Kaikan Nō
Theatre
観世会館能楽堂
34 Backgammon Bar
バックガンモン
38 Bank of Tokyo
東京銀行
39 Kongō Nō Theatre
金岡能楽堂
40 Daimaru Department
Store
大丸デパート
41 Fujii-Daimaru
Department Store
富井大丸デパート
42 Takashimaya
Department Store
高島屋
43 Hankyū Department
Store
阪急デパート
45 Shōren-in Temple
青蓮寺
46 Chion-in Temple
知恩院
47 Yasakajinja Shrine
八坂神社
48 Kyoto Craft Centre
京都クラフトセンター
49 Minami-za Theatre
南座

50 Gion Kōbu Kaburenjō
Theatre
51 Gion Corner
祇園コーナー
55 Kōdaiji Temple
高台寺
56 Kiyomizudera Temple
清水寺
57 Kawai Kanjirō
Memorial Hall
河井寛次郎記念館
58 Kyoto National
Museum
京都国立博物館
59 Sanjūsangen-dō
Temple
三十三間堂
63 Kikokutei Shōseien
Garden
渉成園
67 Costume Museum
風俗博物館
69 Nishi Honganji
Temple
西本願寺
70 Kungyokudō
薫玉堂
71 Higashi Honganji
Temple
東本願寺
73 Kintetsu Department
Store
近鉄デパート
74 Kyoto Minshuku
Reservation Centre
民宿予約センター
75 TIC
80 Porta Shopping
Centre
ポルタショッピング
センター
81 Post Office
中央郵便局
83 Kanchi-in Temple
観智院
84 Tō-ji Temple
東寺

in two buildings opposite Sanjūsangen-dō Temple. There are excellent displays of fine arts, historical artefacts and handicrafts. Admission costs ¥400 but note that a separate charge is made for special exhibitions. It's open daily from 9 am to 4 pm, but is closed on Monday.

Kiyomizu-dera Temple is one of Kyoto's most famous sights. The main hall has a huge verandah, supported on hundreds of pillars, which juts out over the hillside. The steep approach to the temple, known as 'Teapot Lane', is lined with shops selling Kyoto handicrafts, local snacks and souvenirs. Admission to the temple costs ¥300 and it's open from 6 am to 6 pm. To get there from Kyoto station take bus No 207, 206 or 202 and get off at either the Kiyomizu-michi or Gojō-zaka stops. Plod up the hill for 10 minutes to reach the temple.

Gion is the famous entertainment and geisha district on the eastern bank of the Kamo-gawa River. Modern architecture, congested traffic and contemporary nightlife establishments have cut a swathe through the historical beauty, but there are still some places left for an enjoyable walk.

North East Kyoto The **National Museum of Modern Art** is renowned for its collection of contemporary Japanese ceramics and paintings. Exhibits are changed on a regular basis. Admission costs ¥400 and it's open from 10 am to 5 pm daily except Monday.

Heian-jingū Shrine is a sprawling affair close to the museum. It's somewhat gaudy, but the inner garden is worth a visit. Entry to the shrine precincts is free but admission to the garden costs ¥500. It's open from 8.30 am to 5.30 pm (15 March to 31 August), though closing time can be an hour earlier during the rest of the year.

Nanzen-ji Temple began its life as a retirement villa for Emperor Kameyama, but was dedicated as a Zen temple on his death in 1291. It operates now as headquarters for the Rinzai school of Zen. Admission is ¥350 and it's open from 8.30 am to 5 pm. The temple is a 10-minute walk south-east of the Heian-jingū Shrine; from Kyoto station take bus No 5 and get off at the Eikan-dō-mae stop.

Eikan-dō Temple, also known as Zenrin-ji Temple, is interesting by virtue of its architectural diversity and its gardens. The best approach is to follow the arrows and wander slowly along the covered walkways connecting the halls and gardens. The temple is open from 9 am to 4 pm and admission costs ¥400.

The Path of Philosophy is a popular walk from Eikan-dō Temple to **Ginkaku-ji Temple**. Despite the romantic associations of its name, be prepared for the inevitable vending machines and souvenir shops en route – at least it's traffic-free. Ginkaku-ji Temple is a 'must-see'. It's just unfortunate that it is often swamped with bus loads of visitors jamming the narrow pathways. Admission costs ¥400 and it's open from 9 am to 5 pm. An explanatory leaflet in English is provided. From Kyoto station, take bus No 5 and get off at the Ginkaku-ji-mae stop.

North-West Kyoto The north-western part of Kyoto is predominantly residential, but there are a number of superb temples with tranquil gardens in secluded precincts. Zen enthusiasts should visit **Daitoku-ji Temple** and **Ryōan-ji Temple**. **Kinkaku-ji Temple** is another major attraction. The JNTO leaflet on walks also covers this area, but most of the walking is through unremarkable city streets.

Kinkaku-ji Temple, the famed 'Golden Temple', is the most famous of the sights in this part of Kyoto. The original building was constructed in 1397, but in 1950 a young monk consummated his obsession with the temple by burning it to the ground. The monk's story was fictionalised in Mishima Yukio's *The Golden Pavilion*. The temple is open from 9 am to 5.30 pm and admission costs ¥300. To get there from Kyoto station, take bus No 205 and get off at the Kinkaku-ji-michi stop; bus No 59 also stops close to the temple.

The **Takao District** is a secluded district tucked far away in the north-western part of Kyoto. It is famed for autumn foliage and the temples of **Jingo-ji**, **Saimyō-ji** and **Kōzan-ji**. To reach Jingo-ji Temple, take bus No 8 from Shijō-Omiya station; allow one hour for the ride. The other two temples are within easy walking distance.

Western Kyoto Arashiyama and Sagano are two districts worth a visit in this area if you feel like strolling in pleasant natural surroundings and visiting temples tucked into

JAPAN

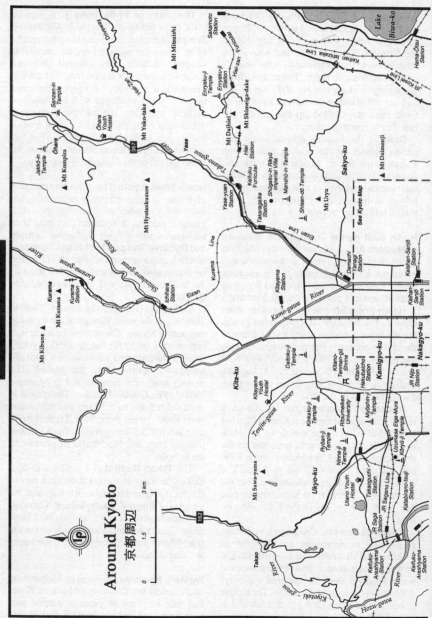

Around Kyoto
京都周辺

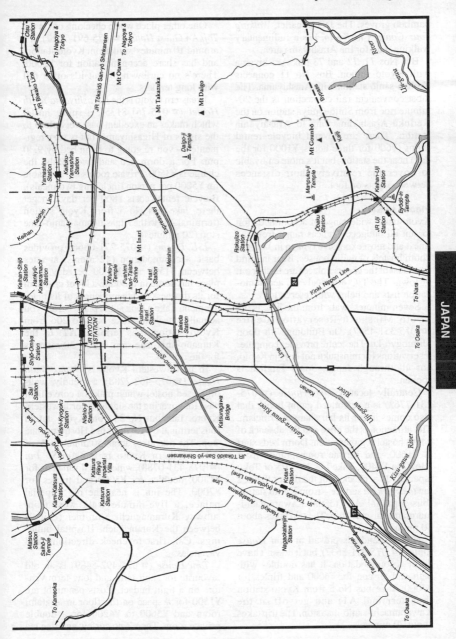

bamboo groves. The JNTO leaflet, *Walking Tour Courses in Kyoto*, has a rudimentary walking map for the Arashiyama area.

Bus Nos 71, 72 and 73 link Arashiyama with Kyoto station. Bus No 11 connects Keihan-sanjō station with Arashiyama. The most convenient rail connection is the 20-minute ride from Shijō-Omiya station on the Keifuku-Arashiyama line to Arashiyama station. There are several bicycle rental shops (¥600 for three hours, ¥1000 for the day) near the station, but it's more enjoyable to cover the relatively short distances between sights on foot.

Places to Stay

Kyoto has a wide range of accommodation to suit all budgets. Choices range from the finest and most expensive ryokan in Japan to youth hostels or gaijin houses. Bear in mind that most of the cheaper places are farther out of town. The TIC offers advice, accommodation lists and helps with reservations.

Seven minutes' walk from the TIC is the Kyoto Minshuku Reservation Centre (☎ 075-351-4547), On Building, 7th floor, Shimogyo-ku. The centre provides computer reservations for minshuku not only in Kyoto, but all through Japan. Some English is spoken.

Centrally located, *Uno House* (☎ 075-231-7763) is a celebrated gaijin house that also comes in for its fair share of criticism. The attraction is the price and the absence of youth hostel regimentation. Dorm beds start at ¥1600, and private rooms range from ¥3600 to ¥5400. Take bus No 205 or Toku (special) 17 – check with the driver that it's the *toku jūnana* service – from Kyoto station (bus terminal A3) to the Kawaramachi-marutamachi-mae stop. The trip takes about 20 minutes.

Higher standards prevail at *Tani House Annex* (☎ 075-211-5637), but it doesn't have dorm accommodation. It has doubles with bath and air-con for ¥6000 and triples for ¥7000. Take bus No 5 from Kyoto station (bus terminal A1) and get off at the Kawaramachi-sanjō-mae stop. The trip takes about 20 minutes.

One other place worth checking out is the *Tōji An Guest House* (☎ 075-691-7017). It's around 10 minutes' walk from Kyoto station, and has share accommodation for ¥2000. There's no curfew here, but it's often full with long termers.

In eastern Kyoto is the *Higashiyama Youth Hostel* (☎ 075-761-8135), a spiffy hostel which makes an excellent base very close to the sights of Higashiyama, but is *very* regimented – you're going to be in bed by 9.30 pm. For a dorm bed and two meals, the charge is ¥3500. Private rooms are available for ¥5000 per person (including two meals). Bicycle rental costs ¥800 per day. To get there, take bus No 5 from Kyoto station (terminal A1) to the Higashiyama-sanjō-mae stop (20 minutes).

ISE Dorm (☎ 075-771-0566) provides basic accommodation (42 rooms) at rates between ¥1500 and ¥3000 per day. This place has come in for quite a lot of criticism for its dirtiness and the rudeness of its management. Take a look at the place before you actually check in. Take bus No 206 from Kyoto station (bus terminal A2) to the Kumano-jinja-mae stop. Allow 30 minutes for the ride.

In north-western Kyoto is *Utano Youth Hostel* (☎ 075-462-2288), a friendly, well-organised hostel which makes a convenient base for covering the sights of north-western Kyoto. Take bus No 26 from Kyoto station (bus terminal C1) to the Yūsu Hosuteru-mae stop. The ride takes about 50 minutes.

In northern Kyoto is the *Aoi-Sō Inn* (☎ 075-431-0788), which has dorm beds for ¥1300, doubles for ¥5000 and triples for ¥7000. The inn is near the old imperial palace, a five-minute walk from subway Kuramaguchi Shin-mei (exit 2) between the Kuramaguchi Hospital buildings. Call first to check directions and vacancies.

Tani House (☎ 075-492-5489) is an old favourite for short-term and long-term visitors on a tight budget. Costs per night are ¥1500 for a space on the floor in a tatami room and ¥3600 to ¥4200 for a double private room. There's no curfew and free tea and coffee are provided. It can become crowded, so book ahead. Take the 45-minute ride on bus No 206 from Kyoto station (bus terminal B4) and get off at the Kenkun-jinja-mae stop.

The *Kitayama Youth Hostel* (☎ 075-492-5345) charges ¥2400 for a dorm bed (without meals) or ¥3500 with two meals. Take bus No 6 from Kyoto station (bus terminal B4) to the Genkoan-mae stop (allow 35 minutes for the trip). Walk west past a school, turn right and continue up the hill to the hostel (five minutes on foot). This hostel would be an excellent base to visit the rural area of Takagamine which has some fine, secluded temples such as Kōetsu-ji Temple, Jōshō-ji Temple and Shōden-ji Temple.

Green Peace (☎ 075-791-9890) is a gaijin house that is really only an option if you are planning to stay three nights or longer as it doesn't take short-term visitors or quote nightly rates. Dorms cost ¥4500 for three nights. Take bus No 4 from Kyoto station (bus terminal A4) to the Nonogami-chō-mae stop. Allow 35 minutes for the ride.

Guest House Kyoto (☎ 075-491-0880) has single rooms for ¥2500 per day. Twin rooms are ¥4000 per day. Take bus No 205 from Kyoto station (bus terminal B3) to the Senbon-kitaoji-mae stop (50 minutes).

Takaya (☎ 075-431-5213) provides private rooms for ¥3000 per day. Take the subway from Kyoto station to Imadegawa station (15 minutes).

Kyoto Ōhara Youth Hostel (☎ 075-744-2528) is a long way north out of town, but the rural surroundings are a bonus if you want to relax or dawdle around Ōhara's beautiful temples. A dorm bed costs ¥2300.

From Kyoto station, you can take the subway to Kitaoji station and then take bus No 'north' 6 to Ōhara (make sure the kanji for 'north' precedes the number or ask for *kita rokku*). Get off at the To-dera stop (near To-dera Temple). The TIC can give precise details for other train or bus routes to get you there.

Places to Eat

At the lower end of the food budget, there are plenty of fast-food eateries, including *Shakey's Pizza, McDonald's, Kentucky Fried Chicken, Mr Donut* etc, all over town.

Coffee shops and noodle restaurants are good for inexpensive meals or snacks. For good value try the chain of *Doutor* coffee shops (big yellow and brown signs), which sell coffee for ¥190 and also have inexpensive snacks like cakes and hotdogs.

Most of the major department stores have restaurants usually offering teishoku (set meals) which are good value at lunch time. Locals favour *Seven-Eight*, the 7th and 8th floors of Hankyū department store, which together form a large complex of inexpensive restaurants and are open until 10 pm. In the Porta shopping centre below Kyoto station there are also rows of restaurants with reasonable prices.

Central Kyoto, in particular the Kawaramachi area, is excellent for digging up reasonably priced alternatives to Japanese fare. To get an idea of what's available, the best starting place is Kiyamachi-dōri (the one with a small canal running through the centre of it) and the lanes that run off it. There's a wide range of international and Japanese restaurants in this area, many with English menus.

For inexpensive Italian food, number one on anyone's list should be *Capricciosa*. This successful chain is renowned throughout Japan for its affordable and authentic pasta and pizza delivered in enormous portions. Two portions here will easily feed three people.

Another place worth a special mention is *Chikyuya*, just around the corner from the Hankyū department store. This is a Kyoto institution, once the favoured haunt of Kyoto's alternative set and now doing a brisk business with a more mainstream clientele. Look for the queue outside.

Things to Buy

Kyoto offers probably the best shopping opportunities for traditional arts and handicrafts in Japan. There are shops scattered all over town. You won't have any trouble finding them.

JAPAN

Getting There & Away

Air Kyoto is served by Osaka Itami Airport, a one-hour bus ride away. As of mid-1994, most international flights should be using the new Kansai International Airport.

Bus JR buses run four times a day between Osaka and Tokyo via Kyoto and Nagoya. Passengers change buses at Nagoya. Travel time for the express buses between Kyoto and Nagoya is about 2½ hours (¥2200). The journey between Nagoya and Tokyo takes about 6¼ hours (¥5000). Other companies competing with JR on the same route include Meihan and Nikkyū. All buses run from the same point.

The overnight bus (JR Dream Bus) runs between Tokyo and Kyoto (departures in both directions). The trip takes about eight hours and there are usually two departures at 10 and 11 pm. Tickets are ¥8030 plus a reservation fee. Buses run either to Yaesu bus terminal close to Tokyo station or to Shinjuku station. Other JR bus possibilities include Kanazawa (¥3990), Tottori (¥3800), Hiroshima (¥5500), Nagasaki (¥11,100), Kumamoto (¥10,500), Fukuoka (¥9500) and Kagoshima (¥12,600).

Train If you are loaded with money, or have a Japan Rail Pass, you can take the JR shinkansen line between Kyoto and Shin-Osaka; the trip takes only 16 minutes. To connect between Shin-Osaka and central Osaka, switch to the Midōsuji subway line for Osaka's Umeda (for JR Osaka station) or Namba districts.

The Japan Rail Pass is also valid on the JR Tōkaidō (San-yō) line which runs via Osaka. The trip between Kyoto and Osaka station takes 45 minutes and is ¥530 for a one-way ticket.

The Hankyū Kyoto line runs between Kyoto (Kawaramachi station) and Osaka (Umeda station – close to JR Osaka station). The fastest trip takes 47 minutes and is ¥330 for a one-way ticket.

The Keihan subway line in the east of Kyoto emerges from underground after Shichijō station and runs to Osaka's Yodoyabashi station, which is on the Midōsuji subway line (convenient for connections with Shin-Osaka, Osaka and Namba). The fastest trip takes 40 minutes and costs ¥330 for a one-way ticket.

Unless you have a Japan Rail Pass, the best option is the Kintetsu line linking Kyoto and Nara (Kintetsu Nara station) in 33 minutes by tokkyū (limited express) for ¥900 one way. If you take a local or express train on this line, the ticket price drops to ¥500 for the 45-minute ride, but you will need to change at Yamato-Saidai-ji, which is a five-minute ride from Nara Kintetsu station. The JR Nara line connects Kyoto with Nara JR station in one hour (¥740 one way).

For getting to Tokyo, the JR shinkansen line is the fastest and most frequent rail link. The Hikari super-express takes two hours and 40 minutes from Tokyo station, and a one-way ticket including surcharges costs ¥12,970.

Unless you're travelling on a Japan Rail Pass or are in an extreme hurry, you'll probably be looking for a cheaper way to make the trip. Travelling by local trains takes around eight hours and involves at least two (often three or four) changes along the way. The fare is ¥7830, and you should call in to the TIC for details on the schedules and where changes are necessary for the particular time you are travelling.

Hitching For long-distance hitching, the best bet is to head for the Kyoto-Minami Interchange of the Meishin expressway, which is about four km south of Kyoto station. Take the Toku No 19 bus (make sure the kanji for 'special' *toku* precedes the number) from Kyoto station and get off when you reach the Meishin expressway signs. From here you can hitch east towards Tokyo or west to southern Japan.

Getting Around

To/From the Airport There are frequent airport limousine buses running between Osaka airport and Kyoto station. Buses also run between the airport and various hotels around town, but on a less regular basis. The journey should take around 55 minutes and the cost is ¥890.

Transport from the new Kansai International Airport will be by rail and will take 85 minutes. No prices were available at the time of writing.

Bus For getting around Kyoto itself, there's an intricate network of bus routes which provides an efficient way of getting around at moderate cost. Many of the bus routes used by foreign visitors have announcements in English. They generally run between 7 am and 9 pm, though a few run earlier or later.

The main bus terminals are Kyoto station, Keihan-sanjō station and Shijō-karasuma station. On the northern side of Kyoto station is a major bus terminus with departure terminals clearly marked with a letter of the alphabet and a number.

The TIC has two bus maps: a simplified map on the reverse of the *Kyoto, Nara* brochure and a bus route map, studded with kanji, for advanced bus explorers.

Entry to the bus is usually through the back door and exit is via the front door. Inner-city buses charge a flat fare (¥180) which you drop into a machine next to the driver. The machine gives change for ¥100 and ¥500 coins or ¥1000 notes, or you can ask the driver. To save time and money, you can buy a *kaisū-ken* (book of six tickets) for ¥1000 at bus terminals or from the driver. There is also a deal offering 11 tickets for the price of 10. Alternatively, there's a *ichinichi jōsha-ken* (one-day pass), which is valid for unlimited travel on city buses, private Kyoto buses and the subway. It costs ¥1050 and is available at bus centres and subway stations. A *futsuka jōshā-ken* (two-day pass) is also available and costs ¥2000. The passes can be picked up in subway stations and the City Information Office.

Bicycle Both the youth hostels at Higashiyama and Utano provide bicycle rental. In Higashiyama you could try Taki Rent-a-Bicycle on Kaminokuchi St, east of Kawaramachi. Arashiyama station has several places for bicycle rental. Nippon Rent-a-Cycle is in front of the southern side of Kyoto station, close to the Hachijō west exit. Expect rental rates of around ¥1100 per day, but different rates apply depending on the kind of bike.

OSAKA 大阪

Osaka (population 2.6 million) is second only to Tokyo in economic importance (third, after Yokohama, in population) and it's a city that suffers from even more of a lack of open spaces, greenery and historical sites than Japan's capital city.

Information

The Osaka Tourist Association has offices at both Shin-Osaka (☎ 06-305-3311) and Osaka (☎ 06-345-2189) stations, though the main office is the one in Osaka station. Both are open from 8 am to 8 pm. Many travellers have problems finding the tourist office in Osaka station. It's in the south-east corner of the station complex, and to find it you should take the Midōsuji exit. Osaka airport also has an information counter (☎ 06-856-6781). All three offices can help with booking accommodation, but you will have to visit the office in person for this service.

Things to See

Osaka's most famous attraction, **Osaka-jō Castle**, is a 1931 concrete reproduction of the original. The castle's exterior retains a certain grandeur but the interior looks like a barn with lifts. The castle is open from 9 am to 5 pm daily and admission is ¥400. The Ōte-mon Gate is about a 10-minute walk north-east of Tanimachi-yonchōme station on the Chūō and Tanimachi subway lines.

Shitennō-ji Temple, founded in 593, has the distinction of being one of the oldest Buddhist temples in Japan, but none of today's buildings are originals. The temple is open from 9 am to 5 pm daily and admission is ¥500. It's most easily reached from Shitennō-ji-mae station on the Tanimachi line.

Kita-ku, the northern ward of central Osaka, where you'll find JR Osaka station, is a little like the east and west sides of

Shinjuku station in Tokyo rolled into one. It's a noisy warren of backstreets punctuated by main thoroughfares and high-rises. Sights worth taking a look at include the **Umeda Sky Building**, just to the north-west of Osaka station, the **Hankyū Grand Building**, a 32-storeyed building next to Osaka station which has a free observatory on its top floor, and the **Umeda Chika Centre**, a labyrinthine underground shopping complex.

Minami-ku, the southern ward of central Osaka centred around Namba and Shinsaibashi stations, is fun just to wander around but it really doesn't come into its own until night falls and the blaze of neon charges the atmosphere. The **Dōtomburi Canal** area makes for a great evening stroll, but by day you can check out **America-Mura**, or America village, a compact enclave of trendy shops and restaurants (with a few discreet love hotels thrown in for good measure).

Places to Stay

The best place to stay when visiting Osaka is Kyoto. It's less than 20 minutes away by shinkansen, or around 40 minutes on the Keihan line, there's a far better choice of accommodation (particularly in the budget bracket) and it's a much nicer place. About 15 minutes from Kita-ku, or 30 minutes from Minami-ku, is the *Osaka-fu Hattori Ryokuchi Youth Hostel* (☎ 06-862-0600), where beds cost ¥1700. Take the Midōsuji line to Ryokuchi-kōen station and leave through the western exit. Enter the park and follow the path straight ahead past a fountain and around to the right alongside the pond. You will find the youth hostel is a little farther on the right.

The *Rinkai Hotel Dejimaten* (☎ 0722-41-3045), the *Rinkai Hotel Kitamise* (☎ 0722-47-1111) and the *Rinkai Hotel Ishizuten* (☎ 0722-44-0088) are close together and good for short or long-term stays; they should be cheaper by the month. Singles start from ¥2200 without bathroom at the Ishizuten and with bathroom for ¥2900 at the Kitamise. Twins are also available at ¥2000

per head. Each of the hotels has cooking facilities and dining areas.

To get to the hotels, the best thing would be to call into one of the Osaka information counters and pick up a map. The hotels are a fair way out of town near Minato station on the Nankai line, which runs out of Namba station – take an express from platform 5 or 6 at Namba station, change to a Nankai line local train at Sakai and get off at the next stop, Minato station.

Places to Eat

Once you get off the main thoroughfares, the backstreets of the Umeda (Kita-ku) area harbour a surprising variety of restaurants. If you just have a brief stop in Osaka (for lunch, for example), head over to the side streets east of Books Asahiya where you'll find rāmen shops, fast-food barns, sushi-ya, they're all well represented.

South of this area is *Canopy*, an open-fronted (at least during the summer months) restaurant with late opening hours. This is the place to pick up reasonably priced pizzas, burgers, fish & chips and anything else generically Western that you've been missing. When we were last in town they were selling beers at ¥300, which is a bargain in Japan.

Minami-ku is also packed with restaurants, but a good starting point is Dōtomburi. If you pick somewhere that is doing brisk business you are unlikely to be disappointed. Dōtomburi has a couple of famous Japanese restaurants whose extensive menus feature some very reasonably priced dishes. You can't miss *Kuidaore* (☎ 06-211-5300) as it has a mechanical clown posted outside its doors, attracting the attention of potential customers by beating a drum. The restaurant has eight floors serving almost every kind of Japanese food, and windows featuring a huge range of plastic replicas. Main-course meals cost from ¥1000.

Entertainment

The *Pig & Whistle* is probably the liveliest of Osaka's expat bars, and does brisk business even on weekday nights. *Sam & Dave*

II, on the 4th floor of a building to the north of the Pig & Whistle, is a popular party spot and has draught beer for ¥300 until 11 pm. *Sam & Dave I* is down by the Kirin Plaza, and is a more intimate spot for a drink. Finally, check out the massive *Bar Isn't It*, on the 5th floor of the first building in the arcade north of Dōtomburi and across from the Kirin Plaza building. All drinks and food cost ¥500 and it's a good place to meet local Japanese and foreigners.

Getting There & Away
Air As well as internal flights, Osaka is a major international air centre. Japan's first 24-hour airport (Kansai International Airport) opened in mid-1994 and will make Osaka a much more important international arrival and departure point.

Train Osaka is the centre of an extensive rail network that sprawls across the Kansai region. Kōbe is a mere 30 minutes away, even quicker by shinkansen, while Kyoto and Nara are each about 50 minutes from Osaka.

Shinkansen services operate between Tokyo station and Shin-Osaka station (just under three hours) via Kyoto, and from Shin-Osaka station onto Hakata in northern Kyūshū (about 3½ hours).

To get to Kyoto from Osaka, the quickest route, other than the shinkansen (just 16 minutes), is with the private Hankyū line, departing from Umeda station. The trip takes around 40 minutes by limited express. See the Kyoto Getting There & Away section earlier in this chapter for more information on other possible routings.

To get to Nara, your best bet is to take the JR Kansai line from Tennō-ji station and get off at Horyu-ji station. The trip takes around 30 minutes. The private Kintetsu line also operates between Namba station and Nara station, taking about 30 minutes.

It is possible to travel between Osaka and Kōya-san from Namba Nankai station via the private Nankai-Kōya line.

Ferry Osaka has a twice-monthly inter-national ferry service to Shanghai (China). The ferries leave from the Osaka Nankō International Ferry Terminal, which can be reached by taking the 'New Tram' service from Suminoe-kōen station to Nankoguchi station. The price for a 2nd-class tatami-style berth is ¥23,000. For further information about Shanghai-bound ferries you can ring the Nitchū Kokusai Ferry company (078-392-1021), though don't expect any English to be spoken. A better source of information on sailing schedules and bookings would be the Kyoto TIC.

Ferries also depart from Nankō, Kanome-futō and Benten-futō piers for various destinations around Honshū, Kyūshū and Shikoku. For Beppu in Kyūshū (via Kōbe) the 2nd-class fare is ¥6900; for Miyazaki in Kyūshū the 2nd class fare is ¥8230. Other possibilities in Kyūshū include Shinmoji in the north of the island near Shimonoseki and Shibushi in the south of the island. For Shikoku, possibilities include Kōchi (¥4530), Matsuyama (¥4900, 2nd class), Takamatsu (¥2800, 2nd class) and Tokushima.

Getting Around
To/From the Airport There are frequent lim-ousine buses running between the airport and various parts of Osaka. To Shin-Osaka station buses run every 15 minutes from 6.50 am to 8.15 pm and cost ¥340. The trip takes around 25 minutes. Buses run at about the same frequency to Osaka and Namba stations (¥440, 30 minutes). There are also direct airport buses to and from Kyoto and Kōbe (see Getting Around in the Kyoto and Kōbe sections for details).

The rail link between Osaka and the new Kansai International Airport will take 35 minutes to Namba and 50 minutes to Umeda.

Train Osaka has a good subway network and, like Tokyo, a JR loop line that circles the city area. In fact, there should be no need to use any other form of transport while you are in Osaka unless you stay out late and miss the last train. Subway and JR stations are clearly marked in English as well as hiragana

JAPAN

and kanji so finding your way is relatively easy.

There are seven subway lines, but the one that most short-term visitors are likely to find most useful is the Midōsuji line, which runs north to south taking in the key areas of Shin-Osaka (shinkansen connection), Umeda (next to JR Osaka station) and Shinsaibashi/Namba, the main commercial and entertainment areas.

If you're going to be using the rail system a lot on any day, it might be worth considering a 'one-day free ticket'. For ¥800 you get unlimited travel on any subway, the so-called New Tram and the buses, unfortunately you cannot use the JR line. You'd really need to be moving around all day to save any money but it might save the headaches of working out fares and where to buy tickets.

KŌBE 神戸

Kōbe (population 1,477,000) is probably one of Japan's most attractive cities, and is a popular holiday destination for Japanese

tourists. Despite this, there's not a lot to hold the average Western traveller, though the city would have to rate as one of the best in Japan to live.

Information & Orientation

The two main entry points into Kōbe are San-no-Miya and Shin-Kōbe stations. Shin-Kōbe station is where the shinkansen pauses, and is in the north-west of town. A subway runs from here to the San-no-Miya station, which has frequent rail connections with Osaka and Kyoto. It's also possible to walk between the two stations in around 15 minutes. San-no-Miya (not Kōbe) station marks the city centre.

There are information centres in both Shin-Kōbe and San-no-miya stations, and English is spoken. At the very least, it's worth picking up a copy of the *Kōbe Guide Map*, which is regularly updated and has listings of restaurants and sights. Both counters are able to assist with accommodation bookings.

Tranquility

Things to See

The **Kitano-chō** area is popular with Japanese visitors for its eclectic architectural styles. This area can also get very busy with Japanese tourists on the weekends. Entry fees soon mount up too. England House, for example, has an entry fee of ¥600, while the viewing platform at the highest point in Kitano is a hefty ¥800.

Kōbe Municipal Museum has a collection of so-called Namban (literally 'Southern Barbarian') art and occasional special exhibits. Entry to the museum is ¥200 and it's open from 10 am to 4.30 pm, closed Monday.

Known as *nankinmachi* by locals, Kōbe's **Chinatown** is nothing to write home about if you've seen Chinatowns elsewhere. It is easy to find: a five-minute walk south of Motomachi station.

Featured prominently in all the tourist literature is 931-metre **Mt Rokko-san**. It's a pleasant trip by cable car (¥560) to the top. To get there, take bus No 25 from Rokko station on the Hankyū line. Get off the bus at the Rokko cable-car station. You can continue onwards on the Arima cable car (¥700). This is also a good area for some hiking. Some people take the cable car up and then hike down. Farther up from the cable-car terminus is the Herb Garden, which gets good reports from locals and visitors alike. Farther up again are good views of Kōbe Harbour and Port Island.

Places to Stay

The *Kōbe Tarumi Youth Hostel* (☎ 078-707-2133) has beds for ¥2100, breakfast for ¥450 and dinner for ¥750, but it's a bit far out of town. Take a San-in line train from Kōbe station and get off after six stops at Tarumi station. The hostel is an eight-minute walk to the east along the road that parallels the south side of the railway tracks.

Unfortunately, with the exception of the youth hostel, there is no moderately priced accommodation in Kōbe. In fact you'll be hard pressed to come up with a single room for less than ¥7000. Accommodation in Kyoto or Osaka is a better idea.

Places to Eat

Kōbe has a reputation as a restaurant city, and the main attractions are *Kōbe Beef* and the city's ethnic restaurants. Most travellers will find both of these overpriced. The best area to search out restaurants is Kitana-chō. You might be lucky and come up with some affordable lunch-time specials. Chinatown has a few restaurants with reasonable prices and the plastic food displays make for easy ordering.

Getting There & Away

Train Shin-Kōbe station is the shinkansen stop for trains to Kyoto, Osaka and Tokyo (three hours 13 minutes) or onto Western Japan and onto Fukuoka (two hours 54 minutes) in Kyūshū. The San-no-Miya station has both JR and some private lines. The JR Sanyō line heads into Western Honshū via the castle town of Himeji. JR trains run also to Kyoto (one hour 15 minutes) and Osaka (20 minutes) on a regular basis, though it's worth bearing in mind that the private Hankyū line does the same journey cheaper, if a little slower. The Hanshin line also runs to Osaka.

Ferry There are ferries from Kōbe to Shikoku, Kyūshū and Awaji-shima Island. There are two departure points for ferries: Naka Pier, next to the port tower, and Higashi-Kōbe Ferry Terminal. Basically, the former has ferries to Matsuyama and Imabari (Shikoku) and Ōita (Kyūshū), while the latter has ferries to Takamatsu (Shikoku). The lowest fares are Takamatsu (¥2370), Imabari (¥3600), Matsuyama (¥4430) and Ōita (¥5870). For information regarding departure times call Japan Travel-Phone (☎ 0120-444-800) or enquire at the TIC in Tokyo or Kyoto.

Getting Around

It is possible to take a bus directly to or from Osaka International Airport. The buses leave the airport every 20 minutes and cost ¥720 for the 40-minute trip. They start and terminate at Kōbe's San-no-Miya station. A high-speed ferry will connect Kōbe with the

JAPAN

new Kansai International Airport in 30 minutes.

JR, Hankyū and Hanshin railway lines run east to west across Kōbe, providing access to most of Kōbe's sights. A subway line also connects Shin-Kōbe station with Sannomiya station (¥160). Buses are frequent and reliable, and because of the fairly low level of traffic, taxis are often a reasonable option in Kōbe.

HIMEJI 姫路

If you see no other castles in Japan you should at least make an effort to visit Himeji-jo Castle, unanimously acclaimed as the most splendid Japanese castle still standing. It is also known as Shirasagi, the 'White Egret', a title which derives from the castle's stately white form. The surrounding town itself has little to offer as a tourist attraction, but there are plenty of places to grab a meal on the way to the castle.

Himeji can be easily visited as a day trip from Kyoto. A couple of hours at the castle, plus the 10 to 15-minute walk from the station is all the time you need there. The only other attraction worth lingering for is Himeji's historical museum, which has some interesting exhibits on Japanese castles. Walk to the castle down one side of the main street and back on the other to see the statuary dotted along both sides.

Places to Stay

There *are* some places to stay in Himeji, but in general they are overpriced and have little to recommend them. Basing yourself elsewhere and visiting Himeji as a day trip would be a far better option. There is no longer a youth hostel convenient to Himeji.

Getting There & Away

The quickest way to get to Himeji is by shinkansen. From Shin-Osaka station the trip takes around 40 minutes, and from Okayama it takes 30 to 40 minutes. JR trains also run between Osaka, Kyoto, Kōbe and Himeji, and the private Hankyū line runs between Kōbe and Himeji.

NARA 奈良

Nara (population 349,000), on first appearance an uninspiring sort of town, has a large number of cultural relics and is, second to Kyoto, the major tourist destination in the Kansai region. Try to choose a fine day for sightseeing as doing the sights in Nara requires a lot of walking, and it's no fun at all in bad weather.

Information

If you are heading for Nara from Kyoto, the TIC in Kyoto has extensive material. In Nara, the best source of information is the Nara City Tourist Centre (☎ 0742-22-3900), which is open from 9 am to 9 pm. It's a short walk from JR Nara and Kintetsu Nara stations. There's a plush lounge for relaxing, a display of handicrafts and helpful staff doling out stacks of maps and literature about transport, sights, accommodation etc.

Things to See

Most of Nara's major attractions are in **Nara-kōen Park**. JNTO publishes a leaflet called *Walking Tour Courses in Nara*, which includes a map for this area. Although walking time is estimated at two hours, you'll need at least half a day to see a selection of the sights and a full day to see the lot.

Kōfuku-ji Temple was transferred here from Kyoto in 710 as the main temple for the Fujiwara family. The National Treasure Hall (Kokuhōkan) contains a variety of statues and art objects salvaged from previous structures. A descriptive leaflet is provided in English. Admission to the Kokuhōkan costs ¥500 and it's open from 9 am to 4.30 pm.

Nara National Museum is devoted to Buddhist art and is divided into two wings. The western gallery exhibits archaeological finds and the eastern gallery has displays of sculptures, paintings and calligraphy. The galleries are linked by an underground passage. Admission costs ¥400 (special exhibitions excepted) and it's open from 9 am to 4.30 pm.

Tōdai-ji Temple is Nara's star attraction. It is the largest wooden building in the world and houses the Great Buddha, which is one

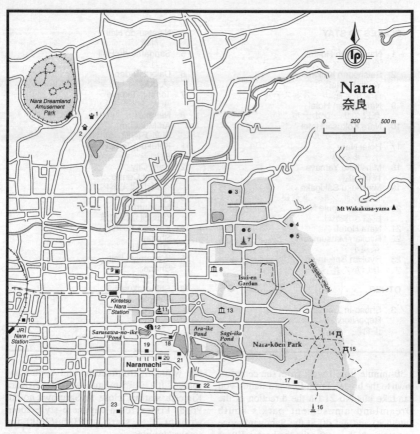

Nara
奈良

0   250   500 m

Nara Dreamland Amusement Park

Mt Wakakusa-yama ▲

Isui-en Garden

Kintetsu Nara Station

JR Nara Station

Sarusawa-no-ike Pond

Ara-ike Pond

Sagi-ike Pond

Nara-kōen Park

Naramachi

JAPAN

of the largest bronze images in the world. The main structure and home to the Buddha is the Daibutsu-den (Hall of the Great Buddha); it is a reconstruction dating from 1709. The Great Buddha itself dates back to 746, and stands just over 16 metres high. Admission to the Daibutsu-den costs ¥400.

Other attractions in the Tōdai-ji complex are the Shōsō-in (Treasure Repository), a short walk north of Daibutsu-den; the Kaidan-in Hall, a short walk west of the entrance gate to the Daibutsu-den (¥400); the Nigatsu-dō and Sangatsu-dō halls; and the Kasuga Taisha Shrine.

Places to Stay

Nara is probably best done as a day trip from Kyoto. Those planning an overnight stay should bear in mind that accommodation can be packed out for festivals, holidays and at weekends. Try and make reservations in advance if you plan to visit at these times. The Nara City Tourist Centre can help with reservations and has extensive lists of hotels, minshuku, pension, ryokan and shukubō.

The *Seishōnen Kaikan Youth Hostel* (☎ 0742-22-5540) is of a nondescript, concrete character, but cheap at ¥2060 per person per night, and the staff are helpful. It's

PLACES TO STAY

1 Nara Youth Hostel
   奈良ユースホステル
2 Seishōnen Kaikan
   Youth Hostel
   青少年会館ユースホステル
9 Nara Green Hotel
   奈良グリーンホテル
10 Nara Kokusai Hotel
   奈良国際ホテル
17 Hotel Nara
   ホテル奈良
18 Minshuku Yamaya
   民宿山屋
19 Minshuku Sakigake
   ホテルサンルート奈良
20 Hotel Sunroute Nara
   民宿さきがけ
21 Nara Hotel
22 Ryokan Matsumae
   奈良ホテル
23 Ryokan Seikan-sō
   せいかん荘

OTHER

3 Shōso-in Treasure
   Repository
   正倉院
4 Nigatsu-dō Hall
   二月堂
5 Sangatsu-dō Hall
   三月堂
6 Daibutsu-den
   大仏殿
7 Tōdai-ji Temple
   東大寺
8 Neiraku
   Art Museum
   寧楽美術館
11 Kōfuku-ji Temple
   興福寺
12 Nara City
   Tourist Centre
   奈良市観光案内所
13 Nara National
   Museum
   奈良国立博物館
14 Kasuga Taisha
   Shrine
   春日大社
15 Wakamiya-jinja
   Shrine
   若宮神社
16 Shin-Yakushi-ji
   Temple
   新薬師寺

a 30-minute uphill walk from the centre of town to the hostel. From JR Nara station you can take bus No 21 (in the direction of the Dreamland amusement park's south entrance) and get off at the Sahoyama-mae bus stop which is opposite the hostel. Buses run about twice an hour between 7 am and 9 pm.

The *Nara Youth Hostel* (☎ 0742-22-1334) is close to Kōno-ike Pond, which is a short walk from the other youth hostel. This is a ritzier hostel which *only* takes guests with a hostel membership card and charges ¥2500 per person per night. It tends to be booked out and is often swarming with schoolkids on excursions. From Nara Kintetsu station, take a bus in the direction of Dreamland, Kamo or Takanohara, and get off at the Yakyūjō-mae stop, which is in front of a baseball stadium beside the hostel.

The *Ryokan Seikan-sō* (☎ 0742-22-2670)

has wooden architecture and a pleasant garden. It's a 15-minute walk from Nara Kintetsu station, close to Sarusawa-no-ike Pond. Prices for a Japanese-style room without bath start at ¥3800/7600 for singles/doubles.

Places to Eat

There are plenty of inexpensive restaurants and fast-food places around both the stations. Opposite Kintetsu station are a couple of fast-food outfits, but the arcade and Marco Polo St, both of which run south from Kintetsu station, are probably the best hunting grounds for foreign and Japanese restaurants. Look out for *TacoDonald's* and *Parie de Rome* on the right side of Marco Polo St.

Getting There & Away

Bus There is an overnight bus service

between Tokyo and Nara which costs ¥8240 one way or ¥14,830 return. The bus leaves Nara at 10.30 pm and reaches Tokyo the next day at 6.20 am. The bus from Tokyo leaves at 11 pm and arrives in Nara the next day at 6.50 am. Check with the Nara City Tourist Office or the Tokyo TIC for further details.

Train On the rail front, unless you have a Japan Rail Pass, the best option is the Kintetsu line (often indicated in English as the Kinki Nippon railway) linking Kyoto and Nara (Kintetsu Nara station) in 30 minutes by direct limited express (¥980 one way). Ordinary trains take 45 minutes and cost ¥540. The JR Nara line connects Kyoto with JR Nara station (¥680 one way, one hour).

The Kintetsu Nara line connects Osaka (Kintetsu Namba station) with Nara (Nara Kintetsu station) in half an hour by limited express (¥920). Express and local trains take about 40 minutes and cost ¥480. The JR Kansai line links Osaka (Tennō-ji station) and Nara (JR Nara station) via Hōryu-ji (¥760, 50 minutes by express).

Getting Around
Most of the area around Nara-kōen Park is covered by two circular bus routes. Bus No 1 runs counter-clockwise and bus No 2 runs clockwise. There's a ¥150 flat fare. You can easily see the main sights in the park on foot and use the bus as an option if you are pushed for time or get tired of walking.

Nara is a convenient size for getting around on a bicycle. The Kintetsu Rent-a-Cycle Centre (☎ 0742-24-3528) is close to the Nara City Tourist Office. From the city centre, walk east down the main street to the first intersection, turn left into Konishi-dōri and walk about 70 metres until you see Supermarket Isokawa on your right. Opposite the supermarket is a small sidestreet on your left – the bicycle rental centre is at the bottom of this street. Prices start at ¥720 for four hours or ¥1030 for the day. There's a discount for two-day rental.

Western Honshū
本州の西部

There are two popular routes from the Kansai District through the western end of Honshū to the island of Kyūshū. Most visitors choose the southern route through the San-yō region. This is a heavily industrialised and densely populated area with a number of important and interesting cities, including Kurashiki and Hiroshima.

The usual alternative to this route is the northern San-in coast. By Japanese standards, the north-coast is comparatively uncrowded and rural. Although there are not as many large cities as on the southern route, the north-coast route takes you to the historically interesting town of Hagi. Matsue, Izumo and Tsuwano are also interesting towns worth a stop.

KURASHIKI 倉敷
Kurashiki's claim to fame is a small quarter of picturesque buildings around a stretch of moat. There are a number of old black-tiled warehouses which have been converted into an eclectic collection of museums.

Orientation
As in so many other Japanese towns, the main street leads straight out from the railway station. It's about one km from the station to the old canal area. If you walk from the station, the typical urban Japanese scenery is enough to make you wonder whether you are in the right town. But when you turn into the canal area, everything changes; Ivy Square is just beyond the canal.

Things to See
The museums and galleries which are the town's major attraction are concentrated along the banks of the canal. The **Ōhara Museum of Art** is undoubtedly Kurashiki's number one museum, housing a predominantly European art collection. Entry is ¥600; opening hours are from 9 am to 5 pm and it's closed on Monday.

Between the Ōhara Museum and the tourist office is the interesting **Kurashiki Ninagawa Museum**, which houses a collection of Greek, Etruscan and Roman antiquities, together with more modern European marbles and other items. Entry is ¥600 and it's open from 8.30 am to 5 pm daily.

There are numerous other museums to browse in. They include the **Kurashiki Museum of Folkcraft** (¥500, 9 am to 4.15 pm, closed Monday); the **Japan Rural Toy Museum** (¥310, 8 am to 5 pm daily); the **Kurashiki Archaeological Museum** (¥300, 9 am to 4.30 pm, closed Monday); the **Kurashiki City Museum of Natural History** (¥100, open from 9 am to 5 pm, closed Monday); and the **Kurashiki City Art Museum** (¥200, same opening hours).

Ivy Square is the former site of the Kurabō textile factories. Their fine old Meiji-era red-brick factory buildings (dating from 1889) now house a hotel, restaurants, shops and yet more museums. Ivy Square, with its ivy-covered walls and open-air café, is the centre of the complex.

Places to Stay

Kurashiki is a good town for staying in a traditional Japanese inn, and the information office at the station can help you do this. The *Kurashiki Youth Hostel* (☎ 0864-22-7355) is south of the canal area and costs ¥2500 per night. It's a long climb to its hilltop location, but the view is great and the staff are friendly. From the station you can take a bus to the shimin kaikan bus stop and then walk uphill to the hostel.

There are several good-value minshuku conveniently close to the canal. The *Tokuchan Kan* (☎ 0864-25-3056) is near Ivy Square and offers a room-only price as well as a room and two meals for ¥6000 per person, though prices go up during the high season. Right by the canal near the toy museum, the small *Kawakami Minshuku*

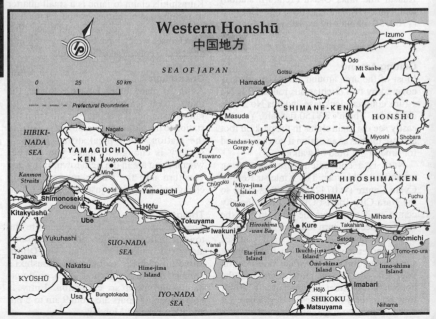

Western Honshū
中国地方

SEA OF JAPAN

0   25   50 km

Prefectural Boundaries

Izumo

Ōdo

Mt Sanbe ▲

Gotsu

Hamada

SHIMANE-KEN

HONSHŪ

Miyoshi   Shobara

Masuda

Sandan-kyō Gorge

HIBIKI-NADA SEA

Nagato

YAMAGUCHI -KEN

Hagi

Akiyoshi-dō

Tsuwano

Chūgoku

Expressway

54

HIROSHIMA-KEN

Kanmon Straits

Mine

Ogōri

Yamaguchi

Miya-jima Island

HIROSHIMA

Fuchu

Shimonoseki

Onoda

Hōfu

Otake

Kure   Takahara

Mihara

Kitakyūshū

Ube

Tokuyama

Iwakuni

Hiroshima -wan Bay

Setoda

Onomichi

Tomo-no-ura

Yukuhashi

SUO-NADA SEA

Yanai

Eta-jima Island

Ikuchi-jima Island

Ōmi-shima Island

Inno-shima Island

Tagawa

Nakatsu

Hime-jima Island

Hōjō

Imabari

KYŪSHŪ

Usa

Bungotokada

IYO-NADA SEA

SHIKOKU

Matsuyama

Niihama

JAPAN

(☎ 0864-24-1221) is slightly cheaper at ¥5150.

The *Young Inn* (☎ 0864-25-8585), behind the Terminal Hotel in the station area, has singles/doubles without bath for ¥3600/6500, which is quite a bargain. There are also slightly more expensive rooms with bathroom in this vaguely hostel-like hotel.

Getting There & Away
If you arrive by shinkansen, the nearest stop is Okayama, a mere 16 km from Kurashiki. From Okayama, take a San-yō line local train to Kurashiki. These operate several times an hour; the trip takes just over 15 minutes and costs ¥470. If you're eastbound, get off at the Shin-Kurashiki station, two stops on the San-yō line from Kurashiki.

HIROSHIMA 広島
Although it's a busy, prosperous, not unattractive industrial city, visitors would have no real reason to leave the shinkansen in Hiroshima (population 1,085,000) were it not for that terrible instant on 6 August 1945 when the city became the world's first atomic bomb target. Hiroshima's Peace Memorial Park is a constant reminder of that tragic day and attracts a steady stream of visitors from all over the world.

Things to See
The symbol of the destruction visited upon Hiroshima is the **A-Bomb Dome** (Gembaku Dōmu) just across the river from **Peace Memorial Park**. The building was previously the Industrial Promotion Hall until the bomb exploded almost directly above it and effectively put a stop to any further promotional activities. Its propped up ruins have been left as an eternal reminder of the tragedy, floodlit at night and fronted with piles of the colourful *origami* cranes which have become a symbol of Hiroshima's plea

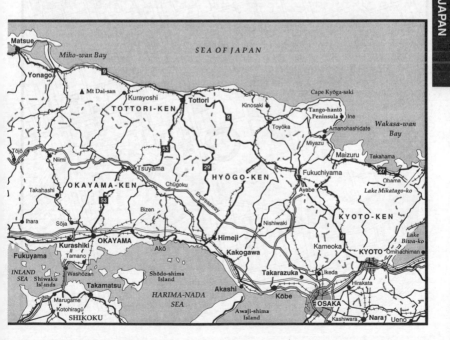

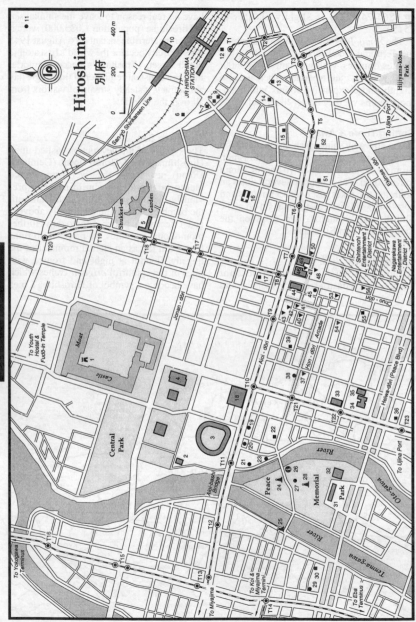

Hiroshima

別府

PLACES TO STAY

6 Hotel New Hiroden
ホテル　ニューヒロデン
7 Hiroshima Ekimae
Green Hotel
広島駅前グリーンホテル
8 Hotel Sun Palace
9 Hotel Yamato
ホテルやまと
10 Hiroshima Terminal
Hotel
広島ターミナルホテル
12 Hiroshima Station
Hotel
広島ステーションホテル
13 Hiroshima Century
City Hotel
広島センチュリーシティ
14 Hiroshima City Hotel
広島シティホテル
15 Mikawa Ryokan
三河旅館
17 Hotel Silk Plaza
ホテルシルクプラザ
22 Hiroshima Green
Hotel
広島グリーンホテル
30 Minshuku Ikedaya
民宿池田屋
34 ANA Hotel Hiroshima
広島全日空ホテル
35 Hokke Club Hotel
法華クラブ広島店
36 Hiroshima Tōkyū Inn
広島東急イン
39 Hiroshima Kokusai
Hotel
広島国際ホテル
51 Hiroshima Central
Hotel
広島セントラルホテル
52 Hiroshima Union
Hotel
ホテルユニオン広島
55 Sera Bekkan Ryokan
世羅別館

PLACES TO EAT

37 Andersen's Bakery
& Restaurant
アンデルセン
40 Spaghetteria San
Mario
サンマリオ
41 Rally's Steakhouse
ラリーズ
42 Yōrō-no-Taki
Restaurant
養老の滝
43 Suehiro Steak
Restaurant
スエヒロ
47 Tokugawa
Okonomayaki
Restaurant
お好み焼き徳川
48 Tonkatsu Tokugawa
とんかつ徳川
50 Kuimonoya & Ottimo
Restaurants
くいものや
53 Chikara Soba
Restaurant
ちから
54 Kumar Indian
Restaurant
くマー
56 Tokugawa
Okonomayaki
Restaurant
お好み焼き徳川

OTHER

1 Hiroshima-jō Castle
広島城
2 Science & Culture
Museum
for Children
こども文化科学館
3 Hiroshima Carp's
Baseball Stadium
広島市民球場
4 Hiroshima Museum
of Art
広島美術館
5 Prefectural Art
Museum
県立美術館
11 Pagoda of Peace
平和塔
16 World Peace
Memorial
Cathedral
世界平和記念聖堂
18 Sogo Department
Store (Sogo Bus
Centre, Kinokuniya
Bookshop)
そごう
19 KDD (International
Telephone)
20 ANA
全日空
21 A-Bomb Dome
原爆ドーム
23 Atomic Bomb
Epicentre
爆心地
24 Children's Peace
Memorial
原爆の子の像
25 Korean A-Bomb
Memorial
26 Tourist Information
Office
観光案内所
27 Peace Flame
平和の灯
28 Cenotaph
原爆慰霊碑
29 Laundrette
コインランドリー
31 Peace Memorial
Museum
平和記念資料館
32 Peace Memorial
Hall
平和記念館
33 Former Bank of
Japan Building
旧日本銀行
38 Maruzen Bookshop
丸善
44 Fukuya Department
Store
福屋百貨店
45 Mac Bar
46 Tenmaya Depart-
ment Store
天満屋
49 Mitsukoshi Depart-
ment Store
三越
50 Harry's Bar
ハリーズ

TRAM STOPS

T1 Hiroshima ekimae
広島駅前
T2 Enkobashi
猿猴橋
T3 Matoba-chō
的場町

JAPAN

T4 Danbara Ohata-chō
     段原大畑町
T5 Inarimachi
     稲荷町
T6 Kanayama-chō
     銀山町
T7 Ebisu-chō
     胡町
T8 Hatchobori
     八丁堀
T9 Tatemachi
     立町
T10 Kamiya-chō
     紙屋町
T11 Genbaku Dōmu-mae
     (A-Bomb Dome)
     原爆ドーム
T12 Honkawa-chō
     本川町
T13 Tokaichimachi
     十日市町
T14 Dobashi
     土橋
T15 Teramachi
     寺町
T16 Betsuin-mae
     別院前
T17 Jogakuin-mae
     女学院前
T18 Shukkeien-mae
     縮景園前
T19 Katei Saibansho-mae
     家庭裁判所前
T20 Hakushima Line Terminus
     白島
T21 Hon-dōri
     本通
T22 Fukuromachi
     袋町
T23 Chuden-mae
     中電前

5343) is about two km north of the city centre; take a bus from platform 22 in front of the JR station or from platform 29 behind it. The hostel is very clearly marked; the nightly cost for members varies seasonally from ¥2090 to ¥2260.

There are two Japanese Inn Group places in Hiroshima. The *Mikawa Ryokan* (☎ 082-261-2719) is a short stroll from the JR Hiroshima station and has singles/doubles for ¥3500/6000, room only. Although the ryokan is convenient for train travellers, and staff are friendly, the rooms are very cramped and gloomy.

In contrast, the *Minshuku Ikedaya* (☎ 082-231-3329) is modern, bright and cheerful. Singles/doubles are ¥4000/7000, room only. The helpful manager speaks good English and if your dirty washing is piling up, there's a laundrette on the corner of the road. The Ikedaya is on the other side of Peace Memorial Park in a quiet area, but an easy walk via the park from the city centre. To get there, take tram No 6 or a Miyajima tram from the station and get off at the Dobashi stop.

Places to Eat

Hiroshima is noted for its seafood, particularly oysters. The familiar assortment of fast-food outlets including *Shakey's Pizza*, *McDonald's* and *Mr Donut* can be found in the Hon-dōri shopping arcade. *Andersen's* on Hon-dōri is a popular restaurant complex with an excellent bakery section – a good place for an economical breakfast watching the world pass by from the tables in the front window. There are a variety of other restaurant sections in the Andersen's complex.

Getting There & Away

Bus Long-distance buses run from the shinkansen exit of Hiroshima station, although there is also a bus terminal on the 3rd floor of Sogo department store. Buses between Hiroshima and Tokyo take around 12 hours and cost ¥11,840; they run from the JR bus terminal next to Tokyo station. Buses to and from Nagoya take around eight hours and cost ¥7700. There are also buses to and

that nuclear weapons should never again be used. Like its equivalent in Nagasaki, the **A-Bomb Museum** wins no awards for architectural inspiration, but its simple message is driven home with sledgehammer force. The museum is open from 9 am to 6 pm (May to November), or until 5 pm (December to April). Entry is ¥50.

Places to Stay

The *Hiroshima Youth Hostel* (☎ 082-221-

from Kyoto (¥5500), Fukuoka (¥4430) and Nagasaki (¥6500).

Train Hiroshima is an important stop on the Tokyo-Osaka-Hakata shinkansen route, with some services originating or terminating in Hiroshima. By shinkansen, it takes about 4½ to five hours to reach Hiroshima from Tokyo (¥11,120 plus a tokkyū charge of ¥6580), 1½ to two hours from Kyoto and slightly less from Hakata.

Boat Hiroshima is an important port with a variety of Inland Sea cruises as well as connections to other cities. The Hiroshima to Matsuyama ferry and hydrofoil services are a popular way of getting to or from Shikoku. (See the Matsuyama entry in the Shikoku section later in this chapter for details.) Ferries also operate to Beppu on Kyūshū and to Imabari on Shikoku. For information on the Imabari service (in Japanese) ring Hiroshima Imabari Kōsoku-sen (☎ 082-254-7555); tickets cost ¥4360. For information on the Beppu service, ring Hirobetsu Kisen (☎ 253-0909); economy-class tickets are ¥4000.

Getting Around

Hiroshima has an easy-to-use tram (streetcar) service which will get you pretty well anywhere you want to go for a flat ¥130 (¥90 on the short No 9 route). There is even a tram which runs all the way to the Miyajima Port for ¥250.

Buses are more difficult to use than the trams as they are not numbered and place names are in kanji only, but the stands outside the station are clearly numbered. Take a bus from stand No 1 to the airport, No 2 to the port.

MIYA-JIMA ISLAND   宮島

Correctly known as Itsuku-shima, Miyajima Island is easily reached from Hiroshima. The famous 'floating' torii of the Itsukushima-jinja Shrine is one of the most photographed tourist attractions in Japan, and with the island's Mt Misen as a backdrop

is classified as one of Japan's 'three best views'. Apart from the shrine, the island has some other interesting temples, some good walks and remarkably tame deer which even wander the streets of the small town.

Things to See

The island's main attraction is **Itsukushima-jinja Shrine**, which dates from the 6th century and in its present form from 1168. Its pier-like construction is a result of the island's holy status. Commoners were not allowed to set foot on the island and had to approach the shrine by boat, entering through the floating torii out in the bay. Much of the time, however, the shrine and torii are surrounded not by water but by mud. The view of the torii immortalised in thousands of travel brochures requires a high tide. The shrine is open from 6 am to sunset and entry is ¥200. The treasure house, west of the shrine, is open from 8 am to 5 pm and entry is ¥250.

Topping the hill immediately east of the Itsukushima Shrine is the **Senjō-kaku** (Pavilion of 1000 Mats). This huge and atmospheric hall (entry ¥50) is constructed with equally massive timber pillars and beams, and the ceiling is hung with paintings. The **Miyajima History & Folklore Museum** combines a 19th-century merchant's home with exhibits concerning trade in the Edo period, a variety of displays connected with the island and a fine garden. The museum is open from 8.30 am to 5 pm, and there's an excellent and informative brochure in English. Entry is ¥250.

The ascent of 530-metre **Mt Misen** is the island's finest walk; the uphill part of the return trip can be avoided by taking the two-stage cable car for ¥800 one way, ¥1400 return. It leaves you about a 15-minute walk from the top. There are superb views from the summit and a variety of routes leading back down. The descent takes a good hour and walking paths also lead to other high points on the island, or you can just follow the gentle stroll through Momiji-dani (Maple Valley) which leads to the cable-car station.

JAPAN

Places to Stay

There is no inexpensive accommodation on Miya-jima Island, although the *Miyajima-guchi Youth Hostel* (☎ 0829-56-1444) is near the ferry terminal and JR Miyajima-guchi station on the mainland. It has rates of ¥2300.

Getting There & Away

The mainland ferry terminal for Miyajima is near the Miyajima-guchi station on the JR San-yō line between Hiroshima and Iwakuni. Miyajima trams from Hiroshima terminate at the Hiroden-Miyajima stop by the ferry terminal. The tram (50 minutes, ¥250) takes longer than the train (25 minutes) but runs more frequently and can be boarded in central Hiroshima. On some trams you may have to transfer at the Hiroden-Hiroshima stop.

From the terminal, ferries shuttle across to Miyajima in just 10 minutes for ¥170. One of the ferries is operated by JR, so Japan Rail Pass holders should make sure they use this one. Ferry services also operate to Miyajima direct from Hiroshima. High-speed ferries (¥1250) do the trip there and back eight times daily and take just over 20 minutes from Hiroshima's Ujina Port. The SKK (Seto Naikaikisen) Inland Sea cruise on the *Akinada* starts and finishes at Miyajima; the Miyajima to Hiroshima leg costs ¥1480.

Getting Around

Bicycles can be rented from the ferry building or you can walk. A free bus operates from in front of the Iwasō Ryokan to the Mt Misen cable-car station.

SHIMONOSEKI 下関

Shimonoseki (population 270,000) is yet another featureless, modern Japanese city, but for travellers it's also an important crossroads, a place through which many people pass and few pause. The town is an important connection to South Korea, with a daily ferry service to and from Pusan.

Places to Stay

The *Hinoyama Youth Hostel* (☎ 0832-22-3753) is at the base of Mt Hino-yama, only 100 metres from the lower cable-car station. There are 52 beds at ¥1800 or ¥1950 depending on the time of year. Take a Hinoyama bus from the station; you can't miss the huge 'YH' sign on top of the building.

Getting There & Away

Train Shinkansen trains stop at the Shin-Shimonoseki station, two stops from the JR Shimonoseki station in the town centre. There are frequent trains and buses between the two stations. By shinkansen, it's half an hour to Hakata, 40 to 80 minutes to Hiroshima and three to four hours to Osaka. The easiest way to cross over to Kyūshū is to take a train from the Shin-Shimonoseki station to Moji-ko and Kitakyūshū.

Ferry The Kampu Ferry Service (☎ 0832-24-3000) operates the Shimonoseki-Pusan ferry service from the terminal a few minutes' walk from the station. Head up to the 2nd floor of this enormous desolate building for bookings. The office closes between noon and 1 pm for lunch. There are daily departures of the *Kampu* or the *Pukwan* at 5 pm from Shimonoseki and Pusan, arriving at the other end at 8.30 am the next morning. You can board from 2 pm. Bookings close on the sailing day at 4.30 pm, but you would have to be snappy about boarding if you book this late as customs and immigration close shortly afterwards. One-way fares start from ¥6800 for students and continue up to ¥8500 for an open, tatami-mat area, ¥10,500 (six-berth cabin), ¥12,000 (four-berth cabin) and ¥14,000 (two-berth cabin). There's a 10% discount on return fares.

Hitching If you're hitchhiking out of Shimonoseki, you'll need to get on the expressway. There's a complicated mass of junctions north of the youth hostel and Mt Hino-yama. Roads diverge in a variety of directions: to Kyūshu by the tunnel or bridge, to Hiroshima by the Chūgoku Expressway and to Yamaguchi by routes 2 and 9.

MATSUE 松江

Matsue (population 143,000), on Western Honshū's northern coast, straddles the Ōhashi-gawa River, which connects Lake Shinji-ko to the Lake Nakanoumi-ko and then the sea. A compact area in the north of the town includes almost all of Matsue's important sites: an original castle, a fine example of a samurai residence, the former home of writer Lafcadio Hearn and a delightful teahouse and garden.

Places to Stay

The *Matsue Youth Hostel* (☎ 0852-36-8620) is about five km from the centre of town in Kososhimachi, on the northern side of the lake at the first station you come to along the Ichihata line from Matsue-onsen station. There are 50 beds at ¥2500 a night. The hostel is closed from 1 to 20 November.

The *Pension Tobita* (☎ 0852-36-6933) in Hamasadamachi is in the same direction as the youth hostel and has Japanese and Western-style rooms for ¥5500 per person with breakfast.

As usual, there are a lot of business hotels around the station, including the unbusinesslike *Business Ishida* (no English sign; ☎ 0852-21-5931), a simple Japanese-style hotel with tatami-mat rooms and shared bathrooms for ¥3600 per person. It's good value and conveniently close to the station: just continue walking past the tourist information office through the bicycle and car parks and it's right beside the elevated railway lines, just past the first road you cross.

Getting There & Away

Matsue is on the JR San-in line, which runs along the north coast. It takes a little over 2½ hours to travel via Yonago to Kurashiki on the south coast.

IZUMO 出雲

Only 33 km west of Matsue, the small town of Izumo Taisha, just north of Izumo itself, has one major attraction, the great **Izumo Taisha Shrine**. Although it's the oldest Shintō shrine in Japan, the actual buildings are not that old. The main shrine dates from 1744, the other important buildings only from 1874. Nevertheless, the wooded grounds are pleasant to wander through and the shrine itself enjoys the 'borrowed scenery' of the Yakumo Hill as a backdrop.

Getting There & Away

Izumo Taisha (as opposed to the rather dull town of Izumo) has two railway stations, the JR one at the end of the street leading down from the shrine and the private Ichihata line station about halfway up the street. The Ichihata line starts from Matsue-onsen station in Matsue and runs on the northern side of Lake Shinji-ko to Izumo Taisha station. The JR line runs from JR Matsue station to JR Izumo station, where you transfer to an Izumo Taisha train. The private-line service also requires a change of train at Kawato, but is more frequent (more than 20 services a day) and also takes you closer to the shrine. The private-line trip takes less than an hour and passes by rows of trees grown as windbreaks.

TSUWANO 津和野

Inland from Masuda is Tsuwano, a pleasant and relaxing mountain town with a fine castle, some interesting old buildings and a wonderful collection of carp swimming in the roadside water channels. The town is noted as a place to get to by the superb old steam-train service from Ogōri and as a place to get around by bicycle, of which there are quite a phenomenal number for rent.

Places to Stay

The information counter at the railway station will help with bookings at the town's many minshuku and ryokan. The cheapest option is, as usual, the local youth hostel: *Tsuwano Youth Hostel* (☎ 08567-2-0373), a couple of km south of the station. It has 28 beds at ¥2300 or ¥2400 per night depending on the season. The cheapest costs in a minshuku or a ryokan will be ¥5500 with two meals.

Getting There & Away

The JR Yamaguchi line runs from Ogōri on the south coast through Yamaguchi to Tsuwano and on to Masuda on the north coast. It takes about one hour 15 minutes by limited express from Ogōri to Tsuwano and about 30 minutes from Masuda to Tsuwano. A bus to Tsuwano from Hagi takes nearly two hours.

During the late April to early May Golden Week holiday, from 20 July to 31 August and on certain other Sundays and national holidays, a steam locomotive service operates between Ogōri and Tsuwano. It takes two hours each way and you should book well ahead.

HAGI 萩

If there was a single reason for travelling along the northern coast of Western Honshū it would have to be to visit Hagi (population 50,000), with its interesting combination of temples and shrines, a fascinating old samurai quarter, some picturesque castle ruins and fine coastal views.

Things to See

Connoisseurs of Japanese pottery rank Hagi-yaki, the pottery of Hagi, second only to Kyoto's raku-yaki. The **Shizuki Kiln** in Horiuchi has particularly fine pieces. The western end of Hagi has several interesting pottery kilns near Shizuki-kōen Park. Hagi-yaki pottery can also be inspected in the **Hagi-yaki Togei Kaikan Museum** near the park; there's a big souvenir area downstairs.

Unfortunately, there's not much of the old Hagi-jō Castle to see, apart from the typically imposing outer walls and its surrounding moat. The grounds have been turned into the pleasant **Shizuki-kōen Park**. The castle is open daily from 8 am to 5.30 pm and entry is ¥200.

Jokamachi, **Horiuchi** and **Teremachi** comprise the old samurai residential area with many streets lined by whitewashed samurai walls. This area is fascinating to wander around and there are a number of interesting houses and temples, particularly in the area known as Jokamachi. Teremachi

is noted especially for its many fine old temples.

Places to Stay

Hagi Youth Hostel (☎ 0838-22-0733) is south of the castle at the western end of the town. It has 120 beds at ¥2300 per night and bicycle rental is available. The hostel is closed from 16 January to 9 February. Tamae is the nearest JR station.

There are ryokan and minshuku in town with affordable prices. East of Shizuki-kōen Park, a big modern place on the riverside, is *Shizuki-sō* (☎ 0838-22-7580), with rooms for ¥3600.

Getting There & Away

Train The JR San-in line runs along the north coast through Tottori, Matsue, Masuda and Hagi to Shimonoseki. The faster expresses take four hours to or from Matsue.

Bus JR buses to Hagi take 1½ hours from Ogōri, south of Hagi on the Tokyo-Osaka-Hakata shinkansen line. The buses go via Akiyoshi-dai, take one hour 10 minutes and cost ¥1900; there are also buses from Yamaguchi. Buses also operate between Tsuwano and Hagi, taking a little under two hours.

Northern Honshū
本州の北部

The northern part of Honshū, known in Japanese as Tōhoku, is the Japanese deep north, a relatively sparsely populated area that has its place in the Japanese popular imagination as a kind of rustic home country. There's little to hold the visitor in the area's urban centres, but rural Tōhoku offers a rare opportunity to sample Japan's lingering past

AIZU WAKAMATSU 会津若松

During feudal times, this castle town developed into a stronghold for the Aizu clan. The family later remained loyal to the shogunate

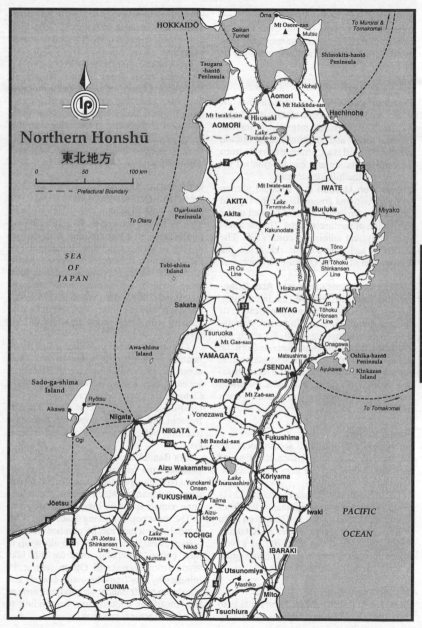

Northern Honshū

東北地方

Prefectural Boundary

HOKKAIDŌ

Ōma
Mt Osore-zan
Mutsu

To Murorai &
Tomakomai

Seikan
Tunnel

Shimokita-hantō
Peninsula

Tsugaru
-hantō
Peninsula

Nohejl

Aomori
Mt Hakkōda-san

Hachinohe

Mt Iwaki-san
Hirosaki

AOMORI

Lake
Towada-ko

45

7   4

Mt Iwate-san

IWATE

AKITA

Lake
Tazawa-ko

Morioka

Miyako

Akita

Oga-hantō
Peninsula

Kakunodate

Tōno

To Otaru

JR Tōhoku
Shinkansen
Line

SEA
OF
JAPAN

Tobi-shima
Island

JR Ōu
Line

Hiraizumi

Sakata

13

7

MIYAG

JR
Tōhoku
Honsen
Line

Tsuruoka

Mt Gas-san

Awa-shima
Island

YAMAGATA

Matsushima

Onagawa

Oshika-hantō
Peninsula

SENDAI

Ayukawa

Kinkazan
Island

Yamagata

Mt Zaō-san

To Tomakomai

Sado-ga-shima
Island

Ryōtsu

Aikawa

Niigata

Yonezawa

Ogi

NIIGATA

49

Mt Bandai-san

Fukushima

Aizu Wakamatsu

Lake
Inawashiro

Kōriyama

Yunokami
Onsen

FUKUSHIMA

Tajima

49

Jōetsu

8

Aizu-
kōgen

Iwaki

PACIFIC
OCEAN

18

JR Jōetsu
Shinkansen
Line

Lake
Ozenuma

TOCHIGI

Nikkō

Numata

IBARAKI

GUNMA

4

Utsunomiya

Mashiko

Mito

Tsuchiura

JAPAN

Tōhoku Expressway

during the Edo period then briefly defied imperial forces in the Boshin Civil War (at the start of the Meiji era). The resistance was swiftly crushed and the town went up in flames.

Things to See

The **limori-yama Hill** is renowned as the spot where teenage members of the Byakkotai (White Tigers Band) retreated from the imperial forces and committed ritual suicide in 1868. The hill is a 15-minute bus ride from the railway station and can be climbed on foot, or use the hillside elevator.

Oyaku-en Garden is a splendid garden complete with tea arbour, large central pond (and huge carp) and a section devoted to the cultivation of medicinal herbs. The garden is open daily and admission costs ¥300. The garden is a 15-minute bus ride from the station – get off at the Oyaku-en Iriguchi bus stop.

Other attractions include the **Aizu Buke-yashiki Samurai House**, an interesting, large-scale reconstruction of the lifestyle of opulent samurai in the Edo period. Admission costs a whopping ¥800. To reach the residence, take a 15-minute bus ride from the station and get off at the Buke-yashiki-mae bus stop. **Tsuruga-jō Castle** is a reconstruction from 1965 and contains a historical museum. Admission costs ¥310 and it's open from 8.30 am to 5 pm.

Places to Stay

For ryokan and minshuku accommodation, the tourist information office has lists of accommodation and can help with reservations.

The *Aizu-no-Sato Youth Hostel* (☎ 0241-27-2054) is only a 10-minute walk from Shiokawa station, which is 10 km from Aizu Wakamatsu and a little closer to Kitakata. Rates are fairly cheap at ¥1700 to ¥1900 depending on the time of year. Bicycle rental is available at the hostel.

Getting There & Away

From Tokyo (Ueno), the quickest route is to take the JR Tōhoku shinkansen line to Koriyama then change to the JR Ban-etsu-Saisen line to Aizu Wakamatsu. The total time for the trip is about 2½ hours; total cost ¥8700.

From Nikkō, there's the option of combining train rides from Shimo-Imaichi to Kinugawa Onsen on the Tōbu Kinugawa line, then changing to the Aizu-Kinugawa line. To get a closer look at the countryside and rural architecture in the valleys on this route, you can also take buses part of the way from Kinugawa Onsen before hopping back onto the train.

MT BANDAI-SAN & BANDAI-KŌGEN PLATEAU
磐梯山・磐梯高原

Mt Bandai-san erupted on 15 July 1888 and in the course of the eruption it destroyed dozens of villages and their inhabitants. At the same time it completely rearranged the landscape to create a plateau and dam local rivers, which then formed numerous lakes and ponds. Now designated as a national park, the whole area offers spectacular scenery with ample scope for walks or long hikes.

The most popular walk, sometimes jammed with hikers from end to end, takes about an hour and follows a trail between a series of lakes known as Goshikinuma (Five Coloured Lakes). The trailheads for the Goshikinuma walk are at Goshikinuma Iriguchi and at Bandai-kōgen-eki, the main transport hub, on the edge of Lake Hibara-ko.

Ura Bandai Youth Hostel is very close to Goshikinuma Iriguchi and makes a convenient base for extended hikes. The hostel has maps in Japanese which outline routes and approximate times for hikes in the areas.

The most popular hiking destination is Mt Bandai-san, which can be climbed in a day – start as early as possible and allow up to nine hours. A popular route for this hike starts from Kawakami Onsen (about 10 minutes by bus from the youth hostel) and climbs up to Mt Bandai-san, looping around the rim of the crater before descending to Bandai-kōgen-eki bus stop.

Places to Stay

For those who want help booking into one of the numerous kokuminshukusha, pensions, minshuku and hotels in the area, the nearest English-speaking tourist information is in Aizu Wakamatsu.

The *Ura Bandai Youth Hostel* (☎ 0241-32-2811) seems a little the worse for wear, but it's in a quiet spot next to one of the trailheads for the Goshikinuma walk. It's also a good base for longer mountain hikes. The hostel manager can provide maps and basic information for hikes in the area. Bicycle rental is also available – much cheaper than the rental at Lake Hibara-ko. Note that this hostel is closed from 1 December to 31 March. A bed for the night is ¥2300.

Take the bus bound for Bandai-kōgen from Inawashiro station and get off 30 minutes later at the Goshikinuma Iriguchi bus stop. The hostel is seven minutes on foot from the bus stop.

Getting There & Away

There are buses from Aizu Wakamatsu station and Inawashiro station to the trailheads for the Goshikinuma walk. Buses from Aizu Wakamatsu to Lake Hibara-ko take 1½ hours (¥1560) and from Inawashiro to Bandai Kōgen-eki 25 minutes (¥810).

Between Bandai-kōgen-eki and Fukushima there is a bus service along two scenic toll roads – Bandai Azuma Lakeline and Bandai Azuma Skyline. The trip provides great views of the mountains and is highly recommended if you are a fan of volcanic panoramas.

The bus makes a scheduled stop (30 minutes) at Jōdodaira, a superb viewpoint, where you can climb to the top of Mt Azumakofuji (1705 metres) in 10 minutes and, if you still feel energetic, scramble down to the bottom of the crater. Across the road is Mt Issaikyō-yama, which belches steam in dramatic contrast to its passive neighbour; a steepish climb of 45 minutes is needed to reach the top with its sweeping views.

The bus fare between Fukushima and Bandai-kōgen-eki is ¥2700; the trip takes

about three hours. This service only operates between late April and late October.

Between Bandai-kōgen-eki and Yonezawa there is another bus service along the scenic Sky Valley toll road. The trip takes two hours and the fare is ¥1700. This service only operates between late April and late October.

SENDAI 仙台

Sendai (population 918,000) is a fairly dull provincial Japanese city, even by dull provincial Japanese city standards.

Places to Stay

The *Sendai Dōchu-an Youth Hostel* (☎ 022-247-0511), just south of Sendai in an old farmhouse, has a high reputation for hospitality to foreigners. From Sendai station, take the subway to Tomizawa station then walk for eight minutes to the hostel. Alternatively, you can walk to the hostel in 18 minutes from Nagamachi station which is one stop south of Sendai station. If you get lost, the hostel manager can give you directions over the phone.

The *Sendai Onnai Youth Hostel* (☎ 022-234-3922) is north of Sendai station. Take bus No 24 bound for Shihei-chō (the stop is in front of the Sendai Hotel, opposite the station) and get off after about 15 minutes at the Tōhokukai Byō-in Shigakubu-mae stop. The hostel is two minutes' walk away. A bed for the night is ¥2300 and bicycle rental is available at reasonable rates.

The *Sendai Akamon Youth Hostel* (☎ 022-264-1405), north-west of Sendai station, is about 15 minutes by bus No 16 to the Nakanose-bashi bus stop then five minutes on foot. A bed for the night is ¥2300, and the hostel is closed from 28 December to 3 January.

The *Japanese Inn Aisaki* (☎ 022-264-0700), a member of the Japanese Inn Group, is behind the post office, a 15-minute walk from Sendai station. It's a friendly place with meals available. Prices for singles/doubles start at ¥4300 per person.

JAPAN

Places to Eat

There are a multitude of dining options in the central city area. The fast-food barns are well represented, with branches of *McDonald's*, *Lotteria*, *Kentucky Fried Chicken* and *Mos Burger* to name a few. There's at least one branch of *Doutor's*, the successful Tokyo discount coffee chain, and also a branch of the equally successful *Italian Tomato* chain on Chūō-dōri. The Japanese gyūdon (beef on rice) chain *Yoshinoya* has a branch up on Hirose-dōri – good economical fare.

Getting There & Away

The Tōhoku Kyūkō (express night bus) runs between Tokyo (Tokyo station) and Sendai (¥5450 one way, 7¾ hours), and reservations are necessary.

The JR Tōhoku shinkansen line takes two hours seven minutes by the Yamabiko service or two hours 34 minutes by the Aoba service between Tokyo (Ueno) and Sendai (¥10,390). Trains run around once every 20 minutes. The Tōhoku shinkansen line also connects Fukushima with Sendai in 26 minutes and continues north to Morioka in 50 minutes.

Sendai is a major port with daily ferries operating to Tomakomai (Hokkaidō). The trip takes just under 17 hours and the passenger fare is ¥8850. There are also ferries operating every second day to Nagoya (¥9580, 21 hours). Japanese speakers can make reservations on ☎ 022-263-9877 or in Tokyo on ☎ 03-3564-4161.

To get to Sendai-futō Pier from Sendai station, take the JR Senseki line to Tagajō station and then a 10-minute taxi ride.

Getting Around

Sendai has a huge, and initially confusing, network of bus services. The present subway system runs from Izumi Chūō in the north to Tomizawa in the south, a route that takes in nothing of interest for the visitor to Sendai. Ticket prices range from ¥180 to ¥260. An extension of the subway is planned to run from east to west.

MATSUSHIMA 松島

Matsushima and the islands in Matsushima-wan Bay are meant to constitute one of the Nihon Sankei, or 'three great sights' of Japan – the other two are the floating torii of Miyajima and the sandspit at Amanohashidate.

Just to confuse things, there's a Matsushima station on the Tōhoku line, but the station that's more convenient to the sights and the harbour is Matsushima-Kaigen, which is on the Senseki line. From Matsushima-Kaigen station, it's only around 500 metres to the harbour, and sights are all within easy walking distance.

Things to See

Founded in 828, **Zuigan-ji Temple** is one of Tōhoku's finest Zen temples. Admission costs ¥500 and includes an English leaflet. The temple is open from 8 am to 5 pm from April to mid-September, though for the rest of the year opening hours are from 8 am to 3.30 pm.

Kanran-tei Pavilion is about five minutes on foot from the dock; bear left after leaving the boat. The garden includes a small museum housing a collection of relics from the Date family. Admission to both the pavilion and museum costs ¥200. It's open from 8.30 am to 5.30 pm (April to October), but closes an hour earlier during the rest of the year.

About five minutes on foot, south of Kanran-tei, **O-jima Island**, connected with the mainland by a red, wooden bridge. It's a pleasant spot for a stroll. The island was once a retreat for priests, and women were forbidden entry until late last century.

Places to Stay

The *Matsushima Youth Hostel* (☎ 0225-88-2220) is at Oku-Matsushima to the east of Matsushima Bay, near Nobiru station. A bed for the night is ¥2500 and bicycle rental is available. The hostel is closed from 5 July to 12 July.

Getting There & Away

The easy way to get to Matsushima is by train from Sendai. Trains run on the Senseki line to Matsushima-kaigan station, take around 40 minutes and cost ¥390. There are only around two services an hour to Matsushima (some of the trains on the Senseki line terminate before they reach Matsushima), though there are three as far as Shiogama. This is important because travelling by train to Shiogama and then travelling onwards by boat to Matsushima is the most popular way of reaching the latter, taking in one of Japan's most self-celebrated strips of coastline on the way. The train fare to Shiogama is ¥310.

Cruises between Shiogama and Matsushima-kaigan usually take about 50 minutes and operate from 8 am to 4 pm. There are hourly departures between April and November, less frequent departures during the rest of the year, and the one-way fare costs ¥1400. The loudspeakers on the boat are cunningly placed so that there is no escape from the full-blast Japanese commentary. Leaping overboard is about the only way of escaping this racket.

KINKAZAN ISLAND　金華山

For those in search of peace and quiet, an overnight stay on Kinkazan Island is highly recommended. The island features a pyramid-shaped mountain (445 metres), an impressive and drowsy shrine, a handful of houses around the boat dock, no cars, droves of deer and monkeys and mostly untended trails.

The island is considered one of the three holiest places in Tōhoku – women were banned until late last century – and you should respect the ban on smoking.

From the boat dock, it's a steep 20-minute walk up the road to **Koganeyama-jinja Shrine**, which has several attractive buildings in its forested precincts.

A steep trail leads from the shrine up the thickly forested slopes, via several wayside shrines, to the summit in about 50 minutes. From the shrine at the summit, there are magnificent views out to sea and across to the peninsula. On the eastern shore of the island is **Senjōjiki** or '1000 Tatami Mats Rock', a large formation of white, level rock.

A map of the island on green paper is provided by the shrine or the tourist information office in Ayukawa. It has neither contour lines nor scale and its only use is to demonstrate that there *are* trails and to provide the kanji for various places on the island (this may be useful when you come across one of the weather-beaten trail markers).

Before setting off for an extended hike, stock up on food and drink either at the dock or at the shrine shop. Apart from the route up to the summit shrine, the trails are mostly untended and you should be cautious with some of the wooden walkways along the summit which are collapsing into rotten pulp. If you do get lost, head downhill towards the sea – there's a dirt road around all but the northern part of the island.

Places to Stay

The *Koganeyama-jinja Shrine* (☎ 022-545-2264), 15 minutes on foot up the steep hill from the dock, has spartan rooms set aside for hostellers and basic meals are served. You can supplement the meals with food purchased from the shop outside the shrine – careful, the deer can mug the unwary! If you get up before 6 am you may be allowed to attend morning prayers. Most Japanese visitors seem to be day trippers, which means the island is virtually deserted in the early morning and late afternoon.

The shrine also has a lodge for pilgrims which provides classier accommodation and food. Near the dock are a couple of unexciting minshuku.

Getting There & Away

Ferries to Kinkazan Island depart hourly from Ayukawa between 8 am and 3.30 pm; the trip takes 25 minutes and costs ¥880. Ferries from Kinkazan to Ayukawa depart hourly between 9 am and 5 pm. Ayukawa can be reached by taking a train from Matsushima-kaigan on the senseki line to Ishinomaki (30 minutes by limited express). From Ishinomaki, buses run to Ayukawa for ¥1850 (90 minutes).

JAPAN

HIRAIZUMI 平泉

Of the few cultural sights in Tōhoku, Hiraizumi is one that should not be missed.

Things to See

The **Chūson-ji Temple** was originally established in 850. A massive fire in 1337 destroyed most of the complex – even so, what you can see now is still most impressive. Admission costs ¥500; the ticket is also valid for admission to Kyōzō Sutra Treasury and Sankōzō Treasury. It is open daily from 8.30 am to 5 pm, but closes 30 minutes earlier from November to March.

Originally established in 850, **Mōtsū-ji Temple** once rivalled Chūson-ji in size and fame. All that remains now are foundation stones and the attractive Jōdo (Paradise) Garden. Admission to the gardens costs ¥500 and they are open from 8 am to 5 pm. Those staying at the youth hostel in the grounds do not have to pay for admission.

Places to Stay

Mōtsū-ji Youth Hostel (☎ 0191-46-2331) is part of Mōtsū-ji Temple and is a pleasant and peaceful place to stay; guests at the hostel are not charged admission to the gardens. The temple is eight minutes on foot from Hiraizumi station.

Getting There & Away

To reach Hiraizumi from Sendai, take a JR Tōhoku shinkansen to Ichinoseki (35 minutes) then the bus which goes via Hiraizumi station to Chūson-ji Temple (¥320, 26 minutes). You can also take a JR Tōhoku Honsen line train from Sendai to Hiraizumi station, but a change of trains is usually necessary at Ichinoseki. The trip takes about two hours.

From Morioka to Ichinoseki on the JR Tōhoku shinkansen line takes 43 minutes. Trains between Ichinoseki and Morioka on the JR Tōhoku Honsen line are less frequent and take about 1¾ hours.

Getting Around

Frequent buses run from Ichinoseki station via Hiraizumi station to Chūson-ji Temple; the 20-minute walk from Hiraizumi station to Chūson-ji Temple is not particularly appealing. From the station, Mōtsū-ji Temple is an easy 10-minute walk. Bicycle rental is available outside the station at ¥500 for two hours and ¥200 for every additional hour thereafter.

MORIOKA 盛岡

Morioka (population 235,000) is capital of Iwate-ken, and dates back to the early Edo period (1600-1868), when it was the castle town of the Nambu clan. As the terminus of the JR Tōhoku shinkansen line, it is a useful staging post for visiting the northern part of Tōhoku, but there's little to see around town.

Information

The Kita Tōhoku Tourist Information counter (☎ 0196-25-2090) is inside the Train Square coffee shop on the south exit of Morioka station on the 2nd floor. There should be at least one English-speaking member of staff on hand, and there is a good supply of information material. It's open from 8.30 am to 7.30 pm.

Places to Stay

Morioka Youth Hostel (☎ 0196-62-2220) is large and a bit bland, but the manager is helpful. A bed for the night is ¥2500. From Morioka station, take a bus from terminal No 11 – not all buses are suitable so check first – and get off after 15 minutes at the Takamatsu-no-ike-guchi stop. It's a three-minute walk from here to the hostel.

The *Ryokan Kumagai* (☎ 0196-51-3020), a member of the Japanese Inn Group, is in a great little building, even if the husband-and-wife team that run it seem to be asleep with the TV on all day. Singles/doubles start at ¥4500/8000; triples from ¥10,000.

Getting There & Away

From Morioka to Tokyo (Ueno) on the JR Tōhoku shinkansen line, the fastest trains take a mere 2¾ hours. If you are heading farther north to Aomori by train, you should change to the JR Tōhoku line for the 2½ hour trip.

Lake Tazawa-ko, just west of Morioka, is reached via the JR Tazawa-ko line. To visit the Hachimantai area, north-west of Morioka, take the JR Hanawa line to either Obuke station or Hachimantai station, then continue by bus. To reach Miyako, on the eastern coast of Tōhoku, take the JR Yamada line.

MT IWATE-SAN 岩手山

The volcanic peak of Mt Iwate-san is a dominating landmark, north-west of Morioka, and a popular destination for hikers. From Morioka station, you can take a bus north-west to Amihari Onsen (¥1240, 65 minutes), which is the start of one of the main trails to the summit. Another popular approach is to take the train north on the JR Tōhoku line to Takizawa station then change to a bus for Yanagisawa where you can join the steep trail to the summit.

MT OSORE-ZAN 恐山

This volcano has been held in awe as a mysterious, sacred place for many centuries – probably long before the founding of the **Entsū-ji Temple** on its slopes in the 9th century.

As you approach Osore-zan by road, the stench of sulphuric gas intensifies. After paying ¥300 admission, you can walk through the temple grounds, past the bath-houses and crunch your way along the trails of volcanic rock crisscrossed by rivulets of green and yellow sludge.

Places to Stay

The staff at the information office inside Mutsu bus terminal don't speak English, but they will do their best to help you book accommodation. There are plenty of minshuku in the drab confines of Mutsu and there are more expensive hotels and ryokan at Yagen Onsen, a scenic hot-spring resort in the mountains, about 80 minutes by bus from Mutsu.

Of the two youth hostels on the peninsula, both in remote locations, you might find that the most useful one is the *Wakinosawa Youth Hostel* (☎ 0175-44-2341). This hostel is well-placed for an excursion along Hotokegaura, the spectacular western coast of the peninsula, and for the ferry connection to Aomori.

Getting There & Away

Bus From Mutsu bus terminal, it's a 35-minute bus ride (¥640) to Mt Osore-zan. The last bus to the mountain is at 3.20 pm and 4.45 pm during the festivals. The service closes down for the winter between November and April.

There are buses running between Aomori and Mutsu bus terminal via Noheji. From Mutsu bus terminal, the centre of transport action for the peninsula, but a real dump of a place otherwise, there are buses to Ōma, where you can catch the ferry to Hokkaidō.

Ferry From Ōma, there are ferries to Hakodate on Hokkaidō. There are three daytime departures (6.30, 11.30 am and 4.10 pm) to Hakodate. The trip takes just over 1½ hours and the cheapest passenger fare is ¥1000. During August, there are also two sailings in the evening (8.35 and 10.20 pm).

There is also a ferry service which takes about an hour for the trip between Aomori and Wakinosawa, for the Shimokita-hantō Peninsula. From Wakinosawa, there are boat excursions via Hotokegaura to Sai. The trip takes 1½ hours (¥2160). A bus service links Sai with the Mutsu bus terminal in 2¼ hours (¥1960).

AOMORI 青森

Aomori (population 287,000) is an important centre for shipping and fishing. It was bombed heavily during WW II and has since been completely rebuilt – as a result, it's of limited appeal to the passing tourist.

Places to Stay

Aomori is a popular place to break the journey between Tokyo and Hokkaidō, and consequently in the peak seasons it's not that uncommon for *all* the accommodation in town to be booked out. Book ahead to be sure.

Right next to the station are a couple of

ryokan with costs of around ¥3500 to ¥4000. They tend to get booked out quickly but should be worth a try. They are the *Fukuya Ryokan* (☎ 0177-22-3521) and the *Mikimoto Ryokan* (☎ 0177-22-7145).

Getting There & Away
JAS operates frequent flights to Tokyo, Osaka and Sapporo. From Aomori station, it's a 35-minute bus ride to the airport (Aomori Kūkō) just south of the city.

JR operates a frequent bus service between mid-April and mid-November from Aomori to Lake Towada-ko (¥2470, three hours). One hour out of Aomori, the bus reaches Hakkōda cable car (ropeway), then continues through a string of hot-spring hamlets to the lake.

For a visit to Mt Osore-zan (Shimokita-hantō Peninsula), you can take a direct bus from Aomori via Noheji to the Mutsu bus terminal in 2¾ hours.

Aomori is connected with Hokkaidō by the JR Tsugaru Kaikyō line which runs via the Seikan Tunnel beneath the Tsugaru Straits to Hakodate in 2½ hours.

The JR Tōhoku Honsen line links Aomori with Morioka in just over two hours by limited express. From Morioka, you can zip back to Tokyo in 2½ hours on the shinkansen.

The JR Ōu line runs from Aomori, via Hirosaki, to Akita then continues down to Yamagata and Fukushima. From Akita, the JR Uetsu Honsen line runs down to Niigata.

MT HAKKŌDA-SAN 八甲田山
Just south of Aomori is a scenic region around Mt Hakkōda-san which is popular with hikers, hot-spring enthusiasts and skiers.

A bus service from Aomori reaches Hakkōda cable car in 70 minutes then continues to Lake Towada-ko. The cable car whisks you up to the summit of Mt Tamoyachi-yama in nine minutes (¥980 one way, ¥1650 return). From there you can follow a network of hiking trails. Some trails in this area are covered in *Hiking in Japan* by Paul Hunt.

To get there, take a JR bus from Aomori station bound for Lake Towada-ko and get off at the Hakkōda Ropeway-eki bus stop. The trip takes around an hour and costs ¥960.

HIROSAKI 弘前
Founded in the 17th century, the castle town of Hirosaki (population 174,000) developed into one of the leading cultural centres in Tōhoku. With the exception of its dreary modern centre, which can be avoided, it has retained much of its original architecture, including a large portion of its castle area, temple districts and even a few buildings from the Meiji era.

Things to See
The **Nebuta-mura Museum** has a fine display of floats used in the Nebuta festival and a man dutifully pops out every 10 minutes to give a drumming demonstration. The museum is open from 9 am to 5 pm (April to mid-November) but closes an hour earlier during the rest of the year. Admission costs ¥500.

Just north of the Nebuta-mura Museum, you can take a stroll around the old **Samurai Quarter**. The traditional layout of the district now contains mostly modern buildings, but a couple of samurai houses have been restored and opened to the public.

Hirosaki-jō Castle was completed in 1611, but the present structure dates from 1812. About a 15-minute walk south of the castle, **Saishō-in Temple** is worth a visit for its Gojū-no-tō Pagoda. About 20 minutes on foot, north of the pagoda, you come to an avenue, flanked by temples on either side, which leads to **Chōshō-ji Temple**.

Places to Stay
The *Hirosaki Youth Hostel* (☎ 0172-33-7066) is in a good location for the sights, but it's a bit drab. From Hirosaki station, take a bus from bus stop No 3 and get off after about 15 minutes at the Daigaku-byōin stop. Walk along the street for five minutes and the hostel is on your left down an alley. Nightly costs are ¥2500.

Getting There & Away

Between mid-April and early November, there are up to six buses from Hirosaki bus terminal to Lake Towada-ko (¥2200). Morioka is linked with Hirosaki by a JR bus service which takes 2¼ hours (¥2880). From mid-April to late October, there are buses from the Hirosaki bus terminal to Mt Iwaki-san.

Hirosaki is connected with Aomori on the JR Ōu line (35 minutes by limited express). On the same line, trains south from Hirosaki to Akita take about 2½ hours by limited express.

MT IWAKI-SAN   岩木山

Soaring above Hirosaki is the sacred volcano of Iwaki-san, which is a popular climb for both pilgrims and hikers.

From mid-April to late October, there are buses from the Hirosaki bus terminal to Mt Iwaki-san. The trip takes 80 minutes to **Hachigōme** at the foot of the cable car below the summit. After a seven-minute ride (¥350) on the cable car, it then takes another 45 minutes to climb to the summit (1625 metres). This route is the shortest and easiest; the youth hostel in **Hirosaki** has maps showing other climbing routes and times.

An autumn festival known as Oyama-sankei is celebrated on the mountain, usually in September. A colourful procession of local farmers wends its way from **Iwaki-san-jinja Shrine** to the summit to complete ancient harvest thanksgiving rites.

KAKUNODATE   角館

This small town with its well-preserved samurai district and avenues of cherry trees is well worth a visit. You can cover the main sights in a few hours or devote a lazy day to browsing around town. Just outside Kakunodate, about 25 minutes away by bus or train (Jindai station), is **Dakigaeri Gorge** with a pleasant four km nature trail.

Things to See

The interior of **Kawarada-ke House** can be viewed from a path leading through the garden. Next door is the **Samurai Shir-**

yōkan, a cramped museum with an interesting assortment of martial equipment. Admission is ¥300 and it's open from 8.30 am to 4.30 pm.

The **Denshōkan Museum** houses exhibits of armour, calligraphy, ceramics and a large section devoted to the tools and products of the cherry-bark craft. In a room to the side is an artisan demonstrating the craft. It is open daily from 9 am to 4.30 pm (April to October), and closes 30 minutes earlier and all day Thursday during the rest of the year. Admission costs ¥300.

Aoyagi-ke House is really a large conglomeration of mini-museums, intriguing in their higgledy-piggledy presentation. Admission costs ¥500 and it's open from 9 am to 5 pm.

Ishiguro-ke House is a fine example of a samurai house with a sweeping thatched roof and meticulously laid out gardens. The house is open from 9 am to 5 pm and admission costs ¥300.

Places to Stay

The tourist information office (☎ 0187-54-2995) at the station can assist with reservations and provide a list of places to stay. Prices tend to be quite high, and budget travellers would be better off visiting Kakunodate as a day trip from Morioka or Akita. A long-time favourite with foreign visitors is *Minshuku Hyakusui-en* (☎ 0187-55-5715), which is an old house, 15 minutes on foot from the station. Prices start around ¥6000 per person without meals or from ¥8000 with two meals.

Getting There & Away

Bus The bus station in Kakunodate is north of the railway station, about 10 minutes on foot. There are six buses daily to Akita; the trip takes 1½ hours (¥1220). From late July to late August there is an infrequent bus service round Lake Tazawa-ko to Tazawako-han.

Train Trains on the JR Tazawako line connect Kakunodate with Tazawako station (access to Lake Tazawa-ko) in about 20 minutes and continue to Morioka in about 45 minutes. A limited express between Morioka and Kakunodate takes around an hour and costs ¥2520. Ordinary services take just under two hours and cost ¥1090. Connections to Akita take about an hour by limited express (¥2190) and usually require a change to the JR Ōu line at Omagari.

TSURUOKA 鶴岡

Tsuruoka (population 99,000) was formerly a castle town and has now developed into a modern city with a couple of sights, but its primary interest is as the main access point for the nearby trio of sacred mountains, known collectively as Dewa Sanzan.

Places to Stay
There are dozens of shukubō at Tōge, a convenient base at the foot of Mt Haguro-san. The tourist information office at the station has lists and can help with reservations. Expect prices to start around ¥5500 per person including two meals – sansai (mountain greens) and vegetarian temple food are a speciality. The bus terminal at Tōge also has an information office which can help with accommodation.

Tsuruoka Youth Hostel (☎ 0235-73-3205) is not in a convenient location. It's a 15-minute walk from Sanze station, which is three stops south-west of JR Tsuruoka station. A bed for the night is ¥2400, and the hostel is closed from 3 to 12 June.

Getting There & Away
Bus Between April and November there is a bus service between Tsuruoka and Yamagata (1¾ hours). Three of the daily departures go via the Yudonosan Hotel, which provides access to Mt Yudono-san. There is also a bus service between Tsuruoka and Sendai which takes 3¾ hours.

Buses to Mt Haguro-san leave from Tsuruoka station and take 35 minutes to reach Haguro bus terminal, in the village of Tōge, then continue for 15 minutes to the terminus at Haguro-sanchō. From July to October, there are a couple of buses which save the sweat of pilgrims by allowing them

to travel from this terminus towards the peak of Mt Gas-san, as far as Hachigōme (Eighth Station) in 50 minutes (¥660).

Between June and late October there are infrequent buses direct to Sennin-Zawa on Mt Yudono-san. The trip takes 80 minutes (¥1390).

Train Tsuruoka is on the JR Uetsu line with connections north to Akita in 1¾ hours by limited express or connections south to Niigata in 2¼ hours by limited express.

DEWA SANZAN 出羽三山

Dewa Sanzan (Three Mountains of Dewa), is the collective title for three sacred peaks (Mt Haguro-san, Mt Gas-san and Mt Yudono-san) that have been worshipped for centuries by yamabushi (mountain priests) and followers of the Shugendō sect.

Mt Haguro-san 羽黒山
This mountain has several attractions and easy access, thus ensuring a busy flow of visitors. From Tsuruoka station, there are buses to **Tōge**, a village consisting mainly of shukubō at the base of the mountain. The orthodox approach to the shrine on the summit of the mountain requires the pilgrim to climb hundreds of steps from here, but the less tiring approach is to take the bus to the top. The climb is well worth the trouble and can be done at a very leisurely pace in about 50 minutes – take your time and enjoy the woods.

The scene at the top is a slight anticlimax. There are several shrines, often crowded with visitors, and a history museum. The museum charges ¥200 admission to see statues, scrolls, plastic replicas of temple food and a large model of Dewa Sanzan.

Mt Gas-san 月山
Mt Gas-san (1980 metres), the highest peak of the three, attracts pilgrims to **Gassan-jinja Shrine** on the peak itself. The peak is linked by a trail from Mt Haguro-san to Mt Yudono-san. The usual hiking route starts from Hachigōme (the Eighth Station on Mt Haguro-san), passes through the alpine

plateau of Midagahara to the Ninth Station (Kyūgōme) in 1¾ hours and then requires an uphill grind for 70 minutes to the shrine. The trail between Hachigōme and Gassan-jinja Shrine is *only* open between 1 July and 10 October.

The descent on the other side to **Yudonosan-jinja Shrine** takes another 2½ hours. After about 40 minutes of this descent, you also have the choice of taking the trail to **Ubazawa**, the main ski resort on Mt Gas-san, which has its own cable car.

Mt Yudono-san　湯殿山

The mountain is approached via a three-km toll road from Yudonosan Hotel to Senninzawa. From there, you can either walk uphill for another three km or pay ¥150 to take the convenient bus (a nice little earner for the shrine management) to the shrine approach. The shrine is then a 10-minute hike farther up the mountain.

Yudonosan-jinja, the sacred shrine on this mountain is not a building, but a large orange rock continuously lapped by water from a hot spring. Admission costs ¥300. Take off your shoes and socks, pay the fee, receive your blessing with a type of feather duster, deposit your prayer slip into a nearby channel of water and then proceed into the inner sanctum where you perform a barefoot circuit of the rock, paddling through the cascading water. You should respect the signs outside the shrine prohibiting photos.

NIIGATA　新潟

Niigata (population 436,000), the capital of the prefecture, is an important industrial centre and functions as a major transport hub. The city itself has few sights and most foreign visitors use Niigata as a gateway for Sado-ga-shima Island or as a connection with Khabarovsk (Russia) as part of a trip on the Trans-Siberian Railway.

Information

The tourist information office (☎ 025-241-7914), on your left as you exit on the north side of Niigata station, has to win top marks for friendly service.

Places to Stay

The tourist information office can suggest accommodation to suit most budgets. There are plenty of business hotels around the station. The *Niigata Green Hotel* (☎ 025-246-0341) has singles from ¥4500 and the *Hotel Kawai* (☎ 025-241-3391) has similar rates.

Ryokan Furukawa-tei Honten (☎ 025-062-2013), a member of the Japanese Inn Group, is on the outskirts of Niigata in the town of Suibara. Prices for singles/doubles start at ¥4000/8000; triples cost from ¥12,000. The ryokan is 15 minutes on foot from Suibara station on the JR Uetsu line.

Getting There & Away

Air Niigata has flights to Khabarovsk (Russia) which connect with departures on the Trans-Siberian Railway. The Aeroflot office (☎ 025-244-5935) is a couple of minutes on foot from the station. Flights link Niigata with Ryōtsu on Sado-ga-shima Island in 25 minutes (¥7400). There are also flights to Tokyo, Osaka, Nagoya, Sendai and Sapporo.

Bus There are long-distance buses to Tokyo (¥5150, five hours), and a night bus to Kyoto (¥8750, 8¼ hours) and Osaka.

Train Niigata is connected with Tokyo (Ueno station) by the JR Jōetsu shinkansen line in between one hour 50 minutes and two hours 20 minutes depending on the service.

Travelling north, Niigata is linked via the JR Uetsu line with Tsuruoka (two hours) and Akita (four hours). Travelling south-west on the JR Hokuriku line, it takes four hours to Kanazawa, and direct trains also continue to Kyoto and Osaka. To travel from Niigata to Matsumoto requires a routing via Nagano which takes 3¾ hours.

Ferry The Shin-Nihonkai Ferry from Niigata to Otaru (Hokkaidō) is excellent value at ¥5150 for a passenger ticket. The trip takes 18 hours and there are six sailings per week. The appropriate port is Niigata-kō which is 20 minutes by bus from Niigata station.

The ferry to Ryōtsu on Sado-ga-shima Island takes 2½ hours, the cheapest passenger fare is ¥1780 and there are between five and seven departures daily. The hydrofoil (also known as the 'jet foil') zips across in a mere hour, but costs a hefty ¥5460. There are at least five departures daily between April and early November and only two or three daily during the rest of the year.

The appropriate port is Sado Kisen terminal which is 10 minutes (¥160) by bus from the station.

Hokkaidō
北海道

Hokkaidō (population 5,644,000) is the northernmost and second-largest of Japan's islands. Although it accounts for over one fifth of Japan's land area, only 5% of the Japanese population lives there. The real beauty of the place lies in the unpopulated, wilderness regions where, in contrast to Honshū, there are no cultural monuments, but superb opportunities for outdoor activities such as hiking, camping, skiing, relaxing in hot springs and observing wildlife.

You should give some thought as to when to visit Hokkaidō. From November onwards the island experiences some five months of frigid weather, and the bulk of visitors at this time are skiers. The season between May and October attracts hikers and campers to Hokkaidō; the peak months for tourism are June, July and August, and transport services are more frequent and extensive at this time of year. The peak months also see accommodation in short supply – a tent is a good idea.

HAKODATE 函館
Hakodate (population 307,200) is a convenient gateway for Hokkaidō, and is a laid-back kind of place with something of a historical heritage.

Information
The Hakodate Tourist Information Office

(☎ 0138-23-5440) is to the right as you exit the station. It's open from 9 am to 7 pm but closes at 5 pm during winter. The office has plenty of detailed maps and brochures in English, and can also help with finding accommodation.

Things to See
The star attraction of Hakodate is the view from the summit of **Mt Hakodate-yama**, preferably enjoyed on a clear night. A cable car whisks you up to the top in a few minutes and relieves you of ¥1130 for the return trip. Operating hours extend into the evening: from 9 am to 9 pm (1 February to 20 April), 9 am to 10 pm (21 April to 10 October), 10 am to 9 pm (11 October to 10 November) and 10 am to 8 pm (11 November to 31 January). To reach the cable-car station from JR Hakodate station, take tram No 2, 3 or 5 and get off at the Jūjigai tram stop (about a six-minute ride). The base station is then a seven-minute walk uphill.

The **Motomachi District**, at the base of Mt Hakodate-yama, has retained several Western-style buildings from the turn of the century and is a pleasant place to stroll around. The easiest building to recognise is the Greek Orthodox Church, an attractive reconstruction dating from 1916 (the original was constructed in 1859). Entry is free.

If you're an early bird, the **Asa-ichi** (morning market) is open from 5 am to noon; closed on Sunday. It's a two-minute walk from the west exit of Hakodate station.

Places to Stay
It's a good idea to visit the tourist information office next to the station as the staff here will know which ryokan, minshuku or hotels, if any, have vacancies. They will also ring ahead and make same-day reservations for you.

Station Area *Minshuku Ryorō* (☎ 0138-26-7652) is a member of the Toho network. Prices start at ¥4500 per person including two meals, ¥3000 without any meals or an additional ¥500 if you only want breakfast. To reach the minshuku, close to the morning market, take the west exit from the station then walk for six minutes keeping to the left of the street until you come to the seventh sidestreet. Go left down the sidestreet and the minshuku is about 30 metres on your right.

One of the cheapest hotels close to the station is the *Business Hotel New Ōte* (☎ 0138-23-4561). It has singles from ¥5000 to ¥5500 and twins from ¥9000 to ¥10,000. The *Miyagi Hotel* (☎ 0138-23-2204), to the north of the Ōte, is really only good for singles, which cost ¥5500.

The recently opened *Hakodate Youth Guesthouse* (☎ 0138-26-7892) is close to Hakodate-kōen Park. It's slightly more expensive than the average youth hostel, but rooms are either doubles or triples; per-person costs are around ¥3500. At the time of writing, the hostel was only accepting parties of two or more, but it would be a good idea to check the current situation over the phone or with the tourist information office next to the station.

The *Ikusanda Ōnuma Youth Hostel* (☎ 0138-67-3419) is a 10-minute walk south of JR Ōnuma-kōen station, about 40 minutes from Hakodate on the JR Hakodate line. Walk out of the station and follow the road for a couple of hundred metres before taking the first right. The hostel is on the left-hand side shortly after you cross the railway tracks. Bicycle rental is available at the hostel and there are hot springs near by.

Getting There & Away
Air ANA and JAL connect Hakodate Airport with Haneda in Tokyo. There are seven flights daily and the one-way fare is ¥21,700, ¥39,240 return.

Train On the rail front, Hakodate is connected with Aomori by the JR Tsugaru Kaikyō line which runs via the Seikan Tunnel beneath the Tsugaru Kaikyō Straits to Hakodate in 2½ hours by limited express. The fare is ¥2880 with ¥2150 limited express surcharge. Limited express sleeper services from Ueno in Tokyo (they continue on to Sapporo) take 14 hours 20 minutes. A combination of limited express and shinkansen

(as far as Morioka) from Tokyo takes around seven to eight hours and costs ¥17,830 with express surcharges.

Sapporo is linked with Hakodate in 3¾ hours by limited express via New Chitose Airport and Tomakomai. The fare is ¥4840 with a ¥2770 limited express surcharge.

Ferry Ferries link Hakodate with ports on Honshū such as Ōma (¥1000, 1¾ hours), Noheji (¥1400, 4¾ hours) and Aomori (¥1400, 3¾ hours). Hakodate-kō Port is not convenient for access to the city centre. The taxi ride to the JR station costs ¥1140. The closest bus stop, Hokkudai-mae, is a seven-minute walk from the ferry terminal; from there you can catch bus No 1 or 19 to the station.

SAPPORO 札幌
Sapporo (population 1.6 million) is Hokkaidō's administrative hub, main population centre and a lively, prosperous city.

Information
If you arrive by train at Sapporo station, pop into the Lilac Paseo International Information Office (☎ 011-213-5062). It's open daily from 9 am to 5 pm and closed the second Wednesday of every month. If you do nothing else, at least pick up a copy of the excellent *Sapporo Visitor's Handbook & Map*. The office is in the west side of the station.

The most useful information centre, however, is the Sapporo International Communication Plaza (☎ 011-211-3678) on the 1st and 3rd floors of the MN building, just opposite the clocktower. The 1st floor office is devoted to the needs of tourists both in Sapporo and farther afield around Hokkaidō.

Things to See
The **Botanical Garden** has more than 5000 varieties of Hokkaidō's flora on a 14-hectare site. In the garden grounds is the **Batchelor Memorial Museum**, which houses the collection of Dr John Batchelor, an English missionary who took a keen interest in the culture of the Ainu and tribes from Siberia.

JAPAN

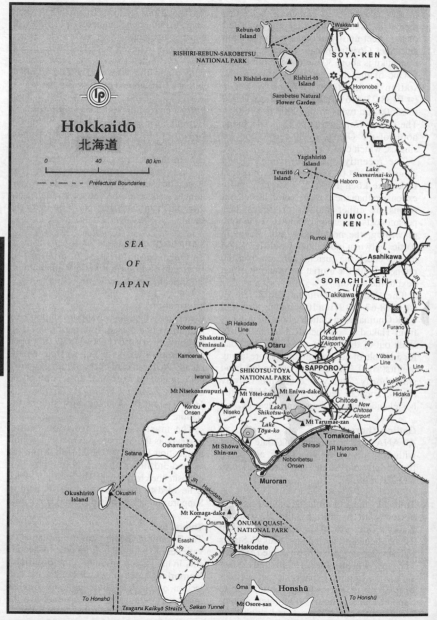

Rebun-tō Island

RISHIRI-REBUN-SAROBETSU NATIONAL PARK

Mt Rishiri-zan

Rishiri-tō Island

Sarobetsu Natural Flower Garden

Wakkanai

SOYA-KEN

Horonobe

JR

Sōya

40 Line

Yagishiritō Island

Teuritō Island

Haboro

Lake Shumarinai-ko

40

Hokkaidō
北海道

0   40   80 km

Prefectural Boundaries

RUMOI-KEN

Rumoi

Asahikawa

12

SORACHI-KEN

SEA

OF

JAPAN

Takikawa

Okadamo Airport

JR

Furano Line

38

Yūbari Line

Furano

Line

Yobetsu

JR Hakodate Line

Shakotan Peninsula

Otaru

SAPPORO

Sekishō

Hidaka

Kamoenai

SHIKOTSU-TŌYA NATIONAL PARK

Iwanai

Mt Nisekoannupuri

Mt Yōtei-zan

Mt Eniwa-dake

Chitose

New Chitose Airport

Konbu Onsen

Niseko

Lake Shikotsu-ko

Oshamambe

Lake Tōya-ko

Mt Tarumae-zan

Tomakomai

Setana

Mt Shōwa Shin-zan

Shiraoi

JR Muroran Line

Noboribetsu Onsen

5

JR Hakodate Line

Muroran

Okushiritō Island

Okushiri

Mt Komaga-dake

Ōnuma

ŌNUMA QUASI-NATIONAL PARK

Esashi

JR Esashi Line

Hakodate

Ōma

Honshū

Mt Osore-san

To Honshū

To Honshū

Tsugaru Kaikyō Straits   Seikan Tunnel

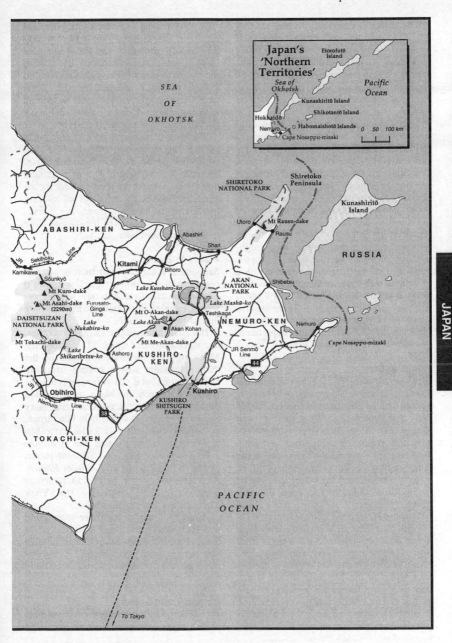

SEA

OF

OKHOTSK

Japan's 'Northern Territories'

Etorofutō Island

Sea of Okhotsk

Pacific Ocean

Kunashiritō Island

Shikotantō Island

Hokkaidō

Nemuro

Habomaishotō Islands

0   50   100 km

Cape Nosappu-misaki

SHIRETOKO NATIONAL PARK

Shiretoko Peninsula

Kunashiritō Island

Utoro

Mt Rausu-dake

Rausu

Abashiri

Shari

RUSSIA

ABASHIRI-KEN

JR Sekihoku Line

Kamikawa

Sōunkyō

Kitami

Bihoro

AKAN NATIONAL PARK

Shibetsu

Mt Kuro-dake

39

Lake Kussharo-ko

Mt Asahi-dake (2290m)

Furusato-Ginga Line

Lake Mashū-ko

DAISETSUZAN NATIONAL PARK

Lake Nukabira-ko

Mt O-Akan-dake

Lake Akan

Akan Kohan

Teshikaga

NEMURO-KEN

Nemuro

Mt Tokachi-dake

Lake Shikaribetsu-ko

Mt Me-Akan-dake

Cape Nosappu-misaki

Ashoro

KUSHIRO-KEN

JR Senmō Line

44

JR Nemuro Line

Obihiro

38

Kushiro

KUSHIRO SHITSUGEN PARK

TOKACHI-KEN

PACIFIC OCEAN

To Tokyo

JAPAN

The garden is open daily from 9 am to 4 pm (29 April to 30 September) but closes half an hour earlier from October to early November and is closed on Monday. Admission is ¥400. Between 4 November and 28 April only the greenhouse is open (10 am to 3 pm); admission is ¥150 and it is closed on Sunday.

The **Tokei-dai Clocktower** was constructed in 1878 and has now become a cherished landmark for Sapporo residents and a useful orientation point for visitors. The **Sapporo Beer Garden and Museum** are on the site of the original Sapporo Brewery. Dating back to 1876, it was the first brewery to be established in Japan. Tours of the museum are free, but reservations are required (☎ 011-731-4368). The tours, lasting about 80 minutes, are given throughout the year from 9 am to 3.40 pm. From the north exit of the station, the brewery is a 15-minute walk east – or take the Higashi 63 bus and get off at the North 8 East 7 *(kita-hachi higashi-nana)* bus stop. There are also special Beer Museum buses running from in front of the Gobankan Seibu department store close to JR Sapporo station.

Places to Stay

Sapporo House (☎ 011-726-4235) is the most convenient of Sapporo's youth hostels, a seven-minute walk from the station, but it's drab and prison-like. When leaving the station, take the south exit (minami-guchi), turn right down the main street and keep walking until you reach the Keiō Hotel at the third intersection. Turn right here, continue under the bridge and the hostel is about 20 metres farther ahead on your right. Beds are ¥2300.

Sapporo Miyagaoka Youth Hostel (☎ 011-611-9016) is close to Maruyama-kōen Park in the west of Sapporo, but it's open from July to late September only. *Sapporo Lions Youth Hostel* (☎ 011-611-4709) is farther west, close to the Miyanomori Ski Jump. Transport from the station to both of these hostels is a bit complicated – a combination of subway, bus and walking – and neither is particularly appealing anyway.

A good alternative to the youth hostels is *Sapporo International Inn Nada* (☎ 011-551-5882), probably the most popular budget place to stay in Sapporo. It's close to the Susukino entertainment area and has no curfew, making it an ideal base for a late night foray into Hokkaidō's most happening nightclub district. Costs are ¥3500 per head, though this will mean sharing a room.

The most popular ryokan with foreigners is the *Yugiri Ryokan* (☎ 011-716-5482), which has per-head costs at around ¥3500 (depends on the room). The management don't speak English but seem to have reconciled themselves to the ways of visiting gaijin and try hard to please. It's a five-minute walk north-west of the station, close to Hokkaidō university.

Places to Eat

Sapporo is a big city and there's a lot to choose from in the dining category. As you'd expect, the fast-food huts are well represented, mainly in Susukino and the shopping district just to the north.

Hokkaidō is famous for its rāmen noodles, and there are rāmen shops all over the city. Many of them have photographs of the dishes outside, which makes ordering slightly easier, but if you're having problems just ask for rāmen, the basic, no-frills (and cheapest) variety. A popular and tasty Sapporo variation is called batā kōn rāmen, or 'butter-corn noodles' – it's a lot better than it sounds. You can try this one at *Rāmen Yokochō*, one of the most popular rāmen places in Susukino or at *Tokei-dai Rāmen*. Another place to try Hokkaidō rāmen is *Sapporo Ichiban*, opposite the York Matsuzakaya department store.

Along with rāmen, there are some good and inexpensive revolving sushi shops in Susukino. *Kuru-Kuro Zushi* has an English sign outside, sushi plates from ¥130 and it is often packed out. *Kaiten Zushi* is a flashy place with the same deal.

Getting There & Away

Air Sapporo has flight connections with most of the major cities on Honshū and even

Okinawa. There are dozens of flights daily from Tokyo; one-way/return fares start at ¥23,850/43,100.

Bus Sapporo is linked with the rest of Hokkaidō by an extensive network of long-distance bus services such as those for Wakkanai (6¼ hours, ¥5850), Asahikawa (two hours, ¥1750), Kushiro (night bus; seven hours, ¥5700), Obihiro (4¾ hours, ¥3800), Kitami (4½ hours, ¥3400) and Hakodate (night bus; six hours, ¥4600).

Train Two of the fastest rail connections from Tokyo include the Hokutōsei Express, which is a direct sleeper to Sapporo in 16 hours, and a combination of the shinkansen to Morioka followed by a limited express via Aomori and Hakodate to Sapporo in 11 hours. In the case of the former, if you are using a Japan Rail Pass, you will have to pay the sleeper supplement. It's also worth bearing in mind that this is a popular service and it only runs three times daily, so book ahead. The cost is ¥13,180 with a ¥3590 limited express surcharge.

From Sapporo to Hakodate takes 3¾ hours by limited express via New Chitose Airport and Tomakomai.

There are frequent trains running northeast on the JR Hakodate line to Asahikawa in 90 minutes (limited express). From Sapporo to Wakkanai, there's a sleeper service that leaves Sapporo around 10 pm and arrives in Wakkanai around 6 am, nicely timed to take the early ferry across to Rishiri-tō or Rebun-tō islands. If you're travelling on a Japan Rail Pass, you'll need to pay about ¥7400 in supplementary charges.

Getting Around

The subway system is the most efficient way to get around Sapporo. There are three lines, the two most useful being the Nanboku line, which runs on a north-south axis and the Tozai line, which runs on an east-west axis. Fares start at ¥180, and special one-day passes are also available for ¥700; they are also valid for Sapporo's buses and trams.

WAKKANAI　稚内

This windswept port on the northernmost fringe of Hokkaidō is visited by travellers heading for Rishiri-tō and Rebun-tō islands. Wakkanai station has an information counter where you can ask for timetables and maps. From the station, it's a 10-minute walk to the ferry terminal. Wakkanai has few sights. Unless your transport arrangements strand you there overnight, there's no compelling reason to stay.

Places to Stay

Hostels *Wakkanai Youth Hostel* (☎ 0162-23-7162) is a 12 minute walk from the southern station for Wakkanai (in Japanese *minami wakkanai eki*). It's open from 1 June to 31 October only. Beds are ¥2500. Bicycle rental is available.

Wakkanai Moshiripa Youth Hostel (☎ 0162-24-0180) is a five-minute walk from Wakkanai station and eight minutes on foot from the Wakkanai-kō Port. Beds are ¥2500, and bicycle rental is available. It's closed during November.

Getting There & Away

Air There are flights from Sapporo's New Chitose Airport and from Sapporo's Okadamo Airport, but most travellers will probably arrive by bus or train. Bus services from Sapporo travel via Asahikawa, take around six hours and cost ¥5850. By train, there's a sleeper service that leaves Sapporo at around 10 pm and arrives in Wakkanai around 6 am, nicely timed to take the early ferry across to Rishiri-tō or Rebun-tō islands. If you're travelling on a Japan Rail Pass, you'll need to pay about ¥7400 in supplementary charges. Other limited express services from Sapporo to Wakkanai take from 5½ hours to eight hours via the JR Hakodate and Sōya lines.

Ferry Wakkanai is linked by ferries travelling to Rishiri-tō and Rebun-tō islands. The ferry to Oshidomari on Rishiri-tō Island departs up to four times daily (between June and the end of August) and takes 90 minutes; the cheapest passenger ticket is ¥1850. From

JAPAN

Oshidomari and Kutsugata there are ferry connections (infrequent) for ¥720 to Rebun-tō Island; these are linked to the arrivals/departures of the Wakkanai service. The trip takes 45 minutes.

There are direct ferries from Wakkanai to Kafuka on Rebun-tō Island up to three times daily (between June and the end of August); the ride takes 2¼ hours (¥2060). There is only one daily service directly from Wakkanai to Funadomari on Rebun-tō Island.

The port at Wakkanai is a 10-minute walk from the station; turn right as you exit the station.

RISHIRI-TŌ ISLAND 利尻島

Part of the Reshiri-Rebun-Sarobetsu National Park, Rishiri-tō Island is dominated by the volcanic peak of Mt Rishiri-zan. A road circles the island and a bus service links the small fishing communities. The main activity for visitors is hiking on the various trails and lakes below the summit of the mountain. Providing you have warm clothes and proper footwear, the hike to the summit can be comfortably completed in a full day. Oshidomari and Kutsugata are the main ports for the island.

Information

Information booths at the ferry terminals of these two ports provide maps and information on transport, sights and hiking, as well as making reservations for accommodation. The booths are opened for the arrival or departure of ferries.

Things to See

There are three trails to the summit of **Mt Rishiri-zan** (1718 metres) but the most reliable ones lead from Oshidomari and Kutsugata. It doesn't make much difference which of these trails you take up, and which one you take down. Prepare properly for a mountain hike, aim for an early start and allow a total of 10 hours for the ascent and descent. Advice and maps in Japanese (excellent hiking details with contour lines)

are available from the information booths at the ports and from the youth hostels.

Places to Stay

The information booth at Oshidomari-kō Port is opened for the arrival and departure of ferries and can help with booking accommodation both on this island and on Rebun-tō Island. There are plenty of minshuku and a couple of youth hostels.

The *Rishiri Green Hill Youth Hostel* (☎ 01638-2-2507) is a five-minute bus ride or 25-minute walk from Oshidomari-kō Port. Beds are ¥2300. Bicycle and scooter rental is available.

Getting There & Away

It's a 20-minute hop with ANK from Wakkanai and the return ticket costs ¥10,580 – there are two flights daily during the peak summer season. The information office (☎ 01638-2-1770) at Rishiri Airfield is open from 9 am to 5 pm.

For details of the service from Oshidomari via Kafuka (Rebun-tō Island) to Wakkanai, see Getting There & Away under Wakkanai earlier in this section.

Getting Around

There are six buses daily which complete a 1¾ hour (¥1880) circuit of the island. Taxis are available in Kutsugata and Oshidomari, though this is an expensive way to do things.

Bicycles are a great way to get around the island and are available for rental at the youth hostels. You can complete a leisurely circuit (53 km) of the island in about five hours.

The cheapest option of all, hitching, is going to require considerable patience, as the island isn't exactly a hive of vehicular activity.

REBUN-TŌ ISLAND 礼文島

Also part of the Rishiri-Rebun-Sarobetsu National Park, in contrast to the conical heights of its neighbour, Rebun-tō is a low, sausage-shaped island which has one major road down the east coast. The main attractions of the island are the hiking trails which follow routes along the west coast past remote fishing communities. Between June and August, the island's alpine flowers, over 300 species, pull out all the stops for a floral extravaganza: a memorable experience.

Kafuka and Funadomari are the main communities and ports, at the southern and northern ends of the island, respectively.

Things to See
The classic hike down the entire length of the western coast is known as the **Hachijikan Haikingu Kōsu** (Eight-Hour Hiking Course). It's a marvellous hike across varied terrain. If you have the extra day, or simply want to pack less into the day, it would be more enjoyable to break the hike into two four-hour sections, **Yonjikan Haikingu Kōsu** (Four-Hour Hiking Course), starting or finishing at Nishi-uedomari.

All the youth hostels and other places to stay on the island provide information on hiking, transport to trailheads and assign hikers to groups.

Places to Stay
The information booth at the port can help find accommodation. There are many minshuku, a couple of hotels and a trio of youth hostels on the island.

The *Rebun Youth Hostel* (☎ 01638-6-1608) in Kafuka is a very friendly place, 13 minutes on foot from Kafuka-kō Port. If you phone ahead, they'll pick you up at the port and when you leave you may be given a lift back to the port. A bed costs ¥2300.

The *Momoiwa-sō Youth Hostel* (☎ 01638-6-1421) is a 15-minute bus ride from Kafuka-kō Port. Take the bus bound for Moto-chi and get off at the Momoiwa Iriguchi stop; the hostel is about a seven-minute walk from there, conveniently close to one of the trailheads for the eight-hour hike. It's open from 1 June to 30 September only. Beds are ¥2300.

The *Rebun-tō Funadomari Youth Hostel* (☎ 01638-7-2717) is a 20-minute walk from Funadomari-kō Port. It's open from 10 May to 15 October only. Beds are ¥2500.

Seikan-sō (☎ 01638-7-2078) is a member of the Toho network, just a couple of minutes

on foot from Funadomari-kō Port. If you speak some Japanese you can ring them up for a lift from the port. Prices start at ¥4500 per person including two meals. It's closed from October until the beginning of May.

Getting There & Away
It's a 20-minute hop with ANK from Wakkanai and the return ticket costs ¥12,080; there are flights twice daily during the peak summer season. The information office (☎ 01638-7-2175) at Rebun Airfield is open from 9 am to 5 pm.

For details of the service from Kafuka providing connections to Oshidomari (Rishiri-tō Island) and to Wakkanai, see Getting There & Away under Wakkanai earlier in this section. There is one daily ferry between Funadomari and Wakkanai.

Getting Around
Most of the time you'll be getting around the island on foot. Youth hostels and other accommodation will usually help with your transport arrangements on arrival or departure. A couple of the minshuku also have bicycles to rent.

The main bus service follows the island's one major road from Kafuka in the south, to Cape Sukoton-misaki in the north. En route it passes Funadomari, the Kūkō-shita (airport) bus stop and Nishi-uedomari. Buses run on this route up to six times daily, but only four go to Cape Sukoton-misaki. Another useful bus service runs five times daily from Kafuka to Moto-chi, a trailhead for the hiking trail along the western coastline of the island. Pick up a copy of the island's bus timetable at the information office in Kafuka-kō Port.

Since there is only one major road, hitching is relatively simple, but most of the rides will be very short.

DAISETSUZAN NATIONAL PARK
大雪山国立公園
This is Japan's largest national park (2309 sq km), consisting of several mountain groups, volcanoes, lakes and forests. It also includes Mt Asahi-dake, which at 2290 metres is

Hokkaidō's highest peak. The park is spectacular hiking and skiing territory, and the main centres of interest are Sōunkyō, Asahidake Onsen, Tenninkyō Onsen, Furano and Tokachidake Onsen. You can pick up maps and information (in English) about the park in Sapporo or try the tourist information offices locally. Only a couple of hikes on the more well-trodden trails are mentioned here, but there are many more routes leading to more remote regions if you have several days or even a week to spare.

Those planning to take a look at the park should bear in mind that at least a few days are needed to get away from the park's tourist traps. It's dubious whether it's worth just heading up to Sōunkyō for an overnight trip. If you have limited time, Asahidake Onsen is a less touristy spot for a quick look at the park.

Things to See

Kamikawa is a useful gateway to Sōunkyō in Daisetsuzan National Park, but it's definitely not an attraction in itself. Local trains from Asahikawa take about 1¼ hours to Kamikawa on the JR Sekihoku line. Buses run from Kamikawa to Sōunkyō in 32 minutes (¥600).

Asahidake Onsen is an unspoilt hot-spring resort consisting of several houses surrounded by forest, which lie at the foot of Mt Asahi-dake, the highest mountain on Hokkaidō. The nearby cable car runs in two stages (12 minutes, ¥1300) to a point within easy hiking distance of the peak.

The base station of the cable car has a restaurant and shop where you can buy *Daisetsuzan Attack* (¥1500), a very detailed map in Japanese. The youth hostel can provide advice on hiking and will loan you a hiking map together with a compass and a jingle-bell. There are *rotemburo* (open-air, natural hot springs) at Yudoku Onsen and Nakadake Onsen along the trails over the peaks. Take warm clothing, appropriate footwear and sufficient food and drink. During the peak hiking seasons, cable cars and lifts operate from as early as 6 am until as late as 7.30 pm.

There are dozens of hiking options in this region; the most popular hike follows trails from the Mt Asahi-dake cable car via several peaks to Sōunkyō; allow about 6½ hours. From the top station of the Mt Asahi-dake cable car, it takes 1¾ hours to climb along a ridge overlooking steaming, volcanic vents to reach the peak of Mt Asahi-dake.

From there, you can continue via Mt Hokkai-dake (1½ hours) to Mt Kurodake Ishimuro (1½ hours) for a pause at the mountain hut and then continue via the peak of Mt Kuro-dake (30 minutes) to the top station of Sōunkyō chair lift (40 minutes). The lift takes 15 minutes to connect with a cable car which whisks you down to Sōunkyō in seven minutes.

From Asahidake Onsen there's a trail through the forest to Tenninkyō Onsen, a small hot-spring resort with a scenic gorge and waterfall, which can be used as a base for extended hiking into the park.

Sōunkyō is the touristic hub of the park and consists of Sōunkyō Onsen, the hot-spring resort with an array of brutally ugly hotels, and Sōun-kyō Gorge itself.

The gorge stretches for about eight km beyond Sōunkyō Onsen and is renowned for its waterfalls – Ryūsei-no-taki and Ginga-no-taki are the main ones – and for two sections of perpendicular columns of rock which give an enclosed feeling, hence their names: Ōbako (Big Box) and Kobako (Little Box).

Since the view from the road is restricted by tunnels, a separate cycling path has been constructed. Local entrepreneurs derive a sizeable income from bicycle rental at ¥1200 per day; the local youth hostels probably offer the best deals for bicycle rental. You could also speed things up by taking a taxi to Ōbako (20-minute ride) and walking back in a couple of hours.

Places to Stay

The *Daisetsuzan Shirakaba-sō* (☎ 0166-97-2246) is an outstanding youth hostel at Asahidake Onsen. There's an indoor hot-spring bath, an outdoor rotemburo where you can soak under the stars and a beautiful

Canadian log cabin with a Japanese tatami-mat interior, and the couple who run the place are well travelled and genuinely hospitable. The charge for a bed is ¥2400.

In Sōunkyō, youth hostellers only have the option of the *Sōunkyō Youth Hostel* (☎ 0165-85-3418), about five to 10 minutes' walk from the bus station in Sōunkyō. The hostel organises early morning hikes to Mt Kuro-dake in the summer months.

Getting There & Away
A bus service runs twice daily from Asahikawa to Tenninkyō Onsen via Asahidake Onsen; from mid-June to mid-October the service increases to three times daily. The last bus to Asahidake Onsen is at 3 pm; the last bus from Asahidake Onsen is at 5 pm. The trip takes 1½ hours and the ticket costs ¥1180.

Buses run from Sōunkyō to Kamikawa in 32 minutes (¥600). The bus service from Sōunkyō to Kitami takes about two hours. The price is a hefty ¥2400, but you get to ride in a deluxe sightseeing bus with plush seats, chandeliers(!), headphones etc, which is a bizarre contrast with the wild scenery outside, especially if you've been out there hiking for a few days.

If you want to head south towards Obihiro, you'll have to use Route 273 which follows a scenic route via Lake Nukabira-ko, but has *no* bus services, so hitch or hire a car. From Obihiro, there's a bus (1¾ hours, ¥1600) to Lake Shikaribetsu-ko which is about 15 km from Lake Nukabira-ko.

SHIRETOKO NATIONAL PARK
知床国立公園
This remote park (386 sq km) features a peninsula with a range of volcanic peaks leading out to the rugged cliffs around Cape Shiretoko-misaki. The main season for visitors is from mid-June to mid-September, and most of the hikes are not recommended outside this season.

Orientation
Shari is the gateway to the peninsula. It has an efficient bus service to the large and rather bland resort of Utoro. However, as Iwaobetsu Youth Hostel is more convenient as a base for hiking, Iwaobetsu is a more viable place to travel to.

Things to See
About 10 minutes by bus from Iwaobetsu Youth Hostel are the **Shiretoko Goko** (Shiretoko Five Lakes), where wooden walkways have been laid out for visitors to stroll around the lakes in an hour or so. You can connect with the buses (there are five a day from Shari) in Shari, Utaro or Iwaobetsu.

Another 45 minutes by bus down the rough road towards the tip of the peninsula, you come to the Shiretoko-ōhashi Bridge just below the spectacular rotemburo which form part of **Kamuiwakka-no-taki Falls**. It takes about 20 minutes to climb up the rocky bed of the stream until you come to cascades of hot water emptying into a succession of pools. Bathers simply strip off and soak in the pools which command a superb panorama across the ocean. A special sightseeing bus service operates to the lakes and the rotemburo once a day between mid-June and mid-September, and passengers are given time to take a dip in the pools.

There are several hikes on the peninsula; Iwaobetsu Youth Hostel can provide more detailed advice on routes, trail conditions and the organisation of transport. Proper footwear and warm clothes are essential.

The hike to the top of **Mt Rausu-dake** starts from the hotel at Iwaobetsu Onsen. There's only one bus a day out to the hotel, so you'll probably have to walk for an hour up the road from Iwaobetsu Youth Hostel to reach the start of the trail; allow 4½ hours from there to reach the top (1660 metres) at a comfortable pace.

The hike to the summit of **Mt Iō-zan** (1562 metres) starts about 500 metres beyond Shiretoko-ōhashi Bridge and requires about eight hours for the return trip.

Places to Stay
Shiretoko Youth Hostel (☎ 01522-4-2764) in Utoro is a massive place with bicycle hire available.

Iwaobetsu is a hamlet, farther up the coast from Utoro, and the *Shiretoko Iwaobetsu Youth Hostel* (☎ 01522-4-2311) deserves recommendation as a friendly and convenient base for exploration of the peninsula. The hostel is closed from 25 October until 1 June. If you are fortunate enough to arrive when the hostel opens for the season, you can expect three consecutive nights of slap-up dinners and partying. Per-person costs are ¥2500.

To reach the hostel, either take a direct bus from Shari or Utoro for Shiretoko Goko (Shiretoko Five Lakes; 70 minutes, ¥1600 from Shari), and get off at Iwaobetsu. The hostel is only one minute from the Iwaobetsu bus stop. If you've missed the bus from Utoro, either hitch (it's only nine km) or phone the cheery and long-suffering hostel manager, who has been known to fetch stranded foreigners.

Getting There & Away

From Shari, there is an efficient bus service to the large and rather bland resort of Utoro, but Iwaobetsu Youth Hostel is a more convenient base for hiking. There are up to eight buses a day from Shari to Utoro, but only three or four continue to Iwaobetsu; the full trip from Shari to Iwaobetsu takes 70 minutes (¥1600). Buses to Rausu operate twice daily from July to mid-October.

Getting Around

Two roads run along each side of the peninsula, but they peter out well before the tip, which can be viewed as part of a long boat excursion from Utoro. Another road crosses the peninsula from Rausu to Utoro. Transport is restricted to infrequent buses and bicycle rental; hitching can prove quite successful.

Between May and early September, two boat excursions are operated from Utoro: one runs once daily out to the soaring cliffs of Cape Shiretoko-misaki (¥4910, 3¾ hours); the other runs up to five times daily for a short cruise along the coastline as far as Kamuiwakka-no-taki Falls (¥1900, 90 minutes).

BIHORO 美幌

Bihoro lies east of Asahikawa and north of Akan National Park. If you're not going to Shiretoko National Park, you can head south from here into Akan National Park.

From Bihoro, the sightseeing buses follow a scenic route to the park, pausing after 50 minutes at Bihoro Pass, which provides a superb view across Lake Kussharo-ko, and then continuing for another 2¾ hours before reaching the terminus at Akan Kohan. It's best to use this expensive service in small doses as the incessant commentary and the sensation of having inadvertently strayed into a pensioners' package tour can be oppressive. The trip from Bihoro to Kawayu Onsen on the shore of Lake Kussharo-ko takes 65 minutes (¥2590).

Places to Stay

The *Bihoro Youth Hostel* (☎ 01527-3-2560) is close to the town centre. From Bihoro station it's a six-minute bus ride followed by a 10-minute walk. Bicycle hire is available, and there are hot springs near by.

KUSHIRO 釧路

Kushiro (population 205,000) is the industrial and economic centre of eastern Hokkaidō and one of the main gateways to Akan National Park.

Places to Stay

The *Kushiro Makiba Youth Hostel* (☎ 0154-23-0852) is a 15-minute walk from the station. Turn left out of the station and walk eastwards for 900 metres and take the first railroad crossing after the bridge. Follow this road for around 500 metres and look out for a small park on your left. The youth hostel is just after the park. Nightly costs are ¥2300, and bicycle and scooter rental are available.

Kushiro Youth Hostel (☎ 0154-41-1676) is a 15-minute bus ride from the station on a No 27 or 30 bus (get off at the Yūsu Hosuteru-mae stop) and then a two-minute walk. It's closed from 16 January to 25 January and from 16 May to 19 May.

Getting There & Away

Air Flights connect Kushiro with Sapporo (40 minutes) and Tokyo (1¾ hours). Kushiro Airport is a 45-minute bus ride (¥800) from Kushiro station.

Bus There are bus services from Kushiro to Akan Kohan (2¼ hours, ¥2440) and to Rausu (3½ hours, ¥2730) on the Shiretoko Peninsula. There's also a night bus to Sapporo (seven hours, ¥5700).

Train The JR Senmō line runs north through Akan National Park to Shari. The JR Nemuro line runs west to Sapporo (4¾ hours by limited express). The fare to Sapporo is ¥5670 with a ¥2970 limited express surcharge. Sapporo also has a night service to Kushiro that leaves at around 11 pm (check for the latest time) and arrives at around 5.30 am in Kushiro.

Ferry A regular ferry service connects Kushiro with Tokyo in 32 hours, the cheapest passenger fare is ¥14,000. Kushiro Nishi-kō Port (also known simply as the Ferii Tāminaru) is a 15-minute bus ride west of Kushiro station. Alternatively, the ferry terminal is just over 500 metres walk south of Shin Fuji station, one stop west of Kushiro station.

AKAN NATIONAL PARK
阿寒国立公園

This large park (905 sq km) in eastern Hokkaidō contains several volcanic peaks, some large caldera lakes and extensive forests.

The main gateways on the fringe of the park are Bihoro in the north and Kushiro in the south. The major centres inside the park are the towns of Teshikaga, Kawayu Onsen and Akan Kohan.

Things to See
Kawayu Onsen makes a convenient base for visiting the nearby sights of Lake Kussharo-ko, Mt Iō-zan and Lake Mashū-ko. Be warned, though, that the place is a bit of a tourist trap.

About three km from Kawayu Onsen is **Lake Kussharo-ko**, the largest inland lake in Hokkaidō and a popular spot for swimming and camping. At Sunayu Onsen on the eastern shore, the hot springs warm the sand on the beach, and at Wakoto Onsen on the southern shore, there are hot springs bubbling into open-air pools.

Mt Iō-zan, just outside Kawayu Onsen, is unmistakable for its steam and distinctive smell. A pleasant nature trail leads from the bus centre through dwarf pines to the mountain and takes 35 minutes. The scene is certainly impressive with hissing vents, billowing clouds of steam and bright yellow sulphur deposits.

Lake Mashū-ko is about 15 km south-east of Kawayu Onsen. Known to the Ainu as the 'Lake of the Devil', there is certainly an unusual atmosphere to this lake, which is surrounded by steep rock walls that reach a height of 300 metres. If you are fortunate enough to visit when the lake is not wreathed in mist, the clarity of the water and its intense blue colour is quite startling.

Akan Kohan is a hot-spring resort on the edge of Lake Akan-ko. You can safely skip the boat trips (¥810) on the lake and the atrocious tourist facilities that purport to be part of an Ainu village, but we'd still recommend using this resort as a base for doing some interesting mountain hikes in the area.

On the eastern edge of the resort is a tourist information office where you can pick up information and hiking maps for the region, but they're mostly in Japanese. Possible hikes include a three-hour ascent and two-hour descent of **Mt O-Akan-dake** (1371 metres). It's around six km south of Akan Kohan and the hiking trail starts at Takiguchi. A more accessible hike is an ascent of **Mt Me-Akan-dake** (1499 metres), an active volcano and the highest peak in the park. Keep a close watch on the weather as conditions can change quickly. Sulphur fumes from volcanic vents can also be a bit of a problem. There is a clear trail up the mountain, which requires 4½ hours for the ascent and 3½ hours for the descent. It's also possible to descend by another trail on the west face of the mountain that connects with the road leading to Nonaka Onsen Youth Hostel. Check with Akan Angel Youth Hostel (☎ 0154-67-2309) for more information on both these hikes.

Places to Stay

The *Mashū Youth Hostel* (☎ 01548-2-3098) is the only youth hostel accommodation available in the area. From Mashū station take a bus bound for Bihoro or Kawayu and get off at the Yūsu-hosuteru-mae stop. If you arrive at Mashū station after 4 pm, ring the hostel for a lift in their minibus. Nightly rates are ¥2500. The hostel is closed from 1 December to 20 December.

A member of the Toho network, *Sanzoku-no-Ie* (☎ 01548-3-2725) is a small minshuku about six minutes on foot from Kawayu Onsen station. Prices start at ¥4500 per person including two meals. It's open from May to late October.

Mashumaro (☎ 01548-2-2027), another member of the Toho network, is a five-minute walk from JR Biruwa station, the stop between Kawayu Onsen and Teshikaga. Prices start at ¥4500 per person including two meals. It's closed during November and April.

The *Akan Angel Youth Hostel* (☎ 0154-67-2309) is a 12-minute walk from the bus terminal at Akan Kohan. If you phone ahead, the friendly owner may offer to fetch you and will give you a lift to the terminal when you leave. He can also provide advice on hiking in the area and often takes groups himself. Bicycle rental and a hot-spring bath (¥150 additional fee) are also available. Nightly costs are ¥2300.

Nonaka Onsen Youth Hostel (☎ 01562-9-7454), about 20 km west of Lake Akan-ko, also provides a base for climbing Mt Me-Akan-dake. The hostel is reached by a very infrequent direct bus service or you can use the more frequent bus service between Akan Kohan and Ashoro station; get off at the Noboriyama-guchi stop (about 55 minutes from Akan Kohan) then take the sideroad south for the 45-minute walk to the hostel. It is located in a nice position beside a small

lake. For an additional fee of ¥75 you can use the hot-spring bath.

Getting There & Away

Bus Sightseeing buses run north-east from Akan Kohan to the main sights in the rest of the park as far as Kawayu Onsen. Other services connect with Ashoro and Obihiro (2¾ hours, ¥3500) to the south-west, Bihoro (1¼ hours, ¥1950) and Kitami to the north and Kushiro (2¼ hours, ¥2440) to the south.

A sightseeing bus service operates from Kawayu Onsen via the main sights in the park to Akan Kohan (2½ hours, ¥3160.

Train The JR Senmō line links Kawayu station with Shari in 55 minutes and with Kushiro in 1½ hours. The Kawayu Onsen bus centre is a 10-minute bus ride from Kawayu station.

SHIKOTSU-TŌYA NATIONAL PARK
支笏洞爺国立公園

Shikotsu-Tōya National Park (983 sq km) is centred around Lake Shikotsu-ko, Lake Tōya-ko and Noboribetsu Onsen. The lakes have the added attractions of mountain hikes or close-up encounters with volcanoes, while Noboribetsu Onsen will appeal to hot-spring enthusiasts. Fast and easy access to the park from Sapporo or New Chitose Airport makes it a favourite with visitors who have only a short time to spend in Hokkaidō.

Information

JNTO publishes a leaflet entitled *Southern Hokkaidō*, which provides a map of the park with information on sights, transport and accommodation.

The information office (☎ 01232-5-2453), close to the bus terminal, is open from 9.30 am to 4.30 pm and has maps and other information.

Things to See

The **Lake Shikotsu-ko** is a caldera lake surrounded by several volcanoes and offers some good hiking opportunities. The lake itself is Japan's second-deepest after Lake Tazawa-ko in Akita-ken. The main centre for transport and information is Shikotsu Kohan, which consists of a bus terminal, a tourist information office, a pier for boat excursions and assorted souvenir shops, restaurants and places to stay.

From the boat pier, there are rather tame sightseeing cruises which stop off at a couple of places around the lake before returning to the pier (1½ hours, ¥1700). If you cross the bridge on your far left as you walk down to the lake shore, you can follow a nature trail around the forested slopes for an hour or so. The Shikotsu-ko Youth Hostel provides bicycle rental (¥250 per hour or ¥800 per day) and this is a good way to follow the road around the edge of the lake as there is no bus service.

The mountain hikes are perhaps the most interesting activities to do around the lake. The youth hostel or tourist information office can give more advice on access, routes and timings.

Mt Eniwa-dake (1320 metres) lies on the western side of the lake. The start of the trail is about 10 minutes on foot from Poropinai, and the Eniwadake Yamaguchi bus stop is near by. It takes about 3½ hours to hike to the summit, where there is a fine panorama of the surrounding lakes and peaks. Don't bother with this hike if it rains as some of the steeper sections of the trail become dangerously slippery.

Mt Tarumae-zan (1038 metres) lies on the southern side of the lake and offers the rugged delights of wandering around the crater of an active volcano. The crater is an easy 40-minute hike from the seventh station, which can be reached from Shikotsu Kohan in three hours on foot; or in 20 minutes if you use the bus service that seems to run only on Sunday. From the crater, you can either return to the seventh station, or follow the trail north-west down the mountain for 2½ hours to **Kokenodō-mon**, a mossy gorge, which is 10 minutes from the car park at Shishamonai on the lake shore. From Shishamonai, you'll have to walk or hitch the 15 km to Shikotsu Kohan.

Places to Stay

There are over a dozen minshuku, ryokan and hotels on the edge of the lake; campgrounds are also available at Morappu, Poropinai and Bifue. The tourist information office can help with booking accommodation.

The *Shikotsu-ko Youth Hostel* (☎ 0123-25-2311) is at Shikotsu Kohan, and just a couple of minutes from the bus terminal. This is a well-organised and friendly hostel which has family rooms as well as the usual dormitory-style accommodation. Bicycle rental and a hot-spring bath (additional fee of ¥150) are also available. Overseas hostellers are eligible for a ¥500 discount. A 'briefing' session is held in the evenings to give advice on hiking in the area and the hostel may be able to help with organising transport to trailheads. Nightly rates are ¥2500. The hostel is closed from 1 December to 10 December and from 16 May to 19 May.

Getting There & Away

There is a bus service from Sapporo (Hokkaidō Chūō bus from in front of Sapporo station) to Lake Shikotsu-ko (80 minutes, ¥1050); other bus services run from New Chitose Airport (47 minutes, ¥700) and Tomakomai (45 minutes, ¥540).

Shikoku
四国

Although Shikoku is Japan's fourth-largest island, it's predominantly rural and very much off the tourist track. Apart from scenery, the Ritsurin-kōen Garden in Takamatsu and four castles (Kōchi, Marugame, Matsuyama and Uwajima), there are no overwhelming attractions.

Shikoku is home to Japan's best known pilgrimage: Kōbō Daishi's 88 Temple Circuit of Shikoku. Kōbō Daishi was born in Shikoku, and it is said he personally selected the 88 temples which make up the circuit. Today, most pilgrims on the circuit travel by

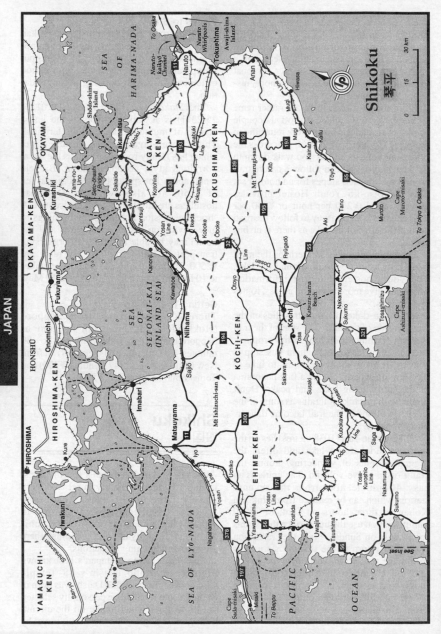

tour bus but some still walk – set aside six weeks and be prepared to walk over 1000 km if you want to join them.

TAKAMATSU 高松

The completion of the Seto-ōhashi Bridge has reinforced Takamatsu's (population 330,000) importance as a major arrival point on Shikoku. Despite the new rail link, it remains an important port for Inland Sea ferry services, particularly to popular Shōdo-shima Island. The town has an important garden, and the nearby Shikoku-mura Village Museum and the very popular Kotohira-gū Shrine is an easy day trip.

Things to See

Although not one of Japan's 'big three' gardens, **Ritsurin-kōen Garden** could easily be a contender for that list. The garden, which was first constructed in the mid-1600s, winds around a series of ponds with lookouts, tearooms, bridges and islands. Entry to the garden is ¥310 and it's open from sunrise to sunset. There's an extra charge for the teahouse. You can get there by Kotoden or JR train, but the easiest way to get there is by a Kotoden bus (¥210) from platform No 2 at the JR station.

The 292-metre high table-top plateau of **Yashima** stands five km from the centre of Takamatsu. Today, it's the site for the Yashima-ji Temple (No 84 on the temple circuit) and offers fine views over the surrounding countryside and the Inland Sea. A funicular railway runs up to the top of Yashima Hill from the left of the shrine at the bottom. The cost is ¥600 one way or ¥1200 return. At the top you can rent a bicycle (¥300 plus ¥1000 deposit) to pedal around the attractions as it's a long walk otherwise.

The two best ways of getting to Yashima are by Kotoden train or by Kotoden bus. From Kotoden Takamatsu Chikkō station it takes around 20 minutes (¥260) to Yashima station. From here you can take the cable car to the top. Kotoden buses run directly to the top from in front of Takamatsu station, take around 30 minutes and cost ¥660.

At the bottom of Yashima Hill is excellent

Shikoku-mura Village, with old buildings brought from all over Shikoku and neighbouring islands. Entry is ¥500; the small museum in the village costs an extra ¥100 and you can safely skip it. The village is open from 8.30 am to 4.30 or 5 pm. If you want to skip Yashima, you can visit Shikoku-mura directly; it's around seven minutes on foot north of Yashima station.

Places to Stay

The *Takamatsu Yashima-sansō Youth Hostel* (☎ 0878-41-2318) is just over five minutes' walk to the north-east of Kotoden Yashima station. The hostel charges ¥2300 per night.

Two of the cheapest alternatives to the youth hostel are the *Business Hotel Japan* (☎ 0878-51-8689), south of the station in the shopping and entertainment district, and the *Business Hotel Marukyu* (☎ 0878-51-7305), which is south-west of Takamatsu station. Both are small and at the grotty end of the business hotel spectrum, but offer singles/twins for ¥4000/7000.

Places to Eat

There are some fast-food outlets in and around the station. A bit of a hike from the station area, one of the cheapest places to slurp back some noodles in town is *Udon House* on Kankō-dōri. Look for the sign outside announcing 'all the rage'. It should be, with prices ranging from ¥300 for a hearty bowl of noodles.

Getting There & Away

Air Japan Air Systems (JAS) have flights to and from Fukuoka and Tokyo; All Nippon Airways (ANA) flies to and from Osaka and Tokyo.

Train The Seto-ōhashi Bridge has brought Takamatsu much closer to the main island of Honshū. From Tokyo, you can take the shinkansen to Okayama, change trains there and be in Takamatsu in five hours. The Okayama-Takamatsu section takes about an hour.

From Takamatsu, the JR Kotoku line runs south-east to Tokushima and the JR Yosan line runs west to Matsuyama. The Yosan line branches off at Tadotsu and becomes the Dosan line, turning south-west to Kotohira and Kōchi. The private Kotoden line also runs direct to Kotohira.

Ferry Takamatsu is also an important ferry terminus with services to ports in the Inland Sea and on Honshū, including Kōbe (4½ hours, ¥2370) and Osaka (5½ hours, ¥2370). Prior to the construction of the bridge, Uno, to the south of Okayama, was the main connection point to Takamatsu. It's still a quick way to make the Honshū-Shikoku trip since Uno-Okayama trains connect with the ferry departures. Takamatsu is also the easiest jumping-off point for visiting attractive Shōdo-shima Island. Takamatsu's ferry terminal buildings are right beside the JR station.

Getting Around
Takamatsu Airport is 16 km from the city and the bus, which departs from outside JR Takamatsu station, takes about half an hour.

Takamatsu has a local bus service, but for most visitors the major attractions, principally the Ritsurin-kōen Garden and Yashima, can easily be reached on the JR Kotoku line or the more frequent Kotoden line service. The main Kotoden junction is Kawaramachi, although the line ends at the Chikko station, just across from the JR Takamatsu station.

KOTOHIRA 琴平
The Kompira-san Shrine at Kotohira is one of Shikoku's major attractions and for anyone in this part of Japan it shouldn't be missed, even if it is a little touristy.

Things to See
The **Kompira-san** or, more correctly, Kotohira-gū, was originally a temple dedicated to the guardian of mariners but became a shrine after the Meiji Restoration. Its hilltop position gives superb views over the outlying country and there are some interesting reminders of its maritime connections.

Near the base of the steps leading up to the shrine is the Kyū Kompira Ōshibai, or

Kanamaru-za, a fine old Kabuki playhouse from the Edo period. It was built in 1835 and became a cinema before being restored to its current elegance in 1976. Inside, you can wander backstage and around the changing rooms, and admire the revolving stage. Entry is ¥300 and it's open from 9 am to 4 pm, closed Tuesday.

Places to Stay
The *Kotohira Seinen-no-Ie Youth Hostel* (☎ 0877-73-3836) costs ¥1700 and is near the kabuki playhouse. Most other options are expensive, but those with some extra cash to lavish on their creature comforts might want to consider the *Kotobuki Ryokan* (☎ 0877-73-3872), right by the riverside along the shopping arcade. It's conveniently situated, clean, comfortable and serves good food. The nightly cost per person with dinner and breakfast is ¥7000.

Getting There & Away
The JR Dosan railway line branches off the Yosan line at Tadotsu and continues through Kotohira and south to Kōchi. There is also a direct Takamatsu to Kotohira private Kotoden line. On either line, the journey takes around an hour from Takamatsu.

TOKUSHIMA 徳島
Tokushima (population 263,000), on Shikoku's east coast, is a pleasant enough modern city, but offers few attractions in its own right. The only real reason for a visit is if you are in transit to somewhere else.

Places to Stay
The *Tokushima Youth Hostel* (☎ 0886-63-1505) is by the beach some distance out of town and costs ¥2500.

Close to the river, in a pleasant and quieter area of town, you'll find the *City Hotel Hamaya* (☎ 0886-22-3411). Although a member of the Japanese Inn Group, it's really just a small business hotel. Singles/doubles with bathroom cost from ¥5500/9100 or from ¥4500/8100 without bathroom. Over on the other side of the river, one of the cheapest around is the *Business Hotel New Tōyō*

(☎ 0886-25-8181), where singles are ¥4700 and twins range from ¥8600.

Getting There & Away

Train Tokushima is less than 1½ hours from Takamatsu by limited express train (tokkyū). There are also railway lines westward to Ikeda on the JR Dosan line (which runs between Kotohira and Kōchi) and south along the coastal Mugi line as far as Kaifu from where you will have to take a bus to continue to Kōchi.

Ferry Ferries connect Tokushima with Tokyo, Osaka and Kōbe on Honshū with Kokura on Kyūshū and with various smaller ports. It only takes two hours to Kōbe by hydrofoil.

Getting Around

It's easy to get around Tokushima on foot; from the railway station to the Mt Bizan cable-car station is only 700 metres. Bicycles can be rented from the underground bicycle park in front of the station.

KŌCHI 高知

Kōchi (population 317,000) was the castle town of what used to be known as the Tosa Province, and the small but original castle still stands. Like Kagoshima in Kyūshū and Hagi in Western Honshū, the town can lay claim to having played an important role in the Meiji Restoration.

The Kōchi area is noted for its fighting dogs and long-tailed roosters. The mastiff-like dogs are ranked like sumō wrestlers and even wear similar aprons. You can see demonstration fights at Katsura-hama Beach, and buy toy fighting dogs from the souvenir shops. Breeders have persuaded the long-tailed rooster to produce tail feathers up to 10 metres long! You can see them at the Nagaodori Centre in the Oshino area of Nankoku City, out towards Kōchi Airport. The JR Gomen station, five stops west of Kōchi, is near by.

Things to See

The **Kōchi-jō Castle** may not be one of the great castles of Japan but it is a real survivor, not a post-war concrete reconstruction. Although a construction on the site dates back to the 14th century, the present castle was built between 1601 and 1611, burnt down in 1727 and rebuilt in 1753. The castle is open from 9 am to 5 pm and entry is ¥350. There's a very informative brochure on the castle available in English.

The hilltop Chikurin-ji Temple and Kōchi's botanical garden are both in **Godaisan-kōen Park**, several km from the town centre. The temple is No 31 on the Shikoku temple circuit, and there's an attractive five-storeyed pagoda at the top of the hill. To get to the park and temple take a bus, marked to the temple, from the Toden Seibu bus station next to the Seibu department store which is at the Harimaya-bashi junction. The journey takes about 20 minutes and the bus stops outside the temple steps. Buses run about once an hour until 5 pm, and the fare is ¥300.

Places to Stay

The Kōchi Ekimae Youth Hostel (☎ 0888-83-5086) is only a few minutes' walk east of the railway station and costs ¥2400. For very basic business hotel accommodation, try the Kōchi Business Hotel Honkan (☎ 0888-83-0221). It has singles from ¥3500 to ¥3900 and twins from ¥7000 to ¥7600. Another place worth trying is the Hotel Tosa (☎ 0888-25-3332), where rooms start at ¥4500. It's not far from the Horizume tram stop.

Getting There & Away

Air ANA connects Kōchi with Osaka, Tokyo and Miyazaki in Kyūshū. Air Nippon Koku (ANK) also flies between Kōchi and Osaka, while JAS flies to Fukuoka, Nagoya and Osaka.

Bus Travel between Kōchi and Matsuyama is faster by bus than by train. These depart hourly from outside the bus station near the JR Kōchi station. If you want to travel right around the southern coast, either westward around Cape Ashizuri-misaki to Uwajima or eastward around Cape Muroto-misaki to

Tokushima, you will have to travel by bus as the railway lines do not extend all the way.

Train Kōchi is on the JR Dosan line which runs from the north coast of Shikoku through Kotohira. It takes about 2½ hours by limited express from Takamatsu. From Kōchi, rail services continue westward to just beyond Kubokawa where the line splits south-west to Nakamura and north-west to Uwajima. From Uwajima, you can continue north to Matsuyama but this is a long and circuitous route.

Getting Around

The tram service running north-south from the station intersects the east-west tram route at the Harimaya-bashi junction. Ask for a *norikaeken* (transfer ticket) if you have to transfer there. You can easily reach the castle on foot, though for the other town attractions, you must take a bus.

CAPE MUROTO-MISAKI　室戸岬

Cape Muroto-misaki, south-east of Kōchi, has a lighthouse topping its wild cliffs. The **Higashi-dera Temple** here is No 24 on the Shikoku temple circuit. Just north of Muroto is a chain of black-sand beaches known by local surfers as 'Little Hawaii'. There's youth hostel accommodation on the cape at the *Hotumisaki-ji Youth Hostel* (☎ 0887-23-2488), where nightly costs are ¥2300.

Getting There & Away

You can reach the cape by bus from Kōchi and you can continue right round to Tokushima on the east coast. Tosa Dentetsu buses for Cape Muroto-misaki run from the Harimaya-bashi intersection, around 10 minutes on foot south of Kōchi station. The journey takes around two hours 20 minutes and costs ¥2650. For those continuing on to Tokushima, the JR Mugi line runs around the east coast from Tokushima as far as Kaifu.

CAPE ASHIZURI-MISAKI　足摺岬

South-west of Kōchi, Cape Ashizuri-misaki, like Cape Muroto-misaki, is a wild and scenic promontory ending with a lighthouse.

As well as the coastal road, there's a central Skyline Rd. Cape Ashizuri-misaki also has a temple (the **Kongōfuku-ji**, No 38 on the temple circuit) which, like the temple at Cape Muroto-misaki, has its own youth hostel (☎ 0880-88-0038).

Getting There & Away

The usual point of access for the cape is Nakamura, from the station of which there are infrequent bus services to the tip of the cape for ¥1870. The cape's main attractions, including Kongōfuku-ji Temple and a wooded 'romance walk', are all within easy walking distance of the Ashizuri-misaki bus centre.

From Tosashimizu, at the northern end of the cape, ferries operate to Kōbe on Honshū. From Kōchi, there is a railway as far as Nakamura; travel from Nakamura around the cape and on to Uwajima is by bus.

MATSUYAMA　松山

Shikoku's largest city, Matsuyama, is a busy north coast town (population 443,000) and an important transport hub with frequent ferry links to Hiroshima.

Things to See

Picturesquely sited atop a hill which virtually erupts in the middle of the town, **Matsuyama-jō Castle** is one of Japan's finest original surviving castles. You don't even have to climb the steep hill up to the castle, a cable car and/or chair lift will whisk you up there for ¥160 one way or ¥310 return. Entry to the castle costs ¥260.

Dōgo Onsen is a popular spa centre, a couple of km east of the town centre, and is easily reached by the regular tram service which terminates at the start of the spa's shopping arcade. The arcade leads to the front of **Dōgo Onsen Honkan**, a rambling old public bathhouse which dates from 1894.

Places to Stay

Matsuyama has three accommodation areas: around the JR station (business hotels); around the centre (business hotels and more expensive hotels); and at Dōgo Onsen (ryokan and Japanese-style hotels).

The *Matsuyama Youth Hostel* (☎ 0899-33-6366), near the Isaniwa Shrine in Dōgo Onsen, costs ¥2500 a night.

In the Matsuyama station area is the *Central Hotel* (☎ 0899-41-4358), a cheaper business hotel with singles/twins from ¥4500/7000. Other hotels within a stone's throw of the station include the *Hotel New Kajiwara* (☎ 0899-41-0402), with singles/twins from ¥5300/8400, and the *City Hotel American* (☎ 0899-33-6660), which is next door and has singles from ¥4500.

Central Matsuyama is dominated by expensive business hotels, but immediately north of the castle hill is a quieter area, conveniently connected to the town centre by a tram line. One of the hotels in this area is the curiously old-fashioned *Business Hotel Taihei* (☎ 0899-43-3560), with rooms from ¥4500/8000; others are the *Hotel Heiwa* (☎ 0899-21-3515) and the *Business Hotel New Kashima* (☎ 0899-47-2100). The New Kashima is the cheaper of the latter two, with singles/twins from ¥4300/8000. Take a tram to Tetsubō-chō tram stop and walk south to the main road to find them.

For Japanese tourists, Dōgo Onsen, east of the town centre, is the big attraction and there are numerous Japanese-style hotels and ryokan in the area. Most of them are overpriced, but *Minshuku Miyoshi* (☎ 0899-77-2581), behind the petrol station near Ishite-ji Temple, is an exception at around ¥5000 per person.

Places to Eat
The long Ginten-gai and Okai-dō shopping arcade in central Matsuyama has *McDonald's*, *Kentucky Fried Chicken* and *Mr Donut*. There's another *Mr Donut* near the Matsuyama city station. There's good Japanese-style fast food just across from Matsushima station at *Nakanoka*, a 24-hour gyūdon specialist. The arcade leading from the Dōgo Onsen tram stop to the Dōgo Onsen Honkan bathhouse also has a number of restaurants with plastic meal replicas.

Next to the post office in the town centre,

Restaurant Goshiki offers sōmen noodles and other dishes. Although there are plastic models in the window and an illustrated menu showing the multi-coloured noodles, this is another place where the artistically scrawled sign looks nothing like the printed kanji. Sōmen and tempura costs ¥850 and you can buy noodles in packets (one colour or mixed) to take home.

Getting There & Away
Air ANA connect Matsuyama with Osaka, Nagoya and Tokyo (both Narita International Airport and Haneda Airport). JAS has connections to Fukuoka, Miyazaki and Kagoshima, all in Kyūshū. JAL also flies to Tokyo while South-West Airlines (SWAL) has direct flights between Matsuyama and Naha in Okinawa.

Train The north coast JR Yosan line connects Matsuyama with Takamatsu, and there are also services across the Seto-ōhashi Bridge to Honshū. Matsuyama to Okayama takes three hours 15 minutes. Another line runs south-west from Matsuyama to Uwajima and then east to Kōchi, though this is a rather circuitous route; it's faster to take a bus directly to Kōchi.

Ferry There are frequent ferry and hydrofoil connections with Hiroshima. Take the Iyotetsudō private railway line from Matsuyama City (Shi-eki) or Otemachi station right to the end of the line at Takahama (¥440 from Otemachi). From Takahama, a connecting bus whisks you the remaining distance to Matsuyama Kankō-kō Port. The hydrofoils zip across to Hiroshima in just over one hour for ¥4950 but there's not much to see en route – the view is much better from the regular ferries. Some services go via Kure, south-west of Hiroshima. The ferry takes from 2¾ to three hours depending on the port in Matsuyama, and costs ¥3710 1st class and ¥1850 2nd class to Hiroshima from Matsuyama Kankō-kō.

Other ferries operate to and from Matsuyama and Beppu, Kokura and Ōita on Kyūshū as well as Iwakuni, Kure, Mihara,

JAPAN

Onomichi and Yanai in Honshū, but check which of the Matsuyama ports services will operate from. From Matsuyama Kankō-kō, a hydrofoil zips across to Ocho (¥2660), Kinoe (¥3070), Omishima (¥3310), Setoda (¥4530) and Onomichi (¥4950).

Getting Around

Matsuyama has the private Iyo-tetsudō railway line and a tram service. The railway line is mainly useful for getting to and from the port for Hiroshima ferries.

The tram services cost a flat ¥150 anywhere in town. There's a loop line and major terminuses at Dōgo Onsen and outside the Matsuyama City station. The Ichiban-chō stop outside the Mitsukoshi department store and ANA Hotel is a good central stopping point.

MT ISHIZUCHI-SAN 石鎚山

Mt Ishizuchi-san (1982 metres), the highest mountain in Shikoku (indeed in all western Japan), is easily reached from Matsuyama. It's also a holy mountain and many pilgrim climbers make the hike, particularly during the July-August climbing season. In winter it's snowcapped.

From Matsuyama, you can take a bus to Tsuchigoya, south-east of the mountain. Alternatively, you can take a bus from the Iyo Saijō station on the Matsuyama-Takamatsu line to the Nishi-no-kawa cable-car station on the northern side. This route passes through the scenic **Omogo-kei Gorge**, an attraction in its own right. Out of season, bus services to the mountain are infrequent. You can climb up one way and down the other or even make a complete circuit from Nishi-no-kawa to the summit, down to Tsuchi Goya and then back to Nishi-no-kawa. Allow all day and an early start for the circuit.

The cable car takes about eight minutes straight up and down and costs ¥900 one way or ¥1700 return. The ride is followed by an optional chair lift (¥200 one way, ¥350 return), which slightly shortens the walk to Jōju, where there is a good view of the mountain from the **Ishizuchi-jinja Shrine**. From

Jōju, it's 3.5 km to the top, first gently downhill through forest, then uphill through forest, across a more open area and finally a steep and rocky ascent. Although there's a path, and often steps, all the way to the top, the fun way to make the final ascent is up a series of *kusari*, heavy chains draped down the very steep rock faces. Clambering up these chains is the approved pilgrimage method. The actual summit, reached by climbing along a sharp ridge, is a little beyond the mountain hut on the top.

UWAJIMA 宇和島

Uwajima (population 68,000) is a relatively quiet and peaceful place with a small but original castle, the shabby remnants of a fine garden, some pleasant temples and a notorious sex shrine. It makes an interesting pause between Kōchi and Matsuyama, although an afternoon or a morning is long enough for a reasonable look around.

Things to See

The **Uwajima-jō Castle** was never a great castle but it's an interesting three-storeyed structure and, dating from 1665, is an original, not a reconstruction. It once stood by the sea and although land reclamation has moved the sea well back, there are still good views over the town. Entry is free and it's open from 6 am to 5 pm, 9 am to 4 pm on Sunday and public holidays.

Once upon a time, many Shintō shrines had a connection to fertility rites but this aspect was comprehensively purged when puritanism was imported from the West following the Meiji Restoration. Nevertheless, a handful of holdouts survived and Uwajima's **Taga-jinja Shrine** is certainly one of them: it's totally dedicated to sex. There's a tree trunk phallus and various other bits and pieces around the temple grounds, but the three-storeyed sex museum is the temple's major attraction. Entry is ¥600.

Places to Stay

The *Uwajima Youth Hostel* (☎ 0895-22-7177) is a long walk from the town centre: when you get to the temples overlooking the town, it's another 650-metre walk uphill. From the shrine, the hostel is a 1.25 km walk, but there are fine views back down to the town. The hostel charges ¥2500 per night.

The *Kiya Ryokan* (☎ 0895-22-0101) is a relaxed and friendly place with per-person costs from ¥5200 without meals, ¥9000 with. It's just south of the shopping arcade.

One of the cheapest business hotels in town is the *Business Hotel Heiwa-sō* (☎ 0895-22-7711), where singles are ¥3000. It's a small place, and definitely at the shabby end of the business hotel spectrum, but it's cheap. It's over by Uwajima-jō Castle, opposite the post office.

Getting There & Away
Train You can reach Uwajima by train from Matsuyama (via Uchiko and Uno), a one hour 40 minute trip by limited express. From Kōchi, it takes 3¾ to 4½ hours by limited express via Kubokawa, where you change trains. If you want to head farther south and on to Cape Ashizuri-misaki, you'll have to resort to buses as the railway line from Kōchi terminates at Nakamura.

Bus & Ferry Direct bus services operate to Honshū from Uwajima, and there is also a ferry connection to Beppu on Kyūshū which travels via Yawatahama.

Getting Around
Uwajima is a good place to explore by bicycle since it's quiet and the traffic is not too bad. The tourist office across from the station rents bicycles for ¥100 an hour.

Kyūshū
九州

Kyūshū (population 14,500,000) is the third-largest and southernmost of the four major islands of Japan. Although somewhat isolated from the Japanese mainstream on Central Honshū, it has been an important entry point for foreign influence and culture.

Kyūshū is the closest island to Korea and China, and it was from Kyūshū that the Yamato tribe extended their power to Honshū. Some of the earliest evidence of Japanese civilisation can be seen at the archaeological excavations around Miyazaki and at the many ancient stone carvings in the Usuki area.

One of Kyūshū's prime attractions is Nagasaki, with its European-influenced history and its atomic tragedy. In the north, Fukuoka/Hakata is a major international arrival point and the terminus for the shinkansen line from Tokyo. In the centre of the island there is the massive volcanic caldera of Mt Aso, while more volcanic activity can be witnessed in the south at Sakurajima. Larger towns like Kagoshima and Kumamoto offer fine gardens and magnificent castles, while Beppu is one of Japan's major hot-spring centres. There are some good walking opportunities, particularly along the Kirishima volcano chain.

FUKUOKA/HAKATA
福岡／博多
Fukuoka/Hakata (population 1.2 million) is a somewhat confusing city as the airport is always referred to as Fukuoka and the shinkansen terminus as Hakata. Today it is the biggest city in Kyūshū but it was originally two separate towns – the lordly Fukuoka to the west of the Naka River and the common folks' Hakata to the east.

Although there are no compelling tourist attractions in Fukuoka, it's a pleasant city and easy to get around.

Places to Stay
Fukuoka itself has no youth hostel, but there is one in nearby Dazaifu, within easy commuting distance of the city (see under Places to Stay in the following Dazaifu section). The information counter in JR Hakata station has a list of inexpensive hotel accommodation in Fukuoka and staff can make reservations.

Getting There & Away
Air Fukuoka has international flights to

JAPAN

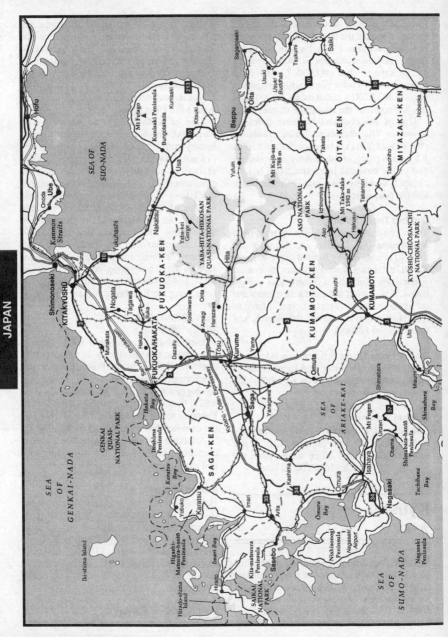

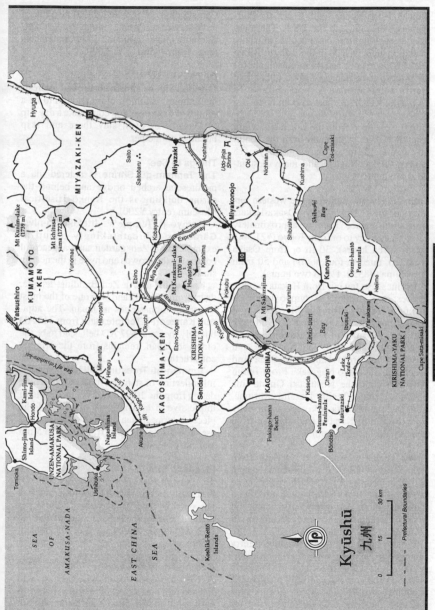

JAPAN

Taiwan, Hong Kong, South Korea, the Philippines, Australia and the USA. There are also internal flights to other centres in Japan, including more than 20 flights a day to Tokyo (¥25,350, one hour and 45 minutes); almost all of these go to Haneda Airport rather than Narita International Airport. Flights to Osaka (¥14,400) take just over an hour.

Bus Buses depart from the Kōtsū bus centre near JR Hakata station and from the Tenjin bus centre. There are buses to Tokyo (15 hours), Osaka, Nagoya and many destinations around Kyūshū.

Train JR Hakata station is the western terminus of the 1177-km Tokyo-Osaka-Hakata shinkansen service. There are approximately 15 services a day to or from Tokyo (¥21,300, six to seven hours), 30 to or from Osaka (¥14,310, three to four hours) and 50 from Hiroshima (¥8530, 1½ to two hours).

JR lines also fan out from Hakata to other centres in Kyūshū. The Nippō line runs through Hakata, Beppu, Miyazaki and Kagoshima; the Kagoshima line through Hakata, Kumamoto, Yatsushiro and Kagoshima; and both the Nagasaki and Sasebo lines from Hakata to Saga and Sasebo or Hakata to Nagasaki. From Tenjin railway station the Nishitetsu Omuta line operates through Tenjin, Dazaifu, Kurume, Yanagawa and Omuta. You can also travel by road or train to Karatsu and continue from there to Nagasaki by train.

Ferry There is also a ferry service from Fukuoka to Okinawa, to Iki-shima Island and other islands off Kyūshū. Ferries operate between the Tokyo ferry terminal and Kokura harbour, taking around 36 hours, and also between Osaka and Shinmonshi harbour, taking around 12 hours.

Fukuoka also offers an international ferry connection, with a high-speed hydrofoil service connecting the city with Pusan in Korea once daily. The hydrofoil is run by JR Kyūshū (☎ 095-281-2315); tickets cost ¥12,400 one way, ¥21,500 return, and the journey takes just under three hours. The

Camellia line (☎ 092-262-2323) also runs a ferry service to Pusan, though it takes considerably longer at around 15 hours. Tickets range from ¥8500 to ¥18,000.

DAZAIFU 太宰府

Dazaifu, with its superb shrine and interesting temples, is almost close enough to be a suburb of Fukuoka. You could take a day trip to Dazaifu or even stay there and skip Fukuoka altogether.

Things to See

The **Tenman-gū Shrine** is entered via a picturesque arched bridge and behind the shrine building is the Kankō Historical Museum (entry ¥200).

Kōmyō-ji Temple's **Ittekikaino-niwa Garden** is a breathtakingly beautiful example of a Zen garden and a peaceful contrast to the crowds and hype in the nearby shrine.

Kaidan-in, now a Zen Buddhist temple, dates from 761 AD and was one of the most important monasteries in Japan. The adjacent **Kanzeon-ji Temple** dates from 746 AD but only the great 697 AD bell, said to be the oldest in Japan, remains from the original construction.

Tenman-gū Treasure Hall has a wonderful collection of statuary, most of it of wood, dating from the 10th to 12th centuries and of impressive size. The style of some of the pieces is more Indian or Tibetan than Japanese. The display is open from 9 am to 5 pm and entry is ¥400.

Places to Stay

The *Dazaifu Youth Hostel* (☎ 092-922-8740) is actually in one of the Dazaifu temples; it has only 24 beds and charges ¥2400 per night. Ryokan and other accommodation can be found in the nearby town of Futsukaichi Onsen.

Getting There & Away

A Nishitetsu line train will take you to Futsukaichi railway station from Tenjin in Fukuoka in 20 to 30 minutes. From Futsukaichi, you'll have to change for the two-station ride to Nishitetsu-Dazaifu railway station. Alternatively, you can take a JR train from JR Hakata station to Kokutetsu-Futsukaichi (the JR station) and then a bus to Nishitetsu-Futsukaichi.

Getting Around
Bicycles can be rented from the information office next to Dazaifu railway station.

NAGASAKI 長崎
Nagasaki is a busy and colourful city (population 450,000) but its unfortunate fate as the second atomic bomb target quite obscures its fascinating early history of contact with the Portuguese and Dutch. The bomb itself actually missed its intended target towards the south of the city and scored a near direct hit on the largest Catholic church in Japan.

Things to See
The **A-Bomb Site** is in Urakami, the epicentre of the atomic explosion. Today it's a prosperous, peaceful suburb with modern shops, restaurants, cafes and even a couple of love hotels just a few steps from the epicentre. The **Hypocentre Park** has a black stone column marking the exact point above which the bomb exploded. Nearby are bomb-blasted relics including a section of the wall of the Urakami Cathedral and a buckled water tower.

The **A-Bomb Museum** is an ugly and badly designed building overlooking the Hypocentre Park. The four floors of photographs, reports, equipment and displays telling the story of the blast are quite enough to leave most visitors decidedly shaken. After that it's worth remembering that Nagasaki's atomic bomb packed only a tiny fraction of the destructive power of the countless nuclear weapons we are so lucky to possess today. Entry to the museum is ¥50 and it is open from 9 am to 6 pm (April to October) and from 9 am to 5 pm (November to March). Behind the museum is the Nagasaki Municipal Museum; entry is ¥100.

Places to Stay
There are four youth hostels in Nagasaki.

The *Nagasaki Youth Hostel* (☎ 0958-23-5032) has 132 beds at ¥2300 and is within walking distance of JR Nagasaki station; it's well signposted in English.

The *Oranda-zaka Youth Hostel* (☎ 0958-22-2730) is south of the city centre on the hilly Dutch Slopes and can be reached by tram No 5; get off at the Shimin-Byōin-mae stop. Beds are ¥2200.

The other two youth hostels are inconveniently located about 20 minutes by bus from JR Nagasaki station. They are the *Nanpōen Youth Hostel* (☎ 0958-23-5526) in Hamahira-chō, which costs ¥2300, and the *Uragami-ga-Oka Youth Hostel* (☎ 0958-47-8473) in Miyoshimachi, also ¥2300.

Central Nagasaki, obviously the best place to be based, has a couple of affordable ryokan. *Miyuki-sō* (☎ 0958-21-3487), five minutes north of the Maruyama entertainment district, has singles/doubles for ¥3300/7000. Slightly more expensive, but still a great deal, is the clean and friendly *Fukumoto Ryokan* (☎ 0958-21-0478) which has singles/doubles for ¥4000/8000.

Minshuku Tanpopo (☎ 0958-61-6230), a Japanese Inn Group member, is north of JR Nagasaki station and near the A-bomb site. Rooms are ¥4000 (singles) or ¥3500 per person in double or triple rooms.

Minshuku Siebold (☎ 0958-22-5623) is a small place with just five rooms from ¥3500 per person without meals. To get there, take tram No 3 from JR Nagasaki station, beyond the Suwa-jinja-mae stop to Shindaikumachi. Follow the road left from the tram stop and take the first right.

Places to Eat
Nagasaki's restaurant centre is around the Hamanomachi arcade and Maruyama entertainment area. For a cheap, quick breakfast in the railway station try the *Train D'Or* bakery.

Getting There & Away
Air There are flights between Nagasaki and Kagoshima, Tokyo (Haneda Airport), Osaka and Okinawa, as well as flights to and from a variety of lesser locations.

JAPAN

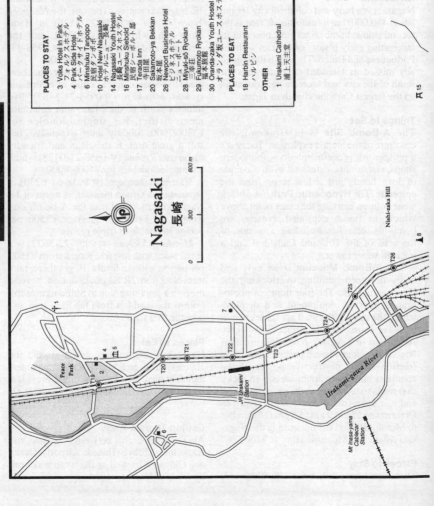

Nagasaki
長崎

PLACES TO STAY

3 Volks Hotel In Park
    フォルクスホテル
4 Park Side Hotel
    パークサイドホテル
6 Minshuku Tanpopo
    民宿タンポポ
10 Hotel New Nagasaki
    ホテルニュー長崎
14 Nagasaki Youth Hostel
    長崎ユースホステル
16 Minshuku Siebold
    民宿シーボルト邸
17 Terada Inn
    寺田屋
20 Sakamoto-ya Bekkan
    坂本屋
26 Newport Business Hotel
    ビジネスホテル
29 Fukumoto Ryokan
    福本旅館
30 Oranda-zaka Youth Hostel
    オランダ坂ユースホステル

PLACES TO EAT

18 Harbin Restaurant
    ハルピン

OTHER

1 Urakami Cathedral
    浦上天主堂
2 Hypocentre (Epicentre)
    Park
    原爆落下中心地
5 A-Bomb Museum
    長崎国際文化会館
7 One-Legged Torii
    片足鳥居
8 Martyrs Memorial
    26 二十六聖人殉教地
9 Prefectural Tourist
    Federation & Ken-ei
    Bus Terminal
    観光案内所
    県営バスターミナル
11 Post Office
    郵便局
12 Fukusaiji Zen Temple
    福済寺
13 Shōfuku-ji Temple
    聖福寺
15 Suwa-jinja Shrine
    諏訪神社
19 NTT
21 Megane-bashi Bridge
    眼鏡橋
22 Kōfuku-ji Temple
    興福寺
23 Enmei-ji Temple
    延命寺
24 Chosho-ji Temple
    長照寺
25 Kotai-ji Temple
    皓台寺
27 Harbour Cruise Office
    観光船大波止発着所

Peace Park

Urakami-gawa River

JR Urakami Station

Nishi-zaka Hill

Mt Inasa-yama Cablecar Station

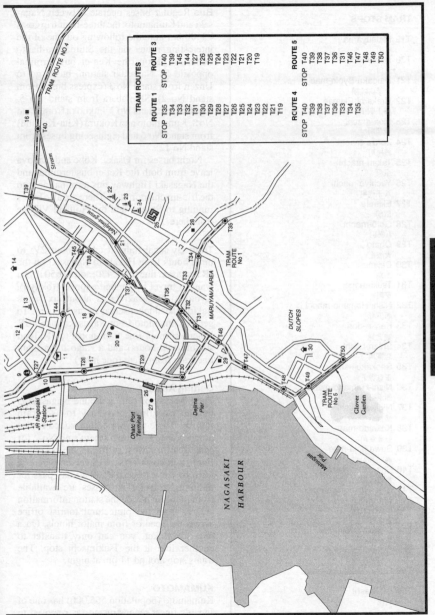

JAPAN

TRAM STOPS

T19 Matsuyama
松山

T20 Hamaguchi
浜口

T21 Daigaku-Byoin-mae
大学病院前

T22 Urakami-Ekimae
浦上駅前

T23 Mori-machi
茂里町

T24 Zenza-machi
銭座町

T25 Takari-machi
宝町

T26 Yachiyo-machi
八千代町

T27 Ekimae
駅前

T28 Gotō-machi
五島町

T29 Ohato
大波止

T30 Dejima
出島

T31 Tsuki-machi
築町

T32 Nishi-Hamano-machi
西浜町

T33 Kanko-dori
観光通

T34 Shian-bashi
思案橋

T35 Shokakuji-shita
正覚寺下

T36 Nishi-Hamano-machi
西浜町

T37 Nigiwai-bashi
眼橋

T38 Kokaido-mae
公会堂前

T39 Suwa-jinja-mae
諏訪神社前

T40 Shindaiku-machi
新大工町

T41 Shin-Nakagawa-machi
新中川町

T46 Irie-machi
入江町

T47 Shimin-Byoin-mae
市民病院前

T48 Ōurakaigan-dori
大浦海岸通

T49 Ōura- Tenshudo-shita
大浦天主堂下

T50 Ishi-bashi
石橋

Bus Regular buses operate between Naga-saki and Kumamoto; the three-hour trip costs ¥3600 but note the following outline of the interesting route via the Shimabara-hantō Peninsula. From the Ken-ei bus terminal opposite JR Nagasaki station, buses go to Unzen from stand No 3 (express buses from stand No 2), Shimabara from stand No 5, Sasebo from stand No 2, Fukuoka from stand No 8, Kumamoto and Kokura (Kita-Kyūshū) from stand No 6 and sightseeing buses from stand No 12.

Night buses for Osaka, Kōbe and Nagoya leave from both the Kei-ei bus terminal and the Nagasaki Highway bus terminal next to the Irie-machi tram stop. There are also buses running to Sasebo and the Holland Village from here.

Train By local train, it takes about 2½ to three hours from Hakata to Nagasaki on the JR Nagasaki line for ¥2470; add ¥1650 if you want to travel by limited express (tokkyū). Kyoto to Nagasaki takes about six hours (taking the shinkansen as far as Hakata). To get to Kumamoto from Nagasaki, take a JR Nagasaki main line train north to JR Tosu station (two hours) and a Kagoshima main line train from there (one hour).

Getting Around
The best way of getting around Nagasaki is on the excellent and easy-to-use tram service. There are four colour-coded routes numbered 1, 3, 4 and 5 (there's no No 2 for some reason). Most stops are signposted in English. It costs ¥100 to travel anywhere in town or you can get a ¥500 all-day pass for unlimited travel. The passes are available from the shop beside the station information centre, from the prefectural tourist office across the road or from major hotels. On a one-ride ticket, you can only transfer to another line at the Tsukimachi stop. The trams stop around 11 pm at night.

KUMAMOTO
Kumamoto (population 565,000) has one of Japan's finest reconstructed (as opposed to

original) castles plus a contender for Japan's 'best garden' title.

Things to See

The **Kumamoto-jō Castle** dominates the centre of town and, like many other castles in Japan, it looks superb at night. Entry to the castle grounds is ¥200, plus another ¥300 for entry into the castle itself. It's open from 8.30 am to 5.30 pm in summer and until 4.30 pm in winter.

Suizenji-kōen Garden is a fine and relatively expansive garden established in 1632. The Momoyama or 'stroll' garden's design is supposed to follow the 53 stations of the Tōkaidō, and the miniature Mt Fuji is certainly instantly recognisable. The garden is open from 7.30 am to 6 pm from March to October and from 8.30 am to 5 pm the rest of the year; entry is ¥200. A route No 2 tram will take you there from JR Kumamoto station or you can take a route No 2 or 3 tram from the central area. Get off at the Suizenji-kōen-mae stop.

Honmyō-ji Temple is to the north-west of the city centre, on the hills sloping up from the river. It's the temple and mausoleum of Kato Kiyomasa, the architect of Kumamoto's great castle. A steep flight of steps lead up to the mausoleum which was designed to be at the same height as the castle's keep. There's a treasure house with exhibits concerning Kiyomasa (open from 9 am to 4.30 pm daily except Monday, entry ¥300). Steps continue up the hill to another temple and then a final steep flight leads to the very top, from where there are good views over the town.

Places to Stay

Kumamoto has two hostels. The *Suizen-ji Youth Hostel* (☎ 096-371-9193) is about halfway between the town centre and Suizen-ji Garden and costs ¥2300 per night. The Misotenjin-mae stop on tram routes No 2 or 3 is close by. The *Kumamoto-Shiritsu Youth Hostel* (☎ 096-352-2441) is west of town, across the Iseri-gawa River, and costs ¥1600 or ¥1800 depending on the time of year. A bus from platform No 36 at the Kumamoto Kōtsu bus centre will take you there.

A 10-minute walk north of the station (crossing the railway lines, walking up the hill and taking the right fork in the road twice) brings you to *Ryokan Hanasato* (☎ 096-354-9445), which costs ¥5300 per person for a Japanese-style room with toilet and washbasin.

Getting There & Away

There are flights to Kumamoto from Tokyo, Osaka, Nagoya and Naha (Okinawa). The JR Kagoshima line between Hakata and Nishi-Kagoshima runs through Kumamoto, and there is also a JR line to Miyazaki on the south-eastern coast. Buses depart from the Kōtsu bus centre for Hakata, taking just over 1½ hours. The cost is ¥1850 for the basic futsū (local train) fare, add ¥1750 for limited express service.

Getting Around

Kumamoto has an effective tram service which will get you to most places of interest. On boarding the tram you take a ticket with your starting tram stop number; when you finish your trip a display panel at the front indicates the fare for each starting point. From the railway station to the castle/town centre costs ¥140. Alternatively you can get a ¥500 one-day pass for unlimited travel.

There are two tram routes. Route No 2 starts from near JR Kumamoto station, runs through the town centre and out past the Suizen-ji-kōen Garden. Route No 3 starts to the north, near Kami-Kumamoto station and merges with route No 2 just before the town centre. Services are frequent, particularly on route No 2.

MT ASO AREA   阿蘇山周辺

In the centre of Kyūshū, halfway between Kumamoto and Beppu, is the gigantic Mt Aso volcano caldera. There have been a series of eruptions over the past 30 million years but the explosion which formed the outer crater about 100,000 years ago must have been a big one. Depending on who is doing the measuring it's 20 to 30 km across

JAPAN

the original crater from north to south, 15 to 20 km east to west and 80 to 130 km in circumference. Inside this huge outer crater there are towns, roads, railways, farms, 100,000 people and a number of smaller volcanoes, some of them still active.

Things to See

Aso-gogaku (**Five Mountains of Aso**) are the five smaller mountains within the outer rim. They are Mt Eboshi-dake (1337 metres), Mt Nishima-dake (1238 metres), Mt Naka-dake (1216 metres), Mt Neko-dake (1408 metres) and Mt Taka-dake (1592 metres). Mt Naka-dake is currently the active volcano in this group. Mt Neko-dake, farthest to the east, is instantly recognisable from its craggy peak but Mt Taka-dake, between Neko-dake and Naka-dake, is the highest.

Recently **Mt Naka-dake** has been very active indeed. The cable car to the summit of Naka-dake was closed from August '89 to March '90 due to eruptions and it had only been opened for a few weeks when the volcano erupted again in April 1990, spewing dust and ash over a large area to the north. When Mt Naka-dake is not misbehaving, the cable car whisks you up to the summit in just four minutes (¥410 one way or ¥820 return). There are departures every eight minutes. The walk to the top takes less than half an hour. The 100-metre deep crater varies in width from 400 metres to 1100 metres, and there's a walk around the southern edge of the crater rim.

There are plenty of interesting walks around **Mt Aso**. You can walk all the way to the Aso-nishi cable-car station from the Aso Youth Hostel in about three hours. From the top of the cable car run you can walk around the crater rim to the peak of Mt Naka-dake and on to the top of Mt Taka-dake. From there you can descend either to Sensui-kyō, the bottom station of the old cable car run on the north-eastern side of Naka-dake, or to the road which runs between Taka-dake and Neko-dake. Either road will then take you to Miyaji, the next railway station east from Aso. The direct descent to Sensui-kyō is very

steep, so it's easier to continue back from Taka-dake to the Naka-dake rim and then follow the old cable-car route down to Sensui-kyō.

Despite the usual shortage of non-Japanese labelling, the **Aso Volcanic Museum** will undoubtedly fill a few gaps in the average person's knowledge of volcanoes. The museum is open from 9 am to 5 pm daily and admission is ¥820.

Places to Stay & Eat

The *Aso Youth Hostel* (☎ 0967-34-0804) is a 15 to 20-minute walk or a three-minute bus ride from JR Aso station and costs ¥1800 or ¥1950 depending on the time of year. There's a campground farther along the road from the hostel. *Aso No Fumoto* (☎ 0967-32-0264) is a good minshuku which costs ¥5600 per person. It is conveniently close to JR Aso station. There are a large number of pensions around Aso, most of them costing ¥7000 per person.

The *Murataya Ryokan Youth Hostel* (☎ 0967-62-0066) costs ¥2200 and is right in Takamori. The *Minami Aso Kokumin Kyūkamura* (☎ 0967-62-2111), a national vacation village, costs ¥7500 per person with two meals and from ¥5200 without; it's crowded in July and August.

The *YMCA/Youth Hostel Aso Camp* (☎ 0967-35-0124) is near JR Akamizu station, the third stop west of JR Aso station. The cost per night is ¥2000. *Minami Aso Kokuminshukusha* (☎ 0967-67-0078) is a people's lodge near the Aso-shimoda private railway station, the third stop west of Takamori. Rooms cost from ¥3600 without meals.

Getting There & Away

Train The JR Hōhi line operates between Kumamoto and Beppu via Aso. From JR Aso station there are buses to the Aso-nishi cable-car station. From Kumamoto to Aso, local trains take 1½ hours (¥930), while limited express trains take one hour and cost ¥1650. The Beppu-Aso limited express service costs ¥2800 and takes 2½ hours. To get to Takamori on the southern side of the crater, transfer from the JR Hōhi line to the Minamiaso private railway line at Tateno.

From March to November the *Aso Boy* steam train makes a daily run from Kumamoto to Aso, terminating at Miyaji railway station. The one-way fare is ¥1730.

Bus Bus No 266 starts from the Sankō bus terminal at JR Kumamoto station, stops at the Kumamoto Kōtsū bus centre then continues right across Kyūshū with an excursion to the Aso volcanic peaks and then along the Yamanami Highway to Beppu. The trip takes seven hours, including a short photo stop at the Kusasenri meadow in front of the Aso Volcanic Museum, and costs from ¥7500. Buses from Beppu to Aso take 2½ to three hours and cost ¥3000, plus another ¥1100 for the services that continue to the Aso-nishi cable-car station.

From Takamori, buses continue south to the mountain resort of Takachiho, a 1½ hour trip along a very scenic route.

Getting Around
Buses operate approximately hourly from JR Aso station via the Aso Youth Hostel to the Aso-nishi cable-car station on the slopes of Mt Naka-dake. The trip takes 40 minutes up, 30 minutes down and costs ¥600. There are less frequent services between Miyaji and Sensui-kyō on the northern side of Mt Naka-dake.

Buses also operate between Aso and Takamori. Cars can be rented at Aso and at Uchinomaki Onsen, one stop west from JR station.

KIRISHIMA NATIONAL PARK
霧島国立公園
The day walk from the village on the Ebino-kōgen Plateau to the summits of a string of volcanoes is one of the finest volcanic hikes in Japan. It's about 15 km from the summit of Mt Karakuni-dake to the summit of Mt Takachiho-no-mine and there's superb scenery all the way. If your time or energy is limited there are shorter alternatives such as a pleasant lake stroll on the plateau or a walk up and down Mt Karakuni-dake or Mt

Takachiho. The area is also noted for its spring wildflowers, fine hot springs and the impressive 75-metre Senriga-taki Waterfall.

Orientation & Information
There are tourist information centres with maps and some information in English at Ebino-kōgen Village and at Takachiho-gawara, the two ends of the volcano walk. There are restaurant facilities at both ends of the walk as well but Ebino-kōgen has most of the hotels, camping facilities etc. Kobayashi to the north and Hayashida, just to the south, are the main towns near Ebino-kōgen.

Things to See
The Ebino-kōgen lake circuit is a pleasantly relaxed stroll around a series of volcanic lakes – **Lake Rokkannon Mi-ike** has the most intense colour, a deep blue-green. Across the road from Lake Fudou, at the base of Mt Karakuni-dake, is a steaming **jigoku** (hot spring). From there you can make the stiff climb to the 1700-metre summit of Mt **Karakuni-dake**, skirting the edge of the volcano's deep crater before arriving at the high point on the eastern side.

The views across the almost lunar landscape from any of the volcano summits is otherworldly. If you have time you can continue from Mt Karakuni-dake to Mt Shishiko, Mt Shinmoe-dake, Mt Naka-dake and Takachiho-gawara, from where you can make the ascent of Mt Takachiho-no-mine.

Places to Stay
Much of the accommodation in Ebino-kōgen Village is expensive, and *Ebino Kōgen-sō* (☎ 0984-33-0161), a kokuminshukusha with accommodation from ¥5700 per person including two meals is about as cheap as it gets. Just north-east of the centre is the *Ebino-kōgen Rotemburo* with basic but cheap huts around a popular series of open-air hot-spring baths. There's also a campground. More accommodation can be found at Hayashida Onsen, between Ebino-kōgen and the Kirishima-jinja Shrine.

JAPAN

Getting There & Away

Train JR Kobayashi station to the north of Ebino-kōgen and Kirishima-jinja station to the south are the main railway junctions. From Miyazaki or Kumamoto take a JR Ebino-go limited express train to Kobayashi on the JR Kitto line, from where buses operate to Ebino. From Kagoshima (around one hour) or Miyazaki (1½ hours) you can take a JR Nippō limited express to Kirishima-jinja railway station. From there buses operate to Takachiho-gawara (about 45 minutes) and Ebino-kōgen.

Bus In many ways a direct bus to Ebino-kōgen is the best way to go. The two main approaches are Kagoshima and Miyazaki, though there are also direct buses from Fukuoka (4½ hours, ¥5000). Buses arrive and depart from Ebino-kōgen (the village on the Ebino Plateau, not to be confused with the town of Ebino down on the plains). You can arrive there from Kobayashi to the north, Miyazaki to the east or Kagoshima to the south and continue on another service. From Nishi-Kagoshima railway station in Kagoshima, buses depart for Kirishima Shrine and Hayashida Onsen at least hourly, and some continue on to Ebino-kōgen. It takes about two hours 10 minutes to Hayashida Onsen (¥1200). There are good views of the volcano scenery from buses driving along the Kirishima Skyline Rd.

KAGOSHIMA 鹿児島

Kagoshima (population 536,000) is the southernmost major city in Kyūshū and is a warm, sunny and relaxed place – at least, as long as Sakurajima's huge cone across Kinkō-wan Bay is behaving itself and not spitting out great clouds of dust and ash.

Things to See

The Shimazu family dominated Kagoshima's history, they also left the city its principal attraction, the beautiful bayside **Iso-teien Garden**. The garden contains the Shimazu Villa, the family home of the powerful Shimazu clan. The garden is north of the city centre (10 minutes by Hayashida line bus No 11 from the stop outside JR Kagoshima station) and is open from 8.30 am to 5.30 pm, except in winter, when it closes half an hour earlier. Entry is ¥800.

The **Shōko Shūseikan Museum**, adjacent to Iso-teien Garden, shows items relating to the Shimazu family and is housed in the building established in the 1850s as Japan's first factory. Entry is included in the garden admission fee, and opening hours are the same for both.

Places to Stay

The only youth hostel close to Kagoshima is the *Sakurajima Youth Hostel*. To get there you have to take the ferry across the bay (see the following Sakurajima section for details).

If you are not in the market for youth hostel accommodation, it is difficult to find inexpensive alternatives. The Nishi-Kagoshima station area is a good hunting ground for business hotels, but it's not where the cheapest places can be found. The cheapest places in town are over the river in central Kagoshima.

The cheapest hotel (only 22 singles) in the station area is the *Business Hotel Suzuya* (☎ 0992-58-2385), which has singles ranging from ¥3900 to ¥4300.

Probably the cheapest business hotel in town is right in the centre, close to a McDonald's and a Dom Dom Hamburger (so you can spend the money you've saved on junk food). The *Business Hotel Nichisenren* (☎ 0992-25-6161) has singles from ¥3000 and twins for ¥5500, but don't expect anything more than the basics. There are no bathrooms in the rooms, so you'll have to seek out the local sento.

The *Business Hotel Satsuma* (☎ 0992-26-1351) is another cheapie just south of the Mitsukoshi department store. It has singles with/without bath for ¥4100/3500 and twins for ¥6400/7400. Moving back down towards the Nishi Kagoshima station area, the *Hokke Club Kagoshima* (☎ 0992-26-0011) has singles/twins from ¥3400/7400.

Getting There & Away

Air Kagoshima's airport has overseas connections with Hong Kong and Seoul, as well as domestic flights to Tokyo, Osaka, Nagoya and a variety of other places in Honshū and Kyūshū.

Bus Hayashida buses to Kirishima and Ebino-kōgen go from the Takashimaya department store in the city centre. A good way of exploring Chiran and Ibusuki, south of Kagoshima, is by rented car, but you can also get there by bus from bus stop No 10 at Nishi-Kagoshima station. Buses also run to Miyazaki (Nishi-Kagoshima station bus stop No 8; 2½ hours; ¥2700), Kumamoto (bus stop No 17; 3½ hours; ¥3600), Fukuoka (bus stop No 16; 4½ hours; ¥5300), Osaka (bus stop No 8; 12½ hours; ¥12,000), Kyoto (bus stop No 16; 13½ hours; ¥12,600) and Nagoya (bus stop No 16; 14½ hours; ¥14,000).

Train Both the Nishi-Kagoshima and Kagoshima stations are arrival and departure points for other areas of Japan. While the Nishi-Kagoshima station is close to a greater choice of accommodation, the Kagoshima station is closer to Iso-teien Garden and the Sakurajima ferry. The stations are about equal distance north and south of the town centre.

It takes about 4½ hours by train from Fukuoka/Hakata via Kumamoto to Kagoshima on the JR Kagoshima line. The local train fare is ¥5150; add ¥2560 for the limited express service. The JR Nippō line connects Kagoshima with Kokura on the north-eastern tip of Kyūshū for ¥7210, plus ¥2780 for limited express. Nippō line trains operate via Miyazaki and Beppu.

Ferry There are car ferry services from Kagoshima to Osaka on Honshū and to a number of the South-West Islands, including Okinawa. For Osaka, ferries take 15½ hours and a 2nd-class ticket costs ¥9270; contact the Blue Highway Line (☎ 0992-22-4511). For ferries to Okinawa, bookings can be made with travel agents, but you can also contact the Queen Coral Marikku Line

(☎ 0992-25-1551), which has daily ferries to Okinawa via Amami Ō-shima, Tokuno-shima, Okino-Erabu-jima and Yoron-jima. The trip takes around 25 hours and costs ¥11,840 2nd class. The Akebono Maru company (☎ 0992-46-4141) does exactly the same route daily for the same price.

Getting Around

As in Nagasaki and Kumamoto, the tram service in Kagoshima is easy to understand, operates frequently and is the best way of getting around town. You can pay by the trip (¥160) or get a one-day unlimited travel pass for ¥500. The pass can also be used on city buses, and can be bought at the Nishi-Kagoshima station tourist information booth.

There are two tram routes. Route No 1 starts from Kagoshima station, goes through the city centre and on past the suburb of Korimoto to Taniyama. Route No 2 follows the same route through the city centre, then diverges at Takamibaba to Nishi-Kagoshima station and terminates at Korimoto.

SAKURAJIMA 桜島

Dominating the skyline from Kagoshima is the brooding cone of this decidedly over-active volcano.

Sakurajima actually has three peaks – Kita-dake (1117 metres), Naka-dake (1060 metres) and Minami-dake (1040 metres) – but at present only Minami is active.

Things to See

The **Sakurajima Visitors' Centre** near the ferry terminal has a variety of exhibits about the volcano, its eruptions and its natural history. The working model showing the volcano's growth over the years is the centre's main attraction. It is open from 9 am to 5 pm daily, except Monday, and entry is free.

Although visitors are not permitted to climb the volcano there are several good lookout points. The **Yunohira lookout** is high on the side of the volcano. The **Arimura lava lookout** is east of Furusato Onsen.

Places to Stay
The *Sakurajima Youth Hostel* (☎ 0992-93-2150) is near the ferry terminal and visitors' centre, and has beds for ¥1850 or ¥2050, depending on the season. The ferry service is so short that it's possible to stay here and commute to Kagoshima.

Getting There & Away
The passenger and car ferry service shuttles back and forth between Kagoshima and Sakurajima. The trip takes 15 minutes and costs ¥150 per person, payable at the Sakurajima end. From Kagoshima station or the Sakurajima Sanbashi-dōri tram stop, the ferry terminal is a short walk through the Nameriwaka market area.

Getting Around
Getting around Sakurajima without your own transport can be difficult. You can rent bicycles from near the ferry terminal but a complete circuit of the volcano would be quite a push, even without the climbs to the various lookouts. Three-hour sightseeing bus tours operate several times daily from the ferry terminal and cost ¥1700. JR buses operate from the Sakurajima ferry terminal up to the Arimura lookout for ¥330.

TAKACHIHO 高千穂
The mountain resort town of Takachiho is about midway between Nobeoka on the coast and Mt Aso in the centre of Kyūshū. It's famed for its beautiful gorge and for a number of interesting shrines. There's a helpful tourist information counter by the tiny train station.

Things to See
The **Takachiho-kyō Gorge**, with its waterfalls, overhanging rocks and sheer walls, is the town's major attraction. There's a one-km walk alongside the gorge, or you can inspect it from below in a rowboat, rented for a pricey ¥1000 for 40 minutes. The gorge is about two km from the town centre, a ¥700 ride by taxi. Buses run to the gorge for ¥210, but they are not that frequent.

Takachiho-jinja Shrine, about a km from

JR Takachiho station, is surrounded by wonderful tall trees. The local Iwato Kagura dances are performed from 8 to 9 pm each evening, and entry is ¥300.

The Iwato-gawa River splits the **Amano Iwato-jinja Shrine** into two parts. The main shrine, Nishi Hongu, is on the western bank of the river, while on the eastern bank is Higashi Hongu, at the actual cave where the sun goddess hid and was lured out by the first performance of the Iwato Kagura dance. From the main shrine it's a 15-minute walk to the cave. The shrine is eight km from Takachiho. Buses leave every 45 minutes from the bus station and cost ¥340; a taxi would cost around ¥1500.

A beautiful short walk from the Amano Iwato Shrine alongside a picture-postcard stretch of stream takes you to the Amano **Yasugawara Cavern**. There, it is said, the gods conferred on how they could persuade the sun goddess to leave her hiding place and thus bring light back to the world. Visitors pile stones into small cairns all around the cave entrance.

Places to Stay
There are three youth hostels in the area, each costing ¥2300 a night. Right in the town centre, the *Yamatoya Ryokan & Youth Hostel* (☎ 0982-72-2243/3808) is immediately recognisable by the huge figure painted on the front. The *Takachiho Youth Hostel* (☎ 0982-2-5152) is a couple of km from the centre, near the JR Amano-Iwato station. The *Iwato Furusato Youth Hostel* (☎ 0982-74-8254/8750) is near the Amano Iwato Shrine. Nightly costs at all three are ¥2300.

Folkcraft Ryokan Kaminoya (☎ 0982-72-2111) is a member of the Japanese Inn Group and just down from the bus station, right in the centre of Takachiho. The friendly owner speaks good English and rooms range from ¥4000 or ¥6500 with two meals. You can get cheaper rates if you do without the meals.

Getting There & Away
The JR Takachiho line runs inland from Nobeoka on the coast, taking just over 1½ hours and costing ¥1300. Alternatively, there

are bus services to Takachiho: buses take about three hours 15 minutes from Kumamoto, 3½ hours from Fukuoka (¥3910), 1½ hours from Noboeka (¥1650) or less than an hour from Takamori near Mt Aso.

Getting Around
Although you can walk to the gorge and the Takachiho Shrine, the other sites are some distance from town and public transport is a problem. Regular tours leave from the bus station: the 'A Course' (¥1100) covers everything, while the 'B Course' (¥750) misses the Amano Iwato Shrine.

Okinawa & the South-West Islands
沖縄・南西諸島

The South-West Islands, or Nansei Shotō as they are known in Japanese, meander for more than 1000 km in the direction their name suggests from the southern tip of Kyūshū to Yonaguni Island, just a strenuous stone's throw (a little over 100 km) from the east coast of Taiwan.

A warm climate, fine beaches, excellent scuba diving and traces of traditional Okinawan culture are the prime attractions. But don't think of these islands as forgotten backwaters with a mere handful of visitors – both ANA and JAL fly tourists to Okinawa from mainland Japan by the 747-load and even the local flights from Okinawa to other islands in the chain are by 737s.

OKINAWA ISLAND 沖縄
Okinawa is the largest and most important island in the Nansei-shotō chain. Okinawa had developed distinct cultural differences to mainland Japan, particularly in architecture, but the destruction of WW II obliterated almost every trace of the old architecture. The USA retained control of Okinawa after the war, handing it back in 1972.

Orientation
Naha (population 300,000) is the capital of Okinawa; it was flattened in WW II and little trace remains of the old Ryūkūan culture. Today Naha is principally a gateway to other destinations.

Okinawa City is the US military centre on Okinawa, centred around the Kadena Air Force Base, which was the initial target of the US invasion. The prewar village has mushroomed into a population of over 100,000. The city has all the hallmarks of American influence, from pizzerias to army surplus stores.

Places to Stay
Naha has two youth hostels. The *Naha Youth Hostel* (☎ 0988-57-0073) is the largest, with room for 80 people at ¥2400 a night. It's south of the Meiji Bridge, near the road to the airport in Onoyama. It's closed from 21 to 30 January. From the airport you can take a No 101 or 24 bus and get off at the Kōenmae stop.

The *Harumi Youth Hostel* (☎ 0988-67-3218/4422) is north of the city towards Route 58. It accommodates 38 people at ¥2400.

Just off Kokusai-dōri is *Hotel Sankyo* (☎ 0988-67-0105), a basic but comfortable enough business hotel with rooms from ¥4000. In an alley just around the corner from the Sankyo are a couple of ryokan with cheaper rates. If you are walking from the Sankyo, they are on the left and have fluorescent signs (no English) outside. The second place has basic rooms for ¥2500.

Places to Eat
The best place to seek out something to eat in Naha is Kokusai-dōri and the sidestreets that run off from it. All the usual fast-food outlets are well represented here and there are plenty of inexpensive Japanese restaurants sporting plastic food displays in their windows.

Okinawa City, no doubt due to the American military presence, is also fast-food city.

JAPAN

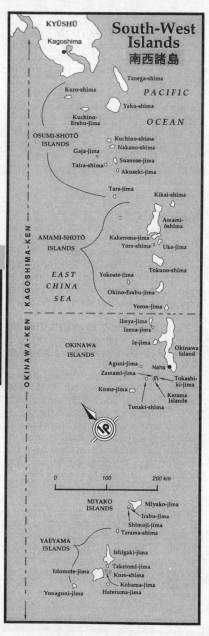

South-West Islands 南西諸島

Getting There & Away

Air Northwest Orient has direct flights from the USA, Continental from Guam, JAL from Hong Kong and China Airlines from Taipei. JAL, ANA, ANK, JAS and South-West Airlines (SWAL) connect major cities on the main islands with Naha, including Fukuoka (1½ hours, ¥23,100), Kagoshima (1½ hours, ¥21,050), Nagoya (two hours, ¥32,750), Osaka (two hours, ¥29,100), Hiroshima (two hours, ¥26,600), Tokyo (2½ hours, ¥34,900) and a number of other centres. SWAL have the most connections to the other South-West Islands.

Boat Various operators have shipping services from Tokyo, Osaka, Kōbe, Kagoshima and other ports to Naha. The schedules are complex and there is a wide variety of fares. From Tokyo it takes about 50 hours (¥20,000 to ¥50,000), from Osaka about 36 hours (¥15,000 to ¥40,000), from Kōbe about 40 hours (¥15,000 for ¥40,000) and from Kagoshima about 24 hours (¥12,000 to ¥30,000). Shipping companies include Arimura Sangyo, Kansai Kisen, Oshima Unyu, Ryūkyū Kaiun (RKK) and Terukuni Yusen. The frequency of services varies from eight to 10 a month from Tokyo to more than 30 a month from Kagoshima.

From Naha Port boats head south to Ishigaki-jima and Miyako-jima islands, north to Yoron-jima Island and Kagoshima. From Naha New Port there are boats to Fukuoka/Hakata, Kagoshima, Kōbe, Osaka and Tokyo, and also to Miyako and Ishigaki islands. From the Tomai Port, boats operate to a number of the smaller islands including Kume, Aguni and the Daito islands.

The Arimura Sangyo shipping company (☎ 0988-68-2191 in Naha, 03-3562-2091 in Tokyo), operates a weekly boat service between Okinawa and Taiwan. Boats depart from Naha Port on Friday and from Keelung (or sometimes Kaohsiung) in Taiwan on Sunday. The service generally operates directly between either Naha and Keelung or Naha and Kaohsiung, but it occasionally (check beforehand) stops at Miyako and

Ishigaki. The trip takes about 19 hours and costs ¥12,000 to ¥24,000.

Getting Around
The busy Naha Airport is only three km from the town centre, and is 10 minutes by taxi for ¥800 to ¥1100 or 12 minutes by bus No 24 or 102 for ¥170. The buses run three to six times an hour (7 am to 10 pm) via the main bus station and then down Kokusai-dōri. The airport has three widely spaced terminals: international, domestic 1 (for mainland Japan) and domestic 2 (for the South-West Islands).

The bus system is relatively easy to use. For local town buses, you simply insert ¥170 into a slot next to the driver as you enter. For longer trips you collect a ticket showing your starting point as you board and pay the appropriate fare as you disembark; a board at the front shows the various starting numbers and the equivalent fares. Buses run from Naha to destinations all over the island.

A number of places rent scooters and motorbikes. A 50cc scooter costs from ¥1500 for three hours to ¥3000 for a day; a 250cc motorbike, ¥4000 to ¥8000. Try Sea Rental Bikes (☎ 0988-64-5116) or Trade (☎ 0988-63-0908).

ISLANDS AROUND OKINAWA
Apart from the islands just a stone's throw from the Okinawan coast, there are three other island groups a little farther away.

Iheya-jima & Izena-jima Islands 伊平屋島・伊是名島
North of Okinawa, these two islands have good beaches and snorkelling and a number of hotels and minshuku. A daily ferry runs from Motobu's port to Izena (1½ hours) and to Iheya (another 20 minutes).

Kerama Islands
There are about 20 islands in this group west of Okinawa, only four of them inhabited. The islands have fine beaches, some good walks, great lookouts and some of the best

scuba diving in Japan. Ferries from Naha take one to 1½ hours; flights are also available.

Kume Island
Farther west of the Kerama Islands is beautiful Kume Island, with its superb scenery, excellent beaches and the long curving sweep of sandbank at Sky Holiday Reef, just east of the island. The **Uezu House** is a samurai-style home dating from 1726.

There are ryokan and minshuku on the island, particularly near **Eef Beach** where there is also a small resort hotel. Day trips can be made from Eef Beach to Sky Holiday Reef.

From Naha, ferries to the island take about 3½ hours, and SWAL has regular daily flights, taking 35 minutes at a cost of ¥5360. You can get around the island by rented car, scooter or bicycle.

OTHER ISLANDS
Miyako Islands 宮古列島
About 300 km south-west of Okinawa, directly en route to the Yaeyama Islands, is the small Miyako group, comprising Miyako itself and, a few km to the west, Irabu-jima and Shimoji-jima islands, plus a scattering of smaller islands.

The prime attraction and entry point for the group is **Miyako-jima Island**. Like the other Okinawan islands, it offers beaches and diving; and, since it escaped the destruction rained down upon Okinawa itself, some traces of Ryūkū culture and architecture remain.

Yaeyama Islands 八重山列島
Ishigaki is the major flight destination for the Yaeyama island group, and boat services fan out from its harbour to the other islands. There are a few sights in the town of Ishigaki itself, and for most visitors it's mainly of interest as a jumping-off point to the other islands. Ishigaki is about 400 km south-west of Okinawa Island.

JAPAN

Appendix – Climate Charts

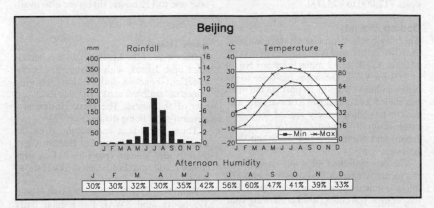

Beijing

Rainfall / Temperature

Afternoon Humidity

J	F	M	A	M	J	J	A	S	O	N	D
30%	30%	32%	30%	35%	42%	56%	60%	47%	41%	39%	33%

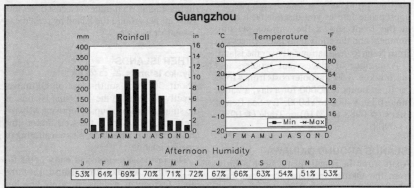

Guangzhou

Rainfall / Temperature

Afternoon Humidity

J	F	M	A	M	J	J	A	S	O	N	D
53%	64%	69%	70%	71%	72%	67%	66%	63%	54%	51%	53%

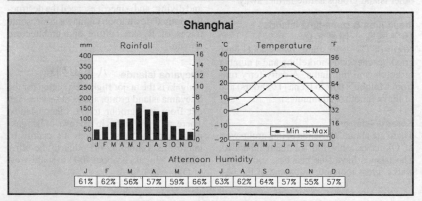

Shanghai

Rainfall / Temperature

Afternoon Humidity

J	F	M	A	M	J	J	A	S	O	N	D
61%	62%	56%	57%	59%	66%	63%	62%	64%	57%	55%	57%

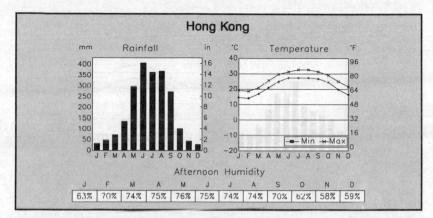

Hong Kong

Rainfall | Temperature

Afternoon Humidity

J	F	M	A	M	J	J	A	S	O	N	D
63%	70%	74%	75%	76%	75%	74%	74%	70%	62%	58%	59%

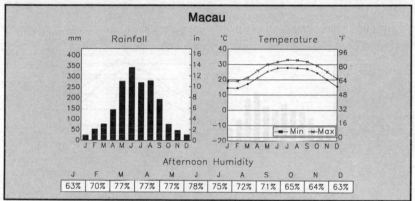

Macau

Rainfall | Temperature

Afternoon Humidity

J	F	M	A	M	J	J	A	S	O	N	D
63%	70%	77%	77%	77%	78%	75%	72%	71%	65%	64%	63%

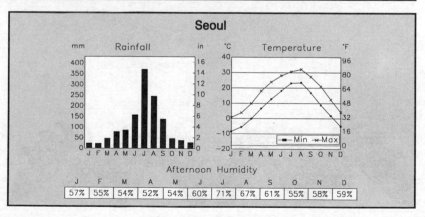

Seoul

Rainfall | Temperature

Afternoon Humidity

J	F	M	A	M	J	J	A	S	O	N	D
57%	55%	54%	52%	54%	60%	71%	67%	61%	55%	58%	59%

Taipei

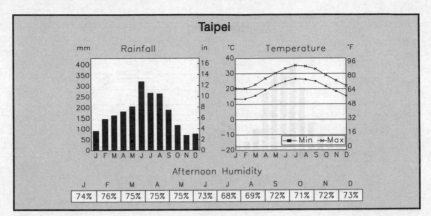

	J	F	M	A	M	J	J	A	S	O	N	D
Afternoon Humidity	74%	76%	75%	75%	75%	73%	68%	69%	72%	71%	72%	73%

Tokyo

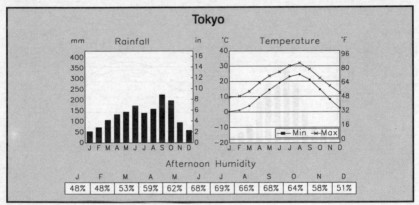

	J	F	M	A	M	J	J	A	S	O	N	D
Afternoon Humidity	48%	48%	53%	59%	62%	68%	69%	66%	68%	64%	58%	51%

Index

ABBREVIATIONS

(Chi)   China
(HK)   Hong Kong
(Jap)   Japan

(Mac)   Macau
(Mon)   Mongolia
(NK)   North Korea

(SK)   South Korea
(Tai)   Taiwan

MAPS

Beijing (Chi) 90-1
  Beijing Bicycle Tour 100
  Central Beijing 94-5

Cheju City (SK) 366-7
Chengdu (Chi) 193
Cheung Chau (HK) 261
Chiayi (Tai) 474-5
China 54-5
  Airfares 86
Chongqing (Chi) 198
Coloane Island (Mac) 390

Dali (Chi) 189

Guangzhou (Chi) 166-7
Guilin (Chi) 178

Hangzhou (Chi) 149
Hiroshima (Jap) 570
Hokkaidō Island (Jap) 590-1
Hong Kong 224-5
  Hong Kong Districts 223
  Hong Kong Island 270-1
  Central Hong Kong 276-7
  New Territories 258-9
  Public Buses 245
Honshū (Jap)
  Central 538
  Northern 577
  Western 568-9
Hualien (Tai) 468-9

International Airfares 44-8

Japan 479
  Domestic Airfares 504
  South West Islands 624

Kansai Region (Jap) 549
Kashgar (Chi) 213
Kowloon (HK) 250
Kunming (Chi) 186
Kyŏngju City (SK) 352
Kyoto (Jap) 550-1
  Around Kyoto 554-5
Kyūshū (Jap) 610-1

Lamma (HK) 262
Lantau Island (HK) 266-7
Lanzhou (Chi) 205
Lhasa (Chi) 216

Macau Peninsula (Mac) 372-3
  Central Macau 378-9
MASS Transit Railway 247
Mokp'o (SK) 362
Mongolia 395
  Airfares 412
Mt Fuji Area (Jap) 531

Nagasaki (Jap) 614-5
Nanjing (Chi) 134-5
Nara City (Jap) 565
Nikkō (Jap) 534
North Korea 284
North-East Asia 10

P'yŏngyang (NK) 298-9
Peng Chau (HK) 264
Pusan (SK) 356
  Subway 359

Qingdao (Chi) 124
Qufu (Chi) 129

Sanya (Chi) 175
Seoul (SK) 334-5

Subway 346
Shanghai (Chi) 140-1
Shikoku Island (Jap) 602
Shinjuku (Jap) 522
Sokch'o (SK) 350
South Korea 306-7
  Airfares 329
Suzhou (Chi) 132

Tai'an (Chi) 126
Taichung (Tai) 460-1
Taipa (Mac) 389
Taipei (Tai) 448
  Central Taipei 450-1
Taitung (Tai) 472
Taiwan 424
  Airfares 445
Tianjin (Chi) 108
Tokyo (Jap) 508-9
  Around Tokyo 528
  Central Tokyo 512
Tsimshatsui (HK) 252-3

Ueno (Jap) 518
Ulaan Baatar (Mon) 414-5
  Ulaan Baatar Environs 420
Ürümqi (Chi) 210

Wanchai-Causeway Bay (HK)
  255
Wuhan (Chi) 158-9

Xi'an (Chi) 118
Xiamen & Gulangyu (Chi) 152

Yangshuo (Chi) 181
Yŏsu (SK) 360

Zhanjiang (Chi) 173

TEXT

Map references are in **bold** type

accommodation 26
air travel 28-34, **44-8**
  air travel glossary 30-31

to/from North-East Asia 28-30,
  31, 32, 33
within North-East Asia 43-6
Aizu Wakamatsu (Jap) 576-8
Akan Kohan (Jap) 599, 600

Akan National Park (Jap)
  599-600
Alishan (Tai) 476-8
Alishan Forest Recreation Area
  (Tai) 477

Amihari Onsen (Jap) 583
Anhui (Chi) 146, 147-8
Anshun (Chi) 183-4
Antu (Chi) 113
Aomori (Jap) 583-4
Asahidake Onsen (Jap) 596
Atami (Jap) 527

Badaling (Chi) 106
Baihe (Chi) 113
Bandai-Kōgen Plateau (Jap)
    578-9
Banpo (Chi) 120
Baoguo (Chi) 197
Beidaihe (Chi) 111
Beijing (Chi) 89-105, **90-1,
    94-5, 100**
    cycling 99-101
    entertainment 103
    getting around 104-5
    information 89-93
    orientation 89
    places to eat 103
    places to stay 101-3
    things to buy 103
    things to see 93-9
Bifue (Jap) 601
Bihoro (Jap) 598
Bingling Si Caves (Chi) 206
Bonsai (Jap) 485
buddhism 60, 226, 309, 375,
    398, 426, 480, 486
bunraku, *see* theatre

calligraphy (Chi) 59
Cape Ashizuri-Misaki (Jap) 606
Cape Irō-zaki (Jap) 527
Cape Muroto-Misaki (Jap) 606
catholicism 60, 375
Central (HK) 251
Central Cross-Island Highway
    (Tai) 458-9
Ch'unch'ŏn (SK) 348-9
Ch'ungmun Beach (SK) 365
Changbaishan Nature Reserve
    (Chi) 113
Changchun (Chi) 112
Changsha (Chi) 161-2
Cheju City (SK) 364-5, **366-7**
Chejudo (Cheju Island) (SK)
    363-8
Chengde (Chi) 110
Chengdu (Chi) 192-6, **193**
Cheung Chau (HK) 260, 273,
    280, 283, **261**
Chiayi (Tai) 473-6, **474-5**
China 53-221, **54-5, 86**
    accommodation 77
    books 74

business hours 71
climate 58
drinks 81
economy 59
electricity 74
embassies 67-8
entertainment 81-2
festivals 72
food 77-81
geography 58
getting around 85-9
getting there & away 82-5
government 58-9
health 75
highlights 76
history 53-8
language 60-7
media 75
money 68-9
photography 75
population 59
post 72
public holidays 71
religion 60
shopping 82
taboos 59
telephones 72-4
time 74
tourist offices 70-1
visas 67-8
women travellers 75
work 76
Chingching Farm (Tai) 465
Chōkoku-no-Mori (Jap) 529
Chongqing (Chi) 197-200, **198**
christianity 226, 309, 426, 486
Chushan (Tai) 477
Clearwater Bay (HK) 260
Climate Charts 626
Coloane (Mac) 387, **390**
confucianism 60, 226, 309, 426,
    486
courses 25
    China 76
    Japan 496
    South Korea 323, 340
    Taiwan 454
cycling 236, 248, 324, 471, 601,
    596

Dadonghai (Chi) 175
Daisetsuzan National Park (Jap)
    595-7
Dalanzadgad (Mon) 421
Dali (Chi) 188-90, **189**
Datong (Chi) 115-6
Dazaifu (Jap) 612-3
Dazu (Chi) 200
Dewa Sanzan (Jap) 586-7

diving (Jap) 625
Dongsheng (Chi) 202-3
Dunhuang (Chi) 207-8

Ebino-kōgen Village (Jap) 619
Eef Beach (Jap) 625
electricity 17
Emei (Chi) 197
Emeishan (Chi) 196-7

Fanling (HK) 257
Fengyuan (Tai) 459
food 26
Fujian (Chi) 151-5
Fujinomiya (Jap) 532
Fukuoka/Hakata (Jap) 609-12
Fuli (Chi) 180
Funadomari (Jap) 595

gagaku 484
Ganlanba (Menghan) (Chi) 191
Gansu (Chi) 204-8
Gokayama (Jap) 542
Golmud (Chi) 220-1
Gongfu (Chi) 59
Gōra (Jap) 529
Goshikinuma (Jap) 578
Gotemba (Jap) 532
Grasslands (Chi) 202
Great Wall (Chi) 105-6
Guangdong (Chi) 162-72
Guangxi (Chi) 176-82
Guangzhou (Canton) (Chi)
    164-71, **166-7**
Guilin (Chi) 176-80, **178**
Guiyang (Chi) 182-3
Guizhou (Chi) 182-4
Gulangyu Island (Chi) 154, 155,
    152
Guling (Chi) 156
Gyantse (Chi) 218

Hac Sa Beach (Mac) 392
Hachigōme (Jap) 585
Hagi (Jap) 576
Haikou (Chi) 172-5
Hainan (Chi) 172-6
Hakodate (Jap) 588-9
Hakone (Jap) 527-30
Hakuba (Jap) 543-4
Hamasadamachi (Jap) 575
Hanging Monastery (Chi) 116
Hangzhou (Chi) 148-51, **149**
Hankou (Chi) 157-60
Happō-one (Jap) 543
Har Us Nuur (Mon) 421
Harbin (Chi) 114
Harhorin (Mon) 420
Hayashida Onsen (Jap) 619

health 18-23
Hebei (Chi) 110-1
Hefei (Chi) 146
Heilongjiang (Chi) 114-5
Henan (Chi) 122-3
hiking 24, 76, 113, 183, 191,
    196, 236, 273, 303, 323-4,
    347, 350, 369, 383, 408, 420,
    438, 463, 465-77, 496, 530-2,
    543-4, 545, 563, 578-9,
    583-7, 584, 585-7, 594-6,
    599, 601, 608, 619
Himeji (Jap) 564
Hiraizumi (Jap) 582
Hirosaki (Jap) 584-5
Hiroshima (Jap) 569-73, 570
Hohhot (Chi) 201-2
Hohuanshan (Tai) 464-5
Hokkaidō (Jap) 588-601, 590-1
Hong Kong 222-83, 223, 224-5,
    245, 247, 276-7
  accommodation 237
  books 233
  business hours 231
  climate 222
  drinks 238-40
  economy 223
  embassies 228
  entertainment 280-3
  fax 233
  festivals 232
  food 238-9
  geography 222
  getting around 244-9
  getting there & away 241-4
  government 223
  health 235
  history 222
  language 226-8
  media 234
  money 229-30
  photography 235
  places to eat 273-80
  places to stay 263-73
  population 223
  post 232
  public holidays 231
  religion 226
  shopping 240-1
  telephones 233
  tourist offices 230-1
  visas 228
  work 235
Hong Kong Island 251-6, 270-1
  entertainment 281-3
  North side 251-4
  places to eat 278-80
  places to stay 269-72
  South side 254-6

Hongdo (SK) 363
Honshū (Jap)
  Central 536-48, 538
  Northern 576-87, 577
  Western 567-76, 568-9
Horiuchi (Jap) 576
Hovd (Mon) 421
Hovsgol Nuur (Mon) 421
Hsiao Yehliu (Tai) 467
Hualien (Tai) 466-7, 468-9
Huangguoshu Falls (Chi) 183
Huangshan (Chi) 146-8
Huashan (Chi) 121
Huangshan City (Chi) 146
Hubei (Chi) 157-61
Hujirt (Mon) 421
Hunan (Chi) 161-2

ice skating, see skating
Iheya-jima Island (Jap) 625
ikebana (Jap) 485
Inner Mongolia 201-3
Irabu-jima Island (Jap) 625
Ishigaki (Jap) 625
Islam 398
Itsukushima-jinja Shrine (Jap)
    573
Iwaobetsu (Jap) 598
Izena-jima Island (Jap) 625
Izu-Hantō Peninsula (Jap) 527
Izumo (Jap) 575
Izumo Taisha (Jap) 575

Japan 479-625, 504, 624
  accommodation 497-9
  bargaining 491
  books 494
  business hours 492
  climate 483
  costs 491
  drinks 499-500
  economy 483
  embassies 489-90
  entertainment 500
  food 499
  gardens 485
  geography 482
  getting around 503-7
  getting there & away 501-3
  government 483
  health 495
  history 480-2
  language 486-9
  media 494-5
  money 490-1
  photography 495
  population 484
  post 492-3
  public holidays 492

religion 486
shopping 500-1
taboos 485
telephones 493
time 493
tipping 491
tourist offices 491-2
visas 489-90
women travellers 495
work 495
Ji'nan (Chi) 127
Jiangsu (Chi) 130-8
Jiangxi (Chi) 155-7
Jilin (Chi) 112-4
Jingbo Lake (Chi) 114-5
Jinghong (Chi) 191
Jiuzhaigou (Chi) 200-1
Jokamachi (Jap) 576

kabuki, see theatre (Jap) 485
Kaesŏng (NK) 302
Kafuka (Jap) 595
Kagoshima (Jap) 620-1
Kaifeng (Chi) 122
Kairaku-en (Jap) 485
Kaiyuan (Tai) 470
Kakunodate (Jap) 585-6
Kamakura (Jap) 535-6
Kamikawa (Jap) 596
Kamikōchi (Jap) 545
Kanazawa (Jap) 546-8
Kansai Region (Jap) 548-67, 549
Karakoram Highway (Chi) 214
karate 486
Kashgar (Chi) 212-4, 213
Kawaguchi-ko (Jap) 532
Kawayu Onsen (Jap) 599
Kayasan National Park (SK) 354
kendō 486
Kenroku-en (Jap) 485
Kenroku-en Garden (Jap) 546
Kenting (Tai) 471-3
Kerama Islands (Jap) 625
Kim Il-sung 286
Kim Jong-il 287
Kinkazan Island (Jap) 581
Kirishima National Park (Jap)
    619-20
Kiso Valley (Jap) 542-3
Kōbe (Jap) 562-4
Kōchi (Jap) 605-6
Kompira-san Shrine (Jap) 604
Kongju (SK) 369
Kōraku-en (Jap) 485
Korea
  East-Central 351-5
  North-East 348-51
  South-East 355-8
  South-West 358-63

Korea *continued*
West-Central 368-70
Korean Folk Village (SK) 348
Kososhimachi (Jap) 575
Kotohira (Jap) 604
Kowloon (HK) 249-51, **250**
Entertainment 280
Places To Eat 274-8
Places To Stay 265-9
Things To See 249-51
Kukuan (Tai) 459-62
Kumamoto (Jap) 616-7
Kume Island (Jap) 625
Kŭmgangsan (NK) 302
Kunming (Chi) 184-8, **186**
Kurashiki (Jap) 567-9
Kushiro (Jap) 598-9
Kutsugata (Jap) 594
Kwangju (SK) 363
Kyŏngju (SK) 351-4, **352**
Kyoto (Jap) 548, **550-1, 554-5**
getting around 558-9
getting there & away 558
information 548
places to eat 557
places to stay 556-7
things to see 548-56
Kyūshū (Jap) 609-23, **610-1**

Lake Ashino-ko (Jap) 529
Lake Kussharo-ko (Jap) 599
Lake Mashū-ko (Jap) 599
Lake Rokkannon Mi-ike (Jap) 619
Lake Shikotsu-ko (Jap) 600
lamaism 398
Lamma (HK) 260, 273, 280, 283, **262**
Lantau (HK) 262-3, 273, 280, **266-7**
Lanyu (Tai) 470-1
Lanzhou (Chi) 204-6, **205**
Leshan (Chi) 197
Lhasa (Chi) 215-8, **216**
Liaoning (Chi) 111-2
Lijiang (Chi) 190
Lintong (Chi) 119
Lishan (Tai) 462-3
Longmen Cave Temples (Chi) 122
Luhuitou Peninsula (Chi) 176
Luoyang (Chi) 122-3
Lushan (Chi) 155-7

Macau 371-93, **378-9**
accommodation 383
books 382

business hours 377
climate 371
drinks 384
economy 371
embassies 376
entertainment 392
fax 382
festivals 380
food 384
geography 371
getting around 385-6
getting there & away 384
government 371
health 383
history 371
language 375-6
media 382
money 376-7
photography 383
places to eat 391-2
places to stay 387-91
population 374
post 380
public holidays 377
religion 375
shopping 384-93
telephones 381
time 382
tourist offices 377
visas 376
women travellers 383
work 383
Macau Peninsula 386-7, **372-3**
Magome (Jap) 542-3
Maisan Provincial Park (SK) 361
Mao Zedong 56-7
Matsue (Jap) 575
Matsumoto (Jap) 544-5
Matsushima (Jap) 580-1
Matsuyama (Jap) 606-8
Mengyang (Chi) 191
Midagahara (Jap) 587
Ming Tombs (Chi) 106
Mishima (Jap) 532
Miya-jima Island (Jap) 573-4
Miyako Islands (Jap) 625
Miyako-jima Island (Jap) 625
Moaksan Provincial Park (SK) 359
Mogao Caves (Chi) 207
Mokp'o (SK) 363, **362**
money 16-7, 36
Mongolia 394-422, **395, 412**
accommodation 408-9
books 406
business hours 405
climate 397
culture 398
drinks 410

economy 397
embassies 401-3
entertainment 410
fax 406
festivals 405
food 409-10
geography 396-7
getting around 411-3
getting there & away 411
government 397
health 407
history 394-6
Inner Mongolia 201-3
language 398-401
media 407
money 403-4
photography 407
population 398
post 405
public holidays 405
religion 398
shopping 410
telephones 405
time 406
tourist offices 404
visas 401-3
work 408
Morappu (Jap) 601
Morioka (Jap) 582
Moto-chi (Jap) 595
Moto-Hakone (Jap) 529
Mt Asahi-dake (Jap) 596
Mt Aso (Jap) 617-9
Mt Bandai-san (Jap) 578-9
Mt Eniwa-dake (Jap) 601
Mt Fuji (Jap) 530-2, **531**
Mt Gas-san (Jap) 586-7
Mt Haguro-san (Jap) 586
Mt Hakkōda-san (Jap) 584
Mt Hakodate-yama (Jap) 588
Mt Hallasan (SK) 365
Mt Hino-yama (Jap) 574
Mt Hokkai-dake (Jap) 596
Mt Hsuehshan (Tai) 463
Mt Iō-zan (Jap) 597, (Jap) 599
Mt Ishizuchi-san (Jap) 608
Mt Iwaki-san (Jap) 585
Mt Iwate-san (Jap) 583
Mt Karakuni-dake (Jap) 619
Mt Karamatsu-dake (Jap) 544
Mt Kuro-dake (Jap) 596
Mt Kurodake Ishimuro (Jap) 596
Mt Maru-yama (Jap) 543
Mt Me-Akan-dake (Jap) 599
Mt Misen (Jap) 573
Mt Naka-dake (Jap) 618
Mt O-Akan-dake (Jap) 599
Mt Osore-zan (Jap) 583
Mt Rausu-dake (Jap) 597

Mt Rishiri-zan (Jap) 594
Mt Rokko-san (Jap) 563
Mt Shirouma-dake (Jap) 543
Mt Takachiho-no-mine (Jap) 619
Mt Tamoyachi-yama (Jap) 584
Mt Tarumae-zan (Jap) 601
Mt Yudono-san (Jap) 587
Mutianyu (Chi) 106
Mutsu (Jap) 583
Myohyangsan (NK) 301-2

Naejangsan National Park (SK)
    361
Nagano (Jap) 543
Nagasaki (Jap) 613-6, **614-5**
Nagoya (Jap) 537-9
Naha (Jap) 623-5
Nakamura (Jap) 606
Naksan (SK) 349
Nanjing (Chi) 135-8, **134-5**
Nara (Jap) 564-7, **565**
New Territories (HK) 256-60
    places to stay 272-3, **258-9**
Ngong Ping (HK) 263, (HK) 273
Niigata (Jap) 587-8
Nikkō (Jap) 532-5, **534**
Ningxia (Chi) 203-4
Nishi-uedomari (Jap) 595
nō, see theatre
Norikura-kōgen Plateau (Jap)
    546
North Korea 284-303, **284**
    accommodation 293
    books 291
    business hours 290
    climate 286
    economy 287
    embassies 288-9
    fax 291
    food 293
    geography 286
    getting around 295-6
    getting there & away 294-5
    government 286-7
    health 292
    history 285-6
    language 287
    media 292
    money 289-90
    photography 292
    population 287
    post 291
    public holidays 290
    religion 287
    telephones 291
    time 291
    tourist offices 290
    visas 288-9
    women travellers 293

Odaesan National Park (SK) 350
Odawara (Jap) 529
Ogimachi (Jap) 541
Okinawa & the South-West
    Islands (Jap) 623-5
Okinawa City (Jap) 623
Okinawa Island (Jap) 623-5
Osaka (Jap) 559-62
Oshidomari (Jap) 594
Outlying Islands 260
overland travel 34-41
    to/from North-East Asia 34-41
    within North-East Asia 46-7

P'anmunjŏm (NK) 302, (SK) 347
P'yŏngyang (NK) 296-301,
    298-9
    entertainment 300
    getting around 301
    orientation 296
    places to eat 300
    places to stay 300
    shopping 300
    things to see 297-300
Paekdusan (NK) 303
Pak Tam Chung (HK) 257
Peng Chau (HK) 263, 280, **264**
Poropinai (Jap) 601
Potala Palace (Chi) 215
Puk'ansan (SK) 347
Pusan (SK) 355-8, **356, 359**

Qiaotou (Chi) 191
Qigong (Chi) 59
Qingdao (Chi) 123-7, **124**
Qinghai (Chi) 219-21
Qinghai Lake (Chi) 220
Qufu (Chi) 128-30, **129**

Rebun-tō Island (Jap) 594-5
Renmin Park (Chi) 192
Reshiri-Rebun-Sarobetsu
    National Park (Jap) 594
Rishiri-tō Island (Jap) 594
roller skating, see skating
running 236, 383

Sai Kung Peninsula (HK) 257
Sai Kung Town (HK) 257
Sakurajima (Jap) 621-2
Sakya (Chi) 218-9
Sangwon Valley (NK) 301
Sanya (Chi) 175-6, **175**
Sapporo (Jap) 589-93
Sarakura-sō (Jap) 543
sea travel
    to/from North-East Asia 42
    within North-East Asia 47-52

Sendai (Jap) 579-80
Senninzawa (Jap) 587
Seoul 332-47, **334-5, 346**
    entertainment 343
    getting around 345-7
    getting there & away 344-5
    information 332-8
    orientation 332
    places to eat 342-3
    places to stay 340-2
    shopping 343-4
    things to see 338-9
Seven Star Mountain (Tai) 454
Shaanxi (Chi) 117-22
shamanism 309
Shamian Island (Chi) 168
Shandong (Chi) 123-30
Shanghai (Chi) 138-46, **140-1**
Shanhaiguan (Chi) 111
Shantou (Chi) 171-2
Shanxi (Chi) 115-6
Shanyuan (Tai) 467
Shaoshan (Chi) 162
Shatin (HK) 257
Shenyang (Chi) 112
Shenzhen (Chi) 162-4
Sheung Shui (HK) 257
Shidu (Chi) 107
Shigatse (Chi) 218
Shikoku (Jap) 601-9, **602**
Shikoku-mura Village (Jap)
    603
Shikotsu Kohan (Jap) 601
Shikotsu-Tōya National Park
    (Jap) 600-1
Shimoda (Jap) 527
Shimoji-jima Island (Jap) 625
Shimonoseki (Jap) 574
Shinjuku 522, **522**
shintō (Jap) 486
Shirahone Onsen (Jap) 546
Shirakawa-gō (Jap) 541
Shiretoko National Park (Jap)
    597-8
Shōkawa Valley (Jap) 541
Sichuan (Chi) 192-201
Silk Route 41
Silver Mine Bay (HK) 263
Silvermine Bay (HK) 273, (HK)
    280
Simatai (Chi) 106
skating 324
    ice 236, 383, 408
    roller 324
skiing 24, 76, 112, 324, 408,
    496, 543-4, 596
Sŏgwip'o (SK) 365
Sok Kwu Wan (HK) 261, 262,
    280

Sokch'o (SK) 349, **350**
Sŏng-ŭp (SK) 365
Songni-dong (SK) 369
Songnisan National Park (SK) 369
Sŏngsan (SK) 365
Sŏnunsan Provincial Park (SK) 361
Sŏrak-dong (SK) 349
Sŏraksan National Park (SK) 349
Sōunkyō (Jap) 596
South Gobi (Mon) 421
South Gobi Tourist Camp (Mon) 421
South Korea 304-70, **306-7, 329**
  accommodation (SK) 325
  books (SK) 321
  business hours (SK) 319
  climate (SK) 308
  customs (SK) 309
  drinks (SK) 327
  economy (SK) 308
  embassies (SK) 316-7
  entertainment (SK) 327
  fax (SK) 321
  festivals (SK) 320
  food (SK) 325-7
  geography (SK) 305
  getting around (SK) 328-32
  getting there & away (SK) 328
  government (SK) 308
  health (SK) 322
  history (SK) 304-5
  language (SK) 309-16
  media 321
  money 317-8
  photography 322
  population 309
  post 320-1
  public holidays 319
  religion 309
  resident certificate 317
  shopping 328
  telephones 320
  time 321
  tourist offices 318
  visas 316-7
  women travellers 322
  work 323
Stanley (HK) 254
Stone Forest (Chi) 188
Subashiri (Jap) 532
Suibara (Jap) 587
Sumō (Jap) 486
surfing 24, 438
Suwon (SK) 348
Suzhou (Chi) 130-3, **132**
swimming 237, 383

Ta'er Lamasery (Chi) 219-20
Taedunsan Provincial Park (SK) 369
Taegu (SK) 354
Taejŏn (SK) 368
taekwondo 324
Tai'an (Chi) 127, **126**
Taichung (Tai) 459, **460-1**
Taijiquan (Chi) 59
Taipa (Mac) 387, **389**
Taipa Village (Mac) 392
Taipei (Tai) 446-58, **448, 450-1**
  entertainment 456
  getting around 458
  getting there & away 457-8
  information 447-9
  orientation 446-7
  places to eat 455
  places to stay 454-5
  shopping 456-7
  things to see 449-54
Taishan (Chi) 127-8
Taitung (Tai) 467, **472**
Taiwan 423-78, **424, 445**
  accommodation 439
  books 437
  business hours 435
  climate 425
  culture 426
  drinks 442-3
  economy 425
  embassies 431-3
  entertainment 443
  fax 436
  festivals 435
  food 439-42
  geography 425
  getting around 444-6
  getting there & away 443-4
  government 425
  health 438
  history 423-5
  language 426-31
  media 437
  money 434
  photography 438
  population 426
  post 435
  public holidays 435
  religion 426
  shopping 443
  telephone 436
  time 436
  tourist offices 434
  visas 431, 433
  women travellers 438
  work 435
Takachiho (Jap) 622-3
Takamatsu (Jap) 603-4

Takamori (Jap) 618
Takayama (Jap) 539-41
Takiguchi (Jap) 599
Tangkou (Chi) 147
taoism 60, 226, 375, 426
Taroko Gorge (Tai) 465
Tayuling (Tai) 464
Tenninkyō Onsen (Jap) 596
Terelj (Mon) 420
Teremachi (Jap) 576
theatre
  bunraku 485
  kabuki 485
  nō 485
The Grand Canal (Chi) 130
Tianchi (Chi) 113-4, (Chi) 212
Tianjin (Chi) 107-10, **108**
Tibet 215-9
Tienhsiang (Tai) 465-6
Tiger Leap Gorge (Chi) 191
Todong (SK) 354
Tōge (Jap) 586
Tokushima (Jap) 604-5, **512**
Tokyo (Jap) 507, **508-9, 528**
  entertainment 521-4
  getting around 525-7
  getting there & away 524-5
  information 507-10
  places to eat 519-21
  places to stay 515-9
  shopping 524
  things to see 510-5
Tongdo village (SK) 358
Tosashimizu (Jap) 606
Trans-Siberian Railway 35-41
  visas 39-40
Tsetseegun (Mon) 420
Tsimshatsui (HK) 249, **252-3**
Tsuen Wan (HK) 256
Tsugaike Natural Park (Jap) 543
Tsuifeng (Tai) 465
Tsumago (Jap) 542-3
Tsuruoka (Jap) 586
Tsuwano (Jap) 575-6
Tuen Mun (HK) 257
Turpan (Chi) 208-9

Ubazawa (Jap) 587
Ueno 518, **518**
Ulaan Baatar (Mon) 413-9, **414-5, 420**
  entertainment 419
  getting around 419
  getting there & away 419
  information 416-7
  orientation 413
  places to eat 419
  places to stay 418-9
  things to see 417-8

Ullŭngdo (SK) 354
Urakami (Jap) 613
Ürümqi (Chi) 209-12, **210**
Utoro (Jap) 597
Uwajima (Jap) 608-9

visas 14-5
    Trans-Siberian Railway 39-40

Wakkanai (Jap) 593-4
Walnut Grove (Chi) 191
Wanchai (HK) 254, **255**
Wando (SK) 363
Western Hills (Chi) 106
whitewater rafting 25, 439, 466
windsurfing 237, 383, 439
work 25-6
Wuhan (Chi) 157-61, **158-9**

Wuling Farm (Tai) 463-4
Wushe (Tai) 465
Wuzhou (Chi) 176

Xi'an (Chi) 117-21, **118**
Xiahe (Chi) 206-7
Xiamen (Chi) 151-5, **152**
Xianyang (Chi) 120
Xindu (Chi) 196
Xining (Chi) 219
Xinjiang (Chi) 208-14
Xishuangbanna (Chi) 191

Yaeyama Islands (Jap) 625
Yagen Onsen (Jap) 583
Yanagisawa (Jap) 583
Yangshuo (Chi) 180-2, **181**
Yangzi River (Chi) 200

Yarlong Valley (Chi) 218
Yashima (Jap) 603
Yinchuan (Chi) 203
Yŏju (SK) 348
Yokohama (Jap) 535
Yongjing (Chi) 206
Yŏsu (SK) 358-9, **360**
Yung Shue Wan (HK) 260, 273, 280
Yungang Caves (Chi) 115
Yunnan (Chi) 184-92
Yushan (Tai) 477

Zhanjiang (Chi) 172, **173**
Zhejiang (Chi) 148-51
Zhuhai (Chi) 164
Zuunmod (Mon) 420

Dear traveller,

Prices go up, good places go bad, bad places go bankrupt...and every guidebook is inevitably outdated in places. Fortunately, many travellers write to us about their experiences, telling us when things have changed. If we reprint a book between editions, we try to include the best of this information in a Stop Press section. We also make travellers' tips immediately available on our World Wide Web Internet site (http://www.lonelyplanet.com) and in a free quarterly newsletter, *Planet Talk*.

Although much of this information has not been verified by our own first-hand research, we believe it can still be very useful. We cannot vouch for its accuracy, however, so bear in mind it could be wrong.

We really enjoy hearing from people out on the road, and apart from guaranteeing that others will benefit from your good and bad experiences, we're prepared to bribe you with the offer of a free book for sending us substantial useful information.

I hope you do find this book useful – and that you let us know when it isn't. Thank you to everyone who has written.

Tony Wheeler

The North-East Asian region is continuing its economic boom. China has the largest growing economy. Travel in the region is still quite safe and crime is low, apart from China where the major problem for foreigners is theft by stealth. The seas in the region are experiencing an increase in piracy with 100 attacks reported in 1995, an increase of 13 on the previous year.

CHINA

China is changing rapidly. Economic growth is running at about 12% annually (much higher in some of the coastal provinces); urban landscapes are being transformed by vast transport infrastructure and construction projects; crime is on the increase; and inflation is running at anywhere between 20% and 30% depending on who is doing the counting.

Inflation has had an impact on all prices, but in particular it has affected hotel rates. While transportation costs have risen on average by about 30% since this edition was researched, you should expect accommodation rates to have jumped from 50% to 100%. In eastern China, widespread hotel renovations have created a shortage of budget accommodation in many cities.

The abolition of the FEC (the foreigners-only currency system) has generally made travel in China easier. The dual-pricing policy inflicted on foreign visitors, however, is still in place for entry tickets, internal flights and railway tickets. In many parts of China, hotels are dropping the dual-pricing system, as are shipping lines.

The political situation is also volatile. There is much uncertainty as to the mechanics of the impending change of power in Hong Kong; US-Sino relations are again at a low point over human rights, tariffs, copyrights and the Taiwan issue; and China's Asian neighbours are concerned by China's growing military might, its incursions and territorial demands in the South China Sea.

Visas & Permits

The telephone number for the Visa Office of the Ministry of Foreign Affairs of the PRC, 5th Floor, Lower Block, 26 Harbour Rd, Wanchai, Hong Kong, has changed to ☎ 2835-3794.

There are Burmese and Lao consulates at the Camellia Hotel, Bldg 3, 1st and 2nd floors, Kunming, Yunnan.

Money & Costs

Galloping inflation and the elimination of the FEC have combined to devalue the yuan by about 33%. The official exchange rate is now US$1 to Y8.31. Although a small black market still exists, the risk of being cheated is so great that it's not worth using. Yuan prices for many tourist purchases have just about doubled – a Y10 tourist entry price may have jumped to Y20, air fares have increased by 90% and many tourist hotels are now twice as expensive in yuan terms.

Customs

Any antiques purchased in China now need an export certificate or they will be confiscated before departure. The only way to recover the item is to return to China and get an export certificate, in which case customs will charge a storage fee.

Dangers & Annoyances

Visitors must be very cautious about theft and rip-offs. Stealing bicycles, particularly from tourists, is increasingly common. Take great care with any large purchase when you are not certain what the cost should be. Beware of rip-offs at window-phone queues, insist on getting the fare in writing before taking an unmetered taxi and don't trust restaurants that won't tell you the cost in advance.

If possible, it's best to flag down taxis on the street, rather than at airports and bus and railway stations. On the street, the driver is more likely to use the meter! However, major airports, such as Shanghai and Canton, have designated taxi ramps where metered taxis wait. Ignore taxi touts and look for the taxi ramp.

Getting There & Away

To/From Pakistan The situation on the overland trip from Pakistan to China has changed. The bus now can be taken only from Sust to Tashkurgan. Both the tourist and local buses cost US$23. The tourist bureau bus is more convenient as the only passengers are tourists, which makes customs processing in Sust and Tashkurgan much faster. The bus can also pick up passengers at their hotel.

To/From Kazakhstan Visas for Kazakhstan are no longer available at the China-Kazakhstan border. You must get your visa from the embassy in Beijing.

The weekly train runs between Ürümqi and Almaty (going as far as Tashkent), takes three days and costs US$65, or US$52 with an ISIC card. The train stops for eight hours at the China-Kazakhstan border. At the Chinese side there is an HIV control centre, but apparently only Russians get asked for their HIV-free certificates. Some Russians proved negativity with US$5! The result of the HIV test was surprisingly known in about one minute!

Alternatively, there is a direct bi-weekly bus between Ürümqi and Almaty that costs US$52, no discounts. There is also a network of local buses and taxis that cross the border and do the same journey in stages, but we have no detailed information on these. There is reportedly a US$10 border tax.

To/From Kyrgyzstan The overland route between Kashgar (China) and Bishkek (Kyrgyzstan) is open to independent travellers and is theoretically possible (though still problematic) for hitch-hikers. There is one Chinese bus with a Russian driver between the towns, but there is no fixed timetable. It just turns around and goes back when it has enough passengers, perhaps three or four times a month in summer, less at other times.

The 1½-day trip includes one overnight stop and is perfectly legal, though passengers must see to their own visas. Tickets cost US$60 to US$70 in Bishkek or Y800 in Kashgar. The Bishkek office (☎ 22-3670) is at Razakov (formerly Pervomayskaya) 7, near the railway station, and is open from 9 am to 5 pm. In Kashgar, it's at the Wuzi Binguan (Wuzi Hotel), half a block south of the post office. Tickets are sold in the lobby but no English is spoken.

Visas for Kyrgyzstan and the other Central Asian republics must be obtained in advance; the closest point in China is

Beijing. Visas for China can be obtained in Bishkek, but only with an invitation – usually with a telex sent to the Chinese Embassy from some officially licensed Chinese agency confirming that they are meeting you on the China side. Otherwise, you should get one at home, preferably including written permission to cross at the Torugart Pass.

Trans-Siberian Railway Travellers have reported that Prague, Czech Republic, is a good place to buy cheap Trans-Siberian Railway tickets. They are available from the main railway station (☎ 2 - 24 21 76 54) or Cedok agency (☎ 2 - 24 19 71 11) Na prikope 18. Booking of the ticket is required at least 40 days prior to commencement of the journey, and tickets are valid from Prague to Beijing.

BEIJING
Forbidden City
Unscrupulous characters approach visitors pretending to be official guides and insisting that the palace can be visited only with a guide. This is not true.

Airport Transport
There are many unmetered taxis at Beijing airport, and they will charge you as much as they think you are willing to pay. However, the increasing competition among taxis has ensured that this is one area which has not suffered price increases. Beijing taxis still cost from Y1 to Y2 per km after the flagfall, and Beijing airport is only 25 km out, so by the meter the fare into town should not be more than Y100. Don't listen to any demands over Y150, but if the taxi is unmetered it is best to agree on a flat fare in advance.

Taxi drivers will deny the existence of the airport bus. The ticket counter is to the right after you pass through customs, but it is not easy buying the Y12 ticket, as the ticket seller ignores customers. If you wish to buy the ticket you need to be forceful. Hold on to your ticket, as it is collected at the end of your journey. The same scenario with taxi drivers will be played out at the Aviation Building in Beijing, where taxi drivers will take tourists

to their hotels at double or triple the normal fare. This can be avoided by getting off the bus when it stops at one of the metro stations along the way from the airport and taking the metro the rest of the way to your hotel.

SICHUAN
Chongqing
Lonely Planet has had reports of touts in Chongqing trying to sell tickets for the trip to Yichang for up to 100% more than the regular boat price. The major complaint was they were shown a photo of a luxury boat, but the boat that they boarded was run-down and dirty.

GUANGXI
Wuzhou
Hovercrafts ply the route three times a day from Dashatou wharf in Guangzhou (about 100 metres from the bus station and the old boat dock) to Wuzhou daily. The first one departs Guangzhou at 8 am and arrives in Wuzhou about 1 pm. The old wharf in Guangzhou still operates slow boats to Wuzhou.

Xingping
The posted rates for ferries along the Li River to Xingping at the ferry dock in Yangshuo are Y30. However, if you go after 9.30 am, when there may be no other passengers, you may end up having to charter the entire boat for Y200. You can get around this by going through CITS, which charges Y30 per person regardless of the number of passengers.

GANSU
Xiahe
The lower bus station does not exist anymore. Buses to Lanzhou and Tongren leave from the bus station next to the market area, not the upper bus station.

YUNNAN
Apart from the road to Tibet, all of Yunnan is open to travellers. It is no longer necessary to go from Dali to Kunming when you want to go to Xishuangbanna. The shortest route

is from Baoshan to Lincang, then to Meng-yang and Jinghong.

It is also possible to travel by bus on the roads along the Myanmar border. From Jinghong there is one bus a day to Menghai. From Menghai there is no public transport to Zhenkang (five hours away), but a taxi costs Y85 for the ride in a six-seater to the first village, from where there is public transport to Zhenkang. The scenery along the way is beautiful.

Myanmar visas for the overland crossing at Ruili are available in Kunming. You can now go all the way into Myanmar legally from China (but not in the reverse direction).

Chenggong County
The bus from Kunming to Chenggong County no longer departs from the Xiaoximen bus station. However, one can still get there by taking the No 5 city bus to its terminal at the Chrysanthemum Village and then transferring to the No 12 bus to Chenggong County.

TIBET & QINGHAI
Visas & Permits
There are no separate visa or permit regulations for Tibet. A Chinese visa is sufficient. The visa application asks a number of questions, including places in China you plan to visit and entry/exit points. You can deviate from these without any problems – the most important point is not to write anything about planning to visit Tibet.

Dangers & Annoyances
Chinese authorities are clamping down on Westerners who distribute photos and tapes of the Dalai Lama. Several travellers have been caught and deported from China for this 'crime'.

MONGOLIA

Despite its magnificent scenery, Mongolia is still not a popular travel destination. The acute shortages reported by the author when he researched this edition are over. Food is available and reportedly there is no widespread starvation. However, there is an acute petrol shortage in the country. Ration cards are required to buy petrol and in remoter parts of the country petrol is used as a tradable item. The economy has shown signs of improvement since 1994. Inflation has greatly decreased to 51% and growth has increased by 8%, but Mongolia and its inhabitants remain poor. The country is still to reap the benefits of privatization and the new capitalist economy.

Visas & Embassies
There are still only two types of visa that are issued to foreigners – a transit and tourist visa. In order to obtain a tourist visa, you either need an invitation from a Mongolian citizen, or purchase a short tour from a travel agent, after which it is possible to stay and see the rest of the country independently.

The telephone number for the US Embassy is ☎ 329606 and 329095.

Money
There are now T500 and T1000 bank notes. All coins are reportedly out of circulation.

The official exchange rate is US$1 to T431.

Postal & Telephone Rates
Rates for airmail letters under 20 grams are T80. Parcels can only be sent by airmail and cost around US$2 per kg.

International telephone rates are about four times higher than what you are used to paying at home. Faxes are now much cheaper to send internationally, about US$3 per page.

What to Bring
One traveller suggested that a tent can be very useful for travelling around Mongolia, no matter what mode of transport is used. Breakdowns and fluid departure times make irregular overnight stops in the middle of the country common. Often there is nowhere to sleep and a tent can provide the only shelter.

Getting Around
There is now a bus that goes to Bayanhongor

from Ulaan Baatar on Monday, Thursday and Saturday mornings. It departs from the front of the Baigal Hotel in Ulaan Baatar.

Ulaan Baatar

SBMI has moved to the north-west corner of the Hudaldaany and Baga Toyruu St crossroads. Local telephone calls now cost T20 to T50. Bus No 22 also goes to the airport.

TAIWAN

The Tourism Bureau, a branch of the Ministry of Communications, has set up a Tourist Information Hotline (☎ (02) 717 3737) that assists travellers with travel information, emergency assistance, accidents, lost and found, language problems and complaints.

Visas

The visa-free entry for the honoured 12 nations has been extended from five to 14 days. All other conditions still apply.

JAPAN

The January 1995 earthquake in Kobe caused much destruction to the city but most of the damage has been repaired. There are no problems for visitors apart from traffic congestion due to restrictions in many places. Japan is still one of the safest countries in the world, despite the isolated incident of the poison gas attack on the Tokyo subway in March 1995, in which 12 people died and about 5000 were injured. One of the new extreme religious sects, Aum Shinrikyo, was responsible and some of its leaders are facing a trial.

Visas & Embassies

The following Japanese embassies and consulates in Australia have changed their telephone numbers: Canberra ☎ 06-273

3244; Brisbane ☎ 07-3221 5188; Melbourne ☎ 03-9639 3244 and Perth ☎ 09-321 7816.

Money & Costs

There is very low inflation and most costs have either stayed the same or only marginally increased. The official exchange rate is US$1 to ¥101.

Tourist Offices

Two of the Tourist Information Centres operated by JNTO offices have new telephone numbers – Narita Airport is now ☎ 0476-346251 and Ginza is ☎ 03-3502 1461.

Three of the overseas offices of JNTO have changed their addresses:

Hong Kong
   37th Floor, Suite 3704-05, Dorset House, Taikoo Place, Quarry Bay (☎ 2968 5688)
UK
   Heathcote House, 20 Savile Row, London W1X 1AE (☎ 0171-734 9638)
USA
   One Rockefeller Plaza, Suite 1250, New York, NY 10111 (☎ 212-757 5640)

Leaving Japan

There is a departure tax from Kansai international airport in Osaka of ¥2600.

ACKNOWLEDGMENTS

The information in this Stop Press was compiled from various sources and reports by the following travellers: Karen Stobbs Aderer (USA), Jonathan Baker (USA), Daniel Bryant, Ludo Jambrich (Slovakia), Wim van Ginkel & Els van Kujk (NL), Elfi Gilissen (D), Heidi Heinzerling, Bart Kleijer (NL), John Kupiec (USA), Simon Nedelke, Tim Nollen, Paco Paconcello (D), Nancy Parshall, Marc Proksch, Mark Swaim (USA) and Roger Young (USA).

Tony Wheeler and one of the authors of this guide, Chris Taylor, made final corrections and additions to parts of the text. Another contribution was made by one of our Central Asia authors, John King.

LONELY PLANET TV SERIES & VIDEOS

Lonely Planet travel guides have been brought to life on television screens around the world. Like our guides, the programmes are based on the joy of independent travel, and look honestly at some of the most exciting, picturesque and frustrating places in the world. Each show is presented by one of three travellers from Australia, England or the USA and combines an innovative mixture of video, Super-8 film, atmospheric soundscapes and original music.

Videos of each episode – containing additional footage not shown on television – are available from good book and video shops, but the availability of individual videos varies with regional screening schedules.

Video destinations include:
Alaska; Australia (Southeast); Brazil; Ecuador & the Galapagos Islands; Indonesia; Israel & the Sinai Desert; Japan; La Ruta Maya (Yucatan, Guatemala & Belize); Morocco; North India (Varanasi to the Himalaya); Pacific Islands; Vietnam; Zimbabwe, Botswana & Namibia.

Coming in 1996:
The Arctic (Norway & Finland); Baja California; Chile & Easter Island; China (Southeast); Costa Rica; East Africa (Tanzania & Zanzibar); Great Barrier Reef (Australia); Jamaica; Papua New Guinea; the Rockies (USA); Syria & Jordan; Turkey.

The Lonely Planet television series is produced by:
Pilot Productions
Duke of Sussex Studios
44 Uxbridge St
London W8 7TG
United Kingdom

Lonely Planet videos are distributed by:
IVN Communications Inc
2246 Camino Ramon, San Ramon
California 94583, USA

107 Power Road, Chiswick
London W4 5PL, UK

For further information on both the television series and the availability of individual videos please contact Lonely Planet.

THE LONELY PLANET TRAVEL ATLAS

Tired of maps that lead you astray?

Sick of maps that fall apart after a few days' travel?

Had enough of maps that get creased and torn in all the wrong places?

**Lonely Planet is proud to announce the solution to all these problems –
the Lonely Planet travel atlas!**

Produced in conjunction with Steinhart Katzir Publishers, a range of atlases designed to complement our guidebooks is now available to travellers worldwide.

Unlike other maps and road atlases, which look good on paper but often lack accuracy, LP's travel atlases have been thoroughly checked on the road by Lonely Planet's experienced team of authors. All details are carefully checked to ensure that the atlas conforms with the equivalent Lonely Planet guidebook.

The handy book format means that the atlas can withstand months of rigorous travelling adventures. So whether you're struggling through an Icelandic gale or packed like a sardine on a backcountry bus in Asia, you'll find it easier to get where you're going with a Lonely Planet travel atlas. (Ideal for armchair travellers too!)

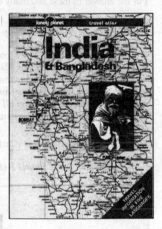

- full colour
- travel information in English, French, German, Spanish and Japanese
- place names keyed to LP guidebooks; no confusing spelling differences
- one country - one atlas. No need to buy five maps to cover large countries
- multilingual atlas legend
- comprehensive index

Available now:
Thailand; India; Zimbabwe, Botswana & Namibia and Vietnam

Coming soon:
Israel; Turkey; Laos and Chile

PLANET TALK
Lonely Planet's FREE quarterly newsletter

We love hearing from you and think you'd like to hear from us.

When...is the right time to see reindeer in Finland?
Where...can you hear the best palm-wine music in Ghana?
How...do you get from Asunción to Areguá by steam train?
What...is the best way to see India?

For the answer to these and many other questions read PLANET TALK.

Every issue is packed with up-to-date travel news and advice including:

- *a letter from Lonely Planet founders Tony and Maureen Wheeler*
- *travel diary from a Lonely Planet author - find out what it's really like out on the road*
- *feature article on an important and topical travel issue*
- *a selection of recent letters from our readers*
- *the latest travel news from all over the world*
- *details on Lonely Planet's new and forthcoming releases*

To join our mailing list contact any Lonely Planet office.

Also available: Lonely Planet T-shirts. 100% heavyweight cotton (S, M, L, XL)

Guides to North-East Asia

Beijing – city guide
Beijing is the hub of a vast nation. This guide will help travellers to find the best this ancient and fascinating city has to offer.

China – a travel survival kit
This book is the recognised authority for independent travellers in the People's Republic. With essential tips for avoiding pitfalls, and comprehensive practical information, it will help you to discover the real China.

Hong Kong, Macau & Canton – a travel survival kit
This practical guide has all the travel facts on these three close but diverse cities, linked by history, culture and geography.

Japan – a travel survival kit
Japan combines modern cities and remote wilderness areas, sophisticated technology and ancient tradition. This guide tells you how to find the Japan that many visitors never see.

Korea – a travel survival kit
South Korea is one of the great undiscovered destinations, with its mountains, ancient temples and lively modern cities. This guide also includes a chapter on reclusive North Korea.

Mongolia – a travel survival kit
Mongolia is truly a destination for the adventurous. This guide gives visitors the first real opportunity to explore this remote but newly accessible country.

Seoul – city guide
It is easy to explore Seoul's ancient royal palaces and bustling market places with this comprehensive guide packed with vital information for leisure and business travellers alike.

Taiwan – a travel survival kit
Traditional Chinese ways survive in prosperous Taiwan. This guide has Chinese script and pinyin throughout.

Tibet – a travel survival kit
The fabled mountain-land of Tibet is slowly becoming accessible to travellers. This guide has full details on this remote and fascinating region, including the border crossing to Nepal.

Tokyo – city guide
Tokyo is a dynamic metropolis and one of the world's leading arbiters of taste and style. This guide will help you to explore the many sides of Tokyo, the modern Japanese miracle rolled into a single fascinating, sometimes startling package.

Also available:
Cantonese phrasebook, **Mandarin Chinese** phrasebook, **Korean** phrasebook, **Tibet** phrasebook, and **Japanese** phrasebook.

Lonely Planet Guidebooks

Lonely Planet guidebooks cover every accessible part of Asia as well as Australia, the Pacific, South America, Africa, the Middle East, Europe and parts of North America. There are seven series: *travel survival kits*, covering a country for a range of budgets; *shoestring guides* with compact information for low-budget travel in a major region; *walking guides*; *city guides*, *phrasebooks, audio packs* and *travel atlases*.

EUROPE

Austria • Baltic States & Kaliningrad • Baltics States phrasebook • Britain • Central Europe on a shoestring • Central Europe phrasebook • Czech & Slovak Republics • Dublin city guide • Eastern Europe on a shoestring • Eastern Europe phrasebook • Finland • France • Greece • Greek phrasebook • Hungary • Iceland, Greenland & the Faroe Islands • Ireland • Italy • Mediterranean Europe on a shoestring • Mediterranean Europe phrasebook • Poland • Prague city guide • Russia, Ukraine & Belarus • Russian phrasebook • Scandinavian & Baltic Europe on a shoestring • Scandinavian Europe phrasebook • Slovenia • St Petersburg city guide • Switzerland • Trekking in Greece • Trekking in Spain • Vienna city guide • Western Europe on a shoestring • Western Europe phrasebook

NORTH AMERICA & MEXICO

Alaska • Backpacking in Alaska •

Baja California • Canada • Hawaii • Honolulu city guide • Los Angeles city guide • Mexico • Pacific Northwest USA • Rocky Mountain States • San Francisco city guide •

CENTRAL AMERICA & THE CARIBBEAN

Central America on a shoestring • Costa Rica • Eastern Caribbean • Guatemala, Belize & Yucatán: La Ruta Maya

SOUTH AMERICA

Argentina, Uruguay & Paraguay • Bolivia • Brazil • Brazilian phrasebook • Chile & Easter Island • Colombia • Ecuador & the Galápagos Islands • Latin American Spanish phrasebook • Peru • Quechua phrasebook • Rio de Janeiro city guide • South America on a shoestring • Trekking in the Patagonian Andes • Venezuela

AFRICA

Africa on a shoestring • Cape Town city guide • Central Africa • East Africa • Trekking in East Africa • Kenya • Swahili phrasebook • Morocco • Arabic (Moroccan) phrasebook • North Africa • South Africa, Lesotho & Swaziland • West Africa • Zimbabwe, Botswana & Namibia • Zimbabwe, Botswana & Namibia travel atlas

Mail Order

Lonely Planet guidebooks are distributed worldwide. They are also available by mail order from Lonely Planet, so if you have difficulty finding a title please write to us. US and Canadian residents should write to Embarcadero West, 155 Filbert St, Suite 251, Oakland CA 94607, USA; European residents should write to 10 Barley Mow Passage, Chiswick, London W4 4PH; and residents of other countries to PO Box 617, Hawthorn, Victoria 3122, Australia.

NORTH-EAST ASIA

Beijing city guide • China • Cantonese phrasebook • Mandarin Chinese phrasebook • Hong Kong, Macau & Canton • Japan • Japanese phrasebook • Japanese audio pack • Korea • Korean phrasebook • Mongolia • Mongolian phrasebook • North-East Asia on a shoestring • Seoul city guide • Taiwan • Tibet • Tibet phrasebook • Tokyo city guide

INDIAN SUBCONTINENT

Bengali phrasebook • Bangladesh • Delhi city guide • India • India & Bangladesh travel atlas • Hindi/Urdu phrasebook • Trekking in the Indian Himalaya • Karakoram Highway • Kashmir, Ladakh & Zanskar • Nepal • Trekking in the Nepal Himalaya • Nepali phrasebook • Pakistan • Sri Lanka • Sri Lanka phrasebook

SOUTH-EAST ASIA

Bali & Lombok • Bangkok city guide • Cambodia • Ho Chi Minh city guide• Indonesia • Indonesian phrasebook • Indonesian audio pack • Jakarta city guide • Java • Laos • Lao phrasebook • Malaysia, Singapore & Brunei • Myanmar (Burma) • Burmese phrasebook • Philippines • Pilipino phrasebook • Singapore city guide • South-East Asia on a shoestring • Thailand • Thailand travel atlas • Thai phrasebook • Thai audio pack • Thai Hill Tribes phrasebook • Vietnam • Vietnamese phrasebook • Vietnam travel atlas

MIDDLE EAST

Arab Gulf States • Egypt & the Sudan • Arabic (Egyptian) phrasebook • Iran • Israel • Jordan & Syria • Middle East • Turkey • Turkish phrasebook • Trekking in Turkey • Yemen

ISLANDS OF THE INDIAN OCEAN

Madagascar & Comoros • Maldives & Islands of the East Indian Ocean • Mauritius, Réunion & Seychelles

AUSTRALIA & THE PACIFIC

Australia • Australian phrasebook • Bushwalking in Australia • Islands of Australia's Great Barrier Reef • Outback Australia • Fiji • Fijian phrasebook • Melbourne city guide • Micronesia • New Caledonia • New South Wales & the ACT • New Zealand • Tramping in New Zealand • Papua New Guinea • Bushwalking in Papua New Guinea • Papua New Guinea phrasebook • Queensland • Rarotonga & the Cook Islands • Samoa • Solomon Islands • Sydney city guide • Tahiti & French Polynesia • Tonga • Vanuatu • Victoria • Western Australia

The Lonely Planet Story

Lonely Planet published its first book in 1973 in response to the numerous 'How did you do it?' questions Maureen and Tony Wheeler were asked after driving, bussing, hitching, sailing and railing their way from England to Australia.

Written at a kitchen table and hand collated, trimmed and stapled, *Across Asia on the Cheap* became an instant local bestseller, inspiring thoughts of another book.

Eighteen months in South-East Asia resulted in their second guide, *South-East Asia on a shoestring*, which they put together in a backstreet Chinese hotel in Singapore in 1975. The 'yellow bible' as it quickly became known to backpackers around the world, soon became *the* guide to the region. It has sold well over half a million copies and is now in its 8th edition, still retaining its familiar yellow cover.

Today there are over 180 titles, including travel guides, walking guides, language kits & phrasebooks, travel atlases and travel literature. The company is one of the largest travel publishers in the world. Although Lonely Planet initially specialised in guides to Asia, we now cover most regions of the world, including the Pacific, North America, South America, Africa, the Middle East and Europe.

The emphasis continues to be on travel for independent travellers. Tony and Maureen still travel for several months of each year and play an active part in the writing, updating and quality control of Lonely Planet's guides.

They have been joined by over 50 authors and 155 staff at our offices in Melbourne (Australia), Oakland (USA), London (UK) and Paris (France). Travellers themselves also make a valuable contribution to the guides through the feedback we receive in thousands of letters each year.

The people at Lonely Planet strongly believe that travellers can make a positive contribution to the countries they visit, both through their appreciation of the countries' culture, wildlife and natural features, and through the money they spend. In addition, the company makes a direct contribution to the countries and regions it covers. Since 1986 a percentage of the income from each book has been donated to ventures such as famine relief in Africa; aid projects in India; agricultural projects in Central America; Greenpeace's efforts to halt French nuclear testing in the Pacific; and Amnesty International.

Lonely Planet's basic travel philosophy is summed up in Tony Wheeler's comment, 'Don't worry about whether your trip will work out. Just go!'